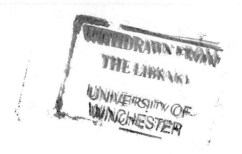

The Encyclopedia of Sculpture

Volume Two

Board of Advisers

The Encyclopedia of Sculpture

Volume Two
G–O

Antonia Boström, editor

Fitzroy Dearborn
New York • London

Published in 2004 by
Fitzroy Dearborn
An imprint of the Taylor & Francis Group
29 West 35th Street
New York, NY 10001

Published in Great Britain by
Fitzroy Dearborn
An imprint of the Taylor & Francis Group
11 New Fetter Lane
London EC4P 4EE

10 9 8 7 6 5 4 3 2 1

Library of Congress Cataloging-in-Publication Data

The encyclopedia of sculpture / Antonia Boström, editor.
    p. cm.
Includes bibliographical references and index.
ISBN 1-57958-248-6 (set : alk. paper)—ISBN 1-57958-428-4 (vol. 1 : alk. paper)—ISBN 1-57958-429-2
(vol. 2 : alk. paper)—ISBN 1-57958-430-6 (vol. 3 : alk. paper) 1. Sculpture, Modern—20th century—
Encyclopedias. I. Title: The encyclopedia of sculpture. II. Boström, Antonia.
NB198.E53 2004
735′.23′03—dc22

                                                                          2003015677

Printed in the United States on acid-free paper.

Contents

G

NAUM GABO 1890–1977 *Russian, active in Britain and United States*

Naum Gabo's sculptural legacy lies in his constructed works. Throughout his career, Gabo avoided carved or modeled work in favor of a constructed manner of sculpture, seen from his small figurative early works to the large-scale abstract creations made late in his life. Together with his brother, Antoine Pevsner, Gabo explored the industrial aesthetic of Russian Constructivism. Straying from many of the ideas of the Constructivists, however, Gabo and Pevsner developed their own ideologies, influenced in part by their extensive time spent living in the West. Gabo's own predictions for the future path of sculpture dictated the characteristics of his unique constructions.

In 1910, at the age of 20, Gabo left Russia to pursue scientific studies in Munich. His interest in constructed sculpture may have had conceptual roots in these early studies. Many of his abstract works, in particular, resemble mathematical models. *Column*, a nonobjective tower of transparent plastic, verged in appearance on a scientific instrument. Gabo also saw this piece as the architectonic culmination of attempts to fuse sculptural and architectural elements. The connection to mathematics was further articulated by Gabo's intention that many of his constructions should be proportionately enlarged to create multiple variations.

Gabo's interest in constructed work was also sparked by visits to his brother in Paris. While in Paris, Gabo was exposed to the work of the Cubists. The Cubist grid developed by Pablo Picasso and Georges Braque, as well as their forays into constructed sculpture, may well have influenced Gabo's subsequent creations. His first major constructed sculpture came in a figurative form and illustrated the Cubist influence: *Constructed Head No. 1* is a series of intersecting wooden planes, as if a three-dimensional translation of Cubist fragmentation. In *Constructed Head No. 1*, Gabo already exhibited an interest that would recur throughout his career: The work displayed volume, through the intersecting planes, but reduced sculptural mass. Variations on the *Constructed Head No. 1* explored media like celluloid. Like other Russian Constructivists, Gabo experimented with such new artistic materials as industrial metals and plastics.

In 1920 Gabo set forth his sculptural insights in the *Realistic Manifesto*, also signed by Pevsner. Their publication signaled a break with other sculptural movements and outlined what Gabo perceived to be the future of sculpture. Although Constructivist ideologues such as Vladimir Tatlin espoused the belief that art must serve a social purpose, Gabo countered that art should serve an independent function in society, as an important means of communication and expression of human experience. In his manifesto, Gabo also addressed his recent artistic predecessors, Cubism and Futurism. Although he praised both movements for their attempted breaks with the past, he ultimately deemed their solutions too obvious and simplistic. In response, Gabo delineated, point by point, the characteristics that he believed would save sculpture from stagnation. In addressing formal elements, Gabo renounced the descriptive value of line and favored instead a line that represents direction and rhythm. Mass, too, he renounced as a sculptural element, turning rather to line and volume as found in intersecting planes. Gabo also asserted the importance of two new elements in sculpture: space and time. His suggestions to incorporate such intangible elements included the enclosure of or projection into space of sculptural components and the deployment of kinetic rhythms to signify time. Only with the involvement of space and time did Gabo believe that sculpture could withstand the pressures of a changing technological society.

Gabo's subsequent sculptural creations followed his manifesto guidelines. In 1920 he created *Kinetic Construction (Standing Wave)*, a motor-controlled vibrating metal rod. The thin line of metal both moved through space and existed within a duration of time. His *Linear Constructions in Space* also demonstrated the inclusion of space as a sculptural element. The web of nylon strings attached to sheets of plastic open up the form and reduce the sculptural mass, focusing on the volume through the extensive use of line and simultaneously enclosing space. By suggesting the void as a positive space, Gabo believed space could be transformed into a malleable, material element.

Gabo furthered his attempts to engage sculptural space through the use of sweeping, curvilinear forms. His stage designs for Sergei Diaghilev's ballet, *La Chatte*, surrounded and projected across the stage, enclosing the dancers and their space. Gabo's many spheric constructions, such as *Spheric Theme Second Variation*, also engage space through the suggestion of constant visual movement.

Gabo not only experimented with new sculptural elements but continually employed nontraditional materials as well. Throughout the 1920s, Gabo incorporated cardboard, plastics, metals, and glass into his creations. Following his move to London in 1936, he was introduced to Perspex, a new plastic developed by Imperial Chemical Industries. While in England, Gabo also began using nylon filament in conjunction with plastic. Both nylon and Perspex became frequent elements in Gabo's work of the next decades.

Gabo repeatedly experimented with variations in size and scale. Some of his works he labeled models, implying continual process and transformation. Following his move to the United States in 1946, he received several public commissions that allowed him to experiment on a monumental scale. His most important public sculpture was *Bijenkorf Construction* for the Bijenkorf building in Rotterdam, the Netherlands. Intending to celebrate the city's postwar reconstruction, Gabo likened the form to a tree soaring into the air but firmly anchored in the ground. *Bijenkorf Construction* continued and enlarged many of Gabo's earlier sculptural concerns. Despite the monumental form, the work displayed a large-scale reduction of mass in favor of linear volume. The former nylon strings were replaced by thin strands of metal surrounding and incorporating the void into the sculpture.

Gabo's constructed sculptures combined a variety of concerns. Interests in mathematics, architectonic forms, and new sculptural elements of space and time all found manifestation in his constructions. His unusual materials and manner of construction have had lasting influence, finding visual echoes in such later movements as Minimalism.

RACHEL EPP BULLER

See also **Pevsner, Antoine**

Biography

Born in Klimovichi, Belarus, 5 August 1890. Brother was sculptor Antoine Pevsner; changed surname to Gabo, *ca.* 1917, for separate identity. Studied science and medicine at University of Munich, 1910–12, and engineering at Technische Hochschule, Munich, 1912–14; lived in Norway, 1914–17, developing ideas in Constructivism; returned to Russia, 1917–22; wrote *Realistic Manifesto*, 1920; moved to Paris, 1933; then settled in London, 1936, and was introduced to new material, Perspex (which he used in his work); designed car for Jowett Car Company in England, 1943; moved to United States and did monumental projects, 1946. Received Guggenheim Fellowship, 1954; elected to National Institute of Arts and Letters, 1965, Royal Academy of Arts, Sweden, 1966, American Academy of Arts and Sciences, 1969, and American Academy of Arts and Letters, 1975. Died in Waterbury, Connecticut, United States, 23 August 1977.

Selected Works

1915   *Constructed Head No. 1*; plywood; private collection, London, England

1920   *Kinetic Construction (Standing Wave)*; metal rod, electric motor; Tate Gallery, London, England

1920–21 *Column*; plastic, glass; Tate Gallery, London, England

1927   Model for stage set of Diaghilev's ballet *La Chatte*; plastic; Tate Gallery, London, England

1937–38 *Spheric Theme, Second Variation*; Perspex; private collection, London, England

1942   *Linear Construction in Space No. 1*; Perspex, nylon monofilament; private collection, England; variation: Perspex and nylon mylofilament, Tate Gallery, London, England

1956–57 *Bijenkorf Construction*; prestressed concrete, steel ribs, stainless steel, bronze wire, marble; N.V. Magazin De Bijenkorf, Rotterdam, the Netherlands

Further Reading

Lodder, Christina, *Russian Constructivism*, New Haven, Connecticut: Yale University Press, 1983

Nash, Steven A., and Jörn Merkert (editors), *Naum Gabo: Sixty Years of Constructivism*, Munich: Prestel-Verlag, 1985

Nash, Steven A., and Michael Compton, *Naum Gabo: Sixty Years of Constructivism*, London: The Tate Gallery, 1987

Olson, Ruth, and Abraham Chanin, *Naum Gabo and Antoine Pevsner*, New York: Museum of Modern Art, 1948

Pevsner, Alexei, *A Biographical Sketch of My Brothers Naum Gabo and Antoine Pevsner*, Amsterdam: Augustin and Schoonman, 1964

LINEAR CONSTRUCTION IN SPACE NO. 1 (VARIATION)

Naum Gabo (1970–1977)

ca. 1942–1943

Perspex, nylon monofilament

h. 34 cm

Tate Gallery, London, England

Linear Construction in Space No. 1 (Variation) exemplifies many of the concerns that permeated Naum Gabo's sculptural career. The work developed through a process of continual revision and modification, mirroring the transformative process Gabo applied to many of his ideas. The piece also realizes some of the proposals for a new brand of sculpture set forth in Gabo's *Realistic Manifesto* and continues an interest in mathematical relationships exhibited earlier in his career.

Because the work is titled a "variation," its background necessarily begins with its predecessor, *Linear Construction in Space No. 1* (1942). This was the first instance in which Gabo employed his famous stringing, a characteristic later to become a near staple of his constructed sculptures. Created while he was living in England, *Linear Construction in Space No. 1* may have been intended as a prototype for a later public sculpture. As with many of his works, Gabo hoped eventually to realize this construction on a much larger scale. There is evidence that the public work based on this original *Linear Construction* would have been designed for a professional corporation, specifically a textile industry. Although *Linear Construction* never developed into a public sculpture, Gabo's original desire may have been a specific reference to his Constructivist roots. Perhaps in an attempt to find a place of social relevance, Gabo looked to public works as a way for the artist to aid in the building of a new society.

Gabo's *Linear Construction in Space No. 1 (Variation)*, conceived a year later, shares many of the formal elements of the original *Linear Construction*. Both are based on a plastic convex form, tall and thin with square-shaped sides. The sides, however, are only partially filled: both works enclose an open, elliptical space cutting diagonally through the center. Strings weave back and forth across the pieces to help define the forms. The compositional difference from the original to the *Variation* exists in the addition of stepped ends, slightly altering the path of the strings. Gabo also modified his materials, shifting from the celluloid and cotton string of his earliest model to the new industrial synthetics of Perspex and nylon.

Although Gabo first made use of stringing in his *Linear Constructions*, he was not the originator of stringed sculpture. Henry Moore employed strings in his sculpture as early as 1937. Gabo, aware of these works, in turn explored stringing, and works by both sculptors soon inspired the stringed works of Barbara Hepworth. Gabo's stringing differed significantly from that of Moore and Hepworth, however. The strings in Gabo's works were much more dominant, serving to define the pieces, rather than simply span open spaces. Gabo's densely packed strings are reminiscent of weaving looms. In the specific case of the *Linear Construction* and its variations, this implication may have been an explicit reference to the potential commission from, and symbolic advertisement for, the textile mill. Gabo's stringing also underwent practical changes during the variations. Although he began with a silk and cotton elasticized thread, after witnessing its fragility he replaced it with the more durable, newly developed nylon thread.

Several aspects of the *Linear Construction in Space No. 1 (Variation)* reflect the ideas set forth in Gabo's *Realistic Manifesto* from 1920. Although line is an important element of the piece, its function is not descriptive. Rather, in accord with Gabo's new sculptural tenets, the line represents rhythm and direction. The repetitive stringing produces a rhythmic motion that follows the contour of the inner ellipse. Similarly, the piece replaces sculptural mass with an emphasis on volume. The intersecting planes of Perspex and the nylon strings delineate the form's volumetric area without imposing weighty mass. The hollow ellipse in the center of the piece also fulfills Gabo's dictate to incorporate the element of space into the new sculpture. By surrounding and tracing the space, the void is given an implicit presence, becoming part of the sculpture and adding to the focus on volume, rather than sculptural mass.

Linear Construction in Space No. 1 (Variation) also echoes Gabo's early sculptural interest in mathematical and scientific models. As noted, Gabo's first use

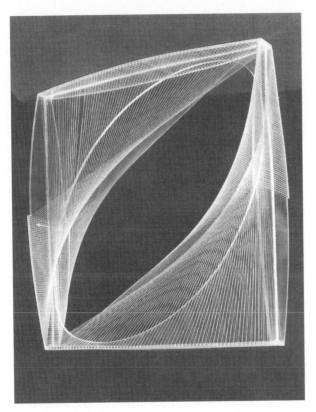

Linear Construction in Space No. 1 (Variation)
© Tate Gallery, London / Art Resource, NY

of string followed his exposure to Moore's work in a visit to Moore's studio. Moore's stringed sculpture derived directly from his study of mathematical models at the London Science Museum. Having connected to such models early in his own career, Gabo may well have found the association compelling. Gabo's stringed sculpture also suggests the appearance of a mathematical model through its emphasis on symmetry. The center ellipse functions as the axis around which the lines of string rotate. Split diagonally, *Linear Construction in Space No. 1 (Variation)* displays two identical halves in reversed opposition. The lines of nylon thread, repetitively circling the plastic form, also imply the mathematical concept of infinity. With no visible beginning or end, the tightly woven strings chart a continuous path.

Gabo went on to make myriad variations on his original *Linear Construction in Space No. 1*. Although none became large-scale public works, Gabo happily produced new versions to meet market demands, most of which he sold for £50 each. In 1946 he sold *Linear Construction in Space No. 1 (Variation)* to Margaret Pulsford, who presented it to the Tate Gallery in 1958.

RACHEL EPP BULLER

Further Reading

Hammer, Martin, and Christina Lodder, *Constructing Modernity: The Art and Career of Naum Gabo*, New Haven, Connecticut: Yale University Press, 2000

DOMENICO GAGGINI *ca.* 1425/30–1492
Italian

Domenico Gaggini (Gagini) was the most prominent member of the Gaggini family, a group of architects, sculptors, and masons who continued for generations from the 15th to the 17th centuries. Domenico Gaggini's activity can be traced from northern Italy in Genoa, to southern Italy in Naples, and ultimately to Sicily, where he established the Sicilian branch of the Gaggini workshop. The Sicilian Gaggini workshop continued into the first half of the 17th century, and Sicilian Renaissance sculpture cannot be mentioned without reference to Gaggini and his workshop.

Gaggini was born around 1425–30 in Bissone, Italy, near Lake Lugano and was trained by his father Pietro. Although he was initially influenced by the northern Gothic sculpture of Lombardy, his work was also shaped by Florentine Renaissance sculpture. Filarete's *Trattato di architettura* (1461–64; Treatise on Architecture) lists Gaggini as a disciple or pupil of the architect Filippo Brunelleschi of Florence. Gaggini's training in Florence exposed him to other Tuscan Renaissance masters, especially the work of Donatello and Ghiberti. Gaggini's contact with these sculptors had a profound impact on his style throughout his career. His style shows his interest in classicism, learned from the Florentine artists, together with a sense of ornament and decorative touches that betray his early encounter with northern Gothic art in Lombardy.

Gaggini returned to northern Italy, probably after the death of Brunelleschi in 1446. In 1448 he received his first and one of his most important commissions, the construction and sculptural decoration of the chapel of S. Giovanni for the Cathedral of San Lorenzo, Genoa. Although his nephew Elia assisted him, the relief sculpture with scenes from the life of St. John the Baptist are mostly by Gaggini. His facade for the chapel, not surprisingly, recalls the Classical facade for Brunelleschi's Pazzi Chapel, Florence, but embellished with decorative detail and ornament. Gaggini's efforts were concentrated on this chapel from 1448 to 1456–57. It is likely that Elia finished the chapel upon Gaggini's departure.

According to a document from 31 January 1458, Gaggini was employed in Naples to work on the triumphal arch of Alfonso of Aragon at the Castelnuovo.

Gaggini is recorded at work on the arch with a number of other sculptors, including Isaia da Pisa, Antonio di Chelino, Paolo da Milano, Francesco Laurana, and Paolo Romano. Questions of attribution have often plagued the work of Gaggini, whose work has frequently been confused with Laurana's. This confusion owes itself in part to the artists' association in Naples, and later in Sicily, and also to an account by Vasari who mistakenly paired the two in Florence in the workshop of Brunelleschi. There is no confusion, however, regarding Gaggini's work on the triumphal arch: a relief of an animated group of life-size musicians carved in high relief and a figure of *Temperance*, often regarded as one of the finest works on the arch. Gaggini departed Naples soon after Alfonso's death in June 1458. Other works completed at this time include the *Virgin and Child* statuette for a chapel at S. Barbara at the Castelnuovo (now Museo di Capodimonte, Naples) and the *Adoration of the Child*, which illustrates the artist's pictorial relief style.

After Naples, Gaggini headed for Palermo, Sicily, where he was responsible for the restoration of medieval mosaics in the Cappella Palatina (restoration *ca.* 1460). A 1463 document records a commission to Gaggini by Pietro Speciale for a sepulchral monument for his son Nicolò Antonio. The tomb and monument rediscovered in 1948 at S. Francesco d'Assisi, Palermo, recall Florentine funerary monuments, with which Gaggini would have become familiar during his apprenticeship in Florence. Some question the attribution, suggesting that its author is Laurana. A bust of Pietro Speciale was probably commissioned at this time and illustrates Gaggini's talents in the genre of the portrait bust.

Apart from a trip to the mainland in 1465, Gaggini spent the remainder of his life in Sicily, where he built a thriving workshop. He is responsible for the *Reliquary of S. Gandolfo*, a significant work from the last years of his life. In 1482 the Chiesa Madre of Polizzi Generosa commissioned from Gaggini the reliquary honoring the Franciscan saint Gandolfo da Binasco, who died in 1260. Even in this late work, the style and form exhibits the influence of Donatello. Another important late commission is the funerary monument to Bishop Giovanni Montaperto in the Cathedral of Mazara del Vallo. The fine quality of these works contrasts with the routine works executed by his workshop, often of the Madonna and child. Like many successful workshops, when the demand and production increased, much of the work was left to other hands, and the quality naturally suffered. Throughout Sicily one can find numerous Madonna and Child statues attributed to the master and/or his workshop. The attribu-

tions of many of these works continue to be challenged.

Gaggini died in September 1492 and was buried in S. Francesco d'Assisi, Palermo. His Sicilian workshop not only continued, but thrived primarily because of the activity of Antonello Gaggini (1478–1536), Domenico's son by his second wife Caterina. Antonello was trained by his father and was also influenced by Benedetto da Maiano, Laurana, and Michelangelo. Although Gaggini worked mainly in marble, Antonello worked in marble, terracotta, and papier mâché. He worked in Calabria and throughout Sicily, where his workshop dominated Sicilian artistic culture in Sicily. Antonello's most significant commission was the sculpture for the chancel of the Cathedral of Palermo.

Gaggini's workshop in Sicily, which thrived under Antonello's direction, was continued by Antonello's own sons, who also became sculptors: Giandomenico, Antonino, Giacomo, Fazio, and Vincenzo. Through several generations of Gaggini sculptors, the legacy of Domenico Gaggini endured into the 17th century.

STEPHANIE MILLER

See also **Benedetto da Maiano; Donatello (Donato di Betto Bardi); Ghiberti, Lorenzo; Laurana, Francesco; Michelangelo (Buonarroti)**

Biography

Born in Bissone, Italy, *ca.* 1425–30. Family included sculptors, masons, and architects. First trained with father, Pietro; other family members include Elia (nephew), Giovanni, Pace, and Antonello (son); trained in Filippo Brunelleschi's workshop in Florence, before 1448; influenced by Donatello; returned to northern Italy, 1448; moved to Naples to work at court of Alfonso of Aragon at Castelnuovo, 1457; after death of Alfonso, moved to Sicily and established branch of family workshop, 1463, and possibly as early as 1458. Died in Palermo, Sicily, 29/30 September 1492.

Selected Works

1448–56/57	Facade; marble; Chapel of S. Giovanni Battista, Cathedral of San Lorenzo, Genoa, Italy
1458	Figures of *Temperance* and musicians; marble; Arch of Castelnuovo, Naples, Italy
1458	*Virgin and Child*; marble; Museo di Capodimonte, Naples, Italy
ca. 1460	*Adoration of the Christ Child*; marble; National Gallery of Art, Washington, D.C., United States

1463   Tomb of Nicolò Antonio Speciale; marble;
         Church of S. Francesco d'Assisi, Palermo,
         Sicily

ca. 1468 Bust of Pietro Speciale; marble; Palazzo
         Speciale-Raffadali, Palermo, Sicily

1482   Reliquary of S. Gandolfo da Binesco;
         marble; Chiesa Madre, Polizzi Generosa,
         Sicily

ca. 1485 Tomb of Bishop Giovanni Montaperto;
         marble; Cathedral, Mazara del Vallo,
         Sicily

Further Reading

Bernini, R., "Gaggini, Domenico," in *Dizionario biografico degli italiani*, vol. 51, Rome: Istituto della Enciclopedia Italiana, 1988

Hersey, George L., *The Aragonese Arch at Naples, 1443–1475*, New Haven, Connecticut: Yale University Press, 1973

Kruft, Hanno-Walter, *Domenico Gagini und seine Werkstatt*, Munich: Bruckmann, 1972

Kruft, Hanno-Walter, "Gagini: Domenico Gagini," in *The Dictionary of Art*, edited by Jane Turner, vol. 11, New York: Grove, and London: Macmillan, 1996

Valentiner, Wilhelm Reinhold, "The Early Development of Domenico Gagini," *The Burlington Magazine* 76 (1940)

GARDEN SCULPTURE/SCULPTURE GARDENS

Sculpture has been an important element in gardens throughout history. During the last part of the 20th century, however, the concept of a *sculpture garden* emerged as distinctly different from a garden with sculpture. In the sculpture garden, sculpture takes a primary role in the garden and is not merely seen as an ornament.

For nearly 3000 years, artists have incorporated sculpture into the design of buildings, gardens, tombs, and public spaces as expressions of a particular society's religious, political, and artistic ideals. Although many of these ancient sites have been pillaged or destroyed, archaeologists have been able to determine much of the extent and location of the use of sculpture. Among the oldest of these sites is Queen Hatshepsut's funerary temple in Egypt near Thebes. Built around 1480 BCE, the design incorporated numerous figures (most were of the queen herself) carved from stone and arranged in rows approaching the temple. Other Egyptian temples were approached by way of long avenues of carved sphinxes protecting the temple precinct.

From 650 to 80 BCE ancient Greeks incorporated impressive statues into their temple complexes that commemorated the gods. The Acropolis in Athens, for example, housed an approximately nine-meter-tall *chryselephantine* statue of Athena that would have been carried from its location in the Parthenon out into the open area of the Acropolis on special occasions. The figure would have been an impressive and startling sight for visitors and enemies approaching Athens from the sea. In addition, Greek marketplaces contained sculptures honoring political and military heroes.

During the Roman Empire, from the 3rd century BCE to the 5th century CE, sculpture had many uses. Archaeologists have found numerous statues in the Roman Forum, the central district of Rome, as well as in courtyards of private residences. From palace courtyards to those of the middle class, statuary formed an essential component of homes in Pompeii. A peristyle walkway surrounded the enclosed courtyards, which often included plantings, a water feature, paintings of imaginary landscapes, and statuary. Statues usually defined the edges of pools and terraces and paid homage to patrons, ancestors, or household gods. Hadrian's Villa in Tivoli contained many statues illustrating Hadrian's extensive travels; the emperor would re-create buildings and gardens at his vast estate as a type of souvenir of his favorite places. Sculpture was an essential component of these tributes.

Sculptural stones of diverse sizes and character held prominent positions in Chinese and Japanese temples and gardens and were seen as sculptures of nature. Gardeners trained trees and shrubs to specific shapes, which, along with stones, were strongly sculptural and symbolic, creating sanctity, mood, and balance in the garden.

The use of stone sculpture during the Middle Ages was not common, but toward the end of the 14th century, the use of topiary—decorative shaping of shrubs, hedges, and borders—became quite popular. As gardeners became more adept at creating these sculptural and often architectural forms from plants, designs became more and more complex. Sculpted fountains in gardens introduced focal points in these spaces.

The 15th century marked the beginning of a dramatic increase of the use of sculpture in the garden, especially in Italy. Looking back at the Roman models of Antiquity, designers of the Renaissance created prominent positions for statues and sculpture in both public squares and private gardens. The great squares in Rome, Florence, and other Italian cities center on monumental statuary or fountains. The Medici Grand Dukes dominated 16th-century Florence, commissioning fountains and garden sculpture within the city and for their Tuscan villas. Villa d'Este in Tivoli is a marvel of fanciful sculpture and waterworks interwoven with the gardens. Some statuary represented mytholog-

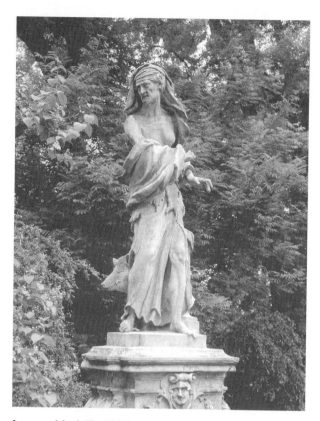

Lorenzo Mattielli, *Old Woman (Vanitas)*, Palais
Schwarzenberg, Vienna, *ca.* 1720
© Erich Lessing / Art Resource, NY

ical figures; other sculpture told the history of Rome.
Nearby Hadrian's Villa heavily influenced Villa
d'Este; some of the sculpture at Villa d'Este was actually taken from the ancient Roman estate. Villa Orsini
in Bomarzo is an excellent example of the Mannerist
response to the Renaissance garden; a large number of
colossal bizarre and primitive stone creatures inhabit
the garden. Among them are giants, two-headed dogs,
and monsters whose open mouths serve as passage-
ways; all of them play with notions of reality, scale,
and fantasy. The element of mystery and surprise is
strong in this garden, and the sculpture seems to take
on a life of its own.

Holland in the early 17th century embraced sculpture to the exclusion of flowers until bulbs came into
vogue. Isola Bella, an island in Italy, became a floating
garden of sculpture ornamenting Lake Maggiore. The
Herrenhausen Royal Gardens at Hanover remain an
extraordinary example of a sculpture-dominated garden. Perhaps in the use of sculpture in gardens, nothing
can surpass France with the great trinity of the Tuileries, Fontainebleau, and Versailles.

The gardens of Versailles (*ca.* 1668) and Vaux-le-
Vicomte (1661) demonstrate the use of sculpture in

the French Baroque garden most clearly; André Le
Nôtre designed both gardens. Work on Versailles was
begun about 1661 but was worked on many years and
completed by Le Nôtre before 1700. Gardens and their
details were designed at a heroic scale, and the domination of nature was evident throughout. Designers used
statuary and fountains in the garden to create focal
points, terminate axes, punctuate space, and create
rhythm in the garden along the wide, long walkways.
These sculptures depicted allegorical and mythological
figures meant to create dignity in the garden, thereby
elevating the status of the patron and reflecting the
patron's own personal imagery.

The English garden style that began to emerge at
the beginning of the 18th century turned its back on
the Italian and French Renaissance styles and created
wholly different landscapes. The use of sculptural elements in the garden was also quite different and took
the form of "follies" or "incidents" set out in the landscape for guests to discover. Designers often created
these follies to appear as ancient ruins and temples, to
provide focal points, and to modulate movement in the
various parts of the pastoral landscape. The gardens
of Stourhead, created in the middle of the 18th century,
provide an excellent example of this style. Structures
with allegorical references offered political commentary and delighted distinguished guests, who were encouraged to move through the garden and discover
each folly. The Temple of Worthies at Stowe also introduced a political message into an Arcadian landscape.

In the United States, although the gardens of Wes-
tover Plantation in Virginia incorporated sculptures as
early as 1726, lead or stones were expensive media
that limited their use. With the invention of Coade
stone in 1769 came a marked increase in the use of
sculpture in gardens. A notable forerunner was the garden created by Governor John Eager Howard at Belvedere in Baltimore, Maryland, in 1783, inspired by
the Vatican Belvedere of Pope Julius II (1504). The
Italian Renaissance had been marked by extensive garden construction, which Americans were copying by
the end of the 18th century. Representations of the
continents, the four seasons, and the five senses competed for pedestals with grazing animals, satyrs, uni-
corns, and other heraldic beasts.

Brookgreen Gardens, founded by sculptor Anna
Hyatt Huntington and her husband Archer Huntington
in 1931 on over 9000 acres of unspoiled land, claims
to be the first public sculpture garden in the United
States. Situated on the coast of South Carolina near
Myrtle Beach, Brookgreen has more than 500 sculptures on display.

The use of sculpture in outdoor spaces in the United
States can first be recognized, however, in conjunction

with the development of the city plaza and public park. Starting in the mid 19th century, sculptors received commissions for monuments of stone and bronze to decorate these spaces. Most were dedicated to Classical figures that represented ideals such as courage and freedom, but later statues emerged that were more realistic portraits of political and cultural heroes. Evidence of this trend is found in the numerous statues of victorious generals astride their horses in cities and towns throughout the United States.

Two influences that developed in the 1960s can be traced quite clearly to the creation of sculpture gardens as they are understood today. One was the requirement imposed by many local governments and the federal government on developers to dedicate a percentage of their project budget to public art. As a result, numerous sculptures have been designed for public outdoor spaces, most of which are more abstract in form than the previous figure compositions. Using modern materials and often bright colors, sculptors moved away from the typical commemorative piece and toward creating pieces that express an idea, convey a message, or explore the relationship between the artwork and its surroundings.

The other significant influence that developed during the 1960s was the emergence of environmental art, following the Minimalist movement. During this time artists began to question the concept of the art "object." They viewed the interior spaces of museums and galleries as limiting and homogenizing because they usually assumed a frontal engagement with the art piece. Artists who wanted to explore the spatial and behavioral aspects of their work found the conventions of interior space restricting. To avoid this confining environment, many artists looked to the outdoors to provide a new setting for their work. The living landscape was a growing, changing entity that offered an entirely different experience than that of the gallery for both artist and viewer. The environmental artist Robert Morris, comparing the spatial qualities of traditional gallery art and environmental art, described them as noun- and verb-type spaces. The gallery, or noun-type space, treats art as an object that is almost always disconnected from its surroundings. The open field, or verb-type space, treats the art as a changing, living form that confronts and integrates itself with its specific site.

Today, sculptures in gardens are no longer an affair of smoothly finished and instantly recognizable lions, centaurs, pineapples, nymphs, and dryads; they are just as likely to be scarred, pitted, and enigmatic. Auguste Rodin's Impressionism marked a watershed, although it was admittedly followed by a reaction epitomized in the sculptures of Carl Milles. The former standard gardening advice to plant bleeding heart or Virginia creeper around the base of a sculpture, thus bringing the sculpture "down to earth," now seems old-fashioned; the scope of garden sculpture has been extended to include almost any scheme involving three-dimensional space and has moved away from permanent exhibits; some collections, such as Hat Hill Copse in England, try to make changes every year. The David Smith collection at the Storm King Art Center in Mountainville, New York, has experimented with a three-year cycle drawn from the permanent collection and from other collections. The Storm King Art Center is perhaps the largest sculpture garden, covering a 500-acre site.

In the contemporary sculpture garden, the sculptor places the artwork with consideration of its natural surroundings as background as well as with an eye to creating relationships between pieces. The more successful sculpture gardens influence viewers' perceptions of the artwork by defining the space and creating views and approaches. These controlled perspectives heighten curiosity and suggest potential discovery, extending the experiential aspects of the garden. The mystery of the three-dimensional object and its relationship to the landscape increases the viewer's desire for discovering the artist's intention. The sculpture may also suggest a literary, mythological, or historical narrative that increases the viewer's interest and appreciation and in turn enhances the sense of place in the garden. The outdoor conditions of weather, light, season, and time also extend the experience of the garden by offering different experiences with each visit.

The Gustav Vigeland display in Frogner Park near Oslo, Norway, is one such example. Vigeland created this 75-acre park over a period of some 20 years (1924–42) to feature more than 200 granite and bronze statues. A three-kilometer walk is intended to parallel life's journey, with sculptures to match, highlighted by an almost 16-meter-high monolith carved with more than 125 figures. The Kröller-Müller Museum in the Netherlands presents a number of experiences through the creation of a variety of enclosures and views related to various pieces. The sculptures in the Henry Moore Sculpture Garden at the Nelson-Atkins Museum in Kansas City, Missouri, seem to inhabit the landscape and respond to Moore's belief that sculpture should be viewed with nature. Ian Hamilton Finlay's garden in Scotland combines sculpture with poetry and guides the viewer through the garden by way of a series of spaces and narratives. At Grizedale Forest in Cumbria, England, artists are invited to create artworks using materials found in the forest; many of these works have a fleeting existence.

Numerous sculpture gardens exist, and new ones are being developed regularly in both public and private realms. A growing number of museums now consider the sculpture garden to be a major and indispensable exhibit area. Many museums hope to attract new and varied audiences to their collections by creating sculpture gardens. The relaxing and natural setting, combined with the creative and skilled display of artwork, helps to achieve this objective by facilitating the introduction of large numbers of visitors to the imaginative forms and ideas of contemporary sculpture.

ELIZABETH R. MESSER DIEHL and PAUL RICH

See also **Chryselephantine; Fountain Sculpture; Milles, Carl; Minimalism; Moore, Henry; Morris, Robert; Public Sculpture; Rodin, Auguste; Smith, David; Vigeland, Gustav**

Further Reading

Bradley-Hole, Christopher, *The Minimalist Garden*, New York: Monacelli Press, 1999

Coffin, David R., "Statuary Gardens," in *Gardens and Gardening in Papal Rome*, by Coffin, Princeton, New Jersey: Princeton University Press, 1991

Farrar, Linda, "Garden Sculpture," in *Ancient Roman Gardens*, by Farrar, Stroud, Gloucestershire: Sutton, 1998

Jashemski, Wilhelmina, *The Gardens of Pompeii, Herculaneum, and the Villas Destroyed by Vesuvius*, 2 vols., New Rochelle, New York: Caratzas Brothers, 1979–93

Lazzaro, Claudia, *The Italian Renaissance Garden: From the Conventions of Planting, Design, and Ornament to the Grand Gardens of Sixteenth-Century Italy*, New Haven, Connecticut: Yale University Press, 1990

MacDougall, Elisabeth B. (editor), *Fons Sapientiae: Renaissance Garden Fountains*, Washington, D.C.: Dumbarton Oaks Trustees, 1978

MacDougall, Elisabeth B. (editor), *Medieval Gardens*, Washington, D.C.: Dumbarton Oaks Research Library and Collection, 1983

MacDougall, Elisabeth B. (editor), *Ancient Roman Villa Gardens*, Washington, D.C.: Dumbarton Oaks Research Library and Collection, 1987

MacDougall, E. B., *Fountains, Statues, and Flowers: Studies in Italian Gardens of the Sixteenth and Seventeenth Centuries*, Washington, D.C.: Dumbarton Oaks Research Library and Collection, 1994

Osmundson, Theodore, "Sculpture Garden Garden Sculpture: Designing the Difference," *Landscape Architecture* 73/1 (1983)

Pereire, Anita, *Gardens for the 21st Century*, London: Aurum, 1999

Ridgway, Brunilde Sismondo, "Greek Antecedents of Garden Sculpture," in *Ancient Roman Gardens*, edited by Elisabeth B. MacDougall and Wilhelmina Mary Feemster Jashemski, Washington, D.C.: Dumbarton Oaks Trustees, 1981

Treib, Marc, "Sculpture and Garden: A Historical Overview," *Design Quarterly* 141 (1988)

HENRI GAUDIER-BRZESKA 1891–1915

French, active in England

During his brief career, Henri Gaudier-Brzeska established himself as one of the leaders of the London prewar avant-garde and a seminal figure in the short-lived Vorticist group. Despite his chameleon-like versatility and the eclecticism of his still-youthful work (which makes him a fascinating barometer of the cultural crosscurrents of the period), he was highly regarded by contemporaries as diverse as Jacob Epstein; the poet, polemicist, and fellow Vorticist Ezra Pound; the Camden Town artists; and the author and critic Roger Fry. Gaudier-Brzeska's pithy advocacy of direct carving proved inspirational to sculptors working in Britain during the 1920s, especially Henry Moore and Frank Dobson. Little known outside London art circles during his lifetime, Gaudier-Brzeska's reputation as a sculptor, polemicist, and draftsman developed posthumously through Pound's *Memoir* (1916) and H.S. Ede's popular *Savage Messiah* (1931). Gaudier-Brzeska's work slowly entered public collections through the dispersal of John Quinn's collection in the United States and through Ede, who acquired the bulk of Gaudier-Brzeska's work following the death of the artist's companion, Sophie Brzeska. Ede subsequently dispersed carvings, posthumous bronzes from uncast plasters, and numerous drawings to public collections in Britain, the United States, and to the artist's native France, where he was virtually unknown until the 1950s. Gaudier-Brzeska is now recognized as a catalytic figure in British 20th-century sculpture based on the strength of his writing and sculptures produced between 1912 and 1914.

Lacking a conventional academic art training, Gaudier-Brzeska learned by sketching from nature, everyday life, museum objects, prints, and magazine illustrations. Life drawings of people, birds, and animals—often executed at speed in fountain pen, his economy of line and eye for movement yielding both mass and intense vitality—provided the essential grounding for the sculpture he began to make from about 1910. In contrast to the hieratic, symmetrical compositions favored by Epstein and Constantin Brancusi and the abstract planar and static effects of early Cubist sculpture, Gaudier-Brzeska's grasp of organic structure imparts dynamism to even his most abstract work.

Modeled pieces such as *Workman Fallen from a Scaffold* and *Self-Portrait (Idiot)* have a Rodinesque fluency that culminates in the sinuous bronze *Dancer*, based on studies of the painter Nina Hamnett; successive movements fuse with seamless grace, as if embodying Henri Bergson's theories on flux and duration, which Gaudier-Brzeska had studied. Produced only a few weeks later, *Red Stone Dancer* is a startlingly modernist treatment of the same theme. Its circular base and rotational movement enhance the tension and physical abandon suggested by the rhythmic torsion of the limbs. In this key work, the dense simplified volumes and motifs culled from African woodcarving and from Brancusi transform an essentially Classical figure composition. *Bird Swallowing Fish*, Gaudier-Brzeska's riposte to Epstein's contemporaneous *Doves*, is enriched by the former's years of studying wildlife. Gaudier-Brzeska conveys the climactic moment of predatory violence largely by the gaping, engulfing throat of the bird, which forms the crux of the composition. He was to go much further in using massed volumes piled in syncopated rhythms in *Stags* (1914) and *Birds Erect*, in which the figurative starting point is almost completely subsumed into an abstract composition.

Gaudier-Brzeska's sculpture underwent rapid metamorphoses as he responded to the artists, writers, and cultures he encountered and associated with different cliques within the London art world. A group of modeled portraits, such as those of his painter friends Alfred Wolmark and Horace Brodzky, reflect his first contacts with Cubism as well as his satirical edge, sharpened by his study of Charles Keene, Jean-Louis Forain, Henri Toulouse-Lautrec, and others. Meeting Epstein in 1912 and seeing that artist's tomb of Oscar Wilde in the studio intensified Gaudier-Brzeska's engagement with direct carving and brought him into a relationship of emulation and rivalry, which is apparent in *Bird Swallowing Fish, Caritas*, the phallic *Doorknocker*, and above all, the *Head of Ezra Pound*, which can be seen as the counterpart of Epstein's *Rock Drill*. During his association with Roger Fry's Omega Workshops, Gaudier-Brzeska designed a number of household articles, and both his drawings and carvings are characterized by simplified, blunted contours, notably the carved plaster *Wrestlers* relief and the alabaster *Boy with Coney*. By early 1914 his increasingly close association with Ezra Pound, Wyndham Lewis, and the nascent Vorticist group stimulated increasingly abstract and aggressively sexual imagery; Gaudier-Brzeska's largest sculpture, the Easter Island–inspired *Head of Ezra Pound*, commissioned by the poet, is a monumental phallic totem. Less commented upon but arguably more original were the small carved semifunctional pieces that require no plinth and can be placed several different ways up. Modeled on the handiness of Japanese netsuke or Maori tiki, rigorously geometric works such as *Torpedo Fish* opened up possibilities more fully explored in Gaudier-Brzeska's sketchbook drawings.

Naturally drawn to debate, Gaudier-Brzeska was a signatory of the Vorticist Manifesto in 1914 and became the most articulate advocate of an uncompromisingly Modernist sculptural program that jettisoned the entire Classical tradition in favor of intuition and admiration for "the savage peoples of the earth." The opening of his bravura Imagist essay on world sculpture in the Vorticist journal *Blast*—"Sculptural energy is the mountain. / Sculptural feeling is the appreciation of masses in relation. / Sculptural ability is the defining of these masses by planes"—established a formal agenda that became something of mantra for Moore and his contemporaries. Gaudier-Brzeska argued for direct carving as *the* modern sculptural technique: "The sculpture I admire is the work of master craftsmen. Every inch is won at the point of the chisel—every stroke of the hammer is a physical and mental effort. No more arbitrary translations of a design in any material" (see Pound, 1960).

Notwithstanding his polemical stance, Gaudier-Brzeska continued to model in clay as well as carve in stone and frequently reengaged with the Classical tradition, as in *Maternity*, his three small *Torsos*, and *Seated Woman*, one of his last works. His ambivalence gave rise to still unresolved, and perhaps unresolvable, controversy about the ultimate direction of his work, Pound asserting the primacy of Vorticist abstraction while others such as Brodzky and Fry saw the Vorticist pieces as a temporary diversion from the naturalistic thrust of Gaudier-Brzeska's talent.

EVELYN SILBER

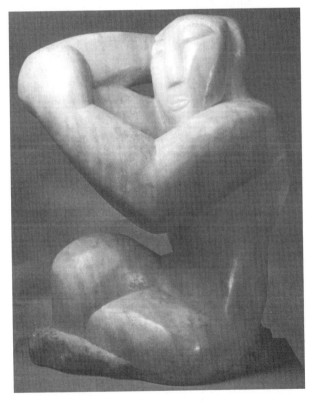

Seated Woman
© Burstein Collection / CORBIS

Biography

Born in Saint-Jean-de-Braye, France, 4 October 1891. Both parents from artisan families, father a carpenter. Educated at the École Municipale Professionelle, Orléans, France; won national scholarship to train for commercial career; attended Merchant Venturers' Technical College, Bristol, England, 1907–08; studied in Nuremberg and Munich for three months in 1909; began creating sculptures, 1910; met Sophie Brzeska in 1910; adopted surname Gaudier-Brzeska and moved to England, January 1911; established studio, January 1913; elected to London Group, 1914; elected chairman of Artists' Committee for the Allied Artists Association, 1914; signatory of the Vorticist Manifesto, 1914; joined French army, September, 1914, and selected for officer training; shot by bullet to the head. Died in Neuville-Saint-Vaast, France, 5 June 1915.

Selected Works

1912   *Self-Portrait (Idiot)*; bronze; casts in Tate Gallery, London, England; Art Gallery of Auckland, New Zealand; Albright-Knox Art Gallery, Buffalo, New York, United States; Scottish National Gallery of Modern Art, Edinburgh, Scotland

1912–13 *Wrestler*; lead; edition of two: City Art Gallery, Leeds, England; Hirshhorn Museum and Sculpture Garden, Washington, D.C., United States; bronze; casts: National Museum of Wales, Cardiff, Wales; Bristol Museum and Art Gallery, England

1913   *Dancer*; plaster, bronze; Tate Gallery, London, England; bronze casts: Christ Church Picture Gallery, Oxford, England; Kettle's Yard, Cambridge, England

1913   *Horace Brodzky*; painted plaster; Fogg Art Museum, Cambridge, Massachusetts, United States; bronze casts: City Art Gallery, Leeds, England; Bristol Museum and Art Gallery, England; Fogg Art Museum, Cambridge, Massachusetts, United States; Tate Gallery, London, England; National Gallery of Canada, Ottawa, Canada

1913   *Maternity*; marble; Musée Nationale d'Art Moderne, Centre Georges Pompidou, Paris, France

1913   *Torso 1*; Sicilian marble; Tate Gallery, London, England

1913   *Wrestlers*; carved plaster relief; Boston Museum of Fine Arts, Massachusetts, United States

1914   *Bird Swallowing Fish*; painted plaster; Kettle's Yard, Cambridge, England; bronze casts: Tate Gallery, London, England; Kunsthalle, Bielefeld, Germany; Kröller-Müller Museum, Otterloo, the Netherlands; Scottish National Gallery of Modern Art, Edinburgh, Scotland; Musée Nationale d'Art Moderne, Centre Georges Pompidou, Paris, France

1914   *Birds Erect*; limestone; Museum of Modern Art, New York City, United States

1914   *Boy with Coney*; alabaster; private collection

1914   *Doorknocker*; cut brass; Kettle's Yard, Cambridge, England

1914   *Head of Ezra Pound* (exhibited in Whitechapel Art Gallery, 1914); Pentelic marble; private collection, Ray Nasher Collection, United States

1914   *Red Stone Dancer*; waxed and polished Mansfield stone; Tate Gallery, London, England

1914   *Seated Woman*; marble; Musée Nationale d'Art Moderne, Centre Georges Pompidou, Paris, France

1914   *Torpedo Fish*; cut bronze; Art Gallery of Ontario, Toronto, Canada

Further Reading

Brodzky, Horace, *Henri Gaudier-Brzeska, 1891–1915*, London: Faber and Faber, 1933

Brodzky, Horace (editor), *Gaudier-Brzeska Drawings*, London: Faber and Faber, 1946

Cole, Roger, *Burning to Speak: The Life and Art of Henri Gaudier-Brzeska*, Oxford: Phaidon, and New York: Dutton, 1978

Cole, Roger, *Gaudier-Brzeska: Artist and Myth*, Bristol, England: Sansom, 1995

Ede, H.S., *A Life of Gaudier-Brzeska*, London: Heinemann, 1930; as *Savage Messiah*, London: Heinemann, and New York: Alfred Knopf, 1931

Gaudier-Brzeska, Henri, *Gaudier-Brzeska: Drawings and Sculpture*, London: Cory Adams and Mackay, 1965

Pound, Ezra, *Gaudier-Brzeska: A Memoir*, London: The Bodley Head, 1916; new edition, Hessle: Marvell Press, and New York: New Directions, 1960

Secrétain, Roger, *Un sculpteur maudit: Gaudier-Brzeska*, Paris: Le Temps, 1979

Silber, Evelyn, *Gaudier-Brzeska: Life and Art*, London and New York: Thames and Hudson, 1996

PAUL GAUGUIN 1848–1903 *French*

Paul Gauguin modeled and carved a variety of two- and three-dimensional sculpture and functional objects throughout his career. His sculptures range from conventional portraits and architectural reliefs to functional objects and ceramics.

Gauguin's first known sculpture is the portrait bust of his wife, Metta, which he executed in 1877 while living in the house of the sculptor and stonecutter Jules Bouillot. That same year Gauguin sculpted a portrait of his son, Emil; a marble version of the same was carved in 1894. These works are close to the style of academic sculpture of the second half of the 19th century.

Gauguin quickly abandoned the academic tradition. He became associated with the Impressionists and began experimenting with materials and techniques that were new to him, using wood, potter's clay, and polychromy. After his early works, Gauguin showed a definite preference for the relief as opposed to sculpture in the round. Wood remained his preferred material for sculpture for the rest of his career.

In 1881 Gauguin exhibited two sculptures in wood, *The Little Parisian Girl* and *La Chanteuse* (the Singer). Their style marks a break with his conventional earlier work, as well as his debut as a woodcarver. In 1886 he began studying ceramics with Ernest Chaplet and created several ceramic pieces until his departure in 1887 to Tahiti, where he became influenced by that nonindustrial culture's carvings. Gauguin referred to his ceramics as ceramic sculpture; he worked with the ceramic clay directly instead of contributing solely to the decoration of ceramic wares. Inspired by pre-Columbian art, Gauguin's early ceramics helped him develop his personal vocabulary.

After the return from his journey in 1887, Gauguin became deeply influenced by Symbolism. Fascinated with the forms of sculpture produced by Mayan and Oceanic cultures, he continued woodcarving by developing Martinican themes through a more sophisticated use of symbols.

One of his major projects in woodcarving, the relief *Be in Love and You Will Be Happy* (*Soyez amoureuses, vous serez heureuse*) in linden-wood, was Gauguin's most ambitious sculpture to date. Carved in Brittany, the relief addresses the theme of love with bitterness and acerbity. In 1890 he carved a companion piece to *Be in Love*, a linden-wood relief called *Be Mysterious* (*Soyez mystérieuses*). Inspired by a fragment from a Javanese building in the Universal Exhibition in 1889, Gauguin produced a carving of a Caribbean woman in painted wood.

The art of nonindustrialized cultures appealed greatly to Gauguin, whose rejection of Western civilization led to his departure to Tahiti and to his efforts to express through his art the life among non-Western, nonindustrial peoples. Gauguin departed for Oceania in a bid to escape the trappings of civilization and rediscover a spiritual simplicity that he had initially sought among the peasants of Brittany. His stay in Tahiti coincided with his artistic maturity. While studying the native arts, Gauguin began to carve works expressing his ideas about Polynesian mythology. His small-scale wooden sculptures combine Oceanic motifs with Asian iconography, expressing his search for a different type of collective spirituality. For example, in his *Idol with Pearl* he carved a seated image of Buddha and two Oceanic anthropomorphic figures.

When Gauguin returned to France in 1893, he hoped that the sculptures he had brought back from the South Seas would have a great success, but the public failed to appreciate these works. Although he meant his second departure to Oceania to be a farewell to his artistic career, his final move to the Pacific Islands coincided with a period of intense creativity. He sculpted five roughly carved panels, *Maison du jouir* (House of Pleasure), for a door frame for his hut in the Marquesas. The theme of these panels harkens back to the two major panels of 1889–90, *Be in Love* and *Soyez mystérieuses*.

Gauguin's art can be divided into the Impressionism of his early work and the synthetism and exotic Symbolism of his mature years. He devoted a large part of his artistic creation to sculpture and renewed the sculptural tradition by focusing on the art of non-European traditions. By embracing arts and crafts, he forged his ideal of an artist-artisan and dissolved the boundaries between sculpture and decorative arts. He did not intend his three-dimensional functional objects (vases, knife handles, spoons, canes, wine casks) for exhibition or sale. They merely helped fulfill his wish that his house be decorated with carved wood. After Gauguin's death, the poet Victor Segalen bought *Maison du jouir*,

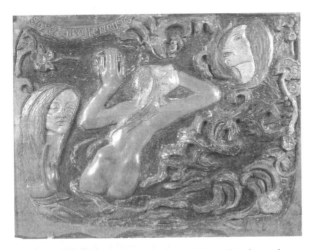

Be Mysterious (Soyez mystérieuses), 1890, painted wood relief, Musée d'Orsay, Paris
© Scala / Art Resource, NY

although the panels today are at the Musée d'Orsay in Paris.

Gauguin visually challenged the constraining narratives of art and artifacts and introduced primitivism into Western European sculpture. His rejection of the industrialized West and his metaphysical inquiries provided a source of inspiration for an entire generation of sculptors in the early 20th century and deeply influenced some of the sculptural accomplishments of Pablo Picasso and Henri Matisse. Indeed, Gauguin's example portends the influence of African sculpture on pre-Cubist Picasso and of pre-Columbian South American sculpture on Henry Moore. An important collection of Gauguin's sculptures resides at the Musée d'Orsay in Paris.

ANNA TAHINCI

Biography

Born in Paris, France, 7 June 1848. Childhood in colonial Lima, Peru; adolescence in Orléans, France, then in Paris; traveled throughout the world with the merchant marine, 1865; settled in Paris as a stockbroker, 1872; met Camille Pissaro, 1874; worked with him at Académie de Colarossi, Paris; exhibited at the Salon for the first time, 1876; showed regularly with the Impressionists in the 1880s; moved around Europe before settling back in France; worked with ceramist Ernest Chaplet then went to Breton village of Pont-Aven, 1886; traveled to Panama, then to Martinique, 1887; spent time in the French provinces in 1888 (in Pont-Aven with Emile Bernard, in Arles with Vincent van Gogh); frequent trips between Brittany and Paris, 1889–91; first move to Tahiti, 1891–93; in Paris, 1893–95; departed for Tahiti again, 1895; attempted suicide, 1898; left Tahiti for Marquesas Islands, 1901. Died in Atuana, Marquesas Islands, 8 May 1903.

Selected Works

1877   *Portrait of Mette Gauguin*; marble; Courtauld Institute of Art, London, England
1881   *La Chanteuse*; wood (location unknown)
1881   *The Little Parisian Girl*; wood; private collection; plaster version: The Detroit Institute of Arts, Michigan, United States
1889   *Caribbean Woman*; painted wood (location unknown)
1889   *Be in Love and You Will be Happy* (*Soyez amoureuses, vous serez heureuse*); linden-wood; Museum of Fine Arts, Boston, Massachusetts, United States
1890   *Be Mysterious* (*Soyez mystérieuses*); painted linden-wood relief, Musée d'Orsay, Paris, France

1894   *Idol with Pearl*; wood; Musée d'Orsay, Paris, France
1894   *Oviri*; stoneware; Musée d'Orsay, Paris, France
1894   *Portrait of Emil Gauguin*; marble; Metropolitan Museum of Art, New York City, United States
1901   *Maison du jouir* (House of Pleasure); wooden relief panels; Musée d'Orsay, Paris, France

Further Reading

Brettell, Richard R., *The Art of Paul Gauguin*, Washington, D.C.: National Gallery of Art, 1988
Cachin, Françoise, *Gauguin: "Ce malgré moi de sauvage,"* Paris: Gallimard, 1989
Gauguin, Pola, *Paul Gauguin*, Oslo: Gyldendal Norsk Forlag, 1937; as *My Father, Paul Gauguin*, translated by Arthur G. Chater, New York: Knopf, 1937
Gray, Christopher, *Sculpture and Ceramics of Paul Gauguin*, Baltimore, Maryland: Johns Hopkins University Press, 1963

BERNARDUS GELDUINUS 11TH CENTURY (dates unknown) *French*

Bernardus Gelduinus is inscribed as the maker of the altar table in the sanctuary of St. Sernin in Toulouse, France. Although no date is inscribed, this altar is accepted as the one dedicated at Toulouse on 24 May 1096 by Pope Urban II, and scholars of Romanesque art have accepted the hypothesis that the inscription names the artist. The top of the altar is carved with lobes and decorative vegetal forms typical of a group of marble altars of the 11th century. The edges, however, are treated in a way unique to this piece. The vertical sides feature decorative rows of imbrications, and the beveled edges below have been carved with figural decoration. On the front a bust of the youthful Christ in a pearled roundel is held by two angels who turn their heads away and whose bodies extend as if flying. Two more angels on the outer ends of the frieze hold a cross and a veil. On the two short sides, heads appear in roundels joined by clusters of leaves, and on the back is a frieze of birds.

The origins of the Gelduinus style remain uncertain. Current scholarship suggests that small-scale art, particularly in ivory and metal, could have been the source for the figural imagery found in his work. Ottonian, and even Carolingian, precedents are cited. However, the skill exhibited in his work at St. Sernin is not consistent with an artist working in an unfamiliar medium. If, as has been suggested, Gelduinus's training was in the small-scale arts of Germany, he was already a practiced stone carver before he received the commission for the Toulouse altar table and reliefs.

Other works at St. Sernin, including seven marble relief slabs now installed in the ambulatory, three capitals reused on the jambs of the Porte Miègeville, and a group of capitals and impost blocks in the transept, are attributed to Gelduinus or, on the basis of stylistic similarities, to his marble-carving workshop. These sculptures carry tremendous importance because they date relatively firmly to the very threshold of the revival of monumental stone sculpture in the Middle Ages. No other work of such plasticity and monumentality can be dated earlier than 1100 with any certainty.

Although the table must originally have served as the main altar of the church, the intended installation of the relief slabs is unknown. Their present location, inserted into the ambulatory walls, is recent. Scholars have suggested a variety of possible uses for the slabs: as cloister piers, reliefs flanking a doorway, a choir screen, or a ciborium constructed around the relics of St. Saturninus. The excellent condition of the relief surfaces suggests that they have always been used indoors, but no documents survive that attest to their locations before the 19th century. A record exists of a donation of four reliefs of angels from demolished churches made to St. Sernin in 1825 by the mayor of Toulouse, but no other documents referring to the reliefs have been uncovered.

The seven reliefs form two groups that differ in scale and show somewhat divergent styles. The first group includes a Christ in majesty, a seraph, and a cherub, each approximately 1.2 meters high. These reliefs show consistent faces with high cheekbones, long, swelling jowls, and smooth, rounded eyes. The drapery is cut with curving double lines for folds and broad, polished surfaces. Parallel vertical folds fall to a nearly straight hemline on the standing figures. There are clear similarities in style, despite the difference in scale, between the heads on the altar table frieze and these three marble figures. The second group consists of four figures of somewhat larger scale, the reliefs measuring over 1.8 meters in height. Two angels form a symmetrical pair, one facing left and pointing right, the other facing right and pointing left. Two saints face the front in the remaining reliefs, each with his right hand raised in blessing. One holds an open book in his left hand, the other a closed volume. The drapery style on these four corresponds closely to that on the group of three. However, the heads are treated differently, with rounder faces and drilled pupils as well as closely fitting caps of hair arranged in tight curls.

Other sculptures at St. Sernin associated with the style of Gelduinus include three capitals now installed on the Porte Miègeville. Two of these were clearly not made for this location because they were carved on all four sides, even though in their current installation only three are visible. One to the left of the portal depicts

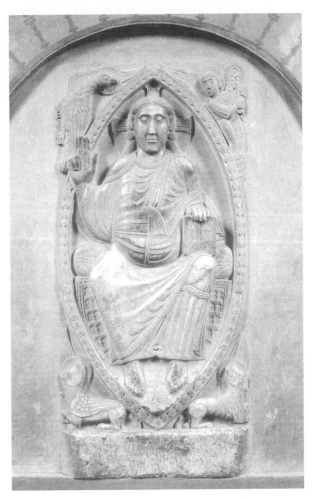

Christ in Majesty, Church of St. Sernin, Toulouse, France
The Conway Library, Courtauld Institute of Art

the Annunciation and the Visitation, whereas the one to the right is carved with the expulsion from the Garden of Eden. On the far left is a third capital, similar in style to the first two but coursed into the masonry, depicting the massacre of the innocents. Thomas W. Lyman has related these capitals to the altar table carvings and has suggested that the two reused ones might have formed a part of the same sanctuary program as the reliefs. Additionally, a series of seven capitals found in the third and fourth bays of the transept triforium share stylistic features with the altar table and reliefs. Especially close are a capital of Christ in a *mandorla* held by angels and flanked by apostles, and one depicting a standing figure holding an open book. An entablature close to the crossing has a particularly interesting subject: two clerics present a square tablet, possibly representing the completed altar table.

The style of the Gelduinus workshop is related to that in a number of locations in southern France and northern Spain in the early years of the 12th century.

Sculptures from Jaca and Saint-Caprais at Agen in the style of the altar table carvers suggest the possibility of sculptors who moved from site to site as work was needed. The influence of the Gelduinus style is visible in the relief slabs from the cloister at Moissac of around 1100, and from the early 12th century in the Porte Miègeville at St. Sernin, the Puerta de las Platerias at Santiago de Compostela, and the portals of San Isidoro in León.

MARJORIE J. HALL

Biography

Active in the south of France in the last years of the 11th century. Known only from an inscription on a marble altar in the Church of St. Sernin in Toulouse, France, which reads, in part, "Bernardus Gelduinus me fec" (Bernardus Gelduinus made me); this altar table, universally accepted as the one dedicated at St. Sernin by Pope Urban II in 1096, provides the only documentary evidence for the sculptor's activity; however, other work at St. Sernin has been attributed to him on the basis of style.

Selected Works

ca. 1096 Altar; marble; Church of St. Sernin, Toulouse, France

ca. 1096 Reliefs of *Christ in Majesty*, a seraph, and a cherub; marble; Church of St. Sernin, Toulouse, France

ca. 1096 Reliefs of two angels and two saints; marble; Church of St. Sernin, Toulouse, France

Further Reading

Cabanot, J., "Le décor sculpté de la basilique Saint-Sernin de Toulouse," *Bulletin monumental* 132 (1974)

Durliat, M., "L'atelier de Bernard Gilduin à Saint-Sernin de Toulouse," *Anuario de estudios medievales* 1 (1964)

Durliat, M., "Les cryptes de Saint-Sernin de Toulouse: Bilan des recherches récentes," *Les monuments historiques de la France* 17 (1971)

Durliat, M., "Les origines de la sculpture romane à Toulouse et à Moissac," *Cahiers de civilisation médiévale* 12 (1969)

Gerke, F., "Der Tischaltar des Bernard Gilduin in Saint-Sernin in Toulouse," *Akademie der Wissenschaften und der Literatur, Abhandlungen der geistes und socialwissenschaftlichen Klasse* 8 (1958)

Hearn, M.F., *Romanesque Sculpture: The Revival of Monumental Stone Sculpture in the Eleventh and Twelfth Centuries*, Ithaca, New York: Cornell University Press, and Oxford: Phaidon, 1981

Lyman, Thomas W., "Arts somptuaires et art monumental: Bilan des influences auliques pré-romanes sur la sculpture romane dans le sud-ouest de la France et en Espagne," *Les cahiers de Saint-Michel de Cuxa* 9 (1978)

Lyman, Thomas W., "Bernardus Gelduinus," in *The Dictionary of Art*, edited by Jane Turner, vol. 3, New York: Grove, and London: Macmillan, 1996

Lyman, Thomas W., "Notes on the Porte Miègeville Capitals and the Construction of Saint-Sernin in Toulouse," *Art Bulletin* 49 (1967)

Lyman, Thomas W., "La table d'autel de Bernard Gilduin et son ambience originelle," *Les cahiers de Saint-Michel de Cuxa* 13 (1982)

Moralejo Alvarez, S., "Une sculpture du style de Bernard Gelduin à Jaca," *Bulletin monumental* 131 (1973)

Terpak, F., "Pilgrimage or Migration? A Case Study of Artistic Movement in the Early Romanesque," *Zeitschrift für Kunstgeschichte* 51 (1988)

VINCENZO GEMITO 1852–1929 *Italian*

Vincenzo Gemito's style defies simple categorization. An accomplished chronicler of quotidian life in Naples who represented street urchins and gypsies with startling verism, Gemito lacked the political sentiment that motivated contemporary social realist sculptors such as Constantin Meunier. Gemito's portraits of friends and fellow artists convey a pulsating immediacy that distances them from the stiff idealization associated with academic Classicism. Nonetheless, he was profoundly inspired by ancient art and frequently emulated Classical sources in his work. Many of his early terracottas and bronzes are distinguished by the vigorous modeling of their almost impressionistic surfaces, in which linear contour dissolves in a play of scattered light, anticipating Medardo Rosso's work of the mid 1880s. Nevertheless, Gemito's use of sinewy, undulating line became a characteristic feature of his late, precisely finished compositions. Combining the influence of antique and Renaissance sculpture with the keen observation of everyday life, Gemito was one of the most talented, enigmatic, and stylistically independent sculptors of late 19th-century Europe.

At the age of nine, Gemito, the adopted son of poor Neapolitan parents, entered the studio of sculptor Emanuele Caggiano, who had won the commission for a winged *Victory* in the Piazza dei Martiri in Naples. There the young boy learned to draw and began a lifelong friendship with the painter Antonio Mancini. A few years later Gemito moved to the workshop of Stanisloa Lista, where he began modeling in clay and wax. Gemito's artistic debut came in 1868 when his statuette *Card Player* was featured in the first exhibition of the Promotrice di Belle Arti and acquired by King Victor Emmanuel II for the royal residence at Capodimonte. Gemito also entered a model of *Brutus* in the annual Academy of Fine Arts competition, which attracted critical notice and earned him a commission to produce it in marble for Cesare Correnti, the minister of public education. By this time Gemito had set up his own studio in an abandoned cloister, working alongside other sculptors of Neapolitan street life such as Achille d'Orsi.

Around 1869–70 Gemito completed a bust of the painter Vincenzo Petrocelli, initiating a remarkable series of portraits that captured the essential psychological and creative spirit of such fellow artists as Domenico Morelli, Francesco Paolo Michetti (1873), Giuseppe Verdi, and Mariano Fortuny. The irregular, jagged truncation of these busts recalls antique fragments and suggests that Gemito's 1877 trip to Paris, where he would have encountered similar works by Jean-Baptiste Carpeaux, only reinforced the independent stylistic inclinations already apparent in his sculpture. While in France, Gemito was a guest of the realist painter Ernest Meissonier, whose granddaughter Charlotte he later portrayed in an intimate portrait that captures the restless movement and soft features of infancy.

At the French Salon of 1877, Gemito exhibited his statue *Little Fisherboy*, a composition he had been developing since 1875. Unlike François Rude's and Carpeaux's earlier, more romanticized versions of this theme, Gemito's *Little Fisherboy* seems plucked off the streets, squatting precariously, with back arched and chin tucked, to examine his catch. The convincing pragmatism of his action contrasts sharply with the more sentimental gesture of Carpeaux's boy holding a shell to his ear and Rude's figure teasing a turtle. The rocky base, matted hair, and faceted surface of the youthful flesh demonstrate Gemito's early preference for sketchy modeling, which helps explain his almost total avoidance of marble, a medium he considered frigid and dull. *Little Fisherboy* also illustrates Gemito's interest in the expressive potential of an instantaneous pose and his combination of animated surface and gesture to create a sense of movement.

Returning to Naples in 1880, Gemito became intensely interested in ancient sculpture, particularly the exquisite bronzes excavated from Pompeii and Herculaneum. His *Water Carrier* refers to Classical prototypes in its nudity and the ancient water trough that serves as a base. However, Gemito tempered the influence of the antique by his realistic rendering of the youth's crooked grin, tousled hair, curled toes, and earthy sensuality. Gemito's 1883 bust of his adoptive mother's second husband, Francesco Jadiccio, *Masto Ciccio* (also called *The Philosopher*), similarly combines inspiration from ancient veristic portraits with the poignant representation of a surrogate father.

In 1883 Gemito set up his own foundry for lost-wax casting with the help of the Belgian industrialist Oscar du Mesnil. In a letter to Ernest Meissonier, Gemito spoke of his rivalry with such famous Renaissance casters as Benvenuto Cellini. In fact, Gemito may be considered one of the last great sculptors to cast using

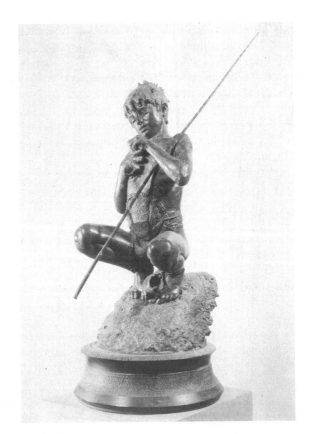

Little Fisherboy
© Scala / Art Resource, NY

the lost-wax process, a highly labor-intensive method that ensured the faithful translation of surface detail from the preparatory model to the final bronze. He also explained his approach to producing multiples, stating that, in the case of one particular object, he would make three signed originals and the rest would be unsigned reproductions made in the foundry without his direct participation.

Gemito's art was intimate rather than monumental in nature, and this aspect of his style ultimately led to his struggle and failure to fulfill state commissions. His involvement in two official projects, a marble statue of Charles V for the Palazzo Reale in Naples and a silver table centerpiece for King Umberto I, ended in disaster. Another sculptor eventually executed the statue from Gemito's model, but the centerpiece never progressed past the preparatory stages, and the artist suffered a mental collapse that kept him in seclusion for the next 20 years. The representation of universal or allegorical concepts, uninformed by direct observation of the living individual, proved antithetical to Gemito's artistic personality.

This conflict may have inspired the persistent, hallucinatory visions of historical and mythological figures that Gemito experienced during his illness, and which he later sought to concretize in his works after 1909, when he came out of seclusion. Just as Masto Ciccio could metamorphose into the iconic philosopher, so could the heroic Alexander the Great or the mythical Medusa be transformed into a vibrant human reality. From 1909 until his death, in addition to reworking such earlier compositions as *The Water Carrier*, Gemito concentrated on portraying legendary ancients, turning his acute gaze from the commonplace to the visionary. In contrast to the expressive sketchiness of his earlier sculptures, many of these late works offer an almost graphic refinement and surface polish evoking the art of Renaissance goldsmiths.

PEGGY FOGELMAN

Biography

Born in Naples, Italy, 16 July 1852. Entered studio of Emanuele Caggiano, sculptor, 1861; received additional training in workshop of Stanislao Lista, sculptor and painter, *ca.* 1864; set up independent studio with Antonio Mancini, Achille D'Orsi, and Giovanni Battista Amendola; exhibited the *Card Player* at Promotrice di Belle Arti, Naples, 1868 (acquired by King Victor Emmanuel II); entered competition with statue of *Brutus* at Instituto di Belle Arti, Naples, and earned commission from Cesare Correnti, minister of public education, to translate model into marble; moved to Paris, 1877; exhibited life-size *Little Fisherboy* and portraits of Ernest Meissonier, Paul Dubois, and Giuseppe Verdi, among others, at Paris Salons, 1877–80; won gold medal for bust of Verdi, Universal Exposition, Trocadero, 1878; returned to Naples, 1880; set up his own bronze foundry with help of Baron Oscar du Mesnil, 1883; won first-class medal, Universal Exposition, Antwerp, 1885; received two state commissions, one for silver table centerpiece for Umberto I's residence at Capodimonte, and one for marble statue *Charles V, Holy Roman Emperor* to decorate the Palazzo Reale in Naples, 1886; suffered mental collapse, *ca.* 1886; committed to a mental institution in 1887; resumed sculpture production, *ca.* 1909; went to Rome, 1920; returned to Paris for last, brief visit, 1924. Died in Naples, Italy, 1 March 1929.

Selected Works

1868   *Card Player*; patinated plaster, Museo Nazionale di Capodimonte, Naples, Italy

1871   *Brutus* (entered in competition at Istituto di Belle Arti, Naples, 1871); terracotta; Museo Nazionale Romano, Rome, Italy

1873   *Domenico Morelli*; terracotta; Museo di San Martino, Naples, Italy; bronze casts: Bank of Naples, Italy; Istituto di Belle Arti, Naples, Italy

1873   *Giuseppe Verdi*; terracotta; Villa Verdi, Bosseto, Italy; bronze casts: Casa di Riposo dei Musicisti, Milan, Italy; La Scala Museum, Milan, Italy; Museo Nazionale Romano, Rome, Italy

1874   *Mariano Fortuny*; terracotta; Palazzo Fortuny, Naples, Italy; wax: Gallery of Modern Art, Milan, Italy; plaster: Istituto di Belle Arti, Naples, Italy; bronze casts: Bank of Naples, Italy; Museo Nazionale Romano, Rome, Italy

1877   *Little Fisherboy* (exhibited at Paris Salon of 1877); bronze; Museo Nazionale del Bargello, Florence, Italy

1879   *Ernest Meissonier*; bronze (two casts): Museo Nazionale Romano, Rome, Italy; Metropolitan Museum of Art, New York City, United States

1880   *Charlotte Meissonier*; terracotta; The Detroit Institute of Arts, Michigan, United States

1880–81 *Water Carrier*; wax; Museo Nazionale Romano, Rome, Italy; bronze: Luxembourg Palace, Paris, France

1883   *Masto Ciccio* (also called *The Philosopher*); bronze; de Mesnil collection; Gallery of Modern Art, Milan, Italy

1886   *Charles V, Holy Roman Emperor*; marble; Palazzo Reale, Naples, Italy

1911   Medusa medallion; parcel-gilt silver; Getty Museum, Los Angeles, California, United States

1912–22 Alexander the Great medallion; plaster; Museo Nazionale Romano, Rome, Italy; silver; County Museum of Art, Los Angeles, California, United States

1926   *Raffaele Viviani*; terracotta; Museo Nazionale di Capodimonte, Naples, Italy

Further Reading

Acito, Alfredo, *Catalogo della mostra di sculture e disegni di Vincenzo Gemito* (exhib. cat.), S.l.: Orsa, 1938

Bellonzi, Fortunato, and Renzo Frattarolo, *Apunti Sull'arte di Vincenzo Gemito*, Rome: De Luca, 1952

Consiglio, Alberto, *Vincenzo Gèmito*, Rome: Istituto Nazionale L.U.C.E., 1932

De Marinis, Maria Simonetta, *Gemito*, L'Aquila, Italy: Leandro Ugo Japadre, 1993

Di Giacomo, Salvatore, *Vincenzo Gemito: La vita, l'opera*, Naples: Minozzi, 1905; reprint, as *Gemito*, Naples: Il Mattino, 1988

Fusco, Peter, "Medusa as a Muse for Vincenzo Gemito (1852–1929)," in *The J. Paul Getty Museum Journal* 16 (1988)

Mantura, Bruno, *Temi di Vincenzo Gemito* (exhib. cat.), Rome: De Luca Edizioni d'Arte, 1989

McArthur, Katherina, and Kate Ganz, *Vincenzo Gemito (1852–1929), Drawings and Sculpture in Naples and Rome* (exhib. cat.), New York: Kate Ganz USA Ltd., 2000

Wardropper, Ian, and Fred Licht, *Chiseled with a Brush: Italian Sculpture, 1860–1925, from the Gilgore Collections* (exhib. cat.), Chicago: The Art Institute of Chicago, 1994

GEMS

See **Engraved Gems**

NIKOLAUS GERHAERT VON LEIDEN
ca. 1410/20–1473 *Netherlandish*

Nikolaus Gerhaert von Leiden was the most important sculptor in the Rhineland, southern Germany, and Austria in the latter part of the 15th century. His style had a lasting influence on the following generation of sculptors, including Veit Stoss and Tilman Riemenschneider. Gerhaert's artistic ideas, rooted in western European traditions, were not only highly esteemed by Emperor Frederick III, who employed him at his court, but also spread into the eastern part of central Europe—into the lands of King Casimir IV of Poland and King Matthias Corvinus of Hungary.

The only remaining documents relating to Gerhaert, as well as his only dated works, exist from the last period of his life. It cannot be determined precisely where he lived previously. It is also unresolved whether his name indicates that Leiden was his place of birth or whether he only kept a workshop there for a time. One piece of evidence for his having resided in the Netherlands at the start of the 1450s may be the stone figure of St. Adrian attributed to him, now in the Musées Royaux d'Art et d'Histoire in Brussels.

Gerhaert's figural style, aimed at clear visualization, and his work's grounding in the close observation of nature—including his grasp of the psyche—indicate that he knew the works of Claus Sluter, likewise from the Netherlands, who had been active at the Burgundian ducal court in Dijon since 1385. In addition, Gerhaert was familiar with the innovative creations of Netherlandish sculpture dating from about 1420 and 1430, for example, the sculptures of Jean Delemer, who created the *Annunciation* group now at Tournai Cathedral (Belgium). Gerhaert's work is stylistically similar to the tomb figures of Duke Charles of Bourbon and his wife Agnes of Burgundy in the abbey church of Souvigny (France) executed by Jacques Morel around 1450. His works also show the influence of the paintings of Jan van Eyck, as well as those of older sculptors in Strasbourg, Alsace, one of the main stations of his life.

The tomb of Jakob von Sierck, Archbishop of Trier, is the earliest of Gerhaert's works authenticated by the sculptor's signature. Originally erected in the choir of the Liebfrauenkirchein Trier (Our Lady's Church), it was originally a two-tiered monument in accordance with French and English models: Gerhaert portrayed the deceased on the preserved tomb slab with open eyes, awaiting salvation, whereas the lower tier, which has been destroyed, depicted him as a cadaver. The recourse to a western type of tomb followed undoubtedly from Jakob von Sierck's own knowledge of such works, as he had stayed in France often as a successful diplomat. Gerhaert may have executed the tomb, presumably commissioned before the Archbishop's death in 1456, while he was also temporarily active in Trier. Jakob von Sierck, a chancellor of the Holy Roman Empire since 1442, may have played a role in Gerhaert's later being summoned to be Emperor Frederick III's court artist. The artist seems to have moved his workshop often around 1460, indicated by the stone sculptures by him in the northern and middle Rhineland, the figures of Christ and Mary in the Hardenrath Chapel to St. Mary in Kapitol in Cologne (although the chapel was built after 1466, the statues were perhaps made already in the late 1450s), and epitaph (before 1459?) of Bishop Siegfried von Venningen with the Annunciation scene in the Cathedral of Speyer. At the same time, figures newly attributed to Gerhaert were carved in wood for the high altar retable, completed in 1462, in the Church of St. George in Nördlingen; they may have been polychromed according to the pattern in Cologne.

Gerhaert's stay in Strasbourg from 1463 to 1467 is well documented. His major works there included the portal and facade of the Chancellery, a newly constructed representational office building for the free imperial city. According to a letter dated 14 July 1464, the sculptor agreed to maintain the work, completed the previous year, for a period of 20 years. From this work, which was damaged by a chancellery fire in 1686 and dismantled during the French Revolution, and whose design has been roughly transmitted in the description by Philipp Ludwig Künast from 1709, three half-length figures remain (two surviving only as fragments), including the busts of Jakob von Lichtenberg and Bärbel von Oppenheim, as they were designated in Strasbourg chronicles. These two figures peered from false windows and probably depicted the theme of the "ill-matched lovers" (*ungleiches Liebespaar*); according to other opinions, however, they represented a prophet and a sibyl. In addition was the half-figure of an introverted man in a melancholic pose, which may have been Gerhaert's self-portrait. Although Gerhaert was certainly already a highly regarded artist, this extensive facade may have prompted his summons to Strasbourg. According to the inscription preserved from his tombstone, previously located in Wiener Neustadt, he was the "Werkmeister des großen Baus zu Straßburg." He seems to have been active after that as an architect for the cathedral; no archival evidence has yet been found for this.

Further stone sculptures from this period include the 1464 epitaph of a canon, probably Conrad von Busnang, in the Cathedral of Strasbourg and the 1467 crucifix formerly in the Old Cemetery in Baden-Baden, for which Hans Ulrich Scherer, a Strasbourg surgeon in the services of the margrave in Baden, was the donor. The epitaph shows the donor and the Virgin as half-length figures portrayed within the same spatial context—a meeting of this world and the beyond, as in a vision—thus exhibiting analogies to Jan van Eyck's Rolin and van der Paele's Madonnas. The athletic Christ figure of the crucifix seems to hover in front of the beams of the cross; his stoic posture indicates his overcoming death. The figure of the crucified Christ, a model for numerous crucifix depictions by Veit Stoss and other artists, is remarkable for its unusually precise representation of the body. Gerhaert also demonstrated his sculptural virtuosity in the 5.6-meter-high cross, which he carved together with the 2.3-meter-high body from a single stone block.

In 1466 Gerhaert produced wood-carved figures for the high altar retable completed for the dedication of the Cathedral of Constance (the resident craftsman Simon Haider was responsible for the carpentry). No more precise indications exist concerning the appearance and conception of this work, which was destroyed during the time of the Reformation.

Already in 1463 Frederick III called on the Strasbourg Council to have Gerhaert move to the imperial court. By 1467 the emperor repeated his call: The sculptor should leave Strasbourg and produce tombstones at the imperial court. That same year he went to Austria, where he created the tomb slab for the imperial sarcophagus erected in St. Stephen's Cathedral at Vienna. It remains unclear how much of this extensive work had been completed by the time of his death in 1473. The choice of materials shows an adherence to imperial traditions of Antiquity. The red marble from Salzburg, for example, was equated—according to the humanist Cuspinianus—with the porphyry reserved for the Roman emperors. The tomb of Empress Eleonora of Portugal in the Neukloster Church in Wiener Neustadt is thought to be from Gerhaert's workshop.

The high altar retable in the Cathedral of Constance demonstrates Gerhaert's ability to work in wood. Four reliquary busts from Wissembourg have also been attributed to him, and recently some major carved works from that same epoch have been connected with the artist. Among these are the figures on the high altar retable in Nördlingen, whose crucifix bears great similarities to the one in Baden-Baden, and the Madonna from Dangolsheim in Alsace (now in the Staatliche Museen, Berlin), one of the most important depictions of the Virgin from the waning Middle Ages.

HARTMUT KROHM

See also **Polychromy; Porphyry; Riemenschneider, Tilman; Sluter, Claus; Stoss, Veit**

Biography

Born *ca.* 1410/20, location unknown. Trained in France, presumably in Jacques Morel's circle, as well as in the Netherlands; active in Trier, perhaps also in Cologne, 1450s; documented in Strasbourg, 1463–67; received full citizenship after serving as mayor (*Schultheissenbürger*), 1464; owned building (Zum Zinneneck) in Strasbourg; served Emperor Frederick III in Vienna and Wiener Neustadt from 1467 until end of life. Died in Vienna, Austria, 28 August 1473.

Selected Works

before 1459?	Epitaph of Bishop Siegfried von Venningen and Nikolaus von Venningen; sandstone; St. Afra Chapel, Speyer Cathedral, Germany
1462	High altar (signed by Friedrich Herlin); wood; Church of St. George, Nördlingen, Germany
1462	Tomb of Jakob von Sierck, Archbishop of Trier, for Liebfrauenkirche (Our Lady's Church), Trier, Germany (dismantled); sandstone; upper tomb slab: Episcopal Cathedral and Diocesan Museum, Trier, Germany
1463	Portal of the Chancellery, Strasbourg; sandstone (destroyed); fragments: Musée de l'Oeuvre Notre-Dame, Strasbourg, France
1464	Epitaph of a priest (Canon Conrad von Busnang?); sandstone; St. John's Chapel, Strasbourg Cathedral, France
ca. 1465	Madonna, from Dangolsheim, Alsace; wood; Staatliche Museen, Berlin, Germany
1467	Crucifix, for the Old Cemetery, Baden-Baden, Germany; sandstone; Church of Saints Peter and Paul, Baden-Baden, Germany
begun 1467	Tomb of Emperor Friedrich III; red marble; Salvator Choir, St. Stephen's Cathedral, Vienna, Austria

Further Reading

Baxandall, Michael, *The Limewood Sculptors of Renaissance Germany*, New Haven, Connecticut: Yale University Press, 1980

Die Dangolsheimer Muttergottes nach ihrer Restaurierung (exhib. cat.), Berlin: Kaiser-Friedrich-Museums-Verein, 1989

"Gerhaert de Leyde, Nicolas," in *Dictionnaire des sculpteurs français du Moyen Age*, edited by Michèle Beaulieu and Victor Beyer, Paris: Picard, 1992

Hilger, Hans Peter, and Borghild Freutag, *Das Jesuskind mit der Weintraube*, Munich: Bayerisches Nationalmuseum, 1991

Krohm, Hartmut, "Zuschreibungen an Niclaus Gerhaert von Leyden: Eine noch längst nicht abgeschlossene Diskussion," in *Skulptur in Süddeutschland, 1400–1770: Festschrift für Alfred Schädler*, edited by Rainer Kahsnitz and Peter Volk, Munich: Deutscher Kunstverlag, 1998

Müller, Theodor, *Sculpture in the Netherlands, Germany, France, and Spain, 1400 to 1500*, translated by Elaine Robson Scott and William Robson Scott, London: Penguin, 1966

Recht, Roland, *Nicolas de Leyde et la sculpture à Strasbourg, 1460–1525*, Strasbourg, France: Presses Universitaires de Strasbourg, 1987

Spätgotik am Oberrhein: Meisterwerke der Plastik und des Kunsthandwerks, 1450–1530 (exhib. cat.), Karlsruhe, Germany: Badisches Landesmuseum Karlsruhe, 1970

Wertheimer, Otto, *Nicolaus Gerhaert: Seine Kunst und seine Wirkung*, Berlin: Deutscher Verein für Kunstwissenschaft, 1929

Zimmermann, Eva, "Gerhaert, Nicolaus," in *The Dictionary of Art*, edited by Jane Turner, vol. 12, New York: Grove, and London: Macmillan, 1996

HUBERT GERHARD *ca.* 1545/50–1620

Dutch, active in Germany

Along with Adriaen De Vries, Hubert Gerhard was the most important mediator of Italian, particularly Florentine, late Mannerism in southern Germany. At the same time, his style reflected his Dutch heritage. Gerhard's work consisted mainly of public fountains as well as religious and secular architectural sculpture in Munich and Augsburg, and it greatly influenced southern German sculpture of the early Baroque period.

Gerhard's contemporaries were always conscious of his Dutch origins, even though he worked exclusively in the region of southern Germany and Austria from 1581. He likely spent his years as an apprentice in the Netherlands and then left for Italy shortly thereafter. In the 1570s and 1580s many Dutch artists left their homeland because of the Eighty Years' War, although ambitious artists and sculptors from other regions also journeyed to Italy for training. As yet, Gerhard has only been recorded on one occasion, in 1581, in the context of the Florentine court workshops.

Along with Carlo di Cesare del Palagio, Gerhard was summoned in 1581 by the Fuggers, a merchant family in Augsburg, to create the bronzes for a grave-altar honoring Christopher Fugger, who had died in 1579. They consisted of two gilded reliefs of the Resurrected Christ and the Ascension of Christ (the latter of which was lost), two standing prophets and two sitting prophets, putti with instruments of the Passion, and two kneeling angels who support the whole structure. As Gerhard's earliest documented works, they are key pieces to our conception of his stylistic heritage. Along with a dependence on Giambologna, the Resurrection relief seems to have been modeled after the designs of Munich court painter Friedrich Sustris. As in other instances of their collaboration, Carlo di Cesare's contribution cannot be methodically and satisfactorily isolated from that of Gerhard.

From 1582 on, the art enthusiast Hans Fugger engaged both sculptors at his newly built castle in Kirchheim (Mindel). Twelve over-life-size terracotta figures of famous men and women were created for the large hall, and three Classical gods were created for the portal. The technique for modeling and firing such figures in terracotta stemmed from the Italian tradition, which Gerhard and Carlo di Cesare introduced north of the Alps.

Smaller works by Gerhard for Duke William V of Bavaria (r. 1579–97) are documented for the first time in 1584. At that time, the Duke was already planning to decorate the Jesuit Church of St. Michael (Michaelskirche) in Munich, which he had founded, with an elaborate series of figures. By 1588 Gerhard's studio had produced about 30 over-life-size terracotta angels with the instruments of the Passion and apostles. After the choir's collapse in 1590, the studio produced another series of apostles, saints, and prophets for the choir. Many of the angels from the 1580s are masterpieces of late Mannerist sculpture and characteristic of Gerhard's style, which gives the figures an emotional, almost Rococo form and distances itself from Giambologna's more severe stylization.

Gerhard remained in the Duke's service until William V's abdication in 1597. The sculptor kept a productive studio in Munich where Hans Krumper and Hans Reichle, among others, are recorded as apprentices. Martin Frey took over the casting of Gerhard's bronzes. As court sculptor, Gerhard did not enjoy free reign over artistic production but was bound to the designs of Friedrich Sustris, who supervised all the craftsmen at court. There are no known original designs by Gerhard. However, it is acknowledged that he created models for goldsmiths, although the silver figures (St. Jacob's Cathedral, Innsbruck, Austria) previously associated with his name are not stylistically convincing.

Gerhard's chief work for the Church of St. Michael is the bronze *St. Michael and Lucifer*, over four meters high, invoked as a powerful image of the church's patron saint on the facade between the two entrances of the church. Enveloped in decoratively flowing garments, Michael is not a martial figure; elegantly sweeping down from above, he slays the devil. One recognizes Sustris's influence in the detailed contours and supple elegance of the figures. The group is among the strongest works of late Mannerism and has become a symbol of the southern German Counter Reformation.

In the later 1580s Gerhard created garden figures for William V's newly built Munich Residenz: a *Bavaria*, with the riches of her country, and the Perseus Fountain in the middle of the Grottenhof (grotto courtyard), decorated after the Italian model. The figures more or less directly reflect Gerhard's and Sustris's Florentine experience: the Perseus Fountain re-creates Benvenuto Cellini's statue (1545–53) in the taste of Sustris's era. For the plastic realization of the figures, Gerhard's interest did not lie in the *figura serpentinata*. Rather, the figures are oriented around a primary perspective and embellished with decorative details.

Gerhard's chief work of the 1590s in Munich has remained unfinished: his patron's tomb for the Church of St. Michael, an impressive structure with 17 life-size bronze figures, reliefs, rows of crests, and other decoration planned by William V, was abandoned when the Duke abdicated in 1597. For this work Giambologna created the figure of the Crucified Christ, and Hans Reichle the grieving Mary Magdalene. The main figures, however, were allocated to Gerhard: the ducal couple with guardian angels, *Angel Bearing the Stoup of Holy Water*, an early Wittelsbach *Duke of Bavaria*, and a *Virgin* suspended above the entire monument on a crescent moon. Gerhard collaborated with Carlo di Cesare on the four knights and four lions. Except for the unrealized figures of the donor couple and the lost angels, all figures have been preserved in different locations in the city. The *Virgin*, placed on a votive pillar (the Mariensäule) in the middle of Munich's marketplace in 1638, has enjoyed a considerable following, particularly among goldsmiths, and has become a trademark of the city. The ancestral statue, *Duke of Bavaria*, crowns Gerhard's so-called Wittelsbach Fountain, which was later moved to the Munich Residenz. The four knights guard Johann (Hans) Krumper's funerary monument for Louis IV the Bavarian in the Cathedral Church of Our Lady (Frauenkirche, Munich), and the lions guard the portal of the Residenz. The holy water angel, four reliefs (not by Gerhard), and the crucifixion group have remained at the Church of St. Michael.

Gerhard received three assignments for monumental fountains, a genre in which his Florentine experience clearly emerged, during the Munich years. About 1586/87 a fountain, the later so-called Wittelsbach

Fountain, was erected for Ferdinand, brother of Duke William, on the square in front of his palace. It met with great appreciation as the first such structure in the region based on the Italian model and influenced the further development of this type of fountain in Germany. The figures on the rim of the basin—four river gods, four standing gods (or the seasons of the year), and eight small putti and grotesque animal groups—are preserved as part of the Wittelsbach Fountain of the Munich Residenz. Their presentation today essentially follows the original, although the fountain was initially crowned by a rider on a horse performing a *courbette* (a curvetting or prancing posture). It has a direct descendant in Caspar Gras's portrayal of Archduke Leopold V of Tirol on a leaping horse that is part of the Leopold fountain (1623–30) in Innsbruck. Gerhard clearly experimented with the horse performing a *courbette* earlier than had either Pietro Tacca or Gras, albeit in a smaller format (approximately 1.4 meters).

The attention received by the fountain for Duke Ferdinand created the impetus for commissioning two further fountains: the Augustus fountain in Augsburg and the fountain for Hans Fugger's Schloss Kirchheim, the middle group of which, *Mars and Venus Playing with Cupid*, was cast in 1590. The group's theme was not only particularly well loved by the Rudolfine (Rudolf II) circle, but also familiar from Netherlandish prints. When considering the somewhat vulgar and erotic appearance of these figures, one should bear in mind the originally eminent position at which they were displayed. Detailed figures reclining on shells are recorded as having been on the octagonal rim of the basin (now lost). The Augustus fountain is one of the few works by Gerhard that is situated near its original location. Crowned by a statue of the city founder, Augustus, the fountain represented a combination of an honorary monument and customary fountain themes that characterized many early monuments in Italy as well.

In 1597 Gerhard lost his position in Munich after William V's son Maximilian I (*r.* 1597–1651) took office. The sculptor then entered the service of Archduke Maximilian III, the grand master of the Teutonic Order (1585–1618), who had ruled in Tirol from 1602 and was a brother of Emperor Rudolf II. Gerhard worked for Maximilian in the residence of the Teutonic Knights in Mergentheim (Franconia) from 1599 to 1602. From the Mergentheim period, it seems that only the equestrian statuette of the Archduke (Städel Institut, Frankfurt am Main, Germany) has been preserved. In 1600 Caspar Gras began an apprenticeship under Gerhard and subsequently became his close assistant.

In contrast to the courts in Prague and Munich, Archduke Maximilian apparently had little interest in monumental projects. At the request of the emperor,

Gerhard sent small bronze groups to Prague in 1602 and 1605, two of which have been preserved in Vienna (*Mars, Venus, and Cupid* and *Hercules and Deianira*). Maximilian's only major commission was for his tomb in the parish church in Innsbruck. The main figures on the monument, the reverently kneeling Archduke and St. George, his patron saint, in armor with his dragon alongside, were apparently already finished in 1608 and therefore attributed to Gerhard himself. After the death of Maximilian in 1618, the bronzes were displayed freestanding in the church, on a slab supported by high arabesque columns, with four mournful cherubs added in the corners by Caspar Gras.

In 1613 Gerhard requested to be released from Innsbruck, for reasons of old age, and returned to Munich; later works that are mentioned by sources have not been preserved.

DOROTHEA DIEMER

See also **Carlo di Cesare del Palagio**

Biography

Born in Hertogenbosch, the Netherlands, *ca.* 1545/50. Completed apprenticeship probably while still in the Netherlands; journeyed afterward to Italy; first documented in Florence, 1581; summoned to Augsburg, Germany, by the Fugger family, 1581, where he worked with Carlo di Cesare del Palagio; also worked for William V, Duke of Bavaria, from *ca.* 1583 as court sculptor until 1597; in the service of Archduke Maximilian III of Tirol, grand master of the Teutonic Order, for whom he worked in the residence of the Teutonic Knights, Mergentheim, 1599–1602; at Innsbruck, 1602–13; returned to his family in Munich, 1613. Died in Munich, Germany, 1620.

Selected Works

1581–82 Relief of the Resurrected Christ, four prophets, two cherubs, and two angels, for the grave of Christopher Fugger; gilded bronze; Victoria and Albert Museum, London, England

1582–84 Twelve statues of famous men and women (with Carlo di Cesare del Palagio); terracotta; Schloss Kirchheim an der Mindel, Swabia, Germany

1584–97 Statues of angels, apostles, saints, and prophets; terracotta; Church of St. Michael, Munich, Germany

ca. 1585–89 *Bavaria*; bronze; Emperor's Hall, Residenz, Munich, Germany

ca. 1585–89 Perseus Fountain; bronze; Residenz, Munich, Germany

1587 Four gods, four river gods, eight groups of grotesque animal figures, and eight putti; bronze; Wittelsbach Fountain, Residenz, Munich, Germany

1588 *St. Michael and Lucifer* (cast by Martin Frey); bronze; facade, Church of St. Michael, Munich, Germany

1589–94 Augustus Fountain; bronze (figures only); Perlachplatz, Augsburg, Germany

1590 *Mars and Venus Playing with Cupid*, from fountain at Schloss Kirchheim; bronze; Bayerisches Nationalmuseum, Munich, Germany

1593–97 Statues for the tomb of William V, Duke of Bavaria; bronze; dispersed: *Angel Bearing the Stoup of Holy Water*, Church of St. Michael, Munich, Germany; *Duke of Bavaria* and two lions, Residenz, Munich, Germany; *Virgin*, Marienplatz, Munich, Germany; two knights carrying banners, Cathedral Church of Our Lady, Munich, Germany

1602–05 *Mars, Venus, and Cupid* and *Hercules and Deianira*; bronze; Kunsthistorisches Museum, Vienna, Austria

ca. 1608 Tomb monument for Archduke Maximilian III of Tirol (with Caspar Gras); bronze; St. Jacob's Cathedral, Innsbruck, Austria (attributed)

Further Reading

Baxandall, Michael, "A Masterpiece by Hubert Gerhard," *Victoria and Albert Museum Bulletin* 1/2 (April 1965)

Diemer, Dorothea, "Quellen und Untersuchungen zum Stiftergrab Herzog Wilhelms V. von Bayern und der Renata von Lothringen in der Münchner Michaelskirche," in *Quellen und Studien zur Kunstpolitik der Wittelsbacher vom 16. bis zum 18. Jahrhundert*, edited by Hubert Glaser, Munich: Hirmer, 1980

Diemer, Dorothea, "Gerhard, Hubert," in *The Dictionary of Art*, edited by Jane Turner, vol. 12, New York: Grove, and London: Macmillan, 1996

Diemer, Dorothea, "Hubert Gerhard in Innsbruck," in *Ruhm und Sinnlichkeit: Innsbrucker Bronzeguss, 1500–1650, von Kaiser Maximilian I. bis Erzherzog Ferdinand Karl* (exhib. cat.), edited by Manfred Leithe-Jasper, Innsbruck, Austria: Tiroler Landesmuseum Ferdinandeum, and Athesia-Tyrolia Druck, 1996

Diemer, Dorothea, "Small Bronzes by Hubert Gerhard," *Studies in the History of Art* 62 (2001)

Leithe-Jasper, Manfred, *Renaissance Master Bronzes: From the Collection of the Kunsthistorisches Museum, Vienna* (exhib. cat.), Washington, D.C.: Scala Books, 1986

Weihrauch, Hans R., "Gerhard, Hubert," in *Neue deutsche Biographie*, vol. 6, Berlin: Duncker und Humblot, 1964

Weihrauch, Hans R., *Europäische Bronzestatuetten*, Braunschweig, Germany: Klinkhardt und Biermann, 1967

AUGUSTUS FOUNTAIN
Hubert Gerhard (ca. 1545/50–1620)
1589–1594
bronze figures
h. ca. 6 m
Perlachplatz, Augsburg, Germany

The Augustus fountain was the first of three renowned fountains with monumental bronze figures that the city elders of Augsburg assigned to nonlocal artists over the course of just ten years. From 1589 to 1594 Hubert Gerhard created his Augustus fountain; in 1599 and 1602 Adriaen de Vries erected his Mercury fountain and Hercules fountain. These three fountains demarcate the central axis of the city, beginning with the Augustus fountain on the square (Perlachplatz) in front of the town hall, and continue to form the city's architectural highlights, as they did 400 years ago. The Augustus fountain is both a fountain and a monument. At the corners of the large rectangular fountain basin lie two women and two older men, unclad and with the attributes of Augsburg's rivers and canals: the Lech, the Wertach, the Singold, and the Brunnbach. The statue of Emperor Augustus appears to contrast with these figures at first glance. Standing high on the central pillar, creating a Classical atmosphere in his magnificent armor with mantle and laurel crown, Augustus has raised his right hand to address his people. The fountain pillar, renewed during a restoration in the 18th century, is still ornamented by the original bronze figures: female herm figures and putti with dolphins.

In terms of the Augsburgers' conception of their own history, the combination of the emperor with the river gods made perfect sense, in addition to the fact that recumbent river gods, dolphin-carrying putti, and so forth, work extremely well as fountain ornamentation. Augustus is considered to be the founder of the city "Augusta Vindelicorum," and the historical self-awareness of the intellectuals of this free imperial city laid great importance, as attested in literature, on the circumstance that the emperor had founded his colony on the precise spot of the city of Augsburg. The city's location in Antiquity, however, was controversial; in the face of such doubts, the personification of the city's rivers at the foot of its founder aimed to reinforce the certainty that the tradition of the city's founding in Antiquity continued uninterrupted. Since then, archaeology has confirmed the story of local historians: the first legion encampment was located on the northern outskirts of the city.

A monumental statue for a historic person had not previously existed in Germany. Even in Italy, this genre first developed during the 16th century, and there as well, the statue of the living ruler combined with a fountain. In the combination of the monumental statue with a fountain, therefore, Gerhard's Augustus Fountain followed the Italian models of his time.

Gerhard worked in the capacity of court artist to the Bavarian Dukes in Munich. Because Duke William V was friendly with several members of the Fugger family, a merchant family in Augsburg, it is easy to understand how the artist could have been commissioned for the fountain. For Gerhard, the 1580s and early 1590s were a time of unceasing work on large projects. The Augustus fountain is particularly notable among them, as it is clearly a work created from his own design, in contrast to the assignments he received at the Munich court, which were carried out according to designs by Friedrich Sustris. With their expressive modeling, which plays intensely with light and shadow, Gerhard's large, recumbent river gods attest to his Dutch heritage as well as his training with the monumental sculpture of Italy. Whereas the representational statue of the emperor allowed for little variation in the stance, the river gods possess many more perspectives. With their naturally twisting movements, they are creations after the Florentine ideal of the *figura serpentinata*.

The total construction of the fountain is utterly Italian in form. Several years after its completion, Gerhard's contemporary, the Württemberg architect Heinrich Schickhardt, protested that the distance between the recumbent figures was too great, that in general the fountain was lacking in ornamentation, and that it stood too low. In these somewhat provincial comments, the difference between the traditional construction of German fountains in the 16th century and the form imported from Italy by Gerhard is clearly expressed. Conventional German fountains were rather narrow and high, with numerous tightly packed figures and detailed ornaments; a prominent example is the Tugendbrunnen (Fountain of the Virtues) in Nuremberg, cast by Benedikt Würzelbauer and erected in 1589. Given that Gerhard was one of a group of sculptors strongly influenced by Florentine late Mannerism and the studio of Giambologna, it is not surprising that Gerhard relied heavily on Italian models for his design of the Augustus fountain; for instance, he borrowed greatly from the broad basin of Bartolomeo Ammanati's Neptune fountain (*ca.* 1560–75) in Florence, with its recumbent naiads and fauns, and especially the figures on the fountain pillar in Giambologna's Neptune fountain (*ca.* 1566) in Bologna. The form of the Augustus fountain's basin, raised in a wide-sweeping, almost Classical profile, which was unusual in Germany, stands in clear contrast to the box-shaped basin usual in the north.

That the Augsburg elders recognized and appreciated Gerhard's innovation is demonstrated by their de-

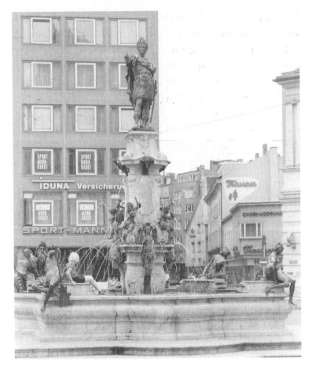

Augustus fountain, Augsburg, Germany
The Conway Library, Courtauld Institute of Art

liberations regarding the optimal location for the fountain, which, strangely enough, only began after Gerhard's fountain was already completed in 1593: "As the fountain has been made from such elegant and splendid masonry work, the likes of which is to be found neither near nor far," they decided that the fountain should be erected in the main square of the city, across from the town hall.

The impetus for ordering such an elaborate fountain was probably driven by two other of Hubert Gerhard's fountains, which had appeared shortly before or simultaneously with the commissioning of the Augustus fountain, and which had aroused the town elders' ambition. In 1586–87 Gerhard had erected in a public square in Munich a similarly constructed fountain, which was ordered by the brother of the reigning duke. The fountain attracted much attention through its abundance of exceptional bronze figures—in particular, the jumping rider in the middle—and through the refined manner employed to direct the fountain water. The other fountain was commissioned by Hans Fugger probably about the same time as that of the Augsburg elders. Gerhard had already furnished the former's castle in Kirchheim (Mindel) with terracotta figures and was now adding to it a fountain with a monumental centerpiece. The Kirchheim *Mars and Venus* group (not by Gerhard) was produced in Augsburg just a few weeks prior to the casting of the Augustus figure,

which, with a height of 2.5 meters and weight in metal of 27 metric hundredweight, was the most significant cast the town caster, Peter Wagner, ever accomplished. Archival accounts of the planning of the Augustus fountain have been collected from the end of 1588 onward. As a three-dimensional model of the fountain pillar was already completed at that time, the assignment and design must have come shortly after Hubert Gerhard's Munich fountain was set up. That the plan for the entire work came from Gerhard himself, and not from the city of Augsburg, for example, is indicated by its Italian form. From the fall of 1589, Gerhard worked in Augsburg on the bronzes. William V would not release him any sooner, as the sculptor first had to complete the ornamentation of the Church of St. Michael, Munich, with terracotta figures. Work on the fountain progressed rapidly. In August 1590 the statue of the emperor was cast; the figures for the rim of the basin and the central pillar were completed by 1592. The sources reflect Gerhard's customary practice of a division of labor, through which he maintained both high efficiency and sculptural quality. His brother Heinrich helped him with the production of the forms for the bronzes; Augsburg goldsmiths took over the painstaking chasing work after the forms were cast. The fountain's bronzes were restored in the 1990s, the figure of Augustus replaced by a replica (the original is in the Maximilianmuseum, Augsburg).

DOROTHEA DIEMER

Further Reading

Bushart, Bruno, "Die Augsburger Brunnen und Denkmale um 1600," in *Welt im Umbruch: Augsburg zwischen Renaissance und Barock*, vol. 3, Augsburg, Germany: Augsburger Druck- and Verlagshaus, 1981

Friedel, Helmut, *Bronze-Bildmonumente in Augsburg, 1589–1606: Bild und Urbanität*, Augsburg, Germany: Mühlberger, 1974

Völkel, Markus, "Marcus Welser und die Augsburger Baukunst der Hollzeit: Einige skeptische Anmerkungen," in *Elias Holl und das Augsburger Rathaus* (exhib. cat.), edited by Wolfram Baer, Hanno-Walter Kruft, and Bernd Roeck, Regensburg, Germany: Pustet, 1985

Weihrauch, Hans R., "Gerhard, Hubert," in *Neue deutsche Biographie*, vol. 6, Berlin: Duncker and Humbolt, 1964

GERMANY: ROMANESQUE

The medievalist Richard Hamann (1924) once quipped that "German sculpture has no history, indeed there has never been such a thing as German sculpture." Many have noted that it is nearly impossible to trace stylistic developments among carvings produced between the years 1000 and 1200 in the region roughly corresponding to present-day Germany. Works often bear little formal resemblance to one another and thus seem to be so many anomolies. In order to deal with this phenomenon, art historians have tended to focus on identifying stylistic and iconographic similarities between German sculpture and that of other regions. The former typically has been described as indebted to outside influences—as derivative. This characterization may help to explain the few studies, especially those written in English, on the subject. Yet there is much that is of interest in German Romanesque sculpture, prompting the question of whether other art-historical models, less rooted in anachronistic conceptions of national identity, may more adequately address this body of work. This question cannot be examined in this short space; only a brief selective survey can be offered here.

Medieval artisans in Germany excelled in the production of small-scale sculptures in precious materials, including ivory and gold. The early 12th-century writings of the monk Theophilus, who is generally identified as the goldsmith Roger of Helmarshausen, attest to the ability of artists to work with various materials. This seems manifest in the multimedia aesthetic of many objects. For example, the portable altar of St. Andrew produced in Trier (*ca.* 990) is decorated with enamels, metal filigree, and a foot modeled in gold. The latter alerts the viewer to a relic housed in the altar, an early example of a "speaking reliquary." Numerous precious antependiums, crucifixes, reliquaries, book covers, and other objects associated with the liturgy, *ars sacra* (sacred art), were produced throughout the period under consideration.

Despite stylistic differences, plasticity stands as a salient feature of much German sculpture produced during the high Middle Ages, particularly when compared with contemporary works from other regions in Europe. Extant sculptures in wood and ivory, which probably represent a small fraction of works produced, manifest this tendency from an early date. On the life-size wooden crucifix associated with Archbishop Gero of Cologne (*ca.* 969–76; Cathedral of Cologne) the dead body of Christ hangs heavily, with a protruding belly that further emphasizes the figure's weight. Similarly, the wooden doors of St. Maria in Kapitol in Cologne, produced before 1065, feature figures, often described as "folkish," that protrude from stagelike backgrounds. The doors' panels illustrate various New Testament scenes, from the Annunciation to Pentecost. Early Christian bronze doors perhaps served as models.

Bearing such objects in mind, one can better understand two bronze doors commissioned by Archbishop Bernward of Hildesheim in 1015 (St. Michael's Church, Hildesheim). Each measures approximately five meters in height and is composed of a single piece of bronze, attesting to the technical virtuosity of the artisans. On the left door, scenes from Genesis are arranged chronologically from top to bottom, from the *Creation of Eve* to the *Murder of Abel*—a visual metaphor of humanity's descent into sin. Salvation history is the subject of the right door, from the *Annunciation* at the bottom to the *Noli me tangere* (literally "touch me not;" describes Christ's appearance to Mary Magdalene after his resurrection) at the top. Visual and thematic parallels between the two doors encourage the viewer to contemplate a number of typologies. The theological sophistication of the program yields insight into the importance of Hildesheim as a center of study in the early 11th century. Other important commissions under Bernward include a bronze column, with scenes of Christ's life arranged in a frieze that spirals upward in a manner probably inspired by Trajan's or Marcus Aurelius's column in Rome and a stone grave marker for the Archbishop.

There are many examples of funereal sculpture, either in bronze or stone, that date to the period under consideration. Beginning in the later part of the 11th century, a likeness of the deceased was often included on tombs. A stone tomb relief in Quedlinburg for the Abbess Adelheid I (*ca.* 1130) is representative. The abbess, who holds a book in her left hand and raises her right, stands before an undifferentiated background framed by two bands; the inner contains an epitaph and the outer is decorated with lush vegetation. This monument provides evidence for the active role of women, particularly ecclesiastics, as patrons of the arts in Germany.

The sudden appearance of accomplished stone sculpture in Germany around 1050 is typically explained as the result of artists trained in other media, such as ivory, taking up the chisel. Three reliefs located in the entryway to the church of St. Emmeram in Regensburg (*ca.* 1050) demonstrate a remarkably plastic conception of forms. Two represent standing saints: *St. Emmeram*, identified by an inscription as the guardian of the church, and *St. Denis*, to whom a chapel in the church was dedicated. On the third an enthroned, *Christ* with a nimbus raises his right hand in a gesture of benediction and holds a book with his left. The figure projects so fully from the background that it seems to be a sculpture in the round. Broad folds arranged asymmetrically across Christ's body lend dynamism to the figure's rather static pose, as does the positioning of his feet on a sloped pedestal. On the front face of this footstool, a roundel contains the bust of *Abbot Reginwardus* (created *ca.* 1048–60?), who is identified by a surrounding inscription that informs the viewer that the abbot ordered this sculpture to be made, thereby providing an approximate date of creation. Another Latin text running along the edges of the relief addresses the appropriateness of the material: "Cum

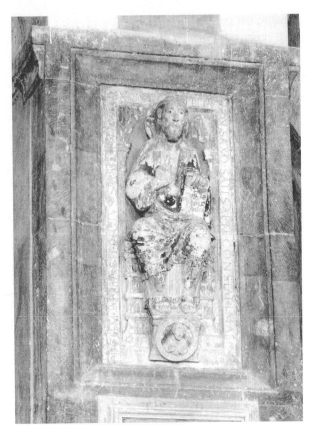

Christ in Majesty with the Bust of Abbot Reginwandus,
mid-11th century; St. Emmeran, Regensburg
The Conway Library, Courtauld Institute of Art

petra sit dictus stabili p[ro] numine / Xps illius / in
saxos satis apte constat imago" (Because Christ is
called "the rock" on account of his immutable divinity,
it is appropriate that his image be fashioned from
stone). The widespread revival of stone sculpture in
the West during the 11th century may be attributed
in part to the material's connotations of permanence,
analogous to the transcendental nature of God's
kingdom.

Other reliefs that probably date to the mid 11th century, although some may be earlier, include those from
Brauweiler, St. Mauritz, Münster, and the Abbey
Church of Werden. A fragment from the latter, which
probably decorated a crypt shrine of St. Luidgur, features an arcade occupied by seated women, whose
identities remain obscure. The treatment of figures and
the large platelike folds recall in a very general way
the reliefs at Regensburg. It is often suggested that
German artists traveled across Europe, from Bari in
southern Italy to León in northern Spain, and perhaps
provided an impetus for the widespread revival of
monumental sculpture in the 11th century.

Capitals carved for an ecclesiastical context were
the most common forms of stone sculpture produced

in Germany during the 11th and 12th centuries. These
often inventively incorporate forms found in antique
sculpture to new effects. On a capital from St. Martin in
Zyfflic, tentatively dated to about 1000, Atlas figures
support an abacus, which is carved from the same
block. The striding postures of these atlantes, figures
not typically featured on ancient capitals, lend dynamism to the composition. Sparsely carved capitals,
cubelike in appearance, may be found throughout Germany, including in the 11th-century crypt of the Cathedral of Speyer. Parallels from Italy and Byzantium
have been cited, but one could state in more positive
terms that the austerity of these works complements
the aesthetic of the surrounding architecture.

Greater numbers of monumental stone sculpture
survive from the 12th century. Worms Cathedral,
which had strong imperial connections, preserves a
rich array of carvings, most of which date to the second
half of the century and which provide insight into the
range of formats employed during this period. A tympanum over the entrance to a chapel dedicated to Nicholas features at its center a bust of the saint, who
seems to be preaching to a group of onlookers, represented by heads or busts. Half-length figures in tympana, although unusual elsewhere in western Europe,
are fairly common in Germany and may be adapted
from Byzantine imagery, such as that of the Christ
Pantokrator. Reliefs incorporated in the walls of
Worms Cathedral represent *Daniel in the Lions' Den*
and a legend of *Juliana*, whom God protected from
demons after she was thrown in prison for her faith.
Elsewhere at Worms, a number of recumbent figures,
both animal and human, support columns in the loggia
of the west facade. Some scholars have cited analogues
in the lions that are incorporated in the portals of Italian
churches, but the wildly grimacing figures at Worms
seem more playful in treatment. A similar attitude may
be observed in a number of carved goats, bears, and
lions that decorate the exterior of many of the window-
sills.

The Externsteine complex at Horn in Westphalia
includes perhaps one of the most idiosyncratic monuments (*ca.* 1100) produced in 12th-century Europe.
This carving in living rock of the *Deposition* is roughly
6 meters in height and decorates the entrance to a
chapel. Joseph of Arimethia is shown receiving the
dead body of Christ from Nicodemus, who stands atop
a small palm that bends under his weight. At left, Mary
proffers a death shroud, and to the right, John the Baptist stands in a posture of mourning. Virtually unique
among medieval Deposition scenes is the presence of
God the Father above the left arm of the cross. The
damaged remains of what appears to be Christ's soul
are visible in the Father's hands. This detail has led
Panofsky and others to liken this scene to Byzantine

representations of the Dormition of the Virgin. In these, Christ stands above his dead mother and cradles her soul in his arms. The significance of the unusual iconography at Horn has yet to be fully explained.

Other important 12th-century sites with monumental sculpture include Brauweiler, Cologne, Erfurt, and Hildesheim. Stylistic and iconographic variations among these works attest to the inventiveness of sculptors during this period.

KIRK AMBROSE

Further Reading

Beenken, Hermann Theodor, *Romanische Skulptur in Deutschland (11. und 12. Jahrhundert)*, Leipzig: Klinkhardt und Biermann Verlag, 1924 (contains a helpful catalogue)

Hearn, M.F., *Romanesque Sculpture: The Revival of Monumental Sculpture in the Eleventh and Twelfth Centuries*, Ithaca, New York: Cornell University Press, and Oxford: Phaidon, 1981

Hotz, Walter, and Günther Binding, *Der Dom zu Worms*, Darmstadt, Germany: Wissenschaftliche Buchgesellschaft, 1998

Lasko, Peter, *Ars Sacra, 800–1200*, London and Baltimore, Maryland: Penguin Books, 1972; 2nd edition, New Haven, Connecticut: Yale University Press, 1994 (good bibliography)

Legner, Anton (editor), *Ornamenta ecclesiae: Kunst und Künstler der Romanik in Köln*, 3 vols., Cologne, Germany: Schnütgen-Museum, 1985

Panofsky, Erwin, *Die deutsche Plastik des elften bis dreizehnten Jahrhunderts*, 2 vols., Munich: Wolff, 1924; reprint, New York: Kraus Reprint, 1969 (pioneering study)

Strobel, Richard, and Markus Weis, *Romanik in Altbayern*, Würzburg, Germany: Zodiaque Echter, 1994

Theophilus, *The Various Arts; De diversis artibus* (ca. 1110–40), edited and translated by C.R. Dodwell, London: Nelson, 1961 (medieval treatise on artistic techniques)

Toman, Rolf, and Achim Bednoz (editors), *Romanesque: Architecture, Sculpture, Painting*, Cologne, Germany: Köneman Verlagsgesellschaft, 1997

Wesenberg, Rudolf, *Bernwardinische Plastik: Zur ottonischen Kunst unter Bischof Bernward von Hildesheim*, Berlin: Deutscher Verein für Kunstwissenschaft, 1955

Wulf, Walter, *Romanik in der Konigslandschaft Sachsen*, Würzburg, Germany: Zodiaque Echter, 1996

GERMANY: GOTHIC–RENAISSANCE

The Gothic and Renaissance periods in Germany can be broken down into the following sub-periods: Early Gothic (1145–1210), High Gothic (1210–1300), Late Gothic (1300–1500), and the Renaissance (1500–1600). These dates serve only as general guidelines, however, since regional developments often interrupt the larger picture. The most important changes in German sculpture appear between the Early and High Gothic phase. Between 1145 and 1210 (Early Gothic period), the influence of French cathedral sculpture had not yet been fully absorbed by the sculptors and artisans in the German cathedral workshops. Consequently, between 1145–1210, German sculpture exhibits a strong adherence to traditional elements based on two-dimensional and flat qualities, where drapery surfaces tend toward the linear and decorative. Facial expressions lack animation, eyes appear lifeless, and movement in the body remains stiff. This resulted in a powerful and expressive frontality of the human figure where all appears frozen, even timeless. Similar qualities appear in Early Gothic French sculpture (ca. 1140–90), most notably the sculpture from the west front of the Cathedral of Chartres. By 1200–1210 rapid changes in sculpture resulted in more naturalism, in which the body turns and moves in space as if reacting to the world around it. In contrast, German sculpture continued the stiff, hierarchic style so prevalent during the Romanesque period.

The High Gothic phase in Germany is thought to have begun around 1210, one year after the Cathedral of Magdeburg was begun. This cathedral represents the first wholehearted adoption of French High Gothic forms. And, although sculpture in wood, stone, and metal was produced during this period, architectural sculpture found its greatest flourish as the newly discovered elements in French cathedral sculpture were deemed worthy of incorporation into German sculptural tradition. It is important to note, however, that the maintenance of a conservative, even Romanesque, style in Germany may not simply reflect lack of skill or talent on behalf of the German artisan but rather a response to a patron's wishes, or a desire to maintain artistic tradition.

High Gothic *ca.* 1210–1300

By the beginning of the 13th century, elaborate sculptural campaigns became common with the construction of a new cathedral. The cathedral workshop (German, *Bauhütte*) was responsible for the construction of the building and creation of sculpture, and its chief architect (German, *Baumeister*; Latin, *magister operis*) oversaw its activities. In some cases the chief architect was also a highly trained sculptor. Through the master sculptor (as well as the chief architect), artistic influences could be transmitted from one cathedral workshop to another, or from one country to another. This was the case with the Cathedral of Bamberg (begun in 1227), where French influence is clearly detected in the Prince's Portal (*Fürstenportal*) and in the famed *Bamberg Rider* from the interior choir (both dated *ca.* 1233–37).

The Prince's Portal contains a series of sculptures that reflect two different stylistic phases. Most of the jamb sculptures display Romanesque features. In contrast, a few other jamb figures on the portal's outermost southern side, and its tympanum depicting the Last

Judgment, are decidedly Gothic. The two styles are the work of two different master sculptors. The conservative style of the first master's figures is stiff and frontal. The second master seized the opportunity to create a considerable variety of poses and highly expressive faces, and he also depicted convincing drapery folds that reveal the underlying human anatomy. Similar qualities are found in the sculptural program at the Cathedral of Reims in France, and it appears that this second Bamberg master worked on the Reims sculptural campaign before Bamberg. Moreover, a comparison of the famous *Bamberg Rider* in the choir with sculpture at Reims reveals strikingly similar features: the hairpin drapery folds, the smooth, idealized face, and the long, slightly curled hair of the youthful rider echo the sculpture of the French cathedral's exterior, specifically the figure of Philip Augustus (now located in the Musée du Tau, Reims, France). Even in the Bamberg tympanum the maniacal faces of the damned to the left of Christ and the piously smug figures to his right appear to be direct adaptations from the Last Judgment portal at Reims.

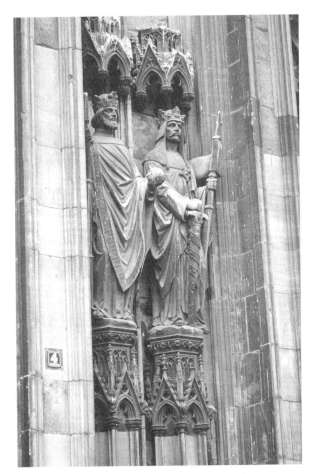

Cathedral of Cologne facade statues
© Ruggero Vanni / CORBIS

The Cathedral of Magdeburg, begun in 1209, also follows French examples both in its architectural plan and in its sculptural campaign. Some of the earliest sculpture, dated to the 1220s, suggests stylistic connections with sculpture from the Cathedral of Notre Dame in Paris and with the Cathedral of Chartres. By 1245, however, it was not French but rather German influences from the Bamberg workshop that are apparent at Magdeburg. The *Wise and Foolish Virgins* (now relocated to the Paradise Portal) exhibit the signature style of the Bamberg workshop. A comparison of these figures with the Last Judgment tympanum from Bamberg shows strong similarities in the exaggerated facial expressions, waves and curls in the hair, and billowing drapery.

Begun in 1248, the Cathedral of Cologne also drew inspiration from nearby France. This time from the interior, located in the choir, 14 figures—the Twelve Apostles and Christ and the Virgin Mary—stand at a height of six meters above the ground, attached to the columns of the piers that align the innermost choir. The immediate predecessor for this apostle cycle is the Sainte Chapelle in Paris, itself finished in 1248. The Cologne choir figures were sculpted between 1270 and 1290, and some scholars suggest that French influence (for example, Cathedral of Reims) was instrumental in their conception. Unlike contemporary French sculpture, however, the choir figures in Cologne are covered in heavy drapery folds, the bodies show an exaggerated sway, and the long beards of apostles become more decorative than representational. They also exhibit an exaggerated and elegant sumptuousness that is truly unique in the course of German Gothic sculpture.

Late Gothic *ca.* 1300–1500

The 13th century is often considered the "Classical" period, or the century of the greatest achievement in German Gothic sculpture. In may ways, artists during the 14th century continued the great sculptural campaigns of the 13th century, but the importance of French influence gave way to the development of regional styles, and the construction of large cathedrals was surpassed by the construction of a number of city and parish churches. Cathedral sculpture of this period is represented by numerous examples, including sculptures from the *Singertor* of St. Stephen's Cathedral in Vienna and the sculptures from the portal of St. Peter from the south tower of Cologne Cathedral. A fine example of parish church sculpture is found in the cycle of Apostles from the west front of the Überwasserkirche in Münster. Carved between 1364 and 1374, the Überwasserkirche figures show stylistic connections to Cologne as well as sculpture to the west of the Rhine, yet they maintain their stylistic independence and integrity: finely carved drapery folds and delicate features of the body contrast with distinct facial types and fluid body poses, whereas a definite mass has been given to the bodies, and fleshiness is depicted in the faces.

The end of the 14th century also witnessed the rise of the individual artisan in the independent workshop. The altarpiece was added to the repertoire of sculptural ornamentation. The abundance of surviving records also allows us to reconstruct the names of individual artisans and their workshops and to illuminate the process of artistic production through surviving contracts. By 1400, and surviving well into the middle of the 16th century, small workshops run by a master craftsman began to flourish. Some celebrated German sculptors from the 15th and 16th centuries include Michael and Gregor Erhart, Hans Multscher, Michael Pacher, Jörg Syrlin, Erasmus Grasser, Tilman Riemenschneider, Adam Kraft, Hans Leinberger, Veit Stoss, and the Vischer family. Individual idiosyncrasies were developed by each craftsman (for example, distinct drapery forms, facial types, and curls of the hair), and during the 15th and 16th centuries these sculptors learned to create more realistic details for sculpted human figures and the environments in which they were placed. Multscher brought a realism into southern German sculpture around 1430, and Riemenschneider introduced unique theatrical backgrounds to heighten the emotive drama of his figures and developed lightly colored varnishes for his wooden sculpture, making them appear unpainted. As one of the first sculptors to use such slight polychromy in his works, Riemenschneider effectively broke the long-standing tradition of fully painted sculpture—both wood and stone.

Characteristic of the 15th and 16th centuries is the importance of engravings and prints for the compositions and designs in carved altarpieces. An engraver, Master H.L. (also known as the Master of the Breisach Altarpiece), signed at least 31 prints, and the similarities of these prints to the Breisach Altarpiece (1523–26) has led scholars to suggest that the same artist is responsible for both works. The prints and sculpture of Master H.L. were distinctive: strong contrasts of light and dark are combined with highly active swirls in the drapery folds and vegetative ornament. No flat surface remains, especially in the Breisach Altarpiece, and the sheer abundance of circular lines creates a carpet of movement.

In secular works, the use of sketches and prints also was important. Sebastian Loscher worked on fountains for the city of Augsburg and is thought to be the sculptor responsible for the decoration in the Fugger Chapel in that city (1509–13)—the first significant burial chapel to use Renaissance forms in Germany. In addition to work for the Fugger Chapel, documents recount that Loscher was paid to produce a sketch before work would begin on a marble fountain in Augsburg.

Prior to 1450, the Netherlands and northern Germany were considered the leading artistic centers because, in large part, of the new realism of Claus Sluter, Nikolaus Gerhaert, and the painters Jan and Hubert Van Eyck. A north German sculptor, Claus Berg of Lübeck, continued the realism of his predecessors yet also sought his training in southern Germany under Veit Stoss before he brought the experiences back to his workshop in Lübeck and Odense, Denmark. The work of Claus Berg parallels that of Master H.L., where fluid vegetative forms create a lively decorative surface and highly animated drapery surfaces bring movement to the figures. The effective combination of these decorative surfaces and lively drapery is particularly noticeable in the high altar from the church of Odense, Denmark, dated to 1517–22.

Renaissance *ca.* 1500–1600

The transition from Late Gothic to Renaissance styles in Germany is unclear. Some suggest that Michael Pacher's interpretation of Italian art marks this change, whereas others claim Albrecht Dürer's immersion in the techniques and methods of Italian art during his trip to Venice in 1505–06 denotes the turning point. German Renaissance sculptors never systematically incorporated Italian Renaissance proportions or ideals into their works and thus remained late Gothic sculptors. The elaborate and dynamic carvings of Master H.L. equal the accomplishments of Italian sculpture, although little or no Italian Renaissance influence is perceptible. For this reason, German sculpture of the late 15th and early 16th century is given the alternate appellation German Renaissance.

KEVIN MCMANAMY

See also **Erhart, Gregor; Erhart, Michel; Gerhaert, Nikolaus; Grasser, Erasmus; Kraft, Adam; Leinberger, Hans; Multscher, Hans; Pacher, Michael; Riemenschneider, Tilman; Sluter, Claus; Stoss, Veit; Syrlin, Jörg, the Elder; Vischer Family**

Further Reading

Baxandall, Michael, *The Limewood Sculptors of Renaissance Germany*, New Haven, Connecticut: Yale University Press, 1980

Müller, Theodor, *Sculpture in the Netherlands, Germany, France, and Spain: 1400 to 1500*, translated by Elaine Robson Scott and William Robson Scott, London and Baltimore, Maryland: Penguin, 1966

Osten, Gert von der, and Horst Vey, *Painting and Sculpture in Germany and the Netherlands, 1500 to 1600*, London and Baltimore, Maryland: Penguin, 1969

Smith, Jeffrey Chipps, *German Sculpture of the Later Renaissance, c. 1520–1580: Art in an Age of Uncertainty*, Princeton, New Jersey: Princeton University Press, 1994
Williamson, Paul, *Gothic Sculpture, 1140–1300*, New Haven, Connecticut: Yale University Press, 1995

GERMANY: BAROQUE– NEOCLASSICAL

Baroque

There is no unified picture of Baroque sculpture in German-speaking countries from the beginning of the 17th century. Of course there were some concerted efforts in the first decades of the 17th century, primarily in the centers of Munich and Augsburg. Those who set the tone were Hans Reichle (who received his training in Florence with Giambologna), Hubert Gerhard, and Adriaen de Vries. In the time that followed, however, no distinguished sculptor emerged who would have been able to propagate what had been started and set new conventions for sculpture. The Thirty Years' War, which depopulated entire stretches of the lands north of the Alps, destroyed all continuity, leaving behind an artistic vacuum that began to be filled only quite slowly up until 1690 and was not uniform in all regions.

Thus in the time that Gianlorenzo Bernini was leading Italian Baroque sculpture to its greatest glory and bringing High Baroque expression to the Catholic faith together with an entire army of unusually talented sculptors, the formal sensibilities of sculptors north of the Alps remained bound for a long time to traditional and regional particularities. Martin Zürn's monumental *Knightly Saints* (1638/39; Staatliche Museen, Berlin, Germany) offers a good example of how artists were bound to what had preceded them locally: The Gothic composition scheme still determined the C-shaped curve of the body and pointed to the longevity of the craftsman-oriented guilds that in many areas formed the urban social basis for artists to receive commissions. It is typical of the ravaged lands north of the Alps that the artistic style of carving went in very different directions at the same time. Although Justus Glesker remained bound to the Italian High Renaissance in his Baroque refurbishing of the Cathedral of Bamberg (beginning in 1648), Georg Petel, who stood under Flemish influence, had already achieved international recognition in Augsburg. Johann Meinrad Guggenbichler, however, who from 1675 stood in the services of the diocese in Mondsee (Austria), developed a language of forms that was bound neither to the Flemish nor the Italian style: The undulations in his garments, his slim figures, and pathetically overdrawn faces informed the style of the Baroque in the Alps and had a decisive influence upon the Rococo.

Although the Mannerist movements of figures of the Italo-Flemish variety remained predominant, and the Zürn brothers and Thomas Schwanthaler (active in the Salzkammergut near Salzburg), among others, strove to rejuvenate the German Gothic, Matthias Rauchmiller (who hailed from the Bodensee [Lake Constance] and trained in Antwerp) introduced a High Baroque figural repertory into German funerary art. In 1675, shortly before moving to Vienna, he created the tomb for Karl von Metternich in Trier (Liebfrauenkirche). Impressed by the art of Peter Paul Rubens's circle as well as of Artus Quellinus, Rauchmiller overcame his own Mannerist style and sought to condense the expression of momentary concentration into the face wrapped in incessant reading. His most important work, however—the *Vienna Trinity Column*—did not get any further than the design stage during his lifetime. By 1692 it was finally realized by the sculptor Paul Strudel after it had been thoroughly reworked by the architects Johann Bernhard Fischer von Erlach and Ludovico Burnacini.

The creation of the Baroque *Gesamtkunstwerk* (total work of art) essentially lay in the melding of architecture and sculpture, which surrendered their particular qualities through their combination with painting and ornamental plasterwork on behalf of a more effective interpenetration of genre. Thus artists such as Fischer von Erlach, Matthias Steinl, and Andreas Schlüter united several talents. Schlüter, for example—who entered the stage of the German late Baroque around 1690 simultaneously with Balthasar Permoser at a time when it was being directed by the tastes set in Paris—was trained in Danzig as a sculptor. In 1694 he started working not only as court sculptor for the elector of Brandenburg but also as an architect, although he remained an autodidact in this latter métier all his life. Before he left his office of master of palace construction in 1707 and—following the call of the Russian czar—went to St. Petersburg, he had already created several of the major works of the Brandenburg Baroque, which provide clear indications of his manifold talents. These include the equestrian statue of the Grand Elector Friedrich Wilhelm I (1696–1709; Schloss Charlottenburg, Berlin, Germany) and the bust of Landgrave Friedrich II (*ca.* 1704; Schloss, Bad Homburg vor der Höhe, Germany), as well as the construction and furnishing of the Zeughaus and the palace in Berlin.

The equestrian statue is not only the most significant but also the very first freestanding monument of its kind erected in Germany. It follows François Girardon's equestrian statue of Louis XIV in Paris (1699; destroyed in the French Revolution and preserved only as a copy in miniature) both in the attitude of the figure as well as in its uniform, and carries the declamatory vocabulary of images of courtly, representational Baroque art. The charismatic ruler presents himself with the reins in the one hand and the staff of command in the other (significantly, Gabriel Grupello depicted his statue of Elector Johann Wilhelm [1703; Düsseldorf, Germany] in the same posture), demonstrating his ability to restrain and direct the elemental energy of the horse as well as the fate of the country.

Permoser, the second luminary of the German Baroque, created an even more decisively dramatic setting for a ruler when he transfigured Prince Eugene of Savoy by wrapping him within the aura of one of the chosen people (1720–1821). As the Hercules of his day, equipped with lion's mane and club, the vanquisher of the Turks supports himself with his right foot on the defeated figure kneeling before him while Fama leads the triumphal trombone call and the winged genius presents the armored hero with the sun of glory. In this allegory overburdened with symbols, Permoser still sought to capture individual facial features and thus avoid sacrificing character for the sake of enunciating imperial rhetoric, as happens in Schlüter's portrait of the Landgrave Friedrich II. Unlike Schlüter, Permoser, who came from Chiemgau, worked for a long time in Italy, and so was able to absorb Bernini's work before he was summoned to the court in Dresden by Elector Johann Georg III. Permoser's art spread throughout Europe in the form of his small-scale ivory figures, which may have been of decisive significance in the rise of German porcelain sculpture. His most important work, however, is the sculptural design for the facade of the Dresden Zwinger (1711–28)—for which Matthäus Daniel Pöppelmann was the main architect—which in its symbiotic relationship to the architecture can be considered a major work of the German Baroque. Through the interplay of ornament and sculpture, the architectural segments begin to flow into one another organically; instead of the usual pilasters, drunken and laughing satyrs are braced against the entablature and form a part of the narrative context of the entire ensemble, thereby transforming the festival ground of the Zwinger into a garden of the Hesperides and transfiguring every prince there into a Hercules or a Paris.

The dissolution of the boundaries between genres typical of the Baroque—a dissolution that allows all the arts to be drawn into the service of a communicative intention—is carried further in the work of the Asam brothers. Both were active as architects in Munich and the surrounding area. Cosmas Damian also worked as a ceiling painter, whereas his brother Egid Quirin was also active as a sculptor and plasterer. In designing the altar for the priory church of Rohr (1723), the younger Quirin gathered his many talents and discovered a satisfying form of expression for the mystery of the Assumption in the illusionist synthesis of architecture, plastering, painting, and sculptures that seem to float in the air. The scenographic staging of the miracle—which reminds one of the ephemeral stage design of the Baroque—was apparently based on the impressions he gathered in Italy, above all those of Bernini's works.

Italian and French models remained an inexhaustible source of inspiration in German-speaking areas; they were propagated either through fruitful student-teacher relationships, as with Permoser and Paul Egell of Mannheim, or by the young talent making its way to the actual locations themselves in order to use the examples set by the masterpieces as models for their own drawing. The art of Georg Raphael Donner, one of the most important representatives of the late Baroque in Austria, grew attuned to Italian styles through his journey there. In his figures for the so-called Grain Market fountain (1737–39), through which he achieved the rank of a European sculptor, body movements and the sway of folds are drawn into an ornamental sense of flow, whereas the limbs are lengthened and the posture of the figures are stylized for the sake of an elegant linear rhythm. Commissioned by the city of Vienna and executed in lead (the material Donner preferred), the fountain contains multiple figures and anticipates the formal repertoire of the late 18th century.

Similar things can be said of Johann Baptist Straub from southern Germany, who received training in the Vienna Academy from Donner and was able to attain the rank of court sculptor in Munich. In his numerous plaster depictions of saints, such as those in the Abbey Church in Ettal (1762), one sees the first glimmer of the rarefied expressive ideal of the southern German Rococo, which reaches full maturity in the work of his student, Franz Ignaz Günther. Although Günther's *Pietà* in St. Ruprecht's Church (1758; Kircheiselfing, near Wasserburg, Germany) still depicts the mother's pain and draws the viewer's sympathy, in the *Pietà* in Weyarn (1764) the embrace that had been so tender and close dissolves into a relation exhibiting equal portions of consternation and distance. The body is presented to the viewer in an elegantly balanced movement, so that it is Christ's body, rather than Mary's complaint, that stands at the center of devotion. The contrasting effects of the abstract depiction of Mary's clothes and the true-to-life execution of the body show that the primary concern of the design is the presentation of the Christ in death. The rarefied formal language of the Rococo is shown in the typical contrasting relationship between the dramatic content and the elegantly stylized depiction; the stylistic refinement is consciously emphasized over the figural narrative and is given its own artistic value.

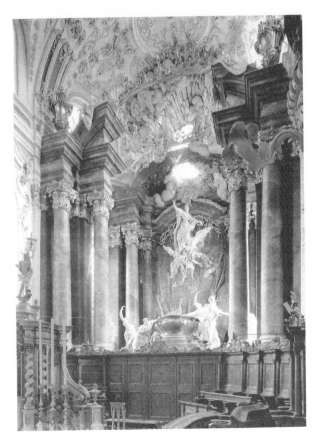

Egid Quirin Asam, *The Assumption,* 1722–23, Abbey
Church, Rohr, Germany
The Conway Library, Courtauld Institute of Art

Neoclassical

Only when the new generations of sculptors appear—
such as Johann Heinrich Dannecker, Johann Gottfried
Schadow, and Christian Daniel Rauch—did sculpting
become characterized by linearly accentuated surfaces
and restrained forms of composition. Following the
strict formal example of Antonio Canova, Bertel Thorvaldsen, and Johan Tobias Sergel in Rome, the German
sculptors in the 1790s also began to renounce the wide
variety of materials used in the Baroque, giving preference instead to marble and seeking to rejuvenate the
ideals of the Greek past. When Dannecker completed
the portrait of Friedrich Schiller in 1794, he followed
canonical forms of expression from antiquity. The profile of the portrait, recurring in herm busts, and the
elevating nakedness of the poet-prince can easily be
associated with antique portraits of philosophers and
contributed to the creation of a form adequate to what
was meant to be seen as the apotheosis of human spirit.

The Classical need to immortalize through commemoration made the portrait, along with funerary and
other monuments, the most important task of sculpture.
The respective requirements of these different types of
work are often combined. Schadow's public commission from Friedrich Wilhelm II to create a marble monument (1796–97) for the Princesses Luise and Friederike of Prussia was, for example, preceded by a private
commission to create two busts of the sisters in plaster
for everyday use years before. Contemporaries praised
the former work due to the predomination of its Classical style, by which they meant not only the richly
folded garments but also the depiction of their inner
communion reminiscent of antique pairings. The sisters thereby become a compositional unit despite the
contrapposto (a natural pose with the weight of one
leg, the shoulder and hip counterbalancing the other)
formation of the figures—one head raised and the other
lowered, one stance relaxed and the other rigid, one
sister's arms bent and the other's outstretched.

Rauch, who stood in the service of the Prussian king
from 1797 and consequently became one of the sculptors in greatest demand in Germany, was the most important student of Schadow. Among his numerous
works, the equestrian statue of Frederick the Great
(1836–51; formerly on Unter den Linden, now in the
park of Schloss Sanssouci, Potsdam, Germany) was
his most important work. It should already have been
built/completed by 1779 following Schlüter's equestrian image, but it was set to fail because, in the opinion
of the king, it was inappropriate to erect a monument
to the field marshall while he was still alive. Frederick
considered the equestrian statue to be a monument to
his personal fame and not a monument of the state
meant to postulate the Enlightenment ideals of a patriotic ethos. When the project was completed 60 years
later, a pedestal with life-size representations of military men as well as civilians important to the state was
erected, on top of which the king sits high on his horse
as the "first servant of the state." The image of a man
who was highly gifted in his rational faculties and
largely free of passions is appropriately rendered
through the distanced realism that is characteristic of
Berlin Neoclassicism.

Although there was no sculptor in German-speaking
countries who had a formative influence upon the Baroque style, and due to territorial divisions there was
no artistic center in the Baroque or constant clientele
for art commissioning (such as the pope in Rome or the
court in Paris), German Classicism does, by contrast,
evince stylistically and geographically unified contours. Schadow, whose public was drawn equally from
the Brandenburg court and the Berlin bourgeoisie, established an artistic ideal that stretched far into the
20th century.

MICHAEL KUHLEMANN

See also **Donner, Georg Raphael; Gerhard, Hubert;
Guggenbichler, Johann Meinrad; Günther, Franz**

Ignaz; Petel, Georg; Permoser, Balthasar; Rauch, Christian Daniel; Reichle, Hans; Schadow, Johann Gottfried; Schlüter, Andreas; Zürn Family

Further Reading

Aschengreen-Piacenti, Kirsten, "Documented Works in Ivory by Balthasar Permoser," *Mitteilungen des Kunsthistorischen Institutes in Florenz* 10/4 (1963)

Bauer, Hermann, *Barock: Kunst einer Epoche*, Berlin: Reiner, 1992

Baxandall, Michael, *German Wood Statuettes, 1500–1800*, London: HMSO, 1967

Bloch, Peter, and Waldemar Grzimek, *Das klassische Berlin*, Frankfurt, Berlin, and Vienna: Propyläen-Verlag, 1987

Bruhns, Thomas P., "Hans Reichle (1565/70–1642): A Reassessment of His Sculpture," (dissertation), Pennsylvania State University, 1981

Hager, Werner, *Barock: Skulptur und Malerei*, Baden-Baden, Germany: 1969

Hempel, Eberhard, *Baroque Art and Architecture in Central Europe*, Baltimore, Maryland: Penguin, 1965

Hitchcock, Henry Russell, *German Rococo: The Zimmerman Brothers*, London: Allen Lane, and Baltimore, Maryland: Penguin, 1968

Hubala, Erich, *Die Kunst des 17. Jahrhundert*, Berlin: Propyläen-Verlag, 1970

Kaufmann, Thomas da Costa, "Schlüter's Fate: Comments on Sculpture, Science, and Patronage in Central and Eastern Europe, c. 1700," in *Künstlerischer Austausch; Artistic Exchange*, edited by Thomas W. Gaehtgens, vol. 2, Berlin: Akademie Verlag, 1993

Keutner, H., *Sculpture: Renaissance to Rococo*, Greenwich, Connecticut: New York Graphic Society, and London: Joseph, 1969

Schönberger, Arno, *Deutsche Plastik des Barock*, Königstein im Taunus, Germany: Koster, 1963

Scholten, Frits (editor), *Adriaen de Vries 1556–1626: Imperial Sculptor* (exhib. cat.), Amsterdam: Rijksmusum, Stockholm: Nationalmuseum, and Los Angeles: Getty Museum, 1998

Smith, Jeffrey Chipps, *German Sculpture of the Later Renaissance, c. 1520–1580*, Princeton, New Jersey: Princeton University Press, 1994

Weihrauch, Hans R., *Europäische Bronzestatuetten, 15.–18. Jahrhundert*, Braunschweig, Germany: Klinkhardt and Biermann, 1967

Woekel, Gerhard P., "An Unknown Early Work by Ignaz Günther 'St. Scholastica,'" *Los Angeles County Museum of Art Bulletin* (1975)

GERMANY: 20TH CENTURY–CONTEMPORARY

German 20th-century sculpture reflects the country's varied history. A great demand for public monuments characterized the last phase of the German Empire (until 1918), while an alternative bourgeois art market developed concurrently with completely different demands. During the Weimar Republic (1918–33) public commissions were largely limited to monuments to those fallen in World War I, while the art market became more international. No free art market existed to speak of during the Third Reich (1933–45), but a private sphere that enabled modern German sculpture to develop further did exist apart from the dictatorial state cultural policy—which was characterized by rejections and by state commissions—for sculptors who did not conform to the government-supported trends. After World War II East and West German sculpture grew distinct from one another. Public and private sponsorship in the Federal Republic of Germany led to a form of sculpture that acquired links with developments in Western Europe and the United States, while sculpture in the German Democratic Republic (GDR) showed connections to developments in other Communist countries.

The clear interrelations between the country's sculpture and its political history have often led scholars to write the history of German sculpture mostly from a political perspective. Such an approach has produced studies in which the value of sculpture is determined solely through either the rejection or the recognition of the political concepts behind it or its political impact. The sculptural traditions and lines of development outside the realm of politics have barely been investigated, although they offer important modes of explication for a genre history that is in part highly contradictory.

The political division of Germany in the 19th century between several royal households led to the development of several centers for sculpture, including Berlin, the Rhineland, Dresden, and Munich. Modern sculpture developed mainly in Berlin, while a more naturalistic tradition persisted in the other centers. An overview of German sculpture in the 20th century has to include an account of these local differences. Sculpture during the Third Reich thus cannot be evaluated without an examination (which is still lacking) of the traditions in Munich (and Austria), while the opposition between the schools in Berlin and Dresden strongly influenced the character of sculpture in the GDR.

German 20th-century sculpture developed out of Neo-Baroque and Neoclassical styles. A late 19th-century German variant of Neoclassicism (called *Neuklassizismus*) originated as a reaction to the lavish Neo-Baroque style of the great monuments appearing mainly in Berlin, arising through the followers of the painter Hans von Marées, who lived in Rome, leading a passionate fight against naturalism and the death of spirit in art. Marées's most important successor was the sculptor Adolf von Hildebrand, whose book *Das Problem der Form in der bildenden Kunst* (1893; English version, *The Problem of Form in Painting and Sculpture*, published in 1907), received throughout Europe, is a theoretical treatment of the foundations of sculpture.

Artists such as Hildebrand, Louis Tuaillon, and the animal sculptor August Gaul developed a sculptural language around the turn of the 20th century whose defining elements were clarity and tectonic construction. For the next generation, including Georg Kolbe, the most popular German sculptor of the time, Auguste Rodin became a great model. The opposition between Hildebrand and Rodin, seen by their German contemporaries as the contrast between theoretical classicism and lively naturalism, would define modern German sculpture until 1914. A second reaction to the Neo-Baroque played out in the area of sculpture related to architecture. Sculptors such as Hugo Lederer and Franz Metzner developed a symbolistic, blocklike monumental sculpture with "Germanic" political connotations. The monument of this movement, which served right-wing political fantasies up until the most recent past, is the *Völkerschlachtdenkmal* (Monument to the Battle of Nations) in Leipzig, dedicated in 1913.

In 1912 the Mannheim Kunsthalle organized the first exhibition of modern German sculpture under the title *Ausdrucksplastik* (Expression Sculpture). These sculptures were meant to depict inner life. The terminology used by these artists shows clear parallels to the contemporaneous German Expressionism, so that the two movements are often treated together. However, applying the notion of Expressionism to greatly varying sculptural approaches, such as the "primitive" works of Expressionist painters, above all those of Ernst Ludwig Kirchner, and to the works of a lone artist such as Ernst Barlach and the early avant-garde—upon which Alexander Archipenko had a formative influence in Germany—is somewhat problematic.

The first abstract German sculptures arose among revolutionary groups of artists after World War I. Artists such as Rudolf Belling and Oswald Herzog developed their abstract language of forms from "vitalist Expressionism" (the typical post-Nietzschian way of thinking of these artists: The main focus is life and not intellect). They continued Expressionist attempts to depict abstract concepts in human figures and directed them toward further formal abstraction. Abstract sculpture played only a small role in the art scene of the Weimar Republic. Another reaction to the pathos of Expressionism proved more important than abstraction: the return to natural models.

For German sculptors of the 1920s the question arises as to the relation between the natural model and its plastic, spatial qualities. Achieving a balance between these two poles became the point of departure for a rejuvenation of the figural tradition oriented toward French sculptors such as Aristide Maillol and Charles Despiau. In comparison, artists in Germany turned to the abstract formal qualities of figural sculpture relatively late. It is also noteworthy that Rudolf Belling, the creator of *Dreiklang* (Chord, 1919), the first German abstract sculpture, once again came to rely on natural forms in the 1920s. Along with another movement oriented more toward Classicism, a small group of socially critical and veristic sculptors from Dresden, including Eugen Hoffmann and Christoph Voll, should also be mentioned.

After 1933 many abstract, avant-garde sculptors could no longer show their works publicly. Some sculptors had to leave the country because of their ancestry or their political persuasions. Contrary to accepted opinion, however, their forced exile was not necessarily connected with their art, as is demonstrated by the examples of two completely different sculptors, Otto Freundlich, one of the most important abstract artists of his time, and the figurative sculptor Bernhard Sopher, who were both forced into exile because of their Jewish ancestry.

An understanding of the figural tradition in the 1920s is imperative to understanding the history of German sculpture in the Third Reich. While further work became impossible for the avant-garde artists, some artists in the figural tradition, which could be considered moderately modern, continued to find an audience. A bourgeois clientele remained faithful to the favored artists of the time, while the new political elite supported on the one hand a highly traditional sculpture and on the other a radically monumental formal language for public commissions. The latter movement defines the image of German sculpture in the 1930s, not least because of the propaganda apparatus that handled this sort of art. Working with varied motives, sculptors such as Arno Breker and Josef Thorak developed a sculpture in which body tension was meant to express political will. Along with these monumental sculptors, a group of figural sculptors depicted a generalized human beauty that could be employed in connection with racist ideology, as in the case of Georg Kolbe.

As an opposition to these tendencies in officially propagated sculpture that put human beauty in the foreground, a group of sculptors in the 1930s oriented themselves more strongly toward archaic models, thereby placing more emphasis on architectonic construction and less on the (idealized) human model. The two most important representatives of this movement, Ludwig Kasper and Hermann Blumenthal, developed a figural sculpture whose audience existed outside of the officially regulated culture. After 1945 critics viewed these artists' work as a possible alternative to the figural tradition tainted by National Socialism.

After the end of World War II, two possibilities seemed to exist for sculptural work in Germany: figural sculpture in the archaic tradition of Blumenthal, Kasper, and Gerhard Marcks, and abstract sculpture connected to the avant-garde notions of the 1920s. The political polarization caused a parting of ways in the realm of sculpture in the 1950s. While the GDR saw an officially instigated dispute with the so-called formalism, figural sculpture in the Federal Republic became ever more marginalized. Beginning in 1949 sculpture in the two countries grew more disparate. Virtually no artistic exchanges took place with the onset of the Cold War.

West German sculptors such as Hans Hartung, Bernhard Heiliger, and Hans Uhlmann took up avant-garde sculptural concepts that had been carried further outside Germany between 1933 and 1945. Hartung's work revealed connections with the forgotten sculptor Richard Haizmann, who was influenced by the mystical language of anthroposophy and had discovered an abstract formal language before 1933 in Hamburg. Uhlmann integrated Cubist elements as well as montages of iron pieces in his sculptures. Whereas these three sculptors remained bound to a broadly conceived figure, Norbert Kricke produced completely nonfigural wire sculptures in the 1950s that bear a resemblance to *art informel* (European abstract expressionist) painting.

In the GDR communist-oriented political sculpture stood in the foreground. The artist Fritz Cremer contributed to the state's political self-understanding with his monument for the concentration camp Buchenwald. Other sculptors, such as Waldemar Grzimek and Gustav Seitz, carried on the figural tradition for the most part without injecting explicit political content. These artists followed a tradition going back to the Berlin sculpture of the 1920s and the sculpture professor Wilhelm Gerstel, whose legacy has been carried on by teachers in the GDR and the eastern German states (after 1990) up to the present.

In the 1960s and 1970s West German sculpture became integrated to a great extent with international developments, particularly contemporaneous developments in England. Sculptors such as Erwin Heerich and Heinz-Günter Prager investigated the fundamental formal elements of sculpture in their works, as well as the relationships of these abstract forms to each other. The figural tradition received new impulses through New Realism, while artists such as Joachim Schmettau and Michael Schoenholtz connected these impulses to a critical social attitude, as was typical of the times. Beginning in the mid 1960s artists such as Joseph Beuys, Wolff Vostell, and Franz Erhard Walther, who made an important international contribution, continued to dissolve the traditional notion of sculpture. The work of Ulrich Rückriem presents some mediation between this expanded notion of art and traditional sculpture.

During the same period an independent figurative tradition arose in the GDR through sculptors such as Wieland Förster and Werner Stötzer; this tradition focused on abstracting the human body to a greater degree. The guidance art received through associations, commissions, and, occasionally, massive political pressure, played an important role here. The great political monuments from around 1970 in the GDR were mostly the creation of sculptors from the Soviet Union, while East German sculptors were in charge of extensive programs for architecture and public spaces. Whereas the Soviet sculptors formed the image of officially sponsored sculpture, sponsorship at a local level exhibits a certain variability that should be further investigated. An art scene developed in Dresden in the 1970s that explored the boundaries of the concept of art in a way similar to that of artists in the West. The government only tolerated groups such as this for a time, however. The work of A.R. Penck, who was exiled from the GDR in 1980, exemplifies the radicalism they achieved.

In the early 1980s a Neo-Expressionism dominated the West German art scene, including sculpture. Painters such as Georg Baselitz created emphatically primitive sculptures, and their work awakened interest in the painter-sculptors of German Expressionism from the first decades of the century. The extent to which these contemporary developments informed the historical picture became apparent when the first great presentation of Expressionist sculpture (in the Los Angeles County Museum of Art, California, in 1983) emphasized the painter-sculptors of the past; our image of this art form thereby became greatly distorted. The prejudice that German art has always been Romantic or Expressionist has made it markedly more difficult for German sculpture's reception to be historically accurate, both in terms of its formally innovative aspects as well as its integration in larger European developments.

When the GDR was absorbed into the Federal Republic in 1990, art worlds that had been largely separate came together. In the following years the East German scene quickly conformed to the West German situation. Stephan Balkenhol has assumed one interesting position, recognized regardless of all the previous boundaries by a broad audience; using photography as well as the conceptual methods of his teacher, Rückriem, he has conceived a form of figuration that has received international attention.

ARIE HARTOG

See also **Balkenhol, Stephan; Barlach, Ernst; Beuys, Joseph; Kolbe, Georg; Lehmbruck, Wilhelm; Marcks, Gerhard**

Further Reading

Barron, Stephanie (editor), *German Expressionist Sculpture*, Chicago: University of Chicago Press, 1983

Beloubek-Hammer, Anita (editor), *Mensch-Figur-Raum: Werke deutsche Bildhauer des 20. Jahrhunderts* (exhib. cat.), East Berlin: Staatliche Museen zu Berlin, 1988

Berger, Ursel, *Figürliche Bildhauerei im Georg-Kolbe-Museum Berlin: Vom ende des 19. bis zur Mitte des 20. Jahrhunderts*, Berlin: Letter-Stiftung, 1994

Bloch, Peter, Sibylle Einholz, and Jutta von Simson (editors), *Ethos und Pathos: Die Berliner Bildhauerschule, 1786–1914*, 2 vols., Berlin: Mann, 1990

Grzimek, Waldemar, *Deutsche Bildhauer des zwanzigsten Jahrhunderts: Leben, Schulen, Wirkungen*, Munich: Moos, 1969

Hartog, Arie, Liesbeth Jans, and Peter van der Coelen (editors), *Entartete beeldhouwkunst: Duitse beeldhouwers, 1900–1945* (exhib. cat.), Zwolle, The Netherlands: Waanders, 1991

Hentzen, Alfred, *Deutsche Bildhauer der Gegenwart*, Berlin: Rembrandt-Verlag, 1934

Koep, Daniel, "Resurrecting the Body: Figurative Sculpture in West-Germany, 1945–1959," (dissertation), London: Courtauld Institute of Art, University of London, 2000

Kuhn, Alfred, *Die neuere Plastik von 1800 bis zur Gegenwart*, Munich: Delphin, 1921

Ohnesorge, Birk, *Bildhauerei zwischen Tradition und Erneuerung. Die Menschendarstellung in der deutschen Skuptur and Plastik nach 1945 im Spiegel repräsentativer Ausstellungen*, Münster, Germany: Lit-Verlag, 2001.

Ranfft, Erich, "Reproduced Sculpture of German Expressionism: Living Objects, Theatrics of Display, and Practical Options," in *Sculpture and Its Reproductions*, edited by Anthony Hughes and Erich Ranfft, London: Reaktion Books, 1997

Skulptur und Macht: Figurative Plastik im Deutschland der 30er und 40er Jahre, Berlin: Akademie der Kunste, 1983

GERO CRUCIFIX

Anonymous

ca. 969–976

polychrome oak

Body: h. 1.87 m; w. 1.66 m

Cross: h. 2.85 m; w. 1.98 m

Cologne Cathedral, Germany

The Gero Crucifix on the Kreuzaltar (crucifix altar) of the Cathedral of Cologne is reputed to be the oldest surviving large-scale sculpture of the Middle Ages. In all likelihood, it is identical to a wooden crucifix documented in literature that Archbishop Gero of Cologne (969–76) commissioned for his cathedral, the predecessor of the Gothic Cathedral of Cologne.

The suffering of Christ is complete. His head is sunken down to the right, and the eyes in his serious, compactly formed face are closed. Because the torso, with its apparent bulk, hangs heavily from the arms, the body bends out slightly to the left. The suffering of the Savior is not beautified, but rather portrayed with statuary precision. It has none of the emotional late medieval pathos, which was unafraid of even extreme contortions; instead it is simply realistic. As with the posture of the figure generally, the individual body parts demonstrate the torture of death on the cross: the stretched skin on the upper body and legs, as well as the protruding stomach.

The sculpture is surprisingly well preserved. It shows the work of a professional both in its detailed artistic composition and in its technical construction. It consists of three pieces of wood, and the arms are attached. The surface work is smooth and uniform; the reverse side was produced more summarily than the rest and is hollowed out in places. Marks on the woodwork indicate that the figure was carved first in rough contours, stored away for a long period of time, then carved to completion.

The present polychromy dates to about 1900. Beneath it, no less than six different painted layers have been identified, the bottom of which (perhaps the original) appears to be relatively well preserved: dark brown on the outside, considerably lighter in damaged places, with a *caput mortuum* (a medieval color) of a pinkish hue. A dark cinnabar red emphasizes the wounds; no other indications of blood have been found. The hair is dark brown. The loin cloth is of a yellow color. The cross itself is still the original; its original coloring (nail marks could signify a layer of gold foil) cannot presently be determined. A crucifixion miniature from Cologne dated to 983–96 from the Sacramentary of St. Gerion (Bibliothèque Nationale de France, Paris, France) resembles the Gero Crucifix in the depiction of Christ's upper body and provides an idea of the latter's coloring.

A date for this work is difficult to verify, but a dendrochronological examination has produced an approximate date between 971 and 1012 when the tree in question was felled for the vertical beam of the cross; for the body, an approximate date of 965 or shortly thereafter is indicated. The halo decorated with rock crystal behind the head of Christ (possibly walnut) could be a later addition, dating probably from the 12th or 13th century (see Schulz-Senger et al., 1976).

The dendrochronological findings confirm both the local belief in Cologne and the testimony of Thietmar von Merseburg (975–1018), who writes in his chronicle:

> The wonderful Archbishop Gero of Cologne had died in the meanwhile. . . . He had the crucifix, which now stands in the middle of church, artistically crafted in wood. When he noticed a crack in the head, he healed it without laying a hand on it himself, but rather employed the following, more potent antidote of the greatest artist of all [God]. He took a piece of the Body of the Lord, our only comfort in times of need, and laid it into

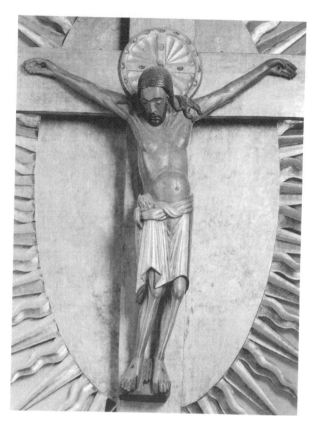

Gero Crucifix, Cologne Cathedral
© Dombauarchiv Köln, Matz und Schnek

the crack. Then he prostrated himself on the floor, and called the name of the Lord through tears, and when he got up again, his humble prayer had caused the damage to disappear.

According to Thietmar, the Gero Crucifix was placed in the old cathedral, one may imagine as a mark of the Kreuzaltar (the exact location of which is unknown), near which Gero may have been buried.

In 1248 the old cathedral burned down and the new Gothic structure began to take shape. By about 1270 Gero's shrine had been erected in the Stephanus Chapel of the new choir ambulatory. The Gero Crucifix was likewise transferred to the new structure and early on seems to have received its present place by the altar on the south side of the choir in the large chapel opposite the sacristy. The altar was referred to as Severin's altar from 1319 and as the Kreuzaltar from 1351. The legend of Blessed Irmgard, probably from the 14th century, localizes the Gero Crucifix there and, grotesquely trumping Thietmar's miracle story, relates a further miracle of this sculpture: It nodded its thanks when Irmgard brought it the greeting of a Romanesque Crucifixion icon.

In 1638, at a time of Counter Reformation piety, attention to tradition, and initial examinations into the

history of the town, the canon Heinrich Mering made the Gero Crucifix centerpiece of a Baroque renovation of the altar, which has been essentially maintained. In artistic terms, the Gero Crucifix appears as a major work practically without precedent, and this is at least in part, although not solely, owing to the high destruction rate of early medieval works of art. The work bears the mark of routine production. As Haussherr has demonstrated, many of its individual stylistic motifs are comparable to older works in ivory and illuminated manuscripts, and thus the Gero Crucifix stands in an artistic tradition (see Haussherr, 1963). The artist assimilated several Byzantine elements into the Western conception of the dying Christ, which show not the majesty and power of the son of God, but rather his suffering. In the Rhineland numerous early medieval sculptures have been preserved or attested to in literature. In addition to the Gero Crucifix, Aegedius Gelenius, a local historian of Early Baroque Cologne, lists "a heavy and very large figure in silver of the mother of God sitting on a silver throne" and a large silver crucifix as being endowments from Gero (see Clemen, 1938). It appears that from the late 10th century, high-quality sculptures, even of larger proportions, were no longer rare in this region.

There has been a tendency to view the expansion of sculpture in the ecclesiastical realm as a consequence of a growing admiration for relics: As relics, the figures are supposed to have served as storage places for the Eucharist. The Gero Crucifix had served as chief witness to this theory, based on the reports by Thietmar and particular to the legend of Blessed Irmgard, which has the Archbishop depositing the host into the miraculous woodwork. However, the Schultz-Senger examination in 1976 indicates that this theory no longer applies to the Gero Crucifix, as it has been proved—counter to all the assertions made in recent literature—that the crucifix does not reveal any sepulchrum for relics. The narrative motif of the "open sculpture" may have originated from the irregular hollowed out portions on the backside, which were technically necessary and unsealable. Little consideration has been given to the fact that the legend of Blessed Irmgard relates not, as the text claims, beliefs from the 11th century, but from the 14th century, when naturalistic head and arm reliquaries were widespread in the Rhineland.

The almost universal loss of early medieval monuments, predominantly crucifixes and Madonnas, renders it impossible to determine the possible artistic contexts of the few remaining pieces. The reverent allusions made in medieval literature lead to the conclusion that the Gero Crucifix was already prominent in its own time and stood out not only because of its size. Although its date can only be approximated, Haedeke has suggested that some later crucifixes depend on the tradition of the Gero Crucifix (see Haedeke, 1958).

PETER DIEMER

Further Reading

Clemen, Paul, *Der Dom zu Köln*, Düsseldorf, Germany: Schwann, 1938

Haedeke, Hanns-Ulrich, "Das Gerokreuz im Dom zu Köln und seine Nachfolge im 11. Jahrhundert," *Kölner Domblatt* 14/15 (1958)

Haussherr, Reiner, *Der tote Christus am Kreuz: Zur Ikonographie des Gerokreuzes*, Bonn: s.n., 1963

Kroos, Renate, "Liturgische Quellen zum Kölner Domchor," *Kölner Domblatt* 44/45 (1979)

Schulz-Senger, Christa, et al., "Das Gero-Kreuz im Kölner Dom: Ergebnisse der restauratorischen und dendrochronologischen Untersuchungen im Jahre 1976," *Kölner Domblatt* 41 (1976)

JEAN-LÉON GÉRÔME 1824–1904 *French*

Although Jean-Léon Gérôme's paintings were more popular than his sculptures during his lifetime, he may arguably be credited now as a greater innovator in the field of sculpture. With the exhibition of a bronze figure of a gladiator (a quotation from an earlier painting of his own) at the Exposition Universelle of 1878, he began a secondary career as a sculptor in which he experimented with many additive and subtractive media, achieving increasingly sophisticated technical effects during the last two decades of his life. His fascination with the pursuit of "truth," his ideal in all aesthetic endeavors, led him to produce his sculpted studies of the human figure in a variety of materials, including tinted marble and ivory (often used to imitate female flesh), bronze (usually reserved for details and drapery), glass paste, and semiprecious and even precious stones. In another curious manifestation of his almost naive respect for the real, he several times depicted his own figurines—themselves quotations of his earlier paintings—as props in scenes of ancient Greek myth and historical genre; and in his oil self-portraits he represented himself as a sculptor (*The End of the Séance*, 1887, and *The Artist and His Mode*, 1895).

As in his best figure paintings, Gérôme's statuary could occasionally boast an eloquence of texture and surface that his rivals could scarcely match and that was an outcome of the artist's tempering of anatomical precision and detail with a flattering "simplification of the planes" (see Ackerman, 1986). The statues satisfy the fin de siècle taste for luxury and decadent subjects and display the sinuous, vegetal rhythms that were a hallmark of Art Nouveau. At the same time, Gérôme made an effort to achieve realism in his figures, as in the stylish but unflatteringly literal bust of Sarah Bernhardt.

Gérôme clearly based one of his best-known paintings, the *Pygmalion and Galatea*, on his own original plaster figure group from which he made the tinted marble version that appeared in the Paris Salon of 1892. He continued to work on variations of the figure's complex *contrapposto* (a natural pose with the weight of one leg, the shoulder, and hip counterbalancing one another) throughout the remainder of his career.

The *Tanagra* was one of Gérôme's many commercial and critical successes of the 1890s, perhaps in part because it displayed to full effect a contemporary ideal of the female form (her marble flesh is tinted with anatomical accuracy: rosy nipples and lips, blonde hair, etc.). The French government was so eager to obtain it that they obliged Gérôme's condition that the money be found from outside the limited budget ordinarily set aside for the purchase of sculpture, so as not to monopolize the fund to the disadvantage of less successful carvers. Other examples of the artist's efforts in mixed media sculpture include a *Seated Woman* and the *Pygmalion and Galatea* group in California.

Concerning his practice of tinting his statues, Gérôme explained in 1892 that he was reviving an ancient

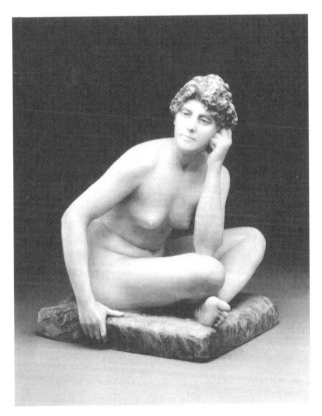

Seated Woman (ca. 1890/95)
Founders Society Purchase, Robert H. Tannahill Foundation Fund
© 1997 Detroit Institute of Arts

Greek tradition and that he "had always been put off by the coldness of statues when, once finished, they were left in their natural state." The tinting of the stone led, he argued, to the attachment to it of "mixed materials, uniting gold, pewter, ivory, etc.," which he also traced to Antiquity. Writing in reference to his almost disquietingly realistic chryselephantine figure of *Bellona*, he concluded,

> To arrive at good results in these matters, be it for the painting of marble or the application of metal to ivory or marble, you have to use taste and temperance. This then is the result of a life of observation in these problematic [areas], so difficult to resolve, and costly too. (Ackerman, 1986)

ANDREW MARVICK

Biography

Born in Vésoul, Haute-Saône, France, 11 May 1824. Began formal training in art at age 16 in studio of painter Paul Delaroche, 1840–43; moved with Delaroche to Italy, 1843; returned to Paris to study with Charles Gleyre, 1844, enrolled at École des Beaux-Arts same year; began a three-year unsuccessful quest to win the Prix-de-Rome, 1846; traveled to Istanbul, 1853, and Egypt, 1856; moved to studio at Rue Notre-Dame-des-Champs in Paris, 1853, which became a meeting center for artists and actors; showed regularly at the Salon, 1857–74; appointed professor at École des Beaux-Arts, 1863; member of the Academie, 1864. Died in Paris, France, 10 January 1904.

Selected Works

1890   *Tanagra*; tinted marble, mixed media; Musée d'Orsay, Paris, France
ca. 1890/95   *Seated Woman*; marble; Detroit Institute of Arts, Michigan, United States
1892   *Pygmalion and Galatea*; tinted marble, ivory, bronze; Hearst Foundation, San Simeon, California, United States
1895   *Bellona*; bronze, ivory; Inn on the Park, Toronto, Canada
1895   Bust of Sarah Bernhardt; patinated plaster, collection of Mr. and Mrs. Joseph M. Tannenbaum, Toronto, Canada

Further Reading

Ackerman, Gerald M., *The Life and Work of Jean-Léon Gérôme: With a Catalogue Raisonné*, New York and London: Sothebys, 1986
Gérôme: Jean-Léon Gérôme, 1824–1904, peintre, sculpteur, et graveur (exhib. cat.), Vésoul, France: Musée Garret, 1981
Hering, Fanny Field, *Gérôme: The Life and Works of Jean Léon Gérôme*, New York: Cassell Publishing, 1892
Isaacson, Robert, *Jean Léon Gérôme and His Pupils* (exhib. cat.), Poughkeepsie, New York: Vassar College Art Gallery, 1967
Jean-Léon Gérôme, 1824–1904: Sculpteur et peintre de l'art officiel, Paris: Galerie Tanagra, 1974

JOCHEN GERZ 1940–   *German*

Jochen Gerz is one of Germany's most innovative and highly respected multimedia artists of the early 21st century. Since the mid 1980s his sculptural works have radically transformed the boundaries of public art. The sculptures are informed by his background as a social activist, concrete poet, performance artist, and Conceptualist. Central to Gerz's aims is the dematerialization of the art object by focusing on the process of production and the objectification of language and dialogue. These aims can be traced to the context of 1970s Conceptual art and artists' critical positions against Minimalist sculpture through the notion of the "counter-monument." The key element for Gerz is collaboration; he often collaborates with a host of targeted and/or random individuals such as art school students to collectively create public art. This recalls the strategies of Christo and Jeanne-Claude, whose grand-scale projects include wrapping and marking landscapes and buildings, as well as the aspirations of German Conceptualist Joseph Beuys, whose work and teachings culminated in what he termed a revolutionary "social sculpture." Finally, much of Gerz's sculptural work has been concerned with the themes of remembrance and memory; he has frequently confronted the painful subject of Europe's fascist past.

Fraught with controversy from its beginnings, the *Monument against Fascism, War, and Violence—for Peace and Human Rights* was a revolutionary work in progress over six years. At an elevated pedestrian crossing in the Hamburg suburb of Harburg, Gerz erected a 12-meter-tall lead stela or column onto which people were invited to engrave their names with a steel stylus. The column was lowered down a shaft on eight occasions, with each lowering making available fresh space for individuals' names (and comments, including graffiti and uncensored racist rhetoric). By 1993 the monument had finally disappeared into the shaft, with only its top surface (now) visible through an observation window. A tablet remains at the site, with these final words: "In the end it is only we ourselves who can rise up against injustice."

Described by James E. Young as a "counter-monument," the Harburg sculpture is, in effect, a self-critical monument: it sought to subvert the traditional notions of the monument (as permanent, mythic, and as a non-invasive image or object for contemplation). The work confronted the conventional process of memorializing by not providing a set of constructed memories (for consolation), but instead asked individuals to add their own voices, words, and memories. Revealing comparisons can be made between this monument and Maya Lin's Vietnam Veterans War Memorial (1982) in Washington, D.C., where visitors have traditionally left trinkets and objects including family photographs, Bibles and prayers, stuffed animals, flowers, even six-pack cartons of beer that have been archived by the Smithsonian as a kind of collective memento mori.

From 1990 to 1993, Gerz courted much controversy with the work *2146 Steine: Mahnmal gegen Rassismus* (2146 Stones—Monument against Racism) in Saarbrücken, Germany. Together with students and Jewish communities, Gerz compiled a list of 2146 Jewish cemeteries in Germany that were in use up to the Nazi dictatorship. The name of each cemetery was inscribed onto the underside of a corresponding paving stone from the square leading to the Saarbrücken Castle. During the course of this clandestine process—there was no authorization for the monument—the project was finally approved and commissioned by the local parliament. With the inscriptions facing into the ground, the sculpture is more "buried" than the Harburg monument. The only textual reminder is the name that replaced "Schlossplatz Saarbrücken" (Saarbrücken Castle Square) after 1993: "Square of the Invisible Monument." Without stones to guide the way back in time, this counter-monument forces the viewer to reconstruct the past invisibly. It cannot give or show anything to the viewer; in the end, the viewer must (and can) create the monument through conceptualization.

Between 1990 and 1995 Gerz undertook a commissioned monument in Bremen, Germany, that was dedicated to the city inhabitants' aspirations for public art. Gerz began *Die Bremer Befragung—sine somno nihil* (The Bremen Questionnaire—nothing without dreams) with a publicized inquiry asking for people's opinions on public art. This resulted in 246 people taking part in public seminars to debate the issues, from which it was agreed that a monument need not be a material object. The resulting "sculpture" consisted of a light projection. A triangle-shaped plate of steel and glass was inserted into the Bürgermeister Smidt Bridge so that the glass surface is reflected out and on to the Weser River. The bridge railing was modified and made to follow the contour of the triangular reflection. The plate on the bridge is engraved with the following text, along with the names of the project participants: "The Bremen Questionnaire is a sculpture which consists of the images in the minds of those who imagine them. All who do so are its authors."

Similar aspirations exist for the commissioned *Le Monument vivant de Biron* (The Living Monument of Biron, 1995–96) in the village of Biron, France,

wherein an old war memorial needed replacement. Gerz erected a blank obelisk, onto which 127 plaques were attached, each inscribed with a statement by one adult villager in response to Gerz's (unpublished) question posed to them. The statements reflect individuals' past memories and thoughts describing their experiences of War World II. *Le Monument vivant* is a permanent work that is continually in progress: A village couple continue to pose the question to all new residents and to the young who grow to adulthood, whereupon their answers will be added to this social sculpture.

Gerz's call for materializing a universal, collaborative dialogue found its most crystallized form in his 1997–98 proposal *Warum ist es geschehen?* (Why Did It Happen?) for the Berlin Holocaust Memorial competition. His memorial, had it been chosen as the successful entrant, would have been a work in progress carried out by visitors answering the question, "Why did it happen?" Their replies would be collected in the "Ear" building, comprised of the rooms of Memory, Replies, and Silence. The answers were to be not only collected in books but also engraved onto the floor of the memorial's expansive square. Throughout the square, 39 lamp posts would bear neon lights spelling out the word "Why?" in the languages of Europe's persecuted Jews.

A last example of Gerz's goals is his turn in recent years to the Internet to produce public art. Appropriately, the first Internet piece was entitled *The Plural Sculpture*, which sought to build a dialogue by soliciting answers to the question, "If art had the power to change your time, what would you ask for?"

ERICH RANFFT

Biography

Born in Berlin, Germany, 4 April 1940. Studied Chinese, English, and German language and literature at University of Cologne, 1958; studied English language, St. Mary's College, London, 1960–61; studied prehistory and palaeontology, University of Basel, 1962–63; translated Ezra Pound and Henri Gaudier-Brzeska, 1959; worked as journalist, London, 1960–61; worked as salesperson and publicist, Basel, 1962–66; formed alternative publishing group *Agentzia*, Paris, 1966; cofounded and worked at *crèches sauvages* (alternative kindergarten), 1969; founded "Society for the Practical Study of Daily Life," Aisne, 1972; taught at Art Academy HBK Saarbrücken, 1990–92; Distinguished Visiting Professor of Art, University of California at Davis, 1992. Received Roland Prize, Bremen, 1990; German Art Critics' Prize, Berlin, 1996; National Order of Merit, Paris, 1996; Peter Weiss Prize, Berlin, 1996; National Grand Prize for the Plastic Arts, Paris, 1998. Exhibited at German Pavilion, Venice Biennale (with Joseph Beuys and Reiner Ruthenbeck), 1976; at *Documenta* 6 and 8, Kassel, 1977 and 1987. Has collaborated with Esther Shalev-Gerz since 1984. Lives and works in Paris, France.

Selected Works

1986–93 *Monument against Fascism, War, and Violence—for Peace and Human Rights* (with Esther Shalev-Gerz); lead, steel; Harburger Ring, Hamburg-Harburg, Germany

1990–93 *2146 Steine: Mahnmal gegen Rassismus* (2146 Stones—Monument against Racism); paving stone; Square of the Invisible Monument, Saarbrücken Castle, Germany

1990–95 *Die Bremer Befragung—sine somno nihil* (The Bremen Questionnaire—nothing without dreams); steel, glass; Bürgermeister Smidt Bridge, Bremen, Germany

1995 *The Plural Sculpture*; Internet questionnaire

1995– *Le Monument vivant de Biron* (The Living present Monument of Biron); sandstone, enamelled plaques; Place Jean Poussou, Biron, France

1997–98 *Warum ist es geschehen?* (Why Did It Happen?), for the Berlin Holocaust Memorial competition, *Monument for the Murdered Jews of Europe*; proposal (text and model) (unrealized)

Further Reading

Butler, Florian von, and Stefanie Endlich, "Build? Wait? Abandon? Notes on the Debate on the Proposed Holocaust Memorial in Berlin," *Domus* 808 (October 1998)

Clark, Toby, *Art and Propaganda in the Twentieth Century: The Political Image in the Age of Mass Culture*, London: Weidenfeld and Nicolson, and New York: Abrams, 1997

Dufour, Gary, *Jochen Gerz: People Speak*, Vancouver, British Columbia: Vancouver Art Gallery, 1994

Gerz, Jochen, *Von der Kunst; De l'art* (bilingual German-French edition), Berlin: Neuer Berliner Kunstverein, 1985

Gerz, Jochen, *2146 Steine: Mahnmal gegen Rassismus Saarbrücken*, Stuttgart, Germany: Hatje, 1993

Gerz, Jochen, *Die Bremer Befragung: The Bremen Questionnaire: Sine Somno Nihil, 1990–1995* (bilingual German-English edition), Ostfildern, Germany: Cantz, 1995

Gerz, Jochen, *Gegenwart der Kunst: Interviews (1970–1995)*, Regensburg, Germany: Lindinger and Schmid, 1995

Gerz, Jochen, *Monument vivant de Biron: La question secrète*, Arles, France: Actes Sud, 1996

Gerz, Jochen, and Esther Shalev-Gerz, *Das Harburger Mahnmal gegen Faschismus; The Hamburg Monument against Facism* (bilingual German-English edition), Ostfildern, Germany: Hatje, 1994

Gerz, Jochen, and Francis Lévy, *Exit: Das Dachau-Projekt*, Frankfurt: Verlag Roter Stern, 1978

Gillen, Eckhart (editor), *German Art: From Beckmann to Richter: Images of a Divided Country*, Cologne, Germany: Dumont Buchverlag, 1997

Jochen Gerz: Life after Humanism: Photo/Text, 1988–1992 (exhib. cat.), edited by Peter Friese, Ostfildern, Germany: Cantz, 1992

Jochen Gerz: Res Publica: The Public Works, 1968–1999 (exhib. cat.), Ostfildern, Germany: Cantz, 1999

Senie, Harriet F., "In Pursuit of Memory: Berlin, Bamberg, and the Specter of History," *Sculpture* 18/3 (April 1999)

Syring, Marie Luise, "Gerz, Jochen," in *Contemporary Artists*, edited by Joann Cerrito, 4th edition, Detroit, Michigan: St. James Press, 1996

Taylor, Brandon, *The Art of Today*, London: Weidenfeld and Nicolson, 1995; as *Avant-Garde and After: Rethinking Art Now*, New York: Abrams, 1995

Young, James E., "The Counter-Monument: Memory against Itself in Germany Today," *Critical Inquiry* 18/2 (Winter 1992)

Young, James E. (editor), *The Art of Memory: Holocaust Memorials in History*, New York and Munich: Prestel-Verlag, 1994

LORENZO GHIBERTI 1378/1381–1455
Italian

As Lorenzo Ghiberti wrote at the end of the second of his three *Commentarii*, a collection of writings on various subjects, "Few important things have been done in our land that I have not drawn and organized myself." Ghiberti understood Florence's preeminent role in the first half of the 15th century, at the beginning of which he was already a fully mature artist. He was a central figure in some of the city's most important enterprises. Although his rival, Filippo Brunelleschi, had conceived and built the dome of the Cathedral of Florence, Ghiberti participated in some manner in that gigantic project (his role cannot be easily defined; it may have been merely honorary). Above all, Ghiberti had created the two doors still lacking at the old Baptistery (to which Florence attributed great symbolic meaning) and the Tomb of St. Zenobius, first Bishop of Florence's ancient cathedral. Moreover, Ghiberti led projects that involved other great sculptors, from Donatello to Michelozzo di Bartolomeo, just as he had summoned important painters such as Benozzo Gozzoli to aid in the final chasing of the Baptistery doors.

Ghiberti originally trained to be a goldsmith but had also been taught painting, thus mastering different forms of expression. The *Commentarii* demonstrate his talents as a writer and confirm his interest in theories of proportion and perspective and knowledge of past literature, from Vitruvius and Pliny the Elder to the medieval Arabs such as Albazen. The first volume contains a history of ancient art, the second a history of contemporary art and Ghiberti's autobiography, and the third a treatise on the theory of vision, anatomy, and proportions. The volumes reveal his capacities as a historian careful to establish the truthfulness of what he recounts. In an era when the modern idea of historiography did not yet exist and accounts of past events were based more on imagination and surmise than on reality, the information Ghiberti provides on 14th-century art is surprisingly reliable. For instance, a statistical study confirms that his writings about Giotto contain a high percentage of proved facts.

In his autobiography Ghiberti writes that he gave many other artists elements that would guarantee the quality of the result (he probably means iconographic indications or suggestions on how to compose scenes). He adds that he made numerous clay and wax models and made many of his drawings available to other painters. Other sculptors could use the clay and wax models for their own works (painters often used such models to study light effects and perspective) or as originals to be cast for serial reproduction. For instance, approximately one hundred copies in a variety of materials, from terracotta to papier mâché, still exist of a *Virgin and Child* usually attributed to Ghiberti's shop. Moreover, as supplier of designs for stained-glass windows (many of those in the Cathedral of Florence were made to his design) and master of a shop that produced bronze objects, he coordinated and supervised assistants and prepared models for works that other people would execute. His enumeration of the kinds of knowledge an artist must have indicates that he understood the new role that the Renaissance artist was called on to play. His writings contain repeated affirmations as to the importance of theory, of "reasoning."

Surviving documents enable us to trace the economic and administrative activities of Ghiberti and the two sons who assisted him. The artist was also a wealthy man. Scholars note that Ghiberti must also have had an uncommon gift for diplomacy, since he kept on good terms with customers despite frequently late deliveries, and he could often recover commissions that had been canceled for that reason. Ghiberti's centrality in Florence during the first half of the 15th century is thus evident from many standpoints. He was the first artist to represent the universality of the Renaissance man, an archetype then continued by Leon Battista Alberti and Leonardo. But unlike Leonardo, Ghiberti began from the exact knowledge and techniques of a craftsman. In fact, he revived the technique of monumental casting in Florence (in the mid 14th century, foundrymen from Venice had had to be summoned to cast the first Baptistery door). His victory over Brunelleschi in the 1401 competition for the sec-

ond Baptistery door was probably due in part to his technical superiority, which enabled him to cast the specimen panel all in one piece, adding only the figure of Isaac, and in the process to save a great deal of costly material. The figure of *St. John the Baptist* he made for Orsanmichele in 1414 was the first monumental statue cast practically all in one piece (only the head and the lower part of the left leg were added) since ancient times. Ghiberti was also one of the artists responsible for the rebirth of terracotta sculpture after centuries of oblivion. Similarly, his bronze reliefs were prototypes that were studied and developed for centuries.

Ghiberti was the only artist to fully incarnate the transition from the Gothic world to the Renaissance in a single career. In the panel depicting the *Sacrifice of Isaac* (with its extraordinary nude of a young man, rather than a boy) for the second (north) Baptistery door, he arranged the movements of the figures, the folds of the garments, and the rock that in a brilliant solution separates the two servants with the ass from the protagonists all in a loose, flowing rhythm of markedly Gothic character. These features identify in general the style of the second door, in which space is represented in an allusive and symbolic way harking back to Giotto, while extremely elegant rhythms animate the scenes, according to the characteristic language of Late Gothic (as epitomized in the painting of the Florentine artist Lorenzo Monaco). The quatrefoil frames are likewise typically Gothic. In the three large statues Ghiberti made for the niches at Orsanmichele (*St. Matthew, St. Stephen*, and the previously mentioned *St. John the Baptist*) at regular intervals over a 15-year period, the great flowing folds of the mantles stand out, as he transferred the refined elegance of the small figures on the second door into monumental dimensions. The head of the figure of *St. Matthew*, based on classic Roman models, also displays Ghiberti's knowledge of ancient statuary.

The third (east) Baptistery door is marked by its inspiration from the Classical world and by the use of linear perspective. The rules of perspective had been formulated only recently in Florence to reproduce the depth of space on a two-dimensional surface, giving a new sense of reality by arranging objects in space according to an exact calculation of their positions. The third door also differs sharply from the second in its overall arrangement. It comprises ten large square panels enclosed in a frame richly decorated with figures strongly inspired by Classical sculpture, instead of 24 in quatrefoil frames.

Ghiberti's Gothic second door and Renaissance third door are each complete works of art that can stand on their own. As Richard Krautheimer points out, Ghiberti cannot be considered a conservative because his Gothic period—which evinces his training as a goldsmith and his familiarity with the great French examples of that craft—represents the most advanced experimentation in Europe at the time. Accordingly, one can also admire Ghiberti for the intelligence with which he chose his models and sources. His artistic career was one of the most extraordinary ever seen in any culture.

GIORGIO BONSANTI

See also **Donatello (Donato di Betto Bardi); Michelozzo di Bartolomeo**

Biography

Born in Pelago (now in Italy), 1378 or 1381. Son of either Cione Ghiberti or of goldsmith Bartolo di Michele. Trained as painter and goldsmith; returned to Florence from Marche (now in Italy) to participate in competition for north doors of Florence Baptistery, 1401; worked in Florence, probably with several short sojourns elsewhere (two in Rome, two in Venice, and one in Siena for two Baptistery panels); created works in gold for Popes Martin V and Eugene IV; won prestigious commission for third door for Florence's Baptistery. Sons Tommaso and Vittorio became assistants, though Tommaso eventually left father's workshop. Died in Florence, Italy, 1 December 1455.

Selected Works

1401	*Sacrifice of Isaac*; bronze; Museo Nazionale del Bargello, Florence, Italy
1401–24	North door; gilded bronze; Baptistery, Florence, Italy
1414	*St. John the Baptist*; bronze; Orsanmichele, Florence, Italy
1420	*St. Matthew*; bronze; Orsanmichele, Florence, Italy
1425–52	*Gate of Paradise* (east door); gilded bronze; Museo dell'Opera del Duomo, Florence, Italy
1427	Reliefs of *St. John the Baptist before Herod* and the *Baptism of Christ*; bronze; Baptistery of the Cathedral of Siena, Italy
1427–29	*St. Stephen*; bronze; Orsanmichele, Florence, Italy
1432–42	Shrine of St. Zenobius; bronze; Cathedral of Florence, Italy

Further Reading

Ghiberti, Lorenzo, *Lorenzo Ghiberti: I commentarii*, edited by Lorenzo Bartoli, Florence: Giunti, 1998

Goldscheider, Ludwig, *Ghiberti*, London: Phaidon Press, 1949

Krautheimer, Richard, and Trude Krautheimer-Hess, *Lorenzo Ghiberti*, Princeton, New Jersey: Princeton University Press, 1956; with new preface, 1982

Istituto Nazionale di Studi sul Rinascimento, *Lorenzo Ghiberti nel suo tempo*, 2 vols., Florence: Olschki, 1980

La Bella, C., "Ghiberti, Lorenzo," in *Dizionario biografico degli Italiani*, Rome: Istituto dell'Enciclopedia Italiana, 2000

Lorenzo Ghiberti: Materia e ragionamenti (exhib. cat.), Florence: Centro Di, 1978

Wundram, Martin, "Ghiberti: Lorenzo (di Cione) Ghiberti," in *The Dictionary of Art*, edited by Jane Turner, New York: Grove, and London: Macmillan, 1996

GATE OF PARADISE
Lorenzo Ghiberti (1378–1455)
1425–1452
gilded bronze
h. 5.06 m
Museo dell'Opera del Duomo, Florence, Italy

On 2 January 1425 the Florentine cloth-merchants' guild (Arte di Calimala), patron of the Baptistery, awarded the commission for the north door to Lorenzo Ghiberti. In April of the previous year, Ghiberti had completed the east door (1401–24), the one facing the cathedral. (The south door, likewise in gilded bronze, was the work of Andrea da Pontedera and dated from the mid 14th century.) When the new door was finished, in 1452, the authorities decided, "because of its beauty," to install it instead on the east side—considered the most important—and shift the older east door to the north side. As scholars have noted, this was the first time in history that a major decision concerning a work of art was made not for iconographic reasons or contingent circumstances, but purely on aesthetic grounds. This is doubtless an extraordinarily modern concept, and it reveals how highly developed Florentine civilization was at the time. From numerous contemporary and later accounts, it is clear that Florence has always attributed great symbolic value to the *Gate of Paradise* as one of the supreme examples of its culture. As to its name, the Baptistery door facing the cathedral was traditionally known as the "Door of Paradise," but in continuing to call Ghiberti's work by that name we are chiefly influenced by the opinion of Michelangelo, who deemed it "truly worthy of Paradise."

The task of preparing the iconographic scheme for the Old Testament stories to be represented on the door was entrusted to the humanist Leonardo Bruni. Following the plan of the first two doors, he proposed a series of 28 panels and described their content in detail. This project was soon rejected, although we have no information thereon except the fact that the actual door is totally different. It consists of ten large panels, each about 80 centimeters square, set in a richly decorated frame. The frame is studded with 24 small heads of prophets and sibyls emerging from circular niches (*clipei*). Flanking each panel are full-length figures of biblical personages. The strips of frame dividing the panels are much wider than the ones Ghiberti used in his first door, which were decorated with heads alone. In consequence, the new door constitutes a powerful, complex system. Even the doorposts are extensively decorated.

We cannot know for certain who was responsible for reducing the number of panels to ten. Most likely Ghiberti himself suggested this crucial change, because in his *Commentaries* he writes, "I was given a free hand to shape the work in whatever manner I thought would make it more perfect, more ornate and richer." In this collection of writings, Ghiberti devotes much more space to the second door than to the first, confirming his particular attachment to the *Door of Paradise*. He emphasizes the fact that the panels were square (as opposed to the multilobed Gothic type) and large ("an ell and a third"), and he dwells on the difficulty of the composition, due to the huge number of figures. In some panels, he notes, "I put in around 100 figures."

Indeed, the most extraordinary aspect of the composition is how Ghiberti fit as many as six or seven episodes into each panel. The procedure in and of itself was hardly unprecedented; the Middle Ages provide innumerable examples. But what is new in Ghiberti's door is the intention of unifying the narratives rather than simply placing different scenes at random in the space of a single panel. When the decision was made to reduce the number of panels, Ghiberti must have already had in mind the possibility of combining several episodes in each to obtain a powerful concentration of expression, in contrast to the minute fragmentation that characterized the two earlier doors. Moreover, the square shape of the panels was conducive to depicting the scenes in a rational perspective that enabled viewers to clearly identify the organization of the internal space. Ghiberti, who had already had experience with the square shape in two panels he had made for the baptismal font in Siena, says he wanted "to imitate nature as far as I was able," as the square—geometrically simple and perfectly regular—enabled him to do. The choice of this shape for the panels of the *Gate of Paradise* is perhaps the most explicit example of a programmatic declaration in favor of the new Renaissance rationality, of the scientific mentality with which artists in Florence were then addressing the problem of how to represent reality in two dimensions. Lastly, Ghiberti demonstrates that even a series of different episodes making up a complex scene can be depicted in low relief: "[T]hey are in very low relief, and on

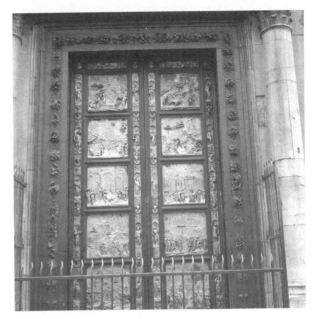

Lorenzo Ghiberti, *Gate of Paradise*
© Paul Almasy / CORBIS

the planes the nearby figures appear larger and the ones farther off appear smaller, as they do in real life."

Ghiberti carefully describes all the episodes represented in the ten panels, which are ordered from left to right, starting at the top. Briefly, their contents are as follows: Creation, the Original Sin, and the Expulsion from Eden; Cain and Abel; stories of Noah; stories of Abraham and the sacrifice of Isaac; Isaac, Esau, and Jacob; stories of Joseph; stories of Moses; stories of Joshua; stories of David; and the meeting between Solomon and the Queen of Sheba (this is the only panel containing only one scene). Stylistically, there is a certain distinction between the more crowded panels, with more figures and less simplified actions (like the story of Solomon), and those that embody a higher synthesis (like the stories of Isaac and his sons). The surviving documents do not enable us to know for certain the order in which Ghiberti designed the panels. Richard Krautheimer believes the artist progressed from the simpler scenes to the more complicated (see Krautheimer, 1971), but Sir John Pope-Hennessy, for one, suggests the reverse. A document from 1437 states that the ten "stories" (i.e., panels) had been cast, but we do not know whether this actually means that all the casting was completed. What is certain is that the finishing process (i.e., cold chiseling after casting) took many more years, and that important artists, such as Michelozzo di Bartolomeo and the young Benozzo Gozzoli, took part in various stages. The door was declared finished on 2 April 1452, and by 16 June the gilding had been completed as well.

As early as the end of the 18th century, Anton Raphael Mengs was urging that the door be restored. It was cleaned in 1948, and the gilding reappeared for the first time, but within a few years it was again covered with black scale due to pollution. Studies by Florence's Opificio delle Pietre Dure in the mid 1980s showed that the gilding rested on an uneven layer of oxidation that was gradually destroying it. A new, extraordinarily difficult conservation effort was undertaken. The panels were detached from the frame, and the process of removing the external deposits began, first with chemical baths, more recently with lasers. At the end of these operations, the door will be installed in a large climatized showcase at the Museo dell'Opera del Duomo. In 1990 a copy of the door replaced the original at the Baptistery.

GIORGIO BONSANTI

Further Reading

Krautheimer, Richard, *Ghiberti's Bronze Doors*, Princeton, New Jersey: Princeton University Press, 1971

Paolucci, Antonio (editor), *Il battistero di San Giovanni a Firenze; The Baptistery of San Giovanni, Florence* (bilingual Italian-English edition), 2 vols., Modena, Italy: Panini, 1994

ALBERTO GIACOMETTI 1901–1966

Swiss, active in France

Although Alberto Giacometti is considered the premier sculptor of the Surrealist movement of the early 1930s, the Swiss artist is best known for the tall, thin figures he produced after World War II. He came to prominence in Paris in the mid 1920s when he began to produce works influenced by contemporary abstract styles and by ancient and non-Western art (particularly African art, which inspired his *Spoon Woman*). From 1926 to 1930 Giacometti created numerous works with the geometric abstraction and spatial emphasis found in Cubist sculpture, and during this same time he began making innovative plaques with extreme abstractions of a head or female figure (for example, *Gazing Head*).

With his work of the late 1920s, Giacometti began to gain serious recognition, and in 1930 the Surrealist leader André Breton invited the artist to join the Surrealist group. This began a very fertile time in Giacometti's career in which he produced a variety of innovative and imaginative works that revolutionized Surrealist sculpture. During this period he contributed to the development of open-form sculpture, kinetic art, and sculptural construction. Among his innovations are "cage sculptures," which consist of objects contained within cage-like structures or models, and table-top works such as the gamelike *No More Play* and the macabre *Point to the Eye*.

Much of Giacometti's work of this time reflects a characteristically Surrealist interest in the unconscious world and dreams as well as the themes of sexuality and violence. The kinetic sculpture *Suspended Ball*, for example, elicits erotic connotations and conveys a sense of sexual frustration, whereas *Woman with Her Throat Cut* suggests not only the Cubist construction of plastic form but with sinister undertones of rape and murder. Evocation of the dream world can be found in the most complex and enigmatic of Giacometti's Surrealist works, *Palace at Four A.M.*, a sculptural construction consisting of seemingly unrelated objects placed in a fragile environment defined by the thin wooden skeletal frame of the "palace." Giacometti once identified the personal experiences that inspired this work, but—as with most Surrealist art—the meaning remains vague (although the sculpture definitely conveys something ominous and suggests an unsettling dream). This highly inventive work had an influence on the open-form constructions prevalent in sculpture after World War II.

In the winter of 1934–35, Giacometti returned to working from the live model, a move that resulted in a split with Breton and the Surrealists who frowned upon such an approach. For the next ten years Giacometti struggled to find his way, at first working from the model and then working from memory. His desire was to capture the reality of a human figure not in a conventionally realistic way but in the way we perceive (at a glance) the whole person in space from a distance. This quest led him to make from memory extremely small sculptures on proportionally large bases.

After World War II, Giacometti found that he could retain that particular sense of reality by making tall figures extremely thin and without detail. Thus he arrived at his mature style, which consisted of tall, attenuated figures with irregular, rough-hewn surfaces. Suffused with existentialist drama and energy, his typical female figures are stiff, frontal, and immobile, whereas male figures act in some way, primarily through walking (as in *Walking Man*) but also by gesturing (as in *Man Pointing*). All of Giacometti's figures are characterized by a dichotomous sense of groundedness that appears to contradict their tenuously thin limbs; this is expressed by their large, heavy feet that are rooted to a base raised only slightly off the floor.

During the postwar period, Giacometti also produced groups of smaller figures, sometimes arranged in planned environments, such as *City Square II*. Many observers of the time interpreted a powerful existential content in these postwar works, and his figures do evoke a sense of alienation and loneliness in the tradition of Jean Paul Sartre, who wrote several critical essays on Giacometti's work. This sensation perhaps most pronounced in figure groups such as *City Square*

II, in which four men walk in aimless futility around a solitary, immobile female figure. It should be noted, however, that Giacometti claimed to have no existential meaning in mind when creating these works, and in more recent years many scholars have seen such interpretations as too narrow and limiting.

The years 1946–52 were productive ones for Giacometti. He developed his mature style and—after many years with few exhibitions and little financial reward—attained success greater than at the height of his Surrealist period. After 1952 Giacometti continued to concentrate on tall walking male and rigid female figures, with the latter being the most common subject. Among the best of his female figures are the *Women of Venice*.

Also important to Giacometti's oeuvre are the many busts he completed, especially those done after 1950. The key model during this time was the artist's brother, Diego, who also served for many years as Giacometti's indispensable assistant. The busts have varying degrees of naturalism, and Giacometti never desired to achieve a conventional individual likeness. However, he did want his portraits to convey to the viewer a lifelike presence, and to do that he felt it important to capture the model's gaze. The 1965 busts of Diego and the photographer Elie Lotar are good examples of this effect. These late busts, along with a series of the artist's wife Annette (from 1962 to 1965), are some of Giacometti's most expressive. Perhaps the most evocative is *Elie Lotar III*. In this bust—the artist's final work—the head rises from a body that looks like it was formed by hardened flowing lava. Lotar gazes at us in silence and creates around himself an almost holy aura, an effect much like that of the ancient Egyptian statues Giacometti so admired.

From 1948 until his death in 1966, Giacometti's stature in the art world kept growing, with several solo exhibitions in Europe and the United States. Since his death admiration for his work has only increased, and today he is recognized not only for his importance to the development of modern sculpture, but also for his unique contribution to the figurative tradition.

JOHN ALFORD

See also **Surrealist Sculpture**

Biography

Born in Borgonovo, Switzerland, 10 October 1901. Father, Giovanni, a Post-Impressionist painter; brother Diego, a sculptor and furniture designer. Studied painting and sculpture in Geneva, 1919–20; studied sculpture in Paris under Émile-Antoine Bourdelle at the Académie de la Grande Chaumière beginning in 1922; moved into Paris studio at Rue Hippolyte-Maindron, 1927; invited by André Breton to join the Surrealists, 1930; left Surrealists, 1934; during World War II lived and worked in Geneva, 1941–45; returned to Paris, 1945, where he lived for rest of his life. Awarded Sculpture Prize, Carnegie Institute's *International Exhibition of Contemporary Painting and Sculpture*, 1961; Sculpture Prize, Venice Biennale, 1962; French Grand Prix National des Arts, 1965. Died in Chur, Switzerland, 11 January 1966.

Selected Works

1926–27 *Spoon Woman*; bronze; Alberto Giacometti Foundation, Zurich, Switzerland

1927–29 *Gazing Head*; marble; Alberto Giacometti Foundation, Zurich, Switzerland

1930 *Suspended Ball*; wood, iron, filament; private collection, Paris, France

1931–32 *No More Play*; marble, wood, bronze; National Gallery of Art, Washington, D.C., United States

1932 *Point to the Eye*; wood, metal; Musée Nationale d'Art Moderne, Centre Georges Pompidou, Paris, France

1932 *Woman with Her Throat Cut*; bronze; Alberto Giacometti Foundation, Zurich, Switzerland

1932–33 *Palace at Four A.M.*; wood, glass, string, wire; Museum of Modern Art, New York City, United States

1934 *The Invisible Object (Hands Holding the Void)*; plaster; Yale University Art Gallery, New Haven, Connecticut, United States; bronze cast: National Gallery of Art, Washington, D.C., United States

1947 *Man Pointing*; bronze; Museum of Modern Art, New York City, United States

1947 *Walking Man*; bronze; Alberto Giacometti Foundation, Zurich, Switzerland

1948 *City Square II*; bronze; private collection, List family, New York City, United States; another version: National Gallery of Art, Washington, D.C., United States

1950 *The Forest (Composition with Seven Figures and a Head)*; bronze; Kunsthaus, Zurich, Switzerland

1954 *Large Head of Diego*; bronze; Alberto Giacometti Foundation, Zurich, Switzerland

1956 *Women of Venice*; bronze; editions of nine different works in various locations, including *Woman of Venice III*, Los Angeles County Museum of Art, California, United States

1965 *Elie Lotar III*; bronze; private collection, Switzerland

Further Reading

Alberto Giacometti: A Retrospective Exhibition (exhib. cat.), New York: Praeger, 1974

Bonnefoy, Yves, *Alberto Giacometti: Biographie d'une oeuvre*, Paris: Flammarion, 1991; as *Alberto Giacometti: A Biography of His Work*, translated by Jean Stewart, Paris: Flammarion, 1991

Dupin, Jacques, *Alberto Giacometti*, Paris: Maeght Editeur, 1962

Hohl, Reinhold, *Alberto Giacometti*, New York: Abrams, 1971

Hohl, Reinhold (editor), *Giacometti: A Biography in Pictures*, Stuttgart, Germany: Hatje, 1998

Juliet, Charles, *Giacometti*, Paris: Hazen, 1985; as *Giacometti*, translated by Charles Lynn Clark, New York: Universe Books, 1986

Lord, James, *Giacometti, a Biography*, New York: Farrar Straus Giroux, 1985

Matter, Herbert, and Mercedes Matter, *Alberto Giacometti*, New York: Abrams, 1987

Prat, Jean-Louis, and Valerie T. Fletcher, *Alberto Giacometti* (exhib. cat.), Montreal, Quebec: Montreal Museum of Fine Arts, 1998

Sartre, Jean Paul, *Les peintures de Giacometti*, Paris, France: Editions Pierre à Feu, 1954

Schneider, Angela (editor), *Alberto Giacometti: Sculpture, Painting, Drawings*, New York: Prestel, 1994

Sylvester, David, *Looking at Giacometti*, New York: Holt, 1996

MAN POINTING

Alberto Giacometti (1901–1966)
1947
bronze
h. 1.79 m
Museum of Modern Art, New York City, United States

Alberto Giacometti created *Man Pointing* during his prolific postwar period, when he began to make his famous tall, thin statues of standing men and women. Although the pose in *Man Pointing* is unique in the artist's oeuvre, the sculpture well reflects the new direction taken by Giacometti at this time, in which he sought to capture the way we perceive a figurative gestalt, all at once and at a distance. Giacometti's figures are painfully attenuated and loosely modeled such that the viewer perceives each figure as thin, light in weight, and void of detail. One would expect such an approach to result in a certain remoteness, and it does. Yet *Man Pointing*, in particular, also has an active sense of vitality and a telling physical presence.

Man Pointing was one of the key sculptures that Giacometti completed for a solo exhibition in 1948 at the Pierre Matisse Gallery in New York City, where for the first time, this work and other postwar sculptures were shown in public. The show was a success, and as a result, Giacometti's new work became well known in the English-speaking world a few years before it did elsewhere, although he lived and worked in Paris.

The gesturing pose of *Man Pointing* resembles that of a speaking figure or—as a photo taken of the work in the street outside Giacometti's studio suggests—a policeman directing traffic. The elongated, slender figure (barely larger than the armature in places) has a rough surface that conveys dynamism, but might also suggest decayed flesh. Although the narrow head has the indistinct facial features of a distant figure, the drooping shapes above the eyes convey sadness, an effect particularly pronounced when strong lighting casts deep shadows. One feature unique to this work among the artist's male figures is an unambiguous male sex organ. Perhaps Giacometti in some sense portrayed himself (a notion strengthened by the resemblance of the figure to the artist, who had a similar thick mass of hair and a furrowed face).

Nobody knows why or for whom the man points. It is known that sometime between 1947 and 1951 Giacometti combined a bronze cast of *Man Pointing* with a plaster male figure of similar height to form a two-figure composition on one plaster base. A photograph exists of *Group of Two Men* (as it was titled), but the sculpture no longer exists. In the composition, *Man Pointing* has his left arm around—although not touching—the other figure, which has an immobile stance very similar to the typical Giacometti female pose. One assumes that the pointing man's gesture is for the other figure, and the grouping implies a relationship of sorts. Interestingly, the pointing figure seems more isolated gesturing for his unresponsive rigid companion than he does alone as *Man Pointing*.

Many observers in the postwar period saw in Giacometti's work a visual expression of existentialist ideas. At the time, the philosophy was very prominent in Paris, and existentialist Jean-Paul Sartre wrote an essay for the artist's 1948 Pierre Matisse Gallery show in New York City. For Sartre and others, Giacometti's works conveyed the despair, futility, and loneliness of the human condition. One can see such solitude and futility in *Man Pointing*, particularly in the way he points in isolation and in the way the figure—with heavy feet that seem imprisoned within the bronze base—seems unable to move, implying permanent separation from others. One also senses sadness in the sagging face, vulnerability in the frail body, and perhaps inner emptiness in the lack of individualized features. One could also argue, however, that the pointing figure (by gesturing) conveys a sense of hope and expectation, rather than despair. Yet even this can be interpreted in existential terms because the striving hints at the existential idea that one can—through taking individual responsibility—find worth in an ultimately meaningless life.

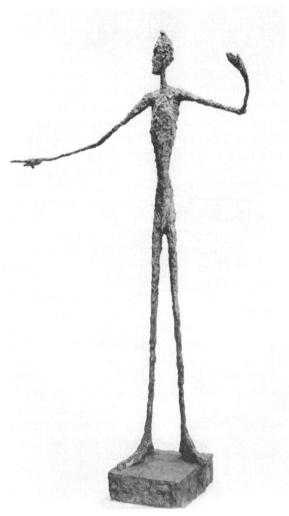

Man Pointing, 1947, bronze, 70 1/2″ × 40 3/4″ × 16 3/8″ at base 12″ × 13 1/4″
Museum of Modern Art, New York. Gift of Mrs. John D. Rockefeller III
Photograph © 2000 The Museum of Modern Art, New York

In more recent years, certain scholars have seen purely existential interpretations as a product of the times and no longer adequate or appropriate. For some, such preoccupations leave little room for other meanings and ignore much of the sculpture's formal aspects. It should be noted that Giacometti said he never intended to convey in his work any particular philosophy or to suggest conditions such as solitude. Many current writers, however, continue to use this langue in their observations of Giacometti's work. The disagreements over interpretation point to the subtle complexity and depth of *Man Pointing*. Indeed, it can be viewed on many levels and can convey seemingly contradictory ideas. The figure appears fragile, remote, and lonely, and his face reveals timidity and doubt, yet he holds his head high and gestures with a certain amount of

confidence and anticipation. He seems grounded and unable to move, yet comforted by his rootedness to the earth.

Man Pointing belongs to the figurative tradition in Western art. Similar poses, for example, are found in certain Classical Greek and Roman statues and in works by Auguste Rodin, particularly his *St. John the Baptist Preaching* (1878). Of course, numerous artists in the history of Western art have used the human figure—just as Giacometti has done here—to convey something significant about the human condition, but one particularly finds the stylistic characteristics of *Man Pointing* (for example, distortion, expressive irregular surfaces, and/or evocative content) in the figurative sculpture of modern or contemporary artists such as Rodin, Medardo Rosso, Wilhelm Lehmbruck, Germaine Richier, César, George Segal, and Magdalena Abakanowicz, among others.

Perhaps more than any other modern artist, however, Giacometti owes much to non-Western and pre-Classical ancient art, which impressed him greatly. He particularly appreciated the stylized and frontal aspects of ancient Egyptian statues, which he thought captured physical reality better than more conventionally realistic works. One sees something similar in *Man Pointing*, where the artist used stylistic means (rather than conventional realism) to portray his own vision of reality.

JOHN ALFORD

Further Reading

Fletcher, Valerie J., *Alberto Giacometti, 1901–1966* (exhib. cat.), Washington, D.C.: Smithsonian Institution Press, 1988
Sartre, Jean-Paul, "The Search for the Absolute," in *Exhibition of Sculptures, Paintings, Drawings [by Alberto Giacometti]*, New York: Pierre Matisse Gallery, 1948

GIAMBOLOGNA 1529–1608 *Flemish, active in Italy*

Giambologna (elided from Giovanni Bologna, the Italianized form of the sculptor's real name, Jean [de] Bologne) was trained as a carver of alabaster by the important sculptor Jacques du Broeucq while in his native French Flanders. Du Broeucq taught Giambologna the technique of carving in an Italianate, classicizing style. This technique was reinforced when Giambologna traveled to Rome in 1550, where he made models of Greco-Roman and Renaissance sculpture. He was particularly impressed by the technical and anatomical skill of Hellenistic statues, such as the Farnese *Bull* (3rd century BCE; excavated as recently as 1545). Michelangelo criticized a model that Giambologna showed him as having been too highly finished before the basic pose had been established. Giambologna never forgot this lesson and always made sketch models in wax or clay when preparing his compositions (several are preserved in the Victoria and Albert Museum, London).

Next Giambologna visited Florence to study the sculpture of the early Renaissance, especially that of Michelangelo. By 1561 he was being paid a salary by Francesco I de' Medici. He went on to a long career as a court sculptor to the grand dukes, producing temporary sculpture for public spectacles and bronze and marble statues on a grand scale and exploiting the potential of bronze statuettes and reliefs. Following the precepts of Michelangelo and the example of his Florentine followers, Niccolò Tribolo and Pierino da Vinci, as well as Benvenuto Cellini, who was creating his masterpiece *Perseus and Medusa* (1545–54), Giambologna began to compose figures with an exaggerated degree of *contrapposto* (a natural pose with the weight of one leg, the shoulder, and hip counterbalancing one another) with a serpentine axis and flamelike contour, which instilled new life into Florentine sculpture.

First of a series of Giambologna's sculptural groups was *Samson Slaying a Philistine*, whose subject and treatment recall a project of Michelangelo's from the 1520s. A 1563 commission for bronze statues to decorate a fountain in Bologna acted as a catalyst, and he invented a pyramidal complex of lively, sensuous figures leading up to an energetic crowning statue of Neptune in a spiraling pose. He also produced there the earliest of several "flying" figures of *Mercury*, which was to become one of his most celebrated compositions. Next of Giambologna's groups was a political allegory, *Florence Triumphant over Pisa*, commissioned for the state wedding of Francesco I de' Medici and Johanna of Austria as a pendant to Michelangelo's group of *Victory* (1532–34). With the help of surviving preliminary models, Giambologna met the challenge with a truly Michelangelesque composition that amalgamates a spiraling axis with a vigorous play of line, all within a conical form.

Giambologna's third great marble group, *Rape of a Sabine*, carved in the 1580s, proved to be the climax of his career. His other major achievement in monumental sculpture was a statue in bronze of Duke Cosimo I de' Medici on horseback in the Piazza della Signoria. In it he met the challenge of all earlier equestrian statues of the Renaissance and set a precedent soon to be commissioned by several foreign heads of state, with statues in Paris, Madrid, and London.

There are few points of reference in the enormous production of bronze statuettes by Giambologna and his principal assistant in this field, the goldsmith Antonio Susini: most were original, small compositions and not reductions from full-scale statuary. Seminal masterpieces are the documented *Apollo* in the Studiolo of Francesco I in the Palazzo Vecchio and a signed figure of *Astronomy* (*ca.* 1573) in Vienna, as well as several other sleek female nudes and variations on the theme of *Mercury*. However, their repertory extended to animals, either life-size, naturalistic birds and monkeys, or miniatures of horses, bulls, and lions; genre figures; and religious subjects, particularly crucifixes. To satisfy the demands of Counter Reformation theology for clear narration, Giambologna also revived the earlier Renaissance system of planning reliefs within a perspectival framework, which had been abandoned by his Mannerist predecessors, Baccio Bandinelli and Cellini (for example, the series of the *Passion of Christ* [*ca.* 1579] in Genoa, Florence, and Munich).

Giambologna exerted enormous influence during his lifetime and for some decades afterward, not only in Italy but also in northern Europe. His statuettes made handsome gifts for distribution to other courts, which disseminated his elegant style. Later his pupils, often Flemish, Dutch, or German by origin, returned north of the Alps to serve the same courts, thus reinforcing his influence, although with personal variations of his style (for example, Adriaen de Vries, Hubert Gerhard, and Hans Reichle in southern Germany and Prague, and Pietro Francavilla in Paris). Giambologna therefore occupies a crucial place in the history of sculpture between Michelangelo, many of whose fundamental ideas he brought to fruition, and Gianlorenzo Bernini, whose invention of the new style in Rome (later called the Baroque) was deeply indebted to him as an intermediary. He died in 1608 and was buried in his own chapel in the Church of Santissima Annunziata, Florence.

CHARLES AVERY

See also **Du Broeucq, Jacques; Michelangelo (Buonarroti); Susini, Antonio**

Biography

Born in Douai, France, 1529. Apprenticed to Jacques Du Broeucq to learn alabaster carving; paid for statues for "joyous entry" of Philip II into Mons, Belgium, 1549; worked in Rome, modeling antiquities and Renaissance sculpture (e.g., by Michelangelo) 1550–52; then moved to Florence, where he was to spend most of the rest of his career; appointed court sculptor the Grand Dukes of Florence; Prince Francesco de' Medici commissioned marble group *Samson Slaying a Philistine*, 1560; worked in Bologna on bronze statues for Neptune Fountain and a statue of Mercury for the university, 1563–66; visited Rome to inspect antiquities, 1572, 1583, and 1588; production of bronze statuettes from his models increased by Antonio Susini; after success of equestrian statue of Cosimo I de' Medici, completed or received several commissions for equestrian monuments for royalty in Liechtenstein, France, and Spain, 1600–1608; made a Knight of Christ, 1599. Died in Florence, Italy, 1608.

Selected Works

1560–62 *Samson Slaying a Philistine*; marble; Victoria and Albert Museum, London, England

1566 *Neptune* and subsidiary statues; bronze; Neptune Fountain, Bologna, Italy

1567 *Turkey, Eagle, Peacock*, and *Owl*, for grotto of the Villa di Castello; bronze; Museo Nazionale del Bargello, Florence, Italy

ca. *Florence Triumphant over Pisa*; white-
1567–72 washed clay; Palazzo Vecchio, Florence, Italy; marble: Museo Nazionale del Bargello, Florence, Italy

ca. 1573 *Psyche/Bathsheba*; marble; J. Paul Getty Museum, Los Angeles, California, United States

1575 *Apollo*; bronze; Studiolo of Francesco I, Palazzo Vecchio, Florence, Italy

1575 *Fountain of Ocean*; marble; Boboli Gardens, Florence, Italy

1577 *Altar of Liberty*; marble; Lucca Cathedral, Lucca, Italy

1580 *Apennine*; brick, volcanic rock, iron; Villa Demidoff, Pratolino, Italy

1581 *Mercury*, for fountain in Villa Medici, Florence, Italy; bronze; Museo Nazionale del Bargello, Florence, Italy

1582 *Rape of a Sabine*; marble; Loggia dei Lanzi, Florence, Italy

1583 Statues of *Virtues*, reliefs of the *Passion of Christ*, for Grimaldi Chapel, San Francesco di Cappelletto, Genoa, Italy; bronze; Great Hall and Chapel, University of Genoa, Italy

1590–92 *Cosimo I*; bronze; Piazza della Signoria, Florence, Italy

1595 *St. Luke*; bronze; Church of Orsanmichele, Florence, Italy

1602–08 *Ferdinando I*; bronze; Piazza Santissima Annunziata, Florence, Italy

Further Reading

Avery, Charles, *Giambologna: The Complete Sculpture*, Oxford: Phaidon Christie's, and Mt. Kisco, New York: Moyer Bell, 1987

Avery, Charles, *Giambologna, An Exhibition of Sculpture by the Master and His Followers, from the Collection of Michael Hall, Esq.* (exhib. cat.), New York: Salander-O'Reilly Galleries, 1998

Avery, Charles, *Jean Bologne: La Belle Endormie; Giambologna: Sleeping Woman with Satyr* (exhib. cat.): Galerie Piltzer, Paris 2000

Bury, Michael, "The Grimaldi Chapel of Giambologna in San Francesco di Castelletto, Genoa," *Mitteilungen des Kunsthistorischen Institutes in Florenz* 26 (1982)

Bury, Michael, "Bernardo Vecchietti, Patron of Giambologna," in *I Tatti Studies: Essays in the Renaissance*, vol. 1, Florence: Villa I Tatti, 1985

Bury, Michael, "The Senarega Chapel in San Lorenzo, Genoa: New Documents about Barocci and Francavilla," *Mitteilungen des Kunsthistorischen Institutes in Florenz* 31 (1987)

Bury, Michael, "Giambologna's *Fata Morgana* Rediscovered," *Apollo* 131/336 (1990)

Corti, Gino, "Two Early Seventeenth-Century Inventories Involving Giambologna," *The Burlington Magazine* 118 (1976)

Dhanens, Élisabeth, *Jean Boulogne, Giovanni Bologna Fiammingo*, Brussels: Paleis der Academiën, 1956

Gibbons, Mary, *Giambologna, Narrator of the Catholic Reformation*, Berkeley: University of California Press, 1995

Holderbaum, James, *The Sculptor Giovanni Bologna*, New York: Garland, 1983

Radcliffe, Anthony, *Giambologna's Cesarini Venus* (exhib. cat.), Washington, D.C.: National Gallery of Art, 1993

Radcliffe, Anthony, "Giambologna's 'Venus' for Giangiorgio Cesarini," in *La scultura: Studi in onore di Andrew S. Ciechanowiecki*, vol. 2, Turin, Italy: Allemandi, 1996

Watson, Katharine, and Charles Avery, "Medici and Stuart: A Grand Ducal Gift of 'Giovanni Bologna' Bronzes for Henry, Prince of Wales," *The Burlington Magazine* 115 (1973)

RAPE OF A SABINE

Giambologna (1529–1608)
1582
marble
h. 4.1 m
Loggia dei Lanzi, Florence, Italy

When Giambologna came to work in Florence, Michelangelo was already a celebrity and his creations were models no artist could ignore. Giambologna's conception of *Rape of a Sabine* is marked by its reference to Michelangelo. Between 1527 and 1530, Michelangelo had wanted to sculpt a grand three-figure marble group of *Samson Defeating the Philistines* for the Piazza della Signoria, but the project had not progressed beyond a famous sketch. Early reverberations of this reference can be seen in *Samson Slaying a Philistine*, a piece Giambologna carved for Prince Francesco de' Medici, the future Grand Duke of Tuscany. In the late 1570s, Giambologna took up Michelangelo's aborted project with the intention of gaining acceptance in academic circles, where the Michelangelo cult was blended with Counter Reformation teachings and a rigorous approach to the study of antiquity. However, Giambologna wanted to change the subject to the erotic one of a young woman being abducted by a young man, which had already been interpreted in Florence by Vincenzo de' Rossi in his sensuous *Theseus Abducting Helen* (1558–60), and which was, moreover, likely to find favor with Francesco I, the greatest art patron of the day.

Giambologna first developed the subject in a small bronze version titled *Rape of a Sabine Woman*, made for Ottavio Farnese. The motif of the youth hoisting the woman was inspired by the Farnese *Bull*, a Hellenistic group discovered about 1545. Even in Giambologna's small bronze, the man's legs are spread so wide that the sculptor could have placed a third figure between them, a crouching man from whom the woman was being seized. The relationship between the figures would have been similar to, and derived from, the one Giambologna had used in *Samson Slaying a Philistine*. In the new piece, he had no specific mythological or historical reference in mind that would have served as a title. He was interested only in displaying his skill in design and technique.

The same concerns underlie the large, three-figure version of *Rape of a Sabine* in marble, which received a title only after its completion. This piece evoked various literary or historical episodes, including the rape of the Sabine women by the early Romans. More important, it gave Giambologna an opportunity to demonstrate proficiency in design and execution, both in the overall arrangement of the masses carved out of the block of stone and in the sensitive details—for instance, the innovative rendering of the woman's soft, fleshy skin. As the contemporary Florentine writer Raffaello Borghini noted in *Il Riposo* (1584), Giambologna wanted to display here "the art of making nude figures (demonstrating the weakness of old age, the strength of youth, and female delicacy) . . . solely to show the excellence of his art, not to tell any story." In effect, the huge group consists of three nudes: an older man, a youth, and a beautiful woman whom the younger man snatches away from the older and weaker man. Abduction for love's sake is expressed with "naturalness"; that is, the subject is treated with a freer approach.

Giambologna was aiming to please Francesco I, who had commissioned many works depicting the ravishing of women for his villa at Pratolino, near Florence, and who might well be expected to buy the grandiose and costly group, which Giambologna may have originally conceived for Pratolino. Nonetheless, the *Rape* does not merely express a banal taste for erotic subjects; it reflects the culture of contemporary academic debates. Attention to the typical features of personages represented in art (in the case of the *Rape*, the young man's strength, the woman's beauty, and the old man's weakness) was an increasingly rigid canon—one dear to Giambologna's mentor, Bernardo

Vecchietti—because it was taken more and more as a standard for judgment. Vecchietti had introduced the Flemish-born Giambologna to the Medici court, and at the time when the artist was working out his idea for the *Rape*, Vecchietti was still hosting him at the Villa del Riposo, the venue for academic discussions influenced by the Counter Reformation and described by Borghini in *Il Riposo*. Giambologna, probably guided by Vecchietti, was thus not interested in depicting a particular story, where he would have had to represent a specific saint or hero in a certain manner; in this way, he was free to concentrate on seeking an expressive naturalness suggested by the nude. Abduction for love was a subject for which nudity was appropriate and would not offend religious proprieties. The strongly Classical rendering of the three figures likewise helped give the impression of simple types and situations present in real life in a natural dimension. Giambologna thus avoided the kind of criticism that upholders of the Counter Reformation had fired at Michelangelo's nudes and creative liberties in the *Last Judgment* (1534–41). Vecchietti and Borghini agreed with that line of criticism, but they praised Michelan-

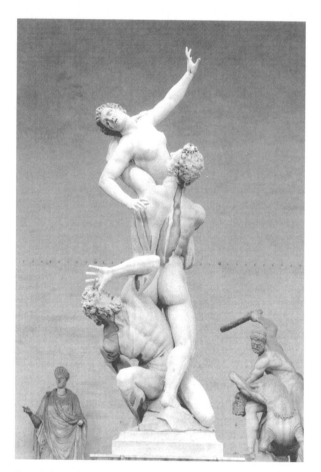

Rape of a Sabine
The Conway Library, Courtauld Institute of Art

gelo's cartoon for the *Battle of Cascina* (1504–05), where the artist had chosen a story suitable for "demonstrating various human attitudes and forms" by means of the nude, in the same way that the *Rape* exhibits the features of weak old age, virile youth, and womanly beauty.

Finished about 1581, the *Rape* did not fail to captivate Francesco I, who wanted it in the Piazza della Signoria, the theater of Renaissance sculpture. The location chosen by the Grand Duke was the Loggia della Signoria, where Benvenuto Cellini's *Perseus and Medusa* (1545–54) was on view in the first bay on the left. Donatello's *Judith Slaying Holofernes* (*ca.* 1459), which had been installed in the right-hand bay since 1506, was removed to make room for the *Rape*, thus altering the whole front view of the loggia. This was certainly not the ideal setting for Giambologna's work; the composition presupposes that the viewer can move freely around it, but the loggia's parapet hinders this. Francesco I chose the location in order to give the work a prime position in Florence, and Giambologna had to adapt it to balance the *Perseus*. His sculpture was higher and wider than Cellini's; to make the two more or less even in height, Giambologna created a base that was lower and wider than the one Cellini had made for his *Perseus*. He modeled it after Michelangelo's base (1504) for *David*.

The Flemish artist showed his knowledge of Florence's sculptural heritage in the base as well, which he decorated with a bronze relief, the *Rape of the Sabine Women*, that followed Cellini's example in the *Perseus* and the tradition initiated by Lorenzo Ghiberti's and Donatello's reliefs. However, although Cellini had depicted *Perseus and Medusa* on the base of his *Perseus* instead of repeating the Medusa story taken from Ovid for the statue, Giambologna's relief illustrates the legend of the Romans and the Sabine women, providing the context for the title suggested by Borghini and approved by the Grand Duke. Thus, Giambologna again paid homage to the Counter Reformation standard of narrative correctness; once the work had been given a name, he created a relief showing the relevant episode from Roman history, a story known to even the least erudite of Florence's citizens.

FRANCESCO VOSSILLA

Further Reading

Avery, Charles, "Giambologna, Sculptor to the Medici (1529–1608): His Style and Its Sources," in *Studies in European Sculpture*, by Avery, London: Christie, 1981

Keutner, Herbert, "Die künstlerische Entwicklung Giambolognas bis zur Aufrichtung der Gruppe der Sabinerinnenraubes," in *Giambologna: Ein Wendepunkt der Europäischen Plastik*, edited by Charles Avery, Anthony Radcliffe, and Manfred Leithe-Jasper, Vienna: Kunsthistorisches Museum, 1978

Radcliffe, Anthony, "Rape of a Sabine (scheda n. 56)," in *Giambologna, 1529–1608: Sculptor to the Medici*, edited by Charles Avery and Anthony Radcliffe, London: Arts Council of Great Britain, 1978

Vossilla, Francesco, *La Loggia della Signoria: Una galleria di scultura*, Florence: Edizioni Medicea, 1995

Vossilla, Francesco, "Il Giambologna e la Loggia della Signoria," in *Giambologna tra Firenze e l'Europa*, Florence: Centro Di, 2000

GRINLING GIBBONS 1648–1721
Anglo-Dutch

Historians universally acknowledge Grinling Gibbons as the outstanding virtuoso ornamental woodcarver of his time—his consummate technical skill was legendary—but they tend to ignore his figural sculpture. Gibbons ran a large workshop and delegated both the design and execution of major commissions, a practice that makes it difficult to attribute works with confidence or to distinguish Gibbons's own hand with precision.

Gibbons probably trained in the studio of Artus I Quellinus of Antwerp, who was working in Amsterdam on decorations for the new town hall and with whose son Gibbons certainly later collaborated in England. Throughout his career, Gibbons benefited enormously from his friendship and contacts with members of the influential Flemish community in London, particularly the painter Sir Peter Lely. Gibbons based his brilliant wood carvings depicting swags of fruit and baskets of flowers, carved so thinly and finely from light wood that they shake realistically in the slightest breeze, on imagery in popular contemporary Dutch and Flemish paintings by Justus van Huysum and Jan Breughel the Younger. Work executed by Gibbons's workshop in the Carved Room at Petworth closely mirror the *Attributes of the Arts* that formed part of the repertoire of Artus I Quellinus's images in the Amsterdam Town Hall more than 40 years before.

The exact date of Gibbons's arrival in England is uncertain, but he seems to have worked first at York and then on ship carving in an isolated studio at Deptford, where John Evelyn recorded encountering him in January 1671. Evelyn introduced Gibbons to King Charles II in March 1671. Sir Christopher Wren, the surveyor-general, noticed Gibbons's remarkable virtuosity in delicate wood reliefs, such as those illustrated in his interpretation of a *Crucifixion* by Jacopo Robusti Tintoretto (1519–94) and an elaborate *Stoning of St. Stephen* in high relief. Wren subsequently became his friend, promoter, and employer. Gibbons's introduction to Wren led to a continuous succession of fruitful commissions. Although Gibbons was not appointed master carver to the crown until 1693, he worked before that under Wren's supervision at Windsor Castle (1677–82), his first major collaboration with Wren and Hugh May, and on the choir stalls at St. Paul's Cathedral in London. Work on other royal palaces at Kensington and Hampton Court, as well as private commissions at Petworth, Dalkeith, and Blenheim, followed.

Gibbon's fine limewood carvings, created with an unprecedented range of fine gouges and specialized chisels for paper-thin undercutting, were so spectacular that the royals used them as ambassadorial gifts to Italian political allies. Charles II sent Gibbons's *Attributes of the Arts* panel (also known as the *Cosimo III Panel*) to Cosimo III, Grand Duke of Tuscany, to commemorate Cosimo's 1669 visit to London and to cement their personal friendship. It is the most opulent of these limewood carvings and ranks as Gibbons's masterpiece. Surmounted by billing doves resting on a fall of fashionable point lace and surrounded by brilliantly carved, undercut fruits of land and sea, a central group of symbols expresses the potency of the arts. A medallion portraying Cosimo's favorite artist, the great Baroque painter and architect Pietro da Cortona, is placed centrally, surrounded by music, instruments, and the quill and signature of Gibbons himself. Behind this joyous affirmation of the arts appear the attributes of power and war—quiver, sword, and scepter; the ducal crown of Cosimo holds the kingly crown of Charles in diagonal balance. James II commissioned from Gibbons a second, more elegant and restrained panel: it includes a medallion portrait of Gibbons as well as the artist's signature.

As with most successful firms, Gibbons ran a versatile business, taking on decorative work in wood, terracotta, plaster, stone, marble, and bronze, such as his work at Trinity College, Cambridge (1689–92). As his workshop developed, he received figural sculpture and monument commissions that were beyond his own personal capabilities. Some ideas Gibbons introduced from the continent, such as his use of military costume for his portrait of *James II*, achieved success, although they were not universally admired by a conservative British public. In 1679 a group of French and Flemish artists, including Artus III Quellinus, the nephew of Artus I, Gibbons's old master, and John Nost of Malines, joined Gibbons to work at Windsor. Quellinus was a highly accomplished figural sculptor, as his terracotta model for a statue of *Charles II* demonstrates. His hand can be traced in many of the finest statues and monuments that came from Gibbons's studio, although they usually went under Gibbons's name, and in at least one case—a finished bronze of *Charles II*—Gibbons, not Quellinus, held the copyright. The Public Record Office in London records the dissolution of

a formal two-year partnership between Quellinus and Gibbons in May 1683, but they may have cooperated informally on monuments until Quellinus's death in 1686. Nost, the foreman, immediately married Quellinus's widow and operated an independent workshop by 1692.

Gibbons's personal strength in stone lay in relief carving, as demonstrated by the exquisite delicacy of his memorial *Robert Cotton* at Conington and his elaborate carving of *Neptune and Galatea* on the fireplace overmantle at Dalkeith Palace (1701). By 1706 his reputation stood so high that John Evelyn praised him in extravagant terms as "our Lysippus." In freestanding figure sculpture, however, Gibbons had varying success: for instance, his bronze *all'antica* (after the antique) *Charles II* in London is more convincing than his marble *Charles Seymour, Sixth Duke of Somerset* in Trinity College, Cambridge, although the pose of each is similar.

Gibbons seemed to be aware of successful figure compositions used on the continent, and his many funerary monuments in Westminster Abbey incorporate French and Italian Baroque imagery. His proposed but unrealized monument for the tomb of Queen Mary (1695) shows a richly inventive and lively Baroque design, full of movement and variety. On the other hand, the essayist Joseph Addison (1672–1719) strongly criticized his monument to Sir Cloudesley Shovel. Although the narrative reliefs depicting the shipwreck of Shovel's crew are lively and naturalistic, the main figure wears an uncomfortable mixture of modern fashion and classical drapes, and the enclosing design, although grand, is rather static in comparison with Quellinus's Thynne monument, with which it is often compared.

Paintings and prints of Gibbons dating from the 1690s onward depict an assured, prosperous, flourishing professional, friend of some of the most famous architects and painters of the age.

J. PATRICIA CAMPBELL

See also **Quellinus Family**

Biography

Born in Rotterdam, present-day Netherlands, 4 April 1648. Parents were English, father a draper from London. Probably trained with Artus I Quellinus at Amsterdam Town Hall. Came to England, *ca.* 1667; worked in York, then Deptford (near London); introduced to King Charles II by John Evelyn in March 1671; befriended by Sir Peter Lely; worked for Sir Christopher Wren and Hugh May; admitted to the Drapers' Company, London, on the basis of patrimony, 19 January 1672; maintained connections and held wardenships throughout life; lived at La Belle Sauvage, Ludgate Hill, London, 1673–84, and at the King's Arms, Bow Street, Covent Garden, where collection displayed and foundry located, until his death; took on Edward Sherwood as apprentice, 1672, and John Hunt in 1675; went into partnership with Artus III Quellinus, 1679–83; appointed Surveyor and Repairer of Carved Work, Windsor, 1682; made Master Sculptor and Master Carver to the Crown, 2 December 1693. Died in London, England, 3 August 1721.

Selected Works

1670–71 *Stoning of St. Stephen*; wood; Victoria and Albert Museum, London, England

ca. 1671 *The Crucifixion*; wood; Victoria and Albert Museum, London, England

ca. 1671 *John Evelyn*; wood; National Maritime Museum, Greenwich, London, England

ca. 1671 *Sir Christopher Wren*; wood; Royal Institute of British Architects, London, England

1680–82 *Attributes of the Arts*; limewood; Museo Nazionale del Bargello, Florence, Italy

1682 *Charles II*; bronze; Royal Hospital Chelsea, London, England

ca. 1685 *The Modena Panel*; limewood; Estense Museum, Modena, Italy

1686 *James II*; bronze; Trafalgar Square, London, England

1691 *Charles Seymour, Sixth Duke of Somerset*; marble; Trinity College, Cambridge, England

1692 Carved Room; wood; Petworth House, West Sussex, England

1697 *Robert Cotton*; marble; Conington, Cambridgeshire, England

1707 Monument to Sir Cloudesley Shovel; marble; Westminster Abbey, London, England

Further Reading

Beard, Geoffrey W., *The Work of Grinling Gibbons*, London: John Murray, 1989

Esterly, David, *Grinling Gibbons and the Art of Carving* (exhib. cat.), London: V and A Publications, and New York: Abrams, 1998

Green, David, *Grinling Gibbons: His Work as Carver and Statuary, 1648–1721*, London: Country Life, 1964

Gunnis, Rupert, *Dictionary of British Sculptors, 1660–1851*, London: Odhams Press, 1953; Cambridge, Massachusetts: Harvard University Press, 1954; revised edition, London: Abbey Library, 1968

Tipping, Henry Avra, *Grinling Gibbons and the Woodwork of His Age, 1648–1720*, London: Country Life, and New York: Scribner, 1914

Vertue, George, *Vertue Note Books*, 7 vols., Oxford: University Press, 1930–55

Whinney, Margaret, *Grinling Gibbons in Cambridge*, Cambridge: Cambridge University Press, 1948

Whinney, Margaret, *Sculpture in Britain, 1530–1830*, Baltimore, Maryland, and London: Penguin, 1964; 2nd edition, revised by John Physick, London and New York: Viking Penguin, 1988

Whinney, Margaret, and Oliver Millar, *English Art, 1625–1724*, Oxford: Clarendon Press, 1957

JOHN GIBSON 1790–1866 *British*

By the time of his death in 1866, having received numerous honors including membership in the Legion of Honor and in 11 academies, John Gibson had become one of the sights of Rome, and a visit to his studio was a fixture on many British and American tourists' itineraries. Patrons from the United States, Australia, India, Italy, Russia, and England had acquired his sculpture. He had also become one of the most materially successful sculptors of his day, leaving more than £32,000 to the Royal Academy inLondon.

Gibson's beginnings were modest. His father, a market gardener from Wales, settled in Liverpool when the sculptor was about nine. Apprenticed to Messrs. Franceys, a leading firm of architectural sculptors, Gibson rose to become their chief designer and carver. Recognizing his talent, William Roscoe, the Liverpool polymath and Renaissance historian, directed Gibson's intellectual education, urging him to base his sculptural style on the pure forms of the Greeks. Roscoe was also an admirer of Michelangelo, whose influence is strongly evident in Gibson's large drawing *The Fall of the Rebel Angels* and in his *Monument to Henry Blundell*.

After the defeat of Napoléon, when Europe again became accessible to travelers, Gibson, with funds provided by his Liverpool friends and ambitious to study antique sculpture in Rome, set out in 1817 with letters of introduction to Antonio Canova, then regarded as the greatest living sculptor. Canova welcomed him into his academy. Although Gibson later had reservations about the Italian's concept of Neoclassicism, he idolized Canova. Under his tutelage, Gibson modeled *Sleeping Shepherd Boy*. Initially inspired by Canova's *Sleeping Endymion* (1819–22), it shows a blend of the rigorous study of both a living model and acknowledged antique masterpieces, including the bas-relief *Endymion on Mount Latmos* (Musei Capitolini, Rome). Throughout his career, Gibson stressed the importance of using an actual incident observed in daily life as the springboard for a work. He based his *Narcissus*, for example, on a boy he saw "sitting on the edge of a fountain with one leg tucked under him looking into the water" (see Matthews, 1911).

Following this pastoral exercise, Canova encouraged Gibson to model a heroic over-life-size group, *Mars and Cupid*. Again, one of Canova's sculptures, of Hector (1808–16), provided the starting point. Canova persuaded the Sixth Duke of Devonshire to commission a marble from the model. Canova's endorsement and the duke's prestigious purchase launched Gibson as the most admired and sought after British sculptor in Rome.

After Canova's death in 1822, Gibson turned for inspiration to the great Danish Neoclassical sculptor in Rome, Bertel Thorvaldsen, regularly submitting new work to him for advice. The gentle, sensuous style of Canova so evident in *Sleeping Shepherd Boy* and *Mars and Cupid* gave way almost entirely to the more rigorously Greek approach pioneered by Thorvaldsen. Increasingly, Gibson's work displayed a frozen calmness and a carefully considered simplicity. Some contemporaries considered that Gibson combined the best qualities of the two masters. Writing of Gibson, John Murray's *Handbook for Rome* (1860) notes, "First amongst our countrymen resident at Rome is this distinguished sculptor who merits the highest praise of having united the styles of the two greatest sculptors of modern Rome, Canova and Thorvaldsen."

In the 1820s and 1830s Gibson benefited from the growing enthusiasm for collecting British art and the declining interest in acquiring antique marbles, which had been such a high priority on any collector's agenda in the 18th century. His patrons included many of the leading collectors of his day: Sir George Beaumont (*Psyche and the Zephyrs*), Lord Prudhoe, later Fourth Duke of Northumberland (*Sleeping Shepherd Boy*), the First Earl of Yarborough (*Nymph Untying Her Sandal* and *Venus and Cupid*), and Joseph Neeld (*Venus*). Later patrons included Queen Victoria and the prince consort and the newly rich, particularly those with connections with Liverpool, notably the Naylor and Sandbach families.

Like Thorvaldsen, Gibson regarded Rome as his spiritual home and had no wish to return to live in England. Visiting Rome was still a must for the wealthy, and the practice of visiting studios and buying contemporary art was well established. In addition, the city had skilled craftsmen able to transfer a work from plaster into marble. To meet the demand for his work, Gibson ran an efficient studio making replicas of either current or older works. His studio repeated some busts, such as *Nymph*, based on the head of *Nymph Untying Her Sandal*, ten or more times. For a sculptor such as Gibson, whose ambition was to produce ideal figures, Rome provided the perfect infrastructure for a successful career.

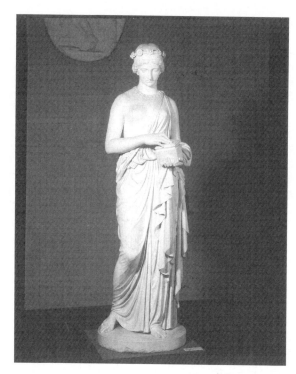

Pandora
© Victoria and Albert Museum, London / Art Resource, NY

The popularity of his work allowed Gibson to be selective over the commissions he undertook for public sculpture and church monuments. The most important was a group for the new Palace of Westminster, *Queen Victoria*. He carved most of his church monuments—which include some of his most inventive work—for friends.

Perhaps sensing that Neoclassicism was effectively dead and that his work now appealed only to the conservative, Gibson showed at the 1862 International Exhibition, London, in a richly colored temple designed by Owen Jones, three tinted figures: *Pandora, Cupid Tormenting the Soul*, and *Venus. Tinted Venus*, an attempt by Gibson to revive the Greek practice of sculptural polychromy, caused a sensation.

His friend Lord Lytton composed the epitaph on Gibson's monument in the Protestant Cemetery in Rome, writing that his character "was in unison with his attributes as an artist, beautiful in its simplicity and truthfulness, noble in its dignity and elevation of purpose." Gibson's career coincided with the last chapter of the dominance of antiquity over European art; Paris now replaced Rome as the center for sculptural innovation.

TIMOTHY STEVENS

See also **Canova, Antonio; Michelangelo (Buonarroti); Thorvaldsen, Bertel**

Biography

Born in Conway, North Wales, before 19 June 1790. Moved with family to Liverpool *ca.* 1799–1800; apprenticed to Southwell and Wilson, cabinetmakers, then from 1805 to Messrs. Franceys, marble carvers; trained under sculptor F.A. Legé; exhibited at the Liverpool Academy, 1810–14; at the Royal Academy, London, 1816–51; left for Rome in 1817 via London, where met John Flaxman; studied under Antonio Canova and at Accademia di San Luca; set up own studio; major commission from Duke of Devonshire led to additional work; leading sculptor in London by 1830; elected associate of the Royal Academy, 1833, and Royal Academician, 1838; showed at London International Exhibition, 1862; granted the Legion of Honor by the French government, 1864. Largest collection of his sculptural works, as well as his sketches and drawings, in the Royal Academy, London; Walker Art Gallery, Liverpool, and the National Museums and Galleries of Wales, Cardiff, hold important collections of his marbles. Died in Rome, Italy, 27 January 1866.

Selected Works

1813   *Monument to Henry Blundell*; marble; Church of St. Helen, Sefton, England

1818   *Sleeping Shepherd Boy*; plaster; Royal Academy, London, England; later marble version: 1830–34, Walker Art Gallery, Liverpool, England

1821   *Mars and Cupid*; marble; Chatsworth House, Derbyshire, England

1822   *Cupid Tormenting the Soul*; marble (untraced); later marble version about 1850: Walker Art Gallery, Liverpool, England

1822   *Psyche and the Zephyrs*; marble (untraced); marble version: 1839, Palazzo Corsini, Rome, Italy

1824–30 *Nymph Untying Her Sandal*; marble; Usher Art Gallery, Lincolnshire, England

1829   *Narcissus*; marble (untraced); marble version: 1838, Royal Academy, London, England

1831   *Venus and Cupid*; marble; Usher Art Gallery, Lincolnshire, England

1838   *Hunter and His Dog*; marble; private collection, England; marble version: date not known, Usher Art Gallery, Lincolnshire, England

1842   *Aurora*; marble; National Museums and Galleries of Wales, Cardiff, Wales

1849   *Venus*; marble; Fitzwilliam Museum, Cambridge, England

1850–55 *Queen Victoria*; marble; Palace of Westminster, London, England

1851–56 *Tinted Venus*; polychromed marble; Walker Art Gallery, Liverpool, England

1856   *Pandora*; marble; Lady Lever Art Gallery, Port Sunlight, Merseyside, England; Victoria and Albert Museum, London, England

Further Reading

Curtis, Penelope (editor), *Patronage and Practice: Sculpture on Merseyside*, Liverpool: Tate Gallery, 1989

Eastlake, Elizabeth Rigby, *Life of John Gibson, R.A., Sculptor*, London: Longmans Green, 1870

Gibson, John, *Engravings from Original Compositions Executed in Marble at Rome*, London: Colnaghi Scott, 1861

Hartman, J.B., "Canova, Thorvaldsen, and Gibson," *English Miscellany* 11 (1955)

Matthews, T. (editor), *The Biography of John Gibson, RA, Sculptor*, London: Heinemann, 1911

Read, B., *Victorian Sculpture*, New Haven, Connecticut: Yale University Press, 1982

ALFRED GILBERT 1854–1934 *British*

Alfred Gilbert was born in 1854 to Alfred Gilbert Sr. and his wife, Charlotte, both accomplished professional musicians. Gilbert's parents did not overtly encourage him to follow an artistic career, although he did attend Aldenham Grammar School between 1865 and 1871. Aldenham was unusual in that its curriculum devoted time to developing its students' skills in the arts.

It was not until 1872 that Gilbert embarked on a formal art education. He then began taking classes at Heatherley's, a well-known London art school that his paternal uncle Herbert had once attended. Gilbert moved on, a year later, to the Royal Academy Schools. As an art student, Gilbert gained a thorough understanding of the human body by studying casts of antique sculpture and by assimilating the Neoclassical works of an older generation of British sculptors that included John Flaxman and Alfred Stevens. Following in the footsteps of many British art students and encouraged by the sculptor Joseph Edgar Boehm, Gilbert moved to Paris in 1876 to refine his visual knowledge at the École des Beaux-Arts.

Paris was not, however, the turning point in Gilbert's years of apprenticeship. In 1878 he moved to Rome in order to see and absorb the history of Renaissance art. While in Italy, he was particularly attracted to the bronze works of Donatello and Benvenuto Cellini. He then set out to learn Renaissance methods of casting, in particular the technique of *cire perdue*, or lost-wax. During the early 1880s in Rome, Gilbert cast his first critically successful works using the lost-wax method: *Perseus Arming* and *Icarus*. Falling into the popular category of ideal figures, these two small statues were perhaps unremarkable for their subject matter—Classical myths—and for being cast in bronze. The size and introspection of the figures, however, was new. Ideal bronze figures intended for exhibition were generally life size; *Perseus Arming* and *Icarus* were both significantly smaller than life size (73.7 cm and 106.7 cm, respectively). Although they were subsequently further reduced in size for reproduction and sale to bourgeois art collectors, their unusual size for exhibition suggests Gilbert's early attention to sculpture's place in intimate domestic spaces. In terms of the subjects' moods, *Perseus Arming* portrays not a hero, but a slightly off-balance mortal with no knowledge of what might come in battle, and *Icarus* belies the possibility of flight with a heavy downward gaze and awkwardly posed, rooted limbs.

When Gilbert returned to London in 1884, he brought with him his knowledge of lost-wax casting and an enthusiasm for the technique, which he shared with his British contemporaries. Since the 18th century, most bronze in Britain had been cast using brick-dust, plaster, or sand techniques; Gilbert's reimportation and popularization of lost-wax casting further expanded the techniques available to British sculptors in the 1880s and 1890s.

Although ideal figures such as *Icarus* were part of the stock expected of a professional sculptor, the chance to solidify a career in sculpture came primarily through the commission of public monuments. Gilbert received just such a commission in 1886. When the Seventh Earl of Shaftesbury died in 1885, a Shaftesbury Memorial Committee formed with the aim of commissioning two public monuments to honor the late Earl's philanthropic works. The committee awarded Joseph Edgar Boehm the first commission of a marble statue of the Earl for Westminster Abbey. At Boehm's urging, the committee gave Gilbert the second commission for a bronze statue, to be erected at a principal London location. Following its formal installation in Piccadilly Circus in 1893, the memorial to Anthony Ashley-Cooper, Seventh Earl of Shaftesbury, became the most popularly known of Gilbert's works and remains familiar today as *Eros*. Gilbert's work on the Shaftesbury memorial was innovative in two ways. First, he interpreted the meaning of a memorial more loosely than any sculptor in the 19th century had done before; rather than sculpting a portrait, he created a symbolic representation of the Earl's charity. The memorial's references to charity are both practical and abstract; Gilbert designed it as a fountain to provide horses and passersby with a place to stop and drink, and the aluminum figure of Anteros, crowning the memorial, personifies selfless love and thus charity. Second, Gilbert made innovative use of materials. Although increasingly in the 1880s and 1890s sculptors juxtaposed industrial materials, such as steel and iron, with bronze, ivory, silver, and gold, Gilbert's casting of the Anteros figure in aluminum was without precedent.

In the course of his career, Gilbert received a number of public and royal commissions, including the Jubilee Memorial to Queen Victoria in Winchester, the Tomb of the Duke of Clarence in the Albert Memorial Chapel at Windsor Castle, and the Memorial to Queen Alexandra at Marlborough Gate in London. All three of these memorials demonstrate the intensity of Gilbert's attention to detail and to the color and properties of different metals. Due to Gilbert's reimaginings, these monuments took years to complete and frequently ended as sources of stress and anxiety for the artist and patrons.

Gilbert extended his vision of sculpture as a play with materials to his interest in the decorative arts. Unlike most other Victorian sculptors, he took on goldsmithing and jewelry commissions. Whereas Gilbert's large-scale commissions were most certainly collaborative studio efforts, he personally undertook all the fine metalwork, thereby fashioning himself as a modern version of a Renaissance court artist. Two of Gilbert's most important goldsmithing commissions were the *Epergne*, presented to Queen Victoria as a golden jubilee gift by the officers of the army, and *The Preston Mayoral Chain*. Made of an eclectic combination of patinated and gilded silver, rock crystal, and shell, the *Epergne* (intended as a centerpiece) combines marine imagery with figural symbols, Saint George and Britannia, to suggest the power of the British Empire. *The Preston Mayoral Chain* is more abstract; it demonstrates Gilbert's keen knowledge of the possibilities of metal, as well as his awareness of the whiplash curves that would come to be known as Art Nouveau.

Although Gilbert was elected professor of sculpture at the Royal Academy in 1900 (he served in this post between 1900 and 1904), his influence on 20th-century British sculpture was tenuous at best. His exile in Bruges, Belgium, beginning in 1901, left him on the periphery of the London art scene, and he had no long-term students. By the time Gilbert returned to London in the late 1920s to create the Memorial for Queen Alexandra, Modernist artists such as Jacob Epstein and Henri Gaudier-Brzeska had long changed British sculpture.

Gilbert is recognized today, however, for his contributions to the so-called New Sculpture, a loosely defined movement between 1880 and around 1900. The New Sculpture was sympathetic to spiritual and symbolist themes and was committed to sculpture's primary physical contexts: domestic spaces and architectural decoration. (Other major sculptors of the New

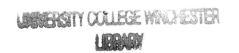

Sculpture included George Frampton, Lord Frederic Leighton, and Hamo Thornycroft.) Gilbert's introduction of the lost-wax casting process and use of polychromy in his sculpture was extremely influential to the ideals of the New Sculpture.

KARA OLSEN THEIDING

Biography

Born in London, England, 12 August 1854. Studied at Heatherley's art school, 1872–73, and then at the Royal Academy Schools, 1873–75; apprenticed to Joseph Edgar Boehm, 1872; went to Paris in 1876 to study with Pierre-Jules Cavelier and Emmanuel Frémiet at the École des Beaux-Arts; worked in Rome, 1878–84, before returning to England; first Englishman to work extensively in the *cire perdue* method in the 19th century; made associate of the Royal Academy, 1886; Royal Academician, 1892; Royal Academy professor of sculpture, 1900–1904; joined the Art Workers' Guild, 1888; awarded Royal Victorian Order (fourth class), 1897; maintained studio in London until forced to declare bankruptcy, August 1901; established art school in Bruges, Belgium, 1903; school closed by 1908; resigned from Royal Academy, 1908; in self-imposed exile in Bruges until 1926, then returned to England; knighted and reinstated as Royal Academician, 1932. Died in London, England, 4 November 1934.

Selected Works

1882 *Perseus Arming*; bronze; Victoria and Albert Museum, London, England
1884 *Icarus*; bronze; National Galleries and Museums of Wales, Cardiff, Wales
1886–93 Memorial to Anthony Ashley-Cooper, Seventh Earl of Shaftesbury (popularly known as *Eros*); bronze, aluminum; Piccadilly Circus, London, England
1887–90 *Epergne*, presented to Queen Victoria as a golden jubilee gift by the officers of the army; patinated and gilded silver, rock crystal, shell; Her Majesty the Queen, on loan to the Victoria and Albert Museum, London, England
1887– Jubilee memorial to Queen Victoria;
1912 bronze, beaten metal, gold paint, crystal; Hall of Winchester Castle, Winchester, England
1888–92 *The Preston Mayoral Chain*; silver gilt inset with diamonds, rubies, sapphires, moonstone, enamel; Town Hall, Preston, England

1892– Tomb of Prince Albert Victor, Duke of
1928 Clarence; bronze, marble, aluminum, ivory, brass; Albert Memorial Chapel, Windsor Castle, Berkshire, England
1895 *St. George*; white metal, ivory; St. Mary Magdalene Church, Sandringham, England
1896 Decorations for the Mortuary Chapel of H.R.H. Prince Henry of Battenberg; bronze; St. Mildred Church, Whippingham, Isle of Wight, England
1899 *St. Elizabeth of Hungary*; bronze, ivory, and tin inlaid with mother-of-pearl, semi-precious stones; Kippen Parish Church, Stirlingshire, Scotland
1899 *The Virgin*; painted bronze; Kippen Parish Church, Stirlingshire, Scotland
1926–32 Memorial to Queen Alexandra; bronze; Marlborough Gate, London, England

Further Reading

Beattie, Susan, *The New Sculpture*, New Haven, Connecticut: Yale University Press, 1983
Bury, Adrian, *Shadow of Eros: A Biographical and Critical Study of the Life and Works of Sir Alfred Gilbert, R.A., M.V.O., D.C.L.*, London: Macdonald and Evans, 1954
Dorment, Richard, *Alfred Gilbert*, New Haven, Connecticut: Yale University Press, 1985
Dorment, Richard, et al., *Alfred Gilbert: Sculptor and Goldsmith*, London: Royal Academy of Arts, 1985
Hatton, Joseph, *The Life and Work of Alfred Gilbert, R.A., M.V.O., LL.D.*, London: The Art Journal, 1903
McAllister, Isabel, *Alfred Gilbert*, London: Black, 1929
Read, Benedict, *Victorian Sculpture*, New Haven, Connecticut: Yale University Press, 1982
Monkhouse, William Cosmo, "Alfred Gilbert, A.R.A.," *Magazine of Art* 12 (1889)
W.T.W., "The Art of the Sculptor Set Forth by Alfred Gilbert, R.A.," *Magazine of Art* 2nd ser., 1 (1903)

TOMB OF PRINCE ALBERT VICTOR (DUKE OF CLARENCE)

Alfred Gilbert (1854–1934)
1892–1928
bronze, marble, aluminium, ivory, and brass
h. 3.2 m; w. 2.0 m
Albert Memorial Chapel, Windsor, England

Prince Albert Victor, Duke of Clarence and Avondale, eldest son of the Prince and Princess of Wales, and eldest grandchild of Queen Victoria, died unexpectedly of influenza in January 1892. Queen Victoria gave the Duke's parents permission to bury him in the Albert Memorial Chapel at Windsor, England, as befitting a man who stood second in line to the British crown. The Prince and Princess of Wales decided that the Duke's tomb should have elaborate sculptural decoration. Thanks to Alfred Gilbert's growing reputation and his long-standing friendship with Queen Victoria's daughter, Princess Louise, the Waleses chose the young English sculptor to execute the Duke's tomb. The favor of a royal commission was a source of pride for Gilbert, but the Duke's memorial proved to be arduous work, fraught with delays and disputes. From beginning to end, the tomb of the Duke of Clarence engaged Gilbert for over three and one-half decades.

Gilbert first designed the tomb as a simple sarcophagus surmounted by an effigy of the Duke. The sarcophagus, made of Mexican onyx, was finished in February 1893, and the Duke's remains were formally laid to rest on 2 March 1893. The year's delay for the entombment bothered the royal family, but Gilbert managed to assuage their anxiety by showing them models that he had completed for the duke's recumbent effigy.

The effigy consists of three major parts: a recumbent effigy figure of the Duke, a kneeling angel at his head holding aloft a crown, and Anteros (the personification of selfless love) at his feet, weeping over a wreath of orange blossoms. The symbolism of the crown is ambiguous, probably consciously so, conflating the English monarch's crown and the crown of eternity. The orange blossoms refer to the Duke's planned wedding to Princess May of Teck, which was to have taken place in the spring of 1892. The Duke's figure, as it was finally cast in 1895, made bold use of polychromy: his uniform of the 10th Hussars is executed in bronze and brass, the lining of his cloak in aluminum, and his face and hands in gleaming white marble. The crisp treatment of the uniform's braiding and buttons contrasts sharply in color and texture with the veiled features of the Duke's waxy, idealized face and his smooth hands.

This profusion of sculptural detail is not, however, accessible to viewers. Gilbert added a final component to the tomb, a bronze grille that surrounds the perimeter of the memorial. Originally conceived as a low railing above which the effigy figures could be seen, the grille evolved into a high and elaborately decorated bronze barrier. It consists of 18 curvilinear uprights, 12 of which are supported by pairs of angels. Above the 12 supported uprights stand 12 stanchions, on which Gilbert designed small statues of saints. Conceptually, the grille owes something to the medieval history of the Albert Memorial Chapel; Henry VIII had intended to be buried on the site in a tomb that had included a high grille decorated with candlesticks, escutcheons, and 12 small saints. The historical context of the site was important to Gilbert, but the grille and its figures also had contemporary symbolic meanings. The saints provided the Duke with an invented spiritual and political genealogy. St. George, St. Edward the Confessor, St. Eth-

elreda of Ely, St. Margaret, and St. Patrick have particular resonance in Britain, and St. Elizabeth of Hungary was believed to be an ancestor of the Duke's grandfather, Prince Albert. Stylistically, the grille demonstrates Gilbert's interest in symbolism and in the Pre-Raphaelites; it conjures up the image of a sleeping prince locked deep within a thicketed realm.

The grille and the first of its figures, *St. George*, were in place by 1898, when Queen Victoria officially dedicated the memorial. Mounted on the west side of the grille on the south corner, *St. George* is cast in aluminum, with face and hands executed in ivory, mirroring the material treatment of the Duke's effigy. Standing languidly with eyes closed, St. George blesses onlookers with his raised right hand. The fluid draping of St. George's fanciful armor and helmet recalls the knights painted by Gilbert's friend Sir Edward Burne-Jones, but the pose of *St. George* owes much to Gilbert's own well-received small bronze of 1884, *Icarus*. Like *Icarus*, *St. George* focuses on the representation of introspection rather than the body's external power.

Although Gilbert spoke out vehemently against Art Nouveau, his works display a visual acknowledgment of contemporary trends in design. The seven saints that Gilbert completed before 1901 provide evidence of this interest in the play of form. The example of *St. Eliza-*

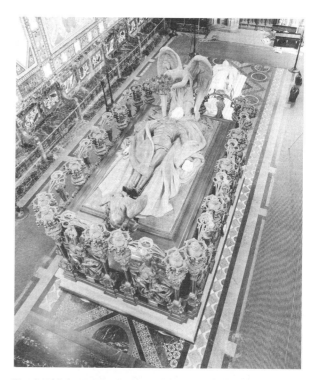

Tomb of Prince Albert Victor (Duke of Clarence)
Photographic Survey of Private Collections, Courtauld Institute of Art

beth of Hungary (located in the west corner of the tomb's north side) is the most compelling. Her billowing cloak is closely related to contemporary work produced by Charles Rennie Mackintosh and his circle in Glasgow and published in the *Studio*; the formal components of St. Elizabeth—especially her long, columnar body, the oval outline of her cloak, and her linear, schematic crown—show that Gilbert had assimilated current trends toward exaggeration and contrast in design and applied them to three-dimensional sculpture.

In 1901 the tomb was finished except for the figures of five saints. The nine years Gilbert had spent on the memorial were full of broken promises for its completion, however, and the delays weighed heavily on the grieving family members. Gilbert, suffering financial reverses, further tried the royal family's patience by selling freestanding copies of the saints from the tomb without royal permission. When Gilbert published the replicas of the tomb saints in the *Magazine of Art*'s Easter issue for 1903, expressly against King Edward VII's wishes, a break between sculptor and patron ensued. It was not until 1926 that King George V invited Gilbert to return from his self-imposed exile in Bruges to complete the tomb. The last five saints, executed in a simpler and more spare style, were at last placed on the tomb in 1928.

KARA OLSEN THEIDING

Further Reading

Beattie, Susan, "The New Sculpture: Aspects of a Nineteenth-Century English Renaissance," *Bulletin of the Detroit Institute of Arts* 62/4 (1987)

Handley-Read, Lavinia, "Alfred Gilbert and Art Nouveau," *Apollo* 85 (January 1967)

Handley-Read, Lavinia, "Alfred Gilbert: A New Assessment," *Connoisseur* 169 (1968)

Roskill, Mark, "Alfred Gilbert's Monument to the Duke of Clarence: A Study in the Sources of Later Victorian Sculpture," *Burlington Magazine* 110 (December 1978)

ERIC GILL 1882–1940 *British*

The son of a clergyman, Arthur Eric Rowton Gill maintained the influence of his religious upbringing throughout his life and work. His early association with the English Arts and Crafts movement also influenced him, although later he would distance himself from it.

Gill began his career as a sculptor in 1909. Until then he had primarily been a calligrapher and stone engraver. Evidence of these early disciplines is apparent in the way he approached sculpting by advocating the practice of "direct carving." He did not favor working from a clay model—a method his patron, Count Harry Kessler, attempted to introduce Gill to in 1910 when he arranged for Gill to travel to France in the hope that he would apprentice himself to Aristide Maillol. This method did not work out, although Gill greatly admired Maillol.

Gill's introduction in 1908 to the Indian art historian Ananda Coomaraswamy was fortuitous. Through him Gill learned about the carvings and frescoes at Ajanta and the erotic temple sculptures of India. Their influence can be seen in *Ecstasy*. Here, the act of lovemaking is celebrated in much the same way as it is on the temples of India. With such references Gill's work shows striking similarities to that of his close friend at the time, Jacob Epstein. Gill's *Votes for Women*, which he carved during the same period, also reflects his interest in the erotic. Carved in relief in stone, it was bought for five pounds by Maynard Keynes.

After Gill moved his family to Ditchling in Sussex, he was commissioned to carve the *Stations of the Cross* at Westminster Cathedral. Fourteen panels in all, they each measure 170 by 170 centimeters and were carved in low relief out of Hoptonwood stone. Considered among his seminal works, they depict Christ's progression along the Via Dolorosa to his crucifixion and later burial. Here, the sculptor's expression is free from the affectation that would manifest itself in his later sculpture and woodcuts.

In 1924 Gill moved with his family to Capel-y-ffin deep in the Welsh highlands. Shortly afterward he carved the *Deposition* in black Hoptonwood stone. Evidently pleased with the results he wrote that it was "about the only carving of mine I'm not sorry about." In 1925 he carved the *Sleeping Christ*, which shows the head of Christ resting in his palm. The attitude is reminiscent of the recumbent sculptures of the Buddha at Ajanta and other Buddhist sites.

In March 1928 Gill had a major exhibition at the Goupil Gallery in London. Among the 15 sculptures in the exhibition was his large kneeling torso of a woman called *Mankind*. The work prompted much adulation, and critics made comparisons with Maillol, Ivan Meštrovic, and even Pheidias. Gill's characteristic style is not as evident in this piece as it is in many of his earlier works. Here, he seemed to restrain his tendency toward the full-figured female, with more of an inclination toward abstraction and Classical design.

The success of the Goupil show coupled with the publication of two books featuring Gill's work, one by John Rothenstein in 1927 and the other by Joseph Thorp in 1929, established him as a major artist. His relocation to "Piggots," near High Wycombe in Buckinghamshire, in 1928 was followed by the offer to

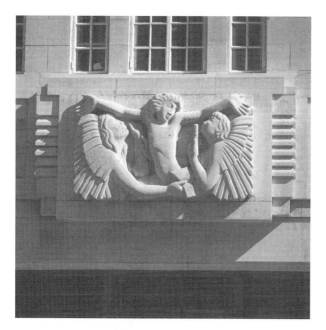

Detail from *Prospero and Ariel* relief from exterior of
Broadcasting House, Portland Place, London
© Angelo Hornak / CORBIS

carve the three "winds" on the London Underground
Electric Railways (now London Transport) headquarters above St. James's Park Station. He was the leader
of a group of six sculptors, Henry Moore and Jacob
Epstein among them.

The early 1930s saw Gill carving *Prospero and
Ariel* over the entrance to Broadcasting House in Portland Place in London. As part of *Prospero and Ariel*
(but not over the entrance) he also carved three panels
in bas-relief showing Ariel being carried by angels,
Ariel piping to children, and Ariel accompanied by
Gaiety and Wisdom. He created a fourth sculpture,
The Sower, for the lobby. Together these are the best-
known examples of Gill's public art. Although Gill
was not especially happy with the project when he
completed it, pedestrians have admired it for its simplicity and narrative qualities—in many respects not
unlike his earlier *Stations of the Cross*.

Gill made brief visits to Jerusalem in 1934 and
1937. He had received a commission to execute a series
of ten small panels for the Palestine Archaeological
Museum. Each panel represents the various cultures
that Palestine had comprised. About this time Gill was
being recognized for his extraordinary contribution to
the world of art with several awards, including one of
the first for "Designer for Industry," given by the Royal
Society of Arts.

In 1935 Gill received a commission to carve three
large panels for the League of Nations building in Ge-

neva, Switzerland. The resulting *Creation* was the last
major work of Gill's career. Two smaller panels flank
the large central panel measuring approximately 9.1
meters by 2.4 meters. They depict the re-creation of
man, a subject chosen by Gill to replace the original
idea put forward by the committee of Christ's rebuke
to Peter, thus avoiding any protest by those who did
not profess the Christian faith.

In 1939 the bishop of Northampton opened a new
Catholic church at Gorleston-on-Sea. This was Gill's
first architectural project and one that garnered much
praise for its revolutionary design. Constructed of red
brick with pointed arches and stark white interior, it
was a departure from traditional church design and
much in keeping with Gill's views on how churches
should be built. The altar was elevated and positioned
in the middle of the church at the intersection of the
cruciform plan. A large crucifix depicting Christ with
red hair and beard hangs over the altar.

By the time of his death at the age of 58, Gill had
achieved a mastery over a wide variety of media.
Along with his friend Jacob Epstein, Gill was responsible for resurrecting issues of human sexuality that had
been discreetly avoided by the puritanical Victorians.
Even so, his doctrine of life and work prompted certain
critics to allege his desire to regress to the Middle
Ages.

ERIC GILL

Biography

Born in Brighton, England, 22 February 1882. Studied
briefly at Chichester Technical and Art School, 1897–
90, before taking apprenticeship with architect William
Douglas Caröe, London, 1899; enrolled in Central
School of Arts and Crafts and influenced by calligrapher Edward Johnston; studied practical masonry at
Westminster Technical Institute, London, 1901;
worked with E.S. Prior at Art Workers' Guild, 1903;
elected to Arts and Crafts Exhibition Society, 1906;
began teaching at Central School and Paddington Institute; visited Rome to study stone-carvings, 1906; first
solo exhibition at Chenil Gallery, Chelsea, 1911; exhibited at Second Post-Impressionist Exhibition, London, 1919–13; designed typefaces for *Perpetua*, 1925,
and *Gill Sans-serif*, 1927; carved *Prospero and Ariel*
at Broadcasting House in London, early 1930s; elected
Honorary Associate of Institute of British Architects,
1935; named Associate of the Royal Academy, 1937.
Won prestigious Designer for Industry award and
named Honorary Associate of the Royal Society of
British Sculptors. Died in Uxbridge, England, 17 November 1940.

Selected Works

1910   *Mother and Child*; Portland stone; National Museum of Wales, Cardiff, Wales

1910   *Votes for Women*; stone

1911   *Ecstasy*; Portland stone; Tate Gallery, London, England

1913   *Boys Boxing*; Portland stone; private collection

1914–18 *Stations of the Cross*; Hoptonwood stone; Westminster Cathedral, Sussex, England

1919   *St. Sebastian*; Portland stone; Tate Gallery, London, England

1924   *Deposition*; black Hoptonwood stone; The King's School, Canterbury, England

1925   *Sleeping Christ*; Caen stone; Manchester City Art Gallery, Manchester, England

1927–28 *Mankind*; Hoptonwood stone; Tate Gallery, London, England

1931   *Prospero and Ariel*; Caen stone; Broadcasting House, London, England

1931   *The Sower*; Corsham stone; Manchester City Art Gallery, Manchester, England

1938   *Creation*; stone; The League of Nations Building, Geneva, Switzerland

Further Reading

Attwater, Donald, *Eric Gill: Workman*, London: Clarke, 1941

Gill, Cecil, Beatrice Warde, and David Kindersley, *The Life and Works of Eric Gill, Papers Read at a Clark Library Symposium, 22 April 1967*, Los Angeles: University of California, 1968

Gill, Eric, *Autobiography*, New York: Adair, 1941

Gill, Eric, *A Holy Tradition of Working: Passages from the Writings of Eric Gill*, Ipswich, Suffolk: Golgonooza, and West Stockbridge, Massachusetts: Lindisfarne Press, 1983

MacCarthy, Fiona, *Eric Gill*, London: Faber and Faber, 1989

Rothenstein, John, *Eric Gill*, London: Ernest Benn, 1929

Speaight, Robert, *The Life of Eric Gill*, London: Methuen, 1966

Strict Delight: The Life and Work of Eric Gill, 1882–1940, Manchester: Manchester University Press, 1980

Thorp, Joseph, *Eric Gill*, London: Jonathan Cape, 1929

BRUNO GIORGI 1905–1993 *Brazilian*

The 20th century witnessed an extraordinary Modernist movement in Brazil. All the fields of art had major contributors: in music there was Heitor Villa-Lobos; in painting, Cândido Portinari; in fiction, Jorge Amado; in poetry, Carlos Drummond de Andrade; in architecture, Oscar Niemeyer and Lúcio Costa; in landscape architecture, Roberto Burle-Marx; and in sculpture, Vítor Brecheret and Bruno Giorgi. The former was identified with early Modernism and the city of São Paulo. The latter represented later Modernism and contributed to the identity of Brasília.

Although of Italian descent and having initially studied sculpture in Italy, Giorgi was essentially rooted in the school of Paris and became very much a part of the international Modernist school. He participated in the Salon d'Automne and the Salon des Tuileries. His initial model was Aristide Maillol, with whom he learned the ample completion of space, especially for the female figure. Progressively, however, Giorgi's work showed the influence of Henry Moore and Alberto Giacometti and a tendency to abstraction. The Stuttgart art critic Max Bense, in fact, declared that Giorgi was the 20th-century Brazilian equivalent of Giacometti and Ossip Zadkine.

Only in the 1940s did Giorgi begin to work in Brazil. Initially he lived in São Paulo and became a member of an artist's movement, the Grupo Santa Helena. It consisted of young artists, often of Italian descent, who worked as artisans, were not part of the art establishment, and painted scenes of local subject matter. During World War II, however, Giorgi moved to the federal capital, Rio de Janeiro. There he came to the attention of one of the most influential ministers of education in modern Brazilian history, Gustavo Capanema.

Giorgi received a contract to build a *Monumento à Juventude* (Monument to Youth) on the plaza in which the new building of the ministry was located. The ministry complex had many important Brazilian artists associated with it, and this sculpture considerably enhanced his reputation. Burle-Marx designed the gardens, Portinari designed the tile panels of the facade, and Niemeyer and Le Corbusier, the Franco-Swiss architect and renowned pioneer of Modernism, planned the building. In it worked not only the minister but also Drummond de Andrade, as the minister's secretary, and Villa-Lobos.

Other public works followed, along with private solicitations. Giorgi now also became associated with a rising generation of Brazilian sculptors consisting of himself, Mateus Fernandes, Ernesto de Fiori, Alfredo Ceschiatti, and Castellane (Arlindo Castellani de Carli). Giorgi participated in the Venice and São Paulo biennials of the early 1950s, and in 1953 he won the national sculptor prize for the third São Paulo Biennial.

In 1956 President Juscelino Kubitschek decided to transfer the Brazilian capital from Rio de Janeiro to the central plateau of the country in a new, planned city, Brasília. Giorgi produced some of the signature pieces for this city. These works not only contributed to the city's identity but comprised the defining works of the artist's career.

For the Ministry of Foreign Relations Giorgi designed *Meteoro* (Meteor), a large, round, white sphere

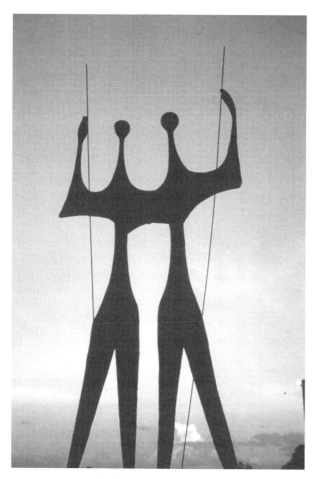

Silhouette of *Two Warriors*
© Julia Waterlow; Eye Ubiquitous / CORBIS

Giorgi held highly successful individual exhibitions in Rio de Janeiro and São Paulo. Numerous critics praised his collective oeuvre. The cataloging of his increasingly valued works in museums and private collections in Latin America, the United States, and Europe followed. In 1989 Giorgi created the marble sculpture *Integração* (Integration) for the Latin American Memorial in São Paulo designed by Niemeyer, marking the culmination of Giorgi's collaboration with this other patriarch of Brazilian Modernism. These exceptions notwithstanding, the overwhelming majority of Giorgi's late work was created for private patrons.

EDWARD A. RIEDINGER

Biography

Born in Mococa, São Paulo, Brazil, 6 August 1905. Moved with family to Rome, 1911; studied sculpture in Rome, 1920–22; moved to Paris, 1935; studied with Aristide Maillol and at Académie de la Grande Chaumière; returned to Brazil, first to São Paulo, 1939–42, then Rio de Janeiro, 1942–49; worked with architect Oscar Niemeyer on sculpture for garden of Ministry of education, 1946, and again in 1960s, producing signature pieces for new capital city of Brasília and a final work with him in 1989; named best national sculptor for 1953 at the São Paulo Biennial. Died in Rio de Janeiro, Brazil, 7 September 1993.

Selected Works

1946   *Monumento à Juventude* (Monument to Youth); stone; Ministry of Education and Culture, Rio de Janeiro, Brazil
1948   *Maternidade* (Maternity); bronze; Banco Safra Collection, São Paulo, Brazil
1960   *À Justica* (To Justice); stone; Praça dos Tres Poderes, Brasília, Brazil
1961   *Dois Guerreiros* (Two Warriors); bronze; Praça dos Tres Poderes, Brasília, Brazil
1968   *Meteoro* (Meteor); marble; Ministry of Foreign Relations, Brasília, Brazil

Further Reading

Amaral, Aracy, *Anotações à proposito de Bruno Giorgi*, São Paulo: Galeria Skultura, 1991

Brazilian Sculpture from 1920 to 1990: A Profile, Washington, D.C.: Cultural Center, Inter-American Development Bank, 1997

Callado, A.C., "Brazilian Sculpture: A Very Vague Outline," *Studio* 607 (October 1943)

Campofiorito, Quirino, "Escultura moderna no Brasil," *Crítica de arte* 1 (1962)

placed at water level on a rectangular reflecting pool that is boarded by tropical vegetation and fronts the glass facade of the ministry building. The marble sculpture and the complex are a stunning example of a balance of elements, producing a modernist reverie of elegance and serenity.

His second work rises in the central square of the capital, standing between the Supreme Court and the executive offices of the presidential palace. *Dois Guerreiros* (Two Warriors) is an abstract metal work, 9 meters high, of two elongated human figures reminiscent of the work of Giacometti. Each figure silhouettes the basic forms of head, torso, arms, and legs and thrusts from its outstretched, distant arm a towering lance. The whole of the work possesses a lyrical, dynamic sense of resolute advance, embodying the spirit that built the city. The work has come to be identified with the *candangos*, the pioneer builders and settlers of Brasília.

Giorgi's later life was not without its accomplishments. In 1985, on the occasion of his 80th birthday,

Louzada, Júlio, "Giorgi, Bruno," in *Artes plásticas: Seu mercado, seus leilões*, by Louzada, vol. 2, *Artes plásticas Brazil*, São Paulo: Inter/Art/Brasil, 1987

Um século de escultura no Brasil, São Paulo: Museu de Arte de São Paulo Assis Chateaubriand, 1982

GIOVANNI DI BALDUCCIO *fl.* 1317/18–1349 *Italian*

Little is known about the life and career of Giovanni di Balduccio. Although his birth and death dates are unknown, it is likely that he was born about 1300 and died shortly after 1349. The factual information regarding his whereabouts and activity is limited to four signed works and his mention in two documents. The Pisan sculptor's first recorded activity is in 1317/18, when he was employed by Cathedral of Pisa's workshop, where Tino di Camaino was *capomaestro* (chief architect) until 1317, when he was succeeded by Lupo di Francesco. Some posit that Giovanni trained in the workshop of Giovanni Pisano, although no evidence exists to suggest his involvement with Pisano's Cathedral of Pisa pulpit (completed 1259–1260). If he did train with Giovanni Pisano, then he was surely born earlier than 1300. Regardless, the influence of Giovanni Pisano, as well as that of Nicola Pisano and Tino di Camaino, on the work of Giovanni is significant. Giovanni is credited with introducing the Tuscan Gothic style learned from these Pisan and Sienese masters to Lombardy, and specifically Milan, where he moved in 1334.

The four signed works by Giovanni help determine the course of his career and style and assist in further attributions. Among these four works, two are dated: the *Arca of Saint Peter Martyr* and the architrave at the Church of S. Maria di Brera, both in Milan. The remaining two, the tomb of Guarniero degli Antelminelli and the pulpit for the Church of S. Maria del Prato at San Casciano, near Florence, certainly date from earlier in the sculptor's career.

The earliest work securely attributed to Giovanni is the tomb of Guarniero degli Antelminelli at the Church of S. Francesco, Sarzana. Some scholars suggest that prior to this work Giovanni may have been responsible for some heads and figures on the exterior of the Campo Santo, Pisa. It has also been suggested that between 1320 and 1325 he executed the high altar of the Church of S. Domenico, Bologna. Although his authorship of the high altar is not universally accepted, this argument may explain how Giovanni became familiar with Nicola Pisano's shrine to S. Dominic (1264–68).

Castruccio Castracane commissioned the tomb of Guarniero degli Antelminelli, which is signed "Iohannes Baldvcii de Pisis" (Giovanni Balducci of Pisa) for

his son, who died in 1327. On 17 November 1327 Emperor Ludwig named Castruccio the Duke of Lucca, and its heraldry is on the tomb, along with the Wittelsbach and Antelminelli family emblems. A tabernacle with a sculpture of the Madonna and Child surmounts the wall tomb with sarcophagus and effigy, all of which is beneath a baldachin. The original *Madonna and Child* (ca. 1327–28), now in the Philadelphia Museum of Art in Pennsylvania, shows the influence of Giovanni Pisano, although Giovanni's early figures tend to have small facial features and are less dramatic. A relatively contemporary work from his Pisan years is a seated *Madonna and Child* at the Church of S. Maria della Spina, Pisa.

After Sarzana and Pisa, Giovanni probably went to San Casciano, near Florence, where he completed his next signed work, the pulpit of the Church of S. Maria del Prato, with Annunciation reliefs. In this signed work Giovanni included the title "magister." Considered among the sculptor's best works, the reliefs are beautifully composed and carved with fine details. Contemporary to the San Casciano pulpit are Giovanni's Florentine works, often described as the most refined examples from his career, showing his exposure to Florentine painters and the sculpture of Andrea Pisano. His Florentine works include the Baroncelli tomb and statues of the Annunciation, both at the Church of Santa Croce, Florence, as well as a series of apostles and virtues for the Church of Orsanmichele, Florence. Scholars attribute the Baroncelli tomb's marble baldachin, not the sarcophagus, to Giovanni. It includes reliefs of the evangelists and apostles with angels standing on each side of the arch. The series of reliefs from the Church of Orsanmichele includes Twelve Apostles and four Virtues (*Charity, Poverty, Truth,* and *Obedience*), although it may have originally included more. All but two reliefs are in the exterior walls of the church, yet this was likely not their original location. *Charity* is now in the National Gallery of Art, and *Poverty* is in the Museo Nazionale del Bargello.

The sculptor likely remained in Tuscany until 1334, when he was called to Milan, presumably to begin work on a Visconti funerary monument at the Church of S. Tecla, of which only fragments remain. He began the most important work of his career shortly after his arrival in Milan, the signed and dated *Arca of Saint Peter Martyr* at the Church of S. Eustorgio, Milan. Nicola Pisano's shrine to Saint Dominic at Bologna directly inspired this Dominican monument. Giovanni's *Arca of Saint Peter Martyr* introduced Lombardy to Tuscan styles and forms based not only on Nicola Pisano's shrine but also on Giovanni Pisano's tomb of Margaret of Luxumbourg and Tino di Camaino's monument for Cardinal Petroni. Giovanni's freestanding monument with sarcophagus rivals its predecessors in its sculptural detail and complex iconography. Like Nicola Pisano's shrine, the sarcophagus for S. Peter Martyr contains carved scenes from the saint's life. The sarcophagus is raised on eight caryatids. Two unique features of the monument are the tomb's sloping trapezoidal lid and a grand tabernacle with statuary of the Virgin and Child and of Saints Peter Martyr and Dominic. Although the form of this sepulchral monument is Tuscan, much of the carving appears Lombardian due to Giovanni's employment of local artisans. Scholars often give credit for the carving of the caryatids and tabernacle figures exclusively to Giovanni.

The *Arca of Saint Peter Martyr* is the apex of Giovanni's career, after which his style loses the clarity, strength, and expressiveness of his Tuscan period. He likely followed the shrine with the tomb of Azzo Visconti (d. 1339), which is often attributed to Giovanni or his workshop. The last work securely attributed to the artist is the signed and dated architrave from the main doorway of the Church of S. Maria di Brera, Milan. It does not recall Giovanni's Tuscan Gothic roots or influences, and the carving and figures lack power and expression. Only that it is signed suggests the hand of Giovanni.

The final reference to Giovanni is in 1349, when the authorities of the Cathedral of Pisa requested his return to his native town to assume the role of *capomaestro*. It is certain he declined the offer and quite possible that he never left Milan and died shortly thereafter. Some scholars believe that he lived longer, suggesting that the shrine of Saint Augustine at Pavia is by the Pisan master. If this is the case, then Giovanni's activity likely continued up to 1360. The shrine of Saint Augustine, however, is more likely by a follower of Giovanni. Nevertheless, it illustrates the influence of Giovanni's Tuscan Gothic style in Lombardy as characterized in his *Arca of St. Peter Martyr*.

STEPHANIE MILLER

See also **Pisano, Giovanni; Pisano, Nicola; Tino di Camaino**

Biography

Born in Pisa, Italy, early 14th century. First documented in 1317/18. Possibly trained in workshop of Giovanni Pisano in Pisa; first documented activity records employment at Pisa's cathedral; in Sarzana to execute tomb for Guarniero degli Antelminelli, 1327–28; worked in and around Florence on such projects as San Casciano pulpit, Baroncelli tomb, and reliefs of *Apostles* and *Virtues* for Orsanmichele, *ca.* 1330–34; moved to Milan to work on Visconti funerary monument, 1334; began work on *Arca of St. Peter Martyr,*

1335; completed, 1339; completed architrave for main portal of S. Maria di Brera, Milan, 1347; remained in Milan at least until 1349, when invited to become *capomaestro* of cathedral works at Pisa (declined position). Died probably in Milan, Italy, after 1349.

Selected Works

ca. 1327–28	Tomb of Guarniero degli Antelminelli; marble; Church of S. Francesco, Sarzana, Italy
ca. 1329	*Madonna and Child*; marble; Church of S. Maria della Spina, Pisa, Italy
ca. 1330	Pulpit; marble; Church of S. Maria del Prato, San Casciano, Italy
ca. 1330	Reliefs of *Apostles* and *Virtues*; marble; Church of Orsanmichele, Florence, Italy; *Charity:* National Gallery of Art, Washington D.C., United States; *Poverty:* Museo Nazionale del Bargello, Florence, Italy
ca. 1330–31	*Annunciation*; marble; Church of Santa Croce, Florence, Italy
ca. 1330–31	Baroncelli Tomb; marble; Church of Santa Croce, Florence, Italy
ca. 1334	Visconti Funeral Monument for Church of S. Tecla, Milan, Italy; marble; fragments: Castello Sforzesco, Milan, Italy
1339	*Arca of St. Peter Martyr*; marble; Church of S. Eustorgio, Milan, Italy
ca. 1339	Tomb of Azzo Visconti; marble; Church of S. Gottardo, Milan, Italy
1347	Architrave; marble; Church of S. Maria di Brera, Milan, Italy

Further Reading

Moskowitz, Anita F., "Giovanni's *Arca di S. Pietro Martire:* Form and Function," *Arte Lombarda* 96–97 (1991)

Moskowitz, Anita F., *Nicola Pisano's Arca di San Domenico and Its Legacy*, University Park: Pennsylvania State University Press, 1994

Paintings and Sculpture from the Samuel H. Kress Collection, Washington, D.C.: National Gallery of Art, 1959

Pope-Hennessy, John, *An Introduction to Italian Sculpture*, 3 vols., London: Phaidon, 1963; 4th edition, 1996; see especially vol. 1, *Italian Gothic Sculpture*

Valentiner, W.R., "Observations on Sienese and Pisan Trecento Sculpture," *Art Bulletin* (March 1927)

Valentiner, W.R., "Notes on Giovanni and Trecento Sculpture," *Art Quarterly* 10 (Winter 1947)

FRANÇOIS GIRARDON 1628–1715
French

François Girardon was one of the key figures of 17th-century French Classical art, and his career reflected the history of artistic taste and movements in the France of his day. Until the final years of the century, Girardon was appreciated and patronized by the arbitrators of French culture, and the decline of his fortunes coincided with the rise of Antoine Coysevox, a dazzling virtuoso who set aside the Classical canons dear to Girardon in favor of grandiloquence and pathos.

Two encounters were crucial to Girardon's training. The first was with Pierre Séguier, who sent the young artist to Rome to study ancient and modern sculpture, then arranged for him to enter François and Michel Anguier's shop. The second was with Charles Le Brun, the king's chief painter and a protégé of Séguier's. Girardon shared Le Brun's Classical and academic ideals, which constituted the solid footing of a long-lasting partnership between the two artists.

Girardon's first important commission, which he shared with Nicolas Legendre, was for the execution of the stucco decoration designed by Le Brun for the château Vaux-le-Vicomte, near Melun. He later worked on the ceiling stuccos, likewise designed by Le Brun, of the Galerie d' Apollon in the Louvre, Paris. Both projects reveal the salient features of Girardon's style: a refined and learned Classicism tempered by the search for a formal and compositional elegance harking back to the Mannerists and expressed above all in the details and the ornamental elements. These were the qualities that made Girardon's style particularly apt for decorating the castles and mansions of the French nobility. He worked at Fontainebleau, with Gaspard and Bathazar Marsy, G. Poissant, Thomas Regnaudin, and Jean-Baptiste Tuby, and on the king's apartments in the Tuileries.

Girardon thus had the ideal qualifications for collaborating on the grandiose project of decorating the royal palace and park at Versailles. There he executed, with the help of T. Regnaudin, the famous group of statues, *Apollo Tended by the Nymphs of Thetis*. While working on it, Girardon made a second journey to Rome to refresh and deepen his knowledge of Classical sculpture. The group, which established the artist's fame, consists of seven white marble statues. Originally placed in the Grotto of Thetis, *Apollo Tended by the Nymphs of Thetis* was part of a larger complex that included the Marsy brothers' and Gilles Guérin's *Horses of the Sun* (ca. 1672) and exemplified the typical Baroque device of telling a story in three distinct but adjacent places. This was the work in which, alongside reminiscences of Classical sculpture, from Hellenistic to the *Apollo Belvedere*, Girardon began to display an interest in contemporary painting, above all in that of Nicolas Poussin, who remained one of his favorite sources of inspiration. Beginning in 1667, Girardon designed many of the Versailles fountains, including the Pyramid fountain and the bas-relief *Bain*

de Nymphes (Bath of Nymphs), a subject that well suited his bent for depicting female figures. His inspiration for *Bain de Nymphes* was Jean Goujon's 16th-century reliefs for the *Fountain of the Innocents* (1547–49) in Paris (now in the Musée du Louvre). In this piece, Girardon abandoned the tenderness and the elegant poses of *Apollo Tended by the Nymphs of Thetis* to tell a lively story, to achieve a more immediate and dynamic representation in which the nymphs seem to be caught unaware of the artist's hidden eye.

The same attention to female figures and skill in investigating and depicting subdued and tender feelings likewise mark two tombs sculpted by Girardon, one dedicated to Anne-Marie de Bourbon, princesse de Conti, and the other to Cardinal de Richelieu. In the partly modified relief, which is the only surviving part of the tomb of Anne-Marie de Bourbon, the emotional impact of the elegantly poised allegorical figure is intensified by the study of light falling on the soft folds of her gown and mantle. The Richelieu tomb, installed in the Chapel of the Sorbonne in Paris, depicts the cardinal on his deathbed supported by Piety and mourned by Christian Doctrine. The three figures were carved with an almost sentimental attention to the drapery, creating an abstract interplay of recesses and projections, light and shadow, that gives the whole tomb an aura of solemn lyricism. As he had done in Versailles, for the Richelieu tomb Girardon carefully studied the setting and the relationship between the figures and the viewer.

Girardon's sculptures did not always stay within these Classical bounds, and his figures were not always as measured and calm in their gestures as noble personages in a world harking back to Antiquity. Sometimes the artist experimented with more Baroque devices and more dynamic and violent actions, as in *Rape of Persephone* created for the park at Versailles (now in the Musée National du Château de Versailles et de Trianon). This freestanding group is composed of three intertwined figures—Pluto, Persephone, and her sister Cynane—carved from a single block of marble. A comparison with Gianlorenzo Bernini's rendition of the same subject (1621–22) and with Giambologna's *Rape of a Sabine* (1582) shows that Girardon probably based his composition on these pieces, but art historians have noted that Poussin also was one of his sources of inspiration.

Girardon's most prestigious commission was the equestrian monument to Louis XIV, which stood in the Place Louis le Grand in Paris but was eventually destroyed during the French Revolution. The surviving bronze models give an idea of how the artist approached his subject, patterning it largely on the 2nd-century Roman statue of Marcus Aurelius.

In the last two decades of the 17th century, Girardon's art evinced a timid and somewhat unsuccessful attempt to depart from the Classicism of his first major works. His interpretation of the dynamism typical of the Baroque style, which he translated chiefly in terms of formal elegance, characterized *Rape of Persephone* and other marble groups he created for Versailles, such as *Hercules at Rest* and *Victory of France over Spain*. However, not even in the numerous busts Girardon carved after 1690 did his Classical training allow him to adhere wholeheartedly to the new style in which the younger Coysevox was coming to the fore in those same years.

Girardon continued to play a leading role in French artistic culture even in the years when his fame was eclipsed by his younger rival's. Girardon directed many decoration projects, including the bâtiments du roi (the King's buildings) at Versailles and the Louvre, and the dome of the Hôtel des Invalides in Paris. His rich collection—paintings, drawings, and some 800 sculptures, including works from Giambologna's shop, copies from Michelangelo, and terracotta pieces by François du Quesnoy—was documented in a series of 13 etchings grouped under the title *La Galerie de Girardon* (*ca.* 1709) in a description written in 1713, and in a posthumous inventory.

In his last years, Girardon led a secluded life far from the official appointments he had once held. His sophisticated and courtly language, imbibed with ancient and Mannerist culture, did not respond to the new Baroque taste that was making headway in France in the late 17th century. His teachings, similar in many respects to du Quesnoy's, were followed by some of his pupils, including Sébastien Soldtz, but imbued with new and different intents. A century after his death, Girardon was again held up as an example in Italy, where Luigi Vanvitelli, in designing the fountains for the royal palace in Caserta, seems to have had in mind the elegant sculpture groups created by Girardon for the park at Versailles.

MADDALENA SPAGNOLO

Biography

Born in Troyes, France, 1628. Father a metalworker. Apprenticed in Troyes to sculptor Claude Baudesson; at age 19 noted by chancellor Pierre Séguier who sent him to Rome to complete his studies; in Rome, met French painter Pierre Mignard; returned to Troyes, 1650, then moved to Paris, 1651, where placed by Séguier in François and Michel Anguier's workshop; became friendly with Charles Le Brun, the king's chief painter; worked with Gilles Guérin, 1653–54; admitted to the Académie Royale de Peinture et de Sculpture, 1656; appointed professor at Académie Royale, 1659; from 1667, lived in the Palais du Louvre, where he kept rich art collection, including ancient and contemporary sculpture; after a second journey to Italy, appointed assistant rector of the Académie, 1672, and rector, 1674; succeeded Pierre Mignard as chancellor in 1695; semiretired by 1700. Died in Paris, France, 1 September 1715.

Selected Works

1659   Decoration, for Château Vaux-le-Vicomte; stucco; Seine-et-Marne, France
1663–64 Decoration, for vault in Galerie d'Apollon, Paris, France; stucco; Musée du Louvre, Paris, France
1666–75 *Apollo Tended by the Nymphs of Thetis*; marble; park, Château, Versailles, Yvelines, France
1667   Pyramid Fountain; lead, formerly gilded; park, Château, Versailles, Yvelines, France
1668–70 *Bain de Nymphes* (Bath of Nymphs); lead, formerly gilded; park, Château, Versailles, Yvelines, France
1672–75 Tomb of Anne-Marie de Bourbon, Princesse de Conti; marble, bronze (destroyed); modified marble relief: Metropolitan Museum of Art, New York City, United States
1675–94 Tomb of Cardinal de Richelieu; marble; Chapel of the Sorbonne, Paris, France
1677–99 *Rape of Persephone*; marble; Musée du Château de Versailles et de Trianon, Yvelines, France
1683–92 Equestrian monument to Louis XIV; bronze (destroyed, 1792); reduction: bronze, Musée du Louvre, Paris, France
1679   *Hercules at Rest*; stone; Château, Versailles, Yvelines, France
1680–82 *Victory of France over Spain*; stone; Château, Versailles, Yvelines, France

Further Reading

Rambaud, M., "Les dernières annés de F. Girardon," *Gazette de Beaux-Arts* 5 (1973)

Souchal, François, "La collection du sculpteur Girardon d'après son inventaire après-décè," *Gazette de Beaux-Arts* 5 (1973)

Souchal, François, "De Giambologna à Foggini à Girardon et à Delvaux," in *Relations artistiques entre le Pays Bas et l'Italie à la Renaissance: Etudes dédicées à Suzanne Sulzberg*, Brussels: Institut Historique Belge de Rome, 1980

Souchal, François, *French Sculptors of the 17th and 18th Centuries: The Reign of Louis XIV*, vols. 1–3, Oxford: Cassirer, 1977–87, and vol. 4, London: Faber and Faber, 1993; see especially vol. 2

Souchal, François, "Girardon, François," in *The Dictionary of Art*, edited by Jane Turner, vol. 12, New York: Grove, and London: Macmillan, 1996

Walker, Dean, "The Early Career of François Girardon, 1628–1686: The History of a Sculptor to Louis XIV during the Superintendance of Jean Baptiste Colbert," (dissertation), University of New York, 1982

APOLLO AND THE NYMPHS OF THETIS

François Girardon (1628–1715)
1666–1675
marble
h. of Apollo 1.77 m; h. of tallest nymph 1.85 m
Château de Versailles, Yvelines, France

> When the Sun is tired, and has finished his task,
> He descends to Tethys, and finds some repose.
> Thus does Louis seek relaxation
> From a toil which must be renewed every day.

This passage from Jean de La Fontaine's "Les Amours de Psyche et de Cupidon" (1669), which refers to a large-scale model of *Apollo and the Nymphs of Thetis* that had been installed in the Grotto of Thetis (Tethys) at Versailles, not only indicates the ensemble's infrequently depicted mythological subject, but also reveals its metaphorical allusion to France's Sun King himself, Louis XIV. According to a brief reference in Ovid's *Metamorphoses* (2.67–69; 2.119–120), Apollo and his horses would descend to the watery palace of the sea goddess Thetis for respite following their daily journey illuminating the world. Thus at the center of the composition sits the majestic yet youthful Apollo, who extends his left arm and right leg to receive the cleansing ministrations of three seminude nymphs, two of whom kneel before him. These foreground figures, along with Apollo, are the work of François Girardon, as documented by the king's historiographer, André Félibien (see Félibien, 1689). The three more fully attired attendants in the background who complete the encircling entourage like so many stars around the sun were carved by Thomas Regnaudin. What visually affirms the metaphorical link to the king, however, is a relief representing the Passage of the Rhine on the vase held by the kneeling nymph at the left. In this way, the Sun King's rest is seen as a reward for virtuous action, such as that leading to the significant military victory scored by Louis XIV and his troops in 1672.

The present location of the ensemble within a rocky formation created by the painter Hubert Robert in 1778 is much different from its original context, which was inherently more magical and wondrous. The Grotto of Thetis was a building just north of the château, and it functioned as a pleasure palace where Louis and his court would frequently come to escape worldly cares and enjoy theatrical and musical performances. The centerpiece of the interior decoration was *Apollo and the Nymphs of Thetis*, the first over-life-size marble figures believed to have been carved by Girardon (marble was at that time an infrequently used medium in France). We know from a 1676 engraving by Jean Le Pautre that this group was located on a shallow base in the centermost of three monumental niches, whereas in the niches to either side were sculpted groups of the horses of Apollo: to the left was a rather docile pair of horses and tritons by Gilles Guérin, and on the right was a more dynamic group of rearing horses and struggling tritons carved by Balthazar and Gaspar Marsy. These ensembles were in semidarkness, set against a blue and pink rocaille wall while water flowed around them and mechanical birds twittered, completing the enchanting atmosphere. Sadly, the Grotto was razed in 1684 in order to construct a north wing for the palace; the sculpted groups were moved to the Bosquet de la Renommée that year, then were transported to the Bosquet du Marais in 1705, where they were placed under gilded baldachins.

When moved to Robert's artificial grotto in the late 18th century, the two nymphs at the far right and left of the central ensemble were interchanged, with one statue placed farther back. The original composition was thus even more integrated yet featured a remarkable diversity of pose and appearance within this unity, as Félibien notes. Because of its harmonious synthesis of varied figures, not to mention the strongly classicizing style, Girardon's *Apollo and the Nymphs of Thetis* has been likened to the paintings of Nicolas Poussin. This equivalence might suggest the intervention of Charles Le Brun, a follower of Poussin and designer of much of the sculpture for the gardens of Versailles. However, Charles Perrault, a member of the Petite Académie responsible for devising the visual rhetoric associated with the reign of Louis XIV, wrote in his

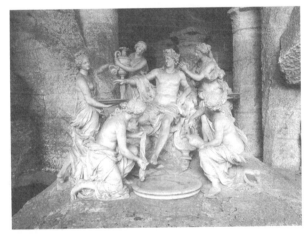

Apollo and the Nymphs of Thetis
© Giraudon / Art Resource, NY

Mémoires (*ca.* 1700) that although he conceived of the theme, the ensemble itself was visually realized by his brother, the architect Claude Perrault; Le Brun is only credited with enlarging these designs.

What rightly brought Girardon much acclaim, however, was his marvelous execution of the figures, which are a textbook example of lyrical French Classicism. The sculptor made a second trip to Italy in 1668–69 to further study such ancient masterpieces as the *Apollo Belvedere* and the Ludovisi *Mars*, which undeniably influenced his work. Yet Girardon's originality in the handling of drapery and fleshy naturalism of the female figures distinguishes the ensemble from being a mere imitation of the antique. *Apollo and the Nymphs of Thetis*, in fact, received the highest praise as a work of modernity by Charles Perrault in his *Paralelle des Anciens & des Modernes* (1688–97): he states that after 2000 years, it would be regarded with perhaps even more veneration than the greatest sculptures of Antiquity.

JULIA DABBS

Further Reading

Berger, Robert, *In the Garden of the Sun King: Studies on the Park of Versailles under Louis XIV*, Washington D.C.: Dumbarton Oaks, 1985

Félibien, André, "Description de la grotte de Versailles," in *Recueil de descriptions de peintures et d'autres ouvrages faits pour le Roy*, by Félibien, Paris: Veuve de S. Mabre-Cramoisy, 1689; reprint, Geneva: Minkoff, 1973

Lange, Liliane, "La grotte de Thétis et le premier Versailles de Louis XIV," *Art de France* 1 (1961)

Rosasco, Betsy, "Bains d'Apollon, Bain de Diane: Masculine and Feminine in the Gardens of Versailles," *Gazette des Beaux-Arts* 117 (January 1991)

GISLEBERTUS *fl.* 1120–1140 *French*

A Burgundian sculptor and leading artist of the French Romanesque period, Gislebertus's name appears in an inscription on the west portal of the Autun Cathedral (1195), founded as a pilgrimage church: "Gislebertvs hoc fecit" (Gislebertus made this). The traditional assumption is that the inscription refers not to the patron but rather to the artist and that Gislebertus was the creator of the tympanum. An attempt to link the sculptor with the hermit of the same name, with whom Abbot Petrus Venerabilis of Cluny corresponded, has not been successful. Similarly, it has been pointed out that about the same time a *capellanus* (chaplain, probably at the old Cathedral of St. Nazaire in Autun) named Gillebertus appears as a witness in a document. In the end, the name proves simply too common to act as the sole basis for identification.

The dating of Gislebertus's sculpture at the church is linked to the dating of the construction of Autun.

Construction in the apse of the choir seems to have begun about 1120. A change of plans occurred soon thereafter, perhaps in reaction to a partial collapse during the construction of the abbey in Cluny in 1125. Along with the new architectural forms based on the Cluny model came Gislebertus's style of architectural sculpture. In 1130 the pope visited the church, but the relics of Lazarus were not transferred to the still-unfinished church until 1146 or 1147. For this reason scholars usually place the time frame of the sculptor's work at Autun between 1125 and 1135/40.

The sculptures of Autun include the capitals of the church's interior. Of the more than 100 capitals, about half are decorated with figures and the others with floral motifs. No recognizable cohesive iconographical agenda is apparent. The area of the choir contains typical pictorial motifs from the repertory of the Cluny sculptors and their entourage, indicating a relatively early production: for example, a three-headed bird, a faun with a bulging buckler, and a siren. Of the same origin are four very carefully decorated capitals, taken down in the 19th century, displaying scenes from Christ's childhood. Most of the remaining depictions are thematically distinct: Old Testament subjects such as *Abraham's Sacrifice*, New Testament subjects such as the *Washing of the Feet*, and hagiography such as the *Death of Stephan*, as well as, for example, a cockfight. The sculptors' models are unknown. Judging by what remains of them, books from the cathedral library did not provide the patterns. Some themes also occur in the almost contemporaneous architectural sculpture at Vézelay in the Church of Ste-Madeleine (including *Moses and the Golden Calf*, *Jacob's Struggle*, the *Death of Judas*, and the *Liberation of St. Peter*). One can conclude therefore that contact and exchange between the artists occurred. Individual capitals in Autun are also thematically connected. For example, the *Rise and Fall of Simon Magus* is situated near the *Baptism of St. Paul* and the *Liberation of St. Peter*. The small cycle may link back to a mural series or to book illustrations of the deeds of the apostles. Gislebertus consistently refashioned his models in his own style, making his sources obscure.

The portal of the north transept was previously the main entrance. Modernized in 1766, the sculpture was largely destroyed. A description from 1482 conveys the pictorial organization: the *Resurrection of Lazarus* in the tympanum, the *Fall of Man* on the lintel, *St. Lazarus* in bishop's garb on the pillar of the door, and "several other old-fashioned images." In addition to the renowned figure of *Eve* and the head of the diabolical tempter in the depiction of the Fall, two angels from the archivolts have been preserved (Metropolitan Museum of Art, New York City; Fogg Art Museum, Cambridge, Massachusetts). Many fragments that have been traditionally assigned to the tympanum probably come from other contexts. The jamb capitals, which remain in their original locations, show the widow of Naim before Christ with her son, who has been raised from the dead, the clothing of the lost son; and the misery and divine reward of the beggar Lazarus, who is obviously being equated here with the church's founder. The scene presents a carefully thought out theological agenda here in the *Resurrection of Lazarus*, Christ's friend, whose remains are honored in Autun. It juxtaposes the Fall, bringing death to man, against the triumph over death through Christ. In addition, there are depictions of St. Lazare's life, as well as two other scenes of resurrection: the bringing back to life of the youth from Naim and Christ's parable of the lost son who experiences a spiritual reawakening, "for this my son was dead, and is alive again" (Luke 15:24).

Despite its large dimensions, the west portal is a side exit leading to a cemetery. The sculptures, which were covered over in stucco in 1766, escaped the iconoclasm of the French Revolution; they were uncovered again in 1842. The theme of the gigantic tympanum is the *Last Judgment*. Gislebertus translates the traditional image of the *Last Judgment* originally and expressively into the large-scale sculpture: An over-life-size Christ dominates as the judge in the middle, similar to the formal schemata of the Maiestas Domini (Majesty of God) customary in Burgundy; on each side a scene from the Last Judgment unfolds. The now-destroyed innermost archivolt contained the elders, and the *Resurrection of the Dead* can be seen on the lintel of the portal. Gislebertus's style of exaggeratedly long, almost abstract figures combines poignantly here with the theme of terror and suffering. All around the scene are images of time and the cosmos: seasons, months, and the zodiac. Only one jamb capital has a direct bearing on the central theme: it shows six elders who apparently had not found a place in the archivolt.

Based on the signature of Gislebertus on the *Last Judgment* tympanum on the west side, historians at one time presumed that Gislebertus was responsible for the entire sculptural decoration of Autun Cathedral. Even if this argument is not compelling, the uniformity of style in the choir after the change of plans suggests that a single studio was at work here. There is no consensus as to the size of this studio and the possible number of workers. Grivot and Zarnecki (1960) emphasize the stylistic uniformity and attribute the production of the two portals as well as the approximately 50 figural capitals of the interior to Gislebertus. Salet, on the other hand, theorizes a studio with a system of divided labor, such as Vézelay presumably had in place at the same time, and names an "Enfance du Christ" master after an artistically significant capital (see Salet,

1961). Sauerländer likewise refutes the theory of Gislebertus as the sole artist (see Sauerländer, 1965). It is clear that other, provincial sculptors worked on the majority of the capitals on the highest jump of the nave, and the artistic accuracy seems to decline as the works extend to the west. In general, however, the studio must have been organized around the goal of strict homogeneity.

The artistic antecedents to Gislebertus's style are thought to be in Cluny. He may have worked as a stonemason there on the abbot church, although the basis for comparison is too meager. Sauerländer has shown how Gislebertus adopted important elements of style from wall paintings such as those in the Cluny Prior's Church of Berzé-la-Ville. This is especially evident in the way he imparted the mobile, elegant forms of the wall paintings with a hardness, flatness, and often even an aggressiveness and in his propensity to attenuate the bodies or limbs. Thus, the characteristic taste for ornamentation, with its many drillings, pearls, and grooves, remains unclear. Since our present knowledge of the beginnings of Romanesque large-scale sculpture in Burgundy and the Rhone Valley is entirely insufficient, the artistic background remains nebulous.

The chief representative work of the Gislebertus style is in Autun, but others can be found on a few other churches in the region. Grivot-Zarnecki ascribed the *Last Judgment* tympanum of the narthex facade in Vézelay, uncovered in 1793, to Gislebertus. The narthex facade was created about 1140, but the traces of sculpture on the tympanum appear archaic for that date. Consequently, Grivot and Zarnecki have supposed that the tympanum was created prior to Autun, about 1120, but put in place much later (see Grivot and Zarnecki, 1960). The attribution to Gislebertus of a fragmentary triangular gable, apparently the remains of the church ornamentation (Musée Lapidaire, Vézelay, France), seems more plausible. Ecclesiastical structures of the surrounding area, including the collegiate churches of St. Andoche in Saulieu and Notre-Dame in Beaune, as well as churches such as La Rochepot and St. Vincent, Chalon-sur-Saône, either copied capital motifs from Autun or made allusions to the Autun decorative style. In the case of Saulieu, which was subordinate to the Autun chapter, a direct reliance may be presumed. In most instances, however, the sheer rate of destruction now renders it impossible to determine the precise relationship to Autun. For example, the Emmaus capital from Moûtiers-Saint-Jean (Fogg Art Museum, Cambridge, Massachusetts, United States) is similar to a capital in Autun in terms of motif and may directly depend on the latter (perhaps through a former assistant of Gislebertus), or the two may share a common source. Here, too, we are hindered by our ignorance of the studio organization and the artistic models of the sculptor's milieu.

PETER DIEMER

Biography

There is virtually no known definitive information on the artist's life. All that is known for certain about Gislebertus is that he worked on sculptures for the Cathedral of St. Lazare (now Autun Cathedral), Autun, France, in the period 1125–ca. 1140, and perhaps for nearby churches in the French towns of Vézelay, Saulieu, Beaune, La Rochepot, and St. Vincent.

Selected Works

ca. Capitals; limestone; Autun Cathedral,
1125–40 Autun, France
ca. *Last Judgment*; limestone; west portal,
1130–40 Autun Cathedral, Autun, France
ca. 1130 Triangular gable; limestone; Musée
Lapidaire, Vézelay, France

Further Reading

Grivot, Denis, and George Zarnecki, *Gislebertus, sculpteur d'Autun*, Paris: Trianon, 1960; 2nd edition, 1965; as *Gislebertus, Sculptor of Autun*, New York: Orion, and London: Trianon, 1961
Oursel, Raymond, "Autun, Cathédrale Saint-Lazare," in *Dictionnaire des églises de France: II, Centre et Sud-Est*, Paris: Robert Laffont, 1966
Salet, Francis (rev. Grivot/Zarnecki), in *Bulletin monumental* 124 (1966)
Sauerländer, Willibald, "Gislebertus von Autun: Ein Beitrag zur Entstehung seines künstlerischen Stils," in *Studien zur Geschichte der europäischen Plastik: Festschrift Theodor Müller*, Munich: Hiermer, 1965
Stratford, Neil, "An Uncovered Document Relating to the West Portal, Untitled," *Bulletin monumental* 134 (1976)
Stratford, Neil, "Romanesque Sculpture in Burgundy: Reflections on Its Geography, on Patronage, on the Status of Sculpture, and on the Working Methods of Sculptors," in *Artistes, artisans et production artistique au moyen âge*, edited by Xavier Barral i Altet, Paris: Picard, 1987
Stratford, Neil, "Gislebertus," in *The Dictionary of Art*, edited by Jane Turner, vol. 12, New York: Grove, and London: Macmillan, 1996
Le Tombeau de Saint Lazare et la sculpture romane à Autun après Gislebertus (exhib. cat.), Autun, France: Musée Rolin, 1985
Werckmeister, Otto Karl, "The Lintel Fragment Representing Eve from Saint-Lazare, Autun," *Journal of the Warburg and Courtauld Institutes* 35 (1972)
Zink, Jochen, "Das Lazarusportel der Kathedrale Saint-Lazare in Autun," in *Kunst in Hauptwerken: Von der Akropolis zu Goya*, edited by Jörg Traeger, Regensburg, Germany: Mittelbayerische Druckerei- und Verlags-Gesellschaft, 1988

GLOUCESTER CANDLESTICK

Anonymous
ca. 1107–1113
copper and iron, with glass inlays
h. 51 cm
Victoria and Albert Museum, London, England

The Gloucester Candlestick is one of the most impressive candlesticks to survive from the Middle Ages and is a major example of English Romanesque art. It is rare for a candlestick on this scale (approximately 51 centimeters in height, excluding the pricket) to have survived from the Medieval period in its entirety. The majority of precious metalwork was melted down for the value of its materials, especially during the Reformation.

The Gloucester Candlestick consists of three main elements: a triangular base supported by dragon feet; a vertical shaft composed of openwork decoration inhabited by beasts and human figures, with the central knop containing symbols of the four Evangelist in beaded medallions; and a hemispherical drip pan supported by three dragons. The candlestick was made in three separate sections using the lost-wax method, and the metal was engraved and inlaid in places with niello (a process of enriching the incised design by filling the incisions with a black metal alloy made of sulfur, silver, and lead) and the figures were inset with glass eyes. An iron rod holds the three sections together. The candlestick itself is made of a copper alloy that has an unusually high silver content.

The candlestick is unusual among medieval artifacts in that one of its inscriptions provides us with information about its donor, the church to which it was given, and its date. This inscription along the stem states that the candlestick was commissioned by Abbot Peter and the monks of the Benedictine Abbey, later Cathedral, at Gloucester (hence its name). Peter was abbot of the abbey from 1107 until his death in 1113, and from this it can be inferred that the candlestick was made between these dates. Gloucester need not, however, have been the place of manufacture. The closest stylistic comparisons have been made with illuminated manuscripts produced at Canterbury in the early 12th century, especially those from the Abbey of St. Augustine, which are frequently inhabited by human figures. This comparison does not, however, prove a Canterbury localization, and it is just as possible that the candlestick was made by an itinerant artist working at Gloucester who was acquainted with recent artistic developments at Canterbury. The general consensus, however, is that the candlestick was made in England.

Another inscription on the Gloucester Candlestick refers to the symbolism of light. It states, "This flood of light, this work of virtue, bright with holy doctrine instructs us, so that man shall not be benighted in vice." All of the figures clamber upward to look at the light of the candle, which would have been inserted in the pricket.

The closest antecedent for the general design of the candlestick, with its triangular base supported by three feet, three-noded shaft, and hemispherical drip pan, can be found in the pair of candlesticks made for Bishop Bernward of Hildesheim a century earlier. But the Gloucester Candlestick significantly differs from these in both its height (51 versus 43 centimeters) and, more importantly, its elaborate technique of pierced hollow casting. The congruence in design can perhaps be explained by the widespread prestige and influence of German art in England in the early 12th century, as can be seen, for example, in the slightly later sculptural reliefs at Chichester Cathedral.

The candlestick's exact location in the abbey at Gloucester and its function must remain conjectural in the absence of documentation. It was probably intended to be placed on an altar, and unlike the Hildesheim candlesticks, it does not appear to have been a member of a pair.

The practice of placing candlesticks on altars began to develop in the 11th century. At an early date (probably in the late 12th century) the Gloucester Candlestick was taken to Le Mans by Thomas of Poche and presented to the cathedral, and it remained there until the French Revolution. It is not known why this was done. In 1861 the Victoria and Albert Museum (then the South Kensington Museum) acquired the candlestick from the Russian collector Prince Soltikoff for £1,000. Its acquisition reflected the renewed interest in early medieval art in the middle of the 19th century. The Gloucester Candlestick is generally regarded as the finest piece of metalwork to have survived from the 12th century in England.

ANDREAS PETZOLD

Further Reading

Borg, Alan, "The Gloucester Cathedral," in *Medieval Art and Architecture at Gloucester and Tewkesbury*, London: British Archaeological Association, 1985

Brandt, Michael, and Arne Eggebrecht (editors), *Bernward von Hildesheim und das Zeitalter der Ottonen* (exhib. cat.), Hildesheim, Germany: Bernward Verlag, and Mainz, Germany: Von Zabern, 1993

Harris, Anabell, "A Romanesque Candlestick in London," *Journal of the British Archaeological Society* 27 (1964)

Oman, Charles, *The Gloucester Candlestick*, London: HMSO, 1958

Zarnecki, George (editor), *English Romanesque Art, 1066–1200* (exhib. cat.), London: Arts Council of Great Britain, 1984

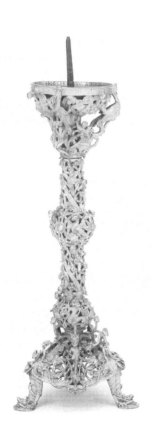

Gloucester Candlestick
© Victoria and Albert Museum, London / Art Resource, NY

GOLD

See **Precious Metal**

GOLDENES RÖSSL (*GOLDEN HORSE*) OF ALTÖTTING

Anonymous

1404

Parisian gold, enamel

h. 62 cm

Treasury of the Holy Chapel, Altötting, Bavaria, Germany

The *Goldenes Rössl* (*Golden Horse*) of Altötting is among the few remaining secular works in gold from the Medieval period that were once synonymous with the splendor, wealth, and luxury of the courts. The group of figures, measuring 62 centimeters, was a New Year's gift for the year 1405 (or 1404 according to the French calendar, in which the year did not begin until Easter) from the French queen Isabeau (Isabella) of

Bavaria to her husband Charles VI. It is also documented in that year's inventories of the royal treasure in the Bastille in Paris. Just a few months later, however, on 30 July 1405, the *Golden Horse* was pawned to Isabeau's brother Louis (Ludwig)—along with another gold Marian statue, *Die Gnad* (Grace) (which was lost but is documented in an 18th-century painting), a gold enamel sculpture of St. Michael (also lost but documented in an 18th-century painting), and a golden brooch—as the royal couple could no longer pay him the high income of 120,000 francs per annum that was promised to him upon his marriage to Anne de Bourbon in 1402.

Upon his return to Bavaria in 1413, Louis took the *Golden Horse* and bequeathed it to the Church of Unserer Lieben Frau in Ingolstadt, to be used for the ornamentation of his tomb. This plan was evidently not carried out. The *Golden Horse* appeared in 1447 in the possession of the Bavaria Landshut line, who pawned it in 1509 to the Altötting cloister as collateral for war loans. There the sculpture remained until, in the midst of the secularization movement (1801), it was brought to the Munich mint, where it barely escaped being melted down. Since 1821, it has remained once again in the treasury of Altötting.

In a manner typical of the late Middle Ages, the *Golden Horse* combines courtly ceremony and private piety. A richly dressed squire stands holding the golden bridle of a white horse below a golden platform supported by four columns. Stairs on either side lead up to the platform, where Charles VI, dressed in gold armor and a blue mantle strewn with golden lilies—the emblem of French kings—is kneeling before a prie-dieu. Instead of a crown, he wears only a diadem. Behind the king stands a doglike animal, which, with the assistance of contemporary reports, can be identified as a tiger, the personal device of the king. On the prie-dieu, which is covered with a golden cloth, lies the king's open prayer book. Across from the king kneels a squire in armor dressed in the same colors as the page. He holds the king's helmet with its crown and lily. Both the king and his companion gaze respectfully at the scene unfolding before their eyes. On a pedestal protected by a merlon and covered by a green meadow strewn with flowers—an emblem of the *hortus conclusus* (garden of paradise), according to the Song of Solomon 4:12—the Virgin Mary is sitting dressed in a white garment with the boy Jesus clad in red on her lap, and a lectern is on her left. The depiction of the Virgin Mary comprises a combination of several iconographic types: the enthroned Madonna, not normally portrayed with a book, and the reading Madonna as the epitome of piety, which are found in representations of the Annunciation, for example. Similar prayer scenes were already established in the tradition of illuminated books.

Behind Mary rises golden foliage ornamented with jewels—*un jardin fait en manière de traille*, as it is described by medieval sources. Situated behind her head is a (restored) sunbeam; two angels float above it carrying a crown decorated with gems and pearls—the emblems of her rank as the Queen of Heaven. Both John the Baptist and John the Evangelist, represented as children clad in white, kneel at the Virgin Mary's feet: John the Baptist with a lamb, and John the Evangelist with a goblet and a few flowers, which he offers up to the child Jesus. The latter, however, has turned his attention to St. Catherine, who is kneeling to the left-hand side behind John the Baptist. Holding a palm branch in her left hand, she extends the middle finger of her right hand toward Jesus so that he may place an engagement ring on it. Charles VI and his companions are thus witnesses to the mystical engagement of Christ.

The *Golden Horse* of Altötting is one of the greatest and most significant masterpieces of Parisian gold and enamel art of the International Gothic period. The number of materials used and the technical perfection of the production lay the foundation for its renown. The *émail en ronde bosse* (enamel on a round relief) merits particular mention. Enamel had been applied strictly to flat or slightly arched surfaces in the past; beginning in the 14th century, it was used more and more to decorate three-dimensional images. In addition to the luminous colors of translucent enamel, beginning around 1380, opaque white (*émail blanc*) also enjoyed a special appreciation, as it could be used for shaping details (such as the eyes of the king and the mane of the horse). Around 1400, this technique reached its peak. In addition to enamel, *opus punctile* should be mentioned; it was an old technique to which even Theophilus Presbyter (also known as Roger von Helmarshausen) dedicated a treatise in his *Schedula Diversarium Artium* (ca. 1060/1090). Inspired perhaps by the punch marks in Italian painting, an increasing fondness for this technique developed in the 14th century, and it appears in numerous variations in the *Golden Horse* of Altötting, such as on the floor board, the horse blanket, the pedestal of the Virgin Mary's throne, and the cover of the king's prie-dieu.

The artists who created the *Golden Horse* of Altötting are unknown. They were probably several goldsmiths, including specialists in enameling, shaping, and the setting of gems and pearls. As masters of the new techniques of the goldsmith craft, they were also well versed in the most current stylistic tendencies of the art. Instead of the more starkly linear figural formations at the end of the 14th century, which were based on contrasts such as long folds against bunches of material and small folds, these figures were done in the already softer style of the new century.

NICOLAS BOCK

See also **Émail en ronde bosse**

Further Reading

Baumstark, Reinhold (editor), *Das Goldene Rössl: Ein Meisterwerk der Pariser Hofkunst um 1400* (exhib. cat.), Munich: Hirmer, 1995

Gauthier, Maria-Madeleine, *Émaux du moyen âge occidental*, Fribourg, Switzerland: Office du Livre, 1972

Lüdke, Dietmar, *Die Statuetten der gotischen Goldschmiede: Studien zu den "autonomen" und vollrunden Bildwerken der Goldschmiedeplastik und den Statuettenreliquiaren in Europa zwischen 1230 und 1530*, 2 vols., Munich: Tuduv-Verlagsgesellschaft, 1983

Meiss, Millard, *French Painting in the Time of Jean De Berry: The Late Fourteenth Century and the Patronage of the Duke*, 2 vols., London: Phaidon, 1967

Müller, Theodor, and Erich Steingräber, "Die französische Goldemailplastik um 1400," *Münchner Jahrbuch der bildenden Kunst* (third series) 5 (1954)

Schatzkammerstücke aus der Herbstzeit des Mittelalters: Das Regensburger Emailkästchen und sein Umkreis, Munich: Bayerisches Nationalmuseum, 1992

ANNA GOLUBKINA 1864–1927 *Russian*

Anna Golubkina entered the Moscow School of Painting, Sculpture, and Architecture in 1891, with little formal education and only minimal training in art. In addition to several years of study in Moscow and St. Petersburg, she made three extended trips to Paris; on the second trip, in 1897–98, she visited Auguste Rodin weekly for advice on sculpture. Her first significant venture outside the classroom was *Age*, a sculpture depicting an elderly female model in a crouching pose suggestive of resignation and despair. The uneven surface recalls Rodin's technique of modeling, although Golubkina was not happy to be designated a "pupil of Rodin." She had, in fact, shown extraordinary impressionistic freedom of technique while still a student at the Moscow School of Painting, Sculpture, and Architecture before she came into contact with Rodin. Along with several other works by Golubkina, *Age* was accepted for exhibition in 1899 at the Spring Salon in Paris.

Upon returning to Russia, Golubkina began a series of sculptures personifying nature. Some, such as *Mist*, reveal a conventional Art Nouveau style and convey an empathetic feeling for the growth, movement, and energy of nature; others were more idiosyncratic.

Golubkina received her first major commission in 1902, when she created a large high-relief sculpture for the facade of the Moscow Art Theater. *Swimmer*, which still occupies its original position over one of the theater's side entrances, is a classic example of Art Nouveau. Undulating movement dominates the composition; human figures—several of them women with long hair that floats in the water—appear to have been caught up by a gigantic cresting wave that surges forward as though threatening to break out of its architectural framework. The central image is a muscular swimmer who lunges forward, half-submerged in the cresting wave but striving to separate himself from it; he does not succumb, as do the other figures, to the rhythms of nature. In his struggle against overwhelming forces, Golubkina's swimmer invites comparison with the storm-tossed figures of Rodin's *Gates of Hell* (1880–1917); Golubkina, like Rodin, has embedded fragments of figures in a vague, amorphous background. Unlike Rodin, however, Golubkina hints in *Swimmer* at possible human triumph over the blind forces of nature. Above the wave—and extremely difficult to see from street level—is a soaring gull; the seagull was the emblem of the Moscow Art Theater and as such embodies references to human creativity and to the liberating power of art.

The bust-length female figure represented in *Earth*—although cast in bronze and relatively modest in scale—has the brutal strength of a mountain rendered in roughly modeled clay. Clay was, in fact, Golubkina's preferred material; she was an eloquent advocate of clay as the most challenging and satisfactory medium for a sculptor. The first section of her brief treatise *Neskol'ko slov o remesle skul'ptora* (A Few Words about the Profession of a Sculptor; 1923) is devoted to discussion of the sculptural properties of clay. Although Golubkina did some work in stone—she even made a special trip to Paris in the summer of 1904 in order to study stone carving with French craftsmen—she argued that because of clay's fluidity and inherent formlessness, working in clay requires greater assurance and experience than working in stone. Yet at the same time, the malleability of wet clay makes it an ideal medium for representing the evanescent effects of nature.

Like other sculptors of her period, Golubkina's stock in trade was portraiture. Nonetheless, many of the sitters were of her own choosing—that is, friends and fellow artists. She sought out outstanding contemporaries such as the writers Viacheslav Ivanov, Andrei Bely, and Alexei Remizov in order to sculpt their portraits. Golubkina's depictions of women are worthy of special note because of their avoidance of the usual clichés of femininity. Her women are strong, forthright, and by no means ingratiating. *Head of a Woman*, for example, follows a pattern established by Rodin in that the artist embedded a smoothly polished head in a rough block stone. Indeed, she accentuated the contrast by employing two different materials, marble for the head and limestone to surround it. Yet Golubkina's woman has none of the youthful delicacy of the girl represented in Rodin's *Thought* (1886; Musée Rodin, Paris, France); instead, she is a mature woman whose uncompromising features and frontal pose signal strength of will rather than Rodin's "immaterial thought."

Soviet-period emphasis on Golubkina's credentials as an artist of the people has obscured her wide-ranging interests and sympathies. She engaged in serious discussions of religion and philosophy with her friends, she was widely read in contemporary literature, and she particularly admired the writing of Anton Chekhov, Henrik Ibsen, and Maurice Maeterlinck. Golubkina's political sympathies did manifest themselves in those works for which she chose "proletarian" models with rough-hewn features; among these are two large freestanding sculptures, *Walking Man* and *Seated Man*. Although the pose of *Walking Man* is obviously a dynamic one (unmistakably indebted to Rodin's sculpture of the same name), Golubkina's *Seated Man* was an attempt to convey "an irresistible will towards movement" in a static, seated figure (see Korovich, 1983). From some viewpoints, it is clear that the arms of *Seated Man* have simply been truncated like those

of an antique statue; from other perspectives, he looks like a bound captive. The reference to Michelangelo's 16th century *Rebellious Slave* (Musée du Louvre, Paris, France) is almost certainly deliberate. Golubkina admired Michelangelo as the dominating genius of sculpture, and she approached the task of figurative sculpture in Michelangelesque terms—that is, employing subtle suggestions of movement to create an impression of spirit animating inert matter.

After the outbreak of World War I, Golubkina's career was overshadowed by ill health and material hardship. No work survives from the period 1914–20. From 1920 to 1923 her only sculptural activity consisted of carving cameos from seashells, these being inexpensive and relatively easy to obtain. From 1918 to 1922 she taught in the new art schools established after the 1917 revolution, the Free Studios (SvoMas) and the Higher Artistic and Technical Workshops (VkhuTeMas). Eventually she lost her post at VkhuTeMas; her friends attributed this to the pernicious influence of avant-gardists who thought her work too conservative. Golubkina's last major work was a bust of Lev Tolstoy, commissioned by the Tolstoy Museum in Moscow.

Because Golubkina supported left-wing political causes (she was briefly imprisoned in 1907 for distributing illegal literature in her hometown of Zaraisk) and because she adhered throughout her life to a style that was, broadly speaking, realist, she was canonized during the Soviet period as an artist of the people. Despite these credentials, her reputation in Soviet times followed a crooked path. At her death in 1927, her family donated the contents of her studio to the Soviet government, and a Golubkina Studio Museum opened in 1932. The bronze casts of her sculpture now found in museums were for the most part made between 1932 and 1941. During the 1950s, however, conservative Soviet officials attacked Golubkina as a potentially negative influence on young artists because of the "impressionism" of her style. In 1952 the Golubkina Studio Museum was closed and the collection transferred to the State Tretyakov Gallery in Moscow and the Russian Museum in Leningrad (now St. Petersburg). Although ranking sculptors such as Vera Mukhina and Ilya Efimov attempted to defend her memory, Golubkina's reputation was not restored until 1964, the centenary of her birth. The Golubkina Studio Museum reopened in 1976.

JANET KENNEDY

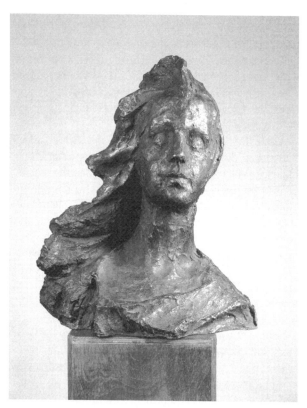

Female Bust
© The State Russian Museum / CORBIS

Biography

Born in Zaraisk, Moscow region, Russia, 28 January 1864. Studied in Moscow with Sergei Volnukhin, 1889–90, and with Sergei Ivanov at Moscow School of

Painting, Sculpture, and Architecture, 1891–94; began work in studio of Vladimir Beklemishev at Higher Art School of the Academy of Arts in St. Petersburg, 1894; lived in Paris, studied sculpture at Académie Colarossi, 1895–96; returned to Paris, 1897–98, received private tuition from Rodin; showed (*Age*, 1898) at Paris Salon, 1899; final visit to Paris, 1904; participated in Russian Revolution of 1905; imprisoned in 1907 for activity against the monarchy; returned to Moscow studio same year; taught at Prechistenka Workers' School, 1913–16, and in the Free Studios and the Higher Artistic and Technological Workshops (VkhuTeMas), 1918–22; in the early 1920s began working on a small scale because of serious illness. Died in Moscow, Russia, 7 September 1927.

Selected Works

1898   *Age*; bronze; Russian Museum, St. Petersburg, Russia

1899   *Mist*; bronze; Russian Museum, St. Petersburg, Russia

1902   *Swimmer* (also known as *Wave*); tinted plaster; Moscow Art Theater, Moscow, Russia

1903   *Walking Man*; plaster; Russian Museum, St. Petersburg, Russia

1904   *Earth*; plaster; Russian Museum, St. Petersburg, Russia

1904   *Head of a Woman*; marble, limestone; Russian Museum, St. Petersburg, Russia

1905   *Karl Marx*; plaster; State Tretyakov Gallery, Moscow, Russia

1912   *Seated Man*; tinted plaster; Russian Museum, St. Petersburg, Russia

1927   *Lev Nikolaevich Tolstoy*; bronze; State Tretyakov Gallery, Moscow, Russia

1927   *Female Bust*; bronze; Russian Museum, St. Petersburg, Russia

Further Reading

Kamenskii, Aleksandr A., *Anna Golubkina: Lichnost', epokha, skul'ptura* (Anna Golubkina: Personality, Epoch, Sculpture), Moscow: Izobrazitelnoe Iskusstvo, 1990

Korovich, N.A. (editor), *A.S. Golubkina: Pis'ma, neskol'ko slov o remesle skul'ptora, vospominaniia sovremennikov* (A.S. Golubkina: Letters, a Few Words about the Profession of a Sculptor, Recollections of Contemporaries), Moscow: Sovetskii Khudozhnik, 1983

Sarab'ianov, Dmtrii Vladimirovich, *Russian Art from Neoclassicism to the Avant-Garde, 1800–1917: Painting, Sculpture, Architecture*, New York: Abrams, and London: Thames and Hudson, 1990

Worrall, Nick, *The Moscow Art Theater*, London and New York: Routledge, 1996

JULIO GONZÁLEZ 1876–1942 *Spanish*

The sculpture of Julio González has many things in common with other art of the 1930s; he was a man of his time. What most clearly distinguishes González's work is his technical handling of his metals and his attitude toward abstraction.

From the beginning of his life, he was subject to the authority of his elder brother, Joan. After Joan's death (1908), he was surrounded by numerous personalities and movements. He was a contemporary of Constantin Brancusi, Raymond Duchamp-Villon, Amedeo Modigliani, Vladimir Tatlin, Alexander Archipenko, Jean (Hans) Arp, and many others. Brancusi, who met González in 1904, was already using the basic elements of his later sculpture by 1907. Modigliani began to cultivate a synthetic, stylized form of sculpture by 1909. Naum Gabo and Antoine Pevsner published the "Realistic Manifesto" in Moscow in 1920, and László Moholy-Nagy and Kemeny published their call for a "Dynamic-constructive system of forces" in 1922. For González, this was a period of exploring different movements, individual personalities, and the rapid succession of innovation. His hypersensitivity, his reserve, and his lack of confidence in his own worth show only a part of his personality.

González began working with jewelry very early with his brother Joan, and in 1892 he won a bronze medal at the international exhibition of handicraft in Chicago and the gold medal at the exhibition for applied arts in Barcelona. His one-man show in 1922 at Galerie Povolovsky in Paris provides an opportunity to appreciate the variety of González's techniques and ideas in his paintings, water colors, drawings, sculptures, jewelry, and different objects made in silver, gold, wrought iron, and hammered iron.

González's experience at the Renault factory, where he worked during World War I and where he learned the use of the oxyacetylene torch, added to the mastery of iron he had acquired in his father's workshop. For González, iron and bronze were not the hard substances with smooth and streamlined surfaces they commonly were for other sculptors. Instead, he used them as malleable and responsive materials in which the imprint of hammer on metal corresponded to the artist's subtle manipulations. González shaped his materials at white heat, which allowed a greater plasticity in the large forms as well as in the surface detail. The gleaming surfaces of Pevsner, Moholy-Nagy, or Brancusi, and the painted disks of Alexander Calder's mobiles, appear in González's creation as pitted, rusted, and oxidized surfaces embellished with odd bits of solder and scrap. These qualities can be found in González's work before and after his artistic collaboration with Picasso.

Working with Picasso was a crucial moment in González's life, particularly for his work with iron. In 1931 he began executing sculptures in iron for Picasso, among them the *Monument to Apollinaire*. Thanks to this collaboration, González found a way to extend the combining of analytical elements with the use of cut-metal forms to the whole figure. Nonetheless, González's great works of the 1930s all deal with the figure or the head, such as *Woman Combing Her Hair* or *Don Quichotte*, which show his liberation from the figurative. He moved toward more and more open construction in space. Although he did not exhibit with the artists' groups "Cercle et Carré" and "Abstraction-Création," he was in contact with these groups and ideas.

Whether in the antique patina of the *Japanese Mask* (1929) and the *Head* (1935) or the surface modulations of the *Grande Trompette* (Big Trumpet) and the *Torso*, González showed a consistency in his technical approach. The early abstract works, such as the *Harlequin* (1930) and the *Tête aigüe* (1930) have a crispness of form that González continued to explore in the large filiform figures of 1934 and 1935. In these larger

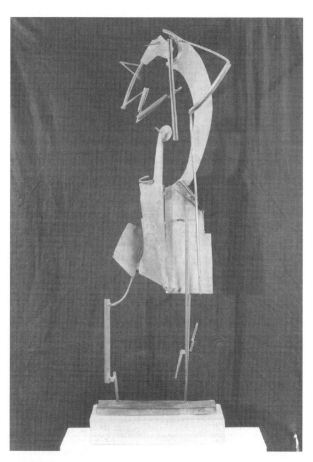

Woman Combing Her Hair I
© 2001 Artists Rights Society (ARS), New York, ADAGP, Paris

works, broken and corroded forms and surfaces replace hard surfaces and precise delineations. The plastic treatment of metal, as with the *repoussé* (the method of producing relief metal by hammering and punding chiefly from behind), masks and decorative pieces, required heating the larger and thicker pieces in the forge until they could be easily hammered, bent, and molded. This technique explains also the creation of the fragile bronze flowers and bibelots in the family workshop, the early bronze repoussé masks, and later sculptures as the *Torso*, the *Grande Trompette*, and the late *Cactus Man*.

González's experience as a craftsman allowed him to acquire a close familiarity with his chosen material and enabled him to transform forged bronze or iron into the airy and skeletal *Giraffe* and *Cactus Man*, and the battered aspect of the *Mask of Crying Montserrat*. For González, the metals did not dictate any one aesthetic: he felt free to use these materials both for abstract and expressive modes. His sculptures are delicate and quiet, creating an intimate spatial ambience. That he also created sculpture in iron and steel suggests that González may have wished to realize them in a monumental scale, but he never completed any works larger than life-size. The clearest indication that González might have been interested in monumental projects are the drawings of the last two years before his death in 1942. In 1935 he stopped welding and modeled few sculptures after this time; almost all his energy was directed toward drawing. All are studies for sculptures which were never to materialize.

González rejected nonobjective art, which at that time was almost exclusively geometric and Constructivist. But he also rejected realism as a satisfactory solution. The very idea of total abstraction was one of the few subjects González felt passion for, but at the same time he never lost touch with what he termed *La Nature*. The debate concerning abstraction and realism was an ongoing controversy among artists, and González tried to maintain his own stylistic equilibrium. The metamorphosis of the image itself became his essential theme, realized in hybrid forms such as *Big Venus*, or even ambiguous forms such as *L'Ange* (The Angel), *Daphné*, or *Woman Combing Her Hair*.

Although for a long period he was not well known, González forged a poetic and gestural style that assured him an important place in 20th-century sculpture. Due to González's hesitation, self-denial, shyness, and personal problems, his sculpture was mostly unknown until the retrospective exhibition at the Musée National d'Art Moderne, Paris, in 1952, and more recently, the exhibition *González-Picasso: Dialogue* organized at Toulouse at the Abattoirs by the Musée National d'Art Moderne in collaboration with the Picasso Museum of Paris (1 June–20 September 1999).

DOÏNA LEMNY

Biography

Born in Barcelona, Spain, 21 September 1876. As a member of the family workshop, exhibited artistic metalwork at the international exhibitions of Chicago and Barcelona, obtaining several distinctions in 1892; moved to Paris, 1900, exhibited at the Salon de la Société Nationale des Beaux-Arts, 1903; learned techniques as apprentice in Renault factory, 1918, that he would use later in the execution of works in iron; showed at Salon d'Automne and Salon de la Société Nationale, 1920–21; solo exhibition of paintings, drawings, sculptures, jewelry, and other objects at the Galerie Povolovsky, 1922; produced first sculpture in iron, 1927; began execution of sculptures in iron for Picasso, 1931, including *Monument to Apollinaire*; solo exhibition at Galerie Percier and Cahiers d'Art in Paris, 1934, and participation in collective exhibition at Kunsthaus in Zurich with Jean Arp, Max Ernst, Joan Miró, and others; showed masterpiece *Montserrat* at Spanish Pavilion at Paris Universal Exhibition, 1937; showed in exhibition *De Cézanne à nos jours* in Musée du Jeu de Paume; work largely unknown until retrospective (and posthumous) exhibition at Musée Nationale d'Art Moderne, Paris, 1952. Died in Arcueil, France, 27 March 1942.

Selected Works

1929–30 *Don Quichotte*; iron; Musée Nationale d'Art Moderne, Centre Georges Pompidou, Paris, France

1930 *Montserrat*; iron; private collection, Mrs. Andrew P. Fuller, New York City, United States

1930 *Harlequin*; iron; Kunsthaus, Zurich, Switzerland

1931 *Woman Combing Her Hair I*; iron; Musée Nationale d'Art Moderne, Centre Georges Pompidou, Paris, France

1934 *The Dream/The Kiss*; iron; Musée Nationale d'Art Moderne, Centre Georges Pompidou, Paris, France

1935 *The Giraffe*; iron; Musée Nationale d'Art Moderne, Centre Georges Pompidou, Paris, France

1935 *L'Ange*; iron; Musée Nationale d'Art Moderne, Centre Georges Pompidou, Paris, France

1936 *Woman Combing Her Hair III*; iron; Museum of Modern Art, New York City, United States

1936 *Torso*; iron; Museum of Modern Art, New York City, United States

1936–37 *Montserrat*; iron; Stedelijk Museum, Amsterdam, The Netherlands

1937 *Daphné*; iron; private collection, Dr. W.A. Bechtler, Zollikon, Switzerland

1938–39 *Mask of Crying Montserrat*; iron; Musée Nationale d'Art Moderne, Centre Georges Pompidou, Paris, France

1939 *Cactus Man*; iron; Musée Nationale d'Art Moderne, Centre Georges Pompidou, Paris, France

1939–40 *Cactus Woman*; iron; Staatliche Kunsthalle, Karlsruhe, Germany

Further Reading

Cassou, Jean, "Julio González," *Cahiers d'art* 22 (1947)

Cassou, Jean, "Foreword," in *Julio González, Sculptures* (exhib. cat.), Paris: Éditions des Musées Nationaux, 1952

Curtis, Penelope, "Julio González: Fact and Fiction," in *Julio González: Sculptures and Drawings* (exhib. cat.), London: South Bank Centre and Whitechapel, 1990

Danieli, Fidel, "Julio González: A Representative Showing at the Landau Gallery," *Artforum* 4/4 (December 1965)

Descargues, Pierre, *Julio González*, Paris: Le Musée de Poche, 1971

Dudley, Dorothy, "Four Post-Moderns," *Magazine of Art* 28, no. 9 (September 1935)

Giedion-Welcker, Carola, "New Roads on Modern Sculpture," *Transition* 23 (February 1935)

Giedion-Welcker, Carola, *Modern Plastic Art: Elements of Reality, Volume, and Disintegration*, Zurich: Girsberger, 1937

González, Roberta, "Julio González, My Father," *Arts* 54/9 (February 1956)

González, Roberta, and Hans Hartung, "Notes on González," in *Julio González* (exhib. cat.), London: Tate Gallery, 1970

Krauss, Rosalind, "The New Art: To Draw in Space," in *Julio González, Sculpture and Drawings, October 2–31, 1981* (exhib. cat.), New York: Pace Gallery, 1981

Llorens, Thomas, *Julio González, las Collectiones del IVAM*, Valencia: IVAM Centre Julio González, and Madrid: Ed. El Viso, 1989

Merkert, Jörn, *Julio González*, Milan: Electa, 1987 (catalogue raisonné)

Rowell, Margit, *Julio González: A Retrospective, the Solomon R. Guggenheim Museum, New York* (exhib. cat.), New York: Solomon R. Guggenheim Foundation, 1983

Tabart, Marielle, "González, Picasso: Échanges réciproques," in González, Picasso, Dialogue, Paris: Centre Georges Pompidou, and Réunions des Musées Nationaux, 1999

Withers, Josephine, "The Artistic Collaboration of Pablo Picasso and Julio González," *Art Journal* 35/2 (Winter 1975–76)

Withers, Josephine, *Julio González: Sculpture in Iron*, New York: New York University Press, 1978

ANTONY GORMLEY 1950– *British*

Born in London of German and Irish descent, British sculptor Antony Gormley is best known for his figurative sculptures in lead cast from molds made of his own body. Additionally, he has worked in a variety of other materials, including clay, steel, iron, concrete, and fiberglass, and in a variety of sizes ranging from the minuscule (the tiny figures of his *Field* series measure 8 to 26 centimeters in height) to the monumental (*Angel of the North* stands 20 meters high).

Gormley studied archaeology, anthropology, and art history at Trinity College in Cambridge. He traveled for the next three years through Turkey, Syria, Afghanistan, Pakistan, Iraq, and Iran, and studied a form of Buddhist meditation called Vipassana in India and Sri Lanka. Upon his return to London in 1974, Gormley spent a year at the Central School of Art, followed by two years at the Goldsmiths School of Art and another two years of postgraduate study at the Slade School of Fine Art.

By his own account, Gormley credits his travels abroad, his involvement with Vipassana, and his upbringing in Roman Catholicism with exerting an immense influence upon his art. His preoccupation lies with body and spirit, with their unity, and with the tensions between them. The lead figures of the 1980s were intentionally cast hollow, with their internally trapped pockets of air acting as an additional sculptural element. Forming a kind of body "container" akin to ancient Egyptian mummy cases and medieval European reliquaries, they suggest a spirit within.

Gormley's sculptural process begins with his studio assistants taking a plaster and burlap mold, made in sections, directly from his own, plastic-covered body. The negative mold is then cast in its final material: lead, iron, fiberglass, and plaster, or welded steel bars. Unlike George Segal (whose figures, although not usually identifiable as individuals, are anchored in historical time and place by their clothing and environment) or Duane Hanson (whose polyester resin and mixed-media forms are hyperreal portraits of his models), Gormley's sculptures are lifelike but featureless. With only the barest essentials of the body represented, they seem strangely solitary, even when engulfed in a crowd. In this sense, his work bears a relationship to the faceless personages of Polish sculptor Magdalena Abakanowicz.

Part of the power of Gormley's work comes from his choice of materials. His use of lead—a metal that is heavy but soft, poisonous if ingested but life-preserving if used as a shield against radiation—creates multiple layers of meaning when combined with the human body. In other instances, solid cast iron acts as metaphor. In the case of *Another Place*—where 100

life-size figures were placed standing in the sea off the shores of Cuxhaven, Germany, and Stavanger, Norway—the rust resulting from the interaction of salt and metal, along with the flowing and ebbing of the tides, suggests the inevitability of aging and the passage of time. The various versions of the *Field* series exploited the tendency of clay to pick up and preserve the fingerprints of those who modeled it. In order to produce 35,000 hand-size terracotta figures, Gormley worked with the Texca family in Cholula, Mexico (brick makers by trade) and residents of St. Helen's, Merseyside (for the *Field for the British Isles*). Their participation remains visible as subtle traces on the surface.

Angel of the North is perhaps Gormley's most notorious work: It is a mammoth figure 20 meters high with a wingspan of 54 meters made of Cor-ten (self-rusting) steel. It is visible from a distance of 48 kilometers and can be seen from both the A1 highway and the main London-to-Edinburgh railway line. Located in the northeastern part of England in Gateshead, an area plagued by unemployment, this commission was controversial from its outset. A number of local residents protested its £800,000 cost, demanding that the money be used instead for social programs. More than 4500 people signed a "Stop the Statue" petition. However, *Angel of the North* was paid for by a national lottery, whose funds are earmarked specifically for the arts and, therefore, may not be diverted to other projects.

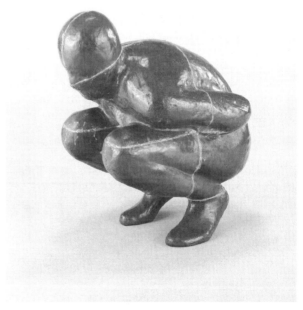

Proof
© Christie's Images / CORBIS

Controversy was sparked again with Gormley's design of a stamp for the Royal Mail's special millennium series. Along with other notable English-born artists such as Bridget Riley and David Hockney, he was invited to create a 63-pence stamp based on a tale of achievement in British medicine. He chose the first successful in vitro fertilization procedure and designed *Test-Tube Baby/Patients' Tale*, using an image of a curled-up, sleeping infant modeled after his own daughter at six days old. However, a number of Roman Catholic and pro-life groups claimed it resembled a dead fetus and unsuccessfully tried to prevent the stamp's publication.

Despite these controversies, Gormley has continued to accept public commissions. *Quantum Cloud* was created to coincide with the opening of London's Millennium Dome. It stands at the edge of the Thames River on an old pier just outside the dome. Made of crisscrossing segments of stainless steel bar and designed with the help of computer technology, it incorporates a shadowy presence of a figure within.

VIRGINIA MAKSYMOWICZ

Biography

Born in London, England, 30 August 1950. Studied archeology, anthropology, and art history, Trinity College, Cambridge, 1968–71; traveled through the Middle East, India, and Sri Lanka and studied Buddhist Vipassana meditation, 1971–74; studied art at Central, Goldsmiths, and Slade Schools of Art, London, 1974–77; first solo exhibitions at Serpentine Gallery and Whitechapel Art Gallery, London, 1981; participated in Venice Bienniale "Aperto," 1982; first solo exhibition in New York City, Salvatore Ala Gallery, 1984; included in "An International Survey of Recent Painting and Sculpture" at Museum of Modern Art, New York City, 1984; received Turner Prize, 1994; completed controversial commission, *Angel of the North*, in Gateshead, England, 1998; continues to exhibit internationally. Lives and works in London, England.

Selected Works

1981 *Natural Selection*; lead; Tate Gallery, London, England
1984 *Proof*; lead, fiberglass, plaster, air; collection of the artist
1986 *Sound II*; lead, fiberglass, water; collection of Winchester Cathedral, Hampshire, England
1993 *European Field*; terracotta (temporary installation); Malmö Konsthall, Sweden
1997 *Another Place*; cast iron (temporary installations); Cuxhaven, Germany, and Stavanger, Norway
1998 *Angel of the North*; reinforced steel; Gateshead, Tyne and Wear, England
2000 *Quantum Cloud*; stainless steel bar; Millennium Dome, London, England

Further Reading

"Commissions: Monumental U.K. Sculpture Raises Controversy," *Sculpture* 17/5 (May/June 1998)
Dault, Gary Michael, "Antony Gormley: One Moment after Another," *Border Crossings* 19/1 (2000)
Dunne, Aidan, "Where Angels Fear to Tread," *The Irish Times* (4 December 2000)
Gormley, Antony, *Making an Angel: Gateshead Council*, London: Booth Clibborn, 1998
Greenberg, Sarah, "Gormley Garners Turner," *Art News* 94/2 (February 1995)
Hutchinson, John, E.H. Gombrich, and Lela B. Njatin, *Antony Gormley*, London: Phaidon Press, 1995; revised and expanded edition, 2000
Roustayi, Mina, "An Interview with Antony Gormley" *Arts Magazine* 62/1 (1987)
Tromp, Ian, "Body and Light: Antony Gormley's 'Quantum Clouds,'" *Modern Painters* 13/1 (Spring 2000)

GOTHIC SCULPTURE

The figural sculpture of the High Gothic period (1140–1300) is distinguished by its naturalistic conception of the human body and its restraint in the rendering of emotional affects. Although fundamentally architectural, the relation of sculpture to its architectural frame appears looser than in the Romanesque period; from the last decades of the 12th century, figures occupy increasingly autonomous spaces in front of columns or inside niches. Bodies, enveloped in richly articulated draperies, are slender and naturally proportioned, with relaxed but elegant postures, restrained gestures, and serene facial expressions. Although typically carved from the same materials as the architecture, usually a local limestone or sandstone, Gothic sculpture was always polychromed. Draperies glistened in brilliant reds and blues, whereas faces gained heightened verisimilitude and expressive power through natural coloration. Independent (or free-standing) sculpture, sometimes made of wood, was likewise painted and often embellished with gold leaf or jewels. Most surviving examples of Gothic sculpture are ecclesiastical; church officials were the most important patrons of these expensive and labor-intensive products.

According to medieval theologians, images possessed both a didactic and a devotional function: they served to teach the unlettered laity of events in sacred history and to stimulate emotional response. This attitude underlies the particular form taken by sculptural programs in the 12th and 13th centuries. The construction of complex iconographic programs on church facades made Christian teachings accessible to a broad and socially variegated public, while the high degree of naturalism in individual figures triggered the identification and empathetic engagement that allowed them to assume personal meaning for their beholders.

It was on the west facade of the Abbey church of Saint-Denis north or Paris, France (ca. 1140) that the characteristic structure of the Gothic sculptured portal was established. However, many figures were destroyed during the French Revolution, and much of what remains represents the labors of restorers—an all too familiar story in the study of Gothic sculpture. The central tympanum, largely intact, shows Christ seated in a *mandorla*, extending his arms over the heads of his apostles, while tiny figures rise from their tombs below. This eschatological scene spills over into the archivolts on either side, where miniature men and women are welcomed into heaven or pushed into hell. Although the life-size figures of kings occupying the jambs are now destroyed, extant drawings suggest that they resembled the figures on the Royal Portal at the Cathedral of Chartres (ca. 1145–50) with elongated limbs, stylized gestures, and thin draperies defined by shallow parallel lines. Although rigidly columnar in proportions, the bodies of the Chartres figures gently swell beneath the long, finely pleated gowns, and the faces gaze outward with unprecedented sensitivity.

A move toward greater plasticity in jamb figures is evident in the portal at the Cathedral of Senlis (ca. 1165–70), where the fluid curves of the bodies are highlighted by swirls of looping drapery folds and project further outward from the supporting columns. In the archivolts, deeply canopied niches frame the figures, amplifying their corporeal volumes through stark contrasts of light and shadow. On the heart-shaped tympanum, a handsome Christ places a crown on the head of his youthful Mother, a reference to the Song of Songs. This emphasis on the Virgin Mary, rather than a patently eschatological theme, represents a shift in devotional patterns that occurred during the 12th century. At this time, the Virgin, in the guise of a courtly lady, became a favorite subject of Gothic sculpture, assuming perhaps her most winsome form in the *Vièrge Dorée* (Golden Virgin) at Cathedral of Amiens (ca. 1260).

Like the Senlis jamb figures, and in contrast to those on the Royal Portal, the figures on the Chartres transept portals (1204–24) appear to move freely in front of their respective columns, twisting their heads and torsos to the side so as to interact with neighboring figures. Some wear heavy draperies that fall in deep, troughlike folds, a convention developed in the goldsmith works of Nicholas of Verdun during the last quarter of the 12th cen-

tury and known today as *Muldenfaltenstil*. The abruptness with which these jagged lines slice across the drapery surface lends energy to the figures, while vigorous *contrapposto* (a natural pose with the weight of one leg, the shoulder, and hips counterbalancing one another) stances give their upright bodies a dynamic curvature (the characteristic "Gothic S curve"). Around 1235, freestanding statues of an entirely different formal vocabulary were added to the newly constructed transept porches. The figure of St. Theodore, depicted as a contemporary knight, leaves behind the blatantly classicizing elements of the *Muldenfaltenstil* while retaining a sense of balanced calm. In its detachment from the architectural support, its relaxed, slightly hip-shot stance, and the easy flow of lines in its limbs and draperies, the figure reveals an elegant, unforced verisimilitude.

The Cathedral of Reims contains the largest, most stylistically varied, and most widely influential assortment of sculptural works of the 13th century. In the jambs of the west façade, heavily classicizing figures with *Muldenfaltenstil* draperies (the *Visitation* group on the center portal, 1225–35) stand juxtaposed with others whose jaunty stances, supple but angular planes of drapery, and expressive faces were more favored after mid century (figures of St. Joseph and smiling angels, 1245–55). Between these stylistic extremes are figures with square, stable body construction, loosely hanging draperies with few internal lines, expressionless faces, and sober gestures. These elements hark back to Byzantine models, probably ivory carvings, widely available to western sculptors after the 1204 conquest of Constantinople and first employed in large scale on the west facade of the Cathedral of Notre Dame in Paris (1210–20). In keeping with Cathedral of Reims's role as coronation church for the French monarchs, its upper levels are peopled with an array of stern kings and graceful angels who gaze outward from the towers and buttresses. Along the clerestory level, far out of normal viewing range, a series of wildly expressive, portraitlike heads serve as corbels and decorative devices. Although their purpose and significance remain a mystery, these "masks" bring to view especially vividly the acute interest in transient appearances that characterizes much Gothic sculpture.

The stylistic diversity at Reims indicates the activity there of several distinct teams of sculptors over the course of nearly 40 years. By contrast, the west facade of the Cathedral of Amiens (ca. 1230–35) was executed within a single decade by one team. The three portals comprise a comprehensive encyclopedia of images from sacred and local history united by a network of interlinked vertical and horizontal axes. A continuous row of jamb figures stretches across the lower facade, integrating the doors with the projecting buttresses between them. As physical types, these apostles and saints closely resemble one another, with stiffly erect bodies; broad, V-shaped drapery folds; and somber, immobile faces. Although this stylistic uniformity may result from new techniques of mass production, it can also be explained as a visualization of the notion of *imitatio Christi* so important in 13th-century Christianity. The figures conform physically to the standard set by the solemn *Beau Dieu* (Beautiful God) on the *trumeau* (pier) of the center portal. The three vertically oriented tympana depict the establishment of the bishopric of Amiens (north), the story of Mary, patron of cathedral and town (south), and the Last Judgment (center), thus tying together local, biblical, and future times. Closer to the ground, lively relief carvings framed by quatrefoils display biblical scenes and anecdotal images of the Virtues and Vices and Labors of the Months, thus incorporating worldly ethics and activities into the vision of sacred history.

The systematic, iconographically cohesive quality of French portal sculpture is closely aligned with developments in 13th-century intellectual history, such as the scholastic drive to catalogue and synthesize all elements of human knowledge. The architectural sculptors of other countries assimilated this model but modified it according to local tastes and needs. In England, the concentration of sculptured imagery around massive doorways was eschewed in favor of uniform distribution of figures across the entire facade. The broad west front of the Cathedral of Wells (1225–40), for example, appears overlaid with a lacy screen of gables and niches framing large, sculptured figures of saints and noblemen.

In Germany, where the main entrance to many churches stood on a flank, rather than the western end, portals were smaller in scale and sculptural programs therefore narrower in scope. Whereas French tympana were typically subdivided into registers containing many small figures, German versions were often filled completely by large figures enacting a single scene. This allowed for the amplification of expressive content characteristic of German Gothic sculpture. The rowdy Last Judgment in the Princes' Portal tympanum at the Cathedral of Bamberg and the sorrowful renditions of the Death and Assumption of the Virgin on the south transept portal at Strasbourg (formerly part of the Holy Roman Empire) exemplify this tendency. Flanking these portals stood female figures representing the triumphant Ecclesia and the vanquished Synagoga, a subject that offered sculptors opportunity to exploit the sensuous, tactile qualities of sculpture in the round. At Bamberg and Strasbourg, Synagoga appears with her head bowed and slender body—wrapped in clingy, nearly transparent draperies—twisted so as to accommodate and, indeed, demand perception from

various viewpoints. Attempts to convey the appearance of bodies and faces in motion were pushed further at the Cathedral of Magdeburg, where an entire portal was devoted to the Wise and Foolish Virgins (*ca.* 1240). Whereas French portals had typically depicted the virgins as tiny figures in low relief tucked into the sides of the doorframe, here they are life-size, emphatically animated figures who stand independently in front of the jambs. Wearing the slinky, belted dresses fashionable in 13th-century courts, the virgins demonstrate an exceptionally rich and varied range of facial and gestural expressions to indicate their respective joy or sadness.

This expressive adaptation of essentially French structures and figural styles characterizes Spanish Gothic sculpture as well. The *Pórtico de la Gloria* of the Cathedral of Santiago de Compostela, ascribed to a Master Mateo and dated to 1168–88, features a lavish array of voluminous, colorful column figures. Although the strongly modeled bodies with curving arrangements of limbs and the looping drapery folds resemble the jamb figures at Senlis, an added dimension of vivacity emerges from the figures' alert facial expressions and the interaction of their gazes. Boundaries between figures and their architectural frames, so strictly observed in French structures, blur; the base of the jambs, for example, is carved into dense conglomerations of squirming beasts, while highly projecting archivolt figures are enthroned upon, and hence mask, the outer edge of the tympanum. More in keeping with French models are the west facade of the Cathedral of León and the *Puerta del Sarmental* on the south transept of the Cathedral of Burgos (1240–45), whose tympanum showing Christ in majesty was executed by a sculptor active at Amiens. A locally trained master, on the other hand, was responsible for more idiosyncratic sculptures in the cloister adjacent to the cathedral. Here, tucked into a deep niche, thickly rounded figures of Gabriel and Mary enact an Annunciation scene of unprecedented intimacy and emotive content.

Independent of the comprehensive portal structure, interior Gothic sculpture tends to be geared toward stimulating affective response among beholders in a more private context through the intensified corporeal and emotional presence of figures. It is surely no accident that some of the most significant experiments with physiognomic variation (the African St. Maurice at Magdeburg, *ca.* 1245) and psychological expression (St. Elizabeth at Bamberg, *ca.* 1235) were executed on autonomous figures meant to be viewed at close range. Comprehensive theological programs did appear, if infrequently, inside churches. The inner west wall (1260–70) at the Cathedral of Reims is filled from floor to ceiling with a vast screen of trefoil niches in which dozens of figures in dense, blocky draperies act out scenes from the Hebrew Scriptures with the expressive gestures of dramatic performers. At Strasbourg, the scene of Judgment that typically crowned an exterior portal was drawn inside. Here, niches on each side of the massive pier supporting the south transept vault (the so-called Angels' Pillar, *ca.* 1230) are occupied by gracefully swaying figures of the four Evangelists, seven angels, and a Judging Christ. Turning toward one another across the colonnettes, these figures, whose elongated limbs and sleek draperies reveal a clear Chartrian influence, direct the beholder's movement around the pier while creating rich, shifting patterns of light and shade.

More frequently, interior figures were displayed as discrete units, punctuating the building with their enactment of transspatial narratives. At the Cathedral of Regensburg, for example, the grinning angel Gabriel salutes Mary across the central vessel of the nave (*ca.* 1260). The monumental Visitation figures in the west choir aisle of the Cathedral of Bamberg, manifestly influenced by sculptures at Reims, are characterized by their remarkably psychological vivacity and a weighty corporeal presence enhanced through deeply cut *Muldenfaltenstil* draperies (*ca.* 1235). High on a crossing pier nearby, a handsome knightly figure on horseback, the so-called *Bamberg Rider* (*ca.* 1235), energizes the space as he gazes intently toward the altar. Whereas these figures orient themselves toward the viewer on the ground, the sculptures in the Angel Choir (1270–80) at the Cathedral of Lincoln animate and organize the interior from high above. Tucked into the spandrels of the choir triforium, highly modeled relief figures serve to reflect and signal the respective significance of the liturgical spaces below. Around the choir's major devotional focus, the now-lost shrine of St. Hugh of Lincoln, appears an orchestra of jubilant angels, whereas the spandrels above the high altar are occupied by a more solemn Judgment sequence.

Large-scale figures were frequently built into the peripheral supports of the choir to distinguish the liturgical preeminence of that space. In the Sainte Chapelle (1241–48), the Twelve Apostles who occupy the median level between the ground and the stained glass windows are characterized by supple and richly variegated drapery folds and refined postures. Tightly curled hair and beards, delicate facial features, and sensitive yet restrained expressions add to the nobility of their appearance. Attached to the choir piers (1280–90) of the Cathedral of Cologne stand figures of the Apostles, visibly based on the Sainte Chapelle sculptures, accompanied by a youthful Mary and Christ. With their exaggerated S-curve postures and the mannered quality of their gestures, however, they signal a move toward the new aesthetic of late Gothic art, which valued expressive affects and dynamic tension over dignified restraint and adherence to natural appearances. In the west choir of the Cathedral of Naumburg (1245–50), whose basic structure was likewise influenced by the Sainte Chapelle, the open gallery level is occupied by 12 life-size, portraitlike sculptures of long-dead noble donors to the church. These exceptionally realistic figures display a novel formal and expressive vocabulary in their robust pipe-fold draperies, individualized physiognomies, and striking variety of facial expressions.

Such standing, active donor figures, examples of which also survive at the Cathedral of Meissen (*ca.* 1260) and the cloister at Burgos (*ca.* 1270), commemorate the depicted individual's donation without presupposing the presence of his or her actual body in the church. They thus differ from tomb sculptures, which marked a person's burial site within a favored building. During their 13th-century fluorescence, tomb effigies portrayed the deceased in attire indicative of his or her social estate, with serene, idealized facial features, prayerfully clasped hands, and feet firmly planted on a console or animal figure in seeming contradiction to the figure's supine position.

Liturgical furnishings such as pulpits and screens, which, in contrast to tomb effigies, were integral to the proper functioning of ritual services, were also embellished with sculptures that emphasized the structure's role as a vehicle of communication. In Italy, Nicola and Giovanni Pisano made a career of *historiating* (embellishing with figural, often narrative imagery) the outer surfaces of marble pulpits with lively reliefs that successfully merged an antique figural style with Christian iconography (for example, in the Pisa Baptistery, 1257–59; at Siena, 1265–68; and at Pistoia, 1298–1301). In northern churches, screens delineating the boundary of nave and choir were likewise embellished with relief sculptures that reinforced the content of the Gospel readings and sermons. Fragments from the demolished choir screens at Chartres, Bourges, and Mainz—and extant programs at Modena, Gelnhausen, and Naumburg—indicate a high level of sophistication in the representation of narratives and a keen awareness of the interests and concerns of lay audiences.

Surmounting the choir screen or rood beam stood the monumental crucifix, the main focal point of liturgical experience. In the beginning of our period, the figure of Christ tended to be displayed transcending the physical pain of the Passion; at Halberstadt (*ca.* 1220), the feet are placed side by side so that the body remains relatively erect, and the face, although downturned, appears calm. A generation later, the designer of the west choir screen at Naumburg lowered his eerily lifelike figure into the doors of the portal and amplified the signs of bodily anguish; the head of Christ droops, the limbs sag, and the body curves painfully. By the close of the period, natural appearances were forsaken altogether as the signs of suffering intensified. In the *crucifixus dolorosus* at St. Maria im Kapitol in Cologne (*ca.* 1310), Christ's body, broken and emaciated, hangs grotesquely from a spiky, forked tree.

In its emphasis on expressive affects rather than corporeal verisimilitude, the Cologne crucifix is representative of trends in sculptural figuration at the end of the Gothic period. In place of the public visual encyclopedias of 12th- and 13th-century church portals, meant to be perceived in a systematic, rational manner, the characteristic product of the 14th century was the sculptured *Andachtsbild*, the small-scale devotional image aimed at stimulating intense emotional response within a private setting. In these images, the formal handling of the sculptural material (usually wood) often reinforced the iconographic content. Softly flowing lines and smooth, tactile modeling made visible a quiet, restful quality in images of St. John resting on the breast of Christ, whereas brash angles, jagged edges, and skewed proportions aptly conveyed Mary's agony while clutching the dead Christ on her lap (the pietà). The formal expressivity of devotional images carried over into monumental stone sculpture as well. Portal programs, such as the west facade sculptures of the Cathedral of Strasbourg, and tomb sculptures, such as the later effigies at St-Denis and the images of bishops at Bamberg, de-emphasize the corporeality of the body, allowing its physical bulk to dissolve into more abstract configurations of curvilinear patterns and elastic proportions.

JACQUELINE E. JUNG

See also **England; Germany; Nicholas of Verdun; Pietà; Pisano, Giovanni; Pisano, Nicola; Polychromy; Pulpit; Screens; Tomb Sculpture**

Further Reading

Beck, Herbert, and Kerstin Hengevoss-Dürkop (editors), *Studien zur Geschichte der europäischen Skulptur im 12./13. Jahrhundert*, 2 vols., Frankfurt: Henrich, 1994

Blum, Pamela Z., *Early Gothic Saint-Denis: Restorations and Survivals*, Berkeley: University of California Press, 1992

Katzenellenbogen, Adolf, *The Sculptural Programs of Chartres Cathedral: Christ, Mary, Ecclesia*, Baltimore, Maryland: Johns Hopkins Press, 1959

Möbius, Friedrich, and Ernst Schubert (editors), *Skulptur des Mittelalters: Funktion und Gestalt*, Weimar, Germany: Böhlau, 1987

Panofsky, Erwin, *Die deutsche Plastik des elften bis dreizehnten Jahrhunderts*, 2 vols., Munich: Wolff, 1924; reprint, New York: Kraus Reprint, 1969

Raguin, Virginia Chieffo, Kathryn Brush, and Peter Draper (editors), *Artistic Integration in Gothic Buildings*, Toronto, Ontario, and Buffalo, New York: University of Toronto Press, 1995

Sauerländer, Willibald, *Gotische Skulptur in Frankreich, 1140–1270*, Munich: Hirmer, 1970; as *Gothic Sculpture in France, 1140–1270*, translated by Janet Sondheimer, New York: Abrams, 1971; London: Thames and Hudson, 1972

Schlink, Wilhelm, *Der Beau-Dieu von Amiens: Der Christusbild der gotischen Kathedrale*, Frankfurt: Insel, 1991

Vöge, Wilhelm, *Bildhauer des Mittelalters: Gesammelte Studien*, Berlin: Mann, 1958

Williamson, Paul, *Gothic Sculpture, 1140–1300*, New Haven, Connecticut: Yale University Press, 1995

JEAN GOUJON *ca.* 1510–*ca.* 1565 *French*

A master of the elegant, fluid line, Jean Goujon achieved in his signature medium, the bas-relief, a synthesis of the Classicism of ancient Greco-Roman art and the mannered art of the French Renaissance school of Fontainebleau. Goujon's style of relief carving—a balanced composition of human figures set against a plain background and animated by the graceful torsion of their bodies—brought him royal patronage during his lifetime and lasting fame over the ensuing centuries. Despite this fame, little is known about the events of his life. From his birth around 1510 until the early 1540s, when his name appears in the municipal papers of Rouen followed by the appellation "ymaiginier et architecteur juré" (skilled image-maker and architect), the course of Goujon's early life is full of conjecture.

A dim picture of his youth can be formed from his earliest known work, the organ loft in the Church of St. Maclou, Rouen, France. Although only two marble columns remain from Goujon's work at St. Maclou, they hint at some of the facts of the sculptor's early biography. That his first works were carved in Rouen suggests that he is probably of Norman descent, perhaps born in Rouen or a nearby village. In addition, the proportions and decorations of the columns demonstrate a perfect assimilation of the Vitruvian rules of the Classical orders, making them two of the earliest examples of Renaissance Classicism in France and raising the possibility that, sometime before his work at St. Maclou, Goujon had traveled to Italy, where he learned firsthand the languages of Classical art and the art of the Italian Renaissance.

By 1544 Goujon had left Rouen for Paris, where he worked on the carving of the rood screen designed by the architect Pierre Lescot for the Church of St. Germain l'Auxerrois, a work that marked the beginning of a decade and a half of collaboration between sculptor and architect. Although the screen was destroyed in 1745, Goujon's five marble bas-reliefs have survived. The largest of the five reliefs, a horizontal scene of the *Deposition*, is remarkable in its transformation of diverse artistic styles into a unified, Classical whole. Goujon borrowed from an engraving of the *Deposition* by Parmigianino and a painting of the *Pietà* by Rosso

Fiorentino, originally from the chapel of the Château d'Ecouen (now Musée du Louvre, Paris). While adopting formal elements from other artists, he transformed the rhetorical gestures of Parmigianino and the feverish agitation of Fiorentino into a vision of transcendent serenity. The supple forms of the figures and the fluid grace of their finely pleated drapery recall the *relievo schiacciato* (relief sculpture emphasizing light and shadow through carving methods) carvings of 15th-century Florence. However, unlike the layering of planes by which Florentine sculptors conveyed the illusion of pictorial depth, Goujon creates a sense of spatial volume in the *Deposition*, and the accompanying four *Evangelists*, through the dramatic foreshortening of the figures.

From 1545 to 1547, Goujon is reputed to have worked for the constable of France, Anne, Duke of Montemorency, as the architect of the Château d'Ecouen. It is difficult to determine exactly what contributions Goujon made to the building of the château. Nonetheless, the dedication of the noted classicist Jean Baptiste Martin's translation of Vitruvius' *De architectura: Architecture, ou, art de bien bastir* (1547; Of Architecture: Architecture, or, The Art of Building Well), a work translated under the patronage of the constable of France, states that Goujon illustrated the volume with 27 woodcuts while he was in the employ of the constable as both architect and sculptor.

Goujon's royal patronage began in 1547 with the accession of Henry II, after the death of Francis I. Much of Goujon's work during that period was marked by collaboration. In partnership with Jean Cousin in 1549, he helped design the ceremonial entry of Henry II into Paris. Together with Lescot, he designed the *Fountain of the Innocents*, a rectangular structure that stood on the corner of the rue Saint-Denis and the rue aux Fers. This structure originally consisted of three arched bays with fluted pilasters. Between these, Goujon carved narrow vertical bas-reliefs of nymphs. Bas-reliefs of tritons and nymphs were also placed above and below each bay, and winged figures of Fame filled the spandrels of the arches. The flowing lines and drapery of the figures of the *Fountain of the Innocents* qualify the monument not only as Goujon's masterpiece but as an artistic pinnacle in French Renaissance sculpture.

From 1547 until his flight from France in 1562, Goujon became involved in the sculptural decoration of Lescot's additions to the Louvre. In addition to providing architectural decoration, Goujon was inspired by the reliefs on Trajan's column in Rome (of which he might have seen Primaticcio's casts [1540]) in the three pairs of female allegories he placed around windows above the three doors of the southwest wing of the Cour Carrée. Goujon's departure from the strict classicism of the *Fountain of the Innocents* is evident in this nod to Mannerism, marked by its fine carving and drapery that create a sense of lyrical movement for the images. Similarly, Goujon's four colossal caryatids (*Tribune des Caryatids*) in the Salle des Caryatids clearly draw inspiration from the caryatids on the porch of the Erechtheion, Athens; but unlike their Classical sisters, Goujon's four women display a sensuousness more typical of French 16th-century taste.

Throughout the 13 or so years that Goujon worked at the Louvre, he steadily moved away from Classicism toward the style established by the florid art of the school of Fontainebleau. For example, the high reliefs on the attic story of Lescot's wing of the Louvre (1552–55) do not belong to the history of Classicism; rather, with their sizable bodies posed in exaggerated *contrapposto* (a natural pose with the weight of one leg, the shoulder, and hips counterbalancing one another) and reaching beyond the building's framework, they align themselves more with such Mannerist follies as the figures adorning Giulio Romano's Palazzo del Te in Mantua. Goujon's workshop, which employed artists such as Étienne Carmoy, Martin Lefort, Pierre Nanyn, and the brothers François and Pierre Lheureux, was closely involved with the decorative carving of the staircase of Henry II in the Louvre.

In September 1562 fear of religious persecution prompted Goujon's flight from France. Like other Protestant artists who contributed to the artistic efflorescence of the French Renaissance—among them Pierre Bontemps, Bernard Palissy, Bartholémy Prieur, and Ligier Richier—Goujon abandoned his work in midproject, leaving the task of completing the sculptures on the south wing of the Cour Carrée to his workshop. The last record of Goujon lists him as one of a group of exiled Huguenots living in Bologna in the early months of 1564. The date, place, and circumstances of his death are unknown; it is likely that he died in Italy sometime between 1565 and 1568.

Goujon left no artistic successor, but his sculpture has found praise throughout the centuries. Gianlorenzo Bernini admired the *Fountain of the Innocents* when he visited Paris under the rule of Louis XIV; in 1787 Quatremère de Quincy initiated the first public campaign to conserve Goujon's sculpture as a part of the national heritage; and the Romantic sculptors of the early 19th century found affinity between their own sculptural aesthetic and the expressive, flowing lines of Goujon's bas-reliefs.

MICHAEL DORSCH

Biography

Born probably in Normandy, France, *ca.* 1510. First record of name found in archives of Rouen as *ymaigi-*

nier et architecteur juré, 1540–42; on the basis of artistic style assumed to have studied in Italy before working in Rouen; carved bas-reliefs on rood screen for Church of St. Germain l'Auxerrois, 1544; illustrated Jean Baptiste Martin's translation of Vitruvius, 1544–47; entered service of Henry II, 1549; fled to France because of religious persecution, *ca.* 1562. Died probably in Bologna, Italy, *ca.* 1565.

Selected Works

1541–42 Organ loft; marble (mostly destroyed, two columns remain *in situ*); Church of St. Maclou, Rouen, France

1544 *Deposition* and *Evangelists*, on rood screen for Church of St. Germain l'Auxerrois, Paris, France; marble; Musée du Louvre, Paris, France

1547–49 *Fountain of the Innocents*, for the corner of rue Saint-Denis and rue aux Fers; marble (dispersed); three bas-reliefs: Musée du Louvre, Paris, France; remainder of fountain: Place des Innocents, Les Halles, Paris, France

1547–55 West facade of Cour Carrée; stone; Musée du Louvre, Paris, France

1550–51 *Tribune des Caryatids*; marble; Musée du Louvre, Paris, France

1550–56 Staircase of Henry II; marble; Musée du Louvre, Paris, France

Further Reading

Blunt, Anthony, *Art and Architecture in France, 1500–1700*, London and Baltimore: Penguin Books, 1953

Brese-Bautier, Geneviève, "La sculpture de l'attique du Louvre par l'atelier de Jean Goujon," *La revue du Louvre et nes musées de France* 2 (1989)

Du Colombier, Pierre, *Jean Goujon*, Paris: Michel, 1949

Jouin, Henri Auguste, *Jean Goujon*, Paris: Librarie de l'Art, 1906

Lister, Reginald, *Jean Goujon, His Life and Work*, London: Duckworth, 1903

Vitry, Paul, *Jean Goujon*, Paris: H. Laurens, 1908

Vitry, Paul, *La Sculpture française classique de Jean Goujon à Rodin*, Paris: Morancé, 1934

FOUNTAIN OF THE INNOCENTS

Jean Goujon (ca. 1510–ca. 1565)

1547–1549

marble

h. over 2.5 m

Les Halles, Paris, France (three reliefs in the Musée du Louvre, Paris, France)

During the early years of the Renaissance, the role that the fountain played within the urban fabric of a city was transformed. Although fountains still served as an important feature of the public water supply, a shift occurred in their design, such that they were no longer simple, pragmatic sources of water, but ornate architectural structures festooned with virtuoso displays of sculpture. For instance, only the merest trickle of water flowed from Jean Goujon's *Fountain of the Innocents*, but the scant supply of water did little to diminish the importance of the work, both as an artistic monument and as a civic structure that played a key role in the politics of French royalty.

Jean Goujon designed the *Fountain of the Innocents* as a vantage point from which to view the festive ceremonial entry of Henry II into Paris following his accession to the throne. Originally built on the corner of the rue Saint-Denis and the rue aux Fers, Goujon's fountain stood beside the traditional route of the procession returning to the Palais du Louvre from the royal coronation at the Abbey of Saint-Denis. The *Fountain of the Innocents* remained *in situ* until 1787, when, as part of a campaign to improve the general salubrity of the city, the Saint-Innocents cemetery adjoining the fountain was deconsecrated and moved outside the city walls, thus clearing a space for the construction of the large marketplace of Les Halles and necessitating the removal of Goujon's fountain.

In the late 18th century, the *Fountain of the Innocents* was again erected, in a public square adjoining Les Halles. However, its original design—a loggia of three arched bays adorned with bas-reliefs of nymphs and tritons—was reconfigured into a freestanding square fountain consisting of four arched bays surmounted by a low dome, with the additional arch decorated with bas-reliefs by Augustin Pajou in the style of Goujon. When in 1810 the channeling of water from the Canal de l'Ourcq increased the amount of fresh water flowing into Paris, the fountain became, for the first time since its creation, a primary source of water for the surrounding neighborhood. Ten years later, one last alteration was made: During the previous decade, the increased water flow had begun to damage some of Goujon's sculpture, so in an effort to preserve the carvings, three bas-reliefs were removed from the lower part of the fountain to the Musée du Louvre. To this day, the *Fountain of the Innocents* remains the focal point of the Place des Innocents, a zenith of French Renaissance sculpture amid the hustle and bustle of modern Paris.

The original design of the *Fountain of the Innocents* is recorded in a 17th-century engraving by Daniel Marot. A loggia consisting of three arches sat atop a tier of masonry adorned with bas-reliefs of nymphs, sea creatures, and a triton. A meager trickle of water flowed from this lowest tier. The loggia was composed of two facades of irregular length, with the short facade

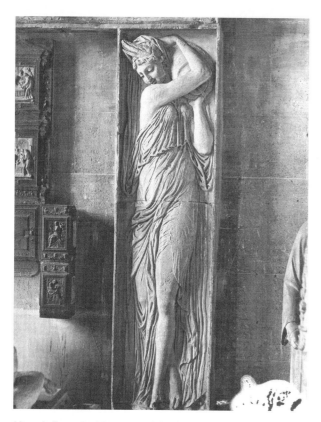

Nymph from the *Fountain of the Innocents*
© Giraudon / Art Resource, NY

during the 16th century. For instance, Goujon's five reliefs of standing nymphs recall Marcantonio's prints after Raphael. More specifically, the relief of *Triton Embracing a Nymph* (one of the three bas-reliefs from the lower tier of the fountain removed to the Musée du Louvre in 1820) draws directly from an ancient sarcophagus that Goujon may well have studied while in Italy in the 1530s. (The sarcophagus is also recorded in the *Codex Escuralensius* [Biblioteca Nacional, Madrid], thus suggesting that its image was in wide circulation during the Renaissance.) However, Goujon consistently translated all the formal elements that he borrowed from other works of art into his own aesthetic language. The great sweeping lines and transparent, clinging drapery of the figures in the bas-reliefs of the Fountain of the Innocents display a sinuous watery grace perfectly in accord with their aquatic theme. Goujon's delicate carvings capture the secrets of the cool undulation of water, revealing his subtle understanding of the sensuous touch and sound of water lapping at the edge of a spring, gurgling over rocks on a streambed, or pouring forth from a vase.

MICHAEL DORSCH

Further Reading

Boudon, Marion, "La fontaine des Innocents," in *Paris et ses fontaines de la Renaissance à nos jours*, edited by Beatrice de Andia et al., Paris: Délégation à l'Action Artistique de la Ville de Paris, 1995

Draper, James David, and Guilhem Scherf, *Pajou: Royal Sculptor, 1730–1809*, New York: The Metropolitan Museum of Art, 1997

Lemonnier, Henry, "La participation de Pajou à la Fontaine des Innocents," *Bulletin de la Société de l'histoire de l'art française* (1907–08)

Miller, Naomi, "The Form and Meaning of the 'Fontaine des Innocents,'" *The Art Bulletin* 50 (1968)

Miller, Naomi, *French Renaissance Fountains*, New York: Garland, 1977

Thirion, Jacques, "La fontaine des Nymphes," in *Les Saints-Innocents*, Paris: Délégation à l'Action Artistique de la Ville de Paris, Commission du Vieux Paris, 1990

(consisting of one arch) fronting the rue Saint-Denis and the longer one (consisting of two arches) facing the rue aux Fers. The arches of the loggia were flanked by Corinthian pilasters, with the spaces between the pilasters adorned with five magnificent bas-reliefs of standing nymphs pouring water from vases. Over each arch was a bas-relief depicting putti frolicking amid the waves with fantastic sea monsters. Although flowing water played a minor role in the design of Goujon's fountain, the theme of water, and more particularly, that of the spirits of the water, dictated its decoration. All of Goujon's bas-reliefs for the *Fountain of the Innocents* conform to a stylistic type: figures of nymphs or sea creatures are presented within a narrow frame, the rhythm of the long sinuous lines of their bodies in contrast to the bare stone backgrounds of the reliefs. The contrast between the smoothly modeled flesh of the figures and the complex system of drapery, which alternately clings to the body in small damp folds and then suddenly billows and twists to create a play of shadows, gives Goujon's bas-reliefs a dramatic sense of animation. Skillful foreshortening in the diagonal lines of the compositions lends the scenes a sense of depth.

Goujon drew inspiration for the fountain's bas-reliefs from a variety of antique works widely known

CASPAR GRAS 1585–1674 *German, active in Austria*

Caspar Gras was the only student, collaborator, and successor of the bronze sculptor Hubert Gerhard to carry on Gerhard's style well into the 17th century in the court of the Archdukes of Tirol in Innsbruck, Austria. Since there were no greater building projects at Innsbruck at that time, there were also no greater sculpture commissions. The only monumental works were the Leopold fountain, which was not erected until the 19th century, and the tomb monument of Archduke Maximillian III in St. Jacob at Innsbruck, executed by Gerhard, and today a cathedral.

Gras was born in Bad Mergentheim in Franconia, the son of the goldsmith Egidius Gras. According to the original apprentice contract, he began his apprenticeship with Gerhard on 2 December 1600. Even in the 18th century, local Innsbruck legend had it that Gras died at close to 90 years of age in 1674 in Schwaz in Tirol. From this, one can deduce a birth date of 1585, and considering that of his education began in 1600, this birth date seems probable.

Gerhard, the man who shaped Gras's artistic career, was one of Giambologna's best-known successors north of the Alps. From 1581 he worked in southern Germany in the city of Augsburg, and between 1584 and 1597 he worked for Duke William V of Bavaria in Munich. During this time, Gerhard accomplished an extensive body of works in bronze and large-scale terracotta sculptures. In 1597 Duke William V abdicated, and because of the Duke's debts, most of Munich's court artists were released from service. Gerhard was hired by Archduke Maximilian III of Tirol, who was a cousin of William V and who held the spiritual title of grand master of the Teutonic Order. Maximilian was at this time at war with Turkey, but upon his return in 1599, Gerhard moved into the residence of the Order of the Teutonic Knights in Mergentheim.

One can assume that the young Gras received his first training before his apprenticeship in his father's goldsmith workshop. His apprentice contract names specifically as a goal that he should learn from Gerhard "the free art of *Possierens*," meaning figure modeling in stucco, clay, and wax.

In 1602 the court of Maximilian III moved to Innsbruck and with it went Gerhard, who was accompanied by Gras. In 1609, after waiting until the completion of his apprenticeship, as was the custom, Gras was married. In 1613, owing to his age, Gerhard left the service of the Innsbruck court, and Gras was able to take over his position, which he held until his death.

Maximilian's first commission for a large-scale bronze sculpture was his own tomb monument, which originally was installed in the choir of St. Jacob's and now can be found in the northern aisle of the same church. Four tall *salomónica*, or twisted, columns decorated with grapevines and small animals, support a platform on which a larger-than-life figure of Maximilian appears clad in armor and kneeling in prayer. Next to him and equally large appears St. George, patron of the Teutonic Order, with a powerful dragon by his side. On the corners sit mournful cherubs with torches. These cherubs as well as the columns were completed in 1619, long after Gerhard's return to Munich. The main group of bronzes was apparently finished in 1608 during the time Gerhard and Gras were active at Innsbruck. It seems logical, therefore, that the main modeling work on this tomb was executed by Gerhard, an

attribution that is further confirmed stylistically. Gras's kneeling figure for the epitaph of Paul Sixt Trautson in Vienna in 1614 is evidently based on his studies of the Maximilian tomb.

In 1618 Archduke Leopold V, bishop of Strasbourg and Passau, succeeded the deceased Maximilian III in Tirol's regency. The ambitious young prince must have commissioned shortly thereafter an ostentatious fountain with bronze figures and his own portrait figure as an equestrian. In four years, materials for the casting had been acquired, and by 1629 the figures were completed. Unfortunately, because of Leopold's death in 1632 and the Thirty Years War, the fountain was never erected and the pieces remained set up individually in a courtyard. It was not until 1894 that the disfigured fountain was restored, misrepresenting the motif and style of Gras's original idea. The bronze work on this fountain represents the pinnacle of Gras's career. It consists of three reclining nautical goddesses and three seated nautical gods, which have been preserved. The remaining figures would have been four putti supporting a large bronze basin that was melted down long ago, over which the image of a horse and rider would have appeared. The originally planned arrangement of nymphs and sea gods is not known. From the number of figures, one would conclude that they were placed on a triangular structure in the same vein as Adriaen De Vries's Hercules fountain (1597–1602) in Augsburg. It is also possible that the Augsburg Fountain served as inspiration. The direct model for this work was a fountain that no longer exists in its original form, one that Gras's teacher Gerhard erected in 1586/87 in Munich for Duke Ferdinand. This work consisted of a fountain basin decorated with sea creatures in the same strange combination with a *kurbettierendem* (a curvetting or prancing pose) horse and rider atop a large bronze shell. Gras's horse and rider are, however, decidedly larger, whereby he was the first to master the technical challenge that had existed since Leonardo da Vinci—to realize a monument of a curvetting horse in such a large format without auxiliary supports.

In these substantial freestanding sculptures, Gras demonstrated the influence of Gerhard long after his mentor's departure from Innsbruck. His figures are smooth and composed, even occasionally dull. The horse's swinging tail is representative of a Baroque and original style that Gras succeeded in creating independently of Gerhard.

Shortly after completing his equestrian image, Gras was called to Konstanz (Constance) by a chapter of the Cathedral of Constance to create the larger-than-life-size *Virgin and Child* for an altar. The statue was cast by the native bronze caster Valentin Algeyer in 1632. This piece is both Gras's last major work and highly characteristic of his style. The inspiration and model for this piece was once again a work done by his teacher, Gerhard: a Madonna for a tomb monument to Duke William V in 1593, which stood from 1606 to 1620 at the main altar of Munich's Cathedral Church of Our Lady (Frauenkirche). In 1638, a few years after the casting of the Konstanz *Virgin and Child*, Gerhard's Madonna became, at Munich's Column of the Virgin Mary (Mariensäule), the central focus of Baroque Marian worship in Bavaria. Gras's Virgin Mary statue follows Gerhard's in the composure, attributes, and dress and in that the heads appear squarer and sturdier. What is for Gerhard's statue a very Classical arrangement of garments appears in Gras's as more lifelike and relaxed. Since 1683, Gras's *Virgin and Child* also has sat atop a column (the Column of the Virgin Mary) in Konstanz's Münsterplatz.

No large bronze works are known from Gras's later years. He most certainly created small bronzes for court and church functions, and the attributional controversy surrounding these works still has not been resolved. A series of equestrian statuettes of Habsburg princes can with certainty be credited to Gras. In this series, the riders, or more specifically, their heads, were cast separately and can be interchanged if the need arises.

DOROTHEA DIEMER

See also **Gerhard, Hubert**

Biography

Born in Bad Mergentheim, Germany, 1585. He was the son of Egidius Gras, a goldsmith. Began his training in his father's workshop; apprenticed to Hubert Gerhard, 2 December 1600; married in 1609, after completing apprenticeship; succeeded Gerhard as court sculptor to Maximilian III, Archduke of Tirol, in Innsbruck, Austria, 1613. Died in Schwaz, Tirol, Austria, 1674.

Selected Works

ca. 1608–19	Tomb monument for Archduke Maximilian III of Tirol (with Hubert Gerhard); bronze; St. Jacob's Cathedral, Innsbruck, Austria
1614	Epitaph for Paul Sixt Trautson; bronze; Church of St. Michael, Vienna, Austria
1619	Four mourning putti and two columns for the tomb monument for Archduke Maximilian III of Tirol; bronze; St. Jacob's Cathedral, Innsbruck, Austria
1620	*The Giant Haymon*; bronze; Wilten Foundation, Innsbruck, Austria
1623–30	Leopold fountain; bronze figures and

upper basin; Tirol Museum, Innsbruck, Austria

| 1632 | *Virgin and Child* (cast by Valentin Algeyer); bronze; Münsterplatz, Konstanz, Germany |

Further Reading

Caramelle, Franz, "Caspar Gras," in *Ruhm und Sinnlichkeit: Innsbrucker Bronzeguss, 1500–1650, von Kaiser Maximilian I. bis Erzherzog Ferdinand Karl* (exhib. cat.), edited by Eleanore Gürtler, Ellen Hastaba, and Anja Seipenbusch, Innsbruck, Austria: Tiroler Landesmuseum Ferdinandeum, and Athesia-Tyrolia Druck, 1996

Doering, Oscar, *Des Augsburger Patriciers Philipp Hainhofer Beziehungen zum Herzog Philipp II. von Pommern-Stettin*, Vienna: Graeser, 1894

Egg, Erich, "Caspar Gras und der Tiroler Bronzeguss des 17. Jahrhunderts," *Veröffentlichungen des Museum Ferdinandeum* 40 (1960)

Leithe-Jasper, Manfred, *Renaissance Master Bronzes: From the Collection of the Kunsthistorisches Museum Vienna* (exhib. cat.), Washington, D.C.: Scala Books, 1986

Scheicher, Elisabeth, "Leopoldsbrunnen," in *Österreichische Kunsttopographie*, vol. 47, *Die profanen Kunstdenkmäler der Stadt Innsbruck: Die Hofbauten*, Vienna: Schroll, 1986

Smith, Jeffrey Chipps, "Gras, Caspar," in *The Dictionary of Art*, edited by Jane Turner, vol. 13, New York: Grove, and London: Macmillan, 1996

Weihrauch, Hans R., "Der Innsbrucker Brunnen des Kaspar Gras," *Pantheon* 31 (1943)

Weihrauch, Hans R., "Die verloren geglaubte Konstanzer Madonna des Kaspar Gras," *Pantheon* 20 (1962)

ERASMUS GRASSER 1445/50–1518
German

It is not just because of its inherent quality that the autograph sculptural oeuvre of Erasmus Grasser, who was also a successful architect and an active hydraulic engineer, surpasses that of the other late Gothic masters in Munich. Grasser and his workshop seem to have loomed above their contemporaries in no small part owing to the extensiveness and importance of the actual commissions they won—from the decoration of the Tanzsaal dance hall in the Alte Rathaus to the choir stalls of the Cathedral Church of Our Lady (Frauenkirche) and the now largely destroyed high altar of the Church of St. Peter. The commission given him for the Holy Spirit altar, originally made for the Cathedral of Salzburg and now nearby in the Benedictine abbey at Nonnberg, indicates that Grasser's importance extended far beyond Munich.

The earliest documentary record of Grasser dates from 1475, when the Painter's, Sculptor's, and Glazier's Guild in Munich filed a protest with the city council objecting to the artist's request to be recognized as a master and to receive tax privileges. The guild accused Grasser of being a "belligerent, muddled, and deceitful knave"; that the city not only ignored the charge and admitted him to the guild but also gave him the Tanzsaal commission by at least 1477 suggests the council's enormous appreciation for his new style. For all of Grasser's success, however, the reconstruction of his oeuvre, which must depend on the Tanzsaal commission as a primary reference point, is made difficult by the fact that only four other documented works exist: the epitaph of Ulrich Aresinger, which bears Grasser's only surviving signature ("Den stain hat gehauen Maister Erasm. Grasser 1482," or "This stone has been hewn by Master Erasmus Grasser 1482"), the *Lamentation* group for the Cathedral of Freising, and the two altars in Reichersdorf. In both invention and execution, moreover, the altars revert to Grasser's earlier work to such a degree that one should take the naming of Grasser in the documents only as a reference to his role as the contractor; his workshop must have carried out these projects largely on its own.

Hans Ramisch has convincingly attributed *St. Mary* and *St. John the Evangelist* of a *Crucifixion* group in Traidendorf to Grasser, dating them to the early 1470s (see Ramisch, 1999). Paul Frankl's suggestion that some of the corbel figures of the Munich Cathedral Church of our Lady are likewise early works by the artist remains an unprovable hypothesis (see Frankl, 1942). About Grasser's previous training, which must have been at least partially completed in a builder's shop, nothing certain is known. His later style shows the influence of Nikolaus Gerhaert von Leiden and his circle, suggesting that Grasser had traveled to Swabia, going perhaps as far as the Upper Rhine. Grasser's statue *St. John the Evangelist* from Traidendorf and the Holy Cross altar at Ramersdorf, among other works, evince

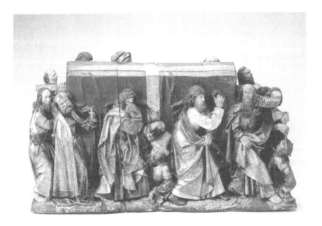

Burial of the Virgin (ca. late 15th century)
© Fine Arts Museums of San Francisco, Gift of Mr. and Mrs. Ralph C. Lee

direct borrowings from the Nördlingen altar, which some scholars attribute to Gerhaert himself and which is in any case closely related to Gerhaert's style. Some of this new Upper Rhenish and Netherlandish formal vocabulary would have been available in contemporary engravings, particularly those of Master E.S. Grasser's works beginning in the 1490s. These, however, also show a marked tendency toward closed volumes and gliding curves and lines, a tendency that recalls the Ulmish tradition stemming from Hans Multscher and which perhaps suggests Grasser's initial training under one of Multscher's followers. If the proposed attribution of the late Gothic tomb of Louis IV the Bavarian in Munich's Cathedral Church of Our Lady to the local sculptor Hans Haldner and the proposed dating of the piece to about 1468 are correct, then this master, too, could be counted as a local source of inspiration for Grasser's works from the late 1470s and 1480s.

Given this multifaceted foundation, Grasser developed an original, highly dynamic, and expressive style, with sculptures that fill space and emphasize the body. The style of constrained movement manifests itself most clearly in his *Morris Dancers*, with slim, dramatically moved bodies, contrasts between tightly applied bits of clothing and freely fluttering draperies, and sharply drawn physiognomic features. It is a style that began with Gerhaert, that characterized all German sculpture of the 1480s, and that found one of its high points in the works of Grasser. Grasser received the commission for the ensemble *Morris Dancers* after he demonstrated his abilities in 1477 with the escutcheons and the images of the sun and moon for the Tanzsaal of the Munich Alte Rathaus. Originally comprising 16 figures, *Morris Dancers* is the most important surviving cycle of German late Gothic secular sculpture. Ten of the figures have survived: Placed on consoles under the barrel vault, they range from 61 to 81 centimeters in height. The moresque, or morris dance, is a grotesque dance, probably originating in Spain and performed by jesters; it symbolized uncontrollable vice in general and the folly of male courtship in particular.

With his epitaph of Ulrich Aresinger, the provost and parson of the Church of St. Peter, Grasser introduced a new type of memorial to Bavaria, in which an effigy of the deceased, placed in a perspectively rendered interior, is nearly the same size as the patron saints beneath whom he kneels in prayer.

The Holy Cross altar from Ramersdorf, which depicts the Crucifixion in the shrine and four scenes from the Passion on the interior of the altar wings, demonstrates in its background a new sort of combination of sculpture and painting, presenting the viewer with a fluid, perspectively correct transition between the two media.

The 1490s marked the calming and the blocklike monumentalization of Grasser's figures, perhaps most clearly seen in the seated figure of St. Peter, on the high altar of the Church of St. Peter in Munich, on which Grasser collaborated with Jan Polack, the most important Munich painter of the time. This development, too, follows a more general stylistic tendency of German sculpture in the period, which Wilhelm Pinder characterized as "quieting," "erasing," and "sharpening" (*Beruhigung, Streckung, Schärfung*; see Pinder, 1929). It is also possible, however, that Grasser's late work shows the influence of the second most important, but nevertheless superb, locally trained sculptor of the time, the anonymous Master of the Blutenburg Apostles.

Grasser's ever more extensive activities as an architect and an engineer for water- and saltworks apparently brought him such a good income in the last decades of his life that he increasingly left the carving of figures to his workshop. After 1506 he apparently accepted no more commissions.

ULRICH PFISTERER

Biography

Born in Schindmühlen, Upper Palatinate, Germany, 1445/50. Presumably traveled in Swabia and Upper Rhineland; in Munich from at least 1475; became master, 1477; large workshop made him into a well-to-do citizen of the city; in later life much in demand as architect and hydraulic engineer; held guild office six times, 1480–1504; made designs for monastery of Mariaberg in Rorschach, Switzerland, 1487–*ca*. 1515; overseer of ducal saltworks at Reichenhall and Weyarn, from 1498; *capomaestro* (chief architect) from 1507, and for service there received from Duke Albert IV of Bavaria yearly salary of 80 gulden; served as adviser to city council for building of a bridge, 1501; *capomaestro* for Church of Our Beloved Lady in Schwaz, North Tirol, 1502–03; member of city's Outer Council, 1512–18; water engineer in Beuerberg (Eurasburg, Upper Bavaria) for Philip, Count Palatine of the Rhineland and Bishop of Freising, 1517. Died in Munich, Germany, between 8 April and 1 June 1518.

Selected Works

1470–73 *St. Mary* and *St. John the Evangelist*, for a *Crucifixion* group; wood; Church of St. Leonhard, Traidendorf, Germany

1477   Escutcheons (coats of arms) and images of the sun and moon, for ceiling of the Tanzsaal, Alte Rathaus, Munich, Germany; limewood; Stadtmuseum, Munich, Germany

1480   *Morris Dancers*, for the Tanzsaal, Alte Rathaus, Munich, Germany; limewood; Stadtmuseum, Munich, Germany

1482   Epitaph of Ulrich Aresinger; marble; Church of St. Peter, Munich, Germany

ca. 1482 Holy Cross altar; wood; Church of St. Maria, Ramersdorf, Germany

ca. 1485 Holy Spirit altar, for Cathedral of Salzburg, Austria; wood; Nonnberg Convent, Salzburg, Austria

1492   *Lamentation*; sandstone; Cathedral of Freising, Freising, Germany

1493–95 High altar (with Jan Polack), for the Church of St. Peter, Munich, Germany; wood (mostly destroyed); figure of St. Peter, *ca.* 1490: wood; *in situ*

1495–   Choir stalls; oak; Cathedral Church of Our
1502   Lady (Frauenkirche), Munich, Germany

late 15th *Burial of the Virgin*; polychromed and gilt
century wood; Fine Arts Museums of San Francisco, California, United States

1502–05 *Virgin and Child, St. Leonhard*, and *St. Eligius*; wood; high altar, Church of St. Leonhard, Reichersdorf, Germany

1503–06 Altar of St. Achatius; wood; Church of St. Leonhard, Reichersdorf, Germany

Further Reading

Baxandall, Michael, *The Limewood Sculptors of Renaissance Germany*, New Haven, Connecticut: Yale University Press, 1980

Frankl, Paul, "The Early Works of Erasmus Grasser," *Art Quarterly*, 5 (1942)

Halm, Philipp Maria, *Studien zur süddeutschen Plastik*, 3 vols., Augsburg, Germany: Filser, 1926–28; see especially vol. 3

Müller, Johanna, "Studien zum Frühwerk des Bildhauers Erasmus Grasser: Die Arbeiten für das Münchner Rathaus und Altarskulptur," (dissertation), University of Munich, 1970

Müller-Meiningen, Johanna, *Die Moriskentänzer und andere Arbeiten des Erasmus Grasser für das Alte Rathaus in München*, Munich: Schnell und Steiner, 1984

Otto, Kornelius, *Erasmus Grasser und der Meister des Blutenburger Apostelzyklus: Studien zur Münchner Plastik des späten 15. Jahrhunderts*, Munich: Kommissionsverlag UNI-Druck, 1988

Otto, Kornelius, "Das Chorgestühl der Frauenkirche im Wandel der Zeit," in *Monachium Sacrum: Festschrift zur 500-Jahr-Feier der Metropolitankirche zu Unserer Lieben Frau in München*, edited by Hans Ramisch and Georg Schwaiger, vol. 2, Munich: Deutscher Kunstverlag, 1994

Pinder, Wilhelm, *Die deutsche Plastik vom ausgehenden Mittelalter bis zum Ende der Renaissance*, vol. 2, Wildpark-Potsdam: Akademische Verlagsgesellschaft Athenaion, 1929

Ramisch, Hans, "Zur Münchner Plastik und Skulptur im späten Mittelalter," in *Münchner Gotik im Freisinger Diözesanmuseum*, edited by Peter Bernhard Steiner, Regensburg, Germany: Schnell und Steiner, 1999

Rohmeder, Jürgen, "Die Wirksamkeit Erasmus Grassers beim Bau von Mariaberg in Rorschach," in *Ulrich Rösch, St.*

Galler Fürstabt, und Landesherr, edited by Werner Vogler, St. Gall, Switzerland: Stiftsarchiv St. Gallen, 1987

GREAT ELEUSINIAN RELIEF

Anonymous

second half of 5th century BCE

marble

2.40 × 1.52 m; Demeter and Kore 1.98 m; boy

1.60 m

National Museum, Athens, Greece

The Great Eleusinian Relief was discovered in four fragments in 1859, approximately 100 meters east of the boundary of the ancient sanctuary at Eleusis. Found near the ruins of a 10th-century Byzantine church, the relief had been taken from its ancient context and reused in the church as a paving stone. It features on its front side three over-life-size figures in low relief, two women and a boy. The low relief would have been enhanced by paint, and certain details were added in metal, as small holes in the surface attest; for instance, a hole in the earlobe of the right figure was used for the insertion of an earring.

The relief should be dated with relative certainty to the last half of the 5th century BCE because of its technical and stylistic similarities to the dated Parthenon frieze. Furthermore, its three figures rely on body types of the middle to late 5th century BCE. The female figures loosely relate to two 5th-century-BCE statue types, the "Cherchel Demeter" and the "Kore Albani," which, clearly famous in Antiquity, are known to us from Roman period copies. The figure of the boy closely resembles a figure on a 5th-century-BCE grave stele from Thespiae. In addition, it was in this period that large reliefs (especially three-figured examples) re-emerged as a monument type in funerary and votive contexts.

There are at least four extant ancient copies of the relief (two in terracotta and two in marble), which implies that the relief remained a prominent monument throughout the Roman period. It may have served as a cult object or may have been a votive offering. The subject of the relief relates to a unique mystery cult, the Eleusinian Mysteries, famous above all others in Antiquity, but the precise subject and purpose of the relief remain open to interpretation. The cult of the Eleusinian Mysteries revolved around the story of Demeter, goddess of grain, and her daughter Kore, who was stolen by Pluto, god of the underworld. While searching for Kore, Demeter spent time in the guise of a nursemaid for the royal family at Eleusis. When the Eleusinians realized her identity, they dedicated a temple to her, and she, in return, taught their kings the mysteries that brought happiness in life after death.

The identity of the two female figures in the relief is clear. The figure to the viewer's left, holding a scepter, is the mistress of the sanctuary, Demeter. Her short hair, which may be interpreted as the hairstyle of a nursemaid or as an allusion to Demeter cutting her hair as a sign of mourning, confirms the identification. The other female figure is her daughter Kore, who is holding the torch that she used to light her way through the underworld. Such torches were used in the mysteries that were held at night.

Between Demeter and Kore is a boy who, facing Demeter, raises his left hand. He wears a mantle draped around his lower body and sandals of interlacing straps. His height—and possibly hairstyle since at least one scholar has argued that a hole in front of the head served for the attachment of a juvenile knot of hair over the brow—indicates that he is intended to be about 12 years old. The modern controversy over the meaning and function of the relief revolves around the identity of this boy.

Among the identities proposed for this figure are Triptolemos, the Eleusinian noble entrusted by Demeter to spread agricultural knowledge (see Schwarz, 1987); Ploutos, the child of Demeter, who symbolized prosper-

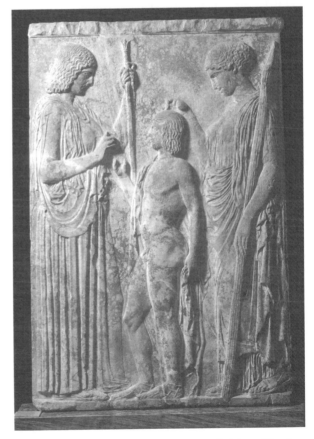

Demeter, Triptolemus, and Kore, votive relief from Eleusis
© Nimatallah / Art Resource, NY

ity and was bestowed on those favored by Demeter (see Clinton, 1994); "the child initiated from the hearth," a boy with priestly functions elected from the local aristocracy (attested by inscriptions as early as 460 BCE); Demophon, the royal child for whom Demeter was nursemaid (see Simon, 1998); and Eumolpos, the first Eleusinian to be initiated by Demeter into the mysteries and the namesake of the hierophants (the chief priests of the Eleusinian Mysteries) (see Harrison, 2000).

The most common interpretation is that the relief shows Demeter handing Triptolemos, crowned by Kore, stalks of grain. The theory is attractive for several reasons: Triptolemos had a shrine at Eleusis; Triptolemos' reception of the grain from Demeter is depicted in contemporary vase painting; and in another standard scene in vase painting Triptolemos appears between the two goddesses. This reading, however, has flaws. Triptolemos rarely (perhaps never) appears without an attribute, naked, or as a child. Also, the relief depicts no grain stalks nor features holes for their addition, and painted stalks would have looked peculiar in the three-dimensional palm of the boy.

Ploutos, who often appears as a boy and half naked, is another possibility. The scene would then be an iconic scene of three divinities. Yet Ploutos here would lack his usual cornucopia, and the action, a material exchange between Ploutos and Demeter, unattested elsewhere, would be without explanation.

The "child initiated from the hearth" interpretation is based on the boy's mortal aspect, especially his knotted hairstyle and shoes, and the appealing idea that the family of a chosen child might erect such a monument as a votive. Yet the hairstyle is a controversial conjecture, and more importantly, mortal initiates were usually depicted fully dressed, barefoot, and holding offerings.

The recent Demophon interpretation is based mainly on the controversial premise that Demeter appears as a nursemaid. This theory has been criticized, however, because the concept of Demeter as nursemaid has a greater connection to her role in women's celebrations than to her role in the Eleusinian Mysteries.

Eumolpos, the first initiate and mythical ancestor of the hierophants, may appear half-draped and beardless in other interpretations. According to this theory, Demeter is shown handing the boy, her protégé, a ribbon, while Kore crowns him with a wreath. The initiation of Eumolpos was a highly important mytho-historical event for all hierophants, who were deemed to be his descendants and might plausibly have been represented on a votive monument set up by such a hierophant. Unlike the boy in the relief, however, Eumolpos is generally shown slightly older and with a sceptor. Without certainty as to the boy's identity, there can be no unanimous scholarly opinion about the relief's message for the ancient viewer.

JULIA LENAGHAN

Further Reading

Beschi, Luigi, "Demeter," in *Lexicon Iconographicum Mythologiae Classicae*, vol. 4, Zurich: Artemis, 1988

Clinton, Kevin, *Myth and Cult: The Iconography of the Eleusinian Mysteries*, Stockholm: Svenska Institutet i Athen, 1992

Clinton, Kevin, "Ploutos," in *Lexicon Iconographicum Mythologiae Classicae*, vol. 7, Zurich: Artemis, 1994

Harrison, Evelyn B., "Eumolpos Arrives in Eleusis," *Hesperia* 69 (2000)

Metzger, Henri, "Le Triptolème du relief d'Eleusis," *Revue archèologique* (1968)

Peschlow-Bindokat, Annaliese, "Demeter und Persephone in der attischen Kunst des 6. bis 4. Jahrhundert," *Jahrbuch des Deutschen Archäologischen Instituts* 87 (1972)

Ridgway, Brunilde S., *Fifth-Century Styles in Greek Sculpture*, Princeton, New Jersey: Princeton University Press, 1981

Ross Holloway, R., "The Date of the Eleusis Relief," *American Journal of Archaeology* 62 (1958)

Ruhland, Max, *Die eleusinischen Göttinnen*, Strassburg: Trübner, 1901

Schneider, Lambert, "Das grosse eleusinische Relief und seine Kopien," *Antike Plastik* 12 (1973)

Schwarz, Gerda, *Triptolemos: Ikonographie einer Agrar- und Mysteriengottheit*, Horn, Austria: Berger, 1987

Simon, Erika, "Neues zum grossen Relief von Eleusis," *Archäologischer Anzeiger* (1998)

Svoronos, J.N., *Das Athener Nationalmuseum*, Athens: Beck und Barth, 1908

GREECE, ANCIENT

Greek sculpture lies at the very heart of Western art. Enshrined as an exemplary ideal by the Romans, it was, until the onset of large-scale discoveries in Greece itself beginning in the early 19th century, chiefly transmitted through the filter of Roman marble copies. Centered on the human figure, it provided the major source of inspiration for artists during the Renaissance (e.g. Michelangelo, Raphael) and Neoclassicism (e.g. Antonio Canova, Bertel Thorvaldsen). Only with a growing awareness of non-European sculptural traditions and the rise of abstract sculpture and its aftermath in the late 19th and early 20th centuries has Greek sculpture lost its force as a dominant point of reference for sculptural art in the West in general.

Greek sculpture was produced over almost a millennium in different media and for different contexts, at first firmly embedded in and influenced by the neighboring cultures of ancient Anatolia, the Near East, and Egypt, before evolving into a distinct form. During this long period it transformed dramatically, each phase providing styles that in their turn stimulated varied modern responses.

A very small section of what originally comprised the whole range of Greek sculpture has been preserved.

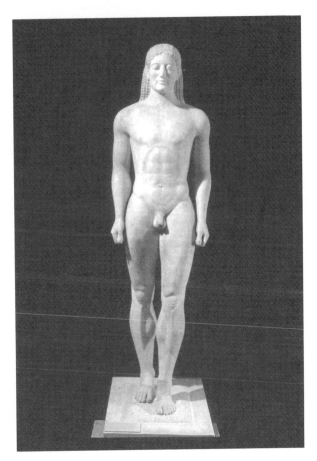

Archaic Greek Kouros figure (*ca.* 525 B.C.E.)
© Gianni Dagli Orti / CORBIS

Ancient literary sources can be used for only some of the evidence. Statues in precious metal or in perishable media such as wood and ivory have rarely survived; once ubiquitous monumental bronzes are lost but for a few dozen examples.

Greek marble sculpture almost throughout the entire history of its production was brightly painted; bronzes were highly polished and enriched with other materials and attributes. None of this is tangible in Roman copies or the casts that played such a major part in the formation of modern Neoclassical taste.

J.J. Winckelmann in the later 18th century pioneered a theoretical, art-historical approach tracing the history of Greek sculptural styles that, with modifications, still determines our understanding of Greek art. Although such a system may be useful to structure the material, the development of Greek sculpture was of course not the natural, predetermined and logical progression it may in retrospect appear to be but owed much to historical and political chance and circumstances and changes in the society it served.

Origins: Dark Ages and Geometric Period

The collapse of the palatial cultures of the Aegean Bronze Age about 1200–1100 BCE brought most sculptural traditions of that period to an end. Although individual monuments (for example, the famous Lion Gate at Mycenae) may have remained visible, the lack of centralized patronage meant that monumental stone sculpture ceased to be produced, and for several generations special skills such as bronze casting may have been lost altogether. Clay figurines of the period exist, with some, especially on Crete, betraying a certain limited continuation of earlier styles.

In the Geometric period (950–700 BCE), small-scale bronzes, terracottas, and, to some extent, ivories were produced in the rigid geometrical forms familiar from contemporary vase painting. A terracotta centaur from Lefkandi on Euboea (before *ca.* 900 BCE; Eretria Archeological Museum) provides a good example of the style. These statuettes (animals, especially horses, and various human figures) were predominantly used as votive offerings and originally often served as decoration of great bronze tripod cauldrons, the most prestigious type of dedication. The casting techniques used for these solid bronze figures had been reintroduced from the Near East. Many of them were found in the major Panhellenic sanctuaries, such as Delphi and Olympia, and distinct local styles can be discerned (e.g. Argive, Attic, Corinthian, Laconian). Human figures in the second half of the 8th century BCE covered a wide range, from individual warriors to small group compositions, such as Hercules and the centaur Nessos (Metropolitan Museum of Art, New York), or a hunter and his dog attacking a lion (Samos Archaeological Museum, Greece). Larger wooden cult images (*xoana*)

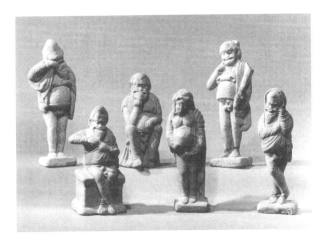

Statuettes (actors) from an Athenian grave, terracotta, probably 4th century BCE
© The Metropolitan Museum of Art, Rogers Fund, 1913

are likely to have existed but have not survived. A group of *sphyrelata* (figures with bronze sheets hammered over a wooden core) representing the gods Apollo, Artemis, and Leto at about half-life-size was found at Dreros on Crete (*ca.* 700 BCE; Heraklion Archaeological Museum, Greece).

This technique too was oriental, and the East provided the major source of inspiration during the following Daedalic period, named after the legendary Cretan sculptor Daidalos. The myth that statues created by Daidalos had to be chained to the ground in order to keep them from moving away, as if they were alive, conveys some sense of the strong impression these sculptures made at the time. Daedalic figures are strictly frontal with heavily stylized forms, flattened heads with triangular faces and prominent eyes, and coiffures horizontally layered in the Syrian and Egyptian fashion or in thick vertical locks. The increasing use of oriental creatures such as griffins, sirens, and lions also strongly shows Near Eastern influence.

Limestone figures from Crete are the first evidence for the revival of larger-scale stone sculpture. An inscribed bronze votive statue from Thebes known as Mantiklos Apollo (Museum of Fine Arts, Boston, Massachusetts, United States) from the first decades of the 7th century BCE shows the concept of orientalizing human figures before the full onset of Daedalic styles. Daedalic terracottas, often made from molds, were widespread. A limestone lintel from Prinias on Crete (Heraklion Archaeological Museum, Greece) from the second half of the 7th century BCE, with two seated female figures on a block decorated with animals on front and back and standing women underneath, and a relief from the Temple of Apollo at Gortyn showing the god striding between two naked goddesses (Heraklion Archaeological Museum, Greece) are among the first examples of reemerging architectural sculpture.

Archaic Period (700–500/480 BCE)

Increasing contact with Egypt and her monumental sculpture in the later 7th century BCE served as a powerful catalyst for the development of the genre in Greece, particularly for the two main formats used for the depiction of the Archaic human form, the kouros and kore types. The kouros was a statue of a young man in peak physical condition standing in a rigid frontal pose, usually nude, with the left leg advanced and the arms by his side. Considered a perfect embodiment of the aristocratic ideal of athletic male prowess and warriorlike virtue that permeated the strata of Greek society wealthy enough to commission sculpture, the format itself remained virtually unchanged throughout the Archaic period. This was helped by its versatile functions as cult image, votive offering, or grave statue, which could be specified through attributes or inscriptions. Kouroi range from statuette format to colossal (for example, the Isches Kouros from Samos [*ca.* 580 BCE], with an original height of *ca.* 4.75 meters); at times people dedicated votive kouroi as a tithe of booty or profit, which may partly explain the variation in size. In general, they were the chief means for the highly competitive aristocracy to express their social standing through sculpture.

Early kouroi seem to have rejected the apparent Egyptian naturalism in favor of strong pattern and ornament and a more theoretical concept of the body. Kouroi, perhaps first originating from Naxos and the neighboring islands, were soon produced in all parts of the Greek world, and distinct regional styles can be discerned. Naxian kouroi were lean and precise with clearly delineated yet stylized anatomy, while Samian examples, some of them colossal, are rounded with smooth transitions and softened anatomical details (the latter may in part be due to particular eastern Greek notions associating corpulence with wealth and high social standing). Attic kouroi appear angular and muscular. Sculptors migrated, however, and ideas traveled quickly. Given the rigidity of the general format, it seems that over time increasing naturalism provided the main means of artistic innovation, with a more realistic anatomy a by-product rather than a conscious aim.

Very early kouroi were still in the Daedalic style (e.g., a small bronze kouros from Delphi, *ca.* 650–625 BCE; Archaeological Museum, Delphi, Greece); the first monumental examples (for example, a kouros from Attica, *ca.* 600 BCE; Metropolitan Museum of Art, New York) seem to have adhered to the standard Egyptian canon of proportions, although sculptors soon dispensed with this. A more important deviation from Egyptian models was the general nudity of Greek kouroi, an outward sign of the ethical qualities associated with a well-trained, muscular male body that came to develop into a defining mark of Greek culture and its expressions in sculpture. A pair of Argive kouroi from Delphi known as Kleobis and Biton, but perhaps representing the Dioskouroi (Archaeological Museum, Delphi, Greece), provides a good example from the first quarter of the 6th century BCE.

The female equivalent of the kouros, the kore, accordingly reflected the norms of aristocratic women, with the statues in a similarly strict format, but richly draped and often adorned with jewelry. Early Daedalic examples from the second half of the 7th century BCE, such as the small kore from Auxerre (Musée du Louvre, Paris, France) and the planklike Nikandre statue from Delos (National Archaeological Museum, Athens, Greece) that to some extent seems reminiscent of wooden images, were soon supplemented by figures such as the recently discovered monumental kore from Santorini. A wooden statuette of a goddess from the Heraion on Samos, presumably Hera (Archaeological Museum, Samos, Greece), provides an exceptional glimpse of sculpture in this otherwise rarely preserved material, but marble now became the preferred medium.

The gradual evolution of stone temple architecture opened up another wide field for sculpture. Metopes, the square panels inserted between the beam heads of the roof, began to be carved in stone rather than being painted on terracotta panels (as had been those from the Temple of Apollo at Thermon, *ca.* 650–625 BCE). A limestone relief with a goddess in the Daedalic style from Mycenae (*ca.* 620 BCE) provides an early sculptured example, while later metopes from the Sikyonian Treasury in Delphi (*ca.* 560 BCE) and temples at Paestum and Selinus (*ca.* 530 BCE) are carved with mythological scenes in increasingly high relief. At the same time, the vast triangular space of the pediments of Doric temples was used to display sculpture. The earliest preserved large-scale example comes from the Temple of Artemis at Corfu (*ca.* 600 BCE), where a fearsome running Gorgon between two panthers in the center is flanked by much smaller mythological groups on either side. Not much later is a limestone pediment from the Athenian Acropolis, with two gigantic lions savaging bulls in the center, the first in a whole series of pediments from that sanctuary. Sculptors gradually adjusted their compositions to the given architectural space, replacing largely symbolic figures of apotropaic character with mythological narratives and over time achieving a unity of theme and scale.

The rapidly narrowing space of triangular pediments in particular required a process of gradual experimentation, resulting eventually in the use of standing, kneeling, and crouching figures that maintained a consistent scale and allowed for a less paratactic composition. A series of temples on the Athenian Acropolis, at Delphi, and on Aegina illustrate this development. Sculptured friezes decorated Ionic buildings. Many Greek poleis erected treasuries, richly adorned with sculpture, to house their votives in the major sanctuaries. The Siphnian Treasury at Delphi (*ca.* 525 BCE) showed a particularly rich display of sculpture and proved very influential through the dynamic narrative of its mythological friezes. Topics such as the fight between gods and giants on the north frieze symbolized the prevalence of the divine order over any challenge and became increasingly used as allegories for specific historic or political contexts.

Cult images, such as the statues of a standing Zeus and a seated Hera from the Temple of Hera at Olympia, are mainly known through literary sources; some very prestigious cult statues were *chryselephantine* (sculptures of wood, ivory, and gold that suggest drapery over flesh). Remains of smaller figures in this technique from the mid 6th century BCE were found at Delphi. A rare example possibly of a cult image was recently discovered *in situ* at Metropolis in Thessaly, where Apollo was represented as a bronze kouros in full armor.

Freestanding sculpture ranged widely in format. The so-called Geneleos group from Samos (*ca.* 560/50 BCE; Staatliche Museen, Berlin, Germany, and Archaeological Museum, Samos, Greece) comprises five members of a family as seated, reclining, or standing kouroi and korai. From about the same time is the Moschophoros from the Athenian Acropolis (Acropolis Museum, Athens, Greece) showing the dedicator [Rh]onbos carrying a calf on his shoulders for sacrifice. Equestrian statues were not uncommon; a fine example is the *Rampin Rider*, also from the Acropolis (Musée du Louvre, Paris, France, and Acropolis Museum, Athens, Greece). Seated statues are known from Didyma and other places. Animals (especially lions and dogs) were frequently depicted; the lion terrace at Delos from the early 6th century BCE still demonstrated a strong influence of Egyptian monuments.

Archaic grave stelae, especially from Attica, were usually tall and narrow with generic kouroslike figures of athletes, hunters, or warriors carved in profile in flat relief, often crowned by apotropaic creatures such as sphinxes. The representation of women in the grave setting was rare, underlining the dominant role of men in society.

Korai by the mid 6th century BCE had largely taken over the eastern Greek fashion of chiton and himation and became ever more refined in the splendor of their luxurious, brightly painted fabrics and rich jewelry. A whole series comes from the Athenian Acropolis. Kouroi, such as the kouros from Anavyssos in Attica, dedicated as a grave statue for a certain Kroisos about 530 BCE, had by then become highly naturalistic and began to look increasingly old-fashioned when compared with the powerful, dynamic poses and narrative of figures carved in relief (for example, the Ballplayer base from Athens, *ca.* 500 BCE; National Museum, Athens, Greece), in architectural sculpture (for example, the Temple of Apollo at Eretria, before 490 BCE), or depicted in contemporary vase painting. A figure such as the Aristodikos Kouros (*ca.* 500/490 BCE; National Museum, Athens, Greece), with its short hair, comparatively slim physique, and arms moving away from the body, reaches the very limits of the format that, as a status symbol of the wealthy elite, remained inherently conservative.

Archaic sculptors remain mostly anonymous, reflecting the relatively low status of their craft. Some names are known from literature, including legendary ones, while a few, such as Geneleos on Samos or Aristion from Paros, who sculpted a kouros and a kore discovered at Merenda in Attica (*ca.* 550; National Archaeological Museum, Athens, Greece), are known through signatures on their work.

Classical Period (500–300 BCE)

By the end of the 6th century BCE, kouroi had become so naturalistic that only the rigid conventions of the format linked them to their predecessors. A number of external factors combined with this internal evolution to serve as a catalyst for what in retrospect has been termed the Classical Revolution. Democratic rule, established at Athens in 510 BCE, introduced sumptuary laws aimed at the aristocratic class that had commissioned kouroi and korai in a funerary context. Athens, under great strain, repelled two Persian invasions, at Marathon in 490 BCE and Salamis ten years later, but the Persian sack of Athens in 480 BCE destroyed much of the extant old-style sculpture in the city. The first commission of the Athenian state after the Persian Wars was a bronze group of the *Tyrant Slayers Harmodios and Aristogeiton* by the sculptors Kritios and Nesiotes in 477/76 BCE, replacing an earlier group that had been carried off by the Persians. The new, early Classical style completely changed the concept of the human figure, being chiefly preoccupied with mobility and action and its expression in the body. The Kritios Boy (Acropolis Museum, Athens, Greece), one of the earliest examples of this new type of sculpture, illustrates this concern with ponderation, now clearly differentiating between a weight-bearing and a relaxed leg. His head is turned to the right and slightly inclined, breaking the strict frontality of Archaic kouroi.

A brightly painted group of Zeus abducting Ganymede from about 480/70 BCE and a slightly earlier head of Athena, both from Olympia (Archaeological Museum, Olympia, Greece), are two rare examples of the otherwise almost completely lost genre of monumental terracottas. Bronze soon became the preferred medium for statuary. The famous Delphi *Charioteer* and the Artemision bronze are important examples of early Classical originals in this material, of which almost nothing has survived.

Between 470 and 456 BCE, a monumental temple for Zeus was built at the important Panhellenic sanctuary of Olympia, one of the most impressive projects in the new style. The east pediment (showing the preparations for a mythical chariot race deciding the future of the sanctuary) and the metopes with the labors of Hercules introduce a radically different narrative, focusing on the moment just before or after the climax of the story told. The figures express a whole range of emotions from pain to anger and fear, and different ages are credibly depicted; hairstyles and dress are different from earlier types, with the thick, woolen Doric peplos on female statues replacing the refined fabrics worn by late Archaic korai. The telltale Archaic smile is replaced by a blank expression that has led to the period being called the Severe Style. Of the same period are the sculptured metopes from Temple E in Selinus (Sicily).

The island of Paros, an important source of high-quality marble, became a major sculptural center and together with other places in Ionia produced remarkable grave reliefs that were widely exported or imitated in other regions, such as Boeotia and Thessaly (e.g. stela with a girl holding doves, *ca.* 460 BCE; Metropolitan Museum of Art, New York).

Many early Classical artists (e.g. Pythagoras, Hageladas, Myron, and Kalamis) are known through later writers, chiefly Pliny the Elder and Pausanias, but their works are only preserved in Roman marbles attributed to them by modern scholars. The spectacular Riace bronzes, two over-life-size statues of Greek warrior heroes from a major dedication, provide a rare glimpse of what has been lost.

Athens itself, by now the head of a league increasingly resembling an empire, initiated under the leadership of Pericles a major building program of which the Parthenon (447–432 BCE) was the main component. Replacing an earlier building of similar but smaller layout, the Periclean Parthenon was designed to outshine any mainland temple in size and in the grandeur of its architecture and sculptural decoration. It has become a lasting icon of the High Classical style. Considerably enlarged to house one of the most famous statues in antiquity, Pheidias's colossal *chryselephantine* image of *Athena Parthenos*, almost every available surface was used to display sculpture praising Athena, Athens's patron goddess, and Attic heroes involved in mythological battles reflecting the triumph of the divine order over chaos and barbarian forces, a clear analogy of Athens's recent victory over its eastern enemies. Pheidias was most renowned for his statues of gods and was also commissioned with the equally colossal *chryselephantine* seated statue of Zeus at Olympia.

On the Peloponnese, Polykleitos of Argos formulated a radically new concept of the nude male form, discussed in a theoretical treatise and illustrated in a statue called the Kanon, probably identical with the so-called Doryphoros or Spear Bearer (*ca.* 440 BCE). Based on an abstract concept defining the human body through the precise mathematical relationship of its individual parts and carefully balanced proportions (*symmetria*), his figures show a fully developed *contrapposto*, (a natural pose with the weight of one leg, the shoulder, and hips counterbalancing one another) with the relaxed leg trailing behind.

Portrait sculpture began to play a more important role; notable are the likenesses of Pindar (*ca.* 440 BCE) and the posthumous portrait of Pericles by Kresilas (*ca.* 425 BCE; British Museum, London, England), but idealizing features still pervaded.

The Temple of Athena *Nike* and its splendid balustrade with its dazzling display of fluid drapery encapsulates the so-called Rich Style of the last quarter of the 5th century BCE. The same "wet" look characterizes the *Nike* of Paionios in Olympia (Archaeological Museum, Olympia, Greece) and the *Aphrodite* from Fréjus (Musée du Louvre, Paris, France).

In Attica the production of grave stelae resumed soon after the Parthenon was finished. The new type of reliefs tended to be wider than their Archaic predecessors, often with an additional architectural frame of a pediment with *akroteria* (crowning ornaments) supported by pillars. Women were depicted much more frequently; in general, the iconography was limited to a range of standard types acceptable for the democratic state, with the deceased and his or her relatives shown as exemplary citizens. Young men were shown as athletes or warriors (for example, grave stela of Dexileos, 394/393 BCE; National Museum, Athens, Greece), mature men as politically active members of the polis, and women in the domestic sphere. Visible links between the figures, such as a handshake (*dexiosis*), underline both the connection of polis and *oikos*, the public and domestic spheres, and the harmony within the family as its basic constituent unit. Multifigured stelae with extended family groups became increasingly popular during the late Classical period (4th century BCE).

After the end of the Peloponnesian War, sculptural production other than grave reliefs in Athens was limited. Foreign patrons began to play a prominent role. The Nereid Monument at Xanthos and hero shrines at Trysa and Limyra from the early 4th century BCE employed Greek iconography and craftsmen for the needs of local dynasts, a trend that culminated in the Mausoleum at Halikarnassos (*ca.* 360–350 BCE; much at the British Museum, London, England).

Praxiteles of Athens, son of the sculptor Kephisodotos whose group of *Eirene and Ploutos* (*ca.* 370 BCE) stood on the Athenian Agora, was one of the first sculptors to again prefer marble as his chief medium. He became particularly famous for creating the first full-scale female nude cult image, the *Aphrodite* of Knidos. Many other sculptors are known from literary sources (for example, Leochares, Naukydes, Skopas, and Timotheos), and scholars have tried to identify their work in Roman copies.

Lysippos of Sikyon is credited with changing the concept of the human form, as Polycleitus had done almost a century before, making more slender figures with longer legs and smaller heads. His famous *Apoxyomenos* (Scraper) replaces the High Classical Polycleitan *contrapposto* with a more tense and vigorous stance, strongly conveying the inherent sense of motion and mobility. Chosen by Alexander the Great for the creation of his portrait, Lysippos stands at the transition to the Hellenistic period. His battle and hunting groups, as well as his representations of allegorical figures such as *Kairos* (Right Moment), set precedents for much of later production, and his sons continued the workshop well into the 3rd century BCE.

Hellenistic Period (323–27 BCE)

The conquests of Alexander the Great opened a vast new field for Greek sculpture. Greek visual styles permeated sculpture from Sicily in the west to India in the east, although some areas saw a fusion between Greek and local traditions. After Alexander's untimely death in 323 BCE, his empire was divided among the successors, with three major (Antigonid Macedonia, Seleucid Syria, and Ptolemaic Egypt) and several smaller kingdoms and independent political units (including Bactria and Pergamon, and the Aitolian and Achaean Leagues) emerging after a prolonged power struggle. Whereas in the old centers Classical styles continued to be produced to some extent, the major new cities were characterized by a different, more cosmopolitan outlook, and kings replaced the old poleis as major patrons.

The Romans largely ignored Hellenistic sculpture (exemplified by Pliny the Elder's polemical statement that art died in 297 BCE and was reborn only in 156 BCE), but some of its major innovations were to have a lasting legacy in Western art. More than ever before, an array of sculptors ranging from mold makers producing terracotta figurines to highly skilled court artists served a vastly expanded market. A great variety of different styles developed for the various classes of product in a much expanded sculptural repertoire replaced the relative stylistic homogeneity of the Classical period.

Individualized portraiture became prominent. Portrait statues of kings were a chief means of communicating the new political ideas, and types pioneered for Alexander set the standard. The so-called Terme Ruler (Museo Nazionale Romano, Rome, Italy) provides a rare over-life-size bronze example for one of the main types, the nude ruler leaning on a spear, but cuirassed and equestrian statues were also common. At Athens the heads of the major philosophical schools received portraits in a variety of styles suited to their teachings, from the elegant, urbane Aristotle to the physically frail, ascetic Chrysippus. The polis honored city politicians and other important figures (e.g. the orator Demosthenes and the playwright Menander), and honorific statues for local benefactors became a staple product of many sculptural workshops. The main medium for these statues was bronze, but whereas the famous leaders and intellectual heroes are preserved chiefly in Roman marble copies, the few originals tend to be of now anonymous local notables.

The various royal courts attracted sculptors for major projects, but the mobility of the artists means that regional styles are generally much harder to distinguish than in the earlier periods. Large victory monuments illustrated royal prestige in a world that over a long period was characterized by military conflict between the main powers. The *Nike* of Samothrace (*ca.* 190 BCE; Musée du Louvre, Paris, France) may commemorate a Rhodian naval victory, while the gigantomachy of the Great Frieze of the Pergamon Altar (*ca.* 170 BCE; Pergamonmuseum, Berlin, Germany) reflects the defeat of Gaulish tribes. Earlier groups of dying Gauls (e.g. the Ludovisi group of *Gaul Killing His Wife* [Museo Nazionale Romano, Rome, Italy] and *Dying Gaul* [Capitoline Museum, Rome, Italy]) belong to a similar context. Sculptors developed a new "baroque" sculptural language for these monuments, with swelling forms, heavily muscled bodies, and ample use of expressive formulae, such as wide-open eyes and mouths. Some of the most famous sculptures from antiquity reflect this style, such as the Belvedere Torso and the *Laocoön* (Vatican Museums, Rome, Italy), a masterful marble translation of a Hellenistic bronze original. Roman variants preserve a small selection of other heroic, mythological groups. The Pasquino Group (Menelaos recovering the body of Patroklos), the Achilles-Penthesilea Group (Achilles with the body of the Amazon Queen), and the Marsyas Group (a hanging Marsyas about to be skinned by a Scythian) all survive in several copies. Excellent imperial marble versions of such groups illustrating episodes from the Trojan War and the *Odyssey* have survived in their Roman setting at Sperlonga in Italy.

A parallel phenomenon, perhaps originating from Alexandria, was the development of genre realism. The urbane upper classes delighted in artful depictions of low-life characters to decorate their parks and gardens. Sculptors portrayed fishermen, peasants, and drunken old women in their decrepit physical state with shocking realism, providing an admirable contrast between the sorry condition of their subjects and its skillful representation in often precious materials. The world

of Dionysos in general provided a powerful outlet for society's fears and anxieties, and statues of satyrs and nymphs, centaurs, hermaphrodites, and the like were ubiquitous.

Statues of athletes continued to be in great demand. Sculptors continued to produce figures in the style of Lysippos' *Apoxyomenos*, but stockier body types were also common. The *Scraper* from Ephesos (Kunsthistorisches Museum, Vienna, Austria) is a bronze copy after such an original of the late fourth or early 3rd century BCE. Wrestling groups were among the innovations in this field. The *Terme Boxer* (Museo Nazionale Romano, Rome, Italy) reflects strong genre realism; the figure's powerfully built, heavily muscled body shows all the cuts and bruises of a professional athlete.

Representations of gods could still be made in Classical styles, soon enriched by baroque elements and expressive formulae (e.g. *Zeus* from Otricoli, Vatican Museums, Rome, Italy). The image of Dionysos, together with Apollo one of the most favored deities of the period, underwent a radical transformation, shedding his beard and taking on a soft, effeminate air. Local divinities, often coupled with their Greek counterparts, received images, and new cults were created. A cult statue for Serapis by Bryaxis in Alexandria was frequently copied as his cult spread rapidly to other regions. Statues of goddesses and women are less clearly differentiated. The Hellenistic image of Aphrodite continued to modulate the theme set by Praxiteles' nude *Aphrodite* of Knidos. The *Crouching Aphrodite* (Museo Nazionale Romano, Rome, Italy) added a new motive, while the famous *Aphrodite* from Melos (Venus de Milo, Musée du Louvre, Paris, France) is a variation of a 4th-century type. The Large and Small Herculaneum Goddesses (*ca.* 300 BCE), probably Demeter and Kore, later became popular types for female portrait statues. New types were created, such as the *Tyche* of Antioch by Eutychides.

Architectural sculpture in the Hellenistic period was less prominent than in the Classical period, while format and subject matter largely followed the earlier precedents. The 3rd-century BCE Belevi tomb, for example, was strongly influenced by the Mausoleum at Halikarnassos, while the 2nd-century temple friezes from Magnesia and Lagina show familiar battles of Greeks versus amazons and centaurs. The Pergamon Altar set new standards for relief sculpture, both with the powerful Gigantomachy and with the interior Telephos frieze, which represents a highly complex continuous narrative.

Votive reliefs display a strong continuity of Classical styles; among the spectacular exceptions is a relief by Archelaos of Priene of the later third or early 2nd century BCE (British Museum, London, England), showing Homer being crowned by King Ptolemy IV and his wife, a reflection of the intellectual milieu at the Alexandrian court.

At Athens, grave monuments had become lavish and grand (e.g. the Kallithea tomb, Archaeological Museum, Piraeus, Greece) by the end of the 4th century, until funerary legislation by Demetrius of Phaleron in 317 BCE put an end to this development. A new type of stela emerged in the 3rd century BCE in the east, smaller and usually carved in one piece with an architectural frame and with the figures occupying a smaller proportion of the relief than on Classical stelae. The deceased are shown as public figures, sometimes heroized, and a distinct type, showing the funerary banquet, continued to be widely popular. The Alexander sarcophagus (*ca.* 300 BCE; Archaeological Museum, Istanbul, Turkey), with its depiction of historical battles and hunts, stands out as an iconographic exception for a foreign ruler.

For certain categories of sculpture, Classical styles always remained in use. Athens in particular, where the sons of Praxiteles were active during the 3rd century BCE, is notable for the continuation of Classical styles and their imitation in truly Neoclassical workshops. A statue of Athena at Elateia by Polykles from the 3rd century BCE held a copy of the shield of the famous *Athena Parthenos* by Pheidias; another free copy of the *Athena Parthenos* was commissioned for the library at Pergamon in the early 2nd century BCE (Pergamonmuseum, Berlin, Germany). Greek, especially Athenian, sculptors increasingly established workshops in Italy to produce statuary in this neo-Attic style for the Roman market. With the major wars of the 2nd century BCE, Rome had become a dominant force in the east and successively took over the Hellenistic kingdoms. The island of Delos, seat of a strong Roman merchant community, provides examples for new sculptural modes, using, for example, highly developed, individualizing Hellenistic portrait styles to cater to the traditional Roman demand for highly specific likenesses. For the remainder of the Hellenistic period, Greek sculptural styles became a universally accepted visual language, and throughout the Roman Empire many genres continued to be produced in formats pioneered in this era, even after the formal end of the Hellenistic age with the fall of the last independent kingdom to Rome in 27 BCE.

THORSTEN OPPER

See also **Apollo Belvedere; Artemision Zeus (Poseidon); Belvedere Torso; Canova, Antonio; Charioteer from the Sanctuary of Apollo at Delphi; Chryselephantine Sculpture; Kore and Kouros; Kritios Boy; Laocoön and His Sons; Lysippos; Parthenon; Pergamon Altar; Pheidias; Polykleitos; Praxiteles; Riace Bronzes; Sarcophagus; Skopas; Stela**

Further Reading

Boardman, John, *Greek Sculpture: The Archaic Period: A Handbook*, London: Thames and Hudson, and New York: Oxford University Press, 1978

Boardman, John, *Greek Sculpture: The Classical Period*, London and New York: Thames and Hudson, 1985

Boardman, John, *Greek Sculpture: The Late Classical Period and Sculpture in Colonies and Overseas*, New York: Thames and Hudson, 1995

Floren, Joseph, *Die griechische Plastik*, vol. 1, *Die geometrische und archaische Plastik*, Munich: Beck, 1987

Pollitt, J.J., *Art and Experience in Classical Greece*, Cambridge: Cambridge University Press, 1972

Pollitt, J.J., *The Ancient View of Greek Art: Criticism, History, and Terminology*, New Haven, Connecticut: Yale University Press, 1974

Pollitt, J.J., *Art in the Hellenistic Age*, New York: Cambridge University Press, 1986

Richter, Gisela M.A., *The Portraits of the Greeks*, 3 vols., London: Phaidon, 1965

Richter, Gisela M.A., *Korai: Archaic Greek Maidens*, London and New York: Phaidon, 1968

Richter, Gisela M.A., and Irma Anne Richter, *Kouroi: A Study of the Development of the Greek Kouros from the Late Seventh to the Early Fifth Century B.C.*, New York: Oxford University Press, 1942; 3rd edition, as *Kouroi: Archaic Greek Youths*, London and New York: Phaidon, 1970

Ridgway, Brunilde Sismondo, *The Severe Style in Greek Sculpture*, Princeton, New Jersey: Princeton University Press, 1970

Ridgway, Brunilde Sismondo, *The Archaic Style in Greek Sculpture*, Princeton, New Jersey: Princeton University Press, 1977

Ridgway, Brunilde Sismondo, *Fifth-Century Styles in Greek Sculpture*, Princeton, New Jersey: Princeton University Press, 1981

Ridgway, Brunilde Sismondo, *Hellenistic Sculpture*, Madison: University of Wisconsin Press, and Bristol, Avon: Bristol Classical Press, 1990–2002

Ridgway, Brunilde Sismondo, *Fourth-Century Styles in Greek Sculpture*, Madison: University of Wisconsin Press, 1997

Robertson, Martin, *A History of Greek Art*, London: Cambridge University Press, 1975

Rolley, Claude, *La sculpture grècque*, vol. 1, *Des origines au milieu du Ve siècle*, Paris: Picard, 1994

Rolley, Claude, *La sculpture grècque*, vol. 2, *La période classique*, Paris: Picard, 1999

Smith, R.R.R., *Hellenistic Sculpture: A Handbook*, New York: Thames and Hudson, 1991

Stewart, Andrew F., *Greek Sculpture: An Exploration*, New Haven, Connecticut: Yale University Press, 1990

HORATIO GREENOUGH 1805–1852

United States

Born in Boston in 1805, Horatio Greenough followed in the footsteps of the great number of European sculptors who had looked to Italy for inspiration, training, and commissions; among American sculptors, however, he was one of the first to study abroad. Although he is usually regarded as the first American sculptor to receive international recognition, he is as well known for his writings on sculpture and architecture and particularly for his views on functionalism.

In his teens Greenough had made copies of casts in the Boston Athenaeum; he learned clay modeling from Solomon Willard and stonecutting from Alpheus Cary. He also made several visits to the studio of the French sculptor John Binon, who was then working in Boston. At his father's insistence Greenough attended Harvard, where his curriculum included German and Italian; he also studied anatomy with the help of Dr. George Parkman. It was his friendship with the painter Washington Allston, however, that proved most instrumental in determining Greenough's future. With Allston's encouragement Greenough continued his study of art and became a member of a circle of students who frequented the painter's studio.

In 1824, again at Allston's urging, Greenough sailed for Italy, which would become his home for most of his remaining years. In Rome, Greenough shared an apartment with the American painter Robert Weir and studied as a provisional apprentice with the Danish sculptor Bertel Thorvaldsen. He also took advantage of the opportunities to draw from life at the French Academy and to model from Rome's many antique works.

After two years in Italy, and partly owing to illness, Greenough returned with Weir to Boston. Greenough arrived in good health and soon began accepting several commissions for portrait busts. During this time he was also elected an honorary member of the National Academy of Design in New York City. Fully recovered and in much greater demand, Greenough set sail for Italy again in 1828. This time he settled in Florence, near the source of his marble at Carrara. Although Greenough had executed portrait busts of several prominent patrons, it was in Florence that he received his first important commission for a mythological subject when in 1830 the American writer James Fenimore Cooper asked him to sculpt *The Chanting Cherubs*. When the work, based on two small angels by Raphael, was sent to the United States, it was criticized by what Greenough considered to be an unsophisticated public who was offended by the cherubs' nudity.

At the recommendation of Cooper and Allston, the U.S. government in 1832 awarded Greenough the first commission it had ever granted for a monumental sculpture. The work, a statue of *George Washington*, was meant to stand in the rotunda of the U.S. Capitol building. As stipulated in the commission, Greenough relied on the bust of *Washington* by the Frenchman Jean-Antoine Houdon in imaging the head. Unlike Houdon, however, who in both the bust and his full-length statue of Washington had depicted the leader

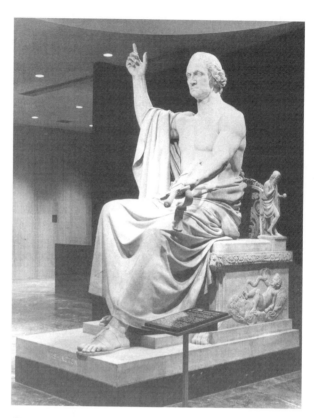

George Washington
© Smithsonian American Art Museum, Washington, D.C. / Art Resource, NY

in military dress, Greenough based his statue at least in part on Antoine-Chrysostome Quatremère de Quincy's 19th-century reconstruction of Pheideas' colossal 5th-century BCE ivory-and-gold statue of Zeus. Greenough's *Washington* is seated with a sheathed sword in his right hand, with his left arm raised in a gesture of address. That the figure was presented as nude from the waist up, however, proved to be its most crucial attribute. Greenough was interested in evoking virtue and nobility rather than portraying any single aspect of Washington's life as a statesman or military leader. Years later in 1853 Henry T. Tuckerman would argue that such a statue of Washington demanded the use of the nude as the most pure form of artistic expression. For Tuckerman and Greenough, the statue of such a man should represent the uncorrupted creation of God, not the holder of a temporary earthly office. Only then could it represent a complete image of the man.

Most Americans, however, lacked the other worldly views of Greenough and Tuckerman. Cooper, as well as other friends, had cautioned against the nude depiction, and Greenough's previous experience with *The Chanting Cherubs* should also have served as a warning. But the sculptor refused to bend to the wishes of an uneducated public, and when the colossal 20-ton statue arrived in the United States in 1841, it immediately provoked controversy and derision. Not only was the public largely offended by its nudity, Greenough himself was disappointed with the sculpture's placement in the rotunda. Poor lighting and an inappropriate pedestal prompted him to insist in 1843 that the statue be moved to another location on the Capitol grounds. It remained on the grounds until 1908 when it was moved to the Smithsonian Institution.

Despite the amount of time Greenough necessarily devoted to the *Washington*, his career continued to flourish throughout the 1830s. Late in the decade he sculpted his *Venus Victrix* which, as the first female nude sculpted by an American, would have a profound effect on the work of future sculptors, particularly that of Hiram Powers. Inspired by the works of the Englishman John Flaxman, Greenough also began executing bas-reliefs at this time. An appreciation of Flaxman's reliefs was likely instrumental in Greenough's decision to include reliefs on the base of his *Washington*.

By 1843 Greenough was back in Florence and occupied with the completion of *The Rescue*, a second government commission and one that he had received before the delivery of his *Washington*. *The Rescue* was part of a sculptural group intended for the east steps of the Capitol. It depicts a frontiersman in combat with a Native American who is threatening a white mother and her children. Despite its blatant portrayal of the subjugation of Native Americans, the sculpture was greeted much more warmly than his *Washington* had been. Greenough returned to live in the United States in 1851 and was possibly suffering from manic depression. Sadly, he succumbed to a fever and died in 1852 before *The Rescue* was installed.

JEFFREY D. HAMILTON

Biography

Born in Boston, Massachusetts, 6 September 1805. Learned sculpting from Solomon Willard and Alpheus Cary; studied with French sculptor, J.B. Binon, in Boston; enrolled at Harvard, 1821; traveled to Italy; arrived in Rome, 1825; studied with Bertel Thorvaldsen; became ill and returned to United States, 1826; received several commissions for portrait busts from prominent Americans, including President John Quincy Adams; settled in Florence, 1828; studied with Lorenzo Bartolini; elected Professor of Sculpture, Accademia di Belle Arti, Florence, 1840; career faltered during 1840s due to negative criticism of nude *George Washington*; returned to live in United States, 1851. Died in Somerville, Massachusetts, 18 December 1852.

Selected Works

1828   *John Quincy Adams*; marble; Library of the Boston Athenaeum, Boston, Massachusetts, United States

1828   *The Chanting Cherubs*; marble (lost)

1832   *George Washington*; marble; The Andalusia Foundation, Andalusia, Pennsylvania, United States

1832–40 *George Washington*; marble; National Museum of American History, Smithsonian Institute, Washington, D.C., United States

1833   *Child and Angel*; marble; Museum of Fine Arts, Boston, Massachusetts, United States

1837   *The Rescue*; marble (dropped, broken into pieces in 1976); government storage facility, Suitland, Maryland, United States

ca. 1847 *Castor and Pollux*; marble; Museum of Fine Arts, Boston, Massachusetts, United States

Further Reading

Crane, Sylvia, *White Silence: Greenough, Powers, and Crawford, American Sculptors in Nineteenth-Century Italy*, Coral Gables, Florida: University of Miami Press, 1972

Craven, Wayne, *Sculpture in America*, New York: Crowell, 1968

Gerdts, William H., *American Neo-Classic Sculpture: The Marble Resurrection*, New York: Viking Press, 1973

Greenough, Horatio, *Form and Function: Remarks on Art, Design, and Architecture*, edited by Harold A. Small, Berkeley: University of California Press, 1947 (contains his most significant writings on art and architecture)

Greenough, Horatio, *Letters of Horatio Greenough, American Sculptor*, edited by Nathalia Wright, Madison: University of Wisconsin Press, 1972

Greenough, Horatio, *Letters of Horatio Greenough to His Brother, Henry Greenough*, edited by Francis Boitt Greenough, Boston: Ticknor, 1887; reprint, New York: AMS Press, 1973

Greenthal, Kathryn, Paula M. Kozol, and Jan Seidler Ramirez (editors), *American Figurative Sculpture in the Museum of Fine Arts, Boston*, Boston: Museum of Fine Arts, 1986

Headley, Janet A., "Horatio Greenough's Heroic Subjects: *Abdiel* and *David*," *Yale University Art Gallery Bulletin* (1991)

Headley, Janet A., " 'Something of My Own Invention': Horatio Greenhough, Sir Joshua Reynolds, and Sculptural Originality," *Sculpture Journal* 4 (2000)

Metzger, Charles R., *Emerson and Greenough: Transcendental Pioneers of an American Esthetic*, Berkeley: University of California Press, 1954

Saunders, Richard H., *Horatio Greenough: An American Sculptor's Drawings*, Middlebury, Vermont: Middlebury College Museum of Art, 1999

Tuckerman, Henry Theodore, *A Memorial of Horatio Greenough: Consisting of a Memoir, Selections from His Writings and Tributes to His Genius*, New York: Putnam, 1853; reprint, New York: Blom, 1968

Wright, Nathalia, *Horatio Greenough: The First American Sculptor*, Philadelphia: University of Pennsylvania Press, 1963

GERHARD GRÖNINGER 1582–1652

German

Gerhard Gröninger was among the most prominent German sculptors of his time. He came from a family of sculptors from Münster and Paderborn that was active between the 16th and 18th centuries. A younger and an older branch of this family existed, although the familial relationship has not been clearly determined. Although they did not reach the level of his importance, three other members of his family were active as artists at the same time as Gerhard: Heinrich, active almost exclusively in Paderborn, and Gerhard's brother and master; Johann Mauritz, court sculptor for the prince bishop of Münster, Gerhard's cousin; and Johann Wilhelm, Johann Mauritz's son.

Presumably born in 1582 in Paderborn, Westphalia, Gerhard Gröninger became an apprentice of his older brother Heinrich after his presumed schooling with the Jesuits from 1599 to 1603. After traveling between 1604 and 1607, Gerhard seems to have gone to the Netherlands, most likely Antwerp, as evidenced in the influence of Dutch Mannerism in his later works. In 1609 he became a citizen of the city of Münster and entered the workshop of the sculptor Hans Lacke, whose daughter he married in 1610. After the death of his father-in-law, Gerhard took over his workshop in 1620 and also followed him in assuming the office of guild master. Due to heavy debts and his subsequent bankruptcy, the artist, who is characterized in the archives as being highly combative and reckless, had to leave Münster in 1639. After many letters of request, he was granted the possibility of returning to the city of Münster in 1647. He was fully restored to his offices by the time he died in 1652.

Gerhard was active almost exclusively for the churches in the bishopric of Münster. In Antwerp, probably schooled in southern Dutch Mannerism, he made the transition to an independent early Baroque style with his characteristic mixture of fantastic and natural forms. His preferred materials were marble, alabaster, Baumberg sandstone (the use of which was especially common in the areas around Münster), and rare woods that were usually polychromed in a coarsely naturalistic way.

No work has been preserved or archivally recorded from the early years of Gerhard's artistic development, nor can anything definitive be said about his level of participation in the works of his brother Heinrich in Paderborn. The records indicate that Gerhard was independent between 1609 and 1620 but that he was also working with his father-in-law in the latter's workshop, making his early style difficult to determine. The epitaph for the Canon Wennemar von Aschebrock, which was erected in 1609 in the Cathedral of Münster, seems to be the first monumental work from Gerhard's own hands. The relationship of architecture, figural sculpture, and ornamental sculpture here demonstrates an expansion of plastic forms that seem to be trying to cover up the architecture completely and to intensify the ornamentation's three-dimensionality. Scholars consider the epitaph for Canon Bernhard von Westerholt (also in the Cathedral of Münster), created about the same time, to be Gerhard's work in its essential features.

Gerhard began his career as an architect in 1612 with the construction of the moated castle at Darfeld, whose gallery is adorned by rich and extremely fine paneling considered to be one of the most remarkable pieces of architecture by a sculptor in the early 17th century in northern Germany. It marks an exciting border area between sculpture and architecture in Gerhard's work.

Sculpture continued to be the main focus of Gerhard's activity. In 1613 he created and dated the statue of *St. Mauritius* for the Cathedral of Münster, one the most beautiful sculptural works of the early Baroque in Westphalia. He followed it with further epitaphs and individual figures. In 1619 he began planning a new high altar for the Cathedral of Münster, for which he sought in vain to persuade Peter Paul Rubens to create the paintings for the side panels. In addition to the sculpted parts of the surmount, Gerhard himself produced two monumental wooden reliefs depicting the *Overthrow of Saul before Damascus* and the *Beheading of the Apostle Paul before the Walls of Rome*; here, he no longer assigned meanings in his work according to medieval custom but achieved a highly expressive perspectival arrangement of figures. Gerhard's high altar of the Church of St. John in Münster (1622), from which two wooden reliefs are still in the bishopric's possession, shows similar characteristics.

After the epitaph altar for the abbess Ottilie von Fürstenberg in the former Premonstratensian Church of St. Peter in Oelinghausen, a tripartite work made of alabaster, sandstone, and multicolored marble, and the altar for the Catholic church of St. John the Baptist in Altenberge, which bears the artist's most mature relief style, Gerhard's art reached its apex in 1625 with the monument to Heidenreich, dean of the Cathedral of Letmathe (completed around 1630). This approximately seven-meter-high work in five sections, meant to be a commemoration of the cleric and to valorize the martyrdom of St. Stephen, fits so precisely into its niche that it seems to have no effect on the surrounding architecture. The work exhibits Gerhard's mastery of the formal vocabulary of his time as well as his extraordinary ability to translate the ethos and the pathos of the depicted sentiments into expressive gestures. It signals a high point in the sculptor's work not only in formal terms but also in terms of the theological treatment of images.

About the same time, Gerhard created other tombs in the Überwasserkirche in Münster. The epitaph here for Bernhard Hausmann and Elisabeth Wetteler is typical of Gerhard, documenting quite well his particular method that employed certain compositions or architectonic structures repeatedly in only slightly varied form. As always, however, his compositions optimally suit the given architectonic space of the surrounding church, so that all the proportions of the compositions or details being reused are correspondingly adjusted. On commission from the Canon Rembert von Ketteler, Gerhard created in 1627 two life-size statues of *St. Peter* and the *Emperor Charlemagne*, which also count among his most important works. They were erected in the galilee of the Cathedral of Münster, whose iconography they complement perfectly.

Gerhard produced only a few significant works in the last decade of his life. The sculptural tradition of Westphalia would not again be revived until his grandchildren's generation, led by Johann Mauritz Gröninger, at the end of the 17th century.

STEPHAN BRAKENSIEK

Biography

Born probably in Paderborn, Westphalia (now in Germany), 1582. Apprenticed to his older brother, Heinrich Gröninger, a sculptor active in Paderborn; traveled abroad, 1604–07; became a citizen of the city of Münster (now in Germany) and entered the workshop of the sculptor Hans Lacke, 1609; married Lacke's daughter, 1610; took charge of Lacke's workshop on his death, 1620; forced by bankruptcy to leave Münster, 1639; permitted to return, 1647; worked almost exclusively for churches in the Münster area. Died probably in Münster, 1652.

Selected Works

1609   Epitaph for Canon Wennemar von Aschebrock; sandstone; Cathedral of Münster, Münster, Germany

1612–16 Relief and sculptural decoration; sandstone; Wasserschloss, Darfeld, Germany

1613   *St. Mauritius*; sandstone; Cathedral of Münster, Münster, Germany

1619   Reliefs of *Overthrow of Saul before Damascus* and the *Beheading of the Apostle Paul before the Walls of Rome*; limewood; Cathedral of Münster, Münster, Germany

1622   Epitaph altar for Abbess Ottilie von Fürstenberg; alabaster, sandstone, multicolored marble; former Premonstratensian Church of St. Peter, Oelinghausen, Germany

1625   Altar; sandstone parish church of St. John the Baptist, Altenberge, Germany

1625   Rummel Epitaph; sandstone; Überwasserkirche, Münster, Germany

1625–30 Stephanus Altar (monument to Heidenreich von Lethmathe); sandstone; Cathedral of Münster, Münster, Germany

1627   Statues of *St. Peter* and *Emperor Charlemagne*; sandstone; Cathedral of Münster, Münster, Germany

Further Reading

Jászai, Géza, *Das Werk des Bildhauers Gerhard Gröninger, 1582–1652*, Münster, Germany: Landschaftsverband Westfalen-Lippe, 1989

Koch, Ferdinand, *Die Gröninger: Ein Beitrag zur Geschichte der Westfälischen Plastik in der Zeit der Spätrenaissance und des Barock*, Münster, Germany: Coppenrath, 1905

Landwehr, Claudia, *Die Bildhauerfamilie Gröninger*, Münster, Germany: Landesbildstelle Westfalen, 1995

Rasmussen, Jörg, *Barockplastik in Norddeutschland*, Mainz, Germany: Von Zabern, 1977

Rickmann, Herbert, "Beiträge zu den Werken des Bildhauers Gerhard Gröninger: Das Architektonische in seinen Altären und Epitaphien und die Benutzung von Vorlagen für figürliche Szenen" (dissertation), Universität Münster, 1963

Stiegemann, Christoph, *Heinrich Gröninger um 1578–1631: Ein Beitrag zur Skulptur zwischen Spätgotik und Barock im Fürstbistum Paderborn*, Paderborn, Germany: Bonifatius Druck-Buch-Verlag, 1989

JOHANN MEINRAD GUGGENBICHLER 1649–1723 *Swiss, active in Austria*

Johann Meinrad Guggenbichler was one of the most gifted and celebrated Baroque sculptors in the Alps area in Upper Austria and Salzburg. His workshop primarily undertook ecclesiastical commissions creating life-size or over-life-size polychromed, gilded wood statues and altars.

Guggenbichler learned the craft from his father, Georg, who had worked for the Benedictine Abbey in Einsiedeln as a sculptor and master builder. Guggenbichler also may have studied in northern Italy. He was already carving foliage ornaments as an assistant woodcarver in the Abbey of St. Florian (near Linz, Upper Austria) in 1670. He must have become acquainted with the wood sculpture tradition of the Innviertel and Salzburg area, mainly the works of Jakob Gerholt, whose art had greatly influenced his early works, such as the high altar of Strasswalchen.

Guggenbichler eventually settled in Mondsee (near Salzburg, Upper Austria) in 1679, where he lived for 44 years. He worked primarily for the Mondsee Benedictine Abbey and on other commissions from the area. He created the following altars for the Mondsee Abbey church: the Holy Ghost, St. Wolfgang, *Speisealtar* (Corpus Christi altar), Poor Souls, and Plague (which was demolished). These carved wooden altars featured polychromed, gilded wood statues placed around a painting. The statues owe a stylistic debt to the area's leading sculptor, Thomas Schwanthaler, but Guggenbichler's own distinct style was already emerging. Following Renaissance tradition, he knew human anatomy intimately, showed facial expressions and movements replete with emotion, and carved the naturally placed draperies in a highly detailed way, as evidenced by the figure of St. Sebastian from the Mondsee Plague altar. Guggenbichler depicted his main figures in characteristic contraposition: turning to face one another almost as if engaged in a conversation, as seen in the figures of St. Benedict and St. Bernhard in the Mondsee Holy Ghost altar, St. Martin and St. Virgil in the Irrsdorf pilgrimage church's high altar (1682–84), and St. Rupert and St. Ulrich from the high altar of the Michaelbeuren (Salzburg) Benedictine Abbey Church (1690–91).

Beyond the sculptural works, Guggenbichler likely designed the entire high altar in Michaelbeuren. He placed his gilded statues of the bishop saints on a silver cloud as if they were floating. The large statues were situated among the gilded, laurel-encased pillars in the black altar construction. Through the window behind the altar, a beam of light among the pillars and ornaments highlighted the vision of floating figures and the heavy gilding. Statues of Benedictine saints Benedict and Scolastica with angels decorated the upper part of the altar. Johann Michael Rottmayr's 1691 painting *Christ's Resurrection* graced its center, while his *St. Michael* was presented just above. In this context, Guggenbichler and Rottmayr created a harmony of the architectural, sculptural, painted, and ornamental details.

Guggenbichler received commissions from a number of churches after the success of his altars in Mondsee and Michaelbeuren. Compared with his earlier sentimental style, his art became more dramatic and pathetic, which probably reflected the needs of his patrons and Late Gothic tradition. Also according to Late Gothic trends, winged altars replaced painting, and a statue or statue group was placed at the center of the altar, such as the figure of St. Lawrence in the

high altar (1699) of the parish church in Abtsdorf, the *Stoning of St. Stephen* group (1699–1701) in the high altar of the parish church in Schleedorf, the *Martyrdom of St. Kilian* group (1708) in the high altar of the parish church in Oberwang, and the *Coronation of the Virgin Mary* group (1709) in the high altar of the parish church in Lochen.

Guggenbichler also created a sequence of outstanding statues for the pilgrimage Church of St. Wolfgang in 1706. Here he was greatly influenced by the fine altars of Michael Pacher and Schwanthaler. He aimed primarily to represent emotions, especially pathos, with mimicry and gestures. The drama and physical and spiritual pain in his statue *Ecce homo* shows that he followed the Flemish and Spanish patterns, with which he probably became acquainted through graphics and small statues. A vital structural change took place with his Altarpiece of St. Anthony, Altarpiece of the Cross, and Altarpiece of the Rosary in St. Wolfgang. The figures were placed as freestanding statues to the sides of the painting and without architectural items in front of the altar.

The representation of emotions and mythical moods remained an important element in Guggenbichler's late works. His figures became slimmer, and their movements were more reserved and suggestive. In his latest period his workshop mainly carried out his commissions, which may be why the surfaces of his late works were not so elaborate and stylization can be observed in the carving of the draperies, such as in the St. Sebastian altar in the Abbey church of Mondsee in 1714 and the St. Leonard altar in the pilgrimage church in Irrsdorf in 1716, as well as in the four statues in the Collegiate Church in Salzburg in 1721–22.

Guggenbichler died in 1723, after which the workshop in Mondsee was closed. His assistants spread the copies and variants of his popular works around the Alps. He had numerous followers—Simeon Friess, J. Georg Baierle, Johann Fenest, Ferdinand Oxner, and Joseph Anton Pfaffinger warrant mention—but none of them could come close to Guggenbichler's level of achievement.

KATALIN HÁMORI

Biography

Born probably in Einsiedeln, Switzerland, before 17 April 1649. Father, Georg Guggenbichler, employed by Einsiedeln Abbey as sculptor and master builder. Studied under his father, and perhaps in northern Italy; worked as assistant woodcarver for Monastery of St. Florian (near Linz), Austria, 1670; received early commission for Strasswalchen parish church, 1675; settled in Mondsee (near Salzburg), 1679, carving wood altars and polychromed, gilded statues with his own workshop; worked for Mondsee's Benedictine Abbey from 1679; received commission for Michaelbeuern Abbey Church, Salzburg, 1690–91; received number of commissions for churches from 1690s including St. Wolfgang, 1706. Died in Mondsee, Austria, 10 May 1723.

Selected Works

1675	High altar; wood; Strasswalchen parish church, Austria
1679–81	Holy Ghost altar; wood; abbey church, Mondsee, Austria
1679–81	St. Wolfgang altar; wood; abbey church, Mondsee, Austria
1682–84	Poor Souls altar; wood; abbey church, Mondsee, Austria
1682–84	*Speisealtar* (Corpus Christi altar); wood; abbey church, Mondsee, Austria
ca. 1682	Plague altar, for abbey church, Mondsee, Austria; wood (destroyed): *St. Sebastian* figure; wood; Heimatmuseum, Mondsee, Austria
1690–91	High altar; wood; Michaelbeuern Abbey church, Salzburg, Austria
1706	Altarpiece of St. Anthony; wood; pilgrimage church, St. Wolfgang, Austria
1706	Altarpiece of the Cross; wood; pilgrimage church, St. Wolfgang, Austria
1706	Altarpiece of the Rosary; wood; pilgrimage church, St. Wolfgang, Austria
1706	*Ecce homo*; wood; pilgrimage church, St. Wolfgang, Austria
1714	St. Sebastian altar; wood; abbey church, Mondsee, Austria
1716	St. Leonhard altar; wood; pilgrimage church, Irrsdorf, Austria

Further Reading

Baum, Elfriede, *Katalog des Österreichischen Barockmuseums im Unteren Belvedere in Wien*, 2 vols., Vienna and Munich: Herold, 1980

Decker, Heinrich, *Barockplastik in den Alpenländern*, Vienna: Andermann, 1943

Decker, Heinrich, *Meinrad Guggenbichler*, Vienna: Schroll, 1949

Decker, Heinrich, "Meinrad Guggenbichler," in *Die Bildhauerfamilie Zürn, 1585–1724: Schwaben, Bayern, Mähren, Österreich* (exhib. cat.), edited by Dietmar Straub, Linz, Austria: Amt. D. OÖ. Landesregierung, Abteilung Kultur, 1979

Ramharter, Johannes, "Johann Meinrad Guggenbichler," in *The Dictionary of Art*, vol. 13, edited by Jane Turner, New York: Grove, and London: Macmillan, 1996

DOMENICO GUIDI 1625–1701 *Italian*

Domenico Guidi transformed Baroque sculpture into a Classical, yet decorative, idiom that influenced numerous 18th-century artists. Guidi, who was born in Torano, went to Naples in 1639 to assist his uncle, Giuliano Finelli, in the execution of a series of statues for the local cathedral. While in Naples, he learned the skills of a founder, casting eight statues representing local patron saints. The statues' sharply defined contours and flat, hard surfaces are typical of Finelli and became an essential element of Guidi's style. After participating in the revolt of Masaniello against the Spanish in 1647–48, Guidi fled to Rome, where he entered the studio of Alessandro Algardi.

Guidi assisted Algardi on two major projects: the monumental relief *Pope Leo the Great Driving Attila from Rome* (1646–53; St. Peter's Basilica, Rome, Italy) and the high altar of the Church of S. Nicola da Tolentino (1653–54; Rome, Italy). Algardi died in 1654 before completing the latter, leaving Guidi, Ercole Ferrata, and Francesco Baratta to carry out his design. The Classical treatment of the figures is a hallmark of Algardi and was quickly adopted by Guidi; the numerous patrons he inherited from Algardi preferred this style to that of Gianlorenzo Bernini and his followers.

The influence of Algardi appears in Guidi's first important independent commission, a marble relief depicting the *Lamentation* for the chapel of the Palazzo del Monte di Pietà in Rome. The tripartite division of the picture recalls the Pope Leo relief, as do the compactness and cohesiveness of the design. A number of the figures are based on works by Algardi, indicative of Guidi's tendency to use the same element in different contexts. For example, the angel standing next to the Virgin Mary is strongly reminiscent of Algardi's *St. Michael Overcoming the Devil* (ca. 1647; Museo Civico, Bologna, Italy). However, Guidi's figures are more angular and picturesque, and his composition does not place the same emphasis on spatial illusion.

Similar characteristics appear in Guidi's other major relief, traditionally referred to as the *Holy Family*. A more accurate description of its subject is the encounter of the Christ child and the infant St. John the Baptist after the return of the Holy Family from Egypt. Although the relief was designed 20 years after the *Lamentation*, its composition is basically the same, the exception being that the figures are more crowded and less defined. This consistency is the result of Guidi's working method, which involved using a set of criteria to produce similar types of monuments. Thus in both the *Lamentation* and the *Holy Family*, the figures are distributed along a curve that rises up from the bottom of the composition where the principal figures are located.

This formulaic approach is most apparent in portraits by Guidi. Artists during this period became increasingly interested in capturing the personality of their subject. Guidi, however, executed his portraits in a standardized manner, reducing the expression of his subjects to a minimum. His compositions show little variation over time, with his figures often assuming the same pose. An example of his style appears in the funerary monuments of Monsignor Marcantonio Oddi, Cardinal Lorenzo Imperiale, and Cardinal Landgraf von Hessen. Executed over the course of 25 years, each monument shows the deceased turned to his right, kneeling atop his tomb, and flanked by allegorical figures celebrating his virtues. The manner in which their drapery is arranged, particularly the complex zigzag pattern formed by the sleeves of their garments, is so distinctive that it appears in no other sculptures except those by Guidi.

Identical patterns appear in papal portraits by Guidi, such as his life-size bust of Alexander VIII. Although Guidi never became an official papal artist, papal circles employed him throughout his career. He executed portrait busts of four other popes besides Alexander VIII and contributed to a number of official monuments, such as the Ponte S. Angelo, for which he carved *Angel Carrying the Lance*. He was also involved with constructing the tomb of Clement IX, which was criticized by Bernini for its austere appearance.

It was precisely the simplicity of Guidi's style, however, that appealed to French patrons and artists, with whom he first came into contact in the mid 1650s when the painter Nicolas Poussin asked him to execute three herms for the Villa of Nicolas Fouquet at Vaux-le-Vicomte (*ca.* 1661; Château, Quinconces del Midi, Versailles, France). In the late 1670s, Guidi received a royal commission to portray *Fame Writing the History of Louis XIV*. The work, based on a design after Charles Le Brun, is a complex allegory celebrating Louis XIV as the ideal monarch. Before this commission, Guidi was already well acquainted with Le Brun, whom he had nominated to succeed him as head of the Accademia di S. Luca in Rome in 1676–77. When Le Brun was unable to leave France, Guidi asked his close friend Charles Errard, director of the French Academy in Rome (established 1666), to serve in his place. In return, he was asked to view and comment on the work of French students at the academy, an honor accorded to only one other sculptor: Bernini.

By these means, Guidi left a strong impression on young French artists working in Rome. This is particularly true of Jean-Baptiste Théodon and Pierre-Étienne Monnot, who worked under Guidi, and of Pierre Legros the Younger, whom he knew through the academy. Both Théodon's *Joseph Distributing Grain* (1705; Chapel of the Monte di Pietà, Rome, Italy) and Legros's *Tobias and the Tax Collector* (1705; Chapel of the Monte di Pietà, Rome, Italy) rely on works by Guidi for their composition. As Guidi's studio produced no notable followers, his artistic legacy lies in the link he provided between the Roman and French sculptors of the late 17th and early 18th centuries.

DAVID L. BERSHAD AND GABRIELLA SZALAY

See also **Algardi, Alessandro**

Biography

Born in Torano, near Carrara, Italy, 6 June 1625. Nephew of the sculptor Guiliano Finelli; nephew of the daughter of painter Giovanni Lanfranco. Moved to Naples, 1639; studied and worked under Finelli; received instruction in casting from Gregorio de' Rossi; participated in revolt against Spanish, 1647–48, and fled to Rome, 1648; entered studio of Alessandro Algardi as an assistant, and remained until Algardi's death, 1654; established independent studio. Member of the Accademia di S. Luca, 1651; elected member of Congregazione dei Virtuosi del Pantheon, 1658; director of Accademia di San Luca, 1669, 1670, 1675; rector of French Academy in Rome, 1676. Died in Rome, Italy, 28 March 1701.

Selected Works

1639–46 *Patron Saints*; bronze (with Giuliano Finelli); Chapel of S. Januarius, Cathedral of Naples, Italy

ca. 1658 Monument of Monsignor Marcantonio Oddi; marble; Church of San Agostino, Perugia, Italy

1659–76 *Lamentation*; marble; Palazzo del Monte di Pietà, Rome, Italy

1661 *Herms (Pan, Pallas, Faunus)*; marble; Quinconces du Midi, Versailles, France

1668–69 *Angel Carrying the Lance*; marble; Ponte S. Angelo, Rome, Italy

1671 Tomb of Clement IX; marble; Basilica of Santa Maria Maggiore, Rome, Italy

ca. 1675 Monument of Cardinal Lorenzo Imperiale; marble; Church of Sant'Agostino, Rome, Italy

1676–83 *Holy Family*; marble; Church of S. Agnese in Agone, Rome, Italy

ca. 1684 Monument of Cardinal Landgraf von Hessen; marble; Cathedral of Wrocław, Wrocław, Poland

ca. 1686 *Fame Writing the History of Louis XIV*; marble; Bassin de Neptune, Versailles, Yvelines, France

ca. 1691 Bust of Alexander VIII; bronze; Victoria and Albert Museum, London, England

Further Reading

Bacchi, Andrea, "A Terracotta Relief by Domenico Guidi," *The Burlington Magazine* 137 (1995)

Bershad, David L., "Domenico Guidi, a 17th-Century Sculptor" (dissertation), University of California, Los Angeles, 1970

Bershad, David L., "A Series of Papal Busts by Domenico Guidi," *The Burlington Magazine* 112 (1970)

Bershad, David L., "Domenico Guidi and Nicolas Poussin," *The Burlington Magazine* 113 (1971)

Bershad, David L., "Some New Documents on the Statues of Domenico Guidi and Ercole Ferrata in the Elizabeth Chapel in the Cathedral of Breslau (now Wrocaław)," *The Burlington Magazine* 118 (1976)

Bershad, David L., "Domenico Guidi: Some New Attributions," *Antologia di Belle Arti* 1 (1977)

Den Broeder, F., "A Drawing by Domenico Guidi for a Monument to Innocent XII," *The Burlington Magazine* 117 (1975)

Ferrari, Oreste, and Serenita Papaldo, *Le sculture del Seicento a Roma*, Rome, Italy: Ugo Bozzi Editore, 1999

Montagu, Jennifer, *Roman Baroque Sculpture*, New Haven, Connecticut: Yale University Press, 1989

Weil, Mark S., *The History and Decoration of the Ponte S. Angelo*, University Park: Pennsylvania State University Press, 1974

GUIDO DA COMO *ca.* late 12TH/early 13TH CENTURY–1257 *Italian*

Guido di Bonagiunta Bigarelli, more commonly referred to as Guido da Como, was a member of a large group of artists from the Canton Ticino (in present-day southern Switzerland). He was among the *magistri marmorum de Lumbardia* (marble masters of Lombardy) who were especially active in western Tuscany between the end of the 12th and the first half of the 13th centuries. Guidetto, a member of the first generation of Ticino artists working around Lucca, and Guidobono are two other Guidos with whom Guido da Como is most often confused by art historians and critics.

Guido was the son of Bonagiunta Bigarelli, a marble cutter for the first *magister* (master) Guidetto at the cloister of S. Ponziano in Lucca (1203) and a nephew of Lanfranco. In 1226 he signed the baptismal font in Pistoia as "Magister Guido de Como." He was from Arogno on Lake Lugano. The earliest reference to him is in 1238 in Barga, near Lucca, and several documents record him in Lucca between 1244 and 1257. The first work known to be his is the octagonal font in the baptistery in Pisa (1246), in which the inscription inside reads "Guido Bigarelli de Cumo fecit opus hoc" (Guido Bigarelli of Como made this work). The baptismal font is a structure made of white Carraran marble and red ammonite with inserts of dark green stone from Prato. It stands in the exact center of the baptistery and consists of an octagonal basin placed on a base constructed with three white marble steps with risers inlaid with green stone in a simple geometric motif. On the inside, four small circular wells proclaim "ad uso dei battezzatori" (for use of the baptizers), just as Dante Alighieri noted about the font at the baptistery in Florence, which was later destroyed. The floor of the basin is white and sea green, and the walls are lined with red marble delimited by white cornices. On the outside, the basin is lined on each side by two slabs of inlaid and carved marble, enclosed in white cornices with an acanthus leaf design, each with a base and a cornice of red marble. The central carving consists of a flower circled by a crown in a plant motif linked by foliage to the cornice border of four human or animal figures placed at the intersections. The remaining spaces are filled with dense geometric marble inlays. This work, enriched by the polychromatic white, red, and green of the elements, appears at a structural, decorative, and, in particular, stylistic level that elaborate the designs previously adopted by Guidetto and the other Lombard masters working in the area. Art historians almost unanimously look at this work as representing the artist's mature style.

The principal components of the repertoire of the Ticino masters remain: plants, animals, and human beings that combine to form hybrids, lions, bears, and eagles; human and animal prototypes; and acanthus leaves turning and spinning with the aid of a compass. The technical perfection of the execution, the chromatic quality of the marble, the exactness of the layout, the lightness of the surfaces, and the smoothness of the carvings deserve to be noted. The ornamentation explodes in the variations of the geometric motifs and in the richness of the carvings of the rosettes: Guido's 16 slabs abandon the rigor of ancient models and exalt the artificial character of invention. The elements of this work alternate in the grids and squares; the only still point in this intricate assemblage of decorative elements is the presence of four small heads in the edges of every rosette.

Guido is mentioned in a document dating from 1248 in Lucca, but in 1250 he was definitely in Pistoia. Other than the Pisan font, the other work that is certainly his is the pulpit in Pistoia at the Church of S. Bartolomeo in Pantano. The design of the pulpit derived from the style that the master Gugliemo had presented in the second half of the 12th century for the pulpit of the Cathedral of Pisa (now in the Cathedral of Cagliari, Sardinia). It consists of a rectangular box supported by three columns, two of which rest on lions and one on a *telamon* dressed in a merchant's period costume. At the edges of the parapet are Sts. Paul, Luke, and John, and anthropomorphic figures representing the Evangelists. The work, however, is still the subject of complex debate regarding its original arrangement. In fact, two inscriptions exist that report the date of 1239 for one part of the sculptural group and 1250 for the other part. Recently the parts signed by Guido have

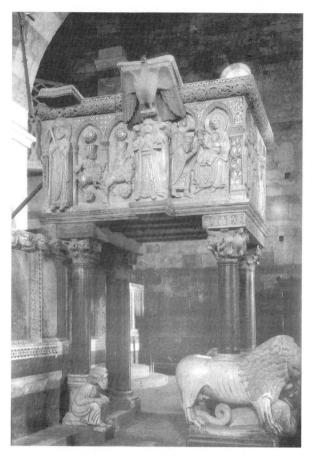

Pulpit, Church of S. Bartolomeo in Pantano, Pistoia, Italy
The Conway Library, Courtauld Institute of Art

acanthus leaves, the same motifs in the inlays, and the two symbols of the Evangelists—the angel and the eagle—on the sides of the door are now recognized as Guido's work and represent an obvious point of contact and development in his previous work. In particular, the modern view is that he began as a decorator but increasingly became a sculptor. The majority of his youthful activity is seen mostly in Pistoia in the *aniconic* slabs of the pulpit (1239) and its figure of St. Andrew, with the regular appearance of the small heads and the simplification of the inlaid designs now definitely attributed to Guido. The Pisan experience of 1246—in which he may have met the Byzantine masters who were then working in the city while he was learning about Roman sarcophagi—signals Guido's mature phase, because the mainstream of ornamental design that tended toward abstraction would have influenced the polished luminosity of his baptismal font. After living in Pisa, Guido gave more vigor and body to the sculptural group in the Pistoian pulpit in 1250, as well as to the sculptures on the central door of the Cathedral of Lucca and the central portal of St. Peter Somaldi, also in Lucca, thereby foretelling an increasingly narrative tendency in sculpture.

LORENZO CARLETTI

Biography

Born in Aragno, near Lugano, Switzerland, late 12th or early 13th century. Flourished in 1238; member of large group of artists from northern Italy who worked mainly in western Tuscany; father (Bonagiunta), a marble cutter, probably worked in the cloister of S. Ponziano, Lucca, 1203, together with Guidetto (with whom Guido was sometimes confused); noted in Barga, near Lucca, 1238; documents record him in Lucca, 1244–57; signed the octagonal font in Pisa baptistery, 1246; signed and dated pulpit, Church of S. Bartolomeo in Pantano, 1250; together with half-brother, Guidobono—the other Guido with whom he was often confused—worked in Lucca, 1257. Died in Lucca, Italy, 1257.

Selected Works

1246   Font; marble, stone; Baptistery, Pisa, Italy
1250   Pulpit; marble; Church of S. Bartolomeo
           in Pantano, Pistoia, Italy

Further Reading

Ascani, Valerio, "La bottega de' Bigarelli: Scultori Tiginesi in Toscana e in Trentino nel Duecento," in *Mario Salmi: Storico dell'arte e umanista*, Spoleto, Italy: Centro Italiano di Studi sull'Alto Medioevo, 1991

been singled out and the pulpit has thus been recomposed. On the rectangular form are four illustrated slabs, each with two stories of the New Testament (four scenes of Christ's infancy dated 1239, and four scenes of Christ after the Resurrection from 1250); three slabs with a geometric decoration, probably from 1239, and two sculptural groups that support the lectern. These sculptures have a particular narrative liveliness of polished and elegant figures, impenetrable faces, and loosely aligned sequences.

On the basis of these two works, and especially on the written records, many scholars have sought to widen Guido's catalogue with other works in Lucca, in the countryside around Lucca, and in Pistoia. A document from 1252 records a "Magister Guido de Como" who, together with his assistants Giannino and Lucano, worked on the northern door of the Cathedral of Pistoia. Other documents record Guido's presence in Lucca between 1252 and 1254. In addition, a simple stylistic analysis of the reliefs on the central door of the Cathedral of Lucca reveals a narrow connection to the reliefs on the Pisan baptismal font and those of the pulpit in Pistoia. The decorative elements on the

Baracchini, Clara, and Antonino Caleca, *Il duomo di Lucca*, Lucca, Italy: Libreria Editrice Baroni, 1973

Caleca, Antonino, "Il battistero: Architettura e scultura romaniche," in *Il duomo di Pisa: Il battistero, il campanile*, edited by Enzo Carli, Florence: Nardini, 1989

Caleca, Antonino, and Aurelio Amendola, *La dotta mano: Il battistero di Pisa*, Bergamo, Italy: Bolis, 1991

Dalli Regoli, Gigetta, "I Guidi Magistri marmorum de Lumbardia," in *Niveo de Marmore: L'uso artistico del marmo di Carrara dall'XI al XV secolo*, edited by Enrico Castelnuovo, Genoa, Italy: Colombo, 1992

Dalli Regoli, Gigetta, *Dai maestri senza nome all'impresa dei Guidi: Contributi per lo studio della scultura medievale a Lucca*, Lucca, Italy: Fazzi, 1986

Garzelli, Annarosa, *Sculture toscane nel Dugento e nel Trecento*, Florence: Marchi and Bertolli, 1969

Kopp-Schmidt, Gabriele, *Die Skulpturen der Fassade von San Martino in Lucca*, Worms, Germany: Werner'sche Verlagsgesellschaft, 1981

Smith, Christine, *The Baptistery of Pisa*, New York: Garland, 1978

FRANZ IGNAZ GÜNTHER 1725–1775

German

Franz Ignaz Günther was the most important Bavarian wood sculptor during the 18th century. He adapted the Rococo idiom to the largely Christian themes of his work. Elaborate drapery, dramatic movement, graceful gestures, and tapering fingers distinguish his work, beginning in the 1750s. These characteristics are evident, for example, in *Christ at the Column*, one of his earliest extant sculptures.

The model for *Christ at the Column* was a processional work of the same theme, made by the Premonstratensian Abbey of Steingaden in Upper Bavaria. Miracles were attributed to this piece (a modest composition with no artistic pretensions), and it attracted thousands of pilgrims every year. Among the many copies and adaptations, Günther's is the most artistically significant. He retained the principal elements of the original work, which depicts Christ wearing a loincloth and chained by the upper arms to a baluster column. Günther's work differs from both the model and other versions, however, through greater compositional logic and increased dramatic tension. In the original, the baluster column is sufficiently high for Christ to rest his elbow on the top, which would have mitigated some of the pain of enchainment. By contrast, in Günther's presentation of the same scene, the column offers no such relief, because it reaches only just above Christ's knee. Moreover, in Günther's version the chains that bind Christ by his upper arms to the column are too short to permit the prisoner to stand erect, thereby justifying a *contrapposto* (a natural pose with the weight of one leg, the shoulder, and hips counterbalancing one another) stance. The drapery, which flares out on the projected left hip, accentuates the

tension of this position. Where in the model Christ is a contemplative figure, he becomes in Günther's work vigorous and agile.

The *Annunciation* at Weyarn is a medley of movement, swirls of fabric, and grace that represents Günther at the height of his powers. His genius for drapery is especially apparent in the Virgin's enveloping garments and scrupulously disheveled head covering. Mary stands in a position of deference. Her head is inclined and turned away, and her knees are bent, a posture that forms her body into an S curve. The gilt-edged blue overgarment wraps around her knees, and the folds in the sleeves of her tunic likewise suggest movement. The angel appears to be still in flight with his right arm raised up and his left leg stretched forward, his voluminous skirt floating behind him. Even the feathers on his wings appear to move slightly. The work as a whole provides a sense of joy and wonder. Günther designed the *Annunciation* as a processional piece, to be seen from below, a perspective that would have accentuated the illusion of flight and movement. His *Resurrected Christ* similarly combines the qualities of majesty and vigor with a sense of ethereality.

Günther also designed ensemble works, such as parts of the interior of the cloister church in Rott am Inn, Bavaria. His contribution to this project included not only the statues, but also the high and side altars. Physical context plays an important role in his work. A kneeling angel, missing its wings, was originally designed as one of a pair to be placed at the side of the tabernacle on a high altar. Because it is no longer *in situ*, its religious or mythological significance is no longer clear.

Although Günther was a virtuoso carver, others in his workshop painted the figures. An example of an unpainted carving by Günther attests to the importance of their work. For example, an unpainted votive Madonna is both simpler and more sensual than his polychromed works.

Günther was principally a sculptor of religious works, a circumstance owing to the political power and wealth of the Romans Catholic Church in Bavaria during the 18th century. Because most of the great Bavarian landowners were prelates, commissions for religious buildings and works of art were common. Among early 20th century critics, the use of the Rococo idiom in a spiritual setting has caused considerable skepticism. To the Anglo-Saxon mind especially, the Rococo is linked with moral frivolity. The *Pietà* at Weyarn, a processional piece, illustrates the perceived conflict between 18th-century polychromed sculpture and religious sincerity. Although technically brilliant, the piece is psychologically unsatisfying for the modern viewer. The dead Christ is too gracefully draped across his mother's lap, his body forming a symmetri-

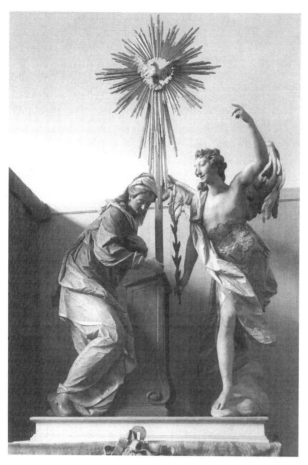

Annunciation Church of Sts. Peter and Paul, Weyarn, Bavaria
© Foto Marburg / Art Resource, NY

first modern art critic to promote Günther in England. However, as late as the mid 20th century, an exhibition in London of Bavarian Rococo art, which included works by Günther, caused considerable controversy.

AMY E. GALE

Biography

Born in Altmannstein, Oberpfalz, Germany, 22 November 1725. Trained with father, Johann Georg Günther; moved to Munich and apprenticed to Johann Baptist Straub, 1743–ca. 1750; traveled to Salzburg, Mannheim, and Moravia as a journeyman, ca. 1750–53; in Mannheim in Paul Egell's workshop, 1751–52; studied at Imperial Kunstakademie, Vienna, May–November 1753; won first prize there for terracotta group; established workshop in Munich, 1754; settled there permanently; appointed court sculptor to Maximilian III Joseph, elector of Bavaria, June 1754; commissions included church interiors, such as cloister church at Rott am Inn, 1760s; commissions declined in late 1760s. Died in Munich, Germany, 26 June 1775.

Selected Works

1754   *Christ at the Column*; polychromed wood; Detroit Institute of Arts, Michigan, United States

1758   *Pietà* (polychromed by Mignolin Demuel); polychromed wood; St. Ruprecht's Church, Kircheiselfing, Bavaria, Germany

1760/70   *Resurrected Christ*; polychromed papier mâché; Bayerisches Nationalmuseum, Munich, Germany

1762   *Annunciation*; polychromed wood; former Collegiate Church (now the Church of Sts. Peter and Paul), Weyarn, Bavaria, Germany

1762   *St. Kunigunde*; wood; Benedictine Cloister Church of Sts. Marinus and Anianus, Rott am Inn, Bavaria, Germany

ca. 1762   Votive Madonna; wood; Bayerisches Nationalmuseum, Munich, Germany

1764   *Pietà*; polychromed wood; former Collegiate Church (now the Church of Sts. Peter and Paul), Weyarn, Bavaria, Germany

1765   Kneeling angel; wood; Städelsches Kunstinstitut und Städtische Galerie, Frankfurt, Germany

1770   *Madonna of the Immaculate Conception*; wood; Cleveland Museum of Art, Ohio, United States

1772   Northwest door; wood; Cathedral Church

cal but improbable arch while waves of colorful fabric contrast with his pallid flesh. The Virgin appears to be displaying her child's corpse. The presence of the putti provides a further detraction. An earlier *Pietà* (1758) is a more successful but less accomplished treatment of the same subject. In this version the Virgin holds her son close, her hands supporting his head, their faces almost touching. Technically, it is not one of Günther's best works. Problems include the lack of definition of Mary's body, which appears to have melted away under the voluminous folds of her garments. Nonetheless, it is a convincing depiction of maternal grief.

Other works by Günther contribute to the assumption that worldliness was the underpinning for 18th-century ecclesiastical art in Bavaria. Thus a pulpit (*ca.* 1765) for the Church of St. Joseph in Starnberg, Bavaria, decorated with the symbols of the four Evangelists, is in the form of an opera box.

As with most Bavarian artists of this period, Günther achieved only regional renown, and after his death he fell into obscurity. Sacheverell Sitwell was the of Our Lady (Frauenkirche), Munich, Germany

Further Reading

Bourke, John, "Bavaria Sancta in the Eighteenth Century," *Apollo* 90 (November 1969)

Hawley, Henry H., "Eighteenth-Century Sculpture from Germany and Austria," *Bulletin of the Cleveland Museum of Art* 51 (January 1964)

Schädler, Alfred, *Exhibition of Rococo Art from Bavaria* (exhib. cat.), London: Victoria and Albert Museum, 1954

Schädler, Alfred, *Rococo Art from Bavaria*, London: Humphries, and New York: Pitman, 1956

Sitwell, Sacheverell, Nikolaus Pevsner, and Anthony Ayscough, *German Baroque Sculpture*, London: Duckworth, 1938

Volk, Peter, "Franz Ignaz Günther's 'Christ at the Column,'" *Bulletin of the Detroit Institute of Arts* 63 (1988)

Volk, Peter, and Wolf-Christian von der Mülbe, *Ignaz Günther: Vollendung des Rokoko*, Regensburg, Germany: Pustet, 1991

Woeckel, Gerhard P., "An Unknown Early Work by Ignaz Günther: 'St. Scholastica,'" *Bulletin of the Los Angeles County Museum of Art* 21 (1975)

Woeckel, Gerhard P., "Der kurbayerische Hofbildhauer Franz Ignaz Günther," in *Bayern im Rokoko: Aspekte einer Epoche im Umbruch*, edited by Herbert Schindler and Alfons Beckenbauer, Munich: Süddeutscher Verlag, 1989

TYREE GUYTON 1955– *United States*

An African-American painter, sculptor, and installation artist, Tyree Guyton is chiefly known for the *Heidelberg Project*. He began this effort in 1986 near downtown Detroit in the neighborhood in which he has lived most of his life—the 3600 block of Heidelberg Street, between Mt. Elliott and Ellery Streets. His use of collage, assemblage, and a raw, junky, found-object aesthetic has complicated the understanding of Guyton's place in art—whether, for example, the *Heidelberg Project* functions as high art, low art, or both or if, despite Guyton's training, it is usefully associated with works by other so-called outsider, visionary, or self-taught artists. The unfinished dynamism of the *Heidelberg Project* further complicates matters. Many ponder whether scholarly efforts sap its performative powers; some critics insist that such works maintain potency for only as long as they exist in the moment—and outside the canon. Despite such difficulties in preservation and reception, one can argue that the *Heidelberg Project* offers enduring testimony of cultural work.

The ongoing *Heidelberg Project* first commanded national attention in the late 1980s with the help of articles in *People* and *Connoisseur* magazines; it also became the focus of an award-winning documentary film, *Come Unto Me: The Faces of Tyree Guyton*, directed by Nicole Cattell (1998). In the years between, Guyton has been both celebrated and ridiculed. Between 1989 and 1992, for example, he annually received prestigious awards from state and city government. In 1990, moreover, The Detroit Institute of Arts featured him in a retrospective exhibit (with exhibition catalogue) (see Jackson, 1990). Nevertheless, the city began demolishing parts of the project in 1989. Although a period of stalemate prevailed through most of the 1990s, tensions resurfaced in 1998, and the city resumed destruction in 1999.

The sight of abandoned and condemned houses combined with immense trees lining spacious, overgrown lots that signify residential neglect or decay became in the case of Guyton's neighborhood the pretext and platform for the *Heidelberg Project*. Guyton has regularly dedicated each "renovation" to a particular theme, sometimes taking cues from dominant materials (such as discarded appliances, timepieces, telephones, wheeled-vehicle parts, street signs, television sets, radios, and old clothing). Early works, now gone, included *Fun House*, *Tire House*, and *Baby Doll House*; the latter focused on a ghetto childhood, symbolized by weathered, broken dolls attached in various configurations to all surfaces of an abandoned residence. Initially focusing on houses that served as active drug trade and prostitution sites, Guyton's project ultimately discouraged such activities from continuing; few could conduct such illegal business under the scrutiny of Guyton and his team or the streams of steady viewers that began arriving to see the *Heidelberg Project*. The project consequently developed a reputation as a sanctuary. After demolition in 1991 Guyton began incorporating additional supports, such as trees and empty lots. A weedy corner, for example, on Heidelberg and Ellery once featured a 1955 yellow passenger bus dedicated to civil rights heroine Rosa Parks.

Houses still standing include the *Dotty Wotty House* (a private residence), the *OJ (Obstruction of Justice)* house (Guyton's studio and education center), and the *Number House* (a private residence). Guyton dedicated the *Dotty Wotty House*, covered in polka dots and other round forms symbolizing jelly beans, to his grandfather and mentor, Sam Mackey, who lived there until his death in 1992 (at age 94). Arriving in Detroit from St. Louis, Missouri, in 1918, Mackey loved jelly beans as much for their taste as for their symbolism of peaceful human coexistence. Mackey believed that variously colored jelly beans are the same on the inside, just as people share a spirit, no matter how different they are on the outside. Also an allusion to growing up poor with hand-me-down clothes, the polka-dot motif that began appearing throughout Detroit in the 1990s has additionally come to stand for protest against the city's treatment of the *Heidelberg Project*. Indeed, some have linked recent city objections to the time when

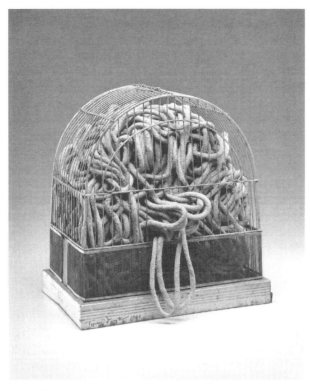

Caged Brain
Founders Society Purchase, Twentieth Century Painting and
Sculpture Fund and Dr. and Mrs. George Kamperman Fund
© 1991 The Detroit Institute of Arts

polka dots began appearing on the political campaign posters that city candidates had themselves affixed to the abandoned buildings.

According to Guyton, Mackey's recollections of lynchings in the South, where he could see only the soles of the lynched men's shoes, inspired the artist to hang footwear from trees. A dominant motif of the *Heidelberg Project*, shoes also formed mounds, recalling World War II scenes of genocide, in sections of an empty lot called *Audience*. Shoes, moreover, lined the sidewalks, representing both the soles and souls of countless individuals standing in unemployment lines or wandering homeless. According to cultural critic Kofi Natambu, after the 1991 demolition Guyton also "litter[ed] the streets of three city blocks with old shoes so that automobile traffic could run over them," a "public protest against the abandonment of the poor and . . . the reactionary nature of the city's response, not only to his work, but to the . . . needs of the community" (see Natambu, 1992).

About 1991 Guyton began suffusing his neighborhood with painted automobile hoods (*Faces in the Hood*) as well as shoe and upside-down flag paintings, many on wooden boards that lean against or are posted on trees, poles, and other surfaces. Sidewalks and streets remain covered in paint, and certain lots continue to offer shifting arrangements of freestanding sculpture, despite the city's most recent actions: bulldozing houses, which destroyed many works in storage; clearing overgrown lots and in the process impounding such works as *Dotty-Wotty Car* and *Noah's Ark* (a landed vessel overflowing with stuffed animals); and felling trees or stripping them bare of material, in which case the trees remain polka-dotted. Guyton has an ongoing commitment to motivate open dialogue about a variety of topics through his projects. Nonetheless, the *Heidelberg Project* remains at odds with the city of Detroit. Recognized as a self-taught and outsider artist, Guyton also belongs to the traditions of African and African diaspora legacies—such as African-American yard show art—whose "unfinished aesthetic" of accumulation and assemblage significantly informs much modern and contemporary art.

MYSOON RIZK

Biography

Born in Detroit, Michigan, United States, 24 August 1955. Served in army, 1970–72; studied art at Wayne County Community and Marygrove Colleges, 1979–84, Center for Creative Studies, 1980–82, as well as with artist Charles McGee and others; worked as inspector at Ford Motor Company in Dearborn, 1972–78, and art teacher at Northern High School, Franklin Adult Education Program, and Marygrove College, 1991; named Michigan Artist of the Year, 1992; major exhibitions included Minnesota Museum of American Art, St. Paul, 1996; Delaware Art Institute, Delaware University, 2000; Harvard University, Cambridge, Massachusetts, 2000; exhibited in Düsseldorf, Germany, 1996; Tokyo, Japan, 1997; Moscow, Russia, 1997; Budapest, Hungary, 1998; and others. Lives and works in Detroit, Michigan, United States.

Selected Works

1986–
present

Heidelberg Project; outdoor art environment including a street, houses, trees, found objects, mixed media; Detroit, Michigan, United States

1986–89 *Baby Doll House*, for *Heidelberg Project*, Detroit, Michigan, United States; mixed media house (destroyed)

1986–89 *Tire House*, for *Heidelberg Project*, Detroit, Michigan, United States; mixed media house (destroyed)

1986–91 *Fun House*, for *Heidelberg Project*, Detroit, Michigan, United States; mixed media house (destroyed)

1990 *Caged Brain*; birdcage, rope; The Detroit
Institute of Arts, Michigan, United States
1991–99 *Audience*, for *Heidelberg Project*, Detroit,
Michigan, United States; shoes (destroyed)
1991–99 *Changing Time*, for *Heidelberg Project*,
Detroit, Michigan, United States; tree with
clocks (destroyed, materials salvaged)
1991–99 *Noah's Ark*, for *Heidelberg Project*,
Detroit, Michigan, United States; mixed
media boat (impounded)
1991–99 *Non-Stop*, for *Heidelberg Project*, Detroit,
Michigan, United States; tree with bicycles
(destroyed)
1991–99 *The Oven*; mixed media; collection of the
artist, Detroit, Michigan, United States
1991–99 *People's Tree*, for *Heidelberg Project*,
Detroit, Michigan, United States; tree with
materials salvaged from 1991 demolition
(destroyed)
1991–99 *Soles of the Most High*, for *Heidelberg
Project*; tree with shoes (destroyed)
1991– *Dotty Wotty House*; mixed media house;
present *Heidelberg Project*, Detroit, Michigan,
United States
1991– *Faces in the Hood*; series of painted
present automobile hoods; traveling, with tour
stops including Harvard University,
Cambridge, Massachusetts, United States;
Ecuador; and Brazil
1991– *Number House*; mixed media house;
present *Heidelberg Project*, Detroit, Michigan,
United States
1991– *OJ* (*Obstruction of Justice*); mixed media
present house; *Heidelberg Project*, Detroit,
Michigan, United States
1991– *Rosa Parks Bus*; 1955 bus and mixed
present media; traveling, with tour stops including
Pittsburgh, Pennsylvania, and South
Carolina

Further Reading

Beardsley, John, *Gardens of Revelation: Environments by Visionary Artists*, New York: Abbeville, 1995
Beardsley, John, "Eyesore or Art? On Tyree Guyton's Heidelberg Project," *Harvard Design Magazine* (Winter–Spring 1999)
Bradsher, Keith, "Art? Maybe. Junk? Perhaps. History? For Sure.," *The New York Times* (6 February 1999)
Come Unto Me: The Faces of Tyree Guyton (videorecording), produced and directed by Nicole Cattell, New York: Naked Eye Productions, 1998
Goldberg, Vicki, "Art by the Block," *Connoisseur* 219/926 (March 1989)
Hall, Michael, "Forward in an Aftermath: Public Art Goes Kitsch," in *Art in the Public Interest*, edited by Arlene Raven, Ann Arbor, Michigan: UMI Research Press, 1989
Heidelberg Project <www.heidelberg.org>
Jackson, Marion Elizabeth, "Tyree Guyton: Listenin' to His Art," in *Tyree Guyton* (exhib. cat.), Detroit, Michigan: The Detroit Institute of Arts, 1990
Natambu, Kofi, "Nostalgia for the Present: Cultural Resistance in Detroit, 1977–1987," in *Black Popular Culture*, edited by Michele Wallace and Gina Dent, Seattle, Washington: Bay Press, 1992
Peterson, Jerry, "Welcome to Heidelberg: A Walk through Detroit's Art Ghetto," *Juxtapoz* 3/4 (Fall 1997)
Plagens, Peter, and Frank Washington, "Come On-a My House: How to Fight City Hall," *Newsweek* (6 August 1990)
Stodghill, Ron, II, "Portrait of the Artist as Polka-Dotter," *Time* (25 August 1997)
The Voodoo Man of Heidelberg Street (videocassette), written and produced by Harvey Ovshinsky, Detroit, Michigan: WTVS-TV, 1989

GYPSUM, ALABASTER, AND "EGYPTIAN" ALABASTER

Gypsum, a common mineral, is a type of sedimentary rock composed of calcium (23.28 percent), hydrogen (2.34 percent), sulfur (18.62 percent), and oxygen (55.76 percent) by molecular weight. Formed by the precipitation of calcium sulfite from seawater in volcanic regions, gypsum is produced by the action of sulfuric acid on calcium-containing minerals (such as limestone) and is found in most clays.

During the Silurian period of the Paleozoic Era, about 300 million years ago, saltwater oceans covered a large portion of the earth. As oceans receded, swamps and "dead" seas formed. Due to the arid climate, the salt concentration increased, and as a result, gypsum was one of first minerals to crystallize. Decaying vegetation and other mineral deposits produced the layers of gypsum and limestone presently found in the earth. In its purest form, gypsum rock is pure white; however, with naturally occurring impurities the rock may appear colorless, gray, brown, beige, orange, pink, yellow, light red, red, green, or black. Gypsum is one of the softest minerals.

Alabaster, the dense, fine-grained form of gypsum used for statuary and ornamental purposes, appears white or yellowish white, translucent, or streaked with reddish brown. Its soft quality lends it to being easily scratched, weathered, and broken. Alabaster is also known as Florentine marble (Italy), Mexican onyx (Mexico), and Oriental alabaster, which is calcium carbonate, or Oriental marble.

Egyptian alabaster is actually calcite, which occurs in a great variety of crystalline forms and is a major constituent of limestone, marble, and chalk. Calcite is known also as travertine and onyx marble (Mexican *tecali*). Selenite, gypsum's crystalline form, is transparent, with a vitreous to pearly luster, and cleaves into thin sheets for applications similar to mica. Satin spar, its fibrous variety, and Desert Rose, a valued crystal form, are used for ornamental purposes.

Gypsum was used by ancient civilizations; the Assyrians and Egyptians carved and polished pure and translucent alabaster into monuments, statuary, and tomb items. Notable examples of Egyptian alabaster include the *Alabaster Human-Headed Sphinx of King Amenophis I Making an Offering of a Libation Jar*, from Karnak, 18th Dynasty (*ca.* 1500 BCE; Egyptian Museum, Cairo, Egypt), the *Alabaster Statue of King Pepi II and His Mother*, Sixth Dynasty (2350 BCE; Brooklyn Museum, New York, United States), *King Phiops I Seated in Jubilee Attire*, Sixth Dynasty (2350 BCE; Brooklyn Museum, New York, United States), objects from the tomb of Tutankhamen, excavated in the Valley of the Tombs of the Kings at Thebes, 18th Dynasty (*ca.* 1350 BCE; Cairo Museum, Egypt), and statue heads from the Fourth Dynasty. Archaeologists also discovered gypsum, made into plaster, in the mud and straw foundations of tomb paintings from the 18th Dynasty. The alabaster of ancient Egypt and Rome was onyx marble or calcium carbonate, a harder stone than ordinary gypsum, which is calcium sulfate.

In the 14th and 15th centuries, a school of carvers in Nottingham, England, known as the Nottingham School, specialized in alabaster wall reliefs, carved altarpieces, and tomb effigies depicting the Passion, the life of the Virgin, saints, and martyrdoms. The gilded and painted reliefs found their way throughout the Christian world, especially to northern Germany, western France, and Spain. Examples include a 14th-century *Christ on the Cross* and 15th-century *Saint Jude* (both Victoria and Albert Museum, London, England) and an early 14th-century *Holy Trinity* (Sankt Maria zur Wiese, Soest [Westphalia], Germany). Other notable examples came from the Netherlands, such as a 15th-century *Head of John the Baptist* (Rijksmuseum, Amsterdam, Netherlands). At Mechelen in the Netherlands, a small group of artists created domestic altarpieces of biblical and mythological subject matter in 10- to 12-centimeter-high framed scenes until the middle of the 17th century. Artists painted and highlighted these alabasters with gold leaf, as in *Africa* (*ca.* 1600; Rijksmuseum, Amsterdam, Netherlands).

Today, gypsum is found in North America, Europe, and the Middle East and is used for commercial and industrial purposes such as cement, chalk, and fertilizer.

ANDREW GRABAR

Further Reading

Aldred, Cyril, *The Development of Ancient Egyptian Art from 3200 to 1315 b.c.*, 3 vols., London: Tiranti, 1952; vol. 3, 2nd edition, revised and enlarged, 1972

Aldred, Cyril, *Egyptian Art in the Days of the Pharaohs, 3100–320 b.c.*, London: Thames and Hudson, and New York: Oxford University Press, 1980

Cheetham, Francis W., *English Medieval Alabasters: With a Catalogue of the Collection in the Victoria and Albert Museum*, Oxford: Phaidon-Christie's, 1984

Hofstätter, Hans Hellmut, *Spätes Mittelalter*, Baden-Baden, Germany: Holle Verlag, 1967; as *Art of the Late Middle Ages*, translated by Robert Erich Wolf, New York: Abrams, 1968

Lange, Kurt, and Max Hirmer, *Aegypten: Architektur, Plastik, Malerei in drei Jahrtausenden*, Munich: Hirmer, 1955; as *Egypt: Architecture, Sculpture, and Painting in Three Thousand Years*, translated by R.H. Boothroyd, New York and London: Phaidon, 1956; 3rd revised edition, London: Phaidon, 1961

Os, Henk van, et al., *Netherlandish Art in the Rijksmuseum, 1400–1600*, New Haven, Connecticut: Yale University Press, 2000

Ranke, Hermann, *Meisterwerke der ägyptischen Kunst*, Basel, Switzerland: Holbein-Verlag, 1948; as *Masterpieces of Egyptian Art*, London: Allen and Unwin, and New York: Beechhurst Press, 1951

H

HAGENAUER FAMILY *German*

Nicholas Hagenauer 1445/86–before 1538

Nicholas Hagenauer, born in Hagenau, Germany, between 1445 and 1486, was one of the most important Late Gothic sculptors of the Upper Rhine. It is believed that he worked with his brothers, contractors Veit and Paul Hagenauer, and ran an important and influential workshop that produced work that became the style for Strasbourg about 1500. He is also presumed to be the father and teacher of Friedrich Hagenauer, one of the greatest portrait medalists of the 1520s. Nicholas was registered as a citizen of Strasbourg in 1493 with evidence placing him there until 1526. His wood and stone sculptures have been characterized as vital, raw, and assertive, with particularized features also favored by Nikolaus von Leiden, who may have been Nicholas Hagenauer's teacher. The faces of Nicholas's figures show his penetrating powers of observation and ability to express intellectual and psychological content. Nicholas also sculpted massive drapery, which added to a sense of majestic grandeur.

One of the only works that securely bore his name (others have been attributed based on style), the Corpus Christi retable (dismantled 1682) for the high altar of the Strasbourg Cathedral, is now lost. Some parts survive, including the predella (a painted panel, usually small, belonging to a series of panels at the bottom of an altarpiece), *Lamentation*, and possibly busts of two prophets. Nicholas was commissioned to carve this piece about 1500, and his brothers, the contractors, were paid 400 florins for the work in 1501. Fragments of wooden altarpieces for the abbey of Saverne, commissioned by Bishop Albrecht of Strasbourg from Nicholas and his two brothers, also survive. But perhaps more important is the tomb for Bishop Albrecht from about 1493–95 (now lost), which included an accurately sculpted skeleton, foreshadowing the mix of art and science during the Renaissance.

Nicholas's most important commission and legacy, however, is known as the Isenheim altarpiece, which consists of great woodcarvings in the Anthonite church at Isenheim, Alsace. The altar is perhaps best known for the paintings, which were done on its wings ten years later by Matthias Grünewald. Created between 1500 and 1510, the predella shows half-length figures of Christ and the 12 apostles, with St. Anthony enthroned and flanked by St. Jerome and St. Augustine. The figure of Jean d'Orliac, the donor, is at St. Augustine's feet. There were originally figures of a country squire and a peasant bearing a cock and piglet as offerings at St. Anthony's side, details of common life grounding the saints back to earth. The figures were carved in lindenwood, and much of the original polychromy has been preserved. Detailed vegetal carvings fill the space above the canopies.

Debatably attributed to Nicholas are the half-length male figure (possibly a self-portrait) above the entrance to St. Andrew's chapel in the south transept of Strasbourg Cathedral; the tabernacle of the Cathedral of Chur in Switzerland and the altar of St. Mary's chapel in Saverne (Zabern), France. Nicholas died between 1526 and 1538.

Friedrich Hagenauer 1490/1500–after 1546

Friedrich Hagenauer was born in Strasbourg between 1490 and 1500 and was active throughout all of south Germany and the Lower Rhine. He trained as a sculptor in Strasbourg, presumably with Nicholas Hagenauer, who is thought to be his father. A renowned woodcarver and among the finest medalists of the 1520s and 1530s, Friedrich was extremely prolific, producing upward of 250 medals and their wooden models, including around 100 that bear his name.

Friedrich left Strasbourg after 1520 to work in a number of cities, including Speyer, Mainz, Frankfurt am Main, Heidelberg, Nuremberg, Salzburg, and Passau, but no works from this period survive. While living in Munich and Landshut between 1525 and 1527, Friedrich executed 20 or so medals, most portraying members of the Munich court and bourgeoisie. His first extant medal, dating from 1525, depicts Matthäus Zaisinger, goldsmith and coin die cutter for the Bavarian court of Wilhelm IV, who may have encouraged Friedrich in medal portraiture work. Another important work from this period is the unusually large (12.4 centimeters) wooden medallion models of the *burgermeister* (mayor) Sebastian Liegsalz and his wife Ursula. The two pieces, probably meant to be showpieces and not cast, were conceived as a pair, with Liegsalz gazing at his wife. Also notable are the *Pfaltzgraf Philipp, Bishop of Freising*, and *Count Palatine*. Friedrich's wood models show great accuracy and precision down to the smallest detail, achieving great admiration as works of art from his patrons and explaining why so many of them survive.

Friedrich then moved to Augsburg, creating 85 medals there, many for the important patron Raymund Fugger. One exemplary work from 1527, a spare, uncluttered portrait, focuses on Fugger's curly hair and full beard, with the reverse displaying an allegory of Charity with a bearded man, perhaps Fugger, offering a jug and dish of fruit to five flying birds. In 1529 Friedrich created perhaps the most beautiful medal portrait of a woman from this period, Margrete von Frundsburg; both the model and the medal survive. A full-length sculpture, *The Virgin and Child*, is attributed to Friedrich based on stylistic details from his models, and a dispute with the local painters and sculptor's guild provides evidence. The guild asserted he abused his situation as a medalist (a craft exempt from guild control) to take work away from sculptors. He replied that in other cities he was recognized as a free artist not subject to guild restrictions.

Leaving Augsburg in 1532, Friedrich created 15 medals of citizens of Alsace as well as his native Strasbourg, working also in Baden and Swabia. Between 1536 and 1544 he worked in Bonn and then Cologne, finding many commissions as the first important medalist to work there. Notable medals from this period include those of Bartolomäus Bruyn, a painter, and Philipp Melanchthon, Martin Bucer, Kaspar Hedio, and Johannes Sturm, important figures during the Reformation.

Few of Friedrich's works after 1536 are signed, and the quality appears not to match his earlier work. During the course of his career, Friedrich reduced the diameter of his models from approximately 70 millimeters to approximately 45 millimeters, mainly concentrating on the profile with a few half-turned faces and frontal views. He may have worked in the Netherlands after 1544, where he is thought to have died.

AMY BERK

Nicholas Hagenauer

Biography

Born in Hagenau, Germany, between 1445 and 1486. Perhaps a pupil of Nikolaus Gerhaert von Leiden, whose style he is said to continue. Worked in Alsace region, mostly in Strasbourg, often with brothers, contractors Veit and Paul; ran influential and important studio; thought to be father and teacher of renowned medalist and sculptor Friedrich Hagenauer; major works include high altar of Strasbourg Cathedral, *ca.* 1501, and altarpiece at Isenheim known as Isenheim altar, 1500–10, later painted by Matthias Grünewald; also created skeleton for tomb of Bishop Albrecht of Strasbourg in abbey of Saverne (Zabern), Alsace. Died before 1538, location unknown.

Selected Works

ca. 1484   Tabernacle; stone; Chur, Switzerland (attributed)

ca. 1486   Altar; St. Mary's chapel, Saverne (Zabern), Alsace, France (attributed)

1493–94   Altarpieces; wood (fragments); Abbey of Notre-Dame, Saverne (Zabern), Alsace, France

ca.   Choir and tomb for Bishop Albrecht (of
1493–95   Strasbourg), including skeleton; wood; Abbey of Notre-Dame, Saverne (Zabern), Alsace, France

1495   Male half-length figure (self-portrait?); wood; balustrade, St. Andrew's chapel, Strasbourg Cathedral, Germany

1500–01   Busts of two prophets, for predella, Corpus Christi retable, Strasbourg Cathedral, Germany; wood; Musée de l'Oeuvre Notre-Dame, Strasbourg, France

1500–01   Corpus Christi retable, for Strasbourg Cathedral, Germany; wood (dismantled 1682)

1500–01 *Lamentation*, for predella, Corpus Christi retable, Strasbourg Cathedral, Germany; limewood; Collège Saint-Étienne, Strasbourg, Germany

ca. 1500–1510 Two peasants bearing offerings, for Isenheim altar, Anthonite Church, Alsace, France; wood; collection of Julius Böhler, Munich, Germany

1505 Statues of *Christ*, *Twelve Apostles*, *St. Anthony*, *St. Augustine*, *St. Jerome*, and *Jean d'Orliac*, for Isenheim altar, Anthonite Church, Alsace, France; wood; Musée d'Unterlinden, Colmar, France

Friedrich Hagenauer

Biography

Born in Strasbourg, Germany, between 1490 and 1500. Thought to be son of sculptor Nicholas Hagenauer, with whom he is thought to have trained. Renowned woodcarver and medalist, particularly known for fine portraiture; worked throughout southern Germany and Lower Rhine; important work in Munich, 1525–27, and Augsburg, 1527–31; left Augsburg after guild dispute, 1532; worked thereafter in Baden, Swabia, Strasbourg, Alsace, Bonn, and Cologne, where he made important late career works; may have worked in the Netherlands after 1544. Died in the Netherlands, after 1546.

Selected Works

1525 *Matthäus Zaisinger*; medal; Vogel Collection, Chemnitz, Germany

ca. 1526 *Pfaltzgraf Phillip, Bishop of Freising*, and *Count Palatine*; medals; Skulpturengalerie, Berlin, Germany

1527 *Raymund Fugger*; stone; Staatliche Münzsammlung, Munich, Germany; stone model: Maximilianmuseum, Augsburg, Germany

1527 Medals of *Sebastian Liegsalz* and *Ursula Liegsalz*; pearwood model; Bayerisches Nationalmuseum, Munich, Germany

ca. 1527 *Anna Rechlinger von Horgau*; boxwood model; Benediktinerabtei, Engelberg, Switzerland

1529 *Margrete von Frundsburg* (von Freudenburg, von Firmian); wooden model; Germanisches Nationalmuseum, Nuremberg, Germany

ca. 1530 *The Virgin and Child*; limestone; Victoria and Albert Museum, London, England

1532 *Joham Heinrich*; Universitatsbibliothek, Strasbourg, France

ca. 1534 *Christoph von Nellenberg*; wooden model; Staatliche Münzsammlung, Munich, Germany

1539 *Bartolomasus Bruyn*; medal; Kaiserliches Hofmuseum, Vienna, Austria

1543 *Johannes Sturm*; medal; Bayerisches Nationalmuseum, Munich, Germany

1543 *Philipp Melanchthon, Martin Bucer*, and *Kaspar Hedio*; medals; Bodemuseum, Berlin, Germany

Further Reading

Baum, Julius, *Meister und Werke Spätmittelalterlicher Kunst in Oberdeutschland und der Schweiz*, Lindau, Germany: Thorbecke, 1957

Baxandall, Michael, *South German Sculpture, 1480–1530*, London: HMSO, 1974

Baxandall, Michael, *The Limewood Sculptors of Renaissance Germany*, New Haven, Connecticut: Yale University Press, 1980

Heck, Christian, and Roland Recht, *Les sculptures de Nicolas de Haguenau: Le retable d'Issenheim avant Grünewald*, Colmar, France: Musée d'Unterlinden, 1987

Müller, Theodor, *Frühe Beispiele der Retrospektive in der deutschen Plastik*, Munich: Beck, 1961

Müller, Theodor, *Sculpture in the Netherlands, Germany, France, and Spain, 1400–1500*, translated by Elaine Robson Scott and William Robson Scott, Baltimore, Maryland: Penguin, 1966

Osten, Gert von der, and Horst Vey, *Painting and Sculpture in Germany and the Netherlands, 1500–1600*, translated by Mary Hottinger, London and Baltimore, Maryland: Penguin, 1969

Recht, Roland, "Les sculptures du retable d'Issenheim," *Cahiers alsaciens d'archéologie, d'art, et d'histoire* (1975–76)

Recht, Roland, *Nicolas de Leyde et la sculpture à Strasbourg (1460–1525)*, Strasbourg, Germany: Presses Universitaires de Strasbourg, 1987

Schädler, Alfred, "Ingolstädter Epitaphe der Spätgotik und Renaissance," in *Ingolstadt: Die Herzogsstadt, die Universitätsstadt, die Festung*, edited by Theodor Müller and Wilhelm Reismüller, 2 vols., Ingolstadt, Germany: Verlag Donau Courier, 1974

Smith, Jeffrey Chipps, *German Sculpture of the Later Renaissance, c. 1520–1580: Art in an Age of Uncertainty*, Princeton, New Jersey: Princeton University Press, 1994

Ullmann, Ernst, editor, *Geschichte der deutschen Kunst, 1470–1550: Architektur und Plastik*, Leipzig: Seemann, 1984

Vöge, Wilhelm, *Niclas Hagnower: Der Meister des Isenheimer Hochaltars und seine Frühwerke*, Freiburg im Breisgau, Germany: Urban-Verlag, 1931

Zeitler, Rudolf, *Einleitender Bericht über die Methode: Fruhe deutsche Medaillen, 1518–1527*, Stockholm: Almquist and Wiksell, 1951

ANN HAMILTON 1956– *American*

Since 1990 Ann Hamilton has conceived, designed, and produced intricately complicated sculptural installations that might be best described as environments that investigate the very nature of sculpture, sculptural materials, and the human body's relation to them. After receiving a BFA in textile design from the University of Kansas, she earned her MFA in sculpture from Yale University and commenced a series of works that combined performance, sculpture and photography, *untitled (body object series)*, 1984–1993. In these works Hamilton interacts with everyday objects and materials to suggest how the interface between animate and inanimate, man and animal, or nature and culture shapes our experience and understanding of the world. In one such piece Hamilton wore a pinstriped suit that she had painstakingly covered with thousands of tiny toothpicks. In another, she photographed herself in profile with a shoe jutting from her nose and mouth, like a muzzle. Another interaction comprised the artist wearing a large, unruly shrub over her head such that the plant engulfed (or nearly replaced) her head, the site of cognition and consciousness. In each of these sculptural performances (all of which are photographed in a relatively unexpressive, almost pseudoscientific style) Hamilton explores her bodily relation to the world of objects; here the body grows an object, or vice versa in a way that is strangely surreal and absurd.

The themes Hamilton mined in the *untitled (body object series)* have remained a vital part of her oeuvre. These include different ways of knowing and perceiving as filtered through the intellect (reason, cognition, knowledge) and the body (corporeality, intuition, irrationality). Hamilton isolated the cultural tendency to value one kind of experience over the other and began to use sculpture as a way to meditate upon and create metaphors for these experiences that question the validity of linear thinking, seeing, and knowing.

In her installation *privation and excesses* (1989), viewers entered the large gallery space at San Francis-

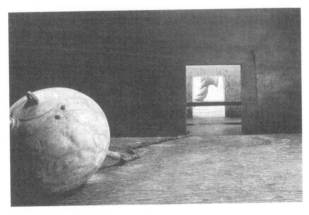

the capacity of absorption (detail)
Courtesy Sean Kelly Gallery, New York. Reproduced with permission of the artist

co's Capp Street Project to find the floor carpeted with 750,000 copper pennies, carefully laid by hand on a bed of fragrant honey. In the corner of the gallery, three sheep quietly grazed in a pen behind a wood grill, as a figure sat nearby, methodically dipping and wringing her hands in a hat filled with honey while two motorized mortar and pestles were at work grinding a bowl of pennies and human teeth. According to the artist, the mortar and pestle was a machine that created an action that imitated the human body and could actually break down or dominate the body (see Hamilton, 1991). The mixture of smells (sheep, copper, honey) and sensations combined to suggest a range of enigmatic metaphors: the labor of humankind (the Sisyphean laying of pennies, the least valuable and most modest of American currency) versus the labor of nature (the sheep grazing, the entropy of human life as symbolized in the grinding of teeth). The connecting thread between Hamilton's choice of materials—pennies and sheep—was the manner in which both have lost their mythical aura or magic over time due to consumption and domestication, respectively. The title, *privation and excesses*, speaks to states of bodily deprivation on the one hand, and decadence or abundance, on the other.

The installation *tropos* (1993) at the Dia Center for the Arts in New York City covered the 5,000-square foot warehouse space with a carpet of hand-sewn horsehair pelts of variegated colors. As the viewer waded through the space he or she became aware of subtle modifications to the surroundings: the floor's elevation had been altered just enough to slightly affect one's gait; the massive gallery windows had had their panes replaced with translucent glass that suffused the interior light; hidden speakers had been installed to fill the room with a hushed murmuring voice that was activated by the viewers' motion. Although one strained to hear a man struggling to speak, the speech remained indecipherable, like the strange poetry of a mental landscape. A person (who Hamilton calls a "sitter" or "tender" and analogous to the figure in *privation and excesses*) silently worked at a small metal table in the corner of the room "erasing" lines of text from stacks of old books using an electric burin. The wafting scent of burnt paper mixed with animal hair filled the space, creating an environment saturated with faint scents, sounds, and sights. The experience of *tropos* (a word derived from *tropism*, that is, the involuntary orientation of an organism to turn, to grow or move, as in the way a plant grows toward the light) cannot be easily interpreted, quantified, or explained through the usual tropes of art history. The title *tropos* is also related to *topos*, or place, site, or landscape. Similar to the manner in which the German artist Joseph Beuys used elemental materials such as fat, honey, felt, and gold to suggest the powers of social healing and transformation, Hamilton relies on the natural or innate qualities of her materials to weave together a subjective narrative of experience that is never singular or prescriptive. Hamilton has said that the power of ritual, transformation, bodily experience, birth, death, and other states of being that perhaps cannot be represented through images or language comprises the subtext of her meditative work. Hamilton desires that her work completely surround the viewer such that the physical, psychological, and emotional borders between body or self and the world, or an other, begin to break down. She stated, "The work is about a rumbling that's underneath everything, the rumbling that's not acknowledged in the cleanness of a place. You don't talk about these desires; you don't talk about longing for a kind of chaos—for to lose a border is to be chaotic" (see Hamilton, 1991). According to curator and critic Lynne Cooke, Hamilton "views verbal language as a deeply limited or flawed vehicle for communication since, with the exception of certain forms of poetry, it remains at best an abstraction, at odds with the immediate affectivity of sensate, visceral experience" (see Cooke, 1993).

According to the poet and writer Susan Stewart, Hamilton's work presents the viewer with an uncanny sense of time and place that is at once familiar, even intimate, and at the same time, strange and awkward in its resistance to explanation or systemization (see Stewart, 1991). Hamilton asks that the viewer traverse the border or boundary between the conscious and unconscious mind, like a somnambulist, examining with wonder and curiosity the things such a journey might turn up. Her sculptural work (best understood as Installation art) offers an intoxicating deluge of effects ranging from the visual and the audio to the olfactory that, like poetry, as opposed to literature, or speech rather than language, present sensations and metaphors for embodiment.

LYNN M. SOMERS

See also **Beuys, Joseph; Bourgeois, Louise; Contemporary Sculpture; Installation; Postmodernism**

Selected Works

1988   *the capacity of absorption*; beeswax, water, twine, crickets, table, linotype, felt, graphite, video; The Temporary Contemporary, The Museum of Contemporary Art, Los Angeles, California, United States; (no longer exists)

1989   *privation and excesses*; pennies, honey, sheep, mortar and pestle, human teeth;

Capp Street Project, San Francisco, California, United States; (no longer exists)

1990   *between taxonomy and communion*; glass, wool, cage, sheep fleece, blood, water, iron table, animal and human teeth, San Diego Museum of Contemporary Art, La Jolla, California, United States; (no longer exists)

1990   *linings*; felt boot liners, woolen blankets, grass, glass, ink on paper, monitor with video loop; collection of the Museum of Contemporary Art, San Diego, California, United States

1992–93 *untitled (aleph)*; color-toned video and LCD screen with sound; edition 3/9, collection of the Guggenheim Museum, New York City, United States

1993   *tropos*; horsehair, glass, metal table, audio component, books; Dia Center for the Arts, New York City, United States; (no longer exists)

1998   *mattering*; red silk, peacocks, ink, graphite, ladder; Musée d'Art Contemporain de Montréal, Canada

2001   *at hand*; 7 compressed air mechanisms, paper with tinted edges, sound; Sean Kelly Gallery, New York City, United States; (no longer exists)

Further Reading

Ann Hamilton (exhib. cat.), with texts by Chris Bruce, Rebecca Solnit, and Buzz Spector, Seattle, Washington: Henry Art Gallery, University of Washington, 1992

Cameron, Dan, *El Jardin Salvaje: The Savage Garden: Landscape as Metaphor in Recent American Installations* (exhib. cat.), Madrid: Fundacion Caja de Pensiones, 1991

Cooke, Lynne, *Ann Hamilton: tropos*, New York: Dia Center for the Arts, 1993

Hamilton, Ann, *Ann Hamilton* (exhib. cat.), edited by Lynda Forsha and Hugh M. Davies, with text by Susan Stewart, La Jolla, California: San Diego Museum of Contemporary Art, 1991

Hamilton, Ann, *Ann Hamilton: present–past, 1984–1994*, Milan, Italy: Skira, 1998

Hamilton, Ann, *Ann Hamilton: whitecloth* (exhib. cat.), Ridgefield, Connecticut: The Aldrich Museum of Contemporary Art, 1999

Hamilton, Ann, *The body and the object: Ann Hamilton, 1984–1996*, Columbus, Ohio: Wexner Center for the Arts and Ohio State University, 1996

Hamilton, Ann, *Mneme* (exhib. cat.), Liverpool, England: The Tate Gallery, 1994

Pagel, David, "Still Life: The Tableaux of Ann Hamilton," *Arts Magazine* (May 1990)

Simon, Joan, *Ann Hamilton*, New York: Harry Abrams, 2002

Stewart, Susan, "As firmament a flame: On the Work of Ann Hamilton," *Ann Hamilton*, La Jolla, California: San Diego Museum of Contemporary Art, 1991

DUANE HANSON 1925–1996 *United States*

The sculptor Duane Hanson was one of the chief proponents of the photorealist style popular from 1969 until the mid 1970s. Artists grouped under this rubric sought to depict people, places, and things with the absolute fidelity of a camera and thereby to call into question the relationship of art and the visual perception of reality. Yet unlike peers such as painters Philip Pearlstein, Chuck Close, Audrey Flack, and Richard Estes, Hanson was more concerned with social ills than with questions of perception. For Hanson realism was a means to an end, helping viewers to identify with a message that over the course of his career moved from commentary to satire.

Frustration and uncertainty marked Hanson's early career, owing in part to his spasmodic art education. Born in Alexandria, Minnesota, he grew up in an isolated farming community, Parkers Prairie, where he hoarded the local library's sole art book. At age 13 he carved and painted a life-size wooden replica of Thomas Gainsborough's 18th-century *Blue Boy*, precociously foreshadowing his mature work. In 1941 Hanson visited an art museum, in Minneapolis, for the first time. Two years later he launched a peripatetic college career that took him from Decorah, Iowa, to Seattle, Washington, to St. Paul, Minnesota, where by 1945 he had enrolled at Macalester College. There, he produced a small soapstone sculpture titled *Woman Spanking Child* (1946), whose exaggerated figures revealed an artist torn between a tendency toward realism and an allegiance to the dominant mode of the day, Abstract Expressionism. The first to graduate with a bachelor's degree in fine arts from Macalester, Hanson continued his studies at the University of Michigan before moving to the studio program at the Cranbrook Academy of Art (also in Michigan), where he attained a master's degree in fine arts.

After a brief time as a high school teacher, Hanson moved to Germany, where he mounted his first solo exhibition in 1958. In the following year, he met George Grygo, a sculptor working with polyester resin and fiberglass. Hanson was impressed with the material, more often used in industry than in art, as it was easily manipulated yet sturdy and lightweight when set. He returned to the United States in 1961 and ultimately settled near Miami, Florida, where his career floundered until he discovered that Pop art had replaced abstraction in the art magazines. To Hanson, this change signaled the renewed legitimacy of realism. The cast plaster figures of George Segal particularly impressed him, although he considered them too generalized and existential. Hanson craved specificity and sought to make sharp social commentary through his art. In 1966 he produced *Abortion*, a white plaster sculpture of a pregnant woman lying dead on a table, draped in a cloth. Local critics were outraged, but Hanson was encouraged and soon produced life-size sculptures of a pauper's corpse, a suicide, and a murdered rape victim. Responding to public dissatisfaction with the Vietnam War, Hanson in 1967 made his most ambitious work to date, *War*, composed of a grisly pile of five dead or dying soldiers, cast in the polyester resin and fiberglass method that henceforth would be his chosen medium. He also began to work with naturalist colors and to add other realistic touches, such as actual clothing and props.

Hanson's sculptures continued to cause controversy in Miami, but he was unknown elsewhere. At a friend's urging, he sent slides of his work to Leo Castelli, whose New York City gallery represented the Pop artists Hanson admired. The gallery's director, Ivan Karp, responded, visiting the artist in 1968 and encouraging him to move to New York. In the following year, Hanson followed Karp's advice and was soon represented there in an exhibition on the theme of infamy at the Whitney Museum of American Art and in his first New York City solo exhibition at Karp's new SoHo gallery, O.K. Harris. Over the next two years, Hanson's art developed rapidly. He continued to produce work intended to goad a visceral response from viewers—a crashed motorcyclist, a race riot, Bowery derelicts sleeping in trash—before moving on to depict pop-culture icons such as boxers, football players, and rock stars in action. By 1971 he had given up headline topics and freeze-frame figures to concentrate on figures of ordinary Americans, in their daily activities, reflecting the banality of postwar consumer culture.

Hanson secured his reputation by producing in rapid succession the sculptures that would become his best-known works. An uncanny sense of mimesis marks his mature work, as he became ever more skilled with the details of mimicking the reality he critiqued. Recreating flesh with oil paint on fiberglass, gluing strands of hair and glass eyes into place, and using clothing and other props, Hanson sought to establish an absolute integrity as he applied artifice to social commentary. *Tourists* is typical of Hanson's blunt satire. A retirement-age couple gazes up at an unseen site; the man is weighted with camera equipment, while his companion carries a quilted bag heavy with brochures. As with many of Hanson's sculptures, it is easy to assume that the artist pointed a finger at such stereotypes in order to ridicule them. But he was also capable of compassion, whether the subject was an exhausted traveling businessman (*Businessman* [*with cigar*]) or an artist with long hair and splattered paints (*Seated Artist*), posed for by a friend in SoHo. Indeed, his best work indicates empathy for senior citizens and working-class subjects.

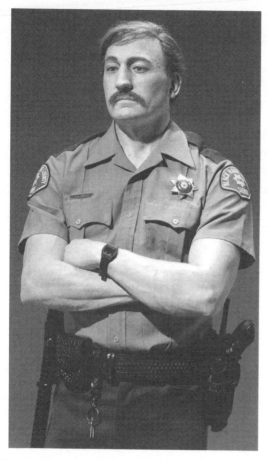

Policeman (detail), 1993
© Christie's Images / CORBIS, and The Estate of Duane
Hansen / Licensed by VAGA, New York, NY

In 1973 Hanson left New York City to settle in Davie, Florida, where he would live for the remainder of his life. He may have left the art world's epicenter, but his work continued to garner critical attention and widespread popularity in the 1970s. His insistence on authenticity led him to use local people as models, subjecting them to an arduous process that transformed them into archetypes. He elicited the life histories of his models for *Janitor* (1973) and *Dishwasher* even as he painstakingly cast their bodies in poses as dispirited workers with diminished aspirations. By way of contrast with his working men, Hanson's women generally enact the grotesquerie of modern consumption. *Florida Shopper* (1973) and *Young Shopper*, for example, show women encumbered by boutique bags and bad taste. By the mid 1970s he had begun to play the stillness of his statues against the viewer's expectations of galleries and museums. *Bank Guard* and *Museum Guard* disappeared into their surroundings and were often mistaken for real guards. A retrospective of Hanson's work traveled to several museums in the years 1976–78; it broke all previous attendance records at the Whitney Museum of American Art, New York

City, and established him as one of the major sculptors of the late 20th century. In the years of his greatest success, Hanson often described his work by quoting Henry David Thoreau's aphorism that "the mass of men lead lives of quiet desperation."

Once the heyday of photorealism ended, interest in Hanson's art began to wane. With only one solo show in New York City between 1985 and 1995, critics considered him and his sculptures irrelevant relics of another era. By the late 1980s he had almost no critical support. However, in the 1990s some critics and historians suggested that Hanson was a precursor to Robert Gober, Charles Ray, and Jake and Dinos Chapman, whose sculptures were similarly intended to create an illusion of reality. Others contended that the later sculptors used realism to entirely different ends, concerned with matters other than satire. After Hanson's death in 1996, a traveling retrospective organized by the Museum of Art in Fort Lauderdale, Florida, garnered new attention for the artist, whose heightened realism continued to astound viewers. However, the exhibition did little to alter critical opinion about Hanson, who is today generally regarded as an anomaly: a gifted vernacular artist who was for a brief moment an art-world wonder.

GRADY T. TURNER

See also **Abstract Expressionism; Segal, George**

Biography

Born in Alexandria, Minnesota, United States, 17 January 1925. Studied art sporadically at Luther College (Decorah, Iowa), 1943, University of Washington (Seattle), 1944, and Macalester College (St. Paul, Minnesota), where he received his BFA, 1946; MFA, Cranbrook Academy of Art (Bloomfield Hills, Michigan), 1951; taught in Germany, 1953–60; returned to United States, 1961; numerous solo exhibitions at O.K. Harris Gallery in New York City, as well as exhibitions at university galleries, such as at Harvard and Yale, and group shows at the Whitney Museum of American Art, New York City; the Corcoran Gallery of Art, Washington, D.C., and Documenta V, Kassel, West Germany, 1970–84; retrospectives organized by Württembergischer Kunstverein, Stuttgart, 1974, Wichita State University (Kansas), 1976, and Museum of Art (Fort Lauderdale, Florida), 1998. Died in Boca Raton, Florida, United States, 6 January 1996.

Selected Works

1966   *Abortion*; plaster (destroyed); smaller
        version: collection of the artist's estate
1967   *War*; polyester resin, fiberglass, paint;

Wilhelm Lehmbruck Museum, Duisburg, Germany

1969 *Bowery Derelicts*; polyester resin and fiberglass, polychromed in oil, with mixed media; Neue Galerie, Aachen, Germany

1970 *Tourists*; polyester resin, fiberglass, paint, hair, glass, clothing, miscellaneous objects; Scottish National Gallery, Edinburgh, Scotland

1971 *Businessman (with cigar)*; polyester resin, fiberglass, paint, hair, glass, clothing, miscellaneous objects; Virginia Museum of Fine Arts, Richmond, Virginia, United States

1971 *Seated Artist*; polyester resin, fiberglass, paint, hair, glass, clothing, miscellaneous objects; private collection of Byron Cohen, Mission Hills, Kansas, United States

1973 *Dishwasher*; polyester resin, fiberglass, paint, hair, glass, clothing, miscellaneous objects; private collection of Ed Cauduro, Portland, Oregon, United States

1973 *Young Shopper*; polyester resin, fiberglass, paint, hair, glass, clothing, miscellaneous objects; Charles Saatchi collection, London, England

1975 *Bank Guard*; polyester resin, fiberglass, paint, hair, glass, clothing, miscellaneous objects; private collection of Max Palevsky, Malibu, California, United States

1976 *Museum Guard*; polyester resin, fiberglass, paint, hair, glass, clothing, miscellaneous objects; Nelson-Atkins Museum of Art, Kansas City, Missouri, United States

1976 *Shoppers*; private collection of Mr. and Mrs. Jerome Nerman, Kansas City, Missouri, United States

Further Reading

Battcock, Gregory, editor, *Super Realism: A Critical Anthology*, New York: Dutton, 1975

Bush, Martin H., *Duane Hanson*, Wichita, Kansas: Edwin A. Ulrich Museum of Art, Wichita State University, 1976

Chase, Linda, and Ted McBurnett, "The Verist Sculptors: Two Interviews," *Art in America* (November/December 1972)

Contemporary American Painting and Sculpture, 1974, Urbana: University of Illinois Press, 1974

Giles, Christine, Elizabeth Hayt, and Katherine Plake Hough, *Duane Hanson: Virtual Reality*, Palm Springs, California: Palm Springs Desert Museum, 2000

Kulterman, Udo, *New Realism*, Greenwich, Connecticut: New York Graphic Society, and London: Mathews Miller Dunbar, 1972

O'Doherty, Brian, "Inside the White Cube," *Artforum* (April 1972)

Pamer, Laurence, and Marco Livingstone, *Duane Hanson: A Survey of His Work from the '30s to the '90s*, Fort Lauderdale, Florida: Museum of Art, 1998

Rose, Barbara, *American Art since 1900*, London: Thames and Hudson, and New York: Praeger, 1967; revised and expanded edition, London: Thames and Hudson, and New York: Holt and Praeger, 1975

Varnedoe, Kirk, "Duane Hanson Retrospective and Recent Work," *Arts Magazine* (January 1975)

HARBAVILLE TRIPTYCH

Anonymous
middle of 10th century CE or middle of 11th century CE
ivory, numerous traces of gilding and red paint; hinges and lock (not original), silver
h. 24.2 cm
Musée du Louvre, Paris, France

Sumptuously carved on front and back, the Harbaville Triptych is one of the most splendid Byzantine ivories. When closed, the exterior wings display four pairs of standing saints and two pairs of busts of saints within medallions separating the upper and lower registers; each saint holds a Gospel book or a cross. When open, the inner sides of the wings show the same arrangement, but here the upper register shows saints in military costume, with lance and sword, while below, saints in court costume hold crosses. The center panel, equal in width to the two wings but thicker and carved in higher relief, is also divided into two registers. The dominant image is the deesis, Christ enthroned flanked by the Virgin Mary and St. John the Baptist, who gesture toward Christ in intercession for the faithful. Christ holds a Gospel book in His left hand and blesses with His right. Two medallions with busts of angels are above the throne. Beneath a central decorative band, five apostles stand on platforms, Peter being in the center beneath Christ. All the figures have their names incised (still encrusted with red paint) next to their heads. Decorative bands of foliate ornament frame the central panel above and below. The upper band includes busts of three prophets.

On the back central panel, a tall Latin cross is flanked by cypress trees, entwined by a grapevine (left) and ivy (right), perhaps symbolizing the tree of life and the tree of knowledge of good and Evil. At the center and the ends of the arms of the cross are rosettes. Below, completing the paradisiacal garden, various animals inhabit the vegetation. Above, 24 stars surround the cross, which is also flanked by the inscription "Jesus Christ conquers" in raised Greek letters.

Different groups of saints assist in the deesis. After John the Baptist and the Virgin come the apostles and then the martyrs and military saints. On the exterior are the church fathers and miracle workers, emphasizing the important role of the church hierarchy as a vehicle of intercession. Additional bishops, apostles, and the medical saints are represented in the medallions. This hierarchical arrangement is also characteristic of monumental art, such as fresco and mosaic decoration, throughout the Byzantine world.

The date of the Harbaville Triptych continues to be a matter of grave scholarly dispute, as it is subject to the dating of the Romanos ivory (Bibliotheque Nationale de France, Paris), thought to have been created in either 945–49 or 1068–71, depending on which Emperor Romanos and which consort Eudokia is believed to be represented. Each passionately argued view in this debate has credibility, based on analysis of historical sources, stylistic analysis, technical examination of the carving, inscriptions, and costume design. The conservative nature of Byzantine ivory carving, and its predilection for reviving earlier conventions, does not help in this matter. The issue is not likely to be resolved until some heretofore undiscovered document can securely date the ivories in question.

The Harbaville Triptych is closely related to two other ivory triptychs, one in the Palazzo Venezia, Rome, and the other in the Vatican Museums. In all three triptychs, the composition of the central part—the deesis above and apostles below—is the same; the arrangement of the saints on the wings is also comparable. Variations on the Harbaville Triptych have been noted: the order of the saints differs slightly from that of the two other triptychs, and St. James the Persian replaces St. Agathonikos of the other two ivories. According to Kalavrezou-Maxeiner, who dates the Harbaville Triptych to the mid 11th century, the composition and arrangement of the Harbaville deesis are based on the 10th-century Palazzo Venezia Triptych, most likely made for Constantine VII Porphyrogennetos (r. 945–59) (see Kalavrezou-Maxeiner, 1997). She views the Harbaville Triptych as a copy in the medieval sense; that is, it incorporates changes in style and iconography that reflect the later period and the patron for whom it was made. Kalavrezou-Maxeiner notes, for example, that the figures in the Harbaville Triptych retain the statuesque quality of the earlier piece, but a restrained plasticity contributes to their controlled elegance.

Although the more widely held scholarly opinion considers the Harbaville Triptych the latest of the three triptychs, Gaborit-Chopin argues that the affinities that it presents with each of the other two triptychs call for an intermediate rank (see Gaborit-Chopin, 1992). The slender proportioned figures project farther from the ground in the Harbaville Triptych than in the Palazzo Venezia Triptych. Proportions are still more elongated in the Vatican Triptych, which also presents the most crowded composition of the three triptychs. Gaborit-Chopin observes further that the faces of the Harbaville Triptych's figures are individualized, many with emotional expression; the flicker of light over the faceted surfaces models the forms.

The Harbaville Triptych is among the most technically accomplished Byzantine ivories. The three decorative bands of the central panel are carefully and deeply undercut to create contrasts of light and shadow. All the details of the clothing, military armor, fringes on the shawl of the Virgin, book covers, and animals and vegetation surrounding the cross are indicated with a remarkable precision and subtlety. An exquisite example of the type of luxury object produced in Constantinople in the 10th and 11th centuries, the Harbaville Triptych functioned as a private icon for personal devotion.

LESLIE BUSSIS TAIT

See also **Ivory Sculpture: Early Christian–Romanesque**

Further Reading

Byzance: L'art byzantin dans les collections publiques françaises (exhib. cat.), Paris: Éditions de la Réunion des Musées Nationaux, 1992

Cutler, Anthony, *The Hand of the Master: Craftsmanship, Ivory, and Society in Byzantium (9th–11th Centuries)*, Princeton, New Jersey: Princeton University Press, 1994

Cutler, Anthony, "The Date and Significance of the Romanos Ivory," in *Byzantine East, Latin West: Art-Historical Studies in Honor of Kurt Weitzmann*, edited by Christopher Moss and Katherine Kiefer, Princeton, New Jersey: Princeton University Press, 1995

Evans, Helen C., and William D. Wixom, editors, *The Glory of Byzantium: Art and Culture of the Middle Byzantine Era, A.D. 843–1261* (exhib. cat.), New York: Metropolitan Museum of Art, 1997

Gaborit-Chopin, Danielle, in *Byzance: L'art byzantin dans les collections publiques françaises* (exhib. cat.: Musée du Louvre, Paris), Paris: Éditions de la Réunion des Musées Nationaux, 1992

Goldschmidt, Adolph, and Kurt Weitzmann, *Die byzantinischen Elfenbeinskulpturen des X.–XIII. Jahrhunderts*, 2 vols., Berlin: Cassirer, 1930–34; 2nd edition, Berlin: Deutscher Verlag für Kunstwissenschaft, 1979; see especially vol. 2

Kalavrezou-Maxeiner, Ioli, "Eudokia Makrembolitissa and the Romanos Ivory," *Dumbarton Oaks Papers* 31 (1977)

Kalavrezou-Maxeiner, Ioli, in *The Glory of Byzantium: Art and Culture of the Middle Byzantine Era A.D.843–1261* (exhib. cat. Metropolitan Museum of Art, New York), New York: Abrams/ Metropolitan Museum of Art, 1997

MICHAEL HEIZER 1944– *United States*

Not content to create portable objects that can be easily exhibited, bought, and sold, Michael Heizer produces monumental earthworks. A Conceptual artist who earned an international reputation in the 1960s, Heizer questions the assumptions of the Western world regarding the fabrication and display of art. Although he started his career as a figural painter, he soon began to experiment with monochromatic, geometrically shaped canvases. These early works highlight the intersection between sculpture and painting. Not only is the palette restricted to white, black, or gray, but the laminar surfaces are polyhedrons that protrude from the wall by more than 0.3 meters. *Negative Painting*, for instance, is a 2.4- meter by 3.6-meter, slate-gray, shaped canvas that circumscribes a void in the shape of an X.

Although Heizer moved to New York in 1966 to be a painter, he made numerous trips back west, particularly to the Mojave Desert and western Nevada, where he began to make art directly on the land. In 1968 Heizer produced *The Mojave Projects*, a series of fugitive sculptures and ground paintings, and *Nine Nevada Depressions*, a series of trenches in the shape of loops, zigzags, and crosses. These "unsculptural" works were studies in subtractive sculptural processes. Unlike chipping away stone to release a sculpture hidden within a block, however, as Michelangelo described his sculptural efforts, Heizer displaces materials to heighten the aesthetic appeal of absence. He deliberately contests the paradigms of European-influenced art traditions and seeks to make an inherently American art. Drawing on traditions of the indigenous peoples of the Americas, Heizer works directly with the land to underscore central aspects of the American identity. He does not romanticize the American landscape, however. Although remote, the sites of much of his work are important only insofar as they exert an influence on the physical forms; the surrounding landscape and its attendant symbolism (freedom, self-reliance, and manifest destiny) is insignificant.

Displaced/Replaced Mass, for example, recalls the efforts of Olmec sculptors who transported large boulders from the mountains to San Lorenzo and La Venta, where they were subsequently carved. Heizer visited these sites as an adolescent with his father, a renowned anthropologist who studied prehistoric efforts of transporting megaliths extreme distances. *Displaced/Replaced Mass* consists of three granite boulders transported from the Sierra Mountains to three rectilinear depressions Heizer dug out of a dry lake in Nevada. This work turns back the clock on the region's geologic activity by returning granite masses extracted at 2,700 meters to their original elevation of 1,200 meters. Unlike the refinement of traditional art materials, Heizer uses materials as he finds them in nature: "The idea of the rocks was that they were surrogate objects, replacement objects, replacement for the art object" (see Brown, 1984).

Heizer's desire to produce a monumental "unsculptural" earthwork was realized in 1969–70 with *Double Negative*. This work illuminates Heizer's interest in revealing the materials of a site and producing an aesthetic "object" out of an absence. Heizer displaced 250,000 tons of soil and rock by carving two aligned, rectilinear incisions across the lip of an eroding draw at the edge of Mormon Mesa in Nevada. The resulting shafts are 9 meters wide, 150 meters top to bottom, and 450 meters long. Across the naturally occurring void, the shaft is implied, as the viewer can see directly into the corresponding space. Even though there are two cuts, they become conceptually one form in the viewer's mind. In this sense, the title is a metaphysical pun: through the negation of earth by the two shafts, a positive presence is ephemerally implicated. As Heizer claimed in an interview, "There is nothing there, yet it is a sculpture" (see Brown, 1984). Heizer's critique of traditional sculpture and its display is implicit here. Longer than the Empire State Building is tall, this work critiques sculpture's traditional status. Previously, sculpture required an architectural context, but in this case, the sculpture is the architecture.

After completing *Double Negative*, Heizer continued to challenge assumptions regarding the display of sculpture by questioning the significance of the pedestal in European traditions. In *Adjacent, Against, Upon*, Heizer offers a sequential work in three elements. The first element consists of a large five-sided granite stone that is placed beside a cement slab that corresponds in shape and size; given the context, the cement slab is an implied pedestal. The second element consists of a trapezoidal granite megalith that leans against a similarly shaped cement slab. The third element is a triangular granite boulder that rests atop a three-sided cement pedestal. Heizer offers here each of the possible relationships a sculpture can have to its base. In a related work, *Elevated, Surface, Depressed* (1982), he placed three large boulders on three bases. The first base inclines at a 45-degree angle, the second one is a horizontal slab, and the third appears to sink beneath the weight of the megalith. *Levitated Mass* also questions the role of pedestals by appearing to be a large stone floating above water.

In 1972 Heizer bought land in Garden Valley, Nevada, where he built a studio and home. At this location, Heizer began working on his magnum opus, *City*, a project that upon completion is to comprise five complexes, covering an expanse greater than 1.61 kilometers at its length. Heizer finished work on *City: Complex I* in 1974. This monumental mound recalls the Egyptian mastaba. It is adorned with L-shaped and T-shaped cantilevered columns that evoke Mayan temples at Chichen Itza. Together, these elements produce a geometric abstraction of the feathered serpent, a Mayan deity. These cross-cultural references reiterate Heizer's avoidance of European tradition by invoking structures he studied while on anthropological travels with his father. In the 1980s Heizer began work on

740

City: Complex II and *City: Complex III*, which also draw on the forms of pre-Columbian architecture. During this time, he designed *Effigy Tumuli*, five earthen mounds at Buffalo Rocks, Illinois, a land-reclamation project at an abandoned strip-mining site. These mounds pay homage to the ancient mound builders of North America and are geometrically abstracted forms in the shape of some of the local animals displaced by the mine—the water strider, frog, turtle, catfish, and snake.

Given their remote locations, many of Heizer's earthworks require great effort to be seen. Most of his works are set in the expansive landscape of the West, but they do not contribute to a romantic, sublime conception of the American West. Heizer is less interested in the symbolic implications of the location of his work than in the relationship that his work strikes with the material found at the site. Instead of working with a chisel or handheld power tools, he uses backhoes, front loaders, and dump trucks to make his ideas reality. He draws on the tradition of pre-Columbian cultures to produce American art uninfluenced by European traditions.

BRIAN WINKENWEDER

See also **Contemporary Sculpture; De Maria, Walter; Long, Richard; Smithson, Robert; Turrell, James**

Biography

Born in Berkeley, California, United States, 4 November 1944. Son of Robert Heizer, pre-Columbian and Egyptian anthropologist. Studied painting at San Francisco Art Institute, 1963–64; moved to New York, 1966; traveled regularly to Mojave Desert, California, and Nevada, to produce large-scale sculptures; first one-man show in Heiner Friedrich Gallery, Munich, Germany, 1969; completed *Double Negative* and showed at Dwan Gallery, New York City, 1970; purchased land in Garden Valley, Nevada, and worked there on *City: Complex I* of his project *City* in 1973–74; continued to paint in New York studio until 1974; in 1980 began work on *City: Complex II*, which he finished in 1988; began working on *Effigy Tumuli* on site overlooking Illinois River, 1983; continued work on *City* and *Effigy Tumuli* throughout 1980s. Cassandra Foundation award, 1968; John Simon Guggenheim Memorial Foundation fellowship, 1983; in 1997, the Dia Foundation and Lannan Foundation provided funds for Heizer to finish *City*. Continues to live and work in Garden Valley, Nevada.

Selected Works

1968	*The Mojave Projects*; fugitive sculptures and ground paintings (deteriorated); El
	Mirage Dry Lake and Coyote Dry Lake, California, United States
1968	*Nine Nevada Depressions*, for Nevada desert; earthwork (deteriorated); private collection
1969	*Munich Depression*; earthwork; private collection, Munich, Germany
1969	*Displaced/Replaced Mass*; earthwork, private collection, Silver Springs, Nevada, United States
1969–70	*Double Negative*; earthwork; Mormon Mesa, Nevada (owned by Los Angeles Museum of Contemporary Art, United States)
1972–74	*City: Complex I*; concrete, steel, compacted earth; collection of the artist, Garden Valley, Nevada, United States
1976	*Adjacent, Against, Upon*; granite and concrete; Myrtle Edwards Park, Seattle, Washington, United States
1980	*Levitated Mass*; granite, stainless steel, and water; IBM Corporation Collection, IBM Building, New York City, United States
1980–88	*City: Complex II*; steel and concrete; collection of the artist, Garden Valley, Nevada, United States
1988	*Effigy Tumuli*; earthwork; Buffalo Rocks, Illinois, United States
1999	*City: Complex III*; steel and concrete; collection of the artist, Garden Valley, Nevada, United States

Further Reading

Brown, Julia, editor, *Sculpture in Reverse*, Los Angeles: Museum of Contemporary Art, 1984

Cowart, Jack, *Michael Heizer: Paintings, 1967–1980*, St. Louis, Missouri: St. Louis Art Museum, 1980

Sonfist, Alan, editor, *Art in the Land: A Critical Anthology of Environmental Art*, New York: Dutton, 1983

Tiberghien, Gilles A., *Land Art*, Paris: Éditions Carré, 1993; as *Land Art*, translated by Caroline Green, New York: Princeton Architectural Press, and London: Art Data, 1995

Tomkins, Calvin, *The Scene: Reports on Post-Modern Art*, New York: Viking Press, 1976

Weiermair, Peter, *Michael Heizer*, Innsbruck, Austria: Galerie im Taxisplais, 1977

Zdenek, Felix, *Michael Heizer*, Essen, Germany: Museum Folkwang, and Otterlo, The Netherlands: Rijksmuseum Kröller-Müller, 1979

HENNEQUIN

See **Jean [Hennequin] de Liège**

DAME BARBARA HEPWORTH 1903–1975 *British*

Barbara Hepworth is usually cited in the company of Henry Moore as one of the first sculptors in England to work in an abstract idiom. In fact, her elegantly simple works in stone, wood, or bronze often go much further than Moore in the direction of nonrepresentational formalism. As biomorphic abstractions, they demonstrate a concentrated attention to the relation of volumes and materials. As she wrote in 1930, "If a pebble or an egg can be enjoyed for the sake of its shape only, it is one step towards a true appreciation of sculpture," adding that "abstract form, the relation of masses and planes, is that which gives sculptural life; this, then, admits that a piece of sculpture can be purely abstract or non-representational." Through such rigorously restricted means, Hepworth's aim was to evoke ineffable truths, particularly the connection between people and nature.

During her time at the Royal College of Art, London, Hepworth became friendly with fellow student Henry Moore, and although their influence was clearly mutual, Moore was to become the inevitable point of reference in critical discussions of Hepworth's work. After graduating in 1924, Hepworth was awarded a traveling scholarship to Siena, Florence, and Rome. At this time, her work was still primarily representational, consisting of monumental torsos inspired by the Egyptian, Assyrian, and pre-Columbian figures that had also begun to intrigue Moore. In the 1930s Hepworth came to be seen as a preeminent representative of the Modernist doctrine of "truth to materials." She favored a direct carving technique, which allowed close concentration on the unique potentialities of a given medium, freeing the object that was felt to be latent in a particular block of wood or stone. Writing in the Constructivist publication *Circle* in 1937, she stressed that "for the imaginative idea to be fully and freely projected into stone, wood or any plastic substance, a complete sensibility to material—an understanding of its inherent quality and character—is required."

Hepworth's activities after she married the painter Ben Nicholson confirmed her tendencies toward abstraction. In 1932–33 they spent time in Paris, where they met artists such as Piet Mondrian, Pablo Picasso, Georges Braque, and Constantin Brancusi. Working in an enclave of prominent Modernist artists in Hampstead, Hepworth also associated with Herbert Read, Naum Gabo, and László Moholy-Nagy, as well as Moore and Mondrian. Mondrian apparently served as a catalyst for Hepworth by suggesting the possibility of a completely abstract sculptural language on the model of "neoplastic" painting, and by the mid 1930s many of her works were making use of pure geometry.

Another (quite literal) breakthrough came in 1931, when she punched a hole through her alabaster *Pierced Form*. This initiated a new exploration of negative space as an integral part of sculptural form, an idiom that was also followed up by Moore.

At the beginning of World War II, Hepworth moved to St. Ives in Cornwall. Here she began a series of open and hollow forms in wood, the concave inner surfaces of which were often painted in unmodulated fields of color. Another major innovation of this period was the addition of tautly stretched strings to her sculptures (*Wave*, *Landscape Sculpture*, and *Pelagos*). The titles of many works of the 1940s and 1950s reflect Hepworth's attempt to invest her sculptures with the experiential qualities of particular landscapes, usually those of Cornwall. She increasingly turned to the medium of bronze in her later years, but even when working in bronze, she was able to retain her favored subtractive technique by carving her models in dry plaster. As her fame grew, her use of bronze facilitated the creation of larger public commissions.

After 1950 Hepworth became intrigued by spatial as well as formal relationships, and many of her sculptures began to make use of two or more contrasting forms, often suggesting groups of people. Such hints of a return to figuration mark several monumental later works, including the *Contrapuntal Forms* of 1949–50, commissioned for the Festival of Britain, and *Monolith (Empyrean)* of 1953, installed next to the new Royal Festival Hall in London. Hepworth returned briefly to representationalism in her *Madonna and Child* for the Lady Chapel of the Church of St. Ives. This was a memorial to her son, who had been killed in 1953 while serving with the Royal Air Force. A much larger memorial work is the colossal bronze *Single Form*, installed at the United Nations in New York and dedicated to the memory of her friend Dag Hammarskjöld, who had also perished in an air crash. Many of Hepworth's tall standing figures of the 1960s and 1970s have a totemic quality, and when set into the landscape, they have not failed to remind critics of the prehistoric standing stones of Cornwall. Her last works tend to eschew the complex curves of organic form in favor of harder, rectilinear, and more geometric shapes. This is typified by the large bronze *Four-Square (Walk Through)* of 1966, which, as its name suggests, was meant to encourage a more dynamic interaction between viewer and sculpture.

Hepworth died in a fire in her Cornwall studio in 1975. The restored studio, located in the center of St. Ives, was opened in 1980 as a museum and sculpture garden under the management of the Tate Gallery. In retrospect, her oeuvre appears as the apotheosis of Modernist formalism and reductivism. The compositional simplicity of her works throws into relief her unflagging devotion to issues of shape, space, and color, as well as to the intrinsic qualities of different materials. To later generations of sculptors, however, her goal of conveying universal human experience through exquisitely crafted abstract forms began to seem overly precious, and younger artists such as Anthony Caro instead took to more aggressive processes of welding and assemblage. Postmodern criticism, predictably, has tended to focus on the relationship of gender issues to her work (a connection that Hepworth herself did not emphasize) and attempts to deconstruct the putatively universal or essentialist nature of her achievement in favor of more complex readings.

CHRISTOPHER PEARSON

See also **Brancusi, Constantin; Caro, Anthony; Gabo, Naum; Modernism; Moholy-Nagy, László; Moore, Henry; Women Sculptors**

Biography

Born in Wakefield, Yorkshire, England, 10 January 1903. Attended Leeds School of Art on scholarship, 1919–20; studied sculpture at the Royal College of Art, London, 1921–24; travel scholarship to Italy, 1924–25; worked in Rome with sculptor John Skeaping, 1924–26; lived in the Mall Studios, Hampstead, 1928–39; first London exhibition, Beaux-Arts Gallery, 1928; visited Paris, 1932–33; met Picasso, Braque, and Brancusi; joined the Abstraction-Création group in Paris, 1933, and was cofounder/member of the Unit One group in London, 1934; moved to St. Ives, Cornwall, England, 1939; first retrospective exhibition, Temple Newsam House, Leeds, 1943; moved into Trewyn studio, St. Ives, 1949; represented British sculpture at the Venice Biennale, 1950; designed sets and costumes for Sophocles's *Electra*, Old Vic Theater, London, 1951, and for Michael Tippett's opera *The Midsummer Marriage*, Royal Opera House, Covent Garden, London, 1954–55; major retrospective shows at Whitechapel Gallery, London, 1954 and 1962; began working in metal, 1956; Grand Prix, São Paolo Biennial, 1959; made a Trustee of Tate Gallery and created Dame of the British Empire, 1965. Died in St. Ives, Cornwall, England, 20 May 1975.

Selected Works

1931 *Pierced Form*; pink alabaster (destroyed World War II)
1935 *Discs in Echelon*; wood; Museum of Modern Art, New York City, United States
1938 *Forms in Echelon*; wood; Hepworth Museum, St. Ives, Cornwall, England
1943–44 *Wave*; wood, string, painted wood; private collection

1944 *Landscape Sculpture*; bronze and strings; Tate Gallery, London, England
1946 *Pelagos*; wood with color and strings; Tate Gallery, London, England
1947 *Pendour*; elmwood with color; Hirshhorn Museum and Sculpture Garden, Washington, D.C., United States
1949–50 *Contrapuntal Forms*; blue limestone; Harlow New Town, Essex, England
1951 *Vertical Forms*; stone; Hatfield Technical College, Hertfordshire, England
1952 *Head (Elegy)*; mahogany wood, strings; Hirshhorn Museum and Sculpture Garden, Washington, D.C., United States
1953 *Monolith (Empyrean)*; blue limestone; Royal Festival Hall, London, England
1954 *Madonna and Child*; stone; Church of St. Ives, Cornwall, England
1955 *Hollow Form (Penwith)*; wood; Museum of Modern Art, New York City, United States
1956 *Theme on Electronics (Orpheus)*; brass with strings; Mullard House, London, England
1958–59 *Sea Form (Porthmeor)*; bronze; Tate Gallery, London, England
1962 *Winged Figure*; aluminum; John Lewis Building, Oxford Street, London, England
1962–63 (unveiled 1964) *Single Form* (memorial to Dag Hammarskjöld); bronze; United Nations, New York City, United States
1966 *Four-Square (Walk Through)*; bronze; edition of three: Churchill College, Cambridge, England; Hepworth Museum, St. Ives, Cornwall, England; Harvard University, Cambridge, Massachusetts, United States
1970 *The Family of Man*; nine bronze pieces; edition of two: First City Bank Corporation of Texas, Houston, United States; Yorkshire Sculpture Park, Wakefield, England

Further Reading

Barbara Hepworth (exhib. cat.), London: Tate Gallery, 1968
Barbara Hepworth: Carvings and Drawings, London: Lund Humphries, 1952
Barbara Hepworth: A Guide to the Tate Gallery Collection at London and St. Ives, Cornwall, London: Tate Gallery, 1982
Bowness, Alan, editor, *The Complete Sculpture of Barbara Hepworth, 1960–69*, New York: Praeger, and London: Lund Humphries, 1971
Curtis, Penelope, *Barbara Hepworth*, London: Tate Gallery, 1998
Curtis, Penelope, and Alan G.Wilkinson, *Barbara Hepworth: A Retrospective*, London: Tate Gallery, 1994

Gale, Matthew, and Chris Stephens, *Barbara Hepworth: Works in the Tate Gallery Collection and the Barbara Hepworth Museum, St. Ives*, London: Tate Gallery, 1999

Gardiner, Margaret, *Barbara Hepworth: A Memoir*, Edinburgh: Salamander Press, 1982

Hammacher, Abraham M., *Barbara Hepworth*, London: Thames and Hudson, and New York: Abrams, 1968; revised edition, London: Thames and Hudson, 1987; New York: Thames and Hudson, 1998

Hodin, Josef P., and Alan Bowness, *Barbara Hepworth*, London: Lund Humphries, and New York: McKay, 1961

Thistlewood, David, editor, *Barbara Hepworth Reconsidered*, Liverpool: Liverpool University Press and Tate Gallery Liverpool, 1996

Wilkinson, Alan G., *Barbara Hepworth: Sculptures from the Estate*, New York: Wildenstein, 1996

SEA FORM (PORTHMEOR)

Barbara Hepworth (1903–1975)

1958–1959

bronze

h. 83 cm; w. 114 cm

Tate Gallery, London, England

(The other six castings in the edition of seven are in the Art Gallery of Ontario, Canada; Yale University Museum, New Haven, Connecticut, United States; the collection of the British Council, London, England; Hirshhorn Museum and Sculpture Garden, Washington D.C., United States; Gemeentemuseum, The Hague, the Netherlands; and Middelheimpark, Antwerp, Belgium. The original plaster, painted green, is at the Hepworth Museum, St. Ives, England.)

Although exemplifying many of her characteristic formal concerns, Barbara Hepworth's bronze *Sea Form (Porthmeor)* is an unexpectedly lyrical presence in the oeuvre of an artist better known for her simpler, more elemental sculptures. The work's pierced silhouette is asymmetrical and organic, a sinuous, involuted piece of sea-green protoplasm that seems to float weightlessly up from its narrow base, flapping and twisting as if moved by unseen currents of wind or water. The suggestion of motion is reinforced by an insistent diagonal axis stretching from lower left to upper right. The rounded edges of the form curve back into its center, loosely defining the open hollow that is a hallmark of Hepworth's works. Anticipating the viewer's urge to interact with the sculpture in a sensuous and tactile way, Hepworth created an effect whereby the curling lips were smoothly polished as if by constant rubbing, contrasting with the more variegated texturing and tonality of the inside and outside surfaces. The patination of the bronze is black, with swirling passages of green and white suggesting the play of spume and waves on the surface of the ocean, or perhaps the traces of water, feet, and birds on a sandy beach.

The sculpture's secondary title refers to a beach at the town of St. Ives in Cornwall, England, where Hepworth had her home and studio. In her *Pictorial Autobiography*, she notes: "I had by this time become bewitched by the Atlantic beach. The form I call *Porthmeor* is the ebb and flow of the Atlantic" (see Hepworth, 1970). Porthmeor beach, now popular with surfers and the site of a new branch of the Tate Gallery, does indeed face out toward the Atlantic, and so receives more substantial swells than the coastline further east. Naturally, the question thus arises: does *Sea Form* represent the rim of a cresting wave, as many critics have suggested?

Sea Form can be fitted into a long series of sculptures by Hepworth—going back to the 1940s—that are named after beaches. Her goal in these works was to express a feeling of connection to the landscapes of Cornwall, and to this end, her forms suggest geographical features—hills, sea caves and tidal pools, eroded coastal rocks, and so on. She described her *Forms in Movement (Pavan)* of 1956, for example, as an encapsulation of the transcendent thrill of facing the open expanse of the Atlantic from the cliffs at the western tip of Cornwall.

In her *Pictorial Autobiography*, Hepworth talks about this ecstatic conflation of landscape and bodily experience: "I wanted to make forms to stand on hillsides and through which to look to the sea. Forms to lie down in, or forms to climb through." Later, she specifies:

> All landscape needs a figure—and when a sculptor is the spectator he is aware that every landscape evokes a special image. In creating this image the artist tries to find a synthesis of his human experience and the quality of the landscape. The forms and piercings, the weight and poise of the concrete image also become evocative—a fusion of experience and myth.

This quasimystical celebration of the spiritual phenomenology of regional landscapes, a goal shared by several other St. Ives artists, is affirmed by the appearance of many Cornish place-names in the titles of her later works.

Regardless of the literalism of this evocation of the marine element, *Sea Form* is the result of a new freedom in Hepworth's work in the 1950s, which breaks away from the static ovoid forms of the previous decade. In 1954 she visited the Aegean and Cyclades Islands of Greece, an experience that proved both exhilarating and liberating, for a new spontaneity, a feeling for light and color, appears in her sketchbook drawings. Two years later, surprising critics who saw her as an unshakable exponent of the Modernist doctrines of direct carving and "truth to materials," Hepworth began working in metal. Her first efforts consisted of curving sheets of copper and brass, but she soon began to create bronze castings, beginning with the parabolic *Curved Form (Trevalgan)* (1956; Tate Gallery).

Critics have placed Hepworth's bronzes of the 1950s in three categories: compact, ovoid, and often highly polished forms; tall architectural commissions with attenuated silhouettes and extensive use of negative space; and, as in the case of *Sea Form*, more varied organic shapes. Hepworth created works in this last category by building up the model in plaster on an armature of bent aluminum mesh. This was then allowed to dry before being carved and ultimately cast in bronze; in this way Hepworth was able to retain the feel of sculpting (rather than modeling), which she so enjoyed. The bronze was cast at the Fulham foundry, London, 1959. The new technique also affected her means of expression, however, for the use of mesh sheets freed her from the closed silhouettes of her earlier sculptures in stone or wood, and her forms could now become linear, transparent, or—as here—planar and warped. The resulting works have been suggestively described by Hammacher as "closed or half-open, like shells, and receptive, with the same delicate female elements which can be seen in *Porthmeor*" (see Hammacher, 1968). The post-Freudian implications of such "female" qualities have become of increasing interest to a more recent generation of Hepworth scholars.

Other bronzes of 1958, such as the tall openwork *Garden Sculpture (Model for Meridian)* and *Cantate Domino* (both at the Tate's Hepworth Museum, St. Ives), share the movement and compositional freedom of *Sea Form*. In addition, the twisting, organic forms of these works of the later 1950s find a counterpart in many of Hepworth's preparatory drawings of this period: these are extremely vigorous and gestural, with thick, looping lines bursting explosively from a central node.

Sea Form has similarities with Hepworth's later and more vertical bronze *Figure for Landscape* (1960) as well as the *Bronze Form (Patmos)* (1962–63) (both at the Hepworth Museum, St. Ives). Its theme (though not its form) was taken up again in the tall bronze *Sea Form (Atlantic)* (1964; Norwich Castle Museum), which is itself part of a series related to the coast around Porthcurno, 2.5 km southeast of Lands End in Cornwall, including the *Oval Form (Trezion)* (1961–63) and *Rock Form (Porthcurno)* (1964).

CHRISTOPHER PEARSON

Further Reading

Hammacher, Abraham M., *Barbara Hepworth*, London: Thames and Hudson, and New York: Abrams, 1968; revised edition, London: Thames and Hudson, 1987; New York: Thames and Hudson, 1998

Hepworth, Barbara, *A Pictorial Autobiography*, Bath, Avon: Adams and Dart, and New York: Praeger, 1970; 2nd edition, revised, Bradford-on-Avon, Wiltshire: Moonraker Press, 1978

LOY HERING *ca.* 1485–*ca.* 1554 *German*

The work of the Swabian-Bavarian sculptor Loy Hering established the new Renaissance style in German stone sculpture. Hering's success as a producer of private tombstones in fashionable Renaissance frames is synonymous with the commercialization of the new Italian style north of the Alps. His remaining works, of which there are about 130, are mostly epitaphs and altar reliefs that he finished together with his workshop during the three decades between about 1520 and 1550. He had a wide-ranging clientele stretching from Vienna to Bamberg-am-Main and into Halle in Thuringia. Hering's workplace was in the northwest Bavarian diocesan city of Eichstätt, and his material was Jura limestone, a stone that was quickly gaining popularity as a substitute for marble in southern Germany during that time. For their pictorial depictions, his reliefs often copied motifs from then-current graphics, including those of Albrecht Dürer, Lucas Cranach, and Heinrich Aldegrever.

Hering learned the craft of sculpting in Augsburg around 1500. Nothing is known about his activities during the next two decades. One must distinguish between two groups of works when discussing his artistic production. The attribution of the work from his productive years in Eichstätt starting about 1520, during which dozens of tombstones left his highly acclaimed stonemasonry shop, is fairly certain. Attribution of the "early work" from the years between 1510 and 1517, however, for which biographical and archival evidence is completely lacking, remains a puzzling and controversial matter. Three of the most excellent stone sculptures of the early Renaissance in Augsburg have been attributed to the young Hering on stylistic grounds: the *Christ the Savior* of the Hörwath altar in the Church of St. George in Augsburg; the stone crucifix—definitely produced in Augsburg—from the parish church in the Tyrolean mining center of Schwaz; and the powerful monument to the founder of the diocese in Eichstätt, St. Willibald, which is located in the cathedral.

In recent research, two contrary positions have competed in regard to these early works. One speaks in favor of the young Hering's authorship (see Reindl, 1977), whereas the other ascribes the Willibald monument and the crucifix in Schwaz to the older, renowned Augsburg sculptor Gregor Erhart (see Schädler, 1975). Admittedly, it is not known for certain whether a single work by Erhart remains. The basic question in this discussion is the following: can we believe that a young sculptor like Hering—who was not yet a master—was capable of the artistic authorship of sculptures bearing the highest quality of those created in their time? Another, intermediate, position looks to Erhart as the directing master sculptor, but grants that Hering participated in its execution as a journeyman (see Gantner, 1997); according to this account, the young Hering is the talented newcomer of the next generation.

At the center of this attribution controversy between Hering and Erhart stands the monument to St. Willibald, which was erected in the choir of the Eichstätt Cathedral in 1514. The figure of St. Willibald, the legendary first bishop of the diocese, sits over–life-size in solitary splendor on a throne in a shell niche. Free of any gestures, the depiction concentrates on conveying the highest degree of dignity. Even the magnificent display of the bishop's vestments seems completely natural. Here the figural attributions predominating in the often symbolic sculpture of the Late Gothic seem to have been entirely overcome, and the human being takes precedence over all *staffage* (garnishes or accessories). There was no precedent in the German-speaking realm for this Willibald figure, with its monumental power of authority and its idealized, although fictitious, portraitlike face of a wise old man. Formally comparable works can be found, at best, in the Roman papal tombstones of the late 15th century, such as Antonio del Pollaiuolo's seated figure of Pope Innocent VIII (completed 1498) in St. Peter's Basilica, Rome.

The Willibald ensemble is justifiably seen as one of the major works of the German High Renaissance. Its disconcertingly "modern" style is similar to secular heroic monuments of the 19th century. Although it was created for a sacred space, it is neither a tombstone nor an altar. Its primary function was to commemorate the founder of the bishopric. The seated figure honors the founder in a secular manner without using him for any liturgical purposes. The Willibald monument thus belongs to a small group of contemporaneously projected commemorative monuments in religious settings that propagated historical traditions primarily in a historical-political, and less hagiographical, vein: the unfinished monument to the German emperors in the Speyer Cathedral (sculpted by Hans Valkenauer, then donated by Emperor Maximilian I in 1514; fragments located in the Museum Carolino Augusteum, Salzburg); Tilman Riemenschneider's tombstone for the imperial couple Heinrich and Kunigunde in Bamberg Cathedral (completed 1513); and the inscription tablet sponsored in 1513 to commemorate Emperor Otto III, with its capital inscription by Hans Daucher, in Augsburg Cathedral.

The conception of the Willibald monument surely stemmed largely from its commissioner, Gabriel von Eyb, who was at that time the highly cultivated bishop of Eichstätt. Its execution, however, required a qualified sculptor who must have been from Augsburg, the nearby center for current styles in stone sculpture. First, several arguments favor the young Hering's having at least participated in its production. Stylistic parallels are noticeable between the architectural ornaments of the monument—for example, around the coats of arms—and the well-known ornamental style of the later epitaphs from Hering's workshop. Second, studies comparing the epigraphic style—for example, the inscription characteristics of the dedication plaque under the seated figure—with the inscriptions on Hering's later works have shown there to be clear similarities between them (see Bornschlegel, 1994). Third, the fact that Hering established himself in Eichstätt immediately afterward can be interpreted as a consequence of his work on the Willibald monument.

Hering directed a master workshop in Eichstätt beginning at the latest in 1518. Commissions followed for sculptures of the three bishops who held office while he was active, as well as for the Eichstätt Cathedral chapter. Even today, the mortuary (the burial room belonging to the cathedral complex) seems to serve as a Hering museum, given the numerous epitaphs from his workshop. In a certain way, Hering can be considered the prototype of a court artist. The lower nobles, the so-called *Reichsritterschaft* (knights of the empire), as well as bishops and cloister abbeys from elsewhere, had him carve their tombstones. Hering's clientele was exclusively Roman Catholic, and it is noteworthy that his career took place just at the time that the contracts for sacred sculpture dried up for his urban colleagues in Augsburg and Nuremberg because the imperial cities were turning toward a Protestantism that was skeptical of images.

Being in a small, conservative diocesan town thus made it possible for Hering to become the most prolific producer of epitaphs, or memorial slabs for the deceased. Hering developed several types of epitaphs with varying degrees of elaborateness. Most common were the portal-like architectural designs with an inscripted socle, flanking pillars, architrave, and tympanum, which together framed a scenic relief. The more elaborate monuments also had flanking wings in the tradition of a three-winged altar. Hering's style of figural relief is marked by his sovereign execution of scenes that were often based on printed graphics: the Coronation of Mary, the Resurrection, the Ascension, and, especially, often, portraits of the deceased in front of the crucifix or with the name patron. His works bear the stamp of the Renaissance above all in the prevalence of central-perspective background architecture and the soft, flowing style of parallel folds in the garments. The figural characteristics are soft and occasionally somewhat unclear. His great number of commissions seems to account for the sculptor's tendency to resort to schematic repetitions in his figural compositions and architectural frames soon after establishing his workshop.

Besides his main body of burial slabs, epitaphs, and altars, Hering also carved in stone two mobile, small-scale reliefs with profane contents: *Rhea Silvia*, a scene from the foundation myth of the city of Rome (in which Romulus and Remus are weaned from their mother Rhea Silvia) and *Der Garten der Lüste* (Garden of Love) as an allegory of the power of love. Their highly modern, iconographically original, humanistic antique motifs attest to his contact with sophisticated clients. Along with the monogram "LH," *Der Garten der Lüste* bears Hering's pictographic signature: a herring fish pointing upward on a slant, within which his family name is inscribed. Otherwise Hering never signed his works.

Scholars have tried to delimit Hering's extensive oeuvre by referring to the finer aspects of his style so as to assign certain works to his workshop. Up to the present day, however, they have not been able to construe who worked in the productive and often-cited Hering workshop. Three of his four sons became sculptors by profession. Georg Hering worked in nearby Regensburg, and Martin Hering, who collaborated with his father and eventually inherited the family shop, worked in neighboring Neuburg an der Donau. Thomas Hering, the most prolific of the three, was established in Munich in the 1530s and 1540s as the court sculptor for the Wittelsbach family. As a *khunstreycher* (artistic) mason, Thomas was called upon to furnish their Landshut city residence, a pioneering construction that enjoys the reputation of being the first German Renaissance palace. The production of this most fruitful German sculpting dynasty in the 16th century ended about 1560, along with the less easily determinable oeuvres of Hering's sons. Reflected in the success of this dynasty is the eruption of a post-medieval world of forms as well as tendencies toward the schematization of Renaissance as an ornamental style.

THOMAS ESER

See also **Erhart, Gregor**

Biography

Born in Kaufbeuren, Germany, *ca.* 1485. Son of Michael Hering, a goldsmith. Began sculpture apprenticeship (as "Leome Hering") with Augsburg sculptor Hans Beierlein, 1499; presumed to be journeyman in workshop of Augsburg sculptor Gregor Erhart; lacking documentation for early work; lived in home of sculptor Jakob Murrmann, Augsburg, 1511–12; referred to as "master" and as living in Eichstätt, 1518; first solidly attributed work documented 1518; rose quickly in Eichstätt society; elected to city council, 1519 and 1522; one of town's four mayors, 1523 and 1533. Had four sons, three of whom were sculptors: Thomas (*ca.* 1510–49); Martin (*ca.* 1515–*ca.* 1553), and Georg (1520/3–1552/4). Loy's testament dated 1 June 1554. Died in Eichstätt, Germany, *ca.* June 1554.

Selected Works

ca. 1511–14   *Christ the Savior*; limestone; Church of St. George, Augsburg, Germany (attributed)

1512–14   Monument to St. Willibald; limestone, marble; Eichstätt Cathedral, Eichstätt, Germany (attributed)

ca. 1515   Crucifix; limestone; Franciscan church, Schwaz, Austria (attributed)

ca. 1517   Monument to Bernhard Arzt; limestone, marble; Eichstätt Cathedral, Eichstätt, Germany

1518–20   Monument to Prince Bishop Georg III von Bamberg; limestone; Bamberg Cathedral, Bamberg, Germany

1521–27   Monument to Georg Truchsess von Wetzhausen, and a tabernacle; limestone, marble, scagliola (polychrome stucco-plasters mixed in wet condition to imitate marble-stones); Protestant parish church, Auhausen near Öttingen, Germany

1524   Portrait of the Count Palatine Philipp (with inscribed dating); limestone; Germanisches Nationalmuseum, Nuremberg, Germany

ca. 1525   Crucifix; limestone; Eichstätt Cathedral, Eichstätt, Germany

ca. 1525–30   *Der Garten der Lüste* (Garden of Love); limestone; Staatliche Museen, Berlin, Germany

ca. 1530   *St. George* (St. George Altar); limestone, marble; Bayerisches Nationalmuseum, Munich, Germany

ca. 1530–35   *Adam und Eva*; limestone; Victoria and Albert Museum, London, England

after 1532   *Rhea Silvia*; limestone; Victoria and Albert Museum, London, England; numerous bronze plaquettes exist in various museums, including Staatliche Museen, Berlin, Germany; Musée des Beaux-Arts, Dijon, France; Victoria and Albert Museum, London, England; and Bayerisches Nationalmuseum, Munich, Germany

1534 Monument to Johannes von Wirsberg and Christoph von Schirnding; limestone, marble; Eichstätt Cathedral, Eichstätt, Germany

1541–43 Monument to Prince Bishop Konrad III von Würzburg; limestone, marble; Würzburg Cathedral, Eichstätt, Germany

Further Reading

Bornschlegel, Franz-Albrecht, "Die Inschriften Loy Herings und seiner Werkstatt," in *Pinxit, sculpsit, fecit: Kunsthistorische Studien: Festschrift für Bruno Bushart*, edited by Bärbel Hamacher, Munich: Deutscher Kunstverlag, 1994

Cannon-Brookes, Peter, "Loy Hering and the Monogrammist DH," *Apollo* 113 (1971)

Gantner, Benno Constantin, "Loy Hering, um 1485/86–1554: Ein schwäbischer Bildhauer in Eichstätt," edited by the Schwäbische Forschungsgemeinschaft, Weissenhorn, Germany: Konrad, 1997

Mader, Felix, *Loy Hering: Ein Beitrag zur Geschichte der deutschen Plastik des 16. Jahrhunderts*, Munich: Ges. für Christliche Kunst, 1905

Reindl, Peter, *Loy Hering: Zur Rezeption der Renaissance in Süddeutschland*, Basel, Switzerland: Historisches Museum, 1977

Schädler, Alflred, "Das Eichstätter Willibalddenkmal und Gregor Erhart," *Münchner Jahrbuch der Bildenden Kunst* 26 (1975)

Smith, Jeffrey Chipps, *German Sculpture of the Later Renaissance, c. 1520–1580: Art in an Age of Uncertainty*, Princeton, New Jersey: Princeton University Press, 1994

EVA HESSE 1936–1970 *German, active in* *United States*

Eva Hesse introduced an innovative formal vocabulary into abstract sculpture that was related to the repetition and structure of Minimalism while also incorporating elements of the human body, organicism, tactility, and the absurd. She began her art studies in New York City at the Art Students League while she attended high school; afterward, she studied at the Cooper Union for the Advancement of Science and Art, transferring in 1957 to the Yale School of Art and Architecture. At Yale she worked with Josef Albers, the venerated German Bauhaus artist and teacher who had shaped the artistic paths of many Abstract Expressionists and New York Minimalists. After college Hesse returned to New York and lived on the Bowery, where she met and befriended many artists and critics, including Claes Oldenburg, Carl Andre, Robert Mangold and Sylvia Plimack Mangold, Lucy Lippard, Robert Ryman, Mel Bochner, and Sol LeWitt. She had her first gallery exhibition at age 25 and received immediate critical attention for her radically eccentric approach to abstraction.

In November 1961, Hesse married sculptor Tom Doyle. She noted in her diaries that she felt professionally dominated by Doyle and personally distressed by the agitated and competitive nature of their relationship. Nonetheless, Hesse's art did not always mirror her life, rather it frequently contradicted it. Her work at this time was characterized by a series of colorful reliefs and related erotic drawings exploring unusual forms and with barely recognizable iconography that married abstraction and organicism.

Hesse's real breakthrough as an artist—her transition from painting into sculpture—occurred in 1964–65 when Doyle was invited to make art for a wealthy German industrialist, F. Arnhard Scheidt, a textile manufacturer. Doyle's large Abstract Expressionist-inspired sculptures were too expansive and expensive to transport, so the collector moved Doyle and Hesse to Kettwig-am-Ruhr in Germany where they could work in studios housed in his massive textile factories. This location proved fortuitous for Hesse's career, stimulating her attraction to three-dimensional forms including variable, soft materials such as string, rope, and cloth.

This stage of her artistic development was influenced if not facilitated by Hesse's memories and associations with her native land, where the threats of war and genocide had splintered her childhood home and family. Born a Jew in 1936 to a German criminal lawyer and his wife, Hesse and her older sister Helen escaped the Nazi terror on a children's train to Amsterdam when the artist was only two. Their parents secretly left Germany and joined the girls and the family, first in London and finally in Washington Heights, an enclave of Eastern European Jewish immigrants in New York City. Initially these memories stymied her production. Doyle suggested that she try something different and experiment with the abandoned materials lying around their studio. Hesse took leftover, discarded elements from the textile factory, including string, cord, and heavy wire, and manipulated these materials into reliefs to produce her first three-dimensional works. *Legs of a Walking Ball*, a painted, and pasted-cord-on-masonite wall relief, is an example of one of these first sculptural investigations. Irregularly abstract with evocative elements of fantasy, Hesse's works were an anomaly among the rigid, regular, symmetrical forms that her peers such as Andre and LeWitt were making.

Hesse rapidly evolved her own intimate imagery and formulated an idiosyncratic style that was both absurd and strangely sensual. Among her primary influences were the preeminent artists of the New York School, especially Jackson Pollock, Willem de Kooning, and Arshile Gorky, and their interest in empathy, chaos, and chance, and the transparency of process in the final product, which was particularly evident in Pollock's drip works. Additionally, she sought elements of Pop art's irony and humor derived from a

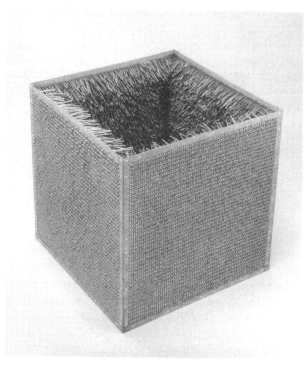

Accession II
Founders Society Purchase, Friends of Modern Art Fund and
Miscellaneous Gifts Fund
© 2001 The Detroit Institute of Arts. Reproduced with the
permission of The Estate of Eva Hesse, Galerie Hauser and
Wirth, Zürich, Switzerland

Neo-Dada aesthetic in the work. The humorous titles
of Hesse's first series of reliefs in Germany from 1965
reflected the playfulness of Pop: *Ringaround Arosie*,
Oomamaboomba, *C-Clamp Blues*, and *Eighter from
Decatur*. Not incidentally, the German Conceptual artist at Düsseldorf Academy, Joseph Beuys—who she
met during her European stay—shaped Hesse's thinking. Beuys's emphasis on the role of art as "social
sculpture" as well as its mystical power to heal trauma
appealed to the collective desire of artists, poets, writers and the broader culture searching for a means to
articulate the experiences of postwar Germany.

While these influences were consequential, Hesse's
milieu provided her with the greatest source of material. One profound motivation lay in her complex and
sophisticated responses to the strong formal influence
of then-current Minimalism and Conceptualism. In
particular, Hesse and her good friend and colleague
Sol LeWitt shared ideas and encouragement as both
explored different aspects of postwar avant-gardism.
Arguably, her reliance on the complicated and eccentric uses of the grid, window, and box forms are a clear
reaction to the primacy and purity of the modular and
cubic forms of Minimal and Conceptual art.

Upon her return to the United States in 1965, Hesse
began making larger sculptures that featured constella-
tions of like forms in monochromatic tones of black
and gray. Characteristic of these playful, black sculptures is *Several* (1965), a cluster of seven papier mâché
sausage-shaped forms painted black and hung on the
wall to reference not only the phallic but animal and
human waste. Some critics interpreted this dark series
as symptomatic of her estrangement from her husband,
yet in typically disjunctive fashion, during this time
Hesse began to make increasingly innovative sculptures in the round that expanded significantly upon the
existing vocabulary of sculpture.

Hesse took the predominant coiled form of her reliefs and translated it into three dimensions, most significantly in January of 1966 when she produced
Hang-Up, which consists of a wrapped stretcher with
a heavy metal wire, also covered, that loops and extends in front of the frame. The work plays on the
notion of a framed object being largely two-dimensional, as the wire projects approximately eight feet in
front of the "frame." The work looks like a painting,
but acts like a sculpture. Hesse herself remarked that
this sculpture represented one of the first times that a
sculpture evidenced her absurd and intense concepts.

The success of *Hang-Up* began a progression into
increased size and scale. Hesse moved on to a freestanding large sculpture in her next major piece, *Laocoön*. Based on the Hellenistic sculpture of the same
name, it is a ladderlike square armature wrapped and
then freely draped with snake forms in a complex web.
In keeping with the desire for rupture from the dominant modes of the 1960s, Hesse's sculpture clearly has
a top and a bottom, but the top is open-ended. This
projection into infinity was a rather bold antiestablish-
ment step for the time it was made, signaling a rebellious defiance of boundaries. The contrast between the
rigid geometry and the relaxed array of snakes signifies
the artist's stress on absurd opposites.

Hesse's major breakthrough came in the much-
touted 1966 group exhibition *Eccentric Abstraction*
curated by Lippard and held at the Fishbach Gallery
in New York City. Lippard demonstrated that these 12
unassociated artists were motivated by the Minimalist
zeitgeist, but all represented a shift away from it. The
work was termed Post-Minimalist or Installation art.
Lippard noted the connection of these artists to Surrealism and its emphasis on eroticism and process, and
she introduced the term "process art." Hesse had three
works in the exhibition, including *Metronomic Irregularity* (1966), a wall-related complex web of wires
attached to two adjoining boards. *Eccentric Abstraction* helped establish Hesse as an important artist. Lippard's role as a major feminist critic in the 1960s and
1970s, in particular, also established Hesse as a nascent

feminist artist, a role with which Hesse had an uneasy relation because of her desire for success on universal terms.

Hesse then moved on to considering the box form in her *Accession I–V* series completed between 1967 and 1968. These five boxes consist of gridded sides and bottom with an open top. Through the holes in the sides, the artist poked rubber hose. These box sculptures are fabulous, weird spaces, with *Accession II* being perhaps the most well known. The work embodies the idea of absurd oppositions, so prevalent in Hesse's work—externally rigid, yet internally soft and pliable.

She made her most radical step in the late 1960s when she began a series of knot and web sculptures related to the ceiling. These sculptures are notable for the disordered structure. *Right After* got its title from its completion coinciding with Hesse's first surgery for a brain tumor. It consists of 15 feet of interlaced casting resin-coated and fiberglass-coated cords. Hesse regarded this work as a failure; the luminous quality of the resin and fiberglass made the work appear delicate and fanciful, like gossamer strands. She quickly went on to make a second tangled sculpture, *Untitled (Rope Piece)*. This time, she used opaque latex instead of translucent fiberglass and dipped the ropes in the latex and then tangled them before hanging them on wire from the ceiling. Each installation changes the work. Hesse felt this work was more successful in its parody of ordered, beautifully woven fabric. Often labeled as a three-dimensional rendering of a Pollock brushstroke, *Untitled (Rope Piece)* truly debunks clarity and traditional order in the conventional criteria of sculpture.

Hesse's art has exerted a strong influence over young women in providing a direction away from rigid, organized forms. Although she is frequently compared with Sylvia Plath and Marilyn Monroe, Hesse did not have a morose sense of life. Instead, she embraced the possibilities of her work and aggressively made art until the end. Her professional career really spanned a few years, yet her malleable and complicated forms have become a source of investigation for any artist interested in abstract sculpture. Her sculptures are entirely abstract and engage the viewer in their subtleties and familiar forms rendered anew and strange. Hesse's willingness to experiment with forms and materials makes her body of work particularly compelling and extremely influential. Since her work had self-referential underpinnings, the artist's life has received a great deal of attention, which has been further promoted by the publication of sections from her diaries. The marriage of Hesse's parents could not withstand so much dislocation and trauma, and they divorced in 1945. Her father remarried soon after; her mother, anguished by the war and the family's displacement, committed suicide in January 1946.

ANNE SWARTZ

See also **Andre, Carl; Beuys, Joseph; Bourgeois, Louise; LeWitt, Sol; Minimalism; Morris, Robert; Serra, Richard**

Biography

Born in Hamburg, Germany, 11 January 1936. Arrived New York City, 1939; studied at Cooper Union for the Advancement of Science and Art, 1954–57, then Yale University School of Art and Architecture under Josef Albers, 1957–59; began career as painter; first group exhibition, 1961; first solo exhibition, 1963; moved from painting to sculpture while living in Europe, 1965; started to produce large-scale sculptures; returned from Germany, and began to achieve fame; contributed to group exhibition *Eccentric Abstraction*, Fischbach Gallery, New York City, 1966, and received significant critical attention; produced greatest body of sculpture work, 1966–70. Died in New York City, United States, 29 May 1970.

Selected Works

1965   *Legs of a Walking Ball*; enamel, tempera, cord, papier-mâché, metal, masonite panel; estate of Eva Hesse, New York City, United States

1966   *Hang-Up*; acrylic, cloth, wood, steel; Art Institute of Chicago, Illinois, United States

1966   *Metronomic Irregularity II*; painted wood, Sculp-Metal, cotton-covered wire (untraced)

1967   *Laocoön*; acrylic paint, cloth-covered cord, wire, papier-mâché, plastic plumber's pipe; Allen Memorial Art Museum, Oberlin, Ohio, United States

1968   *Accession II*; galvanized steel, rubber tubing; The Detroit Institute of Arts, Michigan, United States

1969   *Right After*; casting resin, fiberglass cord, wire hooks; Milwaukee Art Center, Wisconsin, United States

1970   *Untitled (Rope Piece)*; latex, rope, wire, string; Whitney Museum of American Art, New York City, United States

Further Reading

Armstrong, Richard, and Richard Marshall, editors, *The New Sculpture, 1965–1975: Between Geometry and Gesture*, New York: The Whitney Museum of American Art, 1990

Barrette, Bill, *Eva Hesse: Sculpture: Catalogue Raisonné*, New York: Timken Publishers, 1989

Cooper, Helen A., Maurice Berger, and Lesley K. Baier, editors, *Eva Hesse: A Retrospective*, New Haven, Connecticut: Yale University Press, 1992

Eva Hesse: A Memorial Exhibition, New York: The Solomon R. Guggenheim Museum, 1972

Johnson, Ellen H., *Eva Hesse, A Retrospective of the Drawings*, Oberlin, Ohio: Allen Memorial Art Museum, Oberlin College, 1982

Lippard, Lucy R., "Eccentric Abstraction," *Changing: Essays in Art Criticism*, New York: Dutton, 1971

Lippard, Lucy R., *Eva Hesse*, New York: New York University Press, 1976

Nemser, Cindy, *Art Talk: Conversations with Twelve Women Artists*, New York: Scribner, 1975

Wagner, Anne M., *Three Artists (Three Women): Modernism and the Art of Hesse, Krasner, and O'Keeffe*, Berkeley, Los Angeles and London: University of California Press, 1996

ADOLF VON HILDEBRAND 1847–1921

German

Adolf von Hildebrand was one of the formative influences on 20th-century sculpture and aesthetics. A devoted proponent of the Classical, Hildebrand championed a renewed rigor for visual form as the basis for sculpture. Although his sculpture became widely known and appreciated, his greatest impact in this regard was his treatise *Das Problem der Form in der bildende Kunst* (The Problem of Form in Painting and Sculpture; 1893), which went through numerous editions, republications, and translations after its initial publication. In that book and in his sculptural experiments, Hildebrand argued that sculpture presents the most challenging and rewarding medium for aesthetics. Believing that artists' primary sources derive from observations of nature, Hildebrand asserted that the artist's aim was to reconstitute those perceptions in a three-dimensional representational object from which viewers could experience the beauty of pure visual form. Hildebrand's idealized conception of pure form—the harmonious organization of all internal formal elements of a given art object into a perfect visual balance—greatly influenced major German art historians of the period such as Heinrich Wölfflin and Alois Riegl. Interpretations of Hildebrand's ideas and the ubiquity of his own text contributed greatly to the emergence of formalism in the early 20th century. In particular, Hildebrand rooted his argument about pure form in the physiology of vision; much of the first part of *Das Problem der Form* consists of a discussion of the mechanics of the eye. Consequently, Hildebrand shifted the emphasis on beauty and formal harmony away from wishful idealism to a physiological imperative. This assertion of opticality became a central component of the rhetoric of and justification for formalism in the 20th century.

Two of the most influential aspects of *Das Problem der Form* were Hildebrand's arguments about relief sculpture and direct carving. Hildebrand placed relief sculpture at the center of his thesis on vision and form. The "relief conception" entails the belief that people see in planes of relief and that the best sculpture presents the viewer not with variations in views or facets but with a unified frontal image. In other words, the viewer sees such a sculpture as if it were a relief. The dilemma of achieving this ideal in sculpture in the round was fundamental to Hildebrand's argument that sculpture is the crux of aesthetics. In order to work effectively, Hildebrand argued, a sculpture must supersede the potential chaos of being in the round and compel the viewer to perceive it as one whole, unified image, as if it were in relief to its surrounding environment. Hildebrand's theories of vision relied on the belief that retinal images are completely flat and that sculpture must therefore aspire to present in a three-dimensional object visual stimuli that will translate in the eye into a perfect two-dimensional image. Hildebrand went so far as to urge viewers to imagine sculptures as being encased between two planes of glass so that they could adequately envision how well the figure fell into equilibrium across the field of vision.

Closely tied to the question of relief was Hildebrand's emphasis on direct carving. Building on anecdotes about Michelangelo's process, Hildebrand understood the sculptor's process as analogous to the viewer's seeing the figure as in relief. Beginning with a block of marble, the sculptor should ideally create the figure plane by plane by removing the unnecessary stone. Like the relief conception, Hildebrand's emphasis on direct carving was metaphorical and stood as an ideal definition of what sculpture should aspire to be. Although Hildebrand himself executed some statues that were carved without the use of preliminary clay models and pointing machines, he did not in practice explore the extremes of the process of direct carving as did some early 20th-century sculptors in Europe and the United States.

Das Problem der Form exerted such a strong influence during Hildebrand's lifetime because it provided guidance for both artists and viewers. The sometimes ambiguous goal of beauty that had driven aesthetics and art practice for centuries became, in Hildebrand's text, an achievable possibility. Providing the reader with a convincing (although ultimately inaccurate) argument about the mechanics of vision, Hildebrand provided artists and viewers with a manual of how to work within these parameters in order to see or create good art. *Das Problem der Form* made a substantial contribution to the development of Modernist aesthetics through its emphasis on the importance of formal dynamics and their visual reception.

Early in Hildebrand's career the painter Hans von Marées and the philosopher Konrad Fiedler befriended him, and it was in an extended eulogy for his mentor and close companion Marées that Hildebrand first began to synthesize his art theory into a coherent system. With Fiedler's encouragement and support, Hildebrand transformed this text into *Das Problem der Form*. Although closely related to Fiedler's own writings, *Das Problem der Form* became more popularly successful because of its practical applications in art making and art viewing. Hildebrand's own sculpture, however, does not appear on the surface to be informed by the ideas in his treatise, and critics have regularly disregarded it as a mere replication of the Neoclassical format. Hildebrand remained committed to a sculptural style informed by Classical and Renaissance prototypes, but his innovations lie beneath the superficial stylistic level. Works such as his *Standing Man*, however, assert the necessity of planar frontality just as forcefully as *Das Problem der Form*. *Standing Man* is visually unsatisfying from all angles but one, when the composition falls into precise balance. In this work and others, Hildebrand hoped to provide the viewer with an illustration of the importance of form in the construction of artworks. In the process of perceiving the figure, the viewer experiences both the chaotic disorder inherent in three-dimensional objects and its transcendence when the ideal viewing angle is achieved. The sophisticated theoretical system of *Das Problem der Form* largely derives from these earlier experiments in sculpture in which Hildebrand struggled to assert a formal justification for sculpture.

Hildebrand exerted a great influence on the development of sculpture in Germany. In particular, he created ambitious public fountains that combine large numbers of complex elements into a coherent visual and symbolic program. In works such as the Wittelsbach fountain and the Vater Rhein fountain (neither of which exists today in its original form), Hildebrand sought to stage views and experiences of the fountain that would be harmonious with the landscape and surrounding buildings. For the Wittelsbach fountain, Hildebrand shifted emphasis away from the height of the central element to the overall horizontal profile of the entire assemblage, integrating the fountain into the surrounding landscape as opposed to interrupting it. The Vater Rhein fountain, in its original urban setting in Strasbourg, also attested to Hildebrand's interest in the visual picture created by his public sculptures by addressing the manner in which the facades of surrounding buildings visually framed the fountain and its figural sculptures. On a smaller scale, Hildebrand also made a series of highly successful portraits that explored the manner in which the object is perceived. Experimenting with a variety of traditions from the history of art, Hildebrand achieved a sensitive portrayal of his sitter full of expression, without abandoning verisimilitude and an attention to the overall form and profile of the subject. The portrait genre also allowed Hildebrand to explore naturalistic surface rendering that he did not always extend to his ideal figures.

Although the wide range of sculpture Hildebrand produced appears on the surface to be unrelated to the formalism of *Das Problem der Form* and the Modernist aesthetics it engendered, a closer examination of his sculptures reveals a great deal of experimentation within established formats and an unswerving attention to the ways in which the viewer visually apprehends sculptural objects. It was through these rigorous investigations in theory and sculpture that Hildebrand provided a crucial transition between the traditional conceptions of sculpture and the emergence of Modernism.

DAVID GETSY

See also **Germany: Baroque-Neoclassical; Fountain Sculpture**

Biography

Born in Marburg, Germany, 6 October 1847. Studied at Kunstgewerbeschule, Nuremberg, 1864–66; studied with Kaspar Clemens Zumbusch, Munich, 1866–67; met Konrad Fiedler and Hans Reinhard von Marées in Rome, 1867; moved to Italy, 1872; collaborated with Marées on Stazione Zoologica, Naples, 1873; purchased Monastery of San Francesco di Paola, Florence, 1874; won commission for monument to Emperor William I, 1889, but project never executed; received first major commission, Wittelsbach fountain, 1889 (completed 1895); published *Das Problem der Form in der bildende Kunst*, 1893. Died in Munich, Germany, 18 January 1921.

Selected Works

1873   *Drinking Boy*; bronze; Alte Nationalgalerie, Berlin, Germany
1873   *Sleeping Shepherd*; marble; Alte Nationalgalerie, Berlin, Germany
1881   *Julia Brewster*; marble; Wallraf-Richartz-Museum, Cologne, Germany
1882   *Frau Maria Fiedler*; terracotta; Kunsthalle, Hamburg, Germany
1884   *Standing Man*; marble; Alte Nationalgalerie, Berlin, Germany
1886   *Ballplayer*; plaster; Neue Pinakothek, Munich, Germany
1886   *Net Carrier*; marble; Neue Pinakothek, Munich, Germany

1887–88 *Archers and Amazons*; cement; private collections, Wallraf-Richartz-Museum, Cologne, Germany

1889 *Double Portrait*; polychromed terracotta; J. Paul Getty Museum, Los Angeles, California, United States

1890 *Dionysus*; terracotta; Alte Nationalgalerie, Berlin, Germany; replica, Hildebrandhaus, Munich, Germany

1895 Wittelsbach fountain; marble (partially destroyed); restored version (highly altered): Lenbachplatz, Munich, Germany

1899 Johannes Brahms memorial; bronze; Schlosspark, Meiningen, Germany

1902 Reinhard fountain (*Vater Rhein*), for Place Broglie, Strasbourg; marble and bronze; Lenbachplatz, Munich, Germany

Further Reading

Braunfels, Wolfgang, "Adolf von Hildebrand: Artist of Tranquility," *Apollo* 94/117 (November 1971)

Burmeister, Enno, and Christine Hoh-Slodczyk, editors, *Das Hildebrandhaus in München: Sein Erbauer, seine Bewohner*, Munich: Hugendubel, 1981

Esche-Braunfels, Sigrid, *Adolf von Hildebrand (1847–1921)*, Berlin: Deutscher Verlag für Kunstwissenschaft, 1993

Getsy, David J., "Encountering the Male Nude at the Origins of Modern Sculpture," in Angela Hass, *Adolf von Hildebrand: Das plastische Portrait*, Munich: Verlag, 1984

Heilmeyer, Alexander, *Adolf Hildebrand*, Leipzig: Velhagen and Klasing, 1902

Hildebrand, Adolf von, *Das Problem der Form in der bildenden Kunst*, Strassburg: Heitz, 1893; 10th edition, Baden-Baden, Germany: Heitz, 1961; 3rd German edition, as "The Problem of Form in the Fine Arts," in *Empathy, Form, and Space: Problems in German Aesthetics, 1873–1893*, translated by Harry Francis Mallgrave and Eleftherios Ikonomou, Santa Monica, California: J. Paul Getty Center for the History of Art and the Humanities, 1994; 4th German edition, as *The Problem of Form in Painting and Sculpture*, translated by Max Meyer and Robert M. Ogden, New York: Stechert, 1907; reprint, New York: Garland, 1978

Hildebrand, Adolf von, "Zum 'Problem der Form,' 2," *Suddeutsche Monatshefte* 3/2 (July–December 1906); abridged, as "Remarks on the Problem of Form," translated by M. Meyer, *College Art Journal* 11/4 (summer 1952)

Hildebrand, Adolf von, *Adolf von Hildebrands Briefwechsel mit Conrad Fiedler*, Dresden, Germany: Jess, 1927

Hildebrand, Adolf von, *Adolf von Hildebrand und seine Welt: Briefe and Erinnerungen*, Munich: Callwey, 1962

Hildebrand, Adolf von, *Gessamelte Schriften zur Kunst*, edited by H. Bock, Cologne, Germany: Westdeutscher Verlag, 1969

Hildebrand, Adolf von, "Auguste Rodin (1918)," translated by E. Kashey, in *Viewpoints: European Sculpture, 1875–1925*, New York: Shepherd Gallery, 1991

Wittkower, Rudolf, *Sculpture: Processes and Principles*, London: Allen Lane, and New York: Harper and Row, 1977

DAMIEN HIRST 1965– *British*

Damien Hirst first emerged in the British art scene in 1988 with a show he curated titled *Freeze*, which was exhibited in London at an abandoned Surrey Docks warehouse. The exhibition was a watershed for numerous reasons. Of importance was that it consisted of Hirst's fellow Goldsmiths College art students, some of whom would be part of the "Young British Artists" show in 1992, which consequently earned them the moniker of the YBAs. Apart from the attention that *Freeze* brought to these artists, the show's autonomous nature offered the possibility of gaining exposure while circumventing the traditional exhibition routes of the British art establishment. This type of independent spirit would be germane to these young British artists; more emphatic demarcations than their zeal or age that differentiated them from their predecessors were the diverse formal strategies and risqué subject matter that constituted their art. The most publicized member of this group was Hirst.

The publicity surrounding Hirst focused on the controversy of his sculptural materials. Occasionally working in painting, photography, and graphic work, Hirst became internationally known for his monumental sculptures of glass and steel vitrines filled with a formaldehyde solution that contained whole or dissected animals. Apart from using cows, pigs, sharks, lambs, and other animals, Hirst also used medical paraphernalia—trash bags filled with deodorizers, air blowers, and a host of other materials—that when placed in his sleek vitrines made his sculptures immediately recognizable. Hirst's other sculptures, which were just as distinguishable, were cabinets that displayed readymade medications, surgical instruments, and jars of animal organs or fish.

When looking at Hirst's precocious body of work to date, one is struck by its thematic complexity, its visual power, and its subtle attention to art history and unabashed pilfering of both high and low culture. Hirst's intelligent sculptural meshing of form and idea captured a particular zeitgeist of 1990s art while striking an individual and collective resonance by addressing the anxieties of contemporary Western culture. These anxieties manifest in Hirst's ironic narratives, which are concomitantly philosophical and irreverent, poetically conveying for existential questions about life, work, beauty, human relationships, consumer culture, social complacency, and, most important, death.

Prior to *Freeze*, Hirst made two-dimensional assemblage sculptures constructed from everyday refuse. Through their planarity, these works are akin to paintings and are formally reminiscent of Arman's aesthetic of accumulation and the *arte povera* (an Italian movement often characterized by the use of ephemeral materials) of Mario Merz. With titles such as *We're Dying* (1985) and *Hung Up* (1985), these early sculptures hinted at the type of social and psychological subject matter that Hirst would elaborate in his later work. One of his early important pieces, *A Thousand Years*, tapped into these concerns and was one of the first major works bought by YBA patron and advertising giant Charles Saatchi.

A Thousand Years consisted of a putrefying cow's head, flies, maggots, sugar water, and an electric fly-killer all encased within a 1.8-meter-tall vitrine. The work physically narrated the birth, life, and death of flies within the context of annihilation vis-à-vis electrocution, survival via sugar water, and creation by the transition of maggot to fly. The visceral, yet aesthetically powerful, sculpture was only matched by its complex theme of mortality that bordered on the epic. The art-historical sources in *A Thousand Years* range from the Baroque *vanitas* and its iconography of memento mori to the still life or its more apt French appellation of *nature morte*, or dead nature. By way of its pristine presentation in a vitrine, *A Thousand Years* is linked with Minimalists such as Donald Judd. Along with its converging disparate sources, *A Thousand Years* evinced Hirst as a major talent who could simultaneously address difficult subject matter with an abject aesthetic that was paradoxically elegant. Another work from the same year titled *In and Out of Love* showed Hirst's capacity to work with similar themes, but from subtle, even delicate formal material such as live butterflies.

The importance of Saatchi cannot be overstated; apart from being a major collector of Hirst's work, he helped generate international interest in him through sponsored exhibitions. One of the most publicized exhibitions was the 1997 "Sensation: Young British Artists from the Saatchi Collection" in London. This show, like a previous exhibition at which one of Hirst's vitrines was vandalized, caused an uproar because of the material shown and was protested in both London and New York City. And what one first encountered when entering "Sensation"—and which seemed to encapsulate the exhibition's freshness and daring—was Hirst's *The Physical Impossibility of Death in the Mind of Someone Living*.

The Physical Impossibility of Death (as it was popularly called) may possibly be Hirst's best-known sculpture and consists of a tiger shark immersed in a 2.1 meter by 6.4 meter by 2.1-meter vitrine. Working with previous strategies that focused on thematic ambiguity to foster diverse meanings, this piece contained a mimetic quality absent in other sculptures, for the shark, submerged in a formaldehyde solution, is similarly close to its natural habitat. Hirst continued to make vitrines and cabinets throughout the 1990s, and although his spin paintings had a sculptural dimension like his early pre-*Freeze* works, his sculptures began to acquire a Post-Pop aesthetic by way of Jeff Koons, as well as acquiring a more conceptual orientation via their polysemous quality.

Hirst's 2000 exhibition at the Larry Gagosian Gallery in New York City, which included vitrines with gynecological chairs and live fish, sculptures with floating ping-pong balls that mimic lottery games, and a 6-meter-tall painted bronze figure of an anatomy doll, exemplified a different aesthetic sensibility by way of a formal and conceptual redirection that remains anchored in his coherent artistic trajectory. Hirst has proven himself to be an artist of our time. His sculptures have an overwhelming presence that addresses issues of mortality and humankind's increasing alienation in an ever technological world through an honesty that is occasionally brutal, yet visually poetic.

RAÚL ZAMUDIO

See also **Arman; Contemporary Sculpture; Merz, Mario; Postmodernism**

Biography

Born in Bristol, England, 7 June 1965. Began formal art studies with foundation course at Leeds School of Art; after moving to London, studied at program of fine arts at Goldsmiths College, 1986–89; after *Freeze*, group shows in Glasgow, Scotland, and the Institute of Contemporary Art, London, 1989; first solo exhibitions in Paris and London, 1991; participated in "Sensation: Young British Artists from the Saatchi Collection," and "Turner Prize Exhibition," Tate Gallery, London, 1992; participated in Aperto Section, Venice Biennial, Italy, 1993; won Turner Prize at "Turner Prize Exhibition," Tate Gallery, London, 1995. Lives and works in Devon, England.

Selected Works

1989   *God*; glass, steel, MDF (a type of synthetic material similiar to plastic), drug bottles; private collection

1989   *A Thousand Years*; glass, steel, MDF, cow's head, fly-killer, sugar water, maggots, flies; Saatchi Collection, London, England

1991   *The Physical Impossibility of Death in the Mind of Someone Living*; glass, steel, silicone, formaldehyde solution, shark; Saatchi Collection, London, England

1991   *When Logics Die*; color photograph on aluminum, Formica table, medical equipment; private collection

1992   *The Acquired Inability to Escape*; glass, steel, silicone, MDF table, chair, ashtray, lighter, cigarettes; private collection

1994   *I'll Love You Forever*; steel cage, padlock, medical waste instruments, cow's brain, formaldehyde solution; private collection

1996   *Some Comfort Gained from the Acceptance of the Inherent Lies in Everything*; glass, steel, formaldehyde solution, 2 cows in 12 tanks; private collection

1999   *Hymn*; painted bronze; Saatchi Collection, London, England

2000   *Something Solid beneath the Surface of Several Things Wise and Wonderful*; glass, steel, animal skeletons; private collection

Further Reading

Adams, Brooks, et al., *Sensation: Young British Artists from the Saatchi Collection*, London: Royal Academy of Arts, 1997

Garlake, Margaret, *New Art, New World: British Art in Postwar Society*, New Haven, Connecticut: Yale University Press, 1998

Hirst, Damien, *The Acquired Inability to Escape Divided: The Acquired Inability to Escape Inverted and Divided, and Other Works*, Cologne, Germany: Buchhandlung Walther Konig, 1994

Hirst, Damien, and Stuart Morgan, *Damien Hirst: No Sense of Absolute Corruption*, New York: Gagosian Gallery, 1996

Hirst, Damien, *I Want to Spend the Rest of My Life Everywhere, with Everyone, One to One, Always, Forever, Now*, edited by Robert Violette, London: Booth-Clibborn Editions, and New York: Monacelli Press, 1997

Kent, Sarah, *Shark Infested Waters: The Saatchi Collection of British Art in the 90s*, London: Zwemmer, 1994

Kent, Sarah, Richard Cork, and Dick Price, *Young British Art: The Saatchi Decade*, London: Booth-Clibborn Editions, 1999

Renton, Andrew, and Liam Gillick, editors, *Technique Anglaise: Current Trends in British Art*, London, and New York: Thames and Hudson, 1991

Stallabrass, Julian, *High Art Lite: British Art in the 1990s*, London, and New York: Verso, 1999

Young British Artists, London: Saatchi Collection, 1992

MALVINA HOFFMAN 1885–1966 *United States*

Malvina Hoffman was one of the most respected American sculptors of the interwar period. Today she is chiefly remembered for her ethnographic statues at the Field Museum of Natural History in Chicago.

Hoffman's father was a pianist for the New York Philharmonic Orchestra, and her parents nurtured her pursuit of an artistic career. She began her studies under the painter John W. Alexander and the sculptor Herbert Adams. Later, Gutzon Borglum, the sculptor of Mount Rushmore, encouraged her to submit a bust of her recently deceased father, Richard Hoffman, to the National Academy of Design. The success of this emotional portrait, made in the Impressionistic style of contemporary French sculpture, inspired Hoffman to seek the mentorship of Auguste Rodin. In 1910, after the death of her father, Hoffman and her mother traveled to Paris, where she bluffed her way into Rodin's studio and convinced him to accept her as his student for a year. Returning to New York in 1911, she took Rodin's advice and enrolled in anatomy classes at the College of Physicians and Surgeons with Dr. George Huntington. Her studiousness set a precedent that led to the creation of a special department of anatomy for artists in 1912. Hoffman returned to Paris and worked in Rodin's studio frequently in the years before World War I. She also organized a major exhibition of Rodin's sculptures in Dorchester, England (1914), that would become part of the permanent collection at the Victoria and Albert Museum after World War I.

Hoffman's most accomplished work from 1910–20 is distinguished by her careful observation of the dancing body in motion. *Russian Dancers*, which received first prize at the Paris Salon of 1911, depicts the taut and elastic bodies of Mikhail Mordkin and Anna Pavlova draped in thin robes, dancing toward one another in a spiral. This piece was followed by a monumental bronze version, the *Bacchanale Russe*, which shows the same figures running side by side, now unclothed, trailing their garments in the air as if they are preparing to take flight. Pavlova was a frequent subject of Hoffman's work and became a close friend of the sculptor, appearing in numerous portraits. When the ballerina became unsatisfied with film documentation of her choreography, Hoffman stepped up to the challenge, producing *Bacchanale*, a low-relief frieze in 26 panels that interprets segments of Pavlova's signature choreography and was completed in 1924.

In the early 1920s Hoffman established herself in New York as a portraitist and also took on several important public art commissions. Her portraits include a series of bronze busts of the pianist and Polish patriot Ignacy Paderewski, a marble bust of Henry C. Frick, and a marble head of the 19th-century English poet John Keats (1926; University of Pittsburgh). Her first public commission was a war memorial for the Harvard Memorial Chapel, for which she carved a limestone crusader lying at the knees of a woman (*The Sacrifice*). Her second important commission came from Irving Bush, for the Bush House in London, for two monumental male figures representing England and America dedicated *To the Friendship of English-Speaking Peoples*. Despite her successes, Hoffman grew restless and left New York in search of further adventure and different subject matter. In 1926 she traveled to Africa, where she carved the angular features and ornamented hair of a *Senegalese Soldier* in black marble intended to represent the subject's ebony skin. After her trip to Africa, Hoffman studied with the sculptor Ivan Meštrovic in Yugoslavia (1927). Meštrovic encouraged his students to master the craftsmanship of sculpture and inspired her to study the process of bronze casting at the Rudier Foundry in Paris. She later wrote a book, *Sculpture Inside and Out* (1939), which details different sculptural techniques and their application throughout history.

From 1930 to 1933 Hoffman worked on her most ambitious project, the *Races of Mankind:* 101 life-size bronze busts and statues of world racial types for the Chicago Field Museum's hall of physical anthropology. The original commission called for several artists to make plaster figures with glass eyes and real hair, but Hoffman claims to have convinced museum officials that bronze statues by a single artist could accurately document ethnographic details while simultaneously providing a more cohesive, durable, and lifelike display. As chronicled in her popular book, *Heads and Tales* (1936), she first visited the 1931 Paris Exposition Coloniale and then spent two years, together with her husband and an assistant, circumnavigating the globe to make models for the final bronze statues that went

on display during the 1933 Century of Progress Exposition. In *Tamil Man Climbing a Tree* Hoffman simulated the intricately woven basket, rough tree bark, and the lean muscles of the subject to project a sense of objective, factual documentation typical of the project. The best pieces—such as the *Dancing Sara Girl* from Chad, who leans backward while gracefully extending her right arm for balance—retain the dynamic composition of her earlier dance sculptures.

Although intended to promote the unity of humanity, the accuracy of the *Races of Mankind* has been called into question because it places Europeans and white Americans at the peak of a racial hierarchy based on Western conceptions of culture and race. For instance, Hoffman refused to model non-Western subjects that did not conform to her standards of beauty and even then tended to represent them as primitives, whereas her European and white American subjects were modeled in the style of Classical Greek statues. Her collaborators at the Field Museum also arranged the layout of the exhibit with the European and white American figures in the central hall, relegating the racial types from Asia, Africa, and Oceania to side rooms. In the 1960s the exhibition was dismantled because it was deemed unrepresentative and stereotypical, although individual sculptures are scattered throughout the museum and continue to draw the attention of visitors. The original plaster molds were discovered in storage at the Field Museum in 1995.

Hoffman's late work includes the *International Dance Fountain* for the New York World's Fair, a bronze bas-relief (low-raised work) that combined her interests in dance and human diversity.

GREG FOSTER-RICE

See also **Meštrovic, Ivan; Rodin, Auguste**

Biography

Born in New York City, United States, 15 June 1885. Attended classes at Women's School of Applied Design and Arts Students League, New York, 1899–1904; studied sculpture under Herbert Adams and George Grey Bernard at the Vettin School, New York City, 1906, and under Gutzon Borglum, 1909; studied in Auguste Rodin's studio, Paris, 1910–11; enrolled in anatomy classes at College of Physicians and Surgeons at Cornell University, Ithaca, New York, 1911; met Russian dancer Anna Pavlova in New York, 1913, and collaborated with her until 1931; studied sculpture under Yugoslav artist Ivan Meštrovic in Zagreb, Croatia, 1927; retained a studio in Paris starting in 1927 and traveled internationally for the *Races of Mankind* commission from Field Museum of Natural History, Chicago, 1930–33. Recipient of first prize, Société

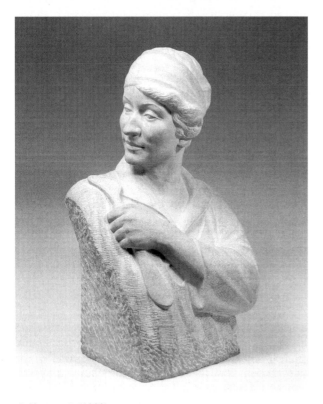

Self-portrait (1929)
© Smithsonian American Art Museum, Washington, D.C. / Art Resource, NY

Nationale des Beaux-Arts, Paris, 1912; first prize, American Art Students Club, Paris, 1913; Julia A. Shaw Memorial Prize, 1917; Helen Foster Barnett prize, 1921; member National Academy of Design, 1931; member American Institute of Arts and Letters, 1937; "Woman of the Year," American Association of University Women, 1957; fellow, National Sculpture Society, 1958; Chevalier of the Legion of Honor, 1951. Died in New York City, United States, 10 July 1966.

Selected Works

1910   Bust of Richard Hoffman; marble; private collection

1911   *Russian Dancers*; bronze; private collection

1915   *Pavlova La Gavotte*; gold bronze casts; The Detroit Institute of Arts, Michigan, United States; Fine Arts Museum of San Francisco, California, United States; wax version: Metropolitan Museum of Art, New York City, United States

1917   *Bacchanale Russe*, in the Luxembourg Gardens, Paris, France; bronze (destroyed, World War I)

1920   *Henry C. Frick*; marble; private collection

1920   *The Sacrifice*; Caen limestone; Harvard Memorial Chapel, Cambridge, Massachusetts, United States

1922   *Paderewski the Artist*; bronze; Cedar Rapids Museum of Art, Iowa, United States

1922   *Paderewski the Statesman*; bronze; Steinway Hall, New York City, United States

1922   *Robert Bacon*; bronze; private collection

1924   *Anna Pavlova*; plaster; Metropolitan Museum of Art, New York City, United States

1924   *Bacchanale* frieze (26 panels); plaster; Cedar Rapids Museum of Art, Iowa, United States

1924–25 *To the Friendship of English-Speaking Peoples*; limestone; Bush House, London, England

1925   *Ivan Meštrovic*; bronze; Brooklyn Museum of Art, New York, United States

1926   *Senegalese Soldier*; Belgian marble; American Museum of Natural History, Washington, D.C., United States

1930–33 *Races of Mankind* (104 pieces); bronze, marble; Field Museum of Natural History, Chicago, Illinois, United States; casts: Cedar Rapids Museum of Art, Iowa, United States

1937   *International Dance Fountain* for the New York World's Fair, New York City, United States; bronze (location unknown)

Further Reading

Bouvé, Pauline Carrington, "The Two Foremost Women Sculptors in America: Anna Vaughn Hyatt and Malvina Hoffman," *Art and Archaeology* 26 (September 1928)

Craven, Wayne, *Sculpture in America*, New York: Crowell, 1968; 2nd edition, new and revised, Newark: University of Delaware Press, 1984

Conner, Janis, *A Dancer in Relief: Works by Malvina Hoffman*, Yonkers, New York: Hudson River Museum, 1984

Decoteau, Pamela Hibbs, "Malvina Hoffman and the 'Races of Man,'" *Woman's Art Journal* 10/2 (1989–90)

Field, Henry, *The Races of Mankind: An Introduction to Chauncey Keep Memorial Hall*, Chicago: Field Museum of Natural History, 1933; 4th edition, 1942

Hill, May Brawley, *The Woman Sculptor: Malvina Hoffman and Her Contemporaries*, New York: Berry-Hill Galleries, 1984

Nochlin, Linda, "Malvina Hoffman: A Life in Sculpture," *Arts Magazine* 59 (November 1984)

Teslow, Tracy, "Reifying Race: Science and Art in *Races of Mankind* at the Field Museum of Natural History," in *The Politics of Display: Museums, Science, Culture*, edited by Sharon MacDonald, London and New York: Routledge, 1998

HOLLAND

See **Netherlands**

HONORIFIC COLUMN

The use of columns as honorific monuments is almost as old as the use of columns themselves. In ancient India, kings erected pillars, often bearing emblems, in imitation of the god Indra, who raised a column after slaying the demons and establishing cosmic order. The Egyptians used pillars, crowned with sphinxes, to guard tombs (see Irwin, 1976). The Greeks used similar columns topped with figures as overseers for sepulchral sites, as votive offerings to particular deities, and as monuments to important contemporaries. Pliny (*Natural History* 34.27) writes that it was in response to the Greeks that the early Romans began introducing statue-topped columns into their own cities. These Roman examples, in turn, became the most familiar reference points for a genre of imagery that flourished in the West for almost 2,500 years.

Roman honorific columns served, as Pliny put it, "to elevate [their subjects] above all other mortals." Frequently they commemorated military victories: the Column of Trajan, around which spirals a long series of reliefs celebrating its namesake's military accomplishments, was but the most elaborate of many similarly dedicated pillars that were once found in Rome and throughout Roman lands. In later centuries, both the triumphal and the imperial associations of these columns were exploited in a variety of ways. Emperor Constantine, who legalized Christianity, had a carving of his own head fitted with the rays of Helios made in the forms of the nails from Christ's cross; the head was placed on the body of Apollo, which topped a Roman porphyry column. The column in turn surmounted the holiest relics in the city of Constantinople (see Haftmann, 1972). The combination honors Constantine's own prowess as a commander, but it also works as a religious monument, celebrating the triumph of Christianity. Thereafter, Christian columns came to be ubiquitous. Many were reduced in form, consisting of a simple shaft topped with a cross, although more elaborate forms were also possible; among the most famous are the *Christus-Säule* at Hildesheim, which includes spiraling reliefs in the manner of Trajan's column and the columns topped with St. Theodore and with St. Mark's lion in the piazzetta in Venice. In the 17th century, the association of the column with victory allowed the invention of the plague column, a monument type that became enormously popular in Hungary, Bohemia, and other Habsburg lands. It celebrated the defeat of pestilence, the aid of the divine, and, implicitly, the administrative skills of the ruler-patron (see Grünberg, 1960; Kaufmann, 1995).

More recent ages have seen the restoration of more properly Roman types. Columns built to General George Washington in Baltimore and to Admiral Horatio Nelson in London have continued to single out war heroes (see Ackerman, 1996), whereas those dedicated to Napoléon in the Place Vendôme in Paris and to Czar Alexander I in St. Petersburg have intentionally drawn on the column's venerable association with the emperor (see Traeger, 1977; Wortman, 1996). In the 19th century, a period as invested in the celebration of armies and nations as of their leaders, allegorical figures sometimes replaced portraits on the column's crown. The column that Wilhelm von Würtemberg sponsored in Stuttgart was topped with a figure of Victory. The same device was used on the nationalistic *Victory Column* erected on the Königsplatz in Berlin several decades later. It might be noted that the winged Victory is itself a familiar character from ancient imperial columns, and that the imperialist overtones of these works were easily exploited: Hitler oversaw the transfer and further elevation of the *Victory Column* in his own Berlin in 1938.

In the tradition of imagery inspired by Roman victory columns, the column often functioned as a giant pedestal, hoisting an honored protector onto the shoulders of the city. Nevertheless, it should not be thought that figure-topped columns were primarily or exclusively honorific. The column reaching from the ground and rising into the sky operates between the mundane and the celestial, and it does so with respect to the figures that ornament it. It is thus significant that columns were frequently used as or in conjunction with funerary structures—it is thought, for example, that Trajan's column itself was intended to serve as the emperor's tomb. When Trajan's effigy was raised on his column, its subject was designated as *divus*, admitted into the pantheon. The lifting of the portrait into the sky could serve as a figurative apotheosis, while those who raised it (in ancient Rome, typically the senate and people, or the family of the person celebrated) could demonstrate their piety (see Settis, 1988). Similar connotations contributed to the popularity of the form in the later Catholic world. In Rome, bronze figures of the apostles Peter and Paul were placed atop the columns of Trajan and Marcus Aurelius. Gianlorenzo Bernini's great Baldacchino (1623–34) essentially consists of four columns topped with angels who in turn support the superstructure covering St. Peter's tomb. Many of the *guglie* (columns topped with holy figures) that populate southern Italy, meanwhile—like the *Mariensäulen* (columns topped with the Virgin, popularized by Jesuits) that were their northern and central European counterparts—featured the Virgin Mary and played on the imagery of the Immaculata: the exalted Virgin was like a vision in the sky.

The column's place between earth and sky could also lend it magical powers. In the ancient world, column monuments were frequently placed in the city's sacred precinct and were associated with outdoor altars. In the Middle Ages, memories and fantasies of the pagan rituals associated with columns remained vivid enough to let the combination of figure and column become the archetypal idol. It may well have been the associated belief that such forms had a sort of talismanic power, which led to their increasing popularity in later centuries. It has been argued, for example, that Donatello's mid 15th-century *David* was intentionally designed as an idol, one that would channel divine strength to the Florentines during their war with the Milanese (see Janson and Lányi, 1963). Donatello's *Judith* from the same period, which also topped a column, was later removed from the city's square because it was allegedly bringing bad fortune on the Florentines. Donatello's *Dovizia*, finally, surmounted a tall column above the Renaissance city's marketplace: its crowning figure may have been intended not only to celebrate the abundance of the market, but also to guarantee it.

The *Dovizia*, which stood at the site of the ancient forum, at the crossing of the *cardo* and the *decumanus*, and at the place believed once to have been marked by a figure of Mars atop a column, highlights the additional importance of column monuments as features in urban planning. Like bell towers and minarets, columns typically counted among the highest structures in a city; they oriented all within its fabric to the city's most important places. Topped with civic patrons, columns could declare a city's allegiances and promise divine protection to its citizens. Providing the equivalent of an *axis mundi*, they focused the city's organization on specific squares and crossroads. Recording engineering feats that proved their patrons' capacities for administrative and technological mobilization, finally, honorific columns stood as monuments to the civic rule represented by one or another regime. Columns created order that was at once visible in its design and cosmological in its implication.

MICHAEL COLE

See also **Column of Marcus Aurelius**

Further Reading

Ackerman, James, "Arch, Column, Equestrian Statue: Three Persistent Forms of Public Monument," in *"Remove Not the Ancient Landmark": Public Monuments and Moral Values: Discourses and Comments in Tribute to Rudolf Wittkower*, edited by Donald Martin Reynolds, Amsterdam: Gordon and Breach, 1996

Grünberg, Alexander, *Pestsäulen in Österreich*, Vienna: Bergland Verlag, 1960

Haftmann, Werner, *Das italienische Säulenmonument*, Leipzig: Teubner, 1939; reprint, Hildesheim: Gerstenberg, 1972

Irwin, John, "'Asokan' Pillars: A Reassessment of the Evidence–IV: Symbolism," *The Burlington Magazine* 118 (1976)

Janson, H.W., and Jenö Lányi, *The Sculpture of Donatello*, Princeton, New Jersey: Princeton University Press, 1963

Karpowicz, Mariusz, "The Column of Sigismund III in Warsaw," *Bulletin du Musée national de Varsovie* 18 (1977)

Kaufmann, Thomas DaCosta, *Court, Cloister and City: The Art and Culture of Central Europe, 1450–1800*, London: Weidenfeld and Nicolson, and Chicago: University of Chicago Press, 1995

Settis, Salvatore, editor, *La Colonna Traiana*, Turin, Italy: Einaudi, 1988

Traeger, Jörg, "Über die Säule der Grossen Armee auf der Place Vendôme in Paris," in *Festschrift Wolfgang Braunfels*, edited by Friedrich Piel and Jörg Traeger, Tübingen, Germany: Wasmuth, 1977

Vogel, Lise, *The Column of Antoninus Pius*, Cambridge, Massachusetts: Harvard University Press, 1973

Wilkins, David, "Donatello's Lost Dovizia for the Mercato Vecchio," *Art Bulletin* 65 (1983)

Wortman, Richard, "Statues of the Tsars and the Redefinition of Russia's Past," in *"Remove Not the Ancient Landmark": Public Monuments and Moral Values: Discourses and Comments in Tribute to Rudolf Wittkower*, edited by Donald Martin Reynolds, Amsterdam: Gordon and Breach, 1996

REBECCA HORN 1944– *German*

Rebecca Horn's art mainly addresses thematic couplings such as body/machine, organic/inorganic, nature/culture, and biology/technology. This dialectical investigation, primarily figured through sculpture, has taken many forms throughout her career. From Horn's early works of a performative nature to her mechanical and robotlike sculptures and her indoor and outdoor installations, she has also conveyed her narratives in cinematic work that is anchored in her myriad sculptural practices. Horn has configured a meshing of disparate themes via conceptual rigor, formal innovation, and a historical understanding of sculpture. These strategies are the foundations of Horn's diverse artistic vocabularies, and through them her art manifests a complexity that evinces her historical importance in late-20th-century sculpture.

Horn first came to prominence with such works as *Arm Extension* (1968), *Overflowing Blood Machine* (1970), and *Measure Box* (1970). Through their vacillation between performance, body art, and sculpture, these works resisted conventional categorization. They each explored the corporeal, but from a sensorial understanding of the world in relation to self as body. In this sense, Horn's early sculptures, although highly visual, subvert modern art's emphasis on the optical, privileging instead other senses as equally important in the transmission and experience of a work of art. Horn's broader sensorial emphasis is apparent in *Paradise Widow*, *Chinese Fiancée*, and *The Feathered Prison Fan*.

In these three works, the body becomes a formal sculptural element. In order to view and hear *Chinese Fiancée*, one enters into it, thus emphasizing the haptic and the aural as well as the visual, amounting to a synesthetic experience. With these three works one also detects the beginnings of Horn's mechanical sculptures and installations, which would establish her as one of the most important sculptors of the post–Joseph Beuys generation of German artists. Horn's formal lineage is broad; she freely culled and transformed sculptural influences from an ample array of artists, including Jean Tinguely, Hans Bellmer, Jannis Kounellis, and Marcel Duchamp, specifically, Duchamp's *Roto-Reliefs* (1935) and his other works that allude to mechanization, such as the *Chocolate Grinder* (1913) and *Large Glass* (1915–23).

With the start of the 1980s, Horn's work became more animated as her sculptures progressively became mechanical and robotic. This formal transformation in lesser artistic hands could have succumbed to gadgetry and the use of the machine as spectacle rather than a conceptual investigation of its role in broader philosophical contexts. This conceptual approach is evident in Horn's thematic integration of anthropomorphic, zoomorphic, and scientific elements played with and against each other. Activated by motors, although they seem to move by their own accord, these sculptures, exhibited as sculpture in the round or on the wall, began to architecturally engage their physical environments. As they increasingly integrated with the architectonic, the sculptures made during this phase eventually veered into the genre of Installation.

As her spatial investigations proceeded from the initial starting point of sculpture, Horn's level of formal and conceptual complexity made it occasionally difficult to discern where her sculptures ended and her installations began. Although Installation is a form of sculpture in that it is its hybrid progeny, sculpture in the traditional sense of the word cannot as equally claim the formal province of Installation. Horn collapsed sculpture into Installation, and articulated her ideas through a rich visual vocabulary constituted from materials that have become her signature trademark. Her use of glass, metal, powdered pigment, motors, feathers, and found objects, as well as a plethora of other materials, amounts to a broad formal arsenal that makes her work easily distinguishable. Yet Horn's sculptures/installations are never formally overloaded but maintain a sparseness and elegance that reflect an astute editorial sensibility that strengthens her work's conceptual force.

By the end of the 1980s, Horn had established herself as an important and internationally renowned sculptor and installation artist, and she began to explore site specificity. In addition to working with existing interior exhibition spaces, Horn also accepted commissions to work outdoors, beginning with her first major outdoor sculptural installation, *The Bath of the Reflected Dew Drops*. She sited this work in a cleared field among trees in Lyons, France. She also created an installation in a crumbling Gothic watchtower-turned-Gestapo interrogation center for the Münster Sculpture Projects in 1987. Titled *Concert in Reverse*, this site-specific installation had less to do with the physicality of the space and more with the social and historical context of the installation's location. Site specificity in this case concerned the buried social and historical memory of the interrogation center that Horn sought to symbolically excavate and incorporate into the work. She also created site-specific installations at an ancient Roman bathhouse in Bath, England (1989), at a converted schoolhouse in Kassel, Germany (1992), and at the Hotel Peninsular in Barcelona, Spain (1992).

At her first U.S. retrospective in 1993, at both the uptown and downtown branches of the Guggenheim Museum in New York City, Horn created her most ambitious sculptural installation to date. This massive exhibition, which included works in the uptown museum's rotunda, contained an installation thematically linked with the museum's downtown satellite. The uptown installation, *Paradisio*, reached from the museum's skylight down to the floor, while the downtown installation, *Inferno*, was located in a shaft of the museum. Horn's cinematic work is equally formally and conceptually complex and as daring as her sculptures, a continuation of her sculptural concerns articulated into the realm of the moving picture. In whatever media she has worked, Horn has attained an importance in modern sculpture through a body of work that addresses grand themes such as life, death, the body, the self, and technology.

RAÚL ZAMUDIO

See also **Bellmer, Hans; Contemporary Sculpture; Duchamp, Marcel; Hamilton, Ann; Installation; Kounellis, Jannis; Tinguely, Jean**

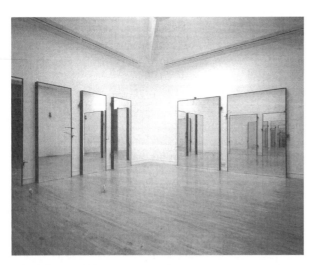

Ballet of the Woodpeckers
© 2001 Artists Rights Society (ARS), New York / VG Bild-Kunst, Bonn

Biography

Born in Michelstadt, Germany, 24 March 1944. Attended Hochschule für Bildende Künste, Hamburg, Germany, 1964–70; awarded a Deutscher Akademischer Austauschdeinst grant, 1971; traveled to London and studied at St. Martin's School of Art, 1971–72; moved to New York City, 1972; participated in *Documenta 5*, Kassel, Germany, 1972, where awarded Anold Bolde Documenta-Preis; participated in *Documenta 6*, 1977; *7*, 1982; *8*, 1986; *9*, 1992; first solo exhibition at Galerie René Block, Berlin, 1973; first U.S. exhibition at René Block Gallery, New York City, 1975; awarded Kunstpreis Glockengasse, Cologne, Germany, 1977; participated at Venice Bieniale, 1980, and Carnegie International, 1988, where awarded Carnegie Prize; began teaching at the Akademie der Künst in Berlin; awarded Trägerin des Kaiserrings Goslar and the Medienkunstpreis, 1992; U.S. retrospective at

Guggenheim Museum of Art, New York City, 1993. Lives and works in Berlin, Germany.

Selected Works

1968   *Arm Extension*; fabric; private collection

1972   *Finger Gloves*; fabric, balsa wood; private collection

1975   *Paradise Widow*; black feathers, metal; collection of Kunstmuseum Bonn-Leihgrabe, Germany

1978   *The Feathered Prison Fan*; white peacock feathers, metal, motor, wood; collection of Thomas Amman, Zurich, Switzerland

1985   *The Bath of the Reflected Dew Drops*; outdoor sculpture/installation: mirrors, glass, metal construction, distilled water; FRAC, Lyons, Rhône-Alpes, France

1986   *Ballet of the Woodpeckers*; mixed media installation; Tate Gallery, London, England

1987   *Lola*; red paint, tap dance shoes, metal, motors; private collection

1988   *An Art Circus*; indoor installation: binoculars, egg, two glass funnels, mercury, pigments, black ink, charcoal, metal, motors; Montreal Museum of Fine Arts, Canada

1991   *Chorus of the Locust I*; 36 typewriters, white cane, metal, motors; Hamburger Kunsthalle, Hamburg, Germany

1992   *High Moon*; two Winchester rifles, two glass funnels, motor, metal, water, dye; Marian Goodman Gallery, New York City, United States

1993   *The Moon, the Child, and the River of Anarchy*; school desks, plastic tubes, ink, glass funnels, lead tubes, mercury; private collection

Further Reading

Baum, Tim, *Rebeccabook 1*, New York: Nadada, 1975

Celant, Germano, et al., *Rebecca Horn* (exhib. cat.), New York: Guggenheim Museum of Art, 1993

David, Jean-Luc, editor, *Actuel Ar*, Geneva: Éditions d'Art Albert Skira, 1980

Haenlein, Carl, editor, *Rebecca Horn: The Glance of Infinity*, Zurich: Scalo, 1997

Horn, Rebecca, *Dialogo della vedova paradisiaca*, Genoa, Italy: Samanedizioni, 1976

Horn, Rebecca, *Rebecca Horn: La lune rebelle*, Stuttgart, Germany: Cantz, 1993

Horn, Rebecca, Sven Nykvist, and Martin Mosebach, *Rebecca Horn: Buster's Bedroom, a Filmbook*, Zurich and New York: Parkett, 1991

Vergine, Lea, editor, *Il corpo come linguaggio (La Body-art e storie simili)*, Milan: Pearo, 1974; 2nd edition, 2000; as *Body Art and Performance: The Body as Language*, Milan: Skira, and London: Thames and Hudson, 2000

HORSES OF SAN MARCO

Anonymous

year unknown, but of ancient, probably Roman, origin

gilded bronze

h. 1.71 m

Church museum, St. Mark's Basilica, Venice, Italy

The four beautiful statues of trotting horses that tower above the symbolic triumphal arch on the facade of St. Mark's Basilica in Venice are known as the Horses of San Marco. Those on display today are modern copies; the originals are preserved in the church museum. As Michael Jacoff has observed, their pagan origin should not disturb anyone since they were intended to symbolize the four Evangelists (see Jacoff, 1993). The horses are far older than St. Mark's, although their history is tortuous and still partially veiled in mystery. We know for certain that they came from the Byzantine Empire and were carried off as war booty by the Venetians in 1204. We also know the names of the protagonists of the Sack of Constantinople: Enrico Dandolo, the doge of Venice; Marino Zeno, first governor of the conquered city; and Domenico Morosini, commander of the ship that brought the horses to Venice. As one perhaps legendary source has it, one of the horses lost a leg during the voyage, and the fragment has been jealously guarded by the Morosini family ever since. That was only the start of the adventures of the precious loot. After reaching Venice, the horses remained at the Arsenal for 50 years. The reason for their quarantine was that the facade of St. Mark's had not been designed to display them, and it took that time to build a suitable loggia from which the masterpieces could be seen from afar. They were installed at St. Mark's during Doge Ranieri Zeno's term of office (1253–68) when the facade took the form we see today, which relates more to the piazza in front than to the church itself.

Art historians have been puzzled over the arrangement of the horses. Many observers maintain that the positions of the horses' legs are not consistent with the direction of their eyes. It may be that their heads were switched. In fact, only the two central horses are looking at each other. For simplicity's sake, scholars have labeled the horses A, B, C, and D, starting from the left. Christiane Pinatel and other scholars argue that if the heads of horses A and D were switched, leaving their bodies as is, the ensemble would become more consistent (see Pinatel, 1997). The movements would be more credible because the head of each horse would appear to be following the motion of its raised forefoot. Conversely, Vittorio Galliazzo believes the proper order would be D, B, C, and A (see Galliazzo, 1984). According to the hippologist Augusto Azzaroli, the motion is elegant but false; in no natural gait can a horse's legs assume the positions they do in these statues (see Azzaroli, 1981).

At this point we must go back to the Sack of Constantinople and try to understand what these four splendid steeds were. During the Renaissance, when humanists were reading Pliny and studying ancient coins and monuments, the idea took hold that the horses were the work of Lysippos and perhaps had pulled the famous *Auriga of the Sun*. The Renaissance attribution to Lysippos was accepted by many scholars in more recent times. In effect, since the Venetian four-horse team is the only one of its kind surviving from Antiquity, the temptation to link it to the name of the greatest sculptor of four-horse chariots is understandable and justifiable.

However, new technologies have been used to compare the horses of San Marco with works commonly attributed to the great Greek sculptor, for instance the Getty bronze. The study found that the horses were cast with a different metal technology and that their surface treatment differs as well. They were cast with the indirect casting technique that came into wide use after the mid 5th century BCE and was used to cast the Riace bronzes and the Piraeus *Apollo*. The alloy is an impure copper that has an extremely high melting point. That it must be heated to temperatures above 1,000–1,300 degrees Celsius (1,832–2,372 degrees Fahrenheit) makes it very hard to cast, and the casting is certain to develop numerous cracks, but the sculptor's choice of this metal doubtless took into account the fact that the statues were to be gilded. In fact, the four horses are literally blanketed with hundreds of irregularly shaped patches that the gilding has concealed for centuries. The study of these patches is what led Licia Vlad Borrelli and other scholars to suggest a Roman origin for the horses, because the Greeks are known to have used only square and rectangular patches (see Vlad Borrelli, 1997). But if the four horses are a Roman work, their dating becomes more uncertain: somewhere between the 4th century BCE and the 4th century CE. Vlad Borrelli has suggested that they came from a four-horse chariot dedicated to Helios, the Sun, which the emperor Septimius Severus ordered to replace the one he had moved from the Tetrasoon to the Temple of the Sun built especially to host them on the Acropolis (see Vlad Borrelli, 1997). This hypothesis is fascinating, but unfortunately there is no documentary evidence for it. It seems beyond dispute

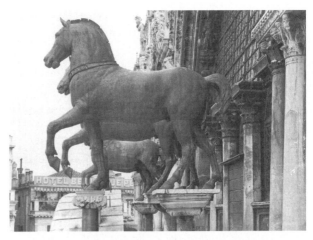

Horses of San Marco, Venice (13th century copy, after original)
© Alinari / Art Resource, NY

that the Horses of San Marco belonged to a four-horse chariot. They are all wearing breast collars, which means they were pulling something; their number obviously implies a four-horse chariot. Originally they may have worn traces, too, which would have been later removed.

The meticulous analyses made of these sculptures revealed several curious details. For one thing, they are nearly 17 hands high (171 centimeters at the withers), which is not rare in today's horses but was decidedly tall for Roman steeds. For another, the pupils of their eyes are rendered by a half-moon incision, as if they were human, not animal. Moreover, the horses' proportions do not correspond to those of any known breed and constitute a deliberate falsity.

Despite these so-called errors, the horses have always been held in the highest esteem. In 1798 the French seized them as war booty and carried them off to Paris, where they remained until 1815. During their sojourn in Paris, they were moved between three locations. In 1815 they were returned to Venice. In 1826 the French, still enamored of the horses, sent a team of expert craftsmen to Venice to take plaster casts of them. The team made casts only of the shaft horses, B and C. The casts, displayed for 150 years at the École des Beaux-Arts in Paris, appear to have influenced François-Joseph Bosio in sculpting the four-horse chariot atop the Arc de Triomphe du Carrousel, as well as a large part of monumental equestrian sculpture in France.

GIOVANNA CHECCHI

Further Reading

Azzaroli, Augusto, "Note ippologiche," in *I cavalli di San Marco*, edited by Guido Perocco and Renzo Zorzi, Milan: Edizioni di Comunità, 1981

Bertoli, Bruno, editor, *La Basilica di San Marco: Arte e simbologia*, Venice: Edizioni Studium Cattolico Veneziano, 1993

Galliazzo, Vittorio, "I cavalli de San Marco: Una quadriga greca o romana?" *Faventia* 6/2 (1984)

Haskell, Francis, and Nicholas Penny, *Taste and the Antique: The Lure of Classical Sculpture, 1500–1900*, New Haven, Connecticut: Yale University Press, 1981

I cavalli di San Marco, Venice: Procuratoria di San Marco, 1977; as *The Horses of San Marco, Venice*, translated by John and Valerie Wilton-Ely, London: Thames and Hudson, and Milan and New York: Olivetti, 1979

Jacoff, Michael, *The Horses of San Marco and the Quadriga of the Lord*, Princeton, New Jersey: Princeton University Press, 1993

Niero, Antonio, editor, *San Marco: Aspetti storici e agiografici*, Venice: Marsilio, 1996

Pinatel, Christiane, "I calchi dei cavalli di San Marco in Francia," in *Storia dell'arte marciana*, edited by Renato Polacco, Venice: Marsilio, 1997

Vlad Borrelli, Licia, "Ipotesi di datazione per i cavalli di San Marco," in *Storia dell'arte marciana*, edited by Renato Polacco, Venice: Marsilio, 1997

HARRIET GOODHUE HOSMER 1830–1908 *United States, active in Italy*

Harriet Hosmer is one of the best known of a group of women artists who lived and worked in Italy during the mid 19th century. This group, famously referred to by the author Henry James as the "white marmorean flock," also included artists such as Mary Edmonia Lewis and Emma Stebbins. Although Hosmer's sculpture was both critically and commercially successful, her enigmatic personality made her one of the more controversial figures of her time.

Hosmer was raised in Watertown, Massachusetts, by her father, a physician, after her mother and three siblings died of tuberculosis. Dr. Hosmer promoted an outdoor, active lifestyle for his daughter out of concern for her health, eschewing Victorian gender conventions. Scholars have often cited this early freedom as the impetus for Hosmer's refusal to conform to traditional female roles throughout her life. At age 15, she was sent to Mrs. Charles Sedgwick's School for Girls, a progressive boarding school. Hosmer stayed there for four years, then returned to Watertown, announcing her plans to become a sculptor. This was, at the time, an extremely unconventional vocation for women, who were credited with neither the creativity nor the physical strength to produce sculpture. Undeterred, Hosmer set up a studio at her father's home and began studying with sculptor Peter Stephenson in Boston. Hosmer's work was halted, however, when she was denied access to anatomy classes in local medical schools because of her sex. Eventually, her father persuaded Dr. Joseph McDowell of the McDowell Medical College in St. Louis, Missouri, to admit her. Hosmer moved to St. Louis, attended classes, and then returned to Watertown.

Back in Watertown, Hosmer began to produce ambitious pieces such as portrait medallions and a bust, *Hesper* (completed in 1852). Inspired by a poem by Alfred, Lord Tennyson, "In Memoriam," this Classical-inspired bust won favorable reviews. Seeking inspiration and further instruction, Hosmer moved to Rome that same year. In the early 19th century, Rome was an artistic center for many American sculptors. Easy access to Greek and Roman masterpieces was one draw, but skilled workmen and wealthy tourists purchasing art while on the grand tour were also powerful incentives for artists to set up a studio. She became a student of John Gibson, who had been a student of the Italian Neoclassical sculptor Antonio Canova and the Danish sculptor Bertel Thorvaldsen.

In 1854 Hosmer completed two original busts, *Daphne* and *Medusa*. *Daphne*'s delicate hair is pulled back in a bun, framing her Classical features. Her eyes are cast downward, and laurel leaves at the base of the bust enfold her arms. Drawn from a Greek myth, the bust depicts Daphne's plight when, fleeing Apollo's amorous pursuits, she begs the gods to save her. Just as Apollo catches her, she is turned into a laurel tree. The bust of *Medusa* represents a similar moment of transition as her hair turns into snakes. Hosmer's skill with the tenets of Classicism is reflected in both works; they also reveal the artist's desire to depict strong and assertive women. Both Daphne and Medusa find independence in a man's world—a notion that certainly had resonance for Hosmer.

In 1855 Hosmer's father informed her that he could no longer support her financially. Instead of returning home, she decided to stay and sculpted a marketable piece, *Puck*. She went on to produce more than 30 variations of the small, fanciful sculpture featuring Puck, a character from William Shakespeare's *A Midsummer Night's Dream*, sitting on a toadstool. This piece and its pendant, *Will-o'-the-Wisp*, secured Hosmer finances and added to her growing reputation. She returned to a more serious subject in her next piece, *Beatrice Cenci*. This work depicts Beatrice on the eve of her execution, in Classical drapery, sleeping with a beaded rosary chain twisted around her hand. The piece, which again attests to Hosmer's interests in portraying feminine fortitude in repressive circumstances, was exhibited to much acclaim at the Royal Academy in London in 1857. During that same year, Hosmer was commissioned, and became the first American, to sculpt a funerary monument in a Roman church.

Hosmer's success in securing commissions and on the international art scene made her the focus of much attention, not all of which was positive. In Rome her unconventional lifestyle and manner had drawn contempt from other American sculptors. She also became the victim of rumors claiming that she was not creating

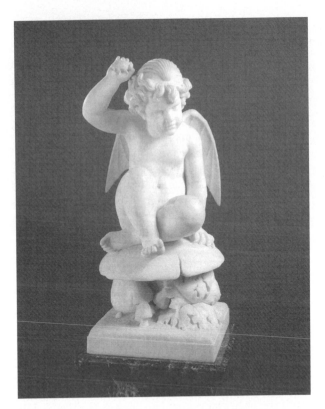

Puck
© Smithsonian American Art Museum, Washington, D.C. /
Art Resource, NY

her own work. In 1862, when Hosmer exhibited her new work *Zenobia* at the International exhibition in London, an article in *Art Journal* insinuated that Italian workmen had created the piece. Hosmer responded with her own article that detailed her creative process. The sculpture was a huge success, and ultimately the notoriety only increased Hosmer's popularity. This episode, nonetheless, reveals that, despite apparent acceptance of Hosmer and her work, there was still hostility toward women artists.

The 1860s continued to be a productive time for Hosmer. While *Zenobia* toured the United States, attracting large crowds, Hosmer was at work on her statue of Thomas Hart Benton, a Missouri senator. Hosmer modeled the over–life-size statue of Benton, with a Classical toga over contemporary dress, in bronze, an exception to her usual work in marble. She returned to more traditional fare with marble pendants *Sleeping Faun* and *Waking Faun*.

In the 1870s Hosmer's artistic production declined after she left Rome and pursued new intellectual interests. Although she withdrew from the art world in her later life, Hosmer's legacy endures. She remains one of the strongest of the American Neoclassical artists. Her work, in particular her images of women, breathed new life into the vocabulary of Classicism. Hosmer's

contribution to the history of female artists is of equal importance. Despite the gendered obstacles that she confronted, Hosmer's devotion to the ideal of the art proved itself exceptional to both her contemporaries and female artists who followed her.

ALEXIS L. BOYLAN

See also **Canova, Antonio; Gibson, John; Lewis, Mary Edmonia; Thorvaldsen, Bertel; Women Sculptors**

Biography

Born in Watertown, Massachusetts, United States, 9 October 1830. Only surviving child of Sarah Grant and Hiram Hosmer, physician. Attended Mrs. Charles Sedgwick's School for Girls in Lenox, Massachusetts, 1845–49; began studying sculpture with Peter Stephenson in Boston, 1849; studied anatomy at McDowell Medical College at St. Louis University, 1850; departed for Italy, 1852, and studied with English sculptor John Gibson, 1852–59; only female sculptor to exhibit in International Exposition in London, 1862; closed studio in Italy in 1875 and moved to England; returned to the United States, 1900. Died in Watertown, Massachusetts, United States, 21 February 1908.

Selected Works

1852   *Hesper*; marble; Watertown Free Public Library, Watertown, Massachusetts, United States

1853   *Hands of Robert and Elizabeth Barrett Browning*; bronze; Newark Museum, New Jersey, United States

1854   *Daphne*; marble; Metropolitan Museum of Art, New York City, United States

1854   *Medusa*; marble; The Detroit Institute of Arts, Michigan, United States

1856   *Puck*; marble; National Museum of American Art, Washington, D.C., United States

1857   *Beatrice Cenci*; marble; St. Louis Mercantile Library Association, Missouri, United States

ca. 1858 *Will-o'-the-Wisp*; marble; Chrysler Museum, Norfolk, Virginia, United States

1859   *Zenobia*; marble (presumed lost)

1859   *Zenobia in Chains* (reduction); marble; Wadsworth Athenaeum, Hartford, Connecticut, United States

1864   *Thomas Hart Benton*; painted bronze; Lafayette Park, St. Louis, Missouri, United States

1865   *Sleeping Faun*; marble; Museum of Fine Arts, Boston, Massachusetts, United States

1866–67 *Waking Faun*; plaster or marble (location unknown)

Further Reading

Clark, Henry Nichols Blake, "Harriet Hosmer," in *A Marble Quarry: The James H. Ricau Collection of Sculpture at the Chrysler Museum of Art*, New York: Hudson Hills Press, 1997

Faxon, Alicia, "Images of Women in the Sculpture of Harriet Hosmer," *Woman's Art Journal* 2 (spring–summer 1981)

Gerdts, William H., "The *Medusa* of Harriet Hosmer," *Bulletin of the Detroit Institute of Arts* 56 (1978)

Hosmer, Harriet, *Harriet Hosmer: Letters and Memories*, edited by Cornelia Carr, New York: Moffat, Yard, 1912

Sherwood, Dolly, *Harriet Hosmer, American Sculptor, 1830–1908*, Columbia: University of Missouri Press, 1991

Zastoupil, Carol, "Creativity, Inspiration, and Scandal: Harriet Hosmer and *Zenobia*," in *The Italian Presence in American Art, 1760–1860*, edited by Irma B. Jaffe, New York: Fordham University Press, and Rome: Istituto della Enciclopedia Italiana, 1989

JEAN-ANTOINE HOUDON 1741–1828
French

The career of Jean-Antoine Houdon, one of the most important sculptors in France at the end of the 18th century, spans the reign of Louis XIV to the late years of the Napoleonic empire. Tied historically to Neoclassicism more than any other movement, he is also closely linked with the art of the Baroque and Gianlorenzo Bernini. Known primarily for his acute and lifelike portraits, Houdon wanted to revive the great age of sculpture of the 16th and 17th centuries, striving for two main goals: anatomical accuracy and technical mastery. Realism was the overarching feature of his work, but a realism informed by his study of Antique and Renaissance models. While he cannot be seen as a true Neoclassicist, his sculpture incorporates a subtle idealism with Classical poses and psychological penetration.

Houdon was born in Versailles, the son of the concierge for the comte de Lamotte, controller-general of the king's parks. Houdon's father was also concierge at Lamotte's Parisian *hôtel*, which housed the École Royale des Élèves Protégés, an elite art school associated with the Royal Academy. By 1756 Houdon was enrolled in school at the Royal Academy of Painting and Sculpture and studied in the studio of sculptor René-Michel Slodtz, as well as with Jean-Baptiste Lemoyne and Jean-Baptiste Pigalle. In that year Houdon took third prize in the Prix de Rome competition, along with Michel Clodion. In 1761 Houdon won the First Prix de Rome (Rome Prize) and entered the École Royale des Élèves Protégés in preparation for his travel to the French Academy in Rome.

Houdon left for Rome in 1764, an important step in the career of all artists, since it enabled them to study the work of the Renaissance masters and also original Greek and Roman works of art. One of his major works in Rome—and his most important religious sculpture—is the *St. Bruno* in the Church of Santa Maria degli Angeli, a monumental marble that served as a response to his teacher Slodtz's *St. Bruno* of 1744 in St. Peter's Basilica, Rome. In contrast to Slodtz's overly refined Rococo version, Houdon's work is more sober and quietly powerful in its stark realism and contemplative attitude, the body a pronounced vertical of smooth drapery relieved only by the saint's praying hands. For a pendant commission for a statue of St. John the Baptist, Houdon produced a full-size, graphically accurate anatomical study, known as *L'Écorché au bras tendu* (*Flayed Man*), after having studied anatomy from corpses in a hospital in Rome. Since that time, art schools have used casts and copies of *L'Écorché* as anatomical models.

In November 1768 Houdon returned to Paris. He was accepted as an *agréé* (admitted) to the Royal Academy in July 1768 and was thereafter allowed to exhibit at the Salon, a privilege reserved for those artists affiliated with the academy. The Salon of 1771 marked Houdon's entry into portraiture with a terracotta portrait head of the Enlightenment philosopher Denis Diderot, depicted without wig, with disheveled hair, and undraped, *à l'antique* (after the antique). Diderot's mouth is slightly open, a device that adds to the bust's spontaneous quality, and the head twists slightly to the right, revealing the age and character of the sitter in the subtly observed folds of the neck. The most important feature of this work is Houdon's treatment of the eyes; he cut out the iris and bored a hole for the pupil, leaving a small piece of marble in place to catch the light and suggest character. Houdon's typical working method was first to model his subject in clay and then make a plaster cast. He kept the original clay (fired to preserve it as a mold) and the plaster cast in his studio as models for later reproductions.

Houdon traveled twice to the court of Saxe-Gotha in Germany, in 1771 and 1773, to execute portraits of four members of the house of Saxe-Gotha (exhibited at the Salon of 1773), classical portraits that reveal the court's affinity for the aesthetic theories of J.J. Winckelmann. In 1776 Houdon produced a plaster of *Diana the Huntress* for the Duke of Saxe-Gotha, depicting the goddess with a half-moon on her forehead, balanced on her left foot, and holding a bow and arrow. Since Antiquity, Diana was depicted either as running and clothed or nude and reclining; Houdon's treatment combines these two characteristics in a work whose realism shocked some of his contemporaries.

Houdon became a full member of the academy in 1777, a decade that saw the growth of his fame as a portraitist. Among the many portrait busts exhibited are the statesmen Turgot, the composer Gluck, the actress-singer Sophie Arnould, and in 1779 alone, Molière, Rousseau, D'Alembert, and Voltaire. Houdon's only royal commission was for comte d'Angiviller's Great Men of France series, a full-size sculpture of the Maréchal de Tourville in contemporary dress, exhibited in 1781, at which time Houdon also showed the original plaster of his *Voltaire Seated*. Houdon's concerns in portrait sculpture included accuracy (even going so far as to make death masks of sitters), psychological penetration, and liveliness, all of which are visible in this depiction of the philosopher and writer.

The most important of Houdon's portraits of U.S. statesmen is the statue of George Washington commissioned by the state assembly of Virginia with the help of Thomas Jefferson, ambassador to France. Houdon traveled to the United States in 1785 to make studies from life. He shipped the work, signed 1788, to the United States in January 1796. Houdon wanted to depict Washington in Classical dress, but Washington refused. The president stands in a restrained *contrapposto*, (a natural pose with the weight of one leg, the shoulder, and hips, counterbalancing one another), his right hand resting on a cane, his left on the fasces

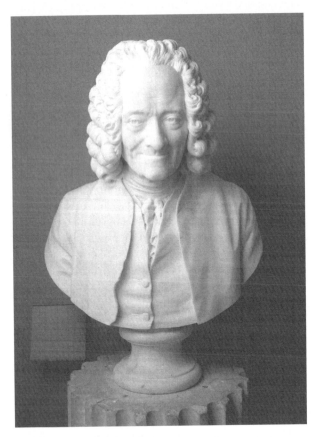

Voltaire
Photo by M. Beck Coppola
© Réunion des Musées Nationaux / Art Resource, NY

(bundle of rods signaling rulership) from which his sword hangs. Behind is a plow, referring to Cincinnatus, the Roman general who returned to his farm during times of peace, like Washington himself. Houdon achieved dignity, command, and elegance through the pose and distribution of attributes, from which the contemporary dress does not detract. Houdon depicted Washington, as he did in his portrait busts of Thomas Jefferson and Napoléon I, as a man of vision and principle, a thinker rather than a man of action.

The 1770s and 1780s proved the most productive years of Houdon's career. By this time Houdon was an established and highly respected master of sculpture. He became a member of the Section of Painting and Sculpture of the Institute of France in 1795 and a professor at the École des Beaux-Arts beginning in 1805. He exhibited at the Salon for the last time in 1814 and died in Paris at the age of 87.

KRISTIN O'ROURKE

See also **Bernini, Gianlorenzo; Lemoyne Family; Pigalle, Jean-Baptiste; Slodtz, René-Michel [Michel-Ange]**

Biography

Born in Versailles, France, 25 March 1741. Enrolled in the School of the Royal Academy of Painting and Sculpture by 1756; studied in the studio of René-Michel Slodtz; also studied with Jean-Baptiste Lemoyne and Jean-Baptiste Pigalle; won third prize for sculpture, 1756; won the Prix de Rome (Rome Prize) in sculpture, 1761; entered École Royale des Elèves Protégés, 1761–64; went to Rome in 1764, where he studied original Greek and Roman art works, along with works by Renaissance masters such as Michelangelo; returned to France, 1768; traveled to court of Saxony, 1771 and 1773; *agréé* (admitted member) of the Royal Academy, 1768; elected member, 1777, and appointed assistant professor of sculpture, 1778; member of the Section of Painting and Sculpture of the Institute of France, 1795; professor at École des Beaux-Arts from 1805; named Chevalier of the Legion of Honor, 1805; exhibited at the Salon throughout his career, first in 1769, last in 1814. Died in Paris, France, 15 July 1828.

Selected Works

1766   *L'Ecorché au bras tendu (Flayed Man)*; plaster; Schloss Friedenstein, Gotha, Germany

1767   *St. Bruno*; marble; Church of Santa Maria degli Angeli, Rome, Italy

1771   *Denis Diderot*; terracotta; examples: Yale University Art Gallery, New Haven,

1776   *Diana the Huntress*; plaster; Schloss Friedenstein, Gotha, Germany; bronze casts: 1782, Huntington Library and Art Gallery, San Marino, California, United States; 1790, Musée du Louvre, Paris, France

1777   *Morpheus*; marble; Musée du Louvre, Paris, France

1778   *Voltaire*; marble, Musée du Louvre, Paris, France

1781   *Maréchal de Tourville*; marble; Château, Versailles, Yvelines, France

1781   *Voltaire Seated*; plaster; Bibliothèque Nationale de France, Paris, France

1786–96 *George Washington*; marble; State Capitol, (signed Richmond, Virginia, United States 1788)

1789   Bust of Thomas Jefferson; marble; Museum of Fine Arts, Boston, Massachusetts, United States

1806   *Napoléon as Emperor*; terracotta; Musée des Beaux-Arts, Dijon, France

Further Reading

Arnason, H.H., *Sculpture by Houdon* (exhib. cat.), Worcester, Massachusetts: Worcester Art Museum, 1964

Arnason, H.H., *The Sculptures of Houdon*, London: Phaidon, and New York: Oxford University Press, 1975

Hart, Charles Henry, and Biddle, Edward, *Memoirs of the Life and Works of Jean-Antoine Houdon, the Sculptor of Voltaire and of Washington*, Philadelphia, Pennsylvania: De Vinne Press, 1911

Houdon, Jean-Antoine, *Réflexions sur les concours en général et sur celui de la statue de J.-J. Rousseau en particulier*, s.l.: s.n., 1791; reprint, in Réau, 1964 (below)

Lami, Stanislas, *Dictionnaire des sculpteurs de l'école française en dix-huitième siècle*, Paris: Champion, 1910

Levey, Michael, *Painting and Sculpture in France, 1700–1789*, New Haven, Connecticut: Yale University Press, 1993

Poulet, Anne, *Jean-Antione Houdon: Sculpture of Enlightenment* (exhib. cat.), Chicago: University of Chicago Press, 2003

Réau, Louis, *Houdon: Sa vie et son oeuvre*, 2 vols., Paris: De Nobele, 1964

VOLTAIRE SEATED

Jean-Antoine Houdon (1741–1828)

1781

plaster

h. 138 cm

Bibliothèque Nationale de France, Paris, France
Marble versions in Comédie Française, Paris,
France; Hermitage, St. Petersburg, Russia

Jean-Antoine Houdon made his most significant contribution to the art of his time through portrait sculpture, in particular portrait busts or portrait heads of some of the most illustrious and important figures from contemporary political and cultural life. His most favored subject, judging by the many versions and copies of the work requested and produced, was the image of the philosopher, playwright, and intellectual Voltaire. Once Houdon had created the original version of a particular subject (based on life studies and often face and shoulder masks and measurements), he frequently went on to produce, upon demand, numerous copies and variations of his figures in different media (terracotta, marble, bronze, and plaster) and of differing dimensions. Students executed many of the copies under his supervision; however, the copies continued to be carried out after his death and can be of varying quality. So popular were his works that Houdon himself believed he had been deprived of a significant amount of money because of the many illegal copies made by forgers.

The Salon of 1779 witnessed Houdon's first *Voltaire*, a portrait head in plaster *à l'antique* (after the antique), depicted without wig, bald, and undraped in a classicizing but highly realistic manner, shown, like the *Denis Diderot* from a few years before, as a modern philosopher. Many variations of this portrait head exist: with and without wig, in contemporary dress, draped and undraped, and in many media. Two years later, at the Salon of 1781, Houdon exhibited the original plaster of his *Voltaire Seated* (now in the Bibliothèque Nationale de France), a statue that he produced without commission but most likely with the hope that it would be taken up as a public monument to the philosopher. The *Voltaire Seated* is Houdon's most monumental undertaking of this subject.

Voltaire, who had been living in a form of exile on the Swiss border, returned to Paris in February 1778. Houdon must have obtained sittings from Voltaire immediately after the philosopher's return to Paris since Voltaire died a few months later, in July 1778. The unsuccessful full-size sculpture of *Voltaire* by Jean-Baptiste Pigalle, shown to overwhelmingly negative response at the Salon of 1776, certainly played a major role in influencing Houdon's depiction of Voltaire. Pigalle's version, which had been commissioned as a public monument by leading intellectuals and businessmen and paid for by subscription, depicted Voltaire in the nude as an aging philosopher. Pigalle studied the head from life but took the body from an aged and decrepit model. Voltaire himself had tried to dissuade Pigalle from a nude image to no avail; the resultant sculpture was universally disliked. Houdon's much-admired version by contrast depicts the 84-year-old Voltaire fully draped in vaguely Antique robes and crowned with a philosopher's headband. He is seated in a Classically styled chair, looking alert and engaged with the space around him. His hands rest anxiously on the arms of the chair, as if about to spring up out of it; although his body is hidden by the voluminous draperies, a subtle attention to anatomical detail and presentation of character assures his physicality and presence. Voltaire's head twists to the right, and his eyes, deeply cut, look slightly down and to the right. He appears as elevated on a pedestal, looking downward and somehow beyond the viewer's space. His facial expression has been the subject of much commentary and mythmaking. While the exact circumstances of Houdon's encounter with Voltaire are not known, one contemporary anecdote relates that, while Voltaire was posing, the "crown of glory" he had received from the Comédie Française was placed suddenly on his head in order to provoke a response that Houdon would then be able to record in his sculpture. Voltaire does wear a form of a ribbon around his forehead, a motif to signify his intellectual standing, but here incorporated artfully as if holding back the scant amount of hair on his head (Voltaire was in fact fully bald by this time). The overall presentation of the figure offers an image of Voltaire as a modern "ancient" philosopher, not withdrawn and contemplative but full of life and defying his many years. The figure suggests Voltaire's wit and sagacity, along with his general curiosity, through the slightly smiling mouth and bright eyes. The *Voltaire Seated* offers not only an image of the man himself but a portrait of the age of Enlightenment.

Voltaire's niece, Mme. Denis, presented a marble version of the *Voltaire Seated* from 1781 to the Comédie Française. She had originally commissioned the marble version as a gift for the Académie Française. However, she became antagonized by satirical comments by members regarding her marriage at a late age and gave the statue instead to the Comédie Française. The members of the Comédie were overjoyed to receive the sculpture and expressed as much in a letter to her. They considered the statue to be perfectly at home at a theater where so many of Voltaire's plays were staged. Voltaire was in fact more popular after the French Revolution than he had been before. By order of the government, Voltaire's plays were produced in revival in Paris at the main theater in the years following the Revolution, themselves inspiring many paintings and sculptures. Busts of Voltaire were even frequently placed on stage during productions of his plays. In 1782 Houdon presented to every member of the Royal Academy a plaster bust of Voltaire, and busts continued to emerge from his studio after his death. The number of portrait busts and heads of Voltaire far exceeds those of any other subject by Houdon, testifying to the currency and appeal of Voltaire at the time; not only private individuals but nearly every theater and university in France wanted a bust of Voltaire.

Houdon produced a second full-size marble of the *Voltaire Seated* (1781) for Catherine II of Russia, which is now in the Hermitage in St. Petersburg. Catherine was an important patron of Houdon, and he took great care in the creation of this version. In addition to the plaster and the two marbles, a life-size terracotta is in the Musée Fabre at Montpellier, France, and a life-size papier mâché version, meant to be carried in a procession, is in Rouen. Also existing are many reduced versions in all materials.

KRISTIN O'ROURKE

Further Reading

Dacier, Emile, *Le Musée de la Comédie-Française, 1680–1905*, Paris: Librarie de l'Art Ancien et Moderne, 1905

Sauerländer, Willibald, *Jean-Antoine Houdon: Voltaire*, Stuttgart, Germany: Reclam, 1963

HUY, JEAN PEPIN DE

See **Pepin de Huy, Jean**

I

INDIA: INDUS VALLEY CIVILIZATION–GUPTA

The history and heritage of Indian sculptures may be traced to about 2500 BCE. Through the ages, with the patronage of the imperial and the lay class, sculptors experimented with numerous sculptural styles and materials that later came to be associated with particular geographical regions. However, the development of Indian sculpture was never an insulated process. Instead, styles and guilds traveled from one region to another. The study of Indian sculpture has been divided into different periods on the basis of region, chronology, and patronage. Sculptural development in India from 2500 BCE to the 6th century CE encompasses the Indus Valley, or Harappa, civilization to the Saisunaga-Nanda, Maurya, Sunga, Andhra, Kusana, and Gupta periods.

Indus Valley Civilization

The Indus Valley civilization, more popularly called the Harappa civilization, is the earliest known civilization of the South Asian subcontinent, extending from 2500 to 1500 BCE. Remnants of this civilization have been excavated from at least three other towns besides the Indus Valley, as well as several villages from the Indian peninsula (Rupar on the upper Satlaj to Rangpur in Kathiawar). Therefore, the term "Indus Valley civilization" is no longer considered truly descriptive.

The sculptural works from the Indus Valley play a vital role in understanding the society of that period because no written history has yet been successfully deciphered. The few stone and metal sculptures that have come to light in excavations reflect a mature stage of artistic development in which problems of proportion, scale, relation of forms, and surface enhancement have been explored. These surviving examples are certainly a tiny fraction of the objects once produced. Over 2,000 seals in the form of small clay tablets with relief figures of various human, animal, and other motifs have been discovered in the Indus cities. These steatite seals remain the most impressive and enigmatic artifacts from the Harappan civilization, revealing the most consummate and delicate perfection of craftsmanship. Numerous terracotta figures and toys have been recovered from Harappa sites, but these differ considerably in style and decoration from the stone and metal pieces. They seem to represent a popular art form and were created more spontaneously. Among human figures are the massive portliness evident in the gray stone *Dancing Male Torso* (Central Asian Antiquities Museum, New Delhi, India) and the slender form in the *Dancing Girl* (National Museum, New Delhi, India). The ambiguous sensuousness of the male statuettes and the wiry vigor of the bronze *Dancing Girl* from Mohenjo-Daro contrast with the dignity of the *Priest Head* (National Museum, Karachi, Pakistan), which is characterized by an attitude of concentration with yoga glance and the corresponding fixation of the mind.

Even though the legs of the *Dancing Male Torso* are broken and only drilled sockets remain where arms and head were fitted, the figure is so full of energy and dynamism that it has been named the *Dancing Male Torso*. The suggestion of movement imparted by

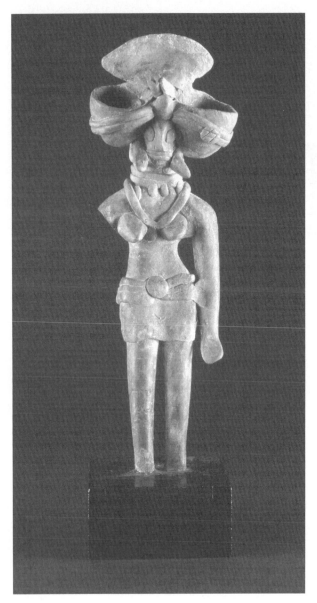

Mother goddess figure from Indus Valley Civilization
© Angelo Hornak / CORBIS

the violent axial dislocation of the head, thorax, and hips further enhances the sense of energy. The modeling is extremely simple but imbued with a vital force. A large cavity in the groin indicates that the figure was originally ithyphallic. The fleshlike treatment of the body and the forceful movement make this piece of work remarkable.

The *Dancing Girl*, a small metal sculpture from Mohenjo-Daro of a young girl with her hair dressed in a complicated coiffure, stands nude except for a short necklace and an arm completely ringed with bangles. Her relaxed body twists so that one hand rests on her right hip while the other holds a small bowl against her left leg. Her provocative posture and stance and

overall disposition have led scholars to conclude that she may represent a temple dancer or prostitute. The elongated limbs, which have none of the softly modeled fleshiness of the *Dancing Male Torso*, seem to show a disregard for naturalistic proportions, yet the overall effect is one of liveliness and animation. The *Dancing Girl* is the single major metal sculpture from Harrapan sites. The other known bronze or copper items include several miniature animal figures and utilitarian objects such as axe heads and fishing hooks.

The *Priest Head*, a male limestone bust from Mohenjo-Daro, was found in one of the later Harappa-period levels. Originally inlaid with red paste, the face sports a carefully barbered beard, shaved upper lip, and hair gathered in a bun behind the head. The wide headband has in its center a flat circular ornament that is duplicated on the bangle worn high on the right arm. The eyes were originally inlaid with shell; one eye still retained its inset when found. The figure reveals some affinities to Mesopotamian imagery; details such as the trefoil design on the togalike garment and the mode of hairdressing may be compared with those from Sumerian sculpture. The half-closed eyes and the overall restraint and dignity of this figure has led scholars to determine that this figure may be a votive portrait of a priest or a shaman.

Saisunaga-Nanda Period

The two dynasties ruling Magadha, an ancient region in the Gangetic valley (modern Bihar State), were the Saisunagas (*ca.* 642–413 BCE) and the Nandas (*ca.* 413–322 BCE). This period is that of the later Vedic literature, the Brahmanas, the Upanisads, and the earlier Sutras. The texts give an overview of the use and advanced knowledge of metals and specifically mention the extensive use of tin, lead, and silver. Organizations of craftsmen in guilds of various trades included leather dressers, woodworkers, and painters. Unfortunately, because the archaeological evidence for this period is scanty and incomplete, one has to rely primarily on textual references.

The major source dealing with the history of this period belongs to the Buddhist and Jain canons; it was during this period that Buddha (*ca.* 563–483 BCE) and Mahavira (*ca.* 540–468 BCE) lived and practiced their religions in Magadha. The various texts pertaining to their lives and the faith they preached contain references to this city. Magadha assumed a leading role in the political and economic spheres of the subcontinent.

The Jataka tales—narratives detailing the many lives of Sakyamuni Buddha prior to his final life—tell of 18 guilds comprising various artists and craftsmen, an indication of the significant role art and craft may have played in the society. However, actual remains from this period are few. A small gold plaque with a figure of a nude female was excavated from what apparently is a Vedic burial mound at Lauriya-Nandangarh (8th–7th century BCE). Scholars have associated this figure with the Earth goddess. Minor antiquities have also been excavated from various sites that can be attributed to this period, such as Nagari, Bhita, Pataliputra, and the Bhir mound at Taxila. The remains from the Taxila site include beads and lathe-turned polished hard stones, as well as terracotta reliefs, some of which are similar to the Earth goddess from Lauriya-Nandangarh. The antiquities from the 5th and 4th centuries BCE indicate a high level of technical accomplishment of cutting and polishing of hard stones, as well as in the field of glassmaking. The polishing of hard stone is suggestive of the Mauryan polish from the next period of Indian sculptural history.

Maurya Period

By the 4th century BCE, the social, political, and economic situations that were in the developing stages in Magadha since Upanisadic times achieved a stable and prosperous status. Candragupta Maurya, who overthrew Mahapadma, the last king of the Nanda dynasty, founded the Mauryan Empire (ca. 323–185 BCE). The most illustrious of the Maurya kings was Asoka (reigned ca. 273–232 BCE), grandson of Candragupta.

Buddhism under Asoka's reign received royal patronage beginning with Asoka's conversion to Buddhism after the wrath of the Kalinga battle. Numerous surviving epigraphs inscribed on rocks and pillars comprise the earliest intelligible corpus of written texts from Asoka's reign. These Asokan edicts provide historical information about the period, glimpses of the personality of the ruler, and insights into the state of religion at that time.

Several stone sculptures of human figures from the Mauryan period have survived. Even though these sculptures lack inscriptional evidence and direct archaeological context, they share technical and stylistic features with those of the Mauryan pillars, capitals, and caves. Scholars identify these sculptures predominantly with this dynasty because of the Mauryan polish. Moreover, these sculptures were discovered at sites within the limits of the ancient city of Pataliputra. In addition to stone sculptures from the Mauryan period are a number of terracotta sculptures. One of the most remarkable of these is a figurine from Bulandibagh, Pataliputra, a rather naturalistically depicted woman garbed in an elaborate dress and headdress.

Pillar capitals are of particular significance in the context of Mauryan sculptures. The best preserved is of a *Seated Lion Capital* from Lauriya Nadangarh (ca. 242/241 BCE), while the most elaborate is the *Lion Capital* from Sarnath (mid 3rd century BCE; Sarnath Site Museum, Sarnath, India), with its distinct Mauryan polish. Carved out of Chunar, tan sandstone, the piece consists of a quartet of lions placed back to back, facing the four cardinal directions, on top of a circular abacus. On the abacus, four other animals alternate with wheels—an elephant, horse, bull, and lion. Each of these animals signifies various aspects of Buddha's life. This work represents the wheel of law that Buddha preached for the first time at Sarnath. Strong evidence of Persian—or, more exactly, Achaemenid—influence can be traced in this sculpture. The elongated petals that form the fluting of the bell, the realism of the animals on the abacus, and the stylized, tense muscles of the lion all seem to have been adapted from Achaemenid sculptures from the great capital city of Persepolis.

The *Cauri Bearer* (Patna Museum, Patna, India), a female figure found at Didarganj and more popularly known as the *Didarganj Yakshi*, wears a diaphanous garment adorned with heavy jewelry. Here, the sculptor has succeeded in almost freeing the figure from the matrix of the stone except around the legs. Her right hand holds a whisk (*cauri*) used to keep flies away from distinguished people, which is an indication of her subservient role. The smooth, glossy surfaces and meticulously carved details of jewels and drapery further heighten the figure's fleshlike quality and smooth, flowing contour. Two male figures in stone excavated at Pataliputra may also be ascribed to the Mauryan period. These sculptures are similar in style to that of the *Cauri Bearer*.

A headless and nude *Male Torso* (Patna Museum, Patna, India), carved out of Chunar sandstone with a distinct Mauryan glossy polish, was found at Lohanipur, near modern Patna. No inscriptional evidence for this work survives, and the purpose of the sculpture is not clear. On the basis of its nudity, scholars have suggested that it portrays a member of the Digambara sect of the Jain faith. The natural treatment of the flesh is in contradiction with the quality of the stone. The sculptor carved both the front and back of the image with the same intensity, indicating that the sculpture was conceived in the round.

Sunga Period

The origin of the Sunga dynasty (2nd–1st century BCE) may be traced to Pusyamitra Sunga, the principal military officer of the Mauryan Empire. He assassinated Brihadratha, the last Mauryan king, about 185 BCE and took over the empire. Throughout his rule until 151 BCE, Pusyamitra maintained much of the empire of the Mauryas. However, only in the beginning was the Sunga empire as extensive as the Mauryan Empire;

therefore, the artworks that can be associated with the Sunga period do not always imply Sunga domination of the region or Sunga patronage. The works brought under this broad umbrella have been excavated from various regions in the Indian subcontinent, including Vidisa, Mathura, Pataliputra, Ahicchattra, Ayodhya, and Kausambi. Numerous terracotta sculptures may be dated to the Sunga period; one of the significant pieces is from Tamluk, West Bengal. Elaborately ornamented and delicately executed, this *Female Figure* (Ashmolean Museum, Oxford, England) wears a very thin pleated garment and a heavy jeweled girdle. She wears a prominent headdress, a typical Sunga feature.

The *Parkham Yaksa* (Mathura Museum, Mathura, India), a colossal sculpture of a standing male, was found at Parkham, near Mathura. The date and origin of this figure is debatable. Stylistically, however, the fullness of the body and the diaphanous treatment of the drapery suggest Sunga origin. The size (three meters), frontality, and heaviness of the body further enhance the image's monumentality. Because both the arms are missing, no iconographic connection can be established. It is identified as a *yaksa* (a male nature spirit who functioned as a wealth diety and guardian of treasure) image on the basis of its massive disposition, suggesting wealth and abundance.

Stupa II at Sanchi is one of the oldest structures from this period. The term *stupa* denotes a dome-shaped or rounded structure that contains a relic of Buddha or another honored individual, and is thus considered to be a type of sepulchral monument. In the case of *Stupa II* both the interior and exterior of the railing are carved with shallow reliefs and medallions. These reliefs typify much of Sunga-period art in their flatness, the way in which the figures and other carved elements seem to be set against a two-dimensional background with little suggestion of depth or natural space. The figures portrayed in these relief panels are not of individual characters but instead of certain types, male or female, that are repeated with variations in gestures and stance. The male figures typically wear large earrings, necklace, elaborate headgear, and clinging garments for the lower portion of the body. Their lively poses provide a sense of animation and spontaneity lacking in sculptures of the Mauryan period.

The *Yaksini Chandra* (ca. 100–80 BCE; Indian Museum, Calcutta, India) was found among the remains of a large stupa at Bharhut in north-central India. She stands gracefully on a *vyala* (composite animal). Her languorous pose, an arm grasping the blossoming branch above and leg embracing the tree trunk below, identifies her with the *shalabhanjika*—a beautiful woman who can, by the mere touch of her foot, cause a tree to bloom. The elaborate headdress, braided hair, jewelry, and auspicious marks tattooed on her cheeks complement her regal bearing. The exquisite carving of details of the tree, the facial features, and the sensitivity with which the flesh has been rendered mark this work as one of the masterpieces of Bharhut. On the whole, the sculptures at Bharhut are more deeply carved than their Sanchi counterparts, thereby imparting a greater sense of three-dimensionality to them.

Buddhist cave complexes were excavated in the 2nd and 1st centuries BCE in the western Ghats. One of the best preserved early Buddhist rock-cut monasteries is at Bhaja. In the monastery known as Vihara 19, two interesting relief panels flank the entrance to the chamber at the right end of the veranda. One has been identified as Surya, the Hindu sun god, in his chariot; to the right is Indra, the god of lightning, on his elephant. This incongruity of Hindu images at a Buddhist site is intriguing. The compositions are freely executed and have an unplanned, random appearance. No consistent ground line or unified perspective is used because the main intention of the sculptor seems to have been to communicate the religious story to the devotee. Similar to other Sunga carvings from Sanchi, the carving is shallow and the scale of the figures is based on the hierarchic order of importance. Other typical Sunga features evident in these sculptures are the elaborate headdress, flat face, and heavy ornaments.

Andhra Period

While in the north artistic developments were occurring under the patronage of the Kusanas, the Satavahanas from west-central India, who were mentioned as subjects of Asoka's empire, patronized artistic endeavors of considerable scale in the Deccan. Later, in the Puranas of the Gupta period, they were called the Andhras. Very little is known about the early Andhras, but eventually the Andhra region became one of the most renowned centers of Buddhism. By the 2nd century CE, they had reached the zenith of their power, dominating the central Deccan from coast to coast and controlling most of India's rich trade routes and seaports. Although most of the sculptures from this period are from the Buddhist faith, traces of Hindu monuments exist. One of the most significant sculptures is that of the *Lingodbhavamurti* from Gudimallam, which dates from around the 1st century BCE.

A *Chakravartin Mandhata* relief panel (Madras Government Museum, Madras, India) recovered from Jagayyapeta displays an early sculptural style and can be dated to around the 1st century BCE. This work is a significant example from this region representing a *chakravartin* (universal monarch). Stylistically, the relief is similar to the works from the Sunga period from Bharhut and Sanchi. The figure, appearing with his seven jewels, has been identified as Chakravartin Mandhata from the Mandhata Jataka. The angular pose of the main figure, the flat treatment, and the elongated arms and legs with oversized feet are all reminiscent of the Sunga sculptural language. The lack of spatial clarity and ground-line reference with regard to the placement of the whole entourage reflect the Sunga vocabulary.

Amravati, the most important Buddhist site in Andhra Pradesh, achieved its final form in the 2nd century CE. This region in ancient times was part of Dhanyakataka, the capital of the later Satavahanas. None of the stupas have survived intact from this period, and therefore the carvings must be studied in isolation. The great stupa from Amravati was decorated with numerous slabs, most of which depicted scenes from various Jataka tales. One of the roundels from this stupa's railings, dated to the beginning of the 3rd century CE, shows Buddha subduing a maddened elephant. A superb example of mature Amravati school, the composition's action is remarkable, as is the organization of space. The composition beautifully accommodates the story, as well as a wealth of architectural and human details.

Numerous changes are apparent in the sculptural style of this period compared with earlier remains from the region. Deeply carved, crowded, active, and more naturalistic works by the 2nd century CE replace the flat, linear, simple carvings of the 1st century BCE. Some of these changes may be attributed to the influence from the western Deccan art schools, manifested at Karli, Nasik, and Kanheri. Contact with Roman trading colonies (Arikamedu and Maisolia) that existed along the east coast of India from the 1st century CE likely had some impact on the art as well. For instance, the perspective and naturalism of Roman art seem to have influenced the art of Andhra Pradesh. A drum slab from this period shows four episodes from the life of Buddha, separated from each other by architectural forms. These architectural elements lend depth and perspective to the composition; the figures in each of these compositions assume lively poses and are deeply carved.

Freestanding votive images of Buddha are common among the late sculptures of the Satavahana rule (end of the second and beginning of the 3rd century BCE). Stylistically, these images have massive bodies wrapped in heavy drapery with prominent folds, similar to the seated Buddha from the Kusana period.

Kusana Period: Gandhara and Mathura

At the beginning of the common era, northern India experienced a series of developments in history and art that may be attributed directly or indirectly to Roman trade with Asia and the great silk route. From Chinese historical sources, one can trace the origin of the Kusana dynasty, initially known as Kuei-shuang, from northwestern China. They were forced to move westward because of the expansionist policies of the Chinese Han dynasty. Having arrived at Bactria, their leader Kujula Kadphises during the early years of the 1st century CE led them across the mountains into Gandhara.

Gandhara is the most famous of the western Asiatic states from this period because of important and revealing archaeological excavations there. The two main spheres of Kusana art that are generally recognized are the broader Bactro-Gandhara region in the northwest, which was strongly Hellenized, and northern India, particularly the Mathura region, where works of more Indian style were produced. The greatest development in the field of art in the Kusana period occurred during the rule of Kanishka. Peshawar, not far from the Khyber Pass, was Kanishka's capital, and Mathura appears to have been a second capital.

Standing Buddha images in stone were the most popular and commonly seen Buddhist images from the northwest region. A typical example shows a frontal Buddha (Lahore Museum, Lahore, India) with a halo behind his head, standing barefoot with one leg slightly bent. He wears a heavy robe that covers both shoulders; his left hand hangs down holding his garment and the right hand in *abhayamudra* (a gesture of protection and reassurance displayed by deities to their worshippers; in most cases, the right hand is held palm outward with the fingers pointing upwards). The sculptures display a strong classicist tradition of Hellenistic and Roman art that includes heavy three-dimensional folds of the drapery—unlike the diaphanous, clinging Indic drapery—well-defined facial features, and wavy hair. A muscular body in keeping with the Classical norm is indicated in all these sculptures by the well-developed torso evident from under the drapery. The bent leg too may be related to the Classical *contrapposto* (a natural pose with the weight of one leg, the shoulder, and hips counterbalancing one another).

Bodhisattava images, in both seated and standing position, are some of the most popular subjects from this period. *Bodhisattava Maitreya* (Lahore Museum, Lahore, Pakistan) from Takht-i-Bahi, Pakistan, may be taken as an archetypal figure. It is a standing male figure with a muscular and well-developed torso and an elaborate hairdo, with locks of hair falling around the shoulders. The style of these images is highly Classical, reflecting the cultural heritage of the Gandhara region in particular. Aside from these sublime images, sculptors also represented bodhisattavas in the most dramatic manner, a reflection of extreme asceticism on the part of the bodhisattavas. In *Fasting Siddartha* (Lahore Museum, Lahore, Pakistan) from Sikri, Pakistan, the bodhisattava is depicted as an emaciated ascetic, with every detail of the skeleton, the structure of the neck, and the wasted flesh of the body carefully carved.

Ivory works, most significantly from Begram, have been excavated, in addition to the stone and metal sculptures. The most remarkable of these are the fragments of a chest with an elaborate border surrounding a composition of four women on its cover, which can be found at the Kabul Museum in Kabul, Afghanistan.

Mathura was the southern capital of the Kusana Empire. Sculptures of this school have been found in Sanchi, Sarnath, and the northwest. The fleshy body and bulky physique of these sculptural images seem to derive from the earlier Indic figure type and contrast strongly with the muscular, athletic male figures from the northwest.

The headless enthroned figure of *King Vima Kadphises* (Mathura Museum, Mathura, India) from Mat Shrine, Tokri Tila, presents a regal presence. Nearly every element of the costume, posture, and throne may be identified as being of foreign origin; however, the workmanship and sculptural style, including the treatment of the body forms in a generalized manner, the fullness of the body forms, and the use of linear detail to indicate three-dimensional elements, such as the folds on the boots, bespeak an Indic craftsmanship. The high, heavy boots and long tunic are marks of the Kusana period. Conceived in a frontal and stiff manner, the figure creates an imposing effect on the viewer.

Another headless image with similar characteristics is the image of Vima Kadphises's *Emperor Kanishka* (Mathura Museum, Mathura, India) from Mat Shrine, Tokri Tila, who is dressed as a scythian nobleman, with boots and a stiff tunic. The body's form does not determine the shape of the garment, a sharp contrast with the diaphanous and clinging style of the Indic art. A static frontality pervades the figure, almost as if it were two-dimensional in conception. The arms are lost, but the hands, at waist level, are positioned aggressively, holding a sword and a club.

Bhiksubala (Sarnath Site Museum, Sarnath, India), an inscribed image of a bodhisattava from Sarnath, dates to the third year of Kanishka's reign. Like the *King Vima Kadphises* and *Emperor Kanishka*, the stance is regal, and a lion stands between the legs, which indicates that the image is that of Sakyamuni.

The *Seated Buddha* (Mathura Museum, Mathura, India), an image dressed in a diaphanous garment and found at Katra, is a typical image of Kusana and post-Kusana sculpture. It depicts a central large image of Buddha seated on a lion throne. The crisply carved facial features and other details demonstrate the high quality of craftsmanship of the Mathura workshops during this phase.

Gupta Period

The Gupta dynasty along with its tributary states dominated most of the northern and north-central part of the Indian subcontinent from the 4th to the 6th centuries CE. Candra Gupta I (*r. ca.* 320–330 CE) was the first to attain significant power and fame in the Gupta dynasty. Very few works of art can be attributed to the early Gupta period, and those that can are not of great consequence. A huge *Horse* (State Museum, Lucknow, India) surviving from Emperor Samudra Gupta's reign may have represented the sacrificial horse for *asvamedha* (Vedic horse sacrifice). Three Jain figures from a slightly later period have been found at Durjanpura, near Vidisa. These sculptures have been attributed to a lesser known Gupta king, Ramagupta, with the aid of inscriptional evidence. The best preserved of these images is that of a seated Jain *tirthankara* (one who has attained perfect knowledge) flanked by *cauri* bearers. The overall composition is similar to the Buddhist images of the Kusana period.

Udaigiri near Vidisa is the most significant Hindu site from this period. Twenty rock-cut caves were excavated that are adorned with numerous Hindu images. One of the most notable sculptural panels is from the Varaha cave (cave 5; early 5th century CE). It is a large-scale representation of Varaha, the boar form of Visnu. Here, Varaha appears in his human form with the head of a boar, lifting the Bhudevi (Earth goddess). The Varaha image exhibits the muscularity that was apparent in the Kusana sculptures of the Mathura school. The colossal power and the slow flowing plasticity of this unique relief blend harmoniously with the delicacy of detail carved in the flowers of the garland, the folds of the *dhoti* (lower garment), and the jewelry of Bhudevi.

The other significant Hindu image is that of Krishna depicted as Govardhandhari (early 5th century CE) from Varanasi, holding Mount Govardhan aloft with his left hand. Here, too, one can trace a relation stylistically with the Kusana sculptures from the Mathura school. The lower torso and stomach display the Sarnath sensitivity, a barely perceptible roll of flesh swelling out above the constricting top of the *dhoti*.

The Mathura region saw a phase of Kusana art activities until about the late 3rd century CE. During the reign of Samudra Gupta, this region was brought under the Gupta domain. However, the Mathura Gupta style evidences the heritage of Kusana art of both the Mathura and the Bactro-Gandhara regions. The Standing Buddha image from Jamalpur, Mathura (Mathura Museum, India), dating to the mid 5th century CE, demonstrates this style. Carved in red sandstone typical of Mathura Gupta images, the body displays a fluid and graceful contour. The relaxed pose, with the right leg slightly bent, the delicate treatment of the halo, and the regular folds of the drapery can be related to the Bactro-Gandhara Kusana style even though the diaphanous clinging quality is typically Indian. Thus the Gupta-period artists seemed to have unified the two traditions into a harmonious synthesis. However, unlike the Kusana images, the images show no trace of the powerful corporeality of the previous centuries. Instead, they are lighter and more ethereal.

Sarnath is the other site that rose to prominence and became a major Buddhist center. The style of sculptures from this region that emerged around the third quarter of the 5th century is distinct from that of the Mathura school. Most of the Sarnath sculptures are carved in buff-colored Chunar sandstone. Three dated images from this region have survived that were all dedicated by a monk named Abhayamitra. The elongated, slender, graceful bodies and the refined execution of the details of the halos, robes, and faces have long been considered a measure of the Gupta art. A significant feature of the late Sarnath Gupta style is the treatment of the drapery. Although fully dressed, the figures are clad in drapery so clinging as to reveal all the forms of the bodies beneath. Downcast eyes, a gently smiling expression, and refined treatment of the individual elements characterize the facial types of these images. Another significant sculpture from about 475 CE is a representation of *Seated Preaching Buddha* at the Deer Park at Sarnath (Sarnath Museum, Sarnath, India).

A number of terracotta sculptures belong to this period. The most impressive examples are life-size *Ganga Yamuna* river goddess figures from Ahicchattra (National Museum, New Delhi, India) that originally flanked the entrance of a Siva temple. The costumes, with heavy drapery folds and tight bodices, and the fully modeled facial features suggest a departure from the more tranquil, delicate forms of Gupta stone sculpture.

Few metal sculptures seem to have survived from this period, although a collection of metal images found at Chausa, Bihar, may be attributed to the Gupta period. One representation of Risabhanatha, the Jain *tirthankara*, especially reveals the grace of form and naturalism associated with Gupta art.

DEEPANJANA DANDA KLEIN

See also **Clay and Terracotta**

Further Reading

Agrawala, Vasudeva Sharana, *Gupta Art*, Lucknow, India: U.P. Historical Society, 1948

Agrawala, Vasudeva Sharana, and Prithvi Kumar Agrawala (editors), *Gupta Art: A History of Indian Art in the Gupta Period, 300–600 AD*, Varanasi, India: Prithvi Prakashan, 1977

Basham, A.L., *The Wonder That Was India*, New Delhi: Rupa, 1954; 3rd revised edition, 1996

Coomaraswamy, Ananda K., *History of Indian and Indonesian Art*, New York: Dover, 1985

Coomaraswamy, Ananda K., and Ratan Devi (editors), *Introduction to Indian Art*, Delhi: Munshiram Manoharlal, 1920; new edition, edited by Mulk Raj Anand, Edinburgh: Aspect, and New Delhi: Arnold, 1991

Craven, Roy C., *Indian Art: A Concise History*, London: Thames and Hudson, 1976

Dehejia, Vidya, *Early Buddhist Rock Temples: A Chronological Study*, London: Thames and Hudson, 1972

Goetz, Hermann, *India: Five Thousand Years of Indian Art*, New York: McGraw-Hill, and London: Methuen, 1959; 2nd edition, 1964

Gupta, Swarajya Prakash, *The Roots of Indian Art: A Detailed Study of the Formative Period of Indian Art and Architecture*, New Delhi: B.R. Publishing, 1980

Hallade, Madeleine, *Gandhara—Art of North India and the Graeco-Buddhist Tradition in India, Persia, and Central Asia*, New York: Abrams, 1968

Harle, James C., *Gupta Sculpture: Indian Sculpture of the 4th to the 6th Centuries*, AD, Oxford: Clarendon Press, 1974

Harle, James C., *The Art and Architecture of the Indian Subcontinent*, New York: Penguin, 1986

Huntington, Susan L., *The Art of Ancient India: Buddhist, Hindu, Jain*, New York: Weatherhill, 1985

Kosambi, Damodar Dharmanaud, *An Introduction to the Study of Indian History*, Bombay: Popular Book Depot, 1956

Kramrisch, Stella, *Indian Sculpture*, London: Oxford University Press, 1933

Kramrisch, Stella, *Exploring India's Sacred Art: Selected Writings of Stella Kramrisch*, edited by Barbara Stoler Miller, Philadelphia: University of Pennsylvania Press, 1983

Marshall, John Hubert, *The Buddhist Art of Gandhara: The Story of the Early School, Its Birth, Its Growth, and Decline*, Cambridge: Cambridge University Press, 1960

Ray, Niharranjan, *Maurya and Sunga Art*, Calcutta: University of Calcutta, 1945; 2nd edition, Calcutta: Indian Studies Past and Present, 1965

Rowland, Benjamin, *The Art and Architecture of India: Buddhist, Hindu, Jain*, Baltimore, Maryland: Penguin, 1954; 3rd edition, 1967

Thapar, Romila, *Asoka and the Decline of the Mauryas*, London: Oxford University Press, 1961

INDIA: MEDIEVAL

The classification of India's art between the 9th and 16th centuries CE as "medieval" is a matter of chronological convenience rather than a qualitative discretion. Indian art achieved artistic excellence in sculpture and architecture during this period. The salient feature of medieval art in India is the germinating of regional idioms in art and architecture. In South India, the enthusiasm of Hindu art initiated by the Pallava dynasty of Kanchi (7th–9th centuries) continued in the Chola dynasty of Tanjavur until the end of the 12th century. The Rashtrakutas dynasty ruling from Malkhed dominated the Deccan region in the 8th to 11th centuries, assimilating the sculpture and architecture styles of the Pallavas and Chalukyans, as evident in the art activity at Ellora. Western Indian art came of age under the Solankis of Patan and Gurjara Pratiharas of Kanouj. The Chandellas of Bundelkhand and Paramaras of Malwa supervised the central Indian affairs. The glory of medieval art was soon followed by its death knell with the Afghan occupation of North India in the 13th century.

The medieval period in India witnessed a tremendous interest in temple-building activity in all regions, exemplified by the magnificence of Kailashnath at Ellora (Maharashtra State), Surya Temple at Modhera (Gujarat State), Kandariya Mahadeva Temple at Khajuraho (Madhya Pradesh State), and Surya Temple at Konarak (Orissa State). Sculptors were in great demand since the new architectural design needed more figural decoration. Many art historians consider this high demand and the shift of focus from quality to quantity the reason for the alleged decline of sculptural styles in medieval India. The lyricism of the narration seen at Mahabalipuram and Kanchipuram (both in Tamil Nadu State) gave way to more iconic forms of representation.

Improvements in carving technique and the use of softer materials resulted in intricate carving and the ostentatious quality that the sculptors of this period are accused of by art historians. The provincial centers of art preferred specific stones for the sculptures and architecture during this period. The Hoysalas favored green schist, and Vijayanagara rulers opted for harder material such as granite, while in North India sculptors used soft materials such as sandstone and marble.

Because temple building was going on in the regional centers simultaneously, it is difficult to cite a precise starting date of the medieval period in India. However, the Rashtrakuta dynasty's activity at Ellora and elsewhere during the 8th to 11th centuries initiated the process of flamboyance and intricacy of the medieval Indian sculpture.

Rashtrakuta Dynasty of Malkhed

The west-facing temple of Kailashnath Temple in Ellora is raised on a solid basement sculpted with a frieze of elephants and lions. Staircases ascend to the upper level, which contains a columned hall with three porches and an antechamber at the rear. A terrace with seven shrines on it is found at the rear of the principal shrine. Sculptures on the projections and recessions adorn the walls of the shrine proper. The conceptual design of the temple may be of the Chalukyan style, but the technique employed was likely imported from the Pallava region. The amalgam of the two traditions visible in architecture would repeat itself in sculpture as well.

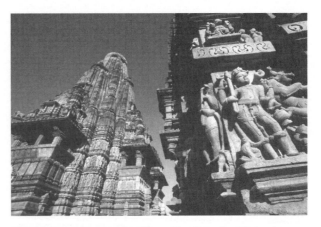

Elaborate carvings on the Visvanatha Temple, Khajuraho, India
© Adam Woolfitt / CORBIS

The temple, which is a monolith hewn out of rock, can be considered as a monumental sculpture placed in the center of a courtyard. The dependence on the syntax of art, especially that of Virupaksha Temple at Pattadakkal (Chalukya; 743) and Kailashnath Temple at Kanchipuram (Pallava; early 8th century), is evident in the relief panels at Ellora.

The sculptures in the Kailashnatha complex at Ellora can be classified into three categories. The Chalukyan-inspired style adorns the outer walls of the shrine proper and the staircase leading to the shrine. The relief sculpture *Ravana Shaking Kailash* on the western plinth wall is an excellent example of this group of sculptures. The similarity in style between Chalukyan and Rashtrakuta idioms is clear in the panel showing the fight between Ravana and Jatayu on the southern wall. The second category is the Pallavan-influenced style, which appears on relief sculptures of the outer walls flanking the cardinal entrance to the complex. The *Mahishasura Mardini* (goddess killing the buffalo demon) on the inner wall of the gateway also shares the Pallavan heredity, evident in its compositional similarity to the *Mahishasura Mardini* panel at Mahabalipuram (Tamil Nadu). The figures of *Narasimha* (Shiva slaying the demon *Andhaka*) and the *Dikpalas* (guardian deities of the cardinal directions) outside the Gopura also fall into this category. The monumental panels of *Gajalakshmi* (goddess of wealth flanked by elephants) and the figure of *Yogesvara Shiva* (Shiva in a meditative mood) in the inner veranda can be categorized under the third group of sculptures, the expressions of local Rashtrakuta carvers assimilating the tradition of Pallavas and Chalukyans.

The magnificent sculpted panel of *Ravana Shaking Kailasha* on the southern side is the temple's magnum opus, revealing the artistry of Rashtrakuta sculptors. The panel is approximately six meters high and five meters wide. The composition is divided into two horizontal panels: the upper panel narrates the action in the abode of Shiva, while Ravana in the lower panel is shown having committed the feat of lifting the mountain. Both the upper and lower portions receive equal attention from the sculptor. The narrative approach to the sculptures, which had been gradually disappearing from the Indian tradition, was revived at the Kailashnath Temple at Ellora.

The sculpture and architecture from other excavations in the Kailashnatha complex, such as the columned veranda at the rear and the subsidiary caves of Lankesvara, Paralanka, and Yagnasala, suggest a later date. The same can be said of the *Nandi mandapa*, a columned hall housing Nandi, the vehicle of Shiva, abutting the cardinal shrine in the front. The sculptural panels of the colonnade encircling the eastern portion of the temple contain a series of sculptures, which appear to belong to the inferior school of sculpture, evident from the low-relief carving. The bas-relief quality, however, should not be considered an indication of an earlier date. Although of lesser quality, the sculptures probe new patterns of iconic representations. The important sculptures on the veranda include *Krishna Killing Kaliya* (south), *Shiva as Lakulisa* (east), and *Ravana Offering His Heads to Shiva* (north).

Except for the *Nataraja* (Dancing Shiva) on the eastern corner of the temple, Lankesvara cave sculptures show a shift already toward the iconic tradition. The figure of *Nataraja* demonstrates that the late Rashtrakuta sculptors had a masterful understanding of the flexion of the human body. The spiral movement obtained here for the first time would become the ideal for the later medieval sculptors of northern India. The marked difference between the *Nataraja* sculpture and rest of the sculptures of Lankesvara makes an art-historical riddle. The figures of *Mahishasura Mardini* and *Gangadhara Murti* on the north side of the cave next to the overhanging portico are placed as part of the square-shafted column. The figures of the southern wall as *Trimurti* (i.e., *Brahma, Visnu,* and *Shiva*) are in the iconic tradition and thus placed later on the chronological scale.

The Yagnasala cave, on the southwest side of the shrine proper, contains seated figures of the *sapta Matrikas* (seven Mother goddesses). While the *Matrikas* occupy the southern portion of the chamber, the images of *Durga* with attendants and *Kali* with her spouse engage the eastern and western sides. These figures appear to be slightly later than the shrine proper and the corridor. With their expanded shoulder and hips, the figures appear closer to the images of cave 32 (Jain Caves) at Ellora. The breasts of the figures are hemispherical, leaving space for the *ekavali* (a single-threaded garland that begins at the left shoulder and

joins with the waistband). The interesting feature of the Yagnasala images is their three-dimensional quality, which is rarely observed in medieval Indian sculpture.

The Nandi Mandapa of the Kailashnath Temple reveals the emergence of medievalism at the site. Although in low relief, the sculptures show the tendency toward accentuated flexions. The *Narasimha* image on the northern niche loses the monumentality observed in the other figures of Kailashnath, such as the aforementioned *Ravana Shaking Kailasa* on the southern side of the temple. Together, the sculptures of Kailashnatha Temple at Ellora present a noteworthy interlude in the formative phase of medieval sculpture in India.

Medieval Sculpture in North India

North Indian medieval sculpture was mainly sponsored by regional dynasties, such as the Pratiharas and Solankis in western India, the Paramaras and Chandellas in central India, the Pala and Senas in Bengal, the Somavamsis and the Gangas in Orissa and Silaharas and Yadavas in the Deccan region.

The Pratihara dynasty (*ca.* 730–1027) ruled from Kanauj (Uttar Pradesh), although their art activity centered around present-day Rajasthan and western Madhya Pradesh. Sculpture under the Pratiharas maintained a palpable and portly quality, with an elaboration of accessories such as highly ornamented headgear and jewelry. The facial expressions remain calm and serene, as shown, for example, on the female figure from Gwalior (now in the National Museum, New Delhi). Another important site that can be attributed to the Pratiharas is Osian (Rajasthan). Osian sculptures maintain the tactile quality of their counterparts in central India but are much more slender. The figures, charged with activity, anticipate the accentuated movements found in the later medieval period. As Huntington notes, "the ninth and tenth centuries saw the dissemination of the Gurjara Pratihara style complex throughout much of North India, as well as a marked change in the sculptural style itself, for the softness and animation previously seen in the figures gave away to a harder, stiffer form" (see Huntington, 1985).

The temples built by the Chandellas of Bundelkhand at the site of Khajuraho (Madhya Pradesh) demonstrate the medieval characteristic of sculpture superseding architecture in India. At Khajuraho the mere quantity of the sculptures adorning the walls of Lakshmana (954), Khandariya Mahadeva (11th century), Visvanatha (11th century), and other minor temples overshadows the architecture. In addition to the cardinal Hindu deities occupying the niches on the cardinal directions, the Khajuraho sculptors introduced other figures such as heavenly damsels (*surasundaris*) and composite animals (*vyala*). While the sculptures of the cardinal deities maintain the austerity of their subject matter, the *surasundaris* indulge themselves in the pleasures of life, preparing for the carnal union with their lovers in the *antarala* (antechamber) portion of the wall. The sculptors engaged in a freedom of expression, depicting the sensuous figures of the *surasundaris* flexing their prodigiously acrobatic bodies. Mundane activities such as putting on an anklet, squeezing water out of their hair, or showing the love marks made by a lover are accordant with the romance poetry of that time and are depicted exquisitely. The *vyalas* presented another opportunity for innovation to the sculptor. The construction of the mythical animal, combining the forms of the lion with that of the elephant (*gaja-vyala*), or even with a parrot (*suka-vyala*), was a formidable task for the sculptor. Placed on the wall, the grotesque nature of the *vyala* figures contrasts with the sensuality of the *surasundaris*.

As in the preceding style of the Pratiharas, the Chandella sculptures also emphasized ornamentation. The facial features have become more schematic and sharp. Prominent eyebrows curved like a bow, following the ancient injunction of the ideal human form. The postures of the sculptures are mostly in *tri bhanga* (triple flexion), although sculptors also frequently used *ati bhanga* (exaggerated flexion). The sculptors moved the figure within their restricted space, thus achieving frontal, profile, and rear views of the figures, in what appears to be a unique feature of Khajuraho sculptures.

Sculptural activity centered on Hindu temples ceased in North India soon after the disruption of Chandella power in Bundelkhand. Such activities continued, however, in the western and eastern regions for a few more centuries until those areas came under the Sultanate of Delhi. In the western region (comprised mainly of the present-day Gujarat state), the Solankis of Gujarat with their capital at Patan began their temple-building activities in the mid 11th century. The Sun Temple at Modhera (1026) and the step-well subterranean water pavilion named Rani ki Vav at Patan (both in Gujarat State) illustrate the intentions of the Solankis. The Gujarat sculpture tradition had a long history beginning in the pre-Gupta period. Although the temple architecture passed through tremendous modulations, sculpture adhered to the tradition. In Modhera the sculptures have enough space to interact with the viewers. *Aditya* (manifestations of the Sun) images adorn the temple wall duly attended by his divine retinue. The projections of the wall of the Sun temple at Modhera is not as complex as at Khajuraho. Thus the number of sculptures is much smaller here. Still, the sculptors used *surasundaris* and *vyalas* to embellish the wall. The figures at Modhera are carved frontally, with less possibility of flexion. The ornamentation on the figures, which is lesser in Modhera,

becomes more complex in the sculptures of Rani ki Vav. The figures at Rani ki Vav are more slender and schematic, with sharp features. The size of the sculptures has also been drastically reduced at Rani ki Vav and in the later Solanki structures.

One of the most ambitious projects achieved in medieval India is that of Konarak (1238–58), executed in eastern India by a medieval dynasty, the Gangas of Orissa (12th–14th centuries). The Gangas continued the art activity in Orissa that had been initiated by the Somavamsis. Although the style of architecture achieved a monumental scale during the Ganga period, the sculptural form remained the same. The Orissan sculptural style is highly ornate with an added slenderness. The figures have drooping shoulders, a tapering torso with broadened hips, and elongated legs. The full breasts are shown close to each other. The flexion of the body is as complex as that used at Khajuraho using the triple and accentuated flexions. The facial features are sharp, with prominent eyebrows. The male figures, especially the Surya images, have elongated crowns, which in turn increase the elongation of the figures. As demanded by the architecture, some of the figures in Konarak are of enormous size. To deal with the scale of the sculptures, the sculptors increased the volume of the figures and reduced the elongation.

Medieval Sculpture in South India

While the Afghan incursion on the northern and western frontiers of India disrupted the temple-building activity and thus the sculptural manifestation in upper India, such building continued in South India almost until the end of the 18th century. The Pallava dynasty inaugurated artistic activity on a large scale in the 7th century in Tamil Nadu. Simultaneously, such art activity occurred in Karnataka under the Chalukyans of Badami. As the Rashtrakutas of Ellora absorbed the style of the Chalukyans, the Cholas of Tanjavur continued the style of the Pallavas, both in architecture and in the tradition of sculpture. The Nagesvarasvamy Temple (10th century) at Kumbhakonam (Tamil Nadu), which was built a century after the waning of Pallava dynasty, exhibits a dominant Pallava influence. These sculptures, identified by some scholars as the portraits of the donors (other scholars maintain that they are the characters of the epic *Ramayana*), are arguably the best among the Chola sculptures in the initial phase.

The sculptors employed naturalism in these early works, demonstrated by the individual characteristics observed in the figures. The schematized form found in other regional styles of medieval sculpture was not present during the early Chola phase. The figures are at ease and do not appear attached to their niches. The niches here materialize as doorways through which figures are passing. The sculptures at Srinivasanallur and Tiruvaranjuli (now in the Thanjavur Museum, India) show this same approach.

The miniature friezes on the plinth of the Nagesvarasvamy Temple, which depict the *Ramayana* story, recall the narrative sculptures of the Ikshvaku-period (1st–3rd century) Buddhist panels in Amaravati and Nagarjunakonda. Here, the Chola sculptors were attempting to revive the narrative tradition that had been losing its popularity during the medieval period. They were not wholly successful in this endeavor as the narrative panels are completely absent in the middle and later Chola period.

Rajaraja I inaugurated the second phase of Chola art activity in the early decades of the 11th century. He and his successors believed in the monumentality of architecture at the expense of sculptural art. The figures in the second phase are schematic in representation and more iconic in character. The naturalism observed in the early phase of Chola art, along with the narrative panels, has completely disappeared. Due to the vastness of the figures in accordance with the dimensions of the temple, at both Brihadeshvara Temples (one at Thanjavur and the other at Gangaikondacholapuram, both in Tamil Nadu), the intimacy between the sculpture and the onlooker is lost. The placement of attending figures around the niche to populate the wall with sculptures, first used by the Pallavas, achieved its culmination during the second phase of the Chola period. The embellishment of columns with figural sculpture is a Chola innovation in South India. This feature would later mold the syntax of sculptural placement in South India during the Vijayanagara and Nayaka periods (14th–18th centuries).

The decline of Rashtrakuta power in the Deccan region gave opportunity to three potential powers to sponsor the temple activity during the medieval period. The Chalukyans of Kalyani ruled over the southern part of present-day Maharashtra, the Kakatiyas of Warrangal reigned over the Andhra region, and the Hoysalas of Dvarasamudra controlled the bulk of the Karnataka region. Although they borrowed from the common stock of Rashtrakuta sculptural style, these dynasties preferred their own regional varieties of sculpture and architecture. The Chalukyans of Kalyani followed the preceding style zealously, while the Hoysalas and Kakatiyas favored contrasting styles. Hoysala sculptures were highly ornamented and profusely adorned with foliage patterns. The softer quality of the stonelike green schist used for the sculptures gave the Hoysalan sculptors at Belur, Halibedu, and Somnathpur ample opportunities to execute intricate carvings. Most of the Hoysala figures have undercuts that enhance the three-dimensional quality of the figures and the embellishing

accessories. Kakatiya sculptors, on the other hand, endorsed severity rather than embellishment. The sculptures of the Ramappa Temple at Palampet, for example, have elongated and schematic figuration.

When the Sangama dynasty established itself as the ruling dynasty of Vijayanagara and virtually all of South India out of the political vacuum created by the onslaught of Malik Kafur (1300), they had two styles to choose from, that of the Chalukyans of Kalyani or that of the Hoysalas. The early rulers of Vijayanagara seem to have preferred the former style until Devaraya I occupied the throne of Vijayanagara. Through the construction of the Ramachandra Temple at Hampi (Karnataka), the capital of Vijayanagara, Devaraya I launched the Tamil style of architecture and sculpture in Karnataka. At the Ramachandra Temple the wall decorations depict scenes from the epic *Ramayana* that are similar to such figures in Tamil Nadu created during the Chola period. The carved panels on the walls and the pillars do not show much detail since the stone used was the much harder granite. Sculptors also carved the monumental monoliths, including the *Lakshmi-Narasimha* and two *Ganapati* figures at Hampi.

Vijayanagara sculptors in the post-Devaraya phase added sculptural embellishment on the columns of the temples, following their Tamil ancestry. Because space limitations restricted the sculptors, many images of the columns are shown frontally and in complete profile, such as the *Hanuman* and *Garuda* in many temples across the Vijayanagara empire.

Krishna Devaraya, the most illustrious ruler of Vijayanagara, took the reins of the empire in the early 16th century. His rule saw the expansion of the Vijayanagara idiom of art beyond the boundaries of Karnataka. Monumental columned halls were added to the basic plan of the temples. Already-existing structures received renovations with added-on *mandapas*. The *mandapas* contained pillars vigorously animated with rearing *vyalas* and, at times, narrative panels. As Michell has observed, "It was during this period that the first attempts were made to liberate carvings from their supports. Figures such as *Krishna* dancing on *Kaliya* and *Narasimha* are fashioned almost three dimensionally on colonnettes of the mid 16th century mandapa extension of the Vittala Temple at Vijayanagara" (see Michell, 1995). This approach to pillar decoration reached its pinnacle of perfection during the Nayaka period in Tamil Nadu.

Although initiated by the Cholas of Thanjavur, South Indian medieval sculpture reached its zenith of esteem during the Vijayanagara period. Unlike North Indian medieval art, which remained regional, the South Indian style under the wings of Vijayanagara imperial expansion spread to almost all regions of

South India. The schematization of the figures, accentuated movements, and the heroic poise found at imperial Vijayanagara continued after the fall of Vijayanagara in 1565 in the sculpture of their loyal vassals, who assumed the title of Nayakas. In the Nayaka period, although sculptors tried to expand their work in terms of size, the basic syntax remained that of Vijayanagara.

JAYARAM PODUVAL

Further Reading

Dahmen-Dallapiccola, Anna Libera, and Anila Verghese, *Sculpture at Vijayanagara*, New Delhi: Manohar, 1998

Huntington, Susan, *The Art of Ancient India: Buddhist, Hindu, Jain*, New York: Weatherhill, 1985

Kannal, Deepak, *Ellora, an Enigma in Sculptural Styles*, New Delhi: Books and Books, 1996

Kramrisch, Stella, *Indian Sculpture*, Calcutta: Y.M.C.A. Publishing House, and New York: Oxford University Press, 1933

Michell, George, *Architecture and Art of Southern India: Vijayanagara and the Successor States*, Cambridge and New York: Cambridge University Press, 1995

INDIA: MADURAI TO MODERN

The age between the Madurai period and the modern period of Indian history saw tremendous political, social, and cultural transformation. The fall of the Vijayanagara dynasty (1565) resulted in the domination of Islamic rule in Deccan. The Mogul regime under the rule of Akbar (1556–1605) reached out to Deccan, which would subsequently succumb to the inroads under Aurangazeb. Except for the restoration of power under the Maratthas led by Shivaji, no other non-Islamic dynasty could establish its hegemony over Deccan. In the case of South India, however, the transfer of power was much smoother, changing from the hands of Vijayanagara rulers to their respective regional chieftains called the Nayakas.

The fall of the Vijayanagara dynasty after the disastrous war of Talikotta (1565) initiated a political vacuum similar to the one that existed prior to the establishment of the dynasty. This time, however, saw many claimants to the land that was once the Vijayanagara Empire. Erstwhile governors of the Vijayanagara Empire, mainly Telugu-speaking officers of the empire, known as Nayakas, took over the regions, especially that of Tamil Nadu. Three major Nayakas came to the forefront from Gingee, Thanjavur, and Madurai and continued their hegemony over Tamil Nadu until the British domination of the country. The most enduring among them were the Nayakas of Madurai. Thus the period between the 17th and 19th centuries is often referred to as the Madurai period.

The salient artistic feature of the Madurai period is the continuation of the Vijayanagara elements in the field of architecture, sculpture, and painting augmenting its vitality, intricacy, and monumentality. The Madurai-period artist had to cope with the political, social, and cultic pressure, which introduced new materials, icons, and aesthetics of adornment. Metal and wooden sculptures became popular, along with those made of stone. Ivory was popular during this time mainly at the centers of Mysore, Tiruchirapally, and Madurai.

New dominant cults demanded the modification of iconography. As George Michell notes, "Cults of some deities, such as Vittala, were imported from outside the region. The importance accorded such divinities extend also to the realm of saints. . . . Virtually all of these gods and saints find their expression in the art of the period" (see Michell, 1995). The patrons were allowed to mingle with the saints and divinities through their sculptural depictions, which were either kept in niches or placed on the columns of the *manda-*

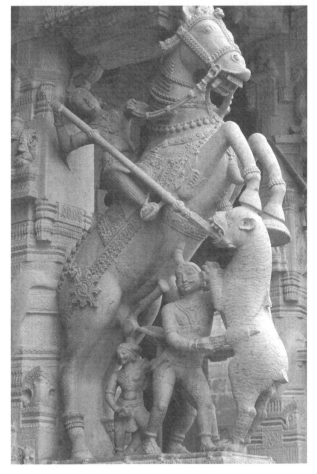

Sculptures at Srirangam Temple at Tamil Nadu, India
© Lindsay Hebberd / CORBIS

pas (hall with many columns) The best example probably is the portrait of the queen of Tirumala at Alagarkoil, north of Madurai.

Sculptures become cardinal figures of architecture during the Madurai period. The architectural exuberance depended entirely on the magnificent carvings on the shafts and the surmounting *vyalis* (mythical lions) of the capital. The columns in the Sheshraya Mandapa at Srirangam contain figures of soldiers riding on the rearing horses duly supported by the warrior figures. In one column alone the sculptor placed about five to six figures. The carving approach is highly three-dimensional, with prominent undercuts. The rearing *vyalis* of the Vaikunthanatha Temple at Srivaikuntham dominate the shaft of the columns apart from the *vyalis* on the bracket. These *vyalis* became the salient feature of the Madurai period, as seen, for example, in the long circumambulatory corridors attended by them at Ramesvaram and many other sacred centers of Tamil Nadu.

Probably as a political statement, all the Nayakas appropriated the sacred centers of Tamil Nadu. They renovated and refurbished the temples built by the previous rulers such as the Pallava, Chola, and Vijayanagara dynasties, adding new structures such as the *kalyanamandapams* (sacred marriage halls) and tanks. The whole complex was enveloped within boundary walls with ceremonial openings called *gopurams*. Sculptors embellished these *gopurams* with sculpted stucco figures, yet another innovation that the Nayakas appropriated from their Vijayanagara overlords. The Nayaka appropriations of the already-existing structures occurred mainly through the sculptural embellishment of the *mandapas*. The *kalyanamandapam* at the Varadarajaperumal Temple at Kanchipuram is an example of this approach.

One innovation of the Nayakas was the merging of architecture into sculpture, as seen, for example, in the Ramasvamy temple at Kumbhakonam and Vishvanatha temple at Tenkasi, where sculpted panels act as the weight-bearing piers. The sculptures thus completely envelop the architecture. This feature had its beginnings in the Vijayanagara period but developed into a finer form during the Madurai period. The restriction that sculptors once faced due to the hardness of materials such as granite stone did not seem to bother the Nayaka carvers. The finer undercuts and defined forms, which were absent in the earlier traditions of the Pallava, Chola, and Vijayanagara, characterize the work of the Madurai-period carvers. The pillars of the Shesharaya Mandapam at Srirangam, the columns of the Visvanatha Temple at Tenkasi and Sri Rama Temple at Kumbhakonam, and the figures on the *mandapams* of the Minakshi Temple at Madurai and Lakshmi

Narayana Temple at Tirukkarangudi all point to a new aesthetic sensibility in the Madurai period, which preferred the monumentality of form but never compromised on the detailing. Madurai sculptors reserved stylization and schematization of the forms for the divinities and mythical animals such as *vyalas*. When dealing with mundane themes such as wars, processions, dancers, and individual portraits, they took care to delineate the characteristic features within the schematization of sculptures acceptable at the time.

The sculptors of the Madurai period has a sense of monumentality, which was last seen in Ellora Caves [9th century] period, although it had its beginnings in the Vijayanagara period through the Lakshmi-Narasimha and Ganapati at Hampi. As the Nayakas of the Madurai period horizontally expanded the temple complex, the sculptors continued the aspect of monumentality of architecture and sculpture, creating over-life-size portraits of the patrons.

Nayaka architecture demanded complete domination over the sacred premise and the devotees. The formal and decorative approach to sculpture aided the Nayaka sculptors and their patrons to achieve this goal. The immensely popular Nayaka idiom is deeply rooted in the culture of the Tamil country, so much so that the architecture and sculpture of modern Hindu temples outside of India are also designed in the Nayaka, or Madurai, style.

While temple building reached its peak in South India, North India was experiencing the power struggle between the Islamic Sultanate and the Rajput chieftains. Temple building virtually came to a halt during this time, especially in the Ganga Jamuna Daub and Deccan, although in centers such as Gujarat (western India) and Bengal (eastern India) such activities continued on a smaller scale. Even in these centers the artists and architects abided by the new requirements of the ruling Islamic powers. Although an architect could still make a living, the sculptor was reduced to the position of the decorator of the architecture.

The political alliance between the Moguls and the Rajput states during Akbar's regime prompted the Rajput chieftains to revive temple-building activities in centers such as Vrindavan (Uttar Pradesh), Jaipur, and Jodhpur, although figurative sculpture betrayed its lack of confidence with figures that look archaically geometric. The Moguls themselves never contributed to the sculptural tradition even though architecture was at its peak. Few jade images of animals and other decorative pieces from this time are extant, but they can be found occasionally in many collections around the world. Many of these works can be placed into the period of Shahjahan. The lack of documentation hampers a full discussion of the sculptural activities from this period.

JAYARAM PODUVAL

Further Reading

Michell, George, *Architecture and Art of Southern India: Vijaya-nagara and the Successor States*, Cambridge and New York: Cambridge University Press, 1995

INDIA: BAROQUE AND COLONIAL

The colonization of India by European powers was initiated by the geographical discoveries under the guidance of Philip the Navigator of Portugal. Barthalomeo Dias reached the Cape of Good Hope at the southern tip of Africa in 1488. Before long, Vasco da Gama's more politically charged expedition commenced and reached the shores of India in 1498.

The Portuguese had two intentions in India: look for spices and propagate Christianity. To his amazement, da Gama discovered that Christianity already existed in the region. According to legend the Apostle Thomas arrived in India in AD 52. It is still unresolved whether he or the descendants of the church he established in the Near Eastern city of Edessa had come to India. According to another tradition, some 400 Christians belonging to seven clans from Baghdad, Nineveah, and Jerusalem migrated to Kerala in AD 345 to escape persecution.

The sculptures of 16th- and 17th-century India, especially Christian icons, betray their roots in the contemporaneous European Baroque traditions. The Portuguese power, centered in Cochin, soon faded away, although the religious fervor of the Portuguese continued through the Jesuit missionaries, active through their headquarters in Goa. The Jesuit activities seem to have influenced the Christianization of South India. Famous among these Jesuit missionaries was St. Francis Xavier, who apparently built 45 churches in Travancore before he left India in 1552.

As part of the Christianization and education of the Kerala Christians, the missionaries surely imported icons from Europe. In addition to these works, sailors carried wooden sculptures from their home countries. Some of the ships had separate chapels on board. A few of the imported sculptures are still preserved in the churches of Kerala and Goa. St. Thomas's Church at Tumboli, Alappuzha district, contains an image of the Virgin Mary that the local people call the *Kappalkkarattiyamma* (the mother who came by ship). The figure of *Saint Sebastian* at Arthungal reputedly came from France. In another route of imports Portuguese nobles or Jesuits commissioned European artists to execute work in India, as was the case for St. Francis

Xavier's mausoleum in Goa, commissioned by the Italian noble Grand Duke Cosimo III de' Medici and executed in 1698 by the Italian artist Placido Francesco Rampani.

Not all the Christian images in India were imports from Europe, although the imported icons acted as models to a different art tradition, divergent in theme and form, from the indigenous Hindu tradition in wood. The regional variations of the icons reveal the differences in the prototypes that followed. The sculptures of churches in Goa, Daman, and Diu are quite different from those in the rest of India, including Kerala. While the Goan style is imperialistic, with immediacy to Italian Baroque, the wood carvings from Kerala are strikingly similar to the wooden sculptures of Germany and the painted figures of the Netherlands. Lacking the grandeur of the Italian Baroque, the sculptures, especially their facial features, contain a medieval gloom. The compositions are mainly frontal, with no attempts to achieve spiral movement. In all, the sculptures are unrefined.

The British period witnessed church-building activities that were entrusted entirely to the non-British missionary societies. Sculptures from the period also show a thematic shift from religious to political. As also happened in painting, sculptors now created naturalistic portraits of rulers as viceroys and governors, as well as portraits of the rulers of England. The rajas, the indigenous rulers of India, picked up the threads from British overlords to support these Neoclassical or academic sculptures. Major cities including Bombay, Calcutta, Madras (presently Mumbai, Kokatta, and Chennai, respectively), and Lahore established institutes of fine arts to train Indian artists in the European academic style. The courses offered were primarily an attempt to "correct" perceived shortcomings of the Indian methods by focusing on Western ideals of proportion, perspective, and anatomy. For this purpose the academies imported large quantities of plaster casts and marble and bronze copies of Greco-Roman and Neoclassical works. The rulers of Indian princely states staunchly supported the academic style, and their European shopping list included the marble and bronze copies of Canova, Michelangelo, and numerous insignificant artists from Europe. The incident of the Aundh maharaja is unique. Having some money left after buying expensive bronze casts during a trip to England, he bought the work of a young sculptor for a few hundred pounds. The young sculptor's name was Henry Moore, and this sculpture remains the only work of a European master sculptor in India.

The colonial rulers also patronized the products of these regional schools. In 1937 G.K. Mhatre received the commission for the portrait of George V at Bombay. M.S. Nagappa (1938) and Hironmay Roy Choudhary (1939) received commissions to do the same at Madras (in bronze) and Lucknow (in marble), respectively. The maharajas patronized many of these academic sculptors as well.

The sculpture of this particular phase also set the trend at the popular level, which still bears traces of the Neoclassical style. The realistic portrait sculpture initiated by the British continued even after they left the Indian shores. National heroes such as Gandhi and Nehru and cultural figures such as Rabindranatha Tagore and Vivekananda replaced the portraits of the "Georges, Williams, and Elizabeths." The pedestals once occupied by the equestrian statues of maharajas and generals now held equestrian portraits of Shivaji and Rani of Jhansi. Sculptors also used nonpolitical and secular themes, delving into the sentimental and romantic subject matters such as *To the Temple* by Mhatre and *Spring* by Hironmoy Chowdhary. The popularization of academic and Neoclassical sculptures was due largely to the establishment of the film industry in India, centered in Bombay. The high art, which was offered to the masses, was the academic style, which continued into the 1960s.

The artist Deviprasad Roychowdhury was one of the few sculptors from this period to successfully go beyond the academic style to encompass the contemporary trends. His characteristic Rodin-like modeling, especially in some of the noncommissioned works, was a harbinger to many of his students in Madras. Nonetheless, the academic/colonial style persists in the portrait sculptures of national and provincial political leaders, as well as in popular cinema and television series.

JAYARAM PODUVAL

INDIA: MODERN

The initial stages of modern Indian sculpture may be traced to the preindependence era around the turn of the 20th century. The cultural milieu of this time in India held a certain duality between British and Indian influences. On the one hand sculptors had the rich sculptural heritage of India to refer to, while on the other hand these artists were now exposed to British academic sculpture with its heightened naturalism. The influx of European sculptures and the establishment of art schools by the British government furthered this exposure. Based on the amalgamation of these two distinct schools, a new trend emerged that broke away from the traditional Indian religious stone sculptures. The style born out of this interaction is often referred to as the Indo-European style.

In the first few decades of the 20th century, Westernized middle- and upper-class urban Indians began to patronize sculptors of the resulting secular works.

Such projects became instrumental in the growth of individual styles that became apparent between 1925 and 1950. Sculptors such as Deviprasad Roychowdhury, S. Pansare, V.P. Karmarkar, and Ramkinkar Baij interacted with modern Western sculpture and its various "isms."

Major sculptural activity during the first 30 years of the 20th century centered around Bombay. During this phase formal portraits and equestrian monuments became the main preoccupation of the sculptors, who now mainly worked on commission. Two of the most significant early sculptors from this period were G.K. Mhatre and B.V. Talim. Both excelled in portraiture, but it is their original compositions that portray the romantic spirit of the age. Mhatre's work shows strong influence of Western antiques and is severely academic. Talim, on the other hand, depicted scenes from his surroundings using academic realism. Mhatre's *To the Temple*, a standing figure of a young Maharashtrian girl carrying an offering, displays the sweet simplicity of the Pre-Raphaelite type. Talim's sculptures have the same romantic appeal but exhibit a somewhat Expressionistic treatment with a heavy touch of sentiment evident, for example, in *Poverty*, a bronze half figure of a poor old man mending his clothes. S. Pansare was one of the significant sculptors working around the same time.

V.P. Karmarkar and Deviprasad, working around the same time, struggled toward a new objectivity in their sculptures. Karmarkar explored within the academic idiom the human body and its gestural movement, but with greater rhythmic expression. The variations in his drawings derived from posed life models or from real life. He was perhaps the most outstanding of the academic sculptors in the second quarter of the 20th century. The most representative of his works is the portrait of *Dr. D.N. Mullah* at the Bombay High-Court. Deviprasad had a marked predilection for Victorian ideals even though he was exposed to the work of some early modern French sculptors and the Bengal School. His works *When Winter Comes* and *The Triumph of Labor* reveal a willingness to experiment and so stand out distinctly from the average academic line.

A rapid change in attitude occurred in the Indian sculptural movement beginning in 1940 that diversified further in the 1960s. The works from the end of 1940s begin to show greater individuality and creativity, as sculptors explored different materials and techniques. The period saw a shift from academic realism to abstraction, a move toward Conceptual art. Sculptors such as Daviervalla and Raghav Kaneria also began experimenting with junk art and the use of welding.

Between the 1930s and 1950s Ram Kinkar Baij, Dhanraj Bhagat, Prodosh Dasgupta, Sankho Chowdhury, Amarnath Sehgal, and Chintamani Kar played significant roles in the development of the modern Indian sculptural movement. The works of Ram Kinkar, a highly independent artist, constitute a turning point in this movement. Although his works are based on Indian life, he conceived his sculptures as independent objects in outdoor settings. Ram Kinkar's works have a dual nature: first, a structural core that is internal and organic and shows itself in the organization of forms and, second, an expressionistic quality that is Baroque, buoyant, and flowering. He created a semblance between his work and nature by giving a furrowed coarse surface to his work, similar to that of tree trunks and rocks. He integrated the natural movements of the human body—stretched legs, gesticulating arms, and thrusting heaving torsos—to give an inner vitality and pulsating life to the sculptural mass, such as seen in his *Santhal Family* and *Way to Market*. He was probably the first Indian sculptor to work with abstract forms, for example, his *Lampstand*.

Dhanraj Bhagat began wood carving around 1950, influenced by the simplicity, abstraction, and naïveté of African art. He developed a type of distortion and stylization in which the figure's proportions are often elongated, with sharp angles and curved body joints. This lyrical stylization is free flowing, and the total sculpture is conceived in linear silhouette. These qualities are apparent in works such as *Three Women* and *Flute*.

Sankho Chowdhury introduced in India the philosophy of returning to fundamentals, as Constantin Brancusi, Naum Gabo, and Henry Moore had done in the West. These sculptors had evolved a new definition of sculpture, the tenets of which are loyalty to material, three-dimensional palpability, the activating of space through juxtaposition of solids and voids, and the belief that a sculptural object is an organism in its own right that possesses its own reality and is not a substitute for any other reality. Chowdhury's carvings and metal sculptures express these qualities.

In 1960 the sculptor Adi Daviervalla began experimenting with new ideas and media, exploring the intrinsic quality of an object or form for its own beauty and balance rather than for any visual and tactile sensations it evokes. His experiments with aluminum, lead, magnets, plastic, and glass produced unconventional forms. Daviervalla's work displays scientific precision in its organization and a keen intellectual sensibility. He considered the basic value of sculpture to be the intrinsic quality of material, that is, heaviness, lightness, balance, magnetic power, and so on, which is apparent in works such as *Genesis, Cosmic Balance,* and *Animated Suspension*.

Different regional schools and trends have arisen, such as the Madras school in the southern part of the country. The works of this school are largely iconic, influenced by folk and tribal objects and traditional craftsmanship. P.V. Janakiram, one of the most significant sculptors from this school, worked around 1962 with beaten copper. His works are single iconic stela-like figures that owe much to Indian imagery, a style that was taken further by S. Nandagopal in the early 1970s.

Figurative sculptures of Sarbari Roychowdhury, Meera Mukherjee, and Somnath Hore and the more abstract works of Ajit Chakraborty and Sushen Ghosh became influential in the eastern part of India. Each of these sculptors has a distinct style. Roychowdhury's works exude a tremendous quality of mass and volume, while Mukherjee's work shows the influence of the folk tradition. Her use of the lost-wax process allows her to create intricate surface decoration, apparent in her 1973 work *Ashoka*. Hore's works speak of human suffering. His *Wound* series, relief cast in paper pulp, and sculptures in the round in bronze show masterly manipulation of these media.

On the western side of the country the Baroda school took shape, with Mahendra Pandya, Raghav Kaneria, and Nagji Patel playing the key role in the sculptural movement. Characteristics of Pandya's works derive from woodcarving and have significance in the context of the iconic and the trends of the 1960s. Kaneria has created fantastic images that arise from the juxtaposition of strange rusty surfaces and found forms. Patel's work, on the other hand, exudes a strongly organic, sensuous feeling. He works mostly in marble with various abstract forms. One of the most monumental of his works is the *Banyan Tree* in Baroda City.

Throughout the country, sculpture from the 1960s displays a certain political consciousness that led to the need for being "Indian" and gave rise to Indigenism. However, this identity crisis gradually diminished in later phases of the art movement. Various shifts and developments in terms of material have occurred, from plaster, bronze, and stone to wood, metal sheet, and terracotta. Thematically as well, a shift took place from portraiture and storytelling to conceptual art.

Sculptors from the last two decades of the 20th century exhibit a diverse range of subject and style. The art critic Jaya Appaswamy has described the modern Indian sculptor as not just a corollary but a collective statement that exists in its own right by virtue of its intrinsic merit. Sculptors from this period include Kanai Kunhiraman from Kerala, Balbir Katt from the Baroda school, and Dhruv Mistry from the Baroda school. Kunhiraman emerged as an experimentalist-Symbolist and perfectionist in the 1970s and 1980s.

His *Yakshi* figure is an erotic, squatting female nude figure. Many consider it to be an artistic profanity or aberration in the name of the ongoing polemic about modernity. Others, however, feel that behind this seemingly outrageous gesture the sculptor's intent was to stir up the desensitized and apathetic attitude of people toward the business of art. Balbir Katt in his *Sun Series* from the 1970s grapples with huge abstract forms that he fills with rhythm and flamboyant life. His main concern is spatial relation of the sculpture and the space around it. Dhruv Mistry's work *Hanuman, Study for a Spatial Metaphor* plays with positive and negative space.

Sculptors who came into the fore in the 1980s include Krishna Kumar, Rimzon, Alex Mathew, and Pushpamala N. Krishna Kumar belonged to the Radical group from Kerala, who believed in essentializing over their selfhood. This crisis is common to the radical subjectivity formation in general that takes various forms of self-projections evident in Krishna Kumar's work *Vasco-da-Gama*. Rimzon, another young sculptor, skillfully models his figures and casts in fiber. One of his works is a life-size nude man portrayed sitting on the floor, savagely pulling his legs apart to expose his genitals. The shock and the invitation are not in the sexual details but in the defiant violence of the gesture, an admission of personal perversion that is also a social malady. The lifelike naturalistic rendering may be compared with those of Dhruv Mistry. The skillful naturalistic modeling in Dhruva's figures generates a loving ritual complete in itself. The figures attempt to renounce contact with reality, both personal and historic, to become metaphysical. They seem more anxious to find their place in museums than to reach out and speak to their people. Rimzon's work seems to directly question Dhruva's figures. In Rimzon's work the nearness of the subject overrides considerations of style and chronicles the real struggle to involve or contain in a single image the hangover of academic training in naturalism and the method of the larger sculptural tradition. Most of Alex Mathew's sculptures are particularized images that slowly expand into archetypes. He incorporates and fuses memories of childhood and adult experiences organically with images of the Kerala countryside.

Art in this phase is often preoccupied with socio-political aspects, and the angst of the realist-Expressionist sensibility seems to be a major concern of contemporary sculptors such as Pushpamala. Pushpamala exploits the direct freshness and plasticity of terracotta, its ability to be pinched, pressed, stretched, and have marks made upon it. She plays constantly with the suggestion and transformation of appearances and through this achieves and explores and chides, mocking and condemning the self and the world through clowns, contortionists, and ventriloquists. Her works are predominantly concerned with the woman: as child, adolescent, and adult; naive, innocent, promiscuous, sensuous, and corrupt. She also addresses the problem of sculpture today, one divorced from its original architectural frame. With the demarcation of niche and pedestal gone, sculpture now must behave as an object among objects, while continuing to extend its technical and thematic repertoire. Therefore, Pushpamala believes that the sculptor must redefine the relations between sculptural forms and their environment. Her work *The Fools Orchestra* may be interpreted as a direct pun on society and the so-called elite class.

Young sculptors are currently working throughout India, exploring the theories and possibilities of abstraction, realism, and Conceptual art. During the second half of the 20th century, the character of both art and artist has changed, with a tremendous thrust toward individualism. The contemporary art scene has provided sculptors with complete freedom in their approach to creative expression, resulting in a breakdown of inhibitions and adherence to the rather limited traditional means of expression.

DEEPANJANA DANDA KLEIN

See also **Brancusi, Constantin; Gabo, Naum; Moore, Henry**

Further Reading

Appasamy, Jaya, *An Introduction to Modern Indian Sculpture*, New Delhi: Indian Council for Cultural Relations, 1970

Appasamy, Jaya, "Contemporary Indian Sculpture," *Lalit Kala Contemporary* 40 (1995)

Dasgupta, Anshuman, and Shivaji Panikkar, "The Transitional Modern: Figuring the Post Modern in India," *Lalit Kala Contemporary* 41 (1996)

Kapur, Geeta, *When Was Modernism: Essays on Contemporary Cultural Practice in India*, New Delhi: Tulika, 2000

Nandakumar, R., "Personal Iconography and Public Art," *India Magazine* (1993)

Narzary, Janak Jhankar, "Modern Indian Sculpture: A Brief History," *Lalit Kala Contemporary* 41 (1996)

Ramachandran, M., "Sculptural Ideas," *Lalit Kala Contemporary* 41 (1996)

INSTALLATION

Installation is one of the more difficult artistic genres to define because it encompasses such a wide range of approaches. Most basically, it is an art form, usually three-dimensional, that has a close relationship with its exhibition space. It might be completely site-specific, that is, created especially for one fixed location, or it might be adaptable to a variety of different environments. It might be a self-contained unit with its own walls or boundaries. It might interact with a particular situation purely on a formal level or generate meaning from historical or conceptual relationships. It might incorporate found objects, make use of text or technological elements, or include sound, smell, or movement. It might present itself as a tableau or diorama, or it might require the viewer to move through it, physically interact with it, or perform a specific activity. It might be highly ephemeral or permanent. What Installation definitely is not, however, is an art of the singular, finely crafted object.

Installation probably began with the Bauhaus's (1919–33) emphasis on the interrelationship of space, form, and function and grew out of the explorations of the Italian Futurists, the Russian Constructivists, the Dutch De Stijl artists, the German Dadaists, and the Surrealists. Contemporary Installation artists and art historians often view Kurt Schwitters's *Merzbau* as a seminal work. He completed several versions during the 1930s and 1940s, constructing the first, which grew out of a column that the artist had begun in 1919, in his own home. The result was room-size structures that dominated their spaces.

Undoubtedly, Marcel Duchamp also exerted a strong influence on what we now term Installation art. A combination Surrealist, Cubist, Futurist, and proto-Conceptualist, he first created controversy with *Nude Descending a Staircase*, a groundbreaking painting exhibited at the 1914 Armory Show in New York City. He later gained notoriety through his use of found objects as sculpture, artworks that he termed readymades.

Duchamp also took part in the transformation of specific exhibition spaces. For a 1938 show of Surrealist painting at the Galerie Beaux Arts in Paris, he designed the large, central hall to include four large beds along with live grass, a pool, and 1200 sacks of coal suspended from the ceiling. During the opening reception the aroma of roasting coffee wafted throughout the hall, German marching-band music played, and a dancer performed around the pool. Four years later, for a Surrealist exhibition in New York City, he strung the gallery with a crisscrossing of twine. A 1947 exhibition in Paris included a room with water falling like rain onto artificial grass.

Duchamp's final artwork, *Given: 1. The Waterfall 2. The Illuminating Gas* (*Étant donnés: 1° la chute d'eau. 2° le gaz d'éclairage*) (1946–66), permanently displayed at the Philadelphia Museum of Art, Pennsylvania, also engages its location and its audience. Located at the far end of the room, it first seems to be nothing more than a wall-like barrier made of rough wood. Upon approaching closely, however, viewers are enticed to peer through a set of peepholes in order to see the diorama behind it.

American artist Allan Kaprow has suggested that Abstract Expressionist painting freed artists to experiment with assemblage and, eventually, three-dimensional space. Kaprow came to call these spatial explorations Environments. These Environments involved transforming spaces as well as designing activities to incorporate the spectator's participation. *An Apple Shrine* (1960), an Environment at Judson Gallery in New York City, required visitors to wind their way through a newspaper-strewn labyrinth. *Yard* (1961) demanded that the audience climb over piles of tires in the backyard of New York's Martha Jackson Gallery. In 1962 and again in 1963 Kaprow presented *Words*, which involved participants turning on record players, rotating rollers, and adding their own words. The action-oriented aspects of these Environments came to be called Happenings.

Other American artists during the 1960s, such as Jim Dine, Claes Oldenburg, and Carolee Schneemann, espoused Environments and Happenings as well. Oldenburg, for example, set up *The Store* (1961–62) in the form of a functional retail business in the front of his storefront studio; the "merchandise" for sale consisted of his funky, mixed-media sculptures of food and everyday objects.

Simultaneously in Europe artists such as Joseph Beuys were conducting their own spatial and experiential experiments. Beuys became known for setting up exhibition spaces with piles of felt, fat, and found objects. His *I Like America and America Likes Me* (1974) at the New York City branch of Rene Block's Berlin gallery used his own body wrapped in felt and a live coyote as "sculptural" elements.

The works of American sculptors George Segal, Red Grooms, Robert Morris, and Carl Andre also show an interest in the interaction of the physical space with the viewer. Segal became known for his stagelike dioramas of ghostly white, life-size figures, made of plasterized gauze, positioned amid real objects such as Coca-Cola vending machines and theater marquees. Grooms's cartoonish constructions out of papier mâché and mixed media often required walking around or through the work. His *Ruckus Manhattan* (1975–76) included a full-scale subway car complete with a crowd of New Yorkers and a rocking floor, which caused those who entered to sway unsteadily from side to side.

Morris and Andre, along with Americans Donald Judd and Dan Flavin, were part of what came to be known as Minimalism. While the visual style of Minimalist sculpture seemed to be the antithesis of the makeshift, often messy, aesthetic of Environments, Minimalist sculptors nonetheless modified their exhibition spaces by involving some sort of viewer interaction. Morris's geometric sculptures and Flavin's colored fluorescent lights, for example, were installed in ways that relied on both the architecture of the room and the movement of the gallery goers. Andre's floor pieces, made of metal tiles, were meant to be walked upon.

During the 1970s American artists such as Yoko Ono, Lucas Samaras, and Yayoi Kusama constructed mirrored- and glass-paneled rooms that were meant to be entered. In Los Angeles Miriam Schapiro and Judy Chicago, together with other female artists, took over an entire building and created Womanhouse (1972). They structured each room to address space and content according to a newly emerging feminist consciousness. On the East Coast Gordon Matta-Clarke was literally splitting houses in half. Subsequently, San Francisco artist David Ireland turned his own house on Capp Street into a self-contained environment. A decade later English artist Rachel Whiteread created *Untitled (House)* (1993), casting the interior of a house in concrete and afterward removing its outside walls.

Earthwork artists such as Americans Michael Heizer and Robert Smithson and British Richard Long expanded their ideas about spatial alteration to include the landscape. They used bulldozers, ditchdiggers, and dump trucks to sculpt the outdoor environment. The public has to journey to, walk along, and climb on Smithson's *Spiral Jetty* (1970; Great Salt Lake, Utah) and *Amarillo Ramp* (1973; Stanley Marsh Ranch, Texas) in order to fully experience them. The same is true for James Turrell's long-term work *Roden Crater* in Arizona's Painted Desert, begun in 1972, which transforms a natural cinder crater into an environment that relates to the surrounding sky and land through the medium of light. The outdoor works of the team of Christo and Jeanne-Claude, such as *Valley Curtain* (1970–72; Rifle, Colorado), *Running Fence* (1972–76; Sonoma and Marin counties, California), and *Surrounded Islands* (1980–83; Biscayne Bay, Florida), also require viewers to take extraordinary means to experience them.

The term *Installation* as its own category did not appear in the *Art Index* until 1993, although it appeared earlier in general reference books. Installation began to assume its present form during the 1980s and has become an accepted form of contemporary art. The genre is so prevalent in London that Installation artists are now being awarded the Tate Gallery's prestigious Turner prize. Young artists from Korea and Japan are well versed in the art form, and Installation artists can be found working everywhere from Canada to Mexico to Brazil to Australia.

Contemporary Installation is often more calculated than the Environments of the 1960s. Even when found objects are used, such as in the case of the American-Canadian artist Jessica Stockholder, French artist Annette Messager, or Russian artist Ilya Kabakov, they are arranged in ways that look premeditated. In addi-

tion, many large-scale installations, such as Judy Chicago's *The Dinner Party* (1979), have required the expertise and handiwork of others. American artists such as Ann Hamilton, Liza Lou, and Sandy Skoglund regularly rely on assistants to put together their labor-intensive pieces. Hamilton's *privation and excesses* (1989) involved the positioning of 750,000 pennies into a bed of honey; Lou's *Kitchen* (1991–95) and *Backyard* (1995–97) entailed the stringing of millions of glass beads. Thousands of individually blown-out eggshells carpeted the floor of Skoglund's *Walking on Eggshells* (1996–97).

Photography, film, video, and computer technologies also play a large part in contemporary Installation art. Korean artist Nam June Paik, who can be considered the "father" of video installation, was among the first to exploit the "objectness" of both the television sets and the images on their screens. American artists such as Bill Viola, Gary Hill, and Tony Oursler have used film, video, and CD-ROMs in conjunction with roomlike constructions and unconventional projection surfaces. The evocative power of French artist Christian Boltanski's installations is based in his use of black-and-white photographs, each illuminated by a single, bare, incandescent bulb.

Installations first developed and were exhibited in a milieu separate from the commercial art market. Any consideration of the genre's development would be incomplete without considering the impact of university art departments and government arts funding programs. For example, Kaprow, Samaras, and Segal all had teaching positions at Rutgers University in New Jersey, and Beuys taught at the Düsseldorf Academy of Art in Germany. During the 1970s and 1980s public funding programs in the United States provided needed monies for research and development. Alternative galleries that encouraged unconventional art forms flourished in New York, Los Angeles, Chicago, and many smaller U.S. cities. In Canada the government-supported Parallel Galleries provided similar venues throughout its provinces. Sheltered somewhat from the normal constraints of the marketplace, artists were encouraged to experiment in the realm of form and idea. The result has been a type of art that cannot easily be packaged.

The acceptance of Installation in the mainstream art world, ironically, has coincided with the dwindling of public funding and diminishing opportunities for university teaching in the United States and Canada. Artists have had more difficulty finding support for the kind of freewheeling experimentation that gave birth to the genre. Often, museums—sometimes those not devoted to exhibiting fine art—have opened their doors to avant-garde endeavors. In 1992–93 the Maryland Historical Society in Baltimore invited Fred Wilson to rearrange the objects in its own collection as an artistic "installation" that would shed new light on how history is viewed. A number of other cultural institutions then adopted Wilson's *Mining the Museum* project. Notably, a few philanthropic organizations have begun to fund art of this sort. For example, Artangel, based in London, sponsored Whiteread's *House*. In addition, the Dia Center for the Arts in New York City has preserved some of the most important Installation artworks of the late 20th century, including Walter de Maria's *Earth Room* (1977) and *Broken Kilometer* (1979), both in New York City, and his *Lightning Field* in New Mexico. The center has also sponsored retrospective re-creations of the work of Beuys and has commissioned new works by Flavin, Hamilton, and Robert Irwin.

VIRGINIA MAKSYMOWICZ

See also **Andre, Carl; Beuys, Joseph; Bourgeois, Louise; Christo and Jeanne-Claude; De Maria, Walter; Dine, James Lewis; Judd, Donald; Long, Richard; Morris, Robert; Oldenburg, Claes; Segal, George; Smithson, Robert; Turrell, James**

Further Reading

Avalanche (fall 1970–summer 1976) (journal of installation and performance art); see especially the special issue on Robert Smithson (summer–fall 1973)

Baele, Nancy, "Artists Pay Homage to the Great Sculptor Brancusi," *Ottawa Citizen* (20 May 1997)

Kabakov, Ilya, Margarita Tupitsyn, and Victor Tupitsyn, "Conversation: About Installation," *Art Journal* 58/4 (winter 1999)

Kaprow, Allan, "The Legacy of Jackson Pollock," *Art News* 57/6 (October 1958)

Kaprow, Allan, *Assemblage, Environments, and Happenings*, New York: Abrams, 1965

Kimmelman, Michael, "Installation Art Moves In, Moves On," *New York Times* (9 August 1998)

Kirby, Michael (editor), *Happenings*, New York: Dutton, and London: Sidgwick and Jackson, 1965

Kultermann, Udo, *Neue Dimensionen der Plastik*, Tübingen, Germany: Wasmuth, 1967; as *The New Sculpture: Environments and Assemblages*, New York: Praeger, 1968

Kultermann, Udo, *Leben und Kunst: Zur Funktionen der Intermedia*, Tübingen, Germany: Wasmuth, 1970; as *Art and Life*, translated by John William Gabriel, New York: Praeger, 1971

Lehmann, Henry, "Views from a Poet of Modern Loneliness," *The Gazette* (Montreal) (27 September 1997)

Lucie-Smith, Edward, *Arte oggi: Dall'espressionismo astratto all'iperrealismo*, Verona, Italy: Mondadori, 1976; as *Art Today: From Abstract Expressionism to Surrealism*, Oxford: Phaidon Press, 1977; 3rd edition, 1989

Molesworth, Charles, "Installations," *Salmagundi—A Quarterly of the Humanities and Social Sciences* 120 (fall 1998)

Reiss, Julie H., *From Margin to Center: The Spaces of Installation Art*, Cambridge, Massachusetts: MIT Press, 1999

Singerman, Howard, *Art Subjects: Making Artists in the American University*, Berkeley: University of California Press, 1999

Smith, Roberta, "In Installation Art, a Bit of the Spoiled Brat," *The New York Times* (3 January 1993)

INTAGLIO

See **Engraved Gems (Intaglios and Cameos)**

IRELAND

Evidence of stone carving in Ireland can be traced to about 2500 BCE in the decoration found in passage graves. A group of such tombs was constructed northwest of Dublin in County Meath, among which Newgrange is the most famous. Many of the stones bear geometric ornamentation, notably the spiral that reappears in early medieval Irish sculpture as a design feature on the Celtic cross. These graves and their decoration are not exclusive to Ireland but exist in several other locations, particularly in Brittany and Wales. Therefore, in the very earliest manifestation of sculptural work in Ireland, a pattern for the understanding and study of Irish sculpture is already established. Although an island nation, artistic expression and style in Ireland are inextricably linked with developments in art outside the country and, if Italy and France are influential in different periods, what is happening in Britain has remained constantly significant.

The earliest examples of three-dimensional carving are the small cult figures dating to the Iron Age, two of which are to be found on Boa Island in County Fermanagh. These pagan images have large heads, with big, bold eyes and sharply pointed chins, perhaps suggesting beards. However, the bodies are truncated, and in the case of one of them, a two-headed figure, the arms and phallus are on one side and the legs on the other. Although the original purpose and meaning of these so-called pagan deities are lost to the contemporary viewer, and like so much public sculpture their context has changed over time, they nonetheless have an inherent primitive fierceness, a rawness of expression, that makes them immediately engaging. The focus on genitalia reemerges more emphatically in the *Shelah-na-Gigs* of the Medieval period. Images of naked females projecting their sexuality carved in high and low relief on rectangular blocks of stone are to be found across Ireland. Making their initial appearance in the Romanesque period, they were incorporated into church and castle buildings from the 13th to the 17th centuries. In a religious context, they serve to warn against the evil of lust and are similar to exhibitionist figures carved on pilgrimage routes in Europe. In a secular location they suggest inherent protective powers, warning off the readily suggested evils. Many

Shelah-na-Gigs are held in the National Museum of Ireland.

It is not without significance that one of the sculptural images most particularly identified with Ireland is the early medieval High Cross, which serves today as a memory of monastic Ireland. These stone crosses are often richly carved with decorative detailing in the form of Celtic spirals, interlacing, and fretwork, and with religious figures and biblical scenes. The Cross of Muiredach at Monasterboice in County Louth, dating to the mid 9th century, is among the most detailed, with many scenes on the shaft, starting with the Fall of Adam and Eve and rising to an image of Christ in Judgment in the center of the cross. Although the individual scenes are not arranged in sequence, they display clarity in the orchestration of details, and the confident carving of the sandstone makes these busy relief scenes highly legible. The medieval crosses, in rural settings, served variously as commemorative objects, places of prayer, and boundary markers. In revivalist form, such imagery proliferated in the 19th and 20th centuries and found its way into more central locations on streets and in graveyards. The Celtic cross has become a familiar sight in towns and villages across the country, particularly in its role as a public memorial commemorating the Rising of 1798. This Celtic Revival work was an intentional projection of Irishness, both Catholic and nationalist, echoing a glorious past, a time before Ireland was invaded.

Colonization in the 17th century brought with it a close, if enforced, association with Britain, as a result of which Irish sculpture for many centuries reflected the stylistic developments that were taking place in England. Also, many of the sculptors working in England in the 17th, 18th, and 19th centuries—for example, Grinling Gibbons, Michael Rysbrack, and E.H. Baily—carried out work for the Crown in Ireland and for the Church of Ireland; therefore, what is found in the country is not always Irish. Late medieval tomb monuments, with kneeling, reclining, or recumbent effigies and often incorporating several figures, are English in character. Some include polychromy, notably the elaborate monuments erected by Richard Boyle, First Earl of Cork, in St. Mary's Church, Youghal, in County Cork (1620) and in St. Patrick's Cathedral in Dublin (1632) to commemorate various members of his family. If these have a primitive formality, Baroque extravagance and pomp can be seen in a monument erected nearly 100 years later in Kilnasoolagh Church in County Clare. Commemorating Sir Donat O'Brien and carved by William Kidwell (1662–1736), who came to Ireland in 1711, it is a theatrical presentation of a solitary figure in white marble set against a black background. Color is again employed in the monument to Provost Baldwin erected in Trinity College Dublin

in 1784, the work of Christopher Hewetson (*ca.* 1739–98). Executed in Rome in the circle of Antonio Canova, it is the finest example of Neoclassical sculpture in Ireland. The three white marble figures, Baldwin accompanied by an angel and the Muse of Science, are emphatically delineated against a red granite pyramid and surmount a black marble sarcophagus. The clarity of the work highlights the restrained emotional expression.

The Roman sojourn was not unusual for Irish sculptors, and many more would visit that city in the 19th century, notably John Hogan (1800–58), who spent 25 years there between 1824 and 1849. Working largely for the Irish market and often producing rather dry religious imagery, Hogan's masterpiece is his statue of *Hibernia with the Bust of Lord Cloncurry* (1844; National Gallery of Ireland, on loan from University College Dublin). Considered the finest sculpture displayed at the Industrial and Art Exhibition in Dublin in 1853, this elegant statue splendidly combines an austere Late Classical manner with Celtic Revival imagery. Hogan's return to practice in Dublin for the last years of his life marked a decline in his career.

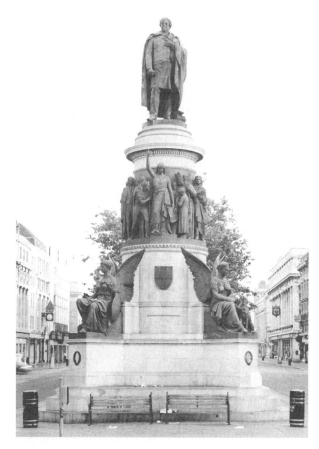

John Henry Foley, O'Connell Monument
© Sarah Cully

The issue of absentee artist was the focus of much debate in 19th-century Ireland, particularly with regard to the many Irish sculptors who worked from studios in London. Several became well known to the point where the comment was made that "the best British sculptors are Irishmen" (*Art Journal*, 1862). Patrick MacDowell (1799–1870) and John Henry Foley (1818–74) established significant practices and were widely commissioned to execute work for English and Irish patrons. Both worked on the Albert Memorial in London's Kensington Gardens, McDowell executing the Europe group and Foley the one representing Asia. Moreover, Foley also modeled the statue of the prince. This was a particularly prestigious commission for an Irish sculptor. Much of the work of these two sculptors in Ireland was public sculpture executed in a century that is identified with statue mania. Propagandist by nature, public statuary in Ireland in this period was often controversial. Dublin, for example, with three 18th-century royal equestrian monuments in place, witnessed the erection of several imperial commemorations in the 19th century, the earliest of which were the Nelson Column dating to 1808, with the portrait likeness carved by Thomas Kirk (1781–1845), and the Wellington Testimonial in the Phoenix Park erected in 1822. However, the nationalist demand for more specifically Irish commemorations encouraged commissions for memorials to Irish literary and political figures. Among these, Foley's monument to Daniel O'Connell, designed in 1867 but not erected until 1882, is the most significant. The three-tiered presentation, with its circular drum depicting the people of Ireland, has a sense of grandeur and uniqueness among the monuments in Dublin.

Foley did not receive the commission for the O'Connell monument without considerable public debate. Nationalists in the country favored a local sculptor to carry out the work, notably Thomas Farrell (1827–1900). Farrell, one of a family of sculptors, had an extensive career, particularly in portraiture, both public and private. One of his earliest commissions, a statue of Archbishop Daniel Murray (1855) for St. Mary's Pro-Cathedral in Dublin, won in competition against strong opposition that included John Hogan, received much acclaim. With its classical clarity, it is at once moving and simple. Appointed the first sculptor president of the Royal Hibernian Academy in 1893, Farrell identified the way in which the memorial portrait kept "the sculptor's art from being extinguished in Ireland," while, at the same time, imaginative sculpture was neglected (*Father Reffe Memorial Booklet*, 1896). All of these Irish Victorian sculptors, whether practicing in England or in Ireland, modeled ideal subjects as well as their portrait works. Typical of the period, the female figure, nude and seminude, biblical and mythological, academic and inexpressive, abounds. Influences from France that liberated artistic expression from Victorian academic constraints crept into Irish sculpture early in the 20th century in the work of Oliver Sheppard (1865–1941) and Andrew O'Connor (1874–1941). Sheppard's vigorously modeled figures of pikemen, erected in County Wexford in the first decade of the 20th century and serving as 1798 memorials, display a dynamic energy that is immediately engaging. O'Connor's complex and troubled *Monument to Christ the King*, in Dun Laoghaire (1926), has all the hallmarks of an artist who has studied the work of Auguste Rodin. Irish art was late adapting to Modernist styles, and in a newly independent country, nationalist concerns found expression in a continuing projection of portrait/commemorative and religious imagery. The Dublin statues of Theobald Wolfe Tone at St. Stephen's Green and Thomas Davis in College Green, modeled by Edward Delaney (*b.* 1930) and unveiled in the 1960s, attempt to marry traditional public portrait imagery with Expressionist modeling techniques. Although the resulting portraits are awkward, the accompanying subject pieces, in both instances, are painfully expressive.

Abstract color sculpture made its appearance in the public spaces in the second half of the 20th century. It was through such new practices in sculpture that Ireland took its position artistically beyond the provincial and the parochial. *Reflections* by Michael Bulfin (*b.* 1939), the painted yellow sculpture placed outside the headquarters of the Bank of Ireland in Baggot Street in Dublin in 1978, remains, in its interaction with the building in both color and form, one of the most eye-catching sculptures in the city. At the turn of the 21st century, Michael Warren (*b.* 1950) has continued this public display of abstract sculpture. In contrast to Bulfin's *Reflections*, Warren's soaring and sinking wooden sculpture in front of the Civic Offices on Wood Quay in Dublin has a silent presence. Sophisticated and elegant, it nonetheless incorporates a natural sense of movement.

If the foregoing names have all been male, there has also been a significant female presence in the practice of sculpture—adopting the broadest understanding of the term *sculpture*—beginning in the late 20th century. Kathy Prendergast, Eilis O'Connell, Alice Maher, Louise Walsh, and Dorothy Cross are just some of the artists who have been enormously experimental in their practice. Working with a range of materials, from bronze to hair, from video to found object, their imagery is exploratory and dynamic. If a focus on the female condition can often be witnessed in their work, their subjects also reach well beyond such limitations. Cross (*b.* 1956) is perhaps the most experimental among these artists, employing a wide range of material to project her ideas, from whole environments, such as *The Power House* (1991), to cow's udders and mortuary slabs. Her *Ghost Ship*, an ephemeral work, was located briefly in Dublin Bay in 1999. Best seen by night, the glowing hull commemorated a life at sea long since passed.

At the beginning of the 21st century, the sculptor-artists in Ireland have the most experimental art practices, and sculpture/environment work is the most widely experienced art form through the proliferation of public art and community work. No longer necessarily delimited within traditional or nationalist constraints, Irish sculptural expression has arrived at a level of sophistication, maturity, imagination, and experimentation that rejects closure and borders and welcomes openness and internationalization.

PAULA MURPHY

Further Reading

Crookshank, Anne, *Irish Sculpture from 1600*, Dublin: Department of Foreign Affairs, 1984

Harbison, Peter, Homan Potterton, and Jeanne Sheehy, *Irish Art and Architecture: From Prehistory to the Present*, London: Thames and Hudson, 1978

Henry, Françoise, *Irish High Crosses*, Dublin: Three Candles, 1964

Hill, Judith, *Irish Public Sculpture: A History*, Dublin and Portland, Oregon: Four Courts Press, 1998

Hunt, John, and Peter Harbison, *Irish Medieval Figure Sculpture, 1200–1600: A Study of Irish Tombs with Notes on Costume and Armor*, 2 vols., Dublin: Irish University Press, 1974

Murphy, Paula, "Thomas Farrell, Sculptor," *Irish Art Review* 9 (1993)

Murphy, Paula, "British Sculpture at the Early Universal Exhibitions: Ireland Sustaining Britain," *Sculpture Journal* 3 (1999)

Potterton, Homan, *Irish Church Monuments, 1570–1880*, Belfast: Ulster Architectural Heritage Society, 1975

Read, Benedict, "John Henry Foley," *Connoisseur* 186/750 (August 1974)

Read, Benedict, *Victorian Sculpture*, New Haven, Connecticut: Yale University Press, 1982

Stalley, Roger, *Architecture and Sculpture in Ireland, 1150–1350*, Dublin: Rose, 1971

Turpin, John, *John Hogan: Irish Neoclassical Sculptor in Rome, 1800–1858*, Dublin: Irish Academic Press, 1982

ITALY: ROMANESQUE–GOTHIC

Romanesque Late 10th Century–Early 13th Century

In sculpture, as in architecture, the Gothic style appeared later in Italy than elsewhere in Europe, and Romanesque sculpture survived longer. The term *Romanesque* was coined in the 19th century to underline the Latin characteristics of Western art from the end of the 10th century to the early 13th century, as opposed to the supposedly Germanic origin of Gothic art and architecture, which dawned at the beginning of the 13th century.

The English term *Romanesque* has the same etymological root as the Italian *romanico*, the French *roman*, and the German *romanik* and recalls the Romance (neo-Latin) languages and literature born in more or less the same period from the 11th to the 12th century. Yet the notion of Romanesque, although universally accepted, is somewhat improper because it has come to include phenomena that are foreign to the propagation of the Romance literature or refer to many other cultural traditions, including the Classical, Byzantine, and Classical revivals promoted by Charlemagne and Otto. Especially in the 20th century, art historical research revealed the conceptual limitations of the definition of Romanesque: geographic and even chronological limitations given that south of the Alps this style lingered on after the end of the 13th century, overlaying in a way the new, so-called Gothic style. Generally speaking, Romanesque art refers to a pan-European artistic spectrum with a common conceptual core and common symbolic meanings, but whose manifestations, although sharing similar underpinnings and intentions, were notably different in the various regions of Italy as well as throughout Europe.

Romanesque sculpture was born and developed with close ties to architecture. The faster circulation of goods, ideas, techniques, and craftsmen fostered the appearance of very similar styles in distant regions. Together with Burgundy, Lombardy offers the oldest examples of Romanesque sculpture from the beginning of the 12th century. Outstanding among these are the decorations in the churches of Sant'Abbondio in Como and Sant'Ambrogio in Milan. The pulpit in the Milanese church presents one of the first narrative sculptures of the time: the *Last Supper*, the figures of which evince a plastic force. The pulpit of San Giulio d'Orta (Novara) from the same period presents still more vigorous modeling. These early examples of Romanesque sculpture were closely linked to the Lombard tradition and appeared in the Lombardy-Emilia region—for instance, in the bas-relief ornamentation on the facade of S. Michele in Pavia. Due in part to Armenian and oriental influences, the repertory of anthropomorphic and zoomorphic motifs and of basket-work bas-reliefs gradually grew livelier. The principal consequence was that the figures became rounder and began to emerge from the surfaces.

As was later the case with Gothic, the Romanesque style reached Italy from the north and developed hybrid languages in which Germanic formal conceptions were adapted to the innate classicism of Italian art.

The interaction between these two forces is easy to understand by observing the early 12th-century reliefs on the facade of the Cathedral of Modena in Emilia. Here also is an early example of the tendency of sculptors to announce their identity. The text on a tablet held up by two prophets reads "Inter scultores quanto sis dignus onore claret scultura nunc Wiligelme tua" (How much honor you deserve among sculptors, O Wiligelmo, is evident here in your sculpture). With these reliefs and the four panels with stories from Genesis, Wiligelmo appears to be the key figure in Romanesque sculpture in Italy and beyond. His language has affinities with Romanesque sculpture in Languedoc and Aquitaine, but in recovering stylistic and iconographic elements from late antiquity, it becomes firm and essential. The outcome is a plastic vision based on the dialectic relationship between figure and background. Two other master sculptors were working at the Cathedral of Modena at the same time as Wiligelmo or not long afterward. One, whose panels depict monsters and contorted figures that seem to evoke ancient Greek sculpture, is known as the Master of the Metopes; the other, known as the Arthur Master, carved the Breton cycle on the Peschiera portal for the first time anywhere south of the Alps.

In Emilia, the leading sculptor who continued the strongly expressive style of these Modena masters was Nicolaus. His name appears in an inscription on the Zodiac Portal leading to Sagra di San Michele in Val di Susa (near Turin). This was probably the first sculptural work by this direct continuer of Wiligelmo's style. Although the iconographic subject came from the French tradition and the work reflects to a degree the language then in vogue in the Toulouse region, Wiligelmo's influence is easy to see. Not long after (ca. 1135), Nicolaus's name reappears in an inscription on the reliefs on the portal of the Cathedral of Ferrara and in a lunette depicting the battle between St. George and the dragon. Still more significant was his work in Verona. His scenes from Genesis on the main portal of the Church of San Zeno and the figures of prophets on the doorposts (1138–41) show the mature artist leaning more toward painterly lines and modeling.

The contemporary sculptural decorations on the portal of the Cathedral of Piacenza (1122–30), the door posts of Cremona Cathedral, and certain sculptures and bas-reliefs in Lodi (near Milan) and Castell'Arquato (near Piacenza) are all close in style to the teachings of Wiligelmo and Nicolaus and show a common language developing along the Po Valley in the first half of the 12th century. The analogies with French Romanesque sculpture were coming closer and closer, partly through direct knowledge of the originals and partly because the new language had taken root on both sides of the Alps.

At the zenith of Romanesque culture in the Po Valley, and nearly at the point of the transition to Gothic, stands the celebrated architect and sculptor Benedetto Antelami. His relations with French art, specifically Provençal, must have been quite close. His name—which probably refers to the construction craftsmen known as Magistri Antelami from their origin in the Intelvi Valley (Como)—is recorded in a Latin inscription on a marble panel in Parma Cathedral depicting the Deposition (1178). What is most striking is the rigidity and Byzantine-like rhythm of the figures to the right of Christ and the more dynamic composition to the left of the cross. The figures have an altogether new plastic sense never attained before in Romanesque sculpture. Likewise, in the decoration of the facade of Fidenza Cathedral designed by Antelami (1180–90), how the Lombard-Emilian tradition evolved under the Classical influence of Byzantine art is evident. But it is back in Parma, at the end of the 12th century, that the most significant developments in this evolutionary process are evident in the decoration of the baptistery. In the stories from the Old and New Testament depicted in the portal reliefs, the Provençal influence, as well as a strong affinity with Gothic sculptures on Chartres Cathedral's Royal Portal, is recognizable. Still more distant from the Romanesque tradition are the personifications, carved by Antelami and his assistants, of the months and the seasons inside the baptistery. These works, evincing the now irresistible striving toward sculpture in the round and a naturalistic treatment of bodies and drapery, anticipate the basic elements of 13th-century Italian sculpture. This is why the figure of Antelami is decisive for an understanding of the origins of Gothic sculpture in Italy.

In many respects, Venice was cut off from sculptural developments in northern Italy and constitutes a separate case. Facing east since its origin, the city was enhanced with a huge quantity of ancient artifacts, especially after the Fourth Crusade and the sack of Constantinople in 1204. In the central portal of St. Mark's Basilica, built and decorated between 1230 and 1240 by artists in contact with Antelami's shop, the strong influence of the Byzantine Classical style is notable. More precisely, the portal is a singular blend of Po Valley Romanesque, French Gothic, and Byzantine Classicism. Its closest cognates are in southern Italy in the portals of the Cathedral of St. Nicolas in Bari and in the sculptural decoration of the cathedrals of Troia and Trani.

In Tuscany local sculpture in the second half of the 12th century was influenced by both the Lombard-Emilian Romanesque tradition and Provençal art. In Pisa—then one of the most important ports in the Mediterranean—contacts with the Byzantine east were the most authoritative source of inspiration. Moreover, the almost exclusive use of marble quarried in the nearby Apuan Alps led to a different approach to stylistic and technical developments than in northern Italy. Sculpture produced south of the Apennines (the mountain chain that separates Tuscany from Emilia) shows practically no interest at all in the fledgling Gothic style of northern Europe; rather, it manifests a stylistic evolution that is based on an increasing virtuosity in working marble. This was the setting in which Byzantine models, and oriental models in general, came into play. Thus the pulpit carved by the master sculptor Guglielmo between 1159 and 1162 for the Cathedral of Pisa (now in the Cathedral of Cagliari) starts from Lombard-Provençal premises but develops in a style closely related to the east. In particular, the two *Lions* that probably supported the rectangular pulpit seem to draw on Asiatic models. The Byzantine style is still more explicit in the reliefs of the eastern portal of the Pisa baptistery (*ca.* 1200). The same attention to detail reappears in the pulpit of San Bartolomeo in Pantano in Pistoia (1235–50), a work by Guido da Como, a Lombard sculptor who operated in Tuscany.

The bronze doors cast by Bonanno Pisano for the Cathedral of Pisa likewise highlight the Byzantine influence in this region. Indeed, the technique of casting large bronzes developed from oriental traditions and spread widely in the 11th and 12th centuries. The main door Bonanno executed in 1180 was destroyed in a 16th-century fire, but the San Ranieri door, in the transept, survives. In the biblical stories it depicts, strongly plastic figures emerge from the background, maintaining a balanced relationship between full and empty spaces, and they are successfully harmonized with the explanatory inscriptions on each panel. Besides references to Byzantine iconography, one notes references to ancient Roman sarcophagi present in Pisa. Bonanno also worked in Monreale, Sicily. As a matter of fact, for some time cities throughout central and southern Italy had been importing many bronze doors directly from Constantinople to decorate important cathedrals, including those of Amalfi, Trioa, Benevento, and Salerno.

Between the 12th and 13th centuries, it was precisely in southern Italy that the taste for the antique gained the most ground. This appears clear from a long series of pulpits and ambos: the ambo of the Cathedral of Salerno (late 12th century)—which combines Classical forms with oriental decorative elements—and the pulpits in the cathedrals of Bitonto, Santa Restituta in Naples, and Sessa Aurunca. Here the reprise of the antique was not only formal, because Classical subjects (such as the figure removing a thorn from his foot, which was taken from a Roman sarcophagus) appear alongside motifs inspired by the theme of the Three Graces or the Ages of Man. But it was above all in

Sicily that the Classical taste was advancing in those years, such as in the splendid, carved-stone paschal candlestick in the Palatine Chapel in Palermo (12th century) and the two slightly later *telamons* supporting King Ruggero's tomb in the Cathedral of Palermo. But the most significant recovery of the Antique is found in the Cathedral of Monreale, where the inside columns were topped with reused Roman capitals carved with busts of matrons, and—as if to put the new language to the test and demonstrate its potential—the same figures were reinterpreted in the Romanesque style on a capital in the cloister. Other capitals and small columns are closely related to motifs on late Roman sarcophagi, and the whole sculptural complex of the Cathedral of Monreale appears to be a free Romanesque interpretation of ancient models.

Analyzing the sculpture—more than the architecture and painting—of this period, it is possible to see the reach of 13th-century artistic innovations in Italy. In the first half of the century, sculpture seems to have been dominated by two different approaches. In the Po Valley it developed along the lines indicated by Wiligelmo, Nicolaus, and Antelami and adorned Emilian, Lombard, Venetian, and Piedmont architecture with an increasingly vibrant naturalism. In southern Italy, a great architectonic-plastic movement destined to renovate the whole of Italian art ripened during the reign of Frederick II of Hohenstaufen before it moved north.

Among the most felicitous expressions of Po Valley sculpture during this period are the *Dream* and the *Adoration of the Magi* in the lunette over the portal at S. Mercuriale in Forlì and the *Months* on the south side of the Cathedral of Ferrara. Because of their arrangement, the high-relief figures in the Forlì lunette recall the carved tympana of the great Gothic cathedrals in France. Likewise, the Ferrara reliefs present bodies that manage to move despite the very limited architectonic space. The humanity and familiarity of these compositions has led some to think of them as late works by Antelami, but the strongly naturalistic imprint shows that the Romanesque representational root has already transmuted into a Gothic outcome.

Especially interesting for gaining an understanding of the definitions of Romanesque and Gothic art and analyzing the gradual transition from one style to the other are the developments of sculptural language in central and southern Italy. Despite the stumpy figures and the thick drapery that denote a fully Romanesque style, the group of *St. Martin and the Beggar* on the facade of Lucca Cathedral (*ca.* 1233) is important for its obvious reprise of Classical models such as the *Marcus Aurelius* group on the Capitol in Rome, as well as for the nearly true proportions of the figures. In this context, the production of sculptures no longer in stone but in wood, especially in Tuscany and Campania, displayed a new interest in three-dimensional analysis of the human figure and growing attention to naturalistic detail, such as in the marvelous *Deposition* groups, including the ones in the cathedrals of Tivoli and Volterra, the latter with its polychrome painting nearly intact. The wooden statues are in natural scale and present themselves in dramatic poses, each independent of the other but forming as a whole a strongly suggestive group. The polychrome painting only increases their realism: the statues appear to be decked in precious garments and thus represent the personages of this scene from the Passion as contemporary believers were invited to imagine it.

Gothic *ca.* Early 13th Century

Still more significant is the development of southern sculpture during the cultural renaissance promoted during the reign of Frederick II of Hohenstaufen under the banner of the rediscovery of Antiquity. In Campania and Apulia, the new sculptural choices were related to architectural monuments such as the Capua Gate, which was evidently modeled on Classical triumphal arches and is crowned by a bust of Frederick II (*ca.* 1239). In its ambition, this monument reflects that of the new style, which is also found in a capital (Metropolitan Museum of Art, New York City) that probably comes from the Cathedral of Troia and in the *telamons* of Castel del Monte (*ca.* 1240). In this reprise of Classical models, the naturalistic faces, with their flowing hair and beards and carefully studied anatomy, so closely resemble decorative elements dating from around the same time in Reims as to suggest that French artists were working in Apulia during the period of Frederick II. In the ideological project of reconstructing the empire, ancient culture was revisited in part for the wealth of details it had reproduced in stone.

This was the cultural environment in which Nicola Pisano came of age. Born in the south, "Nicola de Apulia" moved to Pisa in the second half of the 13th century and soon received commissions in the major artistic cities of Tuscany, Perugia, and Bologna. Pisano diffused the Frederican artistic style beyond southern Italy, which marked a radical transformation of the spectrum of Italian sculpture, and it was hardly by coincidence that Pisa was the place where the new sculptural language came to maturity. Roman antiquities had been recovered there for a century, so Pisano was able to copy and study the numerous sarcophagi grouped outside the cathedral. In these marbles he found the elements he needed to enrich his language. The pulpit of the Pisa baptistery (1255–60), his first signed and dated work, is a true masterpiece and well represents the moment of transition from Romanesque to Gothic.

The hexagonal pulpit renews the usually rectangular structure of earlier pulpits. It is supported by six columns, every other one of which rests on the back of a lion according to the Romanesque tradition. The trilobe arches, the capitals surmounted by personifications of the Virtues, and the pinnacles ensconcing prophets and evangelists are all fully Gothic elements, but it is above all in the reliefs on five sides of the parapet, separated by triple columns and representing the traditional iconographic scenes (Nativity, Adoration, Presentation, Crucifixion, and Last Judgment), that Pisano handled his subjects in a powerful style that brings the marble to life.

The pulpit in Siena Cathedral (1265–69), where Pisano's assistants included his son Giovanni, shows a more controlled classicism than its Pisan predecessor and a stronger influence of French Gothic. All of Pisano's work constituted a refined blend of Classical and Byzantine traditions with Romanesque and Gothic, a junction between the Mediterranean area and northern Europe, and a mediation between the two languages that developed a style of their own in Italy from the 11th to the 13th centuries. The drama and truth incorporated in Pisano's marbles are ancient in their Classical precedents yet modern in taking up the contemporary naturalism of European Gothic sculpture. A new horizon thus opened up for all of Italian art. Pisano's style had enduring influence thanks to his numerous disciples, especially his son Giovanni and Arnolfo di Cambio, who furthered the master's work into the full flower of the Gothic style.

LORENZO CARLETTI

See also **Antelami, Benedetto; Arnolfo di Cambio; Guido da Como; Pisano, Giovanni; Pisano, Nicola; Wiligelmo**

Further Reading

Avril, François, Xavier Barral i Altet, and Danielle Gaborit-Chopin, *Le temps de Croisades*, Paris: Gallimard, 1982

Bony, Jean, " 'Transition' from Romanesque to Gothic: Introduction," in *Romanesque and Gothic Art*, Princeton, New Jersey: Princeton University Press, 1963

Carli, Enzo, *La scultura lignea italiana dal XII al XVI secolo*, Milan: Electa Editrice, 1960; 2nd edition, 1961

Castelnuovo, Enrico (editor), *Niveo de marmore: L'uso artistico del marmo di Carrara dall' XI al XV secolo*, Genoa, Italy: Edizioni Colombo, 1992

Crichton, George Henderson, *Romanesque Sculpture in Italy*, London: Routledge and Paul, 1954

Glass, Dorothy F., *Italian Romanesque Sculpture: An Annotated Bibliography*, Boston, Massachusetts: G.K. Hall, 1983

Pope-Hennessy, John, *An Introduction to Italian Sculpture*, 3 vols., London: Phaidon, 1963; 4th edition, 1996; see especially vol. 1, *Italian Gothic Sculpture*

Schapiro, Meyer, *Romanesque Art*, New York: Braziller, 1977

Williamson, Paul, *Gothic Sculpture, 1140–1300*, New Haven, Connecticut: Yale University Press, 1995

Williamson, Paul (editor), *Catalogue of Romanesque Sculpture*, London: Victoria and Albert Museum, 1983

ITALY: RENAISSANCE–BAROQUE

Early Renaissance *ca.* 1400–1480

The long, curving lines of the Late Gothic style combined with the Classical styles of Greek and Roman Antiquity, together with other cross-currents, eventually led to the Italian Renaissance, which was based on a revival of interest in the sculptures of Classical Antiquity and united with the development of the sciences in a new endeavor to represent nature.

Early Renaissance sculpture existed almost entirely in relation to church architecture, supplying statues and reliefs both for exterior decoration and internally for tomb monuments and altars. An immense program of work on the new cathedral, bell tower, and baptistery in Florence during the 14th and 15th centuries provided opportunities for a gifted new generation of sculptors, including Nanni di Banco, Filippo Brunelleschi, Lorenzo Ghiberti, and Donatello. The form in which the Renaissance style first emerged was the narrative relief, the consequence of a competition in 1401 to design a pair of monumental bronze doors for the baptistery of the new Florence Cathedral. Ghiberti created his winning relief panel, *The Sacrifice of Isaac*, for the north doors of the baptistery in the elegant, richly decorative style of the Late Gothic. The panel is remarkable for its superlative craftsmanship, fluency of narrative design, and realism of detail, as well as the Classical reference in the torso of the young Isaac.

The force for change came during the first decade of the 15th century from Donatello, one of the young Florentine sculptors in Ghiberti's workshop, who was developing a new and expressive style through a reassessment of Classical remains. The first clear signs of this new style appear in Donatello's marble statue of *St. John the Evangelist* (1408–15), which exchanges the swaying and attenuated Gothic figure type for a massive seated figure whose flowing beard and intensity of expression create a new and majestic monumentality.

The next important stage in the development of the freestanding figure in Italy was the decoration of the exterior niches of the market hall (later church) of Orsanmichele, Florence, with statues of the guilds' patron saints. Ghiberti's figures, such as the *St. John the Baptist* (1413–14), are still in the Gothic tradition but are the first monumental statues of this new era in sculpture to be cast in bronze. Donatello's marble armorclad *St. George* (1416–17) was the first to express the states of the soul and actions of the mind through the representation of the movements of the body. Through his earlier association with the architect Filippo Brunelleschi, Donatello had been involved in the application of the new discovery of linear perspective, and for his marble relief of *St. George and the Dragon* (*ca.* 1415–20) beneath his statue, he employed a novel mixture of linear perspective and atmospheric relief, an almost flat relief style (*schiacciato*) whose ethereal effect depends for its recession on a progressive softening of contour. His gilt-bronze relief of *The Feast of Herod* for the font in the baptistery at Pisa (1423–25) creates a dramatic scene that observes the basic rules of linear perspective.

Realism in Donatello's style led him toward portraiture, and he may have provided the bronze effigy of the deceased in his collaboration with the sculptor Michelozzo on the tomb monument of the Antipope John XXIII (*ca.* 1421–28) in the Florence baptistery, which set the format of the 15th-century tomb in Tuscany and Rome. In 1443 Donatello received the opportunity to rival the ancients in the creation of a bronze equestrian monument to the condottiere Erasmus de' Narni, known as *Gattamelata* (1447–53). Other key works include his bronze *David* (*ca.* 1455), the first freestanding, life-size nude statue of the Renaissance, and his statuary and reliefs for the high altar of the Basilica of Sant'Antonio, Padua (1444–49).

Donatello's absence from Florence enabled a very different sculptural style to flower from the mixture of Gothic lyricism and Classical realism of Ghiberti. The earliest significant works in this style are Luca Della Robbia's marble reliefs for *The Singing Gallery* (1428–38) for Florence Cathedral. The sturdy figures of his children reveal Luca's study of Classical sculpture as well as of the ornamental Gothic style of the musician angels of the Porta della Mandorla (1391–*ca.* 1423) by Nanni di Banco on the north side of the cathedral. From the 1440s the workshop of the Rossellino brothers, Bernardo and Antonio, produced elegant and classicizing sculpture of high technical proficiency, mainly for tomb monuments designed by Bernardo, such as the tomb of Leonardo Bruni (1446–48), which harmoniously combines architecture and sculpture and demonstrates his understanding of the Classical vocabulary. The best works of Desiderio da Settignano, a master of the art of carving marble, are in a low-relief style similar to Donatello's atmospheric reliefs, eschewing the latter's expressive vitality for an extreme refinement, sensitivity, and textural appeal. Desiderio's portrait busts of women are, like those of the Dalmatian Francesco Laurana, the most abstracted and spiritual expressions of this genre. With Desiderio's early death, the great era of marble sculpture in 15th-century Florence came to an end, but the work of Benedetto da Maiano bridged the gap until its revival with Andrea Sansovino and the young Michelangelo in the 1490s.

Andrea del Verrocchio, like Donatello, excelled in the casting of bronze; its malleability allowed him to advance the boundaries of dramatic narrative, anatomical movement, and emotional expression in every type of statuary. His greatest masterpiece, the bronze group of the *Incredulity of Thomas* (completed 1483) for the Church of Orsanmichele, Florence, was the most influential early example of a two-figure group in which the figures, through their expressive faces, movements, and gestures, enact an emotionally and spiritually profound drama within the small theater of the niche. In another important development, Verrocchio created the bronze fountain statue of a *Putto with a Dolphin* (*ca.* 1470) in Florence's Palazzo Vecchio to be seen from multiple viewpoints instead of the traditional single frontal viewpoint. Verrocchio's final great work was the equestrian monument to Bartolomeo Colleoni (1480–88). Dressed in contemporary armor, Verrocchio's figure divorces the equestrian monument from its Classical origins and prefigures its Baroque descendants.

Verrocchio's main rival in Florence was Antonio Pollaiuolo, whose iconographic and formal innovations may best be observed in his bronze tomb of Pope Sixtus IV (*ca.* 1484–93). His small bronze group of *Hercules and Antaeus* (1475), which demonstrates his understanding both of anatomy and of the dynamics of a group in violent action, pointed the way to Giambologna's action groups in the 16th century. Leonardo da Vinci entered Verrocchio's workshop about 1469 and was profoundly affected by his experience during the modeling of the Colleoni horse, but his own two projects for equestrian monuments, the *Francesco Sforza* and the *Giangiacomo Trivulzio*, were never carried out and are known only through his drawings. Certain works by Giovanni Francesco Rustici reflect Leonardo's unfinished mural of the *Battle of Anghiari*, such as Rustici's small terracotta groups of *Fighting Horsemen*, important as precursors of the dramatic action group, and in the monumental bronze group of *St. John the Baptist Preaching* (1506–11) over the north door of Florence Baptistery, which was, according to Giorgio Vasari, executed to Leonardo's design and under his close supervision.

The Sienese Jacopo della Quercia's style was transitional, moving via the Late Romanesque style of Nicola Pisano to a reappraisal of Classical Antiquity. His best-known works are the marble tomb monument of Ilaria del Carretto (1405–08) in Lucca Cathedral, the two bronze reliefs for Ghiberti's baptismal font (1427–30) for the Baptistery of Siena Cathedral, and stone reliefs and statuary for the *Porta Magna* of the Church of S. Petronio, Bologna (1425–30). In Siena, Donatello's style influenced the works of Lorenzo di Pietro, known as Il Vecchietta, and Francesco di Giorgio. In Padua, Bartolomeo Bellano proved himself a master of the pictorial relief in a remarkable series in the Santo. His pupil Andrea Riccio made Padua a center for a new genre, the bronze statuette, intended for the humanist scholar's study, poetically reinterpreting pagan themes in the spirit of antiquity.

In Venice the prolonged influence of Byzantine art in the first half of the 15th century delayed the development of a native school, and sculptors from outside the city came to supply its needs. Pietro Lombardo supplied much of Venice's sculptural requirements in the second half of the 15th century and transformed the Tuscan tomb monument into a Venetian style. The distinctive work of the Veronese Antonio Rizzo reveals his study of antique statuary. From the 1490s Pietro Lombardo's sons, Tullio and Antonio, led the family workshop, creating a Venetian interpretation of Classical models wholly different from that of their Florentine contemporaries. Tullio designed the architecture and sculpture of the Cappella dell'Arca di S. Antonio, which was refurbished with a series of nine monumental marble reliefs illustrating the *Miracles of St. Anthony* (*ca.* 1500–32); he is best known for a series of mysterious marble reliefs of bust-length portraits of young couples reflecting the poetic mood of contemporary Venetian paintings of themes from Classical mythology. Antonio Lombardo decorated the private apartments of Alfonso I d'Este, Duke of Ferrara, with a fascinating series of marble reliefs, some mythological, whose learned and esoteric themes imply close collaboration with the Duke's artistic advisers.

High Renaissance *ca.* 1480–1530

In response to rediscovered antiquities in Rome, a strong Classical idealization reappeared in the sculptures of Andrea Sansovino, whose mastery both as designer and carver of marble set new standards. His early works are still deeply rooted in the earlier traditions of Ghiberti and Donatello, but his later works—suave, elegantly designed, and technically refined—exhibit complete conversance with the Classical canons of anatomical proportion and pose. In his marble group of the *Virgin and Child with St. Anne* (1512), inspired by Leonardo da Vinci's cartoon of the same subject (1501), the face and hair of the Virgin clearly derive from antique Roman portraits, but the composition and drapery patterns still relate to the early 15th century. Although famed for his narrative reliefs, Andrea Sansovino's most significant contribution to High Renaissance sculpture came in the genre of the tomb monument, where he harmoniously integrated architecture and sculpture.

Michelangelo's modern reputation has obscured the activity of other important sculptors of his generation in Florence. Chief of these was Jacopo Sansovino, trained in the late 15th-century style of Andrea Sansovino (no relation). Jacopo Sansovino would become the dominant figure in Venetian architecture and sculpture from 1527 to his death in 1570. He acquired a Classical manner in Rome but returned to Florence around 1510, where he created his sinuously composed marble *Bacchus* (1510–11), designed to be studied from several viewpoints. Like Michelangelo's *Bacchus* (ca. 1496–98), it is one of the earliest and most successful attempts by sculptors to rival and even surpass the ancients not only in complexity of design but in anatomical control that enables a greater flexibility of movement, which in turn enhances the statue's expressive qualities.

Michelangelo's genius cast a shadow over a generation of sculptors awed by his seemingly superhuman qualities. Popes and princes offered him great sculptural projects, but unusually, Michelangelo had no large workshop under his direction; his sculpture achieved its extraordinary quality because he carried out almost everything from block to finish himself. Michelangelo's first public success, the marble *Pietà* (1497–99) in St. Peter's Basilica, Rome, demonstrates a new degree of technical excellence and compositional subtlety. His work shows a 15th-century love of detail in the precise chiseling of the Verrocchiesque features and complexity of drapery folds, but his dazzling technical bravura in the carving of intractable marble also anticipates the Baroque of Bernini. Michelangelo's colossal marble statue of *David* (1501–04) shows his ability to express the higher emotions or spiritual states through the nude body, an ability expressed most movingly in the *Times of Day* (*Night*, *Day*, *Dawn*, and *Dusk*) (1526–31), his four marble reclining tomb figures symbolizing the principle of time in the new sacristy of the Church of San Lorenzo, Florence, and the uncompleted statues of *Slaves* created for the tomb monument of Pope Julius II. A *Victory* group (1520s) for the Julius tomb demonstrates the expression of action or power in a serenely poised and elegant pose. Here, Michelangelo created a sculpture of multiple viewpoints whose pyramidal composition, combined with the sinuous *figura serpentinata*, proved highly influential.

In 1527 Jacopo Sansovino moved to Venice, where his Classical manner made him Tullio Lombardo's natural heir. The casting of Verrocchio's Colleoni monument in the 1480s had revived interest in bronze sculpture in Venice, and Sansovino also worked in this medium. The most important sculptures of Sansovino's Venetian period include his four bronze statues (1537–40) for his Loggetta (the civic building that housed the offices of the Venetian Republic) in the Piazza S. Marco, which introduced the Roman High Renaissance ideal of integrated sculptural and architectural forms. The *Apollo* synthesizes Classicism with the elegant attenuated Gothic of Ghiberti and the sinuous grace of Roman Mannerism, anticipating the Mannerist style of Florence. The carving of a colossal standing figure in marble to compare with the fabled colossi of Antiquity was considered the sculptor's highest task, and Sansovino's design for his stone colossus of *Neptune* (1554–67) for the Giants' Staircase of the Palazzo Ducale in Venice reveals the influence of Michelangelo.

Mannerism *ca.* 1530–1600

Guided by their sense of the development or improvement of art, the artists of the Renaissance had eventually created a canon of the art and a system they believed would produce such art; Mannerist art deviates from this Classical canon. Sculptors and patrons alike generally believed that Michelangelo had attained a perfection impossible to surpass, yet his nude figure sculptures often defied the Classical proportions and compositional clarity of the High Renaissance. Vasari wrote of the *maniera* of Michelangelo, and the term *mannerism* has since remained to refer to the range of styles of artists who came to maturity during and after the lifetimes of Michelangelo and Raphael. Michelangelo's use of *contrapposto*, (a natural pose with the weight of one leg, the shoulder, and hips counterbalancing one another), which he learned from studying Classical sculpture, combined with a sinuous silhouette, formed an essential part of the Mannerist sculptor's repertory. A distinction may be made between the evolutionary "anticlassicist" and the consciously "revolutionary" Mannerist sculptor: many of Michelangelo's admirers, misunderstanding his essential qualities, tried to compete with him on a technical level or to outdo his compositions in complexity, often producing effects that have a disturbing, even bizarre, beauty of their own. They believed themselves, however, to be exploring what was to them a new canon of art rather than consciously deviating from the old, although the latter was what in practice often occurred.

The foremost anticlassicist Mannerist sculptor in Florence was Baccio Bandinelli. Benvenuto Cellini derided his colossal marble group of *Hercules and Cacus* (1525–34) as "a bag of melons" for its emphatic musculature, but Bandinelli's bronze statuettes have a preternatural beauty. Michelangelo had combined the representation of movement in sculpture with a multi-viewpoint design in his *Bacchus*, and later Giambologna would succeed in combining this with the suggestion of flight in his *Mercury* (1581). Michelangelo's ability to convey spiritual states, often in combination with active poses, was beyond the powers of most admirers, and many returned to the cool Classicism of Andrea Sansovino. Not so Vincenzo de' Rossi, whose series of the *Labors of Hercules* (1561–87) in violent action is deflated by their emotional vacuity. His marble group of *Theseus Abducting Helen* (1558–60), however, became a prototype for the two-figure groups developed by the 17th-century followers of Giambologna. Pierino da Vinci's marble group of *Samson Conquers a Philistine* (1550–52) is a distinguished variation of Michelangelo's *Victory* (1532–34).

After the Sack of Rome in 1527 the sculptural focus had returned to Florence, and the accession of Duke Alessandro de' Medici in 1530 began a long period of Medici patronage. From this time to Bartolomeo Ammanati's return in 1555, many sculptors and styles flourished in Florence; of these the most interesting were Francesco da Sangallo, Niccolò Tribolo, and Pierino da Vinci. Among the Florentine sculptors who produced interesting work mainly elsewhere was Giovanni Angelo Montorsoli, but the most important of these was Florentine goldsmith and sculptor Cellini, whom Duke Cosimo I de' Medici commissioned to carry out the statue of *Perseus and Medusa* (1545–54), the most important civic statue since Michelangelo's *David* and a classic of the new multiviewpoint figure style. In contrast to the statue's comparatively realistic anatomy, Cellini's statuettes for its base introduced into Florentine bronze sculpture the smoothly abstracted, elongated, often androgynous, and coldly elegant figure style he had acquired from the stucco ornamentation of Fontainebleau by Rosso Fiorentino and others, combined with his refined goldsmith's finish. Of Cellini's assistants on the *Perseus* project, Francesco Ferrucci del Tadda, Domenico Poggini, and Stoldo and Battista Lorenzi became significant figures in the artistic life of Medici Florence.

During the 1550s the artistic environment of Florence underwent radical change: Vasari settled in Florence in 1553 and dominated the artistic life of the city thenceforth, and three more highly important sculptors arrived, two already established—Ammanati and Vincenzo Danti—and the young Flemish student Giambologna. Ammanati, a substantial artist, created coolly classicizing, strong-limbed, and stylish figures imbued with a subtly restless quality of movement. In 1527 he joined Jacopo Sansovino in Venice, and his Paduan sculpture retained a substratum of his Venetian training, eventually amalgamated in his sculptures for the Medici court in Florence with the influence of Michelangelo. The citizens of Florence nicknamed Ammanati's handsome but lifeless colossal marble statue of *Neptune*, surmounting his public fountain (*ca.* 1560–75) in the same square, "the big white fellow,"

unable to avoid comparison with the emotional charge of Michelangelo's nearby *David*.

Born in Perugia, Danti trained as a goldsmith and metal caster and learned to carve marble expertly. His marble group of *Honor Triumphant over Falsehood* (1561), another emulation of Michelangelo's *Victory* group, is among his finest work. *Honor* reflects the effortless action and calm detachment of Michelangelo's group, but the contortions of *Falsehood* outdo those of Cellini's *Medusa*. Danti is perhaps best known for his monumental bronze group of the *Beheading of St. John the Baptist* placed over the south portal of the Florentine Baptistery in 1571.

After Cosimo I's retirement from political life in 1564 in favor of Prince Francesco (Duke Francesco I from 1574), the elegant, artificial style perfected by Cellini came back into fashion and dominated international court taste for the rest of the century. Giambologna became court sculptor to Francesco I and his successors from the 1550s. He followed his sound Flemish formation by studying the Antique and then Michelangelo, but his admiration for the sophisticated style and fine finish of Cellini's bronze works also reflects his appreciation of the school of Fontainebleau. Giambologna based the composition of his first Medici commission, *Samson Conquers a Philistine*, on a model by Michelangelo, using a pyramidal format and helical design combined with an active but emotionally restrained mood. Giambologna preferred bronze for the compositional flexibility it permitted and because it allowed him to give his models to a well-trained workshop to cast and finish. In this medium he produced his great equestrian monuments, colossal statues, and religious statuary and reliefs. He created large bronze statuettes and also revived the genre of the small bronze statuette in Florence. He made some small and larger statuettes for the Medici court as diplomatic gifts but made many more in partnership with the goldsmith Antonio Susini for sale to collectors; the dispersal of these statuettes disseminated the Florentine Mannerist court style throughout Europe. During and after Giambologna's lifetime, his closest associates—including Pietro Tacca, who inherited his workshop, Pietro's son Ferdinando Tacca, and Antonio Susini and his nephew Giovanfrancesco Susini—continued to produce fine versions of these statuettes and to perpetuate his style. Other sculptors of significance in this era in Florence included Rodolfo Sirigatti and the Roman Giovanni Caccini.

In Venice, Alessandro Vittoria, Jacopo Sansovino's pupil and collaborator, was the most distinguished sculptor working in the second half of the 16th century. His marble statue of *St. Sebastian* (*ca.* 1590) reveals an assimilation of Michelangelo, Hellenistic sculpture, and Sansovino into a distinctive personal style. Some of Vittoria's most beautiful designs, for example a *Neptune*, are in bronze statuette form. Other prominent sculptors of this period include Tiziano Aspetti, Girolamo Campagna, Danese Cattaneo, and Nicolò Roccatagliata.

Baroque *ca.* 1600–1750

A new era of opportunity for sculptors opened at the beginning of the 17th century. In Rome, after the Council of Trent, the popes and the great religious orders recognized the power of art to propagate the Counter Reformation, and elsewhere absolutist rulers likewise perceived its value as a propaganda tool. The Roman Catholic Church demanded a new clarity of form and narrative for biblical themes and the lives of saints (which reflected artists' own nostalgia for the certainties of the High Renaissance after the diversity of Mannerism) and a new emphasis on the ecstatic joy of religious experience and the scenographic combination of architecture, painting, sculpture, color, and light. Sculptors received unprecedented opportunities for grand spectacle, and they expanded sculpture's formal language according to the demands of their new tasks and themes. Two styles evolved, one represented by Gianlorenzo Bernini and another, quieter style, reflecting contemporary French classical painting, represented by François du Quesnoy and Alessandro Algardi. By the end of the century a prevailing distaste for the excesses of the High Baroque had engendered a new sense of decorum and restraint and a modified reprise of earlier Classicism. The Baroque style nevertheless lingered in Italian sculpture until the arrival of Neoclassicism around the mid 18th century.

The artist synonymous with the Baroque style is Bernini, but the first sculptor to break new ground was the Tuscan Francesco Mochi, whose dynamic, pictorial, and highly expressive style came from the Venetian tradition through his teacher Camillo Mariani. The fundamental characteristics of the Baroque are already present in his first important work, a marble *Annunciation* group (*ca.* 1603–09) for the Cathedral of Orvieto. Stefano Maderno's unorthodox compositional solutions also made him a precursor of the Baroque. His marble statue of *St. Cecilia* (1599–1600), which touchingly represents the body of the young woman lying on her side just as she was found, was a new and dramatic form of realism that would inspire Bernini's own representations of female saints.

No artist before or after Bernini created so many projects on so large a scale, but Bernini managed a vast workshop in Rome that included substantial independent sculptors, as well as a host of technicians. His most dazzling theatrical spectacle, the Cornaro Chapel in the Church of Santa Maria della Vittoria in Rome (1647–52), contains his marble group of *The Ecstasy of St. Teresa*. The *Pluto and Proserpine* reveals that Bernini understood the dynamics of Giambologna's *Rape of a Sabine* (1582), but Bernini's desire to present his own groups as theatrical tableaux favors only one viewpoint, and his attraction to genrelike naturalism and illusionistic detail undermines its heroic mood. These characteristics become virtues, however, in his tableau of *Apollo and Daphne* (1622–24).

The Bolognese Alessandro Algardi, who arrived in Rome in 1625, followed a comparatively traditional line of development, working predominantly in marble for private patrons. His style, in which Classical and Mannerist influences moderate the Baroque of Bernini, is demonstrated in his masterpiece, an over-life-size marble group of the *Beheading of St. Paul* (1634–48). Algardi's reliefs initiated a new fashion for the decoration of the aristocratic chapel with his richly detailed and exquisitely finished marble relief of *Pope Leo Driving Attila from Rome* (1646–53). Algardi's works were mainly collaborative projects (his best-known assistants were Michel Anguier and Domenico Guidi), and he shared with Bernini the services of sculptors such as Ercole Ferrata and Antonio Raggi. Camillo Rusconi, Melchiorre Caffà, Pierre Legros the Younger, and Edmé Bouchardon also perpetuated his style.

The calm, sweet-tempered Classicism of the Fleming du Quesnoy allied him with Algardi's version of High Baroque sculpture. He created two influential marble statues in Rome, the *St. Susanna* (1629–33) and *St. Andrew* (1629–40). Du Quesnoy was equally known and appreciated for his two bronze statuettes made about 1630–40 for Vincenzo Giustiniani (a *Mercury* and an *Apollo*); they demonstrate a sophisticated reinterpretation of antique statuary mediated through the style and finish of the Giambologna school.

Intellectually gifted sculptors such as Melchiorre Caffà from Malta assimilated and built upon the ideas of Bernini and Algardi. Among the most technically gifted of Bernini's assistants was the Lombard Antonio Raggi, whose stucco statues of allegorical figures in the Church of the Gesù, Rome (1670s), and the life-size marble relief of *The Angel Announcing the Flight into Egypt to St. Joseph* (1671–81) demonstrate his reinterpretation of the fantasy and spirituality of Bernini's late style. Although Caffà's works are far fewer in number, they are artistically more important. The only work completed entirely by him is the marble relief of the *Ecstasy of St. Catherine of Siena* (1667), in which his swaying, ecstatic figure of St. Catherine reinvigorates the language of Bernini's fervidly religious late style. The ideas presented in Caffà's numerous models provided inspiration for Pierre Puget in Genoa and were more directly useful to the Lombard Ercole Ferrata, who came to Rome from the workshops of Cosimo Fanzago and Giuliano Finelli in Naples. Ferrata's association with Algardi and his classicizing direction had important implications for the Late Baroque out of proportion to his gifts: a new generation of sculptors trained in his workshop, and he was also artistic director of the neophytes of the new Florentine Academy in Rome. The tender, lyrical feeling of his marble statue of *Charity* for the tomb of Pope Clement IX (1671) represents him at his most sincere. After the Florentines, the most able of Ferrata's numerous students were Francesco Aprile and Michele Maglia. Of the other sculptors who assisted Algardi, Domenico Guidi became master of a busy studio and produced a body of distinguished work whose influence extended to the end of the 17th century and beyond. His style was not overly Classical—his monument to Cardinal Imperiali (*ca.* 1675) in the Church of Sant'Agostino, Rome, displays his lively imagination in this most extravagantly Berninesque of tombs—but other works show his taste for the academicism of Poussin, and he played much the same role for the French Academy in Rome (founded in 1666) as Ferrata did for the Florentines.

During the 1620s the Florentine artistic establishment, proud of its own traditions, reacted skeptically to the Roman innovations, but the preparations of Grand Duke Ferdinando II de' Medici for his 1637 wedding prompted a reversal of this policy, and the stylistically progressive Domenico Pieratti led the sculptors employed on the renovation and embellishment of Palazzo Pitti and the Boboli Gardens in Florence. Pieratti's theatrical marble statue of *Zeal for the Honor of God* (1635–42) reveals his pursuit of a Florentine Baroque style inspired by Hellenistic statuary and Michelangelo, but his statue of *St. John the Evangelist* (1640s) has the genrelike realism and naturalistic emotional mood of the early Bernini. These features reappear in the scenographic bronze two-figure statuette groups of Ferdinando Tacca in his highly individualized revision of the Mannerism of Giambologna. Grand Duke Cosimo III's establishment in 1673 of a branch of the Florentine Accademia del Disegno in Rome signaled a renewal of cultural policy. The academy was responsible for the blossoming of a Late Baroque style under the last Medici, providing the court with artists able to embellish their palaces and projects in the modern style while retaining artistic traditions peculiar to Florence. The prolific imagination and organizational ability of Giovanni Battista Foggini ensured his leading role at court; the more poetically gifted Massimiliano Soldani Benzi, appointed to the granducal mint, executed fine reliefs and statuary in bronze for the Grand Prince Ferdinando. Two other graduates of the Florentine Academy, Carlo Marcellini and Giuseppe Piamontini, also produced fine work.

In Genoa a wealthy and cultured patriciate provided important projects supporting an intense local artistic activity that attracted foreign artists of the importance of the painter Rubens. Here, too, the Baroque style arrived late, after Filippo Parodi, the most important Genoese sculptor of his day, returned home from Rome in 1661 with a graceful and vivacious sculptural style full of pictorial fantasy, as in his set of four marble garden statues (*ca.* 1680) representing subjects from Ovid's *Metamorphoses*, irreverently mingling references to Bernini and Poussin. Without aspiring to the heroic or sublime aspects of the Baroque style, Parodi was also influenced by the style of Pierre Puget, one of the greatest and most original sculptors of the Baroque era. The French-influenced Genoese Baroque idiom was to mingle with the styles of Bernini's later followers in Rome.

During the 16th century Naples was one of the capitals not only of Spanish south Italy but also of modern Europe. It is famous for its exuberant Baroque style, yet its principal sculptors were not native-born. Two Florentines, Michelangelo Naccherino and Pietro Bernini, supplied the style required by the Counter Reformation; they greatly influenced two other naturalized foreigners, Fanzago and Finelli, each representative of different schools of expression and who determined the character of Neapolitan Baroque sculpture. Fanzago's style was formed in Lombardy; his series of marble busts of Carthusian saints (1623–43) and marble statues of *David* and *The Prophet Jeremiah* (1637–ca. 6) display his high ability and idiosyncratic manner. Finelli, an extraordinarily gifted marble specialist from Carrara, began and ended his career in Naples, but in his Roman interlude, he contributed the most delicate details of Bernini's *Apollo and Daphne*. Among Finelli's finest works in Naples are a series of 13 bronze statues for the cathedral (1638–48). Local sculptors prominent in Naples included Lorenzo Vaccaro and Giandomenico Vinaccia.

The decoration of Andrea Pozzo's altar of St. Ignatius Loyola (1697–99) for the Church of the Gesù opened a new era for Roman sculpture. None of the younger sculptors was a follower of Bernini. Pierre Legros the Younger and Jean-Baptiste Théodon, who synthesized the classicizing manner approved by the French Academy with the influence of Caffà and Berninesque pictorialism, undertook the most important elements. The team also included Lorenzo Ottoni from the older generation and Angelo de' Rossi and Francesco Moratti from the new one. Another significant departure from the High Baroque style emerged in the *Apostles* (designed by Carlo Maratti) for the Basilica of San Giovanni in Laterano, Rome (1703–18), as executed by Camillo Rusconi, Legros, and Pierre Monnot. Two distinguished sculptors of the Late Baroque, the

Florentine Filippo della Valle and Pietro Bracci, shared artistic dominance of 18th-century Rome. Della Valle's most important work is the relief of the *Annunciation* (1750); Bracci's best-known work is the central figure of *Oceanus* (1759–62) for the Trevi fountain in Rome. The most splendid sculptural project of the mid 18th century in Naples is the ornamentation of the Cappella Samsevera for the Church of Santa Maria della Pietà dei Sangro (1749–66), which includes the Genoese Francesco Queirolo's marble *Allegory of Deception Unmasked* (1752–59), a work of dazzling technical bravura. The chapel also includes the marble statue of *Modesty* (*ca.* 1750), the most famous work of Antonio Corradini of Este, whose specialty was the veiled figure. Giuseppe Sanmartino also used the veiled figure to great dramatic effect in his macabre *Dead Christ* (1753). In Palermo the virtuoso stuccoist Giacomo Serpotta provided stupendous effects, as in stucco reliefs *The Battle of Lepanto* and *The Glorious Mysteries of the Rosary* (after 1688), where squadrons of cherubs support a vast cloth of honor.

ANTHEA BROOK

See also **Algardi, Alessandro; Ammanati, Bartolomeo; Aspetti, Tiziano; Benedetto da Maiano; Bernini, Gianlorenzo; Bernini, Pietro; Bouchardon, Edme; Bracci, Pietro; Caffà, Melchiorre; Campagna, Girolamo; Cellini, Benvenuto; Corradini, Antonio; Desiderio da Settignano; Donatello; du Quesnoy, François; Fanzago, Cosimo; Ferrata, Ercole; Finelli, Giuliano; Foggini, Giovanni Battista; Ghiberti, Lorenzo; Giambologna; Guidi, Domenico; Jacopo della Quercia; Laurana, Francesco; Legros II, Pierre; Leoni Family; Lombardo Family; Mochi, Francesco; Nanni di Banco; Parodi, Filippo; Pierino da Vinci; Pollaiuolo, Antonio; Riccio, Andrea; Robbia, Della, Family; Roccatagliata, Nicolò; Rossellino Family; Rossi, Vincenzo de'; Rusconi, Camillo; Rustici, Giovanni Francesco; Sanmartino, Giuseppe; Sansovino, Andrea; Sansovino, Jacopo; Serpotta, Giacomo; Soldani Benzi, Massimiliano; Susini, Antonio; Tacca Family; Tribolo, Niccolò; Valle, Filippo della; Vecchietta (Lorenzo di Pietro); Verrocchio, Andrea del; Vittoria, Alessandro**

Further Reading

Avery, Charles, *Florentine Renaissance Sculpture*, London: Murray, and New York: Harper and Row, 1970

Avery, Charles, *Giambologna: The Complete Sculpture*, Oxford: Phaidon Christie's, and Mt. Kisco, New York: Moyer Bell, 1987

Avery, Charles, *Bernini: Genius of the Baroque*, London: Thames and Hudson, and Boston: Bulfinch, 1997

Boucher, Bruce, *The Sculpture of Jacopo Sansovino*, New Haven, Connecticut: Yale University Press, 1991

Boucher, Bruce, *Italian Baroque Sculpture*, London and New York: Thames and Hudson, 1998

Butterfield, Andrew, *The Sculptures of Andrea del Verrocchio*, New Haven, Connecticut: Yale University Press, 1997

Krahn, Volker (editor), *Von allen Seiten schön: Bronzen der Renaissance und des Barock: Wilhelm von Bode zum 150. Geburtstag* (exhib. cat.), Berlin: Edition Braus, 1995

Montagu, Jennifer, *Alessandro Algardi*, New Haven, Connecticut: Yale University Press, 1985

Nava Cellini, Antonia, *La scultura del Seicento*, Turin: UTET, 1982

Nava Cellini, Antonia, *La scultura del Settecento*, Turin: UTET, 1982

Poeschke, Joachim, *Die Skulptur der Renaissance in Italien*, vol. 1, *Donatello und seine Zeit*; Munich: Hirmer, 1990; as *Donatello and His World: Sculpture of the Italian Renaissance*, translated by Russell Stockman, New York: Abrams, 1993

Poeschke, Joachim, *Die Skulptur der Renaissance in Italien*, vol. 2, *Michelangelo und seine Zeit*, Munich: Hirmer, 1992; as *Michelangelo and His World: Sculpture of the Italian Renaissance*, translated by Russell Stockman, New York: Abrams, 1996

Pope-Hennessy, John, *An Introduction to Italian Sculpture*, 3 vols., London: Phaidon, 1963; 4th edition, 1996; see especially vol. 2, *Italian Renaissance Sculpture*, and vol. 3, *Italian High Renaissance and Baroque Sculpture*

Wittkower, Rudolf, *Art and Architecture in Italy, 1600–1750*, London and Baltimore, Maryland: Penguin, 1958; 6th edition, 3 vols., revised by Joseph Connors and Jennifer Montagu, New Haven, Connecticut: Yale University Press, 1999

ITALY: NEOCLASSICAL–19TH CENTURY

Through the legacy of the German archaeologist and art historian Johann Joachim Winckelmann, Greek Classicism assumed an exemplary role for sculpture from around 1760 until after 1848. The canon of Polykleitus and his seminal *Doryphoros* (Spear Bearer) and its standard of beauty assumed a universal character. The Apollo's form was the model of perfection since the Renaissance, and the Apollonian became a symbol of a formal imperative that opposed itself to the Dionysian—that valued measure over the limitless, control over the unbounded. Neoclassical sculpture searches for truth, clear lines, and simple forms, thus detaching itself from the previous epoch of the sensual Baroque. During this period, it enters the Italian academies as the indisputable pedagogical program.

Another decisive moment for this enthusiasm for Antiquity were the archaeological finds in Pompeii after 1738 and in Herculaneum after 1748, which brought about the conservation as well as the restoration of antiquities. In addition, a bustling art market flourished for authentic antiquities as well as faithful copies and even forgeries. The buyers, who were often advised by artists such as Thomas Jenkins, Gavin Hamilton, Vincenzo Pacetti, and Pietro Camuccini (who also drove the art market in Rome at the end of the eighteenth century), were typically either nobility or the first industrialists in England. This international enthusiasm for antiquities gave rise to the great collections of the so-called contemporary sculpture galleries, like those established in Malmaison by Josephine Beauharnais, Count Devonshire in Chatsworth, Prince Metternich in Vienna, and Count Esterhazy in Hungary, Count Sommariva in Villa Carlotta (Lake Como), the Demidoffs in Florence, and the Torlonias in Rome.

Napoléon's successful absconding of art from 1796 to 1798 brought about strict regulations for the exporting of cultural goods in Rome. In response, two edicts were issued in 1802 and 1816—the "Commissione generale consultiva di belle arti"—that were worked out by a committee in which Carlo Fea, Antonio Canova (President), Antonio d'Este, Bertel Thorvaldsen and Francesco Visconti served as advisors. The subsequent limitations on exports of antiquities created a drastic rise in demand for forgeries and imitations. In the sculptors' workshops there flourished primarily the restoration of antiquities so that the production of one's own work assumed secondary importance in guaranteeing one's living. The first version of an art market was established in the ateliers that were open to art agents who would lead illustrious travelers to them on the obligatory grand tour.

Bartolomeo Cavaceppi (1716–99), who restored the antiquities bought by Cardinal Albani and was an adviser for the Capitoline Museums, came to Rome in 1779. He was the best-known forerunner of Classicism in the plastic arts before Canova and was a close associate of the art historian and critic Anton Raphael Mengs and J.J. Winckelmann. His most influential student, Giuseppe Angelini (1742–1811), resided in England from 1770 to 1787 and was a direct acquaintance of the sculptors Joseph Nollekens and Josiah Wedgewood. The grave memorial constructed by Angelini for the architect and antiquities connoisseur, Giovanni Battista Piranesi in S. Maria del Priorato in Rome (1779–80), which has much in common with the sculptural busts of Jean-Antoine Houdon, also impressed Canova.

Cosmopolitan Rome played host at this time to the English contemporaries John Gibson, John Flaxman, the German-Dane Jacob Asmus Carstens, the Swede Johann Tobias Sergel, and the Swiss Alexander Trippel, who passed on his considerable learning of Antiquity in the name of Enlightenment within an influential private academy in Rome for several years.

Rome: Academies and Workshops

The Accademia del Nudo in Rome, whose founding was owed to Pope Benedict XIV in the eighteenth century, was changed considerably during the course of its reformation under Napoléon that began in 1798–

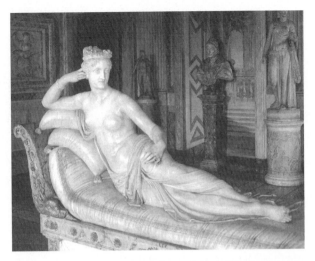

Antonio Canova, *Paolina Borghese*, Galleria Borghese, Rome

99. The reconstituted academy was modeled on the French art academy in Rome, which had been created for Italian artists by Pope Pius VII with the help of Canova.

Napoléon nationalized the Accademia di San Luca, which was directed by the clergy, and the affiliated Accademia del Nudo. This institutionalized Classicism created a transregional model for study and competition in the academies of Milan, Turin, Genoa, Venice, Florence, Bologna, and Naples, from which students would emerge as artists and then continue their studies in Rome with the help of a stipend.

The new accommodations of the academy were in the Palazzo Venezia. The founding of the academy was due primarily to the diplomat and later publisher of the *Giornale Arcadio*, Giusepe Tambroni. The Accademia dell' Italia in Rome took students from all over Italy who were permitted to study there for four years. They were required to exhibit their work on a yearly basis and received prizes for their efforts.

Canova's engagement with young artists, which had been little recognized until this point, manifested itself in both the commissioning of busts of the "uomini illustri [famous men]" for the Pantheon as well as in the establishment of two stipends—the "Concorso del Anonimo" beginning in 1812 and the "Concorso Triennale" beginning in 1817. He encouraged young sculptors to study the writings of Pliny and the athletic figures of Hellenic sculptures, in order to achieve verisimilitude. While Canova remained an adherent of natural beauty as a function of active forms of expression, Thorvaldsen favored Greek Archaicism and Early Classicism. The differences within Neoclassical sculpture in the early nineteenth century in Rome can be followed through the students of both these men well past the middle of the nineteenth century.

When the fate of the kingdom of Italy was called into question after 1814, the money for stipends could no longer be paid. Students were forced to earn their living in workshops or in making copies of antiquities. The following students worked in Canova's workshop: Adamo Tadolini, Alessandro d'Este, Rinaldo Rinaldi, Giovanni Ceccarini, and Cincinnato Baruzzi.

Adamo Tadolini (1788–1868) of Bologna came to Rome on a stipend in 1814, where he entered Canova's atelier on a recommendation from his teacher, Giacomo de Maria, at the Accademia Clementina (founded in 1730) in Bologna. Tadolini had mastered the Classical canon in his early academic studies, and in his later work he introduced feeling and temperament into his expressive sculpture. His figure of the reclining *Venus with Laughing Amor* (1823) or his two variations of *Ganymede with the Eagle* (1818) are works that are still crafted in the manner of his master. His works can be found from Europe to Latin America to India. Tadolini achieved fame as Canova's favorite student, and Canova gave Tadolini a few original sculptures from which Tadolini, with the consent of his master, made copies, that is, his *Amor and Psyche* group (1823) completed for Count Sommariva in Cadenabbia on Lake Como.

Thorvaldsen's atelier operated differently because he allowed his first *bozzetti* (small-scale preparatory studies) to be built by his students in large scale clay models and very often had his master students complete the figures in marble. This technique was discarded in subsequent periods because the process of a sculptor carving from the marble block was supposed to include both design and execution. Next to Luigi Bienaimé, his most famous Italian student was Pietro Tenerani, who was a hostile competitor of Tadolini.

Pietro Tenerani (1798–1868) from Torano near Carrara received his first lessons from Bartolini and came to Rome after 1813. He remained in Thorvaldsen's atelier until 1827. Together with Bienaimé he belonged to the most skilled artisans who constructed Thorvaldsen's large-scale models. His early works like *Psyche abbandonata* (Psyche Abandoned: 1819) are defined more by their softness and similarity to the Canovian style than through the strict Archaicism of his teacher. In his mature period, he distanced himself from the academic school and turned instead to Purism, a direction that can be seen in his grave memorial for Pope Pius VIII. He presents historical personalities realistically and in the fashion of their times, as in his *Pellegrini-Rossi* (1854–56)—a seated figure in a modern chair—and *Simon Bolivar* (1845), a freedom fighter dressed in a general's uniform in Bogotà. Together with the Nazarene Franz Overbeck and the painter

Tommaso Minardi, Tenerani signed a Purist manifesto, *Del purismo nelle arti* (1842), which refers explicitly to the inspiration of religious painting as a divine gift and searches for the expression of "true Christianity" in its themes.

Rome: Sculptural Ensembles

The architecture and interior decoration of the Villa Borghese, which Antonio Asprucci (1723–1808) designed and had decorated in the newly emerging Classical style, can be seen as a prototype of the new art movement, although it also reaches back to the already completed Villa Albani. The commissioner of the project, Marcantonio Borghese, himself a collector of antiquities, strongly supported the new forms of decoration. In the main salon the new and old meet: plaster reliefs by Tommaso Righi (1727–1802), Massimiliano Laboureur (1759–1820), Vincenzo Pacetti (1746–1820), and Francesco Carradori (1757–1825) embraced the discoveries of archaeology and interpreted them anew.

The expansion and renovation of the Quirinal Palace, which Napoléon had redesigned by Raffaele Stern after 1811 as his new seat of government, was equally influential in its combination of the Antique and the Neoclassical. Historical triumphal processions in relief friezes still serve today as testaments to the new power politics. In reference to such triumphal processions, in 1812 Thorvaldsen created the frieze of the renowned *Battle of Alexander*, and Carlo Finelli sculpted the frieze of *Il trionfo di Cesare*.

A further significant decorative program of this time followed with the establishment of the Museo Chiaramonti in the Braccio Nuovo palace of the Vatican, executed by Raffaele Stern between 1816 to 1820. Contemporary reliefs depicting triumphal processions of Titan, Trajan, and Marcus Aurelius and sacrificial and bacchanalian scenes done in an antique style by Massimiliano Laboureur were meaningfully united with the exhibition of antiquities (1820). Shortly afterward works from the Classical collections in the Palazzo Torlonia (1813–14) exhibited leitmotifs of this valorization of Antiquity, whose highpoint is captured in Canova's *Hercules and Lichias* sculptural group. Clear references to the heroism of Classicism (with the themes of Hercules and Alexander the Great) and bucolic and convivial motifs (Theseus and Bacchus, Amor and Psyche, Apollo and the Parnassus Muses) constituted the imagistic program.

The redesign of the Piazza del Popolo with sculptural decorations after 1810–20 until roughly 1840 was planned by the architect Giuseppe Valadier. The sculpture along the fountains was executed according to academic tradition on the one side by Canova's students,

Francesco Massimiliano Laboureur and Giuseppe Ceccarini, and, on the other side, by Thorvaldsen's students, Luigi Bienaime, Filippo Gnaccharini, Alessandro Massimiliano Laboureur, Achille Stocchi, and Pietro Tenerani among others. The design of the garden park of Monte Pincio with the cycle of busts of the *uomini illustri* (famous men) refers back to Valadier as well, yet it was only transformed into a botanical garden under Pius IX (1846–58). The famous cycle of busts from renowned artists, which was exhibited in the Pantheon since the Renaissance, can be seen as a predecessor of the portraits of the great personalities from the fields of literature, history, politics, and the natural sciences, which were exhibited permanently after 1850–53. The cycle of busts was understood as a didactic, patriotic program of the "Repubblica Romana," which was founded on 9 February 1849, and their form corresponded to the historically oriented Neoclassicism.

Neoclassicism: Rome, Turin, Genoa, Venice, Florence, and Naples

Rome

Giuseppe Franchi (1731–1806), who was trained in Rome under Ignazio and Filippo Collino and was an admirer of Canova, grew up in Carrara. He studied the Early Neoclassical achievements and went to Milan in 1776, where he taught at the newly founded Brera Academy under the direction of Giovanni Maria Guidici di Viggiù (1723–1804). He was responsible for the decorations of the Palazzo Reale (Monza) and of the Villa Melzi in Bellagio, which he carried out under the direction of the sculptor Gaetano Callani (1736–1809) and the architects Giuseppe Piermarini and Giocondo Albertolli (one of the first representatives in northern Italy of the vocabulary of Antiquity and sixteenth-century Classicism).

Camillo Paccetti (1758–1826) became Franchi's successor, and his primary accomplishment lay in the design of the architectural ornamentation on the peace arch, *Arco della Pace* in Milan. Pompeo Marchesi (1789–1858), who first studied under Franchi and then lived in Rome between 1805 and 1808 and frequented Canova's atelier, contributed to the *Arco della Pace* with the reliefs *Fondazione del Regno Lombardo Veneto*, *Passaggio del Reno*, and *Vittora di Lipsa*. Marchesi assumed Pacetti's teaching position, and Marchesi was later succeeded by Benedetto Cacciatori (1794–1871), who came from Carrara and was a student of Bartolini. His contribution to the *Arco della Pace* were the colossal figures of the river allegories, *Po* and *Ticino*, and the relief, *Ingresso Ferdinand I* (The entry of Ferdinand I).

Pietro Giordani and Giuseppe Bossi were among the most influential theoreticians and writers on art and set the tone in Brera in the early 1800s. Pietro Giordani (1774–1848) assumed a teaching position between 1800 and 1808 at the University of Bologna. He was an enthusiast of Canova. In 1815 he completed his tenure as codirector of the Biblioteca Italiana in Milan and edited his writings. In 1816 he praised Leopolo Cicognara's *Storia della Scultura*, which he felt represented the highpoint of the "glory of Italian art." Giordani's line of thought was taken up by Giuseppe Bossi (1777–1815), who exerted a reforming influence on the academy in Milan. He was a painter, man of letters, and art collector in one. He came to Rome in 1795 and maintained contact there with the representatives of Neoclassicism, among others Jean-Baptiste-Louis Giorge D'Agincourt, Felice Giani, Angelika Kaufmann, and above all Canova. His guiding principles appeared in his *Discorsi*, which became the model for all Italian academies after 1804.

Turin

Ignazio Collino (1724–93) arrived in Rome in 1748, his brother Filippo Collino came five years later; both were active in the circle of Alessandro Albani. They achieved their fame for their statues depicting mythological themes in the Palazzo Reale in Stupinigi (near Turin)—*Meleagro, Atalanta, Diana, Atteone*. With the figure of *Hercules Battling the Lions* in the Accademia Albertina, Collino anticipated Canova's use of the theme. These works achieved the high level of international Classicism found between Rome and Paris, inspired by the works of Giovanni Battista Maini. The teaching of the Collino brothers as professors at the Accademia Albertina (founded in 1778 in Turin) established important trends that were later taken up and developed by Carlo Marochetti and the following generation of sculptors.

Genoa

Francesco Schiaffino (1691–1765) founded the Ligustica Academy in 1750 in Genoa still under the influence of the Baroque. As Schiaffino's successor, Nicola Traverso (1745–1823) introduced Neoclassicism after staying in Rome from 1771 until 1790, where he not only acquainted himself with the world of Antiquity and its restoration, but also with the new currents of Neoclassicism. His fluctuation between the Baroque and the new style is especially apparent in his high relief of *Santa Agnese in gloria* (St. Agnes' Glory) in the Church of S. Carmine (Genoa). Francesco Ravaschio (1743–1820), a student of Schiaffino, assisted Traverso with the completion of the sculptural decorations for the Palazzo Ducale. Bartolomeo Carrea (1764–1839) and then Giuseppe Gaggini (1791–1867) continued the work of Traverso.

Venice

The history of Venice's academy was subject to the changing politics of the various occupying powers of the city. The Scuola del Nudo (extant since 1768) and the famous collection of Daniele Farsetti, whose antiquities and renowned works from all over Europe were allowed to be copied by artists, constituted the basis of the academic education on which Giovanni Ferrari (1744–1826) would later build. He continued the school of Giuseppe Torretti (Canova's teacher), but distanced himself from Neoclassicism by anticipating romantic trends. His *Monumento del Ammiraglio Emo* (Monument to Admiral Emo) in the Church of S. Biagio in Venice (1792) is considered his most important work.

Count Leopoldo Cicognara (1767–1834), a politically liberal art critic and author from Ferrara who was named the president of the Accademia delle Belle Arti in Venice in 1808, maintained intense friendships with other artists, especially Canova and Pietro Giordani. His monumental historical work, *La storia della scultura dal suo risorgimento in Italia fino al secolo di Canova, per servire di continuazione delle opere di Winckelmann e d'Agincourt*, defined within a particular historical and cultural context the development of sculpture from Nicola Pisano to the age of Neoclassicism. Cicognara committed himself to the construction of a tomb for Canova (1827) and Titian (1837) in the Frari Church in Venice, both were representative of Neoclassical tombs. The sculptures of Luigi Zandomeneghi (1778–1850) and his son Pietro Zandomeneghi (1806–60) mark the transition from Classicism to Romantic verism or naturalism.

Florence

The enthusiasm for Antiquity from Rome to Florence can be witnessed in the decoration of the Palazzo Pitti before 1800. Giocondo Albertolli completed the stucco in the Sala delle Niobe in 1780 and Francesco Carradori (1747–1824), who came to Rome in 1772 on a stipend and copied antiquities under Agostino Penna, completed four medallions there with the *Story of Niobe* and a *Bacchus-Ariadne* sculptural group. He later restored the antiquities of the Medici Collection. In 1768 he was called to the Accademia delle Belle Arti in Florence as the successor to Innocenzo Spinazzi and reformed the academy. Following a strict academic style, Stefano Ricci (1765–1837) completed the tombs of Dante 1829 and Michele Borgovia Skotnicki (1808) in the Church of Santa Croce, and the statue of Ferdinand II (1822) in Arezzo.

The academy in Carrara began in 1769. Starting in 1807, Lorenzo Bartolini taught there. The academy's first honorary members included Napoléon I, Eugène Beauharnais, John Flaxman, Canova, and others.

Naples

The sculptural program and fountain figures in Caserta, whose architectural design goes back to Luigi Vanvitelli, demonstrate the transition from the Baroque to Neoclassicism. The sculptors who participated in this project, Pietro Solari (responsible for the primary figures on the Actaeon fountain), Paolo Persico (designed the blueprint for the Actaeon fountain), Andrea Violani, Gaetano Salomoni, Giuseppe Sammartino, and Angelo Brunelli, represent a cross section of this transitional period.

Giuseppe Sammartino (1720–93), known as a talented carver of Nativity scenes, completed the fountain's figures of *Ceres*, *Eolo*, *Venus*, and *Diana and Attone*. He also worked with Tommaso Arnaud, Angelo Solari, and others in the decoration of the Palazzo Reale.

Angelo Brunelli (1740–1806) completed the Aeolian fountain in Caserta, which was designed in the Baroque style. He then came to Naples in 1790 as a court sculptor and embraced the Neoclassical style. From 1803, along with Andrea Calli, he influenced the reform movement in the reopened Accademia delle Belle Arti in Naples. Antonio Calli (1789–1866), son of Andrea, created the Neoclassical equestrian statue, *Ferdinand I* (1822), on the Piazza del Plebiscito in Naples; the sculpture refers back to the Roman Marcus Aurelius and the model for the horse came from Canova.

Romanticism to Historicism

Pre-Raphaelite tastes appeared at the same time as Purism, which Andrea Bianchini (a student of Tomaso Minardi) introduced as a concept in 1833 and discussed in a manifesto of 1842. Purism emerged from the desire to promote themes from the Renaissance and only those works that were divinely inspired, a move that introduced a decidedly anti-academic attitude. In literature, the theme of religious sentimentality in Heinrich Wackenroder's *Confessions of an Art Loving Friar* (1797) had an exceptionally strong influence on Romantic ideas about art. No less important were the 'romantic poems' of the brothers August Wilhelm and Friedrich von Schlegel that appeared in the journal *Athenaeum* (1798), and that prized the irrational and the fantastic over the rational of the Enlightenment (embodied in Immanuel Kant's *Critique of Judgment* (1790). François-Auguste-René de Chateaubriand's *Genius of Christianity* (1802) reflected on the Christian life in a way that was far from the principles of the Enlightenment. His work released a new found enthusiasm for religious, romantic, and emotion-driven images and themes. The tendency in Romantic sculpture can be described as a belief in the individual and sub-

jectivity, and it is closely associated with funeral and memorial sculptures with their unavoidable pathos.

The repertoire of purist sculpture also includes *Abele morente* (Dying Abel) (1842) by Giovanni Dupré in Florence (Galleria d'Arte Moderna) as well as a sitting figure of Eve by Scipione Tadolini (1867–75) that he reproduced over thirty times. The figure of *Susanna* (1852) by Scipione Tadolini and O. Fantacchiotti (1871) in Florence (Galleria d'Arte Moderna) represents a profaned religious tendency. At a later time, with the proclamation of the dogma of the Immaculate Conception by Pope Pius IX in 1854, the cult of Mary was revived and is visible in the *Monumento della Immacolata* (Monument to the Immaculate Virgin) on the Piazza di Spagna in Rome.

The cult of genius typified by interest in Raphael represented Renaissance artists as modern saints. Their lives and personalities were analyzed. A psychological or historical moment was extracted from the life of the artist in order to place him in the line of *uomini illustri*. The final result of this historicism was the synthesis of Nature and the Ideal. Examples of this are the *Raffaello* (Raphael) (1838) on the Pincio in Rome by Achille Stocchi, a Raphael statue (1847) in the Cathedral of Urbino by Carlo Finelli, and a monument to Raphael (1883–98) by G. Belli also in Urbino.

Romanticism: Rome, Milan, Genoa, Florence, Venice and Naples

Rome

In Florence Giovanni Dupré set the tone for Romantic innovations of verist sculpture. His students Tenerani and Tadolini favored a verism that was more or less in line with academic Neoclassicism.

Funeral sculptures on the Campo Verano in Rome demonstrate both tendencies of the period. On the one hand, one sees the naked, heroic academic figure in the spirit of Canova's *Endymion* on the grave memorial *Cesare Mancini* (1875) by Fabi Altini (1830–1906), a student of Tadolini. On the other hand, there is the sitting figure by Stefano Galletti (1833–1905) on the grave memorial *Erminia Fuà Fudinato* (1876) in which the subject is in the costume of her age.

The Caffé Greco in Rome was a gathering place artists. Its important collection still bears the expression of its time. Tadolini's student, Luigi Amici (1817–97), bequeathed the Caffé his collection of small marble, terracotta, and plaster images of the regulars of Caffé Greco.

Milan

The cultural events in Milan influenced the diversity of themes of sculpture much more innovatively than in Rome. Pietro Magni (1817–77) with his figure, *La*

Leggitrice (The reader) (1856) (Galleria d'Arte Moderna) illustrates this broader sensibility. His monument, *Leonardo da Vinci* (1872), anticipated the verism of the following generation of Vincenzo Vela and Antonio Tandarini (1829–79), whose figures, *La Leggitrice* and *Schiava* (The female slave) were well received at the exhibition of Paris in 1867. Giovanni Strazza (1818–75), who trained under Pietro Tenerani in Rome, was a Purists. His figure *Ismael morente nel deserto* (Ismael dying in the desert) (1845), which recalls G. Dupré's *Abele Morente* (1842), demonstrates an almost anti-academic sensibility.

Genoa

Salvatore Revelli (1816–59), trained under Pietro Tenerani in Rome. He completed a number of works in Turin. His 1855 grave memorial *Maria Adelaide* (the wife of Victor Emmanuel II) in the Basilica of Superga (near Turin) and the reliefs on the monument of *Cristoforo Colombo* in the Piazza Acquaverde in Genoa demonstrate a verist historicist tendency that is more generally visible in the cycles of *uomini illustri*.

Venice

Following the example of Milan and Florence, Venice in 1847 received the first 15 busts (of a projected 60) of the "Pantheon Veneto" for the first floor of the Doge's Palace on which numerous sculptors worked. To name just a few, the most important busts are: *Paulo Paruta* (1847) and *Carlo Alberto* (1874) by Luigi Ferrari; *Angelo Emo* (1863) and *Dante* (1865) by Pietro Zandomeneghi, *Leonardo Loredan* (1862) by Luigi Borró, and *Marco Foscarini* (1847) by Luigi Minisini.

Luigi Ferrari (1810–94) contributed to the grave memorial *Titian* (1837). His verist tendencies can be seen in *Laocoön* (1853) in Brecia (Pinacoteca Tosio Martinengo). He worked between Classicism and Purism, as in his grave relief of *Principessa Jabonowski* (ca. 1840) in the Cathedral of S. Antonio (Padua). His kneeling statue with the lion, *Doge Foscari* (1885) on the facade the Basilica of S. Marco is a conscious citation of the fifteenth century.

Pietro Selvatico Estense, who was president of the art academy between 1851 and 1869 and taught aesthetics, was an absolute proponent of Purism. In addition, he was one of the first to work with photography, which he introduced in his newly founded Scuola di Arti Industriali in Padua in 1867 as a tool to assist in teaching drawing.

Florence

There are two places in Florence where one can stand facing an entire panorama of Classicist, Romantic, and Purist sculpture. One is the Church of Santa Croce and the other is the Portico Vasariano in the Galleria degli

Uffizi. Santa Croce contains the grave memorials *Alfieri* (1804–10) by Canova, *Macchiavelli* (1798) by Innocenzo Spinazzi, and *Sofia Zamoyska* (1836) by Bartolini.

The figural cycle of the *uomini illustri* in the niches of the Portico Vasariano, which were created between 1836 and 1856, was conceived completely in the style of history painting, simply transformed into sculpture. Artists, poets, military leaders, and intellectuals appear before the eyes of the viewer as a *Portico delle Glorie Toscane,* reflecting the patriotic pride of the Florentines during the Renaissance. Among the Tuscan sculptors, who almost always represented their heroes as versatile figures in period costume, were Giovanni Dupré (*Giotto*), Bartolini (*Niccolo Macchiavelli*), Pio Fedi (*Nicola Pisano*), and Luigi Pampaloni (*Leonardo da Vinci*).

Naples

The primary representative of the Romantic sensibility in Naples was Alfonso Balzico (1825–1901) who increasingly oriented himself toward verism and occasionally drew themes from the genre. He received his initial training in Naples under Giuseppe Angelini and Francesco Citarelli, then in Rome and Milan, where he met Pietro Magni and Vincenzo Vela. He was equally prized by the Bourbons and King Victor Emmanuel II. His most famous genre sculpture after a literary model was his naturalist Romantic *Gretchen* (1852) from Johann Wolfgang von Goethe's *Faust*, which was more melodramatic than his figures, *Sposa dei cantici* (1865–70) and *Nello della Pietra and Pia de Tolomei* (1885) in Rome (Galleria d'Arte Moderna). In Turin one can find his verist monuments, including *Massimo d'Azeglio* (1873) and *Duke Ferdinando di Genova* (1863–77), whose depiction of a single moment of movement received great acclaim.

Sculpture in the Second Half of the Nineteenth Century

As Neoclassicism waned in the middle of the nineteenth century, the divide between a genre-based Romantic tradition and the realistic movement of verism only increased. Lorenzo Bartolini and his successor Giovanni Dupré set the tone for Florence, just as Pietro Tenerani and Adamo Tadolini did for Rome. Sculpture was supposed to express a psychological moment and the immediacy of feeling, criteria that had already been applied to portrait and sepulchral sculpture and only later became important for genre sculptures. The double portrait of the kneeling *Queens Maria Adelaide and Elisabetta di Savoia Carignano* (1861) by Vela in the Church of Consolata in Turin marked the beginning of this movement.

The study of models as the basis of the artistic process replaced the study of antiquities as the ascendant realism gained increased significance through its representation of social themes—the milieu of workers and scenes of everyday life. From the spontaneous moment, *gusto episodico,* to the everyday gesture, the new form of expressive sculpture had its origin in Naples with Stanislao Lista and Achille D'Orsi and quickly spread to northern Italy. Thus in *Il primo parto* (The first) (1861) by Giuseppe Trabacchi, *Bambino con il gallo* (Child with a rooster) (1868) by Adriano Cecioni, or *L'avvicinarsi alla procella* (1877) by Roberto Belliazzi, the depiction of poverty as a social critique is artistically accentuated. An excellent example of an anti-academic figure is *The Suicide* (1868) by Adriano Cecioni in Florence (Galleria d'Arte Moderna), which communicates to the viewer doubt and decisiveness in an extreme moment of life. It incited an extremely polemical debate within the academy, which was now considered an institution with rigid values.

The circle of artists of the Macchiaioli in Florence challenged the priorities of the academy. Parallel to this current, a literary movement with a strong orientation toward foreign literature took place in Milan from 1860 to around 1880. The name of the movement, *Scapigliatura* (literally "disheveled"), points to Cletto Arrighi's novel *La Scapigliatura e il 6 febbraio. Un dramma in famiglia: romanzo contemporaneo* (Milan, 1862). Against the background of the workers revolt of 1853, this novel provided the artistic bohemians of Milan the opportunity to pillory the outdated traditions of the Italian academy. Utopia, sentiment, and the exotic were to be the new expressions of sculpture. Giuseppe Grandi's *Ulisses* (1866) and Enrico Butti's *Eleonora d'Este* (1874) mark the beginning of this movement.

In the middle of this new orientation one also encounters the phenomenon of Orientalism. Journeys to the Near East, Egypt, and North Africa gave rise to a curiosity for and incorporation of the foreign along with a growing scholarly interest in research excursions. The exotic gained importance and images of everyday life in the bazaar were valued. Most popular were the depictions of the slave markets or the harems with their odalisques that the painter Jean-Auguste-Dominique Ingres incorporated in his canvases. The politically explosive conflicts between Greece and Turkey (1821–1830) inspired Eugène Delacroix's painting *The Massacre on Chios* (1824), in which Greek Christians fall into the hands of the Turks against whom they are powerless. Hiram Powers's sculpture *Greek Slave* (1844), an oriental version of the Medici Venus, can be interpreted as propaganda for the abolition of slavery in America. Giovanni Strazza's relief *Una barca di schiave* (A boat of slaves) (1848) and G. Dupré's sitting slave woman, *La Riconoscenza*

(1853), both engaged this theme. Even thirty years later, the female slave had lost nothing of its currency; on the contrary, she developed into a prototype of the erotic modern figure of Venus, which Scipione Tadolini copied up to 30 times. The increasingly market oriented nature of art led to more fashionable tendencies, while at the same time, through large national or international exhibitions, the art world measured itself against the achievements of progress and the products of industry, seeking legitimacy in reproducibility. It was here where art developed into a commodity and decorative sculpture dominated.

In the great exhibitions of 1851 in London and 1855 in Paris a spectacle was presented that was supposed to be understood as a "view of all Europe" in a single work of art. Sculptures, valued equally with industrial products, were offered as commodities for sale. Humankind in conflict with its work or with machines dominated the new range of themes. What Gustave Courbet critically depicted in his groundbreaking painting *The Stone Breakers* in 1850 will be represented in Italian sculpture two decades later in Raffaello Belliazzi's detailed realism, for example, in *L'avvicinarsi della porcella* (1877) and *Orfanella* (The orphan) (1873). Going one step further, artists critiqued the belief in progress central to the industrial world in so far as man—having lost his individuality—becomes a victim of the very machines he invents. The appearance of increasing numbers of fashionable genre figures that were easily reproduced and sold were disqualified by contemporaries as a caprice of fashion not to be taken seriously.

Realism: Rome, Milan, Genoa, Florence, Naples

Rome

The first international exhibition, for which a large exhibition hall was exclusively constructed on the Via Nazionale, occurred in 1883 in Rome, almost twenty years after Milan, Turin, and Florence had already initiated an innovative program of exhibitions beginning in 1861. One of the exhibitors, Giulio Monteverde (1837–1917) received his initial training in Genoa and came to Rome in 1865 on a stipend. He excited the public with his Romantic-verist themes, even if they were still bound to a certain academicism. Among his major works are *La giovinezza di Cristoforo Colombo* (The youth of Christopher Columbus) (1870) in the Galleria di Parma and *Eduardo Jenner che inocula il vaccino al proprio figlio* (Edward Jenner inoculating the vaccine on his own son) (1873) in Genoa (Palazzo Bianchi) and the monuments *Garibaldi* and *Marco Minghetti* (1893) in Bologna.

At the same time as Monteverde, Ercole Ferrari (1845–1929) entered the field of sculpture in Rome. A born Roman and trained in the Accademia di San Luca, he garnered attention with his relief *Assunzione della Vergine* (Assumption of the Virgin) (1870) on the Quadriportico des Campo Verano. His monument *Giordano Bruno* (1887) in Rome (Campo di Fiore) and *Garibaldi* (1896) in Rovigo show clear antiacademic tendencies and indicate his embrace of realism.

Giuseppe Trabacchi (1839–1909) exhibited the figure *Il primo parto* (1861) in Florence and belonged to the representatives of verism, evinced in his work on the Campo Verano and his colossal group, *L'arte trionfante fra lo Stato e la Place* (Art triumphing between the State and peace) (1882) on the Palazzo della Esposizione on the Via Nazionale.

Ercole Rosa (1846–1893) won the contest for the monument *Fratelli Cairoli* (1871–77) in Rome and the equestrian statue, *Viktor Emanuels* (1896), in Milan on the Piazza del Duomo.

Milan

Odoardo Tabacchi (1831–1905) received his initial training under Benedetto Cacciatori and Pietro Magni at the Accademia di Belle Arti at Brera in Milan and came to Rome in 1851 on a stipend. Later he lived in Florence, where he entered the artists' circle of the Macchiaioli in Caffé Michelangelo. Tabacchi's major works include *Arnaldo* (1880) and *Cavour* (1865) in Milan and *Garibaldi* (1887), *Paleopcapa* (1871), *Cassinis* (1873) and *Bottero* (1899) in Turin. His most famous student, Giuseppe Grandi (1843–1891), who was trained in Milan and then in Turin, premiered with his work *Ulisses* (1866). He was also counted among the Scapigliati, an intellectual movement that envisioned art and literature as the highest expression of human thought. Monuments to *Cesare Beccaria* (1871), marbles in the Castello Sforzesco, and the veterans memorial *Cinque giornate* (Five days) (1883–91) reflect this spirit of the times. Grandi's impressionism is carried on by Antonio Bezzola (1846–1929) and later by Paolo Troubetzkoy, Ernesto Bazzaro, and even later by Medardo Rosso.

Francesco Barzaghi (1839–92), a student of Tandarini's, thoroughly oriented his work towards Vincenzo Vela. Next to mythological subjects, he also worked on genre depictions (such as *L'innocenzia* [Innocence] 1881) that corresponded closely with the tastes of bourgeois Late Romanticism. He also completed a number of memorial statues, of which his equestrian monument, *Napoleon II* (1881–84), in Milan is considered the most successful.

Genoa

Pietro Costa (1849–1901) studied initially under Santo Varni (1866–70) at the Accademia Ligustica in Genoa. His early works include genre figures like *L'istinto materno* (Maternal instinct) (1870) and *Spazza camino*

(1873–77). Later, he lived in Florence and Rome, where he tended toward the Neopolitan spirit. In Rome he completed the bronze statue, *Vittorio Emanuele II* in 1878 for the council chamber of the Consiglio Provinciale and also the decorative sculpture for the palazzo of the Ministry of Finance. One year later, he emerged as the winner of a competition for the monument of *Vittoria Emanuele II* (1878–99) in Turin, which was only completed after 1899 by other sculptors.

Florence

Antonio Bortone (1844–1938), who studied under Tito Angelini, came to Florence in 1863 and created the mausoleum for Gino Capponi in Santa Croce. He also exercised considerable influence over Adriano Cecioni (1836–86) whose verism could be seen most clearly in his figure *Il suicida* (The suicide) (1866), which uses its antique garb to hide a gruesome spectacle. The tradition of Cecioni, who only received his professorship at the academy two years before his death, was continued by Augusto Rivalta (1837–1925), who came to Florence in 1857 and completed numerous monuments in the wake of Italy's unification. The sitting figure, *Giovanni Battista Niccolini* (Galleria Nazionale d'Arte Moderna, Rome), demonstrates not only a sensitive psychological observation but also a painterly period costume.

Naples

Next to Balzico, Stanilao Lista (1824–1908), who was influenced by the painter Domenico Morelli, made antiacademic sculpture that moved in the direction of verism. His statue *Paisello*, in front of the theater of S. Carlo in Naples is distinguished by a minute, lifelike reproduction of the subject in historical costume. It is depicted as a quasi-nativity scene. From his school emerged Vincenzo Gemito, Costantino Barbella, Antonio Macini, Luigi Fabron, and Vincenzo Migliaro.

With his socially critical figures *L'avvicinarsi della porcella* (1877) and *Orfanella* (1873), Raffaello Belliazzi (1835–1917) worked in a sentimental vein and continued the trends of Stanilao Lista.

Ettore Ximenes (1855–1926) came to Naples from Palermo in 1872 as a student of Pietro Solari and Lista. He associated primarily with Vincenzo Gemito, who was only three years older. From 1874 to 1880 he lived in Florence. The portraits of *Gino Capponi* and the busts of the priest *Antonio Stoppani* are from this period. In Urbino he taught at the Istituto Raffaello, later he embraced Jugendstil, which his home in Rome on the Piazza Galeno still shows today.

In general, one can argue that at the end of the nineteenth century the artist's individual interpretation assumed a crucial position so that the art world splintered

into a number of great individual achievements and lost the universal character that had always been art's essential feature. All forms and contents existed on an equal plane and theoretically everything was allowed. The turn of the century ushered in a pluralism of styles, a repertoire of possibilities that was indebted to neither the patron nor an academy. The new ideal lay in the discovery of a national, but also very individual form of expression.

TAMARA FELICITAS HUFSCHMIDT

See also **Bartolini, Lorenzo; Bienaime, Luigi; Canova, Antonio; Dupré Family; Equestrian Statue; Flaxman, John; Gemito, Vincenzo; Houdon, Jean-Antoine; Neoclassicism and Romanticism; Nollekens, Joseph; Pisano, Nicola; Polykleitos; Polykleitos** *Doryphoros* **(Spear Bearer); Powers, Hiram; Revivalism; Rosso, Medardo; Sanmartino, Giuseppe; Sergel, Johan Tobias; Thorvaldsen, Bertel; Troubetzkoy, Paolo; Vela, Vincenzo**

ITALY: 20TH CENTURY–CONTEMPORARY

At the turn of the 20th century, many of Italy's most talented sculptors were still at work finishing the colossal statues that had been commissioned during the late 19th century to celebrate the heroes and events of the Risorgimento, Italy's unification movement of the 1850s. The most impressive of these projects is the classicizing sculpture that adorns the monument to Victor Emmanuel II in Piazza Venezia, Rome, completed in 1911. Leading the charge against this propagandistic and highly academic sculpture was Medardo Rosso, who, after contacts with the Post-Impressionists in Paris during the 1890s, introduced into Italy a more tactile, psychologically penetrating type of sculpture. His bronze *Ecce Puer* of 1906 (Ca' Pesaro, Venice), which shows the influence of Symbolism, takes advantage of light to disintegrate the simple shape of the child's face. Such formal innovations influenced greatly the theoretical underpinnings of early Futurism. In *Manifesto dei pittori futuristi* (1910), Rosso is listed as one of the several Italian artists who had already succeeded in freeing Italian art from the impasse posed by the monuments of the Risorgimento. A year later, in *La scultura futurista*, Umberto Boccioni also stressed the importance of Rosso's sculpture, calling it "totally modern and revolutionary, deeper and necessarily restricted." He cautioned, however, that "the impressionistic needs of [Rosso's] attempt have limited [his] searches . . . to a sort of high and bas-relief, which demonstrates that figure is still conceived as a world in itself, with a traditional base and episodic purpose."

Boccioni, hoping to dispel with the latent traditionalism that he perceived in Rosso's work, put forth that sculpture "must make objects live by rendering their extension in space sensible and plastic." Thus, in his own sculpture, Boccioni strove to represent—as he called it—an object's "lines of force," that quality of linear dynamism that, he believed, radiates from all things. Standing as the most important manifestations of these ideas are his *Unique Forms of Continuity in Space* and *Development of a Bottle in Space*, both executed in plaster in 1913 (the originals no longer survive, but among the many bronze casts of each, early examples are preserved in the Museum of Modern Art, New York City). Boccioni also relied on mixed media to increase the plasticity of his works, thus presaging the experiments of Giacomo Balla and Fortunato Depero in the mid 1910s. Their manifesto on Futurist art, the *Ricostruzione futurista dell'universo* (1915), outlines their belief that sculpture can make corporal the "invisible, impalpable, imponderable, imperceptible." Encouraged by recent scientific discoveries, Balla, in particular, sought to give three-dimensional form to such natural phenomena as speed and light; documenting one such effort are the sharp, curvilinear contours of his *Lines of Speed + Landscape*, a bas-relief made in 1914 (since destroyed). Depero, meanwhile, used a variety of materials to create "plastic complexes" that soon gave way to inventive stage productions such as the *Balli plastici* (1918), for which he crafted the marionettes. Enrico Pampolini also contributed much to Futurist sculpture while working as a scenographer.

With the advent of World War I, the first phase of Futurism came to end. Not only did Boccioni die during the war, but more important, as a consequence of this "War of Machines," the late 1910s saw a revolt against the progressive, technological ideals championed by the Futurists. Sculptors such as Arturo Martini drew new inspiration from Italy's classical past. Although his early sculpture developed sharply toward expressionism, best seen in works such as *The Prostitute* (1909–13; Ca' Pesaro, Venice), he—along with those associated with the Roman magazine *Valore Plastici*—began to filter their once avant-garde art through an archaistic lens tempered by the Italian quattrocento. As Martini himself writes, with statues such as *The Prodigal Son* (1926–28; private collection, Acqui Terme), "the Italian history of forms seems to be summarized and transfigured." Marino Marini shared in Martini's crude classicism, although he eyed more closely the Etruscan prototypes of his native Tuscany. His cycle of *Riders*, for example, begun in 1936, manifests an archaic litheness and equilibrium of pose seemingly unfazed by Fascist rubric. Many of Marini's contemporaries, however—especially those affiliated with the Novecento Italiano movement—felt increasingly obliged to promote a nationalist art. For such

reasons, the themes of family, state, and religion became central to Adolfo Wildt's later sculpture; his marble *Mother* (1929; collection of Diego Gomiero, Padua, Italy) adopts the conventions of a quattrocento portrait bust, thus embracing Fascist ideas about family and the primacy of Italian culture. A second wave of Futurist sculpture, spearheaded by Mino Rosso in the late 1920s, made similar claims in behalf of the Fascist state.

During the 1930s, in conjunction with the building campaigns of Benito Mussolini, a Fascist style of sculpture eventually took hold in Rome, thanks in large measure to the creative energies of Mario Sironi. Realizing that mural painting was the most effective media for Fascist propaganda, Sironi also experimented with grandiose bas-reliefs, such as the one he executed between 1939 and 1942 for the façade of the Palazzo del Popolo d'Italia, Rome (now the Palazzo dell'Informazione). Like the 60 marble athletes (1938–39) that ring the sporting venues at the Foro Italico in Rome, Sironi's bas-reliefs bear highly stylized—almost Romanesque—figures, all with overt musculature. In opposition to this monumental classicism, sculptors such as Antonietta Raphael, who associated herself with the loosely knit Scuola Romana group, concentrated on more intimate, carefully modeled forms. Then, too, Lucio Fontana began his first experiments with abstractionism. Turning his back on the anachronistic sculpture of the Novecento movement, Fontana created several impressive works of iron during the 1930s, such as *Abstract Sculpture* (1934; Galleria Civica d'Arte Moderna e Contemporanea, Turin, Italy), in which a straight-edged plane charts a meandering course through space.

Although Fontana's earlier abstract works gained rapid notoriety across Europe, many Italian sculptors continued to explore the possibilities of figurative sculpture, often endowing their art with a social meaning. Indeed, the debate between the two sides—abstract versus representational—characterizes the period immediately following World War II. Among Italy's more traditionally minded sculptors, Giacomo Manzù took recourse in religious imagery to voice his views against Fascism and worldwide violence. Ever since his first visit to Rome in 1934, Manzù had come under the spell of the Roman Catholic Church, being especially impressed by the sculptural quality of its solemn processions. Out of such experiences came Manzù's first bronze statue of a cardinal (Galleria Nazionale d'Arte Moderna, Rome), which he later remade in such versions as the *Standing Cardinal* (1954; Hirshhorn Gallery, Washington, D.C.). When Pope Pius XII awarded Manzù the commission for the bronze doors of St. Peter's Basilica in 1947, he again made use of the simple, formalistic language that he had

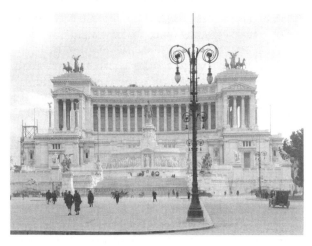

Vittorio Emmanuele II Monument, 1911, Piazza Venezia, Rome
The Conway Library, Courtauld Institute of Art

developed for his cardinal statues—albeit raising it to a harrowing pitch. After convincing the pope that Death, not the Glory of the Saints, should be the theme of the doors, Manzù spent the first years of the 1960s finishing the project's ten bas-reliefs; included among them are traditional subjects such as the Death of Christ, but also more inventive ones such as the *Death of Violence*, which shows a mourning woman next to a man strung up by his feet. Pericle Fazzini, with his prize-winning *Sibyl* (1949; collection of the artist, Rome), and Emilio Greco, who is best known for half-length busts of females such as his bronze *Anna* (1962; Civici Musei d'Arte e Storia, Brescia), practiced a more sensual art that, like Manzù's sculpture, refers back to the Renaissance.

During the postwar era, Fontana and Piero Manzoni established themselves as the most influential practitioners of abstract sculpture in Italy. Fontana's chief accomplishment lies in his articulation of the ideas behind Spazialismo, a movement arising from six manifestos that he authored between 1947 and 1952, which advocate the complete visual synthesis of all environmental factors—sound, light, color, movement, time, and space. His first *Spatial Environment* of 1949 (Galleria del Naviglio, Milan) was a temporary installation consisting of an amorphous mass suspended in a darkened room and bombarded by beams of neon light. Manzoni, meanwhile, explored other types of nontraditional sculpture. In the spring of 1958, he began signing his name on live persons and calling them authentic statues; prefiguring Conceptualism is his *Line 1,000 m Long* (1961; Museum of Modern Art, New York City), in which a roll of paper with an ink line drawn across its 1000-meter length is sealed within a chrome-plated can. Among this period's other abstractionists were

Ettore Cola, who combined geometric forms in large iron assemblages, Emilio Vedova, with his dynamic, light-infused *Cycles of Nature*, and Francesco Lo Spazio, whose *Metals* (1961) anticipate Minimalism. Also important to this phase of Italian sculpture are the great metal spheres that Arnaldo Pomodoro first made during the late 1960s; perhaps the best known of these is *Sphere with Sphere* (1990), which decorates the middle of the Cortile della Pigna at the Vatican Museums.

Despite the many artistic movements—such as Continuità, Forma, and Art informel—which emerged in Italy during the second half of the 20th century, *arte povera* (an Italian art movement often characterized by the use of ephemeral materials) was the most innovative and probably longest lasting, especially with regard to sculpture. The term, coined by the Genoese art critic Germano Celant in 1967, describes a group of Italian artists, who, from the late 1960s, sought to destroy the "dichotomy between art and life" by way of sculpture made from everyday materials. Pino Pascali was one of *arte povera*'s founding members, and with works such as his *Anti-Aircraft Gun* of 1965, he succeeded in giving expression to the anxieties of this politically troubled and war-torn time. Michelangelo Pistoletto, in turn, used reflective materials to force the viewer to see himself as part of his sculpture's meaning; his *Vietnam* (1965; Menil Collection, Houston) has life-size images of antiwar protestors before a reflective background. Some *arte povera* sculptors, such as Mario Merz, sought allusions to non-Western civilizations. From the late 1960s, Merz constructed igloos out of natural and synthetic materials, emphasizing the disparities between modern and nomadic cultures. Jannis Kounellis, too, experimented with the juxtaposition of seemingly antithetical objects, arriving at solutions that reveal his disillusionment with society's growing fragmentation. While artists such as Giovanni Anselmo kept *arte povera* alive throughout the 1980s, the Transavangardia sculptors, including Mimmo Paladino, made moves toward a more figurative—sometimes primitive—art during the last decades of the 20th century.

CLAUDE D. DICKERSON

Further Reading

Baldacci, Paolo, and Gianni Vianello, *Arturo Martini*, edited by Vianello, New York and Milan: Daverio, 1991

Bonito Oliva, Achille, *Minimalia: An Italian Vision in 20th-Century Art* (exhib. cat.), Milan: Electa, 1999

Bossaglia, Rossana (editor), *Giacomo Balla* (exhib. cat.), Milan: Mazzotta, 1994

Braun, Emily (editor), *Italian Art in the 20th Century: Painting and Sculpture, 1900–1988* (exhib. cat.), Munich: Prestel, 1989

Braun, Emily, *Mario Sironi and Italian Modernism: Art and Politics under Fascism*, Cambridge and New York: Cambridge University Press, 2000

Coen, Ester, *Umberto Boccioni* (exhib. cat.), New York: Metropolitan Museum of Art, 1988

Casè, Pierre (editor), *Marino Marini* (exhib. cat.), Milan: Skira, London: Thames and Hudson, and New York: Abbeville Press, 1999

Celant, Germano (editor), *Piero Manzoni* (exhib. cat.), London: Serpentine Gallery, and Milan: Charta, 1998

Crispolti, Enrico, and Rosella Siligato (editors), *Lucio Fontana* (exhib. cat.), Milan: Electa, 1998

De Micheli, Mario, *La scultura del novecento*, Turin, Italy: UTET, 1981

De Sanna, Jole, *Medardo Rosso; o, La creazione dello spazio moderno*, Milan: Mursia, 1985

Fagiolo dell'Arco, Maurizio, *Scuola romana: Pittura e scultura a Roma dal 1919 al 1943*, Rome: De Luca, 1986

Fagiolo dell'Arco, Maurizio (editor), *Balla e i futuristi* (exhib. cat.), Milan: Electa, 1988

IVORY AND BONE

For millennia, ivory was used for objects as diverse as religious images and thimbles, furniture, and jewelry, most often for fine and high-quality sculpture and, more specifically, for luxury artifacts. The subtle and glowing color of this precious and noble material, its delicacy of tone, and the apparent smoothness of ivory-made objects exerted a fascination for centuries, qualities that still are an invitation to take these objects in one's hands. It is probably not by mere chance that most ivory artifacts were made to be touched or caressed, such as Japanese netsukes (carved toggles in the form of a miniature sculpture used to secure hanging objects to the sash of a man's kimono), Mughal chess pieces, and Chinese seals.

It is not really necessary to propose a histology of all raw materials here reviewed, except to state that they are a compound of organic and inorganic elements. Bone, for example, consists of fibrous protein collagen and crystals of hydroxyapatite, a complex of tricalcium and calcium hydroxide. The material is thus light and strong and rather flexible. Ivory, technically known as dentine, also is a mixture of organic and inorganic materials of ossein and hydroxyapatite. Although it is impossible to distinguish bone from ivory through chemical analysis only, their microstructures differ. The cross-section of bone, which is formed by compact tissues enveloping spongy tissues, presents a porous structure of rough grains that are difficult to polish. Ivory, on the contrary, is formed by a compact, hard, and dense tissue (dentine), and its section presents a finer texture offering a certain homogeneous aspect except for the fine ducts that radiate from the pulpar cavity. Ivory can be identified by other characteristics, such as its iridescent color, its brightness, and the fine lines that run along the main tusk's axis. Ivory

is less breakable than bone and presents a brilliant and smooth surface when polished.

True ivory comes from the tusks of the African and Asiatic elephant. Its color and fineness vary according to the species involved, the geographical origin, the animal's age, and the moment of its extraction. The most prized ivory comes from Africa: compared to Indian ivory, African ivory offers a finer grain richer in tone. The Chinese imported tusks from nearby countries, but as early as the 12th century they recognized that African ivory was by far the best. Ivory from West Africa, although it is less white, usually is harder than East African ivory. Green ivory is a translucent ivory extracted from fresh-killed elephants: it will contract itself when drying. Yellow and opaque white ivories denote ancient ivories. Thailand's ivory, which is heavy with fine grains, is particularly sought after, as is Guinea's ivory, which is matte white, pearly, and milklike, and possesses the particularity of whitening with time. Some ivories present a solid color: Ceylon's ivory is pale pink and veined, whereas Cape Town's ivory quickly turns yellow. Although denser, Indian ivory is softer than African ivory but hard to polish and will also quickly yellow. African tusks are normally larger and of better quality than Asian: they measure up to 2 meters long for an average weight of about 23 kilograms. Mammoth ivory is the biggest. Its trade began in the 17th century and increased two centuries later when it was exported from the Arctic tundra of Siberia and Alaska to Europe and the Far East, especially China. It sometimes presents a bluish tone—hence its designation as turquoise ivory—but usually is nutty brown. Once worked, mammoth ivory cannot be distinguished from elephant.

There exists other "ivory," which was used as a raw material for carving. Bone—both human and animal—has been used since ancient times for domestic objects (combs, handles, pins, buttons, dice, etc.) and to inlay furniture. Supply of bone far exceeded demand and was easily available because the species involved generally were identical with those exploited for food. There were bone-based carving industries in Greco-Roman Egypt and northern Italy, where the school of the Embriachi flourished in the 14th and 15th centuries. Long bones of horses and cattle were the raw material for both schools. Bone has also been used as a lower quality substitute for ivory and was often polished to imitate the more costly material.

In northern countries, whaling, known as early as the 6th century, also provided the necessary material for the carvers. From the late 10th to the 12th or 13th centuries, walrus ivory became popular as a raw material for carving into secular and devotional objects. Also known as morse ivory, walrus ivory is the only native source of ivory in Europe, and early Scandinavian ivory artifacts such as weapons were carved from it. Just like the beaver's teeth that were prized as amulets in the Anglo-Saxon period, walrus was believed to have prophylactic powers, probably being taken for the famous unicorn horn along with narwhal tusk. The latter assuredly was one of the most highly prized *mirabilia* (marvels) during the later Medieval period, mainly as a curiosity (complete tusks are thus recorded in royal and church treasuries) and used against poisoning (drinking cups were made out of it). Although its twisted shape leaves very little workable material, the Japanese used narwhal tusks for small objects, including netsuke. Seamen etched scrimshaw on whole sperm whale teeth. Other materials carved during these centuries include hippopotamus (a whiter ivory), boar, and warthog teeth. There exist a lot of substitute materials, such as the casque of the helmeted hornbill, the horn of both the African and Asiatic rhinoceros, and also horns and antlers of rams, deer, and antelope, which were used for small objects, such as handles of weapons and mugs, buttons, and boxes.

Ivory, although a hard substance that requires sharp tools, can easily be sawn or filed. Since the tusk grows outwardly by successive layers, it presents a conical hollow (the pulp) that runs from its base through two-thirds, or more rarely half, of its length, and the remaining portion of the tusk is solid. The hollow portion or proximal end of the tusk is cut up in order to release either plates when cut lengthwise or circular boxes, liturgical buckets, or armlets when crosscut. The other part of the tusk is devoted to the carving in the round and conforms to the tusk's shape: numerous Gothic statuettes thus incorporate the curvature into the design. The techniques employed by the ivory carver have not changed since Antiquity. The tusk is first prepared by sawing out the block or the plate for the appropriate object to carve. Using progressively finer tools, the carver then shapes details with the chisels, gouges, and files. Turned work is produced with the bow lathe, a practice that became more common in the 11th century on, or the ornamental turning lathe with which German virtuoso masterpieces of the 17th century were made. Ivory can also be riveted, clamped, glued, or fixed. Greek *chryselephantine* statues (sculptures of wood, ivory, and gold that suggest drapery over flesh), such as Pheidias's *Zeus* at Olympia (mid 5th century BCE), were made of gold and ivory mounted on a wooden base, ivory being particularly convenient for representing flesh. Pygmalion's statue was so realistic, Ovid tells us (*Metamorphoses* X.243), that he fell in love with her and demanded that Aphrodite give life to her so that he could marry his creature. Yet heavy disadvantages occur when assembling different pieces of ivory: it is indeed difficult to conceal

the joints, which will darken, and to correctly match veins of one piece with the other.

The processes and tools used to cut ivory, bone, and antler are the same as those used to work other hard materials. Tools involved are the same as the wood sculptor's—knives, chisels, gouges, gravers, files—although of smaller dimensions. Saws are the most important implements used in the working of skeletal materials, not only for cutting up the material but also in applying surface patterns (see MacGregor, 1985). As for decoration, traces and marks on the artifacts indicate the wide range of tools used in the process. "Compass-drawn" decorations were probably made with a kind of mortise gauge. For operations of smoothing and polishing, the use of different files is attested, from the rough to the finest one, although some traces on the objects also indicate the use of sharp knives in the process. During Classical and Medieval times, final polishing was executed with a kind of sandpaper, probably made of leather and fine sea sand or crushed chalk or ashes. Traces on objects also reveal the use of the drill and the borer. Ivory can also be gilded, painted, or stained with oils, dyes, and pigments, and it seems that ivory artifacts were likely to have been painted in Antiquity as well as the Classical and Medieval periods (see Connor, 1998). Examples of polychrome ivories survive from the Middle (3rd millennium BCE) and New Kingdom Egypt (14th century BCE) to the end of the Middle Ages. Like wood, ivory contracts and expands according to the variations of humidity and tends to crack or split. This may well explain the complete loss of color over time. Worked ivory, like carved wood and stone sculpture, was most probably painted in Antiquity, although its natural color was occasionally exploited, as with the *chryselephantine* statues. To quote one single example, late Roman consular diptychs were entirely painted, as R. Delbrueck correctly argued (see Connor, 1998).

It is also possible to soften and mold ivory, bone, and antler. Methods differ according to the material involved. When plunged in cold and then boiling water, bone and antler become soft enough to enable shaping and cutting into various forms. Experiments conducted have also shown that when immersed in an acid solution (such as vinegar or a broth of sorrel leaves), bone and antler become soft within two days to six weeks, depending on the acid solution used. But it seems more likely that, to save time, handcrafters have used the former method. Rendering horn malleable and soft is achieved simply by applying it to heat. Horns can thus be redressed or, when appropriately cut, unrolled to form square translucent surfaces. Evidence for softening elephant ivory has been noted since Roman times. In his *De diversis artibus*, composed around 1125, Theophilus gives some recipes for ivory softening, including heating in wine or vinegar, then anointing with oil and wrapping in leather. Ivory irremediably loses some of its particularities in the process. Since ivory is a mixture of organic and inorganic material, it is subject to various causes of damage that will provoke its splitting and warping when exposed to moisture or heat. Ivory that has been recovered from archaeological excavations is degraded to some extent, being porous, breakable, or chalky. Late Antique and Early Medieval ivories such as consular diptychs and book covers were preserved in church treasuries, and this could perhaps explain their nearly perfect state of conservation.

PIERRE ALAIN MARIAUX

See also **Chryselephantine Sculpture; Pheidias**

Further Reading

Barnet, Peter (editor), *Images in Ivory: Precious Objects of the Gothic Age* (exhib. cat.), Princeton, New Jersey: Princeton University Press, and Detroit, Michigan: The Detroit Institute of Arts, 1997

Connor, Carolyn L., *The Color of Ivory: Polychromy on Byzantine Ivories*, Princeton, New Jersey: Princeton University Press, 1998

Cutler, Anthony, *The Craft of Ivory: Sources, Techniques, and Uses in the Mediterranean World*, A.D. 200–1400, Washington, D.C.: Dumbarton Oaks Research Library and Collection, 1985

MacGregor, Arthur, *Bone, Antler, Ivory, and Horn: The Technology of Skeletal Materials since the Roman Period*, London: Croom Helm, and Totowa, New Jersey: Barnes and Noble, 1985

Randall, Richard H., Jr., *Masterpieces of Ivory from the Walters Art Gallery*, New York: Hudson Hills Press, and London: Sotheby's, 1985

Vickers, Michael J., et al., *Ivory: A History and Collector's Guide*, London: Thames and Hudson, 1987

IVORY SCULPTURE: ANCIENT

The archaeological record of the earliest period of human existence in Europe, the Paleolithic Age, which covered an immense span from around 400,000 to about 10,000 BCE, is full of ivory and bone objects. Regional inhabitants during this period used ivory from mammoth tusks, and the people of the Gravettian culture (22,000–18,000 BCE) were the first to use ivory in jewelry, such as in beads, pendants, and bracelets, as well as for female figurines similar to the *Venus of Willendorf* (one such figurine is known from Kostiencki in southern Russia). Ivory figurines dating to the Solutrean or the Magdalenian periods (18,000–8000 BCE) have also been found.

Egypt

Specially designed objects for domestic use, such as handles for spear-throwers or harpoons and arrowheads, have been discovered in Egypt. Tombs from Predynastic and Early Dynastic Egypt (*ca.* 6000–*ca.* 2575 BCE) were rich in ivory and bone funerary equipment. These tombs have furnished the earliest examples of ivory-made objects such as long-toothed combs and hairpins often carved with animals, bangles and pendants, bracelets, necklaces, ointment containers such as the one in the Walters Art Museum (Baltimore, Maryland; made in the form of a swimming duck), game pieces, and amulets in the form of bulls' heads and flies. Objects in ivory are among the earliest Egyptian works of art to survive, thanks to a favorably dry climate. Since the middle of the 5th millennium BCE, the Egyptians developed techniques of cutting and carving ivory, which they sometimes combined with other materials. Hippopotamuses' teeth were extensively used for ivory carving. In the ancient Near East, man produced luxury items in ivory such as small vessels and boxes, spoons, scepters, and drinking horns. Ivory was also used as mosaic inlay and for handles and knobs, small-scale statues of deities (such as the so-called concubines or dwarfs, for instance), and for anatomic details of larger statues (such as faces, hands, or feet). Ivory was frequently gilded and colored. It is interesting to note that the artists had the capacity to capture natural forms like animals, reflecting a careful observation of the subjects that recalls an authentic naturalism, yet still stylized human figures. Some uses of ivory and bone were more prevalent during certain phases of Egyptian history: magic knives, always of hippopotamus ivory, were produced only in the Middle Kingdom and shortly afterward (*ca.* 2000–*ca.* 1600 BCE), whereas ivory furniture inlay was common until the late Dynastic period.

Ancient Near East

The tradition of ivory carving in Egypt had a great influence on the rest of the ancient world. This influence is very noticeable through the adoption of iconographical motifs, such as sphinxes or lion-headed demons, and stylistic formulas. There is evidence that Egyptian pharaohs and Assyrian kings received elephant tusks as tribute from Syria, yet texts state that the Sumerians also received ivory from the island of Dilmun (modern Bahrain). Dilmun's source for ivory may well have been India, with which they were in contact already in the 24th–23rd centuries BCE. As Jeanny Vorys Canby states (see Randall, 1985), if elephants were indigenous to the Near East, it remains unclear why ivory was not used as lavishly as in Egypt. It has been suggested that herds of elephants were periodically exported from India. Although this situation seems not to have fostered a strong tradition of ivory carving in the Near East, excavations have revealed that ivory was widely used there. Syria-Palestine and Anatolia thus had flourishing ivory carving schools in the Bronze Age, which surprisingly enough occur only sporadically, whereas extensive ivory carving is not attested in the Near East until after the 15th century BCE.

Excavations of ivory carvers' workshops near Beersheba in Palestine have revealed statuettes of human figures and ornamental plaques dating to 3500 BCE. These pieces resemble earlier Predynastic figures from Egypt, reflecting not only an obvious stylistic influence but also a direct copying of Egyptian artifacts. Some other pieces present a blend of Egyptian and local styles. In the Late Bronze Age, Egyptian ivories and other luxury artifacts were exported throughout the Near East, and this had a wide influence on ivories found in the Middle East and, from the earlier 2nd millennium BCE until the fall of the Hittite empire around 1120 BCE, in Anatolia (modern Turkey). But in Assyria, as in Anatolia, a more independent school developed (see the Pratt Ivories acquired by the Metropolitan Museum of Art in New York City during the 1930s). The investigation of the palace of Ugarit in northern Syria, a major center of production in the 2nd millennium BCE, produced royal furniture such as beds, chairs, and tables with ivory inlay. In the Assyrian palaces at Nimrud from the 9th to the 7th centuries BCE, rooms full of ivory inlays for furniture and a variety of other objects were discovered. Recent research on this group of artifacts suggests the existence of various schools of carving, leading to the conclusion that the major cultural centers of the Near East had their own styles (see Barnett, 1982).

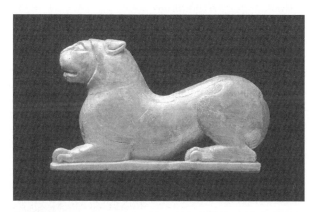

Seated lion
© Araldo de Luca / CORBIS

Greece

The trade of ivory is attested since the Early Bronze Age, but it was from Syria that ivory first came to the Greek world. Excavations at Knossos and in other small palaces at Phaistos and Zakro have yielded caches of unworked tusks as well as ivory chips discarded in the workshops. There is evidence of activity among Cretan craftsmen during the Early Minoan II period (*ca.* 2600 BCE), which continued into the Middle Minoan times (*ca.* 1900–1600 BCE). These craftsmen excelled in carving three-dimensional figures in ivory, but they also used ivory for seals of various forms. Their figurines show the special technique of separately carved torsos and limbs, which were then attached together at the joints with ivory pegs. They also combined ivory with gold to make the hair and the decorative parts. Figurines such as the Snake Goddess or Priestess in the Walters Art Museum can be seen as the forerunners of Classical Greek *chryselephantine* statues (sculptures of wood, ivory, and gold that suggest drapery over flesh). The figure is constructed from five pieces of ivory, whereas elements of the dress are made of thin gold sheets; the raised arms were entwined with gold snakes, and a gold diadem was part of the headdress.

Cretan craftsmen soon exported their skills and techniques and traveled to the mainland. In the 14th and 13th centuries BCE, Mycenaean workshops thus produced combs, pyxes, hairpins, mirror and knife handles, musical instruments, seals, sword pommels, and pieces of furniture with inlaid ivory (a stool made of ebony inlaid with ivory butterflies is known from the palace of Pylos). Many of the ivories found in mainland palaces and tombs were carved by Mycenaean artists. With the collapse of Mycenaean rule in the 12th century BCE, the practice of ivory carving nearly disappeared and survived only in peripheral regions like the island of Cyprus. At Salamis, for instance, ivory thrones and other regal pieces of furniture dating back to 700 BCE have been discovered.

It is most probably from the East that ivory carving reappeared in Greece in the second half of the 8th century BCE. In the course of the following century, craftsmen from the Near East settled in Greece. Much of the evidence about ivory from large urban centers comes from sanctuaries, although it was much in demand. The urban centers had the craftsmen to work the ivory tusks and produce luxury items. Inventory lists from the Parthenon and other temples at Athens and elsewhere thus record ivory lyres, tables, flute cases, animals, and thrones. Caches discovered under the Sacred Way at Delphi and in the foundation deposit of the Artemision at Ephesus contained more than 2000 ivory statuettes classified as oriental in style and reliefs depicting battle scenes and mythological subjects dating to the 7th and 6th centuries BCE. In the Greek world, ivory was considered a suitable material for the gods, either for the realization of divine images or for the confection of objects dedicated to the deities in the sanctuaries. The situation was different in Etruria, where the artifacts recovered from tombs in Cerveteri or Praeneste seem to be personal or private possessions: tools, combs, handles, plaques, and boxes.

Supply of raw material from Syria soon diminished because elephants were probably extinct in that area by the end of the 9th century BCE, and ivory would have had to come from Africa; acquisition of raw ivory took place on the Atlantic coast of Africa in Libya and Egypt, as well as India. Phoenicians exchanged Attic pottery, perfume, and "Egyptian stone" for ivory and animal skins, which traveled further west to North Africa, Spain, and eventually Italy, where local workshops developed the technique of ivory carving along with an ornamental repertoire. Ethiopians also traded gold and ivory. Pausanias informs us (V.12.3) that "the Greeks brought ivory from India and Ethiopia to make statues." He also recorded more than 24 *chryselephantine* statues, the most celebrated of which were the statues of Athena in the Parthenon and of Zeus in the temple of Olympia, both by Pheidias.

The tradition of making pieces of furniture with ivory inlay or veneers obviously continued in the Greek world: ivory couches (such as the one kept in the Hermitage Museum in St. Petersburg, Russia, excavated at Kul Oba in South Russia in 1830), chairs and tables, chests and boxes, and musical instruments, which could be fashioned in part from ivory and bone. There were also swords and daggers inlaid with ivory, as well as fittings, handles, and jewelry (brooches, pins, and rings) made of ivory.

Etruria

From the 7th century BCE, prestige objects were imported from Syria that were also imitated locally on Etruscan soil in the orientalizing and Greek styles: fan handles, goblets, cylindrical caskets, and combs were among the possessions of princes. Among these objects, the Walters Art Museum keeps a pyxis dating to 650–625 BCE found at Cerveteri, which was fashioned from the hollow end of an elephant's tusk. Its surface is divided by four blind bands into three registers on which are figural reliefs. On one side of the lower register, rampant sphinxes frame a group of three women holding hands, whereas on the other side two male figures grasp the tails of two sphinxes that flank a single woman who is holding their raised paws. The middle register offers a frieze of four chariots ready

to parade. Four animals occupy the upper register: a crouching deer looking back, a lion, a bull or deer upside down, and a second feline. A Phoenician palmette separates the deer from the lion. The cover of the pyxis is missing, but its knob, which is carved in the form of a sphinx wearing a Phoenician palmette crown, is preserved. The decor, the shape, and the ivory material of this box indicate that the Etruscan artist copied several different reliefs and that the pyxis was made after a Near Eastern model.

In the last quarter of the 6th century BCE, ivory was no longer imported in tusk form, but in small tablets of standard dimensions. Cut in the form of plaques and carved with a mythological decor, ivory (sometimes substituted by bone) was applied to wooden caskets. Etruscan craftsmen drew on a repertory of eastern Greek forms. By the 3rd century BCE, the craft seems to have been no more innovative, except for mirror handles.

Rome

Contrary to the Etruscans, Romans used ivory sparingly in the 5th and 4th centuries BCE. Ivory indeed played little role in the early republic, and bone was often preferred as a substitute for inlay or for small plaques attached to furniture and boxes. By the late 3rd century BCE, the situation changed when the Carthaginian wars brought the Romans into contact with the Hellenistic cultures of southern Italy and Sicily: spoils of war included gold and silver vessels and coins, which were carried in procession throughout Rome and influenced—some say corrupted—Roman taste. Ivory was no longer reserved for insignia of high office such as scepters or curule chairs, but also for the effigies and statues of leading citizens in the manner of the Greek rulers. The almost life-size ivory face and arm in the Vatican Museums were probably parts of a Roman *chryselephantine* statue of Athena, made after a Greek original. Excavations at Pompeii and elsewhere have brought to light furniture inlaid with ivory and bone, *auloi*, circular boxes, game boards, knife handles, writing tablets and styli, doctors' tools, decorative pins for hairdressings and garments, objects for the table and the dressing-room, ceremonial weapons, and even small pieces such as dice, theatre tokens, or gaming pieces. All these pieces were alternately and equally made of bone and ivory, both materials often seen in the same piece. Whalebone ivory seems not to have been an available substitute in ancient Rome.

PIERRE ALAIN MARIAUX

See also **Chryselephantine Sculpture; Pheidias**

Further Reading

Barnett, Richard David, *Ancient Ivories in the Middle East*, Jerusalem: Institute of Archaeology, Hebrew University of Jerusalem, 1982

Carter, Jane Burr, *Greek Ivory-Carving in the Orientalizing and Archaic Periods*, New York: Garland, 1985

Connor, Carolyn L., *The Color of Ivory: Polychromy on Byzantine Ivories*, Princeton, New Jersey: Princeton University Press, 1998

Delbrueck, Richard, *Die Consulardiptychen und verwandte Denkmäler*, Berlin: De Gruyter, 1929

Drenkhahn, Rosemarie, *Elfenbein im Alten Ägypten: Leihgaben aus dem Petrie-Museum London*, Erbach, Germany: Deutsches Elfenbeinmuseum, 1986

Fitton, J. Lesley (editor), *Ivory in Greece and the Eastern Mediterranean from the Bronze Age to the Hellenistic Period*, London: The British Museum, 1992

Poursat, Jean-Claude, *Les ivoires mycéniens: Essai sur la formation d'un art mycénien*, Athens: École Française d'Athènes, 1977

Randall, Richard H., *Masterpieces of Ivory from the Walters Art Gallery*, New York: Hudson Hills Press, and London: Sotheby's, 1985

Vickers, Michael J., et al., *Ivory: A History and Collector's Guide*, London: Thames and Hudson, 1987

Volbach, Wolfgang Fritz, *Elfenbeinarbeiten der Spätantike und des frühen Mittelalters*, Mainz, Germany: Wilckens, 1916; 3rd edition, Mainz: Von Zabern, 1976

IVORY SCULPTURE: EARLY CHRISTIAN–ROMANESQUE

4th–6th Century

The 4th to the 6th century saw the Roman Empire metamorphose into the Early Byzantine Empire. The Classical religious tradition gave way to Christianity as the capital shifted from Rome in the West to Constantinople in the East. Coincident with this period of political, religious, and social transformation was a great flourishing of ivory carving. *Eborarii*, or ivory carvers, were among the artists exempt from civil obligations in an edict of 337 included in the Theodosian code, the practice of their craft evidently on a par with service to the state. Greater access to sources of ivory and widespread demand by wealthy patrons for objects made from ivory suggest that the skilled labor of ivory carvers was greatly valued indeed. Much of the sculpture of this period continued the Roman practice of using ivory to adorn all manner of household goods. Texts from the 4th and 5th centuries describing lavish decoration with ivory underscore the evidence offered by the extraordinary number of surviving ivory and bone plaques from Byzantine Egypt, many of which were undoubtedly used as inlays for furniture. Some of the finest examples of these plaques were reused on the 11th-century ambo for Henry II (Palace Chapel,

Aachen, Germany). These plaques, 25 centimeters in length and created in Alexandria during the 6th century, show subjects drawn from a Classical decorative repertory: Isis appears in one panel, Bacchus in two, Nereid in another, and military leaders in two others.

Although many of the Egyptian plaques betray the sketchy workmanship associated with "mass" production, contemporary plaques linked to Rome and Constantinople exhibit more meticulous carving, tailored to the specific patrons they commemorate. These pieces attest to the importance of ivory sculpture in the social rituals of the empire's elite. Ivories, particularly diptychs, were commissioned as gifts to friends upon the attainment of a high-ranking post within the empire's elaborate civil hierarchy. Minor officials, such as the suffect consul Lampadius and the vicar of Rome Rufius Probianus, likely commissioned their diptychs for that purpose (Museo Civico dell'Età Cristiana, Brescia, Italy; Staatsbibliothek, Berlin); a letter from the urban prefect Q. Aurelius Symmachus states his intention to send ivory, along with silver bowls, to friends in honor of his son's quaestorian games. The most significant body of ivories involved in the social custom of gift-giving are the large number of diptychs distributed by eastern and western consuls in the 5th and 6th centuries, of which some 40 survive in modern collections. The earliest commemorates Probus's accession to the western consulate in 406 (Cathedral Treasury, Aosta, Italy). The latest, from 541, represents Basilius, the last consul (Castello Sforzesco, Milan). Many show portraits of the official in an architectural setting accompanied by symbols of his rank and largess. Made from long and relatively thick slabs, these were ostentatious works that became increasingly declamatory over time, both in size and iconography. A number of consular diptychs from the 6th century exist as multiples, suggesting they were issued in large numbers with different styles of diptychs perhaps distributed to different classes of recipients.

Although often associated with consular diptychs, "imperial" or five-part diptychs are more ambiguous in terms of function. The Barberini diptych (Musée du Louvre, Paris), which is actually a single, five-part tablet, depicts a victorious emperor receiving tribute from his vanquished foes. A sumptuous object made from a gigantic tusk, this 6th-century tablet would seem a politically motivated commission although it, like the fragments from other five-part diptychs, offers few clues. The Symmachorum and Nichomachorum panels (Victoria and Albert Museum, London; Musée National du Moyen Âge, Paris) provide another instance of ivory sculpture commissioned by Roman nobility as a social ritual. They were likely requested around the year 400 by two senatorial families in order to commemorate a marriage. Each of these elegant panels, carved in low relief, shows a woman, perhaps a priestess, performing pagan rites before an altar. In both style and subject matter, they recall earlier Roman and Greek reliefs. Through their deliberate references to the past, they assert the families' allegiance to ancient ways at a time when the influence of Christianity was growing.

Eborarii from this period hardly restricted their work to secular or pagan themes. Christian iconography appears on ivory sculpture as early as around 370 in the Brescia Casket (Museo Civico dell'Età Cristiana), which shows scenes from the Old and New Testament. An ivory in Munich (Bayerisches Nationalmuseum), around 400, couples a scene of the three women at the tomb with one of the Ascension of Christ. Ecclesiastical furniture made from carved ivory survives in the form a throne for Archbishop Maximianus of Ravenna (Museo Archiepiscopal, Ravenna). Christian attributes, albeit in a secondary role, appear in ostensibly secular ivories as well. A number of consular diptychs, including the Clementinus (Liverpool Museum, England) and the Justinian diptychs (Metropolitan Museum of Art, New York City) include discrete crosses in their decoration. *Pyxides*, small containers made from the cross-section of elephant tusks, abound in this period. Their carved decoration features Christian subject matter as often as pagan. Many ivories with Christian subjects follow the format of secular works. A diptych with Christ on one panel and the Virgin with the Christ Child on another (Museum für Byzantinische Kunst, Berlin) shows the figures seated on a cushioned throne beneath an architectural canopy, reminiscent of the setting often seen in consular diptychs. A Christian diptych from Milan (Cathedral Treasury) features Christian symbols in the central panels surrounded, in the manner of five-part imperial diptychs, by smaller plaques with scenes from the life of Christ.

6th Century

Diminishment in the number and quality of ivories after the mid 6th century suggests a reduction in supply as well as demand, particularly in what had been the great centers of ivory carving, Constantinople and Rome. Few objects can be firmly dated to the 7th century; the inadequate evidence we possess in terms of objects and texts suggests that ivory carving became a marginal enterprise. Earlier ivories were still valued, however, and many, such as the Barberini diptych, found new uses as liturgical diptychs with prayers and names to be recited inscribed on the back. Not until the mid 8th century do we again find instances of accomplished carving in ivory or bone, although they were associated with relatively remote monastic set-

tings, rather than urban centers. The Franks Casket (British Museum, London; Museo Nazionale del Bargello, Florence), carved from whalebone, presents a sophisticated ensemble of scenes from Roman legend, Germanic folklore, and the Bible, alongside runic inscriptions in Old English and Latin. Likely associ-

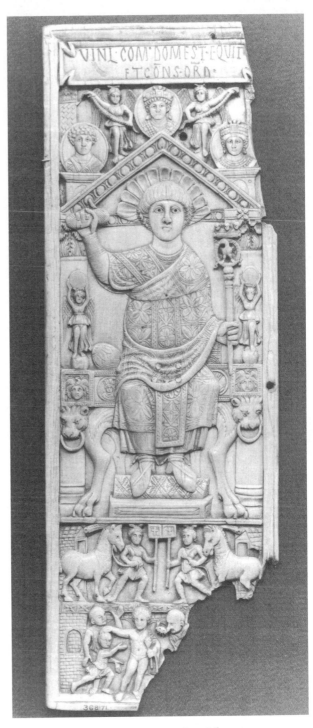

Anastasius Diptych, Victoria and Albert Museum
© Victoria and Albert Museum

ated with an Anglo-Saxon monastery in Northumbria, the piece displays a lively linear style where words and images compete for space on crowded panels. The Werden Portable Reliquary Altar (Saint Luidger Church, Essen-Werden), which blends geometric motifs with charmingly schematic representations of Christ and angels, and the Gandersheim Casket (Herzog Anton Ulrich Museum, Brunswick, Germany), with its dense patchwork of interlace designs, both attest to the virtuosity of Anglo-Saxon sculptors working in bone in the late 8th century.

8th–9th Centuries

In the late 8th and 9th centuries, during the reign of the Carolingians, ivory carving underwent a resurgence in western Europe. The Carolingian court and the wealthy monasteries that supported it all promoted the development of ivory workshops. These workshops, dispersed throughout the Frankish kingdoms, specialized in plaques, which were used primarily as book covers and, to a lesser degree, caskets, and their favored subject matter was narratives from the life of Christ. Although the Carolingians continued the practice of inscribing the back of earlier ivories in order to use them as liturgical diptychs, they also saw fit to cut down, turn over, and plane older ivories to provide an empty field for new carvings. The practice of recarving ivories suggests a shortage of material, yet rarely did Carolingian ivory sculptors turn to inferior materials such as antler or bone. Rather, they became virtuosos in developing compositions suited to plaques of small dimensions and in negotiating panels of remarkable thinness.

Carolingian artists and patrons admired ivory carvings of the Late Roman and Early Byzantine period. Many ivories, such as the Roma and Constantinople Diptych (Kunsthistorisches Museum, Vienna), the Werden plaques (Victoria and Albert Museum, London), and the Andrews Diptych (Victoria and Albert Museum), vacillate between 5th and 9th century dates, as scholars cannot agree on whether they are ancient carvings or scrupulous emulations by Carolingian sculptors. Numerous Carolingian ivories display direct borrowings from earlier pieces. A Crucifixion ivory (Liverpool Museum) draws its scene of the women at Christ's tomb directly from the early 5th-century Munich Ascension plaque, whereas the Bodleian (Oxford) ivory of the resurrected Christ derives its scenes from 5th-century fragments now in Berlin (Museum für Byzantische Kunst), Paris (Musée du Louvre), and Nevers (Musée Municipal Frédéric Blandin de Nevers, France). The five-part format, used in the 6th-century Barberini and Milan diptychs, appears again in the covers of the Lorsch Gospels (Vatican Museums; Victoria and Albert Museum) as well as the Bodleian plaque.

The indebtedness of Carolingian ivory sculptors to earlier ivory carving ought not to obscure their many innovations in iconography and visual narration. The theologically rich iconography of a 9th-century Crucifixion ivory, now on the cover of the Pericopes of Henry II (Bayerische Staatsbibliothek, Munich), was novel in its incorporation of Classical and Christian personifications. The piece proved enormously influential for subsequent images of the Crucifixion in the Carolingian period. A Crucifixion scene from Narbonne (Cathedral Treasury) relies on a complex arrangement of paired scenes of the life of Christ and attests to Carolingian daring in the area of narrative sequencing.

Although the original function and patronage of most Carolingian ivories is now lost, those few ivories that retain evidence of their original context suggest that ivories often participated in the political and social commerce of the day. With its ironic and subtle images of the labors of Hercules, the mid 9th-century St. Peter's throne (St. Peter's Basilica, Rome), according to Lawrence Nees, contributed to the political and intellectual discourses associated with Bishop Hincmar of Reims and Charles the Bald (see Nees, 1991). The ivory plaques that adorned the *Dagulf Psalter* (ca. 795; Musée du Louvre, Paris) were probably intended as part of a package of diplomatic gifts offered to Pope Hadrian II by Charlemagne. Their subject, the transmission of the Psalms, not only suited the book's contents but also flattered the giver and receiver, as is suggested by the two dedicatory poems inside the manuscript. Furthermore, one of the poems, in paying tribute to the sculptor of the ivory covers, makes clear what one must largely surmise: that Carolingian artists and patrons appreciated "the gifted hand [who] has carved marvelously."

10th–11th Centuries

The iconoclastic controversy of the 8th and early 9th centuries undoubtedly dampened even further the already diminished production of ivory in the east. Ivory carving of high quality resumed, however, in the 10th and 11th centuries. Economic stability with an attendant restoration of some trade routes likely encouraged the limited import of ivory, although the supply of ivory seems to have never reached the abundant quantity of the 4th–6th centuries. Many of the finest ivory sculptures were carved from inferior ivory, and bone often appears as a substitute or in conjunction with elephant dentine. Limitations of material notwithstanding, the era produced a large number of finely carved icons and boxes. Ivory icons took the form of single plaques, diptychs, and most characteristically triptychs, and like mosaics, enamels, and paintings, they depicted an array of holy personages. Their small scale made them suitable for private, rather than collective, devotion. An object such as the Harbaville triptych (Musée du Louvre, Paris) is an overt declaration of prayer as it opens to show the *deesis* (Greek for entreaty), that is, a representation of Christ flanked by the intercessory figures of the Virgin and John the Baptist. The five apostles depicted below as well as the 26 saints (hierarchically arranged) that adorn the interior and exterior of the triptych's wings augment the icon's petitionary power.

New narrative themes, linked to liturgical feast days, emerge in this period, with ivory plaques offering some of the earliest surviving examples. The theme of the *Koimesis*, or the "falling asleep" in the death of the Virgin, appears first on ivory icons carved during the 10th century for the wealthy of Constantinople (Metropolitan Museum of Art, New York City). Its comforting vision of the Virgin at the end of her earthly life, surrounded by mourning apostles, her swaddled soul tended by Christ, no doubt contributed to the popularity of the image, which would come to appear in an array of materials on personal icons and in church cycles. The icons of the forty martyrs of Sebasteia offer another instance of an emotionally riveting image that debuts in ivory in the 10th century (State Hermitage Museum, St. Petersburg; Museum für Byzantinische Kunst, Berlin). The poignant scene of forty half-nude men huddled together on an icy lake provided ivory carvers not only with an opportunity to hone their depictions of the male physique but also to explore the stages of anguish and acceptance in the moments before death.

Over 100 boxes, known as "ivory caskets," survive from the Middle Byzantine period. Although some of these boxes are made of elephant ivory, many are of bone, and no small number mix the two. Largely devoted to secular themes, these luxury items were likely the proud possessions of Byzantine courtiers and high officials. Their sizes and shapes vary, but almost all make use of rosette borders that frame, on each side of the casket, a central scene. These scenes might be drawn from Classical mythology, the fantastic, the animal world, or the Bible, and single caskets readily mix different themes. The playful nudes so often featured on the caskets provide a humorous, at times overtly erotic, touch. Many of the boxes were probably readymade for purchase, whereas the most elaborate, such as the *Veroli Casket* (Victoria and Albert Museum, London) or the casket with warriors and "mythological" figures (Metropolitan Museum of Art, New York City) were probably made to order, their subject matter

specifically chosen to match the interests of the owners.

Like the consular diptychs from the earliest period, ivories in the Middle Byzantine period continued to serve political and social functions. Ivory plaques such as Christ crowning Constantine VII Porphyrogennetos (State Pushkin Museum of Fine Arts, Moscow) may have been produced as commemoratives of the imperial coronation and offered as gifts to friends and high officials. The subtle inclusion of Christian symbols seen in the consular diptychs, however, gives way in these images to an explicit evocation of Christ's endorsement of imperial power.

In 968, at roughly the same moment when ivory production was gearing up again in the east, Western sculptors working for the Ottonian royal family in what is present-day Germany produced an ambitious cycle of plaques in all likelihood for the Cathedral of Magdeburg, a favorite of Otto I and his wife Edith. The large group of plaques, of which 16 still survive, were intended for an elaborate piece of church finishing. Each plaque represents a scene from the life of Christ with the exception of the dedication panel (Metropolitan Museum of Art), which shows Otto presenting a model of the church to Christ for his blessing while in the company of patron saints. The openwork plaques were undoubtedly backed by gold foil, making the whole an extraordinary accumulation of sumptuous materials meant to match the grandeur of Otto's church.

The Ottonian imperial family were keen patrons of ivory sculpture, and the relative abundance of material at this time permitted them to commission objects requiring a significant store of ivory, such as the Magdeburg church furnishing. Ivory *situla*s, vessels for holy water requiring a significant cross section of elephant tusk, are rare, but no fewer than three were commissioned by Ottonian royalty. Ottonian emperors prided themselves on their close relations with Byzantium, and a number of high-quality ivories traveled to the West as gifts at this time. There they were almost immediately incorporated into elaborate book covers for imperial patrons. A plaque of the *Koimesis* adorns the Gospel Book of Otto III (Bayerische Staatsbibliothek, Munich). A prayer book for Henry II (Staatsbibliothek, Bamberg) is also outfitted with Byzantine plaques. Ottonian ivory carvers would sometimes directly imitate Byzantine forms, as is the case with a plaque of 982 or 983 depicting Christ crowning Otto II and his Byzantine wife Theophanu (Museé National du Moyen Âge). Additionally, the Ottonian penchant for extensive narrative cycles in the manner of Byzantine manuscripts evidences itself not only in large groups of ivories like the Magdeburg plaques, but also in single ivory objects like the Basilewsky *situla* (Victoria and Albert Museum).

Although no names of ivory sculptors from 11th-century Germany have come down to us, the distinctive style manifested in a group of ivories linked to Trier and Echternach offer evidence of a sculptor working in a highly original, even idiosyncratic manner. The forceful expressiveness of the figures on plaques such as the crucifixion scene on the Codex Aureus from Echternach (Germanisches National-museum, Nuremberg) and the Moses and Doubting Thomas pair (Staatliche Museen Preussischer Kulturbesitz, Berlin) is achieved through the unnatural contortion of their bodies and the unforgiving intensity of their stares. Supple figures distorted for expressive ends are hallmarks of the Romanesque carving that ivories herald.

11th–12th Century

Ivory sculpture in the 11th and early 12th centuries does not lend itself to easy characterization. By the 12th century, very little if any ivory carving was produced in Constantinople. The soft stone of steatite, inexpensive and more easily carved than ivory, came to replace dentine for smaller carved objects. The only dateable ivory from the late Byzantine period is a tiny box from around 1355 or 1403–04, itself subject to much debate, which depicts members of the imperial family (Dumbarton Oaks, Washington, D.C.). Its modest dimensions (4.2 by 3 centimeters) suggest that even the emperor did not have access to an ivory supply of any significance. By this time ivory en route from Africa likely bypassed Constantinople on its way to Paris and other centers of production in the West.

Ivories of exceptional quality appear throughout western Europe at this time, but they defy generalizations regarding their development and style as well as attempts to date or localize them with precision. Indeed many of the most important ivories, such as the whale-bone panel with the *Adoration of the Magi* (Victoria and Albert Museum, London) or the *Deposition from the Cross* (Victoria and Albert Museum, London) have been attributed to both England and Spain. One can only highlight some of the distinctive objects associated with some of the small centers of ivory production scattered in Spain, Italy, England, France, and Germany in attempting to describe the many, often conflicting currents in Romanesque ivory sculpture.

León was one such center during the 11th-century in Spain. A large and splendid crucifixion reliquary (Museo Arqueológico Nacional) originally from the treasury of San Isidoro in León testifies to the bold artistic patronage of Ferdinand I of León and his queen, Sancha. Their names are inscribed on the bottom of the cross, which they gave in 1063. The *Last Judgment* receives a novel treatment on the cross as the resurrected Christ appears at the top while the many awaiting judgment appear as an intricate interlace pattern along the border. Another set of ivories that are traditionally, although not definitively, associated with León once decorated a reliquary (Masaveu Collection, Oviedo, Spain; State Hermitage Museum, St. Petersburg; Metropolitan Museum of Art, New York City). Displaying scenes of the Death and Resurrection of Christ, the panels from the early 12th century employ dynamic figures whose dramatic gestures are underscored by swirling drapery.

In southern Italy, ivory workshops flourished in Amalfi. Extensive commercial relations with Arabs in North Africa not only supplied the city with ivory but also encouraged the production of carved ivories for a sophisticated clientele open to Islamic, Byzantine, and western styles. The Latin inscription on a cylindrical writing box decorated with Islamic motifs (Metropolitan Museum of Art, New York City) suggests that a local family might have commissioned the piece from the Muslim artists. Amalfi was the likely site for the production of a large group of some 38 narrative panels showing scenes from the Old and New Testament that was carved around 1084 for a piece of liturgical furnishing in the Cathedral of Salerno. The crisp Classical forms of the ivories attest to the region's strong ties with Byzantium.

In mid 12th-century England, we find ivory sculpture that is masterfully inventive in its disposition of figural scenes on unlikely forms. On the *St. Nicholas Crozier* (Victoria and Albert Museum, London), three scenes relating to Christ and one to St. Nicholas wrap around the curved volute of the crook. In the case of an altar cross often attributed to Bury St. Edmunds (Metropolitan Museum of Art, Cloisters Collection, New York City), the slender arms of that Christian symbol serve as a field for a dense exegetical commentary on the cross's typological significance.

A group of four appliqué figures (British Museum, London; Musée de l'Hôtel Sandelin, Saint Omer, France; Metropolitan Museum of Art, New York City; Musée des Beaux-Arts, Lille, France), surviving elements from a now-lost object showing the 24 elders of the Apocalypse, displays the happy confluence of bold linear patterns and complex drapery associated with Anglo-Saxon and northern French manuscript painting. The arresting figures, likely made in St. Omer in northern France, demonstrate the strong ties that bound ivory sculptors on both sides of the English Channel.

In Germany, as ivory became increasingly rare in the 12th century, sculptors turned to the more readily available materials of walrus ivory and bone. Eleven related plaques distributed in museums in Europe and the United States attest to the skills brought to the craft of walrus tusk carving during this period. The large square panels, perhaps created for the front of an ambo, are each made up of several smaller pieces of walrus ivory. Characterized by small nicks that emphasize the folds of the drapery, these pieces of the so-called *gestichelte* (pricked) style are variously dated from 1110 to 1170. Cologne was a prominent center for walrus ivory carving during the 12th century, with workshops specializing in book covers, game pieces, reliquaries, and portable altars; the city also had a thriving export business throughout Europe. Some 30 examples of octagonal or tower reliquaries all decorated with figures of the Apostles still survive, a tribute to Cologne's "mass-production" of reliquaries made from bone.

MELANIE HOLCOMB

See also **Carolingian; Harbaville Triptych; Ottonian Sculpture**

Further Reading

Bergman, Robert P., *The Salerno Ivories: Ars Sacra from Medieval Amalfi*, Cambridge, Massachusetts: Harvard University Press, 1980

Cutler, Anthony, "Prolegomena to the Craft of Ivory Carving in Late Antiquity and the Early Middle Ages," in *Commande et travail*, edited by Xavier Barral i Altet, Paris: Picard, 1987

Cutler, Anthony, *The Hand of the Master: Craftsmanship, Ivory, and Society in Byzantium (9th–11th Centuries)*, Princeton, New Jersey: Princeton University Press, 1994

Delbrueck, Richard, *Die Consulardiptychen und verwandte Denkmäler*, Berlin: De Gruyter, 1929

Gaborit-Chopin, Danielle, *Ivoires du moyen age*, Fribourg, Switzerland: Office du Livre, 1978

Goldschmidt, Adolph, Paul Gustave Hübner, and Otto Homburger, *Die Elfenbeinskulpturen aus der Zeit der karolingischen und sächsischen Kaiser, VIII.–XI. Jahrhundertst*, 4 vols., Berlin: Cassirer, 1914–18; reprint, 2 vols., Berlin: Deutscher Verlag für Kunstwissenschaft, 1969

Goldschmidt, Adolph, and Kurt Weitzmann, *Die byzantinischen Elfenbeinskulpturen des X–XIII Jahrhunderts*, 2 vols., Berlin: Cassirer, 1930–34; 2nd edition, Berlin: Deutscher Verlag für Kunstwissenschaft, 1979

Lasko, Peter, *Ars Sacra, 800–1200*, London and Baltimore, Maryland: Penguin, 1972; 2nd edition, New Haven, Connecticut: Yale University Press, 1994

Nees, Lawrence, *A Tainted Mantle: Hercules and the Classical Tradition at the Carolingian Court*, Philadelphia: University of Pennsylvania Press, 1991

Parker, Elizabeth C., and Charles T. Little, *The Cloisters Cross: Its Art and Meaning*, New York: Metropolitan Museum of Art, and London: Miller, 1994

Volbach, Wolfgang Fritz, *Elfenbeinarbeiten der Spätantike und des frühen Mittelalters*, Mainz, Germany: Wilckens, 1916; 3rd edition, Mainz, Germany: Von Zabern, 1976

IVORY SCULPTURE: GOTHIC

13th–14th Centuries

The 1328 extant Gothic ivories catalogued by Raymond Koechlin testify to the success of sculpture carved in ivory during the Late Middle Ages (see Koechlin, 1924). As African elephant ivory became widely available in Europe through Mediterranean trade during the 13th century, prolific professional workshops of ivory carvers developed, coinciding with widespread urbanization. Paris, the preeminent center of church, royalty, and learning by 1300, was the center of ivory production during most of the period.

In contrast to the ivory book covers, portable altars, and plaques carved for altar decorations from the Early Middle Ages, during the Gothic period, sculptors used ivory for a wide range of objects, including statuettes and tabernacles, devotional diptychs and triptychs, writing tablets, mirror backs, combs, and caskets for secular use. Whereas sculptors frequently used walrus ivory and bone as substitutes for elephant ivory prior to the Gothic period, the 13th and 14th centuries saw a steady supply of African elephant ivory. This was a period of expanding horizons for western Europe. The Crusades established Latin forces in the eastern Mediterranean, and travelers such as Marco Polo ventured into Asia during the 13th century. Most significant, archeologists have documented active trade routes for ivory, gold, and other precious materials that ran from the coast of southeastern Africa, through the Red Sea, to the Mediterranean.

Only a few ivories can be dated to the first half of the 13th century. Indicative of changes in devotional practice that were critical to the emergence of ivory carving as a significant art form in the Gothic period,

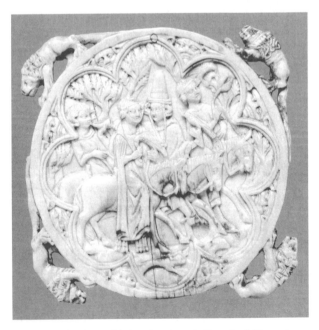

Mirror (back view with hunting scene), French, 14th century
© The Metropolitan Museum of Art, Gift of George Blumenthal, 1941

these are mostly religious in subject matter and were made to serve as private devotional objects. The foundation of private chapels in parish churches and cathedrals, as well as the incorporation of chapels in private homes, increased dramatically during this period. Ivories proved to be ideal small-scale objects with which to furnish these private, sacred spaces. The many statuettes of the Virgin and Child produced during the 13th century testify not only to the increase in personal devotion on the part of lay persons, but also to increasing devotion to the Virgin. Sculptural groups in ivory of the *Coronation of the Virgin* and the *Descent from the Cross*, intended for a larger public, were also new developments.

The Sainte Chapelle in Paris, built as a royal chapel for King Louis IX and dedicated in 1248, is the grandest of 13th-century private chapels. Among its treasures was the ivory statuette of the Virgin and Child (now in the Musée du Louvre, Paris). Standing 41 centimeters tall and datable to about 1250–60, the statuette is among the earliest important ivory sculptures. Like many 13th-century ivory carvings, it can be compared to monumental stone sculptures of the same date produced in and around Paris. As did the sculptors of the north transept portal of the Cathedral of Notre-Dame in Paris and of the south transept portal of Amiens Cathedral, the carver of the Sainte Chapelle ivory conveys the intimate communication between the Virgin and her child. She sways slightly, her right leg bent and her weight on her left leg. The Virgin's mantle gathers in sweeping folds to her left hip and then cascades to the ground in deeply cut folds.

The predilection for portable sculpture in ivory that began in the 13th century became widespread during the 14th century. Ivories provided appropriately luxurious decoration for private chapels patronized by established aristocratic and rising bourgeois families. Throughout the century, private devotion became more widespread, requiring more small-scale objects as the focus of such personal observance. Diptychs and other small relief sculptures intended for private devotion most frequently incorporated scenes from the infancy and the Passion of Christ. As the production of ivories grew, compositions became increasingly schematic, often using a simplified iconography by eliminating many details.

The intimate relationships that can be observed between ivory sculpture, monumental sculpture, and manuscript illumination in the 13th century become increasingly difficult to follow with later works, as ivory production was standardized during the 14th century, more frequently following its own models. While French ivory production grew to meet an international demand, centers outside France also developed. The Rhineland, the Netherlands, Italy, and England con-

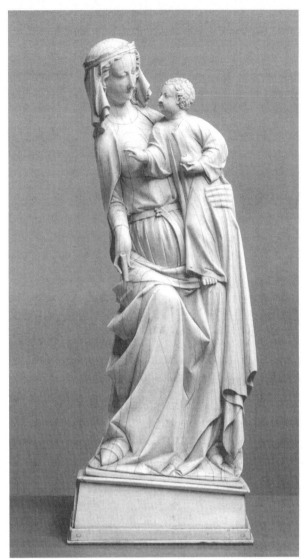

Virgin and Child statuette, French, early 14th century
© Victoria and Albert Museum, London / Art Resource, NY

tributed significantly to the corpus of Gothic ivory, although the forms and style of Paris were preeminent throughout Europe.

Ivories representing scenes from the romance tradition are among the most widely appreciated of all Gothic ivories. Although religious subjects dominated Gothic ivory carving, a clientele for secular carvings among the aristocracy and the wealthy bourgeois also began to grow. Étienne Boileau, who produced a compendium of guild regulations known as the *Livre des métiers* (Book of trades) at the request of King Louis IX in the 1260s, was silent about how the carvers of secular ivories were organized. It is likely, however, that the comb-makers' guild was responsible for the production of mirror cases, because these items were often paired in leather cases. Among the most impressive Gothic ivories are caskets depicting literary themes, which were likely produced in workshops where devotional ivories were also created.

As carvers developed new forms of religious objects in ivory for the private chapel, they also created secular objects such as mirror cases and boxes for the home. They often employed new themes inspired by chivalric subjects popular in vernacular works, such as the Arthurian romances, in the decoration of these personal objects. Many different literary sources can be found, illustrating a variety of narratives combining allegorical themes of love and warfare. The best-known image is the siege of the castle of love, where catapults bombard a lady's fortress with roses. Related ivories depict noble men and women together pursuing leisure pastimes such as chess and hunting. These images of love and leisure activities decorate a variety of objects used in the medieval household, such as mirror cases, combs, and caskets. In their function and decoration, the ivories are significant documents of private life in the Middle Ages. A mirror back in the Metropolitan Museum of Art, New York City, is characteristic of this class of objects. Originally one of a pair of cases that would have enclosed a polished metal disk, Gothic ivory mirror backs have been seen as the forerunner of the modern compact. The New York example, probably carved in Paris during the third quarter of the 14th century, depicts a fashionably dressed, aristocratic couple on horseback. They each hold a falcon, while the man has his right arm around the woman's shoulder, and an attendant accompanies them with a hunting horn and another training falcon.

15th Century

By the beginning of the 15th century, ivory production in France was no longer flourishing. Perhaps owing in part to a diminished economy, ivory appears to have been less widely available during the 15th century than in the preceding period. French production continued along established lines, although in vastly reduced quantities. The prosperity of the Burgundian court, centered in the Netherlands, and the rise of powerful families in northern Italian cities led to new types of production. These areas also emerged as leading centers for painting, metalwork, and other art forms.

With the advent of production in the Netherlands and Italy, carvers altered many of the standard 14th-century French forms and developed new forms of devotional objects. For example, Virgin tabernacles with central ivory statuettes and bone relief plaques on the flanking wings, boxes, and paxes were popular products of the Netherlands. The historical events of the 14th and 15th centuries, such as repeated famines and plagues and the seemingly never-ending conflict of the

Hundred Years' War, affected the spiritual life of the population, bringing an increased devotion to saints. Saints and their legends became popular subjects for diptychs and other objects for private devotion. The new centers also produced secular products in large numbers, with elaborately carved saddles, game boards, and game boxes produced in northern and central Europe. Furthermore, the Embriachi workshop in Venice excelled at making boxes and mirror frames as well as some religious objects decorated with bone carvings.

Recent scholarship has begun to address the evidence for polychrome decoration of Gothic ivories. Modern admiration for the lustrous white surface of ivory has led to the cleaning, even bleaching, of most Gothic ivories, but evidence exists that artists applied surface decoration to ivory during the Gothic period. Surviving traces of paint and gilding have often been overpainted, and scholars must often rely on microscopic samples of surviving polychromy. It is clear that during the 13th and 14th centuries, artists frequently elaborated ivory reliefs and statuettes with paint and gilding, often polychroming details such as pupils of eyes, hair, linings, and hems of garments, as well as architectural elements. It appears that the majority of the ivory surface, however, was most often untouched. Evidence indicates that during the 15th century, when Parisian style no longer dominated, a taste for more extensive polychromy developed, sometimes leaving exposed only the carved surfaces intended to represent skin.

PETER BARNET

See also **Gothic Sculpture**

Further Reading

Barnet, Peter (editor), *Images in Ivory: Precious Objects of the Gothic Age* (exhib. cat.), Princeton, New Jersey: Princeton University Press, and Detroit, Michigan: Detroit Institute of Arts, 1997

Gaborit-Chopin, Danielle, *Ivoires du Moyen Âge*, Fribourg: Office du Livre, 1978 (an excellent overall history)

Koechlin, Raymond, *Les ivoires gothiques français*, 3 vols., Paris: Picard, 1924; reprint, Paris: De Nebele, 1968 (still the most comprehensive catalogue)

Little, C., "Ivoires et art gothique," *Revue de l'art* 46 (1979)

Randall, Richard H., *Masterpieces of Ivory from the Walters Art Gallery*, New York: Hudson Hills Press, and London: Sotheby's, 1985

Randall, Richard H., *The Golden Age of Ivory: Gothic Carvings in North American Collections*, New York: Hudson Hills Press, 1993

IVORY SCULPTURE: RENAISSANCE–MODERN

Ivory carving during the Renaissance played a modest role compared with the great periods of ivory art in the

Gothic and Baroque periods. Renaissance workshops limited themselves to the production of decorative utility objects. Workers specialized in the carving of knife, rapier, and dagger handles as well as powder horns and combs. Artists decorated furniture, board games, weapons, and musical instruments, mostly made of dark wood, with starkly contrasting ivory inlays. The two large ivory reliquary shrines in the Cathedral of Graz, Austria, are among the most important works of the early Italian Renaissance north of the Alps; they carry the coat of arms and mottoes of the House of Gonzaga, and on their front sides are illustrated the Triumphs of Petrach in three relief plates, which exhibit stylistic resonances with the painting of Andrea Mantegna. Artists produced lavish cabinets, small boxes, and caskets in the early 17th century, the wood casings of which were entirely covered with ivory panels. The coin chest covered with rich figural and ornamental reliefs that Christoph Angermair completed between 1618 and 1624 for Elector Maximilian I of Bavaria is a major work of this type. In the High Baroque artists heightened the effect by setting decorative ivory reliefs into dark wood casing, adding accents using sculpturally carved ornaments. An impressive example of such ornaments can be seen in the cabinet for the gallery of the Palazzo Colonna in Rome, which was made by the brothers Dominikus and Franz Stainhart of Munich between 1678 and 1680, after a design by Carlo Fontana.

16th Century

In Germany and Flanders in particular, memento mori depictions played an important role in the 16th century, at first as small pearls on rosaries. These pearls known as the *Dreiköpfe* (three heads) at the beginning of the rosary represent a death's head, the head of a young woman, and the head of Christ. Here, both the symbols and the material itself referred to the transience of all earthly things.

From the second half of the 16th century, ivory lathe work became more important and was part of courtly education and training as a princely mechanical art in many European residences, especially in German-speaking regions, and contributed to the elevation of ivory into a material explicitly associated with the court. Born of a fascination with the machine and the mechanical worldview of the 17th century, in which the sovereign at the lathe saw his work as a reflection of his skill in the craft of statesmanship, artworks with no intended purpose were turned at the lathe and were crafted into increasingly more complex geometrical and abstract shapes. Collectors considered these works highly desirable because of the difficulty in producing them. These virtuoso cabinet pieces, whose beauty un-

ites mathematics with technology, came to carry an artistic statement only when the figural parts became fully integrated and an iconographic frame of reference was thereby created. The 17th-century artist Marcus Heiden's covered goblet with five putti playing music (1631), whose figural decoration was created by a second artist—a sculptor active in the circles of the Master of the Sebastian Martyrs—is perhaps the most convincing example of a piece uniting the two typical techniques for working ivory: turning and carving.

17th Century

After the costly exotic ivory began reaching Europe in larger quantities via ports in Portugal, Spain, Holland, Italy, and the Hanseatic ports in northern Germany, ivory sculpting around 1600 gained new life and immediately became a focal point of interest. The history of small-scale sculpture, and thus also of ivory sculpture—as its most important representative in the 17th century—is closely connected with the history of collecting through all of its preliminary stages. Small-scale sculpture found its appropriate setting in the complex space of the encyclopedic of the *Kunstkammer* as a *theatrum mundi*, even if it did not take center stage there. Similar to the bronze statuette of the Renaissance, the *Helffenbein* (ivory) figure was foremost a collector's item for connoisseurs, kept in the *Kunstkammer* or in a smaller art cabinet among other figures, reliefs, and ivory vessels. The inventories from aristocratic as well as bourgeois collections provide information about the variety of themes as well as the high monetary value of the small-scale ivory sculptures, which were to be viewed up close and therefore had to be carved to perfection. Sculptors carried out these works either after a wax model (for instance, Georg Petel's *Model for a Tankard with Drunken Silenus*), which could at the same time have a contractual function, after a sketch design, or after a living model.

While the statuettes and reliefs were not painted outside of the Spanish cultural sphere, it became quite popular toward the end of the 17th century to combine materials that either contrasted effectively with or underscored the silky shimmer of the ivory. The works known as combination figures (*Kombinationsfiguren*), in which the ivory inlay pieces are connected with the pieces of wood casing, are a particular specialty in this regard. They are often arbitrarily designated as Troger figures, in reference to their most important creator, the Tyrolean Simon Troger, who produced numerous combination figures and combination groups for Elector Maximilian III of Bavaria. Although their provenance is often not entirely clear, their artistic origins are found in Tyrolean Nativity scene carvings.

825

One distinguishing feature of Baroque ivory sculpture is its reproductive character, marked by its unquestioned reliance on printed graphic models, antique sculptures, and Mannerist sculpture. Compositional schemes were thus themselves international, independent of their iconography: certain gestures became the distinguishing signs of certain affects and situations. Contemporaries measured virtuoso ivory carvers not only according to their mastery of the material and ability to cope with the form but also according to their ability to translate a graphic or a single motif from a graphic—that is, a foreign *invenzione* (invention, idea)—into a three-dimensional form. Along with these reproductions, however, artists also produced many original designs that were then copied into other media, for example, into bronze.

The tasks assigned to Baroque ivory sculpture were thus entirely different from those of Gothic ivory sculpture. Gothic ivories were mainly focused on religious functions and motifs. In the religious sphere the tasks were more limited, while in the secular sphere they were greatly expanded. Counter Reformation, post-Tridentine sacred small-scale sculpture concentrated on a few themes, preferably didactic or moralizing ones: artists produced crucifixes as altar crosses or as prayer images for private devotion, and among the various holy statuettes, sculptors frequently depicted the Virgin, as well as Saint Sebastian (for example, Georg Petel's *Saint Sebastian, ca.* 1630) and Christ on the Cross—the latter two providing an opportunity to undertake the nude figure. Protestant patrons especially prized the didactic character of Old Testament motifs.

The forms of profane items with mythological, allegorical, and even antique and contemporary contents were more widely varied. These forms decorated many containers, including tankards, goblets, and bowls. Artists conceived of the works that were ornamented largely with gold-plated silver mountings as representational pieces without any utility. They especially favored such themes as bacchanalias, sea goddesses, and hunting scenes. The most beautiful example of an unframed ornamental vessel was the *Covered Goblet with the Rape of the Sabines* by Matthias Rauchmiller, signed and dated in 1676. Georg Petel's covered goblet from 1629, modeled after compositions by Peter Paul Rubens, is perhaps the most successful creation of this type; he not only repeated it himself, but it also appeared in modified form in the work of many other ivory carvers (as well as goldsmiths) in versions of varying quality.

Ivory hunting paraphernalia, consisting of bowls and flasks and often combined with horn, represent a specifically German contribution to ivory sculpture. The raw dark horn not only produced the desired color

contrast to the silky shimmer of the light ivory but was at the same time a further material reference to the hunt. Members of the Maucher family in Schwäbisch Gmünd were the most important producers of such luxury items.

In the Early Baroque, commemorative portrait medallions arose as an art form typical of the court and were often made to be exquisite gifts. The principal master of this form was the 17th-century itinerant artist Jean Cavalier. David Le Marchand enjoyed great success as a portraitist in ivory in England. The two equestrian statuettes of *Emperor Leopold I as Victor over the Turks* and *King Joseph I as Victor over the Furor*, created about 1690–93 by Matthias Steinl as an allegorical double monument, certainly represent the most impressive contributions to court ivory sculpture. The tremendously complex political and historical demands made upon the artist by these technically virtuosic "indoor monuments" (Saalmonumente) increased their significance beyond purely formal concerns, making them a unique monument to imperial self-representation.

Individual European countries participated to varying degrees in modern ivory sculpting. Italy and France did not measure up to their earlier importance in this area. Noteworthy works from these countries include the sacred statuettes of Francesco Terilli from Feltre, which are strongly oriented toward Venetian Mannerist sculpture. Spain's ivory art was essentially limited to the production of folk Infant Jesus figures with glass eyes. The Capuz family seems to have produced several ivory carvers. In the second half of the 18th century, the Madrid workshop Buen Retiro acquired renown under the direction of Andrea Pozzo. Portugal's contribution included ivory works produced serially under the direction of European missionaries at the center for the East Indian mission in Goa. In the statuettes of Menino Jesus Bom Pastor, Christian, Hindu, and Buddhist representations are bound together within a typically Indo-Portuguese syncretic style. Higher forms of small-scale sculpture did arise in the 17th and 18th centuries, however, in Holland, Germany, and Austria.

The Netherlands made an independent contribution to Baroque ivory art. The easy access to the raw material, which arrived in enormous quantities in the harbors of Amsterdam and Antwerp, aided in the leading role that the southern Netherlands, as well as Germany and Austria, played in ivory art at this time. The works of François du Quesnoy and Francis van Bossuit reveal a heavy orientation toward the art of Antiquity and the Classical tendencies of Baroque sculpture in Rome. Du Quesnoy's main contributions to Baroque ivory art were his putti, which as realistic infants with rounded bodies and fat limbs became the model for generations of sculptors. Rubens had a much greater influence on the sculpture of his time, including small-scale ivory sculpture. The saltcellar that Georg Petel created in 1628 based on a model by Rubens belongs to the great treasures of Baroque ivory art. Among the Flemish sculptors, Artus Quellinus the Elder and Luc Fayd'herbe in particular drew upon Ruben's achievements. Fayd'herbe's statuettes follow one of the main tendencies of Dutch sculpture in the second half of the 17th century, which aimed to intensify the painterly element and to heighten the movement of the whole figure. Artus Quellinus the Elder strove to achieve strong three-dimensional closure in his compactly modeled figures. Gérard van Opstal's fame was founded above all on his Cupic reliefs.

Important trade connections and artistic contacts existed between the Netherlands and Germany in the first half of the 17th century. Under the influence of Georg Petel in Augsburg and David Heschler in Ulm, the stylization of Mannerist figures gradually dissolved in favor of more lifelike effects, which derived from the naturalistic representation of the body, a feeling for materiality and surface effects, an expressive gestural language, and individualistic facial expressions. The collective character of this complex of features often makes it difficult to distinguish between Flemish and southern German sculptures before 1650. Without exception, all the great German sculptors of the 17th century—Georg Petel, Leonhard Kern, Justus Glesker, Matthias Steinl, Matthias Rauchmiller, and Balthasar Permoser, among others—worked in ivory along with other materials. The borders between the craft professions were also not well defined, as, for example, is the case with Bernhard Strauss, active in Augsburg, who signed the sides of his tankards with *aurifaber* (goldsmith).

The dispersion of artistic activity in many small territories prevented the development of an artistic center in Germany, so that significant artistic contributions were often made in remote areas, for example, Leonhard Kern in Franconia in central Germany. During the Thirty Years' War, the number of sculpture commissions decreased in general, and large-scale monuments were practically not commissioned; it was only small-scale sculpture, such as ivory, that profited. Around 1600 artistic energies grew more retrospective with the Dürer Renaissance, a phenomenon that, in recovering Albrecht Dürer's style and motifs, had a formative influence upon the development of German small-scale sculpture and ivory sculpture. The seamless interrelations of Antiquity, the study of nature, and Flemish sensualism also influenced its features. A particular style developed at the Viennese court of Emperor Leopold I, which was the other important center of Baroque ivory art after Augsburg; this style had its roots in the late Mannerist linearity of Seeschwaben, seen, for example, in the work of the 17th-century imperial bone engraver (*Kammerbeinstecher*) Johann Caspar Schenck. Balthasar Griessmann's relief style, by contrast, relies heavily upon the graphic models on which his ornamental vessels were primarily based. Matthias Rauchmiller, Matthias Steinl, Ignaz Elhafen, and Ignaz Bendl emphasized the virtuoso aspect of ivory carving. Magnus Berg, Jakob Dobbermann, and Joachim Hennen were active mainly in northern European royal residences.

18th Century

Ivory sculpture in Germany reached its late apex with the work of Balthasar Permoser in Dresden, who was strongly influenced by Italian artists and who opened up the way to new artistic media. Starting around 1730 porcelain, the "white gold," increasingly replaced ivory as artists' favorite material for small-scale sculpture. In the brief span of time between 1765 and 1795, artists created striking filigree microcarvings with landscapes, seascapes, and pastoral settings, especially in Dieppe (Jean-Antoine Belleteste) and Vienna (Sebastian and Paul Johann Hess). These carvings were generally mounted as decorative pieces or as box lids.

After the Baroque period ivory no longer played a significant role. Only in France (Dieppe), Belgium (Antwerp), and Germany (Erbach im Odenwald) were arts and crafts objects produced that bore some utilitarian value—tobacco boxes, nutmeg graters, and combs—but which do not compare with the great creations of the previous epoch. The Art Deco period saw a revival of combination figures, where the combination of ivory with bronze or gold especially suited the tastes of the time. Through the collaborations of ivory carvers and casting workshops, ivory sculpture transformed from being a precious individual work of art to a figural showpiece whose production became industrialized.

SABINE HAAG

See also **Art Deco; Bossuit, Francis (Frans) van; du Quesnoy, François; Le Marchand, David; Permoser, Balthasar**

Further Reading

Baumstark, Reinhold, Peter Volk, and Philipp P. Fehl, *Apoll schindet Marsyas: Über das Schreckliche in der Kunst, Adam Lenckhardts Elfenbeingruppe* (exhib. cat.), Munich: Bayerisches National Museum, 1995

Christoph Daniel Schenck, 1633–1691 (exhib. cat.), Sigmaringen, Germany: Thorbecke, 1996

Colman, Pierre, *La sculpture au siècle de Rubens* (exhib. cat.), Brussels: Musée d'Art Ancien, 1977

Ehmer, Angelika, *Die Maucher: Eine Kunsthandwerkerfamilie des 17. Jahrhunderts aus Schwäbisch Gmünd*, Schwäbisch Gmünd, Germany: Einhorn-Verlag, 1992

Feuchtmayer, Karl, and Alfred Schädler, *Georg Petel, 1601/2–1634*, Berlin: Deutscher Verlag für Kunstwissenschaft, 1973

Grünwald, Michael D., *Christoph Angermair: Studien zu Leben und Werk des Elfenbeinschnitzers und Bildhauers*, Munich: Schnell und Steiner, 1975

Haag, Sabine, "Studien zur Elfenbeinskulptur des 17. Jahrhunderts. Vorarbeiten für einen systematischen Katalog der Elfenbeinarbeiten des Kunsthistorischen Museums Wien," (dissertation), Universität Wien, 1994

Haag, Sabine, "A Signed and Dated Ivory Goblet by Marcus Heiden," *J. Paul Getty Museum Journal* 24 (1996)

Haag, Sabine, *Masterpieces of the Kunsthistorisches Museum: The Ivory Collection*, Mainz: Philipp von Zabern, 2002

Herzog, Erich, and Anton Ress, "Elfenbein, Elfenbeinplastik," in *Reallexikon zur deutschen Kunstgeschichte*, vol.4, Stuttgart, Germany: Metzler, 1958

Liechtenstein, the Princely Collections (exhib. cat.), New York: Metropolitan Museum of Art, 1985

Philippovich, Eugen von, *Elfenbein: Ein Handbuch für Sammler und Liebhaber*, Braunschweig, Germany: Klinkhardt und Biermann, 1961; 2nd edition, Munich: Klinkhardt und Biermann, 1982

Pühringer-Zwanowetz, Leonore, *Matthias Steinl*, Vienna and Munich: Herold, 1966

Randall, Richard H., *Masterpieces of Ivory from the Walters Art Gallery*, New York: Hudson Hills Press, and London: Sotheby's, 1985

Siebenmorgen, Harald (editor), *Leonhard Kern* (exhib. cat.), Sigmaringen, Germany: Thorbecke, 1988

Theuerkauff, Christian, "Studien zur Elfenbeinplastik des Barock: Matthias Rauchmiller und Ignaz Elhafen," (dissertation), Universität Freiburg, 1964

Theuerkauff, Christian, *Elfenbein: Sammlung Reiner Winkler*, Munich: Kastner und Callwey, 1984

Theuerkauff, Christian, *Die Bildwerke in Elfenbein des 16–19. Jahrhunderts*, Berlin: Mann, 1986

Theuerkauff, Christian, *Elfenbein: Sammlung Reiner Winkler II mit Addenda und Corrigenda zu Teil I, 1984*, Munich: Wolf and Sohn, 1994

J

JACOPO DELLA QUERCIA *ca.* 1374–1438 *Italian*

The Sienese Jacopo della Quercia was the most important non-Florentine sculptor of the 15th century. His works are mainly located in Siena, Lucca, and Bologna. He worked in marble, but also in bronze and wood. His rich and strongly dynamic style differs consistently from that of the early Renaissance in Florence and had a strong influence on later artists, even on Michelangelo.

Jacopo was raised in a family of artists. His father, Piero d'Angelo, was a goldsmith and sculptor, and his brother Priamo was an illuminator. On the basis of various statements in Giorgio Vasari's 16th-century *Lives of the Painters, Sculptors, and Architects*, his birth is dated between 1370 and 1374: on the one hand, he is said to have created an equestrian statue for the burial of Condottiere Giovanni d'Azzo Ubaldini in 1390 at the age of 19; on the other, Jacopo is alleged to have died in 1438 in his 64th year. Presumably, he received his training in the studio of his father, whose only verifiable works are the gilded angel for the high altar in the Cathedral of Siena and an Annunciation of the Virgin (in Benabbio, near Lucca). The work his father performed for the ruler of Lucca, Paolo Guinigi, from 1391 to 1394, may have brought Jacopo his first contacts in the city, where the earliest works attributed to him—*Man of Sorrows* and the Aniello tomb in the Cathedral of Lucca—are found. It has also been speculated that he may have taken trips to France and Bologna and that he may have gained experience through work on the construction of the Cathedral of Florence.

While working on the cathedral's Porta della Mandorla, he may, for example, have met Nanni di Banco and Donatello. In any case, we have the first certain date from there: on 1 January 1401, Jacopo was called upon to participate in the competition for the bronze doors of the baptistery in Florence. That relief is lost today.

The first work clearly attributable to Jacopo is the *Virgin and Child* from 1403, which he created for the Silvestri Chapel in the Cathedral of Ferrara (today in the Museo del Duomo, Ferrara). The fact that he followed Arnolfo di Cambio's works shows how he strove to approximate antique sculpture, which would also decidedly characterize his subsequent works. The treatment of the garments, by contrast, corresponds entirely to the stylistic tendencies that can be observed at the end of the first decade of the 15th century in Florence.

His next work, the tomb of Ilaria del Carretto, the second wife of Paolo Guinigi, moves in an entirely different direction. Whereas the naked putti holding heavy floral garlands on the side of the freestanding sarcophagus refer to models from Antiquity, Jacopo depicted an ideal of beauty from the International Gothic with the fine and elegant recumbent figure of the dead woman. As the monument was completely dismantled after the fall of the Guinigi, we cannot verify whether an arch once belonged to it. The stylistic divergences between the figure of the recumbent woman (*gisant*) and the naked antique putti, however, led to different datings between 1406 to 1413, or even up to 1419.

Between 1408 and his return to Lucca in 1413, Jacopo resided again in Siena, where he had received the commission for a large fountain on the Piazza del Campo in December 1408. The name Fonte Gaia (Fountain of Joy) still communicates the joy from the 14th century when for the first time water could be diverted into the hilly city. Already in January 1409, a change was made in the commission. The commune wanted a new, more elaborate project with more figures and therefore raised the payment to 2,000 florins. A drawing of Jacopo of the time reveals that the statues of Mary and the Christ child, of the three Theological Virtues, and of the four Cardinal Virtues were then to be placed in the niches within the U-shaped wall surrounding the fountain. Two reliefs with the Archangel Gabriel and the Virgin Mary completed the inner decoration of the fountain's basin. On the parapet, the freestanding statues of Rhea Silvia and Acca Laurantia, the natural and the adoptive mothers of the mythical twins Romulus and Remus, refer to the mythic origins of the city founded by Remus. In January 1415 another change affected the plan, in which the relief of the Annunciation of the Virgin Mary (the inner decoration of basin described above) was replaced by two reliefs depicting Adam's creation and the expulsion from Paradise.

The extremely poor condition of the figures, the originals of which are exhibited in the Palazzo Pubblico in Siena, makes it difficult to evaluate them. The strong similarities to antique works again stand out, especially in the Virtues' faces. The robes, however, whose rich and flowing folds no longer adhere to a strict geometry, gain more volume and bear a more dynamic expression.

In the meantime, Jacopo returned to Lucca, where he probably created the statue of St. Luke from the series of the Twelve Apostles on the outside of the cathedral. Possibly he had also received the commission for the decoration of the Trenta family chapel in the Church of San Frediano. The work cannot have progressed very far, however, given that Jacopo and his assistant Giovanni di Francesco da Imola were charged in December 1413 with burglary, rape, and sodomy. Jacopo fled to Siena, where he finally began working on the *Fonte Gaia*. He first received a letter of safe conduct in March 1416, allowing him to return to Lucca.

The Trenta altar follows the model of the great stone altars such as the Delle Massegne at the Church of S. Francesco in Bologna (1388–96) or that of Tommaso Pisano at the Church of S. Francesco in Pisa. Four standing saints in half-relief—Sts. Ursula, Lawrence, Jerome, and Richard—are grouped in narrow niches around the enthroned Madonna and child. An *imago pietatis* (man of sorrows) and the corresponding miracle and martyrdom scenes are depicted in flat relief in the *predella* (a painted panel at the bottom of an altarpiece). The rich, Late Gothic architecture of the retable is crowned by almost three-dimensional half-figures of the prophets. Two burial slabs already finished in 1416, with figures of Lorenzo Trenta (1439) and his wife Isabetta Questi (1426) in front of the altar, complete the ensemble.

Like Donatello and Lorenzo Ghiberti, Jacopo's central artistic activity became the creation of reliefs. This was owing to the commission made by the Siena community in 1417 for two of six bronze reliefs for a baptismal font designed by Ghiberti. A variety of circumstances seem to have prevented Jacopo from working on the project. In 1423 the commission for the relief of the Banquet of Herod was taken from Jacopo and given to Donatello, and there was a legal conflict in which the city demanded Jacopo return the advances paid out to him. Despite these difficulties, Jacopo was named *magister operis* (head of the workshop) in 1427, when the other five reliefs by all participating artists were finally completed. Jacopo was contracted for the completion of the marble carvings on the fountain as well as for a tabernacle forming its upper part; the latter contained bronze reliefs of five prophets and of the Mother of God and was crowned by a marble statue of St. John the Baptist. Jacopo seems to have finished his bronze relief with the annunciation to Zacharias by the time the final payment was made in 1430.

We know of few of Jacopo's works from the time between the Trenta altar in Lucca, completed in 1422, and the start of his work on the Siena baptistery font in 1427, although his reliefs for the Cathedral of St. Petronius in Bologna did begin at this time. In addition, an *Annunciation* scene (1421) in the Collegiata at San Gimignano is attributed to him. Here, Jacopo only carved the figures, which were then painted by the Siena painter Martinus Bartholomei in 1426. The municipality also had him do a gilded leather crown with stone inlay for the Virgin Mary and a silver-plated, iron olive branch with leather leaves for the Angel Gabriel. In contrast to Jacopo's marble works, both figures have a strict and simple posture, thus following Lorenzo Ghiberti's formal ideal. Also ascribed to him are a Madonna and child from San Martino (Museo dell'Opera del Duomo, Siena); a Madonna and child (Musée du Louvre, Paris); and the tombstone of Balduccio Parghia degli Antelminelli (Museo di Villa Guinigi, Lucca).

Beginning in 1435 Jacopo was increasingly busy in Siena. He became the prior of his district and tried in vain to acquire the office of rector of the Ospedale della Scala, but he was finally named responsible for the cathedral construction works. He was knighted in Siena and received the commission for the Loggia della Mercanzia, which would only be completed decades later by Vecchietta and Antonio Federighi. His workshop participated largely in the production of his latest works, especially Cardinal Antonio Casini's private chapel in the Cathedral of Siena (the only remaining evidence of which is a Madonna relief in the cathedral museum) and the tomb of Bentivoglia in S. Giacomo Maggiore in Bologna. After his death on 20 October 1438, Jacopo was buried in S. Agostino in Siena. Charges were brought against his brother Priamo, however, because of Jacopo's misappropriations and his misuse of the cathedral construction for his own purposes.

NICOLAS BOCK

Biography

Born in Siena, Italy, *ca.* 1374. Son of goldsmith and sculptor Piero d'Angelo. Probably trained in father's atelier; first attributed works completed in Lucca, Italy, for the cathedral, *ca.* 1390s; worked in Ferrara, Florence, and Lucca; returned to Siena, 1408; moved back to Lucca, but was forced to return to Siena after being charged with burglary, sodomy, and rape, 1413; focused creative efforts on relief sculpture, from 1417; worked primarily on commissions for churches throughout career. Died in Siena, Italy, 20 October 1438.

Selected Works

1403   *Virgin and Child*, for Cathedral of Ferrara, marble; Museo del Duomo, Ferrara, Italy
1405–08 Tomb of Ilaria del Carretto; marble; Cathedral of Lucca, Italy
1412–22 Trenta Altar; Church of San Frediano, Lucca, Italy
1414–19 *Fonte Gaia* (Fountain of Joy), for Piazza del Campo, Siena; marble; Palazzo Pubblico, Siena, Italy; copy: Piazza del Campo, Siena, Italy
1421   *Annunciation*; wood; Collegiata, San Gimignano, Italy
1425–34 *Virgin and Child* and *St. Petronius*, and reliefs; Istrian stone; Porta Magna, Cathedral of St. Petronius, Bologna, Italy
1427–30 Baptismal font; bronze and marble; Baptistery of Cathedral of Siena, Italy

Further Reading

Beck, James H., *Jacopo della Quercia*, 2 vols., New York: Columbia University Press, 1991

Beck, James H., and Aurelio Amendola, *Ilaria del Carretto di Jacopo Della Quercia*, Milan: Silvana, 1988

Foratti, Aldo, "Jacopo della Quercia," in *Allgemeines Lexikon der bildenden Künstler von der Antike bis zur Gegenwart*, edited by Ulrich Thieme, Felix Becker, and Hans Vollmer, vol. 27, Leipzig: Seemann, 1933; reprint, Leipzig: Seemann, 1978

Hanson, Anne Coffin, *Jacopo della Quercia's Fonte Gaia*, Oxford: Clarendon Press, 1965

Jacopo della Quercia nell'arte del suo tempo (exhib. cat.), Siena, Italy: Palazzo, and Florence: Centro Di, 1975

Krautheimer, Richard, "A Drawing for the Fonte Gaia in Siena," *Bulletin of the Metropolitan Museum of Art* 10 (1952)

Moskowitz, Anne, review of James H. Beck, *Jacopo della Quercia, Speculum* 68 (1993)

Paoletti, John T., *The Siena Baptistry Font: A Study of an Early Renaissance Collaborative Program, 1416–1434*, New York and London: Garland, 1979

Pope-Hennessy, John, *An Introduction to Italian Sculpture*, 3 vols., London: Phaidon, 1963; 4th edition, 1996; see especially vol. 1, *Italian Gothic Sculpture*

Richter, Elinor M., "Jacopo della Quercia," in *The Dictionary of Art*, edited by Jane Turner, vol. 26, New York: Grove, and London: Macmillan, 1996

Scultura Dipinta: Maestri di legname e pittori a Siena, 1250–1450 (exhib. cat.), Florence: Centro Di, 1987

Seymour, Charles, Jr., " 'Fatto di suo Mano': Another Look at the Fonte Gaia Fragments in London and New York," in *Festschrift für Ulrich Middeldorf*, text and photos edited by Antje Kosegarten and Peter Tigler, Berlin: De Gruyter, 1968

Seymour, Charles, Jr., *Jacopo della Quercia: Sculptor*, New Haven, Connecticut: Yale University Press, 1973

PORTAL OF S. PETRONIO
Jacopo della Quercia (1374–1438)
1425–1434
Istrian stone
h. of pilaster 4.55 m; h. of reliefs 99 cm;
h. of statue in lunette 1.8 m
Porta Magna, Cathedral of St. Petronius, Bologna, Italy

On 28 March 1425 Jacopo della Quercia received the commission for an elaborate portal for the Cathedral of St. Petronius in Bologna for a wage of 3,600 florins from the Camera del Papa. What the patron imagined for this commission is described in a greatly detailed drawing by the artist. The height of the portal was set at 15.2–16.3 meters, and its width was half of that, "sia quanto so richiede alla sua proportione" (or what was required by its proportion). Each of the pilasters were to contain seven reliefs showing scenes from the Old Testament; 28 prophets were to frame the portal on the sides, and three New Testament scenes were to be located on the architrave. Figures executed in the round of the Enthroned Madonna and child were planned for the lunette, along with those of St. Petronius with the model of the city of Bologna, as well as the kneeling Cardinal Alamanno, who is presented to the Madonna by Pope Martin V. Two lions were to be set to the side of the portal, and Sts. Peter and Paul were to form the upper end of the pilaster as half-figures.

As can already be seen in the lunette program, the portal was commissioned and sponsored by the papal legate Cardinal Louis Aleman, who ruled Bologna as a possession of the Papal States. His choice of artists probably resulted from his stay in Siena in 1422, during which the cardinal legate had seen the recently completed *Fonte Gaia* (Fountain of Joy). He also wanted to have a monument created by Jacopo, certainly the most modern artist of his time. In 1428, however, when the columns, pilasters, and capitals of the portal exterior were finished, an uprising broke out in Bologna against the papal regiment, and Aleman was chased out of town. As a consequence of these events, it was demanded that the statues of the pope and his representative be replaced by St. Ambrose, the patron of allied Milan. At the same time, the number of Old Testament scenes on the pilasters was reduced to five each, and the number of New Testament scenes on the architrave was increased to five. By 1434 Jacopo had completed the relief scenes on the pilasters, the architrave, and the Madonna and St. Petronius for the lunette (to be placed there only in 1510). Work stopped when Jacopo returned to Siena. After his death, when the portal had to be pushed outward and raised 50 centimeters in 1510 in order to allow new marble paneling on the facade, the sculptures of the lunette were completed with the addition of St. Ambrose, by Domenica da Varigana, and 15 prophets.

The artistic significance of the portal, which Jacopo himself in a letter to the municipality of Siena designated a "laborerio magne sue fame et maximi pretii" (a work [example] of his great fame and highest capacities), rests in the great number of reliefs. By contrast to the illusionist backgrounds of Donatello or Lorenzo Ghiberti's *Gates of Paradise* (1425–52), Jacopo reduced the background to just a few implied architectural or landscape elements. His figures take up almost all of the space available. He looked for vivid and simple solutions emphasizing the dynamism of the event. Through modeling the garments and rendering the people in S-shaped postures, Jacopo underscored the movement and action of the figures.

NICOLAS BOCK

Further Reading

Beck, James H., *Jacopo della Quercia e il portale di San Petronio a Bologna*, Bologna, Italy: Alfa, 1970

Emiliani, A. (editor), *Jacopo della Quercia e la facciata di San Petronio a Bologna: Contributi allo studio della decorazione e notizie sul restauro: Reports on the Conservation Treatment*, Bologna, Italy: Alfa, 1981

Gnudi, Cesare, "Per una revisione critica della documentatione riguardante la 'Porta magna' di San Petronio," *Römisches Jahrbuch für Kunstgeschichte* 20 (1983)

Matteucci, Anna Maria, *La porta magna di San Petronio in Bologna*, Bologna, Italy: Patron, 1966

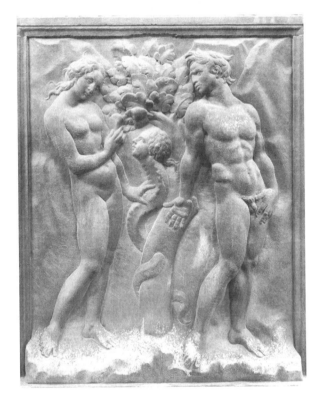

Jacopo della Quercia, *The Original Sin (Adam and Eve)*, relief, Porta Magna, Cathedral of St. Petronius
© Alinari / Art Resource, NY

MATHIEU JACQUET (CALLED GRENOBLE) 1545/46–*ca.* 1611/13 *French*

Of the known sculptors in late 16th-century France, Mathieu Jacquet was the most faithful adherent to the style of Germain Pilon, godfather of his firstborn son, Germain Jacquet (1574–1635). Mathieu Jacquet must have been introduced to sculpture by his father, Antoine Jacquet, who was working at Fontainebleau when, in 1561, he apprenticed the 16-year-old Mathieu to Pilon for three years. Antoine is referred to in documents as a master mason, sculptor, and architect. Edouard Jacques Ciprut has pointed out that he was employed not only at Fontainebleau during the peak of improvements made by Francis I to the château, but also in Paris, where he worked under Pilon's direction on the tomb of Henry II and Catherine de' Medici (*ca.* 1559–85) destined for the Basilica of Saint-Denis (see Ciprut, 1967). At the time, Pilon was finishing his monument for the heart of Henry II and the putti that were eventually incorporated in the monument to the heart of Francis II.

To judge only from Mathieu Jacquet's most famous work, the *Belle Cheminée* (Beautiful Chimney), which was created for the château of Fontainebleau, Pilon's influence remained decisive for Jacquet's style throughout his career. A similar example of Pilon's influence can be found in the mantelpiece from the Château de Villeroy that was at Mennecy (previously attributed to Pilon). Comprising two female Victories that are direct descendants of Pilon's statues of Virtues from the tomb of Henry II and Catherine de' Medici at Saint-Denis, the Villeroy mantelpiece is now attributed to Jacquet not only on stylistic grounds but also because of the continued patronage of Jacquet by the influential de Neufville family, for whom Jacquet carried out several commissions at the Château de Villeroy. (A wood copy of the mantelpiece is in Biltmore, the Vanderbilt mansion near Asheville, North Carolina, United States.)

For the most part, Jacquet's patrons came from within the same court circle as did Pilon's (for example, Françoise de Brézé, Pomponne de Bellièvre, and Philippe Desportes' brother). The remarkable number of funerary monuments, fountains, and mantelpieces that Jacquet produced (most of them destroyed) testify to his success. Documents show that he received commissions for no fewer than 24 mantelpieces. One document specifies that the chimney would be completed according to a design by Jacques Androuet du Cerceau.

Jacquet apparently also worked as an organizing contractor for other artists, overseeing such menial tasks as the demolition of a tomb in the Grands-Augustins (1587) and contracting for a painting after one of Antoine Caron's designs, which was to be carried out in the chapel at the Château de Villeroy in 1588. Jacquet worked with Luc Jacquart, whose atelier and supplies he purchased in 1582. He was also acquainted with Pietro Francavilla and Barthélemy Prieur, and he worked with Nicolas Guillain and Thomas Boudin, who had been apprenticed to him in 1584. Jacquet is referred to in documents as both a sculptor and a painter, which was not unusual for his time.

Jacquet's career reached its peak during the reign of Henry IV. It is probable that Henry IV became aware of Jacquet's work through the commissions for Villeroy. Jacquet's most prestigious commission was the elaborate, large-scale mantelpiece for Fontainebleau popularly called the *Belle Cheminée*, which was dismembered in 1725. It was made of white, black, green, and multicolored marble, with bronze and gilt-bronze details. Its most important surviving element is an equestrian relief of the triumphant Henry IV turning to smile out from the panel. The relief remains at Fontainebleau, as do two allegorical figures separated from it; a smaller relief depicting the king victorious at the Battle of Ivry in 1599 (possibly derived from a drawing by Caron) and other fragments of putti and Victories holding the king's emblem are in the Musée du Louvre, Paris. Jacquet was *sculpteur ordinaire du roi* (sculptor in ordinary to the king) and *garde des antiquitez* (guardian of antiquities). Two wax portraits of Henry IV were inventoried in Jacquet's studio at the time of his wife's death in 1610.

Jacquet's style was more decorative, generalized, and lighthearted (with the exception of the bust of Pomponne de Bellièvre) than Pilon's and lacks the spiritual intensity of his master's work. However, his sculptures are more delicate and animated than Barthélemy Tremblay's.

Although it is often assumed that Jacquet worked on the tomb of the brother of the Duke of Retz, Cardinal de Gondi (1599; Cathedral of Notre Dame, Paris, France), Grodecki points out that no document firmly attributing the *priant* (praying figure) to Jacquet has yet been found (see Grodecki, 1985–86).

MARY L. LEVKOFF

See also **Pilon, Germain**

Biography

Born in Avon near Fontainebleau, France, 1545 or 1546. Son of Antoine Jacquet, a sculptor. Apprenticed at age 16 to Germaine Pilon; received commissions for mantelpieces for Charles de Gondi, 1574; designed tomb for grandchildren of Françoise de Brézé (destroyed), and mantelpieces for Louis d'Ongnies' Château de Chaulnes, 1577; collaborated with Luc Jacquart for tomb of Cardinal de Guise and other works, 1579; designed mantelpieces for Charles du Plessis, 1583; appointed *garde* of funerary sculptures and for abandoned works of Basilica of Saint-Denis, 1590; commissioned to recut a *priant* (praying figure) for tomb of the son-in-law of the Duke of Retz (destroyed), 1592; commissioned for the *Belle Cheminée*, 1597–1600/1601; held title of *sculpteur ordinaire du roi*, 1595; designed tomb of Cardinal de Gondi, 1599, and funerary monument for Philippe Desportes (mostly destroyed), 1607, and for Pomponne de Bellièvre in Church of Saint-Germain-l'Auxerrois, Paris (mostly destroyed). Died presumably in Paris, France, *ca.* 1611–13.

Selected Works

ca. 1575–85   Mantelpiece from the Château de Villeroy; marble; Musée du Louvre, Paris, France (attributed)

1581–82   Bust of Jean d'Alesso; bronze (polychromy lost); Musée du Louvre, Paris, France (attributed)

1597– *Belle Cheminée*, for château of
1600/01 Fontainebleau, France; marble, bronze, gilt bronze (dismantled); fragments: equestrian relief of Henry IV, two allegorical figures; château of Fontainebleau, France; relief of Henry IV at Ivry, putti, and Victories holding royal emblem; Musée du Louvre, Paris, France

1599– *Nicolas III de Neufville* and *Madeleine de*
1602 *l'Aubespine* (wife of Nicolas IV de Neufville); marble; Church of Magny-en-Vexin, France

1607 Portrait medallion of Philippe Desportes; bronze; Musée du Louvre, Paris, France

1608–09 Bust of Pomponne de Bellièvre; marble; Musée du Château, Versailles, France

Further Reading

Beaulieu, Michèle, *Description raisonnée des sculptures du Musée du Louvre*, vol. 2, Paris: Éditions de la Réunion des Musées Nationaux, 1978

Ciprut, Edouard Jacques, *Mathieu Jacquet, sculpteur d'Henri IV*, Paris: Picard et Cie, 1967

Ehrmann, Jean, "La belle cheminée du château de Fontainebleau," in *Actes du colloque international sur l'art de Fontainebleau*, Paris: Cachan, Arts Graphiques de Paris, 1972

Grodecki, Catherine, *Histoire de l'art au XVIᵉ siècle (1540–1600)*, 2 vols., Paris: Archives Nationales, 1985–86

PONCE JACQUIO early 1500s–1570

French

He was incorrectly identified by Giorgio Vasari as "Paolo Ponzio Trebatti," a Tuscan sculptor. In documents he identified himself as a French sculptor: "Io Ponsio Francese." The earliest known works of the French sculptor and painter, about whose development nothing is known, are in fact located in Rome. Ponce probably trained in Italy, perhaps in the circle of Francesco Primaticcio, and he is named as a member of the Accademia di S. Luca in Rome in 1527 and 1535. From 1553 to 1556 he decorated eight halls in the palace of Cardinal Giovanni Ricci (today the Palazzo Sacchetti), one of the most important collectors of antiques in his day, with frescoed friezes framed by sculpted stucco. Each cycle of frescoes is oriented around a hero from antique mythology or history (Odysseus, Alexander the Great, Romulus, and Hannibal). One hall is dedicated to the theme of the Four Seasons; the Stanze di Marmitta contains landscape scenes. Italian and Flemish painters worked under the direction of Ponce, who used drawings by Francesco Salviati, in part, as models for his frescoes. As a painter, Ponce was possibly a student of Salviati and certainly collaborated with him; it was Salviati who, in 1554, furnished the most important hall in the Palazzo Sacchetti, the Sala Grande (di Davide), with frescoes. The art theorist Giovanni Battista Armenini reported the personal contact between the two artists.

Ponce's achievement is most strikingly visible, however, in the decoration of the Salone dei Stucchi or Stanza di Tobia. Here one finds a decorative system in the relation of large stucco figures to frescoed surfaces that Ponce might have been able to learn as a very young man in Primaticcio's workshop. The two artists first collaborated, however, when the sculptor returned to France in the early to mid 1550s. By contrast, there is no stylistic correspondence between these stucco figures, some of which were three-dimensional, and the works of the École de Fontainebleau. The *Satyr-Atlantes* in the corners of the Sala die Tobia are marked by their robust corporeality. The powerful female figures holding wreaths and palm branches stand in calm postures. They are clothed in richly draped antique robes and thereby demonstrate the deep impression that the encounter with antique sculpture left on the young Frenchman. The choice of antique robed figures might also be seen as an homage to the patron and his collection of antiquities.

Charles de Guise, Cardinal de Lorraine, was also impressed by Ponce's plasterwork, and he summoned Salviati and perhaps Ponce as well to France after returning from a stay in Rome in 1555–56. Immediately after Ponce's return, de Guise commissioned the sculptor for stucco figures (destroyed) to decorate a grotto in his palace in Meudon. Ponce collaborated there for the first time with Primaticcio, who in 1559 as the *surintendant des bâtiments du roi* (superintendent of royal buildings) gave Ponce the commission to create eight marble putti for the tomb of Francis I. Germain Pilon, the leading French sculptor of the second half of the 16th century, sculpted eight further putti. The 16 marble figures were not used, however, as originally planned. Three of them were placed at the monument to the heart of Francis II (Basilica of Saint-Denis, Saint-Denis, France), and one is preserved today in the Musée de la Renaissance in the château of Ecouen (Chantily, France). These four works are ascribed to Pilon on stylistic grounds. All eight putti from Ponce's hands, however, have disappeared. Unfortunately, this is also true for most of his documented works for the decade preceding his death in 1570.

Ponce worked during this time for the most varied patrons, and he also undertook less important projects, such as stone fireplace frames. The account books for the association of goldsmiths show that Ponce delivered a design for the high altar of the goldsmith chapel (Chapelle des Orfèvres) in 1560. It was Pilon, however, who received payments for executing the altar.

In the same year, Ponce began with an extensive series of statues for the château of Verneuil, which Philippe de Boulanvilliers had the architect Jacques Androuet Du Cerceau build for him. Twenty-four life-size stone sculptures of the rulers of the four monarchies of Antiquity—Assyrian, Persian, Greek, and Roman—were supposed to be placed in niches in the inner court of the palace. Of this series, the six Assyrian ruler-figures were erected, and in 1601 they were restored and painted bronze along with three further works by the sculptor Matthieu Jacquet. Ponce did not begin the work on 16 three-meter-tall herms (colonnes persiques), since the building was not yet complete at the time of his death. In 1734 Ponce's stone sculptures were destroyed along with the château of Verneuil. It is hardly imaginable that the sculptor would have been able to carry out such an extensive assignment without having a number of assistants. It can therefore be assumed that he directed a large workshop around 1560.

Possibly for that reason, Ponce was included by Primaticcio in the most important project of those years, the tomb of Henry II and Catherine de' Medici, Basilica of Saint-Denis, Saint-Denis, France (1564–65). First he provided terracotta and plaster models for the monument; among these were architectural elements such as capitals. Starting in 1564, he executed two of four over-life-size statues of the Cardinal Virtues *Temperance* and *Prudence*. *Fortitude* and *Justice*, however, are the work of Pilon. In their juxtaposition with the elegant movements of Pilon's bronzes, the peculiarities of Ponce's style become especially apparent. The richly draped, serious figures with powerfully formed bodies are directly reminiscent of antique robed figures. They reach out with powerful movements, but there is also a certain affectation within their gestures. Heavy, complicated coiffures overshadow their broadly shaped and severe facial features. In the overall impression they make, as well as in the individual forms of the drapery, the virtues are reminiscent of the Roman stucco figures in the Palazzo Sacchetti. His years in Paris, and his exposure to the art of the École de Fontainebleau, left no traces in Ponce's style.

Just as other sculptors of his generation, Ponce created smaller scale works along with large sculptures. In the posthumous inventory of his works, some terracotta models are mentioned as well as "a figure of a woman covered in wax," which was preparatory to the bronze casting. There are no known pieces that can be attributed to him with certainty, however. The bronze *Diana with Deer* bears a close stylistic resemblance to the *Temperance* from Henry II's tomb. The strong corporeality, the gesture of reaching out with the right arm, and the relationship of the body and the garment are also reminiscent of the plaster figures in the Palazzo Sacchetti. The calm, self-contained bronze figure of *Kneeling Woman Withdrawing a Thorn from Her Foot* has been counted among his works for a long time. The terracotta model for this work is in the Musée du Louvre in Paris and was part of a Paris collection around 1710.

REGINA SEELIG-TEUWEN

See also **Pilon, Germaine; Primaticcio**

Biography

Born in Rethel in Champagne, France, early 16th century. Probably trained in Italy; member of Accademia di S. Luca, Rome, by 1527; collaborated with Francesco Primaticcio on château of Fontainebleau; also worked together on grotto, château of Meudon, 1552. Returned to Rome, *ca.* 1553; executed stuccowork and frescoes, Palazzo Sacchetti, 1553–56. In Paris to work on tomb of Francis I with Ambroise Perret and Germain Pilon, 1559–62, then tomb of Henry II and Catherine de' Medici, 1563–70; other important patrons included Charles de Guise, Cardinal de Lorraine, and Catherine de' Medici. Died in Paris, France, 1570.

Selected Works

1553–56 Sculpted frames; stucco; Palazzo Sacchetti, Rome, Italy
1560–65 *Diana with Deer*; bronze; Staatliche Kunstsammlungen, Dresden, Germany
1564–65 Statues of *Temperance* and *Prudence*; bronze; tomb of Henry II and Catherine de' Medici, Basilica of Saint-Denis, Saint-Denis, France
ca. *Kneeling Woman Withdrawing a Thorn*
1560–70 *from Her Foot* (attributed); terracotta; Musée du Louvre, Paris, France; bronze: Victoria and Albert Museum, London, England

Further Reading

Boström, Antonia, "Ponce Jacquio," in *The Dictionary of Art*, edited by Jane Turner, New York: Grove, and London: Macmillan, 1996

Goguel, Catherine Mongbeig, "Il disegno di Francesco Salviati," in *Francesco Salviati (1510–1563), o, la Bella Maniera* (exhib. cat.), edited by Goguel, Milan: Electa, and Paris: Réunion des Musée du Louvre, 1998

Jong, Jan de, "An Important Patron and an Unknown Artist: Giovanni Ricci, Ponce Jacquio, and the Decoration of the Palazzo Ricci-Sacchetti in Rome," *Art Bulletin* 74 (1992)

Radcliffe, Anthony, "Ponce et Pilon," in *Germain Pilon et les sculpteurs français de la Renaissance*, edited by Geneviève Bresc-Bautier, Paris: Documentation Française, 1993

CHARLES SARGEANT JAGGER 1885–1934 *British*

Charles Sargeant Jagger was judged by his peers—including Sir William Hamo Thornycroft, Sir William Goscombe John, Gilbert Bayes, and Ivan Meštrovic—to have produced some of the most distinctive and memorable British figurative sculpture of his era. Jagger was particularly praised for the harsh, uncompromising realism he brought to his many World War I memorials. In May 1935 the *London Times* claimed that Jagger's war memorial sculpture was, in terms of emotional impact, on a par with Sir Edwin Lutyens's universally admired *Cenotaph* (1920) in Whitehall. Jagger's war memorial figures were frequently described as uniquely imbued with the emotional reactions to the war that had been felt by the majority of the British people. His premature death was widely perceived as an "irreparable loss" to British sculpture. Many critics correctly predicted that Jagger's hopes for the creation of a "finer, nobler school" of monumental English public sculpture would come to nothing without him.

Although Jagger would later jettison much of the elaborate and intricate Art Nouveau style he had developed while studying at the Royal College of Art (for example, *Bacchanalian Scene*, which won him the British School in Rome's sculpture prize in 1914), he readily acknowledged how much his work owed to the teachings of his mentor Edouard Lanteri. A pupil of Aimé-Jules Dalou, Lanteri instilled in Jagger a lifelong reverence for the work of Auguste Rodin and taught Jagger his own admiration for the skill evident in gigantic ancient Egyptian architectural sculpture in stone. From early in his career, Jagger planned to create works that, in his words, would be as timeless and enduring as the sphinx and the colossal figures of Ramses the Great at Karnak. He perhaps came closest to achieving this goal in his masterpiece, the Royal Artillery Memorial, although he primarily thought of himself as a modeler rather than a stone carver. Lanteri was also instrumental in introducing Jagger to the importance of ancient Assyrian low reliefs carved in stone, depicting lion hunts and battle scenes. Evidence for the influence of such reliefs does not appear in Jagger's own work in low relief until the early 1920s—for example, in the stylized treatment of British World War I soldiers wearing waterproof capes in the panels he carved for the Anglo-Belgian Memorial (1921–23; rue des Quatre Bras, Brussels) and in the Royal Artillery Memorial. It would appear that Jagger greatly benefited from repeated visits to a new gallery of Assyrian sculpture in the British Museum, which opened early in 1920.

Participation in World War I proved to be a watershed in Jagger's life. After traumatic experiences at Gallipoli (Jagger served there October–November 1915) and in Flanders (November 1917–April 1918), which left him with three wounds and a medal, Jagger found that he could not envisage the war in his highly intricate, somewhat overelaborate, prewar Art Nouveau manner. His initial striking low relief, *No Man's Land*, completed soon after the armistice, reveals a new capacity for selective ornamentation of the compositional surface area combined with a talent for compressed expressive detail and vivid facial characterization. *No Man's Land* was recognized and hailed at the time as by far the most devastating and unsparing image of the carnage on the western front produced by any British official war artist.

The work that first brought Jagger widespread and enthusiastic public recognition, however, was *Soldier on Defence* (also known as *Wipers*), created in 1919 for a war memorial at West Kirby, Merseyside. When the full-size model was first exhibited at the Royal Academy in May 1921, it was praised as a heartfelt tribute to the stubborn courage of the ordinary British soldier in the ranks and for its almost overpowering masculine realism, which made all the other war memorial figures present in the exhibition appear feeble and effeminate in comparison. The *Soldier on Defence* type of man—stocky, muscular, unashamedly heroic, and ruggedly idealized—made frequent appearances in Jagger's war memorial work throughout the 1920s: *The Sentry*, *The Ammunition Carrier* from the Royal Artillery Memorial, and in the relief panels for the *Memorial to the Missing of the Battle of Cambrai*. Jagger later told a friend that he would never lose his respect for the ordinary British working man after having fought alongside him in the trenches. His deep admiration for such a type found powerful expression in two of the stone figures he provided for the Imperial Chemical Industries House: *The Builder* and *Marine Transport*.

Nonetheless, there is much more to Jagger's sculpture than brutal, muscle-bound male virility. Some of his works, especially those executed in bronze, reveal surprising depths of subtly and emotionally sophisticated complexity. There is an enigmatic sadness in the face of his hooded female figure *Humanity* on the West Kirby war memorial and a delicately observed, wistful pleasure in the expression of the soldier in *Soldier Reading a Letter*, whereas the pose and features of his portrait-statuette of the *Prince of Wales* conveys an accurate sense of the subject's inner shyness and lack of self-confidence.

Anxious not to be typecast as a war memorial sculptor, Jagger sought commissions for other types of work, such as the lightheartedly decadent bronze relief *Scandal* and garden sculpture on erotic mythological themes (for his long-term patrons the Mond family), as well as his magnificent figure of the heroically un-successful polar explorer *Sir Ernest Shackleton* for the Royal Geographical Society in London. Jagger also proved himself a gifted animal sculptor; his stone elephants for the viceregal court in New Delhi (1929–31) are invested with all that animal's characteristic massive ponderousness and stately dignity. Toward the end of his life, Jagger was eager to work on new subject matter, such as a gigantic, 9-meter-high representation of Jesus in *Christ the King*. (A plastic statuette of this figure was made.) The figure, conceived to present a Christ radiating majesty and authority, was intended to adorn the main facade of a new (and never completed) Roman Catholic cathedral in Liverpool designed by a great admirer of Jagger's talent, Sir Edwin Lutyens.

In the early 1930s Jagger attempted something of a stylistic departure—suppressing detail in favor of ar-chitectural massiveness—with *Saint George* and *Bri-tannia*. The two groups were met with puzzlement and suspicion by the critics, and Jagger himself was un-happy with the results of such experimentation. On the basis of what Jagger left uncompleted at the time of his death, such as the model of *Christ the King*, a 6.5-meter-high statue of *King George V as Emperor of India* (intended for New Delhi) and the colossal head of a *Steel Puddler* (lost), which the critics argued em-phasized massive simplicity and strength at the ex-pense of emotional subtlety, it is quite possible that his future work would have evolved along similar lines to that of socialist realism in the Soviet Union.

JONATHAN BLACK

Biography

Born in Kilnhurst, near Sheffield, England, 17 Decem-ber 1885. Apprenticed for six years to Sheffield firm of Mappin and Webb as metal engraver, 1900; evening classes in sculpture at Sheffield Technical School of Art, 1903–07; taught there as engraving instructor, 1905–07; studied sculpture and modeling under Edou-ard Lanteri at Royal College of Art, London, 1907–11; Lanteri's studio assistant and instructor in modeling at Lambeth School of Art, London, 1912–14; awarded British School at Rome's two-year scholarship in sculpture, July 1914; Official British War Artist for Ministry of Information, 1918–19; numerous war me-morial commissions, 1919–30; elected member of Royal Society of British Sculptors (RBS), 1921; elected Associate Member of Royal Academy and awarded gold medal by RBS, 1926; commissions from Imperial Chemical Industries and the British adminis-tration in India, 1927–34; appointed member of Royal Mint Advisory Committee on Coins and Medals, 1932; awarded second gold medal by the RBS, 1933. Died in London, England, 16 November 1934.

Selected Works

1914   *Bacchanalian Scene*; bronze; private collection
1918–19 *No Man's Land*; bronze; Tate Gallery, London, England
1919   *Soldier on Defence* (also known as *Wipers*); bronze; West Kirby, Merseyside, England
1921   *Soldier Reading a Letter*; bronze; Paddington Station, London, England
1922   *Prince of Wales* (future King Edward VIII); bronze; Sheffield City Art Galleries, England
1923–25 Royal Artillery Memorial; bronze and stone; Hyde Park Corner, London, England
1926–28 *Memorial to the Missing of the Battle of Cambrai*; stone; Louverval, France
1928–30 Four statues: *The Builder, Marine Transport, Agriculture,* and *Chemistry*; stone; Imperial Chemical Industries House, Millbank, London, England
1929–30 *Scandal*; bronze; private collection
1930–31 *Sir Ernest Shackelton*; bronze; Royal Geographical Society, Exhibition Road, London, England
1931–33 *Saint George* and *Britannia*; stone; Thames House, Millbank, London, England
1933–34 *Christ the King*; plaster; private collection

Further Reading

Boorman, Derek, *At the Going Down of the Sun: British First World War Memorials*, York, North Yorkshire: Ebor Press, 1988

Borg, Alan, *War Memorials*, London: Cooper, 1991

Compton, Ann (editor), *Charles Sargeant Jagger: War and Peace Sculpture*, London: Imperial War Museum, 1985 (the standard account of Jagger's work)

Cork, Richard, *A Bitter Truth: Avant-Garde Art and the Great War*, New Haven, Connecticut: Yale University Press, 1994

Harries, Meirion, and Susie Harries, *The War Artists: British Official War Art of the Twentieth Century*, London: M. Jo-seph/Imperial War Museum, 1983

Harrison, Charles, *English Art and Modernism, 1900–1939*, London: Allen Lane, and Bloomington: Indiana University Press, 1981; 2nd edition, New Haven, Connecticut, and Lon-don: Yale University Press, 1994

MacColl, Douglas, "Two of the Young," *The Burlington Maga-zine* 11/227, (February 1922)

Maryon, Herbert, *Modern Sculpture: Its Methods and Ideals*, London: Pitman, 1933

Nairne, Sandy, and Nick Serota (editors), *British Sculpture in the Twentieth Century*, London: Whitechapel Art Gallery, 1981

Parkes, Kineton, *Sculpture of Today*, 2 vols., London: Chapman and Hall, 1921

Read, Benedict, and Peyton Skipwith, *Sculpture in Britain between the Wars*, London: Fine Art Society, 1986

Stamp, Gavin, *Silent Cities: An Exhibition of Memorial and Cemetery Architecture of the Great War*, London: Royal Institute of British Architects, 1977

ROYAL ARTILLERY MEMORIAL

Charles Sargeant Jagger (1885–1934)

1921–1925

bronze and stone

h. 2.4 m (figures)

Hyde Park Corner, London, England

The Royal Artillery Memorial can justly be regarded as the most compelling and memorable British war memorial of the 20th century. Perhaps one of the few World War I memorials to accurately represent the proliferation of new weaponry on the modern battlefield, it not only was hailed as a major achievement by contemporaries but also has been consistently admired by successive generations. The completed memorial resulted from the close collaboration and mutual respect between Sargeant Jagger and the architect Lionel Godfrey Pearson. Pearson displayed an intuitive feel for the use of simple yet grand and imposing architectural forms to complement architectural sculpture. For instance, he designed the setting for Jacob Epstein's tomb of Oscar Wilde in Paris (1909–14). When the war memorial was unveiled, on 18 October 1925, it was widely interpreted as having something new and revelatory to say about the essence of the first war to encompass the entire world and the domination of its course by the systematic processes of industrial mass production.

In February 1921 the Royal Artillery War Commemoration Fund (RAWCF) Executive Committee approached Jagger and Pearson to submit their design for the Royal Artillery Memorial on the understanding that it would be crowned by a life-size representation of an artillery piece. Drawings in the collection of the Royal Institute of British Architects suggest that during March 1921, Pearson and Jagger quickly settled on the essential appearance of the memorial as it was to be unveiled in 1925. Pearson conceived the base as essentially a stubby cross-shaped platform for the gun, built up in a series of steps from rectangular blocks of stone, to be approximately 14 meters long by 7 meters wide. Jagger suggested that this platform be dominated by a replica in Portland stone of a 23-centimeter siege howitzer about a third larger than life-size and positioned as if firing sideways toward the east. The tip of its muzzle would reach about 11 meters above the level of the nearby road. In July 1921, when Jagger was asked why he had specifically selected the 23-centime-

ter howitzer to top the memorial, he replied that, as an infantryman during World War I, he respected the gun for its "terrific power," which had come to represent for him "the last word in force." Overall, he and Pearson had devised the design to radiate "strength, power, and force."

Jagger further envisioned four bronze low-relief panels, depicting the various branches of the Royal Regiment of Artillery (Royal Garrison, Royal Field, and Royal Horse Artillery) in action, being set into the long sides of the platform facing east and west. Two 2.5-meter-tall figures in bronze were to be set into niches at the north and south ends of the platform. From the outset, it would appear that Jagger conceived one of them as assuming the pose of a figure later titled *The Driver*. This figure carries a whip and equestrian harness and would have been responsible for guiding and controlling the two lead horses in a four-horse 18-pounder gun team. In *The Driver*, Jagger sought to exploit maximum artistic effect from a man wearing a waterproof groundcloth as a cape over his uniform. In effect, the man's pose carries with it unmistakable connotations of the crucified Christ. The second figure evolved into *The Battery Commander*.

Toward the end of June 1921, the executive committee provisionally accepted the design submitted by Jagger and Pearson. Approval was still required by King George V as colonel-in-chief of the regiment, and he had grave reservations as to the wisdom of including a figure in the round that looked as if it was being crucified. The monarch's suggestion was put to

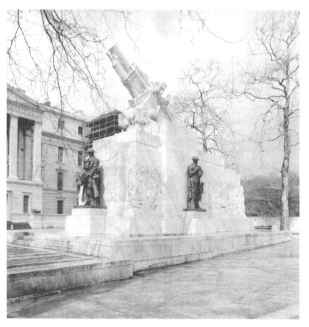

Royal Artillery Memorial
The Conway Library, Courtauld Institute of Art

Jagger that he should try and include some sort of "peacetime" reference in the design, either in the reliefs or in one of the figures in the round. Jagger politely but firmly refused to heed this suggestion, regarding any hint of peacetime conditions as inappropriate in a design conceived to be dedicated to the memory of men who had died in battle and on active service. He argued that his design should be "in every sense of the word . . . a war memorial."

The king dropped his opposition and the design by Pearson and Jagger was accepted. Early in 1923 Jagger persuaded the RAWCF Executive Committee that the memorial required a total of eight relief panels rather than the previously agreed upon four. Each panel, five meters long by two meters wide, would be executed in stone rather than in bronze. When the memorial was unveiled, these reliefs received a particularly positive reception. Many critics were impressed by the way in which Jagger had executed the panels with an angular simplicity reminiscent of Assyrian relief carving from the 7th century BCE. The British World War I gunners he depicted struck observers as radiating a primitive vitality as well as being unmistakably modern and completely in harmony with the technology they were operating with such furious determination.

During the course of 1923–24, a number of alterations and additions were made to the design. At the suggestion of Sir Edwin Lutyens, Jagger changed the position of the gun barrel from firing broadside to facing southward. The sculptor also introduced two more bronze figures (nearly three meters) in the round: *The Ammunition Carrier* and the recumbent figure of a *Dead Artilleryman* on a low platform at the north end of the pedestal. Many on the RAWCF Central and Executive Committees appreciated that Jagger had created for them one of the most stark and uncompromising images of death on a World War I battlefield devised by any British artist either during or after the war. One member of the central committee argued that the figure of the *Dead Artilleryman* was symptomatic of Jagger's uncompromising desire to "force home on the minds of the public the horror and terror of war," which could only cause grieving mothers and widows unnecessary additional heartache.

When the memorial was unveiled, it immediately provoked an extremely heated debate that focused on the justification for including such a prominent representation of an artillery piece. The novelist John Galsworthy, for example, described the memorial as a "barking brute of a thing," squatting like "a great white toad." On the other hand, the *Manchester Guardian* thought Jagger had succeeded, where so many other memorial sculptors had manifestly failed, in confronting the onlooker with "war without the gloss."

JONATHAN BLACK

Further Reading

Black, Jonathan, "War without the Gloss? The Image of the British Soldier in First World War Memorial Sculpture," in *Object Number Two: Postgraduate Research and Reviews in the History of Art and Visual Culture*, edited by Charles Ford, London: University College London, 1999
Casson, Stanley, *XXth Century Sculptors*, London: Oxford University Press, 1930; reprint, Freeport, New York: Books for Libraries Press, 1967
King, Alex, *Memorials of the Great War in Britain: The Symbolism and Politics of Remembrance*, Oxford and New York: Berg, 1998
Parkes, Kineton, *The Art of Carved Sculpture*, 2 vols., London: Chapman and Hall, and New York: Scribner, 1931
Von Donop, Stanley, *The Royal Artillery War Memorial*, London: HMSO, 1925
Whittick, Arnold, *War Memorials*, London: Country Life, 1946

JAPAN

The geographical relationship of Japan to China and Korea has been alternately useful and menacing to the Japanese. Once business developed on a state-to-state level, Japan thrived on the connections, welcomed traders and artisans from the continent, and developed its own culture in tandem. This opened Japan's historic periods, first with Korea (ca. 550–663; the introduction of Buddhism to the Japanese defeat in the Battle of Hakusuki-no-e), then with China (ca. 664–838; exchange of missions and the last mission to China), again with China (ca. 1200–1490; beginning with the Hojo regency to the death of Ashikaga Yoshimasa), and finally with Europe and more recently, the United States (1854–present). These were greatly invigorating stages in the arts, but in the intervening periods, when overt hostility, stagnation, or deterioration characterized the continental cultures, Japan discontinued its formal contacts, built southern fortifications, and created its own unique styles.

Paleolithic–Jomon Periods (to 300 BCE)

The earliest arts in Japan can be traced back to the Upper Paleolithic, with the oldest artwork an ivory figurine between 25,000 and 31,000 years old, made from the core of a Naumann elephant tusk and retrieved from deposits in Lake Nojiri, Nagano prefecture. Called a Venus figure, the work was skillfully carved, with head, torso, and lower body each separated by narrow constrictions. The body is finely shaped and tapered. Unfortunately, the face and front of the torso are sheared off, but such good work was part of a long tradition that moved north Asia. Another early object that survives is a chlorite schist "club" (*sekibo*), a stone phallic symbol, ten centimeters long, resembling a modern wooden *kokeshi* doll (popular wooden dolls made in north Japan with round heads and cylindrical bodies), found with two other rods (both broken) in the Iwato site, Oita prefecture, and dated to around 12,000 BCE; the face details were lightly pecked out. Fertility objects can still be seen at some Shinto shrines dedicated to deities whose powers enhance the continuation of human life.

Major climate changes about 12,000 years ago started a slow rise in temperature and opened the Jomon period (*ca.* 10,000–300 BCE). The land bridge with Korea was lost to rising water, and the four main islands formed. The term for this primarily hunting and gathering stage comes from the handmade, cord-marked (*jo-mon*) pottery that appears in large quantities in thousands of sites. The decoration of these pots reached a striking artistic level, with many late examples in the north bearing both carved and painted patterns.

The production of clay female figurines in distinctive regional styles became especially numerous after the Middle Jomon period. Most typical of this period in the central mountains region were three-dimensional, animal-like faces and large abdomens and buttocks; for the Late Jomon period on the east coast, two-dimensional, more human, but owl-like faces and busted torsos; and for the Latest Jomon period in the north, three-dimensional, often hollow, heavily ornamented, and a few with large, goggle-like eyes. They may have been used as aids in childbirth, and many from the Middle and Late Jomon periods appear to have been intentionally broken as though they were involved in the effigy magic of relieving pains and illness.

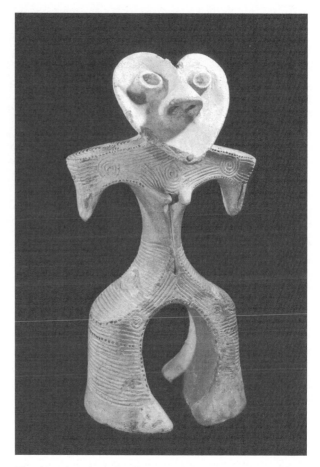

Figurine, clay, from Satohara, Agatsuma-machi, Gumma prefecture, late Jomon period
Courtesy J. Edward Kidder, Jr.

Yayoi Period (*ca.* 300 BCE–250 CE)

After the introduction of rice and the use of iron and bronze to south Japan, ritual practices and consequently the arts changed greatly. Called the Yayoi period (*ca.* 300 BCE–250 CE), this era's pottery lost most of its decoration in favor of simple, utilitarian shapes. A few of the storage pots bear a human face at the top, marked like tattoos and painted red. Bronze bells were cast with fine relief decoration and then buried to protect the crops and the land, and birds were carved from wood, perhaps as grave markers, symbolizing the spirit of the dead.

Kofun Period (*ca.* 250–550)

When the early Yamato rulers took over in the Kinki region (Osaka, Kyoto, Nara, and the surrounding area) and built huge mounded tombs known as *kofun*, from which the Kofun period (*ca.* 250–550) gets its name, the well-stratified society had a military and entrepreneurial class of patrons, an artisan class, and a peasant-farmer class. After about the middle of the 5th century, more immigrants brought new stone-working techniques and a corridor-and-chamber style of tomb; they also brought the practice of painting and carving the interior surface of their walls, the making of Sue pottery, and the use of ornamented horse trappings. Many fine gold pieces were still imported from Korea, but local production of iron and bronze objects was underway, the former for practical tools and the latter for ceremonial objects. They filled their tombs with magnificent grave goods.

A notable Japanese development was the fabrication of *haniwa* (clay rings), clay cylinders in the form of models of inanimate objects, animals, birds, and humans. They stood on the slopes of the mounded tombs; elongated legs or a tube sunk into the earth gave them firm footing. The complete figure with underpinning rarely exceeded 1.5 meters in height. Buildings, military equipment, and ceremonial objects, horses, and birds supplemented the early rows of thousands of cylinders, as did, eventually, male and female peasants and grandly dressed soldiers and elegantly attired ladies. At the large Tonozuka tomb in Shibayama, Chiba prefecture, for example, a mound roughly 100 meters in length, a single row of *haniwa* consisted of a mix of about 80 animals, birds, and human figures, all resembling a funeral procession. A row of cylinders ran above and another below. Because these were visible at only a distance, detail was not a requirement, although this came with time. Facial features are pleasant in their simplicity. One can usually distinguish the farmers from the aristocrats, the civilians from the soldiers, and the commoners from the shamans by the different hairstyles, costumes, trappings, and poses. The shamans may be either male or female and are seated yoga-fashion strumming a *koto* (a stringed instrument). Later *haniwa* tend to be more realistic, and many bear red paint on the front.

Asuka Period (552–645)

Mounded tombs were still built in remote areas as late as the 8th century, but in the middle of the 6th century, a mission from Japan's Korean ally, Paekche, soliciting more help against their common enemy on the peninsula, brought Buddhist articles to the Yamato court (present Asuka village, Nara prefecture) and an articu-

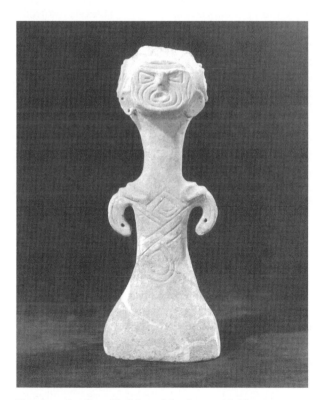

Figurine, clay from Koshigoe, Maruko-machi, Nagano prefecture, Yayoi period
Courtesy J. Edward Kidder, Jr. and the National Museum, Tokyo

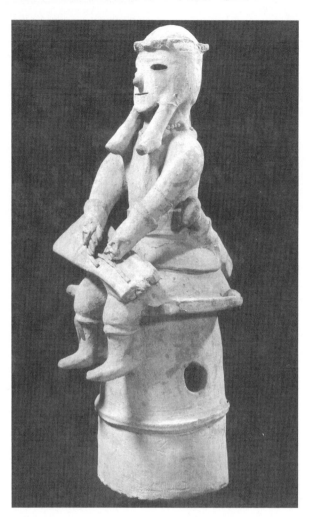

Haniwa figure of female shaman, clay from Furuumi, Gumma prefecture, late Kofun (Tomb) period
Courtesy J. Edward Kidder, Jr. and the National Musuem, Tokyo

late representative who recommended their use. One text suggests for this the date of 538, others 552, when Emperor Kimmei (*r.* 539–571) was on the throne. Not until the Mononobe opposition was destroyed in open battle and the Nakatomi temporarily silenced did the Soga, the supporting family, have the freedom to sponsor the new religion. The arrival of Buddhism opened the Asuka period (552–645).

Emperor Yomei (*r.* 585–587) was the first ruler to follow the Way of Buddha (*Butsu-do*), but the traditional Shinto ceremonies were equally observed. Yomei was the father of the regent, Prince Shotoku (*ca.* 574–622), and the brother of Empress Suiko, who later ruled in her own right (592–628). Together with the Soga kingmakers, they invited teams of Korean architects, sculptors, bronze casters, tile makers, and painters to Japan to build and decorate temples and encouraged family heads to construct their own (*uji-*

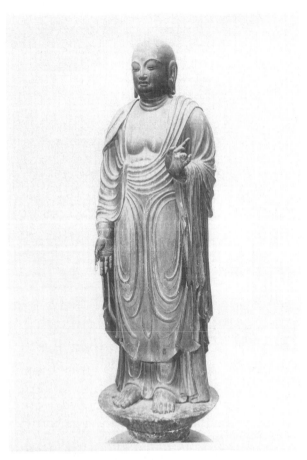

Standing figure of Priest Nichira, wood, in Tachibana-dera, Asuka, Nara prefecture
Courtesy J. Edward Kidder, Jr.

dera, or clan temples). All worked with Chinese translations of Sanskrit texts, and history credits Prince Shotoku with emphasizing the philosophical and devotional content of Japanese Buddhism.

The Soga employed Tori as their court sculptor, a man from the Shiba family, immigrants of Chinese descent who had arrived around 522. They were attached to the saddle makers' (*kuratsukuri*) *be*, one of the specialized occupational groups of the time. The second generation already had some experience in large wooden sculptures, as Shiba Tasuna had made a *joroku* image of Buddha for Emperor Yomei in 587 when the ruler was dying of an unidentified plague. A *joroku* statue (a term that came to be applied loosely to monumental images), then using the north Korean *komajaku* unit, was roughly five meters high. That large statue has disappeared, but according to documents and inscriptions, Tori was the first to have worked in bronze. He cast two images that have survived, the first on order of Empress Suiko (who had a Soga mother) for the Asuka-dera, the temple built by the Soga at the capital in Asuka. The *Nihon-shoki*

(720; *Chronicles of Japan*) describes its construction between 588 and 596.

Tori finished the second image, a large statue of Shaka(muni), the historical Buddha (2.76 meters high), begun in 605, in almost exactly a year. The architects and sculptors failed to communicate, and on the day of dedication they discovered the image to be too large for the main door of the Golden Hall, or the main building for housing sculptures and other icons in a temple. Tori managed to get the piece in without dismantling either, and the empress, who was as pleased with this feat as she was with the statue, appointed Tori to the third of the current 12-rank system and gave him land for rice fields.

The capital moved progressively farther north, leaving Asuka isolated. In 1196 a serious fire destroyed the building housing the Shaka image, the heat deforming it; incompetent restorers magnified the damage. Nevertheless, the Asuka-dera's Shaka Buddha inaugurated a history of casting monumental Buddhas, culminating with the Daibutsu of Nara dedicated in 752 and repeated again when adequate bronze was available with the great Amida Buddha in Kamakura in 1252.

Insufficient supplies of bronze—the copper for which was still largely imported—and the obvious discomfort with *cire perdue* (lost-wax) casting of three-dimensional images led to less ambitious projects. When Prince Shotoku fell ill in 622, his wife and courtiers proposed the making of a statue for his recovery, but he died and the image was completed to "secure the repose of his soul in paradise." Housed in the Golden Hall of the prince's temple, Horyu-ji in Ikaruga, northwest Nara prefecture, the long inscription on the back of the mandorla states that the statue was finished in the third month of 623 by Shiba no Kuratsukuri no obito Tori busshi. "Obito" was an archaic title for a village headman, and "busshi" was the highest rank of distinction given to artists for contributions to the cause of Buddhism.

The inscription also states that the seated Shaka is in the "image of the prince," here taken to mean his size. Two bodhisattvas half his height, standing on iron rods supporting their lotuses, accompany the Shaka, all set before a large boat-shaped mandorla of halo and flame patterns. The Tori style dominated the period, with its emphasis on single viewpoints, frontality, heavy costuming, and linear decoration. The models were the Wei dynasty Buddhist images in north Chinese caves. Most distinctive of the style are the ringlets of hair, archaic smile, long, tubular neck, drooping shoulders, and flattened layers of body-obscuring drapery, which end in cascading folds over the front of the pedestal. The back of the figure lacks details, and the bodhisattvas are only fronts, pushed

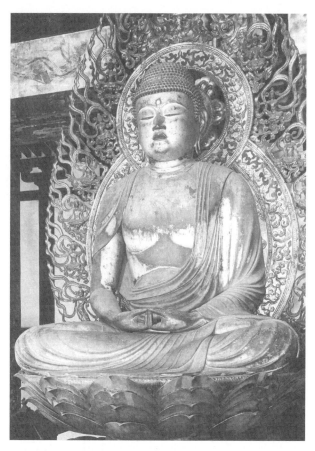

Seated Amida Buddha, gilt wood, in Nishi-daigo, Kyoto
Courtesy J. Edward Kidder, Jr.

against the *mandorla* in an attempt to hide this fact. The artisans, masters of open-face casting, were clearly inexperienced in making large, three-dimensional images.

The smaller Yakushi Buddha in the same hall, with a halo inscription relating it to Emperor Yomei and the year 607, was long regarded as earlier and more important, because for centuries the temple records assert its central position in the Golden Hall. The piece was never attributed to Tori. Recent studies of its casting have indicated its technical superiority, and the piece, loosely modeled after the Shaka, is now regarded as having been made some time after a fire razed the temple in 670. Its casting flaws are only nominal, whereas substantial interior patching of the Shaka was necessary and exterior blemishes were skillfully hidden by postcasting tooling and abrasion.

Seated figures in meditation—one leg crossing the other knee, the elbow resting on the knee, fingers at the cheek, or small variations of the pose—were popular in Korea as bodhisattva types and were adopted as symbolic of the devout Prince Shotoku (as a bodhisattva, never a Buddha; a prince, never an emperor).

Life-size wooden images in the Chugu-ji, the nunnery of the Horyu-ji, and in the Koryu-ji, a temple originally built by the Korean Hata family in the area that became Kyoto, and many small bronze figures, ten in the Imperial Household Collection—an 1876 donation from the Horyu-ji, now in the Tokyo National Museum—demonstrate only minor stylistic differences from their Korean prototypes. Many of these were probably made around 685 when Emperor Temmu ordered all the aristocratic families to install Buddhist altars and images in their homes. Incised inscriptions around the base or on the back of such statuettes show they were dedications to parents, a spouse, or some noted individual or clergyman.

Among other preserved Asuka-period sculptures is the gilt-wood standing Yumedono Kannon (formally, Guze Kannon, the bodhisattva who saves), a tall (2.15 meters), crowned, magnificently haloed, frontal figure with costume flares. The popular name is derived from the hall in which it stands in a black box as the main image, Yumedono (Dream Hall) of the Horyu-ji, erected in 739. Now exposed for special worship only twice a year, it appears to have been hidden or wrapped for centuries. But X rays, which have revealed some 51 Asuka-period nails that hold all of the basic pieces to the body, such as the drapery flares, the so-called fern-frond hair, and boards that cover a hole in the back, show it also received 11 nails during recorded repairs in 1696 and 16 in the Meiji period (1868–1912). Each nail shape is quite distinct. Traditionally said to be in the image of the prince, the Tori influence is strong, except perhaps for its long proportions. Made of camphor wood, several features of the working technique in the statue are abnormal. Three boards hide a large, rotted hollow space in the back. The finished carving was successively covered with clear lacquer, a fine sizing layer of white clay, gold, and, finally again, clear lacquer. The incompatibility of gold on clay should have been well known to such sculptors. In another aberration, a halo was usually supported by a bamboo pole, but in this case, the magnificent, large, but very thin halo is crudely nailed directly to the back of the head.

The Horyu-ji's Four Heavenly Kings (*Shitenno*) in polychromed camphor wood, who stand stiffly in their trim Central Asian armor guarding the four directions of the Buddha platform of the Horyu-ji's Golden Hall, are the oldest in the country (*ca.* 650, on the cusp between the Asuka and Hakuho periods). As a small concession to the worshiping circumambulator, the side flares of their stylized drapery curve forward and so break the rigid single-viewpoint treatment characteristic of Asuka-period sculptures. Under each Heavenly King is a different, strange, mythical beast, all quite unlike the later dwarflike creatures that, together with the king signify, the universal struggle between good and evil. These strange beasts come from the old Indian tradition of the deity and his vehicle, the latter the symbol of his sphere of activity.

Hakuho Period (645–710)

Changes in the arts at this time (after 650) reflected the country's foreign relations. After the Japanese were ejected from Korea, they turned immediately to China, and the influx of early Tang styles and techniques began in the late 660s. During this period, commonly referred to as the Hakuho period (645–710), the centralized political system and Chinese connections stimulated the economy, and the court and families turned to constructing temples dedicated to their ancestors or as an appeal to Buddhist deities for respite from illnesses. Temples proliferated in more remote areas. One text notes the existence of 545 temples when Empress Jito was on the throne (r. 686–697).

Several monumental bronze statues remain today, apparently still cast from imported ores. Most were originally gilded. Their metal contains about 1 percent lead. Not until after local discoveries were made in 708 were Japanese materials used, recognized by a lead content of 5 per cent or more. The best-known set of the period is the Yakushi triad in the Golden Hall of the Yakushi-ji, Nara, which was completed around 697. Emperor Temmu had ordered it as far back as 680 to solicit relief from the Buddha of healing for the empress's ailment, but it was not completed until much later. The full-bodied and thin-draperied Buddha, three times the height of Tori's Shaka (86 centimeters and 2.76 meters), sits on a unique bronze base with decoration that includes the Four Tutelary Deities, creatures of the four directions. His bodhisattvas, Nikko (Sunlight) and Gakko (Moonlight), stand on their own bases, each body in gentle S-shaped curves, their light, flowing drapery enhancing their physical forms. Body shape, elegant drapery, and flesh exposure illustrate Indian influences traceable through Chinese art.

Other cast images of seated Buddhas from life-size to *joroku* size can be seen in various temples, none with their accompanying bodhisattvas today: a Shaka in the Kaniman-ji in Kyoto prefecture (late 7th century); the head of a colossal triad (685) once in the Yamada-dera in Asuka, but removed by militant monks to the Kofuku-ji in Nara in 1187 (only the head is known to have survived a 1411 fire); a Yakushi in the Ryukaku-ji in Chiba prefecture, possibly from the early years of the Nara period; and a somewhat smaller Shaka in the Jindai-ji in Tokyo (late 7th century). The main image of the Taima-dera in Nara prefecture is a large, gilt, unbaked clay Miroku Buddha (ca. 686),

a technique that has left a flaking surface that is an impediment to restorers.

Among the new developments in the enlarging iconography attributed to the arrival of more monks and new sects was the positioning of Buddhas to mark the four directions: Shaka (*Sakyamuni*; south), Amida (*Amitabha*; west), Miroku (*Maitreya*; north), and Yakushi (*Bhaisajya-guru-vaidurya-prabha*; east). This involved the elevation of Miroku from a bodhisattva to a Buddha, the Buddha of the Future. Another new development in the enlarging iconography showed Miroku—and sometimes Yakushi—seated in "western" style, the legs down in front, rather than in the usual yoga or lotus position.

Nara Period (710–784)

Japan thrived on borrowings from the expansive Tang culture, which welcomed foreigners, and adapted styles, techniques, and apparently even costly imported materials to meet the demands of the local elite. The rulers abandoned the checkerboard capital city of Fujiwara (694–710) and occupied the city of Heijo (Nara), a little more than ten kilometers to the north. The Nara period (710–784) was Japan's first golden age of the arts. Some old temples were built anew, retaining a modest establishment in Fujiwara. Workshops now produced in quantity for such huge imperial, two-pagoda temples as the Yakushi-ji, Daian-ji, Todai-ji (745), Shin-yakushi-ji (747), Saidai-ji (765), and Akishino-dera (780). Nara was home to numerous other great family monasteries and nunneries, including, the Fujiwara's Kofuku-ji, the Chinese priests' Toshodai-ji, the second-generation Asuka-dera (called Gango-ji after its transfer), Kairyuo-ji, and Hokke-ji, their staffs of monks and nuns numbering in the thousands. These large, untaxed, sacred institutions became a formidable political force. The country's resources were drained, the government's subsidies became too heavy a burden, the supply of bronze was depleted, and young men avoided forced labor or conscription by entering a monastery.

Before the Nara period opened, the Japanese were making images by use of the Chinese technique of polychromed unbaked clay. Soon they added the technique of dry-lacquer. Imported materials may have been used for both techniques. Along with the traditional bronze, wood, and stone, patrons now had the widest choice of materials in all cost ranges in the history of Japanese sculpture. This phenomenon not only created a hierarchy of sculptors at the top of the pay scales for craftsmen but it dropped other specialists below their normal status. According to old descriptions of workshops, craftsmen in the traditional materials in the old occupational groups—probably all now regarded as native Japanese—were taken for granted, but those working in exotic and scarcer materials enjoyed great respectability and comfortable incomes. From top down—and therefore socially ranked—were sculptors in unbaked clay and dry-lacquer, bronze mirror makers, leather workers, gilders, sculptors in bronze, wood, and stone, painters, bronze casters (such as pagoda spires and beam-end plaques), clay workers (roof-tile makers, potters, etc.), and apprentices and laborers.

Dominating the period was an imperial Nara sculpture style that embraced all materials and which was set by the larger temple workshops. On the basis of contemporary Tang work, changes in China no longer needed a generation to appear in Japan. Unfortunately, fires at the Daian-ji, Shin-yakushi-ji, Saidai-ji, and Akishino-dera do not allow us to fully verify this claim, but survivals at the Kofuku-ji, Todai-ji, and Toshodai-ji allow recognition of the style leaders in the decades of the 730s, 740–750s, and 760s, respectively.

The Kofuku-ji became the headquarters of the Hosso sect temples. It had been moved to Nara from its first location at Yamashina (northeast Kyoto), where Kamatari, the founder of the Fujiwara family, erected it in 669, and it thrived when Fujiwara daughters married royal princes or emperors. At its peak in Medieval times, the huge establishment numbered over 175 buildings and thousands of soldier-monks. Sculptural programs for a main hall of a wealthy Hosso temple could include a large Shaka, Yakushi, or Miroku Buddha seated on the platform facing south, his bodhisattvas (for Shaka, Fugen, and Monju, by the early 8th century) flanking him, and the Four Heavenly Kings on the corners. A pagoda might have the four exoteric Buddhas, placed with their backs to the center pole. In the case of the West Golden Hall (*Saikondo*) of the Kofuku-ji, the "family of Buddha" was arrayed around the platform: images of the Ten Great Disciples (*Judai-deshi*) and the Eight Classes of Heavenly Beings (*Hachi-bushu*). They were made in dry-lacquer and installed in 734 on order of the empress as a memorial to her mother. A text complains that the expense of the statues equaled that of the building.

Dry-lacquer images probably evolved out of a desire to have large but light-weight, portable statues for public exhibition in parades and on other festive occasions. Lacquer, resin of the *Rhus verniciflua* tree, is available throughout most of east Asia, and the Japanese had been using it for waterproofing and decoration for thousands of years. For Buddhist images, a simple wooden, cross-shaped frame supported a rough clay model, over which was placed three to ten layers of hemp or linen cloth, each soaked in lacquer and each allowed to dry separately. The image was then cut open from the back and the clay removed. Finishing materials to give finer details included a mixture of lacquer, incense, clay powder, and sawdust. This surface was covered with black lacquer for gilding or a white clay sizing for polychroming. Called hollow-core dry-lacquer (*dakkatsu kanshitsu*), the practice changed over the decades to wood-core dry-lacquer (*mokushin kanshitsu*), which, as the term implies, involved a roughly shaped wooden figure over which layers of lacquer were built up. By the end of the 8th century, the disadvantages of expense and weight finally won out over the remarkably sensitive details that the material allows, and sculptors discontinued the technique.

Six of the Ten Great Disciples remain (now in the Kofuku-ji Treasure Hall) from the almost life-size set in the West Golden Hall (average height, 1.5 meters), dressed in long monastic robes and in a strikingly new realistic style. The 1923 Great Kanto earthquake destroyed four of the disciples, which had been acquired privately. Simulated rock bases are original for only two that survive. Repairs recorded for 1232 include work on hands and fingers—which are built around copper wires—and repainting. Younger disciples such as Sharihotsu and Subodai, identified with wisdom and the ultimate void, have small heads and delicate features. Brows protrude over deep-set eyes. Older individuals such as Ragora and Furuna, identified with comprehending the esoteric and understanding the Buddhist law, are more intense, their worn faces prominently wrinkled. It has been suggested that deformation resulted from the 1180 fire that destroyed the main images in the hall, but the unusual features are in fact a Kofuku-ji style, recognized for its impressively human qualities: motionless, thoughtful, approachable figures, manneristically elongated, with small features, earnest faces bordering on the quizzical by the presence of the eyebrow pad, and communicating hands.

The Eight Heavenly Beings in the West Golden Hall are ancient personified Indian spirits. Two images retain only their heads. They average just a little larger than the disciples (1.54 meters). Most wear Central Asian armor and have a light scarf from the shoulder or a waist sash, the ends of which hang on either side below the knees, in a rare remnant of the archaic frontal view. The Japanese iconographical scene was slowly accepting distant foreign features: red or very dark brown skin, Indian costumes, bird-headed humans, multiheaded and multiarmed figures, and animal protectors enveloping the head. Ranging from the fierce to the benign, with the exception of Kubanda (a foreign king), Hibakara (a north Chinese bearded face), and Karura (bird head), they tend to share small features and pleasant, almost cherubic faces. The three-headed and six-armed Ashura—a fighting demon—wears only a light shoulder sash and skirt tied at the waist.

Emperor Shomu built the Todai-ji (East Great Temple) on the northeastern edge of the city of Heijo in the years after 745. He wanted to relocate the capital to Shigaraki in Shiga prefecture but was frustrated by the resistance of the temples and the incompetence of his workmen. He therefore put the casting of the Great Buddha on the site of the Todai-ji in the hands of a Korean. Archaeologists discovered the remains of the foundry in 1988, along with scores of wooden tallies (*mokkan*)—the record-keeping system of the time—about 100 of which still bear legible inscriptions. The tallies record the source of the materials, weight of copper, number of workmen, number of furnaces in operation, names of some individuals, the presence of a medical team, and much more. The temple records themselves name a man from Paekche as in charge, called by the Japanese Kuninaka no muraji Kimimaro (*muraji* being the title of a rank), as well as several associated casters. The copper came from the Nagano-bori mine at Mito in Yamaguchi prefecture. The 16-meter-high statue was probably cast in eight horizontal sections (the tallies refer to seven), roughly one section a year, using over 500 tons of copper, 8.5 tons of zinc and lead, and 2.5 tons of mercury. It was dedicated in 752 in a splendid ceremony attended by over 10,000 invited guests. By then the emperor had abdicated to ensure that his daughter, Empress Koken (*r.* 749–758), would be enthroned.

The Todai-ji is the headquarters of the Kegon (Garland) sect; the Big Buddha is Vairocana (Rushana), the chief Buddha of the Lotus-Repository World (*Rengezo sekai*). Natural and man-made catastrophes mistreated it: an earthquake in 855 knocked off the head, and the hall was burned by the Taira in the civil war of 1180. Repairs followed, but another quake in 1567 left it headless again, and restorations in 1692 virtually rebuilt it, thus eliminating evidence of the original casting technique. Among the 56 lotus petals on which it sits, the vast and complicated Lotus World is engraved on the underside of 8, which therefore must have been part of the original base. These illustrations of Shaka Buddha preaching in the midst of 22 bodhisattvas in the 25 heavens, Shumisen (Mt. Sumeru) in the middle, and four continents and great rivers below, show the Japanese treatment of the high Tang style in the use of clustered Buddhas and bodhisattvas, corpulent bodies, and voluminous, fluttering drapery. The outlining is harder, leading toward the so-called steel-line style.

Some time after the willful burning of the temple in the Gempei War (1180–85), several rescued sculptures were consolidated in the Hokke-do (Lotus Sutra Hall) or Sangatsu-do (Third Month Hall, the month when the sutra was read). These are arranged in the east end of the building, the part that was a Kamakura-period addition to the original structure. Currently with 18

images in a variety of techniques, 14 probably date from the 8th century. The main statue is an eight-armed, gilt dry-lacquer Fukukenjaku Kannon (Sanskrit, *Amoghapasa-avalokitesvara*), the bodhisattva who fishes for souls, 3.64 meters high and created in 747. In the center of his magnificent crown of gold work, hung with precious jewels, is a small silver standing Buddha. The production epitomizes the lavish imperial expenditures of the 8th century.

Although the Todai-ji's temple record refers to Four Heavenly Kings of bronze, the only set remaining from the 8th century is the life-size polychromed clay group in the Kaidan-in, which were moved there in 1732 from an unknown building. These statues initiated centuries of production of the type for every respectable temple in the country and were the model for the Two Kings (*Nio*) guarding the gates of temples and for the Twelve Divine Generals (*Juni-shinsho*) of temples dedicated to Yakushi. Their armored suits, facial expressions ranging from disapproving to bellicose, and their S-shaped bodies in a victorious stance over the writhing but subdued dwarflike creatures below vividly dramatize their role as protectors. Unbaked clay serves as the material for the oldest set of Twelve Divine Generals. The generals encircle a seated wooden Early Heian Yakushi Buddha in a secondary building now called the Main Hall (*Hondo*) of the Shin-yakushi-ji in Nara. Fearful and condescending from their elevated positions, they play a powerful role as symbols of the Vows of Yakushi and as protectors of the Buddha.

The Chinese priest known in Japan as Ganjin arrived in 754 to perform an ordination ceremony at the Todai-ji, and his 24 Chinese colleagues built the Toshodai-ji of the Ritsu sect (Sanskrit *Vinaya* [rules]) on the west side of the city. The beginnings of the late Tang style can be narrowed down to the late 750s and early 760s. In the center of the platform of the Toshodai-ji Golden Hall, surrounded by 8th-century images, is the Roshana Buddha of 759, the largest seated hollow dry-lacquer image of the time, some 3 meters in height. Massive and heavyset, modeled in the majestic manner, the face is squarish and the torso broad and ample. The drapery lies lightly over the right shoulder and more fully from the left shoulder across the waist. The wooden halo-mandorla is the Thousand Buddhas arrayed in clusters (864 of the 1000 have survived). On the Buddha's right is the wood-core 1000-armed (*Senju*) and 11-headed (*Juichi-men*) Kannon, 5.5 meters tall, his 953 arms consisting of the 6 regular ones, some 42 in half-arm size, and small ones on copper wires. Acting as the other bodhisattva is a standing wood-core Yakushi Buddha made to scale.

Life-size priest portraiture may predate the making of Ganjin's statue (80 centimeters) in the Toshodai-ji, as the Horyu-ji has a seated polychromed hollow dry-lacquer image (90 centimeters) of Gyoshin (*d.* 750) that is believed to date from no later than 767. Ganjin died in 763, and the extreme degree of realism suggests that the statue is a product of his lifetime. Invited to Japan, he set out in 742, but a series of mishaps prevented his arrival before 754, by which time he had lost his eyesight to sea breezes after a shipwreck. His portrait represents a man of unflagging determination, faithful to his commitment, and content with his religious accomplishments. An early 19th-century fire damaged the image, which was repaired with a surface of papier mâché and repainted.

Early Heian Period (794–893)

Emperor Kammu (*r.* 781–806) decided to isolate the unmanageable temples by moving the capital, after which he reduced their incomes. The first choice, Nagaoka, was a poor site, and ten years later, in 794, Kammu transferred the capital to Heian (Kyoto), which initiated the Early Heian period (794–893). During this time, Japan became disillusioned with stagnating conditions in China, population expansion had exceeded land controls and the ability to tax, and court politics involved endless intrigues.

Most Nara city temple workshops closed, and sculptors found little work in Kyoto during this period. Kammu's refusal to let all but select temples build in the new city impeded the development of the arts. Nonetheless, the emperor sponsored cultural missions to China, from which two great personalities initiated new sectarian practices on their return. Kukai (774–835; posthumously, Kobo Daishi) introduced the esoteric practices of the Shingon (Sanskrit, *Mantra* [true word]) sect and founded the Kongobu-ji on Mt. Koya, Wakayama prefecture; and Saicho (767–822; Dengyo Daishi) brought the Tendai sect (Chinese, *Tientai*), which soon became esoteric, and built the temple later known as the Enryaku-ji northeast of Kyoto. In Tendai the emphasis gravitated toward the worship of Amida Buddha and the principles of the Pure Land (*Jodo*) sect, the other Buddhas (Shaka, Yakushi, and Miroku) all ebbing in popularity.

The emergence of the *shoen* system—family estates—signaled the breakdown of central authority to which had been attributed the relative uniformity of the Nara sculptural style. The rich iconography of esoteric Buddhism now coupled with the new diversity of regional styles. Esoteric Buddhism and Shinto found much in common, and smaller temples were built in old Shinto mountain strongholds. Unlike the expensive materials, wood cost almost nothing to procure and could, in the most stringent cases, be cut, carved, and decorated by one man. Sculptors used the *ichiboku* (one-wood) technique, in which much of the interior

of the image was hollowed out, almost exclusively. Arms, knees and feet were often attached pieces.

Still enjoying the aura of Chineseness, the Toshodai-ji sculptors produced corpulent standing figures of Buddhas and bodhisattvas in wood, in tight-fitting costumes and unimaginatively repeated drapery folds known as *hompa* (rolling waves), which defined bulky torsos and hips. The adoption of a standardized chisel by woodworkers had much to do with this characteristic of the style. A fine example is a seated Shaka Buddha in Muro-ji, in Nara prefecture, for which the carving is sharper and the drapery crisper. The pigment is missing and the sizing (*gofun*) badly flaked. The Toshodai-ji style spread to the provinces, faint features of it surviving for almost two centuries.

Kukai brought painted mandalas (magical diagrams) from China, as well as the principles to apply the theory to both architectural and sculptural groupings. The Lecture Hall (*Ko-do*) of the Kyo-o-gokoku-ji (Realm Protecting Temple; popularly, To-ji, East Temple), the large temple at the south entrance to Kyoto where he had been appointed abbot, contains a huge display of 21 sculptures in mandala plan on its platform, many of which the temple claims to have been the work of Kobo Daishi himself. The middle group of Dainichi Buddha (Sanskrit, *Mahavairocana* [the Great Illuminator]), his Four Esoteric Buddhas, and one other are replacements. The main group on the west surrounds a large seated Fudo (Sanskrit, *Acala* [the Immovable One]), the center of the Godaimyo (Sanskrit, *Vidya-raja* [the Five Great Lords of Light]). The east group is the Five (esoteric) Bodhisattvas. New iconographic types to the Japanese scene include fierce multiheaded, multiarmed, and multilegged figures on exaggerated creatures. Fudo was later adopted by the samurai as their special protector and became one of Japan's most popular deities.

Late Heian Period (894–1185)

Beginning in 857, when the emperor appointed Fujiwara Yoshifusa (804–72) prime minister, the Fujiwara family dominated the era. Daughters married emperors, family heads became regent (*sesho*) and moved up to civil dictator or chancellor (*kampaku*), and Fujiwara men headed governmental departments. During this time, known as the Late Heian period (894–1185), the court set new cultural levels in all of the arts; emperors retired, built magnificent temples, and formed their own "cloistered" (*insei*) governments. The private estates expanded, and armies of peasants were hired for their territorial protection. From the emperor down, people sought penitence as thousands made the pilgrimage to the Seven Great Temples of the Southern

Capital, and many continued to the great Shinto shrines of Kumano.

Temples multiplied in the provinces after the Provincial Temples (*Kokubun-ji*) had paved the way following the imperial order of 741 to build them. A large number of the new temples had a central Amida Buddha and subscribed to the Pure Land philosophy. Called the "easy path," the usual ritual involved reciting the *nembutsu* (the name of the Buddha) 70,000 times a day and visiting temples on special occasions. The demand for images was great, which led to the development of workshops taking contracts, speeding production, and devising a technique to make large, transportable images. The center for this practice was a workshop in Kyoto whose chief personality was Jocho (*d.* 1057), the son of Kosho, a prominent sculptor and workshop owner. Jocho's technicians were already addressing the problems. In a technique known as *yosegi-zukuri*, multiple-block technique, they joined together small blocks of wood, thus allowing much larger and, eventually, more dramatic images to be made. Disassembled images could be moved and reassembled elsewhere—the end of an assembly line organized on the basis of a hierarchy of skills.

Jocho had royal blood and therefore added prestige to the sculptor's craft. His workshop received commissions from the Fujiwara and others on the merit of Jocho's style. Among many that are documented, the only surviving image is the Amida made in 1053 for the Phoenix Hall (*Hoo-do*) of the Byodo-in in Uji, Fujiwara Yorimichi's (*d.* 1074) monastery retreat. The architecture, sculptures, and paintings all contribute to the grand theme of the Amida Buddha coming down to receive the soul of the deceased. As the Pure Land philosophy evolved, the statue became more and more the deity itself rather than the symbol, and Jocho responded with a majestic image of extraordinary physical attractiveness. The round face has a warm expression, the flattish body is lightly adorned with elegant drapery, and the wide-set knees make the frontal proportions almost those of an equilateral triangle. The sense of stability reaffirms the worshiper's feelings of being in the presence of the deity. This had all been made more real by Priest Genshin's exposition of the Pure Land creed in the *Ojoyoshu* (985; variously The Essentials of Salvation, Birth in the Land of Purity), emphasizing the importance of believing, the *nembutsu*, and the compassionate Buddha.

Much like the Toshodai-ji style before it, the Jocho style moved out into the provinces, with each region developing its own characteristics. They adopted the multiple-block technique at a much slower pace, however. The Joruri-ji in Kyoto prefecture is the sole survivor of at least 30 temples that once housed nine gilt statues of Amida, Nine States of Amida's Paradise, in this case probably made a generation later than Jocho's Amida in the Phoenix Hall. All seated, the larger central Buddha is in the traditional *semui-in* (to grant absence of fear) the right palm forward above the waist, the left hand open on the knee, the *mudra* (symbolic hand gestures) of fearlessness and giving; but the other Buddhas are in the *jo-in* (concentration), the two hands cupped together on the lap, the *mudra* of concentration, usually equated with meditation, typical of Amida.

Kamakura Period (1186–1333)

Although wealthy, the Fujiwara had no army of their own and depended on an unstable alliance of families to maintain order. Local rebellions and disputes over appointing the emperor brought their era to a close when Minamoto Yoritomo defeated the Taira in 1185. In his ruthless quest for power, Yoritomo had destroyed his own family, and succession passed to the family of his wife, the Hojo in the Kanto region. The military government (*bakufu*) was set up at Kamakura, from where the Hojo controlled Kyoto and the country. Known as the Kamakura period (1186–1333), centuries of rule dominated by daimyo and the samurai were in store for the Japanese.

During the Kamakura period, the route to China reopened, bringing Zen to Japan. Street-corner preachers from the Tendai sect led a new era of religious pietism. Amida worship spread rapidly throughout the farming class. The peace that followed the destructive wars made possible a frenetic program of temple rebuilding and restoration and replacement of their icons, which was all remarkably accomplished within about one generation. Several sculpture workshops based in Kyoto operated branches in Nara and Kamakura. Competition sharpened their sense of style and ability to deliver their work within deadlines.

Aristocratic patrons in Kyoto tended to ask for replacements in the familiar, traditional styles. Workshops, such as the Sanjo Bussho (Third Block Workshop) or the In School, met their interests. The most progressive workshop of the time was the Shichijo (Seventh Block) Bussho, Jocho's old shop, popularly called the Kei-ha (Kei School) because so many of its known craftsmen had "kei" in their names. Its finest work in terms of style and quantity was done during the time of Kokei (*d. ca.* 1197), Unkei, and Kaikei (both probably died in 1223). Many works of these sculptors remain, especially in locations outside Kyoto, which suffered less damage in the later civil wars. Working in a dramatic, realistic, and colorful style, including inset glass or quartz eyes, and exploiting the multiple-block technique to it fullest, whether in life-size portraits or heroic-size gate guardians, their statues range from a new sense of grandeur to towering, exploding power. Temple records state that the 8.5-meter-high Guardian Kings of the Todai-ji were made in 72 days, by Unkei, Kaikei, two other master sculptors, and 16 shop hands.

Other sculptures by these men and their school can be found in the Kofuku-ji in Nara and in many temples in and around Kyoto and neighboring prefectures. They made hundreds of replacement bodhisattvas and the main image for the Sanjusangen-do, the 33-bay hall in Kyoto, which had burned in 1249.

Minamoto Yoritomo believed that Kamakura should resemble a capital, and whatever its uncertain beginnings, a colossal bronze Amida Buddha, 11.5 meters high, was cast for the Kotoku-in temple in 1252, many years after his death. The work of Ono Goroemon, an otherwise unknown personality, it was built up in large sections brazed together in an unusually sturdy technique. Two buildings collapsed around it, and after the destruction of the second hall in an earthquake in 1494, the statue was left exposed in the open air. Foreshortening gives the worshiper an ideal view of the Amida from the front. The less-than-satisfactory side and back views seen today did not have to be considered when it was housed inside a building with controlled pedestrian traffic patterns.

The huge Zen temples being erected at this time (Kamakura; 1186–1333) in Kamakura and Kyoto were relative sculptural wastelands, as Zen sought the Buddha nature within and not through texts and images. Zen had a crippling effect on the art of sculpture, from which it never recovered. However, one contribution came in the seated wooden statues of the Zen patriarchs, who were elevated to the status of deities. These *chinzo* (portrait of a Zen priest) portraits, in painting and sculpture, continued to be made in later centuries and inspired other sects to memorialize their chief priests. Although replacements of images in temples were always needed, the Kei school had set such high standards that it was impossible to keep up the fervor, and the realistic style led only to successive caricatures.

Muromachi Period (1333/34–1573) and Momoyama Period (1574–1615)

The Muromachi period (1333/34–1573) saw a revival of the civil wars under the Ashikaga, ardent Zen practitioners; and the Momoyama period (1574–1615) saw their termination under the Tokugawa, who gave their name to the last era of military rule (1615–1868). Repairing the great destruction in Kyoto involved replacement of buildings more than images, but the trend toward secular art production in castles and residences led many sculptors into the profitable business of architectural decoration. This practice involved brilliantly painted high-relief ornamentation on structural parts of architecture and screen and transom carvings and can be seen at its most elaborate in the Toshogu complex of buildings associated with the graves of two early Tokugawa shoguns at Nikko in Tochigi prefecture: Ieyasu (1542–1616) and Iemitsu (1604–61). The Ming Chinese influence was strong in the use of colorful decoration, to the point of obscuring the actual architecture.

Many wooden *gigaku* (7th-century music and dance) and some *bugaku* (court dances of Chinese and Korean origin) dance masks survive from the Asuka and Nara periods. Masked dances continued on both the court and folk levels. In Tokugawa cities, No plays were a major aspect of the entertainment world, and fine polychromed wooden masks defining the character of the wearer were—and still are—an important art form. *Netsuke*, pendants or toggles hung from the girdle and made of every conceivable material of every imaginable subject, were especially common among the townspeople of the large cities. The *netsuke* was the practice, after the introduction of tobacco, of attaching the tobacco pouch to the girdle. This practice found its origins in the 16th century but saw its peak in the 17th century. The pouch may have been crafted in ivory, wood, deer horn, coral, metal, or lacquer, representing human figures, animals, birds, fanciful creatures, mythological figures, plants—the entire spectrum of Japanese life.

A rare few creative individuals have made a mark in recent centuries. Enku, an itinerant monk (*d.* 1695), used hastily and roughly carved Buddhist images to pay for his lodging and as demonstration pieces when taking his message to the peasants. In later life he traveled the Hida Road, the Senko-ji in Nibukawa, Gifu prefecture. The fresh primitiveness of these statues has led to many imitations.

Meiji Period (1868–1912)

Japanese artists of the Meiji period (1868–1912) who spent time in France fell under the spell of the Impressionists, and sculptors were particularly attracted to the work of Rodin. One of these was Ogiwara Morie (1879–1910), who pioneered the introduction of Western-style sculpture to Japan. Contemporary Japanese sculptors are less inclined to be as extreme as their Western counterparts but experiment with a wide variety of materials and styles.

J. Edward Kidder, Jr.

See also **China; Kaikei; Unkei; Yosegi-zukuri**

Further Reading

Ishizawa, Masao (editor), *Sculpture*, Tokyo: Toto Shuppan, 1958

Kidder, J. Edward, Jr., *Masterpieces of Japanese Sculpture*, Rutland, Vermont: Tuttle, and Tokyo: Bijutsu Shuppan-sha, 1961

Kidder, J. Edward, Jr., *The Birth of Japanese Art*, London: Allen and Unwin, and New York: Praeger, 1965

Kidder, J. Edward, Jr., *The Lucky Seventh: Early Horyu-ji and Its Time*, Tokyo: International Christian University Hachi-roYuasa Memorial Museum, 1999

Kurata, Bunsaku, *Horyu-ji, Temple of the Exalted Law: Early Buddhist Art from Japan*, New York: Japan Society, 1981

Mason, Penelope E., *History of Japanese Art*, New York: Abrams, 1993

McCallum, Donald F., *Zenkoji and Its Icon: A Study in Medieval Japanese Religious Art*, Princeton, New Jersey: Princeton University Press, 1994

Mori, Hisashi, *Sculpture of the Kamakura Period*, New York: Weatherhill, and Tokyo: Heibonsha, 1974

Nishikawa, Kyotaro, and Emily J. Sano, *The Great Age of Japanese Buddhist Sculpture, AD 600–1300*, Fort Worth, Texas: Kimbell Art Museum, 1982; Seattle and London: University of Washington Press, 1983

Paine, Robert Treat, and Alexander Coburn Soper, *The Art and Architecture of Japan*, Baltimore, Maryland: Penguin, 1955; 2nd edition, London and Baltimore, Maryland: Penguin, 1974

Roberts, Laurance P., *Dictionary of Japanese Artists: Painting, Sculpture, Ceramics, Prints, Lacquer*, Tokyo and New York: Weatherhill, 1976

Saunders, E. Dale, *Mudra: A Study of Symbolic Gestures in Japanese Buddhist Sculpture*, New York: Pantheon Books, and London: Routledge and Paul, 1960

Sawa, Ryuken, *Art in Japanese Esoteric Buddhism*, Tokyo: Heibonsha, and New York: Weatherhill, 1972

Warner, Langdon, *The Craft of the Japanese Sculptor*, New York: McFarlane Warde McFarlane, and Japan Society of New York, 1936

Watson, William, *Sculpture of Japan from the Fifth to the Fifteenth Century*, New York: Viking, and London: The Studio, 1959

JEAN (HENNEQUIN) DE LIÈGE *fl. ca.* 1360–1381 *Netherlandish*

Born in the Netherlands, Jean de Liège established his career in Paris at the royal courts, notably that of Charles V. Only a few works are solidly attributed to Jean; many are lost. A down-to-earth realism typifies his style, strongly flavored by lingering elements of Gothic stylization, which is particularly evident in his simplified and conventional rendering of drapery. The faces of his figures, however, are particularly engaging, often displaying an overlying sweetness imposed on the initially straightforward naturalism.

Jean's earliest known work is the bust of Princess Bonne, daughter of the dauphin Charles (the future Charles V), who died in infancy in 1360. It was originally part of a *gisant* (reclining figure), resting with a companion figure representing Bonne's older sister Jeanne, who died only 17 days before the infant princess (this figure is untraced). The tomb, originally placed in the Cistercian Abbey of St. Antoine-des-Champs, Paris, consisted of a stone base decorated with images of praying nuns, with the *gisants* reclining on a black marble slab and canopies placed above their heads. The bust of Bonne is startlingly realistic. The round face of a two-year-old is softly modeled, with a tiny, sensitive mouth and knobby chin.

Another attribution from around this same time is a *Virgin with the Christ Child Holding a Bird*. The drapery of the Virgin is arranged in broad, sweeping, simplified folds. Her sweetly smiling face is conventional and somewhat masklike, but the head of the Christ child bears great similarity to that of Bonne in its round shape, compressed features, and wan expression.

Several untraced or destroyed works are documented to the 1360s, such as the tomb of Jeanne de Bretagne and figures of Charles V and Jeanne de Bourbon.

In 1366–67 Jean de Liège was in England, where the French-born Queen Philippa of Hanault commissioned him to create her tomb. Originally, the tomb was quite ornate; 32 weeping figures (an innovative element in Jean's tomb designs) were placed on bases projecting out of the sides of the sarcophagus. The figures were polychromed and gilded, as was the *gisant* of Philippa herself. Its drapery folds are typically simplified. The queen's particularized, matronly face, however, departs from the usually idealized tomb effigies of the time. The work was influential in infusing a new realism into English Gothic sculpture. This elaborate tomb design was brought back to France and incorporated, for example, into the tomb of Charles V and Jeanne de Bourbon, which Jean de Liège probably designed.

In an effort to intensify his memory and create powerful reminders of his royal authority, Charles V ordered his heart to be entombed separately from his body. The tomb for his heart (destroyed 1736), commissioned from Jean in 1367–68, was located in the choir of Notre-Dame, Cathedral of Rouen. A surviving drawing shows the *gisant* recumbent on a slab of black marble, his left hand holding a scepter and his right hand a heart. Charles IV had earlier followed this unusual burial practice; his body, heart, and entrails were buried in three different locations. Jean received the commission in 1372 to create statues of Charles IV and his queen, Jeanne d'Evreux, to be placed over their entrails (entombed at the Cistercian abbey of Maubuisson). Less than life-size (just over one meter high), both figures clutch a bag containing their entrails in the left hand. Simple, vertical folds define their robes. Charles's youthful face is smiling, while Jeanne, wearing the wimple and veil of a widow, has a more severe expression. It is difficult to describe the portrayal of Charles IV as naturalistic, especially since it was created decades after his death. Even though the artist probably at some point modeled images of Jeanne d'Evreux from life, this *gisant* image is only mildly compelling, displaying a highly reticent realism.

In later works idealism appears to supersede realism, regardless of whether the artist knew the subject, as, for example, in the tomb sculptures portraying the daughters of Jeanne d'Evreux, Marie de France and Blanche, Duchess of Orléans. Jean received the commission for their double tomb in 1381. The veiled and wimpled face of Blanche's *gisant* is mildly realistic in its depiction of age but highly simplified into broad, sweeping planes. The drapery of this full *gisant* figure is severe in its simplicity. Only the bust of the *gisant* of Marie de France survives. The young woman bears rather particularized features, including a prominent chin and sharp nose. The face is sweet, perhaps even slightly melancholy, but ultimately conventional, as comparisons with portrayals of young women by any number of 14th-century sculptors show.

At Jean's death in 1381, many works were left unfinished in his workshop, attesting to his great popularity. Indeed, he is usually designated as the favorite sculptor of Charles V. Among the unfinished pieces are funerary works as well as various religious subjects and statues for nonfunerary monuments. A former assistant, Robert Loisel, acquired the workshop and completed most of these works, later becoming an established figure. It is only in this sense that a "school" of Jean de Liège can be said to have continued after his death.

Jean's major innovations were in tomb design, particularly his incorporation of weeping figures around the base of the sarcophagus. Regarding his figural style, his realism is reserved and static and for this reason perhaps was seen as highly appropriate to the tomb sculptures for which he received so many commissions.

WALTER SMITH

Biography

Born in the southern Netherlands, date of birth unknown. Possibly a student of Jean Pepin de Huy. Probably settled in Paris, under the patronage of Queen Jeanne de Bourbon, *ca.* 1360; began to receive commissions from the Dauphin Charles (later Charles V), early 1360s; worked for the French-born queen of England, Philippa of Hanault, in England, 1366–67; back in France, working on various other royal commissions, mostly tombs, by 1368. Died in Paris, France, 1381.

Selected Works

ca. 1360 Bust of Princess Bonne, for the Cistercian Abbey of St. Antoine-des-Champs, Paris,

France; marble; Museum Mayer van den Bergh, Antwerp, Belgium

1364 *Virgin with the Christ Child Holding a Bird*; marble; Museum Gulbenkian, Lisbon, Spain

1366–67 Tomb of Philippa of Hanault; marble; Westminster Abbey, London, England

1372 Tomb of the Entrails of Charles IV and Jeanne d'Evreux; marble; Musée du Louvre, Paris, France

1381 Bust of Marie de France; marble; Metropolitan Museum of Art, New York City, United States

1381 Tomb of Blanche, Duchess of Orléans; marble; Basilica of Saint-Denis, Saint-Denis, France

Further Reading

Devigne, M., *La sculpture mosane du XIIe au XVIe siècle: Contribution à l'étude de l'art dans la région de la Meuse moyenne*, Paris and Brussels: Van Oest, 1932

Donzet, Bruno, and Christian Siret, *Les fastes du gothique: Le siècle de Charles V* (exhib. cat.), Paris: Éditions de la Réunion des Musées Nationaux, 1981

"Jean [Hennequin] de Liège," in *The Dictionary of Art*, edited by Jane Turner, vol. 17, New York: Grove, and London: Macmillan, 1996

Stone, Lawrence, *Sculpture in Britain: The Middle Ages*, London: Penguin, 1955; 2nd edition, 1972

JOCHO late 900s–1057 *Japanese*

Jocho was the most innovative Japanese sculptor during the Late Heian period. Breaking away from the traditions of the previously dominant T'ang style, Jocho established a style of sculpture "much more expressive of native Japanese taste" (see Ishizawa et al., 1981). In 1020 he worked as an assistant to his father, Kojo, on a series of nine statues of Amida Buddha for the Nine Amida Hall at Jojoji in Heian. The patron was Fujiwara-no-Michinaga, head of the Fujiwara, the most powerful of all the Heian clans. In recognition of his artistic achievements, Michinaga conferred on Jocho the title of *hokkyo*, Master of the Dharma Bridge, which was a rank within the Buddhist hierarchy never before accorded to a sculptor. In 1023 Jocho received numerous commissions from Michinaga for Jojoji, including 11 statues for the Main Hall, 5 statues for the Hall of the Great Mystic Kings, and 49 statues used in special rites for the well-being of Michinaga in the afterlife.

By 1023 Jocho had established his own workshop, and in 1026 records indicate that his students had grown to include 20 master sculptors each with 5 assistants. Jocho's primary patrons were the Fujiwara family; Michinaga; Michinaga's son, Yorimichi, and daughter, Shosbi; and a few patrons within the Fujiwara social circle. The only commission for Jocho outside of Heian was for replacing damaged statues in Hofukuji, an 8th-century clan temple of the Fujiwara family in Nara. In 1048, Jocho achieved the rank of Hogen for his work at Hofukuji. Unfortunately, none of Jocho's early works survive. The only authenticated extant example is the *Seated Amida (Amida Nyorai)*, commissioned by Yorimichi for the Phoenix Hall (Hoodo) at Byodoin in the Uhi prefecture and consecrated in 1053.

The central image of the Amida Buddha is considered to be Jocho's masterpiece and the epitome of Heian courtly art (see Stanley-Baker, 1984). The statue represents the Buddha of Immeasurable Light and is constructed of red cypress, lacquer cloth, and gold leaf. A flamelike golden aureole adorned with 52 gilded *apsaras* (celestial nymphs) frame the head of the Buddha. These small sculptures attached to the walls adjacent to the Buddha figure represent the Buddha's entourage and appear sitting or standing on clouds and playing musical instruments while others are dancing. The dancing *apsara*, a celestial nymph, is particularly lively and graceful.

The *Seated Amida* is a perfect example of the numerous contributions Jocho made to Late Heian sculpture. In this statue, standing nearly 2.95 meters high including the lotus pedestal and dais, Jocho gave the figure a unique balance of strength and delicacy, of stability and calm, which was praised at the time as being "flawless as the full moon" (see Ishizawa et al., 1981).The vertical proportion of the statue, from the bottom of the legs to the hairline, is exactly equal to the distance between both knees, creating a "superbly balanced whole" (see Ishizawa et al., 1981).

Jocho perfected *yosegi-zukuri*, an assembled woodblock method. Although Early Heian sculptors had used the single wood-block method, *ichiboku-zukuri*, Jocho systematized the *yosegi* technique that had many advantages over the older method. The use of 53 pieces of wood in the *Seated Amida* avoided problems with cracking, which was present in the older wood-block method. In addition, because the wood was hollowed out, a lighter work of sculpture could be produced. Equally important was that the *yosegi* technique allowed several carvers to work in an assembly-line fashion, ensuring that a studio could turn out large-scale images in a short period of time. In this regard, Jocho was instrumental in developing *bussho*, workshops of sculptors who could undertake large commissions under the guidance of a master.

In terms of style, Jocho's *Seated Amida* differs from earlier statues of the Buddha in that the eyes are directed down toward the worshiper, establishing an inti-

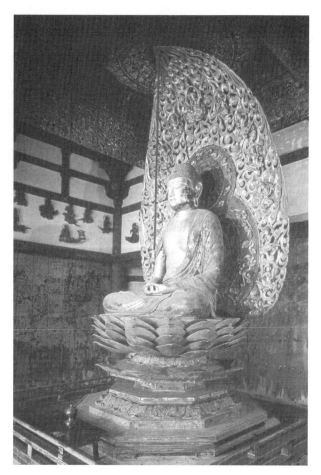

Seated Amida (Amida Nyorai)
© Sakamoto Photo Research Laboratory / CORBIS

mate psychological bond between believer and savior. One further stylistic difference from earlier Buddhist statues is the lack of attendant bodhisattva figures. The much sought-after, elegant courtly style of Jocho became known as the Fujiwara style and was continued by his son, Kakujo, and his main pupil, Chosei, and can be seen in the En, In, and Kei Schools, ateliers established by Jocho's pupils.

MARY ANN STEGGLES

See also **Japan; Yosegi-zukuri**

Biography

Born in Heian (now Kyoto), Japan, late 10th century. Son of Kojo, a sculptor employed by the Fujiwara family; son Kakujo also a sculptor. Studied sculpture in father's studio before opening his own workshop, 1023; by 1026 had 105 sculptors working in his atelier; worked exclusively for Fujiwara family; awarded the title of *hokkyo*, Master of the Dharma Bridge, 1020; given the rank of *hogen*, Master of the Dharma Eye,

1023; traveled briefly to Nara after 1053 to work on the Kofukuji temple; the En, In, and Kei schools developed by pupils of his atelier. Died in Heian, Japan, 1057.

Selected Works

1020	Nine statues of the Amida Buddha, for Nine Amida Hall, Jojoji Temple, Heian (now Kyoto), Japan; red cypress, lacquer cloth, gold leaf (destroyed)
1023	Eleven statues, for Main Hall, Jojoji Temple, Heian (now Kyoto), Japan; red cypress, lacquer cloth, gold leaf (destroyed)
1023	Five statues, for Hall of Great Mystic Kings, Jojoji Temple, Heian (now Kyoto), Japan; red cypress, lacquer cloth, gold leaf (destroyed)
1023–49	Statues, for Jojoji Temple, Heian (now Kyoto), Japan; wood (destroyed)
1053	*Seated Amida (Amida Nyorai)*; red cypress, lacquer cloth, gold leaf; Hoodo (Phoenix Hall), Byodoin, Uji Preferecture, Kyoto, Japan
year unknown	Statues, for Hofukuji Temple, Nara, Japan; wood (destroyed)

Further Reading

Irie, Taikichi, and Jonathan Edward Kidder, Jr., *Masterpieces of Japanese Sculpture*, Tokyo: Bijutsu Shuppan-sha, and Rutland, Vermont: C.E. Tuttle, 1961

Ishizawa, Masao, et al., *The Heritage of Japanese Art*, Tokyo and New York: Kodansha International, 1981

Mason, Penelope, *History of Japanese Art*, New York: Abrams, 1993

Morgan, Sherwood, "Jocho's Amida in Byodoin," *Oriental Art* 2 (Summer 1980)

Morse, Samuel, "Jocho's Amida," *Res* 23 (1993)

Noma, Seiroku, *The Arts of Japan: Ancient and Medieval*, Tokyo: Kodasha, 1966

Roberts, Lawrence, *A Dictionary of Japanese Artists: Painting, Sculpture, Ceramics, Prints, Lacquer*, New York and Tokyo: Weatherhill, 1976

Stanley-Baker, Joan, *Japanese Art*, London: Thames and Hudson, 1984

Tazawa, Uytaka (editor), *Biographical Dictionary of Japanese Art*, New York and Tokyo: Kodansha International, 1981

Yamasaki, Shigehisa (editor), *Chronological Table of Japanese Art*, Tokyo: Geishinsa, 1981

Yashiro, Yukio, *2,000 Years of Japanese Art*, New York: Abrams; and London: Thames and Hudson, 1958

ALLEN JONES 1937– *British*

The oeuvre of Allen Jones contains many more lithographs and paintings than sculptures. However, it was a series of sculptures of female figures he made in 1969 that earned him artistic recognition. This series comprised arresting images of twisted, nearly naked female forms that were manipulated into pieces of human furniture. To some, they are humorous pop culture icons; to others, they are pornographic violations of women's bodies.

Jones's contemporaries at the Royal College of Art in London in the late 1950s included R.B. Kitaj, David Hockney, and Derek Boshier. All were concerned with breaking new ground in art. Jones was expelled from the college apparently because of irreconcilable artistic differences with his professor of painting, but he continued to be active in the London art scene. He held various teaching positions and served as secretary for the aggressive emergent artists' group, the Young Contemporaries.

Jones's work in the early 1960s was informed by his reading of philosophy and psychology, namely Friedrich Nietzsche, Sigmund Freud, and Carl Jung. Jones's earliest sculptures grew out of his interest in the materiality of form. His 1965 work *7th Man*—an abstract sculpture constructed of Plexiglas and painted rope—represented an attempt to fuse the symbolism and form of man into something tangible and spatial. The result was not terribly arresting, but Jones's exploitation of the female figure was spectacular. By the mid 1960s, his immediate inspiration had shifted from philosophy, psychology, and abstract symbols to popular culture images of women.

Each of his life-size women bent and twisted into the forms of a chair, a table, or a hat stand were modeled in clay under the artist's direction before being cast in fiberglass and painted in acrylic. The forms were deliberately distorted to stress the breasts and buttocks, resulting in hyper sexualized and eroticized subject matter. The figures were dressed in black leather fetish gear that evoked sensations of sadism and masochism. In contrast to Jones's brightly colored paintings and lithographs, the black and white palette of these sculptures was enlivened only by the garish makeup on the women's faces. In *Hat Stand*, an erect figure in spidery black leather bondage costume holds out her hands in acquiescence. *Table Sculpture* consists of a passive woman on her hands and knees serving as the base for a glass tabletop. She is naked except for her long black leather gloves, a leather bustier that exposes her breasts, and high-laced, high-heeled boots—all signifiers for either the prostitute or the porn star.

The series of tough-looking sex kittens in demeaning positions set off a maelstrom in England and the United States. Like other Pop artists (and especially those from a British Marxist orientation), Jones was concerned with blurring the boundaries between pop culture and high art within a capitalist, consumer society. The catalogues that accompanied his exhibitions read like consumer catalogues. They included clippings, sketches, and photographs of his plaster casts that demystified the artistic process and made manifest Jones's working methods. He borrowed images and iconography from graphic artists such as John Willie, whose work straddled pulp pornography and the mainstream media. In return, Jones wrote the introduction to the first edition of Willie's cult-classic book, *The Adventures of Sweet Gwendoline* (1974). Jones conceived his images of women as an apposite reflection of the cultural epoch. In an interview, he reasoned that "the gradual hardening of pictorial rendition that culminated in my 'furniture' sculptures of the late 1960s was a legitimate response to the attitudes of that era." Some critics interpreted the work as an extreme and ironic critique of the commodification of women's bodies in the modern era, whereas others saw Jones's images as a reflection of violent personal fantasies that served to reify the masculine domination of the female sex.

Debates about Jones's overtly sexual sculptures were brought to the fore by a decision of the British Arts Council. In the course of publishing a series of artists' books, the council refused a woman artist's exploration of the female genitals, but included a project of Jones's that was rife with explicit but masculine fantasies of women's bodies. Feminist critics, particularly Laura Mulvey and Rozsika Parker (both prominent British writers and critics of the 1970s), used the case to argue that art world access was limited and contradictory, and that it privileged masculinity at the expense of women artists (see Mulvey, 1973; Parker, 1973). Mulvey also effectively disputed Jones's claim that his work reflected the lived experience of women by positing that the real object of representation in his work was not women but remained male desire, fantasy, and fears. In retaliation, but not quite response, Jones suggested that "the feminist movement has more serious issues to debate than the self-expression of one individual. I am bound to say that there is more explicit display in current female fashion on the streets than can be touched in my paintings. I can only hope to make an icon of this reality." In retrospect, some contemporary artists credit Jones with identifying the body, intentionally or not, as a major artistic preoccupation throughout the following decades. After Jones was given a solo exhibition at the Institute of Contemporary Arts in London, two protest feminist exhibitions organized by and featuring the work of women artists followed.

In the 1980s Jones's sculpture shifted to more abstract, less unequivocal subject matter in a variety of media. In *Vision in Pink and Red* Jones cut sheets of steel in order to form curving, abstracted male and female figures. In these sculptures Jones explored how the flat painted surfaces could be manipulated to create twisting, three-dimensional objects. In their conception of flat objects made three-dimensional, the works resemble the 1980s sculpture of Frank Stella, but without that artist's level of art world recognition. In 1988 Ken Johnson in *Art in America* wrote, "Jones's early work was sexist, to be sure, but at least there was something bracingly provocative about it."

While the nature and content of the critiques may have changed, Jones's examination of the disruptive possibilities of sculpture remains a significant issue in contemporary art. Two decades later, sculptors such as Jeff Koons, Mike Kelley, Paul McCarthy, and Damien Hirst aggressively push the boundaries of the taboo in art.

Sarah Watson Parsons

Biography

Born in Southampton, England, 1 September 1937. Attended Hornsey College of Art, London, taking courses in painting and lithography, 1955–59, and Royal College of Art, 1959–60; earned diploma from Hornsey Teacher Training Course, 1961; taught at various art schools around London, 1960–64; remained based in London; lived, worked, and taught in New York, 1964–65, Tampa, Florida, 1968–69, Hamburg, Germany, 1969–70, Los Angeles, 1977, and Berlin, 1982–83. Awarded Prix des Jeunes Artistes at the Paris Biennale, 1963; elected associate of Royal Academy of Arts, London, 1981, and awarded full membership as a printmaker, 1986; elected trustee of British Museum, 1990. Received commissions for International Garden Festival, Liverpool, England, 1984; Frederick R. Weisman Foundation, Los Angeles, 1984–85; St. Martin's

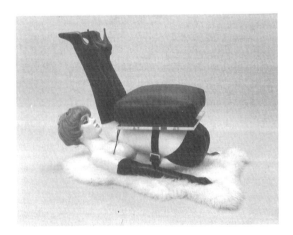

Chair
© Tate Gallery, London / Art Resource, NY

Property Group for Cotton Atrium, London Bridge City, England, 1987; Chelsea and Westminster Hospital, London, 1993; and London Dock Development Corporation, 1994. Currently lives and works in England.

Selected Works

1965   *7th Man*; Plexiglas, rope, collage, paint; private collection, United States
1969   *Table Sculpture*; acrylic paint, fiberglass, leather, hair, glass; Aachen Neue Gallery, Aachen, Germany (edition of six)
1969   *Hat Stand*; acrylic paint, fiberglass, leather, hair, glass; Aachen Neue Gallery, Aachen, Germany (edition of six)
1969   *Chair*; fiberglass; Tate Gallery, London, England
1982–87 *Vision in Pink and Red*; oil enamel on wood
1988   *Artisan* (second variation); painted steel

Further Reading

Gowing, Lawrence, "Allen Jones," *Art and Design* 1 (1985)
"How Would We Discuss Allen Jones' Work in 1995? WAM Takes a Straw Poll," *Women's Art Magazine* 64 (May–June 1995)
Johnson, Kenneth, "Allen Jones at Charles Cowles Gallery, New York," *Art in America* 76 (October 1988)
Lamberth, Andrew, *Allen Jones: Sculpture*, Swansea, Wales: Glynn Vivian Gallery, 1992
Lippard, Lucy, *Pop Art*, New York: Praeger, and London: Thames and Hudson, 1966
Livingstone, Marco, *Allen Jones, Sheer Magic*, New York: Congreve, and London: Thames and Hudson, 1979
Mulvey, Laura, "Fears, Fantasies, and the Male Unconscious; or, 'You Don't Know What Is Happening, Do You, Mr. Jones?'" *Spare Rib* (1973); reprint, in *Visual and Other Pleasures*, by Mulvey, Bloomington: Indiana University Press, and London: Macmillan, 1989
Parker, Rozsika, "Censored: Feminist Art That the Arts Council Is Trying to Hide," *Spare Rib* 54 (January 1973); reprint, in *Looking On: Images of Femininity in the Visual Arts and Media*, edited by Rosemary Betterton, London: Pandora, 1987

JACQUES JONGHELINCK (JONGELING) 1530–1606 *Flemish*

It is only recently that Jacques Jonghelinck has regained his place in the history of sculpture. Nonetheless, during his lifetime he enjoyed fame throughout Europe and was in demand for commissions from Spain to Sweden. Soon after his death, however, he lapsed into obscurity even in his homeland, and it was not until the 19th century that he was partially rediscovered by a few numismatists. His scattered works and unsigned medals fell into anonymity or were the object of erroneous attributions. More than any other artist, Jonghelinck stood in need of a revival.

His life and works are intimately linked to the changing fortunes of the Low Countries during the 16th century. He was born in Antwerp in 1530 into a distinguished family who had produced several directors of the mint; throughout his life, he would be strongly influenced by this background. Nothing is known of Jonghelinck's early training, although it was almost certainly as a goldsmith, much like Benvenuto Cellini, Leone Leoni, and many bronze makers of the period. Indeed there is no reason to suppose that Jonghelinck's family connections helped to develop his artistic gifts, as is often claimed, since the high offices held by his relatives were confined to administrators or financiers, rather than artists. At most, it is known that two of his brothers were members of the Guild of St. Luke, the artists' association in Antwerp.

His family was well connected, however, which certainly led to Jonghelinck's acquaintance with the future Cardinal Granvelle (whose protégé he soon became) and his subsequent recommendation to the "Caesarean" sculptor Leoni, whom he joined in Milan, Italy, in 1552. There Jonghelinck may have witnessed and perhaps assisted in the casting of the famous *Charles V and Fury Restrained* (1549–1555), as well as several large bronzes that the emperor had ordered from Leoni when the latter visited Brussels in 1549.

Upon his return, the young Jonghelinck was commissioned to produce a model for the new Carolus florin. Soon he was chosen to produce the tomb of Charles the Bold at Bruges. The choice of a young man under 30 years of age for such a commission was surprising given that the Netherlands boasted highly talented sculptors such as Jacques Du Broeucq and Cornelis II Floris, a specialist in the field whose fine reputation derived from his mausoleums in Scandinavia. What was needed at Bruges, however, was a counterpart to the existing tomb of Marie de Bourgogne, which was made of gilded copper with enameled coats of arms. Thus it was not a worker in marble that was required, but rather a metal founder who was also a goldsmith. Philip II approved Jonghelinck's design in August 1558, shortly before his final departure for Spain. Notwithstanding the prodigious skill that the artist brought to bear on this delicate project and the ingenuity he displayed in introducing Renaissance motifs into a Gothic scheme, the approach that the commission necessitated was one of imitation and restoration, which does not allow art historians to assess the artist's own style.

Soon afterward Jonghelinck displayed quite different tendencies when his brother Nicolas Jonghelinck—a financier and tax inspector, as well as a patron and collector of the arts—ordered from him a fountain depicting Bacchus and seven large bronzes representing the *Planets* (the sun/Helios, the moon/Diana, Mars, Venus, Mercury, Saturn, and Jupiter) for his sumptuous house in the neighborhood of Antwerp. In these works it was the Italian influence that came to the fore. These bronzes can be compared with their exact contemporaries: the small bronzes by Stoldo Lorenzi and Giovanni Bandini from the Florence *studiolo* of Francesco I de' Medici, as well as with the first versions of Giambologna's *Mercury* (1579). Jonghelinck's group—among the most important of the 16th century—had an eventful history: Ceded to the treasurer general Gaspard Schetz upon Nicolas Jonghelinck's death in 1570, it was then confiscated during the Insurrection as the property of the king of Spain, sold to the king of Sweden, impounded at the point of shipment, and acquired by the municipality of Antwerp, which used it to decorate the city market on the occasion of Alessandro Farnese's triumphal entry after a famous siege on 27 August 1585. Later the group was made a gift to this victorious governor but was subsequently seized by the treasurer general Schetz's heirs. In 1620 it was acquired by the painter Peter Paul Rubens and an alderman of Antwerp, Jaspar Charles, and then by a French refugee, the Duc d'Aumale. Finally, it was sold to Cardinal the Infante Ferdinand, the governor general, who gave it to his brother King Philip IV of Spain in 1637. The *Planets* were set up in the park of Buen Retiro and then in the Alcazar in Madrid, eventually ending up in the royal palace of the Spanish capital, whereas the Bacchus was installed in the gardens at Aranjuez.

Jonghelinck, whose principal clients came from the ruling class, also worked for Margaret of Parma, for whom he produced a fountain for the Parc de la Cour. In 1563 she appointed him sculptor, metal founder, and engraver in ordinary of the king's seals, a title that from 8 November 1565 was accompanied by a pension that doubled in value on 29 May 1572. This role brought him orders for numerous matrices for seals intended for the major state institutions, as well as for many church leaders and dignitaries. In his monumental seals the traditional Gothic design is overshadowed by Renaissance decoration.

When the Duke of Alba wished to celebrate his victory over William of Orange, he called on Jonghelinck to erect a monument in the citadel at Antwerp (1571). This work, which portrayed the fearsome governor trampling the nobility and people of the Netherlands underfoot, aroused an enormous outcry across the whole of Europe and earned its creator fame in the historical literature that had nothing to do with the artistic merits of the work.

Meanwhile, the civil war that raged in the region from 1567 had ruined the collectors, eliminated patronage, put an end to the exportation of works of art, and caused many artists to emigrate. Thanks to his protectors, Jonghelinck was able to concentrate on his art for a few years longer. In December 1572, however, he obtained the position of warden of the Antwerp Mint. Whatever his thoughts on the subject may have been at the time, his career as a sculptor was over. The commissions for a new fountain for the gardens of the palace at Brussels in 1598 and for a Christ for the Pont de Meir in Antwerp in 1605 seem to have consisted merely of casts taken from existing models. For over 30 years he was consumed by his administrative duties in Antwerp. Nonetheless, he continued producing medals and seals for the remainder of his life. This aspect of Jonghelinck's work is not to be overlooked, since as the author of nearly 150 portraits (between 1555 and 1605) he may be considered one of the foremost medallists of the Low Countries in the 16th century.

Jonghelinck's sculptural work epitomizes most of the trends of the period: the Italian influence rubs shoulders with the old tradition of Flemish realism, and the Mannerism of the 1560s is juxtaposed with the style of Floris along with the entire northern European decorative repertoire. In Jonghelinck's works, style was dictated by the commission: he was traditional with the tomb of Charles the Bold, monumental and Italianate with the *Planets*, but realistic and even psychological with the statue and the bust of the Duke of Alba.

Although he allowed his eclecticism free rein, Jonghelinck's inspiration remained somewhat limited. He lacked verve, audacity, and that indefinable quality that makes for genius. Two inhibiting factors constantly held him back: his sense of moderation and his taste for fine workmanship, as though any novelty foreign to the cultured and aristocratic milieu that he frequented would have verged on indecency. The courtly art that he practiced was respectful of hierarchy, enamored of humanism, and addicted to moralizing rhetoric.

His anxiety not to depart from reality (even for the sake of ennobling it) explains why Jonghelinck was especially at home with portraiture. It is this that makes the bust of the Duke of Alba an exceptional work, albeit one sadly not followed by further triumphs in the same genre, although his series of medals constitutes an extraordinary gallery of contemporary leaders.

LUC SMOLDEREN

See also **Leoni Family**

Biography

Born in Antwerp, Belgium, 1530. Family included several directors of the Antwerp Mint; trained probably as a goldsmith; went to Milan, 1552, and worked with the sculptor Leone Leoni; began designing coins back in Antwerp by 1553; worked on sculptures in Brussels, 1555–73; received commission to produce the tomb of Charles the Bold, Bruges, Belgium, 1558; appointed by Margaret of Parma as court sculptor and engraver of the king's seals, 1563, with a pension in 1565 that doubled in 1572; appointed warden of the Antwerp mint, 1572; produced nearly 150 portraits in the form of medals and seals throughout his career. Died in Antwerp, Belgium, 1606.

Selected Works

1559–63   Tomb of the Charles the Bold; bronze; Church of Our Lady, Bruges, Belgium

1564–70   *Bacchus* fountain; bronze; gardens of Palace of Aranjuez, Aranjuez, Spain; seven *Planets*; bronze; Royal Palace, Madrid, Spain

1569–71   Statue of the Duke of Alba, for Citadel of Antwerp, Belgium; bronze (dismantled)

1571   Bust of the Duke of Alba; bronze; Frick Collection, New York City, United States

Further Reading

Buchanan, Iain, "The Collection of Niclaes Jongelinck, I: 'Bacchus and the Planets' by Jacques Jongelinck," *The Burlington Magazine* 132 (1990)

Forrer, L., "Jacques Jonghelinck," in *Biographical Dictionary of Medallists*, compiled by Forrer, vol. 3, London: Spink, 1907, and vol. 7 (supplement), London: Spink, 1923; reprint, New York: Franklin, 1970

Smolderen, Luc, *La statue du duc d'Albe à Anvers par Jacques Jonghelinck*, Brussels: Palais des Académies, 1972

Smolderen, Luc, *Jacques Jonghelinck, sculpteur, médailleur et graveur de sceaux (1530–1606)*, Louvain-la-Neuve, Belgium: Département d'Archéologie et d'Histoire de l'Art, Séminaire de Numismatique Marcel Hoc, 1996

DONALD JUDD 1928–1994 *United States*

Donald Judd has most commonly been categorized as one of the leading figures in the Minimalist movement of the 1960s. Although his works have become icons of Minimalism, his philosophical and art-theoretical concerns differed substantially from other formulations of reductive three-dimensional art offered by artists such as Robert Morris and Carl Andre. Based on his study of philosophy and art history and initially put into practice in his art criticism in the late 1950s and early 1960s, Judd's formulations called for a break with European-derived tradition. Instead, he developed a set of art-theoretical concerns derived from anarchist, positivist, and pragmatist philosophy in which the art-

work was prescribed to be a simple, unified object that did not refer to anything other than itself. In his major 1965 essay "Specific Objects" and his highly influential 1964 interview with Bruce Glaser (along with Frank Stella and Dan Flavin and later abridged as "Questions to Stella and Judd"), Judd called for an art that abandoned the media of painting and sculpture. These categories and the materials out of which they have conventionally been made (oil paint, canvas, bronze, marble, etc.) were, according to Judd, overdetermined and limiting. Instead, Judd put forth the concept of the specific object that would not refer to, signify, or rely on any extrinsic source of meaning. In short, the specific object is what it is.

In addition to his stress on new materials, Judd also emphasized the need to purge the artwork of relational composition. Composing a work part by part—that is, creating an artwork in which internal formal elements are ordered hierarchically—effectively manipulated the viewer by determining the manner in which the work is viewed or experienced. In contrast, Judd sought to avoid hierarchical composition and to create works that frustrated internal formal interpretation. Instead of looking *into* a Judd object, one can only look *at* it as a single, whole entity. In this way, Judd hoped to mitigate the situation in which the viewer is understood as passive recipient for the artist's message (an underlying principle of Abstract Expressionism, the dominant American style of the 1940s and 1950s). Furthermore, the denial of internal composition forces the viewer into a self-conscious physical and perceptual relation with the object itself rather than the conventional attention to internal orderings and patterns. Along with Judd's emphasis on nonrelational composition and externalization, Judd also sought to remove the hand of the artist from the object and had his works fabricated so as to avoid subjective and casual surface incident. Although not industrially produced, they have often been mistaken for mass-produced objects.

Critics have often mistaken the political implications of Judd's mitigation of the authority of the artist for esoteric aestheticism. Such interpretations fail to take into account the anarchist philosophy on which Judd based his work. As David Raskin has shown, Judd's work contains a well-defined political and philosophical basis, and his essays are often overtly political in content. With no extrinsic reference or justifying context, Judd's objects repudiate the authoritative address to the viewer expected from the artist through the artwork. The reductive formal vocabulary of his objects and his erasure of traditional signs of the artist's subjectivity in the work force the viewer to relate directly to the object and the visual experience of it.

In practice, Judd pursued his theoretical aims through a relatively limited group of forms that he created and recreated throughout his career. The most abundant of these are the so-called stacks, progressions, and boxes. The stacks are made up of a series of rectangular boxes vertically lined up between floor and ceiling. Progressions juxtapose a horizontal, square tube with a series of smaller tubes directly below. The lengths and gaps between these lower tubes correlate to preexisting mathematical formulas. Boxes are generally floor-bound and rectangular, often with one or more sides removed or reorganized. Judd's signature materials after the mid 1960s were aluminum and Plexiglas, although he increasingly explored plywood beginning in the mid 1970s.

His intentional constraints on his own output were further components of his art theory. These convenient terms, however, belie the complexity of each individual variation. Although two stacks may appear similar, for instance, no two Judd artworks are ever identical. In each piece he worked out colors, materials, and sizes in minute variations. Believing that each aspect of the artwork should be clearly perceivable as a concrete visual fact, Judd gave all elements of the work a great deal of attention. Furthermore, he determined each artwork in part by the immediate facts of its exhibition context. This approach makes Judd's artworks extremely resistant to conventional modes of art criticism. He understood that most descriptions of art objects projected associations and metaphors onto the art object. By reducing the number of elements and striving for a unitary object, he hoped to block the literary mode of looking (that is, visual narrative) and to compel the viewer to contend directly with the visual facts in front of him or her.

In addition to creating his individual objects, Judd also worked in architectural and furniture design. His most ambitious project combining art, architecture, and furniture developed over the last two decades of his life in his home in Marfa, Texas. Renovating a former military base in this rural Texas town, Judd created one of the largest permanent art installations in the world with his Chinati Foundation. Holding series of works by Judd, Dan Flavin, John Chamberlain, Roni Horn, Ilya Kabakov, and others, the Chinati Foundation is in many ways one of Judd's most enduring legacies. The centerpieces of the Chinati collections are a series of concrete outdoor works and a group of 100 milled-aluminum rectangular solids by Judd. Although at first all of these aluminum objects appear to be identical, each is a unique variation. The vastness of these 100 variations on a limited theme illustrates Judd's attention to how a seemingly simple difference between two objects requires two discrete and thorough acts of perception. Installed in such a way as to alter under the changing light and landscape conditions, the 100 aluminum works also provide a compelling demonstration of the measureless complexity offered even in the most reductive art objects, each of which must be looked at anew each time. Judd's central concern with his art was to provide the situation in which the viewer could recognize that this complexity and richness were the results not of an authoritative voice of the artist or of tradition, but of the direct perceptual encounter with the object itself.

DAVID GETSY

Biography

Born in Excelsior Springs, Missouri, United States, 3 June 1928. Served in U.S. Army (Korea), 1946–47; studied at The Art Students' League, New York, 1948–53; at College of William and Mary, Williamsburg, Virginia, 1948–49; studied philosophy at Columbia University, New York, 1949–53; graduate study in art history, Columbia University, 1957–62; active as art critic for *ArtNews, Arts Magazine*, and *Art International*, 1959–65; taught at Brooklyn Institute of Arts and Sciences, New York, 1962–64; visiting artist at Dartmouth College, 1966, and Yale University, 1967; first museum solo exhibition, Whitney Museum of American Art, 1968; established second permanent residence in Marfa, Texas, 1971; Baldwin Professor of Art, Oberlin College, 1976; established Chinati Foundation in Marfa, 1986; received Skowhegan Medal for Sculpture and Brandeis Medal for Sculpture, 1987; received Stankowski Foundation Prize and Sikkens Foundation Prize, 1993. Died in New York City, United States, 12 February 1994.

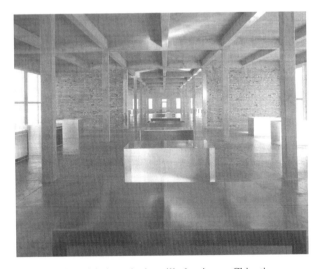

Detail, 100 untitled works in mill aluminum, Chianti Foundation, Marfa, Texas
© 1996 Todd Eberle, The Judd Foundation, and Vaga, New York

Selected Works

The Chinati Foundation and the Judd Foundation, both in Marfa, Texas, collectively hold the largest concentration of Judd's works, including many of the early works

1963   *Light Cadmium Red Oil on Wood*; paint, wood; National Gallery of Canada, Ottawa, Canada

1965   untitled; aluminum and purple lacquer on aluminum; Whitney Museum of American Art, New York City, United States

1966   untitled; blue lacquer on aluminum and galvanized iron, painted aluminum; Norton Simon Museum, Pasadena, California, United States

1968   untitled; brass; Museum of Modern Art, New York City, United States

1969   untitled; galvanized iron, 57 units; Judd Foundation, Marfa, Texas, United States

1971   untitled; blue anodized aluminum, 6 units; Walker Art Center, Minneapolis, Minnesota, United States

1972   untitled; copper, light cadmium red enamel on aluminum; Tate Gallery, London, England

1973–75 untitled; plywood, 6 units; National Gallery of Canada, Ottawa, Canada

1976   untitled; 15 plywood works; Dia Center for the Arts, New York City, United States

1980–84 untitled; milled aluminum, 100 units; Chinati Foundation, Marfa, Texas, United States

1981   untitled; plywood; Saatchi Collection, London, England

1983   untitled; plywood, 4 units; Museum of Contemporary Art, Chicago, Illinois, United States

Further Reading

Agee, William, *Don Judd*, New York: Whitney Museum of American Art, 1968

Donald Judd: Architektur, Münster, Germany: Westfälischer Kunstverein, 1989

Glaser, Bruce, "Questions to Stella and Judd," in *Minimal Art: A Critical Anthology*, edited by Gregory Battcock, Berkeley: University of California Press, 1995

Haskell, Barbara, *Donald Judd*, New York: Whitney Museum of American Art, 1988

Judd, Donald, "Specific Objects," *Arts Yearbook* 8 (1965)

Judd, Donald, *Donald Judd: Complete Writings 1959–1975: Gallery Reviews, Book Reviews, Articles, Letters to the Editor, Reports, Statements, Complaints*, Halifax, Nova Scotia: Press of the Nova Scotia College of Art and Design, and New York: New York University Press, 1975

Judd, Donald, *Donald Judd: Complete Writings, 1975–1986*, Eindhoven, The Netherlands: Van Abbemuseum, 1987

Judd, Donald, "Some Aspects of Color in General and Red and Black in Particular," *Artforum* 32/10 (Summer 1994)

Koepplin, Dieter, *Donald Judd: Zeichnungen; Drawings, 1956–1976*, Basel, Switzerland: Kunstmuseum, and New York: New York University Press, 1976

Meyer, James, *Minimalism: Art and Polemics in the Sixties*, New Haven, Connecticut: Yale University Press, 2001

Poetter, Jochen (editor), *Donald Judd* (exhib. cat.), Stuttgart, Germany: Cantz, 1989

Raskin, David, "Donald Judd's Skepticism," Ph.D. diss., University of Texas at Austin, 1999

Smith, Brydon, *Donald Judd: Catalogue Raisonné of Paintings, Objects, and Woodblocks, 1960–1974*, Ottawa, Ontario: National Gallery of Canada, 1975

JUAN DE JUNI *ca.* 1507–1577 *Spanish*

Juan de Juni's sculpture comprises some of the most dramatic work of 16th-century Spain. Whether in reliefs or figures carved in the round, he evokes powerful emotions through facial expressions, emphatic gestures, and the cascading draperies of his figures. In addition to his distinctive style, with its strong sense of volume, Juni is remarkable for the ease with which he worked in stone, wood, and terracotta.

In his first works in Spain, Juni displayed the accomplished style of a mature artist. Information regarding his career prior to his arrival is scarce. Most scholars believe he came from Burgundy, and some hypothesize that his last name is an adaptation of Joigny; at any rate, a French origin seems certain. Much more difficult to determine is whether he traveled to Italy. Juan José Martín González, the author of the most complete catalogue of the sculptor's work, argues that only such a trip can explain the extensive Italian sources in Juni's oeuvre. Above all, Martín González points to the monumentality and drama of Michelangelo, echoes of the *Laocoön* group, and the example of sculptors of terracotta ensembles, such as Antonio Begarelli, Niccolò dell'Arca, and Guido Mazzoni (see Martín González, 1974). Others have been more cautious, citing the Italian influences available in France and leaving the question open. Over the course of his career, however, Juni abandoned these sources as he developed his own style.

Juni initially appears in Spain in 1533 working in León. The bishop, Alvarez Acosta, may have summoned him, or perhaps the presence of other French sculptors active in the city attracted him, but once there, the sculptor undertook several projects at the Monastery of San Marcos: for the facade, the relief *Descent from the Cross* and medallions with portrait busts of kings ranging from classical heroes to recent Spanish monarchs; in the cloister, the relief *Nativity*; and in the church, a significant share of the upper choir. Although the portrait medallions suffer some wear from exposure, they still demonstrate Juni's characteristic stocky figure types. Similarly, the relief *Descent from the Cross* displays intense emotionalism, vehement postures, and deeply cut drapery, all of which would become a hallmark of his style. The impressive display of one-point perspective that he included in the relief of the Nativity also exhibits Juni's confident mastery of spatial relationships. At a time when few sculptors created such Italianate spatial constructions, this relief, with its range of features carved in low relief to figures carved almost in the round, represents an important development in Spanish sculpture. His work in the upper stalls of the choir, although just as skilled, would have seemed less innovative to a Spanish audience.

By 1537 Juni had left León even though the lower stalls remained to be carved. At this time, he began work in Medina de Rioseco, creating the life-size terracotta statues *St. Jerome* and *Martyrdom of St. Sebastian* for the funerary chapel of the admirals of Castile. Again, Juni's achievement is notable given that few sculptors produced terracotta works in Spain, much less on this scale. Whereas the *St. Jerome* figure has unfortunately lost almost all of its polychromy, the *St. Sebastian* ensemble retains most of its, thereby suggesting how *St. Jerome* might have looked. The ensemble also echoes Italian art: one executioner recalls Giovanni Francesco Rustici's *Baptism of Christ* (1506–11), and the Roman soldier wears the classicizing armor favored by Renaissance artists.

Juni shortly afterward traveled to Salamanca, where he undertook an important funerary ensemble for Gutierre de Castro consisting of a reclining effigy, a terracotta relief of the pietà, and figures of Saint Anne and John the Baptist. Although the effigy no longer exists, the pietà relief and figures survive *in situ*, offering further evidence of Juni's ability to evoke a vivid moment and integrate it within an architectural setting. Juni had by now settled in the city, as evidenced by the will he drew up when he fell ill in 1540. Upon recovering, he carved one of his greatest works, *Entombment* (1541–44), for Alonso de Guevara, Bishop of Modoñedo. Intended for the altar of the bishop's funerary chapel in Valladolid, it consists of freestanding figures arranged in vigorous poses around the dead body of Christ. As a large tableau of dramatic immediacy, the work must have made a great impression on contemporary viewers, particularly because it had few precedents in Spanish sculpture. When creating it, Juni had doubtless drawn on comparable works that he had seen in France and Italy, if indeed he traveled there.

The commission and its subsequent triumph doubtless induced Juni to move to Valladolid. Moreover, the leading sculptor there, Alonso Berruguete, had just settled in Toledo, leaving the field clear. Juni quickly established himself in Valladolid, receiving several major projects in the early 1540s, perhaps none more

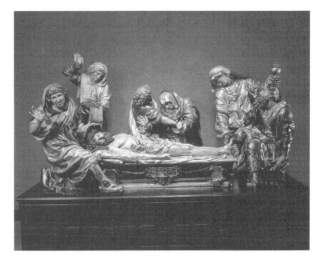

Entombment
© Archivio Iconografico, S.A. / CORBIS

important than that for the high altar of the Church of Santa María la Antigua. The commission, however, proved controversial: although the church awarded it to Juni in 1545, a follower of Berruguete contested the decision, and Juni had to wait five years before the courts ruled in his favor. Throughout the legal proceedings, Berruguete maintained a neutrality, torn between loyalty to his follower and admiration for Juni. In the meantime, Alvarez Acosta, now Bishop of Burgo de Osma, commissioned the high altar of his new cathedral from a team led by Juni. These two altar projects represent Juni's greatest successes in the typically Spanish format combining reliefs and single figures in an architectural framework several stories high. Juni introduced an emphatic Mannerist architecture that provided a more dramatic setting for his vigorous figures and reliefs. Although the size of these projects required a large studio and collaborators, particularly for that at Burgo de Osma, where the division of hands could be established, Juni maintained an impressive quality throughout the works.

The sculptor remained active in his last years, creating remarkable works in various media. For the Church of Santa María in Medina de Rioseco, he carved another altar with vivid figures and compositions constructed with forceful perspective. He sculpted notable single figures, the most famous of which may well be *Virgin of the Angustias*, in which his talent for dramatic expression found an outlet. About 1570, in the Cathedral of Segovia, he returned to the subject of the burial of Christ in a high relief (*Entombment*) of great impact. Perhaps his final masterpiece, the alabaster statue *San Segundo* attests to a technique undiminished by age. Juni again integrated the figure expertly within its setting by depicting the bishop as a freestanding statue praying before the hermitage's altar. Juni died in 1577, leaving his son Isaac, also a sculptor, to carry on his projects and legacy.

PATRICK LENAGHAN

Biography

Probably born in France (Joigny?), *ca.* 1507. Possibly traveled to Italy; in León carved several parts of monastery of San Marcos, *ca.* 1553; worked in Medina de Rioseco, *ca.* 1537; moved to Salamanca, fell ill, and drew up a will; finally settled in Valladolid, by 1543; established himself there and received several major commissions, notably altars for Church of Santa María la Antigua and Cathedral of Burgo de Osma. Son Isaac also sculptor who continued projects left unfinished at father's death. Died in Valladolid, Spain, between 9 and 17 April 1577.

Selected Works

ca. 1533–37	Sculptural decoration, including upper choir stalls, *Descent from the Cross* and medallions and reliefs of historical subjects for the facade, and *Nativity* for the cloister; stone, wood; Monastery of San Marcos, León, Spain
ca. 1537	*St. Jerome* and *Martyrdom of St. Sebastian*; polychromed terracotta; Church of San Francisco, Medina de Rioseco, Spain
ca. 1540–45	*Ecce Homo*; polychromed wood; Museo Diocesano y Catedralicio, Valladolid, Spain
1541–44	*Entombment*, for the former monastery of San Francisco, Valladolid, Spain; polychromed wood; Museo Nacional de Escultura, Valladolid, Spain
1550–54	High altar; polychromed wood; Cathedral of Burgo de Osma, Soria province, Spain
1550–62	High altar, for Church of Santa María la Antigua, Valladolid, Spain; polychromed wood; Cathedral of Valladolid, Spain
after 1561	*Virgin of the Angustias*; polychromed wood; Church of Nuestra Señora de las Angustias, Valladolid, Spain
1567–69	Altarpiece; polychromed wood; Alderete Chapel, Church of San Antolín, Tordesillas, Spain
ca. 1570	*Entombment*; polychromed wood; Cathedral of Segovia, Spain
1572	*San Segundo*; alabaster; Ermita de San Segundo, Ávila, Spain

Further Reading

Azcárate, José María de, *Escultura del siglo XVI*, Madrid: Editorial Plus-Ultra, 1958

Gómez-Moreno, Manuel, *La escultura del renacimiento en España*, Florence: Pantheon Casa Editrice, 1931; as *Renaissance Sculpture in Spain*, translated by Bernard Bevan, Florence: Pantheon Casa Editrice, 1931; reprint, New York: Hacker Art Books, 1971

Gómez-Moreno, Manuel, *The Golden Age of Spanish Sculpture*, London: Thames and Hudson, and Greenwich, Connecticut: New York Graphic Society, 1964

Marías, Fernando, *El largo siglo XVI: Los usos artísticos del renacimiento español*, Madrid: Taurus, 1989

Martín González, Juan José, *Juan de Juni: Vida y obra*, Madrid: Dirección General de Bellas Artes, Ministerio de Educacíon y Ciencia, 1974

Martín González, Juan José, and Joaquín Cruz Solis, *El entierro de Cristo de Juan de Juni: Historia y restauración*, Valladolid, Spain: Institución Cultural Simancas Excma., Diputación Provincial de Valladolid, 1983

Trusted, Marjorie, "Art for the Masses: Spanish Sculpture in the Sixteenth and Seventeenth Centuries," in *Sculpture and Its Reproductions*, edited by Anthony Hughes and Erich Ranfft, London: Reaktion Books, 1997

JUN PAIK, NAM

See **Korea**

K

KAIKEI mid 12th CENTURY–*ca.* 1223

Japanese

Kaikei worked in the Shichijō Bussho (literally, Seventh Avenue Buddhist [images] Work Place) in Kyoto, the major school of sculpture in the 12th and 13th centuries. The workshop had been producing Buddhist images for temples of the aristocracy for at least six generations and had well-established political connections and influence. Kōkei was the director of the workshop—popularly called Kei-ha (Kei school) because of the many artists with *kei* (meaning "rejoice") in their names (Kōkei, Unkei, Kaikei, Tankei, and others)—when, in a decade of appalling violence and destruction, in quick succession the Taira, Minamoto, and finally Hōjo gained control of Kyoto and the right to enthrone the emperor. The wife of Minamoto Yoritomo (1147–99) was a Hōjo, and Yoritomo established his military capital (*bakufu*) in Hōjo family territory, the eastern port city of Kamakura. Military dictatorships remained the political system of Japan for 700 years.

Kōkei adopted Kaikei, as was the custom with outstanding apprentices, who therefore became Unkei's brother. Temple records are surprisingly informative for this era—given the ensuing destruction of temples and their property—and from these sources there is no question that contemporary writers regarded Kaikei as without equal in the field of sculpture. Nevertheless, because Unkei was in the bloodline, he remained Kaikei's senior in every respect, became head of the workshop after Kōkei's death around 1196, and went on to gain a higher place in history. In the titles given

to artists who made exceptional contributions to the church, Kaikei was awarded the title of *hokkyō* (bridge of the law) in 1203 (Unkei's date is unknown) and *hōgen* (eye of the law) sometime between 1208 and 1210 (Unkei received his in 1195); it is not clear whether he became *ho-in* (seal of the law), which Unkei did in 1203. Perhaps only by the vagaries of fate, far more sculptures by Kaikei are preserved today. He was especially close to Priest Chōgen (also called Shunjo Shonin or Shunjōbō [*d.* 1206]), the devout rebuilder of the Tōdai-ji in Nara, who had been won over to the Pure Land (Jōdo) practice of reciting the name of Amida Buddha. Chōgen gave his friends Buddhist names, Kaikei receiving An Amida Butsu. This was abbreviated to An'ami (or Annami), an approbatory term widely used for his style. In the popular mind, his graceful and dignified figures were a projection of his pleasing personality.

Kyoto had other workshops, all apparently offshoots of the original Shichijō group and all retaining conservative reputations. By the end of the Kamakura period, their workshop styles were indistinguishable. The In school (Inson, Injo, Inkaku, Inkei, and others) was located at Shichijō Omiya, with a branch at Rokujo (Sixth Avenue) Marikoji. An earlier group, perhaps distantly related, the En school (Mei-en, Ensei, Choen, Ken-en), had maintained a work place on Sanjo (Third Avenue) from about the end of the 11th century. Rebuilding and restoration work for Kyoto temples was enough to keep all of them busy, but there was intense competition for the more prestigious commissions. The aging nobility of Kyoto preferred their replacements in the old Fujiwara style, the clergy and pilgrims in

Nara were quite willing to see modern variations of traditional subjects, and the rising samurai class of Kamakura were pleased with the new freshness and vitality in the art.

Most of the productions of the Shichijō Bussho were collaborative efforts, with at least the name of the project's manager included in the inscriptions. The rather few cases in which Kaikei and Unkei appear to have worked together suggest that they may have managed branch workshops, joining forces only on the most demanding commissions with short deadlines. Nevertheless, the truly creative sculptors in the group had their own distinctive styles that, with the aid of many inscriptions on their products and documents preserved in temples, can be differentiated to the point of showing the multifaceted, complex nature of the art.

Scholars have divided the changing styles of Kaikei—who was apparently more susceptible to the current influences than Unkei—into roughly three decades of work: his early workshop training in the realism of the Kōkei and Unkei style; a middle stage

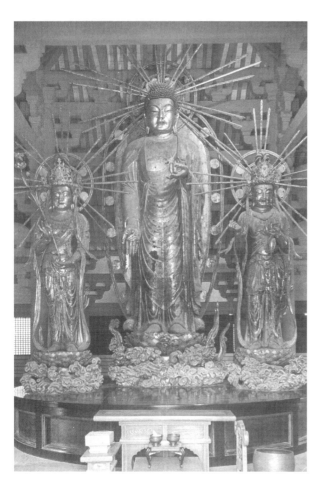

Amida Triad (ca. 1197)
© Sakamoto Photo Research Laboratory / CORBIS

of looser, elegant, more Song dynasty characteristics, sometimes mixed with archaistic features of the Nara (710–94) and Heian (794–1185) periods; and a rather manneristic late stage, with the facial expressions a little moody, the drapery overworked. Kaikei's movements are unclear, but his second style must have been developed when he transferred to the Nara workshop.

The earliest dated image by Kaikei is that of the *Miroku* (Sanskrit, Maitreya) *bodhisattva* carved in 1189. Another *Miroku bodhisattva* is in the Sambo-in of the Daigo-ji, Kyoto (1192). Shaka (Sanskrit, Sakya) Buddha, the historic Buddha, was in the midst of a minor comeback in popularity, and Kaikei made a *Shaka Buddha* for the Empuku-ji in Shiga prefecture, as well as one for the Kengō-in and another for the Bujo-ji, both in Kyoto; all three were created between 1194 and 1199. The Bujo-ji *Shaka Buddha* is shorter on documentation and is only attributed to Kaikei. The Empuku-ji image is in his early style, but the latter two show considerable Song influence, which suggests that the patrons may have had influence on the selection of the style.

Over time, Kaikei produced statues of all the major esoteric Buddhas and the esoteric Dainichi (Sanskrit, Mahāvairocana) Buddha, with the exception of Yakushi (Sanskrit, Bhaisajya-guru-vaidurya-prabha), but the chief demand was for representations of Amida (Sanskrit, Amitabha, Amitayus), reflecting the overwhelming popularity of the belief in Amida and the assured life in the Western Pure Land. These images may be standing or seated. More than a dozen survive. Those dating to the early 13th century are superbly proportioned, realistic to a degree, but idealized through perfectly painted facial details. Gold paint was used for Buddhas and bodhisattvas, polychromy for attendants and monklike figures. The *Jizō* (Sanskrit, Ksitigarbha), a statue of the bodhisattva of compassion, in the Tōdai-ji, is often considered to be Kaikei's finest work. Standing 91 centimeters, in monk's robe, its shaved head, sublime expression, hands forward as though communicating, and handsome curves of drapery folds give a quiet, stately air to the traditionally most popular Japanese deity.

It is no coincidence that Kaikei created an Amida triad for the Jōdo-ji in Hyōgo prefecture (1197) and a single *Amida Buddha* for the Shin-daibutsu-ji in Mie prefecture (1202), because these were two of the three temples that Chōgen founded while canvassing for the reconstruction of the Tōdai-ji. Kaikei alone receives the credit for the huge Monju (Sanskrit, Manjusri) bodhisattva of wisdom, seated on his lion and surrounded by four smaller attendants in the Monju-in (Sakurai city). Kaikei worked together with Unkei to make the immense, overpowering *Niō* (Two Kings; Japanese, Kongojin) that stand as guardians in the Nandai-mon (South Great Gate) of the Tōdai-ji. They are regarded as the Kei school's crowning achievement, yet they seem to have been made almost in passing, as the temple's archives claim their production in 72 days in Kennin 3 (the third year of the Kennin era).

Most of Kaikei's late works are small, often less than a meter in size. Perhaps patronage was moving down the scale and farther from the Kansai as the burst of reconstruction slowed down. These images tend to be florid in detail, overly perfected in technique, and less spirited. Kaikei's name disappeared from inscriptions by 1223. Several rather well-known apprentices continued in his style.

J. Edward Kidder Jr.

See also **Japan; Unkei**

Biography

Born in Nara, Japan, 12th century. Flourished as sculptor, 1183–1223; thought to be disciple of Kōkei; adopted into the family of sculptors operating workshop in Kyoto and a branch in Nara called Shichijō Bussho, popularly known as Kei-ha; supervised by Unkei, workshop director and guardian; became religious disciple of Priest Chōgen, rebuilder of Tōdai-ji in Nara; given name An Amida Butsu, abbreviated to An'ami to describe his style; first dated image is 1189; increased productivity in 1190s, probably in the Kyoto workshop; created images chiefly of Amida, Shaka, and Miroku Buddhas and bodhisattvas for temples; teamed with Unkei for creation of monumental Niō (Two Kings; gate guardians) of Tōdai-ji in Nara, 1203; designed Amida images for two temples Chōgen founded in prefectures Hyōgo, 1197, and Mie, 1202; received rank of *hokkyō* (bridge of the law), 1203, and *hōgen* (eye of the law), 1208–10; name disappeared from inscriptions after 1223. Died probably in Kyoto or Nara, Japan, *ca.* 1223.

Selected Works (all wood, lacquered, gilt, or polychromed)

1189	*Miroku bodhisattva*; Museum of Fine Arts, Boston, Massachusetts, United States
1197	*Amida Buddha* and two bodhisattvas; Jōdo-ji, Ono city, Hyōgo prefecture, Japan
1190s (late)	*Fudo*; Shoju-in, Kyoto, Japan
1190s (late)	*Shikkongo-shin*; Kongo-in, Maizuru city, Kyoto prefecture, Japan
1200	*Kujaku Myo-o* (Peacock King); Kongōbu-ji, Mt. Koya, Wakayama prefecture, Japan
1201	*Shinto deity Hachiman as Buddhist priest*; Tōdai-ji, Nara city, Japan
1201–03	Monju bodhisattva and four attendants; Monju-in, Sakurai city, Nara prefecture, Japan
1202	*Amida Buddha*; Shin-daibutsu-ji, Oyamada village, Mie prefecture, Japan
1203–08	*Jizō*; Tōdai-ji, Nara city, Japan
1211	*Amida Buddha*; Tōju-in (Kobo-ji), Oku town, Okayama prefecture, Japan
1216–20	*Judaideshi (Ten Great Disciples)*; Daiho-on-ji, Kyoto city, Japan
ca. 1221	*Amida Buddha*; Kōdai-in, Mt. Koya, Wakayama prefecture, Japan

Further Reading

Kuno, Takeshi, *Nihon no chokoku* (Sculpture of Japan), Tokyo: Yoshikawa Kobunkan, 1959

Mason, Penelope, *History of Japanese Art*, New York: Abrams, 1993

Mori, Hisashi, *Sculpture of the Kamakura Period*, translated by Katherine Eickmann, New York and Tokyo: Weatherhill, 1974

Nishikawa, Kyotaro, and Emily Sano, *The Great Age of Japanese Buddhist Sculpture, AD 600–1300*, Fort Worth, Texas: Kimbell Art Museum, 1983

Roberts, Laurance, *A Dictionary of Japanese Artists: Painting, Sculpture, Ceramics, Prints, Lacquer*, New York and Tokyo: Weatherhill, 1980

Tokyo National Museum, *Tokubetsu-ten: Kamakura jidai no chokoku* (Special Exhibition: Japanese Sculpture of the Kamakura Period), Tokyo: Tokyo National Museum, 1975

Watson, William, *Sculpture of Japan, from the Fifth to the Fifteenth Century*, London: The Studio Limited, and New York: Viking Press, 1959

ANISH KAPOOR 1954– *Indian, active in England*

Rising to prominence in the 1980s, Anish Kapoor has created works that invoke the sublime and produce spiritual and visceral responses. Born in Bombay, India, to a Hindustan father and Iraqi-Jewish mother, Kapoor studied in England at the Hornsey College of Art, London, and the Chelsea School of Art. Upon graduating from the Chelsea School of Art in 1978, Kapoor traveled to India, where he learned and incorporated into his art the philosophies and aesthetics of his native land. He subsequently returned to England to pursue his artistic career. After his exhibition in 1982 at Aperto (part of the international exhibition at the Venice Biennale), he became associated with other artists under the term New British Sculptors. Although not a coherent group, these British artists sought a greater poetic expression in contemporary art that would question traditional categories of painting and sculpture.

Kapoor's early works combine organic and geometric shapes with vivid color. During the years 1979–81, he worked on a series entitled *1000 Names*, made up of a number of unidentifiable forms positioned on the floor in small groupings with a single form protruding outward from the wall. Acknowledging the mystical impact of color, Kapoor covered each object with loose powder in vibrant hues. Referencing Western and non-Western traditions, the color, material, and shape of the forms produced a gestational quality of being in flux or a process of becoming. Kapoor's interest in the immateriality of the loose powder relates to the artist Yves Klein's idea of art as a potential tool for spiritual transcendence. In India colored powders are associated with Hindu folk rituals that relate to natural elements as well as reference fertility. The theme of the primal in Kapoor's work merges opposing elements of serenity and tension, East and West, ancient and modern, sacred and secular, nature and culture.

Kapoor later began an investigation into the notion of place. He explored its metaphysical qualities, which exist without a particular time, origin, or center. His works took on a more experimental style, using stones, pigment, metals, and other materials. In works such as *Void Field*, for which he represented Britain at the Venice Biennale and was awarded the Premio Duemila, he created 16 large coarse blocks of pinkish sandstone with a black hole on top of each. The material's roughness gave the impression that the blocks had been taken directly from a quarry, and the overall installation created a physical sense of entering into another field of experience. Kapoor also continued here his interest in color as a metaphor for universal themes. For instance, he juxtaposed the reddish color, signifying blood and the circle of life, with the black abyss of the unknown.

Kapoor has also explored the interiority of objects, focusing on the power of womblike interior realms. The body and human sexuality, particularly the female, have also inspired Kapoor. In *The Healing of St. Thomas*, he sliced an approximately 30-centimeter red gash onto a wall reminiscent of the wound in Christ's side. The bodily reference to the shape of the "wound" lends itself to Freudian as well as Hindu interpretations. Referring to the New Testament story that describes the apostle Thomas's doubt about the resurrection of Christ, *The Healing of St. Thomas* conveys a sense of mystically appearing before the viewer without any visible trace of the process. In the words of Kapoor, "The piece draws our attention to the space beyond the wall, and sees the architecture as a metaphor for the self."

In 1991 Kapoor received the prestigious Turner Prize, and he has begun working with materials that reflect his interest in light and reflective materials.

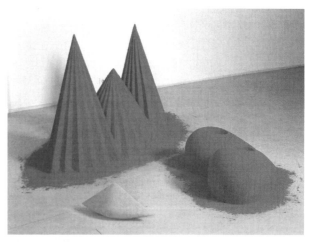

As if to Celebrate, I Discovered a Mountain Blooming with Red Flowers
© 1981 Anish Kapoor. Photo courtesy Tate Gallery, London / Art Resource, NY

Using both chromed and polished aluminum with spills of color, the artist has created works that play with the interactions between light and dark.

Kapoor has also expanded his sculptures and large-scale installations into more organic and anthropomorphic shapes. Always interested in the polarities and convergences between exterior and interior, he explores in his works the sacred act of art. By absorbing both Western and Eastern traditions and aesthetic practices, Kapoor has produced a highly refined body of work that extends the notion of the void, which he first became interested in as an art student.

MIKI GARCIA

See also **Contemporary Sculpture; Klein, Yves**

Biography

Born in Bombay, India, 12 March 1954. Moved to England in early 1970s to study at Hornsey College of Art, London, 1973–77, and Chelsea School of Art, 1977–78; taught art at Wolverhampton Polytechnic, 1979; first solo exhibition at Coracle Press, London, 1981; artist-in-residence at Walker Art Gallery, Liverpool, 1982; represented Great Britain at Venice Biennale, 1990; won the Premio Duemila; solo exhibitions at Barbara Gladstone Gallery, New York City, and Tate Gallery, London, 1990–91; Museum of Contemporary Art, San Diego, 1992–93; collaborated with architect David Connor for Expo'92, Seville, Spain. Awarded Turner Prize, 1991; honorary fellowship from London Institute, 1997; numerous exhibitions and retrospectives throughout the world. Lives and works in London, England.

Selected Works

1981   *As if to Celebrate, I Discovered a Mountain Blooming with Red Flowers*; drawing, wood, mixed media; Tate Gallery, London, England

1989   *Void Field*; four blocks of sandstone, pigment; Art Gallery of New South Wales, Sydney, Australia

1989–90 *The Healing of St. Thomas*; mixed media; Museum of Contemporary Art, San Diego, United States

1990   *A Wing at the Heart of Things*; slate, pigment; Tate Gallery, London, England

1993   Stage design for *River Run*; mixed media; Queen Elizabeth Hall, London, England

1995   *Cast Iron Mountain*; cast iron; Tachikawa Art Project, Japan

2001   Untitled, Millenium Park commission, Chicago, Illinois, United States

Further Reading

"Anish Kapoor at Regen Projects," *Art Issues* 64 (September–October 2000)

Bhabha, Homi K., and Pier Luigi Tazzi, *Anish Kapoor*, London: Hayward Gallery, and Berkeley: University of California Press, 1998

Celant, Germano, *Anish Kapoor*, Milan: Edizioni Charta, Fondazione Prada, 1995, and London: Thames and Hudson, 1996

KEI SCHOOL

See **Japan**

LEONHARD KERN 1588–1662 *German*

Leonhard Kern, one of the most important and diverse figures of the German Early Baroque, was born in Forchtenberg (Hohenlohe, Baden-Württemberg, Germany) in 1588. His father, Michael Kern Sr., was a stonemason and master builder, a profession that four of his sons followed. Leonhard left his father's workshop to continue his sculptural studies in his elder brother Michael Kern Jr.'s workshop in Würzburg from 1603 to 1609.

Kern moved to Italy in 1609 and remained until 1614. He studied life drawing possibly in the Accademia di San Luca and continued his architectural studies in Rome. During his travels that followed, he visited Laibach (now Ljubljana) in 1613, where the bishop of Laibach asked him to build the high altar of the Oberburg (now Gornji Grad) Cathedral. Two polychrome wooden reliefs remain from this work: *The Adoration of the Kings (Epiphany)* and *The Coronation of the Virgin* (both from 1613). These early works reveal the influence of antiquity and the Renaissance, which Kern became acquainted with in Italy.

Kern's early period is dated 1614–20, during which time he worked primarily in his brother's Forchtenberg workshop. Italian influence can be observed in his alabaster *St. Sebastian* (ca. 1615–20). His significant sandstone statues from this era were made for the portals of the Nuremberg Rathaus in 1617. These monumental gable statues are carved after the designs of Cristoph Jamnitzer following Italian exemplars.

Kern's main sculptural period began when he settled in Schwäbisch Hall (near Stuttgart, Baden-Württemberg) in 1620, where he led a successful workshop probably until 1651. In 1648, he worked in Cleve as court sculptor for Frederick William von Hohenzollern, elector of Brandenburg. His works between 1620 and 1651 depended mainly upon 16th- and 17th-century Italian, 16th-century German, and 17th-century Flemish patterns. By this time the typically strong physiognomy of his sculpture had already developed. During this period, Kern worked primarily with ivory, alabaster, soapstone, wood, and sometimes bronze.

In spite of characteristic features, only a few of Kern's works from this fruitful period can be linked to a date or archival records. The bronze statue *Young Sculptor* (or *Allegory of Sculpture*) dates from his works made in Schwäbisch Hall around 1620. The influence of Italian bronze sculpture and the awareness of the traditions of Nuremberg bronze casting reveal themselves strongly in these pieces. Representative of this period are Kern's signed ivory statues *St. Sebastian* (ca. 1620) and *St. Jerome with Lion* (ca. 1620–25), as well as a further series including *Abraham's Offering* (ca. 1645). His walnut-wood *Crucifix* (ca. 1625–30) shows the influence of Albrecht Dürer. Kern carved his monumental, seated, sandstone, female figures of the *Virtues* for the portals of the gables of the Trinity Church in Regensburg (ca. 1630–32).

A series of small statues dating from about 1635 to 1645 depict children; some such as the bronze *Boy with Dog* and the alabaster *Bagpiper Boy* probably represent his own children at play, while others such as the *Children's Bacchanal*, a signed boxwood relief, present children in various forms.

From around 1640 to 1645, Kern was mostly engaged in creating female nudes of biblical and mythological characters, including the signed pear-wood *Eve*, the ivory *Hebe-Temperatia*, the signed boxwood *Standing Female Plaiting Her Hair*, the signed soapstone *Venus and Cupid*, the ivory *Crouching Fortuna*, and the ivory *Abudantia*. About 1640 Kern created his signed plum-wood statue *Gaia* in different versions during the Thirty Years' War (1618–48), probably as an allegory of famine.

One of Kern's most characteristic signed works is the carved and stained limewood sculpture *The Three Graces* (ca. 1640–45). This work demonstrates both the drawing skills and anatomical knowledge learned while studying life drawing in Italy as well as the influence of the female figures by Dürer and Peter Paul Rubens. Of the composition's known multiple variations, the most significant are Kern's Solnhofen-stone relief of about 1645 (Museum für Kunst und Gewerbe, Hamburg), the alabaster relief from before 1650 (Collection Würth, Künzelsau), and the ivory group sequence dated about 1650 (Württembergisches Landesmuseum, Stuttgart).

One of Kern's most significant works of this period, the signed ivory group *Adam and Eve (The Fall of Man)*, exhibits facial traits identical to the portraits of Frederick William, elector of Brandenburg, and his wife, Luise Henriette von Oranien. The biblical-allegorical portrait quality suggests that the work was prepared as a wedding gift for the elector in 1646, or was ordered as a trial work when Kern started working as a court sculptor in 1648. Kern carved an ivory statue of the elector's son, William Henry, who died at the age of one.

Kern moved to Tullau in 1651. His final period of work dating from 1651 to his death in 1662 explored the horrors of war: the alabaster group *Scene of the Thirty Years' War* and ivory statue *Starved Man (Dead Man)*. *Venus, Mars, and Cupid* (ivory, 1657) departed from this motif; instead of isolation, this late-period group presents figures that interconnect. Kern was probably working on the monumental soapstone relief of *Ezekiel's Vision* for the epitaph to Christoph David Stellwag in the Church of St. Michael in Schwäbisch Hall from 1655 until 1662, the end of his life. His nephew Johann Georg Kern and his coworker Johann Jacob Betzoldt, who mainly worked with ivory, were the most talented of Kern's followers.

KATALIN HÁMORI

Biography

Born in Forchtenberg, Hohenlohe (Baden-Württemberg, Germany), 22 November 1588. Son of Michael Kern Sr., a stonemason and master builder. Studied under his elder brother, Michael Kern Jr., in Würzburg, 1603–09; lived in Italy, 1609–14; studied life drawing, possibly at Accademia di San Luca, Rome; also studied architecture there; traveled to Naples, North Africa, and Venice; stayed in Laibach (now Ljubljana), 1613; worked with elder brother in Forchtenberg, 1614–20; received commissions in Forchtenberg, Heidelberg, and Nuremberg, 1614–20; lived and worked with own workshop in Schwäbisch Hall (near Stuttgart, Baden-Württemberg), 1620–51; court sculptor to Frederick William von Hohenzollern, elector of Brandenburg, 1648; moved to Tullau, 1651; fell ill and returned to Schwäbisch Hall, 1661. Died in Schwäbisch Hall, Baden-Württemberg, Germany, 4 April 1662.

Selected Works

ca. 1615–20	*St. Sebastian*; alabaster; Hällisch-Fränkisches Museum, Schwäbisch Hall, Baden-Württemberg, Germany
ca. 1620	*St. Sebastian*; ivory; Schatzkammer, Residenzmuseum, Munich, Germany
ca. 1620	*Young Sculptor* (also known as *Allegory of Sculpture*); bronze; Herzog Anton Ulrich-Museum, Brunswick, Germany
ca. 1620–25	*St. Jerome with Lion*; ivory; Sammlung für Plastik und Kunstgewerbe, Kunsthistorisches Museum, Vienna, Austria
ca. 1625–30	*Crucifix*; walnut-wood; Geistliche Schatzkammer, Kunsthistorisches Museum, Vienna, Austria
ca. 1640	*Gaia*; plumwood; Skulpturengalerie, Staatliche Museen Preussischer Kulturbesitz, Berlin, Germany
ca. 1640–45	*The Three Graces*; limewood; Museum of Fine Arts, Budapest, Hungary
ca. 1645	*Abraham's Offering*; ivory; Victoria and Albert Museum, London, England
ca. 1646–48	*Adam and Eve (The Fall of Man)*; ivory; Skulpturengalerie, Staatliche Museen Preussischer Kulturbesitz, Berlin, Germany
1655–62	*Ezekiel's Vision*; soapstone relief; Church of St. Michael, Schwäbisch Hall, Baden-Württemberg, Germany
1656–59	*Scene of the Thirty Years' War*; alabaster; Sammlung für Plastik und Kunstgewerbe, Kunsthistorisches Museum, Vienna, Austria
1657	*Venus, Mars, and Cupid*; ivory; Staatliche Kunstsammlungen, Kassel, Germany

Further Reading

Fischer, Fritz, "Leonhard Kern," in *The Dictionary of Art*, edited by Jane Turner, vol. 17, New York: Grove, and London: Macmillan, 1996

Grünenwald, Elisabeth, *Leonhard Kern: Ein Bildhauer des Barock*, Schwäbisch Hall, Germany: Eppinger, 1969

Siebenmorgen, Harald, editor, *Leonhard Kern (1588–1622): Meisterwerke der Bildhauerei für die Kunstkammern Europas* (exhib. cat.), Sigmaringen, Germany: Thorbecke, 1988

Siebenmorgen, Harald, editor, *Leonhard Kern (1588–1622): Neue Forschungsbeiträge*, Sigmaringen, Germany: Thorbecke, 1990

Theuerkauff, Christian, *Die Bildwerke in Elfenbein des 16.–19. Jahrhunderts Bildwerke der Skulpturengalerie, Staatliche Museen Preussischer Kulturbesitz*, Berlin: Mann, 1986

WILLEM (GUILLIELMUS) KERRICX
1652–1719 *Netherlandish*

As with many South Netherlandish sculptors, Willem Kerricx came from a family of cabinetmakers/sculptors, including his grandfather Guillaume and his uncle Jan. After his training in Antwerp with Baptist Buys, Kerricx was accepted as master in the guild of St. Luke in 1674–75. One assumes that the young master spent the years between 1674 and 1678 in Paris to perfect his art. Back in his home country, he married Barbara Ogier, who is known as an author of classical plays. From 1678 to his death, 27 pupils were registered with him. Little is known about his activities between 1702 and 1709, a period that he may have spent in England.

The beginning of Kerricx's career was mainly taken up by commissions from several Antwerp churches. Misconceptions about projects attributable to him with any certainty have been all too frequent because his documented works are rare. His collaboration with many other Antwerp sculptors, including Hendrik Frans Verbrugghen, Artus II Quellinus, and Lodewijk Willemssens, makes the question of attribution far more complex. He carried out collaborative work for Antwerp churches, for example, the "altar garden" (a kind of enclosure in front of a garden) with several pierced marble reliefs for the Coopers' guild altar in the cathedral, the twisted columns for the high altar of the Church of St. Jacob, and the temporary festive interior decoration of the Jesuit church.

The confessional in the Zoete Naamkapel (Sweet Name) of the Church of St. Paulus in Antwerp, with personifications of *Penance* and *Meekness*, dates from the late 17th century. This piece of furniture was hitherto attributed to Artus II Quellinus as well as Willem Kerricx. A terracotta sketch for *Penance*, monogrammed G.K., which recently appeared on the art market (now in the Musée Départemental at Cassell, France), allows us to confidently attribute the design of this confessional to Kerricx.

The two pictorial reliefs in marble for the pedestal of the *Rosary Madonna* in the Church of St. Paulus, Antwerp, are very successful. The terracotta models of these medallions are preserved in the Church of St. Jacob. Their composition and the attitude of the figures are unique in their elegance, not just in the oeuvre of Kerricx but more generally in Antwerp sculpture. The source of inspiration may have been found in Paris. A similar courtly style and refined lightheartedness also characterize the marble bust of *Maximilian II Emanuel of Bavaria*, governor of the Spanish Netherlands. Because Flemish 17th-century sculptors generally received commissions for religious subjects, they could not rely on a great tradition of portraiture. This bust is thus not just unique in the oeuvre of Kerricx but also a rarity in the South Netherlandish Baroque as a whole. Court artists such as the Antwerp-trained Gabriel Grupello did not attain Kerricx's technical virtuosity and verve in ruler portraits, even though from 1695 Grupello was court sculptor to the Elector Johan Wilhelm at Düsseldorf, for whom he carried out many official portraits. The twisted composition of *Maximilian II Emanuel of Bavaria*, with its profusion of drapery contrasting with the smooth and refined complexion, is a forerunner of the Rococo. With this bust, Kerricx also had a strong influence on the portrait of Frederick IV of Denmark, at Frederiksborg, which is attributed to Thomas Quellinus.

In 1695 Kerricx collaborated with Hendrik Frans Verbrugghen on the communion rail of the Chapel of the Blessed Sacrament in the Church of St. Jacob at Antwerp; this rail is certainly one of the city's artistic highlights. The artists succeeded in using a narrow marble strip of 12 meters and rendering a harmonious whole of realistically sculpted leaves; the frolicking putti and the remarkable rendition of fabrics are stunning. Verbrugghen's contribution here is superior to that of Kerricx, and it is interesting to note how Kerricx took on Verbrugghen's style. This influence can also be seen in two well-composed confessionals in the Basilica of St. Servatius, the abbey church of Grimbergen (north of Brussels)—a high point in Kerricx's career. These were mistakenly attributed to Hendrik Frans Verbrugghen until 1980. Verbrugghen's influence is also apparent in the altar dedicated to the Virgin in the Church of St. Bartholomeus (1709) at Merksem near Antwerp.

Kerricx received his largest commission from the former abbey church of St. Gertrudis at Leuven. He delivered the high altar with a tomb monument on either side. The altar was destroyed during World War II, but fortunately, fragments of the two monuments are still *in situ*: two marble statues of the abbots C.F. de Fourneau and his successor A.C. de Pallant. The pose of the life-size kneeling figures is rather stiff, but the naturalism of their facial expression is remarkable, and the rendition of fabrics is, as usual with Kerricx, a piece of virtuosity.

The marble tomb monument of the Trazegnies family, commissioned by Albert de Trazegnies to commemorate his brother Fernand, in the Collegiate Church of St. Gertrude at Nivelles (south of Brussels), can be attributed to Kerricx on stylistic grounds. Here too the deceased are represented as a heraldic allusion, kneeling and with hands joined in prayer, their 16 quarters of nobility left and right. Their pose is static, but their facial expressions are extremely realistic—all but flattering—and materials such as lace and fur are naturalistically chiseled.

Kerricx left a number of preparatory drawings, of which the largest collection is kept at the Stedelijk Prentenkabinet at Antwerp. Most of his terracotta models are preserved in the Royal Museums of Fine Arts in Brussels. His graphic and modeling style is often difficult to differentiate from that of his son, Willem Ignatius Kerricx.

Kerricx's works are typical for Late Baroque sculpture: his designs are grander and more theatrical than those of the High Baroque. The stolidly built bodies of the mid 17th century make way to decoratively elongated figures that often give the impression of not obeying the laws of gravity. The contrasting play with light and shadow makes the pictorial effect the prime issue. Kerricx cannot, however, be counted among the innovators or among the leading sculptors of his time. With the numerous and industrious sculptors' workshops, mainly established in Antwerp, it was difficult to vie with sculptors such as Quellinus, Willemssens, and Verbrugghen. Nonetheless, in some works, notably the portrait bust of *Maximilian II Emanuel*, Kerricx demonstrated his refinement and talent.

HELENA BUSSERS

See also **Quellinus Family**

Biography

Baptized at Dendermonde, Spanish Netherlands, 2 July 1652. Born to family of cabinet maker/sculptors; together with his family, moved to Antwerp, 1660, where registered at guild of St. Luke; became a master in the guild, 1674–75; worked primarily on church commissions; probably in Paris between 1674–78; children included the sculptor and painter Willem Ignatius Kerricx (1682–1745); became dean of the guild, 1693–94. Died in Antwerp, present-day Belgium, 22 June 1719.

Selected Works

ca. 1682 Altar garden (enclosure of the Coopers' Guild altar); marble; Antwerp Cathedral, Belgium

late 17th Confessional; oak; Chapel of the Sweet
century Name, Church of St. Paulus, Antwerp, Belgium

1688 Two reliefs on the pedestal of the *Rosary Madonna*; marble; Church of St. Paulus, Antwerp, Belgium

1694 *Maximilian II Emanuel of Bavaria*; marble; Koninklijk Museum voor Schone Kunsten, Antwerp, Belgium

1695 Communion rail (with Hendrik Frans Verbrugghen); marble; Chapel of the

Blessed Sacrament, Church of St. Jacob, Antwerp, Belgium

late 17th Tomb monument of the Trazegnies
century Family; marble; Collegiate Church of St. Gertrude, Nivelles, Belgium

1709 Altar dedicated to the Virgin; marble; Church of St. Bartholomeus, Merksem (Antwerp), Belgium

1710 Two confessionals; oak; Basilica of St. Servatius, Abbey Church of Grimbergen, Belgium

1714 High altar (destroyed), with a tomb monument on either side to the abbots C.F. de Fourneau and A.C. de Pallant; marble; Church of St. Gertrudis, Leuven, Belgium

Further Reading

17th and 18th Century Drawings: The Van Herck Collection, edited by Claire Baisier et al., Brussels: King Baudouin Foundation, 2000

17th and 18th Century Terracottas: The Van Herck Collection, edited by Claire Baisier et al., Brussels: King Baudouin Foundation, 2000

Bussers, Helena, "Guillielmus Kerricx," in *The Dictionary of Art*, edited by Jane Turner, vol. 17, New York: Grove, and London: Macmillan, 1996

La sculpture au siècle de Rubens: Dans les Pays-Bas méridionaux et la principauté de Liège (exhib. cat.), Brussels: Musée d'Art Ancien, 1977

Tentoonstelling van Tekeningen: G. Kerricx en G.I. Kerricx, Maketten en Beeldhouwwerken (exhib. cat.), Antwerp, Belgium: Koninklijke Oudheidkundige Kring van Antwerpen, 1947

HENDRICK DE KEYSER 1565–1621
Dutch

Hendrick de Keyser was the most important and most versatile sculptor in Holland at the beginning of the 17th century. He was born in Utrecht into a family of stonemasons and cabinetmakers. Until his arrival in Amsterdam in 1591, De Keyser's career remains rather obscure. He may have trained in his native town under Jacob Colijn de Nole, but he more likely apprenticed with the Utrecht painter and sculptor Cornelis Bloemaert, who was appointed city mason in Amsterdam in 1591.

After Bloemaert's return to Utrecht in 1594, De Keyser took over his position in Amsterdam as the city's stone carver and sculptor (M. Beeltsnijder ende Steenhouwer). In that capacity, he was responsible for all the official building activities in Amsterdam and thus became instrumental in the modern urbanization of the fast-growing city. He designed several churches for the new Protestant liturgy, but his architectural oeuvre also includes several city towers, city gates and small arches, and townhouses, as well as larger buildings such as the East India House, the Exchange, and the Delft Town Hall. De Keyser and his workshop also produced decorative sculpture for these and other buildings; of these, the decoration of the portal of the former Rasphuis (Correction House) and of the Mason's Guild entrance in the Waag (Weigh House) are still *in situ.*

De Keyser combined an international orientation with a strong sense of artistic and technical innovation. He patented several inventions, including the production of artificial marble. He can also be credited for introducing and using white Carrara marble in Holland. His bust of the wine merchant Vincent Coster (1608) was probably the first Dutch portrait bust made of Italian marble.

As a sculptor, De Keyser was responsible for some of the most original works of his time. In 1618 he received a commission for a bronze statue of *Erasmus* to be erected in Rotterdam. While erecting a public statue for a scholar was in itself an unusual step, the dynamic form De Keyser used underscored the novelty of the *Erasmus* monument. He designed an over life-size bronze figure on a pedestal, showing the scholar walking and leafing through a book. The work was installed in 1622.

De Keyser also played an important role in the development of Dutch portrait sculpture. He produced a few life-size portrait busts in terracotta and marble, representing Dutch burghers such as Vincent Coster, the Leiden burghermaster Van der Werff (now lost), and the Utrecht painter Joachim Wttewael. He also produced several versions of his portrait of William the Silent, prince of Orange, for which there seems to have existed a good market in Holland. De Keyser's portraits, characterized by a strong sense of naturalism and liveliness, are meticulously executed. Most of his busts terminate in grotesque Mannerist masks.

As a sculptor of bronze statuettes, De Keyser was probably inspired by the Delft sculptor Willem van Tetrode, who introduced the bronze statuette to the Netherlands around 1570 and whose models were still circulating. A *Mercury* dated 1611 and signed with De Keyser's monogram (HDK) forms the basis for the attribution of some bronzes to De Keyser, notably an *Orpheus and Cerberus,* a bust of a *Crying Child (ca.* 1618), and a figure of *Mars (ca.* 1610–12). A version of the *Orpheus and Cerberus* group was used in a fountain of the so-called Old Maze (Oude Doolhof) in Amsterdam. Related to these works is the model De Keyser made for the small group of *St. Martin and the Beggar* (1604), which crowns the large silver beaker of the St. Martin's brewers guild in Haarlem.

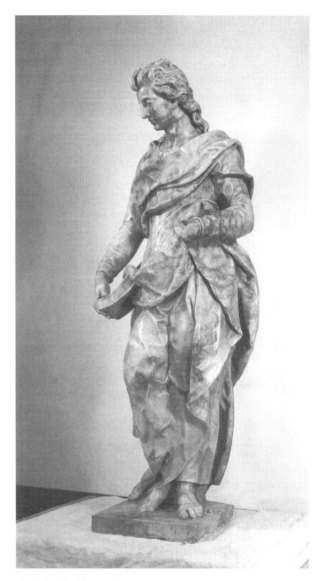

St. John the Evangelist
© Victoria and Albert Museum, London / Art Resource, NY

De Keyser's international reputation is illustrated best by the royal Danish commission to carve a series of statues and reliefs for the Gallery of Frederiksborg Castle near Copenhagen. De Keyser designed the statues, which were executed and installed by his master carver Geraert Lambertsz. The figure of *Jupiter* in particular reflects the influence of models by Giambologna.

Most important for De Keyser's reputation was his opus magnum, the funeral monument to Prince William of Orange—Pater Patriae—in the Nieuwe Kerk (New Church) in Delft. With this prestigious commission by the States-General, De Keyser faced the problem of designing a Protestant, republican monument that could compete with the famous royal tombs in France, England, and Denmark. Basing the monument on the traditional design of a canopied royal tomb, notably Francesco Primaticcio's monument to King Henry II and Catherine de' Medici in the Basilica of Saint-Denis, France, De Keyser introduced several iconographical innovations: four bronze corner figures no longer represented the virtues of the deceased but the more fitting "four fundaments" of the new Dutch republic, *Liberty*, *Religion*, *Justice*, and *Fortitude*. In addition, he represented the effigy of the deceased as an informally reclining body, apparently asleep, wearing his slippers, nightgown, and nightcap. This representation of the dead marks a radical break with the traditional Catholic iconography of representing the dead body in eternal prayer or lying in state. Finally, De Keyser replaced the praying monarchs on top of these royal tombs in the Delft monument with a less Catholic pose of the seated figure of William as commander. At the foot of the effigy of the dead prince, an impressive bronze *Fame* blows her trumpet while balancing on one foot; she was evidently intended as an emulation of the flying Mercury statues by Giambologna, Tetrode, and Adriaen de Vries. For the architecture of the monument, De Keyser used various colorful marbles: white Carrara marble, black Belgian marble, and the yellow-veined Italian portoro, which forms a coloristic link between the stone and the polished bronze figures.

De Keyser did not see the Delft monument completed in 1623; his son Pieter, who took over his father's workshop, finished the piece. De Keyser's son-in-law, Nicholas Stone, who worked in the Amsterdam workshop from 1607 to 1614, successfully continued the De Keyser style in England. In 1630 Salomon de Bray published the *Architectura Moderna*, a compilation of engravings after De Keyser's architectural designs, including some of his sculptural works.

FRITS SCHOLTEN

See also **Giambologna; Netherlands and Belgium; Stone, Nicholas; Vries, Adriaen de**

Biography

Born in Utrecht, the Netherlands, 15 May 1565. Son of a cabinetmaker. Trained possibly under Jacob Colijn de Nole, but more likely apprentice to Cornelis Bloemaert in Utrecht; settled in Amsterdam, 1591; appointed as the city stone carver and sculptor of Amsterdam, 1594; designed buildings in Amsterdam and elsewhere; sculptural oeuvre includes portrait busts in marble and terracotta, bronze statuettes, funeral monuments, and life-size statues in stone and bronze. Died in Amsterdam, the Netherlands, 15 May 1621.

Selected Works

1606   *Bust of a Man* (portrait bust of Joachim Wttewael?); polychromed terracotta; Rijksmuseum, Amsterdam, the Netherlands

1608   *Vincent Jacobsz Coster*; marble; Rijksmuseum, Amsterdam, the Netherlands

1609   Epitaph for Jacobvan Heemskerck; marble; Oude Kerk (Old Church), Amsterdam, the Netherlands

1611   *Mercury*; bronze; Rijksmuseum, Amsterdam, the Netherlands

ca. 1612   *Orpheus and Cerberus*; bronze; Victoria and Albert Museum, London, England

1613   *St. John the Evangelist*; alabaster; Victoria and Albert Museum, London, England

1614–23   Tomb of William the Silent, prince of Orange; marble, bronze; Nieuwe Kerk (New Church), Delft, the Netherlands

1618–22   *Erasmus*; bronze; St. Laurens Square, Rotterdam, the Netherlands

Further Reading

Avery, Charles, "The Rood-Loft from's Hertogenbosch," *Victoria and Albert Museum Yearbook* 1 (1969)

Avery, Charles, "Hendrick de Keyser as a Sculptor of Small Bronzes," *Bulletin van het Rijksmuseum* 21 (1973)

Becker, Jochen, *Hendrick de Keyser: Standbeeld van Desiderius Erasmus in Rotterdam*, Bloemendaal, The Netherlands: Becht, 1993

Jimkes-Verkade, Els, "De Ikonologie van het Grafmonument van Willem I, Prins van Oranje," in *De Stad Delft: Cultuur en maatschappij van 1572 tot 1667* (exhib. cat.), vol. 1, Delft: Stedelijk Museum Het Prinsenhof, 1981

Neurdenburg, Elisabeth, *De zeventiende eeuwsche beeldhouwkunst in de Noordelijke Nederlanden*, Amsterdam: Meulenhoff, 1948

Scholten, Frits, "A Beheaded Bust and a Fountain Statue by Hendrick de Keyser," *The Burlington Magazine* 137 (1995)

Scholten, Frits, "Hele en halve hoofden, kanttekeningen bij terracotta portretten van Hendrick de Keyser," in *Album Discipulorum: J.R.J. Van Asperen de Boer*, Zwolle, the Netherlands: Waanders Uitgevers, 1997

EDWARD KIENHOLZ 1927–1994 AND NANCY REDDIN KIENHOLZ 1943–

American

Edward Kienholz's elaborate sculptural installations, or tableaux, which he created from the early 1960s until his death (in collaboration with his wife, Nancy Reddin Kienholz, beginning in 1972), combine an innovative use of materials with a potent social commentary that has had a broad-reaching impact on contemporary artistic practice.

Kienholz began his career as a painter of abstract work, exploring the material possibilities of the medium to create highly textured surfaces and wall reliefs. By the late 1950s he incorporated figurative imagery in his work, and by 1959 he was creating freestanding sculpture. Kienholz constructed his sculpture from found objects that he transformed and incorporated into his work: in *John Doe* a mannequin sawed in half constitutes the "everyman" male figure; in *The Illegal Operation* a shopping cart and bedpan become the scene of an abortion; in the *Volksempfänger Series, Volkemsempfänger* radios (Bakelite radios bearing the eagle and swastika of German Nazi rule and used for Nazi broadcasts) become the material for a series of works; and in *To Mourn a Dead Horse*, a shell casing becomes a vase for barbed-wire flowers. In Kienholz's process, constituent materials bear the weight of both form and meaning, and the resultant arrangement is politically charged.

Kienholz's work gained widespread recognition in the 1960s, and like the work of many California artists of this period, it existed in contrast to the cool abstract forms of Minimalism or the slick colorful surfaces of Pop art that were prominent in New York at the time. Scholars have aligned his practices with the proto-Pop explorations of paint, material, and content found in the work of Jasper Johns and Robert Rauschenberg and have alternatively related his work to the assemblage practices of West Coast artists such as Bruce Connor. In addition, Kienholz's constructions share similarities with material explorations and constructions of contemporary European artists such as Jean Tinguely. However, Kienholz was not familiar with these practices when he began his own, and his work does not conform easily to any of these associations. The most prominent influence and context for Kienholz's work may be his own reading of social experience, and the strength of his work exists in his placement of realist representations of a less-visible social reality against the images with which society represents itself.

In 1961 Kienholz began to present his sculptural forms as elements of complex environments, further extending both their narrative possibility and social critique. Although the art-historical labels of *environment* and *assemblage* may describe Kienholz's work, his own concept of *tableau* better positions this practice. Tableau proposes a set or scene with narrative content while also evoking the history of the tableau—from its pedagogical role in religious institutions and museums to the spectacular presentation of staged display. In *Roxys*, the first of his tableaux, Kienholz incorporated a cast of characters into a brothel set in 1943. The viewer enters the setting and, existing between voyeur, participant, and spectator, confronts the social commodification of sex that Kienholz relates in visual and material form.

Soon after Kienholz conceived of his tableaux, he produced a series of *Concept Tableaux*. Each work consists of a title engraved on a brass plaque and a framed, one-page typed description. The works were to be purchased in this form, and if the owner was willing to make a further investment, Kienholz would produce a drawing (a small-scale sculptural work related to the piece). For a final investment, he would construct the tableau itself. With these works he addressed certain financial and spatial concerns that large installations presented while also exploring the dynamics of art and its market. Kienholz, who had run two alternative galleries upon his arrival in Los Angeles, included the art world in the spectrum of social activities on which his work commented throughout his career. The tableau *The Art Show*, the most extensive of such works, re-creates a gallery opening in life-size form.

One of the earliest *Concept Tableaux* to be constructed is also one of Kienholz's best-known works. *The State Hospital* consists of a boxlike structure labeled "Ward 19," the interior of which the viewer accesses through the barred window of a closed door. Inside, a naked figure lies strapped into a metal-framed

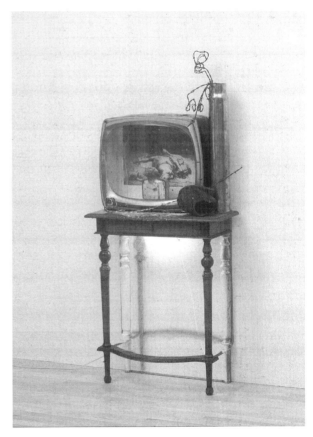

To Mourn a Dead Horse

bed on a filthy, bare mattress. A bedpan sits on the floor, and a naked lightbulb barely lights the space. Above the figure, positioned as a bunk bed, is an exact duplication of the lower bed and figure. The second figure is encircled by a neon speech bubble that rises from the head of the first, indicating that the second figure is a representation of the first figure's mental space. Both figures have translucent bowls for faces in which black fish swim. The fish, as well as the implication that the figure within cannot think beyond the present situation, communicate the claustrophobic and vacant existence of the mental institution. Exemplary of Kienholz's practice, *The State Hospital* produces a potent representation of the underside of American society. Kienholz based this work on his own experience working in a psychiatric hospital for a short period in 1948 and thus makes visible the hidden horrors he had witnessed there.

Earlier in 1966 a retrospective of his work held at the Los Angeles County Museum of Art made apparent the importance and controversial nature of Kienholz's art. The tableaux depicting dark and often sexual elements of human interaction in works such as *Roxys* caused the board of supervisors of Los Angeles County to call for the show's closing. The exhibition and all of its pieces remained and drew record crowds for an exhibition of contemporary art at the museum.

In the early 1970s, Nancy Reddin Kienholz, a photographer by training, began collaborating with her husband to make serial sculptures and life-size installations that melded humor with pop satire. One of the earliest significant pieces was *Pedicord Apartments* (1982–83), in which the artists salvage fragments of a destroyed hotel in Spokane, Washington, to metaphorically re-create a sense of a place of time that draws on sensations of taste, touch, smell, as well as the visual.

In their works, Edward and Nancy Reddin Kienholz remained committed over three decades to the investigation of the social conditions of war, capitalism, media, women, and other variant human interaction. Representing less-visible social forces through material form, their production remains an influential example of sculptural language in 20th-century art.

JANE MCFADDEN

See also **Assemblage; Installation; Segal, George; Tinguely, Jean**

Biography

Born in Fairfield, Washington, United States, 23 October 1927. Attended Eastern Washington College of Education and Whitworth College for short periods, but was a self-taught artist; traveled and worked odd jobs, 1946–52; arrived in Los Angeles, 1953; first solo exhibition, Cafe Galleria, 1955; opened Now Gallery, Los Angeles, 1956; opened Ferus Gallery with Walter Hopps, 1957; met Nancy Reddin and began collaboration, 1972; moved to Berlin, Germany, for Deutscher Akademischer Austauschdienst (DAAD) grant, 1973; began splitting time between Berlin and Hope, Idaho. Died in Hope, Idaho, 10 June 1994.

Selected Works

1959   *John Doe*; paint, resin, mannequin parts, wood, metal, rubber, plastic toys, metal stroller; Menil Collection, Houston, Texas, United States

1961–62 *Roxys*; tableau including paint, resin, mannequin parts, furniture, lamps, various household objects; collection of Reinhard Onnasch, Berlin, Germany

1962   *The Illegal Operation*; paint, resin, shopping cart, furniture, lamp, cloth, bedpan, concrete, medical instruments; Betty and Monte Factor Family Collection, Santa Monica, California, United States

1963–77 *The Art Show*; tableau including plaster casts, clothing, Plexiglas boxes, automobile air conditioning fans and vents, recorded sound, drawings, books, punch bowl, glasses, tablecloth; Berlinische Galerie, Berlin, Germany

1966   *The State Hospital (Concept Tableau)*; engraved brass plaque on walnut, typed description in walnut frame; Moderna Museet, Stockholm, Sweden

1966   *The State Hospital*; tableau including plaster casts, metal bed frames, mattresses, bedpan, fishbowls, live fish, neon tubing, wood, paint; Moderna Museet, Stockholm, Sweden

1968   *The Portable War Memorial*; tableau including plaster casts, tombstone, restaurant furniture, Coca-Cola machine, stuffed dog, photographs, blackboard, wood, metal, fiberglass; Museum Ludwig, Cologne, Germany

1969–72 *Five Car Stud*; tableau including car, plaster casts, clothing, rope, gun, paint, resin, masks, chainsaw, oil pan, Styrofoam rocks, dirt; Kawamura Memorial Museum of Art, Sakura, Japan

1980–81 *Portrait of a Mother with Past Affixed Also* (with Nancy Reddin Kienholz); mixed media; Walker Art Center, Minneapolis, Minnesota, United States

1982–83 *Pedicord Apartments* (with Nancy Reddin Kienholz); mixed media environment; Frederick R. Weisman Art Museum, University of Minnesota, Minneapolis, United States

1985 *The Ozymandias Parade* (with Nancy Reddin Kienholz); tableau including plaster casts, clothing, wood, plastic, mirrored Plexiglas, fiberglass horses, light bulbs, recorded music, wagon, barrel, suitcases, fake money, telephone, toys, miniature flags, metal, galvanized sheet metal, polyester resin, rubber, paint; collection of Nancy Reddin Kienholz, courtesy of LA Louver Gallery, Venice, California, United States

1989 *To Mourn a Dead Horse* (with Nancy Reddin Kienholz); wooden table, television, light, photograph, horse's hoof, cloth, barbed wire, artillery shell, pencil, paint, resin; collection of Nancy Reddin Kienholz, courtesy of LA Louver Gallery, Venice, California, United States

Further Reading

Edward and Nancy Reddin Kienholz: Human Scale (exhib. cat.), San Francisco: San Francisco Museum of Modern Art, 1984

Hopps, Walter, *Edward Kienholz, 1954–1962* (exhib. cat.), Houston, Texas: Menil Foundation, 1995

Hopps, Walter, *Kienholz: A Retrospective*, New York: Whitney Museum of American Art, 1996

Kienholz, Edward, *The Art Show: 1963–1977*, Berlin: Berliner Künstlerprogramm/DADD, and Paris: Centre National d'Art et de Culture Georges Pompidou, 1977

Pincus, Robert L., *On a Scale That Competes with the World: The Art of Edward and Nancy Reddin Kienholz*, Berkeley: University of California Press, 1990

Tuchman, Maurice, "Edward Kienholz," in *Edward Kienholz* (exhib. cat.), Los Angeles: Los Angeles County Museum of Art, 1966

Weschler, Lawrence, "The Subversive Art of Ed Kienholz," *Art News* 83 (September 1984)

YVES KLEIN 1928–1962 *French*

Yves Klein's short but dazzling career was crucial to the advent and development of Conceptual art, which characterized the second half of the 1960s in both western and eastern Europe and America. All his artistic activity was based on a constant esoteric and theosophic quest for the immaterial through the creation of works conceived as vehicles of the absolute.

From 1956 on Klein devoted himself to making sculptures that were three-dimensional versions of his celebrated monochrome paintings. From Marcel Duchamp he took the idea of concentrating the value of a work solely in its concept, thereby erasing the sense of traditional techniques and obliterating the distance between art and life. He reinterpreted the idea of using everyday objects and charged his primary-colored readymades with a strong element of spirituality. *Les Rouleaux*, for instance, was an assembly of Klein's worn-out paintbrushes.

In 1957 he discovered the great dematerializing power of the color blue and realized that his own special hue (which he patented), International Klein Blue (IKB), could potentially transfigure any object. At the opening of a one-man show in Paris that year, he proposed *Aerostatic Sculpture*, releasing 1,001 blue balloons into the sky.

Between 1958 and 1960, Klein's principal tool became the sponge, thanks to its capacity to imbibe any fluid. He created a long series of sculptures using sponges soaked in primary colors, especially blue. *Sponge S E 78*, which consists of a sponge soaked in blue and mounted on an upright with a support, recalls Jean Dubuffet's gestural experiments.

In 1957 Klein and Jean Tinguely joined forces to create an important sculpture titled *Vitesse pure et stabilité monochrome*. This work consists of a rotating blue disk that creates an impression of stability. The motor-driven rotary motion is not perceived as such, but as vibration in the surrounding space. In this way, Klein and Tinguely discovered a kind of speed that, like air pressure, becomes a quality of emptiness, a manifestation of energy.

Klein's intense attraction to emptiness and absence—signs of the metaphysical—reappeared in his crucially important installation *Le Vide*, set up in 1958 at the Galerie Iris Clert in Paris. Klein left the display space completely empty and painted the walls white; his purpose was to give viewers a pure primary perception, erasing all of their previous experience. This important event, to which Fernandez Arman was to reply in 1960 with his *Full-up* installation at the same gallery, is considered the first example of Environmental art, which involves the exhibition space itself through installations or constructions of real environments. The *Spatial Environments* created by Lucio Fontana starting in 1949 can be considered interesting forerunners of these works by Klein.

Klein's *Le Vide* was crucial not only to the development of Environmental art but more generally to much of the conceptual work—Process art, Minimal art, Conceptual art, Land art—that overturned the traditional notion of sculpture in the second half of the 1960s. A forerunner in 1957 was Klein's *Sculpture Tactile*, which involved the viewer directly. The piece consisted of a large cube mounted on a pedestal and pierced by holes on all four sides. Viewers were invited to put their hands through the holes, whereupon they had the sensation of touching human skin.

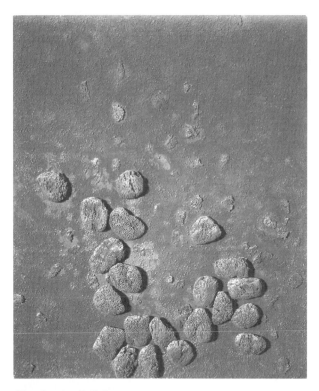

Blue Sponge Relief
© Erich Lessing/Art Resource, NY and © Artists Rights
Society (ARS), NY / ADAGP, Paris

In 1960 Klein created his first series of *Anthropométries*, which made direct use of naked human bodies. These works collapsed the traditional categories or media within the arts, combining sculpture, painting, and music. Klein drew his inspiration partly from the fearsome traces left on the contaminated earth at Hiroshima by atom bomb victims, and partly from those left on judo mats by the sweaty contenders' bodies. He dribbled blue paint over the naked bodies of three female models using a typical action-painting technique. The models then left their body prints on sheets of paper tacked to the wall or spread on the floor as if they were modern winding sheets. Background music gave a rhythmic cadence to the performance.

The Italian artist Piero Manzoni drew directly on these works of Klein's for his own live sculptures. With Klein and Manzoni, sculpture ceased to be a representational art or a way for artists to express themselves. Sculpture became pure tautology, an active object, a being becoming.

In 1960 Klein also founded and took the lead in the French group Nouveau Réalisme, although he was much more conceptual and abstract than the other artists and less fascinated by the physical reality of things. An example of this is the group of highly spiritual casts (blue on a gold background) of the nude bodies, which acted as sponges, of his friends Arman, Martial Raysse, and Claude Pascal.

Klein's interest in the natural elements then blossomed in a series of works that represent the sculptural expression of his cosmic ideas about infinite space. *Blue Rain* consists of 12 wooden rods painted with pure pigment. Inspired by astronaut Yuri Gagarin's description of the earth as a floating blue sphere, Klein created *Relief RP5—Le Mappemonde* by dipping a sphere in his IKB paint and leaving it suspended in the air.

Blue sculptures such as *The Victory of Samothrace* were characteristic of this period. His blue cast of an antique icon belongs entirely to a metaphysical dimension.

Because of the profoundly innovative and revolutionary import of his research, Klein met with much diffidence on the part of critics and the public. He was a brand-new kind of artist/critic who was directly involved—through lectures, articles, and other publications—in supporting and defending the validity of his artistic activity.

His first show in the United States, at the Leo Castelli Gallery in 1961, was greeted with considerable suspicion and perplexity. American reviewers praised the formal qualities of his monochromes but ignored his radical criticism of the basic values of art. The retrospective exhibition jointly organized in the 1980s by the Guggenheim Museum in New York, the Chicago Museum of Contemporary Art, the Houston Museum, and the Centre Georges Pompidou in Paris definitively established Klein's position as an extraordinary precursor of the principal trends in contemporary art.

Celebrated and appreciated for his monochrome paintings, Klein also holds a fundamental place in the history of sculpture because of his decisive contribution in shifting the value of a work to its concept, thereby opening the way to new forms of artistic expression for younger generations oriented toward the exploration of invisible and unconscious worlds.

CATERINA BAY

See also **Arman (Fernandez); Dubuffet, Jean; Duchamp, Marcel; Fontana, Lucio; Manzoni, Piero; Performance Art**

Biography

Born in Nice, France, 28 April 1928. Parents both painters. Attended École Nationale de la Marine Marchande and École Nationale des Langues Orientales, Nice, 1942–46; met artists Arman and Claude Pascal, 1946; traveled through Europe and Japan, 1948–53; painted first monochromes and won black belt in judo at Kodohan Institute in Tokyo, 1952–53; moved to Paris, 1955; same year had first show at Galerie des Solitaires, Paris; aroused public debate with exhibition *Yves: Propositions monochromes*, at Galerie Colette Allendy in Paris, 1956; started his "Blue Period," 1957; collaborated with architect Walther Ruhnau on Gelsenkirchen House in West Germany, 1957–59; lectured at the Sorbonne, 1959. Died in Paris, France, 6 June 1962.

Selected Works

1956   *Les Rouleaux*; mixed media; private collection, Paris, France

1957   *Aerostatic Sculpture*, for Galerie Iris Clert, Paris, France; 1,001 blue balloons (destroyed)

1957   *Tactile Sculpture*; mixed media; private collection, Paris, France

1957   *Vitesse pure et stabilité monochrome* (with Jean Tinguely); blue disk with powered rotary motion; private collection, Paris, France

1958   *Le Vide*, for Galerie Iris Clert, Paris, France; empty gallery space (destroyed)

1960   *Anthropométries of the Blue Period*; body print on paper; private collection, Paris, France

1960   *Sponge S E 78* (from the *Sponge Sculptures* series); blue sponge; private collection, Paris, France

1961   *Blue Rain*; 12 painted wooden rods; private collection, Paris, France

1962   *Arman, Martial Raysse, and Claude Pascal*; polyester casts on gold background; private collection, Paris, France

1962   *Relief RP5—Le Mappemonde*; mixed media; private collection, Paris, France

1962   *Victory of Samothrace*; cast; private collection, Paris, France

Further Reading

Arman, and Tita Reut, *Substitution: Entretien apocryphe d'Yves Klein*, Nice, France: L'Éditions, 1998

Passoni, Aldo, *Yves Klein, 1928–1962*, Turin, Italy: Galleria Civica d'Arte Moderna, 1970

Restany, Pierre, *Yves Klein*, New York: Abrams, and Paris: Hachette, 1982

Restany, Pierre, and François Marthey, *Yves Klein et son mythe*, Brussels: Le Palais, 1966

Stich, Sidra, *Yves Klein*, London: Hayward Gallery, and Stuttgart, Germany: Cantz, 1994

Wember, Paul, *Yves Klein*, Cologne, Germany: DuMont Schauberg, 1972

Yves Klein, Amsterdam: Stedelijk Museum, 1965

Yves Klein, 1928–1962, Paris: Centre National d'Art Contemporain, 1969

Yves Klein, 1928–1962: A Retrospective, Houston, Texas: Institute for the Arts, Rice University, 1982

MAX KLINGER 1857–1920 *German*

Max Klinger began working in sculpture during the 1880s, when he also created his famous graphic suites. His art was decisively influenced by two events in 1884: an exhibit featuring works by sculptor Adolf von Hildebrand and a lecture by Georg Treu, the director of the Dresden Antikensammlung. Von Hildebrand's statue *Adam* awakened Klinger's interest in stone sculpture. Treu's lecture, titled "Should We Paint Our Statues?" drew Klinger's attention to the original polychromy of antique sculpture.

After these experiences, Klinger's first plastic works consisted of sculptures assembled of stone material of various colors, which were then painted in areas. He conceived these pieces during his years in Paris, where he was able to find inspiration in the polychromed works of Charles Cordier, Jean-Léon Gérôme, and others. With his "head studies" of a young Parisian woman in 1886, Klinger began his work on a female figure that was later titled *New Salome*. The stone version was produced in Rome in 1891–93 by using a colored plaster model that was made during 1887/88 in Paris. The young woman, portrayed as a half-figure, holds her arm slung across her breast; underneath lie the heads of two men, both the victims of the woman who gazes challengingly outward. Different varieties of marble characterize the drapery and the color of the flesh; the hair is distinguished through painting. Eyes of inset amber intensify the uncanny appearance of this symbolic sculpture in which Klinger presents his individual version of the femme fatale, a favorite theme of the late 19th century.

Klinger's second famous sculpture, *Cassandra*, also has a threatening effect. The sculpture was planned during numerous drapery studies and design sketches, which sometimes featured a full figure. It was ultimately produced as a half-figure with drapery of a brownish alabaster standing in contrast against the flesh tone of the marble.

When Klinger turned to sculpture in 1883/84, he was occupied with an important assignment: the decoration of the vestibule of the Villa Albers in Berlin/Steglitz (now in the Hamburger Kunsthalle and Museum der bildenden Künste, Leipzig, Germany). Klinger's mural and painted doors complemented a fireplace made of colorful marble and sculptures, which were produced by Artur Volkmann and painted by Hermann Prell, both according to Klinger's designs.

Architecture, painting, and sculpture were united in this pioneering synthesis of the arts. In his programmatic treatise *Painting and Drawing*, which first appeared in 1891, Klinger argued for a connection of the three sibling arts. In his opinion, only colorful sculpture could be integrated well into an "area-artwork."

Klinger's efforts to connect the different genres of the fine arts reveal themselves in two monumental paintings with sculptural frames. The bottom of the *Judgment of Paris* (1885/86; Kunsthistorisches Museum, Vienna, Austria) displays colorful plaster masks. In *Christ on Olympus* (1893–96; Museum der bildenden Künste, Leipzig, Germany), two life-size marble statues are also integrated: *Hope*, Klinger's first torso, and *Remorse*, a highly expressive back-figure.

Klinger's chief work, the monument to Beethoven, also stands in connection with his endeavor for a *Gesamtkunstwerk* (total work of art). The colored plaster model had already been produced in Paris by 1885/86. As the artist recounted, the idea came to him while he was playing the piano. The monument is thus a highly personal expression of his admiration for Ludwig van Beethoven. The figure of the composer, which bears the features of Beethoven's well-known mask (cast from his face during his lifetime), is depicted in a strained posture, suggestive of internal artistic processes; the image of the eagle lifting its wings is also symbolic. The figure is seated on a throne: the artist in the process of creating is majestically, if not divinely, elevated.

Klinger was not able to begin the expensive production of the monumental statue until 1894. He acquired the marble for the bare upper body of the Beethoven figure in Greece, then sculpted the rock pedestal and the eagle of black marble from the Pyrenees—and the drapery of Tyrolean alabaster with a brownish stripe. The throne was cast in bronze and took two years to produce using the lost-wax casting method. The monument to Beethoven was completed in the spring of 1902 and was exhibited in the Vienna Secession in a special room arranged by Gustav Klimt. For the permanent installation in Klinger's hometown of Leipzig, an annex (now destroyed) based on Klinger's own designs was built on the Museum der bildenden Künste. With the monument to Beethoven, Klinger reached the high point of his fame as a sculptor, and the public expressed awe for the monument as though it were a miracle. Some critics, however, found disturbing the cerebral focus, the sheer abundance of motifs, and the richness of the materials.

At the turn of the 20th century, Klinger's sculptures became more reserved in terms of content and form. He created individual figures, such as *Girl Bathing, Looking at Her Reflection in the Water*, or the torso *Amphitrite*, in which paint was used very subtly. Symbolist concepts continued to appear in his monument projects. Klinger's monument for his friend Johannes Brahms, which was completed in 1909, depicts the composer accompanied by two muses. In 1905 and 1914, Klinger created two commemorative busts for philosopher Friedrich Nietzsche. After 1905, Klinger's activity as a sculptor flagged. Although he completed several portraits, larger projects, such as the monument for the composer Richard Wagner that had been planned in 1904, usually remained unfinished.

URSEL BERGER

See also **Hildebrand, Adolf von; Polychromy**

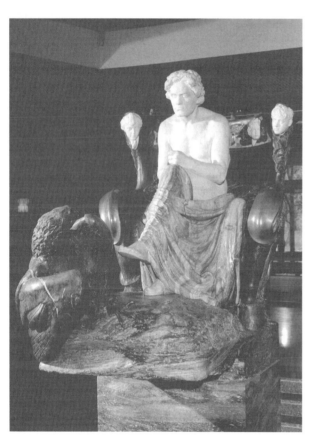

Monument to Beethoven
© Erich Lessing / Art Resource, NY

Biography

Born in Leipzig, Germany, 18 February 1857. Began studies in painting at Art Academy in Karlsruhe under Karl Gussow, 1874; followed Gussow to Berlin the next year; completed studies, 1877; in Brussels, 1879; returned to Berlin, 1881; first trip to Paris, 1883; residence there, 1885–86; graphic suites appear in the 1880s; moved to Rome, 1888; returned to Leipzig, 1893, and in same year, completion of first statue in colored marble, *New Salome*; member of Academy of Fine Arts, Munich, 1891, and Arts Academy, Berlin, 1894; professor at Academy for Graphic Arts in Leipzig from 1897; extended visits to Paris after 1900; exhibited in Vienna Secession, 1902; commissioned by German Artists Association to initiate "Villa Romana," a house for German artists in Florence, 1905; corresponding member of the Vienna Secession from 1897; suffered stroke in 1919. Died in Grossjena, near Naumburg, Germany, 4 July 1920.

Selected Works

1885   Design for the monument to Beethoven; painted plaster; Beethoven-Haus, Bonn, Germany

1891–93 *New Salome*; marble; Museum der bildenden Künste, Leipzig, Germany

1892–95 *Cassandra*; marble; Museum der bildenden Künste, Leipzig, Germany

1894–   Monument to Beethoven; marble, bronze,
1902   ivory; Museum der bildenden Künste, Leipzig, Germany

1896–97 *Girl Bathing, Looking at Her Reflection in the Water*; marble; Museum der bildenden Künste, Leipzig, Germany

1898   *Amphitrite*; marble; Nationalgalerie, Berlin, Germany

1899–   *Elsa Asenijeff*; marble; Neue Pinakothek,
1900   Munich, Germany

1904   *Drama*; marble; Skulpturensammlung, Dresden, Germany

1905–09 Monument to Brahms; marble, Musikhalle, Hamburg, Germany

1904   *Friedrich Nietzsche*; marble; Nietzsche-Archive, Weimar, Germany

Further Reading

Bluhm, Andreas, et al., *The Colour of Sculpture, 1840–1910* (exhib. cat.), Zwolle, The Netherlands: Waanders, 1996

Ehrhardt, Ingrid, and Simon Reynolds (editors), *SeelenReich: Die Entwicklung des deutschen Symbolismus*, Munich: Prestel, 2000; as *Kingdom of the Soul: Symbolist Art in Germany, 1870–1920*, Munich and London: Prestel, 2000

Elsner, Gudrun, and Kordelia Knoll (editors), *Das Albertinum vor 100 Jahren—die Skulpturensammlung Georg Treus*, Dresden: Staatliche Kunstsammlungen Dresden, 1994

Guratzsch, Herwig (editor), *Max Klinger: Bestandskatalog der Bildwerke, Gemälde und Zeichnungen im Museum der bildenden Künste Leipzig*, Leipzig: Seemann, 1995

Klinger, Max, *Max Klinger: Wege zum Gesamtkunstwerk*, Hildesheim, Germany: Roemer- und Pelizaeus-Museum, 1984

Klinger, Max, *Max Klinger, 1857–1920: Ein Handschuh, Traum und künstlerische Wirklichkeit*, Frankfurt: Städtische Galerie in das Städelsche Kunstinstitut, 1992

Lost Paradise: Symbolist Europe (exhib. cat.), Montreal, Quebec: Montreal Museum of Fine Arts, 1995

PYOTR KLODT 1805–1867 *Russian*

Pyotr Klodt was a Classicist in his strict completeness of composition, a Romantic in the emotional expressiveness of his images, and a genuine realist in his remarkably precise portrayal of living reality. He received a military education. Through his subsequent pursuit of art, he went against the prejudices of his social class, which prohibited a nobleman from being a professional artist.

As a youth, Klodt showed an inclination for modeling and carving, as well as a passion for the study of horses in Omsk, Russia, where his father, a celebrated military general, was serving. Klodt began studying in the St. Petersburg Artillery Academy in 1822, where he continued to draw, model, and carve wood figurines of horses and study their habits, poses, movements, and gaits. After a brief period of military service, Klodt resigned his commission with the intent of dedicating himself to sculpture. For two years, he studied independently, working from real life and copying ancient works of plastic art. In 1830 he became a nonmatriculated student at the Academy of Arts in St. Petersburg, where his talent was highly appreciated. Along with the famous sculptors Stepan S. Pimenov and Vasily I. Demut-Malinovsky, Klodt took part in a major government commission in 1831: the sculptural design of the Narva Triumphal Arch in St. Petersburg. Klodt executed the group *Six Horses for the Chariot of Glory*, located on top of the arch. The harnessed horses are depicted in headlong motion, rising up on their hind legs, a departure from the traditional portrayal of this motif in Classical monumental-decorative sculpture. This early work already distinguished itself in its emotional power and in the energy of the sculptural image.

In early 1833 the artist began a project that occupied him for more than ten years and became his lifework: the four bronze horse groups *Horse-tamers* decorating the Anichkov Bridge across the Fontanka River in St. Petersburg. All four groups are united by one theme: man conquers horse, reason restrains the elements. Klodt continued the development of this subject from the famous Roman Dioscuri (copies of which were put on display in 1810 at the Horse Guards Riding School building in St. Petersburg) and the well-known Marly *Horses* by the 18th-century French sculptor Guillaume Coustou. In contrast to his predecessors, Klodt created images from numerous real-life sketches, rather than portraying mythical horses and heroes that are remote from reality, and his artistic synthesis was founded upon a flawless knowledge of anatomy and observance of its laws. Klodt arrived at a formal solution of monumentality and emotional pathos, as the tamer's majestic and confident motions finally curb the impulses of the horse. The sculptural silhouettes are well defined, the forms concise. This unique ensemble unfolds itself to the viewer in a series of successive images. In the first group, the youthful rider, straining with his whole body and firmly seizing the bridle, holds back the rearing horse. The drama of the struggle increases in the next group. The horse breaks forward in untamable impulses, and the man is barely able to rein in the horse. In the third group, the man is toppled to the ground, and the horse almost succeeds in breaking away. Finally, in the fourth group the man subdues the animal. These sculptural works have become symbols of the city and fully harmonize with the architectural panorama of the surrounding parts of the city.

Even before completing the work on *Horse-tamers*, Klodt had already achieved European fame. Czar Nicholas I sent casts of the first two groups as diplomatic gifts: in 1842 to the Prussian king Frederick William IV in Berlin, and in 1846 to the king of the Two Sicilies, Ferdinand II in Naples, where they decorated the royal residences.

From the late 1840s to the early 1850s, Klodt executed an enormous sculptural frieze, almost 70 meters in length, entitled *Horse in the Service of Man*, for the service building of the Marble Palace in St. Petersburg. He created it from a graphic sketch by the architect Aleksandr P. Bryullov, who used the famous frieze of the Parthenon in Athens as his prototype. In this work, Klodt depicts processions on horseback and in chariots, military skirmishes of horsemen, and scenes of hunting.

In 1848 Klodt won a competition to construct a monument to the poet and fabulist Ivan A. Krylov for the Summer Garden in St. Petersburg. The realistic worldview of the sculptor manifests itself in full measure in this work. Departing from Classical conventions and basing his work on real-life observations, he captured the appearance of a man whom he knew well and loved. The poet is dressed in an everyday frock coat with long folds, in a simple, natural pose. Krylov has a book in his hand, as though sitting down to relax, and is surrounded by plots and characters of his fables, included in the high-relief composition of the pedestal. Aleksandr A. Agin, a well-known master draftsman of the period, executed the sketch of the pedestal, under Klodt's supervision.

At the same time as his work on the Krylov monument, Klodt was laboring on another great monumental work: a memorial statue to Prince Vladimir I (St. Vladimir) in Kiev (the architect was K.A. Ton). The sculptor made a colossal statue of the prince using a small sketch model by Demut-Malinovsky and also created a high-relief *Baptism of the Russian People* for the pedestal.

A significant achievement of Klodt in the area of monumental-decorative arts was the equestrian statue

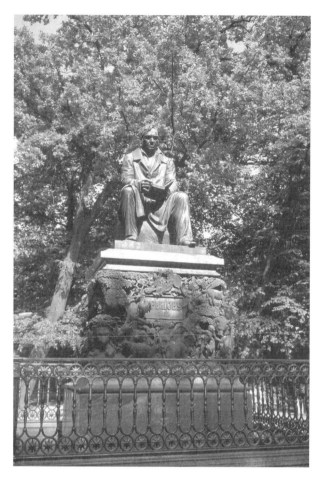

Monument to Ivan A. Krylov
© Cuchi White / CORBIS

of Nicholas I for a monument designed by the architect A. Montferrand. The sculptors N.A. Ramazanov and R.K. Zaleman worked together with Klodt on this project, executing the bas-reliefs and allegorical figures of the pedestal. The triumphal monument is the center of the ensemble of St. Isaac's Square, one of the most beautiful squares in St. Petersburg. The czar, proud and majestic, is portrayed on a galloping horse, its movements rapid and impulsive. Klodt's precise mathematical calculations during the casting enabled him to secure the equestrian statue using two foundations—the hind legs of the horse—without any artificial supports. Klodt was the first in the history of monumental sculpture to solve this complicated technical problem.

The high quality of Klodt's bronze castings also attest to the artistic virtues of his works. From 1838 Klodt was head of the casting workshop at the Academy of Arts and cast the majority of his works himself. His experience as a sculptor and caster allowed him to perfect his technique and raise the level of his execution of both monumental and smaller bronze works.

Klodt's independent studio works played an important role in the establishment and development of the animal genre in Russian sculpture. The names of the pieces alone (*Horse in Watering Place*, *Horse with Colt*, and *Nag*, for example) testify that concrete animals became objects of study and inspiration for the sculptor. Klodt did not simply portray steed, mare, or stallion with naturalistic precision. His works also emphasize the unique grace, plasticity, harmony, and rhythm of the animals' movements and contours. In this way, Klodt imparted a genuinely monumental character to the living form, creating a hymn to the beauty and perfection of nature.

LINA A. TARASOVA

See also **Russia and Soviet Union**

Biography

Born in St. Petersburg, Russia, 5 June 1805. Son of a celebrated military general. Received early education in Omsk, Russia; studied at Artillery Academy in St. Petersburg, 1822–28; enrolled at the Academy of Arts, St. Petersburg, 1830; participated with Stepan S. Pimenov and Vasily I. Demut-Malinovsky in sculptural commission for the Narva Triumphal Arch, 1831–33; won competition for monument to Ivan A. Krylov, 1848; member of Roman Academy of St. Luke, 1852, the Berlin Academy of Arts, and the Paris Academy of Fine Arts. Died in Gute Khalala, Finland, 6 November 1867.

Selected Works

1831–33 *Six Horses for the Chariot of Glory*; bronze; Narva Triumphal Arch, St. Petersburg, Russia

1833–46 *Horse-tamers*; bronze; Anichkov Bridge, St. Petersburg, Russia

1833–53 Monument to Prince Vladimir; bronze (figure), cast iron (pedestal); Kiev, Ukraine

1848–50 Decorative sculpture *Horse in the Service of Man*; plaster of Paris; Service Corps Building of the Marble Palace, St. Petersburg, Russia

1848–55 Monument to Ivan Andreyevich Krylov; bronze; Summer Garden, St. Petersburg, Russia

ca. 1850 *Horse in Watering Place*; wax; State Russian Museum, St. Petersburg, Russia; casts: plaster of Paris, bronze, cast iron

1854–55 *Mare with Stallion*; wax; State Russian Museum, St. Petersburg, Russia; casts: plaster of Paris, bronze, cast iron

1855 *Chariot of Apollo*; copper, galvanized plastic; Bolshoi Theater, Moscow, Russia

1856–59 Equestrian monument to Czar Nicholas I; bronze; St. Isaac's Square, St. Petersburg, Russia

Further Reading

Androssov, Sergei, "Klodt (von Yurgensburg), Pyotr (Karlovich)," in *The Dictionary of Art*, edited by Jane Turner, vol. 18, New York: Grove, and London: Macmillan, 1996

Klodt, Georgii Aleksandrovich, *Lepil i otlival Petr Klodt . . .* (Sculpted and Cast by Pyotr Klodt), Moscow: Sov. Khudozhnik, 1989

Klodt, Georgii Aleksandrovich, *Povest' o moikh predkakh* (The Story of My Ancestors), Moscow: Voenizdat, 1997

Petrov, Vsevolod Nikolaevich, "Ukrotiteli Konei (Horse Tamers)," in *Iz bronzy i marmora* (Made out of Bronze and Marble), Leningrad: Khudozhnik RSFSR, 1965

Petrov, Vsevolod Nikolaevich, *Petr Karlovich Klodt: 1805–1867*, Leningrad: Khudozhnik RSFSR, 1985

Russkaia animalisticheskaia skul'ptura XVIII–nachala XX veka (Russian Animal Sculpture of the 18th–Early 20th Century; exhib. cat.), Leningrad, 1985

Vvedensky, N., "Odna, no plamennaia strast': Petr Karlovich Klodt (A Lone but Fiery Passion: Pyotr Karlovich Klodt)," in *S vekom naravne: Kniga o skul'pture* (Abreast of the Century: Book of Sculpture), vol. 3, Moscow, 1974

GEORG KOLBE 1877–1947 *German*

After studying painting in Dresden, Munich, and (in 1897/98) at the Académie Julian in Paris, Georg Kolbe first became noted for his Symbolist drawings and lithographs. During his stay in Rome, he began making models more by accident, the first examples of which were idealized portraits. After his return to Germany, Kolbe was still painting large frescolike compositions under the influence of Max Klinger, who gave friendly support to the young artist. Kolbe did not abandon painting completely until he resettled in Berlin in 1904, when he started concentrating on sculpture and sculptural drawing.

From the very beginning, the young sculptor distanced himself from the commissioned sculpture of the late 19th century that had led to a much-criticized "monument boom" under Kaiser Wilhelm II. After a rather difficult start, Kolbe developed a distinctive plastic language of forms around 1911/12. The major work of this phase is the *Tänzerin* (Dancer): a slim figure of a girl with closed eyes and arms outstretched immersed in a harmonious dance movement. This bronze figure, a unique work, became one of the best-known German works of art of the 20th century. In this work Kolbe showed that for which he strove: human depictions that are autonomous and timely. In the sculptures of nudes, however, his figures distanced themselves from the everyday world. They were

881

thereby all the more able to reflect the spirit of the times and to embody ideals.

Kolbe became famous with his *Dancer*; his first public commission soon followed: the *Heine-Denkmal* (monument for Heinrich Heine) in Frankfurt-am-Main. The work is crowned by a group of dancers inspired by the performances of the Russian dancers Vaslav Nijinsky and Tamara Karsavina. After that, Kolbe incarnated the much-admired Nijinsky again in a bronze, which was again titled *Dancer*. An extremely thin and elegant Somali also served as his model at the time; the most distinguished of the figures he inspired is the *Somali-Torso*. At that time, however, as well as in the following decade, most of his works were female figures: graceful, gently moving, introverted young girls. After his trip to Egypt in 1913, Kolbe's style developed further—from tender, sensitive modeling to more tectonic construction.

The first successful phase of Kolbe's work was ended by World War I. The sculptor was drafted into military service but was spared being sent to the war front. After the war, he took a leading position in Berlin. As the chairman of the Free Secession, the most important society of artists at the time in Berlin, he fostered novel artistic efforts. He was a friend of Expressionist painters and owned paintings by Karl Schmidt-Rotluff, Ernst Ludwig Kirchner, and Max Pechstein.

After the war, Kolbe reacted to Cubist and Futurist experiments with form by trying to draw natural forms closer to geometrical shapes. This resulted in severe statues like the *Assunta* or highly dynamic, expressive sculptures like the *Little Mermaid* (1921; Georg-Kolbe-Museum, Berlin). Kolbe's style changed once again in the middle of the 1920s during the brief period of political and economic stability in the Weimar Republic. The sculptor distanced himself from stylization and unnatural proportioning; instead, he modeled athletically active female figures with loose, sketchlike surfaces. The bronzes from those years were very well received; they were shown in many individual and group exhibitions in Germany, other European countries, and the United States, and they found their way into numerous public and private collections.

The sculptor's renown can be gathered from the many portraits he produced in the second half of the 1920s. Among others, Kolbe made portraits of his painter colleagues Max Liebermann and Max Slevogt, and the German Reichspräsident Friedrich Ebert. There were also several public commissions in that period, such as the statue *Morning* in Mies van der Rohe's Barcelona pavilion or the Rathenau fountain in Berlin, conceived as an abstract spiral form (inaugurated 1930, demolished 1934, and melted down; reconstructed 1987). In this most successful stage of his ca-

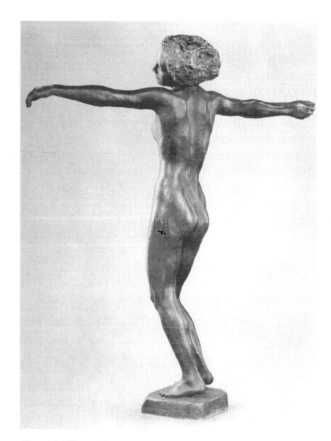

Tänzerin (Dancer)
© Staatliche Museen zu Berlin / Stiftung Preussicher Kulturbesitz, Nationalgalerie

reer, Kolbe was finally able to build his splendid studio-home in the west part of Berlin.

The sharpest transition in Kolbe's creative output was caused by the tragic death of his wife in 1927. No more figures of girls were produced after that, only pictorial works expressive of mourning and abandonment (*Requiem*, *Einsamer* [Lonely Man], *Pietà*; Georg-Kolbe-Museum). Kolbe was then intensely occupied with assignments for memorials—honorary monuments for Ludwig van Beethoven and Friedrich Nietzsche (1931–47; never realized).

Kolbe's human figures from the 1930s were intended to function as exemplars in the Nietzschean sense. Whereas the sculptor had preferred active figures up until then, casual standing figures began to predominate his work. In *Ring der Statuen* (Ring of Statues), Kolbe unified seven female and male figures into a community of chosen people. His new figural ideal, corresponding to powerful, muscular bodies, was usable in National Socialist propaganda. The artist did not, however, let himself be taken in, refusing, for example, a commission to execute a portrait of Adolf Hitler. He was active on behalf of Expressionist artist friends and also in his capacity as the last president of the German Artists Alliance (*Deutscher Künstlerbund*), which was banned in 1936. For Kolbe, however, it was also important during the National Socialist period to show his works in exhibitions, which served to support the regime's artistic policies indirectly. He desired that his *Zarathustra* statue (1932–47) be installed in the Nietzsche Memorial (*Nietzsche-Gedenkhalle*) in Weimar, something Hitler personally prevented.

With the collapsed figure *Der Befreite* (The Liberated Man), Kolbe embodied the Germans' shock after the end of the war. Once again he produced a figure corresponding exactly to the zeitgeist. The artist, who in the last decade of his life suffered from cancer and failing vision, was active to the very end.

Kolbe was the most successful German sculptor in the first half of the 20th century. As the primary proponent of idealizing nude sculpture, he had a formative influence on his generation and had many imitators. In accordance with his will, the Kolbe Museum was opened in his studio-home in 1950, in which the collection gives an overview of the artist's sculptural work and drawings.

URSEL BERGER

See also **Germany: 20th Century–Contemporary; Klinger, Max**

Biography

Born in Waldheim in Saxony, Germany, 15 April 1877. Son of a master painter. Studied painting and drawing, Dresden, 1891–98, Munich, and Académie Julian, Paris; produced first sculptures, Rome, 1899–1901; returned to Germany, 1902, first to Leipzig, then Berlin, 1904; became member of Berlin Secession, 1904; one of the first to receive a stipend at the Villa Romana, Florence, 1905; numerous journeys to Egypt in 1913; drafted for military duty and stationed in Constantinople, 1917, where he remained active as sculptor; received title of professor, 1918; became member of Prussian Academy of the Arts and chairman of Free Secession, 1919; received fewer commissions during National Socialist period; after war damage to studio-home, was evacuated to Silesia, 1943; fled Red Army back to Berlin, 1944. Died in Berlin, Germany, 20 November 1947.

Selected Works

1911–12 *Dancer*; bronze; Nationalgalerie, Berlin, Germany
1912 *Somali-Torso*; bronze; Skulpturensammlung, Dresden, Germany
1912/13 *Heine-Denkmal* (Heine Monument); bronze; Taunusanlage, Frankfurt, Germany

1913 *Dancer*; bronze; Busch-Reisinger Museum, Cambridge, Massachusetts, United States
1920 *Assunta*; bronze; Kunsthalle, Bremen, Germany
1920 *Lucino*; bronze; Cantor Collection, Los Angeles, California, United States
1921 *Wilhelm R. Valentiner*; bronze; Busch-Reisinger Museum, Cambridge, Massachusetts, United States
1922 *Tänzerinnen-Brunnen* (Fountain of Female Dancers); bronze, limestone; Georg-Kolbe-Museum, Berlin, Germany
1924 *Morning*; bronze; Ceciliengärten, Berlin, Germany
1925 *Ruf der Erde* (Call of the Earth); bronze; Georg-Kolbe-Museum, Berlin, Germany
1926 *Kniende* (Kneeling Woman); bronze; Georg-Kolbe-Museum, Berlin, Germany
1926–47 *Beethoven-Denkmal* (Beethoven Monument); bronze; Wallanlagen, Frankfurt, Germany
1927 *Einsamer* (Lonely Man); bronze; Georg-Kolbe-Museum, Berlin, Germany
1933–47 *Ring der Statuen* (Ring of Statues); bronze; Rothschildpark, Frankfurt, Germany
1945 *Der Befreite* (The Liberated Man); bronze; Georg-Kolbe-Museum, Berlin, Germany

Further Reading

Berger, Ursel, *Georg Kolbe, Leben und Werk: Mit dem Katalog der Kolbe-Plastiken im Georg-Kolbe-Museum*, Berlin: Mann-Verlag, 1990

Berger, Ursel, editor, *Georg Kolbe, 1877–1947* (exhib. cat.), Munich: Prestel, 1997

Berger, Ursel, and Josephine Gabler, editors, *Georg Kolbe: Wohn- und Atelierhaus, Architektur und Geschichte*, Berlin: Jovis, 2000

Beucker, Ivo, editor, *Georg Kolbe: Auf Wegen der Kunst: Schriften, Skizzen, Plastiken*, Berlin: Konrad Lemmer, 1949

Binding, Rudolf G., *Vom Leben der Plastik: Inhalt und Schönheit des Werkes von Georg Kolbe*, Berlin: Rembrandt-Verlag, 1933

Justi, Ludwig, *Georg Kolbe*, Berlin: Klinkhardt and Biermann, 1931

Pinder, Wilhelm, *Georg Kolbe: Werke der letzten Jahre*, Berlin: Rembrandt-Verlag, 1937

Pinder, Wilhelm, *Georg Kolbe: Zeichnungen*, Berlin: Rembrandt-Verlag, 1942

Tiesenhausen, Maria Freifrau von, editor, *Georg Kolbe: Briefe und Aufzeichnungen*, Tübingen, Germany: Wasmuth, 1987

KÄTHE KOLLWITZ 1867–1945 *German*

Käthe Kollwitz was initially trained as a painter at private art schools. Influenced by Max Klinger's etchings, she eventually decided to turn instead to graphic design, beginning with lithographs and rubbings. Later, inspired by the art of Ernst Barlach, she created graphics using the woodcut technique.

In 1891 Kollwitz moved to Berlin, where she showed her work for the first time in 1893 at the *Freie Kunstausstellung* (Open Art Exhibition). Her first complete graphic series, *The Weavers Cycle* (1893–98), which was inspired by the play *The Weavers* by Gerhard Hauptmann, was exhibited with great success at the *Grosse Berliner Kunstausstellung* (Great Berlin Art Exhibition; 1898).

Similar in style to Klinger's Symbolism and use of Naturalism, Kollwitz's work exhibited her close connection to the rising workers' movement. In the proletarian milieu of Berlin, she found motifs that presented a social-critical confrontation with the Wilhelmenian age. Her first graphic pieces were influenced by her training as a painter and retained the narrative quality of that genre. In 1903 she turned away stylistically from the characteristics of painting and moved toward those of sculpture, achieving concentrated formulations of human situations that were devoid of any narrative details.

In 1904 Kollwitz left for an extended stay in Paris, where she joined the sculpture class at the Académie Julian. She also paid a visit to Auguste Rodin, whom she greatly admired, and who was to have a great impact on her own sculptural work. Yet Kollwitz never gave up her work as a graphic artist; rather, she integrated sculpture as a stylistic element in her graphic work. Additionally, she developed her acute need to express herself three-dimensionally. The reciprocal influence between her graphic and sculptural art, both in stylistic aspects and in the shared use of pictorial images, is frequently identifiable.

Around 1910 she began to produce sculptures. Only two works have been preserved from her early phase as a sculptor: a group titled *Lovers* and *Woman with Child on Her Shoulder* (1915). Prior to these, it has been presumed that she modeled a portrait relief of her grandfather, Julius Rupp (1909; part of a memorial stone erected in Königsberg), and portraits of her two sons (1909–11); these works are now lost. Three further works have been documented in a photograph, each representing a stage in her long series exploring the themes of mother and child and of lovers. She exhibited these early sculptural works twice: *Lovers* in 1916 at the *Freie Secession* and, a year later, a small selection of sculptures at the Cassirer Gallery exhibition celebrating her 50th birthday.

Generally, Kollwitz worked very slowly, and her process of learning to sculpt was painstaking. Despite her introduction to sculptural work at the Académie Julian, she was essentially self-taught. In the beginning, she modeled in clay and then had these sculptures

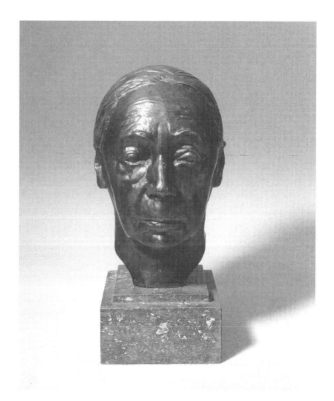

Self-Portrait

cast in plaster, or later in plasticine, after which she continued to work on them. Eventually the works were primarily cast in bronze. Her formal language and motifs, which generally included strong, bold, lines and expressionistic, angular planes and forms, were practically identical in her graphic and sculptural works. As in her graphic work, Kollwitz melded a sociopolitical narrative tradition with bold abstraction.

Kollwitz's themes, such as the mother and child and death and war, always stemmed from personal experience. A prime example is the monument *Grieving Parents*, which she began after the death of her youngest son in 1914 during World War I, but was not able to complete until 1932. Her initial sketches for this work exhibited a Naturalist and narrative style, but over time and an extended working process, she distilled the composition to two reductive, grieving figures with a unified and monumental appearance that offered an impressive memorial for those lost in battle during World War I. Kollwitz was able to realize both the large format and the monumental unity of these figures in one further sculpture: the group *Mother with Twins* (1924–37), with which she succeeded in creating a powerful depiction of motherhood. *Grieving Parents* was carved in granite by stone masons; the first version of *Mother with Twins* was cast in cement. Only later were the forms produced in bronze. Kollwitz's sculptural oeuvre manifests an extensive exploration of self-Portraiture as well. In addition to a realistic portrait of herself at an advancing age (*Self-Portrait*; 1926–36), the artist created several works that have been interpreted as metaphors for the self, and, in particular, reflect her autobiographical image. These include the funerary relief *Rest in the Peace of His Hands* (1935–36) and the relief *Lament* (1938), the latter of which she created following the death of Barlach.

By the late 1930s, because of her age and the circumstances of the time and economy, Kollwitz could work only in a small format. In February 1933, the Nazis ordered Kollwitz to leave the Academy of Arts in Berlin, where she had had the honor of being the first woman elected in 1919. In the wake of the Third Reich's attack on avant-garde and culture (culminating in the 1937 *Entartete Kunst* or *Degenerate Art* exhibition), Kollwitz's pieces were removed from exhibitions and the publication of her work was denied. While she had relied on the graphic medium (posters, lithographs, etchings) as an effective way to disseminate political messages of hope, reform, and activism, her production post–1937 was severely limited. Sculpture therefore began to dominate her work. After completing the graphic series *Death* (1934–37), Kollwitz produced only four more graphic works, but she formed 14 sculptures that made frequent reference to the increasing threat of war.

The sculpture *Mother with Dead Son (Pietà)* (1938) once again presented the painful theme of grief and suffering based on the artist's own loss of her son. Sculptor Harald Hacke enlarged it to a monumental format in 1993, and it was exhibited as a memorial for the victims of war and tyranny in the Neue Wache in Berlin. With works such as *Wives Waving Good-bye* (1937) and *The Tower of Mothers* (1937–38), the artist critically and caustically commented on the state of suffering and poverty in Germany; for this reason, *The Tower of Mothers* was removed from an exhibition by order of the state. Nonetheless, Kollwitz continued to explore personal experiences directly in her work, such as the death of her husband in the sculpture *Parting* (1940–41).

The events of World War II forced Kollwitz to flee Berlin in 1943 when the majority of her works were placed in storage. Nonetheless, numerous pieces were lost in the destruction of her studio and home in November 1943. She died shortly before the end of the war in Moritzburg near Dresden, where a collector of her work had provided her a place of refuge.

JOSEPHINE GABLER

See also **Barlach, Ernst; Klinger, Max; Memorial: War**

Biography

Born in Königsberg, Germany (now Kaliningrad, Russia), 8 July 1867. First art class in Königsberg, 1881; trained as artist under Karl Stauffer-Bern in Berlin, 1885, and under Ludwig Herterich in Munich, 1888; moved to Berlin, 1891; member of Berlin Secession, 1899; trip to Paris, 1904; received Villa-Romana Prize and stayed in Italy, 1907; member of Prussian Academy of Arts in Berlin, 1919; directed master's class for graphic art at the academy, 1928; received Prussian "Pour le Merite" medal from Friedensklasse (Peace Association) for arts and sciences, 1929; participated in petitionary action against the Nazis, 1932; forced resignation from Academy of Arts, 1933; departed Berlin, 1943. Died in Moritzburg, near Dresden, Germany, 22 April 1945.

Selected Works

1912   *Lovers*; plaster; Museum of Fine Arts, Boston, Massachusetts, United States

1914–32 *Grieving Parents*; granite; German Military Cemetery, Vladsloo-Praedbosch, Belgium

1924–37 *Mother with Twins*; bronze; Käthe Kollwitz Museum, Berlin, Germany

1926–36 *Self-Portrait*; bronze; Hirshhorn Museum and Sculpture Garden, Washington D.C., United States

1935–36 *Rest in the Peace of His Hands*; bronze casts; National Gallery, Washington D.C., United States; Friedrichsfelde Cemetery, Berlin, Germany

1937–38 *The Tower of Mothers*; bronze; Baltimore Museum of Art, Maryland, United States

1938   *Lament*; bronze; Hirshhorn Museum and Sculpture Garden, Washington D.C., United States

1938   *Mother with Dead Son (Pietà)*; bronze; Baltimore Museum of Art, Maryland, United States

Further Reading

Bonus, Artur, *Das Käthe Kollwitz-Werk*, Dresden: Carl Reissner Verlag, 1930

Guratzsch, Herwig, editor, *Käthe Kollwitz: Druckgraphik, Handzeichnungen, Plastik*, Stuttgart, Germany: Hatje, 1990

Klipstein, August, *Käthe Kollwitz: Verzeichnis des graphischen Werks*, Bern: Klipstein, 1955

Nagel, Otto, *Käthe Kollwitz*, Dresden: Verlag der Kunst, 1963

Prelinger, Elizabeth, editor, *Käthe Kollwitz* (exhib. cat.), Washington, D.C.: National Gallery of Art, 1992

SERGEI KONYONKOV 1874–1971

Russian

Sergei Konyonkov achieved recognition as a sculptor during the decade leading up to World War I. The earliest of his works, such as *The Stone Breaker*, created during his student days at the Moscow School of Painting, Sculpture, and Architecture, follow the established tradition of Russian realism. As the artist neared the end of his studies, however, his sculpture acquired greater stylistic breadth and expressiveness. As a figurative sculptor, Konyonkov drew on a wide range of source materials: the art of Classical antiquity, the work of Renaissance masters such as Michelangelo, the sculpture of Konyonkov's eminent older contemporary Auguste Rodin, and the indigenous Russian tradition of wood carving.

In 1902 Konyonkov exhibited his first independent work, *Samson*. An over life-size figure 3.2 meters tall, Konyonkov's hero strains dramatically against his fetters. The thwarted energy of Samson's pose clearly derives from Michelangelo's *Rebellious Slave* (Musée du Louvre, Paris), but the pressure of flesh against the containing bonds in Konyonkov's *Samson* is so extreme that its tension seems close to the breaking point. Konyonkov attributed political content to *Samson*, describing it as a depiction of the Russian people in the form of a colossus straining against its chains. The work has become known by the title *Samson Breaking His Fetters*, although when making the work, Konyonkov felt it presumptuous to "forecast" revolution by choosing the moment of liberation; rather, he depicted Samson as a figure still struggling but close to exhaustion.

Konyonkov was directly involved in the street fighting of the 1905 revolution, which occurred in the area of his Moscow studio. His political sympathies are manifest in several works from this period, such as *Ivan Churkin, A Revolutionary Fighter of 1905*. Churkin's rugged head is carved from marble; to underline the figure's impressive strength, Konyonkov left some areas of the stone unpolished or uncarved.

The similarity of Konyonkov's work to that of Rodin is evident in the sensuous surfaces of female nudes such as *Winged Maiden*, which invites comparison with Rodin's *Torso of a Young Woman* (1909; Musée Rodin, Paris). At the same time, Konyonkov's winged figure has a clarity of contour and firmness of pose that allow equally for comparison with female torsos sculpted by Aristide Maillol.

During the first decade of the 1900s, Konyonkov produced bas-reliefs (low-raised work) in a "Greek" style for fashionable Moscow residences. His interest in Greek art eventually broadened to include not only early Classical sculpture but work from the archaic

period as well. *Eos*, although modeled with a sophisticated delicacy, is essentially the face of a kore, complete with archaic smile. A trip to Greece in 1912 solidified Konyonkov's devotion to Greek sculpture. Simultaneously, however, he was also employing roughly carved wood for carvings of folk characters. Wood, a material commonly used in Russian folk art, was his medium of choice for folk subjects: beggars, pilgrims, characters from folktales, and nature deities such as his eerie, smiling *Stribog*, Slavic god of the winds. *Stribog* is carved from wood but incorporates other natural materials (an inlay of pebbles and a pair of ram's horns). Like his contemporary Anna Golubkina, Konyonkov created numerous personifications of natural forces; unlike her, however, he preferred the medium of wood, or occasionally stone, to materials such as clay and plaster from which she derived her more fluid and evanescent effects.

Although Konyonkov was not directly involved with the artists and writers of Russian Symbolism, his general orientation had much in common with theirs, in particular the magical evocation of nature in the writings of Aleksandr Blok and Aleksei Remizov and the paintings of Mikhail Vrubel. Konyonkov also shared in the Symbolist worship of the creative indi-

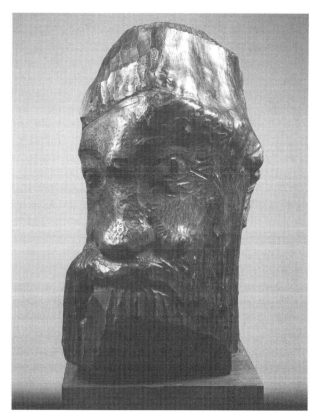

Head of Stenka Razin
© The State Russian Museum / CORBIS

vidual; this assumed concrete form in his portraits of two musicians, Niccolò Paganini and Johann Sebastian Bach. These are not portraits in a conventional sense but rather visualizations of the creative personality. Although he declared Bach his favorite composer, Konyonkov made innumerable versions of Paganini, whom he depicted as a wild and rebellious spirit, as uncontrollable as the wind. Bach, whom he depicted more rarely, is an entirely different character. Eyes closed, in touch with a universal harmony, it is as though he is hearing, literally, the music of the cosmos. Even late in life, during the Soviet period, Konyonkov maintained his conviction that music is a conduit for creative forces that permeate the universe.

After 1917 Konyonkov took part in Lenin's Plan for Monumental Propaganda, a project that aimed for speedy erection of new sculptural monuments dedicated to revolutionary heroes. Konyonkov received the first important commission: a 1918 memorial plaque for the exterior wall of the Moscow Kremlin. This bore the inscription "To Those Who Fell in the Struggle for Peace and Brotherhood"—that is, to those killed in action during the October Revolution of 1917. The plaque represents a winged, half-nude figure of Victory (breasts modestly shielded by a large feather) against a rising sun. The monument was disassembled and removed in 1948, when a passageway was created between the Kremlin and Lenin's tomb; it was repaired, with Konyonkov's help, at the beginning of the 1960s.

At the end of 1923 Konyonkov and a small group of Russian artists traveled to New York City to install an exhibition of painting and sculpture; this opened in the Grand Central Palace in New York on 8 March 1924. Arranged with the approval of the Soviet Committee for Organizing Foreign Exhibitions and Artistic Tours, the exhibition was intended to attract foreign patronage. Konyonkov then remained in the United States for over two decades, executing portrait commissions. His sitters included émigré artists and musicians, prominent members of the American legal profession, and important scientists, including the Russian physiologist Ivan Pavlov, who visited New York's Rockefeller Institute in 1930, and Albert Einstein, about whom Konyonkov wrote at considerable length in his memoirs.

In a succession of Greenwich Village apartments, Konyonkov and his wife, Margarita, created a way of life that reproduced the artist's Russian habits. Their studio home was filled with clay, tools, and giant tree trunks; out of some of these trunks, Konyonkov made magnificent sculptured furniture for their home. The studio also became a social center, often filled with friends and fellow artists.

Konyonkov was, all the same, never entirely happy with life in the United States. In 1945, at 71 years of age, he accepted an invitation from Joseph Stalin and returned with his wife to Moscow. A special ship carried the accumulated contents of the sculptor's studio back to Russia, and until his death, in 1971, Konyonkov occupied a place of honor in the Russian art world, showered with major commissions and awards from the Soviet government.

During this period, excerpts from Konyonkov's autobiographical writings were published in various Russian periodicals, and three books of memoirs appeared. These all served to reinforce Konyonkov's image as an artist dedicated to the cause of revolution and capable of meeting the great and famous on equal terms. What they did not reveal were his interest in the occult, including astrology and numerology, the wisdom of the Egyptian pyramids, and recent research into human immortality. Konyonkov continued to work with wood and particularly favored gnarled stumps and tree roots that imbued his work with qualities of growth, energy, and expansion. The grand project of his final years, left unfinished at his death, was *Cosmos*, a complex installation that stretched from floor to ceiling in his Moscow studio. A complex construction in wood and other materials (string, glass, and pebbles), *Cosmos* incorporates small figures, masks, and cryptic symbols that sum up Konyonkov's vision of the universe.

Because of his return to the Soviet Union and his subsequent establishment as an "official" artist, Konyonkov has received little attention in the West. Most of his work remains in Russia, where it is found in the collections of the State Tretyakov Gallery in Moscow and the Russian Museum in St. Petersburg, as well as in two smaller museums dedicated exclusively to him: the Konyonkov Memorial Museum in Moscow and the Konyonkov Museum of Fine and Applied Arts in Smolensk, near the artist's birthplace.

JANET KENNEDY

See also **Russia and Soviet Union**

Biography

Born in Karakovichi, Smolensk Province, Russia, 28 June 1874. Studied sculpture under Sergei Volnukhin and Sergei Ivanov at the Moscow School of Painting, Sculpture, and Architecture, 1892–96; continued his studies at the St. Petersburg Academy of Arts, 1899–1902; active participant in the revolutionary movement of 1905 in Moscow; traveled to Berlin, Dresden, Paris, and Italy, 1896–97; visited Greece and Egypt, 1912; member of the Russian Academy of Arts, 1916; emigrated to the United States, 1923; lived and worked in New York, 1924–45, and in Italy, 1928–29; returned to USSR at the invitation of Joseph Stalin, 1945; member of the Academy of Arts of the USSR, 1954; People's Artist of the USSR, 1958; Hero of Socialist Labor, 1964. Died in Moscow, 9 October 1971.

Selected Works

1898   *The Stone Breaker*; bronze; State Tretyakov Gallery, Moscow, Russia

1902   *Samson* (also known as *Samson Breaking His Fetters*); plaster (destroyed)

1906   Bust of Nicolò Paganini; plaster; State Russian Museum, St. Petersburg, Russia; Konyonkov Museum, Moscow, Russia

1906   *Ivan Churkin, a Revolutionary Fighter of 1905 (Ivan Churkin the Worker)*; marble; Central Museum of the Revolution, Moscow, Russia

1910   *Johann Sebastian Bach*; marble; private collection, Moscow, Russia

1910   *Stribog (Pagan God)*; wood with inlaid pebbles and ram's horns; State Tretyakov Gallery, Moscow, Russia

1912   *Eos*; tinted marble; private collection, Moscow, Russia

1913   *Sleep*; marble; State Tretyakov Gallery, Moscow, Russia

1913   *Winged Maiden*; wood; State Tretyakov Gallery, Moscow, Russia

1918   *To Those Who Have Fallen for the Peace and Brotherhood of All Nations*, for the wall of the Moscow Kremlin; tinted cement relief; State Russian Museum, St. Petersburg, Russia

1918   *Head of Stenka Razin*; wood; State Russian Museum, St. Petersburg, Russia

1930   *Portrait of the Academician Ivan Pavlov*; bronze; State Russian Museum, St. Petersburg, Russia

1938   *Portrait of Albert Einstein*; bronze; Princeton University, New Jersey, United States

1950–58 *Cosmos*; mixed media; Konyonkov Memorial Museum, Moscow, Russia

Further Reading

Bankovskii, N.N., and N.N. Marenina, editors, *S.T. Konenkov: Vstrechi, vospominaniia sovremennikov o skul'ptore* (S.T. Konyonkov: Meeting and Remembering the Sculptor, by Contemporaries), Moscow: Sovetskii Khudozhnik, 1980

Bychkov, Iu., editor, *S.T. Konenkov: Vospominaniia, stat'i, pis'ma* (S.T. Konyonkov: Memories, Essays, Letters), Moscow: Izobrazitel'noe Iskusstvo, 1984

Kamenskii, Aleksandr A., *S.T. Konenkov*, Moscow: Iskusstvo, 1975

Konenkov, Sergei Timofeevich, *Sergei Konenkov*, compiled by K. Kravchenko, Leningrad: Aurora Art Publishers, 1977

Lampard, Marie Turbow, "Sergei Konenkov and the 'Russian Art Exhibition' of 1924," *Soviet Union/Union Soviétique* 7/1–2 (1980)

Lampard, Marie Turbow, John E. Bowlt, and Wendy R. Salmond, editors, *The Uncommon Vision of Sergei Konenkov 1874–1971*, New Brunswick, New Jersey: Rutgers University Press and The Jane Voorhees Zimmerli Art Museum, 2001

Sarab'ianov, Dmtrii Vladimirovitch, *Russian Art from Neoclassicism to the Avant-Garde, 1800–1917: Painting, Sculpture, Architecture*, New York: Abrams, and London: Thames and Hudson, 1990

JEFF KOONS 1955– *American*

Jeff Koons became widely known in the 1980s for his appropriations of commodity objects and images, for having others make his artwork, and, later, for his extensive self-promotional campaigns. Koons's career to date can be divided into two major periods. The first, terminating in 1987, consists of a series of thematically organized groups of appropriated objects and images: *The New, Equilibrium, Luxury and Degradation*, and *Statuary*. Based on these series, critics initially grouped Koons with other artists exploring commodification and simulation in art and culture as an alternative to the emergence of Neo-Expressionist painting in the early 1980s.

The New, his first major series, consisted primarily of pristine vacuum cleaners encased in vitrines and centered around the concept of newness as an organizing myth of consumerism. These vacuum-cleaner sculptures have become icons of the novelty-driven art world of the 1980s. Insisting on unused, brand-new household appliances, Koons attempted to capture their unsullied condition, making them forever the ideal consumer products inside their Plexiglas cases. Only at the most rudimentary level do Koons's works use the strategy of the readymade. Although appropriated from a nonart context, the act of displacing is secondary to the thematic content of the group. Koons expanded on his manipulation of the appropriated object in his subsequent series that he presented as installations—*Equilibrium, Luxury and Degradation*, and *Statuary*. He exhibited *Equilibrium*'s fish tanks with perfectly buoyed basketballs alongside appropriated sports posters and bronze casts of scuba equipment. The entire installation was, according to Koons, a statement on race and social mobility. He asserted that *Luxury and Degradation* also had a social theme: the connections between various brands of liquor and the social classes for which they are intended. For *Statuary*, Koons cast in stainless steel statues that had traditionally been excluded from serious art-historical consideration—from a big-headed *Bob Hope* to the

Baroque *Louis XIV* to a *Rabbit* cast from an inflatable bunny. In all of these works, Koons appropriated the everyday consumer object with the intention of exposing the ways in which it posited a classed subject. He increasingly became interested in elevating those objects he understood to be directed at the middle and lower classes (i.e., kitsch) to the status of finely crafted art objects.

The first phase of Koons's career terminated in 1987 with the creation of his life-size stainless-steel statue *Kiepenkerl* for the Münster Sculpture Project. According to his own account, the difficulty he encountered in the casting of this statue freed him to move from appropriating consumer objects to creating and manipulating his own works and images (although appropriation remained a central artistic strategy). Coinciding with this break was a transformation in Koons's public persona. After this he began to cultivate an image of the artist as rock star—a parallel often made by critics and journalists in the boom art market of the 1980s. Subsequently, he began to construct and reconstruct his own history, citing 1987 as a turning point.

Koons's new attitude and posturing manifested themselves most infamously in a series of art-magazine advertisements in 1988. These full-page advertisements announced the opening of his new series of works—*Banality*—and featured him attended by bikini-clad women, snuggling a pig, or teaching a class of small children. Although criticized as mere self-aggrandizement, the art-magazine advertisements take on, as their object of appropriation and transformation, the ideal persona of the artist. The booming 1980s art market and the mass-media attention to it had created a number of art-world stars who were achieving widespread fame. Rather than take on the eccentric, intellectual, and sensitive persona many newly made art stars adopted to temper the commercialism of the art world, Koons acquired some of the most debased stereotypes of the artistic persona. He attempted to embody the pop-culture stereotype of the artist rather than the ideal image others were trying to project.

The *Banality* series consisted of large-scale porcelain sculptures of such recognizable figures as Michael Jackson, the Pink Panther, and St. John the Baptist. Inverting the Modernist rejection of kitsch, Koons represented his project as an embrace of lower- and middle-class culture. As with his earlier work, expert craftsmen, rather than Koons himself, meticulously constructed these sculptures. This process ensured that they can be regarded as precious commodity objects as well as the result of his artistic intention. The works were, in other words, museum-quality kitsch. The *Banality* series resulted in a major legal battle for Koons when a greeting-card photographer sued Koons for unattributed use of his work for Koons's *String of Pup-pies* (1988). With far-reaching implications for artistic license and appropriation, the court deemed as plagiarism Koons's translation of the photograph into a polychromed statue.

In response, Koons's next series abandoned appropriation altogether and involved the creation of his own kitsch-inspired works with the extreme self-presentational strategy of *Made in Heaven*. Begun as a collaborative project between Koons and his wife at that time, Ilona Staller, *Made in Heaven* initially encompassed film, sculpture, advertisements, and painting. The film was never made, but controversy erupted over the polychromed wood and porcelain sculptures and oil-ink paintings (mechanically printed from photographs onto canvas so they would have the status and durability of painting). Although the paintings and wood sculptures depicted Staller and Koons having sex, they were not intended to be pornographic. Rather, they were an extension of Koons's embrace of kitsch and self-aggrandizement. Capitalizing on Staller's international reputation as "La Cicciolina," Koons shifted from the appropriation of commodity objects to the appropriation of his artistic persona as commodity. Prior to her involvement with Koons, Staller had been an erotic performance artist (appearing in a number of pornographic films), as well as a member of the Italian parliament. More so than his earlier series, the explicit artworks of the *Made in Heaven* series cannot be divorced from their central theme: Koons himself as object of appropriation.

Following the lukewarm critical reception of the *Made in Heaven* series, coupled with a deluge of media coverage of the works, Koons was not invited to participate in the 1992 international art fair *Documenta* IX. In response, Koons created his monumental *Puppy*, arguably one of his most successful works, for an auxiliary exhibition held at Schloss Arolsen, Germany. The 11.3-meter-high topiary dog encapsulates Koons's interests in making heroic those objects normally excluded from the high-art context. Koons embraced the sweetness of kitsch with *Puppy* but, as with all of his earlier work, did not affect an ironic posture. *Puppy* is both monumental and cute, grandiose and humble. Although rooted in the long tradition of garden design, the medium of topiary has come to be degraded as faux opulence—that is, kitsch. By taking that medium and applying it to the seemingly harmless subject matter of a puppy, Koons did not shy away from those aspects of visual culture normally excluded from the canon of fine art. He venerated them, in fact, through the monumental scale of the piece. *Puppy* is a triumphant celebration of the warm, the fuzzy, and the cute meant to provide an alternative to the ennui and angst that characterize modern definitions of art and the artist.

The most discomforting element of Koons's art and persona has consistently been his lack of irony. Modern art has often exploited kitsch to disparage popular culture, but by affecting earnestness Koons breaks with the assumptions connected with high art. Instead of attempting to dissolve the artificial distinctions between high or low in art or assuming a traditionally avant-garde posture through the ironic substitution of the bad taste for good art, Koons effects the much more radical and disconcerting intervention of naively embracing it all.

DAVID GETSY

See also **Postmodernism**

Biography

Born in York, Pennsylvania, United States, 25 January 1955. Studied at Maryland Institute College of Art, Baltimore, Maryland, 1972–75 (B.A., 1976); studied under Ed Paschke at School of the Art Institute of Chicago, 1975–76; moved to New York, 1976; worked at Museum of Modern Art (selling memberships); became commodities broker on Wall Street beginning in 1979; exhibited window installation at New Museum of Contemporary Art, 1980; first gallery solo exhibition, 1985 (at gallery International with Monument, New York City); first museum solo exhibition, 1988 (Museum of Contemporary Art, Chicago, Illinois). Simultaneous retrospectives presented by San Francisco Museum of Modern Art, California; Stedelijk Museum, Amsterdam; Aarhus Kunstmuseum, Denmark; and Staatsgalerie, Stuttgart, 1992–93. Lives and works in New York City, United States.

Selected Works

1980–86 *The New*; appropriated consumer goods; window installation, New Museum of Contemporary Art, New York

1981 *New Shelton Wet/Dry Tripledecker*; vacuum cleaners, Plexiglas, and fluorescent light; Des Moines Art Center, Iowa, United States

1985 *Lifeboat*; bronze; Museum of Contemporary Art, Chicago, Illinois, United States

1985 *Three Ball Total Equilibrium Tank (Two Dr. J Silver Series, Spalding NBA Tip Off)*; glass, steel, sodium chloride reagent, distilled water, and basketballs; Tate Gallery, London, England

1986 *Rabbit* (edition of three); stainless steel; Broad Art Foundation, Santa Monica, California, United States

1987 *Kiepenkerl*; stainless steel; private collection

1988 *Pink Panther*; porcelain; Museum of Contemporary Art, Chicago, Illinois, United States

1988 *Michael Jackson and Bubbles*; porcelain; San Francisco Museum of Modern Art, California, United States

1988–89 Advertisements for *Artforum, Art in America, Art*, and *Flash Art*; subsequently issued as portfolio of four lithographs, edition of 50

1991 *Self-Portrait*; marble; private collection

1992 *Puppy*, for Arolsen, Germany; steel, live flowers, soil; Guggenheim Museum, Bilbao, Spain

Further Reading

Buskirk, Martha, "Commodification as Censor: Copyrights and Fair Use," *October* 60 (Spring 1992)

Jeff Koons (exhib. cat.), Chicago: Museum of Contemporary Art, 1988

Jeff Koons (exhib. cat.), Amsterdam: Stedelijk Museum, 1992

Jeff Koons (exhib. cat.), San Francisco: San Francisco Museum of Modern Art, 1992

The Jeff Koons Handbook, London: Thames and Hudson, and Anthony d'Offay Gallery, and New York: Rizzoli, 1992

Jeff Koons (exhib. cat.), Aarhus, Denmark: Aarhus Kunstmuseum, 1993

Littlejohn, David, "Who is Jeff Koons and Why Are People Saying Such Terrible Things about Him?" *ArtNews* 92/4 (April 1993)

Lotringer, Sylvère, "Immaculate Conceptualism," *Artscribe* 90 (February–March 1992)

Muthesius, Angelika, editor, *Jeff Koons*, Cologne, Germany: Taschen, 1992

Parkett 19 (March 1989) (special issue on Koons)

Sprinkle, Annie, "Hard-Core Heaven: Unsafe Sex with Jeff Koons," *Arts* 66/7 (March 1992)

Varnedoe, Kirk, and Adam Gopnik, editors, *High and Low: Modern Art and Popular Culture* (exhib. cat.), New York: Museum of Modern Art, 1990

KORE AND KOUROS

The kouros is an Archaic Greek sculpture type that developed after the orientalizing phase, when Greeks colonizing overseas (North Africa, the Black Sea coast, Italy, and Asia Minor) came into contact with the monumental statues of Egypt. Early Greek sculpture before the 7th century BCE were usually small in scale and made of impermanent materials. Exposure to Egyptian art seems to have inspired the Greeks to exploit the rich marble deposits of the mainland and the Aegean Islands and begin to make large-scale works. Large-scale sculpture in bronze did not appear until the end of the Archaic period. Throughout the Archaic period

Greeks used kouroi as grave markers and dedications in sanctuaries. Although the Greek male statues sprang from Egyptian prototypes, they differed greatly from those images that inspired them. Whereas Egyptian male statues in the round were almost always clothed, Greek sculptors most often depicted the kouroi nude and usually beardless. In some of the earliest examples, the figures wear a belt, possibly as an attribute of the god Apollo. The Greek kouroi, derived from Egyptian canons, became the module for experimentation in rendering the human figure.

Later Greek sculpture in the round often depicted deities and mythological figures. In the case of the kouroi, however, the subject is often ambiguous. The kouroi dedicated in sanctuaries could possibly represent the votary as well as the deity to whom the statue is dedicated. Inscriptions associated with kouroi are rare. Some do, however, reveal the function of the statue and give insight into the subject. The inscription associated with the well-known Anavysos Kouros (National Archaeological Museum, Athens, Greece), for example, indicates that the statue represents Kroisos, a youth who perished in battle.

Archaic Greek kouroi vary greatly in scale, from colossal versions to a few that are under life-size. The majority are, however, between 1.5 and 2 meters tall. A larger statue would have made a much richer votive offering to a deity or a grander statement about the man whose burial the statue marked. Differences in scale, however, seem not to have any specific relationship to the subject of the statue or of its function.

The poses of the kouros figures rarely changed over the course of the Archaic period. Like their Egyptian predecessors, the Greek examples are characterized by a stiff and straight posture, with the left leg advanced and arms held to the sides. Rigid frontality is the norm. The step forward with the left leg is not a naturalistic hint of movement. The left foot is set slightly in front of the right, but the rest of the body shows no reaction to support this suggestion of motion; the hips remain rigidly horizontal, as do the shoulders. The sculptors of the Archaic kouroi simply lengthened the left leg in order to suggest that the male figure was advancing that leg. As with all Greek sculpture, artists rendered details of anatomy such as the irises of the eyes and hair color in paint, using the encaustic technique in which pigment is suspended in wax.

Although the stance of the Archaic nude male never changed, the course of the late 7th and 6th centuries BCE shows a linear progression toward greater naturalism. The earliest kouroi demonstrate a distinct patterning in the rendering of the anatomy—ears are volutes, hair is a beaded curtain, and abdominal muscles are strictly horizontal parallel ridges, as in the New York Kouros (Metropolitan Museum of Art). With the de-

velopment of the kouros type came a break with the conceptual nature of the first monumental anthropomorphic statues; sculptors rendering the latest kouroi from the turn of the 5th century BCE were clearly observing the human body and its individual parts. The latest kouroi demonstrate a three-dimensionality unseen in the earlier versions. Sculptors rendered the more archaic kouroi with a foursquare approach; the more mature kouroi reveal a unity of the human form in which the body is seen more as a unified cylinder than an elongated cube. The nude male continued after the Archaic period to serve as the Greek module in experiments in the rendering of anatomy, constantly moving toward naturalism and even superrealism. The end of the kouros type came in the second decade of the 5th century BCE and the Kritios Boy (Acropolis Museum, Athens), whose slight head turn and subtle *contrapposto* (a natural pose with the weight of one leg, the shoulder, and hips counterbalancing one another) stance make a clear break with the Archaic period.

Korai, or "maidens," have much in common with the kouroi. As female figures, however, they were always shown clothed. They served similar votive and funerary functions in the Archaic period. Sculptors often rendered korai serving as a dedication in a sanctuary bearing a gift to the deity—a piece of fruit, a small bird, or a hare, held in an outstretched hand. They exhibit the same rigid posture as their male counterparts, but the korai usually stand with their feet planted together, instead of the left foot forward. The development of style in korai seems to have been somewhat behind that of the kouroi, with a break with the older Daedalic style coming at the end of the 6th century BCE. Whereas the female figures show the same kind of progress toward greater naturalism, the greatest changes emerged in the types of garments worn by the korai. They wore two main garments: a simple peplos, common on the mainland of Greece, shown, for example, on the Peplos Kore (Acropolis Museum, Athens), and the more richly pleated chiton, most often seen on korai from the Ionian Islands and other eastern regions, as in the kore in the Acropolis Museum. Earlier sculptors of the female figures seem to have preferred the heavier peplos; the thinner drapery and complicated folds of the later korai allowed artists to experiment with rendering the suggestion of anatomy under the garment. Paint not only picked out the facial features and hair color of the korai but also added decorative details to the garments rendered in stone.

FRANCESCA C. TRONCHIN

See also **Greece, Ancient**

Further Reading

Boardman, John, *Greek Sculpture: The Archaic Period*, London and New York: Thames and Hudson, 1991

Guralnick, Eleanor, "Proportions of Kouroi," *American Journal of Archaeology* 82 (1978)

Guralnick, Eleanor, "Proportions of Korai," *American Journal of Archaeology* 85 (1981)

Iversen, Erik, "The Egyptian Origin of the Archaic Greek Canon," *Mitteilungen des Deutschen Archäologischen Instituts, Abteilung Kairo* 15 (1975)

Levin, K., "The Male Figure in Egyptian and Greek Sculpture of the Seventh and Sixth Centuries B.C.," *American Journal of Archaeology* 68 (1964)

Payne, Humfry, and Gerard M. Young, *Archaic Marble Sculpture from the Acropolis: A Photographic Catalogue*, London: Cresset, 1936; and New York: Morrow 1951

Richter, Gisela M.A., *Korai: Archaic Greek Maidens*, London: Phaidon, and New York: Praeger, 1968

Richter, Gisela M.A., and Irma Anne Richter, *Kouroi: A Study of the Development of the Greek Kouros from the Late Seventh to the Early Fifth Century B.C.*, New York: Oxford University Press, 1942; 3rd edition, as *Kouroi: Archaic Greek Youths*, London and New York: Phaidon, 1970

KOREA

Three Kingdoms Period (57 BCE–668 CE)

Korea is a mountainous peninsula extending from the Chinese mainland toward the southern islands of Japan. The Koreans who formed into tribal leagues about 3000 or 2000 BCE in this mountainous country were of the Ural-Altaic strain of cultures, which spans north Asia, Siberia, and northern Europe. By the time Buddhism arrived on the peninsula from China in the mid 4th century CE, the only sculptural tradition on the peninsula was the hand molding of technically unsophisticated but highly expressive clay tomb figurines. Artisans in other media, however, were producing high-fired glazed ceramics, bronze mirrors, weapons, glassware, and finely crafted gold jewelry.

Over the two centuries leading to the introduction of Buddhism to Korea in 372 CE, the nation had coalesced from a scattering of tribal leagues into four distinct centralized kingdoms: Koguryo in the north, Paekche in the southwest, Silla in the southeast, and tiny Kaya on the south coast, sandwiched between Silla and Paekche. The Han dynasty of China kept an outpost in Lelang, north of Pyongyang in Koguryo, and this is where Buddhism was probably first introduced to Korea. King Sosurim of Koguryo readily accepted this religion—he emulated all things held in high regard by the Chinese—and began its dissemination.

The oldest extant Buddhist sculptural image in Korea is a bronze statuette (National Museum, Seoul) in a late-4th– to early-5th–century north Chinese style. Almost 5 centimeters high, it represents a seated Bud-

dha on a rectangular pedestal graced by two lions in relief. The image is of the archaic and formal type produced by the Central Asian patrons of Buddhism during the Northern Wei dynasty. The seated posture, unusual mudra (symbolic hand gesture, in this case with hands clasped over the belly), square pedestal containing two lions, and small, knoblike *usnisa* (cranial protuberance signifying a Buddha's transcendental wisdom) are all common to early portable icons, which, by virtue of their portability, clearly trace the spread of Buddhism from China through Korea to Japan. But their portability also makes difficult the tracing of particular objects to their place of origin. This object was found at Ttuksom, in the eastern part of Seoul, in what was then Paekche territory, but whether the Ttuksom statuette is a product imported from north China or of Korean manufacture in this style remains unclear.

The oldest Buddhist statue verifiably made in Korea is a 15-centimeter-high gilt-bronze standing Buddha (National Museum, Seoul). It is a single-cast piece with

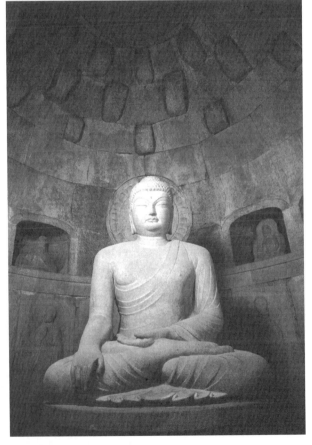

Seated Buddha, Unified Silla, second half of 8th century, Sokkuram Cave Temple, Kyongju, North Kyongsang Province
© Archivo Iconografico, S.A. / CORBIS

a leaf-shaped *mandorla* (body halo). The inscription on the back of the *mandorla* indicates that it was the 29th of a thousand such images commissioned by the head priest of East Lelang Temple in a reign year that corresponds to 539 CE. The U-shaped folds of the inner drapery down the front of the torso, the symmetrical projection of the overdrapery to the sides in a serrated or finlike manner, and the figure's stylized elongation closely follow the contemporary Northern Wei model.

The reproduction of Buddhist images for religious merit—sometimes producing a thousand or more identical images per commission—resulted in the creation of a large number of images of this type from this period: 10- to 15-inch-high (25 to 40 cm) standing Buddhas in the Wei dynasty elongated style, in bronze, framed by a leaf-shaped *mandorla*. They exhibit slight variations in composition and style while clearly remaining under the influence of Chinese prototypes. The large number of triads including Amita and his two bodhisattvas produced toward the end of the 6th century indicates the popularity of Amitist Buddhism in China and Korea at this time.

Paekche

Small-scale imperially or aristocratically commissioned bronze statuettes of Buddhas and bodhisattvas such as those discovered in the Koguryo territory were also popular in Paekche, showing some traces of influence from the Chinese coastal province of Shandung, which is across the sea from Paekche. While no large-scale Buddhist images in metal, earthenware, or wood survive from the Three Kingdoms period, a ceramic base for such an image does survive from Paekche. Large Buddhist images accommodate formalized ritual observances wherein the object may be faced, or circumambulated, sometimes by large assemblies of worshipers, reflecting the further entrenchment of Buddhism into Korean life.

The ceramic base, found at the Ponui-ri kiln site in south Chunhong province, is 99 centimeters tall, suggesting that the Buddha image overall was life size or slightly larger. The form of the pedestal and, more tellingly, the nature of the drapery folds are similar in their rhythm and symmetry to the drapery seen on the pedestal of Torii Busshi's Shaka triad at Horyu-ji in Japan, a form of drapery that originates in the late 5th century in southern China. Busshi was a Japanese-born artisan (a saddle maker turned sculptor) of Paekche descent. This particular drapery is characterized by synthetically balanced folds that lack any errant wrinkles, nested or overlapped in an organ-pipe manner, in shallow relief. The perfect symmetry of fold patterns on both sides of the median of the pedestal is a conspicuous aspect of this style.

Buddhism existed marginally in Japan before 552, but the gift of a gilt-bronze Buddhist image and sacred texts from Paekche to Emperor Kimmei in that year effectively marks the beginning of state-sponsored Buddhism in Japan, and Paekche monks and carpenters built the first Buddhist temples there. The famous Kudara Kannon at Horyuji refers in its name to Paekche, known in Japan as Kudara, although it was doubtless carved in Japan. Whether the artisans who made it were from Paekche, Paekche artisans oversaw the project, or it is a purely Japanese interpretation of Paekche style is the sort of question often raised about objects from this period of sculpture, painting, and temple construction in Japan.

The stylistic characteristics of the famous camphor wood Chugu-ji Miroku (Maitreya) at the Chugu-ji convent near Horyu-ji also indicate Korean origin, via Paekche. All three kingdoms produced images of a seated Maitreya in this posture, rendered in this same delicate, elongated style, which is considered a hallmark of Korean Buddhist sculpture. The popularity of Maitreya, the future Buddha, reached its peak in China in the 5th and 6th centuries and in Korea in the 6th and 7th centuries, enjoying a renaissance during the Koryo period (962–1392 CE) (although in an entirely different sculptural form).

Maitreya is considered to reside in the Manorama paradise of Tusita heaven, where (like the Shakyamuni Buddha, before his advent on earth) he preaches the dharma (Buddhist law) to angels and gods before descending to earth to preach the dharma to worldly beings. Maitreya may be depicted standing or seated, but a recurrent seated disposition for him in Central Asia and China—wherein the bodhisattva is depicted seated on a throne, feet on the ground, ankles crossed—expresses this teaching capacity. Unlike Central Asian and Chinese Maitreya images, the Korean images show Maitreya seated in a pensive pose, with one leg crossed over the other, one hand resting on the crossed leg, and the left hand gently touching the cheek of the gently bowed head. This posture is similar to that used in the famous Koryo dynasty paintings of Water-Moon Kuanum (Chinese: Guanyin; Sanskrit: Avalokitesvara), in which the contemplative bodhisattva of compassion is shown, seated upon his rock on Potalaka (his enchanted island abode) with one leg crossed over the other and one hand gently touching the cheek of his bowed head. Hence, the Three Kingdoms Maitreya images embody his compassion in the act of patiently contemplating the world he will come to save as a Buddha-incarnate.

The contemplative Maitreya figures of the Three Kingdoms period represent the first significant development in the history of Korean Buddhist sculpture. Technically, these images, whose bronze shells are in some cases paper-thin, represent a high achievement in bronze casting. Formally, they are fully in the spirit of elegant Chinese cast-bronze prototypes in their synthetic elongation and subtle adornment of the figure, expressing the bodhisattva's grace in terms of sculptural stylization. Iconographically, the figure shows a complex development of conventional visual and conceptual tropes, so that Korea's Maitreya is depicted as youthful, contemplative, calm, and aristocratic. The technical, formal, and iconographic elements achieve seamless harmony in these images and survive to the present day as icons of national cultural heritage.

Silla

The insular kingdom of Silla accepted Buddhism later than Koguryo and Paekche, and the first temple in Silla, Hwangyong-sa, was built in the capital city Kyongju in 544 CE. Fragments of a large gilt-bronze Buddha image there suggest that artisans created large-scale sculpture early in the history of Silla Buddhism, although early images were among the casualties of 13th-century Mongol invasions, and only fragments, temple foundations, and scant records remain.

Large images in stone from the early 7th century fared better and afford the best picture we have of early Silla Buddhist sculpture. At the base of Namsan, near the capital city Kyongju, stands a triad in granite that reflects the influence in Silla of a style developed in the Qi and Sui dynasties in China. A number of elements in the Namsan triad display the Qi-Sui style: the treatment of the figures is volumetric, rather than thin and elongated (as in the Wei style); and simplified but pronounced sculptural lines conform to and delineate these wide bodies, in contrast to the Wei model wherein the body itself is secondary to sculptural stylization. Naturalistic modeling of bodies and the integration of naturalistic drapery to delineate them are Qi-Sui tendencies that achieved their realization in the naturalism of the Tang style.

Other stylistic characteristics emerged in the 7th century that distinguish Silla images from those in Paekche and Koguryo, for example, Buddha figures with their garments draped over only one shoulder. This manner of draping the Buddha derives directly from India, and it is noteworthy that in the early 7th century, three Indian monks arrived in Silla and resided at Hwangyong-sa. Silla images inspired by Indian (Gupta-period) models also display the *tribangha* (thrice bent; *contrapposto*) posture, which became a characteristic of the Tang International style in the late 7th century.

This posture was one of several characteristic elements of a style that disrupts the rather more static, stylized, full-frontal figures of the Wei period and in-

forms Buddha and bodhisattva figures with a more naturalistic grace. Whereas the elongated Wei style expresses Buddha and bodhisattva figures in terms of symmetry and plasticity, the Gupta and Tang styles adopted in Silla express these figures in terms of their physical, bodily presence, accentuating sensuality in the bodhisattvas and the rounded, organic contours of the Buddha.

Small cast-bronze images reveal these stylistic characteristics more clearly, since the sculptor enjoyed greater control of the materials than did the sculptor in stone. Bodhisattva figures are especially expressive of these characteristics. The earliest renderings of bodhisattvas, such as Avalokitesvara in India, depict these figures as princes, in a metaphorical parallel to the Buddha's royalty prior to his more conservatively rendered Buddhahood. A Silla Kuanum from Sonsan, dated to the 7th century, reflects the cultivation in Silla of the style developing in Sui and early Tang China, a period with which its production is commensurate. Numerous strings of jewels, tassels, clasps, and necklaces drape the figure's body, and where they fall and drape in the negative space between the figure's arm and body further accentuates the complexity and range of these accessories. The cloth that falls beyond the figure's right hand seems to sway naturally to the side, suggesting an animated moment caught in time. The *tribangha* posture and the placement of one foot slightly ahead of the other also animate the figure.

The large number of Kuanum figures from this period reflects the resurgence of belief in Amita, Lord of the Western Paradise, where believers hope to be reborn after death. According to Amitist or Pure Land belief, Amita will descend to the believer's deathbed with Kuanum, who will collect the soul of the deceased in a lotus blossom, in which it will be conveyed to the Western Paradise.

Faith in Amita is often connected to periods of strife and warfare, and such was the Three Kingdoms period, with occasional military campaigns between kingdoms and nations, the threat of brigands and pirates, and a short life span even in the best circumstances. Indeed, the commerce in Buddhist images and styles between countries maps neatly onto the lines of political commerce between nations as the kingdoms sought alliances and paid tribute in the face of war with neighboring nations.

Unified Silla

In 668, in an alliance with Tang China, King Munmu defeated both Paekche and Koguryo, unifying the peninsula. A 7th-century Amita triad in Kunwi-ri, near the capital of Kyungju, embodies the various styles at play in the transition from the Three Kingdoms period to the Unified Silla. Except for the studied drapery and the conservative treatment of the face, the central Buddha is archaically massive and angular, the head disproportionately large for the body, and the hair and *usnisa* represented by a smooth, raised cap, also an archaic element. The face seems dispassionate and of a distant spirituality. The garment, which covers both shoulders, is notably more free and advanced than the face and body overall. The drapery folds over the front of the squarish throne recall pre-Tang stylization and symmetry. In contrast, the rich detail and natural, even animated fall of the folds of the bodhisattvas' drapery, their sensuously animated postures, and the more gentle study of their faces express the Silla adaptation of Tang motifs.

By the early 8th century, the Buddha's drapery had become fixed in a pattern of U-shaped "string folds" draped voluminously over an unarticulated body. In some cases a pair of U folds, separated by a shallow trough between them, mark the legs. This form of drapery originated in Sarnath, of the Gupta kingdom, and became commonplace in the Tang as well as in Unified Silla.

These various tendencies—crisp lines formulating a naturalistic and an organic treatment of figures—achieved crystallization in the sculptural program of the Sokkuram grotto. Construction on the grotto began in 751, concurrently with reconstruction of the Pulguksa Temple on Mount Toham, overlooking Kyongju. The prime minister Kim Taesong was responsible for both projects, which he initiated in memory of his parents in his present and previous lives. The project was not yet completed at the time of his death in 774.

Sokkuram is an artificial grotto constructed of large blocks of white granite that were quarried nearby. The structure consists of a round, domed main chamber, in which a 3.4-meter-high Shakyamuni image—also of local white granite—sits upon an octagonal platform whose capitol and base are carved in a lotus motif. A short passageway connects this chamber to the outside, and a small rectangular transept intermediates the passage between the exterior and the main chamber.

The central Shakyamuni image is the only freestanding sculpture in the shrine, but he is surrounded in the main chamber by two registers of bodhisattvas, arhats (earthly saints), and *devas* (gods derived from the Hindu pantheon). Sculptors carved these figures in relief in 1.8-meter-high stone panels in the wall surrounding the Buddha. Above this register is another register of ten niches, all but two containing seated bodhisattvas.

The lower register of life-size figures begins at the outer entrance to the transept chamber with two guardian figures in martial poses. They wear vigorously flying skirts but are bare chested, their muscular features expressed through a taut anatomical study. More guardian figures lead the worshiper through the transept, and in the main chamber bodhisattvas and arhats dominate the scheme, culminating in the bodhisattvas Manjusri and Samanthabadra, the *devas* Brahma and Indra, and directly behind the Buddha an 11-headed Kuanum.

Iconographically, the choice and arrangement of deities represent the assembly of deities on Vulture Peak to hear the Buddha's sermon described in the influential Lotus Sutra. The inclusion of an 11-headed Kuanum suggests that some form of esoteric Buddhism may have been practiced here. The placement of this bodhisattva behind the Buddha visually suggests that the Buddha is an emanation of the bodhisattva's more fundamental magical powers of protection and compassion. It is clear that one of the functions of the Sokkuram project was national defense, especially in the direction of the East Sea and Japan beyond, which Shakyamuni squarely faces.

Stylistically, the sculpted figures represent a now long-cultivated tradition associated with the Tang dynasty. The posturing of the figures is mannered, as is the slight elongation in their tall, slender frames. The extent to which they seem to be animated derives from the naturalistic treatment of their postures and faces, as well as the garments and jewels that cover their bodies. The incising is crisp and the details complexly studied, so that an ephemeral quality informs these figures emerging in shallow relief from the white granite.

The Buddha figure displays a refinement not seen previously in granite sculpture in Korea. The deft treatment of the face is simplified, but not in an archaic sense. Two long eyebrows arch over two wide, narrowly open eyes. The mouth is narrow but full-lipped, and a subtle suggestion of fleshiness appears about the cheeks and chin. The overall effect is of an intense, grounded, and dignified spirituality.

A thin garment drapes one shoulder—in the Indian manner—and is described with a few, carefully placed folds over the covered arm and over the chest. Creases are described in simple terms also on the covered legs, and the garment terminates in a semicircular gathering between the Buddha's legs.

The overall scheme of the shrine derives from the *chaitya* hall architectural motif in India, in which a large assembly hall, carved into living rock, culminated in an ambulatory around a large stupa in the apse. The position of the Buddha at Sokkuram in the place of a stupa, with an ambulatory around the Buddha (as around a stupa in a *chaitya* hall), suggests that circumambulation was the manner of worship here. The refinement and complexity of the monument—its international influences, the crystallization of technique, the complexity of its architecture, and its neat amalgam of functions and motivations and iconographies—all suggest that it was the product of a prosperous and articulate Buddhist culture.

Koryo

By the 9th century, the government in Kyongju was beginning to collapse. Feuding rival factions of the royal clan weakened the government, and peasants were rebelling under an exorbitant tax burden and disenfranchisement. Moreover, the Tang dynasty had fallen, and China itself was fractured. The merchant-class rebel leader Wang Kon entered the fray and by 918 had toppled the Silla government and established the capital in his hometown, Kaesong, 72 kilometers (45 miles) north of Seoul.

When artisans moved from Kyongju to Kaesong, they brought with them iron casting, a sculptural method begun in the late Unified Silla period. Cast-iron Buddhas became something of a trademark of the Koryo period, although the period is best known for its elegant votive paintings on silk, commonly of Amitist themes and figures. While these paintings, ceramics, printing, and metal arts reflect the refined tastes of the aristocratic patrons of Buddhism in the Koryo, some scholars see the Koryo as the beginning of a degeneration in Buddhist sculpture from which it has not recovered. According to this rising-falling art-historical model, the late Unified Silla period was the apogee of Korean Buddhist sculpture, and the Koryo represents its degeneration toward the static, plastic, inelegant, and unifying modern phase.

Even viewed objectively, the plasticity of these Koryo images is evident in their faces. In terms of the spatial and linear qualities of the face and rather ambiguous index of its spirituality, an example of Amita from Wonju (National Museum, Seoul) falls in the median between other contemporaneous images that are cold, stern, and distant at one extreme and those that are youthful, disproportionate, and in some cases exotic at the other. In short, the faces of the iron Buddhas were poorly realized, but the gold leaf that once covered these images no doubt enhanced their power as icons.

The presence of style elements derived from the Sokkuram Buddha indicates that Koryo sculptors also looked back to Silla style as the classical ideal. Many of the Koryo images wear the Indian-style garment over one shoulder, and the drapery creases follow the same simplified pattern. Also, as in the Sokkuram image, the drapery falls in a semicircle from under the Buddha's ankles.

The construction of large-scale Maitreya images in stone during the Koryo period is worthy of note. Wang Gon Tae Jo, the founder of the dynasty, commissioned the first of a uniquely Koryo style of Maitreya (Kwan-chuk Temple, near Unjin City, South Korea). This monumental form of Maitreya, carved into a tall pillar-shaped stone, is abstractly slender and tall and wears a capstone on its head. The numerous images of this type constructed in the early Koryo period display a broad regional variation in the treatment of the faces, indicating that these images were commissioned by local, wealthy patrons. The manner in which the figures conform to the medium, as well as the free interpretation of the figures represented by these images, suggests that they may better be considered as large-scale folk-art representations of a Buddhist motif.

Chosun and Modern Buddhist Sculpture

In 1388 General Yi Song Gye, while leading the cavalry on an ill-advised expedition against Ming forces, turned back at the Yalu River, returned to Kaesong, and overthrew the government. Like Wang Gon years before, Yi filled the vacuum of a fractious, weakened, and corrupt government and began a new phase in Korean history. He established a conservative government based on neo-Confucian principles. To eliminate the corrupting influence of a powerful Buddhist clergy, he repressed Buddhism, almost eradicating it altogether. The fortunes of Buddhism rose and fell through the Chosun period, its very existence dependent on its ability to address concerns that Confucianism could not: protection of the nation, the appeasement of ghosts, apotropaic ritual for rain and fertility, and thaumaturgy.

Due to the loss of imperial patronage, economic necessity turned the focus of Buddhist ritual from sculpture to painting, and sculptural images become something of an adjunct to these painted images. Especially in modern times, sculpted Buddhist images have a generic, uninspired, almost assembly-line blandness to them, which, some argue, suggests that the rustic simplicity of Korean folk arts—which flourished in the Chosun—is now the stylistic principle informing modern Buddhist sculpture. An Amita dated to 1637 (National Museum, Seoul) displays folkish qualities in its soft, rounded, childlike treatment, common during the Chosun period. Modern images conform to the dimensions and scale of such images, with a youthful face and head bent slightly forward, but harden the features somewhat through a rather more mechanical, less expressive treatment of the face.

Most images of the modern period that grace altars in front of panel paintings are cheaply and rapidly produced of white pine, painted with a coat of black lacquer to protect the wood and provide a smooth surface for the application of gold paint. Once the image is delivered to the temple, the priest performs a highly formalized eye-opening ceremony whereby the pupils of the figure's eyes are painted in order to "animate" it. These images, formally unremarkable, may well reflect in their form and unceremonious manner of production a modern role for such icons: rather than embodiments of Buddhahood, potent protectors of the nation and bringers of rain, they may well serve as mere organizers of space and time in the ritual life of the temple, which entails public assemblies of lay worshipers whose time in the presence of the images is limited and often perfunctory. Modern financial restraints also divert funding from sculptural and painting projects to other necessary sectors of temple upkeep unknown in premodern times.

Two large-scale Buddhist statues of the modern period bear note. One, the 15-meter-tall (49 ft.) granite Kuanum at Naksansa Temple on the east coast, carved by Kwon Chong-hwan and dedicated in 1977, overlooks the East Sea as the tallest granite sculpture in Korea. The other is a 33-meter-high (108 ft.) bronze Maitreya at Popju-sa in the middle of South Korea, cast from a giant single mold in 1988. The statue is hollow inside, and one can ascend a spiral staircase into the figure's head. Both images evidence the continuing prosperity of Buddhism in the modern period, with an occasional large expenditure on the part of patrons producing colossal images, impressive more as technical than as stylistic achievements.

Modern Korean Sculpture

During an exhibition of his work at the Galeria Bonino (New York City) in 1974, Nam June Paik, perhaps the Korean artist best known outside of Korea, rapidly assembled one of his signature pieces to fill a gap in the gallery space. He situated a meditating Buddha image in front of a television monitor, whose mounted camera was trained on the Buddha, so that the Buddha's impassive image reflected back at him. Although Korean by birth, Nam has spent most of his professional life outside of the country, and his influences and collaborators include John Cage, Joseph Beuys, and the Fluxus movement in Europe. The story of modern Korean art is very much that of Korean or Asian themes embodied in international styles and media, and much contemporary Korean sculpture—indeed like Nam's TV Buddha—addresses the tensions inherent in classifications such as Eastern and Western, high and low art, stasis and time.

The story of modern art in Korea began during Japan's colonization of the peninsula between 1910 and 1945. During this period, Korean painters and sculptors studied at the Tokyo School of Fine Arts, where they learned Western styles and media, and the notion of art for art's sake, new in Japan as well, became more common in Korea, with private and corporate sponsors and public galleries becoming significant elements in the development of Korean arts. Kim Pokchin, considered Korea's first modern sculptor, studied in Japan in 1920, and other Korean sculptors began to produce representational sculptures—busts, figures, and nudes—in plaster, bronze, and wood in the early 20th century.

The Korean War brought artistic enterprises to a halt, but by the end of the 1950s, with the nation slowly regathering after the war, the art community in South Korea was thriving to the extent that it experienced movements, rifts, and controversies. The Informal movement of painters and sculptors in the early 1960s fostered abstraction, and sculptors in iron and steel more often used the random elements of their media—rough edges and weld seams, pits, and rust—in their work.

The imperfections achieved by such techniques reference the rusticity of Korean folk arts, appreciated as unique and aesthetically sound in their own right by Chinese and Japanese collectors. Such manipulations, however, are for the Korean artist also an expression of the fragility and harshness that has been the lot of the Korean people throughout its fractious history. Modern Korean art—both literary and visual—is often informed with melancholy and stoicism, and by the 1980s artists expressed these sentiments in a more socially and politically informed idiom.

By the 1980s, with the growth of its economy, South Korea was emerging as a world economic power, although tensions between the military government and labor and human rights groups was reaching a pitch. A trend toward social consciousness and national independence in art developed among progressive artists, who decried politically uninvolved art and the slavish incorporation of foreign style and media.

Lee Young-hak's Standing Figure (1990) embodies modern Korean artistic sensibilities in its conflation of the folkish and modern. As folk art it is a genre scene in a traditional medium-stone—of a woman carrying a bundle on her head, a common scene even in modern Korea. Its execution conforms the media, with an antique approximation, to the subject. That it is displayed among works of less equivocally "contemporary" sculpture casts the object in an ambiguous light, straddling the boundaries of classification that much contemporary Korean art addresses, while still passionately embodying native themes and the nation's long, illustrious heritage of sculptural production. The range of themes and styles encountered in modern Korean sculpture—represented by Nam June Paik's video assemblages at one extreme and rustic images such as

Lee's figure at the other—evidence a vital and innovative perpetuation of this heritage.

LOU MORRISON

See also **Beuys, Joseph**

Further Reading

Ch'oe, Sun-u, *5000 Years of Korean Art*, Seoul: Hyonam, 1979

Han, U-gun, *The History of Korea*, Seoul: Eul-yoo, 1970

Inmul ro ponun Han'guk misul: Sae ch'onnyon t'ukpyol kihoek; Koreans by Koreans: Portraits from Prehistory to Modern Times (bilingual Korean-English edition), Seoul: Samsong Munhwa Chaedan, 1999

Kim, Wonyong, *Art and Archaeology of Ancient Korea*, Seoul: Taekwang, 1986

McCune, Evelyn B., *The Arts of Korea: An Illustrated History*, Tokyo and Rutland, Vermont: C.E. Tuttle, 1962

Smith, Judith, editor, *Arts of Korea*, New York: Metropolitan Museum of Art, 1998

Stooss, Toni, and Thomas Kellein, *Nam June Paik: Video Time/Video Space*, New York: Abrams, 1993

Whitfield, Roderick, editor, *Treasures from Korea: Art through 5000 Years*, London: The British Museum, 1984

KOSHO late 12th or early 13th CENTURY–after 1250 *Japanese*

Kosho apprenticed with his father, Unkei, the founder of the Kei school of sculpture. When Unkei died in 1223, Kosho's older brother, Tankei, inherited his father's sculpture workshop. Kosho continued to work in the family studio. The sculpture produced by the atelier was heavily influenced by Chinese Song sculpture. Typical was the emphasis placed on portraiture during the Kamakura period. Indeed, during this time, portraits of Buddhist priests, such as Kosho's *Kuya Preaching*, were more revered than effigies of the Buddhist gods. Kosho assisted in the replacement of 845 statues for Sanjusangendo Temple in Kyoto. The replacement statues were commissioned in 1251 following a fire in 1249.

Kosho's most famous work of sculpture is the 117.5-centimeter-high statue of *Kuya Preaching*, which dates from the early 13th century. The statue is an excellent example of the new naturalism present in the sculpture of the Kamakura period following the precedents of Song China. This is reflected in the realistic rendering, as opposed to the idealism of the earlier Heian period, of the facial features and details of the clothing.

Kuya was a devout adherent of Amidism, an early expression of Pure Land Buddhism, and founder of the Rokyharamitsu-ji in Kyoto. Kuya traveled extensively throughout Honshu, preaching and chanting the *Namu Anzicki Butsu* while dancing to the accompaniment of drums and bells. In this charming portrait statue,

Kosho illustrates a famous, perhaps apocryphal, story of the priest's conversion to Amidism after he killed a deer and then realized the enormity of his act. Kosho depicted Kuya with his pilgrim's walking staff affixed with one of the deer's antlers to the top and the deerskin wrapped around his waist, a reminder of why Kuya became a priest.

The figure, constructed using the *yosegi* woodblock method, is in a walking stance with the back stooped. A gong is held to the chest by a yoke over the shoulders. Attached to a wire coming out of the priest's mouth are six tiny standing Amida figures symbolizing the *Namu Anzicki Butsu* chant. The statue is considered the climax of Kamakura realism, which sought not only a representation of the physical actions of the individual but also their inner essence in addition to trying "to express the very words which Kuya taught" (see Paine and Soper, 1955).

MARY ANN STEGGLES

See also **China; Unkei; Yosegi-zukuri**

Biography

Born in Heian (now Kyoto), Japan, late 12th or early 13th century. Grandson of the sculptor Kokei and great grandson of the late Heian sculptor, Jocho; fourth son of Unkei, famous Kamakura period sculptor; brothers Tankei, Koun, Koben, Unka, and Unjo also active as Buddhist sculptors. Worked in Heian; additional biographical information scarce. Died after 1250, place of death unclear.

Selected Works

Before 1207	*Kuya Preaching*; painted wood; Rokuhara Mitsu-ji Temple, Kyoto, Japan
1230s	*Amida Buddha*; bronze; Horyu-ji Temple, Kyoto, Japan
1230s	*Koho-Daishi*; painted wood; Toji Temple, Kyoto, Japan
1250s	Replacement statues; painted wood; Sanjusangendo Temple, Kyoto, Japan

Further Reading

Irie, Taikichi, and Jonathan Edward Kidder, Jr., *Masterpieces of Japanese Sculpture*, Tokyo: Bijutsu Shuppan-sha, and Rutland, Vermont: C.E. Tuttle, 1961

"Kosho," in *Kodansha Encyclopedia of Japan*, New York and Tokyo: Kodansha, 1983

Masao, Ishizawa, et al., *The Heritage of Japanese Art*, Tokyo and New York: Kodansha International, 1982

Mason, Penelope, *History of Japanese Art*, New York: Abrams, 1993

Paine, Robert Treat, and Alexander Soper, *The Art and Architecture of Japan*, Harmondsworth, England, and Baltimore, Maryland: Penguin, 1955; 3rd edition, 1981

Roberts, Lawrence, *A Dictionary of Japanese Artists: Painting, Sculpture, Ceramics, Prints, Lacquer*, New York and Tokyo: Weatherhill, 1976

Tazawa, Uytaka, editor, *Biographical Dictionary of Japanese Art*, New York and Tokyo: Kodansha International, 1981

Yamasaki, Shigehisa, editor, *Chronological Table of Japanese Art*, Tokyo: Geishinsa, 1981

Yashiro, Yukio, *2,000 Years of Japanese Art*, New York: Abrams, and London: Thames and Hudson, 1958

JANNIS KOUNELLIS 1936– *Greek*

Jannis Kounellis's oeuvre is tied to his fundamental experience with the *arte povera* (an Italian movement often characterized by the use of ephemeral materials) group active in Italy between 1967 and 1970. While the *arte povera* movement was associated with the artists' use of not only discarded but decrepit, anti-aesthetic materials such as manure and food, Kounellis did not aim to present a violent or aggressive image of reality. Rather, in his multimedia installations he attempted to create a space where nature and artist intermingle, exploring and recovering the primordial and mythical elements.

In common with the international tendencies of Process art (Robert Morris, Bruce Nauman, Richard Serra) and Land art (Michael Heizer, Walter de Maria, Robert Smithson), both of which are rooted in a broadly conceived Conceptualism, Kounellis and the other artists of *arte povera*, including Michelangelo Pistoletto, Mario Merz, and Alighiero Boetti, used various natural and industrial materials to exalt the primary expressiveness of the materials' physical properties: weight, hardness, elasticity, transparency, fluidity, luminosity, and so on. The recovery of material as the primary element allowed a radical redefinition of the traditional borders of art, open to the direct involvement of reality in the work. The artist's intervention involved how these materials were placed and arranged in their exhibition space, whether in a gallery, museum, or outside environment as part of an Environment, Installation, or Happening.

Within the *arte povera* group Kounellis concentrated on attempting to rediscover a general *Mediterraneità* (Mediterraneaness) and a more precise *Grecità* (Greekness) in radical opposition to the modern capitalist society. During the late 1960s, a period of overt social and political tension, the German Joseph Beuys, who wielded a notable influence on Kounellis with his theory of *Scultura sociale* (social sculpture), theorized the functions of the artist as stimulating a spiritual catharsis, as well as serving as a kind of shaman or prophet of a new civilization through the creation of "actions" equivalent to life. Searching for a radical critique of consumer society, Kounellis gravitated around 1965 to the Italian Pop art movement, where he abandoned the language of the urban pop culture and the mass media for that of myth.

In 1967 Kounellis participated in the first exhibition of *arte povera* at La Bertesca Gallery in Genoa, Italy, presenting a container of coal. The contrast between organic elements and metal structures used as containers-exhibitors is a constant in all of his work. Coal recalls the archetype of fire. Much of Kounellis's work revolves around the central theme of fire; he used lit propane gas torches in 1969, and trails of smoke became a constant in his work beginning in 1976. For Kounellis fire is doubly symbolic. It recalls shepherds' bivouacs, symbolizing Mediterranean agricultural-pastoral civilizations, which can be interpreted as fitting antagonists of bourgeois society. In addition, in the Hellenic religion fire symbolized life in dialectical opposition to death. In Kounellis, therefore, the recovery of myth is not nostalgic or intellectual but a reemergence of concrete elements that evoke pastoral civilization: coal, cotton, spindles of wool. Similarly, he frequently used jute sacks filled with grain, rice, coffee, and lentils. For Kounellis these elements resurfaced from the deep reservoir of an authentic collective unconscious as they were lived in his childhood, and then they were raised to a general symbolic level.

Marcel Duchamp, the forerunner of Conceptual art in the 1960s and 1970s, had already used coal in an installation with 1,200 sacks suspended above a brazier for the staging of a Surrealist show in 1938. In turn Kounellis added symbolic significance to the choice of common materials taken from everyday life.

Kounellis's work reached its most extreme consequences when he presented a garden of cactus plants at L'Attico Gallery in Rome in 1967 and 12 live horses in 1969. These works identified completely with life in its continuous variations, the artist working to organize living things so as to exalt their essence, directly attaining the substance of a natural event, such as the inexorability of a growing plant or the instability of an animal's behavior. Kounellis often crossed over into performance art by presenting himself and his activities as a part of the work.

In the 1970s Kounellis turned his attention to the memory of Greek culture. He inserted into his installations fragments of Classical works. Alongside fire, the symbol of vitality, Kounellis placed fragments of a statue, symbols of a lost language essential to the comprehension of the present. Classicism, which in antiquity meant a clear form and an equilibrated interpretation of reality, became in Kounellis an obscure and indecipherable language.

In all of Kounellis's installations objects and actions relate within a fluid relationship, never by rigid opposition. The air acts as a vital link, materializing as emptiness, silence, absence, or fear. Kounellis often uses music and dance to underline the movements of the continuous relationships between objects and actions.

In 1973 Kounellis presented *Apollo* at the Sonnabend Gallery in New York. He placed on a table fragments of a cast of a Classical sculpture as well as a stuffed raven, symbolizing death. Kounellis appeared in Apollo's mask while a flutist performed a Mozart work. In the 1980s Kounellis frequently used steel panels of various sizes contrasting with crude or coarse materials from everyday life such as coal, wood, meat, jute sacks filled with grains, and flowers or synthetic materials such as wax, gold, and lead. He again often included fire or fragments of Classical works.

Kounellis's artistic vicissitudes are emblematic of the crisis regarding the traditional conception of art in the 1960s and 1970s. Art in the second half of the century, profoundly influenced by Postmodern thought, philosophy, and literature, challenged much of Modernism's preconceived notions of historical meaning. Kounellis's performances and installations often provoked public scandal because of the difficulty in understanding his work, which was so completely removed from the conventional notions of sculpture. In spite of the critics committed to supporting the avant-garde work of various groups, the official criticism judged these experiments negatively. This harsh criticism was in fact becoming a new type of academicism; the most serious accusation in regard to Kounellis, as with many other artists of his generation, was that he pillaged the inexhaustible mine of Duchamp's brilliant ideas.

In the late 20th century critics recognized in Kounellis a notable poetic intensity capable of overcoming the most acute crisis in sculpture; his 1986 retrospective at the Museum of Contemporary Art in Chicago was vital in this regard. Kounellis has built a corpus of visionary and imaginative work that is reflective of the poetic force of his generation.

CATERINA BAY

See also **Beuys, Joseph; De Maria, Walter; Duchamp, Marcel; Heizer, Michael; Installation; Merz, Mario; Serra, Richard; Smithson, Robert**

Biography

Born in Piraeus, Greece, 21 March 1936. Studied in Athens until 1956, at which time he moved to Rome where he completed his studies at Accademia di Belle Arti; first one-person show at La Tartaruga Gallery, Rome, 1960; associated with *arte povera*, starting 1967; first solo show at Sonnabend Gallery, New York City, 1972; participated in Venice Biennale, 1976,

1978, and 1984; major exhibitions and retrospectives at Stedelijk Museum, Amsterdam, 1982; Musée d'Art Contemporain, Bordeaux, 1985; Museum of Contemporary Art, Chicago, and Musee d'Art Contemporain, Montreal, 1986; the Art Institute of Chicago, 1990. Awarded fifth Milan Prize, 1974; fifth "Pino Pascali" National Prize in Bari, 1979. Lives and works in Rome, Italy.

Selected Works

1967   *Coal Yard*; coal; temporary installation realized at La Bertesca Gallery, Genoa, Italy

1967   *The Garden*; mixed media; temporary installation realized at L'Attico Gallery, Rome, Italy

1967   *Parrot*; live parrot; temporary installation realized at L'Attico Gallery, Rome, Italy

1969   *Fires*; lit propane gas torches; performance sculpture realized at Iolas Gallery, Paris, France

1969   *Horses*; live horses; temporary installation realized at L'Attico Gallery, Rome, Italy

1969   *Seed bags*; jute, seeds; Kunsthalle, Bern, Switzerland

1970   *My Love*; performance realized at Ricci Palace, Montepulciano, Italy

1973   *Apollo*; plaster, stuffed raven; performance sculpture realized at the Sonnabend Gallery, New York City, United States

Further Reading

Briganti, Giuliano, Willem A.L. Beeren, and Jannis Kounellis, *Kounellis: Via del mare*, Amsterdam: Stedelijk Museum, 1990

Celant, Germano, *Arte povera*, Milan: Mazzotta, 1969; as *Art Povera*, New York: Praeger, 1969

Corà, Bruno, *Jannis Kounellis* (exhib. cat.), Paris: ARC/Musée d'Art Modern de la Ville de Paris, 1980

Corà, Bruno, editor, *Kounellis: Esposizione di paesaggi invernali*, Milan: Charta, 1993

Fuchs, Rudolf Herman, *Jannis Kounellis* (exhib. cat.), Eindhoven, Netherlands: Stedelijk Van Abbemuseum, and London: Whitechapel Art Gallery, 1981

Jacob, Mary Jane, Arnoldo Mondadori, and Thomas McEvilley, *Jannis Kounellis*, Chicago: Museum of Contemporary Art, 1986

Jannis Kounellis (exhib. cat.), s.l.: s.n., 1977

Jannis Kounellis: Oeuvres de 1983 à 1985 (exhib. cat.), Bordeaux, France: Musée d'Art Contemporain, 1985

Kounellis: Il giardino i giuochi (exhib. cat.), Rome: Galleria L'Attico, 1967

Kounellis, Jannis, *Odyssée Lagunaire: Écrits et entretiens, 1966–1989*, Paris: Lelong, 1990

Reviews: Jannis Kounellis (exhib. cat.), New York: Galerie Sonnabend, 1973

Rose, Bernice, *Allegories of Modernism: Contemporary Drawing* (exhib. cat.), New York: The Museum of Modern Art, 1992

MIKHAIL (IVANOVICH) KOZLOVSKY
1753–1802 *Russian*

One of the outstanding masters of the Russian Enlightenment, Mikhail (Ivanovich) Kozlovsky expressed elevated humanistic ideals with a special fervor. The mythological and historical subjects of his works are unified by the themes of heroic exploit, self-sacrifice, and faithful patriotic duty. Stylistically, Kozlovsky's art exemplifies early Russian Classicism, whose orientation toward antiquity was compatible both with Baroque reminiscences and the obvious trends of sentimentalism and romanticism.

At the age of 11, Kozlovsky enrolled in St. Petersburg's Imperial Academy of Arts, which was founded in 1757. He entered the sculpture class of Nicolas-François Gillet, who had been invited to St. Petersburg from Paris and who, in the course of his 20 years of teaching, followed the pedagogical system of the French artistic school. The talented painter and master of academic drawing, Anton (Pavlovich) Losenko, who arrived from Rome in 1769 and headed the life drawing class, played an equally important role in Kozlovsky's education. Having received various awards for his studies, Kozlovsky was honored with a gold medal and a scholarship to study abroad in 1773.

The sculptor perfected his craft in Italy (1773–80) through copying antique art, attending classes at the French Academy and the Academy of St. Luke, and studying celebrated paintings and sculptures in the galleries, palaces, and churches of Rome. All of these activities found reflection in Kozlovsky's journal, which he sent to his homeland and which has been preserved in the archives of the Academy of Arts (see Petrov, 1977). He was most profoundly impressed by the creations of Michelangelo. It is no accident that in his written request for an extension of his Italian scholarship, Kozlovsky mentioned his desire "to learn more from Michelangelo." Evidence of this influence can also be found in the drawing *Russian Bath* (1778), which depicts a multitude of naked male and female figures, seemingly inspired by the titanic power of the images at the Vatican's Sistine Chapel. One must also note that his contemporaries, as well as art critics of the first third of the 19th century, often compared the Russian sculptor to Michelangelo. "Kozlovsky was a true genius," wrote Vasily Ivanovich Grigorovich, conference-secretary of the St. Petersburg Academy of Arts in 1826. "Fiery imagination, intelligent composition, and decisive execution distinguished everything emerging from the hand of this famous artist. He was

a renowned draftsman. An admirer and imitator of Michelangelo, Kozlovsky, like that celebrated sculptor, was sometimes carried away by the desire to display his knowledge of anatomy and was excessive in his portrayal of muscles."

Kozlovsky's period of creative flowering began in the 1780s, when he executed bas-reliefs and allegorical figures to decorate the interiors of the Marble Palace in St. Petersburg and the marble statues *Catherine II as Minerva* and *Vigil of Alexander of Macedon*. During his stay in Paris (1788–90), the sculptor created such famous works as *Apollo* (*Shepherd with a Hare*) and *Polycrates*. In these works, Kozlovsky displayed a wide creative range and the ability to convey with equal mastery a state of idyllic harmony and dramatic incandescence of passions. Such characteristics appear more clearly in his maquettes, which reside now in the State Russian Museum, St. Petersburg. These compositions in terracotta (*Mercury Brings Bacchus to a Nymph for Upbringing*, *The Death of Astyanax*, and *Ajax Shielding the Body of Patroclus*) are considered to be the artist's masterpieces. The compositions *Rinaldo Abandons Armide* and *The Ruin of Ippolit*, carved on wooden boards, are distinguished by Kozlovsky's genuine virtuoso execution.

The statue *Yakov Dolgoruky Destroying an Imperial Decree*, executed twice by Kozlovsky in marble, serves as one of the most interesting examples of Russian Enlightenment Classicism. The subject, who lived in the epoch of Peter I, is surrounded here by a multitude of allegorical attributes, which underscore the heroic significance of the legendary story of how the courageous and just senator decided to destroy an order that was burdensome for the nation. The bronze monument to the distinguished military leader Alexander Vasilievich Suvorov continued Kozlovsky's patriotic theme; it became one of the most famous monuments in St. Petersburg, second to the equestrian statue of Peter I (the Great) by Étienne-Maurice Falconet, and entered the ranks of great Russian art.

ELENA V. KARPOVA

See also **Falconet, Étienne-Maurice; Russia and Soviet Union**

Biography

Born in St. Petersburg, Russia, 26 November 1753. Studied at Imperial Academy of Arts in St. Petersburg, 1764–73, under Nicolas-François Gillet; received gold medal and scholarship to study abroad, 1773; in France received title of academician at the Marseilles Academy of Painting and Sculpture, 1780; in Paris, 1788–90, as commissioner for exchange students on scholarship from St. Petersburg Academy of Arts; returned to Russia; received title of academician, 1794; taught sculpture at Academy of Arts, became professor, 1795, then senior professor, 1799. Died in St. Petersburg, Russia, 18 September 1802.

Selected Works

1785   *Catherine II as Minerva*; marble; State Russian Museum, St. Petersburg, Russia

ca.   *Vigil of Alexander of Macedon*; marble;
1785–88 State Russian Museum, St. Petersburg, Russia

1789   *Apollo* (*Shepherd with a Hare*); marble; Pavlovsk Palace, Pavlovsk, Russia; Hermitage, St. Petersburg, Russia

1790   *Polycrates*; bronze; State Russian Museum, St. Petersburg, Russia

mid   Maquettes for subjects of Homer's *Iliad*:
1790s   *The Death of Astyanax* and *Ajax Shielding the Body of Patroclus*; terracotta; State Russian Museum, St. Petersburg, Russia

1796   *Hymen*; marble; State Russian Museum, St. Petersburg, Russia

1796   *Minerva and the Genius of the Arts*; bronze; State Russian Museum, St. Petersburg, Russia

1797   *Cupid with an Arrow*; marble; State Russian Museum, St. Petersburg, Russia

1797   *Yakov Dolgoruky Destroying an Imperial Decree*; marble; State Russian Museum, St. Petersburg, Russia; another version: State Tretyakov Gallery, Moscow, Russia

1799   *Hercules on Horseback*; bronze; State Russian Museum, St. Petersburg, Russia

1800   Tombstone of P.I. Melissino; bronze; Alexander Nevsky Lavra, St. Petersburg, Russia

1801   Monument to Alexander Vasilievich Suvorov; bronze; Suvorov Square, St. Petersburg, Russia

1801   *Psyche*; marble; State Russian Museum, St. Petersburg, Russia

Further Reading

Androssov, Sergei, "Kozlovsky, Mikhail (Ivanovich)," in *The Dictionary of Art*, edited by Jane Turner, New York: Grove, and London: Macmillan, 1996

Gosudarstvennyi Russkii Muzei (Russian State Museum), *Skul'ptura, XVIII–nachalo XX veka: Katalog* (Sculpture, 18th–Early 20th Centuries: Catalogue), Leningrad: Iskusstvo, 1988

Kovalenskaia, Nataliia Nikolaevna, *Russkii klassitsizm: Zhivopis', skul'ptura, grafika* (Russian Classicism: Painting, Sculpture, Graphic Art), Moskow: Iskusstvo, 1964

Petrov, Vsevolod Nikolaevich, *Mikhail Ivanovich Kozlovskii*, Moscow: Iskusstvo, 1977

Riazantsev, I.V., "Novoe o tvorchestve M.I. Kozlovskogo (New Findings on the Works of M.I. Kozlovsky)," in *Sovetskaia skul'ptura* (Soviet Sculpture), vol. 8, Moscow: Sovetskii Khudozhnik, 1984

Riazantsev, I.V., "Ikonografiia i atribut v rabotakh M.I. Kozlovskogo (Iconography and Attributes in the Works of M.I. Kozlovsky)," in *Trudy Akademii Khudozhestv SSSR* (Works of the Academy of Arts of the USSR), vol. 3, Moscow: 1985

Russkaia terrakota epokhi klassitsizma (Russian Terracotta of the Classical Period; exhib. cat.), Leningrad: Gos. Russkii Muzei, 1988

ADAM KRAFT *ca.* 1455/1460–1509 *German*

In contrast to other Nuremberg artists of his day, relatively little is known about Adam Kraft. The oldest references to him come from Johann Neudörfer, the city writing master and arithmetician. He mentioned Kraft in his *Report on Nuremberg Artists and Artisans*, which appeared in 1547. Kraft was probably born between 1455 and 1460 in Nuremberg. Since he did not need to apply for Nuremberg citizenship, his parents may have been from Nuremberg.

According to legend, which cannot be verified, Kraft was connected to the future bronze caster Peter Vischer the Elder and the future woodcarver Sebastian Lindenast through a childhood friendship. As it is told, the three began drawing together as boys. Kraft probably completed his training as a stone mason with the construction of the east choir of St. Lorenz, one of the two large parish churches in the city, which was completed in 1477. He probably began his apprenticeship—which lasted approximately five years—at the age of 14, as was customary at the time; he was then a journeyman for two years. It is assumed that Kraft also received training as a sculptor and master builder so he could create sketches, draw plans, and produce ground plans and drafts. Only with these abilities could he have had the opportunity to assume a supervisory role in construction. Another period as a journeyman, this one lasting about a decade, followed. Kraft traveled to Swabia, probably in the Neckar River region; perhaps to Ulm, where work on the cathedral was underway at the time; and to the upper Rhine region. It is presumed that he was in Strasbourg as well. The Cathedral of Strasbourg was among the major construction sites of the time, so the blossoming church masons' guild in Strasbourg—which was the most significant of its kind in the German empire—was in great demand.

Sources confirm that Kraft returned to Nuremberg in 1490 when he got married. A fountain on the facade, which used a dragon as a waterspout, distinguished his large residence. It is assumed that the figure of the animal, now lost, was created by Kraft.

His first major work in his hometown was the Schreyer-Landauer monument, produced between

1490 and 1492 on the facade of the east choir in the Church of St. Sebaldus. At the commission by councilman Hans Imhof the Elder, Kraft also produced the tabernacle in the choir of the Church of St. Lorenz. The structure was more than 60 meters high and reached up into the vaults. In terms of beauty and size, it is equal, if not superior, to its predecessors in the Cathedrals of Ulm and Strasbourg. This type of towerlike tabernacle was widespread from the beginning of the 13th century and is represented in the Swabian-Allemanic region more than anywhere else. A contract between the donor and Kraft established the exact iconography and mode of representation. In fact, it even set provisions for the care and storage of the filigree after its completion. The architectonic scaffolding, which tapers in toward the top, displays a series of reliefs of the Passion of Christ and numerous figures of the apostles, prophets, saints, and angels. The collection of images symbolizes the salvation brought about by Christ's sacrificial death. The entire structure is supported by three almost life-size, kneeling male figures that are realistically sculpted and are without precedent in older Nuremberg sculpture. One of the figures is considered to be a self-portrait of Kraft, and the other two are interpreted as representations of his journeymen. The integration of the figures in the holy story depicted in the sculpture, and their significance as bearers of the sacrarium with its great ritualistic meaning, documents the artists' newfound sense of their own worth during this time. Kraft received 700 ducats for the production, as well as 70 ducats as "honorarium," which clearly indicates the thorough satisfaction of the patron.

In the following years, he took on a series of sculptural assignments for heraldic panels and inscribed cartouches for the city. Some remain today, such as the relief from 1494/95 on the imperial stable of the Nuremberg castle; the sculptural work for the city weighing house from 1497; and the 1501/03 decoration of the portal of the Mauthalle, a large warehouse and customs office in the city. In addition, he produced a tabernacle in 1500 for the Cistercian Convent Church of Kaisheim near Donauwörth in Swabia, which is now lost. In Nuremberg, Kraft was also entrusted with the composition of entire courtyard architecture projects and tracery galleries, including figural decoration for bourgeois residences. In addition, a series of figures was created by private assignment for the facades of the houses in the city, such as the almost life-size Annunciation group created in 1499 for the residence of Sigmund Oertel. The Peringsdörffer family ordered an epitaph for the transept of the Augustine monastery; for the Rebeck family, Kraft chiseled a pictorial stone epitaph in 1500. Both are now on display in the Church of Our Lady. In 1503 he created at the commission of Matthäus Landauer a multifigured epitaph depicting the crowning of the Virgin Mary. Around 1500, Hans Imhoff donated a relief featuring the scene of the strangulation of St. Beatrice for the Church of St. Lorenz. In 1504, Kraft produced a tympanum relief for the Church of St. Sebaldus, which depicts the finding of the Holy Cross by St. Helena, and in 1506 he completed some carved work for the armory representing Christ's bearing of the cross, which has since been moved to the Church of St. Sebaldus.

With one or two journeymen, Kraft headed a small trade business, which developed amazing production power around the turn of the century. Around 1503, he began experiencing financial difficulties. His wife died in August of that year, and although he remarried, his financial situation continued to worsen. In 1505, Kraft was in debt to Imhof, and he apparently had a child out of wedlock. During this time, his physical health also began to deteriorate, and on 25 February 1508, the church master in charge of accounts at the Church of Our Lady reported that Kraft was no longer capable of working because of physical weakness. He had been assigned to create the gable for the small choir of St. Michael on the west side of the church. In all likelihood, the job was completed by his journeymen; because of the lack of documentation and the fundamental renovation of this architectural portion, it remains unclear which accomplishments may be attributed to Kraft.

Between 1506 and 1508, the *Seven Stations of the Cross* were produced in Kraft's studio; they consisted of reliefs decorated with free sculptural figures that lined the path from the city wall to the St. Johannis Friedhof (St. John's Cemetery), which was situated outside the city. Whereas the first three pictorial works were characterized by closely placed figures, the remaining ones are characterized by a reduced number of figures and a newfound clarity and penetration in the representation.

Despite his persistent illness and the weakness of old age, Kraft was consulted one last time for a building assignment. The wealthy master of the mint, Hans Rosenberg from Schwabach, had donated a chapel dedicated to St. Anne as an extension of the north side of the nave in the parish church of that city. The dome was slated for 1509. The construction presented unforeseen technical difficulties, and Kraft's counsel was sought for a solution. He was brought to Schwabach in January of 1509 and died shortly thereafter. His body was transported to Nuremberg and buried on 21 January 1509. In memorial, the death knells of the Church of St. Lorenz and the Church of St. Sebaldus rang on that day. Even before his burial, Imhof, to whom Kraft had mortgaged his house in 1505, had his claim on the property legally filed. On 20 February it was awarded to him by the city judge. The sources provide no information as to the fate of Kraft's widow.

Kraft's work distinguishes itself through its breadth and diversity. It employed a repertory of forms still strongly influenced by the late Gothic period and combined it with modern innovations of sculptural three dimensionality to achieve a new quality in plastic composition. Kraft was an artist who acted as an arbitrator in the field of sculpture between the late Gothic and Renaissance periods.

FRANK MATTHIAS KAMMEL

See also **Germany: Gothic–Renaissance; Vischer Family**

Biography

Born probably in Nuremberg, Franconia, Germany, *ca.* 1455/1460. Training probably in Nuremberg, in Swabia and upper Rhine region; after many years as journeyman, returned to Nuremberg, *ca.* 1490, where he worked from then on; known primarily for religious commissions, including Schreyer-Landauer monument and tabernacle for Church of St. Lorenz, Nuremberg. Died in Schwabach near Nuremberg, Franconia, Germany, January 1509.

Selected Works

1490–92   Schreyer-Landauer monument; sandstone; Church of St. Sebaldus, Nuremberg, Germany

1493–96   Tabernacle; sandstone; Church of St. Lorenz, Nuremberg, Germany

1497   Relief for city weighing house; sandstone; Germanisches Nationalmuseum, Nuremberg, Germany

1498/99   Peringsdörffer epitaph; sandstone; Church of Our Lady, Nuremberg, Germany

1506–08   *Seven Stations of the Cross*; sandstone; Germanisches Nationalmuseum, Nuremberg, Germany

Further Reading

Bauer, Hans, and Georg Stolz, *Engelsgruss und Sakramentshaus in St. Lorenz in Nürnberg*, Königstein im Taunus, Germany: Langewiesche, 1974

Kammel, Frank Matthias (editor), *Adam Kraft*, Nuremberg, Germany: Germanisches Nationalmuseum, 2001

Schleif, Corine, "The Many Wives of Adam Kraft: Early Modern Workshop in Legal Documents, Art-Historical Scholarship, and Historical Fiction," *Georges-Bloch-Jahrbuch des Kunsthistorischen Institutes der Universität Zürich* 5 (1998)

Schwemmer, Wilhelm, *Adam Kraft*, Nuremberg, Germany: Carl, 1958

SCHREYER-LANDAUER MONUMENT
Adam Kraft (ca. 1455/1460–1509)
1490–1492
sandstone, originally polychromed
h. 2.5 m
Church of St. Sebaldus, Nuremberg, Germany

The Schreyer-Landauer monument is the oldest documented work by Adam Kraft. The work was a donation by local Nuremberger Matthäus Landauer and his uncle Sebald Schreyer, an influential merchant and respected supporter of the arts and sciences in the imperial-free city. Landauer's house was a meeting point for many scholars, and together with Sebastian Cammermeister he published the famous *Schedel's World Chronicle* (1493).

Since 1453, the Landauer and Schreyer families had owned burial plots between two buttresses on the exterior wall of the east choir in the Church of St. Sebaldus. At first, the walls above the gravestones were decorated with painted scenes from the Passion. However, in the year 1490 both families decided to have the dilapidated fresco replaced with stone reliefs representing the suffering and the glorification of Christ. They assigned Kraft this task, which, amazingly, he was able to accomplish in approximately 20 months. Kraft received the sum of 200 florins in compensation, as well as 4 additional florins for his wife, which suggests that the clients were highly satisfied with the results.

Similar to a winged altar, the monument consists of a large slab resting against the wall of the choir as well as two smaller side pieces on the buttresses. In front of the center of the main slab, a stone arm holds a tall iron lantern with a pyramidal top, which represents the eternal light. Chiseled into the arm itself is the year the work was finished, 1492. In the corners of the three relief surfaces, figures of prophets stand atop small columns. The image of Christ carrying the cross appears on the viewer's right-hand side. The figure of Christ collapsing under the weight of the cross is effectively raised from the surface, which is filled with compressed figures and landscape elements. Several of the individuals depicted are directly involved in Christ's suffering: although he has fallen to his knees, they pull him farther along by a cord wrapped around his loins, pull at his hair, and brutally beat him. Other figures, however, appear rather unconcerned and talk among themselves. The exemplary role of the pious observer is assigned to the group surrounding the Virgin Mary, who is forced to watch the scene from an elevated ledge. The middle tablet shows the descent from the cross in the background of a nature landscape; in the foreground two men appear simultaneously returning home from the hill of Golgotha and the burial scene itself. The crosses on the hill are already vacant. The ladder, with which Christ's body was being concealed, is just being pulled away, and the people—Nicodemus and Joseph of Arimathea are particularly singled out—return once again to the valley. On the left-hand side of the picture, Nicodemus and Joseph of Arimathea grasp Christ's body firmly and lower it into the grave. The women protagonists and St. John wring their hands mournfully. The Resurrection of Christ appears in the tablet on the left-hand side. Various scenes of the reappearance of the risen Christ are depicted in the background, although dominant among them is the figure of the risen Christ between two soldiers. As in the carrying of the cross, the central perspective of the scene concentrates itself on the Son of God.

With its narrative series of scenes from the Passion and the image of the Resurrection, the monument assumes a special place within its genre during the Late Medieval period, as devotional motifs such as the "Man of Sorrows," the Mass of St. Gregory, and images of the Virgin Mary and the saints were more customary. The series of images must be read from right to left, counter to the Western tradition, because the columns of the Church of St. Sebaldus were already decorated with images chronologically depicting Christ's suffering, beginning on the north side and continuing over the east side of the church onto its south front, which were taken into account during the planning. The images on the tomb had to follow the same direction, particularly since the path around the church, which was surrounded by a cemetery at that time, was also used as a processional path. Even while it was being built, the wall of reliefs was protected by a roof and closed off with an iron gate. On the bottom edge

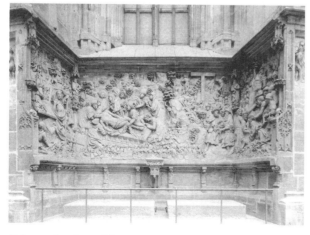

Schreyer-Landauer Monument
The Conway Library, Courtauld Institute of Art

of all three reliefs, the benefactors, their relatives, and family crests are depicted in a smaller scale to reflect their lesser significance within the relief.

Kraft's reliefs are narrative and have been imbued with certain qualities from painting. The overabundance of details, as well as the turbulent interplay of light and shadow, is among the standards that characterized relief sculpture at the end of the Medieval period. The sculptor probably used graphic models. A particularly striking similarity exists between the relief of the bearing of the cross and Martin Schongauer's copper engraving of the same subject.

In terms of style, the tremendous work reveals both a knowledge of the most modern achievements of sculpture in the Upper Rhine region and the fact that Kraft was a part of the Nuremberg sculptural tradition, which combined established themes and styles optimally with skills gained outside the region. In the Schreyer-Landauer monument, a great master announced his arrival on the sculptural scene: he was capable of composing with both clarity and scope and possessed a remarkably natural sense of space as well as an understanding of corporeality and volume. Strength and dramatic energy characterize his sculptural forms. Both Kraft's architectural skills and his facility for decorative composition are shown at their best in this work of his early career.

The figures of the two men engaged in conversation in the middle relief have sparked debate. Both of the superbly portrayed old men, Nicodemus with his tool and Joseph of Arimathea with the crown of thorns, are returning from the mount of Calvary and appear as the primary figures in a hitherto unknown scene. Within the context of the customary pictorial language, this homecoming presents a significant part of the iconography, as the scene replaces the usual depiction of the Crucifixion. Among others, comparisons with the presumed self-portrait of Kraft on the tabernacle in the Nuremberg Church of St. Lorenz and with portraits of Landauer by Albrecht Dürer have led to the conclusion that both figures were endowed with the physical traits of the sculptor himself and one of the patrons. The very size of these figures within the scenery of the Passion supports this theory. However, since there is no definitive proof to this end, the scene remains a subject of contention.

The function of this sort of memorial epitaph erected over graves was to inspire the viewer both to linger before a pictorial representation of the holy story and to pray for the deceased. In this instance, the need of a proud bourgeoisie for representation comes together with the desire for reverence and the forgiveness of one's sins. This is made particularly clear by the donors' arrangements with the Bishop of Bamberg, Heinrich III, which offered a pardon of sins to all those who prayed for the dead at this location on particular days.

FRANK MATTHIAS KAMMEL

Further Reading

500 Jahre Grabmal der Familien Schreyer und Landauer von Adam Kraft, Nuremberg, Germany: Bauhütte St. Sebald, 1992

Schleif, Corine, "Nicodemus and Sculptors: Self-Reflexivity in Works by Adam Kraft and Tilman Riemenschneider," *The Art Bulletin* 75/4 (1993)

KRITIOS BOY

Anonymous/ca. 480 BCE

marble

h. 1.16 m

Acropolis Museum, Athens, Greece

By an accident of archaeological preservation, the two-thirds life-size marble statue of a naked young man known as the Kritios Boy is the earliest preserved free-standing statue to exhibit the characteristic stance that art historians call *contrapposto* (a natural pose with the weight of one leg, the shoulder, and hips counterbalancing one another), and thus is the first known work to be conceived in the "Classical tradition." It may not, in fact, have been the earliest, nor need its anonymous master have been the one who invented the pose; there is evidence to suggest that vase painters may have discovered it first. The significance of this discovery, whoever made it, cannot be overestimated; with the *contrapposto* of the Kritios Boy went the idealized aesthetic of the human figure in the art of the High Classical period and ultimately the whole course of the Western figural tradition. From the *Augustus of Prima Porta* to Michelangelo's *David* and Rodin's *Age of Bronze*, every figure that assumes a *contrapposto* stance would now strike the eye as Classical, thereby forbidding us ever to consider the Kritios Boy as anything but Classical, even though in reality he is as much the last of one line (of archaic kouroi) as the first of another.

There is some question about the Kritios Boy's precise provenance on the Athenian acropolis, which underwent major excavation in the latter portion of the 19th century. It had long been assumed that the statue was found in the so-called Persian destruction debris (*Perserschutt*), a stratigraphic level that contained the material destroyed by the Persians during their sacks of the acropolis in 480/79 BCE and which was deliberately buried by the Athenians soon after the "barbarian" had been repelled. This is the same debris field that yielded the majority of archaic statuary from the acropolis, in-cluding most of the korai figures. If this is the case, then the advanced style of the Kritios Boy suggests that it had been freshly created and erected on the acropolis when the Persians came and that, accordingly, it should be dated close to the Persian destruction—hence the date of about 480 BCE. However, a recent theory (Hurwit, the most complete study of the Kritios Boy to date) argues that the statue was not found in the *Perserschutt* and that it dates to just after the Persian Wars. Give or take a few years either side of 480 BCE for its date, it is clear that the piece is transitional between two distinct styles, the Archaic and the Early Classical.

The statue as it now exists is incomplete, missing its arms below the biceps, its right leg below the knee, and both of its feet and ankles. The wrong head had once been attached and later removed; the present head is more in keeping with the proportions and style of the figure, and surely belongs, although it was repositioned in the mid 1980s. The vacuous expression for which this statue is frequently faulted is owed to the fact that its once-inlaid eyeballs are missing; when in place, the figure would no doubt have seemed alert and uncannily lifelike. The hair is long, like that of the kouroi, but worn rolled up around a fillet, in a fashion typical for boys in the Early Classical period. The finely engraved hair suggests that the sculptor may also have worked in bronze; if so, his interest in conveying a sense of potential for movement would be all the more explicable because bronze lends itself more readily to the portrayal of figures in movement than does marble. The misnomer "Kritios Boy" is due to the one-time attribution of this statue to Kritios, who, with Nesiotes, sculpted the *Tyrannicides*, a famous Early Classical bronze statuary group that is preserved only in Roman copies. There remains a rather superficial resemblance to the younger tyrant slayer, but the association with Kritios has generally been abandoned, although the appellation has stuck. The statue's identity and purpose are unknown. He has been identified both as a victorious athlete and as Theseus; the latter theory has received little support. What is certain is that the statue functioned as a votive dedication, probably to Athena, much like other objects, including all of the korai, which crowded the acropolis during the Archaic period.

The most important aspect of the statue, its *contrapposto* pose, consists of a subtle asymmetrical reordering of various body parts to reflect a shift in weight that naturally occurs when a person stands at ease. (Those who persist in describing the *contrapposto* as a descriptive shorthand for "walking" ignore the fact that the line of the hips does not perceptively shift as one is walking; it rotates slightly but remains parallel to the ground.) The line of the hip shifts to an oblique angle, raised just slightly over the "weight leg" (the

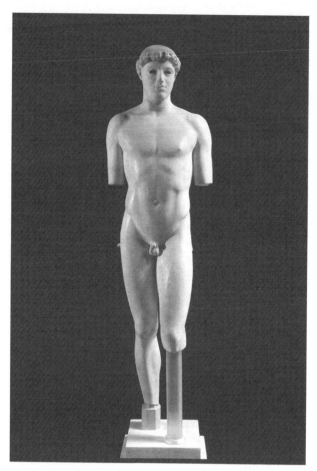

Kritios Boy
© Nimatallah / Art Resource, NY

boy's left), which is straightened, and correspondingly dropped just slightly over the "free leg" (the boy's right), which is allowed to bend. To compensate, the upper body shifts as well: the shoulder over the weight leg/raised hip compensates by dropping, whereas the shoulder over the free leg/lowered hip compensates by rising. The resulting pattern of body parts responding to body parts can be summarized as chiasmatic (X-shaped); the intangible effect is an uncanny bestowal of apparent life that had not previously been seen in sculpture. In the Kritios Boy, the lifelikeness is further enhanced by the slight tilt to the side of both the shoulders and the head, marking a final, irreversible break with the rigid pose of the kouros, itself a format almost certainly borrowed from Egypt, and thereby resulting in a definitive, new, purely Greek statement. Add to this the effect of the marble's translucency, especially when properly lighted, which causes the stone surface to appear soft and pliable to the touch, and the mimicking of life is complete.

How and why did this discovery (or so it seems after the fact, but which at the time was an invention

in every sense) occur, when it had not occurred in 2,500 years of a continuing monumental figurative tradition in Egypt and the Near East? The phenomenon of the drive toward perfect naturalism between about 600 and 480 BCE has inspired hyperbolic expressions from Gombrich's "The Greek Revolution" to "The Greek Miracle," the title of an exhibition that included the Kritios Boy. This question is ultimately unanswerable; attempts to credit enlightened patrons or the political zeitgeist rather than the artists themselves are subject to the criticism of being circular arguments. However it came about, it will always remain an impressive fact that, among advanced ancient civilizations, only the Greeks thought (or dared) to make monumental statues that possessed no godlike qualities, unless beauty be considered godlike, to justify their presence; for the first time, they created statues that looked just like the creators' vainglorious selves at one nondescript, unselfconscious moment of their existence.

MARY STIEBER

See also **Greece, Ancient; Kore and Kouros**

Further Reading

Boardman, John, *Greek Sculpture: The Classical Period: A Handbook*, London and New York: Thames and Hudson, 1985
Buitron-Oliver, Diana, et al., *The Greek Miracle: Classical Sculpture from the Dawn of Democracy: The Fifth Century B.C.*, Washington, D.C.: National Gallery of Art, 1992
Gombrich, E.H., *Art and Illusion: A Study in the Psychology of Pictorial Representation*, New York: Pantheon Books, 1960; 2nd edition, Princeton, New Jersey: Princeton University Press, 1969
Hurwit, Jeffrey M., "The Kritios Boy: Discovery, Reconstruction, and Date," *American Journal of Archaeology* 93 (1989)
Hurwit, Jeffrey M., *The Athenian Acropolis: History, Mythology, and Archaeology from the Neolithic Era to the Present*, Cambridge and New York: Cambridge University Press, 1999

JOHANN (HANS) KRUMPER *ca.* 1570–1634 *German*

As a bronze sculptor and designer of architecture and architectural decor, Johann Krumper had a formative influence on art in the Bavarian ducal court during the transition from late Mannerism to Early Baroque. Among his sculptures, the *Madonna and Child* on the facade of the Munich Residenz, Germany, and the statues of the tomb of Louis IV in the Cathedral of Our Lady in Munich are his best-known works. Their orientation toward simpler local formal traditions demarcates the turn of southern German Early Baroque artists away from Mannerism.

Krumper came from a family of woodcarvers in Weilheim, and he entered into an apprenticeship under Hubert Gerhard at the Munich court in 1584. As an apprentice, Krumper took part in the decoration of the new wing of the Residenz around the Grottenhof (grotto courtyard) and probably in the production of Gerhard's over-life-size terracotta figures for the Church of St. Michael in Munich. In 1590 Krumper was granted a traveling scholarship, while committing himself at the same time to a lifetime of service under Duke William V (*r.* 1579–97; *d.* 1626). From 1594 on, Krumper received a yearly salary from the court. After the abdication of William V in 1597, however, the only engagement he was able to procure was that of William's private architect and sculptor. Finally, in 1609, he was engaged by the successor to the throne, Duke Maximilian I (*r.* 1597–1651), for whom he worked until about 1630.

Krumper's training in court service taught him to emulate the model of the artist capable of working in many areas, which individuals such as Friedrich Sustris embodied at the Munich court. Krumper worked not only as a sculptor in stucco, wax, and bronze, but equally as a designer for goldsmith's work and as a painter, interior designer, and, occasionally, as an architect. William V seems to have availed himself of this versatility, particularly before Krumper entered into court service in 1609.

The period of Krumper's large sculptural assignments began in 1609. Maximilian employed him primarily as the bronze sculptor and interior designer for the construction of his new Residenz, which had been in planning since 1606. Designs for stucco decorations and ornamental painting and architectural sculpture also fell in Krumper's domain, yet he did not hold a position within the court workshops comparable to that of his predecessor Sustris, whose designs were mandatory for all court artists, and Krumper had no directorial function outside of his own sculpture workshop. The series of bronzes produced on the duke's assignment began with the funerary monument, erected in 1611, for Cardinal-Bishop Philip William of Regensburg, a son of William V who had died young. The cardinal is shown kneeling, clad in broadly sweeping vestments, and with a pleading gaze turned upward toward Christ on the cross. Krumper succeeded in animating a traditional tomb theme with human intensity and warmth. The noble portraiture and the garment's finely detailed surface, shaped by many flat depressions to achieve an almost glittering effect, are characteristic of his style.

Duke Maximilian had the facade of the newly built wing of the Residenz, which faced the city, ornamented with a programmatic series of figures in bronze. In the center is the *Madonna and Child*, with the Madonna portrayed as the lady and protectress of Bavaria, or *patrona Boiariae*. The eternal light at her feet confers upon her the character of a house altar facing outward. On the portal gables recline the four cardinal virtues, Prudence, Justice, Fortitude, and Temperance, which, given Maximilian's early absolutist political agenda and sense of duty, assumed a central position along with crests, emblems, and ornamentation. Krumper created these monumental bronzes in 1614–16. In the Virtues, Krumper's predilection for the Classical modeling of his figures in both motion and their proportions generally emerges clearly. The Madonna no longer shows the formal language of Mannerism in her calm, broadly attenuated figure, but is closer to local traditions, in which Krumper was rooted through his own heritage.

Krumper's most outstanding monument in terms of dynastic political representation is the tomb of Emperor Louis IV the Bavarian, with its great number of figures. Louis IV (*d.* 1347) was the only native of Wittelsbach to achieve imperial honors. Because Louis had died in excommunication, Maximilian, as one of the most adamant fighters for the Counter Reformation, considered it his personal cause to honor and reestablish this ancestor. Krumper's assignment was to integrate the marble slab of the Gothic tomb visibly and to introduce portrait statues of Duke William V's father and grandfather. The funerary monument, with its dark and dramatic color combination of bronze and black marble, characteristic for the Early Baroque period, was erected in 1622 in the central location of the choir entrance of the Cathedral Church of Our Lady. Older bronze sculptures from a tomb monument, which William V had wanted to display at the Church of St. Michael in Munich, were recycled for the occasion: the four standard-bearing knights on bended knee by Gerhard and Carlo di Cesare del Palagio. The personi-

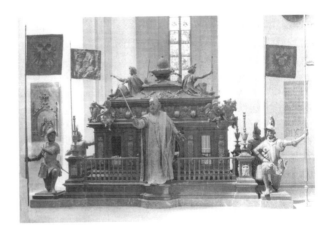

Tomb of Ludwig the Bavarian, (Emperor Ludwig IV), Cathedral Church of Our Lady, Munich
The Conway Library, Courtauld Institute of Art

fication of imperial power in war and peace, which crown the monument, and the over-life-size portrait statues of William IV and Albert V, with their tranquil, representative standing motif, are among Krumper's most impressive figures.

Krumper was also commissioned for smaller bronze sculptures for the Residenz's interior. Among them the four fountain figures representing the four seasons for the Grottenhof merit particular attention.

Already in the 16th century, bronze reliefs were sought after for epitaphs. Krumper created a couple of such reliefs, primarily for the tombs of courtiers. These include the predella-like (a predella is a painted panel, usually small, belonging to a series of panels at the bottom of an altarpiece) commemorative plaque for the bronze caster Martin Frey (*d.* 1603), tomb monuments for the conductor of court music Wilhelm di Lasso and the ducal physician Jakob Burchardt, and additional reliefs for the grave of Councillor Philipp Götz (*d.* 1627), ordered during the latter's lifetime. The reliefs depict traditional funerary themes such as the lamentation and the resurrection of Lazarus in a detailed and striking manner, as if Krumper had faithfully translated his graphic models into relief. The nuanced modeling and simple, psychologically penetrating figure formation lend these pieces a calm intensity that is far removed from the taste in reliefs held by the generation of his teachers.

Several designs document Krumper's activity in the construction of new wings of Maximilian's Residenz. In addition to the preparatory drawings for the *patrona Boiariae* and a portal cornice with personifications of the cardinal virtues, small, rather sketchlike designs, often of figural details for stucco decorations, have been preserved and attest to Krumper's authorship of the stucco pieces in the wings of the imperial court. The figural stuccos of the so-called *Kaisertreppe* (Imperial Staircase), the main vault of the court chapel, and the stuccos on the ceiling of the Reiche Kapelle can be convincingly connected with Krumper. A collection of designs from the Munich court workshops, discovered in 1921, pertain mainly to commissions for Sustris, Gerhard, and Krumper (Krumpers Nachlass, Stadtmuseum, Munich). Among other architectural and decorative designs are a conspicuous number of designs for bronze pieces commissioned by Maximilian that have been preserved (the Four Season Fountains [Ferdinandeum, Innsbruck, Austria]; Martin Frey epitaph [Städtische Kunstsammlungen, Augsburg, Germany]; and funerary monuments for Duke Ferdinand and Emperor Louis IV, as well as figures on the facade of the Residenz [Stadtmuseum, Munich]).

Krumper's work as a designer for goldsmiths has also been documented elsewhere, but only a single relief, depicting the annunciation of the shepherds, has been identified. Two wax figures on reliquaries (St. Tiburtius and St. Valerianus) were probably modeled by Krumper himself. Krumper is widely recorded as creating wax figures—which usually served as votive gifts after births, for example—although cabinet pieces and reliquaries have also been documented.

DOROTHEA DIEMER

Biography

Born in Weilheim, Upper Bavaria, Germany, *ca.* 1570. Apprenticed to Hubert Gerhard, at the Munich court, from 1584; committed himself to lifetime service in the ducal house, 1590; traveled to Italy, with trip financed by the court; received official salary from the court, from 1594; became private architect and sculptor of William V, Duke of Bavaria, after the duke's resignation in 1597; taken into service at the court of his successor, Maximilian I, Duke of Bavaria, 1609; worked for the court as a sculptor and designer of interior decoration, until *ca.* 1630. Died in Munich, Germany, 1634.

Selected Works

1611 Figures of the four seasons, for Grottenhof fountain, Residenz, Munich, Germany; bronze; Bayerisches Nationalmuseum, Munich, Germany

1611 Tomb of Cardinal-Bishop Philip William of Regensburg; bronze; Regensburg Cathedral, Bavaria, Germany

1612 Relief for tomb of Wilhelm di Lasso; bronze; Church of St. Peter, Munich, Germany

1614–16 *Madonna and Child* and *Four Cardinal Virtues as Portal Crowning*; bronze; west facade, Residenz, Munich, Germany

1615 Tomb of Dr. Jakob Burchardt; bronze; Cathedral of Our Lady, Munich, Germany

1615–17 Tomb of Sigismund Lösch; bronze; parish church, Hilgertshausen, Germany

ca. 1616 Decoration of the *Kaisertreppe* (Imperial Staircase) and the Reiche Kapelle ceiling; stucco; Residenz, Munich, Germany

1622 Tomb of Emperor Louis IV (Ludwig IV) the Bavarian; bronze; Cathedral of Our Lady, Munich, Germany

Further Reading

Berg, Karin, *Der "Bennobogen" der Münchner Frauenkirche: Geschichte, Rekonstruktion, und Analyse der frühbarocken Binnenchoranlage*, Munich: Tuduv-Verlagsgesellschaft, 1979

JOHANN (HANS) KRUMPER *ca.* 1570–1634

Diemer, Dorothea, "Hans Krumper," in *Wittelsbach und Bayern* (exhib. cat.), edited by Hubert Glaser, vol. 2, part 1, *Um Glauben und Reich: Kurfürst Maximilian I*, Munich: Hirmer, Piper, 1980

Diemer, Dorothea, "Bronzeplastik um 1600 in München: Neue Quellen und Forschungen, Teil II," *Jahrbuch des Zentralinstituts für Kunstgeschichte* 3 (1987)

Diemer, Dorothea, "Krumper, Hans," in *The Dictionary of Art*, edited by Jane Turner, New York: Grove, and London: Macmillan, 1996

Dischinger, Gabriele, "Quellen zur Planung und Ausführung der Weilheimer Stadtpfarrkirche," *Ars bavarica* 33/34 (1935)

Feuchtmayr, Karl, "Krumper, Hans," in *Allgemeines Lexikon der bildenden Künstler von der Antike bis zur Gegenwart*, edited by Ulrich Thieme, Felix Becker, and Hans Vollmer, vol. 22, Leipzig: Engelmann, 1928; reprint, Leipzig: Seemann, 1978

Feulner, Adolf, "Hans Krumpers Nachlaß: Risse und Zeichnungen von Friedrich Sustris, Hubert Gerhard, und Hans Krumper," *Münchner Jahrbuch der bildenden Kunst* 12 (1922)

Geissler, Heinrich, editor, *Zeichnung in Deutschland: Deutsche Zeichner, 1540–1640* (exhib. cat.), Stuttgart, Germany: Staatsgalerie Stuttgart, 1979

L

GASTON LACHAISE 1882–1935 *French-American*

Gaston Lachaise was a complex and daring sculptor whose singular vision was, and remains, highly controversial. Extraordinarily driven, he concentrated on many themes, including standing and reclining women, acrobats, and floating figures. He also completed numerous portraits, bas-reliefs, and abstracts. Described by many as obsessed with the glorification of the female and the vitality of Eros, Lachaise deified through distortion the primal powers of the archetypal woman, with original modern-primitive representations of pendulous breasts and mountainous flesh. Critics acknowledge his standing women as his greatest works and his most significant contributions to modern sculpture.

Born in Paris, Lachaise was a recognized prodigy at an early age, having begun to carve wood at his father's cabinetmaking shop at age five. He entered the École Bernard Palissy at 13 and the prestigious Académie Nationale des Beaux-Arts at 16, often exhibiting his work at the Salon des Artistes Français, where he was frequently a finalist for the prestigious Prix de Rome.

Strongly influenced by the Symbolists, Lachaise read Paul Verlaine, Arthur Rimbaud, and Charles Baudelaire and spoke of his early "driftings" through the Montmartre section of Paris. He also found inspiration as a youth in the erotic and monumental works of Auguste Rodin, then greatly revered by the French avant-garde.

At 20 Lachaise met Isabel Nagle, an American woman temporarily in Paris, who quickly became the singularly most significant influence in his life. Lachaise explained that Nagle was "the primary inspiration which awakened my vision and the leading influence that has directed my forces" (see Cummings, 1928). Abandoning his studies, Lachaise worked for renowned jeweler and glassmaker René Lalique to earn money for passage to join Nagle in the United States.

In January 1906 Lachaise arrived in Boston, where he remained for six years, working closely under the supervision of academic sculptor Henry Hudson Kitson on a variety of Civil War monuments. Independently, he also began to carry out his own sculptural experiments in clay during this time. These small pieces can be seen as modern interpretations of the Paleolithic fertility statues such as the *Venus of Willendorf* and *Venus of Lespurges*, and the later formal poses and gestures of Hindu goddess statues, all with Isabel as muse. One major work completed during these early years was the sensual bronze statuette *Woman Arranging Hair* (1910–12).

Lachaise followed Kitson to New York in 1912 and in so doing fully launched his career. Through Kitson he met Arthur B. Davies, who invited Lachaise to exhibit his *Nude with Coat* (1912) in the famous Armory Show of 1913. This small piece, perhaps stylistically influenced by Rodin's monumental *Balzac*, is a dramatic depiction of a mature woman whose nude body is exposed through the front opening of a full-length cloak clasped together at her hip.

Shortly following the Armory Show, Lachaise began a long working relationship with the highly regarded sculptor Paul Manship, assisting him on several works, including the J. Pierpont Morgan Memorial, in

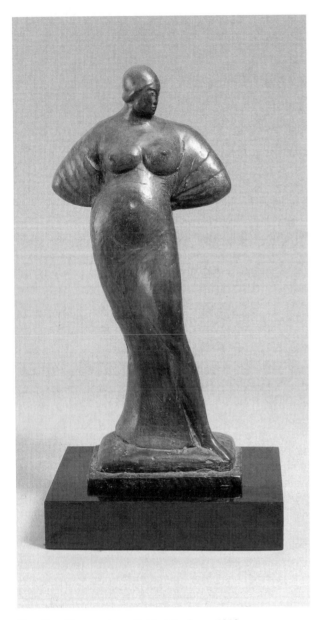

Standing Woman, Arms Behind Back, ca. 1918
Courtesy of The Lachaise Foundation, Photograph Courtesy
of Salander-O'Reilly Galleries, New York

the Metropolitan Museum of Art in New York City.
Through this association Lachaise received numerous
commissions for decorative work, including a frieze
of singing and dancing youths for the American Telephone and Telegraph Building in New York. Later architectural reliefs include panels for the RCA Building
and the International Building at Rockefeller Center
(1931).

Often working all day and into the evening at the
Manship studios, Lachaise developed on his own time
a series of exotic statues of standing women, all approximately 30 centimeters in height, including *La*

Force Éternelle/Woman with Beads (1917), and *Standing Woman with Arms behind Her Back* (1918). His
most important statue from this time is the life-size,
then-patinated plaster called *Elevation*, which he began
in 1912. He continued to rework this piece through to
its final bronzed state in 1927, fully destroying it at
least once.

Lachaise had his first solo exhibition February
through March 1918, at the Stephan Bourgeois Gallery
in New York. A landmark, critically praised exhibition, it included an early version of *Elevation* and a
series of animal pieces. It was followed by a second
exhibition two years later. Bourgeois continued to represent Lachaise until 1922, when low sales convinced
the sculptor to move to the Kraushaar Gallery, where
his work appeared in a group exhibition from January
through February 1924. By 1927 Alfred Stieglitz represented Lachaise at The Intimate Gallery, first exhibiting the final bronze *Elevation* and the large-scale
plaster *Floating Woman*, one of a series of floating and
acrobatic figures.

Throughout the 1920s members of New York's
avant-garde embraced Lachaise, particularly Scofield
Thayer and James Sibley Watson, publishers of the
influential literary and artistic journal *The Dial*. Partly
to finance the increasing demands of his family during
this period, Lachaise produced a number of commissioned portrait busts, most of which are now recognized as significant contributions to the art form. These
include *Scofield Thayer* (1923), *E.E. Cummings*
(1924), *Georgia O'Keeffe* (1927), *Marianne Moore*
(1924), and *John Marin* (1928).

One of Lachaise's most significant contributions in
the 1930s was the bronze *Heroic Woman*, which can be
seen as a triumphant culmination of all of the Lachaise
goddess figures. At 2.25 meters, it is a powerful and
forceful representation of the female archetype, with
feet firmly on the ground, head high, and hands de-
fiantly on her hips.

In his final years Lachaise concentrated on a series
of reclining women, several with a metaphorical
mountain theme materialized by organically shaping
the torso in stone to represent a landscape form. In
1934 he created the monumental cement *La Montagne
Héroique* for the George L.K. Morris estate in Lenox,
Massachusetts, in which the artist fully realized this
theme for outdoor display.

Lachaise also focused on a series of Expressionist
abstracts with overtly sexual themes in the 1930s, most
of which could not be exhibited during his lifetime.
Significant among these are the bronzes *Dynamo
Mother* (1933) and *In Extremis* (1934). Reminiscent of
Rodin's *Iris, Flying Figure* in their sexual explicitness,
these rarely shown sculptures remain highly controversial.

From January through February 1935 the Museum of Modern Art in New York City mounted a retrospective of Lachaise's work, the first of his lifetime. This long awaited exhibition displayed all his major works, including *Elevation, Floating Woman, Heroic Woman, La Montagne Héroique*, and *Man*, along with numerous drawings.

LINDA PASACHNIK

See also **Manship, Paul; Rodin, Auguste**

Biography

Born in Paris, France, 19 March 1882. Fourth son of renowned cabinetmaker Jean Lachaise. Won entrance to École Bernard Palissy, 1895; studied sculpture under Alphonse Emmanuel Moncel and director Jean-Paul Aube; entered Académie Nationale des Beaux-Arts, 1898; studied in atelier of sculptor Gabriel Jules Thomas; exhibited in Salon des Artistes, and briefly conscripted into military, 1899–1903; left Beaux-Arts to work for René Lalique, 1904–05; arrived in Boston, January 1906; worked for Henry Hudson Kitson, 1906–12; moved to New York, 1912; worked with Kitson and Paul Manship, eventually became Manship's assistant; exhibition, the Armory Show, 1913; became United States citizen, 1916; first American exhibition, Stephan Bourgeois Galleries, 1918; second exhibition, Stephan Bourgeois Galleries, 1920; joined C.W. Kraushaar Gallery, 1922; first exhibit there, 1924; Art Institute of Chicago exhibit, 1925–26; Alfred Stieglitz exhibited work in The Intimate Gallery, 1927; exhibition at Brummer Gallery, 1928; Museum of Modern Art (New York) retrospective, 1935. Died in New York City, United States, 17 October 1935.

Selected Works

1910–12 *Woman Arranging Hair*; bronze; Lachaise Foundation, Boston, and Salander-O'Reilly Galleries, New York City, United States

1912 *Nude with Coat*; bronze; Lachaise Foundation, Boston, and Salander-O'Reilly Galleries, New York City, United States

1912–17 *Elevation*; bronze; Albright-Knox Art Gallery, Buffalo, New York, United States; Art Institute of Chicago, Chicago, Illinois, United States; Metropolitan Museum of Art, New York City, United States; St. Louis Art Museum, St. Louis, Missouri, United States

1917 *La Force Éternelle/Woman with Beads*; bronze; Smith College Museum of Art, Northampton, Massachusetts, United States

1918 *Equestrienne*; bronze; Corcoran Gallery of Art, Washington, D.C., United States

1918 *Standing Woman with Arms behind Her Back*; Lachaise Foundation, Boston, and Salander-O'Reilly Galleries, New York City, United States

1922 *The Peacocks*; bronze, gilt with basalt base; Metropolitan Museum of Art, New York City, United States

1923 *Scofield Thayer*; bronze; Metropolitan Museum of Art, New York City, United States

1924 *E.E. Cummings*; bronze; Estate of Marion Cummings, Fogg Art Museum, Cambridge, Massachusetts, United States

1924 *Marianne Moore*; bronze; Metropolitan Museum of Art, New York City, United States

1927 *Floating Woman*; bronze (cast 1935); Museum of Modern Art, New York City, United States

1927 *Acrobat/Upside Down Figure*; bronze; Fogg Art Museum, Cambridge, Massachusetts, United States

1927 *Georgia O'Keeffe*; alabaster; Metropolitan Museum of Art, New York City, United States

1928 *John Marin*; bronze; Museum of Modern Art, New York City, United States

1930–35 *Man*; bronze (cast 1938); Chrysler Museum, Norfolk, Virginia; Kykuit, Rockefeller Estate, Pocantico Hills, New York, United States; New Orleans Museum of Art, New Orleans, Louisiana, United States

1931 Architectural relief; limestone; RCA Building, Rockefeller Center, New York City, United States

1932 *Heroic Woman*; bronze; Franklin D. Murphy Sculpture Garden, University of California at Los Angeles, Los Angeles, California, United States; Museum of Modern Art, New York City, United States; Hirshhorn Museum and Sculpture Garden, Smithsonian Institution, Washington, D.C., United States

1933 *Dynamo Mother*; bronze; Museum of Modern Art, New York City, United States; Lachaise Foundation, Boston and Salander-O'Reilly Galleries, New York City, United States

1934 Architectural relief; limestone; International Building, Rockefeller Center, New York City, United States

1934 *In Extremis*; bronze; Lachaise Foundation,

Boston, and Salander-O'Reilly Galleries,
New York City, United States
1934   *La Montagne Héroique*; cement;
Frelinghuysen-Morris Museum, Lenox,
Massachusetts, United States

Further Reading

Ames, Winslow, "Gaston Lachaise, 1882–1935," *Parnassus* 8 (April 1936)

Bourgeois, Louise, "Obsession of Gaston Lachaise," *Artforum* 30 (April 1992)

Carr, Carolyn Kinder, and Margaret C.S. Christman, *Gaston Lachaise: Portrait Sculpture*, Washington, D.C.: National Portrait Gallery, Smithsonian Institution, 1985

Cummings, E.E., "Gaston Lachaise," *Creative Art* 3 (August 1928)

Eglinton, Laura, "Exhibition Review," *Art News* 33 (February 1935)

Gallatin, Albert Eugene, *Gaston Lachaise: Sixteen Reproductions in Collotype of the Sculptor's Work*, New York: Dutton, 1924

Goodall, Donald B., "Gaston Lachaise, Sculptor," (dissertation), Harvard University, 1969

Hobhouse, Janet, *The Bride Stripped Bare: The Artist and the Female Nude in the Twentieth Century*, New York: Weidenfeld and Nicolson, and London: Cape, 1988

Hunter, Sam, and David Finn, *Lachaise*, New York: Cross River Press, 1993

Kirstein, Lincoln, *Gaston Lachaise, Retrospective Exhibition* (exhib. cat.), New York: Museum of Modern Art, 1935

Kramer, Hilton, "On Gaston Lachaise," in *Gaston Lachaise: Sculpture and Drawings* (exhib. cat.), New York: Salander-O'Reilly Galleries, 1998

Nordland, Gerald, *Gaston Lachaise: The Man and His Work*, New York: Braziller, 1974

The Sculpture of Gaston Lachaise, New York: Eakins Press, 1967

Seldes, Gilbert, "Hewer of Stone," *The New Yorker* (4 April 1931)

LAMENTATION AND DEPOSITION GROUPS

Sculptors have treated the subject of the Deposition (or Descent from the Cross) and the Lamentation over the body of Christ in Christian sculpture, although not as often as the Crucifixion. From the standpoint of theological history, its popularity throughout western Europe at the end of the Middle Ages was probably due to the diffusion of texts such as the *Meditations* of Pseudo-Bonaventura. Beghard communities in the Low Countries and numerous French communities found the theme particularly appealing. In Spain, too, a close correlation existed between the presence of certain theological texts and the diffusion of these iconographic subjects, as witnessed by the wooden sculptures made in Catalonia. But unlike elsewhere in Europe, Spanish artists also often used the subject in monumental funerary art and in the tympanums of church portals. In Italian art the term *pietà* is sometimes used to define Deposition scenes (as in the case of works by Guido Mazzoni and Niccolò dell'Arca). This discussion focuses on only those pietàs that are truly Deposition groups—that is, several figures grieving over the dead body of Christ—and does not consider those (such as Michelangelo's) with only two figures, the Virgin Mary and Christ.

Marble, stone, and wood are the most common materials used in renditions of this subject, but rare examples exist in alabaster, ivory, and metal. Liturgical and devotional objects such as reliquaries also present the subject. In Italy sculptors executed many such groups in terracotta, both glazed and unglazed.

The Lamentation has a standard set of characters: the Virgin Mary, Saint John the Evangelist, Mary Magdalene, Joseph of Arimathea (a member of the Sanhedrin who did not vote for the execution of Christ), and Nicodemus. According to Christian tradition Nicodemus, aided by Joseph, gathered Christ's lifeless body in his arms. Some sculptures also include men using tongs to pull out the nails that fixed the body to the cross. Only rarely do Lamentation groups show the two thieves crucified with Jesus. One such example is the Catalonian-style wooden group known as the *Deposition of Erille-La-Vall* (12th century, Museo Episcopal de Vich, Barcelona). With the presence of the two thieves, a Lamentation group can include eight figures. The number of characters appearing in a Lamentation, as well as other aspects of the group, has differed across time and place.

One of the best-known early examples of Western artistic culture is the *Deposition* sculpted by Benedetto Antelami around 1178 for the cathedral in the northern Italian city of Parma. The work's composition (perhaps part of a pulpit, or more likely a parapet) still reflects the Byzantine scheme, and the symmetrical ordering of the various elements, particularly the close parallel folds of the drapery, is also typically Byzantine. But some iconographic elements (for instance, the small central figures representing the Roman Catholic Church and the Jewish community) reflect French influence, and the clypeate images of the sun and moon circumscribed by corollas and of flying angels resembling winged Victories are of Classical origin. However, the sculptor's taste for elegant vegetal ornamentation—on the corollas, in the refined polychrome intaglio work on the border, and even on the cross, in which an acanthus leaf replaces the traditional board supporting Christ's feet—seems already Gothic. The style of the figures—their vigorous modeling, the fullness of the massive strong-jawed heads, broad hands, and big feet emerging from the grooved drapery—is altogether original. The scene's dramatic composition, underlined by the movement of the lateral figures toward the center, is most effective. This movement heightens the tension around the deposition and channels the viewer's gaze to the immense long-armed figure of Christ; oddly, his arms are longer than those of the cross. The most interesting figures are placed closest to him. From the statically composed lateral figures, the viewer's gaze is gradually drawn to the central group's powerful but restrained dynamism. The poignant gesture by which the Virgin's hand touches her son's right hand expresses her tender love. This gesture can be interpreted in two ways; she seems to be supporting his body for an instant, but perhaps it is Jesus who is caressing Mary's suffering face for the last time.

The early-13th-century *Deposition* in the Cathedral of Tivoli, not far from Rome, is made of wood. Although unfinished, it displays a finely modeled structural arrangement. The figures seem unrelated to other local art but close to northern Romanesque. Likewise, the beautiful *Deposition* (13th century) in the Cathedral of Volterra in polychrome wood seems influenced by the northern Italian style and shows an analogy with the art of Benedetto Antelami. This group has only five figures: Jesus in the center, two men lifting him down from the cross, the Virgin Mary on the left, and Saint John the Evangelist on the right. The tenderness of Mary's and John's gestures recalls the detail in the Parma marble. The beautifully colored and carefully arranged drapery draws the viewer's attention away from the dramatic event. The composure of the gestures, the spirituality of the faces, and the beauty of the seemingly sleeping Christ give this group an inner serenity, the attitude that Christians are supposed to take in the face of death.

Another interesting piece is a small ivory diptych carved in France or Germany around 1350 with six scenes from the *Passion of Christ*. The stories are to be read clockwise, starting from the lower left-hand corner. One depicts the *Deposition*, and the next the *Lamentation over the Dead Christ*.

One of Europe's major art centers around 1400 was the city of Pilsen, in western Bohemia. Strategically situated, Pilsen was a crossroads between east and west, linking Nuremberg and Prague, the Danube valley and Saxony. An important artistic tradition originated in the region in the 13th century due to the presence of several important monasteries: the Cistercians at Plasy and Nepomuk to the south and north and the Benedictines at Kladruby to the west. The turn of the 15th century saw an explosion of sculpture portraying the Virgin Mary, the saints, and the Deposition. In the late 14th century sculptors often portrayed Mary with a sweet face and characteristically serpentine body. Such statues, for instance, the Pilsen Madonna carved around 1384 by the Master of the Madonna of Krumlov, combine idealism and realism. But in a radical

change that began in 1420, naturalism won out over formal perfection, and the emphasis switched to Christ's suffering. Master sculptors trained in Prague who moved to Pilsen in those years may have precipitated the shift. The monumental *Crucifixion* by the Master of *The Crucifixion of Saint Bartholomew* illustrates the new manner and was probably the work of two or three sculptors. The artist who sculpted the Christ must have been familiar with mystical 14th-century crucifixions and with the works of the Master of the Church of Tyn, who was executing a Calvary about 1420. Another hand probably created the statue of the Virgin Mary, whose style reflects Netherlandish influence. The figure of Saint John differs from both of these and is accordingly attributed to a third anonymous sculptor. The Master of *The Crucifixion of Saint Bartholomew*, together with Hans Multscher of Ulm and Jacob Kaschauer of Vienna, was one of the most important sculptors working in central Europe in the first half of the 15th century.

The *Tájó Pietà* (preserved in Budapest) dates from 1480 to 1490. This relatively small composition in painted wood shows the influence of Netherlandish painting. Christ's body is positioned on a diagonal line, as it is in a Veit Stoss engraving and in a relief on the high altar in Kraków Cathedral. The Hungarian group comprises four characters. The Virgin Mary and Mary Magdalene support Christ's left arm while Saint John supports his body. An intense dynamism animates John's windswept mantle and Mary Magdalene's body, which leans toward Christ. Also noteworthy is the careful rendering of the drapery.

An example from the Italian Renaissance is the marble and glazed terracotta *Tabernacle* created by Luca della Robbia between 1441 and 1443 for St. Luke's chapel in the Florentine hospital of Santa Maria Nuova. This work contains several architectural elements. In the tympanum God is shown with an open book on which appear the Greek letters alpha and omega. Below a polychrome frieze decorated with three cherubs is a lunette containing a pietà composed of four figures. At the center is the dead Christ, supported by an angel; the Virgin Mary is on the left and Saint John is on the right. Mary faces forward, looking directly at the viewer, as her right hand indicates her son's body. Her face is serene, as though she understands the mystery of death. John is shown in profile, turning toward his master; his expression is pained and his hands are clasped in prayer.

Guido Mazzoni's terracotta *Pietà*, created in 1480 and preserved in Modena at the Church of S. Giovanni della Buona Morte, includes eight polychrome figures divided into three distinct and balanced groups: two figures on the left, four in the center, and two on the right. Rendered realistically, they are contemplating the dead Christ. The Virgin Mary is on her right knee, as if she had suddenly collapsed, and is aided by John and Mary Magdalene.

Among the most famous sculptural groups of the Italian Renaissance is Niccolò dell'Arca's terracotta *Pietà* at the Church of S. Maria della Vita in Bologna. Dell'Arca arranged the seven figures in a different order than they are now. This group differs from all the others in the dramatic expressions of the faces, which are contracted in pained grimaces. All four women are open-mouthed, as though screaming rather than sorrowing. The garments of the two on the right, one of whom is certainly Mary Magdalene, are in wild disarray, as if the women had been racing in a high wind. The composed attitudes of the two men temper the pathos of the female figures. The figure of Saint John is beautiful, grief-stricken and almost lost in his thoughts, his right hand under his chin. The whole human tragedy is erased in the contemplation of the dead Christ, who has been laid out in a dignified manner on a rectangular support. The serene face, the head lying delicately on a fine pillow, and the hands clasped over the loincloth all give Jesus a dignity that transcends the human dimension. The subject itself relates the sculptures directly to the northern tradition, and in them the crude naturalism of the Ferrara school of painting combines with a dynamic Burgundian-style expressionism. Based on the Ferrara influence, many scholars ascribe this group to the artist's late period, the last decade of the 15th century.

The passage of time and the succession of styles saw a gradual reduction of the characters in the lamentation scene.

In the 16th century many Italian sculptors treated this subject. One of the most noteworthy was the southern artist Giovanni da Nola, who worked from 1540 to 1549 on the crowded *Deposition* at the Church of S. Maria della Grazia in Naples. A group of nine characters appears in the foreground, in the lower part of the composition. Above, the three crosses stand out in a landscape overcast by storm clouds.

European Mannerism produced equally interesting statues, in particular the beautiful works created by Juan de Juni in the first half of the 16th century. Dating slightly later is Baccio Bandinelli's group *The Dead Christ Supported by Nicodemus* (begun in 1554 by Baccio's son Clemente). This unusual composition, made for the artist's tomb and now in the Church of Santissima Annuziata in Florence, is based on rigorously geometric forms but is pervaded by emotion.

A work from Mexico probably from the late 16th or early 17th century and now in the collection of the Hispanic Society of America in New York ranks as the most bizarre and original *Deposition*. It consists of a tiny wooden skull that opens on a golden hinge, revealing two tiny but perfectly clear sculptures. Only five centimeters high, the skull is actually a rosary bead. Inside, the scene on the left side is a *Crucifixion*; the one on the right is a *Deposition*. The *Crucifixion* appears here because it is the last of the five Sorrowful Mysteries of the rosary. The Deposition is not usually included among the 15 Mysteries but often appears in prayer beads. Here it is represented by an animated scene in the upper part, as if the greatest sorrow for the death of Christ were felt in Heaven. In the lower part are four figures: Christ, the Virgin Mary, Saint John, and Mary Magdalene.

GIOVANNA CHECCHI

See also **Antelami, Benedetto; Bandinelli, Baccio; Juni, Juan de; Mazzoni, Guido; Michelangelo (Buonarroti); Multscher, Hans; Niccolò dell'Arca; Reliquary Sculpture; Robbia, Della, Family; Stoss, Veit**

Further Reading

L'art roman (exhib. cat.), Barcelona: Conservatoire des Arts du Livre, 1961

Clifton, James, *The Body of Christ in the Art of Europe and New Spain, 1150–1800* (exhib. cat.), Munich and New York: Prestel, 1997

Forsyth, William H., *The Pietà in French Late Gothic Sculpture: Regional Variations*, New York: Metropolitan Museum of Art, 1995

Kreuzzieger, Milan, "Gothic Art in Western Bohemia," *Apollo* 13 (May 1996)

Kuhn, Charles Louis, *German and Netherlandish Sculpture, 1280–1800: The Harvard Collections* (exhib. cat.), Cambridge, Massachusetts: Harvard University Press, 1965

Mojzer, Miklós (editor), *A Magyar Nemzeti Galéria Régi Gyujteményei*, Budapest: Corvina, 1984; as *The Hungarian National Gallery: The Old Collections*, translated by Elizabeth Hoch, translation revised by Elizabeth West, Budapest: Corvina Kiadò, 1984

Museu, Frederic Marès, *Catàleg d'escultura i pintura dels segles XVI, XVII, i XVIII: Època del Renaixement i el Barroc*, Barcelona: Ajuntament de Barcelona, 1996

Nash, Steven A., *Painting and Sculpture from Antiquity to 1942*, New York: Rizzoli International, 1979

Pope-Hennessy, John, *An Introduction to Italian Sculpture*, 3 vols., London: Phaidon, 1963; 4th edition, 1996

Szmodis-Eszláry, Éva, *The Treasures of the Old Sculpture Collection*, Budapest: Museum of Fine Arts, 1994

Trésors des abbayes Normandes (exhib. cat.), Rouen, France: Musée des Antiquités, 1979

LAOCOÖN AND HIS SONS

Hagesandros, Polydoros, and Athenodoros of Rhodes late 1st century BCE–early 1st century CE (Roman copy after an original from the 2nd century BCE) marble
h. 2.44 m
Vatican Museums, Rome, Italy

The monumental marble statue known as the *Laocoön* group represents the Trojan priest Laocoön struggling to free himself and his two young sons from the pair of snakes sent to punish him. The statue is the only large-scale sculptural representation of Laocoön's punishment to survive from Antiquity, although the subject was depicted in other media, such as Greek vase painting, Pompeian wall painting, and gems. It is generally accepted today that the *Laocoön* group was carved during the late 1st century BCE or early 1st century CE and was based on a lost Hellenistic bronze group of a similar composition.

The fate of the Trojan priest was the subject of a tragedy by Sophocles in the 5th century BCE. The story also appeared in works by Arctinus, Bacchylides, and Euphorion. None of these works is extant, but brief accounts are known from later sources. In the Greek literary tradition, Laocoön, who served the god Apollo, married and fathered children, although these pursuits were forbidden by the god. Apollo punished him for his disobedience and hubris.

The Roman poet Virgil provides a different (and more fully preserved) account of the Laocoön story in the *Aeneid* (*ca.* 26–19 BCE). Laocoön, here a priest of Neptune, is punished not for his moral transgressions but rather for his attempt to alter destiny. During the Trojan War the Achaeans, unable to capture Troy by military force, devised a plan by which they could trick the Trojans into capitulation, constructing a hollow wooden horse in which the soldiers could hide. Laocoön warned the Trojans of the dangers of the wooden horse and was punished for his mistrust by Minerva, who sent a pair of large serpents that mortally wounded the priest and his sons while they were sacrificing at an altar. For fear of offending the goddess further, the Trojans brought the wooden horse into the city, thus ensuring their downfall.

The ill-fated Laocoön and his sons are carved in a style that is conventionally known as Hellenistic Baroque. This style, used primarily for the representation of gods and heroes, is characterized by figures that are arranged in complex groupings and that display intense emotion. The statue represents Laocoön and his sons at the height of their agony. In front of an altar the highly muscled nude figure of the bearded priest contorts as he attempts to disentangle himself from the snakes that are entwined around his own arms and legs as well as around those of the two boys that flank him. The three figures are inextricably bound by the writhing serpents, and the theatrical poses and the anguished facial expressions convey the pathos of the scene.

The Roman author Pliny the Elder provides the names of the sculptors responsible for carving the marble group in his *Natural History* (77 CE) in a passage discussing how the fame of artists who work alone overshadows that of those who work in teams. Pliny cites as an example the *Laocoön* (a sculpture belonging to his patron, the future emperor Titus), a work that he singles out as "superior to all others of painting and sculpture, carved by the eminent artists Hagesandros, Polydoros, and Athenodoros of Rhodes, from one block of stone, according to a plan agreed upon in advance." The *Laocoön* group in the Vatican collection is generally considered to be the same as that discussed by Pliny, although it is not carved from one block of stone but from several pieces that were carefully joined. The three Rhodians mentioned by Pliny were virtuoso marble carvers who specialized in the production of large-scale mythological groups in the Hellenistic Baroque style. They were also responsible for the Sperlonga sculptures, an ensemble of four mythological groups found during the excavation of a seaside villa at Sperlonga (south of Rome), one of which bears the inscribed names of the artists.

The villa in which the Sperlonga sculptures were found is known to have belonged to the Emperor Tiberius (*r.* 14–37 CE), and as a result many scholars date the workshop of Hagesandros, Polydoros, and Athenodoros to the early 1st century CE. A Tiberian date for the Sperlonga sculptures and the *Laocoön* group, how-

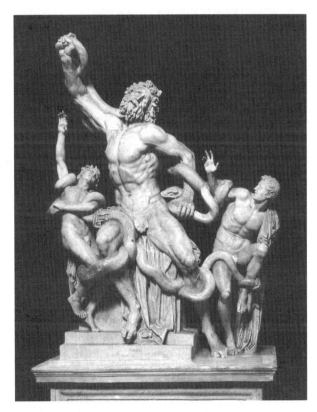

Laocoön and His Sons, Roman copy, perhaps after Agesander, Athenodorus, and Polydorus of Rhodes (former state of restoration)
© Giraudon / Art Resource, NY

ever, cannot be determined with certainty, and it is possible that both ensembles are earlier works. The block of Luna marble that is incorporated into the statue provides the earliest possible date for the *Laocoön* group, as these quarries, which are located outside Rome, were not exploited until the 30s BCE.

The *Laocoön* group was discovered on 14 January 1506 on the Esquiline hill in Rome, near the sites of the imperial palaces of Nero and Titus. Among the first to view the *Laocoön* group were Michelangelo and the architect Giuliano da Sangallo, who immediately identified it as the statue described by Pliny. Pope Julius II purchased the statue and installed it in the Belvedere courtyard at the Vatican, where, except for a brief tenure in France between 1797 and 1816, it has remained. Although generally well preserved, the newly found statue lacked several of its extremities, of which the right arm of the priest was the most significant loss. Soon after the recovery of the statue, the priest's arm was restored extending upward, a restoration that eventually proved to be erroneous. The ancient arm, which was recovered in 1906 and reattached to the statue in 1942, is sharply bent over Laocoön's head.

The *Laocoön* group was well known outside of Rome not only through drawings and engravings but also through sculptural copies of various sizes, ranging from full size to miniature, made from bronze, marble, plaster, and terracotta. The naturalistic anatomy and agonized expressions of the figures were highly praised by and profoundly influential for Michelangelo and his contemporaries, as well as for successive generations of artists and writers. The statue was the subject of Gotthold Ephraim Lessing's critical essay of the same title concerning the distinct limits of the visual and literary arts (1766), and the precise nature of the emotion expressed by Laocoön was debated throughout the 18th and 19th centuries.

JULIE VAN VOORHIS

Further Reading

Andreae, Bernard, *Laokoon und die Gründung Roms*, Mainz, Germany: Von Zabern, 1988
Bieber, Margarete, *Laocoön: The Influence of the Group since Its Rediscovery*, New York: Columbia University Press, 1942; revised and enlarged edition, Detroit: Wayne State University Press, 1967
Brummer, Hans Henrik, *The Statue Court in the Vatican Belvedere*, Stockholm: Almqvist and Wiksell, 1970
de Grummond, Nancy T., and Brunilde S. Ridgeway (editors), *From Pergamon to Sperlonga: Sculpture and Context*, Berkeley: University of California Press, 2000
Haskell, Francis, and Nicholas Penny, *Taste and the Antique: The Lure of Classical Sculpture, 1500–1900*, New Haven, Connecticut: Yale University Press, 1981 (for the post-antique history of the statue)
Magi, F., "Il ripristino del Laokoonte," *Atti della Pontificia Accademia Romana d'Archeologia* 3/9 (1960)
Winner, Matthias, Bernard Andreae, and Carlo Pietrangeli (editors), *Il Cortile delle Statue: Der Statuenhof des Belvedere im Vatikan*, Mainz: Philipp von Zabern, 1998

LATIN AMERICA

When Europeans arrived in the Caribbean in the late 15th century, they encountered a multiplicity of native populations whose cultures ranged from sedentary agricultural to fully nomadic. Some of the semisedentary groups—in particular, the Taino from Cuba, Jamaica, and other islands—boasted sophisticated sculptural traditions that included figural and abstract fiber, stone, and ceramic forms associated with farming and ritualized propitiation.

Spaniards came upon an even more dramatic range of mainland sculptural traditions. The Aztec culture in central Mexico, dominated by the Mexica at Tenochtitlán (site of present-day Mexico City), possessed a strong sculptural heritage. While the ruling Mexica probably produced no sculpture themselves, they gathered at Tenochtitlán specialized artisans from throughout the empire who worked in a variety of materials and techniques. These artists produced monumental abstract and symbolic stone sculpture—the archetypal *Coatlicue* ("She of the serpent skirt"), for example—as well as highly naturalistic and representational imagery, such as stone conch shells and lifelike coiled serpents. They also created architectural ornamentation, sculpted ceramics, gold and silver castings, jade and other semiprecious stone carvings, and wooden sculpture and furnishings.

The Inca of the Andean Highlands, centered at what would become the colonial city of Cuzco, Peru, fashioned intricate hammered and cast-silver and gold figures and jewelry, as well as small symbolic stone fetishes. They also constructed massive stone architecture intrinsically sculptural in concept.

The artistic output of these more densely inhabited regions stands in stark contrast to those areas with smaller resident native populations, such as the region around modern-day Buenos Aires, Argentina, the area in Latin America with the fewest indigenes at the time of contact, a group without a discernible sculptural tradition. This range of local talent affected regional sculptural production in colonial Latin America. In general, where a resident population already had a thriving sculptural tradition, especially in stone and wood, the subsequent early colonial output tended to be more rigorous and complex. (Exceptions are the Caribbean and some parts of South America where native populations were all but wiped out by 1600.) However, by the 18th century throughout much of

Latin America vigorous regional sculptural traditions had emerged.

In the 16th century the construction of hundreds of mendicant mission complexes (*conventos*) created an immediate and widespread demand for religious imagery, subject matter that would dominate Latin American sculpture through the 18th century and even into the 19th century in some areas. Many early works, especially paintings and sculptures in late Renaissance or Mannerist styles, were imported directly from Spain. Exceptional examples by well-known sculptors include the late Renaissance *Virgin of the Evangelization* in the Cathedral of Lima by the Flemish artist Roque de Balduque and the *Christ Child* by the Spanish artist Jerónimo Hernández in the Museo de Arte Colonial, Caracas, Venezuela. In the first half of the 17th century, the most influential imports in Central and South America came from the Sevillian workshop of Juan Martínez Montañés. Several sculpted images in Quito produced by anonymous Spanish artists with whom he probably collaborated clearly show Montañés's influence (e.g., *San Diego de Alcalá*, Convent of S. Diego, and *San Francisco de Asís*, Church of S. Francisco). In Venezuela the Dominican and Franciscan orders commissioned eight altarpieces from Montañés. Guatemalan imagery also clearly expresses his influence. Works associated with him are known for their heightened realism and finely modeled, robust, idealized figures imbued with an intense spirituality.

Most early imports, however, remain anonymous. Some achieved cultlike status when miracles were ascribed to them, such as the portable 16th-century *Virgen de los Remedios* of Mexico City. Local artists reproduced many cult images. To assume the religious currency, a copy adhered to the original as closely as possible in both content and style. This process forced a conservative persistence of *retardataire* tendencies, primarily Mannerist, in some regional Latin American sculpture even into the 19th century. Latent Mannerism also resulted from a continued reliance on European print sources, many of them dating to the 16th and early 17th centuries.

Two groups of Latin American sculptors emerged to fill the burgeoning need for religious imagery in the first century of colonization. The first group consisted of hundreds if not thousands of native artists, including some women perhaps, trained in the missions by the mendicant friars, especially the Franciscans, Augustinians, and Dominicans beginning in the mid 1520s and the Jesuits by the end of the century. Many of these native sculptors, most of whom remain anonymous, descended from families who engaged in various forms of sculpture in the precontact period. Some of them were certainly of petty nobility lineage, the cacique class, who retained elite status under Spanish rule.

They learned their craft either in formal schools built near the main Spanish cities, such as San José de los Naturales begun by the Franciscan Pedro de Gante, in Mexico City, and the Colegio de S. Juan, at Quito, Ecuador, run by the Franciscan Pedro Gosseal, both founded in the 1530s, or in smaller *convento* schools established in the native villages, the pueblos.

Under the tutelage of friars, some with formal artistic training, others guided by a memory of religious art in Europe, and through the direct influence of imported print sources, native sculptors executed impressive stone carvings marked by a certain eclecticism. The mix—in Mexico, labeled *tequitqui* (tributary) by José Moreno Villa in 1942 and also referred to as mestizo (a blend of Spanish and Indian) in South America—translated motifs and forms from Spanish late Gothic, Islamic (Mudéjar), Spanish, Italian, and Flemish Renaissance and Mannerist styles into the vernacular. It is most apparent in 16th-century *convento* facade decoration, baptismal fonts, a few images of saints, and, in Mexico especially, atrial crosses, large stone crosses placed in the center of the walled forecourt of many *convento* complexes, as at Acolman, Mexico. The style exhibits a tendency to abstraction combined with planar, cookie-cutter type relief, repetitive patterning, and strong light/dark contrast, characteristics also ascribed to some precontact sculpture. Representative examples in Mexico include the Plateresque (Spanish Renaissance) church facade of Huejotzingo, Puebla, with a single, slender fluted Doric column on either side of the doorway. In the friezes of La Trinidad, Paraguay (begun 1706), executed by Guaraní natives under Jesuit direction, angels play Paraguayan harps, and local flora and fauna appear in doorway ornamentation. In Brazilian cities the lack of a precontact sculptural tradition combined with the Portuguese colonial preference for interior over exterior decoration stifled the development of monumental stone carving. When Portuguese patrons wanted to embellish Brazilian doorways and windows, they imported architectural ornaments, and even whole facades, directly from Lisbon.

In the 16th century, too, *caña de maiz* (corn pith) and maguey (cactus) paste sculpture evolved to fill the pressing need for religious sculpture in the form of lightweight processional images, processions being at the core of period Catholic ritual. This paste sculpture represented a blend of sources: Christian subject matter and Late Renaissance and Mannerist style with precontact indigenous materials (Aztec warriors purportedly carried sculpted corn-pith deities into battle). In 1538 Vasco de Quiroga, the first bishop of Michoacán, Mexico, where it is said the technology originated, ordered a corn-pith image of the *Virgen de la Salud de Pátzcuaro* from an Indian sculptor named Juan de Berrio.

Among the first Europeans to adapt the indigenous technique to Christian imagery were Matías de la Cerda and his mestizo son, Luis. Matías, perhaps from Seville, began sculpting in corn pith in Pátzcuaro. The process started with a paste made from the heart of dried cornstalks mixed with glue derived from certain orchids that come from the lakes around Pátzcuaro. The paste was modeled on an armature of bundled and glued cornstalks, rolls of European paper, or lightweight wood. The artist then covered the sculpture with wet fabric or paper finished with a fine layer of plaster that when dried was sanded and painted in a manner similar to that of contemporary sculpture in wood. The best-known and largest example is the 16th-century *Crucified Christ* (the favored processional subject) of the Church of San Francisco, Tlaxcala, Mexico. Corn-pith sculptures were exported from Michoacán to other parts of the Spanish Empire: the image of Christ on the main altar of Telde, Canary Islands, and the *Ecce Homo* of the Descalces Reales, Madrid, are prime examples.

In Bolivia native artists working at Copacabana, La Plata (now Sucre), Oruro, and Potosí used maguey fiber in a related technique; the form persisted there through the 18th century. Jesuit friars, artistically the most influential religious order in the region, encouraged its use for religious processional sculpture in Bolivia. Examples include the figures of *Saint Bartholomew* at the Church of S. Miguel de la Ranchería, Oruro, and *Saint Sebastian*, at the Church of Jerusalem, Potosí, both from the early 17th century.

The second group of early sculptors consisted of European-trained professionals, primarily Spanish but also Flemish and Italian in origin. They trickled into the various Spanish cities after early colonization. Many are known by name from period documents, but few extant works are attributed to them. Their numbers increased significantly after 1560 when the focus of the Spanish government shifted from the pueblos under the protection of mendicant friars to the Spanish cities ministered by a burgeoning secular clergy and civil authority. Their numbers were proportional to the yield of local mines and regional economic potential. Mexico City, especially, welcomed a wave of post-1560s artists, whereas Quito, Ecuador, at that time comparatively less developed, experienced only modest immigration. These sculptors produced works comparable to contemporary European, particularly Spanish, examples. Major sculpture commissions through the end of the century, however, continued to come from the pueblos. In 1584–85 the Spanish artist Pedro de Riqueña executed much of the sculpture for the main altarpiece, or retable, of the Franciscan church at Huejotzingo, Puebla (with paintings by the Flemish artist Simón Pereyns). An underlying Classicism, natural but restrained drapery, finely executed and well-proportioned hands and heads, and contemplative, individualized faces, essentially late Renaissance in style, characterize the sculpted pieces that depict the Fathers of the Church and saints associated with the Franciscan order.

Toward the end of the 16th century, significant commissions were also associated with the newly built (or under construction) churches and cathedrals in the main Spanish and Portuguese cities. These works reflected the tastes of a small, emergent upper class. By this time, too, Creole (Spaniards born in Latin America) and mestizo sculptors trained in the established workshops of immigrant European masters who controlled local sculptural production through law or lineage or both. In Mexico City, for example, the bylaws of the woodworkers' guild of carpenters, sculptors (*entalladores*), joiners (*ensambladores*, essentially retable makers), and makers of wooden musical instruments were passed in 1568. Following the mandate of the Council of Trent (1562–63), these rules ensured that members produced iconographically correct religious imagery. They also established masters' examinations to guarantee that *ensambladores* could organize, draw, and plan retables that conformed to good architectural principles accurate in the use of the five orders of columns. New bylaws of 1589 separated sculptors, defined as image makers, from *entalladores*, carvers who produced architectural elements, but the distinction was never fully clarified. Each had independent examinations overseen by a master in their respective field. Sculptors were examined on their ability to draw a well-proportioned, graceful human figure, both nude and clothed; *entalladores* had to know how to cut wood, draw, and fashion a Corinthian capital and a column decorated with foliage, a seraphim, and a bird. These bylaws did not directly exclude Indian (or for that matter, African or Asian) artists, but they did sanction masters from buying or reselling sculpture made by unexamined Indians. However, period contracts document that native artists worked alongside peninsular Spaniards, Creoles, and mestizos alike on the most important commission in Mexico City, the construction of a new cathedral, begun in 1563. In 1704 sculptors officially separated from carpenters into their own guild subdivided into sculptors and *ensambladores*.

Contrary to the situation in Mexico City, sculptors' guilds were less formally organized in other parts of Latin America. Scant documentary evidence suggests that guilds formed in Quito, Ecuador, around 1560, but specific mention of the guild of sculptors and gilders does not occur until 1742. Sculptors and *ensambladores* in Guatemala, perhaps the most prolific sculpture production area during the colonial period, apparently never formed officially sanctioned guilds with requisite masters' examinations. Instead, Guatemalan sculptors worked out of the various studios attached to dynastic families of sculptors, such as the 18th-century Galvéz line. Nor did guilds with fixed rules ever materialize in Caracas, Venezuela, where beginning in the mid-17th century a close network of artists formed workshops based on intermarriage. These shops engaged in a full range of artistic production—painting, sculpture, gilding, ornamentation, carpentry—all under one roof.

Colonial sculptors produced four basic types of wood sculpture in the colonial period: retables, sculpted figures, figures in relief, and *artesonado* ceiling mosaics. Retables were the most significant art form of the colonial period, a collaboration between architects, carpenters, painters, sculptors, and gilders. Together, these artists produced lavish gilt ensembles that incorporated canvas and panel paintings, relief panels, and life-size polychrome statues of saints set within architectural frameworks. Owing to their complexity, artists produced most retables in the workshops of the main Spanish cities, their parts then exported and assembled on the spot.

Retables are subdivided into two types: the main retable, essentially didactic, an architectural construction designed to organize church history, which often filled the apse end of the church; and the side or lateral altar, a smaller, more intimate composition usually dedicated to a single saint. By the end of the 17th century, churches typically had a number of side altars that spilled down the nave walls and filled the transept arms of the church. *Cofradías*, lay organizations that included guilds, cared for the side altars.

Late Renaissance through Early Baroque main retables balanced two or three horizontal tiers (*cuerpos*), delimited by the architraves, against three, five, or even seven vertical bands (*calles*), defined by the columns. An attic story (*remate*) crowned the composition; a *predella* (*banco*) formed its base. Paintings, reliefs, or three-dimensional sculptures filled the niches between the columns. By the 18th century compositions became increasingly centralized and ascensional while the framing elements of tiers and bands, now filled predominantly with sculpture or relief, were less easily defined.

Cuba and other islands in the Caribbean developed no significant local retable tradition; instead, patrons imported most of them directly from Spain. Mexico and Peru in the 16th century and Guatemala, Ecuador, and parts of Brazil in the 17th century initiated strong retable traditions that referenced Spanish (and Portuguese in the case of Brazil) examples in style, composition, and iconography but at the same time remained distinctly regional with respect to surface ornamentation and elaboration. Local retable production spread finally to Venezuela, Colombia, and other areas in the 18th century.

Few altarpieces remain from the first 125 years of colonization because of the devastating effects of earthquakes and other natural disasters, combined with the Pan–Latin American inclination to periodically remodel outdated retables. The most complete early retables from this period are in Mexico. These retables are marked by the presence of classic columns, either fully fluted or divided into thirds, the lower third often heavily ornamented, and a balance of horizontal and vertical members coupled with Plateresque surface ornamentation, as evidenced in the main retables of Huejotzingo and Cuauhtinchán, both in the state of Puebla. Early-17th-century South American examples include the well-documented side retable in the Church of Copacabana (1618), a single-tiered retable with fluted columns patterned on the lower third, by Sebastián Acosta Túpac Inca, a native artist, and the Spanish import by Martínez Montañés in the Cathedral of S. Juan Bautista, originally intended for the Church of La Concepción (1607), both in Lima.

In Brazil the earliest surviving altarpieces, primarily Jesuit, are Mannerist and date from the first quarter of the 17th century. Only a few Jesuit retables escaped destruction after the order was expelled in 1759, and none apparently survive in their original locations. The one preserved in the Church of Nossa Senhora do Bomsucesso, Rio de Janeiro, is strictly Mannerist in style but constructed in tropical wood, made therefore by a European-trained sculptor active in Brazil. It contrasts sharply with a retable housed in the Salvador Cathedral, a native reinterpretation of Mannerist elements.

By the mid 1650s, in response to a shift in European aesthetics, the form of the column began to move from the vertical shaft to the spiraling or "Solomonic" column, a reference to the biblical description of the twisting supports of King Solomon's Temple. Gianlorenzo Bernini commemorated them in his gilt-bronze baldachin (1623–34) for St. Peter's Basilica, Rome, known in Spain through mid-1620s print sources. By 1650 in Spain the Solomonic column was standard on both main and lateral retables. They appeared first on Mexican retables in the Puebla-Tlaxcala region in the 1650s, but by the 1690s Solomonic columns were the main signifiers of Baroque style across Latin America. Mexican examples include the main retables at Metztitlán, Hidalgo (1698), by Salvador de Ocampo, and at the Church of S. Agustín (1690s), Mexico City, by Tomás Xuárez, the only celebrated 17th-century Indian sculptor from Mexico. Although the spiraling support fell out of Mexican fashion by the second decade of the 18th century, it reigned supreme in much of the rest of Latin America through the last quarter of the century.

Guatemala was an important regional center for retable production in the colonial period, but few extant altarpieces predate the 1773 earthquake at Santiago de Guatemala (now Antigua). Their appearance may be theorized, however, from a study of period retable facades (Solomonic by the 1690s) of Guatemalan churches, crafted by the same sculptors who made retables.

The primary artistic centers in colonial Peru were Lima, where, as in the earlier period, many altarpieces continued to be imported from Spain, and Cuzco, where the Solomonic column may have made its Peruvian debut. In the second half of the 17th century, Cuzco assumed a pivotal role in retable production, stimulated first by post-1650 earthquake artistic fervor and then by the avid patronage of Archbishop Mollinedo, who arrived in 1673. The use of the ubiquitous Solomonic column and the regionalized application of surface mirrors embedded in the architectural framing that serve to dematerialize the form (e.g. the main retable, Church of S. Clara, 1660) characterize Cuzco's Baroque retables. The epitome of Cuzco's early Baroque is the main altar of the Church of La Compañia, composed of interrupted stories, multiple architectonic elements, curved and broken pediments, and rich surface decoration. Its form echoes in Bolivia in the main retable of Copacabana (1656), Lake Titicaca, and in numerous examples in Potosí.

In Brazil the Franciscans were the major patrons of Early Baroque retables, also characterized by the use of Solomonic columns, but here they link at the capital by concentric archivolts. The oldest examples—seven in all—are located in the Golden Chapel of the Monastery of Recife (1698–ca. 1724), by the sculptor Antônio M. Santiago. These fully gilded compositions with their foliated but reserved surfaces, labeled Portuguese "national style" by Robert C. Smith, had no equivalent in the rest of Latin America and remained constant in form for at least three decades across Portugal's dominions.

A common element linking many High Baroque retables, beginning in the 1730s in Mexico, is their sheer size: they spread across the entire presbytery, invade the ceiling, sometimes spill into crossing arms and chapels, and often become indistinguishable from the architecture. Frequently, they employ colossal supports two or three tiers high, profuse decoration, and recessive and projecting elements. In contrast, retables of 18th-century Venezuela are modestly proportioned constructions one or two tiers high that remain independent of the architecture.

In some areas, such as in Bolivia and Brazil, columns remained Solomonic but boasted increasingly agitated surfaces. Bolivian High Baroque retables are characterized by their *horror vacui*—a plethora of si-rens, animals, angels, and tropical and liturgical fruits scatter across every imaginable surface—mixed with archaic themes and stylistic elements appropriated from precontact, medieval, and Mannerist sources. Urban examples include the main retables of La Merced, Sucre, and San Pedro, La Paz; rural ones are found in Puna and Ilabaya, in the states of Potosí and La Paz, respectively. Contemporary Brazilian retables, increasingly unified and theatrical, bear fully rounded Solomonic supports, multiple canopies, and broken pediments and cornices, as in that of the Ordem Terceira da Penitência, Rio de Janeiro, by the Portuguese collaborators Manuel and Francisco Xavier de Brito.

Columns anthropomorphized in other areas. In Mexico they assumed the form of elongated, inverted pyramids, called *estípites*, and resemble human torsos. Foliate details bite into their angled surfaces to visually negate their architectural function. The Spanish artist Jerónimo Balbás introduced *estípites*, derived from Spanish prototypes, into Mexico on the Altar of the Kings (1718–30s), the main altarpiece in the Cathedral of Mexico City. Eagerly adopted by local architects and makers of retables alike, the *estípite* became the hallmark of Mexican High Baroque. The *estípite* pilaster appeared on Venezuelan retables in 1739, but here it retained its supporting function and is more reserved, planar, and pyramidal in form. It remained in vogue until about 1780. In Lima half- and full-length figures replaced the column supports on several examples, as in the High Baroque retable of the Church of S. José, in La Merced, and the Rococo (identifiable by the use of C- and S-curve elements) altarpiece in the Church of S. Francisco de Paula Nuevo, Rímac.

Rococo ornamentation appeared in Mexico in the 1760s and had crept south by the 1780s. Where the vertical support element persisted, Rococo decoration camouflaged its structure, as in the retable of the Church of El Hospital, in Quito, Ecuador. Spanish and Portuguese carvers brought the Rococo and then the Neoclassical styles to Buenos Aires in the years immediately following its elevation to capital city of the New Viceroyalty of Río de la Plata in 1776. The number of carvers, sculptors, and gilders increased sharply in response to a doubling of the number of chapels and churches in Buenos Aires by the end of the 18th century. In Mexico the *estípite* diminished in size while the space between, the *interestípite*, an elaborated multipaneled niche, increased in dimension and finally supplanted the support altogether, as in the altar of the Church of S. Rosa de Viterbo (1780s), Querétaro. The period was short-lived, however, and the column returned in its pure form in Neoclassical-period retables, beginning about 1780 in Mexico and slightly later across Central and South America. Massive retables all but ceased to be constructed by the second decade of the 19th century when religious patronage began to wane.

Sculpted figures are the second type of colonial sculpture. With the exception of a few 18th-century secular funerary portraits and crèche animals, all depict religious subjects. Carlos Duarte (1979) classifies them as fully sculpted wooden figures; *imágenes de vestir*, literally, figures to be dressed; wooden relief figures; and figures made of materials other than wood.

Fully sculpted wooden figures feature gilt detailing, called *estofado*, which imitates rich period textiles, and carefully applied and modeled flesh tones, termed *encarnación*. Larger figures, 1.5 meters high and taller, were designed to fill retable niches. Smaller, similarly finished examples, especially popular in the 17th and 18th centuries, were reserved for domestic devotion. Added elements—fabric cuffs, real hair lashes, brows and wigs, and glass eyes, together with articulated limbs (particularly common on depictions of Christ)—maximized image realism, a motive increasingly important as the colonial period progressed. The most common themes included images of the Virgin and of Christ, followed by individual saints, martyrs, Fathers of the Church, God the Father, and angels and archangels. Each subject was ideally identifiable by its associated attributes. For instance, the image of the Virgin of the Immaculate Conception wears a crown of 12 stars and a pink gown and blue mantle, stands on a crescent moon above a serpent, opens her hands in an orant position, and, in the Baroque period, bows her head slightly in response to the elegant S curve of her body. Examples include the 18th-century *Virgin of the Immaculate Conception* by a follower of Luis Espíndola, in the Cathedral of Trujillo, Peru, and another by Bernardo de Legardo in the Museo de Arte Religioso in Popayán, Colombia.

Imágenes de vestir were lightweight mannequins intended for use in public procession and featured a sculpted head, hands, and sometimes feet. Often life-size and made either of wood grown locally or imported from Europe or of fine Philippine or European porcelain, these sculptures attached to a pyramidal wooden armature left unfinished or overlaid with gessoed and painted fabric. These images were in contemporary dress and often wore stylish wigs of human hair. Individual images, especially those of the Virgin, could have dozens of costumes and were the recipients of jewels and other precious gifts. A prime example of the porcelain type is the *Virgin of Solitude* (1620) in the Church of La Soledad, Oaxaca, Mexico.

To create figures in relief, artists would usually carve half-round figures and then glue them to a flat support board, sometimes elaborated with background details or iconographic information. They applied these reliefs to retables, choir stalls, pulpits, and other types of furnishings, including domestics that incorporated limited secular and mythological imagery. On retables they were finished with *estofado* and *encarnación*, in imitation of fully sculpted figures, as in the *banco* figures of the Huejotzingo and Cuauhtinchán retables. More often they were only waxed or varnished when applied to other furnishings, such as the figural reliefs incorporated on church furnishings in the Cathedral of Lima, as in Juan Martínez de Arrona's Renaissance sacristy box (1608) and Pedro de Noguera's Mannerist choir stall (1623).

Sculptors also fashioned figures from materials other than wood, including stone, clay, bone, jet, metal (silver, gold, copper, bronze, iron, tin), and paper. They imported some materials, such as marble from the Philippines, whereas others became local specialties (Venezuela was noted for its copper and bronze images that measured a mere "six fingers high").

Wooden ceiling mosaics, primarily geometric in pattern and made of short, interlaced and decorated pieces of wood, were common in earthquake-prone parts of Latin America through the 16th and 17th centuries. Stone or brick vaults and domes replaced these mosaics only as the technology and financing became available. Moorish in origin and found especially in parts of Spain, the form spread from the Caribbean (House of Diego Columbus, Santo Domingo, 16th century) to Mexico (Church of S. Francisco, Tlaxcala, 17th century), Colombia (Church of S. Francisco, Bogotá, 17th century), Peru (Church of Andahuayillias, near Cuzco, 17th century), and Bolivia (Church of S. Miguel, Sucre, 17th century).

The discovery of rich ore deposits in various parts of Latin America in the 18th century stimulated localized sculptural activity, and with it emerged several noteworthy regional sculptors. Among the best known is Antônio Francisco Lisboa (also known as Aleijadinho), active in the gold-mining region of Minas Gerais, Brazil, beginning about 1760. The illegitimate son of a Portuguese architect, Manoel Francisco Lisboa, and his African slave, he contracted a mysterious disease after 1777 (his most important works postdate the disease) that resulted in severe limb deformation and the loss of some digits, thus the nickname *O Aleijadinho*, the "little cripple." He executed a variety of sculpted works, including altarpieces, portals, pulpits, banisters, and freestanding statues. His undisputed masterworks, however, are his two sculptural programs for the Pilgrimage Church of Bom Jesus do Matozinhos in Congonhas do Campo. The first, dated between 1796 and 1799, consists of 64 life-size wooden sculptures arranged in seven scenes from the Passion of Christ: *Last Supper, Agony in the Garden, Betrayal, Flagellation, Crowning with Thorns, Road to Calvary,* and *Crucifixion*. Unevenly executed with the help of assistants of varying degrees of skill, the series is nevertheless eloquently cohesive. The second, dated between 1800 and 1805, consists of a group of 12 theatrical monumental stone statues of Old Testament figures, which lines the atrium of the church and processes up its great stone stair, also designed by the artist. These works straddle the divide between High Baroque and Neoclassical sculpture.

Neoclassicism's influence in art was felt in Mexico, via intellectual circles, by the end of the 18th century. There was little opportunity for its development in the rest of Latin America, however, due to the various wars of independence from Spain through the 1820s followed by civil wars that waged into the next decade. In the 1840s, 1850s, and even later, sculpture in some areas—Uruguay, interior Argentina, Venezuela, and Bolivia, especially—remained essentially colonial in style and religious in theme; a localized tradition of image making, the art of the *santero*, developed in Puerto Rico and other parts of the Catholic Caribbean, as well as in New Mexico (part of Mexico until 1848).

By the middle of the 19th century, government-supported academies based on French and Spanish models began to replace traditional craft workshops in some major cities. Arts patronage shifted from the Roman Catholic Church and its need for religious polychromed wood sculpture to the autonomous nations with their swelling demands for civic secular marble, plaster, and bronze images. One of the earliest and certainly among the most spectacular bronze sculptures was the equestrian portrait of *Charles IV* (erected 1803), originally designed for Mexico City's main plaza, by the Spaniard Manuel Tolsá, director of the Mexican Academy of San Carlos. Several well-known Neoclassical native sculptors emerged in Mexico about the same time. The most notable, Pedro Patiño Ixtolinque, a student of Tolsá, became the director of the academy in 1826. His best-known official sculptures include personifications of *America* and *Liberty*. Neoclassicism persisted in Mexico through the end of the century, best exemplified by the government-sanctioned bronze statue *Cuauhtémoc* (1878) by the Mexican sculptor Miguel Noreña.

Following the Mexican lead, monumental portraits, many by foreigners, of national heroic figures became de rigueur in cities throughout much of Latin America after 1850. An early example is the image of *Simón de Bolívar* (1859) for Lima's Plaza del Congreso, by the Italian Adamo Tadolini; a late expression is the depiction of *Christopher Columbus* (1896) by the Spaniard Tomás Mur for Guatemala City. At this time, too, a few young Latin American artists, including sculptors, began to make student sojourns to Europe, funded primarily by state grants. Many remained in Europe—Peru, for example, was essentially devoid of native artists between 1890 and 1910—while others returned home. Among the latter were the Brazilian Rodolfo Bernardelli and the Argentine Francisco Cafferata. Bernardelli spent his childhood in Mexico and Chile and studied sculpture in Brazil. Awarded a trip to Europe, he remained there almost ten years, primarily in Rome where he worked under Achille Monteverde and executed his best-known Neoclassical work, the marble *Christ and the Adulteress* (1884). Bernardelli returned to Brazil in 1885, was named director of the National School five years later, and became the most prominent Brazilian sculptor of the period. Cafferata studied in Buenos Aires and in 1877 went to Italy. His bronze Neoclassical *Slave* received the gold medal at Buenos Aires's Continental Exposition of 1882. Returning to Argentina three years later, he was among the first of the Latin American sculptors to move away from academic subject matter in his Argentine depictions of African descendants.

By the early 20th century a few young Latin American sculptors broke stylistically with academism, influenced especially by the works of Auguste Rodin, which they encountered in Paris. One of the first was Jesús F. Contreras of Mexico, whose emotional female nude allegories, such as *Malgré tout* (1898), recall the Impressionistic surfaces of Rodin's sculptures. Rogelio Yrurtia, who studied under a follower of Cafferata and then in the Parisian studio of Jules-Félix Coutan, is recognized as the first great Argentine sculptor. His *Sinners* (1903), compositionally and emotively indebted to Rodin's *The Burghers of Calais* (1884), won a major prize at the Saint Louis World's Fair in 1904. His counterpart in Uruguay was Juan Manuel Ferrari, the son of an Italian sculptor. Ferrari studied in Buenos Aires and then in Rome but returned to Montevideo in 1897. His monumental works include the *Monument to General San Martin's Liberation Army* (1914), also influenced by Rodin. In general, however, sculpture remained strictly academic under conservative regimes, as in Peru, or languished with the lack of government support, as in Guatemala and Paraguay, through the 1930s, and 1940s.

New subject matter began to appear in the sculpted works of the Social Realists of Argentina, such as Agustín Riganelli, who in the 1920s depicted working-class subjects. Pre-Columbian themes and motifs and indigenist sentiment informed the work of some Mexican sculptors of the 1930s, who explored direct carving in stone or wood. Such was also the case in Costa Rica, among the few Caribbean countries to develop a strong sculptural tradition.

Modernism, critical to the development of Latin American painting in the early 20th century, had little immediate stylistic influence on sculpture. The sculptors who did respond included a few trained in Europe, such as Victor Brecheret from Brazil. Brecheret had studied in Rome (1913–19) and was influenced by the Symbolists. He returned to São Paulo in 1919, where he inspired younger artists. Although he returned to Europe two years later, he continued to send work home, now informed by the works of Constantin Brancusi. Brecheret settled permanently in São Paulo in the 1930s but remained connected to European currents. His late works, such as his bronze *Indian and Sauçuapara* (1951), combine abstracted forms with indigenous content, a combination that also characterizes the work of a few of his contemporaries. In Peru Joaquín Roca Rey collaborated with Fernando de Szyslo, the important abstract painter who explored Andean themes, to create *Angel of Judgment* (1957). Chilean Marta Colvin studied in both Paris and London, and later returned to Chile, where she was profoundly affected by pre-Columbian art. In Bolivia highly stylized indigenist themes distinguish the work, in a variety of materials, of Marina Nuñez del Prado. Slightly later, similar indigenist themes persist in sculptures by Ted Carrasco. Carrasco's work became increasingly abstract into the 1970s when he lived in Europe and then more figure-bound after he returned to Bolivia later in the decade.

During the 1940s and 1950s public support for the arts increased, a few museums of modern art were established, and a new appreciation for European movements evolved in some Latin American countries. In Argentina, for example, the Asociación Arte Concreto Invención included the Constructivist sculptor Ennio Iommi. Other Argentine developments included Grupo Madí, involved with technology, new materials, and viewer participation, and Spazialismo, a concept developed in Italy by Argentine native Lucio Fontana in 1947 that he explored in his amoebalike temporary installation *Ambiente spaziali* (Spatial Environment; 1949). Brazilian Lygia Clark studied in Paris from 1950 to 1954 under Fernand Léger and was influenced by Soviet Constructivism and the Bauhaus. She turned from figuration to geometric abstraction in two series of concrete constructions, *Modulated Surfaces* and *Counter-Reliefs*, executed in Rio de Janeiro between 1954 and 1958.

In Mexico abstraction developed under the tutelage of the Mexican Germán Cueto and the German Mathias Goeritz. Essentially self-taught, Cueto visited the studios of some of the most important French and Spanish sculptors of the 1920s and 1930s and experimented with varied techniques and materials. His experimental spirit informed the Mexican avant-garde after 1950. Goeritz, who moved to Mexico in 1949, was a leader of Mexican modern art into the 1970s via his sculptures, teaching, writing, and especially through his collaboration on Mexico City's large out-door sculpture complex at the Ciudad Universitaria, completed in 1979.

During the 1960s and early 1970s, virtually all of the European and American movements were at play in Latin American art, yet artists asserted their individual voices and affirmed their national differences. Art in the 1970s could also be politically responsive. Brazilian artists consciously employed Conceptual art in protest of the repressive military regime established in 1964, as did artists in Chile following the ascendancy of its military government in 1973. The work of Mario Irarrázabal, for example, uses the human body to express injustice, helplessness, and torture. Contemporary Latin American artists continue to work in a variety of media and styles, some informed by pre-Columbian and indigenous motifs and themes and much of it politically and socially charged.

KELLEN KEE MCINTYRE

See also **Aleijadinho; Brecheret, Victor; Fontana, Lucio; Montañés, Juan Martínez**

Further Reading

Barnitz, Jacqueline, *Twentieth-Century Art of Latin America*, Austin: University of Texas Press, 2001

Bayón, Damián, and Murillo Marx, *Historia del arte colonial sudamericano*, Barcelona, Spain: Ediciones Polígrafa, 1989; as *History of South American Colonial Art and Architecture*, New York: Rizzoli, 1992

Bernales Ballesteros, Jorge, et al., *Escultura en el Perú*, Lima: Banco del Crédito del Perú, 1991

Duarte, Carlos F., *Historia de la escultura en Venezuela: Época colonial*, Caracas, Venezuela: Castro, 1979

La escuela mexicana de escultura: Maestros fundadores (exhib. cat.), Mexico City: Instituto Nacional de Bellas Artes, 1990

Gutiérrez, Ramón (compiler), *Pintura, escultura y artes útiles en Iberoamérica, 1500–1825*, Madrid: Cátedra, 1995

Luján Muñoz, Luis, and Miguel Alvarez Arévalo, *Imágenes de Oro*, Guatemala: Corporación G and T, 1993

Mesa, José de, and Teresa Gisbert, *Escultura virreinal en Bolivia*, La Paz: Academia Nacional de Sciencias de Bolivia, 1972

Palmer, Gabrielle G., *Sculpture in the Kingdom of Quito*, Albuquerque: University of New Mexico Press, 1987

Ramírez, Fausto, *La plástica del siglo de la independencia*, Mexico City: Fundo Editorial de la Plástica Mexicana, 1985

Rodríguez, Belgica, *Breve historia de la escultura contemporánea en Venezuela*, Caracas, Venezuela: Fundarte, 1979

Rubiano Caballero, Germán, *La escultura en América Latina (siglo XX)*, Bogotá: Universidad Nacional de Colombia, 1986

Sullivan, Edward J., *Latin American Art in the Twentieth Century*, London: Phaidon Press, 1996

Traba, Marta, *Arte de América Latina, 1900–1980*, Washington, D.C.: Banco Interamericano de Desarrollo, 1994; as *Art of Latin America, 1900–1980*, Washington, D.C.: Inter-American Development Bank, 1994

Turner, Jane, *Encyclopedia of Latin American and Caribbean Art*, New York: Grove, and London: Macmillan Reference, 2000

Weismann, Elizabeth Wilder, *Mexico in Sculpture, 1521–1821*, Cambridge, Massachusetts: Harvard University Press, 1950

FRANCESCO LAURANA *ca.* 1430–1502
Dalmatian

The artistic career of Francesco Laurana has not yet been entirely reconstructed. The lack of documents concerning his life renders it particularly difficult to determine the beginning of his career or to trace with certainty his numerous travels. Giorgio Vasari incorrectly named Laurana as one of Brunelleschi's followers, with Domenico Gagini and Geremia da Cremona, contributing to the misunderstanding of the sculptor's presumed Tuscany formation. Rolfs assumed Laurana to be among Gagini's disciples (see Rolfs, 1907), whereas Venturi identified him among Matteo de' Pasti's collaborators in the workshop of the Tempio Malatestiano in Rimini (see Venturi, 1925). Laurana's early artistic development probably occurred in Zadar, at a goldsmith's workshop. The geometric surfaces and the nearly graphical treatment of some details typical of the reliquary busts are important characteristics of the rarefied beauty of Laurana's female busts.

A coupon (notification of payment) dated 17 July 1453 is the first known documentary source attesting to the presence of the sculptor among the artists active in the decoration of the Arch of Castelnuovo in Naples; the wording *mestre* (master) presupposes an important role inside the sculpture yard, which included Paolo Romano, Isaia da Pisa, and Pietro da Milano.

Laurana had probably already collaborated with Peitro da Milano in Dubrovnik at the Rector's Palace on the reliefs of the Little fountain. The left-hand relief depicting *Alfonso and His Suite* (1453–58) has been attributed to Laurana. The perspective organization is uncertain; the figures are constructed on divergent axes, with a proportional canon based on the unit of measure of the head (1:5 or 1:4.5). Typical of Laurana's taste is the treatment of the cloth, which is rendered with wide folds. His participation in the relief depicting *The Tunisian Embassy* and in some figures for the relief depicting *Ferrante and His Suite* in the Arch of Castelnuovo, Naples, attributed to Pietro da Milano, has also been established. In 1458, perhaps because of the plague, work on the Arch of Castelnuovo stopped.

Between 1461 and 1466, Laurana was in Provence at René d'Anjou's court. During his first stay in France, Laurana produced a series of medals. Among the many he produced is one depicting René d'Anjou and Jeanne De Laval, whom he also represented in one of his first portrait busts. Some affinities have confirmed a connection between the artist and Matteo de'

Pasti's circle. The presence of Laurana in Sicily is documented from 1468. A document dated 22 May 1468 relates to a controversy with Baron Graffeo of Partanna concerning payment. The facts relating to the artist's arrival and first periods of activity on the island are not entirely known. His career in Sicily may have begun in 1467, between Sciacca and nearby Partanna, famous for its quarry of alabaster marble.

The 1468 commission for the Mastrantonio Chapel in the Church of San Francesco d'Assisi in Palermo marks the transfer of Laurana to that city. The articulated decorative system has been lost; only the entrance arch remains. According to some interpretations, the reliefs are a representation of Faith, through the writings of the Old and New Testament. In the panels executed by Laurana, the empty space allows the figures to emerge.

The *Virgin and Child*, created in 1471 for the Church of the Crucifixion of Noto, is Laurana's only signed and dated work and is one of his series of full reliefs depicting the Virgin and Child. The artist revised the pose of the *hanchement* (unbalanced position of Virgin holding Child on her arm and turning to him) favored during the French Late Gothic, transforming the nervous stretching of the figure into a serene equilibrium of movement. The folds of the Virgin's mantle

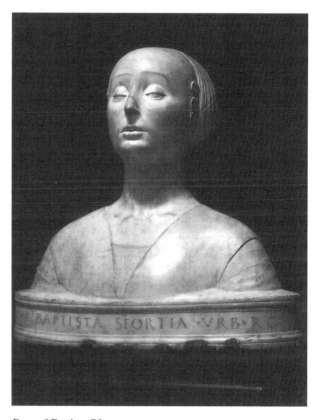

Bust of Battista Sforza
© Alinari / Art Resource, NY

suggest the light inclination of her torso, a last allusion to the sinuous movements characteristic of the French Late Gothic, remains in the cloth's fold on the arm and in the tapering fingers.

No document has been found regarding the portrait bust of Battista Sforza to explain the circumstances relating to the commission and execution of this work. Laurana probably met Federico da Montefeltro in Naples, where he had returned after his stay in Sicily, and he decided to follow Montefeltro, stopping for a period in Urbino. Laurana's bust of Battista Sforza is an ethereal figure whose wide, smooth surfaces seem to come from an ideal world and respond to contact with light. The head, neck, and shoulders are created from pure solids or sections, and the joining of the parts is flawless. The ovoid face rests on the cylindrical neck, which inclines back in a simple balance, constructed on an angle. The physical traits render the face recognizable; nevertheless, in the shapes of the eyes, in the curve of the lips, and in all that determines the figure's individuality, the ephemeral has been eliminated. In this, Battista Sforza becomes a goddess.

Elisabeth Mognetti has assigned to Laurana a statue of *Saint Anne Trinitaire* dating to 1476. It is conceived as a whole mass, in which the Virgin and Child's bodies are welded to Saint Anne's. In Laurana's relief *Christ Carrying the Cross*, the figures crowd in an apparently visually upset composition. Laurana explored here the possibilities of an expressionist language.

The artist's presence in France is documented between 1476 and 1483, but the next 15 years remain a mystery. He may have returned to Sicily, but this hypothesis cannot be confirmed. In 1498 he was in Marseilles; he died in Avignon in 1502.

Controversy surrounds a number of female busts attributed to Laurana, and the lack of documents makes if difficult to determine the identity of the subjects and the dates of some sculptures. A significant case is the three portrait busts of Eleonora of Aragon, Alfonso II's sister (now in the Palazzo Altabellis, Palermo). Patera assumes that Laurana returned to Sicily between 1483 and 1498 and that he executed three versions of the bust for Count Carlo Luna of Caltabellotta (see Patera, 1992), but this hypothesis and others formed previously are not universally accepted. The problem is that nobody has reconstructed what happened during the years from 1484 to 1498, a mystery that is not solved by examination of the Eleonora busts alone.

MARIA CRISTINA BASTANTE

See also **Gaggini, Domenico**

Biography

Born in La Vrana, near Zadar in Dalmatia (present-day Croatia), probably *ca.* 1430. Received instruction in goldsmith's workshop; presence in Dubrovnik as collaborator with Pietro da Milano on Rector's Palace and Little fountain assumed *ca.* 1450; called *mestre* (master) on notification of payment, Naples, 1453; worked there with Pietro da Milano, Isaia da Pisa, Paolo Romano, and others on reliefs for Arch of Castel Nuovo, 1453–58; moved to Provence, 1461; worked as medallist at court of René d'Anjou until 1466; in Sicily, probably first in Sciacca, then in Palermo, 1468–71; contract for decoration of Mastrantonio Chapel (with Pietro di Bonitate), dated 2 June 1468; returned to Naples, *ca.* 1474; in Urbino, at Federico da Montefeltro's court, 1475; carved there posthumous portrait bust of Battista Sforza; in south of France to collaborate with Tommaso Malvito, 1476; presence in France is documented until 1483; then 15-year lull in documentation follows; active in Marseilles, 1498. Died in Avignon, France, before 12 March 1502.

Selected Works

1453–58 Sculptures for the Arch of Castel Nuovo; marble; Naples, Italy

1458–61 *Virgin and Child*; marble; Church of S. Agostino della Zecca, Naples, Italy

1458–61 *Virgin and Child*; marble; portal lunette, Chapel of S. Barbara, Castel Nuovo, Naples, Italy

1468 *Madonna Libera Inferni*; marble; Palermo Cathedral, Italy

1468 Tomb (untraced), entrance arch, and *Virgin and Child*; marble; Mastrantonio Chapel, Church of San Francesco d'Assisi, Palermo, Italy

1471 *Virgin and Child* for Noto Antico, Sicily; marble; Church of the Crucifixion, Noto (Syracuse), Italy

1471? *Virgin and Child*; marble; S. Maria della Medaglia, Palazzolo Acreide, Syracuse, Italy

before 1476 Bust of Battista Sforza; marble; Museo Nazionale del Bargello, Florence, Italy

before 1476 Bust of Beatrice of Aragon; marble; Frick Collection, New York City, United States

1476 *Sainte Anne Trinitaire*; marble; Parish Church, Les Pennes-Mirabeau, France

1476 Tomb of Jean Cossa; marble; Church of Santa Marta, Tarascon, France

1478–81 *Christ Carrying the Cross* for Chapel of the Celestines, Avignon, France; marble; Church of Saint Didier, Avignon, France

Further Reading

Burger, Fritz, *Francesco Laurana: Eine Studie zur Italienischen Quattrocento Skulptur*, Strasbourg, France: Heitz, 1907

Goss (Gvodzanovic), Vladimir, "The Dalmatian Work of Pietro da Milano and Francesco Laurana," *Arte Lombarda* 42–43 (1975)

Kruft, Hanno-Walter, *Francesco Laurana: Ein Bildhauer der Frührenaissance*, Munich: Beck, 1994

Kruft, Hanno-Walter, and Magne Malmanger, "Francesco Laurana Beginnings in Naples," *The Burlington Magazine* 850 (1974)

Kruft, Hanno-Walter, and Ulrich Middeldorf, "Three Male Portrait Busts by Francesco Laurana," *The Burlington Magazine* 818 (1971)

Patera, Benedetto, *Francesco Laurana in Sicilia*, Palermo, Italy: Novecento, 1992

Rolfs, Wilhelm, *Franz Laurana*, Berlin: Bong, 1907

Valentiner, Wilhelm R., "A Portrait Bust of King Alphonso I of Naples," *Art Quarterly* 1 (1938)

Valentiner, Wilhelm R., "Laurana's Portrait Busts of Women," *Art Quarterly* 4 (1942)

Venturi, Adolfo, *Grandi Artisti Italiani*, Bologna: Zanichelli, 1925

HENRI LAURENS 1885–1954 *French*

Henri Laurens holds a unique position as a core member of Cubism's fledgling group, a painter-sculptor whose refined craftsmanship equaled that of his friend Georges Braque and whose originality in his use of materials significantly extended the Cubist vocabulary. His constructions of wood, sheet metal, plaster, and tin comprised elegant exercises in poetic metaphor, proclaiming sculpture's independence and expressive facility with great wit and aplomb. Their language was one of abbreviation, allusion, and trompe l'oeil (extreme realism in art; literally "deception of the eye"), inventively using color, texture, and rhyming forms to create "new" objects that made reference to the everyday—to pipes, bottles, newspapers, and domestic interiors—but that operated in a realm of shifting meanings and continuous metamorphosis.

Laurens was a thoroughly French sculptor by both training and inclination. Even at his most subversive, his instinct was always to work with an eye to the great traditions of French sculpture. It is his special contribution to modern sculpture that he was able to fuse fertile experimentation seamlessly with an evident and fruitful engagement with tradition, expressed through a profound empathy for ancient Greek and Romanesque statuary in particular. It was for this that he was prized by his contemporaries, as indeed he was for his personality, which seemed also to express this continuity with the past—his consistency and calm, steady, assured way of working.

The many accolades Laurens received during his lifetime expressed the general view that his work epitomized all that was most French—an innate harmony and balance, sensibility coupled with measured reason, and an imagery rooted in the cycles of nature. Laurens's work was felt to provide an anchor, suggesting enduring and incorruptible values, particularly when, in the wake of World War I and through the sociopolitical upheavals of the 1930s, French artists and intellectuals were most rife with self-doubt and insecurity.

Laurens's style underwent a radical, albeit gradual, transition. By the late 1920s, he replaced his analytical constructions and collages, with their angularity and crisp planar intersections, with an altogether softer and more fluid idiom; still lifes were supplanted by rounded, reclining nudes. Henceforth, Laurens would be exclusively identified with the tradition of the female nude and with a gently naive, sensuous rendering of the body that related to what he called "the ripeness of form," a sense of organic, "active" volume that not so much occupies space as takes possession of it.

The medium in which Laurens excelled as a figurative sculptor was terracotta. Varying its color and tone by the way he mixed and fired the clay, he produced warm, fleshy hues of great subtlety, and through his understanding of simplification and construction, learned during his Cubist years, he gave the most modest of figures a sense of much greater scale and monumentality.

Laurens's evolution of this distinctive style owed much to particular physical and geographic circumstances. During World War I and into the 1930s, Laurens spent much time at L'Étang-la-Ville, a quiet rural location not far from the home of his friend Aristide Maillol. This proximity to Maillol undoubtedly made its mark on Laurens's sculpture, impressing him by, as he said of the older man's work in 1925, an intuitive closeness to nature and a potent three-dimensionality, a luxurious sensuousness that Laurens associated with the generous forms of Romanesque figuration and Parisian city sculpture by, for example, the 16th-century sculptor Jean Goujon. It was a sensuousness that used distortion of the body to emphasize its energy and

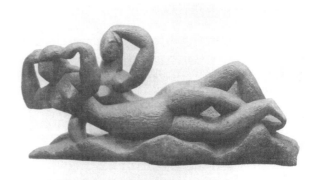

Les Ondines
The Conway Library, Courtauld Institute of Art
© Artists Rights Society (ARS), New York

928

uniqueness. By the 1920s Laurens too was creating female icons of great presence, such as *Woman with a Basket of Fruit*. The work's exaggerated volumes are compacted to suggest ripeness and fertility. Laurens's admiration for the Romanesque had intensified in 1918 with his first visit to Chartres Cathedral. The forms of the figures around the royal portal made a deep impression on him for the way they suggested timeless serenity and seemed to arise spontaneously out of the stone itself.

A different landscape, that of the sea, was to mark Laurens's imagery profoundly. In the mid to late 1920s, Laurens worked on a commission for Charles de Noailles's villa at Hyères, on the Mediterranean. Those frequenting the villa included the members of "Les Six"—a group of six young French composers that included Arthur Honneger, Darius Milhaud, and Francis Poulenc—with whom Laurens was already in contact. The combination of musical and maritime influences inspired not only *Standing Woman with Drapery*, created for the grounds of the villa, a figure that stood staring out to sea like a siren from Antiquity, but also one of Laurens's most memorable sculptures, *Les Ondines* (1933–34). Two figures gaze into the distance, their bodies undulating as if buoyed by water. They recall the legend of the undine, goddess of the seas, a female water sprite whose story had inspired composers from Sibelius to Ravel. Laurens's work of the 1930s and 1940s is peopled by legendary figures who are mysterious and yet retain a certain earthiness. *Les Ondines'* limbs evoke the textured bark of those woods to the west of Paris where Laurens liked to wander.

Among all of Laurens's influences and acquaintances, Braque remained a lifelong ally and cohort. Just as in the early 1940s Braque explored mythology through his graphic work, illustrating the exploits of Ulysses and Hercules, so Laurens had studied the myth of Amphion, whose lyre-playing protected Thebes; later, in the 1940s and 1950s, Laurens produced wood engravings and etchings based on classics by Theocritus and Homer. Laurens's poor health also meant that drawing and engraving were often more manageable than sculpture. His graphic dexterity was again posited as a characteristically French talent.

CATHERINE PÜTZ

See also **Maillol, Aristide**

Biography

Born in Paris, France, 18 February 1885. Trained under stonemason working on city sites; studied academic drawing with sculptor Jacques Perrin; moved to Montmartre, 1902; contracted tuberculosis of the bone resulting in amputation of one leg and poor health for remainder of life, 1909; settled in La Ruche, Montparnasse, Paris; befriended Georges Braque, 1911; established studio same year and made first attempts at Cubist sculpture; exhibited at the Salon des Indépendants, 1913 and 1914; made first *papiers collés* (glued papers, or collage), 1914; first solo show in Galerie de l'Effort Moderne, Paris, 1916. Exhibited at Rosenberg's Gallery, 1918; produced first modeled sculpture, 1918–19; moved to L'Étang-la-Ville, 1921, and received first major architectural commission from Jacques Doucet; moved to Villa Brune, Porte de Châtillon, 1927; awarded Helena Rubinstein prize, 1935; showed in Cubism and Abstract Art exhibit, Museum of Modern Art, New York City, 1936; showed with Pablo Picasso, Braque, and Henri Matisse in Oslo, Stockholm, and Copenhagen, 1938; worked in seclusion in Paris, 1940–44; exhibited at the Venice Biennale, 1948 and 1950; major retrospective at Musée National d'Art Moderne, Paris, 1951; awarded Grand Prix at the São Paulo Biennial, 1953. Died in Paris, France, 5 May 1954.

Selected Works

1915   *Clown*; painted wood; Wilhelm Lehmbruck Museum, Duisburg, Germany; another version: Moderna Museet, Stockholm, Sweden

1917   *Guitar*; painted stone; Galerie Louise Leiris, Paris, France

1917–18   *Guitar*; painted tin; Museum Ludwig, Cologne, Germany

1918   *Dish with Grapes*; painted wood, sheet metal; Collection of M. and Mme. Claude Laurens, Paris, France

1919   *Reclining Woman with Fan*; bronze; Galerie Louise Leiris, Paris, France

1924   *Woman with a Basket of Fruit*; stone; Galerie Louise Leiris, Paris, France

1927   *Standing Woman with Drapery*; bronze; Galerie Louise Leiris, Paris, France; another version: marble, Galerie Louise Leiris, Paris, France

1929   *Cariatid*; bronze; Musée National d'Art Moderne, Centre Georges Pompidou, Paris, France (on display at Villeneuve d'Ascq)

1932   *Large Maternity*; bronze; Galerie Louise Leiris, Paris, France; smaller version: bronze, Hirshhorn Museum and Sculpture Garden, Washington, D.C., United States

1933–34   *Les Ondines*; bronze; Galerie Louise Leiris, Paris, France

1937   *Amphion*; bronze; private collection

1940   *L'Adieu*; stone; Galerie Louise Leiris,
        Paris, France
1947   *Bather*; bronze; Centre Georges Pompidou,
        Paris, France; larger version: bronze,
        Baltimore Museum of Art, Maryland,
        United States
1948   *Autumn*; bronze; Centre Georges
        Pompidou, Paris, France; Tate Gallery,
        London, England

Further Reading

Harrison, Michael, "Introduction," in *Henri Laurens: Bronzes, Collages, Drawings, Prints*, London: Arts Council of Great Britain, 1980

Henri Laurens: Rétrospective, Paris: Réunion des Musées Nationaux, 1992

Hofmann, Werner, *The Sculpture of Henri Laurens*, New York: Abrams, 1970

Kuthy, Sandor, *Henri Laurens, 1885–1954* (bilingual German-French edition), Bern, Switzerland: Kunstmuseum, and Fribourg, Switzerland: Office du Livre Fribourg, 1985

Lichtenstern, Christa, "Der Amphion von Laurens: Plastischer Prozess und Mythos," in *Henri Laurens (1885–1954): Skulpturen, Collagen, Zeichnungen, Aquarelle, Druckgraphik*, edited by Norbert Nobis, Hanover, Germany: Sprengel Museum, 1985

Menier-Fourniau, Mady, *L'oeuvre sculpté d'Henri Laurens*, Paris: Publications de la Sorbonne, 1993

Monod-Fontaine, Isabelle, *Henri Laurens: Le cubisme, constructions et papiers collés, 1915–1919*, Paris: Éditions du Centre Georges Pompidou, 1985; abridged as *Henri Laurens: Cubist Constructions and Collages, 1915–1918*, Fort Worth, Texas: Fort Worth Art Museum, 1986

PIERRE LEGROS II 1666–1719 *Franco-Roman*

Pierre Legros was the most significant and innovative of the French sculptors to rise to prominence in Rome during the later 17th and early 18th centuries. Gianlorenzo Bernini's death in 1680 had left the field of sculpture without a dominant heir, and the discontinuation of great papal commissions caused a shift in patronage to the wealthy religious orders and other prominent secular and ecclesiastic individuals. Yet far from stifling sculptural production, this situation allowed talented newcomers such as Legros a chance to make their mark. The 24-year-old Legros arrived in Rome in 1690 with an ideal pedigree, having learned his art from his father, Pierre Legros I, and his uncles, the Marsy brothers, all sculptors for the royal works in Paris and Versailles. The younger Legros had shown such talent as a student at the Royal Academy in Paris that the academy sent him to its Roman outpost with a prestigious stipend despite Louis XIV's financial difficulties at the time. After five years of study, Legros emerged as the surprise winner of one of the top commissions available: the large sculptural group of *Religion Overthrowing Heresy* on the altar of St. Ignatius in the Chapel of St. Ignatius of Loyola at Il Gesù, Rome, the mother church of the Jesuit order. This feat brought him both instant fame and the immediate dismissal from the academy for circumventing the king's prerogative as a patron. Subsequently, Legros, giving up any further royal support, embarked on an extremely successful independent career. He followed the novel conception of the *Religion* group, a relieflike composition set on a sharp diagonal and integrated with its architectural base, with other equally creative reconsiderations of familiar sculptural genres.

Among his early reliefs, the sarcophagus of Pius V, *St. Pius V on His Deathbed*, at the Church of Santa Maria Maggiore seems to recall works by Germain Pilon in its extremely sensitive low relief in gilt bronze, with rippling draperies and gentle but precise modeling. *The Apotheosis of the Blessed Aloysius Gonzaga* in the Church of Sant'Ignazio is a stunning tour de force, capturing painterly effects in sculpture on a monumental scale. The gleaming figure of the youthful saint seems hardly attached to the cloudy relief background with groups of angels gesturing toward him from above and below. In his later reliefs, such as *Tobit Lending Money to Gabael* and *St. Francis of Paola Imploring the Virgin*, Legros proved himself a master of multifigure compositions that combine narrative power and ornamental detail.

Between 1697 and 1707 Legros created the major sculptural components for the ambitious and elaborate De La Tour–Bouillon family tomb in France, a project instigated by Cardinal Bouillon, who was then residing in Rome. Although the disastrous political and dynastic pretensions of Bouillon ultimately prevented the erection of the monument, Legros's sculptures survive—the life-size portraits of the cardinal's parents, a battle relief, and a heraldic tower with a winged figure emerging from it—as does documentation proving the sculptor's contribution to the overall conception. Legros, who used the tower to take the place of the more traditional obelisk or pyramid behind the deceased, posed the couple engaged in an active dialogue, instead of merely side by side. His later tomb of Pope Gregory XV at the Church of Sant'Ignazio compares in sumptuousness and grand design. Legros adapted its most striking motif, a huge drapery and baldachin of alabaster arranged over and around the enthroned pope, directly from the ephemeral catafalques that were so popular at the time.

Legros also carved a number of large statues—most notably *St. Dominic* at St. Peter's Basilica, Rome, and *St. Thomas* and *St. Bartholomew*, both at the Basilica of San Giovanni in Laterano—each carefully designed in consideration of its location and exact position relative to lighting and viewpoints. He generally selected simple poses or gestures for his figures that retain their effectiveness at a great distance and arranged the drapery into large areas of dramatic light and dark. He directed greatest attention, however, to a consistently sensitive and detailed articulation of the surface that allows the viewer at a closer range to experience an astonishing variety of textures and hues.

Most of the larger architectural and sculptural ensembles to which Legros contributed were collaborative projects under the supervision of an architect or designer, but the sculptor managed to maintain a distinct independence while adhering to general agreed-upon guidelines. Perhaps his most felicitous partnership occurred with Filippo Juvarra in the Antamori Chapel in the Church of San Girolamo della Carità between 1708 and 1710. Legros sculpted the statue of *St. Philip Neri in Glory* shown in religious rapture, transported from earthly existence and supported by two angels and a cloud bank. Despite severe limitations regarding space and lighting, the architectural design enhances the ecstatic vision of the saint by placing the figure before an oval window whose glass panes are articulated like an off-center halo. By obscuring the base, the saint seems to hover in a removed sphere; the celestial light emanating around his head further diminishes the marble's material presence. The gestures, the light on the textured sculptural surface, and the architectural framing coordinate perfectly to produce not only a familiar expression of Baroque rhetoric but also one of new emotional subtlety.

The considerable number of surviving terracotta *bozzetti* (small sculptures made as preparatory studies or models for full-scale works) shows that Legros was also a masterful and admired modeler who worked swiftly in wet clay, imbuing it with the same sophisticated effects as his marbles. Although his French roots remain palpable, Legros's sculptures also reflect Italian influences from Bernini and Alessandro Algardi, as well as certain compositional motifs adapted from Ercole Ferrata and Melchiorre Caffà. However his personal style found no direct following in Rome. While he was on a trip to Paris in 1715, jealous sculptors refused him Royal Academy membership, which embittered the famous artist, who promptly returned to Italy for good. Yet his sweet-faced, heavy-lidded figures and his emphasis on the sculptural surface suited the trends of the new century and were further developed in the works of younger Frenchmen, such as his student Guillaume Coustou.

STEFANIE WALKER

See also **Baroque and Rococo; Bernini, Gianlorenzo; Caffà, Melchiorre; Ferrata, Ercole; Italy: Renaissance–Baroque; Pilon, Germain**

Biography

Born in Paris, France, 12 April 1666. Son of Pierre I a sculptor for the French crown. Studied at Académie Royale in Paris from early 1680s; won prizes, 1685 and 1686. In Rome, first as resident member at Royal French Academy, from 28 June 1690, independent after 1695; member of Accademia di San Luca, Rome, 10 October 1700. Collaborated with painter-designers Andrea Pozzo and Carlo Maratti; architects Filippo Juvarra and Carlo Fontana; sculptors Pierre-Etienne Monnot, and Camillo Rusconi, among others. Major patrons included the Jesuit and Dominican orders, Cardinal Bouillon, Congregation of the Monte di Pietà, lawyer Tommaso Antamori, and banker Pierre Crozat. Died in Rome, Italy, 3 May 1719.

Selected Works

1692–95   *Vetturia* (after the antique); marble; Tuileries Gardens, Paris, France

1695–99   *Religion Overthrowing Heresy*; marble; Chapel of St. Ignatius of Loyola, Il Gesù, Rome, Italy

1697–98   *The Apotheosis of the Blessed Luigi Gonzaga*; marble; Lancellotti Chapel, Church of Sant'Ignazio, Rome, Italy

1697–98   *St. Pius V on His Deathbed*; gilt bronze; Basilica of Santa Maria Maggiore, Rome, Italy

1697–99   *The Apotheosis of Ignatius of Loyola*; silver, bronze (largely reconstructed); Chapel of St. Ignatius of Loyola, Il Gesù, Rome, Italy

1697– before 1708   *Frédéric-Maurice de la Tour d'Auvergne*; marble; Hotel-Dieu, Cluny, France

1701–03   Tomb of Cardinal Girolamo Casanata; marble; Basilica of San Giovanni in Laterano, Rome, Italy

1702   *Clement XI and the Arts*; terracotta; Accademia di San Luca, Rome, Italy

1702   *St. Dominic*; marble; St. Peter's Basilica, Rome, Italy

1702–03   *St. Stanilas Kostka*; marble; Cappellette di Santo Stanislao, Rome, Italy

1702–05   *Tobit Lending Money to Gabael*; marble; Church of Monte di Pietà, Rome, Italy

1705–12   *St. Thomas* and *St. Bartholomew*; marble; Basilica of San Giovanni in Laterano, Rome, Italy

1706–08   *Cardinal Girolamo Casanata*; marble; Biblioteca Casanatense, Rome, Italy

1708–10   *St. Philip Neri in Glory*; marble; Antamoro Chapel, Church of San Girolamo della Carità, Rome, Italy

1709–14 Tomb of Pope Gregory XV; marble, colored stones, gilt bronze; Church of Sant'Ignazio, Rome, Italy

1714–19 *Gregory the Great* and *Emperor Henry II*; marble; Chiostro dei Benefattori, Montecassino, Italy

ca. 1716 *St. Francis of Paola Imploring the Virgin*; marble; San Giacomo degli Incurabili, Rome, Italy

Further Reading

Bissell, Gerhard, *Pierre Legros, 1666–1719*, Reading, Berkshire: Si Vede, 1997

Enggass, Robert, *Early Eighteenth-Century Sculpture in Rome: An Illustrated Catalogue Raisonné*, 2 vols., University Park: Pennsylvania State University Press, 1976

Nava-Cellini, Antonia, *La scultura del Settecento*, Turin, Italy: UTET, 1982

Souchal, François, *French Sculptors of the 17th and 18th Centuries: The Reign of Louis XIV*, vols. 1–3, Oxford: Cassirer, 1977–87, and vol. 4, London: Faber and Faber, 1993; see especially vols. 2 and 4

ST. STANISLAS KOSTKA

Pierre Legros II (1666–1719)

1702–03

marble

life-size

Cappellette di Santo Stanislao, Rome, Italy

Even today's visitors to the chapel of St. Stanislas Kostka, with its striking figure by Pierre Legros II, experience a mild shock and a lingering sense of the surreal. Both reactions are remarkably similar to those expressed by 18th-century viewers: "the devotion that [the statue] arouses . . . where in the light and dark of the room those who enter seem to see a deceased on his deathbed . . . one is struck by terror at the first sight of this figure, [but] no one fails to admire it, as one examines its beauties" (see Bissell, 1997). The main reason for this is the unique way one encounters the recumbent statue of Stanislas and the manner in which it is sculpted and staged.

Although the chapel area experienced several alterations, one still sees Legros's sculpture much as it was originally intended. After passing through a series of modest domestic rooms, a small, unobtrusive doorway opens the view toward the foot of the saint's freestanding bed. Upon entering, the visitor is led by the twisting pose of the figure around to the lateral and main view of the work. The saint is shown on a low bed and propped by two pillows with his left knee slightly lifted. His head rolls to his right in the direction of the chapel's altar, but his eyes are veiled and his lips parted, expressing impending death and religious ecstasy. No barriers, only a low platform, hold the viewer's physical proximity in check (thin iron railings visible in 18th-century prints have been removed). The result is an astounding sense of intimacy that is only heightened by the figure's lifelike scale and coloring. The head, hands, and feet, as well as collar of his shirt, are of white marble; the habit, laid into ridges and waves, is of shiny black touchstone, whereas the mattress and drape of the bier are of striated ochre marble with a fringe of gilt bronze. As has been noted by Bissell (1997), the brownish gold of the bed would have picked up the tones of a gilt bronze halo, now missing from the statue, and the framed Madonna picture in his left hand (also gilt), as well as parts of the crucifix and rosary that once nestled in his right arm and hand.

A short explanation of the life and significance of this rather obscure saint helps to clarify the genesis and appearance of the sculpture. Stanislas Kostka, born of Polish nobility, overcame the vigorous resistance of his family and other hardships to join the Jesuit order. By 1567 the sickly 17-year-old had survived what should have been fatal illness through visions of the Virgin and of angels bearing the Eucharist. Taken ill again in 1568 and hospitalized at the Novitiate of Sant'Andrea, he died there on 15 August in what was considered an exemplary manner of humble acceptance and religious observance amid further visions of the Virgin among angels. Admiration for his youthful purity and depth of religious conviction, as well as numerous miracles credited to his intercession, eventually led to his beatification under Pope Clement X in 1670 and his canonization under Benedict XIII in 1726. He became the first adolescent saint and a patron of both the Polish nation and religious youth in general.

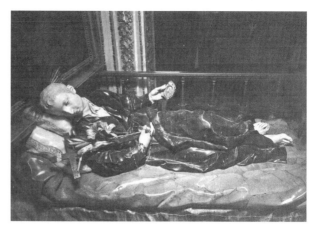

St. Stanislas Kostka
© Alinari / Art Resource, NY

The promotion of Stanislas as a saint was actively pursued by the Jesuits in the 17th century and belongs to a series of similar efforts to advance the cult of prominent figures from their order, such as St. Ignatius, St. Francis Xavier, and St. Aloysius Gonzaga. At the turn to the 18th century, all of the major artistic projects, mainly altars and statues, that were commissioned by the Jesuits for each of these new saints involved Legros, making him a kind of house sculptor. In August 1702, the Jesuit general Thyrso Gonzalez, one of Legros's most active supporters, ordered the renovation of the chapel and contiguous rooms on the basis of the newly discovered location of Stanislas's chamber next to a dilapidated chapel in the Novitiate. In 1703 he donated 300 *scudi* of his own funds, and the new chapel with Legros's statue was consecrated that year by Cardinal Santacroce on the saint's feast day, 13 November. The reigning pope, Clement XI, visited the chapel on the following day and praised the sculpture warmly.

An early print of the new chapel in 1703 indicates that a fresco on the wall behind the top of the bed represented Stanislas's last vision, the Madonna accompanied by angels gesturing toward the statue. The limited light, cited by the earliest visitors, further enhanced the illusion. The entire chapel area, therefore, tried to persuade the visitor to suspend the present and experience the past and the otherworldly as real. Gianlorenzo Bernini's *Ecstasy of St. Teresa* (1647–52) and *Blessed Ludovica Albertoni in Ecstasy* (1671–74) are important precursors for such attempts, but in these examples, the main figure remains elevated and removed from the viewer, seen through an architectural opening beyond a balustrade. In a sense, Legros's *St. Stanislas* is more related to effigies under altars that could be viewed closely, such as Stefano Maderno's *St. Cecilia* (1600), and to more internalized representations, such as Melchiorre Caffà's *St. Rosa of Lima* (1668). More than any explicit action of the figure, its aura and that of the entire room, its realistic colors, and its quiet intimacy produce the strongest effect (see Bissell, 1997).

The various aspects of the sculpture and its singular mise-en-scène appear carefully calculated, yet the documentary evidence makes it unlikely that there was a single designer for the entire site. Legros certainly was a master at maximizing the potential of given spaces and sources of light, but one might question whether he was the sole originator of this staged environment, the revolutionary idea of a sculptural representation without any distance to or boundaries for the viewer. There is a certain didactic component and degree of illusionism that suggest Jesuit methods and preferences of education and persuasion. Supporting the possibility of a Jesuit contribution is the interesting contro-

versy about the relocation of the statue to the Church of Sant'Andrea in 1713 (see Haskell, 1955). Legros took great pains to support such a move; he clearly preferred to have his statue placed above an altar in a much more traditional fashion. Despite his eloquent arguments, the Jesuits decided to leave it where it was, citing the statue's proven effectiveness. The committee realized that they had a winning combination that perfectly served their intentions of emotional persuasion. Expansions and "renovations" in the chapel in the 1730s and the 19th century may have further altered the space, but Legros's *St. Stanislas Kostka* maintains an aura all its own.

STEFANIE WALKER

Further Reading

Bissell, Gerhard, *Pierre Legros, 1666–1719*, Reading, Berkshire: Si Vede, 1997
Haskell, Francis, "Pierre Legros and a Statue of the Blessed Stanislas Kostka," *The Burlington Magazine* 97 (1955)

WILHELM LEHMBRUCK 1881–1919
German

At 14 years old Wilhelm Lehmbruck began his more than ten-year study of art. He was trained primarily as a craftsman at the School for Arts and Crafts and the Art Academy, both in Düsseldorf. His early sculptures and designs corresponded to the genres that were in demand: portraiture, tombs, and architectural sculpture. A thematic focus of the Düsseldorf Art Academy was to offer representations of the working world. Lehmbruck, the son of a miner, revealed the influence of this naturalistic direction in his early work. He achieved his first success in 1902 with the opulent femininity of his neo-Baroque *Woman Bathing*. Before 1910, however, Lehmbruck did not distinguish himself significantly from the obsolete traditions of Wilhelminian Germany.

In 1904 he became acquainted with the work of Auguste Rodin at a major exhibition in Düsseldorf. He began taking trips to Paris in 1906 and participating in the exhibitions of the Société Nationale des Beaux-Arts, the traditional salon (as opposed to the Salon d'Automne). His dramatic monumental figure *Mankind* clearly reflected his examination of Rodin.

When Lehmbruck moved to Paris in 1910, he met Rodin. The direct encounter was a disappointment to Lehmbruck, which is why he distanced himself from his former idol. His first Parisian works, above all the *Standing Female Figure* (1910) underscore his break from Rodin. This self-contained, larger than life-size female figure was influenced far more by the German painter Hans von Marées, whose work had been rediscovered about 1908/10. The figures in Marées's paintings, which seem to live in an Arcadian past rather than the present day, were the models for a Neoclassical style in painting and sculpture that dissociated itself from Naturalism and Impressionism. Under Marées's influence, Lehmbruck was able to free himself from his early work not only in sculpture but also in his painting and graphic work.

The large *Standing Female Figure* (1910), Lehmbruck's first masterpiece, was the starting point for his artistic development in various directions. Immediately after its completion, Lehmbruck—following the example set by Rodin—experimented with torsos. He created *Female Torso* without the typical features of dangling arms and legs covered by drapery. The compact trunk and soulful head form a concentrated unity. With the *Hagen Torso*, also known as the *Small Female Torso*, Lehmbruck formed for the first time a sculpture that was intended as a torso from the beginning.

In the early Parisian years, Lehmbruck began experimenting with cement casts, testing out various color tones and surface structures. The sculptor's initial notion that these casts would be just as permanent as the expensive sculptures in precious bronze and marble did not prove true. Many of Lehmbruck's stone casts

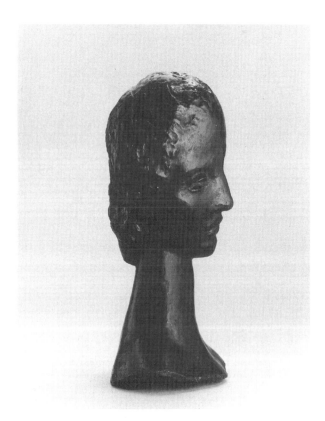

Head of a Woman (1913–14)
Bequest of Robert H. Tannahill
© 1985 The Detroit Institute of Arts

are now damaged or destroyed. He did continue to use bronze and even marble in addition to the stone casts; however, he could only afford the expensive bronze casts for small sculptures.

In 1911 Lehmbruck created his most famous statue, *Woman Kneeling.* The extremely overattenuated, large female figure is distinguished clearly from his earlier works. Lehmbruck was inspired by his friend Alexander Archipenko, who had produced a similarly composed *Kneeling Woman* in 1910; however, Archipenko's work lacked the animation typical of Lehmbruck's work. Lehmbruck's figure was shown in 1911 in the Salon d'Automne in Paris and appeared subsequently at important exhibitions of avant-garde art, including in 1912 at the Sonderbund in Cologne, and in 1913 at the Armory Show in New York.

The sculptor transferred the protracted proportions of *Kneeling Woman* onto his following large statues: *Rising Youth* and *Woman Thinking.* There are also torsos of these figures. For the torso of the *Woman Thinking,* Lehmbruck made the exception of omitting the head as well. Unlike the female figures, Lehmbruck did not exhibit *Rising Youth* in Paris, rather, he showed this very bulky, severe statue for the first time in Berlin.

For the last figures of his Parisian period, such as *Girl Gazing Back over Her Shoulder,* Lehmbruck turned away from lean, overelongated proportions and returned to a more serene, harmonious modeling of the figures. When he presented his first solo exhibition in the Galerie Levesque in Paris, writer André Salmon described him in the introduction of the catalogue as a sculptor striving for Classical representation and order. In German art criticism, however, Lehmbruck's work after 1911 was described as Expressionist.

The outbreak of World War I compelled Lehmbruck to leave Paris and move to Berlin. He was spared service at the front and became an ambulance man in a Berlin hospital for a short time. In 1916 he was released from war duty and traveled to neutral Switzerland. Although Lehmbruck was not personally and directly confronted with the events of the war, he grappled with them through his art. The impetus was the invitation to enter a contest to create a warrior monument in Duisburg, Germany. Although Lehmbruck did not participate in the competition, the figure of the *Fallen Man* was created in this context. The piece is an overelongated masculine nude kneeling and bending so far forward that his head touches the ground.

Various titles have been given to the second large masculine figure created during those years: *Seated Youth*; *Man, Bending Over*; *The Friend*; or *The Thinker.* These play on different layers of meaning: despondency and grief, probably over a dead friend, as well as a clear allusion to Rodin's *The Thinker* (*ca.*

1880). Both of these large masculine figures have been posthumously interpreted as obvious antiwar statements.

Most of Lehmbruck's works begun in Switzerland were not completed. The sculptor had fallen into a serious artistic and personal crisis. He developed an unhappy passion for the young actress Elisabeth Bergner, whose portrait he modeled (*Portrait Bust of Miss B.* and *Betende—Woman Praying*: 1918; Wilhelm Lehmbruck Museum, Duisburg). Illness and professional failure compounded his crisis. At the end of March 1919, Lehmbruck took his own life in his Berlin studio.

Lehmbruck's unfinished works are highly divergent. His extensive work in drawing and painting reveal a clear affiliation with Symbolism, the subject matter of which was translated into Expressionist forms. Although his famous individual statues arise out of the same context, they leave the weight of content behind. Lehmbruck succeeded in creating several figures that embody serenity or inspiration, but also grief and desperation in an impressive manner. His masterpieces were perceived by his contemporaries as exemplary representations of man; he stands as one of the most significant German sculptors of his time.

URSEL BERGER

See also **Archipenko, Alexander Porfirevich; Rodin, Auguste**

Biography

Born in Meiderich (now a quarter of Duisburg), Germany, 4 January 1881. Began studies in 1895 at the Kunstgewerbeschule (School for Arts and Crafts) in Düsseldorf; at the Kunstakademie there under Karl Janssen, 1901–06; became a freelance artist in Düsseldorf, where worked on assignments for portraits and tombs; traveled to the Netherlands and England, 1904; first trip to Italy, 1905; went to Paris by 1910, where he exhibited at the Salon of the Société Nationale des Beaux-Arts; visited Rodin; participated in many exhibitions in Paris and Germany; first solo exhibition at Galerie Levesque, Paris, 1914; second trip to Italy, 1913; returned to Berlin after the outbreak of World War I, 1914; served as an ambulance man; released from duty; relocated to Zurich, Switzerland, 1916; elected into the Prussian Akademie der Künste, 1919. Died in Berlin, Germany, 25 March 1919.

Selected Works

1902   *Woman Bathing*; bronze; Kunstmuseum Düsseldorf, Germany

1910   *Female Torso*; bronze;
Skulpturensammlung, Dresden, Germany

1910   *Portrait of Mrs. L.*; bronze; Städtische Kunsthalle, Mannheim, Germany

1910   *Standing Female Figure*; cast stone; Kröller-Müller Museum, Otterlo, the Netherlands

1910–11 *Hagen Torso (Small Female Torso)*; cast stone; Museum Folkwang, Essen, Germany

1910–12 *Standing Female Figure*; marble; Wilhelm Lehmbruck Museum, Duisburg, Germany

1911   *Woman Kneeling*; stone; Museum of Modern Art, New York City, United States

1913   *Rising Youth*; stone; Museum of Modern Art, New York City, United States

1913–14 *Woman Thinking*; cast stone; Staatsgalerie, Stuttgart, Germany

1914   *Girl Gazing Back over Her Shoulder*; cast stone; Wilhelm Lehmbruck Museum, Duisberg, Germany

1914–17 Torso of *Woman Thinking*; cast stone; Städtische Kunsthalle, Mannheim, Germany

1915–16 *Fallen Man*; cast stone; Wilhelm Lehmbruck Museum, Duisburg, Germany

1916   *Seated Youth*; colored plaster; National Gallery of Art, Washington, D.C., United States

1918   *Head of a Thinker*; cast stone; Nationalgalerie, Berlin, Germany

1918   *Woman Praying*; plaster; Wilhelm Lehmbruck Museum, Duisburg, Germany

Further Reading

Händler, Gerhard, *Wilhelm-Lehmbruck-Sammlung*, 2 vols., Recklinghausen, Germany: Verlag Aurel Bongers, 1964; see especially vol. 1, *Plastik-Malerei*

Heller, Reinhold (editor), *The Art of Wilhelm Lehmbruck*, Washington, D.C.: National Gallery of Art, 1972

Hoff, August, *Wilhelm Lehmbruck, seine Sendung und sein Werk*, Berlin: Rembrandt-Verlag, 1936; as *Wilhelm Lehmbruck: Life and Work*, London: Pall Mall, 1969

The Museum of Modern Art, New York, *Wilhelm Lehmbruck, Aristide Maillol: Sculpture*, New York: Plandome Press, 1930

Rudloff, Martina, and Dietrich Schubert (editors), *Wilhelm Lehmbruck*, Bremen, Germany: Gerhard Marcks-Stiftung, 2000

Salzmann, Siegfried, *Das Wilhelm Lehmbruck Museum Duisburg*, Recklinghausen, Germany: Aurel Bongers, 1981

Salzmann, Siegfried, and Karl-Egon Vester (editors), *Hommage à Lehmbruck, Lehmbruck in seiner Zeit*, Duisburg: Wilhelm-Lehmbruck-Museums, 1981

Schubert, Dietrich, *Die Kunst Lehmbrucks*, Worms, Germany: Werner, 1981; 2nd edition, Worms: Wernersche Verlaggesellschaft, 1990

Schubert, Dietrich, *Wilhelm Lehmbruck: Catalogue raisonné der Skulpturen, 1898–1919*, Worms, Germany: Wernersche Verlagsgesellschaft, 2001

Stiftung und Sammlung Sally Falk, Mannheim, Germany: Städtische Kunsthalle Mannheim, 1994

Wilhelm Lehmbruck (1881–1919): Plastik, Malerei, Graphik, Duisburg, Germany: Wilhelm-Lehmbruck-Museum der Stadt Duisburg, 1987

LORD FREDERIC LEIGHTON 1830–1896 *British*

Although the painter Frederic Leighton exhibited only three statues in his long career, he occupies a pivotal position in the history of British sculpture. As president of the Royal Academy, Leighton instituted a number of reforms and fostered the neglected art of sculpture, paving the way for the movement commonly known as the "New Sculpture." His first work in sculpture, *Athlete Wrestling with a Python* (1877), is usually considered the inaugural work of the revival in interest in and production of sculpture in Britain.

During Leighton's lifetime it became commonplace to refer to the "sculpturesque" qualities of his paintings, which focused on the rendering of figural mass and solidity. Well-schooled in ancient art as well as in Continental developments, Leighton decided to make his own entry into sculpture with *Athlete Wrestling with a Python*. The initial idea for the statue arose from his work on the monumental processional painting *Daphnephoria*, a work that occupied Leighton from 1874 to 1876 and that contains numerous allusions and references to Classical statuary and its figure types. Leighton developed the poses for many of these painted figures with the aid of small statuettes. These *modellos* allowed him to better visualize the figures in order to best translate them to the two-dimensional painted surface. Manipulating these small handheld sculptures, Leighton became increasingly interested in the challenges of three-dimensional representation.

Athlete Wrestling with a Python grew out of this method of working with statuettes. Leighton exhibited the life-size sculpture in bronze at the Royal Academy summer exhibition in 1877 to almost universal acclaim. The statue depicts a nude athlete struggling head to toe with a python. Remarkable for its full nudity and naturalistic treatment of anatomy, the statue also employs a dynamic spiral composition that encourages the viewer to circumambulate around the work, mirroring Leighton's own process of rotating his sketch models. Through this strategy Leighton urged the viewer to experience the sculpture fully as a three-dimensional object from all sides. The work seemed to critics far more lifelike than the frontal, standardized Neoclassical style that characterized most contemporary sculpture. Exhibited in the year before Leighton's election as president of the Royal Academy, *Athlete Wrestling with a Python* effectively functioned both as a testament to the sculptor's artistic ability to work successfully in various media and as a challenge to the existing conventions of sculpture. It became one of the first purchases for the British state under the Chantrey Bequest; Leighton was elected to the presidency of the Royal Academy the following year.

Athlete Wrestling with a Python marks a watershed in the history of British sculpture and proved inspirational to other artists, such as Hamo Thornycroft, Alfred Gilbert, and William Blake Richmond—all of whom created statues that respond to aspects of Leighton's statue. Leighton himself further explored the spiral composition in *Sluggard* (1886). This detailed male nude demonstrates Leighton's knowledge of male anatomy as well as the artist's highly complex compositional aims. The spiral organization of the earlier *Athlete Wrestling with a Python* fused with traditional *contrapposto* (a natural pose with the weight of one leg, the shoulder, and hips counterbalancing one another), resulting in a naturalistic rendering of body and pose that nevertheless avoids singular frontality and encourages circumambulation. In the same year, Leighton also exhibited the statuette *Needless Alarms* (1886), in which he attempted to apply the same bodily organization to the female nude. Later, statuette versions of these three statues were produced. The sketch model for the *Sluggard* became one of the most influential and popular statuettes of the Late Victorian era after Arthur Collie presented it in 1890.

In his capacity as president of the Royal Academy from 1878 until 1896, Leighton supported many of the young sculptors who would become the central figures of the New Sculpture movement, including Thornycroft, Gilbert, and Thomas Brock. Improving the training of sculptors in the Royal Academy, orchestrating key public commissions, and publicly arguing for the importance of sculpture, Leighton played a substantial role in the Late Victorian sculptural renaissance in England. He personally initiated a campaign to have Alfred Stevens's monument to the Duke of Wellington moved to its originally intended location in St. Paul's and completed according to the sculptor's plan, even going so far as to pay a substantial portion of the costs. Leighton bought and commissioned works by many of the main sculptors of the day, including Thornycroft, Gilbert, and Auguste Rodin, and was one of Rodin's first patrons in England.

Over the course of Leighton's presidency of the Royal Academy, British sculpture achieved a higher degree of international reputation than it had previously. Shepherded by Leighton, many of the practitioners of the New Sculpture served on international selection committees and organized large exhibitions in

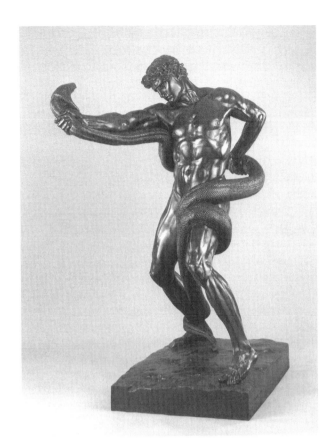

Athlete Wrestling with a Python
© Tate Gallery, London / Art Resource, NY

Selected Works

1877   *Athlete Wrestling with a Python*; bronze; Tate Gallery, London, England
1886   *Needless Alarms*; bronze; private collection
1886   *Sluggard*; bronze; Tate Gallery, London, England
1890   *Sluggard* (sketch model); bronze statuette; various collections
1891   *Athlete Wrestling with a Python*; marble; Forbes Collection, Old Battersea House, London, England

Further Reading

Barringer, T.J., and Elizabeth Prettejohn (editors), *Frederic Leighton: Antiquity, Renaissance, Modernity*, New Haven, Connecticut: Yale University Press, 1999

Barrington, Emilie, *The Life, Letters, and Work of Frederic Leighton*, 2 vols., London: Allen, and New York: Macmillan, 1906; reprint, New York: AMS Press, 1973

Getsy, David J., "Encountering the Male Nude at the Origins of Modern Sculpture: Rodin, Leighton, Hildebrand, and the Negotiation of Physicality and Temporality," in *Look, See, Behold: The Spectator's Time*, edited by Antoinette Roesler-Friedenthal and Johannes Nathan, Berlin: Mann, 2001

Jones, Stephen (editor), *Frederic, Lord Leighton: Eminent Victorian Artist*, London: Royal Academy of Arts, and New York: Abrams, 1996

Leighton, Frederic, *Addresses Delivered to the Students of the Royal Academy*, London: Kegan Paul Trench Trübner, and New York: Longmans, Green, 1896

Ormond, Leonée, and Richard Ormond, *Lord Leighton*, New Haven, Connecticut: Yale University Press, 1975

Prettejohn, Elizabeth, "The Modernism of Frederic Leighton," in *English Art, 1860–1914: Modern Artists and Identity*, edited by David Peters Corbett and Lara Perry, Manchester: Manchester University Press, 2000; New Brunswick, New Jersey: Rutgers University Press, 2001

Read, Benedict, *Victorian Sculpture*, New Haven, Connecticut: Yale University Press, 1982

Read, Benedict, "Leighton as a Sculptor: Releasing Sculpture from Convention," in *Lord Leighton, 1830–1896, and Leighton House: A Centenary Celebration*, edited by Robin Simon, London: Apollo Magazine, 1996

Read, Benedict, and Alexander Kader, *Leighton and His Sculptural Legacy: British Sculpture, 1875–1930*, London: Joanna Barnes Fine Arts, 1996

Britain. From both the exemplary sculptures Leighton created and his institutional encouragement, Late Victorian sculpture owed a substantial portion of its renewed vitality and public acclaim to Leighton.

DAVID GETSY

See also **Stevens, Alfred; Thornycroft Family**

Biography

Born in Scarborough, North Yorkshire, England, 3 December 1830. Moved to Florence and enrolled at the Accademia di Belle Arti, 1845; moved to Frankfurt am Main, Germany, 1846, and studied at the Städelsches Kunstinstitut; after two years in Brussels and Paris, returned to Frankfurt and the Städelsches Kunstinstitut, where he studied under Edward von Steinle, 1850–52; moved to Rome, 1852, then Paris; returned to London, 1859; elected associate of the Royal Academy, 1864; elected full Royal Academician, 1868; known primarily for his paintings, exhibited first sculpture in 1877; president of the Royal Academy, 1878–96; knighted, 1878; created a baronet, 1886; became first artist raised to peerage, as Baron Leighton of Stretton, 1896. Died in London, England, 25 January 1896.

HANS LEINBERGER *fl.* 1511–1531
German

The Bavarian cities of Munich, Regensburg, and Passau form an art-geographical triangle whose sacred 16th-century wood sculpture was closely connected with the name, workshop, circle, and school of the sculptor Hans Leinberger. His work marks the apex of Late Gothic sculpture in the Bavarian/Austrian artistic realm. Leinberger's work is typified by over life-size

Madonna sculptures with thick, billowing garments and wide, furrowed heads that exude a rural vitality; along with them stand figures of young saints with disheveled hair who trip along in a fitful, jerky manner. His reliefs describe Christ's catastrophic sufferings and the martyrdom of the saints as dramatic tragedies played out in groups of protagonists engaged in frenetic activity. Leinberger was a master of figural effects: the massiveness and folding in the draping of his garments are so unsettlingly and impetuously arbitrary and they have such a plastic vehemence and physical presence that the observer is simply forced to make an aesthetic judgment about these figures over and above his cultic veneration of them. Among the contemporaneous Late Gothic Mannerists of German sculpture—Veit Stoss from Nuremberg, Meister H.L. from the upper Rhine Valley, and Meister von Ottobeuren from Swabia—Leinberger produced by far the most monumental and dramatic stylistic novelties. Never fine, courtly, or modern in the sense of the Italian-oriented Renaissance, his work is characterized by a refined coarseness that has a certain style.

The number of Leinberger's remaining documented works is admittedly rather low and is limited to two altar ensembles in Moosburg and Polling, as well as a few small-scale signed reliefs. The individual style appearing in these, however, allows a large number of further wood sculptures to be attributed to him without any doubt. Today, two altar ensembles consisting of several figures, as well as 15 large-scale wood sculptures, are unquestionably attributable to him, to which can be added some small-scale reliefs and a few bronze sculptures.

Nothing is known about Leinberger's training and early work. In 1513/14, he was already commissioned as "Meister Hans Pildschnitzer" from Landshut to do the carving for the great altar of the convent church in Moosburg (between Munich and Landshut). There he completed one of the last, great winged altars of the pre-Reformation period. Soon afterward he carved an over life-size cast model of the Habsburg Landgrave Albrecht IV for the tomb of Emperor Maximilian I in the Hofkirche (Court Church) in Innsbruck. Albrecht Dürer created the design sketch for this work. The drawing (Berlin) and the bronze casting (Innsbruck) have been preserved. Leinberger's casting model, however, has been lost. For this project, Leinberger was involved with artists from Swabia, Franconia, and Austria. His reputation had apparently grown beyond Lower Bavaria already in his early years. He made at least two further attempts in bronze sculpture: a *Mary and Child* in Berlin and a small-scale *St. John in Mourning* (*ca.* 1515) in Hamburg are, for the most part, failures from the perspective of the bronze casting technique, but they do document his engagement with the most valued of sculptural genres, the bronze cast, or at least with its technical challenges.

It is known that the ducal court in Landshut made numerous payments to Leinberger, but up to now not a single work from these commissions has been identified aside from the Moosburg altar. The rest of his known oeuvre consists entirely of religious iconography. Among his Madonnas, the *Virgin and Child* in the Church of St. Martin in Landshut is the most distinguished. Very similar to the Madonna in the Moosburg shrine, but free of influence from the antiquated Lukas-type Madonna typical of Moosburg, this over 2-meter-high Landshut *Virgin and Child* was once surrounded by a rosary. The high, slim, dignified Madonna is captured in a thickly bulging frame composed of circular folds that are the clearest mark of Leinberger's style.

A third sculpture of the Virgin Mary registers Leinberger's late style: his activity from 1526 to 1528 is documented by sources concerning the parish church in Polling, near Weilheim in Upper Bavaria, which was the sculpture's original location. Leinberger created three figures for an altar there, of which the enthroned *Mary and Child* (*Pollinger Madonna*) deserves special mention. Just as surely to be included among his late works are the imposing *St. George* in the Church of Our Lady, Munich, and the enthroned apostle *St. James the Elder*, in which the uncommonly fissured carving of the garments has been compared with "furrows" (see Lill, 1942).

Leinberger's production of crucifixes is also significant; it includes a group (entirely attributed) spanning the range from over life-size examples to small-scale pieces. His depictions of *Christ at Rest* seem to have had similar popularity—a favorite motif of Christ's sufferings in the devotional pictures venerated in the late Middle Ages, for which Dürer's small woodcut of the Passion became an important model.

Leinberger's style was rooted in various precedents. The arrangements of the figures and the gestures they make toward one another are similar to the altar figures of his Tyrolian predecessor, Michael Pacher. The same dramatic figural composition and the same sketchlike, stormy landscapes, as seen especially in Leinberger's reliefs, can be found in the paintings and graphic work of the so-called Danube School—Albrecht Altdorffer, Lucas Cranach the Elder, and Wolfgang Huber. Leinberger has accordingly been called the main representative of the Danube School of sculpture (see Legner, 1965). Even analogies to the preponderance of drapery popular in the so-called soft style (*weicher Stil*) around 1400 cannot be dismissed outright. This may be interpreted as a conscious, retrospective quotation on Leinberger's part, lending his cult images a representative dignity by falling back on old-fashioned and venerable styles.

Leinberger has correctly been identified as the author of several small-scale wood reliefs, some of which bear the sealed monogram "HL." The *Death as Skeleton* (also known as *Little Ambras Death*) belongs already to the modern genre of small-scale cabinet pieces: a meager, partially decomposed personification of Death, whose elegant, dancelike posture contrasts effectively with the repulsive motif of the depiction.

Local regional research has primarily investigated Leinberger's works from the usual standpoint of the connoisseur: about 70–80 items are being discussed today, as well as the reconstruction of biographical facts and the chronological order of his oeuvre. Closely related works are appropriately ascribed to his workshop or school, and provisional names have even been created for those in his circle. His elevation to the status of "one of the greatest German sculptors" (see Lill, 1942) served to stimulate research.

Leinberger research has been receiving new attention since the last decades of the 20th century and the result has been to place his work into a broader context according to more current art historical perspectives regarding the history of form and function. In the various effects they achieve from close up and from a distance, Leinberger's sculptures call for a basic self-awareness of sculpture over and above its simple perception. "A Leinberger sculpture is a permanent possibility of cumulative sensation" (see Baxandall, 1980), whether with regard to various distances from up close to far away or with regard to the change from front to side perspectives. These different perspectives between close and far and front and side invite the observer to move around the sculpture out of sheer curiosity—behavior on the part of the observer that runs entirely contrary to that of static devotion before the cult image.

Leinberger's work also stands as the break in tradition between the official cult image of the Middle Ages and a worldly, individual need for images on the part of the art consumer at the beginning of Modernity. The sculptor systematically quotes the older style of the *schöner-Stil* (Beautiful style) Madonna from the International style, the latter of which, around 1400, depicted figures wearing billowing, richly folded robes. He combined it with other, likewise traditional types of cult images, such as that of the legendary *Madonna* of St. Luke, to form particular stylistic variations. Leinberger thereby introduced a historical moment of retrospective and period-conscious art into the ahistorical craft of sculpting. As a consequence, Leinberger's art is associated with the "end of the medieval cultic image" (see Decker, 1985).

THOMAS ESER

See also **Germany: Gothic–Renaissance; Pacher, Michael; Stoss, Veit**

Biography

Born probably between 1475 and 1490; location unknown, but likely Landshut or Nuremberg, Germany. Training probably in Vienna or Regensburg; active in Landshut, Lower Bavaria, from 1510; worked regularly for court of Bavarian dukes (payments from the court in 1516, 1519, 1522, 1524, 1529–31); worked on Moosburg altar, erected 1514, and altar sculptures at nearby Regensburg, *ca.* 1520; last work for which there is archival evidence in accounts at the Landshut court, recorded February 1531; accounts of city treasurer in Munich, however, name a sculptor Hans from Landshut, suggesting he may have lived until 1535. Died in Germany, precise city and date unknown.

Selected Works

1511–14 High altar (including *Mary and Child, St. Castulus, St. John the Baptist, St. John the Evangelist, Emperor St. Henry II, Crucifixion of Christ, Mourning Virgin and St. John, St. Corbinian, St. Sigismund,* and reliefs of the martyrdom of St. Castulus); linden wood; Church of St. Castulus, Moosburg, Bavaria, Germany

1514–15 *Albrecht IV von Habsburg,* for the tomb of Emperor Maximilian I (based on a design by Albrecht Dürer, cast by Stefan Godl); bronze; Hofkirche (Court Church), Innsbruck, Austria

ca. 1515 *Mary and Child*; bronze; Staatliche Museen, Skulpturensammlung, Berlin, Germany (attributed)

ca. 1515–20 *Virgin and Child*; linden wood; Church of St. Martin, Landshut, Germany

1516 *Calvary*; boxwood; Bayerisches Nationalmuseum, Munich, Germany

1516 *Deposition from the Cross and Lamentation*; boxwood; Staatliche Museen, Skulpturensammlung, Berlin, Germany

ca. 1520 *Death as Skeleton* (also known as *Little Ambras Death*); pear wood; Schloss Ambras, Innsbruck, Austria (attributed)

ca. 1520–30 *Christ at Rest*; linden wood; Staatliche Museen, Berlin, Germany

ca. 1525 *St. James the Elder*; linden wood; Bayerisches Nationalmuseum, Munich, Germany

ca. 1525–30 Crucifix; linden wood; Cleveland Museum of Art, Cleveland, Ohio, United States (attributed)

ca.   *St. George*; linden wood; Church of Our
1525–30 Lady, Munich, Germany
1526–27 Altar sculptures for Church of Our Lady;
                  linden wood (mostly destroyed); *Mary and
                  Child*, also known as *Pollinger Madonna*:
                  convent church, Polling, Germany

Further Reading

Arnold, Paul M., *Der unbekannte Hans Leinberger: Unbekannte und verkannte Werke des Landshuter Bildschnitzers: Zuschreibungen, Analysen und Interpretationen, Abgrenzung gegen den Umkreis*, Landshut, Germany: Hans-Leinberger-Verein, 1991

Baxandall, Michael, *The Limewood Sculptors of Renaissance Germany*, New Haven, Connecticut: Yale University Press, 1980

Behle, Claudia, *Hans Leinberger: Leben und Eigenart des Künstlers, stilistische Entwicklung, Rekonstruktion der Gruppen und Altäre*, Munich: Kommissionsverlag UNI-Druck, 1984

Buchheit, Hans, and Georg Lill, *Hans Leinberger, Hans Stethaimer* (exhib. cat.), Munich: Wolf, 1932

Decker, Bernhard, *Das Ende des mittelalterlichen Kultbildes und die Plastik Hans Leinbergers*, Bamberg, Germany: Lehrstuhl für Kunstgeschichte und Aufbaustudium Denkmalpflege an der Universität Bamberg, 1985

Emmerling, Erwin, Hans Portsteffen, and Markus Weiss, *Die Pollinger Madonna von Hans Leinberger*, Munich: Bayerisches Landesamt für Denkmalpflege, 1990

Legner, Anton, "Plastik," in *Die Kunst der Donauschule: 1490–1540* (exhib. cat.), Linz, Austria: Oberösterreichischer Landesverlag, 1965

Liedke, Volker, *Hans Leinberger: Marginalien zur künstlerischen und genealogischen Herkunft des grossen Landshuter Bildschnitzers*, Munich: Kunstbuchverlag Weber, 1976

Lill, Georg, *Hans Leinberger, der Bildschnitzer von Landshut: Welt und Umwelt des Künstlers*, Munich: Bruckmann, 1942

MARY AND CHILD

Hans Leinberger (fl. 1511–1531)

1511–1514

linden wood

h. 2.12 m; with retable, 14.5 m

High altar, Church of St. Castulus, Moosburg, Bavaria, Germany

In early 1514, one of the last large-scale winged altars of the Late Gothic period was erected in what was then the convent church of Moosburg. It has been preserved *in situ* within what is now the Church of St. Castulus. The church was founded by the Moosburg provost Theoderich Mair together with the Bavarian dukes, whose members are represented along with the provost on a portrait of the founders in the altar predella (a painted panel at the bottom of an altarpiece).

The convent's accounts mention a "Meister Hannsen Pildschnitzer" from Landshut several times be-tween 1513 and 1514 as the artist was carrying out the altar, and there is no doubt that this artist was Hans Leinberger. The present Moosburg altar includes ten remaining large figural wood sculptures made of painted (or polychromed) linden wood: five in the area of the shrine, where the over life-size, central Madonna figure is framed by *St. Castulus* and *Emperor St. Henry II*; two biblical figures—*St. John the Baptist* (left) and *St. John the Evangelist* (right; previously St. Sebastian, then reworked in the 18th century to depict St. John)—serve to guard the shrine; and five figures in the altar crest, which includes a *Crucifixion of Christ*, the *Virgin*, and *St. John*, as well as the founders of the diocese, *St. Corbinian* and *St. Sigismund*. Next to those were numerous smaller figures of other saints and angels, bringing the number of figures originally comprising the sculptural ensemble to 25.

The furniture and sculpture of the altar underwent considerable changes in the late 18th century. Some figures were recarved or completely remade by the workshop of the Baroque sculptor Christian Jorhan the Elder (see Schmidt, 1989). The color composition was also changed several times, leading to numerous speculative reconstructions of the details of its original appearance. Also removed from the altar in the Late Baroque, but still in the church today, are four shallowly carved wooden reliefs that unquestionably once formed the hinged wings of the altar. They depict scenes from the life and martyrdom of the church patron, St. Castulus, a saint from Roman Antiquity who suffered his martyrdom under Emperor Diocletian. Castulus' relics had been located in Moosburg since 826. In the Late Middle Ages there was a brief tide of pilgrims to the church.

With a height of 14.5 meters, the Moosburg altar is, architecturally, one of the most powerful altar artifacts of its time. When Leinberger created the Moosburg altar, the so-called winged altar or polyptych had developed over two centuries to become the central liturgical fixture of German church interiors. The most impressive exemplars of its type had come into being since about 1450: Hans Multscher's Sterzing altar (1456–58/59) in southern Tyrol, Veit Stoss's altar (1477–89) at the Church of St. Mary in Kraków, and Michael Pacher's St. Wolfgang altarpiece (1471–81) near Salzburg. Along with their monumental size and synthesis of architecture, painting, and sculpture, these altars were characterized by their "transformability": over the course of the church calendar, the wings could be opened or closed to achieve various effects. Like a changing stage set, they offered the observer an ever-renewed experience of the images they contained.

In the middle of the shrine, towering at a height of 212 centimeters over all of the sculptures, stands the powerful figures of the *Mary and Child*, often referred to as the *Moosburg Madonna*. It is one of the major works of German wood sculpture from the years between the Late Gothic and Renaissance periods. Within its stylistic appearance, Leinberger combined the contrary phenomena of tradition and innovation in such an ingenious way that a very particular and highly original "cult image style" emerged, which would become the sculptor's trademark.

At first sight, the Mother and Child pair follows a proven and venerated model namely, that of the famous Lukas-type Madonna (supposedly a portrait of Mary made by the Evangelist St. Luke himself), which was manifest in several Byzantine icons (such as the miraculous picture of Santa Maria del Popolo in Rome). Not only the antiquated infant figure—clothed in thick material, raising his right hand as "world ruler," and supporting the other hand on a globe—has been handed down from this type, but also the style of Mary's clothes refer to the ancient, and therefore "authentic," image of the Mother of God. This Byzantine type was transformed into a Bavarian-Baroque *regina coeli* (queen of heaven) only through a partial change made in the late 18th century, which altered the position of Mary's right hand and gave her the

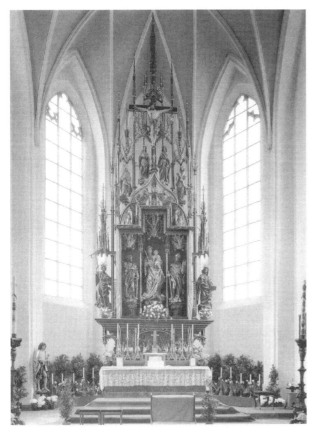

Mary and Child, High Altar
The Conway Library, Courtauld Institute of Art

scepter. In Leinberger's design, the hand that was originally held closer to the body instead points to the infant, which was entirely in accordance with the model of the Lukas-type Madonna.

There had not been a sculpture in the round of the St. Luke *Madonna* until Leinberger's (see Decker, 1985). His artistic accomplishment thus consists in his having transferred an iconic type from painting into the three-dimensional genre of sculpture in order to lend the already highly representative relief sculpture of his huge altar an ever greater representational power by means of the archaic image. This effect of "overtowering" is heightened even more by the four figures of angels on the lower hem of Mary's cloak, figures that—all equally awash in the mass of the garment—try in vain to control the dramatic waves in the drapery.

Leinberger fell back on a style far behind that of the contemporary fashion in a second, more stylistic manner. The powerful play of folds in the Mother and child's cloaks is oriented toward the so-called International or Beautiful style (*schöner-Stil*), characterized by billowing, richly folding robes. This historical style of folding, which by 1500 was completely unfashionable, was exaggerated by Leinberger to such an extent that it conveys a certain pathos. Although the Madonnas of the Beautiful style, caught up within fine cascades of folds, tend toward preciosity, Leinberger's garments gather an almost brutal dominance. Their massive and deep fold structure consists of two levels: as the main motif, three masses reaching far forward form a large Y, behind which lie deep folds. This basic Y-shaped corset is calculated for its effect from a distance. The Y, comprised of a few hasty lines, accentuates the fertile womb of the ancient Greek Theotokos, the *Gottesgebererin* (she who gave birth to God), as can be read on an inscription in the hem of Mary's hood.

The figure was intended to have different effects when viewed from different distances, namely, a coarse structure for the distant gaze and a fine structure for the near observer. Leinberger structured the figures on several foliolike levels. From a closer distance, smaller partitioned areas of creasing, spiral formations, and ear-shaped swirls underlie the macrostructure of massive folds and frayed hems. When one finally walks around the figure, the Virgin's abdomen becomes more pronounced from the side through the pointedly arched folds reaching far outward. The figure is perceived through a series of impressions that supplement and build upon one another.

Leinberger's Madonna type was a great success. After he created the Moosburg prototype in 1514, there followed a bronze figure of *Mary and Child* (today in the Staatliche Museen, Berlin) around 1515, and shortly thereafter came his monumental *Virgin and*

Child in Landshut; then, around 1520, he created the figure of the *Schöne Maria* (Beautiful Mary) for the high altar of the pilgrimage church in Regensburg (the figure is now lost). All of these follow the St. Luke *Madonna* type, and all render this type more emotive through a dramatic rendering of the clothes, which reach out into space, exude power, and harness the body.

Irritated art historians have felt Leinberger's Madonna represents a *Vergewaltigung des Natürlichen* (a mutilation of nature) (see Feulner, 1923). There is an eclectic "historicism" expressed in the radical instrumentalization of historical models and older styles that had been overcome, an instrumentalization that tends toward the production of cheap effects; such a historicism contains a certain Postmodern distance from the present. While the Italian sculpture of the times was falling back on Antiquity as a historical gesture, Leinberger appealed to styles north of the Alps from past epochs and to dogmatic age-old images. He did this with a great consciousness of style and great artistic capacity. However refined this instrumentalization of traditions was, it was just this spirit of eclecticism around 1510/20 that indicated a crisis regarding the cult image. When the sculptor ranges so freely among sacred traditions, the cult image comes to lose its sacrosanct, eternal validity and becomes an art image.

THOMAS ESER

Further Reading

Arnold, Paul M., *Hans Leinbergers Moosburger Hochaltar: Höhepunkt bayerischer Altarbaukunst*, Landshut: Hans-Leinberger-Verein, 1990

Decker, Bernhard, *Das Ende des mittelalterlichen Kultbildes und die Plastik Hans Leinbergers*, Bamberg: Lehrstuhl für Kunstgeschichte und Aufbaustudium Denkmalpflege an der Universität Bamberg, 1985

Feulner, Adolf, *Hans Leinbergers Moosburger Altar*, Munich: Riehn und Reusch, 1923

Schmidt, Otto, "Hans Leinberger oder Christian Jorhan der Ältere? Überlegungen zum Moosburger Altar," *Städel-Jahrbuch* 12 (1989)

DAVID LE MARCHAND 1674–1726

French, active in England and Scotland

Few details are known about the life of David Le Marchand, a celebrated ivory carver. He probably received his training in Dieppe, a seaport in northern France on the English Channel famous for its ivory-carving tradition. A Huguenot, he emigrated with his family to Edinburgh, Scotland, to avoid religious persecution of Protestants in France. Later, in England, Le Marchand acquired the patronage of several prominent families affiliated with the Whig (anti-Catholic) party,

some of whom were also Huguenots. Most of his commissions came in the form of portrait medallions or ivory busts. He also carved portraits and religious subjects in relief on ivory plaques, as well as freestanding renderings of conventional mythological, religious, and allegorical subjects. His style is often described as idiosyncratic, his handling of ivory (a substance that is hard and relatively difficult to carve) characterized by a soft and fluid modeling and a sinuous line quality, particularly in the drapery. Le Marchand almost always based the finished carvings on wax models; working in the soft, malleable material lent itself easily to a fluid rendering of form. The use of wax models was also practical: the time-consuming and laborious process of carving ivory could not have been done in the presence of the subject. Remarkably, Le Marchand was able to preserve the fluid spontaneity of the wax model in the finished ivory carving.

Dating Le Marchand's body of work is difficult; although most of his works are signed, only a few are dated or bear inferences that determine a date (such as the age of a sitter whose date of birth is known).

That Le Marchand had not only attained a technical maturity but also had evolved his personal style at a relatively early age can be discerned in his bust of John Locke, datable to 1697 and the artist's earliest known work. The philosopher bears a dreamy, almost visionary expression, with wide eyes set beneath a knitted brow. His shoulders are swathed in characteristic Le Marchand drapery; the simple, circularly arranged folds are deeply cut and almost buttery in their fluid treatment. The hair, arranged in gently flowing waves, complements the prominent jaw and powerfully outlined nose. Although the bust is a three-dimensional work, the line is the primary bearer of expressivity.

A similarly rendered, although less dramatic, bust portrays Sir Isaac Newton. Probably a much later work, it was either acquired or commissioned by Matthew Raper II, a wealthy merchant and banker (and possibly a Huguenot), whose family was one of Le Marchand's most faithful patrons. The portrait bust of an Unknown Lady is one of the most flamboyant examples of Le Marchand's work in this genre. The proud head, with its ropes of wavy hair tumbling down to meet equally tumultuous drapery, is reminiscent of the work of Gianlorenzo Bernini.

Medallion portraits by Le Marchand exist of Matthew Raper II and his wife, Elizabeth Raper (only in modern ceramic casts of the lost originals). Particularly notable among the artist's surviving original ivory medallions are the portraits of the Huguenots Michael Garnault and Mrs. Anne Dacier. These four works demonstrate Le Marchand's formula for such portraits. The figures, posed in profile, wear stern or neutral expressions. Fluidly sweeping drapery engulfs the shoulders. The men usually wear elaborate periwigs falling in cascading waves. Other medallions by Le Marchand in this genre portray such prominent Whig contemporaries as John Churchill, first duke of Marlborough, and Sir Christopher Wren.

A particularly engaging and sympathetic portrait outside the medallion format depicts Matthew Raper III at the age of 15. The serious youth is shown full length, standing at a table and demonstrating a problem in geometry. A swathe of smooth, waxy drapery arranged over his waistcoat gives the work a Classical veneer. Although the table is rendered in foreshortened perspective, the setting, meant to evoke a library or study, is curiously flat, with a bookshelf of incised lines and a drawn curtain rendered flush to the surface in the background, as if ribbons were pasted to the surface.

Several of Le Marchand's works other than portraiture are of particular interest. An ivory plaque presents a New Testament scene, *The Miracle of the Man with the Withered Hand* (*ca.* 1720). Like the portrait of young Matthew Raper, the scene takes place in a shallow space. There is little indication of setting, but the figures stand on a floor marked as a perspective grid. The figures show great animation and facial expression. Their varying degrees of relief give a sense of recession into space. A *Crucified Christ* (only the corpus survives) is an intense portrayal of the suffering Christ. The sinewy musculature strains against the downward pull of gravity. The face avoids both theatricality and sentimentality, portraying real human agony.

Le Marchand's allegorical figure group *Time with Opportunity and Penitence* (*ca.* 1720) shows the artist's versatility as a copyist. He adapted the work from a group created in 1678 by Thomas Régnaudin for Versailles. Le Marchand reduced the original monumental grouping to less than 30 centimeters high, yet the work retains the clarity and detail of the original. Equally impressive is how Le Marchand fit the serpentine composition of three figures into the format of a single ivory tusk, without additions.

An artist of virtuosity and considerable expressive power, Le Marchand established no school and had no real followers. He partook of a somewhat academic Baroque realism, upon which he succeeded in imposing the stamp of his individuality.

WALTER SMITH

See also **Bernini, Gianlorenzo; Ivory Sculpture: Renaissance–Modern; Wax**

Biography

Born in Dieppe, France, 12 October 1674. Son of a painter, Guillaume le Marchand. Probably trained in Dieppe, a center of ivory carving at the time; emigrated to Edinburgh, Scotland, 1685; opened shop, 1696; moved to London by 1705; became naturalized British citizen, 1709; specialized primarily in portraiture (busts and relief medallions) but also produced statuettes. Died in London, England, 17 March 1726.

Selected Works

The most representative collections of Le Marchand's works are housed at the British Museum, the Victoria and Albert Museum in London, and at the Art Gallery of Ontario, Canada.

1697	Bust of John Locke; ivory (untraced)
1701	Bust of an Unknown Lady; ivory; private collection
ca. 1704	Bust of a Gentleman; ivory; Detroit Institute of Arts, Michigan United States
ca. 1710	John Churchill, first duke of Marlborough; ivory; Victoria and Albert Museum, London, England
1720	*Matthew Raper III*; ivory; Victoria and Albert Museum, London, England
ca. 1720	*Crucified Christ*; ivory; Victoria and Albert Museum, London, England
ca. 1720	*Elizabeth Raper*; ivory (lost); ceramic cast: Wedgwood Museum, Barlaston, England
ca. 1720	*Matthew Raper II*; ivory (lost); ceramic cast: Wedgwood Museum, Barlaston, England
ca. 1720	*Michael Garnault*; ivory; private collection
ca. 1720	*The Miracle of the Man with the Withered Hand*; ivory; National Museum of Wales, Cardiff, Wales
ca. 1720	*Mrs. Anne Dacier*; ivory; British Museum, London, England
ca. 1720	*Time with Opportunity and Penitence*; ivory; Victoria and Albert Museum, London, England

Further Reading

Avery, Charles , "David Le Marchand—Huguenot Ivory Carver (1674–1726)," in *Studies in European Sculpture II*, London: Christie's, 1988

Hodgkinson, Terence, "An Ingenious Man for Carving in Ivory," *Victoria and Albert Museum Bulletin* 1 (2 April 1965)

Houfe, S.R., "A Whig Artist in Ivory: David Le Marchand (1674–1726)," *Antique Collector* (April 1971)

Longhurst, Margaret H., *Catalogue of Carvings in Ivory*, 2 vols., London: Victoria and Albert Museum Board of Education, 1927; see especially vol. 2

The Quiet Conquest: The Huguenots, 1685–1985 (exhib. cat.), London: Museum of London, 1985

ANTOINE LE MOITURIER *ca.* 1425–after 1495 *French*

Although today a somewhat obscure figure in the history of sculpture, Antoine Le Moiturier was celebrated in his own time, as witnessed by another sculptor, Michel Colombe, who in 1511 spoke in the same breath of "Master Claus [Sluter] and Master Antoine [Le Moiturier]." Indeed, Le Moiturier stands as the artistic descendant of Sluter, being the last exponent of the Late Gothic Burgundian school. Symbolic of this connection with Sluter is that two of Le Moiturier's major works, the *gisants* (reclining figures) from the tomb of Duke John the Fearless and Margaret of Bavaria, were originally placed in the Charterhouse of Champmol in Dijon, as was Sluter's *Well of Moses* (*ca.* 1396–1406).

Le Moiturier's earliest documented works are from Avignon: two figures of angels, all that remain from a monumental Last Judgment altarpiece made for the Church of St. Pierre (most of the altarpiece was destroyed during the 17th century). The angels originally stood, one behind the other, at the right hand of the figure of Christ. The first angel originally held a cross bearing the instruments of the Passion. Posed in profile, the angel's head turns as though about to look over his shoulder, which, along with the pensive facial expression, makes the figure strikingly realistic, despite the overall stiffness of pose and the heavy, static folds of drapery. The wings too are hard and static, inert, and almost completely vertical. The second angel gives a somewhat greater sense of movement. Also posed in profile, he bends forward slightly, with the wings responding in a gentle curve, echoing the bend of his back. The hands of this trumpet-blowing angel are broken, but his puffed-out cheeks and intent, concentrated expression vividly indicate his activity.

In 1439 Philip the Good (Philip III, duke of Burgundy) commissioned the Spanish sculptor Juan de la Huerta for the tomb of his parents, Duke John the Fearless and Margaret of Bavaria. When after four years de la Huerta abandoned it, Le Moiturier received the project. Originally placed in the Charterhouse of Champmol, only the *gisants* are considered to be by Le Moiturier. Badly damaged during the French Revolution, the figures have been much restored; only the hands and heads appear to be original. The polychromy is also probably modern. An assessment of Le Moiturier's style from these figures, then, is difficult.

Similarities between the Last Judgment angels and angels originally part of a magnificent sculptural tableau titled *Entombment*, at Semur-en-Auxois (45 miles northwest of Dijon), lend great weight to the attribution of the latter work to Le Moiturier. These angels have the same overall facial cast and similar caps of long wavy hair as the Last Judgment figures. In addition, the approach to drapery is similar. The folds are hard and stiff, giving a frozen, static effect, even though the angels are depicted in flight. One of the Semur angels possesses a particularly interesting composition. Posed horizontally, both the torso and the feet are upraised, the latter meeting the characteristically stiff wings so that the overall composition is circular. The feet, however, are lost in a mass of drapery, constructed of harsh, broken triangular folds. These angels, however, were only decorative accents for the monumental *Entombment* at Semur. Given that the back sides of the angel figures are flat, they were probably originally placed on the wall directly behind the sculptural tableau.

The *Entombment* group consists of several figures arranged around the dead Christ, who is being lowered on a shroud into the tomb by Joseph of Arimathea and Nicodemus. A group of five figures is on a raised platform behind the dead Christ. The Virgin Mary is at the center, flanked by Saint John and a woman disciple while two mourning women holding the instruments of the Passion stand at the far left and right (with the crown of thorns and the nails, respectively). The whole group portrays tenderness and emotion. The two old men lowering the shroud bend slightly forward and inward, drawing attention to the supine figure of Jesus. Mary's placement at the exact center of the group of mourning figures is unusual for Gothic entombment scenes. She further becomes a focal point by the manner in which she is distinctively shrouded, her face obscured by her head covering. The tenderly attentive figures on either side of her, supporting her with their hands and gazing directly at her, strengthen this psychological focus.

As in Le Moiturier's other works, drapery is a primary vehicle of expression in the *Entombment* scene. Overall, the drapery is broad and planar, falling heavily into triangular folds. The bodies underneath are heavily obscured, but as in much Gothic sculpture, he used facial expressions and the positions and gestures of hands as the vehicles for conveying lifelikeness. Much of the surviving polychromy, discovered when the statues were cleaned of their whitewash, further strengthens the realistic effect. Nonetheless, some aspects of drapery treatment may strike the modern viewer as illogical. For example, no real relationship exists between the body of Christ and the shroud underneath him. Stiff and horizontal, the body appears to float above the curved folds of cloth.

The heavy, dramatic drapery of his *Entombment* also appears in another Le Moiturier attribution, the tomb of Philippe Pot, originally in the Chapel of John the Baptist in the Abbey of Cîteaux. Eight robed and hooded mourners, who also bear shields, support a bier holding the *gisant* of Philippe. The tragic and dignified bearing of the mourners fits well with that of the *Entombment* figures. The lowered heads covered with hoods obscure the grave faces. The drapery is typical of Le Moiturier—hard, angular, and heavy, but highly expressive.

Since the early 1970s, scholars have attributed numerous detached sculptures to Le Moiturier, largely on the basis of comparison with the works already attributed. These new attributions, consisting of various figures of saints and angels, indicate an oeuvre and sphere of influence much greater than previously thought.

WALTER SMITH

See also **Sluter, Claus**

Biography

Born in Avignon, France, *ca.* 1425. Probably studied with uncle, sculptor Jacques Morel; received commissions in Avignon by 1461; lived in Saint-Antoine-en-Viennois, probably working at abbey church there, 1462–63; worked at Charterhouse of Champmol on tomb of Duke John the Fearless and Margaret of Bavaria, 1463–69; lived mainly in Dijon from 1469. Died in an unknown location after 1495.

Selected Works

ca. 1463   Two angels, for the Last Judgment altarpiece (destroyed), Church of St. Pierre, Avignon, France; stone; Musée du Petit Palais, Avignon, France

1463–69   Tomb of Duke John the Fearless and Margaret of Bavaria (begun by Juan de la Huerta), for Charterhouse of Champmol, Dijon, France; alabaster, marble; Musée des Beaux-Arts, Dijon, France

ca. 1480–83   Tomb of Philippe Pot; stone; Musée du Louvre, Paris, France

1490   *Entombment*; stone (some elements dispersed); Church of Notre Dame, Semur-en-Auxois, France; two angels: Musée Municipal, Semur-en-Auxois, France; two angels: Musée du Louvre, Paris, France

Further Reading

Antoine Le Moiturier: Le dernier des grands imagiers des ducs de Bourgogne (exhib. cat.), Dijon, France: Musée de Dijon, 1973

Block, Jane, "Le Moiturier, Antoine," in *The Dictionary of Art*, edited by Jane Turner, New York: Grove, and London: Macmillan, 1996

David, Henri, *De Sluter à Sambin: Essai critique sur la sculpture et le décor monumental en Bourgogne au XVe et au XVIe siècles*, 2 vols., Paris: Leroux, 1933

Forsyth, William H., *The Entombment of Christ: French Sculptures of the Fifteenth and Sixteenth Centuries*, Cambridge, Massachusetts: Harvard University Press, 1970

Müller, Theodor, *Sculpture in the Netherlands, Germany, France, and Spain, 1400 to 1500*, translated by Elaine Robson Scott and William Robson Scott, London: Penguin, 1966

LEMOYNE FAMILY   *French*

Three sculptors are usually associated with the Lemoyne family name: Jean-Louis Lemoyne; Jean-Baptiste I Lemoyne, also referred to as John-Baptiste the Elder; and Jean-Baptiste II Lemoyne, known as Jean-Baptiste the Younger. The Lemoyne name was spelled variously Le Moine, Lemoine, Le Moyne, and Lemoigne. The notable painter François Le Moine (Le Moyne) may or may not have been related.

In 1632 Louis Lemoyne married Catherine Guillain, daughter of Simon Guillain, one of the foremost sculptors of the age and himself the son of a notable maker of polychrome tombs, Nicolas Guillain. The Lemoyne family thus had links to notable sculptors working during the reign of Louis XIII. Louis and Catherine's son, Jean Lemoyne, was an ornamental painter. His marriage to a cousin, Geneviève LeBlond, produced Jean-Louis Lemoyne and Jean-Baptiste I Lemoyne, both sculptors who would leave their mark.

From the next generation came the most notable sculptor to bear the Lemoyne family name, Jean-Baptiste II Lemoyne, whom Réau described as a gifted progeny of a distinguished and talented family lineage (see Réau, 1927). He was the son of Jean-Louis Lemoyne and Armide Monnoyer, a landscape painter and daughter of a notable flower painter J.B. Monnoyer, who had also worked at Versailles. Although Diderot dismissed Jean-Baptiste II as a mediocre talent, others, most notably Réau, considered Jean-Baptiste II to have been an underappreciated artist while Levey highly valued his theatricality (see Levey, 1992).

Jean-Louis Lemoyne 1665–1755

Jean-Louis Lemoyne, a pupil of Antoine Coysevox, won the Prix de Rome in 1687 with a low-relief carving titled *The Flood* (now lost). Instead of traveling to Rome, however, Jean-Louis set out for Bordeaux and received additional art instruction at a provincial academy. From these years dates a bust of Louis XIV (1692; now lost) in wood, which was the sculptor's reception piece, and a posthumous portrait of an influential local architect, Pierre-Michel Du Plessis, whom the artist had also known in life. His portrait of Du Plessis is signed "Lemoyne fesit Parisien" (Lemoyne the Parisian made it) and dated. About 1700 Jean-Louis returned to Paris, where in 1703 he was received into

945

the Académie Royale de Peinture et de Sculpture upon presentation of a large bust of royal architect Jules Hardouin-Mansart. Soon, Jean-Louis took part in numerous royal projects working with other notable sculptors, on what have been characterized as *des grandes entreprises collectives*, at various sites, including Versailles, Marly, Yvelines and Meudon, and Hauts-de-Seine. He designed vases, worked on fountains, executed figure sculpture for both inside and outside disposition, and, as the situation required, worked in stone, stucco, or marble and in low and high relief, much as his teacher Coysevox had done before him. Jean-Louis's elegant and graceful *Companion of Diana* echoes Coysevox's own representation of Marie-Adelaide of Savoy, *Duchess of Bourgogne as Diana.*

Jean-Louis also executed religious commissions, and at Versailles he received the commission for two of the 28 statues of saints for the balustrade around the outer roofline of the palace's chapel. Inside the chapel he executed two bas-reliefs, both titled *The Carrying of the Cross.* He modeled the first, a figure of an angel, in higher relief; the second focuses on Jesus and portrays the event, a narrative scratched onto the stone's surface. An elaborate funerary monument meant for Cambrai Cathedral survives only in the posthumous portrait bust of the writer François de Salignac de la Mothe-Fénelon, who was archbishop there.

Jean-Baptiste I Lemoyne 1679–1731

Jean-Baptiste followed a similar educational path as Jean-Louis, his older brother. In 1705 he won a second prize in an academy contest with a bas-relief titled *Judith Led by Soldiers into the Tent of Holofernes* (now lost). He was received into the Académie Royale de Peinture et de Sculpture in 1710 with a plaster model of *Andromeda Chained to the Rock* and became a full member of the academy in 1715 following the submission of a statuette entitled the *Fall of Hippolytus.* Jean-Baptiste I is usually credited with roughing out the marble statue of *Saint John the Baptist* that was part of the *Baptism of Christ* group now in the Church of Saint Roch, Paris, and which was completed by his nephew Jean-Baptiste II.

Jean-Baptiste II Lemoyne 1704–1778

Jean-Baptiste II, son of Jean-Louis Lemoyne, was heir through his father to the traditions and formulas that had come to represent French sculpture in the 17th and early 18th centuries. He began working as a sculptor while still a teenager. Deprived of an opportunity to travel to Rome, he nevertheless became an influential

and popular sculptor with a particular affinity for portraiture. He was a favorite of Louis XV, whom he portrayed in a series of busts that spanned 40 years and in which he recorded the subtle changes to the king wrought by time. In association with his father, Jean-Baptiste II executed an equestrian statue of Louis XV for Bordeaux (now destroyed) and planned other complex monuments to the king's glory for Rouen and Rennes (destroyed).

Jean-Baptiste II's most impressive tomb commission, the monument to Pierre Mignard, survives only in an engraving and a fragment, the mourning figure with the face of Mignard's daughter, Madame de Feuquières, who had commissioned the work. A polychrome extravaganza, it was, according to Levey, "the site of a drama, a clash between the imploring woman at its base and inexorable Time with his prominent

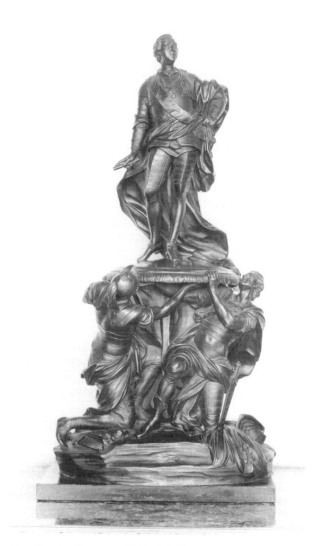

Jean-Baptiste Lemoyne II, Louis XV
Photographic Survey of Private Collections, Courtauld Institute of Art

scythe. The two were connected compositionally by the tremendous twist of fringed drapery which curled around the obelisk and cascaded right down behind the tomb to touch the floor" (see Levey, 1992).

Among Jean-Baptiste II's best-known works are his quieter pieces that seem to epitomize the delicate touch of a Rococo sensibility. In his *Vertumnus and Pomone*, for example, a tableau contemporaries understood to refer to the relationship of the Marquise de Pompadour and Louis XV, the artist caught his subjects in an exquisitely fleeting moment. A portrait bust of the Marquise de Pompadour (commissioned 1758) was shown at the Salon of 1761; ten years later Lemoyne portrayed the Comtesse Du Barry, the king's current favorite. A bust of the young Marie-Antoinette, intended for the Austrian court, is an admirable likeness of the dauphine not yet out of her teens. Among Jean-Baptiste's last activities was delivering bronze reductions of statues he had made of Louis XV to his new royal patron, Louis XVI.

MARILYN BAKER

See also **Caffiéri Family; Coysevox, Antoine; Falconet, Étienne-Maurice; Pajou, Augustin; Pigalle, Jean-Baptiste**

Jean-Louis Lemoyne

Biography

Born in Paris, France, 1665. Instruction with Antoine Coysevox, about 1687, study at École Academique in Bordeaux beginning in 1692, and reception in Paris as an academician, 1703, laid groundwork for career; associate professor at the Academy, 1715; full professor, 1724; a favorite of regent Philippe D'Orléans, whose portrait he produced, 1715; exhibited at the Salon, 1704, 1725, and 1737; also collaborated with son on projects, including equestrian statue of Louis XV, Bordeaux (now destroyed); ceased work as sculptor, *ca.* 1740; became an associate at the Academy, 1744; became rector, a position he held only briefly, 1746; later years difficult because of poor physical condition and impoverished circumstances. Died in Paris, France, 31 May 1755.

Selected Works

1694	Bust of Pierre-Michel Du Plessis; marble; Musée D'Aquitaine, Bordeaux, France
1703	Bust of Jules Hardouin-Mansart; marble; Musée du Louvre, Paris, France
1707	Statues of *St. Simon* and *St. Thaddeus*; stone; balustrade, Chapel of the Château, Versailles, Yvelines, France

1707–09	*The Carrying of the Cross* (allegorical); interior, Chapel of the Château, Versailles, Yvelines, France
1707–09	*The Carrying of the Cross* (realistic); interior, Chapel of the Château, Versailles, Yvelines, France
1710–24	*Companion of Diana*; marble; National Gallery of Art, Washington, D.C., United States
1715	Bust of Regent Philippe D'Orléans; marble; Musée du Château, Versailles, France
1724	Bust of François de Salignac de la Mothe-Fénelon, Archbishop of Cambrai, for Cambrai Cathedral, France; marble; Museé du Cambrai, France

Jean-Baptiste I Lemoyne

Biography

Born in Paris, France, 14 September 1679. Brother of Jean-Louis Lemoyne; often confused with nephew of same name. Studied at Académie Royal de Peinture et de Sculpture; became a full academician, 1715; though at one time wrongly attributed to his nephew, *The Fall of Hippolytus* is the work most firmly associated with his name. Died in Paris, France, 20 October 1731.

Selected Works

1715	*Fall of Hippolytus*; marble; Musée du Louvre, Paris, France

Jean-Baptiste II Lemoyne

Biography

Born in Paris, France, 19 February 1704. Trained with father Jean-Louis Lemoyne and Robert Le Lorrain. Won Prix de Rome (Rome Prize), 1725, approved by Académie Royal de Peinture et de Sculpture, 1728; became full academician, 1738; despite not studying in Italy, achieved considerable success as monument maker; was even more prolific portrait artist; executed many images of Louis XV, a great admirer; worked at Versailles, Hôtel de Soubise, and École Militaire, Paris; *Baptism of Christ* begun by uncle for high altar of St. Jean-en-Grève, Paris, one of his notable intact groupings; became an associate of the academy, 1761; rector and director, 1768; further significance confirmed by role as teacher and mentor to many notable 18th-century French sculptors, including Jean-Baptiste Pigalle, Etienne-Maurice Falconet, Augustin Pajou, and Jean Guillaume Moitte. Died in Paris, France, 25 May 1778.

Selected Works

1715   *Louis XV*; marble; Metropolitan Museum of Art, New York City, United States

1731   *Baptism of Christ* for high altar, Saint-Jean-en-Grève, Paris, France (begun by Jean-Baptiste I); marble; Church of Saint Roch, Paris, France

1742   *Louis XV* (with Jean-Baptiste II) ; bronze (destroyed); bronze reduction currently in Palace Royale, Bordeaux, France

1743   Monument to Pierre Mignard for Jacobin Church, Paris, France; marble, lead (dismantled, partially rebuilt); Church of Saint Roch, Paris, France

1751   Bust of Louis XV; bronze; Musée du Louvre, Paris, France

1760   *Vertumnus and Pomone*; stone; Musée du Louvre, Paris, France

1769   Bust of Louis XV; marble; Musée du Louvre, Paris, France

1772   *Marie-Antoinette the Dauphine*; marble; Kunsthistorisches Museum, Vienna, Austria

Further Reading

Lami, Stanislas, *Dictionnaire des sculpteurs de l'école française du Moyen Âge au règne de Louis XIV*, Paris: Champion, 1898; reprint, Nendeln, Lichtenstein: Kraus, 1970

Lami, Stanislas, *Dictionnaire des sculpteurs de l'école française au dix huitième siècle*, 2 vols., Paris: Champion, 1910–11; reprint, Nendeln, Lichtenstein: Kraus, 1970

Levey, Michael, *Painting and Sculpture in France, 1700–1789*, New Haven, Connecticut: Yale University Press, 1992

Réau, Louis, *Une dynastie de sculpteurs au XVIIIe siècle, les Lemoyne*, Paris: Les Beaux-Arts, 1927

Souchal, François, *French Sculptors of the 17th and 18th Centuries: The Reign of Louis XIV*, vols. 1–3, Oxford: Cassirer, 1977–87, and vol. 4, London: Faber and Faber, 1993

Souchal, François, et al., "The Lemoyne Family," in *The Dictionary of Art*, edited by Jane Turner, New York: Grove, and London: Macmillan, 1996

Tapié, Victor Lucien, *Baroque et classicisme*, Paris: Plon, 1957; as *The Age of Grandeur: Baroque Art and Architecture*, translated by A. Ross Williamson, London: Weidenfeld and Nicolson, and New York: Praeger, 1961; 2nd edition, New York: Praeger, 1966

LEONI FAMILY *Italian*

Leone Leoni *ca.* 1509–1590

New archival evidence indicates that Leone Leoni was born about 1509 and educated in Arezzo, not Menaggio on Lake Como. Sometime in 1533 Leone is recorded as having been in Venice living under the protection of Pietro Aretino, where he made medals and statuettes (none of which have been identified). Leone's talent and connections soon won him a position at the mint in Ferrara. Unfortunately, he was forced to flee the city after being accused of counterfeiting, the first of many brushes with the law that were to plague him throughout his life.

By the fall of 1537, Leone was in Rome, where he remained for the next three years. This was a highly formative period in his life, which laid the groundwork for his career. In Rome he became acquainted with the major artists of the papal court, especially Michelangelo and Baccio Bandinelli, both of whom had a strong influence on his work. He also studied the city's ancient and contemporary art, steeping himself in the latest artistic developments. Leone's time in Rome was not only one of intense study but also one of renewed controversy. In 1538 he was a prime witness against Benvenuto Cellini, who had been charged with stealing papal jewels during the sack of Rome (1527). According to Cellini, while he was imprisoned in the Castel Sant'Angelo, Leone had attempted to kill him by sprinkling a ground diamond on his salad. In 1540 a knife attack on the papal jeweler caused Leone to be sentenced to having his right hand cut off. Only the timely intervention of powerful friends saved him. Resentenced to serve as a galley slave in the papal fleet, he remained chained to an oar for one year, until he was released in Genoa by the admiral of the imperial fleet, Andrea Doria. Leone produced a number of medals of Doria as well as a medallic self-portrait showing him liberated from the papal galley.

Early in 1542 Leone moved to Milan to work in the imperial mint. Here his career as a coiner and medallist flourished, and, by 1546, he had been named master general of the mint of Parma and Piacenza and enjoyed a growing reputation for his medallic portraits. Milan was under the control of the Holy Roman Emperor Charles V; after the emperor's victory over the Protestant princes at the Battle of Mühlberg in 1547, Leone proposed to the governor of Milan the erection of an equestrian statue. In 1548 Antoine Perrenot de Granvelle, the bishop of Arras and adviser to Charles V, invited Leone to discuss his proposal at the imperial court in Brussels. Leone arrived in 1549 and received a commission for a number of portrait busts and statues, the most important of which is the over life-size bronze group *Charles V and Fury Restrained*.

For the emperor and his sister, Mary of Hungary, Leone produced the following works: the bronze bust *Charles V Supported by an Eagle*; the bronze bust *Mary Queen of Hungary* (1552); and the bronze statues *Empress Isabella of Portugal*, *Mary Queen of Hungary*, and *Philip II*. Leone gave form to the idea of the Holy Roman Empire renewed in a Respublica Christiana, uniting all of Europe by creating a visual language rich in iconographic and stylistic references to Roman imperial art and to the art of Titian. Thus both Charles and his son Philip were celebrated as legitimate heirs of Caesar Augustus.

With the death of Charles V in 1558, Leone's patronage shifted to Italy. In 1560 he received a commission from Pope Pius IV, on the recommendation of Michelangelo, to erect a tomb in Milan Cathedral for the latter's brother, Gian Giacomo de' Medici. In the same year, he received a commission honoring the former governor of Milan, Ferrante Gonzaga. This classicizing bronze two-figured group now stands in the center of Piazza Roma, Guastalla. Sometime thereafter, Leone prepared an over life-size seated bronze portrait statue for Vespasiano Gonzaga, which was installed before the ducal palace in Sabbioneta in 1588. Leone's last major commission was for 15 gilt-bronze statues for the high altar retable of the Capilla Mayor and a lesser number of small bronze figures for the tabernacle at the Monastery of S. Lorenzo el Real, Escorial, Madrid. Undertaken with his son Pompeo, they were the crowning achievement of his career, anticipating in their broad muscularity and heroic vigor later stylistic developments in Rome. This style also spread north

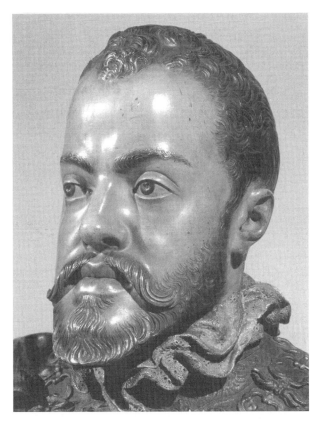

Leoni Family, King Philip II of Spain (*ca.* 1556–60), Kunsthistorisches Museum, Vienna
© Erich Lessing / Art Resource, NY

across the Alps thanks to sculptors such as Jacques Jonghelinck and Adriaen de Vries, who worked with Leone.

Between 1565 and 1567 Leone undertook the reconstruction of a house given to him in 1549 by Charles V. Now known as the Casa degli Omenoni ("House of the Big Men" in Milanese dialect), it remains one of Milan's most distinctive architectural landmarks with its six double life-size barbarian prisoners on the facade. According to art historian Giorgio Vasari, the house was dedicated to Marcus Aurelius, the emperor and Stoic philosopher. Through its program, Leone's impressive collection of art and plaster casts, and his membership in the scholarly Accademia dei Fenici, Leone presented himself not solely as an artist, both knighted and ennobled, but as a "prince," thus significantly raising the status of the artist in 16th-century Italian society. He died in Milan on 22 July 1590.

Pompeo Leoni *ca.* 1533–1608

Pompeo Leoni was born possibly in Venice around 1533, the son of Leone Leoni. He later became an accomplished sculptor in his own right who produced an impressive body of work. Pompeo was trained by his father and assisted him throughout his life. In 1556 he accompanied the statues of the Habsburg family members to Spain, where he remained, finishing them in 1564. During the 1570s, he had several important commissions from Spanish patrons, but in 1579 all private work stopped when Leone received the commission for 15 bronze figures for the retable of the Capilla Mayor at the Monastery of S. Lorenzo el Real, Escorial, Madrid. Pompeo traveled to Milan in 1582 to collaborate on the project, returned in 1589, and installed the statues in 1591. His last commission was from Philip II of Spain for the effigies of the king, his father, and eight other members of the Habsburg family, who kneel in perpetual veneration toward the sacrament tabernacle on the altar. This spectacular ensemble (funerary figures of Charles V and his family, 1592–98; funerary figures of Philip II and his family, 1567–1600) was the crowning achievement of his career. Like his father, Pompeo was also an avid art collector. He assembled an impressive number of paintings, as well as notebooks by Leonardo da Vinci. He died in Madrid on 13 October 1608.

MICHAEL MEZZATESTA

See also **Bandinelli, Baccio; Michelangelo (Buonarroti)**

Leone Leoni

Biography

Born in Arezzo, Italy, *ca.* 1509. Son of Giovanni Battista, a mason from Lombardy. Trained in Arezzo as a goldsmith; possibly traveled to Rome in 1525 with relative Pietro Aretino and met major artistic figures; recorded in Venice in 1533 with wife Diamanta de Martinis and infant son Pompeo; met Titian and designed medals and bronze statuettes; worked in the mint at Ferrara, *ca.* 1536, but fled when charged with counterfeiting; met Pietro Bembo and designed medal for him, 1537; in Rome, worked at papal mint and met Michelangelo and Baccio Bandinelli; sentenced to indefinite term as a papal galley slave, 1540; freed in 1541 by Andrea Doria in Genoa, for whom he designed medals; moved to Milan and began work in imperial mint, 1542; arrived in Brussels with Antoine Perrenot de Granvelle to discuss sculptural commissions with Holy Roman Emperor Charles V, 1549; granted house in Milan, knighted, and made imperial sculptor, 1549; received commissions from Pope Pius IV and Ferrante Gonzaga, 1560; rebuilt his own house, now called Casa degli Omenoni, 1565–67; received major commission from Philip II of Spain for 15 colossal bronze figures for high altar retable at the Monastery of S. Lorenzo el Real, Escorial, Madrid, 1579. Died in Milan, Italy, 22 July 1590.

Selected Works

1549–55 *Charles V Supported by an Eagle*; bronze; Museo del Prado, Madrid, Spain

1549–64 *Charles V and Fury Restrained*; bronze; Museo del Prado, Madrid, Spain

1549–64 *Empress Isabella of Portugal*; bronze; Museo del Prado, Madrid, Spain

1549–64 *Mary Queen of Hungary*; bronze; Museo del Prado, Madrid, Spain

1549–64 *Philip II*; bronze; Museo del Prado, Madrid, Spain

1560 Medal of Michelangelo; bronze; Museo del Prado, Madrid, Spain

1560–63 Tomb of Gian Giacomo and Gabrielle de' Medici; Milan Cathedral, Italy

1560–65 *Ferrante Gonzaga Triumphant over Envy* (installed 1594); bronze; Piazza Roma, Guastalla, Italy

1565–67 House of Leone Leoni (Casa degli Omenoni); Milan, Italy

1570–77 *Vespasiano Gonzaga* (installed 1588); bronze; Church of the Incoronata, Sabbioneta, Italy

1579–90 Statues for Capilla Mayor high altar retable (with Pompeo Leoni); bronze; Monastery of S. Lorenzo el Real, Escorial, Madrid, Spain

Pompeo Leoni

Biography

Born in Venice, Italy, *ca.* 1533. Trained by father Leone, whom he assisted throughout his life. Accom-panied his father's statues and busts from Brussels to Spain with the Holy Roman Emperor Charles V and his retinue, 1556; entered service of the regent, Joanna of Austria, producing several medals in 1557; sentenced by the Inquisition for one year's confinement in a monastery for unorthodox views, 1558; received important series of commissions for marble effigies in Spain; received commission from Philip II of Spain for bronze figures for the Capilla Mayor at the Monastery of S. Lorenzo el Real, Escorial, Madrid, 1579; statues installed, 1591; collected works by Michelangelo and Correggio and notebooks by Leonardo da Vinci. Died in Madrid, Spain, 13 October 1608.

Selected Works

1574 *Joanna of Austria*; marble; Convent of Las Descalzas Reales, Madrid, Spain

1576 Tomb of Fernando de Valdés; marble; Collegiate Church, Salas, Spain

1577 *Cardinal Diego de Espinosa*; marble; Church of Martín Muñoz de las Posadas, Segovia, Spain

1579–90 Statues for Capilla Mayor high altar retable (with Leone Leoni); bronze; Monastery of S. Lorenzo el Real, Escorial, Madrid, Spain

Further Reading

Attwood, Phillip, "Leone Leoni," in *The Currency of Fame: Portrait Medals of the Renaissance*, edited by Steven Scher, New York: Abrams, and London: Thames and Hudson, 1994

Helmstutler, Kelley, " 'To Demonstrate the Greatness of His Spirit': Leone Leoni and the Casa degli Omenoni," (dissertation), Rutgers University, 2000

Los Leoni, 1509–1608: Escultores del renascimento italiano al servicio de la Corte de España (exhib. cat.), edited by J. Urrea, Madrid: Museo del Prado, 1994

Mezzatesta, Michael, "Imperial Themes in the Sculpture of Leone Leoni," (dissertation), New York University, 1980

Mezzatesta, Michael, "Marcus Aurelius, Fra Antonio de Guevara, and the Ideal of the Perfect Prince in the Sixteenth Century," *Art Bulletin* 66 (December 1984)

Mezzatesta, Michael, "The Façade of Leone Leoni's House in Milan, the Casa degli Omenoni: The Artist and the Public," *Journal of the Society of Architectural Historians* 44 (1985)

Mulcahy, Rosemarie, *The Decoration of the Royal Basilica of El Escorial*, New York: Cambridge University Press, 1994

Pope-Hennessy, John, *An Introduction to Italian Sculpture*, 3 vols., London: Phaidon, 1963; 4th edition, 1996; see especially *Italian High Renaissance and Baroque Sculpture*

CHARLES V AND FURY RESTRAINED

Leone Leoni (1509–1590)

1549–1564

bronze

h. 2.51 m

Museo del Prado, Madrid, Spain

Sometime in the fall of 1548, Antoine Perrenot de Granvelle, bishop of Arras and adviser to Emperor

Charles V, invited Leone Leoni to visit the imperial court in Brussels to discuss the proposal advanced by Leone and Ferrante Gonzaga, governor of Milan, to erect an equestrian portrait of the emperor in honor of his recent victory at Mühlberg over the German Protestants. For Leone the invitation represented the achievement of a lifetime goal; he had been working for over two decades as a medalist and coiner attempting to obtain a sculptural commission. Leoni arrived at the imperial court in Brussels in March 1549, where his idea for the equestrian statue was well received; the court ordered him to make a model. The project continued for at least five years but never advanced very far, being abandoned upon the emperor's abdication in 1555. Nonetheless, the visit did result in commissions directly from the emperor for portrait statues and busts—the most important being a bronze portrait of Charles V himself. This work, ultimately realized as *Charles V and Fury Restrained*, was the first project Leone undertook for the emperor and the one on which he expended the most effort. The commission represented an important moment in Leone's career; he had never attempted a life-size statue, let alone the more complicated two-figure group. With this commission he sought to announce his abilities as a sculptor, or as Leone wrote to Granvelle, to show "un altro animo che da medaglista" (a spirit other than that of a medalist).

The statue of *Charles V* stands calmly in a graceful *contrapposto* (a natural pose with the weight of one leg, the shoulder, and hips counterbalancing one another) above a figure identified by the inscription as *Fury*. The emperor holds a short sword decorated with an eagle-headed hilt in his left hand and a lance, or *hasta*, with his right and wears lion-head *pauldrons* (shoulder guards) and boots of the type worn by Roman emperors. The heavily muscled *Fury* is seated and twists its torso violently in reaction to the dominating figure above. *Fury*'s mouth is open in a scream and its face contorts in rage, with beads of perspiration streaming down the forehead. Chained at wrists, ankles, and head to a ring at the side of the base, it grasps a firebrand in its right hand and raises its left arm in anguish. Leone set both statues on a circular pile of arms comprised of instruments of war: cuirasses, a quiver of arrows, a club, a trumpet, sword, trident, fasces, two helmets, and a shield. He skillfully combined the two figures on a small base, organizing the composition clearly from the four major points of view and modeling both figures and weapons with assurance. He brought the cast, a technical tour de force, to an extraordinary level of finish by crisp, sharp chasing and a meticulous attention to detail. The group's impact is powerful and dramatic.

Leone's achievement is all the more astonishing because Charles's armor may be removed to reveal the emperor in heroic nudity. As far as is known, this is the first time in the history of European sculpture that bronze armor was used this way. The sculptor dramatically combined through the use of removable armor two sculptural types mentioned by Pliny the Elder in *Natural History* (77 CE): the nude state or Achillean effigy favored by the Greeks and the warrior wearing armor favored by the ancient Romans.

Leone actually added the armor at a later date; he had originally planned the portrait to be nude. In fact, he conceived *Charles V and Fury Restrained* in three stages over a period of slightly more than a year. The first phase was a nude portrait of the emperor, the commission Leone received in Brussels in 1549; the second called for expanding the commission to a two-figured group by the addition of *Fury* (December 1550); and the third, first broached in a letter of June 1551, sought the emperor's permission for adding armor. The figure of the emperor was cast in Milan in July 1551, *Fury* was cast in November 1553, and the armor was reported near completion in August 1555. Leone did not undertake the final chasing until 1564 when he made a brief trip to Spain. The group remained in his son Pompeo's Madrid studio until Pompeo's death in 1608, and so it was never seen in public during the lifetime of Charles V or Philip II. It is not known where the group was planned to be located or when it would have been seen nude and when armed. After Pompeo's death the group was moved between a number of royal palaces until finally entering the collection of the Museo del Prado in 1830.

Charles V commissioned the statue at the zenith of his power to celebrate his decisive victory at Mühlberg over his Protestant adversaries. In keeping with his Christian piety, Charles wanted the statue to portray that credit for the triumph did not belong to him but to God. Leone solved the problem by crafting a statue that was at once an anonymous allegorical representation of both ancient and Christian virtue and an identifiable portrait of the emperor. He took inspiration from several Roman numismatic sources well known in the 16th century. One shows Trajan as the allegorical representation of *Virus* standing triumphant over a conquered province and holding the attributes of Virtus herself—a short sword and the *hasta*. The second, from the reign of Galba, depicts a nude male holding the same attributes. The inscription on this coin reads "Virtus." Thus Leone conceived the nude statue as an allegorical representation of ancient moral Virtus standing over chained Fury, while the identity of the figure as Charles V is clear. The figure's restrained pose and demeanor, both pensive and modest, clearly illustrate his Christian virtue, a message also signaled by the Christian allegorical tradition of Virtue standing triumphant over Vice.

Armed, the statue reflects another aspect of ancient Virtus, military prowess, although Charles wears contemporary armor. Charles V, Holy Roman Emperor, symbol of ancient and Christian virtue, military and moral, stands triumphant over the defeated representation of war, as the inscription on the base notes: "Caesaris virtute Domitus furor" (Through the virtue of the emperor fury is dominated). The image of *Fury* chained and seated on arms and armor comes from Virgil's *Aeneid*, signaling the end of armed conflict and the dawn of a new golden age established by Augustus.

The figure of *Charles V* stands as a timely and timeless victor, the very embodiment of ancient and Christian virtue, the legitimate heir of the Roman emperors, and, like Augustus, the founder of a new golden age. Charles's subsequent reversal of fortune and the rise of the Counter Reformation may explain why *Charles V and Fury Restrained* was never exhibited during the reigns of Charles V or Philip II.

MICHAEL P. MEZZATESTA

Further Reading

Edelstein, Bruce, "Leone Leoni, Benvenuto Cellini, and Francesco Vinta: A Medici Agent in Milan," *The Sculpture Journal* 4 (2000)

HUBERT LE SUEUR ca. 1580–ca. 1660
French

Hubert Le Sueur was born into a family of Parisian metalworkers and probably was trained by them. Subsequent claims about a period of training with Giambologna in Florence are unwarranted. Le Sueur could also have learned from the other court sculptors, notably Pietro Francavilla (Pierre Francqueville), Francesco Bordoni, Barthélemy Prieur, and Guillaume Dupré. His first major commission, a statue of the constable of Montmorency, would be placed on a preexisting bronze horse at the constable's château of Chantilly—only the constable's head survives. Appointed sculptor in ordinary to King Louis XIII in 1614, Le Sueur proceeded to make some bronze statuettes of the young monarch (large and small) and of his father, Henry IV (large). Various grand commissions ensued, including in 1617 four bronze angels and other elements for the high altar of the Church of the Grands Augustins, Paris (demolished 1674), and in 1622 a monument mostly in marble for the keeper of the royal seal, Guillaume du Vair. Contracts followed for four monumental tombs with varicolored marble components and praying portrait statues (*priants*), none of which survived the French Revolution. Although not highly imaginative, Le Sueur was clearly a competent and successful master mason and sculptor who could manage the various technical aspects of the business.

The marriage in 1625 of the princess royal of France, Henrietta Maria, to King Charles I provided an opportunity for Le Sueur to move to London. He was immediately employed by Inigo Jones to make statues of the late king, James I. This stimulated two prestigious commissions for monuments in side chapels off the Chapel of King Henry VII in Westminster Abbey, with its Tudor tombs in gilt bronze by Pietro Torrigiano. The first of these commissions, for which Le Sueur used bronze caryatids supporting a canopy and topped with a "flying" figure of Fame, commemorated the Duke and Duchess of Lennox and Richmond; the faces demonstrate the artist's lack of feeling for characterization, although repetitive ornamental detail on his armor and her dress serves to distract attention from this shortcoming. However, the general effect impressed the British public. The same is true of the almost contemporaneous monument to the Duke and Duchess of Buckingham (the duke was the erstwhile royal favorite, who was assassinated in 1628, and his widow died in 1634). Here, the deceased are flanked by four effective, although coarsely modeled, seated mourners in bronze; an impression of majesty is conveyed by a towering reredos in marble crowned with statues of their children in prayer.

About Christmas 1629 Le Sueur received a momentous commission for an equestrian statue of King Charles I. When unveiled in 1633, the statue was hailed as a success. Nothing like it had been seen in England and, along with a series of statues and busts after the antique cast for the king's gardens from molds taken expressly for this purpose in Rome in 1631, it secured Le Sueur's reputation. Not only did he take to signing himself "Praxiteles" (after the Greek sculptor), but by 1634 Henry Peacham could proclaim him as the creator of "the most excellent Statuary that ever this country enjoyed." A century later George Vertue uncritically noted, "Brass works are his doing which will eternalize his name so long as the material shall endure."

In 1631 Le Sueur began a series of portraits of King Charles I with an example in marble, which he signed. The figure, clad in armor (as was the norm for monarchs), was rigidly frontal and made no concessions to lifelike characterization. Casts in bronze, with minor variations in regalia, were produced for nobles and cities loyal to the crown, but Charles was deeply dissatisfied, realizing that his court sculptor lacked real talent for portraiture. Charles himself sometimes struck out the exorbitant prices Le Sueur quoted and once wrote crossly, "This I will not have!" The best of Le Sueur's portraits of the king, kept at the time in the royal collection, shows the king in the martial guise of St. George, patron saint of England, wearing a classical helmet with a dragon crest. Full-length statues in bronze of

Charles and of his father, James I, and Charles's wife, Henrietta Maria, were manufactured for display in prominent places in London and outside (for example, the Canterbury Quadrangle, St. John's College, Oxford, and Winchester Cathedral). Those in the capital fell victim to the fury of the Puritan mob during the English civil war. Several portraits of nobility and gentry were made to honor those engaged in this conflict, mostly of figures with armored shoulders similar to those of the king (e.g., a statue of the First Earl of Pembroke [*ca.* 1630, Schools' Quadrangle, Oxford]). An exception is one of Archbishop Laud, who, rather than wearing ecclesiastical garb, appears with bare head and shoulders, in the guise of a Greek or Roman philosopher. Some of the portraits form part of further grand tombs, two in Westminster Abbey and one in Wolverhampton. All betray Le Sueur's limited imagination and his reliance on what were by then outdated formulas.

An opportunity to rival his predecessor, Giambologna, came with a command from the queen for two fountains for her residence in London, Somerset House. The smaller, which cost £100 in 1639, was crowned with a bronze statue of Mercury; at this date, such a figure would almost certainly have implied a derivative, if not an aftercast or direct copy, of Giambologna's celebrated composition. The principal fountain that dominated the queen's formal garden survives, although altered in its arrangement, in the middle of a pond in Bushy Park, near Hampton Court (where it had been reerected under the rule of Oliver Cromwell). The pyramidal design was copied from the Fountain of Neptune erected in Bologna by Giambologna in the 1560s. The crowning statue, a diaphanously draped figure of the nymph Arethusa, is Le Sueur's own invention, but the eight subsidiary, life-size bronze figures showing putti holding up spouting dolphins and sirens expressing jets of water from their breasts correspond with Giambologna's. Even so, their faces and bodies are all modeled with the disappointing blandness that was the best Le Sueur could offer; yet, the ensemble made a brave impression on most contemporary beholders.

In 1635 Charles recruited Francesco Fanelli, a more gifted Italian sculptor, also specializing in bronze casting, thus terminating Le Sueur's unmerited preeminence in London. The balance owed him on a number of works was received from the crown in 1638, and he left London shortly after January 1641. By 1643 he was in Paris, where his expertise as a founder stood him in good stead. He cast four examples of a bust by Jean Warin of Cardinal Richelieu (1643) and copies of certain ancient masterpieces to decorate some courtiers' gardens (1648). Le Sueur died between 1658 and 1668. His youthful endeavors in Paris and his career

as a sculptor at the court of Charles I may be considered a success, even though he failed to join the ranks of the great creative artists.

CHARLES AVERY

See also **Fanelli, Francesco; Francavilla, Pietro; Giambologna; Prieur, Barthélemy**

Biography

Born in Paris, France, *ca.* 1580. Son of Pierre Le Sueur, a master-armorer; other relatives also worked with metal as founders or goldsmiths. Trained in Paris, where appointed sculptor in ordinary to the king, 1614; worked in London as a court sculptor, 1625–39, in the service of King Charles I; executed two major tombs for Westminster Abbey, *ca.* 1628; while in England, worked mainly on life-size busts and tomb portraiture; last payment from the crown known to have been received in 1639; last recorded in London in 1641, and by 1643, upon the outbreak of civil war, returned to native Paris; received commissions for bronze castings, 1643–48, but not for original works, because his style considered out of date. Died in Paris, France, between 1658 and 1668.

Selected Works

1612   *The Constable of Montmorency* (only fragments survive); bronze; Musée du Louvre, Paris, France

ca. 1615   Equestrian King Louis XIII (small); bronze; Victoria and Albert Museum, London, England

ca. 1615   Equestrian King Louis XIII and Equestrian King Henry IV; bronze; Victoria and Albert Museum, London, England

ca. 1620   *Martin Freminet*; bronze; Musée du Louvre, Paris, France (attributed)

1622   *Marseille* and *Lisieux*, for monument to Bishop Guillaume du Vair; marble; Abbey of Saint-Denis, Paris, France

1626–28   Monument to the Duke and Duchess of Lennox and Richmond; marble and bronze; Westminster Abbey, London, England

1628–34   Monument to the Duke and Duchess of Buckingham; marble and bronze; Westminster Abbey, London, England

1630s   Busts of King Charles I in armor; bronze; Bodleian Library, Oxford, England; Woburn Abbey, England

1630s   Bust of King Charles I in helmet; bronze; Stourhead House, Wiltshire, England

1630s   Busts of King Charles I with ermine cape;

bronze; St. Paul's Church, Hammersmith, London, England; Market Cross, Chichester, England

1630s   Statues of King Charles I and Queen Henrietta Maria; bronze; Canterbury Quadrangle, St. John's College, Oxford, England

1631   Bust of King Charles I; marble; Victoria and Albert Museum, London, England

1631   Casts of classical statues; bronze; Windsor Castle, Berkshire, England; Hampton Court, Middlesex, England; Henry E. Huntington Library, San Marino, California, United States

1631   *Robert Bertie, 1st Earl of Lindsey*; bronze; Yale Center for British Art, New Haven, Connecticut, United States

1631   *Sir Peter Le Maire*; bronze; St. Margaret's Lothbury, London, England

1633   Equestrian Statue of Charles I; bronze; Trafalgar Square, London, England

1634   Monument of Lord and Lady Cottington; bronze, marble; Westminster Abbey, London, England

1635   *Archbishop William Laud*; bronze; St. John's College, Oxford, England

1635   Monument of Sir Thomas Richardson; bronze, black touchstone; Westminster Abbey, London, England

1638   Bust of King James I; bronze; Banqueting House, Whitehall, London, England

1638   Statues of King Charles I and King James I; bronze; Winchester Cathedral, Winchester, England

1639   Fountain of Arethusa (also known as *Diana*); bronze, limestone; Bushy Park, Middlesex, England

1643   Bust of Cardinal Richelieu (after Jean Warin); bronze; five casts: Bibliothèque Mazarine, Paris, France; Musée Jacquemart-André, Paris, France; Barber Institute, Birmingham, England; Windsor Castle, Berkshire, England; Staatliche Sammlungen, Dresden, Germany

Further Reading

Avery, Charles, "Hubert Le Sueur's Portraits of King Charles I in Bronze at Stourhead, Ickworth, and Elsewhere," *National Trust Studies* 1 (1979); reprint, in *Studies in European Sculpture*, by Avery, London: Christie's, 1981

Avery, Charles, "Hubert Le Sueur, the Unworthy Praxiteles of King Charles I," *The Walpole Society* 48 (1982); reprint, in *Studies in European Sculpture II*, by Avery, London: Christie's, 1988

Avery, Charles, "Le Sueur, Hubert," in *The Dictionary of Art*, edited by Jane Turner, New York: Grove, and London: Macmillan, 1996

Marsden, Jonathan, "A Note on Portrait Busts," in *The King's Head: Charles I, King and Martyr*, edited by Jane Roberts, London: Royal Collection, 1999

Whinney, Margaret, *Sculpture in Britain, 1530–1830*, London and Baltimore, Maryland: Penguin, 1964; 2nd edition, revised by John Physick, London and New York: Penguin, 1988

EQUESTRIAN STATUE OF CHARLES I
Hubert Le Sueur (ca. 1580–ca. 1660)
1633 bronze
h. 2.9; w. 2.6 m
Trafalgar Square, London, England

In December 1629 Richard Weston, who had been chancellor and under treasurer of the exchequer (1621–28), commissioned an equestrian monument to King Charles I for his new house at Roehampton, southwest of London. In the middle of January 1630, Le Sueur went to determine the location of the statue, whose material, unprecedented in England, was to be bronze. In the contract the statue was described in Latin as "Carolus Magnus" (Charles the Great), an allusion not only to the monarch's status and the statue's size but also to the medieval Holy Roman Emperor, Charlemagne. The sculptor was to complete it within a year and a half and be paid £600. He was instructed to "take the advice of the King's riders of great horses for the shape and action both of the horse and his Majesty's figure on the same." This was not only to ensure authenticity but also to convey a proper regard for the art of equitation, highly prized as a courtly attribute at this period. Furthermore, a monarch controlling his steed was an allegory of good government.

The obvious prototype for such a statue, which was among the first ten of its type in Europe, was one showing Henry IV of France, father-in-law of the monarch, on the Pont Neuf in Paris, which had been cast by Pietro Tacca in Florence and shipped to Paris in 1612. No details of the modeling or casting are recorded, although there exists a bronze statuette that may have been made for presentation to Le Sueur's patron or to the monarch, for there was such an item in Charles's collection (Ickworth House, Suffolk). In any case the date of 1633 inscribed with Le Sueur's signature around a metal plate that anchors one forehoof to the pedestal indicates that he took twice as long as provided for in the contract. This was not unusual for a large sculptural project at the time, owing to the vagaries of casting, and it seems not to have excited criticism. It is perhaps no coincidence that Weston was made earl of Portland on 17 February 1633. The statue was praised in print the following year by Henry Peacham in *The Compleat Gentleman* (1634) and half a century later by E. Chamberlayne in *Angliae Notitia* (1687). The statue was generally admired until the advent of photography enabled invidious comparisons to be made with its various predecessors by Giambologna and his school, making the bland treatment of the horse and rider apparent. The work has been elegantly criticized by Margaret Whinney: "[F]rom a distance [it] has some air of majesty, though detailed inspection reveals the deplorable emptiness of modelling in the head" (see Whinney, 1964). Nevertheless, the statue played an important role in introducing the concept of equestrian portraiture into Great Britain, where it was to have many successors. Once moved from Roehampton to Charing Cross, it became a landmark of the city of Westminster, featuring in an engraving by Wenceslas Hollar, as well as in many subsequent views showing the Strand and Northumberland House.

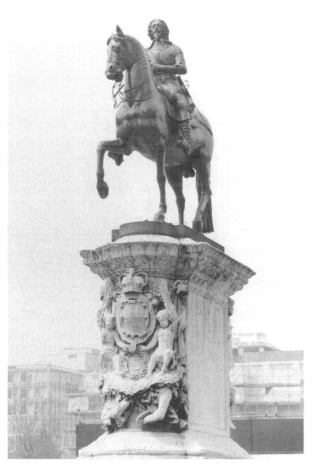

Equestrian Statue of Charles I
The Conway Library, Courtauld Institute of Art

The statue has had an eventful career because of its monarchist imagery; in September 1644, during the English civil war, Parliament ordered the statue to be sold at auction as part of the Second Earl of Portland's assessment. On 1 November officials came to Roehampton "at 2 a clock abowt praysing [appraising] againe ye brasse statue." The wording implies that an earlier valuation had been challenged and that a site visit was now required. On 7 November the House of Commons gave the first reading to an ordinance concerning the "proceed" of "the brasse Horse and Statue," and about 20 December "the brasse statue was carried from Roughampton garden to London Covent Garden by order of the House of Commons." It was sold as scrap metal to one John Rivett, a brazier, "with strict orders to break it in pieces."

Rivett, a covert loyalist, disobeyed the order and secreted the horse and rider in his yard, then proceeded to market trinkets and souvenirs that he pretended were made from its melted-down metal. After the Restoration in 1661 he produced the statue, doubtless seeking to find favor with the new monarch, Charles II, but it was reclaimed by the Second Earl of Portland. His widow eventually sold it for £1600 to Charles II, who provided for its erection in public in memory of his father. Its location at Charing Cross was doubly meaningful: Queen Eleanor's cross (*ca.* 1294) had stood there until its destruction as a "monument of superstition and idolatry" in 1647; and at the Restoration Thomas Harrison and other regicides had been executed there. A pedestal was carved for the statue by Joshua Marshall, master mason to the Crown. It was said that "Marvell made it for London what the celebrated statue of Pasquin[o] was for Rome, a vehicle for lampoons against the government." The statue was thus deemed to be participating significantly in British public life.

CHARLES AVERY

Further Reading

Evelyn, Peta, "Hubert Le Sueur's Equestrian Bronzes at the Victoria and Albert Museum," *The Burlington Magazine* 137 (1995)

Evelyn, Peta, "The Equestrian Bronzes of Hubert le Sueur," in *Giambologna tra Firenze e l'Europa*, edited by Sabine Eiche et al., Florence: Centro Di, 2000

Howarth, David, "Charles I, Sculpture and Sculptors," in *The Late King's Goods: Collections, Possessions, and Patronage of Charles I in Light of Commonwealth Sale Inventories*, edited by Arthur MacGregor, London: Alistair McAlpine, and Oxford: Oxford University Press, 1989

Whinney, Margaret, *Sculpture in Britain, 1530–1830*, London and Baltimore, Maryland: Penguin, 1964; 2nd edition, revised by John Physick, London and New York: Penguin, 1988

MARY EDMONIA LEWIS *ca. 1843/45–ca.* 1911 *United States, active in Italy*

Contemporary critics quickly identified Mary Edmonia Lewis, the first professional American female sculptor of color, with the conditions of her difference. Henry James, in his biography *William Wetmore Story and His Friends* (1903), noted that one of the "white, marmorean flock" of American women sculptors in Rome "was a negress, whose colour, picturesquely contrasting with that of her plastic material, was the pleading agent of her fame." Henry Tuckerman described her "[i]n her coarse but appropriate attire, with her black hair loose, and grasping in her tiny hand the chisel with which she does not disdain—perhaps with which she is obliged—to work," and suggested that "with her large, black, sympathetic eyes brimful of simple, unaffected enthusiasm, Miss Lewis is unquestionably the most interesting representative of our country in Europe" (see Tuckerman, 1867). While Lewis's status as a "black Indian woman . . . offered a tempting opportunity to those eager to demonstrate their support of human rights" (see Hartigan, 1985), critics have typically used her biography to read her works, a phenomenon that at times has trivialized and obscured a clear picture of Lewis's sculptural practice and career.

Progressive New Englanders who hoped to assist the cause of emancipation by supporting Lewis reacted favorably to her first works of 1864–65—clay and plaster portrait busts and medallions of prominent abolitionists, including *John Browne* and *Colonel Robert Gould Shaw* (later portraits included, among others, *Anna Quincy Waterston, Abraham Lincoln*, and African American businessman *James P. Thomas* [1874]). While pursuing a career as a sculptor, Lewis had to negotiate the public interest shown in her gender and dual heritage. Tracing the roots of her creativity to her Chippewa mother's inventive embroidery patterns, Lewis qualified this heritage by suggesting that "perhaps the same thing is coming out in me in a more civilized form" (see Hartigan, 1985). In reference to her African American father, she described in *The Revolution* of 1871 her first work made in Italy, *Freed Woman and Her Child* (1866) as "a humble one, but my first thought was for my poor father's people, how I could do them good in my small way."

Ambivalence among her supporters tempered Lewis's early progress. While she was sculpting the portrait bust of Colonel Robert Gould Shaw, the sale of which funded her trip to Rome, abolitionist Lydia Maria Child, skeptical of Lewis's ability to model the Boston hero's features adequately, neglected to share the photographs she owned of Shaw with the artist in an attempt to dissuade her from what Child considered an overly ambitious undertaking. Active promotion of Lewis's work came later in Rome, when actress Charlotte Cushman, a patron of the pioneering women sculptors there, and sculptor Emma Stebbins raised funds to purchase Lewis's group *Wooing of Hiawatha* (1867) before donating it to the Boston YMCA. Nonetheless, they qualified this support of Lewis by the demand that, according to Cushman, it be couched in terms of Lewis's "praiseworthy efforts at improvement" rather than her "estimable character" (quoted in Lisa Merrill's *When Romeo Was a Woman: Charlotte Cushman and Her Circle of Female Spectators* [1999]).

Lewis completed her Neoclassical apprenticeship in Boston with the sculptor Edward Augustus Brackett, but neither these credentials nor the pathos of her racial and economic position paved the way for easy integration into the Roman artistic community. Despite the warm reception by Harriet Hosmer and Cushman, among others, Lewis was all too aware of her vulnerability to gender and racial prejudices. She reportedly refused to hire marble carvers, according to the accepted practice of the day, for fear of being accused of not producing her own work—charges that had been leveled against Hosmer and Vinnie Ream. Sculptor Anne Whitney related that for the same reason Lewis rejected recourse to the instruction and criticism of her peers. It should be noted, however, that early American sculptors, with no true art academy available at home, frequently pursued and succeeded in their profession with minimal or no formal instruction.

Lewis seems to have made Rome her permanent home soon after arriving there. Around 1868 she joined the Catholic Church and shortly thereafter executed a marble altarpiece of a *Madonna and Child with Angels* (1867) for the marquis of Bute and in 1883 an *Adoration of the Magi* for a church in Baltimore, Maryland, this her last known commission (both works are untraced). As was the case for many 19th-century women sculptors, she used the Classical and classicizing works in Rome as sources for both art and anatomy instruction. Her study copies included a small-scale marble version of Michelangelo's *Moses* and the bust of *Young Octavian* after the ancient original in the Capitoline Museums. Visiting American Elisabeth Buffum Chace greatly admired Lewis's *Young Octavian* and purchased the head, pronouncing it the "best reproduction of the original then offered by any artist in Rome" (see Porter, 1992).

Lewis's faithful study of Michelangelo's *Moses* may have inspired the long, twisting curls of another life-size figure of the same year, *Hagar*. Although nothing in the rendering associates Hagar with an African slave, Lewis represented her after her expulsion into the wilderness by her jealous mistress, Sarah. Hagar looks up in midstride, with her hands clasped

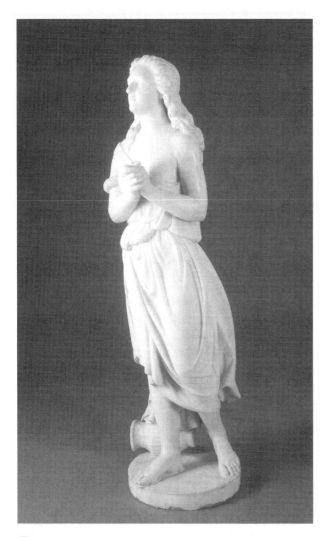

Hagar
© Smithsonian American Art Museum, Washington, D.C. /
Art Resource, NY

in prayer, the agitated movement of her drapery and the overturned pitcher at her feet testifying to her desperation. Long, coarse, thick locks of hair repeat the highly textured patterns of light and shadow in her gown, lending the figure a sense of movement that defies both the rigidly vertical Neoclassical pose of the body and preference for figures in idealized, "transcendental" repose.

Critics have frequently identified Lewis's Native American heritage as the reason for her choice of subject matter from *The Song of Hiawatha* (1855) by Longfellow, whom she also sculpted in 1871 during his visit to Rome. Her three small groups modeled in clay (1865–66), the *Wooing of Hiawatha*, *Marriage of Hiawatha*, and *Departure of Hiawatha and Minnehaha*, bear a strong resemblance in size and sentiment to the celebrated small anecdotal "parlor groups" of contemporary John Rogers. Small marble busts of *Minnehaha* and

Hiawatha and a marble version of the *Marriage of Hiawatha* followed. A later group, *The Old Arrow Maker and His Daughter*, recalls stories Lewis told of a nomadic childhood spent with her mother's tribe, making baskets and embroidering moccasins. While critics define both Lewis and her work as bearers of cultural heritage, her choice to depict subject matter from Longfellow's immensely popular poem also shows a perceptive understanding of the art market.

Crawford (1979) identifies Lewis's representation of the freed man in her life-size group *Forever Free* as a reference to Giovan Angelo Montorsoli's restoration of the *Laocoön*, and the kneeling female figure as a possible adaptation of Doidalses's *Crouching Aphrodite*. Lewis made the basic forms of these ancient works contemporary by the use of modern dress, non-Classical racial types, unidealized proportions, and reference to contemporary events. As her studies of Michelangelo, the *Laocoön*, and the *Octavian*, among others, indicate, Lewis gave particular attention to the historical and art-historical research of her works and could well have learned this convention from Roman art collections such as the celebrated Albani collection of Greek vases, held in the Capitoline Museums in the 19th century.

The Classical world provided Lewis with the subjects for two of her most important works, the colossal marble *Death of Cleopatra* (exhibited at the 1876 Philadelphia Centennial Exposition), and *Hygieia*, a monument for the grave of Dr. Harriot Kezia Hunt, one of the first female physicians in the United States. While Lewis's *Death of Cleopatra* has fortunately been brought back to light and conservation work continues on other of her works, *Hygieia* is slowly eroding in Mount Auburn Cemetery in Cambridge, Massachusetts. Despite the obviously lamentable damage, the weather has given the marble *Hygieia* a strikingly ancient-looking patina and surface texture that reveals, perhaps just as well as its pristine state, Lewis's classicizing touch.

Nancy Proctor and Miranda Mason

See also **Hosmer, Harriet Goodhue;** *Laocoön and His Sons***; Ream, Vinnie; United States: 18th Century– 1900; Whitney, Anne; Women Sculptors**

Biography

Born in either Ohio or New York between 1843 and 1845. Of African American and Chippewa (Objwa) Native American parentage. Enrolled at Oberlin College, Ohio, with the support of her brother, 1859–62, but did not graduate; moved to Boston, 1863; became involved with abolitionists; studied sculpture under Edward Brackett; worked in her own studio; sailed to Europe, 1865, visiting London, Paris, and Florence;

established studio in Rome, winter 1865–66; associated with artistic and literary expatriate circles; revisited United States to exhibit and sell work; converted to Catholicism, *ca.* 1868; last recorded living in Rome, 1911. Died probably in Rome, Italy, *ca.* 1911.

Selected Works

1866   *The Old Arrow Maker and His Daughter*; marble; Tuskegee University, Alabama, United States; *ca.* 1872: National Museum of American Art, Smithsonian Institution, Washington, D.C., United States

ca. 1866   *Anna Quincy Waterston*; marble; National Museum of American Art, Smithsonian Institution, Washington, D.C., United States

1867   *Colonel Robert Gould Shaw*; marble; Museum of Afro-American History, Boston, Massachusetts, United States

1867   *Forever Free*; marble; Howard University Gallery of Art, Washington, D.C., United States

1867   *Minnehaha*; marble; Howard University Gallery of Art, Washington, D.C., United States

1868   *Hiawatha*; marble; Howard University Gallery of Art, Washington, D.C., United States

ca. 1870   *Abraham Lincoln*; marble; San Jose Public Library, California, United States

1871   *Marriage of Hiawatha*; marble; Cincinnati Art Museum, Ohio, United States

ca. 1873   *Young Octavian*; marble; National Museum of American Art, Smithsonian Institution, Washington, D.C., United States

1874   *Hygieia*; marble; Mount Auburn Cemetery, Cambridge, Massachusetts, United States

1875   *Hagar*; marble; National Museum of American Art, Smithsonian Institution, Washington, D.C., United States

1875   *Moses* (after Michelangelo); marble; National Museum of American Art, Smithsonian Institution, Washington, D.C., United States

1876   *Death of Cleopatra*; National Museum of American Art, Smithsonian Institution, Washington, D.C., United States

1876   *Poor Cupid*; marble; National Museum of American Art, Smithsonian Institution, Washington, D.C., United States

Further Reading

Bearden, Romare, and Harry Henderson, *A History of African-American Artists from 1792 to the Present*, New York: Pantheon Books, 1993

Bontemps, Arna Alexander (editor), *Forever Free: Art by African-American Women, 1862–1980*, Alexandria, Virginia: Stephenson, 1980

Buick, Kirsten P., "The Ideal Works of Edmonia Lewis: Invoking and Inverting Autobiography," *American Art* 9 (Summer 1995)

Cikovsky, Nicolai, Jr., Marie H. Morrison, and Carol Ockman, *Nineteenth-Century American Women Neoclassical Sculptors* (exhib. cat.), Poughkeepsie, New York: Merchants Press, 1972

Crawford, John S., "The Classical Tradition in American Sculpture: Structure and Surface," *American Art Journal* 11 (July 1979)

"Edmonia Lewis," *The Revolution* (20 April 1871)

Hartigan, Lynda Roscoe (editor), *Sharing Traditions: Five Black Artists in Nineteenth-Century America: From the Collections of the National Museum of American Art*, Washington, D.C.: Smithsonian Institution Press, 1985

Holland, Juanita Marie, "Mary Edmonia Lewis's *Minnehaha*: Gender, Race, and the 'Indian Maid,' " in *Diaspora and Visual Culture: Representing Africans and Jews*, edited by Nicholas Mirzoeff, London and New York: Routledge, 2000

Porter, James Amos, *Modern Negro Art*, New York: Dryden Press, 1943; 3rd edition, Washington, D.C.: Howard University Press, 1992

Powell, Richard J., and Jock Reynolds (editors), *To Conserve a Legacy: American Art from Historically Black Colleges and Universities*, New York: Studio Museum in Harlem, 1999

Richardson, Marilyn, "Edmonia Lewis' *The Death of Cleopatra*: Myth and Identity," *The International Review of African American Art* 12 (1995)

Tuckerman, Henry T., *Book of the Artists: American Artists Life*, New York: Putnam and London: Sampson Low, 1867; reprint, New York: Carr, 1966

SOL LEWITT 1928–   *United States*

With a formal basis in Minimalism, characterized by the use of repetition and permutation, Sol LeWitt's three-dimensional works are best described as structures rather than sculptures. Minimalist and Conceptualist artists of the late 1960s advocated a radical approach to making "new" work that discarded the formal language of conventional sculpture, which included composition, narrative, surface texture, and so on. With similar commitment, LeWitt referred to all of his murals as "wall drawings," although many are painted. The nondescript, factual language that LeWitt employed to describe his art has been mirrored in his preference for inexpensive materials: walls are covered with pencil lead, colored crayons, or, on occasion, painted torn pieces of Styrofoam; structures are made of steel, aluminum, or wood, or, most prosaic of all, concrete cinder block. LeWitt's straightforward materials allow his ideas to assume center stage. For him, art is first and foremost a vehicle for ideas (as opposed to emotive expression or narrative, for example). This celebration of mind is what allies LeWitt to the Conceptual philosophy of art-making.

Emerging in the 1960s, the Conceptual movement offered a new approach to art. As a pioneer of this avant-garde thinking, LeWitt articulated its vision in his "Paragraphs on Conceptual Art" (1967) first published in *Artforum* magazine. In this seminal essay, LeWitt proposed that the idea behind a work of art was more important than its execution. According to this view, artists are responsible for supplying ideas but not for making their own work. The work is thus "free from the dependence on the skill of the artist as a craftsman" (see LeWitt, 1967). LeWitt's working method reflects this philosophy: his sculptures are fabricated and his wall drawings are executed by a team of trained assistants. Despite LeWitt's apparent rejection of aestheticism, he maintained that the role of art in culture ought to remain nonfunctional, intuitive, and perceptual.

This radical new definition of art-making emerged in part from lunchtime conversations LeWitt had while working at the Museum of Modern Art in New York City from 1960 to 1964. At the time, fellow artists Dan Flavin, Robert Mangold, and Robert Ryman were employed as guards, and Lucy Lippard, the future art writer and important feminist critic, worked in the library. With Jackson Pollock's death in 1956, the mythologies of Abstract Expressionism had since waned. Together LeWitt and his contemporaries sought a new path, namely to re-create art starting at ground zero.

LeWitt's initial exercises in sculpture were simple wood constructions, often painted in bold primary colors. In 1964, LeWitt produced *Standing Open Structure Black*. In this pivotal early work, LeWitt experimented with a basic rectangular solid, removing its "skin" to expose the skeletal framework beneath. Although LeWitt quickly jettisoned black for a less expressive white and began working with cubes instead of rectangles, *Standing Open Structure Black* set a precedent. As a result of this decisive piece, the open cube became a fundamental building block for LeWitt's structures—a role it continued to play well into the 1980s.

Typical of the artist's working method, which is true regardless of media, LeWitt began with a form or idea distilled to its simplest, purest expression and used it to create works of unexpected beauty and complexity. In the wall drawings, one line becomes 10,000. In the three-dimensional work, the cube multiplies to create an endless stream of configured and reconfigured forms.

Serial Project #1 (ABCD) marks LeWitt's first attempt to produce a visually complex sculpture. Whereas *Standing Open Structure Black* was Minimalist in spirit and form, *Serial Project #1 (ABCD)* reflected the Conceptualism that LeWitt is best known for. In this work, solid and open forms are set within one another on a grid that is placed directly on the floor, often abutting the walls. At first glance the shapes appear to be arranged arbitrarily on the grid, like random buildings on a street. Closer inspection,

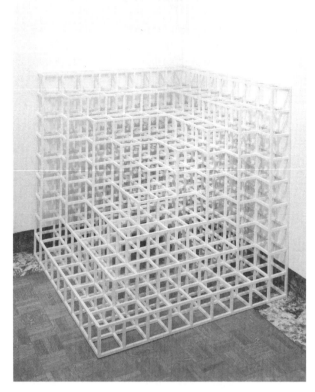

Modular Open Cube Pieces (9 × 9 × 9), Floor/Corner 2 (1976)
Founders Society Purchase, Friends of Modern Art Fund and National Endowment for the Arts Matching Museum Purchase Grant
© 1994 The Detroit Institute of Arts, (1993) Sol LeWitt and Artists Rights Society (ARS), New York

however, reveals that logic dictates their placement. One quadrant features solid forms enclosed by other solid forms. The other three quadrants include all the remaining possible configurations of forms—solid within open, open within solid, and open within open. As suggested by its title, *Serial Project #1 (ABCD)* illustrates LeWitt's absorption with seriality, or the sequential development of ideas using systems. The artist credits his interest in systems to a perhaps unanticipated source: 19th-century photographer Eadweard Muybridge, credited for his photographic studies of motion and time, which he documented using multiple cameras designed with specially rigged shutters that would shoot sequential frames. Muybridge turned these experiments into flipbook-style photographs that captured men, women, and horses in motion, and his work would later profoundly influence the development of cinema. LeWitt learned of Muybridge's groundbreaking studies in 1953, when he moved into an apartment in New York and discovered a book on Muybridge that was accidentally left behind by the previous tenant.

LeWitt's use of seriality reached its apogee in *Incomplete Open Cubes*. Large enough to fill a room, this immensely elaborate structure reveals the 122 possible ways of creating an incomplete cube. LeWitt considered only one-of-a-kind variations, disregarding possible duplicates that would result solely from rotation. The 122 permutations are expressed in three-dimensional form as wood models on a grid and by photographs and drawings on the surrounding walls. In each case, the incomplete cubes are arranged in groupings, according to the number of edges, from least (3) to greatest (11). Among the numerous systems he devised to arrive at 122 permutations, LeWitt bent paperclips into miniature models. Testament to the work's visual and conceptual complexity, the artist also consulted with mathematicians to ensure that every possible configuration had been considered—and with good reason, as he initially had come up a few short.

Significant developments manifest in LeWitt's work after 1980. These changes can in part be attributed to LeWitt's move to Italy in 1980 with his then wife-to-be, Carol Androccio. For the wall drawings and works on paper, lines yield to circles, squares, stars, and triangles, and with the inauguration of vibrant ink wall drawings in 1980, LeWitt's range of colors expanded tremendously. The open cube structures recorded noticeable changes as well. Although the modular cube remains his starting point, LeWitt's structures evolved into elaborate versions of their stoic predecessors. Individual pieces began to possess distinct associations and references. Some mimic towers or ancient monuments, whereas others assume the setback profile of Art Deco skyscrapers. Others suspend from the ceiling. Regardless of individual shape, these white modular cube structures cast delicate, lacy patterns of shadows and offer constantly shifting perspectives as the viewer looks into and through them. They provide some of the best examples of LeWitt's ability to produce works that are both intellectually and visually satisfying.

In 1986, while still making these airy, white modular cube structures, LeWitt began to produce clusters of weighty concrete blocks. These earthbound masses of masonry pay tribute to LeWitt's dedication to his original precepts of the 1960s: his continued commitment to an art that relies on ideas instead of slick materials.

In the late 1990s, he introduced bold acrylic wall drawings and glossy fiberglass sculptures painted in bright acrylics. These recent structures, known as "Non-Geometric Forms" or "Splotches" represent a sharp departure from the modular cube structures of the 1970s and 1980s: systems appear to evaporate and the cubes seem to melt. As with all of his structures, however, LeWitt entrusts a fabricator with making these unusual works. He draws what is called a "footprint" for the sculpture, designating the outline of its base. On paper these footprints look remarkably similar to the irregular amoebalike shapes that appear in many of his recent gouaches. After tracing the footprint LeWitt divides the sculpture into sections and randomly assigns a number to each. The numbers on the drawing indicate to the fabricator the height of each section. LeWitt enjoys not knowing in advance how the structures will appear. As one of the most important and influential postwar American artists, LeWitt has remained true to the principles he established at the onset of his career while continually engaging viewers with new ideas and directions.

VERONICA ROBERTS

See also **Andre, Carl; Hesse, Eva; Judd, Donald; Minimalism; Morris, Robert; Serra, Richard**

Biography

Born in Hartford, Connecticut, United States, 9 September 1928. Studied art at Syracuse University, New York, 1945–49; served in United States Army in Japan and Korea, 1951–52; moved to New York, 1953, and attended Cartoonists and Illustrators School (now known as the School of Visual Arts); employed in design department of *Seventeen* magazine, 1954–55; worked as graphic artist for architect I.M. Pei, 1955–56; worked at Museum of Modern Art, New York City, 1960–65, and met fellow museum employees and artists Robert Ryman, Robert Mangold, Dan Flavin, and writer-critic Lucy Lippard; period of great artistic activity in 1970s, primarily centered around serial and modular works; moved to Spoleto, Italy, 1980. Lives and works in Chester, Connecticut, United States, and Spoleto, Italy.

Selected Works

1964　*Standing Open Structure Black*; painted wood; LeWitt Collection, Chester, Connecticut, United States

1964　*Wall Piece (Hockey Stick)*; painted wood; Museum of Fine Arts, Museum of New Mexico, Santa Fe, New Mexico, United States

1966　*Serial Project #1 (ABCD)*; baked enamel on aluminum; Museum of Modern Art, New York City, United States

1974　*Incomplete Open Cubes*; painted wood structures on a painted wooden base, framed black and white photographs and drawings on paper; San Francisco Museum of Modern Art, California, United States

1986   *Cube*; concrete block; the Bechtler Foundation, Zurich, Switzerland

1988   *Complex Form #8*; painted wood; Bonnefanten Museum, Maastricht, the Netherlands

1999   *Non-Geometric Form #8*; painted fiberglass; collection of the artist

Further Reading

Friedman, Martin, "Construction Sights," in *Sol LeWitt: A Retrospective*, edited by Gary Garrels, San Francisco and New Haven: San Francisco Museum of Modern Art and Yale University Press, 2000

Iles, Chrissie, *Sol LeWitt Structures, 1962–1993*, Oxford: Museum of Modern Art Oxford, 1993

Legg, Alicia, et al., *Sol LeWitt* (exhib. cat.), New York: Museum of Modern Art, 1978

LeWitt, Sol, "Paragraphs on Conceptual Art," *Artforum* 5/10 (June 1967)

LeWitt, Sol, "Sentences on Conceptual Art," *Art-Language* 1/1 (May 1969)

Zevi, Adachiara (editor), *Sol LeWitt Critical Texts*, Rome: Incontri Internazionali d'Arte, 1994

MAYA LIN 1959– *United States*

Maya Lin is a sculptor and an architect best known for her public monuments, most notably the Vietnam Veterans War Memorial, which was dedicated in 1982 on the National Mall in Washington, D.C. Lin attended Yale University, where she earned a bachelor's degree and later a master's degree in architecture.

In her senior year, Lin took a course on funerary architecture. Each student was required to submit a plan for the competition to design a memorial honoring Vietnam veterans, which was to be built in Washington, D.C., between the Lincoln Memorial and the Washington Monument. The competition rules specified that the designs for the memorial be apolitical in tone and include the names of all the servicemen who died or were missing in action during the Vietnam War. In addition, the competition called for a design that was integrated with the surrounding landscape and emphasized more horizontal, rather than vertical, elements. As a result of this assignment, Lin's plan was chosen from among 1420 entries as the design that best fit the spirit and formal requirements of the commission.

Lin's design called for two low, polished black granite walls that seem to grow out of the earth and converge in a shallow V at a height of ten feet at the center of the monument. The names of the more than 58,000 veterans who are dead or missing as a result of their involvement in the Vietnam War are inscribed on each of the two wall faces in chronological order of the date they were recorded as dead or missing.

Critics and historians have traced the powerful effect of Lin's monument to its very reductive and abstract forms; although war memorials are traditionally figurative, the restrained, almost classical minimalism of the Vietnam Veterans War Memorial is neither didactic nor prescriptive. The experience of the work and the work itself remain open to multiple interpretations.

Although this monument is today one of the most popular and visited sites on the National Mall, Lin's design was not without initial controversy. The form of her design created a potent metaphor for the nation's conflict over Vietnam. It was not until after the memorial was dedicated that the full impact and the ultimate success of Lin's design were realized and acknowledged.

Lin's next project, the Civil Rights Memorial at the Southern Poverty Law Center in Montgomery, Alabama, is related to the Vietnam Veterans War Memorial in that it is composed of black granite and is imbued with meaning in the form of inscribed text. The memorial, dedicated in 1989, commemorates central events in the struggle for racial equality and honors those who lost their lives in the struggle. The Civil Rights Memorial is composed of two related parts. The first, a 9-foot-high black granite wall, is etched with the phrase, "Until justice rolls down like waters and righteousness like a mighty stream," a quote from Dr. Martin Luther King Jr.'s famous "I Have a Dream" speech. Water cascades down over the wall from a small hidden pool above the wall. The second component is a black granite disk over which water flows from an off-center font. Inscribed on the surface of the disk are the names of 40 people who lost their lives in the struggle for racial equality, as well as 21 major events associated with the civil rights struggle.

Women's Table, Lin's third public monument, which was dedicated in 1993 at Yale University, can

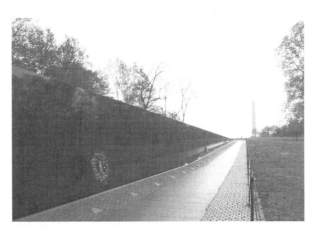

Vietnam Veterans War Memorial
© James P. Blair / CORBIS

be seen as a culmination of the elements found in both the Vietnam Veterans and Montgomery, Alabama, Civil Rights memorials. *Women's Table*, commissioned to recognize the tradition of coeducation at Yale, comprised a dark green granite "table" over which water flows. Inscribed on the surface in a spiral that expands outward from the center is a series of numerals representing the number of women enrolled each year at Yale since 1701. More abstract than her earlier monuments, a label at the base of the monument bears the title of the piece and provides the only textual clue to the subject of the monument.

In addition to her public monuments, Lin has also worked on several large-scale sculptural installations. *Groundswell*, created in 1993 and now permanently installed at the Wexner Center for the Arts in Columbus, Ohio, is constructed of 40 tons of crushed glass. A kinetic sculpture installation, *Eclipsed Time*, in the glass ceiling at the Long Island Railroad Terminal at Pennsylvania Station in New York City, is the result of a 1994 commission. *Wave Field*, an earthwork, was created in 1995 at the University of Michigan in Ann Arbor.

However diverse the project, there are several common threads that run through Lin's work. Above all, her formal training as an architect serves as the framework for much of her sculpture. Her forms bear a simplicity and sensitivity that Lin herself has related to her own inclinations toward more Eastern modes of thinking, rather than the more Western notion of Minimalism with which her works are often associated. Whether she is working directly with the landscape, as in the Vietnam Veterans War Memorial, or using elements such as glass or water, nature is a constant source of inspiration and a key conveyor of meaning in Lin's work. The sculptor's public monuments are united by the fact that in all of them, she seeks to engage the viewer by presenting text and allowing the viewer to come to his or her own conclusions about the subject presented.

Lin's innovative design, in the spirit of the Vietnam Veterans War Memorial program and design competition, not only served as a catalyst for her career but also heralded a shift in the focus of the war memorial genre as a whole. Individuals are singularly honored by the presence of the name of each soldier lost, and at the same time, the tragedy of the entire war is emphasized as one contemplates the sheer number of names that seems to pile up on the walls of the memorial. This same focus on the individual within the larger issue is seen throughout Lin's other public monuments, and along with the sculptor's success in engaging the viewer in the memorial's space, it serves as Lin's lasting contribution to the field.

ELIZABETH PETERS

See also **Contemporary Sculpture; Memorial: War; Minimalism; Public Sculpture**

Biography

Born in Athens, Ohio, United States, 5 October 1959. Studied architecture at Yale University, New Haven, Connecticut, B.A. 1981, M.A. 1986; worked as design consultant for Cooper-Lecky Partnership, Washington, D.C., 1981–82; continued as architectural designer at Peter Forbes and Associates, Boston, 1983, and at Batey and Mack, San Francisco, 1984; architectural apprentice at Fumihiko Maki and Associates, Tokyo, 1985, and design associate at Peter Forbes and Associates, New York, 1986–87; held teaching positions at Phillips Exeter Academy, 1982, Yale University, 1986, and Harvard University, 1988; has operated Maya Lin Studio, New York, since 1987; received honorary doctorate from Yale University, 1987, and visual artists fellowship from National Endowment for the Arts, 1988. Lives and works in New York City, United States.

Selected Works

1981–82 Vietnam Veterans War Memorial; granite; Washington, D.C., United States

1989 Civil Rights Memorial; granite, water; Southern Poverty Law Center, Montgomery, Alabama, United States

1991 *The Playing Field*; stone, grass, Burundi holly bushes; Charlotte Coliseum, North Carolina, United States

1993 *Groundswell*; shattered glass, concrete; Wexner Center for the Arts, Columbus, Ohio, United States

1993 *Women's Table*; granite, water; Yale University, New Haven, Connecticut, United States

1994 *Eclipsed Time*; glass, aluminum, fiber-optic light; Long Island Railroad Terminal, Pennsylvania Station, New York City, United States

1995 *Wave Field*; landscaped earth; University of Michigan, Ann Arbor, Michigan, United States

1998 *Reading a Garden*; stainless steel, granite, crushed stone, bronze; Eastman Reading Garden, Cleveland, Ohio, United States

Further Reading

Abramson, Daniel, "Maya Lin and the 1960's: Monuments, Time Lines, and Minimalism," *Critical Inquiry* 22/4 (Summer 1999)

Branch, Mark Alden, "Maya Lin: After the Wall," *Progressive Architecture* 75 (August 1994)

Bremmer, Ann, *Maya Lin: Public/Private* (exhib. cat.), Columbus: Wexner Center for the Arts, Ohio State University, 1994

Finkelpearl, Tom, "The Anti-Monumental Work of Maya Lin," *Public Art Review* 8 (fall/winter 1996)

Fleming, Jeff, *Maya Lin: Topologies* (exhib. cat.), Winston-Salem, North Carolina: Southeastern Center for Contemporary Art, 1998

Ling, Bettina, *Maya Lin*, Austin, Texas: Raintree Steck-Vaughn, 1997

Malone, Mary, *Maya Lin: Architect and Artist*, Springfield, New Jersey: Enslow Publishers, 1995

Scruggs, Jan, *To Heal a Nation: The Vietnam Veterans Memorial*, New York: Harper and Row, 1985

Swerdlow, Joel L., "Vietnam Veterans Memorial: America Remembers," *National Geographic* 167 (May 1985)

JACQUES LIPCHITZ 1891–1973

Lithuanian, active throughout Europe and United States

Jacques Lipchitz was considered by his contemporaries to be the principal proponent of Cubist sculpture and was one of the most highly regarded, successful, and vocal of the Parisian avant-garde interwar artists. His prodigious facility, forceful personality, and accomplished connoisseurship not only won him a central position within his group of artist friends, which included Pablo Picasso, Juan Gris, Amedeo Modigliani, and Chaim Soutine, but also secured him the respect and good offices of those who were key influencers of the period, among them Jean Cocteau, Coco Chanel, Jacques Doucet, and Albert Barnes. His success with wealthy collectors such as Barnes and Doucet and his status as a Jewish immigrant combined to antagonize a number of vociferous xenophobes within the French art establishment. However, this did not dent his reputation as one of the most important French Modernists, celebrated notably within the context of the 1937 Paris World's Fair in a room at the Petit Palais dedicated exclusively to his sculpture.

The scope of Lipchitz's work during his early career spanned small decorative bronzes, semiabstract reliefs, classical portraiture, and wooden "demountable" constructions (which could literally be taken down and reassembled). His style appeared infinitely variable as he grappled with the spatial innovations of Cubism and the formal inventiveness of African and Oceanic art and as he revisited the great traditions that he most admired, from the ancient Egyptian, archaic Greek, and Roman to the Baroque and the 18th-century elegance of Jean-Antoine Watteau. Throughout his life he was by preference a modeler who worked with bronze. He saw the activity of sculpture as a battle to conquer and manipulate light. Thus his work uses strong masses, deep planes, and accentuated hollows

and voids in a spiral development to draw light and space into the construction and to lead the viewer's gaze around the figure. As his friend Maurice Raynal described it, the forms worked like a fan or concertina, cutting through space and suggesting continuous movement. In his early Cubist masterpiece, the bronze *Sailor with Guitar*, this radical technique is used to create a sharp caricature of a young man Lipchitz had seen in Spain, evoking his jaunty bravado through the twist of the hips and legs, winking gaze, and solid torso.

The enduring imperative behind Lipchitz's work was his desire to create a human-centered art, and although many antagonists derided Cubism for its impenetrable abstraction, Lipchitz proclaimed himself to be "the optimistic Cubist" whose work proved that Cubism was all about humankind's positive and fruitful intervention in the universe. While working closely with Gris around 1918, he was drawn with his friend to the mathematical theories of the ancients, golden section geometry, mystical philosophers such as Louis Claude de Saint-Martin, and alchemy for what they suggested about the potency of human creativity. They revealed the artist's capacity to "rearrange" the forms perceived in nature according to the imagination while still respecting nature's hidden principles of construction and harmony.

Lipchitz's bronze *Head* of 1915 immediately followed a moment of crisis, when Lipchitz had feared that his art was becoming too distanced from the external world and organic life. In this sculpture, he reasserts the balance between formal innovation and representation: the sculptor reassembles the facial features so that they are still recognizable as such but in a highly reduced format that equally suggests other references—the elevations of a building, a stem and leaf. Multiple readings accumulate as the *Head* is seen from different angles. It works like a complex, expansive metaphor. At this early moment of crisis, Lipchitz also called upon the lessons learned from his father, whose understanding of architecture convinced the young sculptor that his work too needed a balanced distribution of masses and clearly delineated "skeleton" through which every part was interconnected.

Probably Lipchitz's most radical innovation was literally to lay that skeleton bare. In the mid 1920s Lipchitz created a new technique for making and casting sculpture through the production of what he called his "transparents." Nothing quite like them had been seen before, and his fellow artists Picasso and Julio González were intrigued. By use of tiny models made of ribbons and fine tubes of wax that were then cast in bronze, Lipchitz invented a sculpture that worked like epigrammatic calligraphy. The rich array of acrobats, pierrots, harlequins, and musicians were not only in-

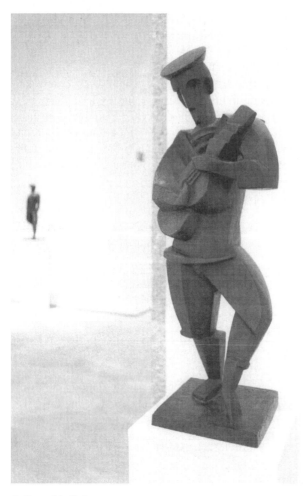

Sailor with Guitar
© Estate of Jacques Lipchitz, courtesy Marlborough Gallery,
New York

geniously animated and witty but they also technically opened up a vast new landscape for sculpture. In *Pierrot*, the figure's body is described by a void; space becomes more expressive than solidity, and one sign is isolated and magnified—the diamond of *Pierrot*'s costume—to act as a psychological index that highlights *Pierrot*'s love of concealment and his feelings of apartness and difference. Lipchitz identified his *Man with Guitar* as the first sculpture to draw space so literally into its construction and into the very core of the human figure. In his later career, in his powerful monumental sculpture, beginning with the *Joy of Life* and *Song of the Vowels* and then in the major commissions of his American years such as *Bellerophon Taming Pegasus* (1964–73) and *Peace on Earth* (1967–69), he continued to enclose "active" space as a means of heightening the emotional complexity of his work and engaging the viewer's imagination.

Beginning in the late 1920s the themes of Lipchitz's work, still deeply humanistic, increasingly used narra-

tive and the drama of myth. As he explored the expressive potential of subjects such as *Prometheus Strangling the Vulture* and *David and Goliath* (1933) his style became increasingly vigorous, the masses heavier, the movement more pronounced. Conflict runs as a constant through his work, revealing often deeply personal anxieties with gusto, even violence. In his later years he produced his most fantastic imagery in a series of small expressionistic studies—the transparents of the forties, the "series-automatics" of the fifties, the sequence *À la limite du possible* (1958–59), and *Images of Italy* (1962–63)—where the animation of the modeling and the intensity of emotion drive the material he works with to the limits of its expressive capacity. The mythic conflicts he represented throughout his career, although not intended as overtly political, were deeply symbolic for his contemporaries, evoking fundamental struggles between good and evil, light and darkness. In the 1930s and 1940s those struggles were unresolved, shown at a moment of high tension. By the end of his career, his figures are still enmeshed, but, as in his *Study for the Government of the People*, their engagement is one of solidarity. To Lipchitz, confrontation and conflict were not at odds with his Cubist convictions; rather, they were tensions also present in the most cerebral and measured Cubist work.

CATHERINE PÜTZ

See also **González, Julio; Modernism; Picasso, Pablo**

Biography

Born Druskininkai, Lithuania, 22 August 1891. Moved to Paris, 1909, and studied under Jean Antoine Injalbert at the École des Beaux-Arts; left to join courses at Académie Julian and Académie Colarossi; followed with two years of anatomy classes at École des Beaux-Arts; brief visit to St. Petersburg, Russia, 1912, then settled in Montparnasse, Paris; befriended Diego Rivera, met Pablo Picasso, and showed at the Salon d' Automne, 1913; visited Spain and Majorca, 1914; befriended Juan Gris, 1916; first solo show at Léonce Rosenberg Gallery, 1920; commissioned for works for Barnes Foundation at Merion Station, Pennsylvania, 1922; first major show in United States at Brummer Gallery, New York City, 1935; visited Paris and made Chevalier of the Legion of Honor, 1946; much work destroyed by fire in Manhattan studio, January 1952; retrospectives at Museum of Modern Art, New York City, Walker Art Gallery, Minneapolis, and Cleveland Museum of Art, 1954; large traveling exhibition in Europe, 1958; award for cultural achievement from Boston University, 1965; gold medal from the Academy of Arts and Letters, New York City, 1966; important retrospectives in Europe, New York City, and Jerusalem, 1970–72. Died in Italy, on the island of Capri, 26 May 1973.

Selected Works

1914   *Sailor with Guitar*; bronze; casts in Musée National d'Art Moderne, Centre Georges Pompidou, Paris, France; Philadelphia Museum of Art, Pennsylvania, United States; Barnes Foundation, Merion, Pennsylvania, United States

1915   *Detachable Figure (Dancer)*; ebony, oak; Cleveland Museum of Art, Ohio, United States

1915   *Head*; bronze; casts in Tate Gallery, London, England; Hirshhorn Museum and Sculpture Garden, Washington, D.C., United States

1915   *Man with Guitar*; limestone; Museum of Modern Art, New York City, United States

1917   *Bather III*; bronze; casts in Art Gallery of Ontario, Toronto, Canada; Norton Simon Museum, Pasadena, California, United States; Tate Gallery, London, England; Centre Georges Pompidou, Paris, France.

1918   *Seated Man with Guitar*; bronze; casts in Wilhelm Lehmbruck Museum, Duisberg, Germany; County Museum of Art, Los Angeles, California, United States; private collection, Dallas, Texas, United States

1925   *Pierrot*; bronze "transparent"; Marlborough Gallery, New York City, United States

1926–30 *Figure*; bronze; casts in Art Gallery of Ontario, Toronto, Canada; Hirshhorn Museum and Sculpture Garden, Washington, D.C., United States; Museum of Modern Art, New York City, United States; St. Louis Art Museum, Missouri, United States; Norton Simon Museum, Pasadena, California, United States

1927   *Joy of Life*; bronze; casts in Israel Museum, Jerusalem, Israel; Forest Park, St. Louis, Missouri, United States; The Meadows Museum, Southern Methodist University, Dallas, Texas, United States

1928–29 *The Couple (The Cry)*; bronze; cast in Kröller-Müller Museum, Otterlo, The Netherlands

1932   *Song of the Vowels*; bronze; edition of seven, including Centre Georges Pompidou, Paris, France; Kröller-Müller Museum, Otterlo, The Netherlands;

Kunsthaus, Zurich, Switzerland; Art Museum, Princeton University, New Jersey, United States

1936–37 *Prometheus Strangling the Vulture*; plaster (destroyed)

1941–45 *Mother and Child II*; bronze; casts in Art Gallery of Ontario, Toronto, Canada; Museum of Modern Art, New York City, United States

1941–45 *Our Lady of Joy (Notre Dame de Liesse)*; bronze; casts in Church of Notre-Dame-de-Liesse, Assy, France; Abbey of St. Columba, Iona, Scotland; Roofless Church of New Harmony, New Harmony, Indiana, United States

1967   *Study for the Government of the People*; bronze; Marlborough Gallery, New York City, United States

Further Reading

Elsen, Albert E., "The Humanism of Rodin and Lipchitz," *College Art Journal* 17/3 (Spring 1958)
Hope, Henry R., *The Sculpture of Jacques Lipchitz*, New York: Plantin Press, 1954
Patai, Irene, *Encounters: The Life of Jacques Lipchitz*, New York: Funk and Wagnalls, 1961
Pütz, Catherine, "Cubist Sculpture and the Circularity of Time," (dissertation), Courtauld Institute of Art, University of London, 1999
Raynal, Maurice, *Jacques Lipchitz*, Paris: Bucher, 1947
Stott, Deborah A., *Jacques Lipchitz and Cubism*, New York: Garland, 1978
Vitrac, Roger, *Jacques Lipchitz*, Paris: Nouvelle Revue Française, 1927
Wilkinson, Alan, *Jacques Lipchitz: A Life in Sculpture*, Toronto: Art Gallery of Ontario, 1989
Ybarra, Lucia (editor), *Lipchitz: Un mundo sorprendido en el espacio*, Madrid: Museo Nacional Reina Sofia, 1997

LISBOA, ANTÔNIO FRANCISCO

See **Aleijadinho**

LOMBARDO FAMILY *Italian*

Pietro Lombardo *ca.* 1435–1515

Pietro Lombardo achieved preeminence among the Lombard sculptors lured to 15th-century Venice by a demand for their skills so great that citizenship was offered for settling there. The dynasty that he founded produced important public and private sculpture in stone and bronze for four generations.

Pietro first proved his mastery of a sought-after Venetian sculptural type, the wall tomb, in the Antonio

Roselli monument in Padua. For this Tuscan-born patron, he introduced a composition based on Florentine tomb sculpture by Desiderio da Settignano and Bernardo Rossellino. Soon Pietro began to win commissions for ducal tombs in Venice and for construction and decoration of churches and chapels. By about 1471, he was working on the chancel (Cappella Maggiore) of the Church of San Giobbe in Venice with a growing workshop that soon included his young sons Tullio and Antonio.

Pietro's decorative and figural sculpture earned the admiration of Sicilian humanist Matteo Collaccio in 1475, when Pietro's sons were old enough to rate mention as *surgentes* (rising) in the profession. His patrons included not only ducal families and the state but also private patrons like Bernardo Bembo, a Venetian humanist and diplomat who commissioned the tomb of Dante at Ravenna and its relief portrait. A *Madonna* for Bembo's villa near Padua is among the best such reliefs attributed to Pietro.

Pietro revised the traditional vocabulary of the great Venetian sculptural form, the public tomb monument, according to his experiences in Florence and Padua. Donatello and Andrea Mantegna influenced his figure types. The statues and reliefs by his fellow Lombard and contemporary Giovanni Antonio Amadeo at the Colleoni Chapel (*ca.* 1470–75) in Bergamo also seem relevant for the tomb of Doge Pietro Mocenigo in Venice. Progressing from the Venetian suspended wall tomb with a canopied bier, as in the Paquale Malipiero monument, Pietro developed variations on triumphal arch architecture with high bases and increasingly deep soffits (undersides) and projecting columns. In the process, he contributed to the secularization of tomb iconography. The Mocenigo tomb reduces overtly Christian subject matter to distant figures at the top. Above all, it celebrates personal and state military triumph, as summed up in the standing statue of the doge in armor and in the personification of virtue, not by traditional statues of draped maidens but by two reliefs of a nude Hercules overcoming monsters on the base. A visiting German friar, Felix Faber, saw this tomb in 1483 and complained of "idols . . . and symbols of paganism inserted among those of our redemption."

Pietro's human types, as on the Mocenigo tomb, are solemn, dignified, and sometimes stiff, with characteristic clinging drapery articulated in flat pleats and broken, angular ridge folds. His best figures exert a stern presence with impressive naturalism, as in the wrinkly skin and boldly veined hands of the signed *St. Jerome* (1490) at S. Stefano. He practiced a severe and forceful portrait style for the lined faces of aged doges on tombs, at its best in the statue of the militant doge Mocenigo. But certain figures of boys and young men show a dawning lyricism, such as the figures of the

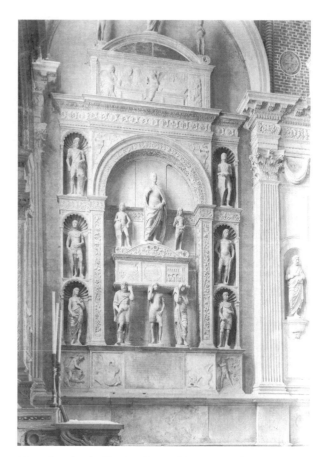

Pietro Lombardo, Tomb of Doge Pietro Mocenigo
The Conway Library, Courtauld Institute of Art

San Giobbe angels of the Cappella Maggiore and the garlanded pages and young caryatid on the Mocenigo tomb.

Experiments with antiquarian ornament harken back to ancient Roman remains, as in the trophy reliefs at the base of the Mocenigo tomb, but especially in the combination of antiquarian fantasy with nature study in botanical and figural ornament. Beginning at San Giobbe, Pietro, or a gifted assistant, carved vine scroll ornament with a sense of burgeoning vitality. Pietro and his workshop, which must have included carvers who worked at the ducal palace at Urbino before 1482, continued variations on this style for decades. A cast of mythical marine hybrids was introduced at the Church of Santa Maria dei Miracoli, Venice, and Treviso Cathedral. Another of Pietro's preferred ornamental types, with bands of smooth botanical ornament in low relief against a stippled background, was later used extensively by his sons.

The size of his shop, which by 1496 could offer 25 workers for a project in Mantua, inevitably makes it difficult to sort out specific hands at work under Pietro's direction. Projects such as the relief decoration in the Giustiniani Chapel at the Church of San Francesco della Vigna in Venice (probably late 1490s), for instance, occupied various hands, none of which have been documented, but evidently included Pietro, Tullio, and Antonio. In 1498, Pietro took over as architectural foreman of the Palazzo Ducale when his chief rival, Antonio Rizzo, fled Venice after being accused of embezzlement. Pietro continued to work with his sons primarily as an adviser and agent.

As a master of stone, Pietro obtained wide varieties for his commissions and practiced as an architectural designer and foreman. In addition to San Giobbe, Santa Maria dei Miracoli, and Treviso Cathedral, he was active at the Church of S. Lio, the Scuola di San Marco, and probably the Scuola di S. Giovanni Evangelista (all three in Venice) and at Cividale Cathedral. His years as foreman at the Palazzo Ducale also resulted in decorative sculpture for the interior rooms, which was possibly executed by his sons.

Tullio Lombardo *ca.* 1455–1532 and Antonio Lombardo *ca.* 1458–1516

Pietro Lombardo's sons Tullio and Antonio achieved an assimilation of antique models that surpassed even that of their Florentine contemporaries. Their grasp of Late Antique expressive formulas is evident in their characteristic carving of eyes with outlined irises, deeply cut pupils, and highlights reserved in relief rising into the upper lid. They also contributed to a renewal of monumental classicizing relief in marble, enlisting this ancient Roman art form to convey Christian narrative, beginning on the facade of the Scuola di San Marco in Venice and reaching its apogee in the reliefs of miracles of Saint Anthony at the Basilica of Sant'Antonio (Il Santo), Padua, where Tullio and Antonio set the standard for the team of sculptors who worked on the project through 1577.

The emergence of Tullio and Antonio Lombardo as recognizable sculptors seems most convincing in the 1480s. At the Zanetti tomb at Treviso Cathedral, both brothers probably shared in creating statues and the relief ornament for the sarcophagus of 1485–88, with its marine monsters. Reliefs of tritons, sirens, and putti on the socles of the triumphal arch at the Church of Santa Maria dei Miracoli in Venice are also convincingly assigned to them. A fully mature style is evident in the reliefs (*ca.* 1490)—*Baptism of Anianus and Healing of Anianus*—on the facade of the Scuola di San Marco, attributed by Francesco Sansovino to Tullio but probably the work of both brothers. The Vendramin monument, the tomb of Doge Andrea Vendramin, well underway in 1493, when the splendor of its "worthy marbles" was praised by Marin Sanudo, is generally recognized as Tullio's masterpiece of tomb

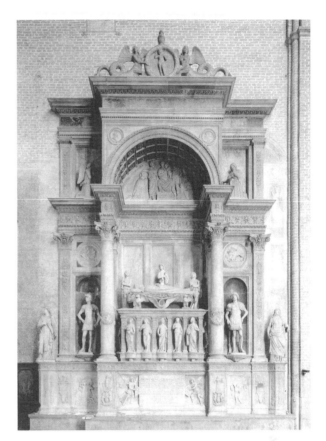

Tullio Lombardo, Tomb of Doge Andrea Vendramin
The Conway Library, Courtauld Institute of Art

design, with several autograph statues among the former total of 18. Conceived as both a triumphal arch and a gate of paradise, it was the grandest and most assertively Classical tomb in Venice in its time.

Among the works that constitute the touchstones for Tullio's style confirmed by documents and/or signature inscriptions are the Vendramin tomb's *Adam* and *Warriors* (probably *ca.* 1490/94); the Ca' d'Oro (Venice) relief *A Couple*; *Coronation of the Virgin* in the Church of S. Giovanni Crisostomo, Venice; and the reliefs in Il Santo in Padua (*Miracle of the Reattached Leg* and *Miracle of the Miser's Heart*). The key works for Antonio are the Padua relief *Miracle of the Newborn Child*; the bronze statue of *Madonna and Child* and relief *God the Father with Child Angels* in the funerary chapel of Cardinal Zen at the Basilica of San Marco, Venice, for which Antonio in 1504–06 provided models that were later repaired and cast by others; and the marble reliefs for Alfonso d'Este, duke of Ferrara, executed around 1507–11, especially *The Forge of Vulcan (The Birth of Athena)* and *The Contest of Athena and Poseidon*. Comparisons with these works support stylistic distinctions and further attributions.

The work of the Lombardo brothers shows intensive study of ancient sculpture of many periods, including early Christian and Byzantine manifestations. This is apparent in their choices of human types, drapery forms, relief compositions, and expressive language. In addition, their subjects and humanist connections suggest some level of Classical learning. The art of Rome and Milan mark the Scuola di San Marco reliefs, which testify to familiarity with, on the one hand, monumental Roman relief sculpture (for example, the Marcus Aurelius reliefs of 176 CE in the Musei Capitolini, Rome) and, on the other hand, Donato Bramante's 1482 experiments with low-relief architectural perspective at the Church of Sta. Maria presso San Satiro, Milan. The roundels on the Vendramin tomb reflect study of the reliefs in similar positions on the Arch of Constantine (312–15) in Rome. Tullio and Antonio also studied late Antonine and Severan portrait sculpture, in which intricately carved eyes suggest luminosity and restless emotion. Tullio's double portraits indicate study of Roman funerary reliefs as well as carved gems. Tullio probably also restored ancient sculpture, including a Muse turned into a Cleopatra in the Museo Archeologico, Venice. He owned an ancient statue of a draped woman without head or hands, and he used it as a model for several works, according to Marcantonio Michiel, who saw it in 1532, when it had been passed to Andrea Odoni. Antonio was greatly influenced by the *Laocoön* group (late 1st century BCE– early 1st century CE) and ancient gems when producing his mythological reliefs for Alfonso d'Este.

In the Vendramin tomb, Tullio Lombardo reduced his father's extensive use of polychromy (as on the tomb of Doge Pietro Mocenigo) to selective gilding. His striking contrasts of black and white include the choice of dark stone backgrounds for niches occupied by the two principal statues. The background of his relief of a couple at the Ca' d'Oro was also once painted a dark color, and the figures' lips were reddened and pupils blackened. By about 1510, Tullio pursued a more Classical austerity; in the tomb of Doge Giovanni Mocenigo, ornamental detail is played down and the principal colors come from the natural hues of gray, white, and orange-gray marble.

Tullio's work and a few surviving letters suggest a contentious personality that battled vigorously for the cause of modern sculpture as private, not just public, art and as a medium that stood as a worthy competitor with both Antiquity and contemporary painting for the attention of connoisseurs. In about 1504, his humanist friend Pomponius Gauricus declared him the greatest of all marble sculptors and intoned, "Are not the genius and miracles of the past returned?" The same author also praised Antonio, the younger brother with whom Tullio "competed in fervent rivalry."

Tullio's particular interest in physiognomy and expression is evident in his invention of ideal portrait reliefs that suggest drama and emotion through single or paired bust-length figures whose identities are now uncertain. Their parted lips and mobile eyes evoke states of reverie, longing, or anxiety. Their combination of nudity with modern costume elements, along with their idealization, leaves doubt as to whether they were ever meant as contemporary portraits. These works must have been destined for discerning private collectors. Tullio experimented further with varieties of facial expression in the low-relief ornament of the Vendramin warriors' armor and in human types that suggest an artistic dialogue with Leonardo da Vinci. The apprehensive scowl of his helmeted warrior seems to be echoed later in Michelangelo's *David* (1501–04). Tullio's expressive vocabulary went beyond faces to nervously flexed, angular hands and the pent-up, rippling movement of hair. His emotionally charged images of beautiful youths in fanciful dress, full of ambiguities that invite imaginative meditation, probably helped prepare the ground for the paintings by Giorgione in Venice. Tullio has been both praised and blamed for the cool, smooth, Classical-like, and sometimes melodramatic qualities of his work. But his brilliant carving, his capacity for amalgamating antique with modern style, and his gift for engaging, haunting expression have been increasingly appreciated, as has his role as a designer of major architectural/sculptural ensembles like the Cappella dell'Arca di S. Antonio at the Basilica of Sant'Antonio (Il Santo) in Padua.

Like his father, Tullio was also an architect, and he took over for his father at the Treviso Cathedral and for his brother at the Zen funerary chapel. Buildings ascribed to him include the Benedictine abbey complex at Praglia (*ca.* 1490) and the Villa Giustinian at Roncade (*ca.* 1495–1510). He also worked at Cividale Cathedral and at the Church of San Salvatore in Venice. Tullio's son Sante (1504–60) worked as an architect in Venice beginning in 1524.

Antonio Lombardo's figure style, close to Tullio's, is often more naturalistic in approach to human types, clothing, and depiction of space. His carving or modeling is more delicately detailed and less rhythmically curvilinear than Tullio's; Antonio used broken drapery folds that suggest the weight of cloth and its response to underlying forms, movement, and gravity. He often rendered hair with impressionistic drill work or silky softness. His facial expressions, more restrained than Tullio's, can appear formulaically dreamy but at their best (*Miracle of the Newborn Child* and the bronzes in the Zen funerary chapel) hint at a warmth, compassion, and even humor distinct from his brother's troubled reverie. In his Padua relief (*Miracle of the Newborn Child*) and the smaller narrative panels for the duke of Ferrara, Antonio created pictorially layered spatial settings by means of low-relief background elements with successive planes of architecture, suspended curtains, and figures in profile crossing behind the high-relief foreground actors.

The Lombardo style of ornamental carving, with burgeoning vegetation and active mythical creatures, took on new life in Antonio's marble panels for the duke of Ferrara. Antonio is also the only Lombardo brother known to have made models for bronze. The style of the Zen funerary chapel figures suggests that he is responsible for a group of small bronze ideal busts (*ca.* 1505–08) of young women and boys (some of which are infant John the Baptist figures), possibly cast by Severo da Ravenna, to be found in Modena (Galleria e Museo Estense), London (the Wallace Collection), Vienna (Kunsthistorisches Museum), Houston (Museum of Fine Arts), New York (Metropolitan Museum of Art), and Oxford (Ashmolean Museum). Thus he carried his brother's experiments with ideal ancient portrait types into a form appropriate to a private *studiolo*.

Another group of objects suited to a humanist's study, the small marble reliefs showing single figures of antique heroes or heroines or scenes from ancient or biblical history, have been attributed to Antonio. The best of these "moral exemplars" (*Philoctetes, ca.* 1508/16, at the Hermitage in St. Petersburg, for instance) are probably autograph, whereas others were produced by sculptors from Antonio's workshop or by followers, including Gianmaria Mosca.

Aurelio Lombardo *ca.* 1501–1564/65, Girolamo Lombardo *ca.* 1505/06–*ca.* 1584/89, and Ludovico Lombardo *ca.* 1509–1575

Three sons of Antonio Lombardo—Aurelio, Girolamo, and Ludovico—carried on the family tradition, chiefly in the Marches region of central Italy. All three undertook carvings for the basilica and shrine of the Santa Casa at Loreto, one of the most important sculptural complexes of the 16th century. Extensive collaboration complicates definitions of their individual personalities. Aurelio Lombardo, the eldest, carved at least one monumental statue under Michelangelo's influence and with his brother Girolamo's assistance, the brooding *Geremia*. Aurelio's marble reliefs of God the Father and angels from the chapel of the Holy Sacrament tabernacle at Loreto recall Antonio's work at the funerary chapel of Cardinal Giovanni Battista Zen in Venice, as do the bronze putti added to the Loreto chandelier of 1547–50. Aurelio was evidently most active as a bronze designer.

Aurelio's younger brother Girolamo Lombardo, the most prolific of the three brothers in work and in life,

raised another generation of sculptors. Ludovico Lombardo continued an exploration of antiquarian portraiture, producing bronze busts of Brutus and Hadrian for private collectors. The three brothers (Antonio's sons) jointly signed the 1559–60 bronze sacrament tabernacle for Milan Cathedral, the only work in which the Lombardi are known to have claimed the name Solari, the name of a family of stone carvers from Carona, a town that is also the birthplace of Pietro Lombardo.

Adaptation by Girolamo and Ludovico of the Milan tabernacle models of the scenes from the Life of Christ for a second tabernacle in Fermo, and for the bronze side doors of the chapel/shrine of the Holy House, inside the Basilica of the Santa Casa at Loreto, indicates both their popularity and the expediency of a busy workshop. From about 1570 on, Girolamo and Ludovico were papal bronze casters, making decorated cannons and other arms. The Recanati school founded by the brothers produced monumental bronze works for the sanctuary of Loreto, as well as numerous bronze functional objects, such as candlesticks and inkwells, for a broad range of patrons.

ALISON LUCHS

See also **Donatello (Donato di Betto Bardi); Desiderio da Settignano;** *Laocoön and His Sons*; **Rossellino Family; Severo di Domenico Calzetta da Ravenna**

Pietro Lombardo

Biography

Born at Carona (Lombardy), Italy, *ca.* 1435. Active in Bologna at San Petronio, 1462–63, but designs suggest visited Florence probably before 1464; produced Roselli tomb, Padua, 1464–67; working in Venice by 1474; directed large workshop, involving sons Tullio and Antonio, for series of marble tomb monuments and chapel decorations for Venetian churches; built and renovated churches and designed architecture for Venetian *scuole* (confraternities); active in Treviso, 1480s, Ravenna, early 1480s, Bergamo, 1488–90, Mantua, 1495; appointed Protomagister of Palazzo Ducale, 1498–1511; head of Venetian stonemasons' guild, 1514. Died probably in Venice, Italy, June 1515.

Selected Works

1464–67 Monument of Antonio Roselli; stone; Basilica of Sant'Antonio (Il Santo), Padua, Italy

mid–   Tomb of Doge Pasquale Malipiero; Istrian
1460s   stone; Church of Santi Giovanni e Paolo, Venice, Italy

ca.   Cappella Maggiore and renovation,
1471–85 including decorative sculpture; various materials; Church of San Giobbe, Venice, Italy

ca. 1476–81	Tomb of Doge Pietro Mocenigo; polychromed Istrian stone; Church of Santi Giovanni e Paolo, Venice, Italy
ca. 1478	Gussoni Chapel; various materials; Church of S. Lio, Venice, Italy
ca. 1481	*Madonna* relief for Bernardo Bembo; *pietra tennera* (limestone); private collection, Padua, Italy
ca. 1481–85	Tomb of Doge Niccolò Marcello, for Sta. Marina; Istrian stone, marble; Church of Santi Giovanni e Paolo, Venice, Italy
1481–89	Church of Santa Maria dei Miracoli, architecture and sculptural decoration (with Tullio and Antonio); marble; Venice, Italy
ca. 1483	Tomb of Dante; *pietra tennera* (limestone), marble; Church of San Francesco, Ravenna, Italy
ca. 1485–88	Zanetti Tomb (with Tullio and Antonio); marble; Treviso Cathedral, Italy
1488–90	Scuola di San Marco (lower part of new facade); marble and Istrian stone; Venice, Italy
1488–90	*Saints John the Baptist, Bartholomew,* and *Mark*; marble; Colleoni Chapel, Church of Santa Maria Maggiore, Bergamo, Italy

Tullio Lombardo

Biography

Born in Padua, Italy, *ca.* 1455 or later. Trained in workshop of father Pietro; assisted with father's projects through 1515; probably visited Milan and Rome before 1490; emerged as recognizable sculptor in 1480s; active as sculptor and architect primarily in Venice; also worked in Padua, *ca.* 1499–1532; in Ravenna, 1515 and 1520–25; in Mantua, 1517, 1523, and 1527; in Rovigo, 1526; and in Feltre, 1528. Died in Venice, Italy, 17 November 1532.

Selected Works

ca. 1485–89	Reliefs and statues (with Pietro and Antonio); marble; Church of Santa Maria dei Miracoli, Venice, Italy
ca. 1485–88	Zanetti Tomb (with Pietro and Antonio); marble; Treviso Cathedral, Italy
1489–90	*Baptism of Anianus*; Istrian stone; Scuola di San Marco, Venice, Italy (attributed)
beginning 1489	Tomb of Doge Andrea Vendramin (with Antonio and workshop), for Sta. Maria dei Servi; marble with gilding; Church of Santi Giovanni e Paolo, Venice, Italy

ca. 1495	*A Couple*; marble; Galleria Giorgio Franchetti, Ca' d'Oro, Venice, Italy
1500–02	*Coronation of the Virgin*; marble; Bernabò Chapel, Church of S. Giovanni Crisostomo, Venice, Italy
1500–04	*Miracle of the Reattached Leg*; marble; Chapel of the Arca of St. Anthony, Basilica of Sant'Antonio, Padua, Italy
ca. 1505–10	*Bacchus and Ariadne*; marble; Kunsthistorisches Museum, Vienna, Austria
ca. 1500–11	*Four Angels*; marble; Church of S. Martino, Venice, Italy (attributed)
ca. 1500–22	Tomb of Doge Giovanni Mocenigo; marble; Church of Santi Giovanni e Paolo, Venice, Italy
1520–25	*Miracle of the Miser's Heart*; marble; Chapel of the Arca of St. Anthony, Basilica of Sant'Antonio, Padua, Italy
1526	*Pietà and Two Saints*; marble; Church of San Francesco, Rovigo, Italy
1528	Tomb of Matteo Bellati; marble; Feltre Cathedral, Italy

Antonio Lombardo

Biography

Born in Padua, Italy, *ca.* 1458 or later. Trained along with older brother in father's workshop; assisted father and brother Tullio with projects through 1506; worked in sculpture with bronze as well as marble; active in Venice, Treviso, and Padua; moved to Ferrara in 1506 to work for the d'Este court. Father of sculptors Aurelio, Girolamo, and Ludovico. Died in Ferrara, Italy, before March 1516.

Selected Works

ca. 1485–89	Reliefs and statues (with Pietro and Tullio); marble; Church of Santa Maria dei Miracoli, Venice, Italy
ca. 1485–88	Zanetti Tomb (with Pietro and Tullio); marble; Treviso Cathedral, Italy
1489–90	*Healing of Anianus*; Istrian stone; Scuola di San Marco, Venice, Italy (attributed)
1500–04	*Miracle of the Newborn Child*; marble; Chapel of the Arca of St. Anthony, Basilica of Sant'Antonio, Padua, Italy
ca. 1504–06	Models: *Madonna and Child (Madonna della Scarpa)*; bronze; and *God the Father with Child Angels*; bronze; funerary chapel of Cardinal Giovanni Battista Zen, Basilica of San Marco, Venice, Italy
ca.	Reliefs for ducal apartment of Alfonso

1507–11 d'Este, Ferrara; marble; State Heritage Museum, St. Petersburg, Russia; Musée du Louvre, Paris, France; Bargello, Florence, Italy; private collections, Liechtenstein

Aurelio Lombardo

Biography

Born probably in Venice, Italy, *ca.* 1501. Moved to Ferrara with father Antonio, 1506; a friar in Ferrara by 1528; settled in Loreto, 1539, to work on sculptural adornment of the Santa Casa; moved to San Vito quarter at Recanati, 1552, and with his brothers established bronze foundry and workshop for sculptors; named chaplain of Confraternity of Corpus Christi in Church of San Vito, Recanati, 1555. Died in Recanati, Italy, 9 September 1563.

Selected Works

1539–42 Prophet *Geremia* (assisted by Girolamo); marble; Basilica della Santa Casa, Loreto, Italy

1542 Chapel of the Holy Sacrament tabernacle; marble; fragments in the Basilica della Santa Casa, Loreto, Italy

1540s? Base for *Idolino*; bronze; Museo Archeologico, Florence, Italy (attributed to both Aurelio and Girolamo)

1547–48 Candlestick (with Girolamo and Ludovico); bronze; Chapel of the Holy Sacrament, Basilica della Santa Casa, Loreto, Italy

1547–50 Chandelier (with Girolamo and Ludovico); bronze; Chapel of the Holy Sacrament, Basilica della Santa Casa, Loreto, Italy

1559–60 Tabernacle (with Girolamo and Ludovico); bronze; Milan Cathedral, Italy

Girolamo Lombardo

Biography

Born in Ferrara, Italy, *ca.* 1505–06. Second son of Antonio Lombardo. Active with Jacopo Sansovino, *ca.* 1535, in Venice, assisting until 1542 with sculptural decoration of Marciana Library and the Loggetta; worked with his brothers Aurelio and Ludovico at the Santa Casa of Loreto from 1542; became a master of bronze casting at Recanati, 1552; lived in Rome *ca.* 1560; granted citizenship in Recanati, 1566; father of sculptors Antonio the Younger (1564–1609), Pietro the Younger (1566–1607), Paolo (1571–1645), and Giacomo (1574–1621). Died in Loreto, Italy, between 17 January 1584 and 12 June 1589.

Selected Works

1540s Base for *Idolino*; bronze; Museo Archeologico, Florence, Italy (attributed to both Aurelio and Girolamo)

1543–47 Statues (probably *Ezechiel* and *Malachi*); marble; Basilica della Santa Casa, Loreto, Italy

1547–48 Cornucopia/lamp (with Aurelio); bronze; Chapel of the Holy Sacrament, Basilica della Santa Casa, Loreto, Italy; copy: 1581, Marilla Chapel of Basilica della Santa Casa

1548 Statue (probably *Daniel*); marble; Basilica della Santa Casa, Loreto, Italy

1550–51 Statue (probably *Zaccaria*; with Ludovico); marble; Basilica della Santa Casa, Loreto, Italy

1559–60 Tabernacle (with Aurelio and Ludovico); bronze; Milan Cathedral, Italy

1560 Statue (possibly *Moses*); marble; Basilica della Santa Casa, Loreto, Italy

1568–73 Doors (north and south, with narrative scenes from Life of Christ; with Ludovico); bronze; Chapel/shrine of the Holy House, Basilica della Santa Casa, Loreto, Italy

ca. Tabernacle (with Ludovico); marble; Altar
1570–71 of the Holy Sacrament, Fermo Cathedral, Italy

1578–79 *Amos*; marble; Basilica della Santa Casa, Loreto, Italy

1582–83 *Madonna and Child* (with son Antonio, Tiburzio Vergelli, and other pupils); bronze; facade of Basilica della Santa Casa, Loreto, Italy

Ludovico Lombardo

Biography

Born in Ferrara, Italy, *ca.* 1509. Worked in Rome on metal faldstool for Chapel of Pope Paul III, 1546; worked on bronze busts for the Ridolfi family of Florence, 1550; arrived in Loreto, *ca.* 1550, to work on sculpture for Basilica della Santa Casa; worked in Rome on base for *Young Caesar*, 1559; granted citizenship in Recanati, 1566; accepted commission for bronze statue of Pope Gregory XIII for Ascoli Piceno in 1573, which remained incomplete at his death. Died in Ascoli, Italy, before 31 July 1575.

Selected Works

1546 Faldstool for the Chapel of Pope Paul III; bronze (lost)

ca. 1550 *Brutus*; bronze casts; collection of the

princes of Liechtenstein, Vaduz; Musée du Louvre, Paris, France; private collection, New York City, United States

ca. 1550 Bust of Hadrian; bronze casts; National Gallery of Art, Washington, D.C., United States; Museo Archeologico, Venice, Italy; Bayerisches Nationalmuseum, Munich, Germany

1559–60 Tabernacle (with Aurelio and Girolamo); bronze; Milan Cathedral, Italy

1568–73 Doors (north and south, with narrative scenes from Life of Christ; with Girolamo); Chapel/shrine of the Holy House, Basilica della Santa Casa, Loreto, Italy

1573–75 Statue of Pope Gregory XIII (completed in 1576 by Antonio Calcagni), for Ascoli Piceno, Italy; bronze (destroyed); plaster mask; Museo Civico, Ascoli Piceno, Italy

Further Reading

Callegari, Raimondo, "Bernardo Bembo and Pietro Lombardo: News from the 'Nonianum,' " *The Burlington Magazine* 139 (December 1997)

Giannatiempo López, Maria, "I Lombardi-Solari e la porta centrale di Loreto," in *Le Arti nelle Marche al tempo di Sisto V*, edited by Paolo Dal Poggetto, Cinisello Balsamo, Italy: Silvana, 1992

Grimaldi, Floriano, *L'ornamento Marmoreo della Santa Cappella di Loreto*, Loreto, Italy: Carilo, 1999

Grimaldi, Floriano, and Katy Sordi, *Scultori a Loreto: Fratelli Lombardi, Antonio Calcagno e Tiburzio Vergelli*, Ancona, Italy: Soprintendenza per i Beni Ambientali e Architettonici delle Marci, 1987

Jestaz, Bertrand, *La chapelle Zen à Saint-Marc de Venise: D'Antonio à Tullio Lombardo*, Stuttgart, Germany: Steiner, 1986

Luchs, Alison, *Tullio Lombardo and Ideal Portrait Sculpture in Renaissance Venice, 1490–1530*, Cambridge and New York: Cambridge University Press, 1995

McHam, Sarah Blake, *The Chapel of St. Anthony at the Santo and the Development of Venetian Renaissance Sculpture*, Cambridge: Cambridge University Press, 1994

Poeschke, Joachim, *Die Skulptur der Renaissance in Italien*, vol. 1, *Donatello und seine Zeit*, Munich: Hirmer, 1990; as *Donatello and His World: Sculpture of the Italian Renaissance*, translated by Russell Stockman, New York: Abrams, 1993

Poeschke, Joachim, *Die Skulptur der Renaissance in Italien*, vol. 2, *Michelangelo und seine Zeit*, Munich: Hirmer, 1992; as *Michelangelo and His World: Sculpture of the Italian Renaissance*, translated by Russell Stockman, New York: Abrams, 1996

Pope-Hennessy, John Wyndham, *An Introduction to Italian Sculpture*, 3 vols., London: Phaidon, 1963; 4th edition, 1996; see especially vol. 2, *Italian Renaissance Sculpture*

Sarchi, Alessandra, "Per Antonio Lombardo: Fortuna e collezionismo: I rilievi per Alfonso I d'Este," *Arte Lombarda* 132 (2001/02)

Sheard, Wendy Stedman, "The Tomb of Doge Andrea Vendramin in Venice by Tullio Lombardo," (dissertation), Yale University, 1971

Sheard, Wendy Stedman, "Antonio Lombardo's Reliefs for Alfonso d'Este's Studio di Marmi: Their Significance and Impact on Titian," in *Titian 500*, edited by Joseph Manca, Washington, D.C.: National Gallery of Art, 1993

Wilk, Sarah Blake, *The Sculpture of Tullio Lombardo: Studies in Sources and Meaning*, New York: Garland, 1978

RICHARD LONG 1945– *British*

Richard Long's first solo exhibition, at Konrad Fischer's gallery in Düsseldorf in 1968, already encapsulated many of the concerns that have continued to preoccupy his work: a formal arrangement of natural elements (in this case, sticks) placed on the floor of the gallery and a connection with a place in the landscape. In this instance, the landscape link was made via the exhibition announcement card—an ordinary picture postcard showing the place where the sticks were collected—appropriated for the purpose and overprinted with the artist's name. The postcard shows the Clifton suspension bridge in Bristol, close to Long's home and birthplace and in the city where he still lives and works.

At the heart of Long's practice, then as now, are the walks he makes in the landscape. These walks—their trajectories, the experiences, and the materials found and rearranged into shapes along the way—and the representation of these activities in words, in photographs, and on maps are the essential components of Long's work. The outdoor works are complemented by gallery sculptures made from locally obtainable or easily transportable materials (including sticks, turf, coal, and mud) or various types of stone, generally taken from quarries. These sculptures take the form of simple geometric shapes—usually lines and circles, although he has also used squares, rectangles, crosses, spirals, zigzags, arcs, and ellipses—formed by placing material directly on the floor. In the case of works made from more liquid materials, such as mud, these may be splashed or hand- or foot-printed onto floor or wall.

The simple shapes made from stones or other natural materials often subtly relate to or reveal their surroundings, whether these are outdoor locations or museum and gallery spaces. In *Circle in the Andes* (1972), contrasts of rough and smooth surfaces and clean and ragged outlines in both the material and form of the work emphasize similar contrasts in the dramatic surrounding landscape. In the simple restraint of the near-contemporaneous work *Three Circles of Stones*, shown at the Hayward Gallery London in the same year, the three concentric circles of rounded pebbles relate the sculpture to the clean-lined uniformity and yet materially raw architectural aesthetic of the Hayward Gallery's interior.

Variation, repetition, and relationships across time and space are key elements of Long's creative vocabulary. This is seen, for example, in the repetition of a few simple shapes in his outdoor and indoor works and in his strategy of reproducing early works in exhibition catalogues and other publications to contextualize new works or, conversely, to allow early works to be reinterpreted by new works. A number of key early works in particular, such as *England 1968* (a cross made by removing daisy heads) or *A Ten Mile Walk England 1968* (represented as a straight line drawn across a section of an Ordinance Survey map), are revisited regularly and can be seen as establishing a set of preconditions and procedures in relation to which subsequent works are realized.

The moment of Long's entrance into the art world was a formative one, both in terms of his own development as an artist and in terms of the perception and categorization of his work in subsequent art historical accounts. His work was included in a number of groundbreaking exhibitions toward the close of the 1960s that inaugurated terms now familiar in the history of art and sculpture, such as Conceptual art, *arte povera* (an Italian movement often characterized by the use of ephemeral materials), and Land or Earth art. Long's work was located in the midst of an international scene where the parameters of art practice and theory were being questioned and reformulated. Long's attendance at St. Martin's School of Art in London (1966–68) placed his student activities and subsequent moves in the context of a debate about what sculpture was and could be. Anthony Caro, who was teaching at the school at that time, famously claimed that "sculpture could be anything," later adding that he meant "it doesn't have to be bronze and stone" (quoted in "Anthony Caro, His Work and His Views," *Art Monthly* 23 [1979]), and that he did not hold himself responsible for the actions of those students who took him at his word and made sculpture from "breathing and walking." Demonstrating that a walk could be sculpture is often seen as Long's most original contribution to sculpture.

By the late 1970s and early 1980s, Long's work was provoking disquiet among critics and art historians, who detected a latent imperialist agenda in Long's worldwide walking and an unacceptable reticence in his silence regarding his work's motives and agenda. Breaking a silence he had maintained almost without exception from the beginning of his public career, Long made two series of statements in 1980 and 1982, followed by a reply to a critic published in *Art Monthly* magazine in 1983; subsequently, he granted a number of interviews and gave more extended commentaries.

These have become increasingly personal and less aphoristic; at the same time, his bodily presence in his work, almost entirely absent or effaced in his earlier works, has in the later 1990s become more visceral, including, for example, such activities as eating, drinking, and urinating.

Long once described one of his works as an attempt to be "absolutely equally modern and pastoral," and this is a fitting description of his work in general. Subtle shifts in his practice can be seen to parallel developments in sculpture and art more generally, from the debates about what sculpture can be in the 1960s through the plethora of sculptural activity outside the confines of the gallery from the late 1960s on; from the eruption of words into the field of the visual associated with so-called Postmodernism in the 1980s to the concern with the role of performance, the performative, and the body in the 1990s. At the same time, Long's work can be seen as embodying and continuing a dialogue with a particularly British—or, more specifically, English—landscape sensibility. Thus his work can be seen to draw on and continue the rich indigenous culture of walking, hiking, and journeying with all its attendant historical, political, and philosophical connotations.

ALISON SLEEMAN

See also **Caro, Anthony; Contemporary Sculpture; De Maria, Walter; Heizer, Michael; Postmodernism; Serra, Richard; Smithson, Robert**

Biography

Born in Bristol, England, 2 June 1945. Studied at the West of England College of Art, Bristol, 1962–65, and with artists working to redefine sculpture in England; attended St. Martin's School of Art, London, 1966–68; closely associated with emergence of a new art form, Land art; represented Britain at the Venice Biennale of 1976. Kunstpreis Aachen, Neue Galerie–Sammlung, 1988; Turner Prize, Patrons of New Art, Tate Gallery, London, 1989; Chevalier of the Order of Arts and Letters, 1990; Wilhelm Lehmbruck Prize, Germany, 1995. Presently living and working in Bristol, England.

Selected Works

1966   *Turf Circle England 1966*; photography and text; public freehold
1967   *A Line Made by Walking England 1967*; photography and text; Tate Gallery, London, England
1968   *England 1968*; photography and text; Tate Gallery, London, England

1968   *A Ten Mile Walk England 1968*; map and text; private collection of Konrad Fischer, Düsseldorf, Germany

1968   *Untitled*; sticks; private collection of Berta Fischer, Düsseldorf, Germany

1971   *A Line the Length of a Straight Walk from the Bottom to the Top of Silbury Hill 1970*; photography and text; private collection of Pier Luigi, Pero, Italy

1972   *Circle in the Andes*; photography and text; private collection, Art and Project gallery, Amsterdam

1972   *Three Circles of Stones*, for Hayward Gallery, London; photography and text; private collection

1972   *Walking a Line in Peru*; photography and text; private collection

1974   *A Line in Ireland*; photography and text; public freehold

Further Reading

Beardsley, John, *Earthworks and Beyond: Contemporary Art in the Landscape*, New York: Abbeville Press, 1984; 3rd edition, 1998

Christov-Bakargiev, Carolyn, *Arte Povera*, London: Phaidon, 1999

Compton, Susan (editor), *British Art in the 20th Century: The Modern Movement*, Munich: Prestel-Verlag, 1986

Godfrey, Tony, *Conceptual Art*, London: Phaidon, 1998

Kastner, Jeffrey (editor), *Land and Environmental Art*, London: Phaidon, 1998

Neff, Terry A. (editor), *A Quiet Revolution: British Sculpture since 1965*, London: Thames and Hudson, 1987

Un siècle de sculpture anglaise (exhib. cat.), Paris: Galerie Nationale du Jeu de Paume, 1996

Tiberghien, Gilles A., *Land Art*, London: Art Data, 1995

A LINE MADE BY WALKING ENGLAND 1967

Richard Long (1945–)

1967

a long trace left in a grass field by walking, photographed

h. 37.5 cm; w. 32.4 cm (image)

Tate Gallery, London, England

A Line Made by Walking England 1967 is perhaps the most frequently reproduced of Richard Long's works. Seen in its reproduced form, the piece consists of a black-and-white photograph in portrait orientation showing what looks to be a parkland setting. The grass is scattered with daisies, and there are trees in the distance, the tops of some of which are cropped by the upper framing edge of the photograph; between the treetops, some patches of sky can be seen. Running vertically across the center of the photograph is a line of flattened grass. Beneath the photograph is a caption in Gill Sans Serif typeface (the typeface used almost exclusively by Long in text works in exhibitions and in publications). The caption, arranged on two lines and centered slightly below the framing edge of the photograph, establishes how, where, and when the line came into existence, with an economy of phrase that is at once both precise and enigmatic.

The caption and the photograph together establish and present the line they ostensibly depict and describe. But what is the sculpture here? Is it the line itself walked in the grass somewhere in England sometime in 1967, or is it the photograph and text that represent it? These are more than incidental questions about this particular work; they are far-ranging and important questions for Long's work, as well as about the practice of sculpture since the 1960s. In his catalogue essay to the major exhibition of Long's work at the Guggenheim Museum in New York in 1986, R.H. Fuchs went so far as to suggest that *A Line Made by Walking England 1967* was "a revelation of how to make sculpture." While this bold claim has historically held up to critical scrutiny, Fuchs's subsequent assertion that "[t]he *Line Made by Walking* became classic the moment it was done" has been interpreted as problematic.

The photograph has not always looked the same, and the caption has not been constant either in typeface or wording. Early captions in published presentations of the work included *Richard Long sculpture March 1967* (1969); *Sculpture 1967 / track in grass / made by walking / England* (1969); *Sculpture by Walking (67)* (1971); and *Walking* (1972). The photograph of the line has not always been presented with the line centered vertically; it was positioned diagonally in versions published in 1969 and off-center to the left in versions published in 1971 and 1972. The "classic" version of the line and caption, as described at the beginning of this essay, seems to have become the standard presentation for this work in the mid 1970s. By 1976, when Long was the British representative at the Venice Biennale, *A Line Made by Walking England 1967* had come to play an important explanatory role in relation to Long's sculptural practice, accordingly being given a full-page reproduction in the accompanying publication, "Some Notes on the Work of Richard Long" (see Compton, 1976). When the work has been displayed in exhibitions, it is presented as a framed photographic print, with the photograph mounted in a large landscape-oriented mount and the caption beneath it rendered in pencil-written text with the ruled guide lines still visible.

When he created *A Line Made by Walking England 1967*, Long was still a student at St. Martin's School of Art in London. At the outset within Long's oeuvre, it was one of a range of strategies for making sculpture, which also included more traditional modes such as modeling and casting with plaster and assembling works from materials such as sticks and stones. It became a touchstone of Long's most basic sculptural procedure—walking—and of the pared-down and spare forms of its representation in photographs and words. As such, it became a revelation about how Long makes sculpture.

As well as marking changes and performing shifting explanatory functions in relation to Long's work, the changes wrought in *A Line Made by Walking England 1967* embody changes occurring more globally in the field of sculpture. The emphatic incantation of "sculpture" in the captions of its early appearances are a strategy of affiliation to a discipline and medium—sculpture—and to its creations as sculptural objects, however unsculptural they may be in a traditional sense. The shifting of the photograph from documentary status to primary artwork is indicative of a shift in sculptural enterprise that could posit a photograph as a work of sculpture rather than as a record of a sculpture. For works that existed in remote locations, the photograph was first a necessary form of transmission between the work made by the artist and the viewer in the gallery. In subsequent art theory, the pho-

tograph became an analogy for the process of making itself, an indexical mark on the grass recorded by photography, itself considered an indexical process. The democratic potential of the work's making and the suppression of the personal pronoun has led others to posit *A Line Made by Walking England 1967* as a profoundly political work (see Godfrey, 1998). The physical status of the work raises questions about originality, reproduction, and conservation, all important and pressing concerns in sculpture more generally.

A Line Made by Walking England 1967 can also be seen as a sculpture in a highly traditional way and as an engagement with long-standing themes in the history of sculpture theory. It inhabits three-dimensional space, evoking in its use of walking the potential perambulation around a sculptural object in the round. At the same time, in its photographic form, framing a single point of view, it presents a temporal action in a resolved form that can be comprehended in a single glance. This is a theme explored in the history of sculpture by theorists as diverse as Sir Joshua Reynolds, Adolf von Hildebrand, and Michael Fried. *A Line Made by Walking England 1967* also has a kind of monumentality and could be seen as a commemorative representation of one of the simplest human activities, walking, and of this activity's importance in its particular place, in the archetypal English landscape.

ALISON SLEEMAN

See also **Contemporary Sculpture; De Maria, Walter**

Further Reading

Bann, Stephen, "From Land Art to Garden Landscape," *Art and Design Profile* 57 (1997)

Bann, Stephen, "The Map as Index of the Real: Land Art and the Authentication of Travel," in *Land and Environmental Art*, edited by Jeffrey Kastner, London: Phaidon, 1998

Compton, Michael, "Some Notes on the Work of Richard Long," *British Pavilion XXXVII*; Venice Biennale, London: Lund Humphries, 1976

Fuchs, Rudolf H., "Walking the Line," in *Richard Long*, by Fuchs, New York: Thames and Hudson, 1986

Godfrey, Tony, "The Dematerialized Object, Almost," in *Conceptual Art*, by Godfrey, London: Phaidon, 1998

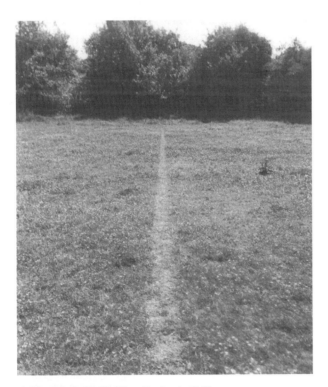

A Line Made by Walking England, 1967
© Richard Long. Photo courtesy the Tate Gallery, London / Art Resource, NY

LONGOBARD SCULPTURE

Longobard sculptural production has long remained obscured by the idea of decadence that has been prejudicially tied to the entire early Medieval period. In addition, the fragmentary evidence and removal of the preserved archaeological finds from their original context make an accurate reading of the original function and destination of these works particularly difficult.

Originating in north-central Europe, the Longobards invaded Italy in 568 and founded their first duchy in Cividale del Friuli in northeast Italy. After establishing their capital in Pavia in 772, they headed south, occupying a large part of the Italian Peninsula. They remained in Italy until 774, when they were defeated by the Franks. The Longobards claimed a solid cultural background, so their contribution to the formation of new techniques and artistic languages melded with the local traditions in Italy and with those of eastern derivation. The metalworking and woodworking talents of the Longobards and of the Germanic populations in general facilitated the assimilation of the widespread style of the ancient east and of the late Romans. The resumption of intertwining and zoomorphic motifs in 7th-century northern Italy can be better understood in this context, even if they lack the naturalism typical of older works. The meeting of different cultures and styles gave rise to a rich artistic production for which it is difficult, and historically inaccurate, to distinguish the Longobard elements from those that are more authentically local.

In Longobardia Major (north-central Italy occupied by the Longobards) and in Longobardia Minor (the Longobard duchies of southern Italy) artists produced many sculpted slabs or paving stones decorated with zoomorphic, plant, and geometric ornamental motifs; comparable works have been found not in the Longobard world but rather in eastern Europe. The classical Byzantine tradition, characterized by plant motifs, mixed with the Germanic tradition, whose zoomorphic repertoire was absorbed into the intertwining plants, thus creating sometimes inextricable weavings. The geometric honeycomb decoration prevailed until the end of the 6th and the beginning of the 7th centuries (e.g., Aldo's Tombstone [Civiche Raccolte di Arte Antica, Sforzesco Castle, Milan]); the transposition to a monumental scale of the type of honeycomb goldwork is not an exclusive Longobard trait but is also found in many contemporary sculptural examples in other areas of Europe. Only under Agilulf's wife, Queen Theodolinda, in the late 6th and early 7th centuries, did artists produce works of various symbols in a late ancient pattern, at least in their choice of iconography, next to the geometric works. With the help of Pope Gregory the Great, Theodolinda obtained the conversion of the Longobard court and a large part of the population; therefore, Christological symbols of paleo-Christian ancestry appeared beginning in the 7th century, reproduced with an archaic and linear style obtained with techniques acquired from goldsmiths and from works in ivory and bone (for example, *Theodolindian Paving Stone* [Treasures of the Cathedral, Monza] and the Tombstones of Odelberto and Manfredo [Civiche Raccolte di Arte Antica, Sforzesco Castle, Milan]). The so-called *Little Head of Theodolinda* (Civiche Raccolte di Arte Antica, Sforzesco Castle,

Milan), in dark-green porphyry, is a singular example of portraiture in the Classical tradition. Among the surviving works in gold are the *Lamina of King Agilulf's Helmet* (Museo Nazionale del Bargello, Florence), in gold and copper with aligned figures, and *Theodolinda's Crown* (ca. 600; Treasures of the Cathedral, Monza), on which are regularly spaced sapphires, aquamarine, and mother of pearl. Together with the *Binding of the Gospels* (ca. 603; Treasury of the Cathedral, Monza), these works display an equilibrium in their compositions that is more comparable to imperial Roman art than to that of the Germanic world.

The period of greatest Longobard artistic splendor came under the Catholic king Liutprand in the 8th century, at the time when the eastern emperor issued his decree against the cult of images. Religious subjects and symbols prevailed during Liutprand's reign. During this period the different artistic centers—connected by networks of exchange—became important, creating homogeneous works of art. Pavia produced the highest number of paving stones or slabs with dated epigraphs that present a pure classicism of Byzantine origin (*Pluteo Adorned with Chalices and Two Peacocks*; *Pluteo Adorned with the Tree of Life among Winged Dragons* [Musei Civici, Pavia]). The dating of the *plutei* (vertical slabs) to the beginning of the 8th century is confirmed by the comparison to the analogous *girali* (scrolls) of the *Paving Stone of Saint Cumiano* (Museo dell'abbazia di San Colombano, Bobbio), in which King Liutprand's name also appears. This type of decoration spread throughout almost all of the Italian territory beginning in the age of Liutprand and ending with the disappearance of the Longobards. Among the many Longobard sculptural works of this period, one of the most refined examples is the trapezoidal paving stone with a peacock (Museo di Santa Giulia, Brescia) belonging to an ambo of the Church of San Salvatore. The peacock, symbol of the resurrection and immortality of the soul, walks stately inside a twisting grapevine, below which is an intertwined band of ribbons. High medieval ornamental motifs meet a Byzantine elegance and a late antique naturalism in the rendering of the peacock's plumage and other anatomical particularities.

The artistic center of Cividale del Friuli was at the apex of Longobard production. Here was created the stone bas-reliefs of the *Altar of Duke Ratchis* (Cathedral, Cividale del Friuli), datable to between 734 and 744, which portray scenes from the life of Christ; the figures are strongly stylized, and the scenes are framed by intertwining motifs. The octagonal *Baptismal Font of the Patriarch Callisto* (Museo Archeologico, Cividale) shows all the decorative variety of sculpture from Cividale, above all in the ciborium, in the decorative arches with geometrical and zoomorphic motifs, and in the capitals, which appear to return to the Corinthian patterns. The base of the font of the Tombstone of Sigwald (Museo Archeologico, Cividale) contains stylized symbols of the evangelists inserted inside four circles arranged at angles of the *pluteo*. The circles are made of and tied together by ribbon that divides the stone horizontally. At the center symmetrically above and below this horizontal line are the cross and the candlesticks, as well as griffins and peacocks around the tree of life. Despite the essential style of the work and the lack of volume in its figures, the language is nonetheless strongly evocative of Christianity.

The stucco decoration of the *Little Temple of Saint Mary in the Valley*, also in Cividale del Friuli, is worthy of mention. Built after 750, the building's interior shows an architrave and an archivolt with rich plant decorations in stucco that create the effect of refined fretwork. Above this decoration six saints emerge from the stucco background; the two central saints turn toward the window that flanks them while the other four face the front. The theme is a rare example of monumental figurative sculpture, and scholars date it alternatively as Longobard, Carolingian, or even from the age of Otto the Great. The combination of stuccos and frescoes in the same building is suggestive of the Carolingian Church of San Salvatore in Brescia and Church of San Benedetto in Malles; indeed, most scholarship places the work at the moment of passage from the Longobard to the Carolingian age at the second half of the 8th century, or at the passage from the "Longobard rebirth" to the "Carolingian rebirth."

LORENZO CARLETTI

See also **Ambo; Carolingian Sculpture; Porphyry**

Further Reading

Brozzi, Mario, and Amelio Tagliaferri, *Arte longobarda: La scultura figurativa su marmo e su metallo*, 2 vols., Cividale, Italy: Fulvio, 1960

Casadio, Paolo, "Zur Stuckdekoration des 'Tempietto Longobardo' in Cividale," in *Stuck des frühen und hohen Mittelalters: Geschichte, Technologie, Konservierung*, edited by Matthias Exner, Munich: Lipp, 1996

De Francovich, Géza, "Il problema delle origini della scultura cosiddetta 'longobarda,' " in *Atti del i congresso internazionale di studi longobardi, Spoleto*, Spoleto, Italy: Presso l'Accademia Spoletina, 1952

De Francovich, Géza, "Osservazioni sull'altare di Ratchis a Cividale e sui rapporti tra Occidente e Oriente nei secoli VII e VIII d. C.," in *Scritti di storia dell'arte in onore di Mario Salmi*, edited by Valentino Martinelli and Filippa M. Aliberti Gaudioso, 3 vols., Rome: De Luca, 1961–63

Haseloff, Arthur, *Die vorromanische Plastik in Italien*, Florence: Pantheon, 1930; reprint, as *Pre-Romanesque Sculpture in Italy*, translated by Ronald Boothroyd, Paris: Pegasus Press, 1930; New York: Harcourt Brace, 1931; reprint, New York: Hacker Art Books, 1971

Romanini, Angiola Maria, "Problemi di scultura e plastica altomedievali," in *Artigianato e tecnica nella società dell'Alto Medioevo occidentale*, 2 vols., Spoleto, Italy: Presso la Sede del Centro, 1971

Tavano, Sergio, *Il tempietto longobardo di Cividale*, Udine, Italy: Longobarde, 1990

LORO JONGGRANG TEMPLE COMPLEX *Central Java, Indonesia, second half of 9th–early 10th century* CE

The Loro Jonggrang Temple Complex, the most magnificent Hindu site of the Central Javanese period, is just one of a dozen *candi* (religious monument or shrine) areas found on the Prambanan Plain in the Opak River valley, east of the modern-day city of Yogyakarta. Dedicated to the god Śiwa, its construction is credited to the Sanjayas, a ruling family who reigned over this region from the second half of the 9th century through the first third of the 10th century.

Loro Jonggrang has been particularly associated with the ruler Rakai Pikatan. This connection was established on the basis of a lengthy Old Javanese inscription dated 856 CE that tells of several events related to this leader, including his patronage of a temple complex similar in plan to Loro Jonggrang. The consensus of scholars has been to accept this mid 9th-century date for the complex, thereby assigning Loro Jonggrang as the sole representative of late Central Javanese architectural and sculptural styles. However, the present lack of comparative examples inhibits any confirmation of this dating, and the somewhat unique features of Loro Jonggrang, such as the emphasized verticality of its architectural structures and their ornate *śikaras* (superstructures), offer additional challenges to placing this series of monuments in art and architectural history. Similarly, Loro Jonggrang's sculptural components are without any contemporaneous counterparts.

Loro Jonggrang's main architectural plan is a tripartite division of concentric square areas. This may serve as a parallel for the centrally emanating order of the three cosmic levels of the universe, one that is common to Indian beliefs and associated with later East Javanese and Balinese temples. The complex is entered from the east and contained by an outer courtyard that spans precisely 390 by 390 meters. Within its borders is an area of 222 by 222 meters reserved for the *jaba tengah*, or middle enclosure. Here one finds the remains of 224 *perwaras* (ladies-in-waiting shrines), small *candis* that may have been donated by members of the nobility. Since there is evidence that each originally enshrined a sculpture of a deity, it is believed that these *perwaras* served as individual family shrines. The innermost sanctuary of Loro Jonggrang,

977

comprising an area 110 meters by 110 meters, is the *jeroan* (central courtyard). It is here that the major *candis* are situated, and, once more according to indirect literary evidence, it is believed that this precinct was accessible only to members of the royal family. Most significant are the three *candis* dedicated to the gods of the Hindu Trinity: Śiwa, Brahmā, and Wisnu. Each of these shrines is comprised of a terrace and balustrade surmounted by the *garbhagriha* (*cella*, or inner chamber) and *śikara*. Across from the main shrines are three smaller *candis* that house sculptures of the *vahanas* (mounts) of these gods: Nandi, Angsa, and Garuda. Two additional *candis*, known as the *apit* (flanking) shrines, are found at the north and south ends of the *jeroan*, whereas four *kelir* (surrounding) shrines are situated at the back of its four entrances. Further, at each corner of this courtyard is a *menara sudut* (corner tower) shrine.

Candi Śiwa is the preeminent monument of the Loro Jonggrang complex. Flanked on the left by *Candi Brahmā* and *Candi Wisnu* on the right, its height of 47 meters also makes it Loro Jonggrang's tallest edifice. The monument is located in the center of the *jeroan*; however, the exact center of the complex is not the *garbhagriha* housing the statue of Śiwa, but instead a small enclosure on the right side of the east staircase of the *candi*. This *candi* is also the architecturally most complex, and its significance is underscored by multiple *cellas* located at each of the cardinal directions. These chambers are individually reached by means of a staircase that bifurcates each side of the main terrace. In the eastern *cella* is an image of Śiwa Mahādewa that is approximately 3 meters in height. The southern chamber contains a sculpture of Śiwa Mahāguru (Agastya), a form of the deity as a great Hindu spiritual teacher that was celebrated in both southern India and

Classical Java. A sculpture of Ganeśa, the elephant-headed son of Śiwa and regarded as the Hindu god of good fortune, is found in the western *cella*. The northern chamber enshrines a sculpture of Durgā Mahāsuramardini. In comparison with other examples of sculptural deities from Central Javanese sites, those of Loro Jonggrang are relatively squat in their proportions and finely embellished with ornate jewelry. In particular, these full-figured images appear to have some correspondence to contemporaneous temple sculpture of Tamilnadu in South India.

In addition to the three-dimensional images of deities, Loro Jonggrang well represents other categories of sculpture, including narrative panels, relief sculptures, and ornamental motifs. *Kālamakara* topped with superstructures frame the gateways of the main *candis*. Unusual to this site, however, is the three-dimensional motif of the fluted *ratna* (jewel) resembling a bell or Buddhist stupa. This form is placed in rows along the top of the balustrades, as well as on the receding stories and pinnacles of the shrines' *śikaras*. The bases of the main *candis* feature a series of the "Prambanan Motif," a compilation of imagery centering on a lion in a central niche framed by an abstracted *kālamakara* and flanked by *kalpavrkshas* (celestial wishing trees) that are themselves accompanied by a set of supernatural or natural animals.

Candi Śiwa presents a more detailed sculptural relief program. A group of 62 celestial dancers and musicians are depicted around its base. These images were patterned after the formulated postures and movements of ancient India's performing arts. On the terrace level of this *candi*, its *cella*'s outer walls are devoted to depictions of the *Astadikpālakas* (guardian deities of the eight directions) and their attendants.

Loro Jonggrang is probably best known for its narrative relief series. These are found along the inner balustrades of the complex's three main *candis*. Although the tradition of sculpting incidents from religious epic literature on Hindu temples appears to have a precedence in ancient India, nothing compares to the narrative complexity and diversity of those of Loro Jonggrang. The sculptors employed all methods of narrative interpretation, including continuous, cyclic, monoscenic, and simultaneous methods. Seventy-two scenes of the *Rāmāyana*, the story of the god Wisnu's incarnation as Prince Rama, are depicted at Loro Jonggrang, making this series the most extensive rendering of this sacred epic created in stone in all of Asia. The first 42 scenes are found on *Candi Śiwa*; the story continues on the balustrade of *Candi Brahmā* with 30 panels visually relating the remaining episodes. Despite the diverse and proliferous nature of the *Rāmāyana* tradition, which still thrives in written, performance, and oral forms, the narratives at Loro

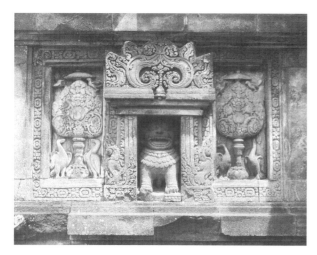

Relief from Loro Jonggrang Temple
© Werner Forman / CORBIS

Jonggrang defy any counterpart in either the Indic or old Javanese literary traditions. The same holds true for the reliefs of the *Kresnayana*, the story of another avatar of Wisnu, which is told in 30 panels lining the balustrade of *Candi Wisnu*. Similar to the images of dancing celestials, the narrative reliefs of Loro Jonggrang reflect an array of narrative formulas based on Indian theatrical traditions and, furthermore, suggest a knowledge of Indian poetics and *rasa* theory (in which a certain emotion or sentiment is evoked by a particular work of art). They are highly valued for their animated and naturalistic qualities, created by means of a specificity of the depicted flora and the incorporation of a bestiary of animal characters that are used as a Greek chorus to enforce the dramatic situations of the protagonists. Moreover, the inclusion of a cloudlike motif among these forms may be emblematic of supernatural or magical powers associated with particular characters. In terms of their technical style, the narratives at Loro Jonggrang are relatively low or shallow when compared with other examples from the Central Javanese period, and their fluid, curvilinear forms suggest a painterly approach to the sculptural medium.

Candi Śiwa and its sculptural components appear to repeat the significance of the tripartite arrangement of Loro Jonggrang. The base may be considered symbolic of *bhuraloka*, or the Realm of Man, whereas, above, the area of the main *cella* is emblematic of *bhurwaloka*, the Realm of the Purified. The superstructure may then be perceived as *swarloka*, the Realm of the Gods. A further meaning may be assigned to the tripartite centrifugal arrangement that directly carries the function of *Candi Śiwa* as a royal ancestral shrine and memorial to the deceased ruler's divine transformation. His deeds and virtues while in his earthly form are coded in the *Rāmāyaṇa* epic on the balustrade. Further to the center, on the exterior walls of the *cella*, the ancestor-ruler is symbolized by the corporeal embodiment of the *Astadikpālaka*. These deities were believed to be inherent in the body of a king and infused him with greater-than-earthly powers. This imagery then coalesces with the main cult statue of Siwa at the *candi*'s locus, which is emblematic of the postmortem deification of the ruler as this supreme god.

CECELIA LEVIN

Further Reading

Bernet Kempers, A.J., *Ancient Indonesian Art*, Cambridge, Massachusetts: Harvard University Press, 1959
Chihara, Daigoro, "Hindu-Buddhist Architecture in Southeast Asia," Leiden, The Netherlands: Brill, 1996
Fontein, Jan, "Preliminary Notes on the Narrative Reliefs of Candi Brahma and Candi Visnu at Loro Jonggrang, Prambanan," in *Living a Life in Accord with Dhamma: Papers in Honor of Jean Boisselier on His Eightieth Birthday*, edited by Natasha Eilenberg, M.C. Subhadradis Diskul, and Robert L. Brown, Bangkok: Silpakorn University, 1997
Fontein, Jan, R. Soekmono, and Edi Sedyawati, *The Sculpture of Indonesia*, Washington, D.C.: National Gallery of Art, and New York: Abrams, 1990
Holt, Claire, *Art in Indonesia: Continuities and Change*, Ithaca, New York: Cornell University Press, 1967
Iyer, Alessandra, *Prambanan: Sculpture and Dance in Ancient Java: A Study in Dance Iconography*, Bangkok: White Lotus Co., 1997
Klokke: Marijke J. (editor), *Narrative Sculpture and Literary Traditions in South and Southeast Asia*, Boston: Brill, 2000
Moertjipto, and Bambang Prasetyo, *Mengenal Candi Ciwa Prambanan dari dekat*, Yogyakarta: Penerbit Kanisius, 1991; as *The Ciwa Temple of Prambanan*, Yogyakarta: Penerbit Kanisius, 1992
Moertjipto, et al., *The Ramayana Reliefs of Prambanan*, Yogyakarta: Penerbit Kanisius, 1991
Soekmono, R., *The Javanese Candi, Function and Meaning*, Leiden, The Netherlands, and New York: Brill, 1995
Stutterheim, Willem F., *Rama-legenden und Rama-reliefs in Indonesien*, 2 vols., Munich: Müller, 1925; as *Rama-Legends and Rama-Reliefs in Indonesia*, translated by C.D. Paliwal and R.P. Jain, New Delhi: Abhinav Publications, 1989

LORSCH GOSPEL COVERS

Anonymous

ca. 810

ivory

front cover: h. 38.1 cm

back cover: h. 38.5 cm

front cover: Victoria and Albert Museum, London, England

back cover: Vatican Museums, Rome, Italy

The two ivory panels known as the Lorsch Gospel covers once served as bookbinding to a Gospel manuscript written around 810 at the court school of Charlemagne in Aachen. This *codex aureus* (golden book) is likely the one mentioned in the library catalogue of Lorsch Abbey drawn up slightly after the middle of the 9th century and there described as "evangelium scriptum cum auro pictum habens tabulas eburneas" (a written Gospel painted with gold and having ivory panels). It was still at St. Nazarius in Lorsch in 1479, but the manuscript and its bookbinding underwent various misfortunes afterward and then separated at an unknown date. As part of the Palatine Library, then in Heidelberg, the manuscript reached the Vatican Library in 1623, where both Gospels of St. Luke and St. John and the back cover, the Christ ivory panel, are still kept. Toward the end of the 18th century, the remaining Gospels belonged to Cardinal Migazzi in Vienna, then to the Bishop of Siebenbürgen through whom Count Ignaz Batthyány acquired them for his library (Alba Julia, Biblioteca Batthyáneum, part of the National Library of Bucharest). The front ivory panel reappeared in the Leven Collection (Cologne, 1853) and passed on to the Soltykoff Collection (Paris, 1861), from where it was acquired by John Webb and finally given to the South Kensington Museum (today, Victoria and Albert Museum) in London in 1866.

It has been assumed that the Lorsch Gospel covers are contemporary with the manuscript and that they were carved in the same school at Aachen, also around 810. Their composition reproduces an antique model, namely, an early-6th-century Constantinopolitan imperial diptych such as the Barberini ivory (Musée du Louvre, Paris). Both leaves present the same structure consisting of five plaques joined together, a scheme that has been used for other Carolingian and post-Carolingian ivories as well as the Oxford and Dole bookbindings (see Gaborit-Chopin, 1978). The back cover presents Christ at the center, treading the beasts according to Psalm 91:13: "super aspidem et basiliscum ambulabis, et conculcabis leonem et draconem" (Thou shalt tread upon the lion and the adder: the young lion and the dragon shalt thou trample under feet). He blesses with his right hand in the Greek manner and holds a book in his left. On either side stand two archangels looking toward Christ, both holding a scepter and a *volumen* (scroll). Above Christ, two angels sustain a circular medallion decorated with a jewelled cross. The lower panel shows the Adoration of the Magi on the right and the Magi before Herod on the left. The front cover uses the same scheme. At the center Mary sits on a throne and holds the Christ Child on her lap. The last two prophets who announced Christ's coming frame her. On her right Saint John the Baptist unrolls a scroll and points to the child, while Zachariah on her left holds a censer and an incense box. The presence of St. John the Baptist is explained by his words (from John 1:29) "ecce agnus Dei qui tollit peccatum mundi" (Behold the Lamb of God which taketh away the sin of the world). The presence of Zachariah is more problematic but may be due to his prophecy (Luke 1:68–79). Above the central scene, as on the back cover, two hovering angels sustain a circular medallion, here decorated with a bust portrait of Christ blessing. The lower panel shows the Nativity and the Annunciation to the Shepherds.

Although some of the figures recall reliefs such as the Maximianus throne in Ravenna (*ca.* 545–53), the best stylistic comparisons are with the very manuscript the ivory panels once covered. Details, such as round faces, staring eyes, expressions of the hands with their long curved fingers, and formal aspects such as shell-like haloes or the architectural arcades within which the figures stand, also appear in the miniatures of the so-called Ada group to which the Lorsch Gospel belongs. This is not surprising since the ivory carvers and illuminators, if not the same, used identical models

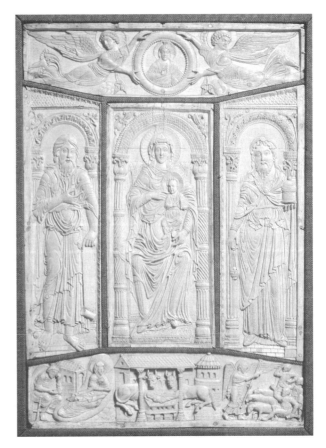

Lorsch Gospel Cover (front), Virgin and Child enthroned with Saint John the Baptist and Saint Zachariah
© Victoria and Albert Museum, London / Art Resource, NY

and likely worked together. The carvers employed by Charlemagne seem to have had some difficulty in finding the material they needed and reused antique pieces of ivory. The Magi panel on the back cover is in fact a leaf of a consular diptych. Its reverse preserves an inscription and a monogram that point to Flavius Anastasius, consul in Constantinople in 517. The former front was obviously abraded, and the Carolingian artist carved a new set of reliefs on the back. The policy of reusing antique material was rather common in Carolingian and post-Carolingian times, especially under Charles the Bald. This policy certainly favored the borrowing of antique forms, as well as the copying of particular details. The artifact that served as model and the product of the Carolingian revival show a close stylistic continuity, which may explain the difficulty at times in differentiating them. Charles Rufus Morey, for example, concluded that the upper panel on the back cover's Vatican leaf was an original piece dating from about 500 and that Carolingian hands reworked the four remaining panels to fit it. Although his hypothesis has neither been proved nor refuted, a close examination of the irregular cutting of the different panels shows that the original planning and assemblage of the book cover changed over time for an unknown reason.

Other ivories attributed to the same workshop include the Leipzig Archangel Michael (also a reuse of an antique consular diptych from 470) and the Darmstadt Ascension. All these pieces share formal details with the Lorsch covers, such as the delicate folding system that develops into an intricate surface design, in which illusionism subordinates to a love of pattern. The Lorsch book cover is probably one of the most significant pieces of Charlemagne's court school, and both panels, although cut by different hands, magnificently testify to the Carolingian revival.

PIERRE ALAIN MARIAUX

See also **Carolingian Sculpture; Diptych and Tripytch**

Further Reading

799: Kunst und Kultur der Karolingerzeit: Karl der Grosse und Papst Leo III. in Paderborn (exhib. cat.), 2 vols., Mainz, Germany: Von Zabern, 1999; see especially vol. 2
Braunfels, Wolfgang, *Das Lorscher Evangeliar*, Munich: Prestel, 1967
Gaborit-Chopin, Danielle, *Ivoires du Moyen Âge*, Fribourg, Switzerland: Office du Livre, 1978
Longhurst, Margaret H., and Charles Rufus Morey, "The Covers of the Lorsch Gospels, I: The Vatican Cover," *Speculum* 3/1 (1928)
Morey, Charles Rufus, "The Covers of the Lorsch Gospels, II: The Cover in the Victoria and Albert Museum," *Speculum* 4/4 (1929)

LUDOVISI THRONE

Anonymous

ca. 470–450 BCE

marble

h. 1.04 m; w. 1.44 m

Museo Nazionale Romano, Rome, Italy

The Ludovisi Throne, a Greek marble relief of the Early Classical period, came to light by chance in 1887 during construction work on the grounds of the former Villa Ludovisi (the ancient Gardens of Sallust) in Rome. Placed first in the Ludovisi collection, from which it takes its name, it was then sold to the Italian state in 1901. A three-sided marble relief with sculptural decoration, the Ludovisi Throne was in all likelihood in Antiquity the crowning element of an altar or some sort of architectural element rather than a throne. It is in many ways a singular monument, and scholars continue to debate its precise context and meaning.

The relief is carved of Thasian marble. The upper middle section of the front side with the heads of the two outer figures is now missing; originally it took the form of a gable sloping down from the center. The side panels equally slope down toward the outside. On the bottom of each corner of the monument are plain, arched sections of relief ground that were originally filled with volutes and palmettes. The marble on the back of the relief is only roughly picked.

The main scene on the front of the relief depicts a frontal female figure, clad in a tight-fitting and long-sleeved, almost-diaphanous chiton. She rises from the ground, flanked on either side by a female figure in profile. These attendants lean forward in a symmetrical position and with the hand closest to the relief ground support the central figure under her armpits, while in their other hand they hold out a large cloth in front of her, covering her groin. The central figure gazes upward to the figure on her right, her head with long hair held by a band turned into profile. The attendant on the left wears a peplos, the one on the right a chiton with short sleeves. Both garments reveal the position of the legs beneath; the figures stand with their outer leg set forward and the inner leg set back on downward-sloping, pebbly ground.

The short sides of the relief depict one figure each, both facing away from the central scene. On the left a nude female, her long hair wrapped in a *sakkos* (cloth), sits with her legs crossed on a thick cushion and plays a double flute with both hands. On the right another female figure sits on a similar cushion; she wears a long chiton and sandals and is tightly wrapped in a himation that also covers her head. Her left hand holds a small box from which she takes something with her right hand, perhaps incense, as an incense burner is depicted in front of her.

Scholars have advanced a number of theories for the interpretation of the relief decor. The central scene has been explained most often as the birth of Aphrodite from the sea in the presence of the Horai, as it is described in the sixth Homeric Hymn. The main figure's clinging drapery and the pebbled ground reminiscent of a beach are the main arguments for this proposal, but other theories have also been suggested, such as the birth of Pandora, the return of Persephone, or even a scene of a goddess giving birth.

If the central figure is Aphrodite, then one can interpret the figure on the left-side panel as a hetaera, a highly cultivated courtesan, or a hierodule, a temple prostitute, both closely connected to the cult of the goddess. The veiled figure on the right panel would then be a priestess or, because of her relaxed pose, perhaps more likely a bride, giving an offering.

The Ludovisi Throne, made of marble from the Greek island of Thasos, clearly bears the sign of Greek craftsmanship. Stylistically, it seems to be best paralleled by works of the Early Classical period of about 470–450 BCE; many historians feel it to be close to

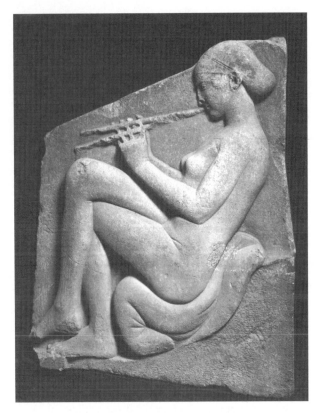

Woman playing the flute, from the Ludovisi Throne
© Alinari / Art Resource, NY

sculptures from *Magna Graecia*, particularly a series of terracotta reliefs from Locri in southern Italy.

Nonetheless, the Ludovisi Throne was discovered in Rome (in the southern part of an area delineated by the modern streets via Piemonte, via Abruzzi, via Buoncompagni, and via Sicilia), on land that in Antiquity belonged to the famous gardens of Sallust. These huge parklands, later imperial property, contained a great number of artworks, and several imported Classical Greek reliefs were found there. When the Ludovisi Throne was dug up, it was found in an upright position with no fragments or built structures around it, strongly indicating that it had been moved there from its previous position. A few hundred meters to the east, however, archaeologists discovered traces of a round building possibly identified as the Temple of Venus Erucina (later Venus Hortorum Sallustiarum), and it has been proposed that the relief came from there. This temple was founded in 181 BCE, and some have speculated that the Ludovisi Throne was then brought to Rome to decorate it, either from Eryx itself, a place on the western tip of Sicily, or perhaps from Locri. Much remains speculative.

Many elements of the Ludovisi Throne are without clear parallel, so that some have even doubted its authenticity, which is even more the case with the monu-

ment it can be best compared with, the so-called Boston Throne. The Boston Throne is a similar three-sided relief that surfaced in 1894 in Rome, said to have been discovered only a few hundred meters to the east of the place in which the Ludovisi Throne came to light. Depicted is a *psychostasia* (the weighing of souls) by a nude, youthful winged figure flanked by draped women on either side in the center and an elderly woman and a nude lyre player on the side panels. The Boston Throne, too, was carved from Thasian marble, and the coloring of the stone and root marks are similar on both monuments, so that the Boston relief appears to be almost a pendant to the Ludovisi Throne. Scientific tests have not revealed any traces that could point to a modern date for either monument. Their obscure origins have to be seen within the context of massive building in Rome in the late 19th century that brought to light countless archaeological treasures. A subsequent financial crisis then forced many established noble Roman families to sell large parts of their collections, including the recent finds, in a sometimes highly secretive manner.

The Ludovisi Throne is a masterpiece of Early Classical Greek sculpture. Future finds will undoubtedly help to place it more precisely within this great tradition.

THORSTEN OPPER

See also **Greece, Ancient**

Further Reading

Giuliano, Antonio (editor), *Museo Nazionale Romano: I, Le sculture*, Rome: De Luca, 1979–

Helbig, Wolfgang, *Führer durch die öffentlichen Sammlungen klassischer Altertümer in Rom*, 4th revised edition, 4 vols., edited by Hermine Speier, Tübingen, Germany: Wasmuth, 1963–72; see especially vol. 3, page 2340

Herrmann, John, *Il trono Ludovisi e il trono di Boston: Quaderni di Palazzo Grassi*, Venice: Palazzo Grassi, 1996 (with an exhaustive bibliography)

Nash, E., "Über die Auffindung und den Erwerb des 'Bostoner Thrones,'" *Mitteilungen des deutschen archäologischen Institutes, Römische Abteilung* 46 (1959)

Talamo, E., "Gli Horti di Sallustio a Porta Collina," in *Horti Romani*, edited by Maddalena Cima and Eugenio la Rocca, Rome: "L'Erma" di Bretschneider, 1998

LUPA

See **Capitoline Wolf**

LYSIPPOS *fl. ca.* 370–315 BCE *Greek*

A native of Sikyon in the northern Peloponnese, Lysippos was renowned not only for his prolific production, apparently exclusively in bronze, but also, and perhaps more importantly, for his connection with King Alexander III ("the Great") of Macedon. The ancient biographer Plutarch wrote:

> Alexander gave orders that Lysippos alone should make portraits of him, since Lysippos alone, it seemed, truly revealed his nature in bronze and portrayed his courage in visible form, while others in their anxiety to reproduce the bend of the neck and the melting look of the eyes failed to preserve his masculine and leonine aspect. (Plutarch, *Life of Alexander* 2.2)

Indeed, although ancient authors record Lysippos' (or rather his workshop's) prodigious output in various genres (images of athletes and public figures, heroes, gods, action groups, animals, and even metal vessels), it was as a portraitist that he was most celebrated in Antiquity. He is said to have been scrupulous in his attention to minute details, and his less famous brother Lysistratos is credited with being the first to take plaster life masks from his subjects and employ them in the production of realistic portraiture (Pliny, *Natural History* 35.153, 34.65).

Writing over 300 years after the sculptor's death, the elder Pliny related that Lysippos alone is said to have produced 1500 works, all of such artistic value that each would have sufficed by itself to make him famous. The number became known after his death, when his heir broke open his strongbox, since it had been his custom to set aside a piece of gold from the price of each statue (Pliny the Elder, *Natural History* 34.37).

Although such anecdotes are to be trusted no more than those that report that he died of starvation on account of his absorption with the formal problems of a statue (Petronius, *Satyricon* 88), they do convey not only the abundance of Lysippos' works but also his wealth, which, like his fame, must have derived from his association with Alexander and the king's companions and successors. He produced hunt and battle groups of and for the Macedonian elite and is said to have designed for Kasander a distinctive amphora to commemorate the founding of Kasandreia.

Lysippos' early training is unknown. He called Polykleitos' *Doryphoros* (*ca.* 440–435 BCE) his master (Cicero, *Brutus* 86.296), but this remark was ironic. Pliny comments on his independence and reports that he rejected the heavy "four-square" proportions of Polykleitan figures in favor of a slimmer body type with a smaller head that gave his statues the appearance of greater height (*Natural History* 34.61). Other ancient writers explicitly state that he was nobody's pupil, but looked instead to nature. His inclination toward illusionism, however, is reflected—as Pliny asserted—in the fact that "he used to say publicly that while other sculptors made men as they were, he made them as they appeared to be."

Many of his statues were transferred to Rome (and eventually to Constantinople), where they were favorites of emperors and other elite collectors. An equestrian statue of Alexander was converted into a portrait of Caesar; Tiberius removed the *Apoxyomenos* (Man Scraping Himself with a Strigil) to his private bedchamber; and Nero marred a portrait of the young Alexander by gilding it, but it was still considered beautiful, despite the scars that remained after the gold was removed. Numerous other images provided subjects for epigrams and literary descriptions. His works were widely copied and imitated, and in Antiquity (as well as today) many statues were over optimistically ascribed to him.

Although no original works by Lysippos survive, inscribed statue bases have been recovered. From descriptions by ancient authors, numerous lost statues have been recognized in ancient "copies" in the round and in representations in other media (such as on reliefs, coins, engraved gemstones, and painting), although some of these attributions result from wishful thinking. Most reliable are the *Kairos* (Opportunity), *Eros*, *Apoxyomenos*, *Alexander*, and the Farnese-type Hercules. He is also credited with a posthumous portrait of Socrates.

The copious written tradition and preserved visual evidence, despite its unreliability, leave little doubt that Lysippos experimented in depicting motion, exploiting the third dimension, and altering proportions, all at a variety of scales. He transformed the Classical tradition, and his career marks the beginning of the Hellenistic period in sculpture, which he influenced through pupils such as Chares and Eutychides. The foremost sculptor in an age of self-promotion, he left no written texts but was soon enrolled among the greatest sculptors of the Greeks alongside Pheidias, Polykleitos, and Praxiteles.

KENNETH D.S. LAPATIN

See also **Greece, Ancient; Pheidias; Polykleitos; Praxiteles**

Biography

Born probably in Sikyon, Greece, early 4th century BCE. Early training not known; became court sculptor to Alexander the Great; known for his prodigious output, traditionally said to number 1500 sculptures, although not a single original work has survived; worked in many genres, including the representation of athletes, public figures, heroes, gods, action groups, and animals; also became known for his great wealth, acquired through his association with Alexander and in

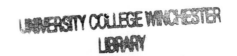

producing hunt and battle groups of and for the Macedonian elite. Date and place of death unknown.

Selected Works

(known from ancient literary sources; ancient copies, some attributed with more certainty than others, also listed below)

ca. 338– *Agias*, at Pharsalos, Greece; bronze? (lost);
ca. 334   Roman copy: marble; Daochos monument,
BCE   Archaeological Museum, Delphi, Greece

ca. 334   Alexander with companions at the Battle
BCE   of the River Granikos, at Dion, Greece
           (also known as the Granikos Monument);
           bronze? (lost); Roman copy: bronze;
           Museo Archeologico Nazionale, Naples,
           Italy

ca. 330   *Apoxyomenos* (Man Scraping Himself with
BCE   a Strigil); bronze? (lost); Roman copy:
           marble; Vatican Museums, Rome, Italy

4th   Alexander and Krateros hunting lions, at
century   Delphi, Greece; bronze? (lost); copy, 3rd
BCE   century BCE: gold medallion, Bibliothèque
           Nationale de France, Paris, France

4th   Alexander with lance; bronze? (lost);
century   bronze copy: Musée du Louvre, Paris,
BCE   France; marble copy of head: Glyptothek,
           Munich, Germany

4th   *Eros*, at Thespiae, Greece; bronze? (lost);
century   Roman copies: marble; Museo
BCE   Archeologico, Venice, Italy; Musei
           Capitolini, Rome, Italy; Vatican Museums,
           Rome, Italy

4th   Farnese-type Hercules, at Sikyon, Greece;
century   bronze? (lost); marble copies: Museo
BCE   Archeologico Nazionale, Naples, Italy;
           Argos Museum, Athens, Greece; National
           Museum, Athens, Greece

4th   *Helios on a Chariot*, at Rhodes, Greece;
century   bronze? (lost); (later Rome)
BCE

4th   *Hercules*, at Tarentum; bronze? (lost);
century   bronze copy: Ny Carlsberg Glyptotek,
BCE   Copenhagen, Denmark

4th   *Hercules Epitrapezios*; bronze (lost);
century   bronze copies: Kunsthistorisches Museum,
BCE   Vienna, Austria; British Museum, London,
           England

4th   *Kairos* (Opportunity), at Sikyon, Greece;
century   bronze? (lost); marble copy: Museo di
BCE   Antichità, Torino, Italy

4th   Poulydamas of Kotoussa, at Olympia,
century   Greece; stone; base: Archaeological
BCE   Museum, Olympia, Greece

4th   *Praxilla* (A tipsy pipe player); bronze?
century   (lost); bronze copy: Santa Barbara
BCE   Museum of Art, California, United States

4th   Sokrates in Pompeion, at Athens, Greece;
century   bronze? (lost); marble copies: Museo
BCE   Archeologico Nazionale, Naples, Italy;
           Musée du Louvre, Paris, France; Musei
           Capitolini, Rome, Italy

4th   *Zeus*, at Tarentum; bronze (lost)
century
BCE

Further Reading

Jones, Henry Stuart, *Select Passages from Ancient Writers Illustrative of the History of Greek Sculpture*, London and New York: Macmillan, 1895, reprint, 1966

Mattusch, Carol C., *The Victorious Youth*, Los Angeles: Getty Museum, 1997

Moreno, Paolo, *Lisippo: L'arte e la fortuna*, Milan: Fabbri, 1995

Pollitt, J.J., *Art in the Hellenistic Age*, Cambridge and New York: Cambridge University Press, 1986

Ridgway, Brunilde Sismondo, *Hellenistic Sculpture*, Madison: University of Wisconsin Press, 1990– ; see especially vol. 1, *The Styles of ca. 331–200 B.C.*

Ridgway, Brunilde Sismondo, *4th-Century Styles in Greek Sculpture*, Madison: University of Wisconsin Press, 1997

Smith, R.R.R., *Hellenistic Royal Portraits*, Oxford: Clarendon, and New York: Oxford University Press, 1988

Smith, R.R.R., *Hellenistic Sculpture*, London: Thames and Hudson, 1991

Stewart, Andrew F., *Greek Sculpture: An Exploration*, New Haven, Connecticut: Yale University Press, 1990

Stewart, Andrew F., *Faces of Power: Alexander's Image and Hellenistic Politics*, Berkeley: University of California Press, 1993

APOXYOMENOS (MAN SCRAPING HIMSELF WITH A STRIGIL)

ca. 330 BCE

bronze

h. of copy 2.1 m (dimensions of original unknown)

Roman copy in marble: 1st to 3rd centuries CE;

Vatican Museums, Rome, Italy

Lysippos' original bronze statue *Apoxyomenos* is lost. Although discussed briefly by the elder Pliny in his *Natural History* (34.62), the work is not mentioned explicitly by any other ancient author, and other statues depicting scrapers are known from Antiquity. Various statues, including the famous *Spinario* in the Palazzo dei Conservatori, had been identified as the Lysippan type prior to the discovery of the Vatican marble in the Trastevere quarter of Rome on the Vicolo delle Palme (now appropriately renamed Vicolo dell'Atleta) on 3 October 1849. In fact, the marble itself was initially thought to copy a statue by Polykleitos, but the German scholar Emil Braun soon recognized it as a Lysippan work.

Restored by Pietro Tenerani, a pupil of Antonio Canova and collaborator of Bertel Thorvaldsen (and restored again in 1994), the Vatican statue is the best preserved, and thus the most often illustrated, version of the type. It is variously dated by specialists: from as early as the reign of Claudius (*r.* 10 BCE to 54 CE) to as late as the 3rd century CE. Other, more fragmentary examples of the type also survive, some of them reversed and, in the opinion of many scholars, better representing the composition of the original. Although a monumental marble in the Villa Medici di Castello near Florence was known as early as 1635, it was misrestored as a gladiator. The work stands some 3 meters tall, and its Roman core seems to date to the mid 2nd century CE. The type appears on ancient gems and has been recognized on painted pots, as well as in marble copies and adaptations. Lysippos' bronze original, unlike the stone versions, would have been free of the distracting struts and the stump necessary to support the weight of the extended limbs. The fig leaf is post-antique.

The identification of this *Apoxyomenos* type with a Sikyonian sculptor is relatively secure thanks not only to its iconography but also to the comments of other ancient authors regarding the style of Lysippos, namely, that he made the heads of his figures smaller and their bodies more slender, and he applied greater naturalism to anatomical details than did earlier sculptors. Such features characterize the Vatican *Apoxyomenos*, with its subtle rendering of musculature, lifelike hair, individualized face, and especially its momentary pose. The youthful male figure is caught in the midst of a complex movement, shifting his weight back from his straight left leg to his relaxed right just as he pushes the strigil (or scraper) forward along his extended right arm. Though not mentioned explicitly by Pliny, this last feature seems typical of the sculptor's interest in representing motion in real time and in three-dimensional space. In the *Kairos* (now lost, but known from ancient representations), Lysippos depicted the personification of Opportunity (or the "Right Moment") as a winged figure running tip-toe on a sphere while balancing scales on a razor in his extended hand; in the Farnese-type Hercules, the sculptor encouraged the viewer to move all the way around the exhausted hero to view the right hand, the only hidden element, which constitutes the key to understanding the statue: the hero casually holds the Golden Apples of the Hesperides, which guarantee his immortality.

The *Apoxyomenos*, which depicts a youthful athlete cleansing himself, is less fraught with iconographical

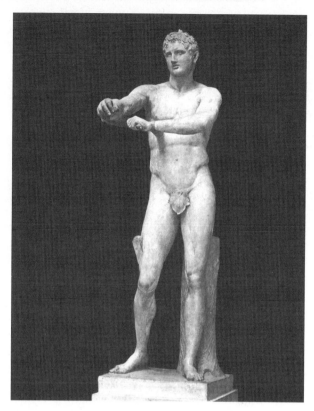

Apoxyomenos (Man Scraping Himself with a Strigil), Roman copy
© Alinari / Art Resource, NY

significance: after exercise, the Greeks oiled their bodies and then scraped away the excess along with dirt and sweat. Compositionally, however, this statue displays more force than the Hercules, for Lysippos took full advantage of the three-dimensional potential of sculpture not hitherto exploited by Greek sculptors by extending the arms forward and the left foot back and to the side. Thus the figure breaks out of a limited space and simultaneously encourages the viewer to move to one side and then the other in order to obtain multiple viewpoints necessary for comprehension.

We do not know precisely when in his long career Lysippos produced the *Apoxyomenos*, or where the original bronze statue stood. Pliny reports that Marcus Agrippa, the lieutenant and sometime heir of the Emperor Augustus, dedicated the statue (which he must have removed from Greece, southern Italy, or, most likely, Asia Minor) in front of the baths he built in Rome not far from the Pantheon. These were the first of the city's great public bathing establishments. Construction began about 25 BCE and seems to have been complete by 19 BCE. At his death in 12 BCE, Agrippa willed to the Roman people free use of the complex, which was further adorned with paintings, terracottas, and stuccoes. Their subjects are not recorded, but it is likely that they, like the *Apoxyomenos*, were thematically appropriate to the building's function.

Augustus' successor Tiberius, according to the elder Pliny, became "astonishingly fond" of Lysippos' statue, and:

> [A]lthough at the beginning of his reign he kept control of himself, in this case he was unable to resist temptation, and had the statue removed to his bedroom, substituting another in its place. But the Roman people became so obstinately opposed to this that they raised an outcry at the theater, shouting, "Give us back the *Apoxyomenos!*" So although he had fallen quite in love with the statue, the emperor had to restore it. (Pliny the Elder, *Natural History* 34.62)

Whether Tiberius' substitute statue was a copy of the *Apoxyomenos* or some other image is not clear from Pliny's text. Agrippa's baths and, presumably, Lysippos' bronze suffered destruction by fire in 80 CE, yet copies of the statue continued to be made thereafter, apparently from casts of the original statue. Since its recovery, restoration, and identification in the mid 19th century, the Vatican statue also has become famous. Plaster casts were immediately made and dispatched to art academies throughout Europe and the United States; the Italian sculptor Carlo Marochetti fashioned *de luxe* bronze replicas at two-thirds scale; and the Fratelli Alinari and others added photographs of the piece to their repertories of art masterpieces. Thus the *Apoxyomenos* quickly became part of mainstream art history and has been quoted by modern artists as diverse as Sir Lawrence Alma-Tadema and Edvard Munch.

KENNETH D.S. LAPATIN

Further Reading

Berman, Patricia G., "Body and Body Politic in Edvard Munch's *Bathing Men*," in *The Body Imaged: The Human Form and Visual Culture since the Renaissance*, edited by Kathleen Adler and Marcia R. Pointer, Cambridge and New York: Cambridge University Press, 1993

Isager, Jacob, *Pliny on Art and Society: The Elder Pliny's Chapters on the History of Art*, Odense, Denmark: Odense University Press, and London and New York: Routledge, 1991

Moreno, Paolo, "Apoxyomenos," in *Enciclopedia dell'arte antica, classica e orientale: Secondo Supplemento, 1971–1994*, vol. 1, Rome: Istituto della Enciclopedia Italiana, 1994

Richardson, Lawrence, *A New Topographical Dictionary of Ancient Rome*, Baltimore, Maryland: Johns Hopkins University Press, 1992

Stewart, Andrew, "Lysippan Studies," *American Journal of Archaeology* 82 (1978)

M

ARISTIDE MAILLOL 1861–1944 *French*

Aristide Maillol, a major French sculptor of his time, began his career as a painter who trained under Alexandre Cabanel, a prominent Salon artist and teacher. Maillol gave up painting in 1893 and immersed himself entirely in the production of embroidered tapestries.

In 1895 Maillol became acquainted with the group of artists known as the Nabis. These young naïf artists were particularly interested in craft techniques. Maillol not only produced tapestries at that time but also worked in wood and clay and began carving reliefs and figures and producing models. The first plastic works by the dilettante sculptor were flat, decorative reliefs, such as *Dancer* (1895), and columnar, severe wood statuettes, such as *Bather* (1899).

Maillol was soon able to master three-dimensional works. Around the turn of the century, he modeled a large number of small sculptures of the female form. His art dealer, Ambroise Vollard, acquired a number of these statuettes in order to have them cast in bronze. These editions were very well received. To this day, Maillol's early bronze statues have remained among his most popular and well-known works: *Léda; Young Woman Crouching*; and *Young Girl Seated, Covering Her Eyes* (*ca.* 1900).

These diminutive masterpieces depict ordinary, but not naturalistically portrayed, young women. They are neither generic nor anecdotal, but rather self-contained. In this way, they distinguish themselves clearly from both Auguste Rodin's works of pathos and the decorative salon sculptures of the time. Maillol's young wife, Clotilde, was the model for all of his figures around the turn of the century. A small woman from the south of France with a compact body, she corresponded entirely to the sculptor's ideal of beauty.

Working in small format did not satisfy Maillol in the long term. After the turn of the century, he pursued large sculptural projects in stone. He received his first assignment in 1904 from Harry Graf Kessler, the German-English art collector who was to become Maillol's most important patron. His chief work was produced for Kessler: *Méditerranée* (The Mediterranean). The plaster model was exhibited in 1905 in the Salon d'Automne to great success. In his review of the exhibition, author André Gide praised not only the beauty and simplicity of the figure but also that it "didn't represent anything." Maillol had left the traditional encumbrance of mythology, allegory, and formula for pathos behind him. For this reason, *Méditerranée* stands at the beginning of modern French sculpture of the 20th century.

Maillol's artistic focus lay in the solid construction of the figure, for which he employed geometric, almost architectonic, compositional elements. The personal production in limestone of *Méditerranée* took at least until 1910; and with it, Maillol achieved clarity without severity. In 1905 the sculptor received his first assignment for a monument; the work is dedicated to social revolutionary Louis Auguste Blanqui and was erected in Blanqui's hometown of Puget-Théniers. As a symbol of Blanqui's efforts, Maillol did not create a portrait figure, but rather the dramatic nude statue *Action in Chains*. Maillol was thereby one of the first artists to distance himself from the traditional monument of the 19th century. Not surprisingly, contemporaries expressed a lack of appreciation for this unusual monument.

Maillol found a larger audience abroad than within France; almost all of his major early works were associated with collections in other countries. Kessler commissioned two more important sculptures in 1907: the stone relief *Desire* and the bronze figure of a young bicycle rider, *Young Cyclist*. Both of these works assume an isolated position in Maillol's oeuvre, as he was working according to the patron's special requests.

His chief interest at this time was the motif of the seated woman, which he varied in two large-format stone sculptures after his completion of *Méditerranée*. *Night* (1905–10) revealed a more contained composition in which the woman's face is buried between her arms. The upright posture of *Serenity*, on the other hand, conveyed a festive gaiety. The latter sculpture, created between 1905 and 1910 for German art collector Karl Ernst Osthaus, was destroyed in 1945. As early as 1907, Maillol conceptualized a fourth large seated figure: the monument for Paul Cézanne. When the stone sculpture was finally finished in 1925, it was rejected by the city of Aix-en-Provence, the painter's birthplace.

Around 1908 Maillol began working on *Pomona*, his first large, tranquil standing figure. The voluptuous female figure holds fruit in her raised arms; she embodies sensuality and fecundity. For this work, Maillol transferred his stringent geometric compositional style onto a standing figure; afterward, he repeatedly varied this type of figure. Through the mediation of the artist

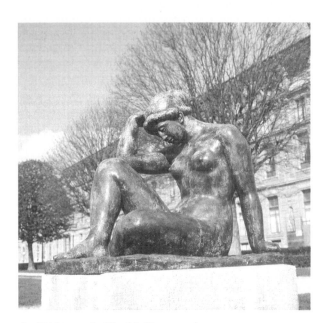

La Méditerranée (The Mediterranean)
© Giraudon / Art Resource, NY and (2003) Artists Rights Society (ARS), New York, ADAGP, Paris

Maurice Denis, Ivan Morosow, a major collector from Moscow, ordered four larger-than-life-size statues in 1908. In addition to *Pomona*, a model of which had already been produced, Maillol created the female figures of *Flora*, *Summer*, and *Spring*. These works were displayed in Morosow's music room, which was decorated with paintings by Denis.

The quartet of figures showed that Maillol no longer favored exclusively compact female figures. *Flora* and *Spring* are slender, elegant figures, as is *Île de France*, a statue that he had already been planning in 1907 but did not finish until 1925. Prior to this, Maillol had a torso version cast, which stands in the Museum of Modern Art, New York City. In general, he accepted few torsos as completed works; numerous torso varieties were edited posthumously.

Maillol's innovative phase occurred during the first decade of the 20th century. In the 1920s his figures took on an almost Classical appearance. Nonetheless, he received public honors and, at last, some public assignments in France during this time. The first, in 1923, was a marble copy of *Méditerranée*, which is now in the Musée d'Orsay, Paris. The work is characteristic of Maillol's style, as the artist had begun his own self-imitations. For example, he developed new large sculptures out of existing ones by altering and disassembling older plaster models in order to reassemble them in new ways. *Air* was created from the Cézanne monument, and *Mountain* (1937) was transformed into *River* (Tuileries Gardens, Paris). Because of World War II, Maillol's last major projects, such as the statue *Harmony*, could not be completed.

Maillol is remembered above all for his groundbreaking statues from the beginning of the 20th century, with which he showed a generation of young sculptors—not merely in France—the way into the new century. His works can be found in numerous museums in Europe, the United States, and Asia, as well as in the Musée Maillol, Paris, which was opened in 1995.

URSEL BERGER

See also **France: Mid–Late 19th Century; France: 20th Century–Contemporary; Rodin, Auguste**

Biography

Born in Banyuls-sur-Mer, France, 8 December 1861. Moved to Paris in 1881; began studies in art at École des Beaux-Arts under Alexandre Cabanel, 1885; initially worked as a painter and artisan; first sculptures (carved wood), 1895; first solo exhibition at the Galerie Vollard, Paris, 1902; showed bronzes as well; lived alternately in Marly-le-Roi, near Paris, and in Banyuls-sur-Mer, from 1903; trip to Greece with most important patron, Harry Graf Kessler, 1908; public rec-ognition in France, honors and assignments by the state, from 1920s; warrior monuments for several cities in southern France; first large exhibition, 1937; after the outbreak of the war, returned to Banylus-sur-Mer. Died in Perpignan, France, 24 September 1944.

Selected Works

1895   *Dancer*; wood; Musée d'Orsay, Paris, France
1899   *Bather*; wood; Stedelijk Museum, Amsterdam, the Netherlands
ca. 1900 *Leda*; bronze; Oskar Reinhart Collection, Winterthur, Switzerland
ca. 1900 *Young Woman Crouching*; bronze; Pushkin Museum, Moscow, Russia
1905–10 *Méditerranée*; limestone; Oskar Reinhart Collection, Winterthur, Switzerland; marble version: 1923, Musée d'Orsay, Paris, France
1905–07 *Desire*; limestone; private collection, Switzerland
1905–08 *Action in Chains*; bronze; Monument to Blanqui, Puget-Théniers, France
1907–25 Monument to Cézanne; marble; Musée d'Orsay, Paris, France
1908–12 *Pomona*, *Spring*, *Summer*, and *Flora*; gilded bronze; Pushkin Museum, Moscow, Russia
1909   *Young Cyclist*; bronze; Kunstmuseum, Basel, Switzerland
1910–25 *Île de France*; bronze; Musée du Petit Palais, Paris, France
1918–28 *Venus*; bronze; Hahnloser Collection, Winterthur, Switzerland
1919–21 *Douleur* (Grief); limestone; Céret, France
1930–37 *Nymphs of the Meadow*; lead; Tuileries Gardens, Paris, France
1939   *Air* (monument to Airmen); stone; Toulouse, France
1940–44 *Harmony*; bronze; Musée Maillol, Paris, France

Further Reading

Aristide Maillol, 1861–1944 (exhib. cat.), New York: Solomon R. Guggenheim Foundation, 1975
Berger, Ursel, and Jörg Zutter, editors, *Aristide Maillol* (exhib. cat.), Paris: Flammarion, and Lausanne: Musée des Beaux-Arts de Lausanne, 1996
Breker, Arno, *Im Strahlungsfeld der Ereignisse*, Preussisch Old-endorf, Germany: Schütz, 1972
Bresc-Bautier, Geneviève, and Anne Pingeot, *Sculptures des jardins du Louvre, du Caroussel et des Tuileries*, 2 vols., Paris: Ministère de la culture, Éditions de la Réunion des Musées Nationaux, 1986
Frèches-Thory, Claire, and Ursula Perucchi-Petri, editors, *Die Nabis, Propheten der Moderne* (exhib. cat.), Munich: Prestel, 1993
Frère, Henri, *Conversations de Maillol et l'âme de la sculpture*, Geneva : Cailler, 1956
Linnenkamp, Rolf, *Aristide Maillol, die grossen Plastiken*, Munich: Bruckmann, 1960
Lorquin, Bertrand, *Aristide Maillol*, Genève: Skira, 1994; as *Aristide Maillol*, translated by Michael Taylor, London and New York: Skira, 1995
Maillol (exhib. cat.), Saint Tropez, France: Musée de l'Annonci-ade, 1994
Maillol au Palais des Rois de Majorque (exhib. cat.), Perpignan, France: Musée Hyacinthe-Rigaud, 1979
Peters, Hans Albert, editor, *Maillol* (exhib. cat.), Baden-Baden, Germany: Staatliche Kunsthalle, 1978
Rewald, John, *Maillol*, edited by André Gloeckner, Paris: Hyperion, 1939; as *Maillol*, London and New York: Hyperion, 1939
Vierny, Dina, *Fondation Dina Vierny-Musée Maillol*, Paris: Fondation Dina Vierny-Musée Maillol: Réunion des Musées Nationaux, 1995
Vollard, Ambroise, *Recollections of a Picture Dealer*, Boston: Little Brown, and London: Constable, 1936
Wilhelm Lehmbruck, Aristide Maillol (exhib. cat.), New York: Plandome Press, 1930

LORENZO MAITANI *ca.* 1270–1330 *Italian*

Lorenzo Maitani, a Sienese architect largely active and esteemed in the first half of the 14th century, is usually connected to Orvieto Cathedral and the bronzes and reliefs on its facade. However, to this day his sculptural activity remains a rather complex critical problem.

The son of the woodmaster Vitale di Lorenzo, also called "Maitano," Maitani's name appears for the first time in a cadastral document of 1290, from which we can deduce that he was born about 1270. Maitani traveled from Siena to Orvieto in 1308 to perform some restructuring work on the cathedral, and from then on he remained connected to Orvieto. In a resolution of the Commune of Orvieto's captain and Council of Consuls, dated 16 September 1310, Maitani was mentioned as the *universalis caput magister* (master of the cathedral works); such a position guaranteed him exemptions from customs for about 15 years. He held this position for 20 years until his death in June 1330. This sort of contract that connected Maitani to Orvieto for such a long time—despite brief interruptions for architectural works in Siena, Perugia, and surrounding areas—shows his ample influence on the sculptural decoration of the cathedral's facade.

There are no known documents that refer explicitly to Maitani's activity as a sculptor, but it is presumed that he was involved in the planning and realization of all artistic elements, including sculpture, associated with the cathedral in the years he supervised the work as the *universalis caput magister*. A 1310 resolution authorized Maitani to appoint others to design and sculpt the facade; it can be presumed, observing the variation in workmanship in the reliefs of the facade's lower levels, that he often availed himself of this option. The problem of establishing precisely who sculpted the facade's marbles and bronzes, as well as their stylistic classification, is one of the most intricate puzzles in the history of Italian sculpture. However, there is proof in an autographed drawing of the facade, conserved in the Museo dell'Opera del Duomo, Orvieto, that the sculptural cycle was in fact planned by Maitani himself. When the necessary marble was procured in 1310, Maitani had probably already designed the facade and decided the iconography of the sculptures for the entire complex, which were then sculpted by various others. In 1329 the metal to cast the eagle located next to the other symbols of the Evangelists on the first-tier frieze was delivered to him; a year later, when Maitani died, the facade was already expanded above that ledge. Today the sculptural group of the central door's lunette—the bronze angels that support the edge of the canopy where the marble *Virgin and Child* is located, the bronze Evangelists' symbols, and the famous marble reliefs of the buttresses with *Genesis* and the *Last Judgment*—is more or less unanimously attributed to him. The compositional fantasy and the energetic lines, in particular in the reliefs of the *Last Judgment* with the figures that emerge from the background and become dramatically entangled, almost slipping away, are reminiscent of the Gothic sensibility that is close to the Sienese figurative tradition of the period.

It was Orvieto, before Siena or Pisa, that was the center from which the new Gothic modes of sculpture (particularly in wood) spread to other cities because of the presence of French and Franco-Flemish artists who were working there at the end of the 13th century. Three splendid wooden crucifixes, which are almost unanimously attributed to Maitani, are still preserved in Orvieto. They have been compared with some ivory reliefs in France because of the precision and technical delicateness that characterize them. The oldest is found in the Church of S. Francesco and shows a more dramatic and restless spirit: the arms of the Redeemer are held high and, by contrast, the body weighs heavily toward the bottom and is twisted so that the prominence of the knees is sharpened and the left foot rests on the right. This work seems similar to the crucifixes by Giovanni Pisano in the pulpits of Pisa and Pistoia and is attributed to Maitani's early years in Orvieto. The second crucifix, on the contrary, is in the first sacristy of Orvieto Cathedral. Here the Redeemer resembles one of the damned figures in the *Last Judgment*, both in the posture as well as in the hollow or sunken chest, but, above all, the figures resemble one another in their dramatic intensity that is transformed

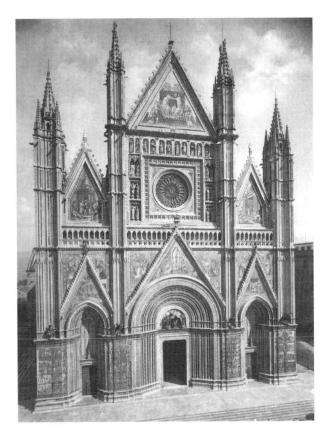

Facade Reliefs, Orvieto Cathedral
© Alinari / Art Resource, NY

into a refined lyricism; accordingly, this work is seen as a later one and is dated to about 1330. The third crucifix, in the canonicals' sacristy of Orvieto Cathedral, is thought to have been sculpted between 1315 and 1330, but there are some doubts as to whether it is by Maitani. It is now thought that the artist might have been one of the sculptors who collaborated with Maitani on the reliefs of the cathedral's facade.

The attributions of other wooden sculptures to Maitani are also not convincing. Among these is the *Christ Giving a Blessing* at the Museo dell'Opera del Duomo in Orvieto, whose head, although characterized by a certain lyricism typical of Maitani, contrasts excessively with the heavy drapery in the lower part of the statue. Geza De Francovich's proposal that the *Annunciation* in the Sangiorgi Gallery in Rome is by Maitani is even less convincing (see De Francovich, 1929).

The facade of Siena Cathedral, realized at the end of the 13th century by Giovanni Pisano, evidently served as an example for Orvieto Cathedral; Pisano's influence is also evident in other works by Maitani. But the use of bronze and a pictorial and linear style signal the distance between the two men and help place Maitani closer to the French Gothic style. According to today's most respected criticism, Maitani's last works are those that best manifest the greatness of his stylistic language and his originality; the refined elegance of his linear rhythms and volumes are energetically modeled with an impetus that stretches them in a sort of formal preciosity. Any risk of virtuosity is avoided, however: the three crucifixes see to this in the pathetic content of their faces and in their refined and almost aristocratic features in which one can see the artist's intimate participation in the human tragedy. For this they are considered to be "the highest and most intense plastic representations of the Crucifix of the entire 14th century in Italy" (see Carli, 1960).

LORENZO CARLETTI

See also **Gothic Sculpture**

Biography

Born in Siena, Italy, probably *ca.* 1270. Son of Vitale di Lorenzo (called "Maitano"), a Sienese sculptor and master woodworker. Requested to help build Orvieto Cathedral, 1308; became *universalis caput magister* (master of the cathedral works), 1310, and held position until his death; also worked in Orvieto on refacing of Communal Palace, arrangement of fountains, and consolidation of walls (1326–27); worked in Perugia on repair of aqueducts; in Siena, studied extension of cathedral (1322); planned castle of Montefalco and worked on restoration of castle in Castiglion del Lago (1323–25). Died in Orvieto, Italy, June 1330.

Selected Works

1310–30 *Genesis* and the *Last Judgment*; marble; facade of Orvieto Cathedral, Italy (attributed)

ca. 1315 Crucifix; wood; Church of S. Francesco, Orvieto, Italy (attributed)

1315–30 Crucifix; wood; canonicals' sacristy of Orvieto Cathedral, Italy (attributed)

1320–30 *Virgin and Child*; marble; facade of Orvieto Cathedral, Italy (attributed)

1325–30 Angels and evangelists' symbols; bronze; facade of Orvieto Cathedral, Italy (attributed)

ca. 1330 Crucifix; wood; first sacristy of Orvieto Cathedral, Italy (attributed)

Further Reading

Carli, Enzo, *La scultura lignea italiana, dal XII al XIV secolo*, Milan: Electa Editrice, 1960

Carli, Enzo, *Gli scultori senesi*, Milan: Electa, 1981

De Francovich, Géza, "Lorenzo Maitani scultore e i bassorilievi della facciata del duomo di Orvieto," *Bollettino d'arte* 7 (1927–28)

De Francovich, Géza, "Un'annunciazione in legno di Lorenzo Maitani," *La Diana* 4 (1929)

Lisner, Margrit, *Holzkruzifixe in Florenz und in der Toskana von der Zeit um 1300 bis zum frühen Cinquecento*, Munich: Bruckmann, 1970

Middeldorf Kosegarten, Antje, *Die Domfassade in Orvieto: Studien zur Architektur und Skulptur 1290–1330*, Munich: Deutscher Kunstverlag, 1996

Pope-Hennessy, John, *An Introduction to Italian Sculpture*, 3 vols., London: Phaidon, 1963; 4th edition, 1996; see especially vol. 1, *Italian Gothic Sculpture*

Valentiner, Wilhelm Reinhold, "Observations on Sienese and Pisan Trecento Sculpture," *Art Bulletin* (1927)

FACADE RELIEFS, ORVIETO CATHEDRAL
Lorenzo Maitani (ca. 1270–1330)
Early 14th century
Orvieto, Italy

The marble panels of relief sculpture that decorate the four piers on the west facade of the Orvieto Cathedral have long been an enigma to art historians. The extent of Lorenzo Maitani's personal involvement in the actual execution of the narrative scenes illustrating (from left to right) Genesis, the Tree of Jesse and other Old Testament prophecies of the Redemption, the life of Christ and the prophets, and the Last Judgment is still a topic of open debate. It is generally accepted, however, that the team of medieval craftsmen responsible for the extensive decorative program on the first level of the facade worked under the supervision of the *capomaestro* (chief architect) Maitani until his death in Orvieto in 1330. The momentum of the works seems to have faltered at this point and probably ground to a halt during the following brief period in which the cathedral works were directed by Maitani's sons Vitale and Lorenzo, together with Meo da Siena.

Maitani's presence in Orvieto is first documented on 16 September 1310 in a contract that declares him to be *universalis caput magister* (master of the cathedral works) of Orvieto Cathedral. Although the document describes him as being experienced in buttressing and making roofs and "walls figured with beauty," it is at best an interpretation to conclude that Maitani was actually a sculptor. Neither does this document provide any real indication of an initial date that the decoration of the facade piers was begun, as there is no reference to Maitani being the designer of the project.

There are in fact two existing drawings (Museo dell'Opera del Duomo, Orvieto) that are thought to be preliminary schemes of the cathedral facade. Studies support earlier attributions of the single-gabled drawing to the Sienese artist Ramo di Paganello, whose presence in Orvieto is documented in the last decade of the 13th century. A Sienese document of 1281 describing Ramo as being "de partibus ultramontanis" (having left Siena to travel north of the Alps) supports this theory, as the drawing combines French elements from the Gothic *rayonnant* style with typically Italian motifs. The second drawing is generally attributed to Maitani and is thought to follow the first by only a few years. This three-gabled plan is clearly influenced by existing Italian cathedral designs, in particular Giovanni Pisano's scheme for the Siena Cathedral facade (1287–97) and Arnolfo di Cambio's drawing for the Florence Cathedral facade (1294–1302). It is characterized by flat, smooth walls and a Classical rapport between geometrical elements; in addition, it demonstrates a knowledge of recent spatial developments at the Cathedral of Assisi.

That the reliefs decorating the four lower piers of the facade are unfinished provides a rare opportunity for an analysis of working proceedings in a medieval sculptural workshop. The panels are incomplete from about halfway up on all four piers, therefore making the workshop's various phases of execution apparent. Although scholars tend to agree that Maitani undoubtedly coordinated the design and decoration of the four piers, there are two theories as to the division of labor among the pool of sculptors who worked under him. The more traditional hypothesis seeks to identify the number of artists involved on the lower front of the west facade. The second widely accepted theory sees a highly sophisticated organization of the division of work within the sculpture workshop in which each artist was charged with a distinct phase of the creation of the reliefs. This specialization entailed that individual sculptors be limited to carving details such as hair and drapery and could also correspond to the individual's use of specific instruments. The commission's complex nature probably determined this highly structured

organizational solution. It certainly provided the *capo-maestro* with a system for controlling his individual workers that enabled them to work rapidly and efficiently, leading them to obtain an overall sense of stylistic unity in the resulting panels of reliefs.

The third, or right central, pier, devoted to the life of Christ, demonstrates most succinctly the various phases of work. Workshop drawings that no longer survive may have been transferred to the irregular component slabs of marble and would have been roughly blocked out using adzes, trimming hammers, chisels, and punches. Increasingly fine claw chisels were then used to further refine the resulting coarse surface. Finally, the forms were finished with straight-edged chisels and polished with abrasives. A number of different phases of transition can be seen in the *Baptism of Christ* on the third pier.

Two distinct styles are generally recognized in the narrative panels on the lower level of the facade. These have been attributed to the work of two different teams of sculptors and have been linked to the personalities identified with the two existing preparatory drawings of the cathedral's western front. The main workshop is thought to have created the Genesis reliefs, the lower part of the *Last Judgment* pier, and possibly the upper parts of the two central piers. This group can be identified by its well-integrated compositions, natural landscapes, a figure style that demonstrates a firm knowledge of natural forms, and the use of soft transparent drapery that anatomically defines the body beneath. A second group is apparent in the sculpting style of the lower reliefs on the two central piers. Here the figures are heavier, harder draperies are marked by deeper cuts in the marble, the figures and their backgrounds are not always in close compositional rapport, and at times the narrative scenes show a fussy attention to detail.

The influence of Giovanni Pisano can be seen in the style of both teams of sculptors. The major workshop's ability to express a vast emotional range and violent action in its figures, particularly in the scenes of *Cain and Abel* and the *Last Judgment*, reflects Pisano's work. The *Visitation* scene sculpted by the second group on the third pier is probably dependent on the similar scene on Pisano's Pisan pulpit, finished in 1310. Both teams of sculptors probably worked together on the facade at some stage, illustrated by evident overlapping of the two styles in the reliefs on the third pier.

Stylistic comparisons have resulted in Maitani's name being associated with the reliefs on the two outer piers. Figures in the *Genesis* and the *Last Judgment* reliefs, in particular certain angels, closely resemble the bronze angels and the Evangelists' symbols situated above the sculpted panels. The attribution of these later sculptures to Maitani is supported by a document

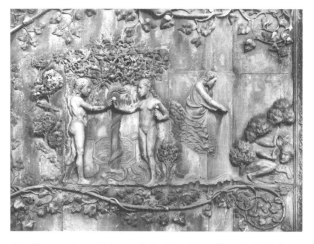

The Temptation of Man and the Expulsion, Facade Reliefs, Orvieto Cathedral
© Alinari / Art Resource, NY

of 1330 that notes the provision of the bronze for casting the eagle. The document is not, however, firm proof that Maitani was personally responsible for the sculpture; as *capomaestro* of the cathedral, he may simply have received the bronze and consigned it to the teams of sculptors he directed.

PIPPA SALONIUS

See also **Arnolfo di Cambio; Gothic Sculpture; Pisano, Giovanni; Relief Sculpture**

Further Reading

Bonelli, Renato, *Il Duomo di Orvieto e l'architettura italiana del duecento–Trecento*, Rome: Officina, 1972

Carli, Enzo, *Le sculture del Duomo di Orvieto*, Bergamo: Istituto Italiano di Arte Grafiche, 1947

Gillerman, David M., "La facciata: Introduzione al rapporto tra scultura e architettura," in *Il Duomo di Orvieto*, edited by Lucio Riccetti, Rome: Laterza, 1988

Harding, Catherine, "Maitani, Lorenzo" in *The Dictionary of Art*, edited by Jane Turner, vol. 20, New York: Grove, and London: Macmillan, 1996

Harding, Catherine, "Orvieto," in *The Dictionary of Art*, edited by Jane Turner, vol. 23, New York: Grove, and London: Macmillan, 1996

Martellotti, Giovanna, and Peter Rockwell, "Osservazioni sugli strumenti della scultura nei rilievi della facciata," in *Il Duomo di Orvieto*, edited by Lucio Riccetti, Rome: Laterza, 1988

Middeldorf Kosegarten, Antje, *Die Domfassade in Orvieto: Studien zur Architektur und Skulptur, 1290–1330*, Munich: Deutscher Kunstverlag, 1996

Ricetti, Lucio, *Le origini dell'Opera: Lorenzo Maitani e l'architettura del Duomo di Orvieto: In margine al disegno di una storiografia*, Florence: Olschki Editore, 1996

White, John, "The Reliefs on the Facade of the Duomo at Orvieto," *Journal of the Warburg and Courtauld Institutes* 22/3–4 (July–December 1959)

MANNERISM

See **Renaissance and Mannerism**

PAUL MANSHIP 1885–1966 *United States, active in France*

The son of a Confederate soldier who had come north following the war, Paul Manship was born in St. Paul, Minnesota, where he received his earliest art education and began his career as a commercial artist. For further art instruction he moved to New York City in 1905. Manship also worked as a studio assistant to Solon Borglum, under Charles Grafly at the Pennsylvania Academy of Art, in Philadelphia, and with Hungarian-born sculptor Isidore Konti. It was Konti who encouraged Manship—by this time determined to make his career in sculpture—to compete for a scholarship offered by the prestigious American Academy in Rome (AAR). He won the prize in a competition adjudicated by Daniel Chester French. His assigned topic included a family grouping—a mother, father, and child—titled *Rest after Toil* (whereabouts unknown).

Following three years in Rome, Manship returned in 1912 to the United States where he began to exhibit, win garden and architectural commissions, and gain recognition among New York's cultural elite. Kenyon Cox, a traditionalist painter and art critic, was among those who saw promise in Manship's work, as did Frank Crowninshield, the influential editor of *Vanity Fair* and son of a former director of the AAR. Soon Manship was a highly paid sculptor who in order to keep up with his obligations employed studio assistants, including Gaston Lachaise, already a skilled artist, and Reuben Nakian, whom Manship helped train.

Over the years Manship won many prizes and honors, including a gold medal at the Panama Pacific Exposition in San Francisco in 1915 for his much-admired sculptural groupings in the Court of the Universe, and inclusion, as early as 1914, in the collections of the Metropolitan Museum of Art in New York City.

Early in his career Manship had begun to make portrait and commemorative medals. A medal featuring images of Joan of Arc was produced in aid of the Italian War Relief committee. Following American entry into the war, Manship produced another notable medallion, the *Kultur Medal* (1918), which sold well at ten dollars. With this medal he intended to fuel the flames of patriotic ardor by using an image of the fearsome German kaiser sporting a skull-encrusted necklace (his rosary) on one side of the coin, and a bestial-looking German soldier carrying off his struggling victim on the other. *Vanity Fair* described the medal portraying the rape of Belgium as "a wonderful bit of sculptured hate."

Some of Manship's most notable early works were portraiture: of his daughter, *Pauline Frances, Three Weeks Old* (1914), and an equally striking but very different bust of philanthropist and captain of industry John D. Rockefeller (1918). Manship's friend John Singer Sargent, who painted his own portrait of Rockefeller around this same time, had recommended Manship for the assignment. A monument to J.P. Morgan, the John Pierpont Morgan Memorial (1915–20), which, however, did not include a likeness of Morgan, was commissioned by the Metropolitan Museum of Art after Morgan's death in 1913 and carved by Lachaise from Manship's designs.

Despite the generally positive response to his sculpture at home, Manship decided to seek exhibitions and recognition abroad. After a period in England, where he exhibited in 1921 (and again in 1935 in a solo exhibition at the Tate Gallery), he relocated to Paris and set up a studio. In 1923 he had his first Paris exhibition.

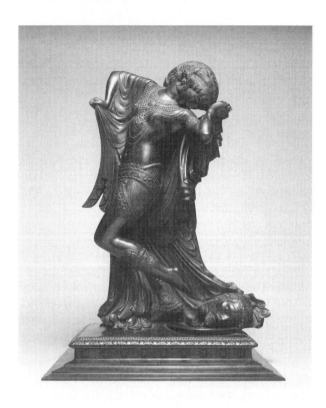

Salome
© Smithsonian American Art Museum, Washington, D.C. /
Art Resource, NY

In 1925 he exhibited a work at the Exposition Internationale des Arts Décoratifs et Industriels Modernes, a showcase of the Art Deco style. Manship's streamlined formulations of ideal beauty are embodied in his *Diana* (1925) and *Actaeon* (1925). His *Cycle of Life* (1924) was displayed in the garden sculpture area of the International Exposition in Paris (1925). It contains a family group reminiscent of his earlier AAR competition submission *Rest after Toil* within the armature of a skeletal sphere.

Manship did portraits of the wealthy and well connected, including one of an American, Grace Rainey Rogers. This association paved the way for one of his most significant and successful commissions of the 1920s: the decorative bronze gates for the Bronx Zoo, a memorial to Rogers's brother Paul J. Rainey, a noted explorer. This project required the efforts of 15 assistants from 1926 through 1934 and cost approximately $250,000. Through other Paris connections Manship met the curator of sculpture at the Musée du Louvre, Paul Vitry, who in 1927 wrote a monograph on Manship. Two years later Manship was also honored with membership in the French Legion of Honor.

Among Manship's notable works of the 1920s are *Indian Hunter and His Dog* (a variation on a theme done often by him), a war monument (the Thrasher-

Ward Memorial) in the courtyard of the AAR, and separate statues of the fleet-footed *Diana* and *Actaeon*, of which a number of versions exist. He also produced several variations on the theme of *Europa and the Bull*, which he continued to rework and revise throughout the 1930s.

Although Manship maintained a studio in Paris until at least 1937, he traveled constantly and vied for important commissions at home, including one for a heroic bronze statue of the young Abraham Lincoln—*Abraham Lincoln, The Hoosier Youth with Four Medallions* (1932)—for the Lincoln Life Insurance Company in Fort Wayne, Indiana. Unlike French's or George Grey Barnard's full-length statues, all of a mature Lincoln, Manship's Lincoln is still a young man, his face untroubled, his person yet untested.

No discussion of Manship's sculpture would be complete without reference to his most famous large-scale commission—the Prometheus Fountain—for the Radio Corporation of America (RCA) building at Rockefeller Center in New York that he worked on from 1933–38. Manship returned to the Prometheus theme again in 1950 when he produced a series of drawings and small-scale sculpture groupings chronicling additional episodes in Prometheus's life. Known as the *Prometheus Trilogy*, it included *Prometheus Bringing Fire*, *Prometheus Bound*, and *Prometheus Freed by Hercules*.

MARILYN BAKER

See also **Art Deco; Lachaise, Gaston; Public Sculpture; United States: 1900–1960**

Biography

Born in St. Paul, Minnesota, United States, 25 December 1885. Attended St. Paul Institute of Art; studied at Art Students League in New York, 1905, and at Pennsylvania Academy of Fine Art, 1906; won Prix de Rome, 1909; traveled to Italy, Greece, and Egypt; continued education at American Academy in Rome, 1909–12; returned to United States, 1912; established studio in Paris until 1937. Member of National Academy of Design, National Sculpture Society, American Academy of Arts and Letters, and Alumni Association, all in New York City, as well as the American Academy in Rome; National Fine Arts Commission; and American Academy of Arts and Sciences; popularity declined after World War II. Died in New York City, United States, 31 January 1966.

Selected Works

1914   *Pauline Frances, Three Weeks Old*;
        marble, polychromed bronze; Metropolitan

Museum of Art, New York City, United States

1915 Jeanne d'Arc medal; bronze; Minnesota Museum of Art, St. Paul, Minnesota, United States

1915 *Salome*; bronze; Smithsonian American Art Museum, Washington, D.C., United States

1915–20 John Pierpont Morgan Memorial; limestone; Metropolitan Museum of Art, New York City, United States

1918 *John D. Rockefeller, 1918*; marble; Rockefeller Archive Center, North Tarrytown, New York City, United States

1918 *Kultur Medal*; bronze; Minnesota Museum of Art, St. Paul, Minnesota, United States

1924 *Actaeon*; gilded bronze; Brookgreen Gardens, Brookgreen, South Carolina, United States

1924 *Europa and the Bull*; bronze, marble base; Minnesota Museum of Art, St. Paul, United States

1925 *Flight of Europa*; gilded bronze, marble base; National Museum of American Art, Smithsonian Institution, Washington, D.C., United States

1926–34 *Paul J. Rainey Memorial Gateway*; bronze; New York Zoological Park, Brooklyn, New York City, United States

1932 *Abraham Lincoln, The Hoosier Youth with Four Medallions*; bronze; Lincoln National Life Insurance Company, Fort Wayne, Indiana, United States

1933–38 Prometheus Fountain; gilded bronze; Rockefeller Center, New York City, United States

1950 *Prometheus Trilogy (Prometheus Bringing Fire, Prometheus Bound*, and *Prometheus Freed by Hercules)*; bronze; Minnesota Museum of Art, St. Paul, Minnesota, United States

Further Reading

Canfield, Mary Cass, "The Sculpture of Paul Manship," *Vanity Fair* (October 1918)

Cox, Kenyon, "A New Sculpture," *Nation* (13 February 1913)

Craven, Wayne, *Sculpture in America*, New York: Crowell, 1968

Gallatin, Albert Eugene, *Paul Manship: A Critical Essay on His Sculpture and an Iconography*, New York: Lane, 1917

"The Kultur Medal," *Vanity Fair* (April 1918)

Manship, John, *Paul Manship*, New York: Abbeville Press, 1989

Proske, Beatrice Gilman, *Brookgreen Gardens Catalogue of Sculpture*, Brookgreen, South Carolina: s.n., 1936; new edition, 1968

Rather, Susan, *Archaism, Modernism, and the Art of Paul Manship*, Austin: University of Texas Press, 1993

Salmon, Robin R., *Brookgreen Gardens Sculpture*, Murrells Inlet, South Carolina: Brookgreen Gardens, 1993

Smith, Carol Hynning, *Drawings by Paul Manship: The Minnesota Museum of Art Collection*, Saint Paul: Minnesota Museum of Art, 1987

Taft, Lorado, *The History of American Sculpture*, New York: Arno Press, 1969

Valentine, Lucia, and Alan Valentine, *The American Academy in Rome, 1894–1969*, Charlottesville: University Press of Virginia, 1973

CRISTOFORO MANTEGAZZA early to mid 15th CENTURY–1480 AND ANTONIO MANTEGAZZA early to mid 15th CENTURY–1495 *Italian*

To separate the works of Cristoforo Mantegazza from those of his younger brother, Antonio, is one of the central problems of Milanese Renaissance sculpture. The literature recognizes them as leading sculptors of the Certosa di Pavia, but there is little agreement on how to distinguish their styles. Nineteenth-century scholars inferred that Cristoforo was the great artist whose style is characterized by passionate expression, undercut low relief, and "cartaceous" drapery (resembling crumpled paper). However, many of the sculptures in this Mantegazzesque style were made after 1480, the year of Cristoforo's death.

The key to solving this attribution problem is the document of 12 October 1478, according to which the Mantegazza brothers and Giovanni Antonio Amadeo agreed to have certain works they had done for the Certosa estimated. The Mantegazzas are said to have made two "doctors" for the *tiburio*, a marble pietà, and an image of the Virgin Mary, made of Angera stone, for a keystone. This keystone has been identified in the seventh chapel at the right of the nave, and it displays an old-fashioned, curvilinear, International Gothic style, different from that called Mantegazzesque. This keystone is in the same style as most of the 130 corbels of the Certosa's large cloister, and documents prove that Cristoforo made many of them. Therefore, this keystone and most of the large cloister corbels (none of which is Mantegazzesque) were made by Cristoforo. The two doctors of the 1478 document have been identified, and one of them, *St. Augustine*, exemplifies the Mantegazzesque style. The pietà mentioned in the document can be identified as the *Lamentation* in the Victoria and Albert Museum (London, England), and it, too, is of the Mantegazzesque style. Therefore, this must be the style of Antonio. He worked until 1495, so the chronology of his style extends from about 1474 to 1495.

A large, homogeneous group of sculptures can be attributed to each brother. For Cristoforo, there have been identified, in addition to the large cloister corbels already mentioned, three keystones in the vaults of the Certosa church. The *Adoration of the Magi* in the Capitolo dei Padri is Cristoforo's greatest masterpiece. The *St. Jerome Roundel* of the *tiburio* is the second of the two doctors attributed to the Mantegazza in the 1478 document, and it seems to have been a collaboration between the two brothers.

In a document of 7 October 1473, the Certosa gave the Mantegazza brothers a contract to execute the entire Certosa facade. However, on 20 August 1474 the prior allotted half of the work of the facade to Amadeo and the other half to the Mantegazza brothers. The most significant sculpture made for the facade between 1474 and 1480 is the series of Old Testament panels, intended for the socle but now partly mounted high on the facade and partly elsewhere in the monastery. About half of these panels display the mannered, angular, flattened Mantegazzesque style and are attributable to Antonio, whereas the other half reveal the more traditional style of Cristoforo.

The following works at the Certosa, all homogeneously Mantegazzesque in style, can also be attributed to Antonio: the pietà lunette on the interior of the small cloister portal; the Resurrection lunette and statue on the portal leading from the cemetery to the Capitolo dei Fratelli; 12 socle medallions with imaginative numismatic portraits of ancient rulers on the right half of the facade; two panels of angels supporting heraldic crests, also on the right-hand socle of the facade; the *St. William* medallion on the reverse side of the right corner buttress of the facade; six New Testament panels on the right of the facade; and the gigantic *Lamentation* relief in the altarpiece in the Capitolo dei Fratelli, Pavia, which is Antonio's finest masterpiece. Also attributable to Antonio are the *Faith, Hope, and Charity* relief in the Musée du Louvre (Paris) and the *Creation of Adam, Creation of Eve*, and two *Sibyls*, now in the Castello Sforzesco Museum (Milan).

A recently published document of 1491 states that one Francesco Mantegazza donated to the monastery of Campomorto a marble *ancona* (altarpiece), which he had contracted to be sculpted ("que ipse dominus donator sculpi fecit") by Antonio. This altarpiece is composed of relief panels that show no resemblance to the Mantegazzesque style. Some scholars have concluded that these panels are unquestionably the work of Antonio, and therefore he could not have executed the above-mentioned Mantegazzesque works. This argument fails to recognize the possibility that while Antonio oversaw the making of this altarpiece, the component parts were made by an associate. This associate can be identified. The style and composition of the Campomorto panels

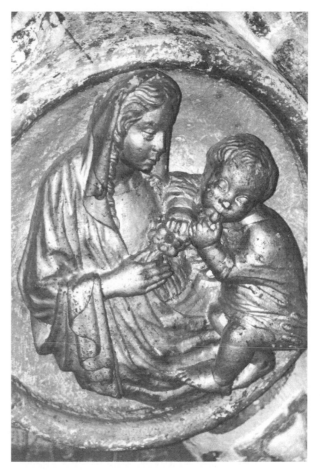

Cristoforo Mantegazza, *Madonna and Child*, from Certosa di Pavia
Photo courtesy of Charles Morscheck

are so similar to New Testament reliefs on the left of the Certosa facade (opposite the Mantegazzesque works on the right) that they have been called imitations of these facade panels. Comparison of the Campomorto panels with these reliefs reveals that the former were executed earlier but by the same sculptor, identified as Antonio della Porta, called Tamagnino. Many sculptures attributed to Tamagnino, at the Certosa and elsewhere, show stylistic affinities with the Campomorto reliefs, which appear to be his earliest known works, probably made in the mid to late 1480s. Moreover, the style of the Campomorto reliefs and the left-hand facade New Testament reliefs is close, but not identical, to that of Cristoforo Mantegazza. These similarities suggest that Tamagnino was an apprentice or an assistant to Cristoforo in the late 1470s and carried on his more traditional style into the 1490s.

In a document dated 12 May 1492, Amadeo associated himself with Antonio and Tamagnino for the purpose of finishing the Certosa facade. This association, together with the similarity of the Campomorto reliefs to the left-hand facade New Testament reliefs, suggests that Tamagnino had been associated with the Mantegazza brothers before 1492.

In conclusion, the older Mantegazza brother, Cristoforo, had a conservative, International Gothic style; the younger brother, Antonio, had the more innovative Mantegazzesque style; and Tamagnino, a follower of Cristoforo, became the associate of Antonio. Of these three, Antonio Mantegazza may be regarded as the greatest genius.

CHARLES MORSCHECK

See also **Certosa di Pavia; Lamentation and Deposition Groups**

Biography

Brothers Cristoforo and Antonio born in Milan, Italy, early to mid 15th century. Sons of Galeazzo, official of Fabbrica of Duomo (cathedral workshop), resident in parish of Santa Babila, 1428–50; brothers Giovanni and Giorgio were goldsmiths and sculptors. Cristoforo a stonecutter for the Milan Cathedral, 1448–51; Antonio also a stonecutter there in 1458. Cristoforo did sculpture for Certosa di Pavia, 1464–66; Antonio documented there in 1465. Cristoforo took a sculptural apprentice in 1469; Cristoforo and Antonio jointly took apprentices in drawing and sculpture, as well as making terracotta reliefs, one each in 1470 and 1472. Cristoforo and his brothers, called goldsmiths, offered to make bronze equestrian monument of Francesco Sforza, 1473. The prior of the Certosa assigned the two brothers half of the church facade, and Giovanni Antonio Amadeo the other half, 1474. In 1481, after Cristoforo's death, brother Giovanni and Cristoforo's daughter and heir, Costanza, rented Cristoforo's share of Certosa facade to Gabriele and Giovanni Pietro da Rho. Amadeo agreed to collaborate with Antonio and Antonio della Porta (Tamagnino) to finish facade, 1492. Brothers died probably in or near Milan, Cristoforo in 1480 and Antonio in October 1495.

Selected Works

Cristoforo Mantegazza

ca.   Most of 130 corbels; Angera stone;
1464–70 Certosa di Pavia, Pavia, Italy

ca.   Three keystones; Angera stone; Certosa di
1467–73 Pavia, Pavia, Italy

ca.   *Madonna and Child* keystone; Angera
1476–78 stone; Certosa di Pavia, Pavia, Italy

ca.   *Adoration of the Magi*; marble; Capitolo
1476–80 dei Padri, Certosa di Pavia, Pavia, Italy

Antonio Mantegazza

ca.   *Pietà* lunette; Angera stone; Certosa di
1470–78 Pavia, Pavia, Italy

ca.   *Resurrection* lunette and statue; marble;
1470–78 Capitolo dei Padri, Certosa di Pavia, Pavia, Italy

ca.   *St. Augustine* roundel; Angera stone;
1476–78 Certosa di Pavia, Pavia, Italy

ca.   *Lamentation*; marble; Victoria and Albert
1476–78 Museum, London, England

ca.   *Angel Holding a Crown of Thorns*;
1476–82 marble; Museum of the Fabbrica of the Duomo, Milan, Italy

ca.   *Faith, Hope, and Charity*; marble; Musée
1476–82 du Louvre, Paris, France

ca.   Twelve socle medallions; marble; Certosa
1476–95 di Pavia, Pavia, Italy

ca.   *Creation of Adam, Creation of Eve*, and
1486–90 two *Sibyls*; marble; Castello Sforzesco Museum, Milan, Italy

ca.   Two panels of angels supporting heraldic
1486–95 crests; marble; Certosa di Pavia, Pavia, Italy

ca.   Six New Testament panels; marble;
1486–95 Certosa di Pavia, Pavia, Italy

ca.   *St. William* medallion; marble; Certosa di
1486–95 Pavia, Pavia, Italy

ca.   *Lamentation*; marble; Capitolo dei Fratelli,
1490–95 Certosa di Pavia, Pavia, Italy

Cristoforo and Antonio Mantegazza

ca.   Thirty-four Old Testament panels; marble;
1474–80 Certosa di Pavia, Pavia, Italy; one panel: Castello Sforzesco Museum, Milan, Italy

ca.   *St. Jerome* roundel; Angera stone; Certosa
1476–78 di Pavia, Pavia, Italy

Further Reading

Bernstein, JoAnne Gitlin, "The Architectural Sculpture of the Cloisters of the Certosa di Pavia," Ph.D. diss., New York University, 1972

Fadda, Elisabetta, "Ancora sui Mantegazza," *Nuovi studi* 4 (1997)

Morscheck, Charles R., *Relief Sculpture for the Facade of the Certosa di Pavia, 1473–1499*, New York: Garland, 1978

Morscheck, Charles R., "Keystones by Amadeo and Cristoforo Mantegazza in the Church of the Certosa di Pavia," *Arte Lombarda* 69–70 (1984)

Morscheck, Charles R., "The Certosa Medallions in Perspective," *Arte Lombarda* 123 (1998)

Norris, Andrea S., "Mantegazza," in *The Dictionary of Art*, edited by Jane Turner, vol. 20, New York: Grove, and London: Macmillan, 1996

Pope-Hennessy, John, *An Introduction to Italian Sculpture*, 3 vols., London: Phaidon, 1963; 4th ed., 1996; see especially vol. 2, *Italian Renaissance Sculpture*

Shell, Janice, "The Mantegazza Brothers, Martino Benzoni, and the Colleoni Tomb," *Arte Lombarda* 100 (1992)

Shell, Janice, "Amadeo, the Mantegazza, and the Facade of the Certosa di Pavia," in *Giovanni Antonio Amadeo: Scultura e architettura del suo tempo*, edited by Janice Shell and Liana Castelfranchi Vegas, Milan: Cisalpino, 1993

PIERO MANZONI 1933–1963 *Italian*

Piero Manzoni's iconoclastic career, which lasted only from 1956 to 1963, called into question the language and the nature of art and heralded the Conceptual art movement of the second half of the 1960s. With clairvoyance and an ironic spirit akin to Marcel Duchamp's, Manzoni severely criticized the way art was turning into an invasive industry. His main targets were the commodification of aesthetic objects and the commercialization of artists' signatures. The serial nature of his artistic output and the prices he always put on his works testify to Manzoni's obsession about the way art was equated with merchandise.

Yves Klein's 1957 exhibition at the Galleria Apollinaire in Milan was crucial in shaping Manzoni's ideas about art. However, Manzoni's work differed from Klein's in being closely tied to the body and physical substance and lacking any transcendental or spiritual implications.

Beginning in 1959 with his series of *Lines*, Manzoni took his place beside Klein as a precursor of the avant-garde movements of the 1960s. These constructions consist of cardboard tubes or metal boxes bearing labels that describe in detail the length of the lines they contain or attest to their "infinite length." By hiding his lines in a box or tube, Manzoni asserted the primacy of concept over visual form.

In 1959 and 1960, Manzoni made a series of 45 *Air Bodies*, which were inspired by Klein's *Aerostatic Sculpture* (1957) but lacked any ascetic implication. This was the start of an experimental program aimed at exalting the body and its waste products, which turn into three-dimensional solids: breath, feces, fingerprints, blood. By using his own body as the source of ready-made materials, by presenting the traces of his fleeting passage in boxes closed like works of art, he broke down any remaining barrier between art and life.

Manzoni's *Air Bodies*—pneumatic sculptures of up to 80 centimeters in diameter—were made in series, sold in a wooden case, and priced at 3,000 lire (about five dollars). The case contained a tripod and a balloon that could be blown up by the buyer or the artist. In the latter case, the work was titled *Artist's Breath*. Manzoni priced his own breath at 200 lire (about 30 cents), thereby ridiculing the noble, spiritual value people have always attributed to breath as an expression of the soul.

In that same period, Manzoni created his first *Sculpture in Space*, in dialogue with Klein's *Vitesse Pure et Stabilité Monochrome*. The piece consisted of a sphere suspended in space by a circular air jet provided by a two-cycle motor. Manzoni applied the same principle in a series of *Air Bodies of Absolute Light*, where spheroids turning on their own axes at dizzying speed created a virtual volume.

Manzoni's balloons containing the artist's breath recalled the sealed bottle of Parisian air proffered in 1919 by Duchamp, the recognized leader of all conceptual research. Duchamp had realized the huge advantage of using containers to conceptualize artworks, because they made the object invisible. However, Manzoni's criticism of consumer society and the commercialization of the artist's signature was much more biting than Duchamp's. Manzoni's three-dimensional boxes have the same radically polemical value as Andy Warhol's two-dimensional soup cans and Jasper Johns's sculpted ale cans.

In his *Artist's Shit* series, Manzoni took the idea behind Duchamp's *Urinal*—which had produced a scandal in the 1920s—to an extreme by focusing on the abject bodily substance. The 90 boxes Manzoni made beginning in 1961 contained 30 grams of the "naturally preserved" matter. Each box, signed by the artist on the cover, was to be sold by the gram at the going price of gold. Manzoni was succinctly and shockingly equating money, art, and excrement, thus damning the modern belief that artistic work is not alienated work.

Also in 1961 Manzoni presented the nude bodies of models as *Live Sculptures* at the Galleria La Tartaruga in Rome. Drawing inspiration from Klein's contemporary *Anthrométries*, Manzoni nullified the traditional sense of sculpture as representational art or a way for artists to express themselves and presented it as pure tautology. Each signed model received an "authenticity certificate." Relying on the ephemeral concept of artistic aura, Manzoni's signature certified even the most banal objects, such as a scarf that had belonged to his friend the painter Mario Schifano, as works of art.

In a 1960 performance titled *Audience Consumption of Dynamic Art—Devour Art*, at the Galleria Azimut in Milan, and the series of *Magic Bases* created from 1961 on, Manzoni experimented with direct involvement of the audience, a key part of Conceptual art. In his 70-minute performance at the Azimut, Manzoni invited the spectators to eat eggs he had cooked himself and marked with his own fingerprint. In *Magic Bases*, a person or object standing or placed on top of the structure is to be considered a work of art. *Socle of the World (Foundation of the World No. 3—Tribute to Galileo)*, Manzoni's most monumental work, was part of this series. It consists of an upside-down iron box that is supposed to hold up the entire world, transforming every single thing into a work of art.

In 1961 Manzoni made a box-shaped *Straw Sculpture* and a spherical *Rabbit-Skin Sculpture*, each mounted on a burnt-wood base. The straw sculpture was supposed to be covered with small reflecting balls made of the material used for road signs. Here Manzoni was experimenting with the way luminosity changes as time passes.

Among the projects Manzoni thought up were a line traced around the earth along the Greenwich meridian, vials containing his blood, and an exhibition of cadavers in transparent boxes. He described these impossible projects in numerous articles and manifestos written in parallel with his enormous output of objects. Like all Conceptual artists, he continually produced theoretical documents intended to support and defend the validity of his own work.

Manzoni was initially dismissed as a playful iconoclast, but critics have now come to see him as a rediscoverer of the languages of art and have recognized his role as precursor of the major avant-garde movements. The first retrospective devoted to him by an Italian museum was the 1971 show at the National Gallery of Modern Art in Rome; it was followed by exhibitions in Germany, the Netherlands, and England. In 1972 the Sonnabend Gallery in New York City presented a small retrospective that was completely ignored by the public and the critics. At the beginning of the 1990s, an important retrospective that traveled to museums in Paris, Herning (Denmark), Madrid, and Turin (Italy), plus a show at the Hirschl and Adler Gallery in New York City, definitively enshrined Manzoni's work as a critical point in the crisis of contemporary art, capable of revealing the conflict between aesthetic and commercial value.

CATERINA BAY

See also **Beuys, Joseph; Duchamp, Marcel; Klein, Yves; Performance Art**

Biography

Born in Soncino (near Cremona), Italy, 13 July 1933. Attended Brera Academy but soon dropped out; signed the manifesto "Toward the Discovery of an Image Zone" and began to show paintings, 1956; participated in 60 exhibitions in Milan alone, including 23 group and seven solo by 1962; member of the Nuclear Group, 1957–59; spent summers in Albisola, a gathering place for Lucio Fontana, Emilio Scanavino, and the Cobra group; came in contact with the Zero Group, 1959; founded the review *Azimut* with Vincenzo Agnetti and Enrico Castellani; opened Galleria Azimut in Milan; spent time in Herning, Denmark, 1960; visited the Nouveau Réalisme show in Paris and met Arman, Jean Tinguely, and Yves Klein, 1961; showed at Stedelijk Museum, Amsterdam, 1962; participated in a Zero Group show in Bern, at the Schindeler Gallery; held last show in Brussels, 1963. Died in Milan, Italy, 6 February 1963.

Selected Works

1959   *Air Body*; wood, balloon, metal, paper; private collection, Florence, Italy

1960   *Air Body of Absolute Light*; balloon, compressed air (destroyed)

1960   *Audience Consumption of Dynamic Art—Devour Art*; performance (boiled eggs signed with the artist's thumb); Galleria Azimut, Milan, Italy

1960   *Sculpture in Space*; balloon, compressed air (destroyed)

1961   *Artist's Shit* no. 033; metal box; Kunstmuseum, Herning, Denmark

1961   *Line 1,000 m Long*; cardboard, paper, ink; Museum of Modern Art, New York City, United States

1961   *Live Sculpture*; performance (live nude models signed by the artist); Galleria La Tartaruga, Rome, Italy

1961   *Rabbit-Skin Sculpture*; pelt, burnt wood; Kunstmuseum, Herning, Denmark

1961   *Socle of the World*; iron block; Angligården Park, Herning, Denmark

1961   *Straw Sculpture*; straw, burnt wood; Kunstmuseum, Herning, Denmark

Further Reading

Bodyworks (exhib. cat.), Chicago: Museum of Contemporary Art, 1975

Celant, Germano, *Piero Manzoni*, Turin, Italy: Sonnabend Press, 1972

Celant, Germano, *Piero Manzoni: Catalogo generale*, Milan: Prearo, 1975

Celant, Germano, editor, *Piero Manzoni*, Milan: Electa, and Rivoli, Italy: Museo d'Arte Contemporanea, 1992

Celant, Germano, editor, *Piero Manzoni* (exhib. cat.), London: Serpentine Gallery, and Milan: Charta, 1998

Piero Manzoni (exhib. cat.), Eindhoven, The Netherlands: Stedelijk Van Abbemuseum, 1969

Rubey, D., "Review of Exhibitions at Marisa Del Re Gallery," *Art News* (January 1990)

Ruiz, Alma, and Angela Vattese, *Piero Manzoni: Linee*, Ravenna, Italy: Montanari, and Los Angeles: Museum of Contemporary Art, 1995

San Martin, Francisco Javier, *Piero Manzoni*, Madrid: Nerea Editorial, 1998

Van Der Marck, Jan, "Piero Manzoni," *Art in America* (February 1973)

GIACOMO MANZÙ 1908–1991 *Italian*

Giacomo Manzù focused on a few core themes in his art that he developed with many variations. His works display an intense expressive force that was foreign to the formalisms and experiments of so many contemporary art styles. At their center is an investigation of humankind's deepest values as they appear in daily life, without rhetoric or academic styling.

After working in a gilding shop and a stucco craftsman's shop, Manzù moved to Milan in 1930 and began work on his first sculptures. His style in this early period, between 1929 and 1933, shows a strong influence of the archaic-like suggestions of Modernist primitivism. His fascination with Egyptian, Etruscan, and Romanesque models impelled him toward a forceful simplification of form. His archaism should be understood not only as a formal pursuit, but as an attempt to find an unaffected response to the Classical style promoted by the Fascist regime, which was characterized by pseudo-heroic monumentality.

The Guitarist, a small bronze from 1929, expresses the artist's striving for pure and rigid forms, which translates into an essential geometry. A pervasive sensibility that infuses the figure with a subtle breath of life mitigates the tendency toward concision.

In this early period Manzù's doubts and uncertainties led him to destroy many of his works. He finally found an important point of reference in the Impressionistic sculpture of Medardo Rosso. Between 1934 and 1937 Manzù created a series of small female heads in wax. He did not simply copy Rosso's light effects but began to immerse his works in a constant quiet light. In this way the form does not disintegrate but defines itself subtly. Through his study of Rosso, Manzù connected with the ancient Lombard tradition, characterized by its Leonardesque treatment of light.

The wax *Susanna* of 1937 already evinces these elements. The intense natural light that wraps the tender nude reveals every detail yet softens the fluid outlines. The naturalistic content thus transforms into spiritual content, imparting to the sculpture the infinite tenderness typical of all Manzù's works. This *Susanna* can be seen as the ascendant of a host of female figures at the center of Manzù's artistic endeavor.

His bronze *David* is an early masterpiece. Light is the essential basis of the form, which is perfectly defined. This sculpture is the first of many biblical and evangelical figures whom Manzù, in keeping with the oldest Lombard artistic tradition, portrayed as people one might meet in daily life. *David* appears as a boy from the streets, and in his compressed pose the viewer perceives the imminence of a vital action.

From 1936 to 1938 Manzù explored other themes to which he would return many times. Bronze was his favorite medium, but he also created versions of some works in marble. He began what was to be a 30-year series of cardinals of the Roman Catholic Church and created the first versions of *The Painter and the Model* (a series that continued until the mid 1960s) and of

The Girl on a Chair (repeated many times and culminating with the bronze masterpiece of 1955).

A rigorous pyramid-shaped formal structure characterizes the series dedicated to seated cardinals, where body and vestments join in an indissoluble whole. The folds of the clothing enliven the geometric rigor, preventing staticism and assuring tension and dynamism. Over this long series Manzù tended increasingly to contain the subject in rigid compact forms that look increasingly like funerary pyramids or pillars.

During World War II Manzù began his series of *Crucifixions* expressing violent social denunciation. He eventually collected these pieces in a cycle of reliefs titled *Christ of Our Humanity*. Manzù's intention was to imbue the traditional sacred theme with present-day meaning—opposition to Fascism—by introducing suitable iconographic changes. Identifying the divine with the human, he transformed the religious theme into a secular one. The formal reference is Donatello's ultra-low relief, but Manzù's works never stop at the purely formal. In the 1942 *Deposition* the woman supporting the Christ-like body of the partisan raises her arm in summons and shouts a cry to revolt.

Between 1952 and 1968 Manzù created three important monumental cycles: the *Door of Love* in Salzburg, the *Door of Death* at St. Peter's Basilica in Rome, and the *Door of Peace and War* in Rotterdam. Manzù perfected his low-relief technique, reaching the apex of his poetic inspiration of secular religious feeling founded on a strong narrative capacity.

Manzù met his future wife, Inge, in 1954, which was to prove decisive for a new representation of the female figure. After the first versions of timid young nudes in the *Girl on a Chair* series, he went on in the postwar years to the first delicate ballerinas of the *Dance Step* series and in 1957 to the *Skaters*. Manzù sculpted numerous versions of his wife. In these portrayals her body is enveloped in a vase- or bottle-shaped form—a sort of container of life from which her animated face emerges. Manzù had already experimented earlier with this type of composition in his spindle-shaped *Grand Portrait of a Lady*.

With fatherhood, Manzù returned to the subject of children's games, which he had addressed in the 1940s. The versions of *Giulia and Mileto in the Carriage* date from 1966. He also treated the theme of tenderness between mother and child in a series of bas-reliefs.

Starting in the 1960s Manzù developed a triumphant female figure, full-fleshed and vital. Beginning in 1965 he incorporated this figure in a long series of *Lovers*. In these increasingly open and dynamic compositions, the outward projection of the figures' bodies in different directions expresses their vital energy. He produced some versions in bronze and others in marble or ebony.

Another important theme was *Guantanamera*, which Manzù began in 1968, in which a full-bodied sensual nude stretches out languidly in an armchair. In the interesting series *Folds*, created in fiberglass between 1971 and 1974, Manzù perfected his technique for depicting drapery, which he had already addressed in the *Door of Death*. He patterned his study of rigidly crumpled cloth on the Classical examples of Michelangelo and Gianlorenzo Bernini but gradually assumed formal autonomy and grandeur. In the *Striptease* series from 1967, he experimented with the effect of contrast between the smooth flesh of the figures and the busy capricious drapery.

In the 1980s Manzù replaced *Guantanamera* with *Tebe* in his portrayals of sensual nudes seated in armchairs and returned to the *Dance Step* theme and the domestic subject of the chair. Beginning in the mid 1960s he combined chairs with commonplace objects such as grapevine shoots, pears, and lobsters.

The chair motif recurs in iconographically different variants throughout Manzù's career; he used it as a symbol of daily life, both in religious themes identified as earthly stories and in works expressing his love of family life. A deep interest in humanity, investigated in its indissoluble unity of form and spirit, informs all of his work.

CATERINA BAY

See also **Rosso, Medardo**

Biography

Born in Bergamo, Italy, 22 December 1908. Family was poor; worked in gilding shop and stucco craftsman's shop; went to Paris, 1928, but repatriated shortly thereafter when police found him unconscious from hunger; moved to Milan, 1929; had great success with ten works at 21st Venice Biennale, 1938; taught as professor of sculpture at the Accademia di Brera, Milan, 1940–54; won Grand Prize at fourth Rome Quadriennale, 1942, and Italian Sculpture Prize at 24th Venice Biennale, 1948; held first solo exhibition abroad, at Hanover Gallery, London, 1953; taught at International Summer Academy, Salzburg, Austria, 1954–66; elected to Accademia di San Luca, Rome, Italy, and Belgian Royal Academy, 1954; successfully exhibited at 28th Venice Biennale, 1956; showed for first time in New York, 1957; won commission for two fountains in New York, 1961; named honorary member of American Academy of Arts and Letters, New York, and of Argentina's National Academy of Fine Arts, Buenos Aires; created sets and costumes for Stravinsky's *Oedipus Rex*, 1964; became honorary member of Britain's Royal Academy of Arts and received honorary doctorate from the Royal College of Art, 1970; named honorary foreign member of American Academy of Arts and Science, Boston, 1978. Died in Rome, Italy, 17 January 1991.

Selected Works

1929   *The Guitarist*; bronze; private collection, Milan, Italy

1937   *Susanna*; wax; Galleria Nazionale d'Arte Moderna, Rome, Italy

1938   *David*; bronze; Raccolta Amici di Manzù, Ardea, Italy

1942   *Deposition*; bronze; Collezione Zorzi, Bari, Italy

1946   *Grand Portrait of a Lady*; bronze; A. Conger Goodyear Collection, Museum of Modern Art, New York City, United States

1952–64 *Door of Death*; bronze; St. Peter's Basilica, Rome, Italy

1954   *Dance Step*; bronze; Städtische Kunsthalle, Mannheim, Germany

1955   *Grand Cardinal*; bronze; private collection, Mr. and Mrs. Nathan Cummings, Chicago, Illinois, United States

1957–58 *Door of Love*; bronze; central door of the Salzburg Cathedral, Austria

1965–68 *Door of Peace and War*; bronze; Church of St. Laurence, Rotterdam, the Netherlands

1966   Bust of Inge; bronze; Paul Rosemberg Gallery, New York City, United States

1966   *The Lovers*; bronze; Paul Rosemberg Gallery, New York City, United States

1968   *Guantanamera*; bronze; Paul Rosemberg Gallery, New York City, United States

1987   *Chair*; bronze; Raccolta degli Amici di Manzù, Ardea, Italy

Further Reading

Bossaglia, Rossana, editor, *Manzù* (exhib. cat.), Milan: Electa, 1988

Carrà, Massimo, *Giacomo Manzù*, Milan: Fabbri, 1966

De Micheli, Mario, editor, *Giacomo Manzù*, Milan: Fabbri, 1971; as *Giacomo Manzù*, New York: Abrams, 1974

Eccher, Danilo, editor, *Giacomo Manzù* (exhib. cat.), Calliano, Italy: Manfrini, 1991

Milesi, Silvana, *Manzù*, Bergamo, Italy: Corponove, 1987

Pacchioni, Anna, editor, *Giacomo Manzù*, Milan: Edizioni del Milione, 1948; 2nd edition, as *Giacomo Manzù: Scultore*, edited by Carlo Ludovico Ragghianti, 1957

Pepper, Curtis Bill, *An Artist and the Pope: Based upon the Personal Recollections of Giacomo Manzù*, New York: Grosset and Dunlap, and London: Davies, 1968

Recent Bronzes by Giacomo Manzù (exhib. cat.), New York: Rosenberg, 1985

Rewald, John, *Giacomo Manzù*, London: Thames and Hudson, 1966; Greenwich, Connecticut: New York Graphic Society, 1967

DOOR OF DEATH

Giacomo Manzù (1908–1991)

1952–1964

bronze

h. 7.65 m

St. Peter's Basilica, Vatican City

On 1 July 1947 the Vatican announced a competition for the door at St. Peter's Basilica, and Manzù submitted a design. The following year the jury invited him to enter a second competition, together with 11 other selected artists. In January 1952 he received the commission, the subject being "Triumph of the Saints and Martyrs of the Church."

Manzù immediately encountered many problems treating this theme, which he felt overly rhetorical. He began several sketches, but the work proceeded fitfully and with many changes. The greatest impediment was the Church's insistence on adherence to Roman Catholic dogma.

To solve the impasse Manzù asked to change the subject; in 1961 he received permission from Pope John XXIII to make a "Door of Death." The change enabled him to bend the religious iconography to reflect everyday reality. At the center of the composition is a meditation on the meaning of life and history, on the rejection of violence, and on pain.

Work then proceeded rapidly and without interruption. Manzù created ten panels to be mounted on the front of the door and a strip for the back. The eight lower panels are grouped in four for each side, forming two squares. The spaces among the panels are so narrow that the whole composition seems to be formed by only two panels.

The scene in the left upper corner is the *Death of the Virgin*. Manzù treated the theme like an ordinary death of a woman, with relatives mourning. The angels appear as kind comforters rather than divine creatures. In the right upper corner is the *Deposition*, where Christ, in the fragility of his flesh, is seen as a human victim of violence.

The identification of the divine and the human becomes still more explicit in the lower panels. The first scene on the left portrays Cain's murder of Abel as a deadly brawl between modern-day youth in blue jeans. Below this scene is an image (from Manzù's series of reliefs titled *Christ of Our Humanity*) of a dead partisan hanging upside down, shown together with a grieving girl.

To the right, above and below, are portrayed the deaths of Joseph and of Pope John XXIII, so that two natural deaths are juxtaposed with two violent deaths. The pope kneels in prayer, his hands joined. The large vestment draped from the shoulders covers the entire figure. The image reveals the deep admiration and affection Manzù had for John XXIII. During the period when Manzù was modeling this portrait, the two men had established a unique relationship based on their deep humanity.

The upper part of the other door depicts the lapidation (stoning) of St. Stephen and Gregory VII before the young Robert Guiscard. Below are two ordinary deaths, one in space and the other on the earth: a woman falls to her death, and a mother is struck dead in her chair as her weeping child watches from a small window.

Manzù eliminated friezes, frames, and moldings. The panels attach straight onto the doors; their borders are not squared and polished but notched and uneven. The two symbols of the Eucharist—sheaves of wheat and grapevine shoots—dividing the upper panels from

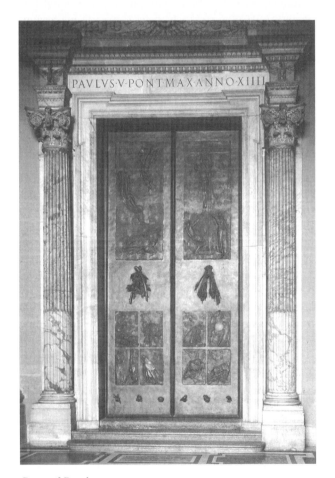

Door of Death
© Scala / Art Resource, NY

the lower are part of the same rigorous conception that characterizes the entire composition.

The same principle informs the images of six animals (a dead bird, dormouse, owl, hedgehog, tortoise biting a snake, crow) placed in sets of three at the foot of the doors, instead of socles. Likewise, the strip stretching across the back of the two doors is simple and unadorned, depicting a line of priests, nuns, bishops, and cardinals. The last image on the left is a young woman, gentle and grieving, who resembles Manzù's many portrayals of women beside martyred Christ figures hanging upside down. On the other end Pope John XXIII seated on his throne is receiving homage from Cardinal Rugambwa, one of the leaders of the Second Vatican Council.

What strikes the viewer most in this extraordinary complex is its simplicity, which eschews sumptuousness. This principle coincides not only with the need of formal rigor but also with the intention of giving an opulent church an image of pure human truth, neither rhetorical nor acclamatory.

In designing the *Door of Death*, Manzù drew on the four reliefs he had done in 1957–58 for the *Door of Love* at Salzburg Cathedral. Both works reflect his desire to simplify the scenes and avoid crowding. The overall image thus acquires enormous power from the relationship between the empty spaces and the panels, which depict no more than two people each. Manzù had used the same compositional scheme in his *Crucifixion* reliefs (later collected in the *Christ of Our Humanity* series), in which the figures act in empty, undescribed spaces. This conception contrasts decidedly with the long sculptural tradition, from Ghiberti to Rodin, which wanted the entire surface of the church door to be bustling with figures.

Compared with his Salzburg doors, Manzù's doors at St. Peter's Basilica display a greater attention to the figures' rich drapery, which fades pictorially into the background. He developed his relief technique still further in his last great cycle, the *Door of Peace and War*, for the Church of St. Laurence in Rotterdam (1965–68). Here he did not divide the scenes into individual panels; the images cover the entire portal, which is crowned by a tympanum.

Religious iconography identified as earthly stories was a recurring theme in the works of Italian painters working in Milan during World War II. Tragedy and the need of social denunciation led painters such as Renato Guttuso and Aligi Sassu—both very close to Manzù—to cast religious iconography in modern terms, with appropriate variations.

Although no direct comparison can be made with contemporary sculptors because they have rarely received such demanding commissions, Manzù accomplished the task of decorating the door at St. Peter's

Basilica brilliantly. The preparatory drawings, models, and final panels constitute one of the greatest artistic complexes in contemporary art, devoid of any rhetoric or academic devices. The narrative power that emerges from them, absent any formalism for its own sake, is capable of investigating man's deepest values—beyond any dogmatic conception—with great perceptiveness and humanity.

CATERINA BAY

Further Reading

Il bozzetto per le porte di San Pietro in Vaticano, Rome: Istituto Grafico Tiberino, 1949

Brandi, Cesare, *Studi per la porta di San Pietro: Bozzetti e varianti esposti alla 32 biennale internazionale di Venezia*, Milan: Edizioni del Milione, 1964

Fuhrmann, Franz, *Giacomo Manzù: Entwürfe zum Salzburger Domtor, 1955–1958*, Salzburg: Verlag Galerie Welz, 1958

Heynold von Graefe, Blida, *Das portal von Manzù fur die Grosse Oper Sankt Laurenskirke zu Rotterdam*, Rotterdam: Pakoed Holding N.V., 1968

Michels, Thomas, *Die Salzburger Domtore*, Salzburg: Verlag Galerie Welz, 1960

Sandri, Giuseppe, *La porta della morte di Giacomo Manzù: San Pietro in Vaticano*, Rome: Edizioni di Storia e Letteratura, 1966

MAORI

see New Zealand

Marathon Boy

Anonymous
late 4th century BCE
bronze
h. 1.30 m
National Archaeological Museum of Athens, Greece

Greek fishermen accidentally discovered the statue of the *Marathon Boy*, an original Greek bronze statue of the later 4th century BCE, in the bay of Marathon (northern Attica) in 1925. Scholars long assumed that it belonged to the cargo of a lost ship (such as the bearded god and horse and jockey from nearby Cape Artemision, or the sculptures from Antikythera and Mahdia), but a reexamination of the underwater site in 1976 did not yield any further artifacts or traces of a wreck.

Represented is a naked youth, probably Hermes or a young, victorious athlete, near life size for a boy aged 12 to 16. He stands in a relaxed pose with the weight on his left leg and the left hip curved outward. The right leg trails behind, with the heel raised from the ground. His left arm is held close to the body and bent forward at the elbow and turned, so that the outstretched left palm faces upward. The right arm by contrast is raised up high and held forward, with the fingers stretched and only the thumb and index finger slightly touching. The inclined head turns toward the left hand. The whole body thus portrays a smooth S curve. A narrow band, knotted in the back and with a leaflike forward-curving tongue at the top, encircles the short curly hair. The sensuous, slender form without pubic hair and developed but not overly prominent musculature indicates the figure's comparatively young age.

The statue is in an excellent state of preservation; only the separately cast frontal section of the right foot is missing (it is now restored), and the left foot is slightly damaged below the ankle. The eyes were inlaid in different material, of which only the pupils are missing. Conservators discovered traces of a black patina when the incrustations caused by its long exposure to seawater were removed.

The figure originally held a large, separately cast object in his left hand. A circular hole in the palm with a bronze pin for attachment is all that remains of this object; the extent of the flattened surface on the left lower arm and palm suggests that it measured at least 20 centimeters in diameter. The figure's gaze was fixed on this lost object, which is crucial for the correct identification of the statue. In its absence the peculiar band worn in the youth's hair provides the best evidence for interpretation. Detailed iconographic studies have shown that it was predominantly athletes in the gymnasium and their god, Hermes, who wore bands of this type, with a spiky central tongue.

Suggested identifications abound, but nothing certain can be stated. The gesture of the right hand in particular is difficult to explain. Scholars have suggested anything from playfully snipping the fingers to holding various objects. Proposals for the left hand include a tortoise for Hermes (out of whose shell he would later create a lyre) or some sort of sacrificial tray for an athlete, onto which he might pour something or reach toward with a branch. A box has also been suggested, from which the figure would have pulled a fillet with his right hand.

Stylistically, the *Marathon Boy* is close to works of the 4th century BCE, especially two statues ascribed to the Athenian sculptor Praxiteles, the *Pouring Satyr* and the youthful *Apollo Sauroktonos* (Lizard Slayer). With the Satyr in particular, a statue frequently copied in the Roman period, the *Marathon Boy* shares the pose and attitude of the arms and head. Although it does not seem that the figure leaned against a tree or support in the manner of the Apollo, the motif of a playful, young god seems appropriate—if the interpretation as

Hermes, particularly one holding a tortoise, were correct.

The similarities between these statues have led many scholars to consider the *Marathon Boy* a work of Praxiteles or his circle from the later 4th century BCE. Some have claimed, however, that the *Marathon Boy* was substantially altered in the Roman period in order to turn it into a decorative figure, such as a tray or lamp bearer (*lychnouchos*), which were popular at that time and of which several examples have been found. It seems that ultimately this claim is solely based on a preliminary description by one scholar (Wrede) who speculated that both arms were attached below the shoulders after a violent break. His note was published in 1926, before the first full report by K.A. Rhomaios on the statue. The lack of a comprehensive scientific study of the *Marathon Boy* precludes final judgment, but the currently known facts suggest that the figure in its entirety is an original 4th-century BCE work.

The statue was cast in several pieces. The alloy used for the bronze contains almost no lead, which in general is typical of Greek bronzes of the Classical period. Similarly, other Classical bronzes (e.g., the Riace statues, *Antikythera Youth*, *Artemision God*) precisely parallel the technique used to strengthen the joints between some of the separately cast sections, in this case, the neck and left arm joints. In this particular technique the bronze caster would cut shallow half ovals into the outer surface of the bronze on either side of the joint in order to create a larger surface that could be filled with welding metal and thus form a stronger joint. The traces of this process seem to have been mistaken for signs of a break and subsequent repair, leading to the unfounded theory about the statue's later adjustment.

Further speculation that the statue came from the grounds of the villa at Marathon of the 2nd-century CE Athenian magnate Herodes Atticus is also unfounded. The *Marathon Boy* therefore remains a fine example of late 4th-century BCE Athenian bronze sculpture. It varies a design that was apparently popular for Late Classical votive statues and was widely appreciated in the Roman period.

THORSTEN OPPER

See also **Greece, Ancient; Praxiteles**

Further Reading

Calligas, P.G., "Statue of a Young Athlete," in *Mind and Body: Athletic Contests in Ancient Greece* (exhib. cat.), no. 71, edited by Olga Tzachou-Alexandri, Athens: Ministry of Culture, National Hellenic Committee, 1988

Haynes, Denys Eyre Lankester, *The Technique of Greek Bronze Statuary*, Mainz, Germany: Von Zabern, 1992

Houser, Caroline, *Greek Monumental Bronze Sculpture of the Fifth and Fourth Centuries B.C.*, New York: Garland, 1987

Picard, Charles, *Manuel d'archéologie grecque: La sculpture*, 5 vols., Paris: Éditions Auguste Picard, 1935–66; see especially vol. 3, 1948

Ridgway, Brunilde Sismondo, *Fourth-Century Styles in Greek Sculpture*, Madison: University of Wisconsin Press, 1997

Rhomaios, K.A., "Ho ephebos tuo Marathonos," *Archaiologikon Deltion* 9 (1924–25)

Rolley, Claude, *La sculpture grecque*, vol. 2, *La période classique*, Paris: Picard, 1999

Schuchhardt, Walter-Herwig, "Der Jüngling von Marathon," *Die Antike* 6 (1930)

Wrede, Henning, "Archäologische Funde des Jahres 1925 in Griechenland," *Archäologischer Anzeiger* 41 (1926)

MARBLE

See **Stone**

MARCELLO (ADÈLE D'AFFRY) 1836–1879 *Swiss, active in France*

One of the most successful woman sculptors of the 19th century, Marcello was born Adèle d'Affry on 6 July 1836 to aristocratic parents in the small town of Givisiez, near Fribourg, Switzerland. Her father, Comte Louis d'Affry, was a lieutenant in the Swiss National Guard and had a penchant for art, creating small watercolors and drawings; her mother was Lucie, the marquise de Maillardoz. Both parents came from important political and long-established Swiss families. Marcello had one sister, Cécile d'Affry, who later became the baronne d'Ottenfels. (Marcello was childless; it is Cécile's children and their descendants who have preserved and protected her legacy). After the death of their father in 1841, their mother provided both children with a classical and advanced education, in which they were privately tutored.

Marcello studied drawing with landscape painter Joseph Fricero, watercolor with the Nazarene painter Peter Cornelius, and sculpture with Heinrich Max Imhof, the latter a follower of Bertel Thorvaldsen. While studying sculpture in Rome with Imhof, she met and married Don Carlo Colonna, Duke of Castiglione Altibranti (sometimes spelled Aldovrandi), in 1856; he died that same year from typhoid fever, which he contracted in Paris. After her husband's death, Marcello went home to Givisiez, then returned to Rome in 1858 to resume her study of sculpture. She stayed at Trinità dei Monte, the grand church atop the Spanish Steps in a neighborhood where a large, international sculptural community had developed by midcentury.

While in Rome she made important contacts, including the painter Henri Regnault and the sculptors Auguste Clésinger and Jean-Baptiste Carpeaux, the latter with whom she shared an enthusiasm for Michelangelo. Although her gender prevented her from attending the École des Beaux-Arts in Paris, she did receive permission to study anatomy and view dissections at the École Pratique de Médecine. She set up a studio in Paris in 1861 at 1, rue Bayard, a building owned by Léon Riesener (a painter and cousin of Eugène Delacroix). According to some sources, she worked in the studio of the sculptor Marie Lefévre-Deumier in the early 1860s.

In 1863 Marcello submitted three works to the Paris Salon exhibition, all of which were accepted. To avoid receiving special consideration because of her title and high social rank (and also to avoid the male chauvinism of the Salon jury), she exhibited her work under the pseudonym by which she is now best known, Marcello, so that her work would be judged on its own merit. Marcello's sculptures were exhibited in 7 of the 13 Paris Salon exhibitions held between 1863 and 1876—an excellent success rate for any artist of the period. Along with these successes, she also exhibited her work at other venues, including the Royal Academy, London (in 1865, 1866, and 1867), and at the Universal Expositions in Paris (1867), Munich (1869), and Vienna (1873).

Marcello was invited by Napoléon III and Empress Eugénie to their infamous *séries* at Fontainebleau in 1863 and at Compiègne in 1864, yet it is important that she not be confused with the emperor's mistress, Virginia Odoini, comtesse de Castiglione. Thus Marcello obtained some imperial commissions, such as for *Bianca Cappello* (now in the Musée de Marseille, France), busts of Marie-Antoinette at Versailles and in prison (for example, *Marie-Antoinette au Temple*), and *Hecate and Cerberus* in 1866. She also created seven busts of the empress, one of which is now in the collection of the Château Musée de Compiègne near Paris. Two of her works were purchased during the Third Republic by its first president, Adolphe Thiers, for the Musée du Luxembourg, a museum of contemporary French works: *Chef Abyssin* and *Bianca Cappello*, thus making Marcello one of only five women artists to have their works included in the museum's collection during the 19th century. Following her death, Marcello's works were removed from the Musée du Luxembourg as those of a foreigner when her Swiss origins came to light.

In 1868 the architect Charles Garnier commissioned Marcello for a sculpture for his Paris Opéra, which opened in 1875. After she exhibited the *Pythian Sybil* in the Salon of 1870, Garnier commissioned Marcello to create a life-size version for permanent location under the grand staircase of the opera, where it remains a tour de force of 19th-century site specificity and an example of Marcello's anticipation of Art Nouveau. Many of her bronze works were cast by the foundry of Ferdinand Barbedienne, certainly the most important

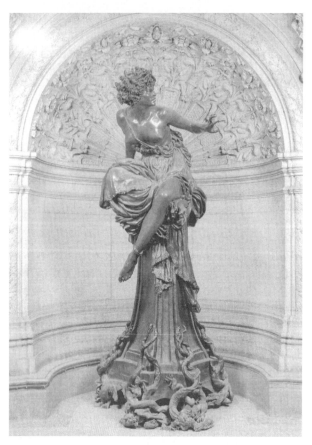

Pythian Sibyl, Opéra, Paris
The Conway Library, Courtauld Institute of Art

bronze foundry of the age, but she was also known to have used Thiébaut Frères.

She counted many important cultural figures among her friends, but she was quite an influential figure in her own right, inspiring painters such as Berthe Morisot and Gustave Courbet to try their hand at sculpture. She shared advice with Carpeaux until his death in 1875, shared models with Regnault in 1868–70, and also helped smooth the way for Courbet's self-imposed exile into Switzerland in 1873.

After 1875 the disease that would finally kill her, tuberculosis, began to take its toll. She concentrated on painting, which was less strenuous for her physically, but she had difficulty finding venues for her paintings. In 1878, before moving to Naples, where she would spend her final days, she prepared for her death admirably, creating her own tombstone and bequeathing a number of her most important works in marble (and some works by her friends in her private collection) to the canton of Fribourg. These works became part of the Musée Marcello, established in 1881, and were arranged, at Marcello's request, in the style of a salon, or reception room. In the 20th century, the museum and its works were disassembled and became

part of the Musée d'Art et d'Histoire in Fribourg, Switzerland, where they remain today.

CATERINA Y. PIERRE

See also **Carpeaux, Jean-Baptiste; Clésinger, Auguste**

Biography

Born in Givisiez (near Fribourg), Switzerland, 6 July 1836. Given name Adèle d'Affry. Parents were Comte Louis d'Affry and Lucie, Marquise de Maillardoz. Studied sculpture in Rome with the Swiss sculptor Heinrich Max Imhof, *ca.* 1853–56, 1858–61; studied anatomy and took first independent studio in Paris, 1861; presented eight works at Exposition Universelle, Paris, 1867; divided time between Fribourg, Nice, and Paris, 1858–76, except during the Franco-Prussian War and the Commune, when she remained in Givisiez. Died in Castellammare (near Naples), Italy, 14 July 1879.

Selected Works

1858	*Self-Portrait*; plaster; Marcello Foundation, Givisiez, Switzerland
1863	*Bianca Capello*; marble; Musée d'Art et d'Histoire, Fribourg, Switzerland
1865	*La gorgone*; bronze; Victoria and Albert Museum, London, England
1866	*Marie-Antoinette au Temple*; marble; Musée d'Orsay, Paris, France
1866	*Hecate and Cerberus*; marble; Montpellier, France
1866	*Portrait of the Empress Eugénie*; wax; Château Musée de Compiègne, Paris, France
1867	*Goethe's Marguerite*; marble; Musée d'Art et d'Histoire, Fribourg, Switzerland
1867–70	*Pythian Sibyl*; bronze; Opéra (Palais Garnier), Paris, France
1869	*Chef Abyssin*; marble; Musée d'Orsay, Paris, France
1870	*Pythian Sibyl*; bronze; Philadelphia Museum of Art, Pennsylvania, United States
1872	*Pythian Sibyl*; marble; Musée Carnavalet, Paris, France
1872	*Adolphe Thiers*; marble; Fondation Marcello, Givisiez, Switzerland

Further Reading

Alcantara, Odette d', *Marcello, Adèle d'Affry, duchesse Castiglione Colonna, 1836–1879: Sa vie, son oeuvre, sa pensée et ses amis*, Geneva: Éditions Générales, 1961

Bessis, Henriette, *Marcello sculpteur*, Fribourg, Switzerland: Musée d'Art et d'Histoire, 1980 (contains an extensive bibliography to 1980)

Bessis, Henriette, "Pourquoi une telle résonance de la *Bianca Capello* de Marcello dans les dernières années du XIXᵉ siècle?" *Gazette des Beaux-Arts* (1982)

Diesbach, Ghislain de, *La double vie de la duchesse Colonna, 1836–1879*, Paris: Perrin, 1988

Easterday, Anastasia Louise, "Charting a Course in an Intractable Profession: Women Sculptors in 19th-Century France," Ph.D. diss., University of California at Los Angeles, 1996

Laurent, Monique, *Marcello: Adèle d'Affry, duchesse Castiglione Colonna* (exhib. cat.), Paris: Musée Rodin, 1980

Loliée, Frédéric, *Les femmes du Second Empire (papiers intimes)*, Paris: Juven, 1906; as *The Gilded Beauties of the Second Empire*, adapted by Bryan O'Donnell, New York: Brentano, and London: Long, 1910

Marcello (1836–1879): Adèle d'Affry, Duchesse Castiglione-Colonna (exhib. cat.), Fribourg, Switzerland: Musée d'Art et d'Histoire de Fribourg, 1980

Pierre, Caterina Y., "Marcello's Heroic Sculpture," *Woman's Art Journal* 22/1 (spring/summer 2001)

Terrapon, Michel, "Questions de métier: A propos de l'oeuvre sculpté de Marcello," *Zeitschrift für Schweizerische Archäologie und Kuntsgeschichte* 38 (1981)

GERHARD MARCKS 1889–1981 *German*

The work of Gerhard Marcks was founded on sculpture created around 1900 in Berlin. Whereas the first generation of modern Berlin sculptors, such as Georg Kolbe, strove to create a harmonious image of man, the autodidactic sculptor Marcks turned away from beauty, harmony, and naturalness quite early. He began working for porcelain manufacturers in 1910 and developed through this experience a great interest in the contemporary efforts to regenerate art through a revival of craft. It was the architect Walter Gropius who introduced Marcks to the Bauhaus in Weimar in 1919 following their initial meeting in Berlin.

As the head of the Bauhaus ceramics workshop in Dornburg, Marcks pursued the ideal of a simple, natural life. In the search for the archetypal, which was typical of the Expressionist era, the sculptor found important sources in medieval and non-European art, as well as in folk art. As with many of his German contemporaries, the opposition, as delineated by art historian Wilhelm Worringer, between a Gothic style as the specific artistic sensibility of a Nordic people and a Classical style rooted in the south lay at the center of Marcks's conception of art. The exploration of Gothic examples and imaginings about medieval society culminated in Marcks's Expressionist ceramic and wood sculptures, as well as in his wood carvings. For Marcks, craft was a step away from the alienation of modern industrial society. He stood among the Bauhaus artists who attempted to think of life holistically. When Gropius wanted to turn the school in the direc-

tion of industry, Marcks stood firmly by the original Bauhaus ideal of the crafts.

Marcks broke away from the Bauhaus in 1925 and accepted a position at Burg Giebichenstein in Halle, a school in which he found a continued veneration for his ideal of craft. During this time, the sculptor increasingly turned away from the formal language of Expressionism. Thus he belonged among the group of sculptors who directed their interest toward a calm objective form where, instead of Gothic art, the art of Antiquity became the focal point of their interest. These sculptors of the 1920s and 1930s did not orient themselves based upon Classical or Hellenistic sculpture, but rather upon archaic sculpture. For the German archaeologists and artists in Marcks's circle, the archaic era was not a predecessor to the Classical period, but rather an independent epoch in which the strict art of the Orient became filled with human life without either of these aspects being dominant. The *Kunstwollen* (literally the will/force that drives the evolution of style) of this archaic time was, according to Marcks, not aimed toward progress (this clearly revealed an antimodern view), but rather toward the completion of the individual work of art.

Marcks's so-called classicism was founded on this reception of the Greek archaic period. He was interested in the combination of strict form and verisimilitude to the model as a way to make modern sculpture that was neither ecstatic (Expressionist) nor sterile (Classicist). In 1930 Marcks created his *chef d'oeuvre* (most important work), the *Thuringian Venus*. In the title itself, two frames of reference are connected: the Thuringian servant girl, Frieda Kronberg, is portrayed with an apple as a Classical Venus. Marcks combined a Classical *contrapposto* (a natural pose with the weight of one leg, the shoulder, and hips counterbalancing one another) with a faithful depiction of the corpulent woman. This sculpture revealed how Marcks used the idea of the "unity of opposites" from the Greek philosopher, Heraclitus, and popularized by Arthur Schopenhauer, as the launching point for thinking about his sculpture.

Marcks's contemporaries praised him for creating a balance in his works that fell between apparent opposites: Gothic (German) plainness and Classical tranquility. After the Nazi rise to power in 1933, Marcks was fired from the teaching faculty. Although some of his works were confiscated, a circle of middle-class art enthusiasts continued to support him. Marcks's conflictual stand during the Third Reich was made evident by his monument *War and Peace* in Bleicherode, Germany. He created this monument for a conservative client in a small town, and it stands as a rare highlight in the monumental art of the 1930s. Although the sculpture remained outside the Nazi discourse, it was

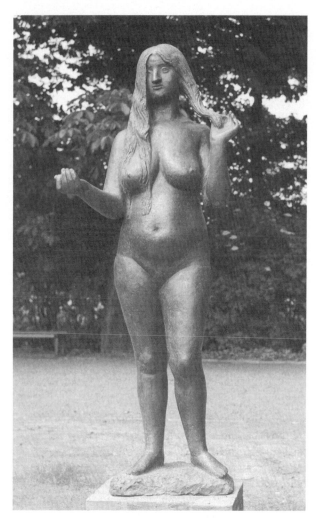

Thuringian Venus
© Gerhard-Marcks-Stiftung, Bremen, Germany

termining which victims were worth memorializing, Marcks dedicated his monuments to all of the war's victims—a remarkable position during the period directly following the war. The claim to universality, which is concealed behind these works, also played a significant role in the discourse on figural or abstract art in Germany. In this debate, Marcks initially displayed a tolerant attitude for all directions, whereas later, after 1953, he emphatically took the side of figural art. Because of this attitude, he headed increasingly toward the margins of West German cultural life, whereas in East Germany he was one of the few respected West German sculptors.

ARIE HARTOG

See also **Germany: 20th Century–Contemporary; Kolbe, Georg**

Biography

Born in Berlin, Germany, 18 February 1889. First exposed to sculpture through August Gaul and Georg Kolbe; shared a studio with Richard Scheibe, 1908–12; founded and led the Bauhaus ceramics studio in Dornburg near Weimar, 1919–24; appointed sculptor at the Burg Giebichenstein in Halle, 1925; traveled to Greece with archaeologist Herbert Koch, 1928; representative director of Burg Giebichenstein, 1928–33; dismissed from teaching position by the Nazis, 1933, because of support for Jewish colleagues; moved to Klosterstrasse studio community in Berlin, 1936; showed at the exhibition *Entartete Kunst* (Degenerate Art), Berlin, 1937; professor at Landeskunstschule in Hamburg, 1945–50; traveled to Spain, Africa, United States, Mexico, Greece; moved to Cologne, 1950. Died in Burgbrohl, Germany, 13 November 1981.

Selected Works

1910 *Standing Man*; bronze; Gerhard-Marcks-Haus, Bremen, Germany
1914 *Relief Workers*, for Modelfactory of Walter Gropius, Cologne, Germany; cement (destroyed)
1920 *Large Thuringian Mother*; maple; private collection, Germany
1930 *Thuringian Venus*; bronze; Gerhard-Marcks-Haus, Bremen, Germany
1932 *Pomona;* marble; Museum of Fine Arts, Boston, Massachusetts, United States
1938 *War and Peace*; bronze; Bleicherode, Germany
1942 *Maya*; bronze; Museum of Modern Art, New York City, United States
1943 *Ver Sacrum;* bronze; Gerhard-Marcks-Haus, Bremen, Germany

still erected in a public space during the Third Reich. Marcks's example shows that a one-dimensional equation of figural art with Nazism is not historically tenable. Art historians have yet to approach a nuanced examination of this topic, as scholarship scarcely differentiates between the diverse cultural groups that formed German cultural life from the 1920s to the 1950s. Marcks could well be one of the most interesting examples of the continuities that exist outside the parameters of the changing political eras in the history of German art.

After World War II, Marcks became a sought-after sculptor for monuments in Germany. Through these monuments, he increasingly came into conflict with the new political and artistic ideas in West Germany. His war monuments displayed a very general Christian or Classical iconography. The motifs were only symbolically connected with the cause of the monuments and appeared to be an attempt to withdraw from political chiasms. In this debate, which centered around de-

1947	Frieze for the Church of St. Catherine; terracotta; Lübeck, Germany
1948	*Prometheus in Chains*; bronze; two casts: Busch-Reisinger-Museum, Cambridge, Massachusetts, United States; Baltimore Museum of Art, Maryland, United States
1949	*Mourning Angel*; marble; St. Maria im Kapitol, Cologne, Germany
1950	*Charon* (Monument to Hamburg); marble; Hamburg-Ohlsdorf Cemetery, Germany
1955	*Herero Woman*; bronze; Gerhard-Marcks-Haus, Bremen, Germany
1960	*Oedipus and Antigone*; bronze; Luther College, Decorah, Iowa, United States

Further Reading

Busch, Günter, editor, *Gerhard Marcks, das plastische Werk*, Frankfurt, Berlin, and Vienna: Propyläen Verlag, 1977

Finkeldey, Bernd, editor, *Gerhard Marcks: Statuen: Plastiken und Zeichnungen aus dem Gerhard-Marcks-Haus Bremen*, Bedburg-Hau, Germany: Stiftung Museum Schloss Moyland, 1999

Frenzel, Ursula, editor, *Gerhard Marcks, 1889–1981: Briefe und Werke*, Munich: Prestel-Verlag, 1989

Gerhard Marcks: A Retrospective Exhibition, Los Angeles: University of California, 1969

Guenther, Peter W., "Gerhard Marcks," in *German Expressionist Sculpture*, edited by Stephanie Barron, Los Angeles: Los Angeles County Museum of Art, 1983

Kath, Ruth R., and Lawrence J. Thornton, compilers, *The Letters of Gerhard Marcks and Marguerite Wildenhain, 1970–1981: A Mingling of Souls*, Ames: Iowa State University Press and Luther College Press, 1991

Rudloff, Martina, editor, *Gerhard Marcks, 1889–1981: Retrospektive*, Munich: Hirmer, 1989

Schierz, Kai Uwe, " '. . . wo man selig ist, da ist auch heute noch Kunst möglich,' Gerhard Marcks und die Suche nach dem Urbild," in *Expressionismus in Thüringen: Facetten eines kulturellen Aufbrucks*, edited by Cornelia Nowak, Schierz, and Justus H. Ulbricht, Jena, Germany: Glaux, 1999

Scott, Yvonne, "The Iconography of Mythological Themes in German Art, c. 1920–1950," thesis, University of Dublin, 2000

Semrau, Jens, editor, *Durchs dunkle Deutschland: Gerhard Marcks, Briefwechsel, 1933 bis 1980*, Leipzig: Seemann, 1995

ORAZIO MARINALI 1643–1720 *Italian*

The Marinali family was from the town of Angarano, near Vicenza, Italy. Surviving sources indicate that Orazio Marinali received his early training from his father, a woodcarver. In 1667 the family moved to Vicenza. According to his first biographer, Giovan Battista Verci, Marinali traveled to Rome not long after, but his artistic development seems to bear no trace of this experience. Much more evident are the traces of a sojourn in Venice, where he appears to have continued his training with Josse de Corte (Giusto de Court), who held sway in Venice until his death in 1679. Marinali interpreted the language of the great Flemish sculptor and adapted it to the cultural climate of the new century. As Semenzato notes, "For this reason, the activity of Orazio Marinali appears decisive for the evolution of Venetian sculpture . . . in the late 17th and early 18th century" (see Semenzato, 1966).

Marinali's first documented work dates from 1675, when he initialed a relief depicting the *Meeting of Christ and Saint Veronica* for an altar in the Church of Santa Maria delle Vergini in Venice. The piece clearly shows his adherence to the formal rhythms that characterized de Court's shop, but it also includes what was to become one of Marinali's leitmotivs: a large knot in the robe. This element reappears in nearly identical form in many of his sculptures, even in the last works he did for the Chapel of the Holy Sacrament at the Church of San Giovanni Battista in Bassano.

Other documented works soon followed for the Church of San Nicolò in Treviso and Vicenza Cathedral, all of them visibly indebted to de Court's solutions. A few years later, in 1680, Marinali and his brothers worked on the great works at the Basilica of Santa Giustina in Padua. All the most highly regarded sculptors of the Venetian area were involved in this enterprise, which implies that Marinali already had a solid reputation.

In the early 1680s Marinali received several important commissions from the city of Bassano, including in 1681 a commission for a statue of St. Bassiano, the city's patron saint, to be set up on a high pedestal in the main square. In an official document written for the occasion, the sculptor and his brothers are called "natives of Bassano and illustrious sculptors from the city of Venice," certifying that Marinali still maintained close relations with Venice. With time, he worked increasingly apart from his brothers, becoming decidedly independent from a stylistic standpoint as well.

The Marinali shop's most important public enterprise was undoubtedly the sculptural decoration of the Monte Berico sanctuary, just outside Vicenza. The commission involved a complex of over 40 statues carved in local stone. Marinali's monogram appears often in this crowded parterre of saints, biblical characters, and moralizing allegories. As well as carving many of the figures himself, he evidently directed the work as a whole.

Although Marinali and his shop produced a quantity of religious sculptures, his most interesting works are garden sculptures, a genre in which he could manifest his greatest inventiveness (also shown in numerous Marinali drawings preserved at the Museo Civico in Bassano). He originated certain decorative typologies that enjoyed ever-increasing success during the 18th

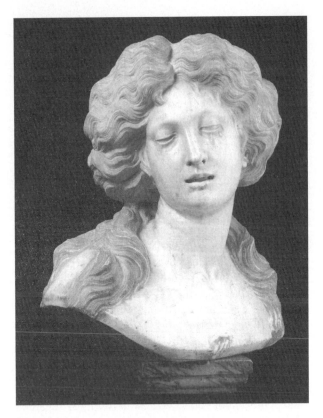

Lucretia
© Araldo de Luca / CORBIS

century and reached their height in Bonazza's enterprises.

In the grand ensembles he designed for a number of great country houses in the Vicenza area, Marinali created truly theatrical scenes crowded with divinities and mythological characters, some involving over a hundred statues. Country houses were traditionally places where people could enjoy pleasures that were forbidden elsewhere, and consequently there was often a great display of nudity in the garden statuary of these residences. Later, in the park of the Conti-Lampertico Villa at Montegaldella, he included a complex stage machine and stock characters from commedia dell'arte to underline the continuously close connection with the theatrical world. Unfortunately, much of the scenographic effect described by contemporaries has been lost because many of the statues (carved from soft stone) have been lost or repositioned, although at least 300 have survived. Marinali's numerous assistants probably carved most of these figures under his supervision, but he certainly did some himself, for instance, the self-portrait and the other statues installed in niches in an unusual grotto created in the garden of Villa Garzadori in Costozza.

Another important part of Marinali's work—the part that remained closest to the 17th-century tradition and harked back to the style of the Tenebrist painters—consisted of character busts and heads. Most of these pieces were intended for the decoration of palaces and villas, but some were for private meditation, such as the extraordinary *Head of Holofernes*. The work's extremely fine anatomical rendering and crude realism presuppose careful studies from real life. Executed with virtuoso skill, it most clearly evinces Marinali's training in Venice, a direct descendant of de Court's finest works.

Less exaggeratedly naturalistic but just as powerful are works such as the well-known *Bravos* and numerous busts of philosophers. A fine example of the latter is the series of nine busts commissioned for the Summer Garden in St. Petersburg, Russia.

Marinali's influence continued to be felt in the Vicenza area for many years after his death, due above all to the activities of his pupils, in particular Giacomo Cassetti. In 1775 Giovan Battista Verci called attention to the importance of Marinali and published a first inventory of his work, which was supplemented in 1779 with a multiauthor volume describing architecture, paintings, and sculpture in Vicenza. In the 19th century, when most art historians were uninterested in Baroque culture, local publications mentioned Marinali only briefly. Only in the 1930s was he rediscovered in a series of publications by Carmela Tua and Giovani Fasolo, which were followed in the 1950s by Franco Barbieri's studies of Vicenza's art heritage. More recent studies continue to throw more complete light on this important artist.

MASSIMO DE GRASSI

See also **Corte, Josse de (Giusto Le Court)**

Biography

Born in Angarano, near Vicenza, Italy, 24 February 1643. Son of a woodcarver, brother of the sculptor Angelo Marinali. Received early training from father; moved to Vicenza (now in Italy) with his family, 1667, where they established a workshop; lived in Vicenza until his death; trained under the Flemish sculptor Josse de Court, until 1679; enrolled in the local stonecarvers' guild, 1674; received important commissions from city of Bassano del Grappa, early 1680s; elected head of the stonecarvers' guild, 1714. Died in Vicenza, 7 April 1720.

Selected Works

1675   *Meeting of Christ and St. Veronica*;
        marble; Staatliche Museen, Berlin,
        Germany
1680   *St. Paul and Angel*; marble; Church of
        Santa Giustina, Padua, Italy

ca. 1690	Allegorical and mythological sculptures; stone; Villa Revedin-Bolasco, Castelfranco Veneto, Treviso, Italy
1690–1703	Allegorical and religious sculptures; *pietra tenera* (limestone); Church of Santa Maria di Monte Berico, Vicenza, Italy
ca. 1695	Allegorical and mythological sculptures; stone; Villa Lampertico Montegaldella, Vicenza, Italy
1697	*Virgin and Child with SS. Dominic and Catherine*; marble; Church of San Nicolò, Treviso, Italy
1710	Self-portrait; marble; Museo Civico d'Arte e Storia, Vicenza, Italy
ca. 1715	Nine allegorical sculptures; marble; Summer Garden, St. Petersburg, Russia

Further Reading

Androssov, Sergei, *Pietro il Grande: Collezionista d'arte veneta* (exhib. cat.), translated by Benedetta Sforza, Venice: Canal, 1999

Barbieri, Franco, *L'attività dei Marinali per la decorazione della Basilica di Monte Berico*, Vicenza, Italy: Rumor, 1960

Galasso, Giovanna, "Orazio Marinali e la sua bottega: Opere sacre," in *Scultura a Vicenza*, edited by Chiara Rigoni, Verona, Italy: Cariverona, 1999

Saccardo, Mario, *Notizie d'arte e di artisti vicentini*, Vicenza, Italy: LIEF, 1981

Semenzato, Camillo, *La scultura veneta del Seicento e del Settecento*, Venice: Alfieri, 1966

Verci, Giambattista, *Notizie intorno alla vita e alle opere de' pittori, scultori e intagliatori della città di Bassano*, Venice: Gatti, 1775; reprint, as *Pittori, scultori e intagliatori della città di Bassano*, Sala Bolognese, Italy: Forni, 1975

MARINO MARINI 1901–1980 *Italian*

At 16 Marino Marini enrolled at the Fine Arts Academy in Florence. He initially studied painting, but in 1922 he began studying sculpture with Domenico Trentacoste. From the start Marini experimented with the different media, creating works in glazed terracotta (*People* 1929), painted wood (*Ersilia*, 1930–49), plaster (*Youth*, 1928–30), and bronze (*Bas-Relief*, 1932).

His discovery of the art of the ancient Mediterranean peoples, particularly the Etruscans, was a crucial step in Marini's artistic development. In 1929, struck by Marini's interest in ancient art, the sculptor and teacher Arturo Martini designated Marini as his successor at the Villa Reale Art School in Monza. Shortly after moving to Milan, Marini exhibited at the second Tuscan Novecento Show. In the 1930s he moved away from the Novecento group; the bare essentiality of his sculpture and his archaic-like approach were at odds with the soft atmospheres its members preferred. In this period the young artist traveled throughout Italy and Europe. In 1930 he met Pablo Picasso, Georges Braque, Henri Laurens, Jacques Lipchitz, and Aristide Maillol in Paris, but his encounter with the major figures in the European avant-garde was not decisive for Marini's artistic development; he continued along paths of his own. His use of a variety of materials remained constant throughout his work, as did his use of color, for him an indispensable means of expression, seen, for example, in his polychrome bronze *Juggler* (1939). Marini ceaselessly explored the possibilities of sculptural language, playing infinite variations on an extremely short thematic range. Indeed, his sculptures revolve around only three subjects: the female nude, portraits, and horses. With these themes—the canonical genres of Classical sculpture—and working incessantly on form, he found he could express himself completely. The joy of nature expressed in the series of *Pomonas*, the anguish of wartime in the *Prisoner* (1943), and anxiety for the future in *The Cry* (1962) all emerge forcefully from this small thematic core.

Marini found inspiration not only in ancient Mediterranean sources—Etruscan terracottas and sarcophagi and ancient Greek sculpture—but also in medieval Tuscan sculpture and the figures of German Gothic. In 1934 Marini saw the equestrian statue of Henry II (although some have speculated it was Frederick II), known as the Bamberg *Rider* (*ca.* 1230), in Bamberg Cathedral in Germany. This experience engendered Marini's most fertile vein of production: starting in 1936, men on horseback became his favorite subject. Through his *Riders* one can trace both his artistic path and his human experience. A symbol of the relationship between humankind and nature, the age-old image of the horseback rider boasts an impressive iconographic success and a powerful symbolic force. Marini bent it to his own expressive needs, making it into a modern figure, a representation of humanity's anxiety and tragedy. His riders are not victorious captains but small, sometimes even mutilated, men unable to dominate increasingly untrustworthy horses. Yet Marini was also capable of irony, as witness his 1937 *Gentleman on Horseback*, which ridicules the Fascist regime's militaristic rhetoric.

Marini also intensified his production of portraits in the 1930s, creating works that hold the greatest interest for their psychological penetration and sculptural form, such as his 1937 bronze *Portrait of Fausto Melotti*. He devoted himself constantly to portraiture, and over time he put together an extraordinary gallery of personages—chiefly artists and intellectuals and including his *Portrait of Mies Van de Rohe*—that has no parallel in contemporary sculpture.

In 1938 Marini married Mercedes Predazzi (nicknamed "Marina"). After teaching for a year at the Turin Academy, in 1941 he was appointed to the sculpture

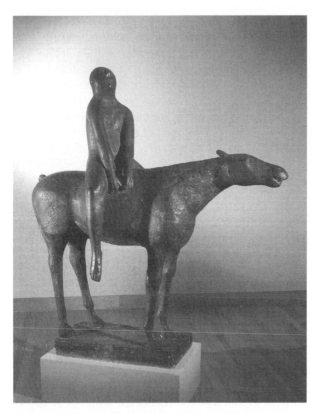

Horseman (*Il cavaliere*, 1947, Tate Gallery, London)
© 2001 Artists Rights Society (ARS), New York / SIAE, Rome

chair at the Brera Academy in Milan. Italy had already entered the war, and the couple took refuge in Locarno, Switzerland, after Marini's studio was bombed. Here Marini met many artists, including Alberto Giacometti, Fritz Wotruba, Otto Baenninger, Hermann Haller, and Germaine Richier. His sculptures from this period, such as the 1943 *Dancer*, are sad and inwardly troubled, severe, and dark. In 1946 Marini returned to Milan, and in 1948 he exhibited at the 24th Venice Biennale, where he met Henry Moore and the American art dealer Curt Valentin.

The war left a deep mark on Marini. His *Riders* became cripples thrown by increasingly skittish mounts, such as the 1953 bronze *Miracle*. With the exception of *Angel of the City* (also known as *Rider*), which is pervaded by a limitless vital force, Marini's postwar sculptures display a tragic pattern. Horses and riders, traversed by deep fissures, writhe in highly dramatic positions. Likewise, the circus people that had previously been among Marini's favorite subjects acquired a tragic sense. *Jugglers* and *Dancers* reappeared but were now joyless, with mutilated limbs and sad faces.

Valentin organized a one-man show for Marini in New York in 1950, which helped the artist make a name for himself in the American market and achieve international success. In the United States he associated with renowned artists such as Alexander Calder and Jean (Hans) Arp. In 1952 he won the sculpture prize at the Venice Biennale; two years later Rome's Lincei Academy awarded him the Feltrinelli Grand International Sculpture Prize. Beginning in the late 1950s Marini received a number of important European commissions for large works; one was the six-meter-high bronze *Rider* created in 1957–58 for The Hague. In Italy he received in 1966 a grand exhibition at Palazzo Venezia in Rome.

In the early 1970s Marini virtually stopped working; he had fallen sick, and his doctors prescribed rest and long periods of solitude. He died in Viareggio, near Lucca, on 6 August 1980. But his *Riders*, from the height of their grim monumentality, continue to stand as a grave warning for modern man, projecting dark and disquieting shadows across city squares around the world.

LUCIA CARDONE

See also **Etruscan Sculpture; Giacometti, Alberto; Italy: 20th Century–Contemporary; Laurens, Henri; Lipchitz, Jacques; Maillol, Aristide; Picasso, Pablo; Richier, Germaine**

Biography

Born in Pistoia, Italy, 27 February 1901. Enrolled at Accademia di Belle Arti, Florence, 1917, to study painting, then switched to sculpture under Domenico Trentacoste, 1922; designated by Arturo Martini to take sculpture chair at Scuola d'Arte della Villa Reale, Monza, Italy, 1929; moved to Milan, 1929; won first prize for sculpture at 2nd Rome Quadriennale, 1935; met Picasso, Braque, Laurens, Lipchitz, and Maillol, Paris, 1920s and later in 1930s; taught for one year at Turin Academy, then obtained sculpture chair at Accademia di Brera, Milan, 1941; spent war years in Locarno, Switzerland; returned to Milan, 1946; exhibited at 24th Venice Biennale, 1948, and met Henry Moore and Curt Valentin, 1950; won sculpture prize at 26th Venice Biennale, 1952; awarded Feltrinelli Grand International Sculpture Prize by Accademia dei Lincei, Rome, 1954. Died in Viareggio, Italy, 6 August 1980.

Selected Works

1929   *People*; colored terracotta; Galleria d'Arte Moderna, Marino Marini Museum, Milan, Italy

1935   *Pomona*; bronze; San Pancrazio Museum, Florence, Italy

1937   *Gentleman on Horseback*; polychrome plaster; San Pancrazio Museum, Florence, Italy; cast: bronze; National Gallery of Canada, Ottawa, Ontario, Canada

1939   *Juggler*; polychrome bronze; San Pancrazio Museum, Florence, Italy

1940   *Portrait of Mies Van der Rohe*; polychrome plaster; San Pancrazio Museum, Florence, Italy

1942   *Rider*; polychrome terracotta; Marino Marini Foundation, Pistoia, Italy

ca. 1948 *Angel of the City* (also known as *Rider*); bronze; Peggy Guggenheim Collection, Venice, Italy; another bronze cast: *ca.* 1950, Solomon R. Guggenheim Foundation, New York City, United States

1951   *Horse*; bronze; National Trust for Historic Preservation, Nelson A. Rockefeller bequest, Pocantico Historic Property, New York City, United States

1953   *Miracle*; bronze; City Hall, Pistoia, Italy

1959–60 *Miracle*; bronze; San Pancrazio Museum, Florence, Italy

1976–77 *Portrait of Oskar Kokoschka*; colored plaster; San Pancrazio Museum, Florence, Italy

Further Reading

Busignani, Alberto, *Marino Marini*, Florence: Sadea/Sansoni, 1968; as *Marini*, London and New York: Hamlyn, 1971

Casé, Pierre, editor, *Marino Marini*, Milan: Skira, London: Thames and Hudson, and New York: Abbeville Press, 1999

Exhibition Marino Marini (exhib. cat.), Tokyo: The National Museum of Modern Art, 1978

Guastalla, Giorgio, and Guido Guastalla, editors, *Centro di documentazione dell'opera di Marino Marini*, Pistoia, Italy: Comune di Pistoia, and Livorno, Italy: Graphis Arte, 1979

Hammacher, Abraham Marie, *Marino Marini: Sculpture, Painting, Drawing*, New York: Abrams, and London: Thames and Hudson, 1970

Hunter, Sam, *Marino Marini: The Sculpture*, New York: Abrams, 1993

Roditi, Edouard, "Marino Marini," in *Dialogues on Art*, by Roditi, London: Secker and Warburg, 1960; New York: Horizon Press, 1961

Waldberg, Patrick, *Marino Marini: Complete Works*, New York: Tudor, 1970

ANGEL OF THE CITY (RIDER)

Marino Marini (1901–1980)

ca. 1948

bronze

h. 2.48 m

Peggy Guggenheim Collection, Venice, Italy (another bronze cast, ca. 1950, at Solomon R. Guggenheim Foundation, New York City, United States)

Angel of the City, or *Rider*, is a typical yet unique example of Marini's sculpture. The work was origi-nally installed on the terrace of Peggy Guggenheim's home in Venice. It stands high, looking over the city, displaying the confident authority of a protective fig-ure, hence the title.

The forms are juxtaposed in a cross: the animal stretches out horizontally, and the rider's position com-pletes and underlines the cruciform composition. With its legs planted firmly on the ground, the horse is breaking into a run with its head forward and a fearless expression. The man's head turns to the sky with an expression of joy and vitality that is reaffirmed by an explicit reference to sexual potency. The solidity of the composition and the compact volumes impose themselves forcefully on the viewer. The surfaces are smooth, without fissures or wrinkles. Produced not long after World War II, the figure of the rider looks forward to the future with no inner wounds or anguish. The rider spreads his arms out and opens his lungs to breathe once again after a long fearful period. *Angel of the City* can be read as an outburst of will, a victory of reason and hope over the absurd brutality of war.

Men on horseback were unquestionably Marini's favorite subject and the most frequent in his vast pro-duction. The image of the rider appeared for the first time in 1936, two years after he saw the equestrian statue of Henry II (known as the Bamberg *Rider*) in the Bamberg Cathedral, Germany. Although familiar with the Roman iconography of Marcus Aurelius and the sculptures of Donatello and Verrocchio, he was deeply impressed by the almost magical figure, sus-pended in time, of this enigmatic northern cavalier. Nonetheless, he eschewed the solemn monumentality that traditionally characterized the subject in Italian art and sought to interpret it in a nonrhetorical mode. In the late 1930s the Tuscan artist began work on a series of works titled *Pilgrim* or *Rider*, which constitute a kind of Mediterranean response to the Nordic sugges-tions of Bamberg.

Marini produced variations on the Classical theme of the horseback rider with a modern perspective and spirit. He sought images capable of reproposing the sense of myth in the context of contemporary society. Although tied to the very origins of sculpture, his equestrian compositions acquire new symbolic conno-tations in Marini's universe. They are firmly rooted in the present. They often give vent to a sincere sense of humor that can also reveal a critical vein. For example, in the *Gentleman on Horseback* the awkwardness of the personage, combined with the archaic style and the openly antiheroic tone, seems intended to ridicule the idea of the bellicose leader propounded in the Fascist regime's pompous rhetoric.

The horror Marini felt from the war is especially apparent in many of his riders. In contrast to *Angel of the City*, they are small men, sometimes mutilated, sometimes reduced to lifeless skeletons, or inept riders who cannot control their mounts, which rear in dizzying twists and throw them to the ground. The tragic progression culminates in the series of desperately gesticulating riders thrown from their horses. Even in their form they differ greatly from *Angel of the City*'s polished strength. The surfaces wrinkle and the volumes become contorted. In a 1949 *Rider* Marini echoed the composition of the *Angel of the City*—the horse's head is extended forward and the rider's arms are outspread, exactly as they are in the *Angel of the City*—but the meaning and visual impact differ altogether. The 1949 piece looks like the fossilized remains of its luminous predecessor. The horse's legs are thin and unsteady; the man is mutilated and wounded. The surface is rough and uneven, as if the material were breaking down. The compact strength of the *Angel of the City* has disappeared; the great hope expressed the year before seems transformed into bitter disappointment.

The names Marini chose for his sculptures in the postwar years were bleak and ominous, for example, *Miracle* and *Warrior*. These new titles testify explicitly to the artist's concerns, his fears for humankind and the fate of the world. His riders took on fanciful colors and odd shapes in an ever more precarious equilibrium between man and horse. Nonetheless, Marini's gaze was never one of surrender. To the contrary, the terrifying images of his postwar riders impose themselves with force, as a resolute warning to plan a better future. The clearest example of this will to change the world is unquestionably the vigorous rider in *Angel of the City*.

The artist's vision became intensely dramatic in the postwar years and remained so. The image of the man on horseback, traditionally associated with triumphant military parades, became a tragic symbol of defeat and the seal of an obscure prophecy. Marini's riders rise up as severe warnings for modern humanity, projecting eerie and disquieting shadows. In the midst of this vast series, his *Angel of the City* is an exceptional figure of hope and joy.

LUCIA CARDONE

Further Reading

Busignani, Alberto, "I cavalli di Bamberg," in *Marino Marini*, by Busignani, Florence: Sadea/Sansoni, 1968

Haftmann, Werner, "Sul contenuto mitico dell'arte di Marino Marini," in *Marino Marini*, edited by Carlo Pirovano, Milan: Electa, 1988

Hunter, Sam, "Equestrians, Warriors, and Miracles," in *Marino Marini: The Sculpture*, New York: Abrams, 1993

Meneguzzo, Marco, editor, *Marino Marini: Cavalli e cavalieri*, Milan: Skira, 1997

ARTURO MARTINI 1889–1947 *Italian*

Arturo Martini is considered one of Italy's most important and problematic 20th-century sculptors, a many-sided artist whose output was rich and variegated. His restlessness—typical of a deeply mystical man who expressed himself through physical matter—is reflected in his artworks, in his writings, and above all in his biography. In fact, Martini moved about from one city to another, from one milieu to another, and from one medium to another. He wondered continually about art, and in the last years of his life, this ceaseless questioning led him to reject sculpture altogether.

He was born in 1889 in Treviso, not far from Venice, and his family was very poor and large. At 16 he was already apprenticed to a goldsmith. At the same time, he studied modeling with Giorgio Martini, father of the etcher Alberto Martini. His first sculpture, in terracotta, dates from 1905. In 1909, thanks to a scholarship received from his employer in Treviso, the Gregorio Gregorij pottery works, he was able to spend some time in Munich and attend Adolf von Hildebrand's lectures on sculpture.

In 1912 Martini showed several works at the Salon d'Automne in Paris, but his name began to circulate only a year later, when he exhibited a piece—a ceramic head titled *Child Full of Love*—at Ca' Pesaro in Venice. The title itself seemed a provocation. Although inspired by the decorativeness of the Viennese Secession, Martini's sculpture, modeled in clay and replicated in seven ceramic castings, alluded clearly to Amadeo Modigliani's contemporary stone heads. Despite polemics, all seven pieces were sold.

Martini continued to seek new experiences and a style of his own. The outbreak of World War I was a crucial event that left a deep mark on his whole life. He was drafted in 1916 but asked to contribute to the war effort as a worker. Accordingly, he was sent to work in Vado Ligure as a foundryman at a weapons factory. In Liguria he learned the art of hot casting and met Brigida Persano, whom he married in 1920. During the war he was hurt and discharged. During his convalescence, Martini published his first book, *Contemplazioni* (1918). The work is unique in that it does not contain written text, but a sort of musical score with a series of vertical lines. The book was probably conceived as a thanksgiving offering for having survived the war and his afflictions, and its mystical message is heightened by a circle containing an alpha and an omega, the two Greek letters that symbolize the beginning and the end. The same letters appear in another work of Martini's from the same period, the baptismal font in the church of Rivalta. Significantly, this piece was executed in cement, a commonplace but very modern material.

After the war, Martini became fascinated with Futurism, although not for long. His attachment to the movement seemed so sincere that he came to write the *Manifesto of Futurist Sculpture* in 1920. Nonetheless, the next year he was side by side with the artists who congregated around *Valori Plastici*, a review published in Rome by Mario Broglio. During this time, he became friends with Carlo Carrà and the brothers Giorgio De Chirico and Alberto Savinio.

Martini's intense production during the 1920s and 1930s included *Maternity* (1921), which revealed his love of Gothic sculpture; *The Dead Lover*, a multicolored plaster statue that recalls Etruscan terracottas; *Woman from Pisa*, an intense, moving bronze that ranks as one of his masterpieces; another *Maternity* (1930) carved in wood that calls to mind sculptures by Jacopo della Quercia and Tino di Camaino; and a beautiful *Virgin Mary and Child* (1930), also in wood and reflecting the style of Benedetto Antelami in the baptistery at Parma (see Nonveiller, 1993).

Martini's most original statue, *Woman Swimming under Water*, dates from 1941. This monumental work, which the sculptor called "the flower of my research," was exhibited at the Venice Biennale in 1942. Its importance lies essentially in its singular dynamism, which Martini derived from the cinema. He loved the movies and confessed that he had been inspired for this piece by the swimmers in W.S. Van Dyke's 1928 film *White Shadows in the South Seas*. His most experimental period culminated in 1943–44. His production during these two years reveals a singular affinity among painting, sculpture, and drawing.

Asked about his favorite painters, Martini named two who had possessed a special feeling for plastic forms: Giotto (see Vallese, 1997) and Paul Cézanne (see Nonveiller, 1994). His favorite sculptor was Michelangelo, who he said "knew the secret of how to put muscles in the right place, as counterweights" (see Mazzolà and Mazzolà, 1968). Every time he intended to work in marble, Martini followed in the Tuscan master's footsteps, nearly always choosing Carrara marble from the same quarries as Michelangelo had used.

In 1945 Martini published his famous book *La Scultura Lingua Morta* (Sculpture Is a Dead Language), based on posthumously published talks with Gino Scarpa.

GIOVANNA CHECCHI

Biography

Born in Treviso, Italy, 11 August 1889. Major formative experiences in Venice, Munich, Paris, and Milan; published book, *Contemplazioni*, 1918; joined the Plastic Values group on Carlo Carrà's invitation, 1920s; traveled to United States with Maurice Stern to execute monument, 1927; won first prize for sculpture at 1st Quadriennale, Rome, 1931; first biography published, 1933; worked on reliefs of the Arengario, Milan, 1941–43. Died in Milan, Italy, 22 March 1947.

Selected Works

1913   *Child Full of Love*; ceramic; Galleria d'Arte Moderna di Ca' Pesaro, Venice, Italy

1921   *The Dead Lover*; painted plaster; private collection, Fernando Vignanelli, Arnoldo Becchini

1928   *Woman from Pisa*; bronze; Museo Civico, Treviso, Italy

1930   *The Happy Bride*; plaster; private collection, Florence, Italy

1930   *Maternity Venturi*; wood; Civica Galleria d'Arte Moderna, Turin, Italy

1931   *Woman at the Window*; terracotta; Galleria Nazionale d'Arte Moderna, Rome, Italy

1932   *Sisters (Stars)*; terracotta; Galleria Nazionale d'Arte Moderna, Rome, Italy

1932   *Venus of the Harbors*; terracotta; Museo Civico, Treviso, Italy

1935   *Sprinter*; plaster; Banca Popolare Vicentina, Vicenza, Italy

1941   *Woman Swimming under Water*; bronze; Museo Civico, Treviso, Italy

1942   *Livy*; marble; Università degli Studi, Facoltà di Lettere, Padua, Italy

1946   *Palinurus*; marble; Università degli Studi, Palazzo del Bo, Padua, Italy

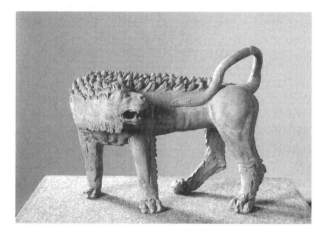

Chimera (ca. 1935)
© Elio Ciol / CORBIS

Further Reading

Benzi, Fabio, editor, *Arturo Martini: Gli anni di Anticoli Corrado*, Rome: Quasar, 1991

Bossaglia, Rossana, *Da Wildt a Martini: I grandi scultori italiani del Novecento*, Milan: Skira, 1999

De Micheli, Mario, and Claudia Gian Ferrari, editors, *Arturo Martini: Il gesto e l'anima; Le geste et l'âme; The Gesture and the Soul*, Milan: Electa, 1989

Manzanato, Eugenia, and Nico Stringa, *Il giovane Arturo Martini: Opere dal 1905 al 1921*, Rome: De Luca Edizioni d'Arte, 1989

Mazzola, Maria, and Natale Mazzola, editors, *Gino Scarpa: Colloqui con Arturo Martini*, Milan: Rizzoli, 1968

Nonveiller, Giorgio, "La scultura di Arturo Martini tra la fine degli anni '20 e i primi anni '30 e il confronto con l'antico," *Arte documento* (1993)

Nonveiller, Giorgio, "Il problema dell'ombra nei disegni di Arturo Martini del 1943–44, con un inedito," *Arte documento* (1994)

Mazzolà, Maria, and Natale Mazzolà, editors, *Gino Scarpa: Colloqui con Arturo Martini*, Milan: Rizzoli, 1968

Stringa, Nico, editor, *Arturo Martini: Opere degli anni quaranta*, Milan: Electa, 1989

Stringa, Nico, editor, *Arturo Martini: La scultura interrogata. Opere dal 1934 al 1947*, Venice: Marsilio, 1999

Vallese, Gloria, "Arturo Martini intimo e segreto," *Arte* (December 1997)

Vianello, Gianni, Nico Stringa, and Claudia Gian Ferrari, *Arturo Martini: Catalogo ragionato delle sculture*, Vicenza, Italy: Neri Pozza, 1998

IVAN (PETROVICH) MARTOS 1754–1835 *Ukrainian, active in Russia*

A contemporary of Antonio Canova and Bertel Thorvaldsen, Ivan (Petrovich) Martos was for all practical purposes the head of the Russian sculptural school over the course of several decades. His most significant creative achievements occurred in the field of memorial and monumental plastic art. From the beginning of the 1780s, Martos was a consistent proponent of Classicism, and to the end of his life, he remained devoted to the "style of the epoch," reflecting all stages of its evolution in his works.

After graduating from the St. Petersburg Academy of Arts, Martos perfected his craft in Rome for six years, studying antique sculpture and attending the French Academy and the Academy of St. Luke. His works from this period were not preserved, but it is known that Martos closely heeded the counsel of the painters Pompeo Batoni and Carlo Albacini, as well as that of Anton Raphael Mengs, with whom he associated in the last years of his scholarship.

The Classical foundation of Martos's art was formed from the artistic impetus he received in Italy. Not inclined toward any divergences of method, he single-mindedly polished a style oriented toward Antiquity. Tombstones became his favorite area of activity during his early years. Many of these are located in the necropolises of Alexander Nevsky Lavra (St. Petersburg) and the Donskoi Monastery (Moscow). Working with equal mastery in marble and bronze,

Martos strove unfailingly to attain harmonious spatial and linear forms. He was uniquely able to fill sculptural forms with the energy of restrained mourning. "I saw here how the marble weeps, as if tears are flowing! It seemed to me that I also heard groans, so much life did the artist pour into his tomb sculpture," wrote Martos's contemporary, Feodor Nikolaevich Glinka, after visiting the mausoleum of Paul I in the park of his country residence. Other gravestones constructed by Martos for members of the imperial family were also installed in Pavlovsk. Among them is a monument, extolled by poets, to the Grand Princess Alexandra Pavlovna, who was given in marriage to the heir of the Austrian throne and died unexpectedly at the age of 18.

The statue of *Actaeon* for the Grand Cascade in Peterhof, recast several times in bronze, and an enormous 15-meter frieze *Moses Striking Water from the Rocks*, which decorates the attic of Kazan Cathedral and is pointed toward Nevsky Prospekt, in St. Petersburg, are also among Martos's best works. However, his most famous monumental work is the memorial to Kuz'ma Minin and Prince Dmitry Pozharsky, erected in 1818 on Moscow's Red Square. Work on the monument lasted many years and was interrupted by the War of 1812. It must be noted, however, that the fervor of Russia's victory over Napoléon (1814) contributed greatly to the extraordinary public response to Martos's monument. Historical parallels inevitably arose in the people's consciousness because Minin and Pozharsky, heroes of 17th-century Russian history, also liberated Moscow from an enemy invasion.

During his late creative period, Martos continued to construct monuments for city squares, acting as a founder of one of the most popular genres of 19th-century Russian sculpture. Many definite stylistic changes were occurring in his monumental projects of the 1820s. Starting from the ideas characteristic of Late Classicism—modeling subjects after personages of Antiquity and using traditional allegories (such as in the monument to the Russian scientist and scholar Mikhail V. Lomonosov in Arkhangel'sk and the monument to the Duke of Richelieu in Odessa)—Martos moved on to the solution of new creative problems involving the execution of strictly portrait statues in contemporary costume, such as the monument to Alexander I in Taganrog. One of his students, Boris (Ivanovich) Orlovsky, proved to be a worthy follower in this line of developing Russian monumental art.

ELENA V. KARPOVA

See also **Canova, Antonio; Orlovsky, Boris (Ivanovich); Russia and Soviet Union; Thorvaldsen, Bertel**

Biography

Born in Ichnya, Chernihiv province, Ukraine, Russian Empire, 1754. Admitted to the St. Petersburg Academy of Arts, 1764; studied with Louis Rollan and Nicolas-François Gillet; received two gold medals, 1772–73; sent to Rome on a scholarship, 1773–79; upon his return taught a sculpture course at the Academy of Arts. Titles conferred: academician (1782), adjunct professor (1785), senior professor (1794), adjunct rector (1799), rector of sculpture (1814), distinguished rector (1831); honorary member of Vilnius University, Lithuania, Russian Empire (1818), Antwerp Academy of Arts, Belgium (1827), the Russian Academy (1829). Died in St. Petersburg, Russia, 5 April 1835.

Selected Works

1782　　Tombstone for M.P. Sobakina; marble; Museum of Architecture, Donskoi Monastery, Moscow, Russia

1782　　Tombstone for S.S. Volkonskaya; marble; State Tretyakov Gallery, Moscow, Russia

1783–90　Tombstone for N.I. Panin; marble; State Museum of Urban Sculpture, St. Petersburg, Russia

1792　　Tombstone for Y.S. Kurakina; marble; State Museum of Urban Sculpture, St. Petersburg, Russia

1803　　Tombstone for E.I. Gagarina; bronze; State Museum of Urban Sculpture, St. Petersburg, Russia

1804–06　*Moses Striking Water from the Rocks*; Pudozh stone; Kazan Cathedral, St. Petersburg, Russia

1804–18　Monument to K. Minin and D. Pozharsky; bronze; Red Square, Moscow, Russia

1805–07　Tombstone for Paul I, "Spouse-benefactor"; marble; Pavlovsk, St. Petersburg, Russia

1807–15　Monument to the Grand Princess Alexandra Pavlovna; marble; Pavlovsk, St. Petersburg, Russia; variant: State Russian Museum, St. Petersburg, Russia

1823–28　Monument to Armand Emmanuel Richelieu; bronze; Primorsky Boulevard, Odessa, Ukraine

1826–28　Monument to M.V. Lomonosov; bronze; Arkhangel'sk, Russia

1829–31　Monument to Alexander I; plaster; State Russian Museum, St. Petersburg, Russia; cast (original destroyed 1917; recast 1998): bronze; Taganrog, Russia

Further Reading

Androssov, Sergei, "Martos, Ivan," in *The Dictionary of Art*, edited by Jane Turner, vol. 20, New York: Grove, and London: Macmillan, 1996

Ermonskaia, V.V., G.D. Netunakhina, and T.F. Popova, *Russkaia memorial'naia skul'ptura: K istorii khudozhestvennogo nadgrobiia v Rossii XI–nachala XX v.* (Russian Memorial Sculpture: Toward a History of Artistic Tombstones in Russia, 11th–Early 20th Centuries), Moscow: Iskusstvo, 1978

Gosudarstvennyi Russkii Muzei (Russian State Museum), *Skul'ptura, XVIII–nachalo XX veka: Katalog* (Sculpture, 18th–Early 20th Centuries: Catalogue), Leningrad: Iskusstvo, 1988

Russkaia terrakota epokhi klassitsizma (Russian Terracotta of the Classical Period; exhib. cat.), Leningrad: Gos. Russkii Muzei, 1988

Kovalenskaia, N.N., *Martos*, Moscow, Leningrad: Iskusstvo, 1938

Kovalenskaia, N.N., *Russkii Klassitsizm: Zhivopis', skul'ptura, grafika* (Russian Classicism: Painting, Sculpture, Graphic Art), Moscow: Iskusstvo, 1964

Kudriavtsev, A.I., and G.N. Shkoda, *Aleksandro-Nevskaia Lavra: Arkhitekturnyi ansambl' i pamiatniki nekropolei* (Alexander Nevsky Lavra: Architectural Ensemble and Monuments of the Necropolises), Leningrad: Khudozhnik RSFSR, 1986

MASEGNE, DALLE, FAMILY *Italian*

Jacobello and Pierpaolo dalle Masegne worked in a naturalistic style typical of northern Europe and were instrumental in the development of the International Gothic style in Italy. Whereas Jacobello responded to the descriptive character of northern sculpture, Pierpaolo preferred the fluid line of the courtly style filtered through the work of Nino Pisano. Their masterpieces, the high altar of the Church of S. Francesco in Bologna and the iconostasis of the Basilica of S. Marco in Venice, influenced the sculpture of northern and central Italy and particularly the early career of Jacopo della Quercia.

Little is known about the brothers before 1383, although they identified themselves in their inscriptions with the phrase *de Venetiis* (from Venice). Their training probably began in the workshop of their father, Antonio dalle Masegne, a stonemason, which may explain the numerous commissions they received for architectural decoration. In terms of the craft of sculpture, Andriolo de Sanctis has been suggested as a possible teacher. Nino Pisano's influence is evident in the work of Pierpaolo, but it is uncertain whether Pierpaolo studied or worked with the Tuscan master in Venice or absorbed Pisano's graceful line and courtly elegance in Tuscany itself. Although the brothers signed commissions jointly in the 1380s and 1390s, the style of one of the brothers tends to dominate individual monuments, which has led to the supposition that their joint signature should be considered more as a trademark than as proof of joint authorship. In the commissions for the Gonzaga family, for example, documents show that work was undertaken by Jacobello but later completed by Pierpaolo. In the case of the facade of Mantua Cathedral, Pierpaolo had the option to change his brother's design.

Jacobello dalle Masegne before 1383–after 1409

An intense, expressive naturalism is the hallmark of Jacobello's style. His hand has been recognized in the central portion of the iconostasis of the Basilica of S. Marco. The best preserved of the works of the brothers, the iconostasis replaced a 13th-century screen with relief panels. Although the intervals between the eight columns conform to the proportions of a Byzantine iconostasis, the Gothic screen supports an architrave that serves as a base for freestanding sculpture, rather than framing painted icons. Arranged symmetrically on either side of a silver crucifix by Jacopo di Marco Benato are the figures of the *Virgin Mary*, *St. John the Evangelist*, and the *Apostles*. About 136 centimeters high, the figures are impressive for the compelling immediacy of their glance and gesture. Today, a dark brown patina obscures the original polychrome decoration along the hem of their garments that once complemented the rich colored marble of the screen itself and harmonized with the opulent revetment of the interior. Lateral sections of the screen extend in front of the chapels of S. Clemente and S. Pietro. Dated to 1397, the figures of these sections show the hand of Pierpaolo in the softer planes of the faces and the gentler cadence of the smooth loops of fabric.

Pierpaolo dalle Masegne before 1383–after 1403

Pierpaolo's style pervades the earlier sculpture of the high altar of the Church of S. Francesco in Bologna, begun in 1388. Dense with images of saints framed by polygonal canopies and flanked by pilasters composed of smaller tabernacles containing figures of angels and saints, the altar has the appearance of a monumental polyptych in stone. The central image of the altar is the *Coronation of the Virgin*. In the octagonal canopy above is a seated figure of *God the Father*. To either side of the *Coronation* group are two rows of saints. The superstructure consists of a series of pinnacles of alternating width and height, articulated at the ends by slender aedicules that frame the figures of *Gabriel* and the *Annunciate Virgin*. A larger aedicule in the center becomes a support for a *Crucifixion* group. Lively half-length figures of the prophets spring from the large foliate finials atop the taller pinnacles. Here perhaps is a trace of the work of Jacobello. Between the pedestals of the base are reliefs depicting the life of St. Fran-

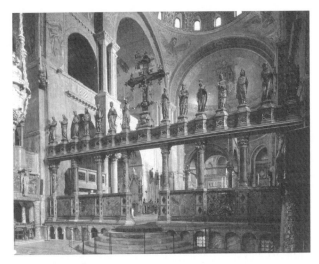

Dalle Masegne family, Iconostasis (choir screen), Basilica of S. Marco, Venice
© Erich Lessing / Art Resource, NY

cis. The large number of figures required assistants; Jacopo della Quercia may have been one of them, as the fluid style of the drapery and the prophet finials are recognizable in Jacopo's design for the Trenta Altar in the Church of S. Frediano in Lucca begun in 1416. Unfortunately, an earthquake damaged the high altar of the Church of S. Francesco, which has also been moved several times, necessitating both restoration and replacement of figures.

Domenico Morone's painting *The Expulsion of the Buonacolsi from Mantua* (1494) records the general appearance of the destroyed facade for Mantua Cathedral. The round arch of the central door was framed by narrow columns supporting two tiers of five tabernacles covered by a triangular gable and flanked by aedicules much in the manner of the high altar. Aedicules also mark the ends of the facade's central portion, revetted in white stone punctuated by horizontal bands of a different color, reminiscent of Tuscan architecture. The alternately curved and straight outline of the superstructure, however, is clearly Venetian.

In 1400 Pierpaolo received a commission to decorate the balcony window of the Great Counsel Hall of the Palazzo Ducale in Venice, overlooking the water. The contract specified 13 figures, which Pierpaolo again grouped in bands of tabernacles and crowned with an elaborate finial. Assistants may have done much of the actual carving because the decoration was complete in 1404. Only the figure of *St. Theodore* is attributed to Pierpaolo. Alessandro Vittoria replaced the figure of *Justice*, destroyed by a 1511 earthquake. Also replaced at a later date were the figures of *Charity* and *St. George*. Less is known about the late works of Jacobello. Documents suggest that he worked on the facade of Milan Cathedral, but no sculpture has been securely attributed to him. He is last documented in Bologna asking for the remaining payments of the high altar of the Church of S. Francesco.

NANCY KIPP SMITH

See also **Jacopo della Quercia; Pisano, Nino; Vittoria, Alessandro**

Jacobello dalle Masegne

Biography

Born in Venice, Italy (date unknown). Career flourished from 1383. Son of Antonio dalle Masegne, a stonemason. Probably trained in Venice; worked in northern Italy, principally in Venice, Bologna, Mantua, and perhaps Milan. Died after 1409, location unknown.

Selected Works

ca. 1380 *St. John the Baptist* and *St. Anthony of Padua*; marble; sacristy, Church of S. Stefano, Venice, Italy

ca. 1383 Tomb of Giovanni da Legnano (with Pierpaolo), for Church of S. Domenico, Bologna, Italy; marble and white stone; Museo Civico Medievale e del Rinascimento (in Palazzo Fava Ghisilardi), Bologna, Italy

1388 High altar (with Pierpaolo); marble; Church of S. Francesco, Bologna, Italy

1394 Iconostasis (choir screen) (with Pierpaolo); marble; Basilica of S. Marco, Venice, Italy

Pierpaolo dalle Masegne

Biography

Born in Venice, Italy (date unknown). Career flourished from 1383. Son of Antonio dalle Masegne, a stonemason. Probably trained in Venice, but may have studied or worked with Nino Pisano in Venice or Tuscany; worked in northern Italy, principally in Venice, Bologna, Mantua, and perhaps Milan. Made his will 10 May 1403 and is thought to have died shortly thereafter, location unknown.

Selected Works

ca. 1383 Tomb of Giovanni da Legnano (with Jacobello), for Church of S. Domenico, Bologna, Italy; marble and white stone; Museo Civico Medievale e del Rinascimento (in Palazzo Fava Ghisilardi), Bologna, Italy

1388 High altar (with Jacobello); marble; Church of S. Francesco, Bologna, Italy

1391 Pilaster bases; stone; facade, Church of S. Petronio, Bologna, Italy

1394 Iconostasis (choir screen) (with Jacobello) marble; Basilica of S. Marco, Venice, Italy

1395–1403 Facade for Mantua Cathedral, Italy; stone (destroyed)

1400 Sculptural frame for balcony window; marble; Palazzo Ducale, Venice, Italy

1400 Tomb of Margherita Malatesta, in Church of S. Francesco, Mantua, Italy; marble; Palazzo Ducale, Mantua, Italy (only effigy remains)

ca. 1400 Tomb of Antonio Venier; marble; Church of Santi Giovanni e Paolo, Venice, Italy

Further Reading

Arslan, Edoardo, *Venezia gotica*, Milan: Electa, 1970; as *Gothic Architecture in Venice*, translated by Anne Engel, London: Phaidon, 1972

Krautheimer, Richard, *Lorenzo Ghiberti*, Princeton, New Jersey: Princeton University Press, 1970

Pope-Hennessy, John, *An Introduction to Italian Sculpture*, 3 vols., London: Phaidon, 1963; 4th edition, 1996; see especially vol. 1, *Italian Gothic Sculpture*

Roli, Renato, *La Pala Marmorea di San Francesco in Bologna*, Bologna, Italy: Patron, 1964

Roli, Renato, *I Dalle Masegne*, Milan: Fratelli Fabbri, 1966

Seymour, Charles, Jr., *Sculpture in Italy, 1400–1500*, London and Baltimore, Maryland: Penguin, 1966

Wolters, Wolfgang, *La scultura veneziana gotica (1300–1460)*, 2 vols., Venice: Alfieri, 1976

RAYMOND MASON 1922– *British*

Raymond Mason's distinction in a century of abstraction lies in his insistence on modern man and woman as the central subjects of contemporary sculpture and on the inclusion of color as an integral part of it. By creating a unique form of high relief and giving his figures varying degrees of emotion, Mason also issued a challenge to Gotthold Ephraim Lessing, whose influential 18th century treatises on aesthetics relegated the sculptor as having limited capability for human expression. In order to give form to these concerns, Mason took as his subject the metropolitan crowd, which he describes as "myself or man multiplied" and which previously was largely the province of the Modern painter. Indeed, Mason's sculpture, like that of his friend and mentor Alberto Giacometti, bears the distinct mark of the draftsman and painter, genres in which he was first trained.

In London and then in Paris, Mason first produced abstract polychrome sculptures, which have been either lost or destroyed. His first low-relief sculptures, *Man in a Street* and *Place Saint-Germain-des-Près*, owe something to Giacometti, but the boxed high-relief *Barcelona Tram*, which includes freestanding figures in the foreground, already suggests Mason's ambition for his sculpture. After two panoramic views of *Paris* and *London* in low relief, which are notable for their absence of human life, Mason made the relief sculpture *Place de l'Opéra*, in which he integrated the passersby of Paris perspectively with the architecture and street as a modern Donatello might have represented the urban bustle of a great city. The modern street as a subject for relief sculpture evokes comparisons with the quattrocento and thus suggests the significance of the painter Balthus, whose importance for Mason was second only to that of Giacometti. Soon after meeting the engimatic painter, Mason created the relief *Crossroads at the Odéon*, which takes as its subject one close to Balthus's historically haunted streetscape of Paris, *Passage du Commerce—Saint André*.

Beginning in the mid 1950s, Mason regularly exhibited at Helen Lessore's Beaux Arts Gallery in London, and in a distinct sense Mason's subjects can be associated with those of the English painters who later became known as members of "L'Ecole de Londres" (London School). During this time Mason met the painter Francis Bacon, whose subject matter is echoed in the emotionally gesturing figures of *Les Epouvantées* (*The Terror-Stricken*) and especially in the three-part torso fragments *The Falling Man*, a work that Giacometti particularly admired. Mason created in the early 1960s drawings of Paris street life that eventually resulted in the conception of the 99-figure *The Crowd*, which was exhibited in plaster at the Claude Bernard Gallery in 1965. Mason has described the generic subject of the crowd as the "torrent of life" and his own sculpture as "the crowd of history"; in 1986, the French government permanently installed one of two bronze versions of *The Crowd* on the steps leading down to the Tuileries Gardens from the Jeu de Paume, where the guillotine once stood and the revolutionary crowd surged.

After the casting of *The Crowd* in 1968, Mason became disenchanted with what he considered to be the monochrome uniformity of bronze. Together with the French molder Robert Haligon, he evolved sculpture in white epoxy resin that could then be painted in acrylic. The first major polychrome work in the new medium, *The Departure of Fruit and Vegetables from the Heart of Paris, 28 February 1969*, commemorates the closure of the eight-century-old Parisian market Les Halles in 1969. Although the figures are in modern dress, their robust realism has the recognizable vitality of a Pieter Brueghel or a William Hogarth canvas; the brimming fruit and vegetables recall the profusion of a Dutch painting suddenly come to life. Despite such precedents, however consciously sought, the work also evokes the playful raucousness of Claes Oldenburg, a sculptor particularly admired by Mason in the 1970s.

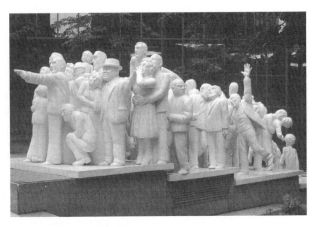

An Illuminated Crowd
© Lee Snider / CORBIS and (2003) Artists Rights Society (ARS), New York and ADAGP, Paris

The sculpture now stands in the Saint Eustache Church near Les Halles, its social and cultural meaning enhanced for Parisians who see it there.

A second major narrative sculpture, *Tragedy in the North. Winter, Rain, and Tears*, more overtly expresses the emotions of modern men and women; it depicts the grieving witnesses of a mining disaster in Liévin, a small town in the Pas de Calais in northern France. Also from the mid 1970s is an extraordinary series of colored landscape reliefs of the Midi in southern France, where Mason had a house; it is the only occasion in which modern sculpture has represented clouds and the sun with an intensity equal to that achieved by Van Gogh in paint. Equally remarkable is the culminating high-relief of the series, *The Grape-pickers*.

Mason has also attained international prominence as a sculptor of public monuments. His 65-figure monochrome *An Illuminated Crowd*, in central Montreal, is set on four levels of steps. Two high-relief monuments placed in 1988 in Georgetown Plaza, Washington D.C., commemorate the history of Georgetown, and in 1990 the second bronze cast of *The Crowd* acquired its permanent home at 527 Madison Avenue, New York. In 1988 Mason received a commission to create a monumental sculpture for Centenary Square in his home city of Birmingham, England; in 1991 he completed the sculpture *Forward. A Monument to Birmingham*, which commemorates the politicians, scientists, and anonymous men and women who contributed to the city's industry. In 1994 the French town of Vézelay installed the original plaster relief of *The Grape-pickers*; and in the same decade Mason made further panoramic reliefs of world cities, including Hong Kong and Edinburgh, as well as figure reliefs of the street and architecture of Paris, a series that also includes a set of finely executed watercolor drawings of the city.

ROBIN SPENCER

See also **Donatello (Donato di Betto Bardi); Giacometti, Alberto; Oldenburg, Claes; Public Sculpture**

Biography

Born in Birmingham, England, 2 March 1922. Student at Birmingham College of Arts and Crafts, 1937–39, and the Royal College of Art, London, 1942; established studio in Birmingham; studied at Slade School of Fine Art, London and Ruskin School of Drawing and Fine Art, Oxford, 1943–44; returned to London, 1945–46; moved to Paris; worked briefly in atelier of Marcel Gimond, École Nationale Supérieur des Beaux-Arts; met and formed life-long friendship with Alberto Giacometti, 1948; first solo exhibition at Helen Lessore's Beaux Arts Gallery, London, 1954; received William and Noma Copley Foundation Award, 1962; showed at *Exposition internationale*, Vienna Secession, and the Arts Club, Chicago, 1969; exhibited at the Venice Biennale, 1982 and 1995; major retrospective exhibitions: the Serpentine Gallery, London, and Museum of Modern Art, Oxford, 1982; Centre Georges Pompidou, Paris, and Musée Cantini, Marseilles, 1985–86; Birmingham, Manchester, and Edinburgh, 1989; Musée Maillol, Paris, 2000. Chevalier des Arts et des Lettres, 1979; Officier de l'Ordre des Arts et des Lettres, 1989. Lives and works in Paris, France.

Selected Works

1953   *Barcelona Tram*; bronze; edition of eight, including Tate Gallery, London, England

1958–59   *Crossroads at the Odéon*; bronze; edition of eight, including Musée Nationale d'Art Moderne, Centre Georges Pompidou, Paris, France

1962–63   *The Falling Man*; bronze; edition of six, including Hirshhorn Museum and Sculpture Garden, Washington, D.C., United States

1965–69   *The Crowd*; bronze; edition of two, including Tuileries Gardens, Paris, France, and 527 Madison Avenue, New York City, United States

1969–71   *The Departure of Fruit and Vegetables from the Heart of Paris, 28 February 1969*; epoxy resin, acrylic; edition of six, including Tate Gallery, London, England, and Fonds National d'Art Contemporain, Paris, France

1972   *St. Mark's Place, East Village, New York City*; epoxy resin, acrylic; edition of six, including Tate Gallery, London, England

1975–77   *Tragedy in the North. Winter, Rain, and Tears*; epoxy resin, acrylic; edition of six,

including Gallerie Claude Bernard, Paris, France, and Birmingham Museums and Art Gallery, Birmingham, England

1976–88   Twin sculptures; stratified polyester resin, polyurethane paint; Georgetown Plaza, Washington D.C., United States

1982   *The Grape-pickers*; polyester resin, acrylic; edition of four, including Marlborough Gallery, New York City, United States

1983–86   *An Illuminated Crowd*; stratified polyester resin, polyurethane paint; Esplanade of 1981, Avenue McGill College, Montreal, Canada

1988–91   *Forward. A Monument to Birmingham*; stratified polyester resin, polyurethane paint; Centenary Square, Birmingham, England

1992   *Rue Monsieur-le-Prince, No 2.*; polyester resin, acrylic; edition of eight, including Marlborough Fine Art, London, England

Further Reading

Bonnefoy, Yves, "In Speaking of Chateaubriand . . .," in *Raymond Mason* (exhib. cat.), by Bonnefoy, translated by Anthony Rudolf, New York: Pierre Matisse Gallery, 1969

Edwards, Michael, *Raymond Mason*, London and New York: Thames and Hudson, 1994

Farrington, Jane, and Evelyn Silber, editors, *Raymond Mason, Sculptures and Drawings* (exhib. cat.), London: Lund Humphries, 1989

Mason, Raymond, "British Art Schools: Augustus John," *New Phineas* (Autumn 1945)

Mason, Raymond, "The Departure of the Fruits and Vegetables from the Heart of Paris, 28 February 1969," in *Le depart des fruits et legumes du coeur de Paris le 28 fuerier 1969* (exhib. cat.), translated by Patricia Southgate, New York: Pierre Matisse Gallery, 1971

Mason, Raymond, "Les mains éblouies," *Derrière le miroir* 9 (April 1948); reprint, *Raymond Mason* (exhib. cat.), Paris: Musée National d'Art Moderne, Centre Georges Pompidou, 1985

Mason, Raymond, *"The Crowd,"* New York: Marlborough Gallery, 1990

Raymond Mason (exhib. cat.), Paris: Fondation Dina Vierny— Musée Maillol, 2000

Raymond Mason: Coloured Sculptures, Bronzes, and Drawings, 1952–1982 (exhib. cat.), London: Arts Council of Great Britain, 1982

HENRI (-EMILE-BENOÎT) MATISSE
1869–1954 *French*

Although renowned for his brilliant and lyrical Fauvist paintings of the early 20th century, Henri Matisse also produced a sizable body of sculpture. His three-dimensional works are distinguished by their small scale, informality, and private function. He created his first sculptures, two small portrait medallions, in 1894, before he enrolled in sculpture classes, sketching ancient

Greek and Roman works and consulting Auguste Rodin and Émile-Antoine Bourdelle.

In 1899 Matisse purchased from the Modernist dealer Ambroise Vollard the plaster model of Rodin's bust of *Henri Rochefort*, which he studied and drew. One of his early sculptural exercises, the *Jaguar Devouring a Hare* (1899–1901), is an interpretation of Antoine-Louis Barye's *animalier* sculpture, and the *Slave* shows the influence of Rodin's *Walking Man* (1900). Based on detailed observation of the human body, with an obvious freedom in the handling of the surface, the *Slave* (1900–03) renewed the tradition of the *bozzetto* (small-scale preparatory study). Matisse accepted Rodin's fragmentation of the human figure, which subordinated detail to the overall effect, but he criticized Rodin for neglecting the wholeness in his quest for an assemblage of carefully sculpted parts and details. Matisse was indeed in search of harmony, of what he called the *arabesque*, to escape from mass and volume toward motion and action. His first arabesque conception was *Madeleine I*, a human body with its arms removed in order to emphasize its sinuous curves. In 1903 he undertook a paraphrase of a Florentine 16th-century *Ecorché* (*Flayed Figure*), which at the time was attributed to Michelangelo. Matisse's trips to Italy and North Africa, combined with the influence of André Derain, resulted in a series of statuettes, such as *Serpentine* and the *Jeanette* busts.

Matisse's most ambitious sculpture, the *Large Seated Nude* (1924–25), forecasted his later major accomplishments, such as the *Reclining Nudes*, the two *Torsos* of 1929, and the *Henriette* portraits. Instead of developing a greater resemblance to the model and a psychological portrait, Matisse in this series gave his model a new character that accorded with his artistic expression. Thus, *Henriette II* is more stylized and formal than its precursor, and Matisse further remade *Henriette III*, closing her eyes and constructing a more assertive profile. After a trip to Tahiti, Matisse created an evocative and Gauguin-inflected head titled *Tiari* (1930–31). Inspired by a Tahitian white gardenia worn by women, it is close to the purity and accomplishments of Jean (Hans) Arp and Constantin Brancusi.

Matisse generally used sculpture as a three-dimensional approach to revive him from his struggle with painting's two dimensions. In his series *Back*, he experimented with bringing the two genres together. In 1930 he completed the final version of this series of monumental female nudes in relief on which he had been working since 1909. These nudes represent a simplification of form, illustrate the expressionistic tendency in his sculpture, and bring to decorative sculpture a new monumentality. *Back 0*, completed in 1909 and only known through a photograph by

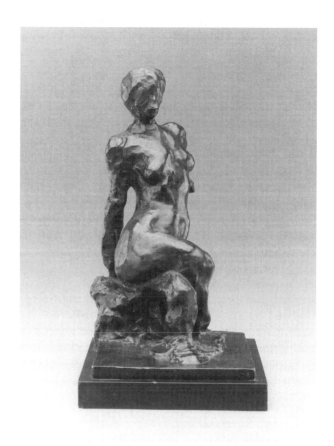

Seated Nude (1909)
Bequest of Robert H. Tannahill
© 2001 Detroit Institute of Arts, the (2003) Succession H. Paris Matisse, Artists Rights Society (ARS), New York

Eugène Druet, is the closest representation of the model who posed for it. *Back I*, completed the same year, is an almost naturalistic depiction of a nude female back. *Back II* is a progressive simplification of the form, and *Back III* grew more stylized and powerfully abstract. *Back IV* represents the epitome of Matisse's thinking on the representation of a human figure, with a radical simplification of the female back, reduced to two columns divided by a third, a thick tress of hair. From the interpretation of a specific model in the first version, the identity progressively disappears, and the final work represents roughly the shape of an unknown woman, the vertical position of her nude body contrasting with the diagonal of her upraised left arm.

Among his later sculptures is the bronze crucifix for the Vence Chapel, which is the most abstract of his three-dimensional works. At the end of his life, Matisse discovered through his late paper cutouts a new personal mixture of painting, drawing, and sculpture.

Matisse's concepts of altering and rearranging parts of a human figure strongly influenced 20th-century sculpture. Although he was quoted as saying, "I did my sculpture as a painter; I did not work as a sculptor," the aesthetic distortion developed by later sculptors originated in his concepts and artistic creations. His later collages acquired a special significance in the 1960s because they accomplished the exemplary aim the art critic Clement Greenberg suggested of sculpture as an extension of collage.

ANNA TAHINCI

See also **Arp, Jean (Hans); Barye, Antoine-Louis; Bourdelle, Émile-Antoine; Brancusi, Constantin; France: 20th Century–Contemporary; Gauguin, Paul; Michelangelo (Buonarroti); Modernism; Rodin, Auguste**

Biography

Born in Le Cateau-Cambrésis, Picardy, France, 31 December 1869. Moved to Paris to become professional artist, 1891; studied first at Académie Julian, then École des Beaux-Arts in atelier of Gustave Moreau; evening courses in sculpture at the workshop of Émile-Antoine Bourdelle, 1899; trips to North Africa and Italy, 1904–07; exhibited three sculptures at Galerie Druet, 1906–07; exhibited 13 sculptures at Salon d'Automne, 1908–09; traveled to United States and Tahiti, 1930s; surgery rendered him a partial invalid, 1941; exhibition of sculptures at Curt Valentin Gallery, New York, 1953. Died in Nice, France, 3 November 1954.

Selected Works

Important collections of Matisse's sculptures are housed at the Musée Matisse in Nice, France, and at the Baltimore Museum of Art, Maryland, United States.

1899– *Jaguar Devouring a Hare*; bronze; private
1901 collection
1900–63 *Slave (Le Serf)*; bronze; Fogg Art Museum, Cambridge, Massachusetts, United States
1907 *Reclining Nude I*; bronze; two versions: Baltimore Museum of Art, Maryland, United States; Musée Nationale d'Art Moderne, Centre Georges Pompidou, Paris, France
1909 *Back I*; bronze; two versions: Tate Gallery, London; Guggenheim Museum of Art, New York City, United States
1913 *Back II*; bronze; two versions: Tate Gallery, London; Guggenheim Museum of Art, New York City, United States

1917 *Back III*; bronze; two versions: Tate Gallery, London; Guggenheim Museum of Art, New York City, United States
1924–25 *Large Seated Nude*; bronze; Baltimore Museum of Art, Maryland, United States
1927 *Henriette II*; bronze; San Francisco Museum of Art, California, United States
1929 *Back IV*; bronze; two versions: Tate Gallery, London; Guggenheim Museum of Art, New York City, United States
1929 *Henriette III*; bronze; private collection
1929 *Reclining Nude II*; bronze; two versions: Tate Gallery, London; Musée Matisse, Nice, France
1929 *Reclining Nude III*; bronze; two versions: Baltimore Museum of Art, Maryland, United States; Musée Matisse, Nice, France
1930–31 *Tiari* (with necklace); marble; Musée Matisse, Nice, France; bronze: Baltimore Museum of Art, Maryland, United States

Further Reading

Elsen, Albert Edward, *The Sculpture of Henri Matisse*, New York: Abrams, 1971
Monod-Fontaine, Isabelle, *The Sculpture of Henri Matisse*, London and New York: Thames and Hudson, 1984
Tucker, W., "Matisse's Sculpture: The Grasped and the Seen," *Art in America*, 13/4 (1975)

ALEKSANDR MATVEYEV 1878–1960
Russian

Aleksandr Terentevich Matveyev occupied a significant place in the development of Russian sculpture in the early 20th century. Working in a variety of materials throughout his career, including marble, wood, bronze, and various types of stone, Matveyev concentrated primarily on the human figure. He imbued his often generalized, highly refined images with a Classical sense of proportion and harmony and put forth a type of modern Classicism that rejected the academicism of the past yet expressed the goals of achieving unity, simplicity, and a harmonious sense of an indivisible whole.

Born in Saratov in 1878, Matveyev was closely identified early in his career with the Blue Rose, a group of painters and sculptors concerned with articulating a Symbolist aesthetic in the visual arts. Matveyev exhibited with the group in 1907 alongside Pavel Kuznetsov, Piotr Utkin, Martiros Saryan, and Kuzma Petrov-Vodkin (although never officially a member, Petrov-Vodkin shared the artistic aims of his Saratov colleagues). The Blue Rose, whose members included several artists from Saratov, owed a substantial debt to the two great Russian Symbolists of the late 19th century, Mikhail Vrubel and Viktor Borisov-Musatov.

Matveyev entered the Moscow School of Painting, Sculpture, and Architecture in 1899. There, the teaching of sculptor Paolo Troubetzkoy, who had just arrived in Russia from Italy, exerted the greatest influence on the young Matveyev. From Troubetzkoy he learned to approach the figure with spontaneity and vitality. Troubetzkoy's practice of creating rough and uneven surfaces, with vigorous and energetic modeling, created a sculptural equivalent of Impressionism. Among the first sculptors in Russia to pursue an Impressionistic style, Troubetzkoy provided an important example to younger artists in breaking with established academic style. Although Matveyev's mature style departed from Troubetzkoy's Impressionism, he learned invaluable lessons from his teacher's practice of working directly from nature and belief in respecting the qualities of the material.

After finishing his studies in 1902 Matveyev established himself among the progressive artists who gathered at the country estate of Savva and Elizaveta Mamontov just outside Moscow at Abramtsevo. Matveyev had the opportunity to work at the ceramics workshop, then directed by the artist Vrubel. Inspired not only by Vrubel's unique Symbolist vision but also by his innovative treatment of majolica and other materials, Matveyev gained much from the Abramtsevo experience. Moreover, the revival of native folk arts and crafts promoted by the Mamontovs acted as a catalyst in Matveyev's later turn to wood carving.

Partly at the urging of his Saratov mentor, Borisov-Musatov, Matveyev left for Paris in 1906. He spent a year seeing firsthand the work of the French Modernists. Paul Gauguin's large retrospective exhibition in 1906 made a lasting impression in both the blocky and thick figures seen in the painter's South Sea works and the carved wooden sculptures Gauguin executed. Matveyev was less taken with Auguste Rodin, whose Impressionistic style he regarded as outdated. Interestingly, it was Aristide Maillol's work that had the most influence on his own development. He responded particularly to the sense of proportion, contour, and Classical restraint found in Maillol's female figures; indeed, numerous comparisons between the two prompted several critics to refer to Matveyev as "the Russian Maillol."

Returning to Russia in 1907, Matveyev reached his mature style in works such as *Sleeping Boy*, *Seated Boy, Dream, Awakening Boy*, and *Youth*. These works feature nude male youths, generalized in form and often retaining the rough surface of the stone or plaster, shown in solitary activities—sleeping, dreaming, meditating, or relaxing. The introspective mood common to all these figures reflects the Symbolist aesthetic dominant among the circle of Russian writers and artists associated with the journals the *Golden Fleece* and *Apollon*. One of Matveyev's most accomplished works from this period is his design for the grave monument of the writer Borisov-Musatov, in which a reclining young boy, rendered in a sweeping, languid pose, has gracefully fallen asleep, alluding to the youthful, elegiac sadness conveyed in much of Borisov-Musatov's own work. Like Borisov-Musatov, Matveyev expressed a timeless quality in his figures by transcending a particular place and time to evoke a lost Classical age.

Another important inspiration for Matveyev was the example of Michelangelo, whose *Slaves* (*ca.* 1517) convey the human drama of struggling against material bondage to find inner spiritual freedom. In subject as well as in carving technique and feeling for material, the relationship to Michelangelo's *Slaves* is clear: figures literally emerge from the natural block of stone, expressing the timeless struggle between body and soul. By the early 1910s Matveyev favored a simplified style based on paring away unnecessary detail to create generalized form. Although he often presented his figures in complex poses of twisting and turning with arms and legs crossed, his overall tendency was toward conveying a sense of calm and repose rather than movement or agitation.

After moving to St. Petersburg in 1912, Matveyev turned increasingly toward Maillol's brand of Classicism. Like Maillol, he focused on the female nude. In two works of 1913, *Girl Arranging Hair* and *Female Figure*, and in a work from 1916, *Girl with Towel*, he achieved a sense of Classical balance and clarity with figures that nonetheless possessed the potential for life and movement. A trip to Italy in 1914, where he studied Classical monuments firsthand, intensified Matveyev's turn to Classicism, as did a general interest in Classicism among Russian critics, chief among them Aleksandr Benois, who expressed his views in the journal *Apollon*. Breaking away from the earlier generation of Symbolists with its message of malaise and decay, the critics and artists in St. Petersburg associated with *Apollon* turned to Classicism as a way to restore beauty and clarity in a living art.

After the Bolshevik Revolution, Matveyev participated in the general restructuring of artistic and educational institutions in Russia. He began teaching at the State Free Studios in 1918 and then took a position at the Academy of Arts, where he remained until 1948. One of Matveyev's most important portraits immediately after the revolution was a full-length statue of Karl Marx for the Smolnyi Institute in St. Petersburg, completed in 1918 on the first anniversary of the revolution. Between 1923 and 1925 Matveyev also returned to the female figure in a series of delicate, small-scale works produced at the Lomonosov ceramics factory. By the late 1920s, as the work of Russian artists turned increasingly to a realist style, Matveyev produced sculptures that would satisfy a growing need for realistic, heroic subjects. He showed *October*, featuring three large-scale figures representing a worker, peasant, and soldier, in 1928 at an exhibition marking the tenth anniversary of the revolution. The work signaled Matveyev's ability to create monumental pieces that accommodated the desire for recognizable, mythical heroes of the Soviet state. Matveyev's last major works were portraits, including those of Lenin, Maxim Gorky, Mikhail Lermontov, Anton Chekhov, and Aleksandr Pushkin; he began the latter in 1938 when the state organized a celebration marking the 100th anniversary of the writer's death. Matveyev turned his attention to producing several busts and full-length versions of Pushkin between 1938 and 1940, and then again between 1948 and 1960.

TAMARA MACHMUT-JHASHI

See also **Maillol, Aristide; Russia and Soviet Union; Troubetzkoy, Paolo**

Biography

Born in Saratov, Russia, 25 August 1878. Studied at Bogoliubskii School of Drawing, Saratov, 1896–1899; attended Moscow School of Painting, Sculpture, and Architecture under sculptor Paolo Troubetzkoy, 1899–1902; worked at ceramics workshop at Abramtsevo headed by Mikhail Vrubel after 1902; in Paris, 1906; exhibited at the Blue Rose and *Golden Fleece*, 1907–10; established studio in Kikerino, near St. Petersburg, Russia, 1907; created large-scale sculptural ensemble for a park in Kuchuk-Koi in the Crimea. Moved to studio in St. Petersburg on Vasilevskii Island, 1912; after the revolution in 1917 began teaching career in Leningrad (now St. Petersburg); taught at the Academy of Arts, 1918–48; created small- and large-scale portraits of revolutionary heroes and famous Russian writers, from the mid 1920s. Died in Moscow, Russia, 22 October 1960.

Selected Works

1907   *Awakening Boy*; plaster; Russian Museum, St. Petersburg, Russia
1907   *Sleeping Boy*; plaster; Russian Museum, St. Petersburg, Russia
1909   *Seated Boy*; plaster; Russian Museum, St. Petersburg, Russia
1910   Study for memorial to Viktor Borisov-

Musatov; plaster; Russian Museum, St. Petersburg, Russia
1910–12   Memorial to Viktor Borisov-Musatov; granite; Tarus, Russia
1913   *Girl Arranging Hair*; plaster; Russian Museum, St. Petersburg, Russia
1916   *Girl with Towel*; wood; Russian Museum, St. Petersburg, Russia
1918   Monument to Karl Marx, for Smolnyi Institute, St. Petersburg, Russia; bronze (destroyed)
1927   *October*; bronze; Russian Museum, St. Petersburg, Russia
1938–40   *A.C. Pushkin*; bronze; Russian Museum, St. Petersburg, Russia

Further Reading

Bassekhes, Alfred, *Aleksandr Terent'evich Matveev*, Moscow: Sovetskii Khudozhnik, 1960
Manturova, Tat'iana Borisovna, *Aleksandr Matveev*, Moscow: Izobrazitelnoe Iskusstvo, 1974
Murina, Elena Borisovna, *Aleksandr Terent'evich Matveev*, Moscow: Iskusstvo, 1964
Murina, Elena Borisovna, *Aleksandr Matveev*, Moscow: Sovetskii Khudozhnik, 1979 (with an English summary)
Sokolov, M.N., "Matveyev, Aleksandr (Terent'yevich)," in *The Dictionary of Art*, edited by Jane Turner, New York: Grove, and London: Macmillan, 1996

GUIDO MAZZONI *ca.* 1450–1518 *Italian, also active in France*

Guido Mazzoni is chiefly known for his life-size groups of polychrome terracotta figures. The use of terracotta reveals the artist's strict adherence to the aesthetic of Renaissance art, which placed a humanist value on modeling, reviving a technique that was known and practiced in Antiquity. This reevaluation of clay modeling was mainly concentrated in Florence, where it was supported by scholars such as Lorenzo Ghiberti, Leon Battista Alberti, and Gaurico Paduan, and was particularly championed by Donatello. However, terracotta was also much used in Emilia, where its chief exponent was Niccolò dell'Arca. In portraiture, the humanistic genre par excellence, where the individual's features had to be recognizable, the life mask, adopted by Andrea del Verrocchio and Donatello, became an indispensable instrument when combined with other modeling and finishing techniques; an incomparable use of this approach can be seen in Donatello's bust of *Niccolò da Uzzano* (*ca.* 1432; Museo Nazionale del Bargello, Florence). Mazzoni followed this practice not only for the portraits in his group but also for other features, such as hands, to achieve a truly realistic effect.

Outside portraiture, this extreme realism and the taste for terracotta, which suffered a decline at the end of the 15th century and became a medium limited to producing devotional images, are the two features that lie at the heart of the originality of Mazzoni's art and are, at the same time, the reasons for the artist's lack of critical acclaim during the following centuries. The sculptor's work can be divided into two clear phases. The first was carried out between Emilia and the Veneto and drew to an end at the Aragon court in Naples. The surviving *Lamentations*, which made him famous, in Busseto, Modena, Ferrara, Padua, and Naples, as well as other subjects, such as the *Madonna della pappa* in Modena Cathedral and the *Virgin and Child* in the Basilica of the Pieve in Guastalla, all show a relationship to the painting of the period.

Almost nothing remains from Mazzoni's French period at the court of Charles VIII, where the artist is recorded as a painter and illuminator, because of the destruction that occurred during the French Revolution. This lack of surviving examples makes it more difficult to assess his development. Sources record major works that reveal how highly his art was considered, such as the tomb of Charles VIII in the Basilica of Saint-Denis, France (bronze and marble) and an equestrian statue of Louis XII (stone) at the entrance to the castle of Blois. In what remains of the marble decoration of the castle of Gaillon, it is difficult to recognize Mazzoni's style.

The *Bust of Child* (possibly Henry VIII) in polychrome terracotta is unanimously attributed to Mazzoni and is thus the sole surviving work from his time in France. This work is possible evidence of the artist's contact with the English court and plans for Henry VII's funerary monument, which was subsequently produced in a different manner by Pietro Torrigiani.

Both these periods of Mazzoni's work found a following in contemporary sculpture, although he had no direct pupils. Echoes of his style reverberate in 16th century Bolognese examples of the *Pietà* by Alfonso Lombardi and Vincenzo Onofri and in the work of Venetian sculptors such as Andrea Briosco, known as Riccio. Both Agostino de' Fondulis and the anonymous artist of the *Lamentation* in the Church of the Carmine in Brescia reveal their familiarity with Mazzoni's lost works in Lombardy, such as that in the Church of San Lorenzo in Cremona.

In France, where Mazzoni ran a workshop, his chief role was to introduce Italian Renaissance models. For example, in the funerary monument for Charles VIII, known through a drawing (Bodleian Library, Oxford, England), in place of the traditional French manner of presenting the deceased as *gisant* (reclining figure), Mazzoni used an iconography more common in Spain and southern Italy, with the deceased praying on the tomb.

In 1543, well after the sculptor's death, Tommasino Bianchi de' Lancillotto's Modenese chronicle records Mazzoni's particular gift for modeling terracotta figures, giving them natural coloration and achieving amazingly realistic results. This fidelity in reproducing the human figure can be related to the young artist's occupation as a maker of masks, for which it seems that he was widely known.

The artist was also greatly admired during his lifetime. Gaurico describes him as "in Italia laudatissimus" (highly commended in Italy), portraying Mazzoni as one of the leading exponents of Renaissance sculpture who had brought clay modeling back into fashion. Although Sabba da Castiglione speaks of him no less highly, Giorgio Vasari only mentions him in connection with his presumed rivalry with Giuliano da Maiano.

Some critics have blamed the scant attention paid to Mazzoni in Vasari's 16th century *Lives of the Painters, Sculptors, and Architects* for the artist's lack of critical acclaim in subsequent centuries. In truth, the decline of clay modeling was one of the consequences of the hierarchy of artistic forms established by the academies, which was an undiscriminating extension of Michelangelo's preference for sculpture that involved subtractive techniques (such as carving), unlike additive techniques such as modeling.

Mazzoni only received a critical reappraisal in the 19th century, first by local art historians and later in international circles, where appreciation of the artist was nevertheless combined with a negative view of his strongly emotive quality. His extreme realism has not been fully understood and has indeed long been considered a limitation, leading the artist to be assigned a minor role in 15th-century Italian art.

Over the last decades, critical and exhaustive monographs have been published, studies analyzing both the iconographic aspects and the artist's relationship with the courts for which he worked (see Gramaccini, 1983), and it has now been established, with convincing argumentation, that Mazzoni was very much part of the artistic context of the Renaissance, moving between the imitation of nature and leanings toward Classical art (see Verdon, 1978, and Lugli, 1990).

MARIA GRAZIA VACCARI

See also **Donatello (Donato di Betto Bardi); Ghiberti, Lorenzo; Michelangelo (Buonarroti); Riccio (Andrea Briosco); Torrigiani, Pietro; Verrocchio, Andrea del**

Biography

Born in Modena, Italy, probably in 1450. Documented early work as a painter and decorator for the Dukes of Este in 1472 and 1476; also recorded as a goldsmith; moved to the Aragon court in Naples, 1489; *Lamentation* of Sant'Anna dei Lombardi completed, 1492; immigrated to France, 1496; worked at the court of Charles VIII and court of Louis XII in Paris; appointed chevalier and received other marks of respect; returned to Modena, 1516. Died in Modena, Italy, 15 September 1518.

Selected Works

ca. 1475   *Lamentation*; polychrome terracotta; Santa Maria degli Angeli, Busseto, Italy

1477–79   *Lamentation*; polychrome terracotta; S. Giovanni Battista, Modena, Italy

ca. 1480   *Madonna della pappa*; polychrome terracotta; Modena Cathedral, Italy

before 1485   *Lamentation*; polychrome terracotta; Church of Jesus (formerly St. Mary of the Rose), Ferrara, Italy

1485–89   *Lamentation* (fragments of four figures); polychrome terracotta; Civic Museum, Padua, Italy

ca. 1489   *Bust of Man* (Alfonso of Aragon?); chiseled bronze with gilding traces; Museo e Gallerie Nazionali di Capodimonte, Naples, Italy

1492   *Lamentation*; polychrome terracotta; Sant'Anna dei Lombardi, Naples, Italy

late 15th century   *Bust of Child* (Henry VIII?); polychrome terracotta; Royal Collection, Windsor Castle, Berkshire, England

Further Reading

Gramaccini, Niccolò, "Guido Mazzonis Beweinungsgruppen," *Städel-Jahrbuch* 9 (1983)

Larson, John, "A Polychrome Terracotta Bust of a Laughing Child at Windsor Castle," *The Burlington Magazine* 131 (September 1989)

Lugli, Adalgisa, *Guido Mazzoni e la rinascita della terracotta nel Quattrocento*, Turin: Allemandi, 1990

Vasari, Giorgio, *Le vite de più eccellenti architetti, pittori, e scultori italiani*, 3 vols., Florence: Torrentino, 1550; 2nd edition, Florence: Apresso i Giunti, 1568; as *Lives of the Painters, Sculptors, and Architects*, 2 vols., translated by Gaston du C. de Vere (1912), edited by David Ekserdjian, New York: Knopf, and London: Campbell, 1996

Venturi, Adolfo, *Storia dell'arte italiana*, 11 vols., Milan: Hoepli, 1901; reprint, Millwood, New York: Kraus Reprint, 1983; see especially vol. 6, *La scultura del Quattrocento*

Verdon, Timothy, *The Art of Guido Mazzoni*, New York: Garland, 1978

Lamentation

Guido Mazzoni (ca. 1450–1518)

1492

terracotta with traces of polychrome

h. 182 cm

Church of Sant'Anna dei Lombardi (known as the Church of Monteoliveto), Naples, Italy

Guido Mazzoni's *Lamentation* of Sant'Anna dei Lombardi was commissioned by Alfonso II, Duke of Cala-

bria, when the artist was living at the Aragon court in Naples, where he settled in 1489. On 27 December 1492 the artist received a first payment of 60 ducats. In a letter to Marcantonio Michiel in 1524, the Neapolitan humanist Pietro Summonte mentions the group in the Church of Monteoliveto. Later, Vasari's *Lives of the Painters, Sculptors, and Architects* reports Duke Alfonso's great admiration of Mazzoni.

The *Lamentation* marks Mazzoni's mature period, which followed an extremely coherent course, adopting an idiom that was free of the overemphatic gestures of the groups he had produced before. The result is certainly one of high realism, but with more fluid forms and calmer, more restrained gestures, and it displays the artist's fine eye for detail.

The composition differs from that of the earlier *Lamentation* groups, which were installed in smaller and shallower spaces with a low central viewing point and figures gathered in a semicircle around the figure of Christ. Here, instead, Christ is not level with the viewer and is no longer the emotional fulcrum of the composition, now widened and arranged in a circle. The chapel holding this group seems out of scale with the figures, which must originally have had a different setting, perhaps changed during the alterations to the church in the 16th century.

The Naples *Lamentation* group, like the others, was painted with lifelike colors, minimal traces of which remain. This has led to the illusionistic features being diminished, but since the material has been revealed, it has been possible to appreciate the fine sensitivity of the modeling that the color once highlighted.

According to 16th-century sources, interest in this group lay chiefly in the portraits that Mazzoni introduced into the composition, following a well-established practice in Emilian sculpture. During the 16th century the duke was already identified as one of the two figures kneeling at the sides; only Vasari and Pietro Summonte suggested that the mirror-image figure could be identified as Ferrante, Duke Alfonso's father. Historians in the 17th century suggested that the group included other figures, portraying the humanists Giovanni Pontano and Jacopo Sannazaro. This hypothesis engendered considerable confusion. On the basis of iconographic comparisons, art historians today tend to believe that Joseph of Arimathaea (the figure on the left) is a portrait of Alfonso II (see Hersey, 1969). The duke is shown wearing a monk's habit; his head is shaven and he is performing a penance.

It is more difficult to identify Nicodemus, whom 17th-century writers rather unconvincingly propose bears a likeness to Jacopo Sannazaro. Summonte's and Vasari's suggestions that Ferrante d'Aragona is presented as Nicodemus are more convincing.

From an iconographic point of view, the Lamentation takes place in the series of visual scenes in the

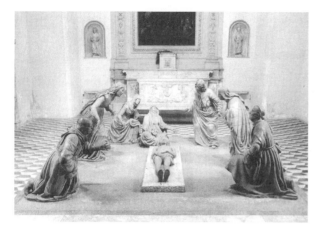

Lamentation
The Conway Library, Courtauld Institute of Art

Passion of Christ, between the deposition from the cross and the entombment. This is a moment of pause, when the dead Christ is displayed to the gaze of the onlookers. The theme was originally Byzantine, and in the Middle Ages it was spread to the West with the aim of encouraging penitence as a path to spiritual salvation.

In Italian art, the image of Christ stretched on the tomb, on the slab, or on the Virgin's lap surrounded by other figures prevailed over the pietà or *Vesperbild* better known in northern Europe, which only included the two central figures of the Virgin and Christ. Images of this kind were already produced in Italian sculpture during the 14th century, but terracotta was not used until the early 15th century. It was during this period that clay modeling became increasingly successful, earning recognition as an independent genre. The reading of Classical writers, especially Pliny the Elder, further encouraged the return to modeling in clay, which had its great flowering in Florence during the 15th century.

The reintroduction of polychrome sculpture, chiefly for themes concerning the Passion for places of worship, was fostered by the preaching of the monastic orders between the late 15th and early 16th centuries, especially the Franciscans, who were extremely active in Lombardy.

Mazzoni's sculptural groups were indeed created with the aim of inspiring compassion among the faithful through the Christian story and its sorrows in forms that were extremely realistic. Thus the naturalistic colors, details of contemporary dress, and distinctive gestures were of importance in imparting the spiritual message to unlearned people. Indeed, Mazzoni's work could be described as popular art. Furthermore, the inclusion of the portraits of patrons, often dressed as Joseph of Arimathaea or Nicodemus, gave these

groups the value of an *ex voto*, an expression of the patron's compassion. Full participation in the sacred event was enacted by the figure-portraits, mediators between fact and fiction.

The use of terracotta became widespread in Emilia and in the Po Valley in the 15th century. The Church of Santa Maria della Vita in Bologna holds one of the earliest and most splendid examples of a terracotta *Lamentation*, made by Niccolò dell'Arca. This was obviously the source for some Emilian groups, although the powerful emotive quality became more moderate. But Mazzoni's relationship to Niccolò is difficult to grasp and cannot be reduced to the terms of one's dependence on the other. The two artists created personal interpretations of the same theme, starting from their different cultural experience. Niccolò dell'Arca's background encompassed southern Italian and Burgundian sculpture and transformed naturalistic detail into an abstract and dynamic image. Mazzoni's training was more homogeneous and entirely Lombard, and his search for illusionistic realism was combined with his personal participation in the religious theme. His works have a more highly dramatic quality.

MARIA GRAZIA VACCARI

See also **Lamentation and Deposition Groups; Niccolò dell'Arca**

Further Reading

Hersey, George L., *Alfonso II and the Artistic Renewal of Naples, 1485–1495*, New Haven, Connecticut: Yale University Press, 1969

Lugli, Adalgisa, *Guido Mazzoni e la rinascita della terracotta nel Quattrocento*, Turin: Allemandi, 1991

Pane, Roberto, "Guido Mazzoni e la Pietà di Monteoliveto," *Napoli Nobilisima* 11 (1972)

GIUSEPPE MAZZUOLI 1644–1725 *Italian*

Giuseppe Mazzuoli stands at the threshold between Roman High Baroque and Late Baroque sculpture. Although strongly influenced by the work of Gianlorenzo Bernini and his contemporaries, a new impetus of formal expression materialized in Mazzuoli's later works. His artistic production was confined to works in marble. Although he spent his career almost exclusively in Rome, he is also regarded as a Sienese sculptor, with good reason: a considerable portion of his works were intended for Siena, where they enjoyed an influence and reception of which his works in Rome were largely deprived.

Although born in Volterra, Mazzuoli grew up in the shadow of Siena Cathedral. From the 1650s, his father, Dionyisio, held the position of *capomaestro* (chief architect) and manager for the cathedral workshops. His elder brothers, Francesco (architect and stonemason), Giovanni Antonio (sculptor), and Agostino (stonemason), likewise entered into service there. This environment was to become a critical factor for Giuseppe's own career; with the promotion of the Sienese Fabio Chigi to the papacy as Alexander VII (*r.* 1655–67), Siena began an extraordinarily productive period in the areas of sculpture, architecture, and city planning, during which the small provincial town gained access to the newest directions in Roman art. At this time, the Chigi Chapel was created in Siena Cathedral, for which Bernini, Ercole Ferrata, and Antonio Raggi produced statues. Together with Melchiorre Caffà, Bernini, Ferrata, and Raggi represent the entirety of the young Mazzuoli's artistic field of reference. The families Chigi and DeVecchi in turn represent the primary patrons who fostered the sculptor's career throughout his life.

As a teacher—along with Bernini—Caffà exercised the greatest influence on the young Mazzuoli; the artistic temperament of this master, only a few years older than Mazzuoli, and his tendency toward elegance and sedate expressiveness corresponded with Mazzuoli's own artistic disposition far more than did Bernini's psychologically saturated and intense style. Mazzuoli's oeuvre repeatedly demonstrates a close connection to Caffà's techniques and compositions. A commission from Prince Agostino Chigi for the church altar at the Santa Maria della Scala Hospital in Siena illustrates this connection: it portrays the marble *Dead Christ* in high relief, mounted on a base of a lifelike veined alabaster, thereby achieving an extraordinary artistic effect. The nearly contemporaneous model for this work is Caffà's large altar relief in the Roman church Santa Caterina da Siena a Magnanapoli, *Ecstasy of Saint Catherine*, which makes similar use of the chromatic values of various materials to impart a pictorial effect.

If Mazzuoli laid the foundation for his artistic fame in Siena with *Dead Christ*, he strove to achieve the same effect in Rome through his collaboration on the tomb of Pope Alexander VII in St. Peter's Basilica. Cardinal Flavio Chigi had conferred the responsibility for designing and managing this prestigious assignment upon Bernini, encouraging the sculptor to entrust the young Mazzuoli with the allegorical figure *Caritas* (Charity) on the base of the monument. Mazzuoli had to adhere to a small terracotta model done by the master, first creating it to scale using inexpensive materials and then carving the figure. The result—the decidedly Berninesque character of a vivacious young woman in a spontaneous walking position—was met with general admiration. From this point on, Mazzuoli received numerous assignments, producing statues for both Roman and Sienese churches. Depending on the as-

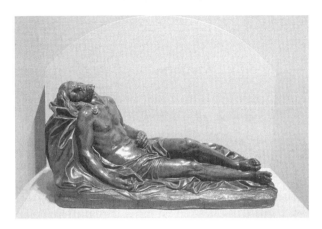

Deposed Christ, Giuseppe Mazzuoli *ca.* 1670–1680
© North Carolina Museum of Art, Raleigh, North Carolina, Purchased with funds from the State of North Carolina and various donors, by exchange / CORBIS

signment, his work either expressed the Berninesque aspects of his training, as in his statues of two kneeling angels holding candles for the high altar of the Church of Sant'Agostino in Siena, or manifested Caffà's influence, as in the lyrical bearing of the *Immacolata* for the Church of San Martino in Siena. The use of different stylistic elements in this phase appears to be less an indication of Mazzuoli's artistic development than a conscious choice of the mode of expression. As his career progressed, Bernini's influence continually diminished.

In 1679 Mazzuoli received the most extensive assignment of his career, one that occupied him for a decade: the production of *The Twelve Apostles* for Siena Cathedral. As the over-life-size figures were to be placed before the columns of the church without any sort of frame, the statues had to remain fully legible in profile. With the *Apostle* statues, for the first time, the now-seasoned master employed numerous assistants in his own workshop.

Of the works from the 1690s, the throne figure *Pope Pius II* for Siena Cathedral draws directly, in terms of composition, on Caffà's throne figure of *Pope Alexander III*, created a quarter of a century earlier for the same location. Other important works from this period include the often-copied praying *Angel* (ca. 1694/95) on the high altar of the Church of San Donato in Siena and the beautiful altar relief with Beato Ambrogio Sansedoni in the Sienese palace of the Sansedoni family.

When Caffà died in 1667, he had been working on the high altar group depicting the *Baptism of Christ* for the main church of the Knights of Malta. Around 1700 the assignment was passed to Mazzuoli, who, with serious modifications to Caffà's original plan, finished the group in 1703. Mazzuoli was by this time increasingly engaged for tombs, for which he could exhibit his abilities as a talented portraitist, cultivated since his early career: these include the Altieri tombs in the Church of Santa Maria in Campitelli and the Pallavicini-Rospigliosi tombs in the Church of San Francesco a Ripa, both in Rome. His important assignment of the first decade of the 18th century was the colossal statue *Apostle Philippus* for the apostle series at the Basilica of San Giovanni in Laterano. This work has met almost uniformly with harsh criticism, although the verdict becomes somewhat more positive when one considers the 96-centimeter marble model for the statue's benefactor, the archbishop of Würzburg, which was probably completed entirely by Mazzuoli. The question remains to what degree the workshop assistants were responsible for the distorted proportions and resulting negative reception of the version at the Basilica of San Giovanni in Laterano in Rome. Mazzuoli was over 60 years old at that time and leaving the transfer of his designs to marble increasingly to his students and assistants. In the case of the statues *Christ and Mary* in Siena Cathedral, the sculptor only created the models; the marble carving belonged entirely to his nephew Bartolomeo Mazzuoli. A similar arrangement with Roman assistants certainly occurred for *Caritas with Three Children* in the Chapel of the Monte di Pietà in Rome, although Mazzuoli signed the statue, giving his age as 79. Of his last work, the monument for Marc'Antonio Zondadari, only the model of the kneeling figure of the grand master of the Knights of Malta is probably Mazzuoli's work, and the execution of the entire monument is attributed to his nephew Bartolomeo.

According to Pascoli, Mazzuoli created two works for his own pleasure (see Pascoli, 1730–36). Like most sculptors of his generation, Mazzuoli was active in the restoration of ancient relics and dealt throughout his career with themes of Classical mythology. His interest manifested itself, however, almost exclusively in small-scale clay models never transferred into monumental sculpture. Only two groups created out of this personal interest, *Adonis with the Boar* (1709) and *The Dying Cleopatra*, were ever realized in marble. The sculptor is said to have worked for 31 years on the *Adonis* group, which would mean that he conceived of the project around 1678. Such an early date, scarcely after the young sculptor had left Bernini's studio, is believable, as the imagery bears the Berninesque style. *The Dying Cleopatra* group, a decade later, lacks such an impetus; as a domestic-intimate scene portrayed elegiacally, it is a child of the 18th century. Both groups are well suited to illuminate the broad spectrum of Mazzuoli's oeuvre.

MONIKA BUTZEK

See also **Bernini, Gianlorenzo; Caffà, Melchiorre; Ferrata, Ercole**

Biography

Baptized in Tuscan city of Volterra, Italy, 1 January 1644. Fourth son of architect and stonemason Dionysio Mazzuoli of Cortona. Moved with family to Siena; elder brothers Francesco, Giovanni Antonio, and Agostino entered into their father's career and together formed, after the latter's death, the family company of Francesco Mazzuoli and brothers, serving Siena and its surroundings and as a base in Siena for Giuseppe; younger brother Annibale a painter; Giuseppe completed primary studies as a sculptor under his brother Giovanni Antonio; moved to Rome to continue his training, *ca.* 1662; worked initially under Antonio Raggi, possibly in the studio of Ercole Ferrata; opened his own studio, 1667; entire career spent in Rome but traveled frequently to Siena; member of the Congregazione dei Virtuosi of the Pantheon, 1675; accepted as member of the Accademia di San Luca, 1679. Died in Rome, Italy, 7 March 1725.

Selected Works

An extensive collection of Mazzuoli's terracotta models can be found in the Chigi Saraceni collection in Siena, Italy.

1669–72	A saint (San Remigio?); travertine; colonnades of St. Peter's Basilica, Rome, Italy
ca. 1670–72	*Carlo de' Vecchi and Giulia Verdelli*; marble; Church of San Vigilio, Siena, Italy
ca. 1671/73	*Dead Christ*; marble, alabaster; Church of the Santa Maria della Scala Hospital, Siena, Italy
ca. 1672–75	*Caritas* (Charity) (after a model by Bernini); marble; tomb of Pope Alexander VII, St. Peter's Basilica, Rome, Italy
1677–78	*Immacolata*; marble; Church of San Martino, Siena, Italy
1677–78?	*Cardinal Flavio Chigi*; marble; Vatican Museums, Rome, Italy
1677–79	Two kneeling angels holding candles; marble; Church of Sant'Agostino, Siena, Italy
1678–80	*Saint John the Baptist* and *Saint John the Evangelist*; marble; Church of Gesù e Maria, Rome, Italy
1679–89	*The Twelve Apostles*; marble; Siena Cathedral, Italy
1686–87	*Clementa*; marble; tomb of Pope Clement X, St. Peter's Basilica, Rome, Italy

1691–94 *Pope Pius II*; marble; Siena Cathedral, Italy

1694 Altar relief (with Beato Ambrogio Sansedoni); Palace of the Sansedoni, Siena, Italy

1700– Alteri tombs; Church of Santa Maria, 1710 Campetelli, Rome, Italy

1700– *Apostle Philippus*; marble; Basilica of San 1710 Giovanni in Laterano, Rome, Italy

ca. *Maria Camilla Pallavicini, Giovan Battista* 1710–19 *Rospigliosi*, and four Virtue allegories; marble; Cappella Pallavicini Rospigliosi, Church of San Francesco a Ripa, Rome, Italy

ca. *The Dying Cleopatra*; marble; garden of 1713–21 the Hospital do Ultramar, Lisbon, Spain

1714 *Cardinal Bandino Panciatichi*; marble; Victoria and Albert Museum, London, England

1717/ *Christ and Mary*; marble (lost) 18–21

1721–23 *Caritas with Three Children*; marble; Chapel of the Monte di Pietà, Rome, Italy

1722–25 *The Grandmaster of the Knights of Malta Marc'Antoni Zondadari*; marble; Siena Cathedral, Italy

Further Reading

Angelini, Alessandro, "Giuseppe Mazzuoli, la bottega dei fratelli e la committenza della famigli De'Vecchi," *Prospettiva* 79 (1995)

Angelini, Alessandro, *Gian Lorenzo Bernini e i Chigi tra Roma e Siena*, Siena, Italy: Banca Monte dei Paschi de Siena, 1998

Angelini, Alessandro, Monika Butzek, and Bernardina Sani, editors, *Alessandro VII Chigi (1599–1667): Il papa senese de Roma moderna*, Siena, Italy: Maschietto i Musolino, 2000

Avery, Charles, assisted by Alastair Laing, *Fingerprints of the Artist: European Terra-cotta Sculpture from the Arthur M. Sackler Collections*, Washington, D.C.: Arthur M. Sackler Foundation, 1981

Draper, James David, "Some Mazzuoli Angels," in *La scultura: Studi in onore di Andrew S. Ciechanowiecki*, Turin, Italy: Allemandi, 1994

Gentilini, Giancarlo, and Carlo Sisi, *La scultura: Bozzetti in terracotta, piccoli marmi e altresculture dal XIV al XX secolo* (exhib. cat.), 2 vols., Florence: S.P.E.S., 1989; see especially vol. 2

Hyde Minor, Vernon, "Mazzuoli, Giuseppe" in *The Dictionary of Art*, edited by Jane Turner, New York: Grove, and London: Macmillan, 1996

Pascoli, Lione, *Vite de' pittori, scultori ed architetti moderni*, 2 vols., Rome: de' Rossi, 1730–36; reprint, 1 vol., Perugia, Italy: Electa Editori Umbri, 1992 (the fundamental biography)

Schlegel, Ursula, "Some Statuettes of Giuseppe Mazzuoli," *The Burlington Magazine* 109 (1967)

Suboff, Valentin, "Mazzuoli, Giuseppe," in *Allgemeines Lexicon der bildenden Künstler von der Antike bis zur Gegenwart*, edited by Ulrich Thieme, Felix Becker, and Hans Vollmer, vol. 24, Leipzig: Engelmann, 1930; reprinted, Leipzig: Seemann, 1978

Westin, Robert, and Jean Westin, "Contributions to the Late Chronology of Giuseppe Mazzuoli," *The Burlington Magazine* 116 (1974)

MEDALS

Inspired by the coins and medallions of imperial Rome, the commemorative portrait medal has its roots in the Italian Renaissance and, with modern exceptions, remains essentially unchanged from its initial appearance about 1438–40. Medals are commonly palm-size or smaller disks of metal, usually of a copper alloy such as bronze or brass, but one also finds examples in lead, silver, and gold. The obverse shows a portrait of the patron (or sitter) surrounded by an inscription, whereas the reverse often holds some sort of allegory, narrative, coat of arms, impresa, or heraldic device accompanied by an inscription. The attraction of the medal lies not only on the immortality provided by its indelible nature or on its tactile qualities that could be enjoyed on an intimate level. The extended visual and textual interplay afforded by such a double-sided object, allowing several levels of interpretation and dualities of meaning, also makes them intellectually stimulating items of discussion and powerful tools of both positive and slanderous propaganda. Portrait medals and coins are often collected under the misleading rubric of numismatics. Although they share a number of similarities with coinage, medals are not currency, and their commission and production are not restricted to governmental agencies.

Portrait medals are either cast or struck. In 15th-century Italy medalists usually built up models in wax, whereas medalists north of the Alps in the following century preferred to cut the model out of a hard, tightly grained wood (such as boxwood) or stone. The medalist took a mold in a fine material (recipes differ, but include ash, salt, tufa, pumice, and a bonding agent) of the model. After carving pouring channels and escape vents into the hardened mold, the medalist joined the two *in cavo* (concave) sides and poured the molten metal. After the medal cooled, the artist chiseled imperfections (or remaining details) on the medals, polished the surface, and added a lacquer.

Struck medals became popular in the 16th century. Striking a medal follows the same technique as coining currency: dies are cut in intaglio in hardened steel, the upper die (trussel) descends—either by hammering or by means of a large screw—upon the fixed, lower die (pile), which holds a softer metal blank (planchet or flan), and impresses both obverse and reverse simultaneously. Struck medals are often smaller, in lower relief, and stiffer in execution than cast medals but allow sharper detail and almost unlimited production runs.

In 1438 the penultimate Byzantine emperor, John VIII Paleologus, visited Ferrara, and Antonio di Puccio Pisano, called Pisanello, a prominent painter in the International Gothic style, commemorated the event with a two-sided, bronze portrait disk. With this medal of the emperor, Pisanello effectively revived and revised the Roman imperial medallion and created an art form that found an immediate following. Although his portraits are certainly elegant accounts of the sitters' dignity, Pisanello's creative facility, especially with allegorical and narrative reverses, has never been surpassed in the medium. Particularly beautiful are the reverses to his medals for Cecilia Gonzaga, with *Innocence Taming the Unicorn*, and Leonello d'Este's medal showing *Love Teaching a Lion to Sing*.

Matteo de' Pasti was among the earliest followers of Pisanello, and his medals, such as those for *Sigismondo Malatesta*, lord of Rimini, reflect the debt. Mantua was the locus for much of the early talent, although many medalists in the 15th century spent much of their careers in distant cities, including Cristoforo di Geremia and Lysippus the Younger, who worked primarily in Rome and whose medals carry elegant Latin epigraphy. Also from Mantua was Sperandio Savelli, who cast a large number of boldly modeled medals for patrons throughout Italy, followed by the sharper, classicizing aesthetics of Pier Jacopo di Antonio Alari Bonacolsi, called Antico, and Galeazzo Mondella, called Moderno.

In Venice several skilled artists in the late 15th and early 16th centuries, including Giovanni Boldù, Vittore Gambello, called Camelio, and Fra Antonio da Brescia, produced finely modeled medals for the Venetian patriciate. Medals became popular in Florence at a surprisingly late date. Bertoldo di Giovanni, bronze sculptor to the Medici and teacher of the young Michelangelo, was among the earliest artists to make medals, although most of them date from the 1480s. His medal commemorating the Pazzi Conspiracy (1478), which shows the murder of Giuliano de' Medici and the wounding of his brother Lorenzo "il Magnifico," illustrates one of the most turbulent and intriguing events in late 15th-century Florence. Florence's dominant medalist of the 15th century was Niccolò di Forzore Spinelli, called Niccolò Fiorentino, who combined large, sensitive portraits with indifferent, repetitive reverse compositions largely appropriated from the antique.

Although the production of medals was almost exclusively restricted to Italy in the 15th century, the 16th century found medalists throughout Western Europe. In Italy medalists increasingly struck or pressed medals, rather than casting, due primarily to technological innovations such as the screw press by Benvenuto Cellini in Rome. The ducal court of Florence supported several medalists, including Giampaolo and Domenico Poggini, Pietro Paolo Galeotti, and Gaspare Mola. One of the most prolific medalists, Pastorino de' Pastorini worked primarily in Ferrara and Florence and cast over 200 portraits (many uniface, or one-sided) of the leading citizens in Italy. In Padua Giovanni Cavino cast and struck medals usually paraphrased from Roman sesterces. Milan surfaced as the center for medallic activity in 16th-century Italy, largely due to the workshop of the sculptor Leone Leoni, whose profound influence on artists can be traced throughout Europe, particularly those regions controlled by or sympathetic to the Habsburgs. The most surprising medals of the 16th century come from the Reggio Emilia region, where artists such as Alfonso Ruspagiari and Bombarda (probably Andrea Cambi) cast whimsical, extremely thin uniface portraits in lead.

Medals first appeared in Germany in the 16th century and reflect an uncompromising attention to detail and naturalistic portraiture. Medallic production in Germany centered on the cities of Nuremberg and Augsburg. In Augsburg Hans Daucher cast a number of exceptional medals in the 1520s, and his contemporary Hans Schwartz may be counted among the greatest of the early German medalists. Also dominant in Augsburg were the wood sculptors Christof Weiditz and Friedrich Hagenauer, who sometimes eschewed the profile for three-quarter portraits. Mathes Gebel dominated the medallic community in Nuremberg, particularly in the second quarter of the century, followed by the substantial talents of Joachim Deschler and Hans Bolsterer. In Saxony Hans Reinhart cast a series of adequate portraits but is particularly remembered for the spectacular, silver high-relief *Trinity* medal, dated 1544.

France produced few medals of distinction in the 16th century, with the exception of the sculptor Germain Pilon's large cast medals for the Valois kings. Artists from Italy, Germany, and the Netherlands designed the vast majority of medals produced in England during this period. Jacques Jonghelinck and Steven van Herwijck worked in Antwerp and Utrecht; the latter produced a large number of exceptional medals informed with the stylistic tendencies of the Milanese school.

The most important and influential medalists of the 17th century in France were Guillaume Dupré and the sculptor Jean Warin. Dupré cast all of his medals, whose sharp clarity and excellent portraits reflect certain influences of Dutch and German artists, as well as those of Italian medalists such as Leone Leoni and Jacopo da Trezzo. His style in turn had a profound impact on Italian medalists for the better part of the

17th century. Warin produced a large body of struck medals (and coins), ranging in style from those revealing Mannerist tendencies to medals that anticipate Neoclassical solutions. Warin oversaw production of the *Medallic Histories*, which were issued in several versions and editions between the 1660s and 1723, as part of the vast propaganda program meticulously planned and governed by Louis XIV (the 1702 and 1723 series included some 300 medals). The format of the *Medallic Histories* influenced later French medalists such as the prolific Jean Duvivier and Joseph Roettier.

In Rome Gaspare Mola was among the most distinguished medalists in the early 17th century, and his medals, although struck, share a stylistic affinity with the work of Dupré. Francesco Travani, Giovanni Battista Gugliemada, and the Hamerani family (Giovanni and his sons Ermenegildo and Ottone) created medals for various popes, ambassadors, and leaders of state. In Florence the large cast medals by Massimiliano Soldani-Benzi for the Medici family and others combined lively portraits with sprawling allegorical reverses replete with finely modeled figures barely covered by carefully described drapery. Soldani-Benzi had numerous students and disciples, including Antonio Selvi and Lorenzo Maria Weber, a transplanted German.

Although their predominance waned toward the end of the 17th century, Augsburg and Nuremberg continued as the centers for German medallic production, with work by Christian Maler, Sebastian Dadler, and Johann Blum. The late 17th and early 18th centuries saw medalists Philipp Heinrich Müller and Martin Brunner producing large numbers of medals to commemorate various events such as Müller's *Battle of La Hogue* (1692). Christian Wermuth struck hundreds of medals for various ducal houses, as well as a series on the Roman emperors. The medals by G. van Bijlaer from the Netherlands often dispensed with the portrait and commemorated military conflicts and alliances, and later in the 17th century, medals by his compatriots Jan Boskam and Jan Smeltzing aggressively satirized Louis XIV. In England Nicolas Briot (from Paris) worked at the London mint and struck medals for Charles I, and Abraham Simon and Thomas Simon's cast medals of politicians and diplomats are among the best to come out of England from the 17th and 18th centuries. Jan Roettier was Dutch, but he and his family worked extensively for the British crown. Much of the rest of Europe, including Arvid Karlsteen of Sweden and Anton Meybusch of Denmark, remained indebted to French medallic sensibilities.

Medalists struck the majority of medals produced in the first half of the 19th century with a clean, sometimes clinical, application of Neoclassical ideals to portraiture and reverse design. The *Histoire Métallique*

(1804–14) recalls the medallic programs of Louis XIV and commemorates the Napoleonic Wars and the emperor in a series of 90 medals. Not to be outdone, England commissioned a series of medals to commemorate British military successes, many of which were, ironically, designed and engraved by French artists such as André Brenet.

In England Neoclassicism's greatest exponent was William Wyon, who came from a well-established family of medalists and designed more than 200 medals distinguished by excellent portraits, elegant reverse compositions, and a subtle mastery of the figure. Wyon became chief engraver at the royal mint only in 1828, after a long disagreement with his primary adversary, the Italian gem engraver cum medalist, Benedetto Pistrucci. Several Italian medalists followed Pistrucci's Neoclassical tendencies, including Luigi Manfredini and Giovanni Antonio Santarelli. Dependence on Neoclassical models continued for much of the 19th century in France, evidenced in artists such as Emile Rogat and Jean-Jacques Barré, and remained the dominant influence on artists in much of Europe such as Wilhelm Kullrich in Berlin, Joseph Daniel Boehm in Vienna, and Léopold Wiener, with his architectural medals, in Belgium.

Concurrent with but directly opposed to the increasingly mass-produced struck medals in the 19th century was a return to the cast medal. The celebrated French sculptor David d'Angers led this revival and cast portraits from the 1820s to the 1850s, but it was a revival of technique only: the loose, romantic portraits and lettering (often incised), such as David's medals of *Napoléon* and *Juliette Récamier*, represented a freedom of experimentation with the medium not previously seen. The cast medal became popular again in the latter decades of the 19th century with artists such as Auguste Préault and Alexandre Charpentier in France and Alphonse Legros and Edward John Poynter in England.

The reducing machine, which allowed the mechanical reduction and reproduction of a model without the need of an engraver, decidedly influenced the final decades of the 19th century. By the end of the century the reducing machine was commonplace, and several artists used the technique with tremendous skill, including Jules-Clément Chaplain and Oscar Roty in France. Their compositions depart from the formal rigidity of Neoclassicism: figures are bathed in an iridescent, misty light and recede almost imperceptibly into their backgrounds. The velvety, ephemeral compositions of French artists from the turn of the 20th century such as Hubert Ponscarme, Daniel Dupuis, and Ovid Yencesse echoed elements of the Art Nouveau movement, whereas the objects themselves, sometimes serving no commemorative function whatsoever, often blurred the lines between medals and plaquettes. Also working at the turn of the century were medalists of exceptional talent throughout Europe, such as Erik Lindberg of Sweden, Philippe Wolfers in Holland, and Lancelot-Croce (French but working in Italy). In Prague Heinrich Kautsch, Stanislas Sucharda, and Sucharda's student Bohumil Kafka created medals that reflect the predominant style in France but which also reveal the Austro-Hungarian Secession style (especially evident in the lettering) and the formal and compositional influences of decorative painters such as Gustav Klimt.

Medals in the early years of the 20th century continued to be influenced by the work of Roty and Chaplain and the Art Nouveau style. Noteworthy is the work of Lithuanian-born Victor David Brenner, who studied under Roty and Charpentier in Paris but worked mainly in the United States, where he designed dies for many medals, as well as the Lincoln cent. After World War I German medalists such as Karl Goetz, Walther Eberbach, and Ludwig Gies sought a language to describe the horrors of war and departed from their contemporaries with brutal and sometimes massive force. German Expressionism did not strike a particularly resonant chord in France, but the gauzy, diaphanous textures of artists such as Yencesse and the vernal, decorative nature of Art Nouveau were unsuitable for dealing with the aftermath of the war. Art Deco prevailed as the dominant tendency in the 1920s and 1930s in many media, often revealing a fascination with modern technology. French Art Deco medalists such as Pierre Turin returned to hard edges of Neoclassicism but ground their work in geometrical forms and decisive, angular lines. The Art Deco movement also found sympathetic medalists in Sir Robert Johnson in England and in industrial designer Norman Bel Geddes, Paul Manship, and Laura Gardin Fraser in the United States.

Since World War II medals have increasingly pushed the limits of the medium by experimenting in subject matter, technique, format, and materials. This period also has seen a significant increase in interest in the medal worldwide. Artists working in France, including Roger Bezombes, Henri-Georges Adam, and Swedish-born Siv Holme, often keep portraiture central to their medals, even if the portrait assumes an extremely novel approach. Other artists have abandoned the portrait altogether. Medalists such as Fritz Nuss in Germany have explored the styles of artists such as Paul Klee and Pablo Picasso. Others, including Hungarian-born Mariá Lugossy and Italians Gianfranco Zanetti and Pino Mucchuit, have moved past the representational, and the Hungarian Tamás Asszonyi has examined compositional issues sometimes based on the shape of the medal itself. The design of medals was also influenced by talents outside of Europe and the United States, such as Ken Kakuyama's work in Japan. In its varied forms, the medal continues to be a vibrant art form around the world, enjoying strong support from both governmental sources and private societies.

ARNE R. FLATEN

See also **Bertoldo di Giovanni; David d'Angers; Dupré Family; Leoni Family; Pisanello; Warin, Jean**

Further Reading

Brown, Laurence A., *British Historical Medals*, 2 vols., London: Seaby, 1980–87
Fischer, Jacques, and Gay Seagrim, *Sculpture in Miniature: The Andrew S. Ciechanowiecki Collection of Gilt and Gold Medals and Plaquettes*, Houston, Texas: Museum of Fine Arts, and Louisville, Kentucky: J.B. Speed Museum, 1969
Goldenberg, Yvonne, *La médaille en France de Ponscarme à la fin de la Belle Époque* (exhib. cat.), Paris: Hôtel de la Monnaie, 1967
Hill, George F., *A Corpus of Italian Medals of the Renaissance before Cellini*, 2 vols., London: British Museum, 1930; reprint, with new preface and appendix by J. Graham Pollard and Ulrich Middeldorf, Florence: Studio per Edizioni Scelte, 1984
Hill, George F., and Graham Pollard, *Renaissance Medals: From the Samuel H. Kress Collection at the National Gallery of Art*, London: Phaidon, 1967
Jones, Mark, *The Art of the Medal*, London: British Museum, 1979
Jones, Mark, *A Catalogue of the French Medals in the British Museum*, London: British Museum Press, 1982–88
Loubat, Joseph F., *The Medallic History of the United States of America, 1776–1876*, 2 vols., New York: s.n., 1878; reprint, New Milford, Connecticut: Flayderman, 1967
Luftschein, Susan, *One Hundred Years of American Medallic Art, 1845–1945*, Ithaca, New York: Herbert F. Johnson Museum of Art, 1995
Middeldorf, Ulrich Alexander, and Dagmar Stiebral, *Renaissance Medals and Plaquettes: Catalogue*, Florence: Studio per Edizioni Scelte, 1983
Norris, Andrea, and Ingrid Weber, *Medals and Plaquettes from the Molinari Collection at Bowdoin College*, Brunswick, Maine: Bowdoin College Museum of Art, 1976
Pollard, J. Graham, editor, *Italian Medals*, Washington, D.C.: National Gallery of Art, 1987
Scher, Stephen, editor, *The Currency of Fame: Portrait Medals of the Renaissance*, New York: Harry Abrams, 1994
Scher, Stephen, Christopher Eitmer, and Philip Attwood, "Medal," in *The Dictionary of Art*, edited by Jane Turner, New York: Grove, and London: Macmillan, 1996
Taylor, Jeremy, *The Architectural Medal: England in the Nineteenth Century*, London: British Museum, 1978
Trusted, Marjorie, *German Renaissance Medals: A Catalogue of the Collection in the Victoria and Albert Museum*, London: Victoria and Albert Museum, 1990
Vannel, Fiorenza, and Giuseppe Toderi, *La medaglia barocca in Toscana*, Florence: Studio per Edizioni Scelte, 1987
Whitman, Nathan, and John Varriano, *Roma Resurgens: Papal Medals from the Age of the Baroque*, Ann Arbor: University of Michigan Museum of Art, 1983

MEDICI VENUS

attributed to Kleomenes, the son of Apollodoros,
from Athens (fl. 1st century BCE)
ca. 60 BCE
marble (perhaps Parian)
h. 1.53 m
Galleria degli Uffizi, Florence, Italy

The *Medici Venus* was found in or near Rome, probably in the 16th century. The exact location of the find is a matter of controversy. It is likely that the sculpture entered the Valle-Rustici-Bufalo collection in Rome, was bought by Ferdinando de' Medici in 1585, and was then housed in Rome in the Villa Medici. The Medici family took the statue to Florence in 1677, and by 1688 it had been placed in the Tribuna of the Galleria degli Uffizi. In 1802 it was taken to Paris (Musée Napoléon); it was returned to Florence in 1816. Since then it has resided in the Galleria degli Uffizi. From the 17th to the 19th centuries, the *Medici Venus* was one of the most widely admired ancient statues.

The statue itself has been recomposed from many fragments. The main modern restorations are the whole of the right arm and the left arm from the elbow. The goddess rises from the sea, the setting indicated by the dolphin ridden by two childish Cupids placed near Venus's left leg. Startled by a beholder, she shields her breasts and her pubis with her arms in a gesture of modesty, turning her head (which had been broken off and restored) to the left so as to avoid the gaze of the intruder. The firm and high breasts suggest a young, teenage Venus. The wavy hair, held by a ribbon and collected in a bow on the top of the head and in a knot on the nape, is also intended to contribute to the young grace of the body.

Around 40 copies of this style of Venus are known. The most superb copy stands in the Metropolitan Museum of Art in New York City. This particular copy is important because the head is preserved unbroken on the body, thus confirming that the position of the restored head on the Medici copy is correct. This Venus-type sculpture was inspired by Praxiteles' masterpiece, the naked *Knidian Aphrodite* of around 360 BCE, who also shielded her pubis with her right hand.

The original statue of the Medici-type *Venus* is perhaps represented on a coin from Sikyon in the northwestern Peloponnese, Greece. Written sources state that the Sikyonian sculptor Lysippos made a sculpture of a naked Venus with a dolphin at her feet. This has led to the attribution of the original statue of this type to Lysippos, specifically to the period of his activity around 330 BCE.

Indeed, the *Medici Venus* has many features that are common to the art of the great Lysippos: the slender body, the small head, and the lack of frontality due to the forward inclination of the torso and the turning of the head to the side. The sinuous side views are similar to those of Lysippos's *Apoxyomenos*, and the head is similar to that of his *Eros*, the *Apoxyomenos*, and the Copenhagen-type *Alexander*, creations all attributed to Lysippos.

The anatomy of the *Medici Venus*, characterized by the slightness of the bone and the fullness of the flesh, is in keeping with the style of Lysippos. The position of the arms across the body is also characteristic of his work. This creation should thus be regarded as earlier than the original statue of the *Capitoline Aphrodite*, who also shields her graces with her arms. It appears much closer to the Praxitelean heritage, with a predilection for surfaces characterized by plays of light and shade. For this reason, the original creation of the *Capitoline Aphrodite* is usually attributed to Kephisodotos the Elder, the son of Praxiteles, active around 300 BCE.

Kleomenes, whose signature is on the Florentine copy, was the son of Apollodoros and a member of a well-known family of Athenian sculptors. He is probably the same Kleomenes who signed an unpublished base of a colossal statue from the Acropolis of Athens, now in the Epigraphical Museum of that city. This signature suggests that he was based in Athens. Other works of his are a group of Muses known as the *Thespiades*, mentioned by the Roman writer Pliny the Elder (*Natural History*, 77 CE) and inspired by Praxiteles' *Thespiades* group; an altar with the carved representation of the *Sacrifice of Iphigenia*, now also in the Galleria degli Uffizi of Florence and probably a variation of the late 5th-century painting on the same subject by Timantes; a statue found in the northern Italian city of Piacenza; and a Herm of Eros derived from Praxiteles' *Centocelle Eros*, found in Rome and drawn by the 16th-century Roman antiquarian Pirro Ligorio.

The last three works listed above are attributed to Kleomenes because his signature has been found on them. This Kleomenes, active during the Caesarian period, was thus influenced by Late Classical Greek style, which was then in fashion. In the *Medici Venus*, we see his use of the Late Hellenistic style, especially in his research of strong chiaroscuro effects, and in particular in the deep carving of the buttocks and the cavernous navel. The copy in Florence, when compared with the copies that are closer to the Late Classical original, and in particular the one in New York, seems cooler and more academic, the three-dimensionality of the original statue having been moderated in favor of the bidimensional conception of sculpture that was typical of the neo-Attic workshops of the 1st century BCE.

Kleomenes' son, also named Kleomenes, was active during the Augustan period. His signature can be found on a 5th-century-BCE Hermes type with a portrait head of the Julio-Claudian prince Marcellus (the so-called *Germanicus*), now in the Musée du Louvre, Paris, and a copy of the 5th-century-BCE statue of the *Wounded Warrior*, also now in the Galleria degli Uffizi (his signature was erased in modern times, presumably to suggest that the statue had been made by a more renowned ancient sculptor). This second Kleomenes was thus more interested in Early Classical Greek sculpture, in keeping with the admiration for the legacy of Polykleitos held by Augustus's circle.

ANTONIO CORSO

Further Reading

Alexander, Christine, "A Statue of Aphrodite," *The Metropolitan Museum of Art Bulletin* 11 (1953)

Beschi, Luigi, and Giancarlo Susini, *La statua del Guerriero Ferito*, edited by Piera Bocci, Florence: Centro Di, 1992

Cittadini, Rita, "Figure femminili di Lisippo," *Bollettino d'Arte* 100 (1997)

Haskell, Francis, and Nicholas Penny, *Taste and the Antique: The Lure of Classical Sculpture, 1500–1900*, New Haven, Connecticut: Yale University Press, 1981

Havelock, Christine, *The Aphrodite of Knidos and Her Successors: A Historical Review of the Female Nude in Greek Art*, Ann Arbor: University of Michigan Press, 1995

Mansuelli, Guido, editor, *Galleria degli Uffizi: Le sculture*, 2 vols., Rome: Istituto Poligrafico dello Stato, 1958–61; see especially vol. 1

Neumer-Pfau, Wiltrud, *Studien zur Ikonographie und Gesellschaftlichen Funktion Hellenistischer Aphrodite-Statuen*, Bonn: Habelt, 1982

CONRAT MEIT 1470/1485 (?)–1550/1551

German

In the diary of his Netherlandish journey of 1520/21, Albrecht Dürer praised Conrat Meit as "the good image carver named Conrad, the like I have never seen." Highly esteemed by his contemporaries but forgotten soon after his death, Meit is considered one of the preeminent northern European Renaissance sculptors in the first half of the 16th century. Born in Worms at an unknown date, the formation of his artistic personality in the upper Rhine region and a possible trip to Italy remain major problems of Meit studies. The origins of his style, however, can best be considered within the dominant tradition of the Nikolaus Gerhaert school, which at the end of the 15th century underwent a transformation from intricately agitated and folded figure compositions toward a monumental, statuary, and more balanced style with stricter contours.

Meit's first documented (now lost) commission— a complex, double-sided image of the Madonna accompanied by Forty Angels for the castle church at Wittenberg for Frederick III the Wise, Elector of Saxony—which he sculpted in the newly founded workshop of Lucas Cranach the Elder, placed him in a progressive artistic milieu in which basic elements of German Renaissance art were available. Meit's Renaissance interest in nude figures may have originated from his collaboration with Cranach and the paradigmatic example of Dürer, whom he might have known there.

Meit had already been paid for works done in the service of Archduchess Margaret of Austria, governess of the Netherlands, when he was first recorded as court sculptor in Mechelen in 1514. The governess had expressed in a letter to an unidentified cousin in 1512 that she wished to borrow his good German sculptor for the carving of a stone portrait of her deceased husband, Duke Philibert II of Savoy. The circumstances expressed in the letter can be related to some of Meit's earliest recorded works, such as the lost pair of life-size marble portrait busts of Margaret and her late husband that were first documented in 1517.

From 1514 until his death in 1550–51, Meit's career can be followed with fragmented documentary evidence. Securely dated works survive only from this part of his life, whereas all attempts to ascribe anonymous Late Gothic statuary to the young Meit have not been entirely convincing. With the masters of Late Gothic German statuary, Meit shared the competence of sculpting works in stone and wood. A major part of his surviving oeuvre, especially the small-scale portraits and nude statuettes, show the secular and humanist spirit of his patrons and their interest and taste in the antique, which is also exemplified in the unpolychromed life-size alabaster *all'antica* (after the antique) *Head of a Man* (J. Paul Getty Museum, Los Angeles), which is considered to be a portrait of Cicero. Partially polychromed, the small-scale objects, obviously conscious of their art status, were made for early collectors. Like Meit's life-size sculptures, these are characterized by the monumentality of conception, the infinite rendering of the smallest detail, and the virtuosity in depicting the surface textures of the human body and facial features.

Payment records mention a number of works that Margaret of Austria commissioned until 1526. These include a wooden *Hercules* (possibly the model for the following statuettes; 1518); two metal statuettes of *Hercules* (one of which was a gift to Hendrick III, count of Nassau-Breda; 1518); two wooden miniature portraits of Margaret as a widow (1518); a wooden tower and a stag's head that was to be placed on the chimneypiece in Margaret's library (1518); a wooden pietà for the convent of the Annonciades in Bruges, which was polychromed by the court painter Bernard van Orley (1519); a gilt metal pair of Adam and Eve statuettes (1519); a polychromed wooden figure of Christ as Gardener (*Noli me tangere*, 1526); and a

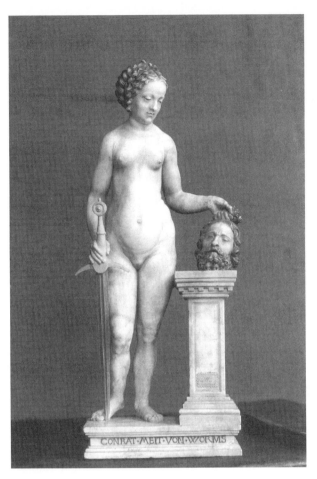

Judith with the Head of Holofernes
© Foto Marburg / Art Resource, NY

polychromed wooden image of Philibert of Savoy (1526). Most of the sculptural works listed in the detailed inventories of Margaret of Austria's residence are small-scale sculptures, the earliest a wooden statuette of Christ and a wooden statuette of Lucretia in 1516. In the same year the first small-scale sculptures are mentioned with reference to Meit's authorship, a wooden self-portrait of Meit—although lost, the fact itself is an extraordinary sign of the changing status of the artist—and a wooden horse. Later works mentioned in the inventories without reference to Meit's name include a marble statuette of the *Spinario*, a pair of small portrait busts of Margaret and Philibert in wood, a wooden *Man Holding a Dog and a Baton*, a metal statuette of a child sitting on a horse, and a metal statuette of Hercules, which must be identical with the aforementioned commission of 1518.

Although most of the recorded works are lost, the extant small-scale portraits certainly were made for Margaret. The Munich miniature bust of Margaret as a widow can be connected with the above-mentioned payment from 1518. With the exception of a wooden

pair of statuettes that could have functioned as a model for the documented metal statuettes of *Adam and Eve*, the extant statuettes cannot directly be connected with documents. The group consists of two wooden pairs of *Adam and Eve* that are in Gotha and Vienna, a bronze group called *Mars and Venus* in Nuremberg, a bronze female nude in Cologne, and the wooden *Fortitudo* in Écouen. They show all the idiosyncrasies of Meit's style; the female bodies and their coiffure closely resemble the only signed work by Meit, the alabaster statuette of *Judith with the Head of Holofernes*, which can be dated close to the alabaster putti in Brou, which were executed between 1526 and 1528.

A documented trip to Brou, near Bourg-en-Bresse, in 1524 antedated Meit's move to Brou in 1526. For the three single tomb structures in the Church of St. Nicolas of Tolentino, Meit and his workshop, to which his brother Thomas belonged, executed five lifesize effigies: two of Margaret of Austria and two of her last husband Philibert of Savoy (both depicted as alive and dead on the different levels of their tombs), and one of Margaret's mother-in-law, Margaret of Bourbon (depicted as alive), guarding animals at the feet of the upper figures and 16 putti. Two putti from the tomb of Margaret of Bourbon vanished during the French Revolution. The almost perfectly preserved ensemble shows the three upper effigies in an animated state, turning toward each other in prayer. The two lower effigies, the representations *de la mort* (of death), of the ducal couple depart from the tradition of depicting the dead in a state of decay. Instead, Margaret and Philibert are shown young and beautifully idealized, almost as if to suggest they might resurrect at any moment.

It is difficult to determine exactly to what extent Meit had to follow preexisting plans while executing the commission. The three single architectural tomb structures and the adorning statuettes were already completed when Meit began his work in Brou. Because of a delay in obtaining the marble, which arrived from Carrara in 1528, the alabaster sculptures were carved first. Therefore, the effigy of Margaret of Bourbon and a guarding greyhound, six putti of the recessed wall tomb, and the representations of the dead Margaret and Philibert were finished by Meit before the two marble representations of Margaret and Philibert shown alive and dressed in ceremonial vestments, depicted in an advanced age, and the marble putti were begun.

Although there is much debate as to Meit's involvement, the faces and hands of all five effigies are certainly by him. The extent of work done on the upper effigies' clothing by his workshop sculptors is unknown and not easy to distinguish. Only the marble putti show different individual sculptors at work in

Brou while the earlier alabaster putti can be attributed to Meit.

It appears that the unfinished, life-size alabaster group of the *Pietà* was only begun by Meit. In 1532 Antoine de Montcut, the former confessor of Margaret of Austria, ordered the *Pietà* (now in St. Jean's Cathedral in Besançon) to be placed on the altar of his chapel in St. Vincent's Church (destroyed) in Besançon. Principally based on a lost work by Andrea del Sarto (the Puccini Madonna), which was known through a graphic reproduction by Agostino Veneziano, the sculptural composition significantly changes the underlying model. Until 1534 Meit is documented working with assistants on more than a dozen life-size alabaster statues for a monumental tomb structure that never was installed. In 1531 Meit had signed a contract with Duchess Philiberte of Luxembourg for the tomb of her late son, Philibert of Chalon, prince of Orange, in Lons-le-Saunier. Although kept in Lons until the 18th century, no single sculpture for the tomb, which comprised several portraitlike depictions of the prince, members of his family, and allegorical and religious representations, has ever been found.

Changing from his earlier status as court sculptor, Meit in 1536 inscribed as a member of the painters' and sculptors' Guild of St. Luke in Antwerp. More than 16 life-size sculptures are documented during Meit's late years. He was also recorded as being engaged in the decoration of the Antwerp Cathedral, which had burned in 1533. The fragmentary accounts document work on a side altar with a miraculous image of the Virgin Mary. Meit must have been the head of a considerable workshop in Antwerp, for in 1536 he accepted another major commission for the Norbertine Abbey of Tongerloo, where he carved the life-size alabaster statues of three sibyls that were to be placed on the lower level of the imposing sacramental tabernacle. Meit's last documented commission of 1540, a Holy Sepulcher with 13 life-size figures (destroyed), also for Tongerloo and finished in 1542, included a portrait of the abbey's prelate in the guise of one of the attendants.

Apparently, all of Meit's late sculptures and many works of his contemporaries in the Lowlands were destroyed or vanished in the iconoclastic devastation of the Protestant Reformation of the 16th century or later in the course of the French Revolution. An assessment of his supposedly strong influence on Netherlandish sculpture in the period between his move to Antwerp and the iconoclasm of 1566 and the question of a late style, therefore, lacks a material basis.

JENS LUDWIG BURK

See also **Gerhaert von Leiden, Nikolaus**

Biography

Born in Worms, Germany, between 1470 and 1485. First mentioned as employed by Frederick III the Wise, elector of Saxony in 1511; created *Double-sided Madonna with 40 Angels* (destroyed) in Lucas Cranach's workshop in Wittenberg, Germany, before 1510; court sculptor to archduchess Margaret of Austria, in Mechelen (now in Belgium), before 1514 until 1530; worked on the archduchess's tomb complex near Bourg-en-Bresse (now in France), 1526–31; commissioned by Duchess Philiberte of Luxembourg to execute sculptures for tomb of her son in Lons-le-Saunier, France, 1531; acquired house in Antwerp, 1534; became member of Guild of St. Luke, Antwerp, 1536; received commission for Antwerp Cathedral, 1536–39, and for the Norbertine Abbey of Tongerloo, 1536–42. Died in Antwerp (now in Belgium), between September 1550 and June 1551.

Selected Works

ca. 1510 *Adam and Eve*; wood; Schlossmuseum, Gotha, Germany

1515–20 *Mars* and *Venus*; bronze; Germanisches Nationalmuseum, Nuremberg, Germany

1518? *Margaret of Austria*; wood; Bayerisches Nationalmuseum, Munich, Germany

1525–28 *Judith with the Head of Holofernes*; alabaster; Bayerisches Nationalmuseum, Munich, Germany

before 1523/24 *Philibert of Savoy*; wood; Skulpturengalerie (currently on loan to Kunstgewerbemuseum), Berlin, Germany

before 1526 *Margaret of Austria* and *Philibert of Savoy*; boxwood; British Museum, London, England

1526–31 Tomb effigies of Philibert of Savoy, Margaret of Bourbon, and Margaret of Austria; marble, alabaster; and alabaster putti for the tomb of Margaret of Bourbon; Church of St. Nicolas of Tolentino (Musée de Brou), Brou, near Bourg-en-Bresse, France

before 1532 *Pietà*; alabaster; Cathedral of St. Jean, Besançon, France

after 1530 *Adam and Eve*; wood; Kunsthistorisches Museum, Vienna, Austria

after 1530 *Fortitude*; wood; Musée de la Renaissance, Écouen, France

after 1530 *Madonna with Child*; marble; St. Michel's Cathedral, Brussels, Belgium

Further Reading

Bode, Wilhelm, "Die bemalte Thonbüste eines lachenden Kindes im Buckingham Palace und Meister Konrad Meit," *Jahr-*

buch der Königlich Preuszischen Kunstsammlungen 22 (1901)

Borchgrave d'Altena, J., "A propos d'une madonne de Contrat Meijt," *Revue belge d'archéologie et d'histoire de l'art* 23 (1954)

Duverger, Jozef, *Conrat Meijt (ca. 1480–1551)*, Brussels: Hayaz, 1934

Lowenthal, Constance, "Conrat Meit," Dissertation, New York University, 1976

Osten, Gert von der, and Horst Vey, *Painting and Sculpture in Germany and the Netherlands, 1500–1600*, London and Baltimore, Maryland: Penguin, 1969

Rasmussen, Jörg, "Eine Gruppe kleinplastischer Bildwerke aus dem Stilkreis Conrat Meits," *Städel-Jahrbuch*, n.s., 4 (1973)

Troescher, Georg, *Conrat Meit von Worms—ein rheinischer Bildhauer der Renaissance*, Freiburg im Breisgau: Urban, 1927

Vöge, Wilhelm, "Konrad Meit und die Grabdenkmäler in Brou," *Jahrbuch der Königlich Preuszischen Kunstsammlungen* 29 (1908)

Vöge, Wilhelm, "Zu Konrad Meit," *Monatshefte für Kunstwissenschaft* 8 (1915)

MELANESIA

Melanesia is one of the principal cultural groups of Oceania. Located in the South Pacific between the equator and the tropic of Capricorn, east of New Guinea, Melanesia can be outlined in general as a grouping of islands and archipelagoes comprised of the Admiralty Islands, New Ireland, New Britain, the Solomon Islands, the Banks Islands, and New Caledonia. A variety of sculptural traditions dominate the arts, ranging from complete figures in the round to relief carving on ceremonial house posts and lintels to elaborate masks of mixed-media construction.

To define a strict geographical area as Melanesia is problematic. For example, to the southwest the Torres Strait Islands are included within the administration of Australia but are culturally aligned with Melanesia. To the southeast the islands of Fiji are at times either included with Melanesia or Polynesia. Some of the Vanuatu and Solomon Islands also have connections across political and cultural lines. New Guinea is often also included within Melanesia due to its coastal interactions and similarities with the nearby smaller islands, although the majority of its various art traditions do not have strong affinities with Melanesian traditions.

Attempting to delineate Melanesia through language is also problematic because the islands include a variety of languages with disparate historical origins. In terms of human population Melanesia has nearly no unity. The region has a complex prehistory consisting of more than one major period of Asian migration.

The earliest migration into this region took place possibly 50,000 years ago during the last Ice Age. At that time the oceans were as much as 120 meters lower than they are now. The lower water levels exposed the continental shelves that created the landmasses of Sahul and Sunda. Sahul included the regions of Australia, New Guinea, and Tasmania. Sunda encompassed the Malay Peninsula, the Philippines, Borneo, Sumatra, Java, and Sulawesi.

The first migration from Southeast Asia could have been accomplished on foot, with the stretches of ocean and rivers, which were considerably shorter than today, separating Sahul and its nearby islands of New Britain and New Ireland being traversed by small canoes or rafts by 35,000 years ago. The longer voyages to the Solomon Islands were accomplished by 28,000 years ago, and to the Admiralty Islands by approximately 20,000 years ago. Some evidence suggests that the earliest migrations into New Guinea may have included groups from earlier populations established in Australia.

After the Pleistocene era the rising ocean waters between 11,000 and 8,000 years ago covered the exposed continental shelves, creating the landmasses as

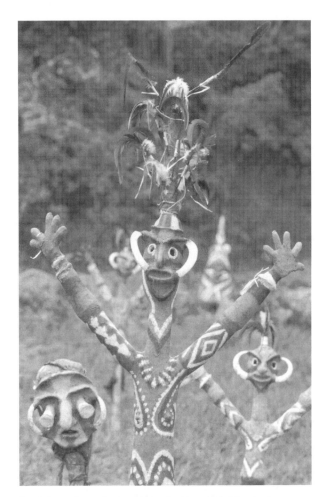

Lagiol carvings, Ambryn Islands, New Hebrides (today Republic of Vanuatu), Melanesia
© Jack Fields / CORBIS

they are known today. This process not only increased the divide between the islands of Southeast Asia, New Guinea, and Australia but also decreased the size of the islands of Melanesia considerably. The greater distance between the islands and their smaller size would have made the prospect of ocean voyage less likely without increased maritime skill. Contact between these regions may have continued, although on a considerably smaller scale.

The second sizable migration into Melanesia from Southeast Asia may have begun some time between 6,000 years ago and 1,000 years ago. Much of the evidence for these migrations is linguistic and connected to the dispersal of Austronesian speakers from Southeast Asia throughout Oceania. The seafaring migrations of these people and their contact and blending with the prehistoric settlements account for more than a thousand languages and cultures. Resistance to these migrants is evident in areas where the prehistoric populations may have been well entrenched. In New Guinea the Austronesian settlements seem to have never reached the highlands and only established themselves along the coast and rivers.

Pottery along the Sepik coast of New Guinea first appeared approximately 5,700 years ago. Linguistically and archaeologically, the origin of pottery in both Asia and Oceania has been linked to Austronesian languages, although New Guinea samples suggest that pottery may have predated this contact in Oceania. If the latter is true, the origins of pottery in Melanesia may be from New Guinea prior to Austronesian contact.

Approximately 3,600 years ago a culture known as Lapita, named after a site in New Caledonia, arose in the Bismarck Archipelago. Whether the Lapita culture originated there, from the nearby New Guinea pottery traditions, or from the immigration of Southeast Asian Austronesian speakers is still debated. The Lapita culture, with its distinct pottery and obsidian artifacts, spread from about 3,200 years ago through Melanesia and eventually into western Polynesia about 2,000 years ago. Regardless of the absolute origins of pottery in Melanesia, the strong connection between the coastal Lapita culture and Austronesian languages was an important factor in establishing Melanesian art traditions, much more so than in New Guinea. Lapita pottery fragments have been discovered with incised geometric motifs and, less frequently, anthropomorphic forms. The patterns have some general similarities to those found in later bark-cloth and tattooing arts of Oceania.

The artistic traditions that have developed over the last several millennia in Melanesia do not easily fit Western categories of visual art and art production. The most prolific art form is sculpture of both carved and constructed types. One can see the sculptural elements of Melanesian art throughout the island cultures in the forms of canoe prow and stern figures, boat hangers, carved door posts and roof finials, figurines, modeled staves, bas-relief carved shields, battle and ritual dance clubs, slit gongs, masks and headdresses, agricultural and house implements, *malanggan*-style carvings of New Ireland, and mobile structures of the Admiralty Islands.

Important features of sculpture in Melanesia, and many areas of Oceania, are the ephemeral and mobile aspects of the art. In many cases, in addition to the wood carvings and sculptures most readily accepted by the Western eye as art, the attached ephemeral elements and their movements either in battle or through dance and ritual in conjunction with music and chant were the most important attributes given to a sculpture. Some of the many materials used in the construction and ornamentation of the sculptural arts included wood and leaves from various types of trees, beaten bark, seeds, fruit, colored earth and clay, shells, birds of paradise and other bird plumage, pelts of tree-dwelling mammals, spiderwebs, sloughed skins, and human hair. For many sculptures the loss of these elements or immobility due to a lack of use would render the sculpture irrelevant and powerless to the society. After a work of art has lost its ritual significance, it may be burned or discarded in the jungle to be reclaimed by the environment that provided the elements used for its construction.

Most representations of traditional art are of either a nature or human spirit, or some combination of the two. The nature spirits inhabit the different aspects of the environment and some animals. The human images commonly depict culture heroes. They can be in the form either of remembered real ancestors or of mythical origin ancestors.

With the long history of settlement, migration, and trade through the modern day, tracing specific iconographic patterns through time can be problematic. The great diversity of languages and worldviews also makes forming broad generalizations to categorize sculpture types, their use, and development in Melanesia nearly impossible and ill advised. Within a smaller regional distribution one can make some limited delineation between the various island groups.

Admiralty Islands

The Admiralty Islands make up the Manus province of Papua New Guinea. The region consists roughly of three major groups speaking several Austronesian languages. The Matankol make up the majority of the islands and coasts. The Ussiai populate the Great Admiralty further inland, and the Manus live along the southeast coast.

Many everyday objects, such as sculpted ladle handles, cup handles, wooden lime spatulas, and lime gourds, have artistic components. The Matankol were the primary producers of wood carvings and other decorated objects, but they did not have a masking tradition. Each island tended toward its own specialty objects. For example, the Lou were known for their obsidian blades, while the Baluan made ladles, spatulas, and bird-shaped bowls. One distinctive aspect of Matankol bowls is the intricate openwork scroll handles carved separately and attached with bindings. Artisans often only partially decorate wooden objects, such as adding bands of geometric patterns. They seem to have used decorative motifs for both ritual and secular objects.

Sculptures of the human figure are most often represented standing, arms at its sides, and incised with decorative patterns. In addition to figurines, artisans used the human form, commonly interchanged with animals such as the crocodile and birds, to decorate canoe prows and sterns, ladders, bed frames, and slit gongs.

The period after World War II saw a rejection of the traditional material culture in the region. At this time nearly all of what remained of the traditional culture was lost. Today many parts of Oceania have begun an attempt at the revival of traditional art forms.

New Ireland

Human occupation of New Ireland, a province of Papua New Guinea, dates back nearly 35,000 years. It played an important role in the early distribution of the Lapita culture. New Ireland is most well-known for its *malanggan* art tradition.

The *malanggan* cycle of mortuary ceremonies, which this art form comes from, likely had its origins in the Tabars of the nearby coral islands. The ceremonies, comprised of feasting, ritual performances, and gift exchanges, concluded with the display of a *malanggan* sculpture created in secrecy specifically for the occasion. The sculpture provided not merely a physical representation of but also an interpretive commentary on the deceased individual's family ties and lineage. The *malanggan* ceremony could last as long as several years.

Performance-related objects include several dance mask categories, such as masks with fiber-crested headpieces used for specific types of line dances, other types used to represent bush spirits, and the intricate *malanggan*-style masks.

Even though the *malanggan* art objects may take on various forms, they show a common stylistic use of carved openwork, interest in the use of negative space, the combination of animal and human forms, the use of snail opercula for eyes, and the use of black, red, and white pigments leaving areas of the natural wood exposed. Drawings dating to 1643 attest to the existence of intricate *malanggan*-style art prior to the introduction of metal tools to the island. The *malanggan* art traditions saw a revival over the last few decades of the 20th century, after nearly being wiped out in the wake of World War II.

New Britain

The earliest known art on New Britain, situated between New Ireland and New Guinea, is Lapita pottery from approximately 2,500 years ago. The island has a complex linguistic structure, with certain areas having Papuan and Austronesian languages mixed. New Britain is now a part of the state of Papua New Guinea.

New Britain is renowned as the center for Melanesian mask making and for its canoe making. The masking tradition incorporates a variety of mask types, although few are carved from wood. Most of the masks are constructed of fragile, ephemeral materials. The best-known type of mask consists of painted bark cloth, woven pith, and netting over a cane frame. In some cases artisans attach feathers and wood-carved accessories to the exterior of the mask. These masks are used by the Baining in day and night dance ceremonies to celebrate harvest and youth initiations and to honor the deceased.

An initiation dance of the Iniet men's society uses masks modeled over skulls of ancestors. New members of the society also receive small limestone and chalk carved figures. Similar small chalk figures are also found in the south of New Ireland.

Solomon Islands

The Solomon Islands, comprised of nearly 40 islands, lie at the geographic center of Melanesia. The traditions, ideas, and art forms now present on the Solomon Islands have grown from gradual and repeated interaction with New Guinea, its Melanesian neighbors, and the later Micronesia and Polynesia centers. The elaborate sculptures and other art forms of the Solomon Islands predominantly use the color black, which the artist creates by coating a surface with a resin-based pigment. Artists often accent the black surface in red and with small linear patterns in white of inlaid fragments of mother-of-pearl shell.

The central Solomon Islands are known for their small sculptures and carvings attached to canoe prows. The prow and stern posts in this area may reach as tall as three meters. Small carvings and shell inlays decorate the entire length of the posts. These sculptures, as well as those in other parts of Oceania, place great emphasis on the head. In part this refers to the headhunting tradition of the area. One type of canoe prow figure, the *nguzu nguza*, consists of a head and arms holding in their hands a small human head.

Overmodeled ancestor skulls with inlaid shell work also demonstrate a high level of craftsmanship. Artists modeled the skulls in a paste of parinarium nuts and decorated them with shells to replicate the jewelry worn by the deceased. The skill and materials required for decorating the skull reflected the importance of the ancestor being honored.

Banks Islands

The Banks Islands comprise part of the state of Vanuatu. Several Lapita pottery sites there have been archaeologically dated to about 3,500 years ago.

The painted tree-fern sculptures and figurines of the Banks Islands represent a fine example of Melanesian sculpture tradition. The sculptures consisted of carving in fern wood and modeling in clay, vegetable compost, and spiderweb. These figures were placed at the front outside corners of the ceremonial houses.

New Caledonia

The Melanesia prehistory associated with Lapita pottery also existed in New Caledonia. The island region has a tradition of fine wood sculptures of figurines, roof finials, and masks. The majority of the sculptures were to decorate the conical roofed men's ceremonial houses. Human faces generally adorn the finials, upper doorjambs, and interior posts. The lintels and lower doorjambs are carved in relief with a repetitive diamond motif.

New Caledonia also has a tradition of adorning lengths of bamboo with engraved groups of humans, often demonstrating an activity, which is unusual in the canon of Melanesian art.

Modern Influence

Outside contact and influence on the inhabitants of Melanesia during the modern era has had noticeable and sometimes considerable impact on the visual art traditions of these cultures. Brief contacts between Melanesian Islanders and Europeans began in the 16th century and reached a state of continuous contact by the late 18th century. Explorers' relations with these islands had diverse ramifications. The importation of items such as iron tools, guns, and cloth to the islands became new sources of power, often undermining cen-

turies of established power structure. The increase in maritime contact created not only intensified relations between islanders and explorers but contact between remote island groups as well. Europeans would at times trade items they gathered from one island with a group on a distant island. Representatives of an island would also join a ship's crew and sail to another island, thus participating in the first direct contact between two island groups.

With European contact came Christian missionaries. In some cases missionaries caused the destruction of art objects that they saw as idols and suppressed many forms of ritual activity and warfare, while they viewed other art objects, such as pottery, bark cloth, baskets, and decorative ornaments as potentially valuable in commerce and trade. Some missionaries encouraged conversion of islanders by incorporating Christian iconography into traditional settings, for example, replacing a ceremonial house finial with a Christian cross.

Most Oceanic islands to some extent have also undergone a period of colonization. The introduced commercial activities of a colonial power transformed some societies; mining, logging, fishing, nuclear testing, and tourism have all had an effect on the island cultures. Artists are divided between creating traditional objects for rituals or ceremonial exchange and making items for the tourist market. This situation has created both a loss of some traditional arts and the adaptation of others. Some regions have adapted by creating a tourist art separate from the traditional ritual arts. Other communities, possibly in need of funds, consider selling ritual objects to museums or private collectors.

Toward the end of the colonial era and into the present, the islands have had a growing interest in preserving remaining traditional arts and reviving those that were no longer practiced. In this process a variety of internal and external variables influence the final form and purpose of the art object. In addition to the revival of traditional arts, and the transition of a once-traditional art into a new tourist art, the creation of new art forms draws on both indigenous and Western materials and beliefs.

JOHN L. MACHADO JR.

See also **New Guinea**

Further Reading

Gathercole, Peter, Adrienne L. Kaeppler, and Douglas Newton, *The Art of the Pacific Islands*, Washington, D.C.: National Gallery of Art, 1979

Kaeppler, Adrienne L., Christian Kaufmann, and Douglas Newton, *Oceanic Art*, New York: Abrams, 1997

Meyer, Anthony J.P., *Oceanic Art*, 2 vols., Edison, New Jersey: Knickerbocker Press, 1996

Newton, Douglas, editor, *Arts of the South Seas: Island Southeast Asia, Melanesia, Polynesia, Micronesia; The Collections of the Musée Barbier-Mueller*, New York: Prestel, 1999

Thomas, Nicholas, *Oceanic Art*, New York: Thames and Hudson, 1995

Wardwell, Allen, *Island Ancestors: Oceanic Art from the Masco Collection*, Seattle: University of Washington Press, 1994

MEMORIAL: OTHER THAN WAR

Memorials are signs of remembrance. They can take the form of statues, buildings, festivals, plaques, and medals, among others. They can be private or public. Private memorials are erected by individuals mourning the loss of a friend or loved one. The range of expression varies by circumstance and financial means. Public memorials are raised by either public funds or erected within the public realm, or both. They honor individuals whose lives were significant to a wider audience than just family and friends, individuals who gave their lives to advance a particular area of human endeavor and who are deemed worthy of public commemoration. From the simple slab on a grave or a white cross marking the site of an accident to the elaborate funerary tomb or public monument, each type of commemoration serves to keep the memory of a person or event alive.

Funeral Memorials

The earliest memorials were probably simple stones erected at the place of burial or at a significant site. Dolmens from the Celtic word *doi*, meaning "table," were chambers or enclosures consisting of two or more vertical stones supporting a large single stone. They were built as tombs, each enclosing an individual burial. Many of those erected in the Carnac region of Brittany, France, were decorated on their interiors with either carvings or paintings. These stone monuments functioned as a link between the present and eternity. Their stone structure, as opposed to the wood used on domestic architecture, was intended to last forever, protecting the body of the deceased and serving as a place of remembrance. On the Indian subcontinent, similar burial mounds covered the burial sites of Hindu royalty. These evolved into the mounds over sacred relics such as the Great Stupa at Sanchi. Over time this act of remembrance developed into funerary markers, tombs, church memorials, gravestones, and the organization of public cemeteries. One of the largest burial tombs unearthed in the 1970s was that of Qin Shi Huangdi, the first emperor of the Qin dynasty (221–210 BCE). The pits of the tomb located at Lingtong near the modern city of Xi'an have revealed the replication on a massive scale of the emperor's army, his guards, and entourage in terracotta. It is estimated that when the entire site is excavated that there will be in excess of 7,000 figures. It is interesting that prior to this time, individuals were buried alive with their ruler, so the change to figures in clay, the facial features of each individualized, was a dramatic break from previous traditions.

During the Classical period elaborate stelae served as memorials. Many included incised carvings of female allegorical figures offering libations, while others were kore or kouros figures erected above burial sites in temples.

Typical of the memorials from the Celtic and Norse periods are the carved cross slabs. The carving usually included a simple representation of the Christian cross, and the slabs were normally memorials to the dead. Several examples from the Isle of Man include the Ogham form of writing, a script thought to have originated in southern Ireland in the 5th century. Others are runes that contain a Germanic form of script adapted from the Latin alphabet and used on Scandinavian memorial stones. Runes were in use from the 3rd century until the Middle Ages. The Isle of Man contains over 200 carved Manx crosses that served as memorials, erected in the vicinity of the Celtic *keeills*, simple small chapels. In later centuries people appropriated the cross slabs for use in other building works without regard to their original memorial purpose.

Beginning in the 7th or 8th century, Christians buried their dead inside parish churches or within adjacent or neighboring parish cemeteries. Burial within a parish church soon became a sign of social status as well as an expression of piety. The wealthier preferred a sepulcher close to the main altar or, alternately, within a chapel or under the *charnier*.

Accompanying this burial was the need to erect a memorial for the deceased. Many took the form of slab floor markers for those buried underneath the nave; other often more elaborate memorials were erected on the walls of the churches. These funerary tablets ranged from a simple tablet often accompanied by a portrait medallion of the deceased and acanthus decoration to a large multifigured allegorical grouping. These memorials rely heavily on Christian belief, the deceased lying on their deathbed surrounded by friends and family, looking toward heaven, with angels appearing ready to carry their souls to heaven. Soon, however, the church walls were filled, and memorials began to take the form of small brass plaques or stained-glass windows.

In the late 14th and early 15th centuries, the memento mori entered the public space of the city. Wealthy individuals began to embellish their cemeteries with distinguished burial structures. These structures became private chapels amid the assembled piles of skulls and bones, such as the Cemetery of the Holy Innocents in Paris, as images to represent the folly of human vanity. Pictures and inscriptions on the cemetery walls reinforced the idea that life was only mortal and that salvation rested in Christian faith. Many of these decorations included the danse macabre, in which a skeleton, representing either the dead person or Death incarnate, compels an unwilling partner to join him in the dance of death. Most were sardonically grinning figures on huge catafalques erected within the church for the funeral and then later placed on the mausoleum erected to perpetuate the memory of the deceased. The most famous of these dramatic images on 17th-century funerary tombs come from the Italian sculptor Gianlorenzo Bernini. During the 15th century, sculptors were commissioned to create monumental wall tombs that celebrated individual achievement. These are often referred to as the humanist tomb. One example is the tomb to Leonardo Bruni by Bernardo Rossellino in the Church of Santa Croce, Florence, Italy, dated 1444. The design for Bruni's tomb became the prototype of Renaissance wall tombs. Significant changes occurred in burial practices when exhumation of the skeletal remains after decomposition followed the burying in mass graves. The bones and skulls were stored under the roofs of the parish churches.

The combined impact of increased population and the plague prompted innovations in burial practices. The dead were seen not only as dangerous to the living but as defiling the church. Reformers during the 17th century, such as Jean-François Sobry, sought to separate the two sides of existence. The Parliament of Paris in 1765 ordered the restriction of burials inside parish churches. The result was the eventual forbidding of burials within the city. The new cemetery that the Parliament of Paris envisaged was a place of distinction in which the Christian portrayal of death and the humanist celebration of worthy accomplishments could coincide. The earliest designs were based on the ancient Roman walled garden, such as the Horti Bassiani Antonini, popular between the 3rd century BCE and the 1st century CE. Combined with this garden design, with its walls, arched openings, and freestanding columns, was the wish to accommodate the Christian vision of death. A memorial statue of Death normally rose above the entire complex, the skeletal figure modeled after the symbol of Death in Cesare Ripa's popular *Iconologia* (first edition, unillustrated, 1593; four subsequent editions published during Ripa's lifetime), the standard handbook for artists, writers, and sculptors for the previous two centuries, or a newer version of Death as Chronos. In this version sculptors carved a figure straddling a globe on top of the central chapel. Like the earlier danse macabre, the sculpted figure was a reminder of fleeting time and of human mortality.

The 18th-century concept of the cemetery as a landscape of virtue and achievement fostered the growth of sculpted memorials. Now not only were kings remembered in the public square or isolated memorials to heroes erected, but the cemeteries recognized the honors of all classes of society. While grand mausoleums, often in the favored shape of the pyramid, were still erected, sculptors began to be called upon to design individual memorials or markers for the graves in these formal landscape gardens representing the Elysian Fields. Deathbed scenes were particularly popular. The growth in popularity of cemeteries such as Père-Lachaise (Paris), Mount Auburn (Cambridge, Massachusetts), or Highgate (London) greatly increased the amount of sculpture commissions. Sculpted memorials became a part of these pastoral landscapes where individuals could sit on benches, stroll, and meditate.

Many sculptors, such as John Bacon (1740–1799) in England, offered clients pattern books from which to select a suitable memorial. The range was extensive, only depending on the space allocated and the finances of the individual family. Of the grandiose funerary memorials, many alluded to the vocation of the individual, as well as to the inherent religious beliefs of the community. For example, the figure of the French painter Theodore Géricault in Père-Lachaise Cemetery in Paris depicts the painter reclining, holding his easel.

By the end of the 19th century, the situation had entirely reversed itself. Public opinion previously having banished cemeteries from the city now desired a pastoral area to remember their dead within the city. The 20th century, however, saw a decline in the demand for private sculpted memorials. This was because of the cost of memorials as well as the cost of the management of cemeteries.

Notwithstanding traditional beliefs that kept funerary customs from rapidly changing, new memorials nonetheless arose in the latter part of the 20th century and early 21st century. Concern for space, the environment, and ease of maintenance led to a diminishing of three-dimensional sculpture over burial sites. The flat slab with the name of the deceased, the birth and death dates, and on occasion, a small verse is now common. Concurrent with this has been an increase in cremations with or without interment of the ashes. Again, this practice has led to a decrease in funerary sculpture. Becoming more prominent are the virtual memorials on the Internet as a replacement for permanent markers. Today, less formality is also common, as is the secularization of the rites of passage reflecting Western society's complex relationships and increasing religious, racial, ethnic, and cultural diversity.

Public Memorials

The modern tradition of erecting a commemorative sculpture as a metaphorical way of keeping a person's memory alive began in imperial Rome. Portrait busts, portrait statues, and equestrian monuments alongside triumphal arches and obelisks established the standards from which later sculptors took their inspiration. Typical of the Roman period is the bust of *Julius Caesar* dating from the 1st century BCE. Sculptors usually carved busts in marble, often from a wax death mask, so that specific physiognomic details of the individual were preserved. Portrait statues during the Roman era tend to be idealized. The standing marble figure of Augustus commonly known as the *Augustus of Prima Porta* is an example of idealized portraiture. Here the 76-year-old statesman and military ruler appears as a young man. The decorative motifs on the breastplate commemorate his military conquests and the pacification of Gaul while the right hand is raised in a gesture characteristic of orators.

The Romans were the first to aggrandize their heroes with bronze equestrian memorials. The only surviving example is the equestrian statue of Marcus Aurelius at the Piazza del Campidoglio in Rome. The victorious military leader extends his right arm as if speaking to the crowd while concurrently suggesting domination and conquest. Single freestanding columns commemorating individual achievement began to appear during the Hellenistic period. The Romans added a continuous narrative relief that served as a historical document of achievement.

The enthusiasm for erecting memorials to worthy individuals reached its zenith during the 19th century, a phenomenon commonly referred to as one of "statumania." Committees ready to immortalize with a sculpture individuals who died for their country would appear almost immediately after their death. It was the age of the cult of the hero both in art and in literature. Memorial statues placed in the public realm were seen as an effective means of inspiring patriotism. These sculptural commissions were thus undertaken not only to enshrine personal sacrifice but also to promote heroic ideals.

One of the most popular public figures to receive worldwide recognition in the form of memorials was Queen Victoria. Her death in 1901 resulted in a plethora of memorial statues, institutes, and charitable organizations throughout the British Empire. Typical was the intercity or interregional rivalry to erect the most prestigious memorial. On the Indian subcontinent alone, more than 50 statues were raised in the Queen's memory. Public donations funded most of the memorials.

Memorials erected to international, national, or local heroes are almost always placed in full view of the public, often erected on the most conspicuous site available. Funded through the public purse, public subscriptions, or by an individual benefactor, they adorn the fronts of buildings, town squares, and boulevards. The largest and most prestigious monuments within the urban capitals recognize individuals who were considered national worthies; often, various sites throughout a nation commemorate these same heroes. Local heroes tend to receive smaller and less costly recognition on the local level.

One of the biggest problems with erecting a public memorial is deciding who is deserving of such an honor. Controversy has always surrounded the commemoration of individual worth in the public arena. In its traditional form public sculpture represents the values of the ruling classes, who viewed it as an extension of their authority. As symbols of a particular political ideology, these public images changed with political rule. The destruction of public memorials erected to leaders of the Communist regime in the former Soviet Union was not new to the history of the public memorial. Images of Stalin and Lenin being hoisted from their pedestals by cranes or public memorials to Enver Hoxta being torn down in Tirana, Albania, in the 1990s were reminiscent of the controversy and removal of statues of the French monarchy during the French Revolution.

One of the most dramatic changes to public memorials came at the end of the 1960s, when social and political upheavals in the United States seriously challenged the power structure. As an outgrowth of the Civil Rights movement, the women's movement, and Vietnam War protests, the United States embarked on a new program of public art.

It is no longer deemed acceptable to memorialize only war or its heroes; instead, the public consciousness desires to remember the innocent victims of war as well as the "average" person whose life touched that of others. In Canada, near the city of Thunder Bay, for example, the memorial to Terry Fox, raised in 1981, commemorates the young man who led the Marathon of Hope only to succumb to cancer.

Today, the many complex social forces that respond to erecting memorials have resulted in a richness, diversity, and pluralism in such structures. Catastrophes and disasters have emerged as legitimate subjects for public memorials. Previously, battles, famine, disease, and genocide were not usually remembered as such, although many became part of oral traditions of premodern society or later entered the accounts of literature. Exceptionally, many parts of Europe erected memorials to victims of the plague. For example, the town of Maribor, Slovenia, was ravaged by the plague five times during 1680, with more than a third of the population wiped out. In 1743 the sculptor Joseph Straub completed a new memorial for the town square in memory of the victims of the plague. The memorial takes the form of a victory column surmounted by a figure of the Virgin Mary. Surrounding the base, which is in the shape of an altar, are figures of saints invoked to protect against further occurrences. These include St. Francis of Assisi, Bostjam, Jacob the Elder, Anton of Padovaanski, Rok, and St. Francis Xavier.

There are numerous examples from around the world that would suggest an increasing demand for a more formal recognition of catastrophes or great tragedies. Significant examples include the numerous Holocaust memorials or the Monument to the Coffin Ships erected in 1997 at the foot of Croaghpatrick in County Mayo in remembrance of those who tried to escape the Irish famine by immigrating to the United States. In Hiroshima and Nagasaki, Japan, numerous memorials to victims have been erected. These include the Monument to the 26 Saints erected in Nagasaki honoring the 26 Catholics on the ill-fated Spanish galleon, the *San Felipe*, which wrecked off the coast of Shikoku in 1596. All the survivors were forced to march to Nagasaki, where they were crucified on 5 February 1597. The monument was erected in 1962 in honor of the 100th anniversary of their canonization by Pope Pius IX. Memorials to the victims of the U.S. atomic bombings of Hiroshima and Nagasaki include the colossal figure *Peace* by Kitamura Seibo, which was completed in 1955 to mark the tenth anniversary of the event. In the United States, Ed Hamilton's *Amistad Memorial*, completed in 1992 for New Haven, Connecticut, commemorates victims of the slave trade.

The tragic events of 11 September 2001 provided venues for both spontaneous and planned memorials. Besides digital memorials, photo essays, flag relays, and personal tributes that took place across the United States and the world, permanent memorials were planned for all three crash sites, as well as for cities throughout the United States who lost citizens.

Neil Dawson's 15-meter aluminum and steel sculpture *Chalice* was unveiled in Christchurch's Cathedral Square, Christchurch, New Zealand, a week before 11 September 2001. One week later spontaneous offerings of flowers were placed at its base suggesting that artworks, seemingly unrelated, had taken on a new iconographic significance following the attacks on the World Trade Center in New York City and the Pentagon in Washington, D.C.

MARY ANN STEGGLES

See also **Bacon, John; Bernini, Gianlorenzo; Equestrian Statue; Gerz, Jochen; Honorific Column; Kore and Kouros; Lin, Maya; Portrait; Public Sculpture; Rome, Ancient; Triumphal Arch**

Further Reading

Baigall, M., "Sega's Holocaust Memorial," *Art in America* (summer 1983)

Beattie, Susan, *The New Sculpture*, New Haven, Connecticut: Yale University Press, 1983

Controversial Public Art, from Rodin to Di Suvero, Milwaukee, Wisconsin: Milwaukee Art Museum, 1983

Hannah, N.B., "The Open Book Memorial," *National Review* (11 December 1981)

Hess, E., "A Tale of Two Memorials," *Art in America* (April 1983)

Jackson, John Brinckerhoff, *The Necessity for Ruins, and Other Topics*, Amherst: University of Massachusetts Press, 1980

Read, Benedict, *Victorian Sculpture*, New Haven, Connecticut: Yale University Press, 1982

Richards, Maureen Costain, *The Manx Crosses Illuminated*, Port St. Mary, Isle of Man: Croshag, 1988

Senie, Harriet F., *Contemporary Public Sculpture: Tradition, Transformation, and Controversy*, New York: Oxford University Press, 1992

Young, James Edward, "Holocaust Memorials: The Art of Memory, the Permanence of Monuments," *The Journal of Art* (February 1990)

Young, James Edward, *The Texture of Memory: Holocaust Memorials and Meaning*, New Haven, Connecticut: Yale University Press, 1993

MEMORIAL: WAR

Wars, momentous events in human history, have been commemorated from ancient times to the present. Memorials may be built to mark victory over an enemy, a particular war or campaign, the achievements of great generals or admirals, the countless deaths of ordinary servicemen and servicewomen, or the tragedy of civilians caught up in warfare. Whatever the scale of the conflict, or whether the memorial commemorates an individual or a nation's losses, the erection of structures that mark humanity's destructive capabilities has long provided scope for sculptural endeavor.

The desire to remember, whether it stems from personal grief or political expediency, manifests itself in the need for structures created from enduring materials to evoke a diversity of sentiments, from honor, glory, and sacrifice to sorrow and anger. Memorials may have a utilitarian architectural function, but it is the need to remember that has often driven the commissioning of sculptors to evoke in plastic form the memory of war and its victims.

A war memorial may be a rough-hewn cross on a rural roadside or an elaborate group of statuary in a capital city. Although the former provides testimony of private grief and the local impact of war, the latter is a graphic statement of national values and identity. Many memorial forms are of ancient origin and comprise a distinct sculptural vocabulary; they are closely allied to the architecture that was adopted at particular times for public monuments and to bury and commemorate the dead. The sculptor was engaged in the embellishment of the underlying structure through the addition of narrative reliefs, motifs, or trophies, surmounting figures or equestrian statues, or the carving of names and inscriptions.

Obelisk

Obelisks erected by the ancient Egyptians remain one of the most striking forms built to denote power. The divine status of the pharaohs was equated with military prowess, and some obelisks possess inscriptions detailing particular battles as well as reliefs that provide invaluable information on the conduct of military campaigns. Similarly, although Assyrian narrative sculpture can portray generic scenes of war that symbolize the power of the ruler, there are examples that provide accurate accounts of particular conflicts, the sequence of battles, and the arms and tactics employed—for example, the stone panels from the Palace of Sennacherib (British Museum, London) that record the siege and capture of Lachish in 701 BCE. The drama and detail of such works have greatly influenced the way battle has been represented sculpturally ever since.

The ancient Greeks erected stelae listing those who were killed in battle, but most memorials celebrated particular victories or great military leaders. The monument and its sculpture were intended to depict the power of one civilization, nation, state, or tribe over another. The tomb of King Mausolos at Halicarnassus, erected about 350 BCE, was surmounted by a bronze statue of the king in a chariot and included friezes of battle scenes. Here, sculptors were employed to emphasize military achievement as an element of the king's greatness. Similarly, the tomb of Alexander from Sidon includes sculptural reliefs around a sarcophagus that illustrate the victory of Alexander over the Persians in 334 BCE. The military leaders, foot soldiers, and the enemy are represented in a dynamic composition that possesses an expressiveness and emotional content that was remarkable for its time. Greek sculptors employed the same techniques to represent contemporary battles as they did conflict in myths; rulers and generals were depicted in the same way as the gods. In this way, Greek military campaigns and their leaders were imbued with heroic status, as were athletes, poets, and politicians.

Victory Figure

Another significant memorial form derived from the Greeks is that of the winged Nike. The floating *Victory* by Paeonius, excavated from Olympia, was set up to mark the military success of the Athenians and their allies at Sphacteria in 425 BCE. Figures of Victory were to become a standard component of Roman triumphal projects. Indeed, throughout the Roman Empire, sculptors had an important role in the construction and embellishment of monuments to victory in war and to military leaders. Statues of generals were placed on columns, and the supporting structures were inscribed or decorated, the most elaborate example being Trajan's Column of the 1st century CE in Rome. In later eras, statues of generals and kings and representations of the archangels Michael and Gabriel have exerted a great influence on the ways in which the hero in war has been commemorated. The conquering hero on horseback—for example, Andrea del Verrocchio's powerful and emotionally charged monument to Bartolomeo Colleoni in Venice (1480–88)—is a motif that has ancient precedents, for instance in the equestrian monument to Marcus Aurelius (180–161 BCE), and that has endured despite changes in the technology of warfare.

Triumphal Arch

The triumphal arch is perhaps the most distinctive structure associated with the commemoration of war; the Arch of Titus in Rome marked the capture of Jerusalem in 70 CE and included panels depicting scenes from this campaign. Later examples can be found across Europe from the 17th century to the most enduring example from the 19th century: the Arc de Triomphe in Paris was completed in 1836 and records Napoléon's military campaigns with illustrative friezes and panels by François Rude, among other sculptors, on the piers.

Despite the formal and geographical diversity of war memorials, one thing common to their sculptors before the 19th century was their employment by the state, and later the church, as a means of reinforcing the power of particular regimes and ideologies. This pattern continued, but changes in attitude to those killed in conflict and the huge increase in the scale of deaths in war shifted the meaning of war memorials significantly, with emphasis now placed on combatants and victims. More war memorials were built in the 20th century than in any other. A product of modern warfare, they serve to remind spectators of the scale of death induced by the collision of mass citizen armies and civilians with technologically advanced armaments. They convey the values of the political regimes of both the victors and the vanquished, as well as the ambiguities of "undeclared" wars.

For centuries, professional soldiers were buried on the battlefield and sailors at sea; only great generals or admirals were deemed worthy of public commemoration in cathedrals and civic spaces. Although monuments such as the Colonne Vendôme, Paris, with its surmounting statue of Napoléon (1810) or Nelson's Column, London (1843), depict the ordinary soldier and sailor, these remain anonymous characters largely serving to illustrate the achievements of their leaders. Gradually during the 19th century, attitudes toward soldiering changed. As ordinary citizens began to enlist for particular conflicts, a need arose to commemorate the losses of all ranks. Memorials to the Crimean War (1853–56) were erected in many British towns to mark the local cost of this war. The American Civil War (1861–65) brought about the establishment of the National Cemetery System to honor the rank and file. It was at this time that representations of the ordinary soldier were elevated from their illustrative function to become the sole subject. Monuments to the Spanish American War (1898–1901) are indicative of this sculptural shift that forms one of the key, and certainly most popular, types of modern war memorial: the soldier statue.

World War I Memorials

The unprecedented scale of loss during World War I led to a surge of memorial building across all combatant nations in the postwar years. No one memorial could list the hundreds of thousands of dead from each country; consequently, the commemoration of individuals was fragmented and localized, with the building of thousands of small community memorials. Nationally, the commemoration of total casualties called for symbolic interpretation. In London the Cenotaph was erected in July 1919 to commemorate the dead of the British Empire. Designed by Sir Edwin Lutyens, this empty tomb was an appropriate device to represent those who were buried elsewhere. The bereaved all around the globe were experiencing the absence of their dead, and the appeal of the burial of unknown warriors testifies to the intensity of this experience. By returning one anonymous body from the battlefields, a symbolic commemorative trope was activated, which played on the possibility that the returned soldier could be one's own son, brother, husband, or friend. The burial of the British Empire's Unknown Warrior in Westminster Abbey and the French *Inconnu* below the Arc de Triomphe in Paris coincided with the second anniversary of Armistice Day in 1920. In 1921 the American Unknown Soldier was interred at Arlington National Cemetery. Subsequent burials across the world reflect the adaptability of this formula.

The World War I dead were buried in mass cemeteries overseen by institutions established solely for this purpose. In Great Britain the Imperial War Graves Commission, now the Commonwealth War Graves Commission, was formed in 1917 to commemorate the dead of the British Empire, and the American Battle Monuments Commission was established in 1923. Vast expense, resources, and artistic talent were used for complex and ambitious commemorative programs. Eminent architects and sculptors were employed to devise a restrained, egalitarian system of commemoration that would treat all ranks, religions, and nationalities equally. Blatant triumphalism was avoided, yet the resulting aesthetic, although moving, speaks of sanitizing order and imperial power.

Official commemorative structures built after World War I were mirrored by a surge of memorial-building by communities throughout the world seeking to remember their local dead. Communities required a means of publicly displaying the names of the dead in a manner that was deemed acceptable to the subscribing public. Inevitably, innovative or avant-garde solutions were avoided. In Great Britain the use of crosses and other religious imagery were popular because they equated the sacrifice of the war dead with Christ's sacrifice. In France, where crosses were banned in public spaces, *monuments aux morts*, secular in character with a tendency toward melodramatic narrative statuary, were constructed. French communities were eligible to apply to the ministry of the interior for a grant toward the cost of a memorial. As in Great Britain, commercially produced memorials were criticized and the use of professional sculptors encouraged. Yet for many towns and villages, catalogues of designs enabled communities to see exactly what they would receive for their careful accumulation of subscriptions. They could be confident that the design they chose conformed to a conventional commemorative vocabulary, be it a Tommy or Digger or Doughboy surmounting a pedestal, or an obelisk with wreaths, cock, eagle, flame, urn, Victory, or flags.

For many sculptors, memorial projects meant the opportunity to obtain public commissions, regarded as a prestigious step forward in their careers, marking the transition from *sculpteur* to *statuaire*. Some older artists, experienced in the creation of statues depicting politicians and other figures that adorned late 19th- and early 20th-century city centers or who had worked on monuments to earlier conflicts—the creators of "souvenir art," as Albert Elsen has described them—adapted their skills to commemorate the World War I dead. The sheer quantity of work, with competitions announced almost every week in the art press, enabled many other sculptors, for whom public commissions would previously have been out of reach, to realize their ambitions. In addition, many popular and established sculptors had no reservations about producing variations on a theme, rearranging various monumental elements and materials to suit different budgets.

World War II Memorials

Up until World War II, the legitimizing function of memorials necessitated the use of an established monumental language that spoke of honor, glory, and sacrifice in a way that could be readily understood by a public audience. After 1945 the iconography mobilized to commemorate the earlier conflict was widely regarded as anachronistic and inappropriate. Sculptors were less concerned about public commissions because sculpture's space had moved from the public square to the gallery. Sculptors sought to respond to their own creative instincts rather than the whims of a commissioning committee.

The British public expressed widespread antipathy toward monuments and statues, and projects for regeneration rather than commemoration were favored—for example, projects to benefit future generations and schemes to preserve and restore the landscape. Instead of commissioning separate monuments, many communities added the names of the dead to existing World War I memorials. Most new memorials commemorated civilian and air force casualties.

Hiroshima and Holocaust Memorials

Although the Allies were able to adapt established practices in order to commemorate their military dead, triumphalist monumental forms were entirely inappropriate for addressing the horrors of the atom bomb and the Holocaust. In 1946 a competition was organized for the building of a Peace Center at Hiroshima directly below where the first atomic bomb had been detonated. Comprising a museum and a community center, Kenzo Tange's starkly elegant memorial was opened in 1953. In July 1944 the Soviets had decided that the concentration camp at Majdanek should remain as a memorial museum, and in 1947 the Polish government declared that Auschwitz-Birkenau should be similarly preserved. In 1957 the first open competition for a memorial at Auschwitz-Birkenau was held, chaired by Henry Moore, who expressed the dilemma underlying all artists' involvement with the commemoration of war and suffering: "Is it in fact possible to create a work of art that can express the emotions engendered by Auschwitz?" The Treblinka monument of 1964 by the Polish architect Franciszek Duszenko and sculptor Adam Haupt powerfully evokes the theme of absence and gravelessness. It is a symbolic cemetery of granite stones inscribed with the names of Jewish communities throughout Poland that were destroyed during the Holocaust. From the first decisions to preserve sites of extermination through the building of Yad Vashem in Jerusalem to memorial museums in the United States, debates about appropriate sites of remembrance have continued, highlighted by initiatives in the 1990s to commemorate the Holocaust within the changing political map of Europe, particularly in a unified Germany.

Vietnam War Memorials

Traditionally, war memorials enforced official, legitimizing memories of war by means of didactic representations and patriotic inscriptions. Their intrinsically retrospective function always placed them at odds with the sculptural activity of modernists. In the last two decades of the 20th century, however, the creators of memorials have attempted to acknowledge the diversity of spectators' memories and experiences by providing a catalyst to memory or a site of memory rather than by prescribing what should or should not be remembered. This emphasis on the spectator underpins the National Vietnam Veteran's Memorial in Washington, D.C. Unveiled in 1982 and designed by Maya Lin, it was a controversial commission. Objectors commented on its difference from other monuments: it was primarily black and horizontal, and it was designed by a woman. Yet the inclusion of over 58,000 names of the dead and missing, listed chronologically by date of death, links it with earlier memorials in which the structure becomes subordinate to the task of recalling the absent. The reflective black granite implicates the spectator in the act of remembering; one cannot see the dead without seeing oneself. A similar attempt to deny a unifying image and to confront the spectator was the aim of Jochen Gerz and Esther Shalev-Gerz's Monument against Fascism, in Harburg, Germany (1986–93). The winning entry of a competition organized by the local council, their 12-meter-high square column was covered in soft lead, allowing the public to inscribe their names in a personal commitment against fascism. Gradually, as the inscriptions filled up the accessible carving space, the monument was lowered into the ground, to leave an emptiness intended to reveal that the responsibility for injustice lies within oneself. Impermanent, changing, and adaptable, this monument contradicted almost every aspect of a conventional memorial. Yet its links with past monuments, the emphasis on inscribed names—be they those of its audience rather than the dead—and its public setting were essential to its meaning.

Attempts to adapt new artistic and conceptual understanding for the monumental genre have grown even as conventional solutions have persisted. Over 300 local memorials to the Vietnam War have been erected across the United States by towns and states and at air bases, most in the mid 1980s. The majority depended on public donations, revealing the coming to terms of American communities with the Vietnam War and, crucially, the acceptance of veterans whom they were intended to honor, if belatedly, as much as the dead. They range from simple plaques to elaborate architectural or sculptural compositions. Figurative depictions of soldiers, such as those in Washington, D.C., tend toward the sentimental or glamorous. Thus, the pattern of local and national commissioning, characteristic of World War I, continues, emphasizing the ongoing dichotomy between the commemorative needs of the bereaved and home communities and those of the state.

Anniversaries and the need to commemorate those who were overlooked in immediate postwar years have led to new memorials elsewhere as well. Some are inspired by a political desire to recall a significant moment in a nation's past or by pressure from ex-servicemen and servicewomen; others have a cathartic function. It has also been argued that memorials have become a heritage asset, their solidity opposing the temporal and their permanence the transient.

Sculptors who have successfully managed to work around the restrictions of a commissioning body and the expectations of the subscribing public or government sponsors are exceptional. Memorial museums are now popular options. By placing emphasis on their educational value, the controversy of commissioning too radical or conservative a work of art may be avoided.

A report from the unveiling of the World War I memorial at Bangor, Northern Ireland, in 1927 noted, "No monument, however costly or magnificent, no parade of pomp or circumstance, bears any relation to the human loss that a war memorial connotes." Yet as wars persist, so will the need for sites of remembrance, by the state, combatants, victims, and the bereaved.

CATHERINE MORIARTY

See also **Equestrian Statue; Gerz, Jochen; Lin, Maya; Moore, Henry; Obelisk; Public Sculpture; Rude, François;** *Departure of the Volunteers of 1792 (La Marseillaise)***; Stele; Triumphal Arch; Verrocchio, Andrea del**

Further Reading

Borg, Alan, *War Memorials: From Antiquity to the Present*, London: Cooper, 1991
Inglis, Kenneth Stanley, and Jan Brazier, *Sacred Places: War Memorials in the Australian Landscape*, Carlton, Victoria: Melbourne University Press, 1998
King, Alex, *Memorials of the Great War in Britain: The Symbolism and Politics of Remembrance*, Oxford and New York: Berg, 1998
Longworth, Philip, *The Unending Vigil: A History of the Commonwealth War Graves Commission, 1917–1967*, London: Constable, 1967; revised and updated edition, as *The Unending Vigil: A History of the Commonwealth War Graves Commission, 1917–1984*, London: Cooper, 1985
Michalski, Sergiusz, *Public Monuments: Art in Political Bondage, 1870–1997*, London: Reaktion Books, 1998
Moriarty, Catherine, "The Absent Dead and Figurative First World War Memorials," *Transactions of the Ancient Monuments Society* 39 (1995)
Sherman, Daniel J., "Art, Commerce, and the Production of Memory in France after World War I," in *Commemorations: The Politics of National Identity*, edited by John R. Gillis, Princeton, New Jersey: Princeton University Press, 1994
Strait, Jerry L., and Sandra S. Strait, *Vietnam War Memorials: An Illustrated Reference to Veterans Tributes throughout the United States*, Jefferson, North Carolina: McFarland, 1988
Winter, Jay M., *Sites of Memory, Sites of Mourning: The Great War in European Cultural History*, Cambridge and New York: Cambridge University Press, 1995
Young, James Edward, editor, *The Art of Memory: Holocaust Memorials in History*, Munich and New York: Prestel-Verlag, 1994

PEDRO DE MENA (Y MEDRANO) 1628–1688 *Spanish*

One of the most celebrated sculptors of the Spanish Baroque, Pedro de Mena y Medrano worked principally in Granada and Málaga, exerting a significant influence throughout his native Andalusia and to a lesser extent, Castile. He primarily carved single figures—most notably depicting the *Ecce Homo*, the *Mater Dolorosa* (Grieving Mother), the *Penitent Mary Magdalene*, and *Saint Francis*—whose emotional intensity earned him considerable renown. In fact, Mena received an extended biography in the Spanish painter and author Antonio Palomino's *El parnaso español pintoresco laureado con las vidas de los pintores y estatuarios eminentes españoles*, which appeared in the volume of his *El museo pictórico* published in 1724.

Pedro de Mena was baptized in Granada. His father, Alonso de Mena, was a leading sculptor there, and the family was related by marriage to the other major artistic dynasties of the city. Alonso trained his son, who then took over the family workshop as an 18-year old when his father died in 1646. At this stage the young man probably looked to collaborate with his relatives in the Mora family, particularly Bernardo de Mora. In the following year Pedro de Mena married Catalina de Victoria y Urquijo, with whom he had several children. Of the 13 who are documented, 5 survived and entered religious life, but not before Mena trained two of his daughters, Andrea and Claudia, in sculpture.

In 1652 Pedro de Mena's career, like that of all artists in Granada, changed with the arrival of the talented painter and sculptor Alonso Cano. As Cano received several projects, he turned to Bernardo de Mora and Pedro de Mena for assistance in sculpture, an association that decisively influenced Mena's style. For example, when Cano designed four figures for the Convent of Angel Custodia—*St. Anthony of Padua*, *St. Joseph*, *San Diego of Alcalá*, and *St. Peter of Alcántara*—he engaged Mena to help him. The two artists collaborated so seamlessly that scholars disagree on the division between the two hands. Some argue that Mena sculpted all of the figures following Cano's design, whereas others have attempted to distinguish between the two hands in the various statues. The figures reflect Cano's style, but they also recur throughout Mena's career. At the same time, Mena also created several figures that offer further evidence of his debt to Cano, one of the most celebrated of which is his *Immaculate Conception*.

Collaboration with Cano may have helped Mena win the commission to complete the choir stalls of Málaga Cathedral in 1658. At that time Pedro de Mena transferred his workshop to Málaga, and apart from a brief trip to Castile, he spent the rest of his life there. The project had been begun 25 years earlier, but the first sculptor, Luis Ortiz de Vargas, and his successor, José Alfaro y Micael, died before they could finish it. Thus the bishop turned to Mena, first for a test relief of St. Luke; the chapter then awarded him the contract for the 40 remaining saints, for which Mena had to conform with the broad design for the choir established by Luis Ortiz. In addition to his relief of St. Luke, the program called on Mena to depict saints ranging from historical and medieval figures such as St. Mark, St. Catherine of Alexandria, and St. Bernard to relative contemporaries such as St. Teresa of Avila, St. John of God, St. Philip Neri, and St. Thomas Villanueva. In these reliefs, Mena carved the figures almost fully in the round and set them against a flat background. The work offers a sculptural tour de force, as Mena took advantage of the different types and varied the faces, draperies, and poses to create an impressive ensemble that established his reputation.

Soon after completing this project, Mena visited Castile. The trip was probably short but its impact notable. For Toledo Cathedral he carved the *St. Francis of Assisi*, a statue of the saint's body standing upright as, according to legend, it had been found when his tomb was opened. The subject had been previously painted by Francisco de Zurbarán and carved by Gregorio Fernández. Although Mena followed Fernández's model, his version became the one that subsequent sculptors emulated. The work achieved such success that the cathedral named Mena its official sculptor. Mena's time in Castile led to other prestigious commissions, including a statue of the Virgin for the king's half-brother, Don Juan José of Austria, and a crucifixion for Prince Doria, both now lost.

After he returned to Málaga, Mena carved one of his most famous images, the penitent *Magdalene* for

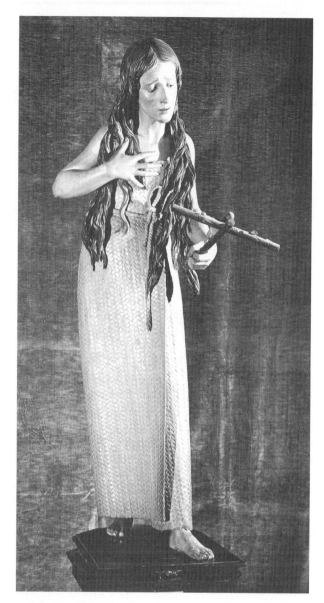

Magdalene, Madrid, Spain
© Scala / Art Resource, NY

a Jesuit convent in Madrid. His statue of the beautiful woman dressed in sackcloth and lost in contemplation of the cross she holds became the model for subsequent artists, just as his *St. Francis* had done. Again, Mena drew on an extant type, in this case a work in the Convent of Descalzas Reales (Madrid) that some scholars have attributed to Fernández. The ensuing decades proved Mena's most productive as he sculpted numerous statues of the *Ecce Homo*, the *Mater Dolorosa*, and saints. With their powerful yet restrained expressions and gestures, these works established his reputation as an artist of religious figures of great impact. He created such a pair of an *Ecce Homo* and *Mater Dolorosa* for his funerary chapel at the Church of Santa Anna del Cister of the Cistercian convent in Málaga. He occasionally carved images of other subjects, such as the charming *Saint John the Baptist*, in which the subject is depicted as a child, and his two versions (dated 1675–77 and 1676–78) of the Catholic monarchs, King Ferdinand and Queen Isabella of Castile, which attest to the breadth of his talent.

In December 1679 Mena fell so ill that he made his last testament, but he recovered and lived for another nine years, dying in 1688. The documents reveal that he had become a rich man, holding a certificate of nobility and owning both slaves and property that included houses and perhaps palaces. His legacy to Spanish sculpture lies not only in his distinctive style but also in a series of types that sculptors in Granada, such as the Mora family and José Risueño, would develop. Mena's workshop, which had executed many statues during the artist's life, continued, but the pieces associated with his principal follower, Miguel de Zaya, are generally considered of lesser quality.

PATRICK LENAGHAN

See also **Cano, Alonso; Fernández, Gregorio; Spain: Renaissance and Baroque**

Biography

Born in Granada, Spain, before 20 August 1628. Son of Alonso de Mena a leading sculptor. Trained by father; inherited family workshop when father died, 1646; style matured working with Alonso Cano, 1652–57; moved to Málaga to work on cathedral's choir stalls, 1658; after completing Málaga choir stalls, traveled to Madrid, *ca.* 1662–64; received numerous commissions in Spanish court and at Toledo; carved statue for Toledo Cathedral, on basis of which probably named *escultor de la catedral* (sculptor of the cathedral), 7 May 1663; returned to Málaga and spent rest of life there; made last will 7 December 1679. Died in Málaga, Spain, 10 May 1688.

Selected Works

ca. 1652–56 *Immaculate Conception*; polychromed wood; Church of Nuestra Señora de la Concepción, Alhendín, Granada, Spain

ca. 1653–57 Statues *St. Anthony of Padua, St. Joseph, San Diego of Alcalá,* and *St. Peter of Alcántara* (with Alonso Cano), for Convent of Angel Custodia, Granada, Spain; polychromed wood; Alhambra, Granada, Spain

1658–62 Choir stalls (begun in 1630s by Luis Ortiz de Vargas); wood; Málaga Cathedral, Spain

ca. 1663 *St. Francis of Assisi*, for Toledo Cathedral, Spain; polychromed wood; Museo Catedralico, Toledo, Spain

1664 *Magdalene*, for Casa Profesa, Madrid, Spain; polychromed wood; Museo del Prado, Madrid, Spain

1673 *Ecce Homo*; polychromed wood; Convent of Descalzas Reales, Madrid, Spain

1673 *Mater Dolorosa*; polychromed wood; Convent of Descalzas Reales, Madrid, Spain

1674 *St. John the Baptist*; polychromed wood; Museo Provincial de Bellas Artes, Seville, Spain

1675–77 Statues of Catholic monarchs King Ferdinand and Queen Isabella of Castile; polychromed wood; Granada Cathedral, Spain

1676 *Ecce Homo*; polychromed wood; Church of Santa Ana del Cister, Málaga, Spain

1676 *Mater Dolorosa*; polychromed wood; Church of Santa Ana del Cister, Málaga, Spain

1676–78 Statues of Catholic monarchs King Ferdinand and Queen Isabella of Castile; polychromed wood; Málaga Cathedral, Spain

Further Reading

Anderson, Janet Alice, *Pedro de Mena, Seventeenth-Century Spanish Sculptor*, Lewiston, New York: Edwin Mellen Press, 1998

Martín González, Juan José, *Escultura barroca en España, 1600–1770*, Madrid: Cátedra, 1983; 3rd edition, 1998

McDonald, Mark P., " 'So As to Avoid Confusion': A Contract Drawing for a Sculpture by Pedro de Mena y Medrano," *Sculpture Journal* 4 (2000)

Orueta y Duarte, Ricardo de, *La vida y la obra de Pedro de Mena y Medrano*, Madrid: Blass, 1914

Palomino de Castro y Velasco, Antonio, *El parnaso español pintoresco laureado con las vidas de los pintores y estatuarios eminentes españoles*, in *El museo pictórico*, Madrid, 1724; as *Lives of the Eminent Spanish Painters and Sculptors*, translated by Nina Ayala Mallory, Cambridge and New York: Cambridge University Press, 1987

Pedro de Mena y Castilla (exhib. cat.), Madrid: Ministerio de Cultura, Dirección General de Bellas Artes y Archivos, Dirección de los Museos Estatales, and Valladolid, Spain: Museo Nacional de Escultura, 1989

Pedro de Mena y su época: Simposio nacional, Málaga, Spain: Junta de Andalucía, 1990

Sánchez-Mesa Martín, Domingo, *El arte del Barroco: Escultura-pintura artes decorativas*, Seville, Spain: Ediciones Gever, 1991

MARIO MERZ 1925– *Italian*

Influenced by the French movement *Nouveau Réalisme* and the American New Dada, in 1966 Mario

Merz abandoned the traditional modes of artistic expression and began to present everyday objects as works of art. His found object sculptures featured neon tubes that passed through and vitalized ordinary objects such as bottles, cushions, umbrellas, and newspapers. Many artists in the 1960s, in particular those of the Mimimalist, Process art, and Conceptual schools, such as Dan Flavin, Bruce Nauman, James Rosenquist, Keith Sonnier and Richard Serra, often incorporated neon in their works. Lucio Fontana had pioneered the use of neon in a 1951 work titled *Spatial Environment in Neon*.

Merz's neon works stood out for their intense organic and vitalistic message. In *Raincoat* he assembled a mix of objects of contrasting structures and materials and used neon to connect them all in a single, unending, vital flow; his purpose was to recover the elementary energy that governs nature. Merz joined the *arte povera* (an Italian movement often characterized by the use of ephemeral materials) group (which included Jannis Kounellis, Giulio Paolini, and Michelangelo Pistoletto) in 1968–69. He abandoned the readymade technique and devoted himself to creating works with moral and social messages, often proffered outright via political slogans or literary quotations written in neon letters.

Merz's *Igloos*, of which he did a long series, became the leitmotiv of his career. They are suspended between the past and the future by a combination of "poor" materials, such as earth, sticks, clay, and wax, and sophisticated modern materials, such as neon, wire mesh, and glass panels. He aimed to show the spirit of primitive nomadic cultures returning in the electronic future, to wipe out temporal differences in a single, unending, vital flow. *Giap's Igloo* is an iron structure clad with garbage bags and surmounted by the neon lettering of a quotation (translated into Italian) from General Giap: "If the enemy masses his forces he loses ground; if he scatters he loses strength." Merz drew inspiration from Giap's quotation to capture natural energy in a core of force. In 1969 Merz presented an installation called *What's to Be Done?* at the L'Attico Gallery in Rome. He spread out a number of metal igloos beside faggots of chestnut firewood, a "poor" material used by shepherds and peasants. The opaque but translucent surface of the igloos made the enclosed energy field visible from outside.

In 1969 Merz became transfixed by the idea of the spiral shape, the geometric translation of a mathematical series discovered by the 13th-century Italian theorist Leonardo Fibonacci, in which each number is the sum of the previous two (1, 1, 2, 3, 5, 8, 13, 21, etc.). Merz wanted to show how Fibonacci's series explains spiral shapes in all plants, animals, and minerals and reveals the secret of growth and universal order. In

Proliferating Spiral, for example, the shape enabled Merz to visualize the infinite expansion of energy while maintaining an exact center of gravity. (In many of his preparatory drawings, the center of the spiral is occupied by a snail.) Neon numbers made Fibonacci's mathematical principle immediately visible. From this point Merz featured neon numbers in all of his installations, strengthening the conceptual direction of his work, although he balanced them by his constant attention to natural elements.

Beginning in 1972 Merz used spiral tables, often covered with tropical fruit, in many of his works as the geometric translation of Fibonacci's series and a symbol of the will of human beings to relate to each other, transcending cultural barriers and limitations. In 1976 Merz presented an installation titled *Proliferation of Fibonacci* at the Galleria Mario Pieroni in Pescara. High on the outside of the building, he placed the numbers of the Fibonacci series; inside, he indicated their numerical proliferation by means of a long spiral table winding through the rooms and covered with fruit and vegetables.

In *Crocodile*, Merz placed the numerical series in neon beside a stuffed crocodile. As with igloos and tropical fruit, stuffed animals, especially prehistoric or fierce species, appear frequently in his installations. His fascination with these objects reflects his will to connect to a mythical primitive era in which humans were fully integrated in nature and had not yet interrupted the incessant vital flow with the barriers of rigid rational thought.

Merz returned in the 1980s to his interest in color, images, and manual values, now renovated by conceptual schemes based on the constant use of neon. His installations now included large, thickly colored paintings of prehistoric animals on unstretched canvas or sheets of cloth. At the Durand-Dessert Gallery in Paris, he presented a bamboo construction in which neon tubes pierced through paintings of prehistoric animals. In *Portrait of a Gecko, Portraits of a Gallinacean Raptor and a Sphinx that Should Have Been Done 50,000 Years before 1983*, a neon text issues forth from a thicket that evokes a fanciful forest. Because of their reflective nature, long, elaborate writings with ironic overtones were a fixture in Conceptual art.

In 1990 Merz carried out an idea he had been cultivating since 1970 for Mies van der Rohe's museum in Krefeld, Germany. At the Museo Pecci di Arte Contemporanea in Prato, he wrapped the modern building's rational, geometric structure in a 300-meter long spiral made of metal, neon, and beech and chestnut twigs, thereby incorporating the entire space in a single work of art. The museum's rectilinear space dissolved in the fluid coils, which became a gigantic energy vector in unstoppable expansion. In 1997 he took on the medieval structures of the Tuscan town of San Casciano Val di Pesa. Here, he installed a stuffed deer and the Fibonacci series above the ancient town walls, wiping out temporal differences in a continuous vital flow. With these two installations Merz concluded the experimentation in which he had been engaged since the second half of the 1960s and brought to a height his conception of space as ceaseless energy in perpetual motion, overcoming physical and temporal barriers in an infinite embrace.

CATERINA BAY

See also **Duchamp, Marcel; Fontana, Lucio; Klein, Yves; Kounellis, Jannis; Minimalism; Postmodernism; Serra, Richard**

Biography

Born in Milan, Italy, 1 January 1925. Attended classical high school; moved to Turin and began painting "informal" pictures as a self-taught artist, 1950; first exhibition at Bussola Gallery, Turin, 1953; married Marisa Merz, a member of *arte povera* group; showed at Sonnabend Gallery, Paris, 1969, and New York City, 1971; exhibited first time at Venice Biennale, 1972; solo show, Kunsthalle Museum, Basel, 1975; Folkwang Museum, Essen, organized first important retrospective, 1979; showed at Musée d'Art Moderne, Centre Georges Pompidou, Paris, 1981; at Guggenheim Museum, New York City, organized major retrospective, 1989; last showed at Venice Biennale, 1997. Lives and works in Milan, Italy.

Selected Works

1967   *Raincoat*; raincoat, neon, wood, spray paint; artist's collection
1968   *Giap's Igloo*; iron, plastic bags, garbage, neon; Musée Nationale d'Art Moderne, Centre Georges Pompidou, Paris, France
1969   *What's to Be Done?* igloo, glass, glue, wood; L'Attico Gallery, Rome, Italy
1976   *Proliferation of Fibonacci*; metal tubes, glass, clamps, glue, crystal, rock, neon, fruit, vegetables, wood, newspapers; Galleria Mario Pieroni, Pescara, Italy
1979   *Crocodile*; stuffed crocodile, neon; private collection
1979   Untitled; bamboo, canvas, neon; Durand-Dessert Gallery, Paris, France
1980   *Proliferating Spiral*; iron pipes, wood; artist's collection
1983   *Portrait of a Gecko, Portraits of a Gallinacean Raptor and a Sphinx that Should Have Been Done 50,000 Years*

before 1983; neon; Buchmann Gallery, St. Gall, Switzerland
1990   *The Spiral Appears*; metal, beech and chestnut wood, neon, newspapers; Museo Pecci di Arte Contemporanea, Prato, Italy
1997   *Deer*; stuffed deer, neon numbers; San Casciano Val di Pesa, Italy

Further Reading

Celant, Germano, *Mario Merz*, Milan: Mazzotta, 1983
Celant, Germano, *Mario Merz*, New York: Solomon R. Guggenheim Museum and Rizzoli, 1989
Corà, Bruno, and Mary Jane Jacob, *Mario Merz at MOCA*, Milan: Fabbri Editori, 1989
Mario Merz: ARC/Musée d'art moderne de la ville de Paris (exhib. cat.), Paris: Kunsthalle Basel, 1981
Mario Merz (exhib. cat.), Basel, Switzerland: Sekretariat des Basler Kunstvereins, 1975
Mario Merz (exhib. cat.), Essen, Germany: Museum Folkwang, Eindhoven, The Netherlands: Stedelijk Van Abbemuseum, and London: Whitechapel Art Gallery, 1980
Mario Merz (exhib. cat.), Florence: Hopefulmonster, 1990
Merz, Mario, *Fibonacci 1202*, Turin, Italy: Sperone, 1972

JUAN DE MESA 1583–1627 *Spanish*

Juan de Mesa, an accomplished sculptor, was famous for his Passion images created for religious institutions in Spain. He worked in a realistic and highly emotional style inspired by his teacher Juan Martínez Montañés. He created sculptures for retables, as well as processional images for confraternities. His religious subjects evoked the spirituality of the Counter Reformation.

Mesa sculpted a *Virgin and Child* and *St. John the Baptist* for the Monastery of S. Maria de las Cuevas; the Carthusians had originally ordered the sculptures from Montañés, but Mesa signed the contract at a lower price. The two works show a similarity in naturalism and spirit to those for the Church of S. Isidoro del Campo, Santiponce, created by Montañés in 1610. Mesa's work distinguishes itself from his master's in the drier modeling and sweeter character. The most notable derivation in Mesa's sculpture is John the Baptist's confrontational glance.

Mesa sculpted many dramatic crucifixes throughout his career. One of his earliest surviving sculptures is the *Crucifix of Love* for the Sevillian Confraternity of Love. Montañés's *Christ of Clemency* (1603–06) in the Cathedral of Seville inspired Mesa's *Christ of the Good Death* for the Jesuit Casa Profesa in Seville. Montañés based his sculpture on the formula set forth by Francisco Pacheco, the inspector of paintings for the Inquisition in Seville. According to Pacheco, Christ should be in a standing position in order to eliminate the curve of the body, which he thought lessened the dignity of the image. Pacheco suggested that artists use a total of four nails, one in each hand and one in each foot, and that the feet should be crossed. Mesa depicted Christ in the crucifix in frontal position, with his head looking downward on the faithful as he dies. The work departs from the model, however, by using three nails, an older iconographic form that his master also used in some works. Mesa also used only the Latin initials INRI (Jesus of Nazareth, King of the Jews) rather than the entire title written in Hebrew, Greek, and Latin. Another crucifixion titled *Christ of the Conversion of the Good Thief*, created for the Confraternity of Montserrat and Jesús of Nazareth and Holy Cross in Jerusalem, follows the iconography of his sculpture for the Jesuits, excepting the position of the head, which turns in the direction of the good thief.

Mesa created many processional images for confraternities, which were to be carried during Holy Week. In an effort to engage and provoke the public, he made such sculptures realistic, emphasizing the suffering of Christ. In *Christ the Almighty* for the Confraternity of Nazarenos in the Basilica del Gran Poder, Seville, Mesa referred to similar images done by his master, in which the facial expression and physical weakening as Christ bears the weight of the cross indicate Christ's suffering. Nazarenos was a penitential confraternity and as such was dedicated to a particular moment in Christ's Passion. Mesa created a number of other sculptures of Christ and saints for penitential confraternities.

In his short life Juan de Mesa became one of the most important followers of Montañés; had he lived to a mature age, he would have surely developed a more individual style.

JENNIFER OLSON-RUDENKO

See also **Montañés, Juan Martínez; Spain: Renaissance and Baroque**

Biography

Born in Córdoba, Spain, on or before 26 June 1583. Apprenticed to Juan Martínez Montañés and lived in his house, Seville, Spain, 1606–10; followed the style of his master, as an independent sculptor; member of the Confraternity of Montserrat and Jesús of Nazareth and Holy Cross in Jerusalem; produced many freestanding images for religious institutions in Spain, from 1618 until his death. Died in Seville, Spain, 26 November 1627.

Selected Works

1618–20 *Crucifix of Love*; polychrome wood; Confraternity of Love, Church of the Savior, Seville, Spain

ca. 1619 *Christ of the Good Death*; polychrome wood; chapel, University of Seville, Spain

1619–20 *Christ of the Conversion of the Good Thief*; polychrome wood; Montserrat Chapel, Royal Monastery of San Pablo, Seville, Spain

1620 *Christ the Almighty*; polychrome wood; Basilica del Gran Poder, Seville, Spain

1621 *St. John the Baptist*; polychrome wood; Museo Provincial de Bellas Artes, Seville, Spain

1621 *Virgin and Child*; polychrome wood; Museo Provincial de Bellas Artes, Seville, Spain

Further Reading

Gilman, Beatrice, *Catalogue of Sculpture in the Collection of the Hispanic Society of America*, New York: Hispanic Society of America, 1932

Hernández Díaz, José, *Juan de Mesa: Escultor de imaginería, 1583–1627*, Seville: Excma, Diputación Provincial de Sevilla, 1972; 2nd revised edition, 1983

Kubler, George, and Martin Soria, *Art and Architecture in Spain and Portugal and Their American Dominions, 1500–1800*, Baltimore, Maryland: Penguin, 1959

Proske, Beatrice Gilman, *Juan Martínez Montañés*, New York: Hispanic Society of America, 1967

Webster, Susan Verdi, *Art and Ritual in Golden-Age Spain: Sevillian Confraternities and the Processional Sculpture of Holy Week*, Princeton, New Jersey: Princeton University Press, 1998

MESOAMERICA

Mesoamerica is a region now occupied by parts of Mexico, Guatemala, Belize, and Honduras. From the appearance of the first villages to the fall of the Aztecs at the hands of the Spanish conquistadors in 1521, Mesoamerica gave rise to numerous sculptural traditions as rich and diverse in technique and media as they are in imagery and iconography. Nevertheless, cross-cultural appropriation and reinterpretation of stylistic and iconographic elements resulted in contacts and continuities between regions and across time periods. Recurring themes of Mesoamerican sculpture include historical events, warfare, maize and creation mythology, the underworld, and the activities and divinity of deities, kings, and ancestors. Sculptures often served as the locus of contact between the mythological and earthly worlds.

Time periods are divided into several phases: Formative and Protoclassic (2000 BCE–250 CE), Early Classic (250 CE–600 CE), Late Classic (600–900), and Terminal and Post-Classic (900–1521). Major regional divisions include central Mexico, Gulf Coast/Veracruz, west Mexico, southern Mexico/Oaxaca, and the

Maya region (lowlands of northern Guatemala, Chiapas, Tabasco, the Yucatán Peninsula, Belize, and Honduras).

Materials for monumental sculpture included wood and stone such as limestone, sandstone, volcanic tuff, granite, andesite, and basalt. Sculptors crafted architectural sculpture from stone and plaster made from burned limestone and produced smaller, portable sculpture in ceramic, wood, shell, bone, limestone, and fine greenstones. In later epochs sculptors sometimes made small sculptures out of gold. Sculptural techniques included chipping, incising, cutting, polishing, molding, and modeling, primarily with stone tools and abrasives. Sculptural surfaces may bear colors from clay slips and natural pigments, although many of these colors no longer remain. Some Mesoamerican sculpture is site specific, including freestanding monuments that relate to buildings or plazas, as well as sculpture on architectural facades. Funerary sculpture included items specifically made for the tomb and other objects that found a new use within the funerary context.

Formative and Protoclassic Period

During the Formative period (2000–250 BCE) the foundations of Mesoamerican sculptural traditions were established. Sculptors of various regions created a wide range of figurines and other sculpture in ceramic and stone that appear to relate to the basic concern of agricultural fertility. Elites concentrated on the Gulf Coast propagated a more international style known today as Olmec. This style was the first major pan-Mesoamerican art tradition and had a significant influence on contemporary and later cultures.

Two of the hallmarks of Olmec monumental sculpture—colossal heads and tabletop altars or thrones—come primarily from the Gulf Coast sites of San Lorenzo and La Venta. Workers transported basalt boulders from the nearby Tuxtla Mountains, which sculptors then carved, drilled, and abraded with simple stone tools. Sculpted with a high degree of realism, each head depicts a different individual with distinctive headgear that likely relates to the Mesoamerican ballgame. The heads defined sacred spaces within sites and also may have functioned within broader sculptural programs including thrones, stelae, and smaller freestanding sculptures. High- and low-relief carvings on both the stelae and the thrones often emphasize the centrality of one human figure surrounded by subordinates or motifs defining the figure's supernatural location such as the sky, the earth, or a cave. The degree of articulation, from outlines to three dimensions, may have indicated the figure's relative importance in the overall composition.

Numerous smaller figurines, masks, and accoutrements in the Olmec style exist, created with greenstone and jade imported from certain areas of Guerrero, southern Guatemala, and Costa Rica. Many exhibit elaborate iconographic programs that convey an ideology of shamanic rulership shared by elites of these regions. The ubiquity of the objects and motifs makes it difficult to discern if the ideology they represent was mandated from a central location such as the Gulf Coast or if it developed as a more synthetic blend of local and pan-Mesoamerican traditions.

The trade networks that brought these greenstones to the Gulf Coast included the sites of Chalcatzingo, Morelos, and Teopantecuanitlan, Guerrero. Chalcatzingo features the only known tabletop throne outside the Gulf Coast, as well as a remarkable program of reliefs carved into the living rock of a towering volcanic stone plug. Teopantecuanitlan has four monuments with the hallmark Olmec "were-jaguar" face: almond-shaped eyes, flattened nose, and down-turned mouth. As at the Gulf Coast centers, these individual monuments function within larger programs reflecting themes of rulership, sacred space, and ritual.

The Olmec style also appears in a wooden mask and a series of small wooden busts from the swampy Gulf Coast site of El Manatí. These busts probably represent a prototypical physical ideal: an elongated head, slanted eyes, and down-turned mouth. This same type can be seen in the numerous ceramic "hollow babies" allegedly from the site of Las Bocas, Puebla, and other parts of central Mexico. Contemporaneous sculptures from central Mexico and Guerrero include the "pretty ladies" of Tlatilco that depict female figures, often with distended buttocks and elaborate headdresses. Objects from Tlapacoya also include ceramic male figures wearing ballgame equipment. An extraordinary group of ceramic sculptures from Xochipala, Guerrero, is remarkable for their naturalism, although they convey little overt symbolic content.

Large-scale architecture, although little monumental sculpture, is present at Early Formative sites in Oaxaca such as San Jose Mogote. Monte Albán, Oaxaca, was a major center through the Classic period, but its famous *danzantes* date to the Protoclassic phase of its history. Carved on approximately 50 slabs, the *danzantes* depict human figures in a variety of standing, seated, and floating positions. The relief technique emphasizes overall outline rather than physical volume. Many figures appear with glyphs that probably indicate names. Although 20th-century scholars named these figures *danzantes*, or dancers, their flaccid postures and maimed bodies indicate that these figures were prisoners; their display on buildings may have been incorporated into rituals celebrating the military victories of Monte Albán's rulers.

The artistic traditions of western Mexico (Colima, Nayarit, Jalisco) constitute some of the most varied ceramic sculptural traditions in Mesoamerica. The excavated sculptures probably come from the region's shaft tombs and range from miniature figurines to nearly monumental hollow figures. Poses range from stiff and formal to the intimate and casual. Artists also depicted complicated household and village scenes with numerous figures and structures, which scholars believe may symbolize shamanic belief systems, rulership, feasting rituals, and the ballgame.

After the abandonment of the major Gulf Coast Olmec sites, a new regional style emerged. Although its exact parameters remain unclear, parallels exist between the one known stela from La Mojarra, Veracruz, and those of Izapa, El Baúl, and Kaminaljuyu on the Pacific coast of Guatemala. These monuments add a new ingredient—hieroglyphic writing—to the earlier Olmec tradition of low-relief stela carving that emphasized a central ruling figure, usually shown in profile and in elaborate costume. At the site of Izapa the stelae are devoted to mythological narratives.

In the Maya region during this period, sculpture and architecture often melded into complex integrated programs. Large stucco facades depicting mythological creatures flank the central staircases of most major temples to a degree that these temples appear to support such sculptural facades rather than the sculptures serving as architectural decoration. Early examples of monumental sculpture such as the Hauberg Stela (197 CE) suggest an attempt to fix transient ritual moments forever in stone. The Maya centers of the lowlands (El Mirador, Nakbe, Rio Azul) and their contemporaries on the Pacific slope (El Baúl, Abaj Takalik) may have imported the concept of the stela along with a variety of trade goods. The Maya quickly adopted this form throughout the lowlands; its development marks the beginning of the Classic period in the region.

Early Classic and Late Classic

On the Gulf Coast, Classic-period Veracruz sculpture (400–900 CE) largely consists of portable stone objects in the shapes of Mesoamerican ballgame equipment. Players likely wore these stone equipment effigies, carved in hard and fine stones, in rituals related to the ballgame. Their volumetrically sculpted or incised surfaces often bear elaborate zoomorphic and anthropomorphic figures. Artists often sculpted yokes, U-shaped objects worn at the ballplayer's waist, into stylized animals such as felines and amphibians. Details of the animal's physiognomy often appear in high relief; further adornment in low relief features human faces and zoomorphic forms surrounded by interlocking volutes similar in style to stone carvings at El Tajín. The

palma, a fan-shaped object with a long, slender neck, attached to the yoke and protruded upward and outward from the player's waist. These may be plainly polished or elaborately carved and include individual humans or animals as well as complex narrative scenes often related to ballgame mythology and ritual.

Ball-court and sacrificial imagery are also common at El Tajín (Late and Terminal Classic periods). Six elaborately carved panels on the inner faces of El Tajín's main ball court depict narrative friezes of humans and supernatural beings involved in ballgame decapitation sacrifice and other activities. These panels are carved with the distinctive double-outline characteristic of Classic Veracruz stone sculpture. Another ball court and the Pyramid of the Niches also include relief-carved panels, and Structure 5 holds a freestanding stela. Basalt doorjambs from El Aparicio, Veracruz, also include images of ballgame sacrifice.

Classic Veracruz sculpture includes a variety of small- and large-scale hollow ceramic figurines made in molds and with modeled clay. These include the *Smiling Figures*, small hollow clay figures—many from the site of Las Remojadas—that commonly have youthful triangular faces emphasized by a decorated cap. Other accoutrements such as ear spools, necklaces, and decorated skirts may have embellished the figures. Sculptors also produced small sculptures of animals on wheels, the only known use of the wheel in pre-Hispanic Mesoamerica, as well as large-scale figures of humans and supernaturals, often adorned with *chapapote*—a shiny black, naturally occurring petroleum asphalt. The tradition of monumental hollow ceramic sculpture continued into the Postclassic period with the larger and more elaborate figures of the Huastec tradition.

In Classic-period Oaxaca, another independent style of sculpture flourished at the Zapotec hilltop site of Monte Albán. Middle and Late Classic Monte Albán stone sculpture primarily appeared as architectural panels, carved in medium and low relief. In the tradition of the earlier *danzante* reliefs, many depict captives with place-name glyphs. However, these captives are still alive, active, and dressed in ritual or warfare regalia. After the decline of Monte Albán, sites such as Zaachila and Etla carried on the tradition of stone panels. The images usually include a seated male–female pair, a type that continued in Oaxaca, appearing repeatedly in Late Postclassic and Early Colonial Mixtec and Zapotec manuscripts for marriage events and dynastic lists.

Classic-period Oaxaca, especially at Monte Albán, had a tradition of ceramic cylindrical censers, decorated with pieces formed in molds or by hand-modeling, constituting a single anthropomorphic figure wearing an elaborate headdress. These urns possibly grew out of the censer tradition of Teotihuacan, although the Zapotec versions are fuller, with more naturalistic body parts.

Toward the end of the Formative period, the central Mexican site of Teotihuacan began accumulating power and influence over a large part of Mesoamerica. Although the ethnic identity of its inhabitants remains a mystery, Teotihuacan eventually became the most important urban center of the Early Classic period. After its destruction in the 7th century CE, cultures throughout Mesoamerica continued to draw upon Teotihuacan iconography and ideology. At Teotihuacan, sculpture included ceramic figurines, finely carved stone masks free of decoration or iconography, and occasional monumental sculpture. The two former categories tend to depict the same physical type—a human face with broad forehead, elliptical eyes, and slightly open mouth. These faces were once probably attached to the fronts of funerary bundles displayed in apartment complexes along the Avenue of the Dead, the heart of the city. Larger sculpture tends to depict mythological subjects; the facade of the famous Pyramid of the Feathered Serpent is punctuated by a number of tenoned heads depicting a stylized head of a serpent, its feathered body in lower relief. The tail, also tenoned, carries a depiction of the mosaic mask with goggle eyes that soon became the primary symbol of warfare throughout Mesoamerica. The colossal Great Goddess sculpture, depicting a standing female figure, evokes the graphic delineation of Teotihuacan's numerous painted apartments.

Another distinctive monumental sculptural style is the localized and limited style of the region around Santa Lucia Cotzumalhuapa near the Pacific coast of Guatemala. This sculptural tradition (*ca.* 400–700 CE) is the work of an unidentified people whose artistic style and subject matter drew upon those of Teotihuacan, Veracruz, and the Maya region. Carved in medium relief, stela 1 depicts a ballplayer who, wearing a Veracruz-style yoke and other ballgame regalia, makes an offering to a sun deity or ancestor above, who emerges from a serpent maw. The ceramic sculpture of this region also bears influence from other Mesoamerican regional styles. Ceramic censers from Escuintla, for example, are closely modeled after Teotihuacan censers.

The first stone sculptures of the Early Classic Maya (250–600 CE) were limestone stelae at central Petén sites including Tikal and Uaxactún, featuring elaborate images and hieroglyphic texts concerning historical events and rulers. Tikal stela 29 (292 CE) features a standing profile ruler bedecked in elaborate costume, which became the prototypical pose for public representations of Classic Maya rulers. A significant anomaly is Tikal stela 4 (379 CE), whose frontal representation harkens to frontal representations from Teotihuacan. An invasion probably brought Teotihuacanos into Tikal. The most eloquent attempt to integrate the ancient Maya past with new foreign elements appears on Tikal stela 31 (445 CE). Although later smashed and cached, this monument had great artistic repercussions in later works of the region.

In Late Classic Maya art (600–900 CE) naturalism and idealization predominated. Portraiture provided specificity otherwise available only from costume elements and hieroglyphic texts. Maya sculptors of the Late Classic primarily carved in relief and solved many problems of visual representation, such as foreshortening. They also experimented with depicting narrative and the passage of time. Their sculpture deals with the king and his family, events in their lives, wars against other Maya sites, and their intimate relationship to ancestors, deities, and mythological events.

The beginning of the Late Classic saw a temporary decline of the Maya cities of the Petén and contemporaneous growth and prosperity in cities of the western Maya realm, such as Palenque, Toniná, Piedras Negras, and Yaxchilán. Painterly, curvilinear lines in deep relief characterize Palenque stone sculpture, carved from soft, fine-grained local limestone, with attention to the supple curves of the human body. Palenque artists moved away from the freestanding-stela tradition of the central Petén, placing innovative sculptural forms into diverse architectural surfaces of interior and exterior space.

The greatest sculptural program of Palenque's grandest king, Pakal, comes from his funerary building, the Temple of the Inscriptions (*ca.* 675–90 CE). The upper surface of his enormous sarcophagus bears a low-relief image of a youthful, idealized king dressed in the costume of the Maya maize god. The king falls in death down the World Tree and into the skeletal jaws of the Underworld in a characteristic pose of birth, thus paralleling the death and resurrection of the maize god. Other sculpture in the chamber includes nine figures in stucco, a medium used for much architectural sculpture at Palenque.

Yaxchilán reached its sculptural apogee in the late 7th and early 8th centuries. The site's corpus includes stelae, carved lintels, and hieroglyphic stairways. Lintels 24, 25, and 26 feature the king's wife, Lady Xok, participating in different phases of a bloodletting and ancestor-conjuring ritual. Although presented as a narrative progression of the same ritual, the panels actually record three ceremonies, in the years 709, 723, and 726 CE. At the juncture of text and image, then, the lintels play with the concept of the passage of time and its expression in a fixed image.

The sculpture of Piedras Negras includes varying depths of relief and three-dimensionality and is renowned for its innovative multifigural compositions from its earliest monument, panel 12 (514 CE), to the latest, stela 12 (795 CE). Many Piedras Negras monuments include the sculptor's signatures, a tradition seen elsewhere in the Usumacinta drainage yet extremely rare in pre-Hispanic Mesoamerica. The monuments generally deal with accession, rituals performed by rulers, and victories in war. The standard accession monument presents the king upon a litter or scaffold. Carved partially in the round, the king emerges from the niche in which he is seated. This play in depth focuses attention on the figure of the king. The warrior stelae show the king in a frontal position in full military regalia replete with Teotihuacan warrior iconography. Teotihuacan iconography also appears in relation to warfare in Late Classic sculpture from other sites such as Yaxchilán, Tikal, Aguateca, and Dos Pilas.

Tikal resumed its sculptural tradition in the late 7th century under the aegis of Hasaw Chan K'awil, who acceded to the Tikal throne in 682. The conservative artistic program of his reign closely modeled the sculpture from Tikal's earlier history. Stelae, carved in low relief, primarily consisted of a single, static figure—the elaborately dressed king. An altar of varying design accompanied some of these stelae in a new type of architectural complex—the twin-pyramid complex—that celebrated the completion of each 20-year period. Sculpture included wooden lintels with intricate low-relief carvings of fantastic, innovative design on panels of dense wood from the sapodilla tree.

At Copán sculptors carved stone sculpture from volcanic tuff. During the reign of Waxaklahun Ubah K'awil (r. 695–738 CE), sculptors studded the city's Great Plaza with stelae carved in the round, depicting over-life-size images of the king adorned with grand costumes and accoutrements of rulership and deities. Altars carved in three-dimensional forms accompanied these stelae. Many stelae at nearby Quiriguá are near copies of Copán stelae, although much taller. Quiriguá sculptors created these after Quiriguá captured the Copán king. The Copán sculptural tradition also includes architectural sculptures of deities and mythological places.

In the Yucatán Peninsula to the north, the primary sculptural expression of the Chenes and Río Bec styles consisted of stone mosaic monster-mouth facades that engulf doorways. The most abundant sculptural form of the Puuc Hills at sites such as Uxmal and Kabah also included stone mosaic architectural sculpture, commonly using repeating masks of deities such as the long-nosed god, as well as freestanding stelae with carved two-dimensional images and hieroglyphic texts in the style of the southern lowlands.

Small ceramic figurines from funerary contexts in the burial island of Jaina, Campeche, comprise the most significant tradition of Maya ceramic sculpture during this period. Small-scale sculpture in jade, flint, shell, and human and animal bone often appear in caches and funerary contexts. Carved objects of jade throughout the Maya realm, including figurines, funerary masks, and costume elements, often include imagery of rulership.

Terminal Classic

The Terminal Classic period, a period of transition from the Late Classic to the Postclassic, was a time of great change throughout Mesoamerica. With the gradual collapse of the greatest cities of the previous era, new centers of power in new territories arose, and unprecedented communication occurred among cultures across Mesoamerica. The process of cosmopolitan stylistic formation became the hallmark of Postclassic Mesoamerica. Sculptures at sites such as Xochicalco, Chichén Itzá, and Tula are quintessential examples of the cultural and artistic contact and innovation between the 9th and 11th centuries.

Xochicalco's eclectic architectural and sculptural styles combined elements of art from Teotihuacan, Monte Albán, Veracruz, and the Maya region. The pyramid of the Feathered Serpent is architecturally similar—although with different proportions—to the *talud-tablero* buildings of Teotihuacan and bears deeply cut relief sculptures on each face. On the lowest level are undulating serpents with seated figures in Maya pose and dress who occupy the spaces between the serpent coils. Xochicalco sculpture also includes three stone stelae—carved in relief—whose images relate to rulership, the rain deity, and the planet Venus.

Chichén Itzá, in the northern Yucatán, rose to power in the second half of the 9th century and drew upon ancient Classic Maya roots in addition to Gulf Coast and central Mexican traditions. Abundant commonalities in architecture and sculpture at Chichén Itzá and Tula, Hidalgo, suggest contact and artistic influence between them, although the materials and artistic flair vary greatly between the two sculptural corpuses. The more purely Maya art of Chichén Itzá includes architectural facades with stone mosaic long-nosed masks that resemble those of the Puuc sites. Carved stone lintels include hieroglyphs that clearly are Maya but are written in a different calligraphic style than those of the Late Classic. Sculptures differing from the traditions of Maya sculpture of the southern lowlands but referring to Maya cosmology characterize the northern part of the site.

The relief-carved column is a fertile sculptural form at Chichén Itzá for the depiction of deities and warriors, although three-dimensional sculpture also abounds. These include the *chacmool*, an innovative sculptural form featuring a reclining or fallen warrior or sacrificial victim. *Chacmools* are also common at Tula, Hidalgo, although these are crudely cut with awkward body proportions and show nothing of the volumetric bounty of those from Chichén Itzá. *Chacmools* often appear in front of ruler thrones, a sculptural juxtaposition that visually exemplifies the intimate link between rulers and the sacrifice essential to maintenance of the position of rulership. The sculpture of the Great Ball Court of Chichén Itzá contains other examples of sacrifice imagery on six massive sculptural panels that depict victorious and defeated ballplayers. Characteristic of both Chichén Itzá and Tula, Hidalgo, is the feathered-serpent column, comprised of stacked cylindrical drums with incised feather and scale elements attached to a three-dimensional serpent head below. Artists at Chichén Itzá also used gold—a new material for the Maya—to produce disks bearing narrative historical and mythological scenes.

Postclassic

Three-dimensional Huastec monumental stone and ceramic sculpture comprise the most significant sculptural tradition of Postclassic Veracruz (1000–1300). Huastec stone figural sculpture is highly polished, with smooth surfaces and fine relief and incising; body positions and facial expressions imbue a sense of movement. A common type features a living human with a skeletal figure or baby that rides on its back, a visual embodiment of life-and-death duality. The Huastecs also produced stone sculptures of female fertility and agricultural deities and at least one stela, that of Huelozintla, Veracruz, which resembles those of the Late Classic Maya and which appears to have been influenced by the artistic style and carving technique of El Tajín.

After the fall of Classic-period Zapotec Monte Albán, little production of monumental sculpture occurred in the valley of Oaxaca. The Mixtec culture held great sway in this region from the 14th century and into the Colonial period; its primary artistic expressions were codex painting and small-scale sculpture in fine stones, gold, and bone. The Mixtecs also crafted turquoise mosaic into funerary masks on wooden frames.

The last pre-Hispanic civilization of central Mexico was the Aztec (also called Mexica or Nahua; 1325–1521). The Aztecs had extensive contacts through trade and conquest with other cultures of Mesoamerica, which influenced the art of those regions. Aztec imperial artists also appropriated and transformed these "conquered" styles into an imperial style of their own. The earliest Aztec art drew upon cultures already in ruins, especially of Teotihuacan and Tula, Hidalgo,

reusing their objects and ideas to recapture the power of those legendary centers. Some early sculptures, including a polychrome *chacmool* and a relief-carved image of priests, eagles, and jaguars, both from the Great Temple of Tenochtitlán, show striking similarities to Tula sculpture.

Later Aztec sculpture is characterized by finer artisanship, polish, and more complexity in iconography and figural compositions. The cylindrical relief Stone of Tizoc depicts 15 pairs of figures, each with a victorious Mexica warrior holding a captive by the hair. The greenstone head of Coyolxauhqui, carved in the round with naturalistic modeling, is the largest Aztec monument in a precious stone. With imagery related to myths of sacrifice and warfare, it is a poignant presentation of the empire's wealth and history. Sculptures from the reign of Motecuzoma II (*r.* 1502–20) show increasing complexity and emphasis on the expression of Mexica conceptions of time and space. On the upper surface of the Calendar Stone (1502) is the central ring of the sun-disk with the face of the earth monster inside the date glyph "4-Ollin," the future mythical date of the destruction of the current world. Combined with other elements organized in concentric rings, the entire image visually expresses Mexica conceptions of the passage of time in relation to space, the creation of the universe, and sacrificial responsibilities for ensuring its continuation.

Sculptors of the Aztec Empire also produced smaller-scale stone sculpture with images of deities of fecundity and fertility. The Aztecs also created small sculptures, masks, and carved musical instruments in wood and finer materials such as greenstone, turquoise, and gold for temple and house shrines and cached in funerary contexts and offerings. The richest concentration of Aztec sculpture is in the caches of the Great Temple of Tenochtitlán. The Aztecs also produced naturalistic monumental ceramic sculpture, whose technical and design roots likely stemmed from the ceramic traditions of the Huastecs of Veracruz.

Aztec sculpture for architectural surfaces—for instance, at the site of Malinalco and on the Great Temple of Tenochtitlán—served to honor particular deities and re-create mythological spaces. The feathered-serpent sculptures at the base of the pyramid are reminiscent of those of Tula and Chichén Itzá and define this place as the mythical Serpent Hill. At the foot of the stairs of construction phase IVb lies the Coyolxauhqui Stone, an enormous ovoid basalt sculpture depicting an image of a nude, decapitated, and dismembered female with golden bells on her cheeks, clearly relating to the mythic defeat of the moon goddess Coyolxauhqui and the founding of the Aztec Empire. Other architectural and sculptural complexes include the Precinct of the

Eagle and Jaguar Warriors and the stone *tzompantli* or skull rack similar to those of Tula and Chichén Itzá.

After the decline of Chichén Itzá in the 11th century, little sculptural production occurred in the northern Yucatán. Nevertheless, with the 13th-century founding of Mayapán came a revival of ancient traditions from Chichén Itzá and the southern Maya lowlands such as stelae. Tulum, on the east coast of the Yucatán Peninsula, includes architectural sculpture in stucco. The Postclassic Maya of the Yucatán also produced large ceramic censers decorated with humans and deities. The Guatemalan highlands produced large ceramic censers and burial urns with images of deities, humans, and animals.

MEGAN O'NEIL AND MATTHEW ROBB

Further Reading

Berrin, Kathleen, and Esther Pasztory, editors, *Teotihuacan: Art from the City of the Gods*, New York: Thames and Hudson, and San Francisco: Fine Arts Museums of San Francisco, 1994

Clark, John E., editor, *Las Olmecas en Mesoamérica*, Mexico City: El Equilibrista, and Madrid: Turner Libros, 1994

Coe, Michael D., *Mexico*, London: Thames and Hudson, 1957; New York: Praeger, 1962; 4th edition, as *Mexico: From the Olmecs to the Aztecs*, New York: Thames and Hudson, 1994

Kubler, George, *The Art and Architecture of the Ancient Americas: The Mexican, Maya, and Andean Peoples*, Baltimore, Maryland: Penguin, 1962; 3rd edition, London and New York: Penguin, 1990

Matos Moctezuma, Eduardo, *The Great Temple of the Aztecs: Treasures of Tenochtitlan*, translated by Doris Heyden, New York: Thames and Hudson, 1988

Miller, Mary Ellen, *The Art of Mesoamerica from Olmec to Aztec*, New York: Thames and Hudson, 1986; revised edition, 1996

Miller, Mary Ellen, *Maya Art and Architecture*, London and New York: Thames and Hudson, 1999

The Olmec World: Ritual and Rulership, Princeton, New Jersey: Art Museum, Princeton University, and New York: Abrams, 1995

Pasztory, Esther, *Aztec Art*, New York: Abrams, 1983

Schele, Linda, and Mary Ellen Miller, *The Blood of Kings: Dynasty and Ritual in Maya Art*, New York: Braziller, and Fort Worth, Texas: Kimbell Art Museum, 1986

Schmidt, Peter J., Mercedes de la Garza, and Enrique Nalda, editors, *Maya*, New York: Rizzoli, and Milan: Bompiani, 1998

Townsend, Richard F., editor, *Ancient West Mexico: Art and Archaeology of the Unknown Past*, Chicago: Art Institute of Chicago, and New York: Thames and Hudson, 1998

FRANZ XAVER MESSERSCHMIDT
1736–1783 *Austrian*

Franz Xaver Messerschmidt was an outstanding sculptor of 18th-century Central Europe. He had a unique style, independent character, and an intense commitment to his work. A number of legends are associated with him owing to his lifestyle and alleged mental illness, making objective evaluation of his works somewhat difficult.

After studying under his sculptor uncles in Munich and Graz, Messerschmidt moved to Vienna, where he attended the Viennese Academy of Fine Arts. As a disciple of Matthäus Donner, Jakob Christoph Schletterer, and Balthasar Ferdinand Moll, he was introduced to Georg Raphael Donner's Late Baroque formal style and techniques. Through the mediation of Martin van Meytens, rector of the Academy of Fine Arts, Messerschmidt was employed as a stuccoist (*Stuckverschneider*) and gun-founding assistant at the Imperial Arsenal (Zeughaus) where he realized his first independent sculptural works.

During this time in Vienna in 1760–65, Messerschmidt worked in the Late Baroque–Rococo court style. Commissioned by Prince Joseph Wenzel von Lichtenstein Marshall, he created his first known works for the Viennese Arsenal, including the life-size pendant gilded bronze busts of Empress Maria Theresa and her husband Emperor Franz I Stephan von Lothringen (1760), as well as the busts on oval, signed pendant bronze reliefs of their son Joseph II as Archduke and his first wife Maria Isabella von Parma (1760–63). In the wake of the success of these works, Messerschmidt received several commissions from the Viennese imperial court and aristocracy. His most significant early works, *Empress Maria Theresa as Hungarian Queen* and *Emperor Franz I Stephan von Lothringen* (1764–66), are full-figure, over-life-size, signed pendant statues made from zinc-copper alloy to the order of the empress. These official portrait statues of the imperial couple were erected in the Imperial Painting Gallery in Stallburg. Following the representative style of court artists Balthasar Ferdinand Moll and Martin van Meytens, Messerschmidt depicted the empress in Hungarian national dress; her husband was modeled in a heroic posture, with idealized features, in his posthumous portrait.

Again commissioned by the empress, Messerschmidt made the life-size zinc-copper portrait bust of Emperor Joseph II for the Cabinet of Natural Curiosities in Hofburg, and the signed gilded lead-zinc alloy bust of Gerard van Swieten, court physician for the Medical Faculty of the Viennese University. In each of these works the sculptor complied with the court requirements for the decorative nature of portraits. A change in style can be traced in his Neoclassicist portraits depicting the followers of the Viennese Enlightenment. The signed lead bust of Franz von Scheyb (1769) was one of those works that enabled Messerschmidt to become a member of the Viennese Academy of Fine Arts. With this portrait, he emphasized features and character representation rather than decorative elements. He placed the bust on a simple cube socle. Several Neoclassicist signed busts followed this one, among them Franz Anton Mesmer in lead (1770), Johann Cristoph von Kessler in lead (1770–71), and a second bust of Gerard van Swieten in marble (1770–72). The recently found, signed alabaster bust titled *A Bearded Old Man* (*ca.* 1770–72) also belongs to Messerschmidt's Neoclassicist works that were inspired by ancient Roman and Egyptian busts studied and copied during his survey journey to Rome.

Messerschmidt also created a number of significant works with religious subjects. Commissioned by Princess Maria Theresa Felicitas von Savoyen-Carignan, he ornamented the facade of the princess's Viennese palace with a large-size *Maria Immaculata* zinc-lead group. Also on the princess's commission, he carved in marble the signed, over-life-size statues of *Mater Dolorosa* and *Saint John the Evangelist* as the side figures of the Holy Cross Altar in the Savoy burial chapel of St. Stephen's Cathedral in Vienna. Messerschmidt cast the zinc-lead group *Eliseus and the Miracle of the Widow's Oil jug* on a court wall fountain in the princess's palace in Vienna in 1769–70. On these works, Donner's Late Baroque influence predominates.

His career ascending, Messerschmidt became a recognized and popular artist. Nominated deputy professor under Schletterer at the Viennese Academy of Fine Arts in 1769, he purchased a house in 1770 where he established his own workshop. At this point, an abrupt change took place in his life. He scarcely was given any commissions and entered into conflicts with his friends and colleagues. According to unverifiable anecdotes and allegations, Messerschmidt began presenting the symptoms of a mental illness beginning in 1770, which was also the time he started working on the so-called *Charakterköpfe*, or *Character Heads*, series, which absorbed him until his death. After Schletterer's death, Messerschmidt was rejected for the vacant professorial position and dismissed with a low pension owing to charges that he was mentally unstable. The background events of this situation cannot be reconstructed; historians can only surmise that his mental illness or perhaps the rivalry of his competitors caused his state of neglect. Leaving Vienna disappointed, he returned to his birthplace, Wiesensteig, in 1775 and then traveled to Munich upon the invitation of the elector's court, where he waited in vain for the promised commissions and permanent employment. The only work surviving from his Munich period is a female marble bust called *Religion* carved for the tomb of Johann Baptist Straub's wife and which is stylistically similar to his allegorical Neoclassicist works.

Messerschmidt lived in the house of his sculptor brother in Bratislava from 1777 until 1780, after which he lived in his own house secluded in poverty until his death, making his living by producing portraits for the local aristocracy and citizens. In 1777–80 he made a signed lead bust of his most important commissioner, Albert, Duke of Saxe-Teschen, the governor of Hungary, as well as a life-size bust from marble, around 1780. Messerschmidt created a delicately elaborated, small-sized medallion portrait series out of alabaster, most of which he signed. On these he also depicted Albert, Duke of Saxe-Teschen, and his wife, the daughter of Empress Maria Theresa, Archduchess Maria Christina. The medallion series can be dated to about 1780 on the basis of the medallion *Joseph II with the Holy Crown of Hungary*; this representation could only have been made in 1780, shortly after the death of Empress Maria Theresa, when it was still not known that her son would not be crowned with the Hungarian crown. Among the medallions are Messerschmidt's *Laughing Self-Portrait* and *Serious Self-Portrait* in caricature-like representation. All the above-mentioned medallions, together with several others, he gave as gifts to his friend József Kiss, who was also represented on one of the medallions. The medallion portrait of Count Franz Balassa also belongs to this series, among several other unidentified portraits. Messerschmidt's signed zinc-lead bust titled *Capuchin Monk*, presumably representing Ignaz Aurel Fessler, a Freemason, dates to 1780–83. The Hungarian Freemason historian Márton György Kovachich was exceedingly pleased with his bust ordered for himself, for which the sculptor modeled him wearing the typical outfit of the Hungarian Josephinians in 1782. Messerschmidt's signed zinc-lead bust conveyed the self-confident, critical, slightly ironic character of the leading figure of the Hungarian Enlightenment, complete with a highly sarcastic expression.

Messerschmidt's portraits made in about 1780 are frontally set Neoclassicist portraits, but the modeling of the features is severe as compared to those a decade earlier, and he also elaborated on the characteristic dress of his sitters. During this period, he devoted most of his time and energy to the *Character Heads*. The grimacing heads, really physiognomic and proportion-system studies, were unique in Central Europe. Because of the unusual subject and his secluded life, contemporaries considered the artist to be idiosyncratic, and his figure became the target of rumors and legends. Ten years after his death, in 1793, his most famous and most widely disputed works, the *Character Heads*, were exhibited for the first time in Vienna.

KATALIN HÁMORI

See also **Central Europe; Donner, Georg Raphael; Portrait**

Biography

Born in Wiesensteig (Württemberg), Germany, 6 February 1736. Studied under his two sculptor uncles, Johann Baptist Straub in Munich, 1746, and Philipp Jakob Straub in Graz, Austria, 1752–54. Moved to Vienna, 1754; studied at the Viennese Academy of Fine Arts under Matthäus Donner, Jakob Christoph Schletterer, and Balthasar Ferdinand Moll from the end of 1755; worked at the Imperial Arsenal (Zeughaus) in Vienna; first known works in Vienna, 1760; received commissions from the Viennese court and aristocracy, 1760–65; traveled to Rome, Paris, and London, 1765; commissions in Vienna, 1766–74; appointed deputy professor of sculpture at Viennese Academy of Fine Arts, 1769; first symptoms of mental illness appeared, *ca.* 1770; started work on series of *Character Heads*, *ca.* 1770; traveled to Wiesensteig and Munich, 1775; moved to Bratislava (Hungarian Pozsony, German Pressburg; then capital of the Hungarian Kingdom, current capital of Slovakia), 1777; lived with his sculptor brother, Johann Adam Messerschmidt, 1777–80; purchased house on the outskirts of Bratislava, 1781; lived in isolation and poverty working on portraits and *Character Heads* during this period. Died in Bratislava, Slovakia, 19 August 1783.

Selected Works

1760   Busts of Empress Maria Theresa and Emperor Franz I Stephan von Lothringen; gilded bronze; Österreichische Galerie, Vienna, Austria

1760–63 Busts of Joseph II as archduke and Maria Isabella von Parma; bronze; Österreichische Galerie, Vienna, Austria

1764–66 *Empress Maria Theresa as Hungarian Queen* and *Emperor Franz I Stephan von Lothringen*; zinc-copper; Österreichische Galerie, Vienna, Austria

1766–67 *Maria Immaculata*; zinc-lead alloy; Savoysches Damenstift, Vienna, Austria

1767   Bust of Emperor Joseph II; zinc-copper; Kunsthistorisches Museum, Vienna, Austria

1768   *Mater Dolorosa* and *Saint John the Evangelist*; marble; St. Stephen's Cathedral, Vienna, Austria

1769   Bust of Franz von Scheyb; lead; Historisches Museum der Stadt Wien, Vienna, Austria

1769   Bust of Gerard van Swieten; gilded lead-zinc; Österreichische Galerie, Vienna, Austria; marble version: 1770–72, Kunsthistorisches Museum, Vienna, Austria

1769–70 *Eliseus and the Miracle of the Widow's Oil jug*; zinc-lead; Savoysches Damenstift, Vienna, Austria

ca.   *A Bearded Old Man*; alabaster;
1770–72 Liebieghaus, Frankfurt, Germany

ca.   *Character Heads*; mostly lead-zinc alloy
1770–83 or alabaster; some lost, others in various collections, most predominantly Österreichische Galerie, Vienna, Austria; Museum of Fine Arts, Budapest, Hungary; Historisches Museum der Stadt Wien, Vienna, Austria; and private collections

1775–77 *Religion*; marble; Bayerisches Nationalmuseum, Munich, Germany

1777–80 Bust of Albert Duke of Saxe-Teschen; lead; Bayerisches Nationalmuseum, Munich, Germany; marble version: *ca.* 1780, Graphische Sammlung Albertina, Vienna, Austria

ca. 1780 Series of medallion portraits, e.g., *Joseph II with the Holy Crown of Hungary*; Albert, Duke of Saxe-Teschen; Archduchess Maria Christina; *Laughing Self-Portrait; Serious Self-Portrait*; József Kiss; alabaster; Museum of Fine Arts, Budapest, Hungary; Count Franz Balassa; alabaster; Porijesmi Muzej Hrvatske, Zagreb, Croatia

1780–83 *Capuchin Monk*; lead-zinc; Galéria Hl. Mesta, Bratislava, Slovakia

1782   Bust of Márton György Kovachich; zinc-lead; Museum of Fine Arts, Budapest, Hungary

Further Reading

Balogh, Jolán, *Katalog der ausländischen Bildwerke des Museums der Bildenden Künste in Budapest, IV–XVIII Jahrhundert*, 2 vols., Budapest: Akadémia Kiadó, 1975

Baum, Elfriede, *Katalog des Österreichischen Barockmuseums im Unteren Belvedere in Wien*, 2 vols., Vienna, Austria and Munich, Germany: Herold, 1980

Kraph, Michael (editor), *Franz Xavier Messerschmidt 1736–1783*, Hatje Cantz, 2003

Merkwürdige Lebensgeschichte des Franz Xaver Messerschmidt, k. k. öffentlichen Lehrer der Bildhauerkunst (1793), Vienna: Wiener Bibliophilen-Gesellschaft, 1982

Pötzl-Malikova, Maria, *Franz Xaver Messerschmidt*, Vienna: Jugend und Volk, 1982

Pötzl-Malikova, Maria, "Messerschmidt, Franz Xaver," in *The Dictionary of Art*, edited by Jane Turner, New York: Grove, and London: Macmillan, 1996

Wittkower, Rudolf, and Margot Wittkower, "Was Franz Xaver Messerschmidt Insane?" in *Born under Saturn: The Character and Conduct of Artists: A Documented History from Antiquity to the French Revolution*, London: Weidenfeld and Nicholson, and New York: Random House, 1963

CHARACTER HEADS

Franz Xaver Messerschmidt (1736–1783)
ca. 1770–1783
mostly lead-zinc alloy or alabaster
h. ca. 30–48 cm
Some lost, others in various locations, most predominantly Österreichische Galerie, Vienna, Austria; Museum of Fine Arts, Budapest, Hungary; Historisches Museum der Stadt Wien, Vienna, Austria; and private collections

The legendary *Character Heads* assume a peculiar, popular, and disputed place in Franz Xaver Messerschmidt's oeuvre. The naming of the series and of the individual heads does not come from the artist; we know nothing of his original intentions and specific prototypes regarding these works. None of the heads were made on commission; he never signed them and he never parted with them.

Messerschmidt worked on the series continuously and with extreme intensity from about 1770 until his death. In 1775 he took five completed heads with him to Wiesensteig, Austria where he made additional pieces. In a 1777 letter to his brother, Johann Adam Messerschmidt, he mentions 12 finished heads, which he took with him when moving to Bratislava in 1777. According to the memoirs of Friedrich Nicolai, he saw the sculptor working on the sixty-first head in 1781. On Messerschmidt's death 69 heads were found in his workshop. According to the legacy files the series came into the possession of Richter Anton Reichard, from whom Johann Adam Messerschmidt bought the heads in 1785 and sold them after 1791 to a person called Strantz or Strontz, the cook of the Citizens' Hospital (*Bürgerspital*) in Vienna. Strantz exhibited the heads in the hospital in 1793. The series was presented to readers as *Charakterköpfe*, or *Character Heads*, for the first time in an article of the 6 November 1793 issue of the *Wiener Zeitung*. At this time 49 heads were known; the missing 20 must have already been lost or damaged. The naming of the specific heads can be traced to a thus-far anonymous author who assembled a brochure titled *Merkwürdige Lebensgeschichte des Franz Xaver Messerschmidt, k. k. öffentlichen Lehrer der Bildhauerkunst* (1793), in which he issued a biography of the sculptor and numbered, named, and briefly described the specific heads. The work was published in several versions. The names included in the brochure, although inaccurate and ambiguous, became standard and are still in use. The heads can be identified by the number carved into their socle (base) presumably in 1793 and according to the lithography published in the Viennese periodical *Der Adler* in 1839, in which M.R. Thoma presented the 49 heads arranged into six rows. After changing owners several times most of the series pieces came into the possession of the Österreichische Galerie, Vienna; the rest are scattered among various collections. Several variants and reproductions of the *Character Heads* survive; most noteworthy of these are the series of copied castings in the Österreichische Galerie, Vienna, and in the Slovenská Národná Galéria in Bratislava, Slovakia.

Various hypotheses have been advanced to explain the form and content of the *Character Heads*. The fundamental starting point of all these hypotheses is Nicolai's guidebook-like 1785 memoirs, in which he describes his 1781 visit to the sculptor's studio in detail. Although inaccurate and anecdotal at points, the text is nonetheless a vital source. Nicolai represents Messerschmidt as a remarkable artist and strong man, although eccentric, fanatically active, and solitary, whose sources included an old Italian book on human proportions and a drawing of an Egyptian statue without arms. According to Nicolai the artist was mentally ill and fighting visions, recording his own grimaces on his life-size busts. The sculptor allegedly told Nicolai that spirits of proportions were chasing him and that the making of grimacing faces helped him to keep the evil ghosts at bay. Nicolai named the heads *caricatures* and divided them into three groups: natural heads, grimacing faces, and *Schnabelköpfe* (Beak Heads). Into the first group he included, for example, the artist's laughing self-portrait, likely the lead bust *Der Künstler, so wie er sich lachend vorgestellt hat* (no. 1; The Artist Imagining Himself Laughing), from a private collection, Los Angeles, California; and a lead-zinc self-portrait with the tongue poking out, probably the lead-zinc bust *Der Gähner* (no. 5; The Yawner), in the Museum of Fine Arts, Budapest, Hungary. In the second group Nicolai classified 54 grimacing faces, and in the third group, two heads with beak-shaped facial features. One of these is lost; the other, the alabaster bust *Zweiter Schnabelkopf* (no. 6; Second Beakhead) is in the Österreichische Galerie, Vienna.

Attempts at interpreting these busts have included psychological, typological, and physiognomic analyses. Psychological analyses postulate a direct relation between Messerschmidt's alleged mental illness and the series, which began about the same time (*ca.* 1770). The most remarkable psychological study was published in 1932 by Ernst Kris, an art historian and practicing psychiatrist. Applying the methods of psychoanalysis, Kris astutely diagnosed the sculptor with schizophrenia and suggested that Messerschmidt made the grimacing busts in part as a response to his disease. Messerschmidt's diagnosis, or whether he was ill at all and not simply deemed ill because he was different from his contemporaries, remains, however, unverifiable. Nonetheless, the theory that Messerschmidt suffered from schizophrenia or paranoid schizophrenia is a constantly-reappearing topic in the literature due to Kris's remarkable analysis. The essence of the psychological analyses is that the *Character Heads* had a defensive or sublimatory function for the sculptor, who thought that by portraying his own frightening facial expressions he could keep the so-called spirits at a distance and protect himself against the fantasized or imagined fatal dangers.

Maria Pötzl-Malikova mostly accepts Kris's study, supplementing it with a formal classification of the *Character Heads*. She established seven typological groups for the 49 heads and their newly found variants based on various combinations of head shape, type of hair (or lack of it), mouth shape, breast section, and so on (see Pötzl-Malikova, 1982). While Pötzl-Malikova's classification seems logical, within the sevenfold classification specific heads can be assigned to several different groups simultaneously, and, in fact, it is possible to form further variations and combinations. Presumably Messerschmidt was not working on the basis of strictly designated typologies.

Every interpretation concerning the heads accepts that the *Character Heads* are physiognomic and proportion-system studies. Of the physiognomic studies so popular during the 18th century, Messerschmidt's works are usually linked to the ideas of the mystic and theologian Johann Caspar Lavater, a contemporary of Messerschmidt who was examining the connection between the exterior self and internal character. Although the sculptor may have been familiar with Lavater's ideas, he began his series of heads independently from Lavater. Messerschmidt's most probable prototype was James Parsons, an English physician who published lectures he delivered in 1746 in London, illustrated with engravings made after his own drawings. Parsons demonstrated the different facial expressions formed as a result of the motions of facial muscles on the same head. Messerschmidt must have been dealing with a topic similar to Parsons's, as evidenced by his Italian book on human proportions, and his depictions of proportion studies and facial expressions observed on his own face. Messerschmidt's features (as a younger as well as an older man) can be recognized in the heads, but a sequence of the heads according to age is difficult to establish due to the stylized nature of the self-portrait busts. Regarding their form, the heads are set frontally, axially symmetrical, and with no drapery on their short or elongated chest areas in keeping with early Neoclassical portraits following the antique Roman and Egyptian busts. The *Character Heads* are usually life-size, their material is mostly lead-zinc alloy or alabaster, and their technical elaboration is consistently of superior quality. It is not possible (and surely reductive) to draw a dividing line between the "sane" works of the sculptor and those heads considered to be the product of a "psychotic" artist. Their exceptional quality and massive quantity speak to the artist's unbroken creative capacity. The *Character Heads* can be defined as one of the best physiognomic and proportion-system studies of the Enlightenment.

KATALIN HÁMORI

See also **Portrait**

Further Reading

Bücherl, Barbara, "Franz Xaver Messerschmidt—Charakterköpfe," in *Wunderblock: Eine Geschichte der modernen Seele* (exhib. cat.), edited by Jean Clair, Cathrin Pichler, and Wolfgang Pichler, Vienna: Löcker, 1989
Glandien, Otto, *Franz Xaver Messerschmidt (1736–1783): Ausdrucksstudien und Charakterköpfe*, Cologne, Germany: Forschungsstelle des Instituts für Geschichte der Medizin der Universität zu Köln, 1981
Kris, Ernst, "Die Charakterköpfe des Franz Xaver Messerschmidt: Versuch einer historischen und psychologischen Deutung," *Jahrbuch der Kunsthistorischen Sammlungen in Wien* (N.F.) 6 (1932)
Kris, Ernst, *Psychoanalytic Explorations in Art*, New York: International Universities Press, 1952
Lloyd, Jill, "Franz Xaver Messerschmidt 'Character Heads': Reception, Revival, Renewal," in *Franz Xaver Messerschmidt Character-Heads, 1770–1783—Arnulf Rainer Overdrawings Franz Xaver Messerschmidt* (exhib. cat.), London: Institute of Contemporary Arts, 1987
Pötzl-Malikova, Maria, *Franz Xaver Messerschmidt*, Vienna: Jugend und Volk, 1982
Wittkower, Rudolf, and Margot Wittkower, "Was Franz Xaver Messerschmidt Insane?" in *Born under Saturn: The Character and Conduct of Artists: A Documented History from Antiquity to the French Revolution*, London: Weidenfeld and Nicholson, and New York: Random House, 1963

IVAN MEŠTROVIĆ 1883–1962 *Croatian*

Ivan Meštrović, Croatia's most celebrated sculptor, was born in 1883 to a peasant family of shepherds. He later lived and worked in Vienna; Rome; Paris; London; Syracuse, New York; and South Bend, Indiana. He incorporated Impressionistic, Secessionist, and Romanesque styles into his work, as well as Gothic, Byzantine, Archaic Greek, Assyrian, and Egyptian influences.

As a boy, Meštrović's sculptural talent emerged in his figures of equestrian heroes from folktales. He was apprenticed to a stonemason in Split (Croatia), excelled in his work, and was sent to Vienna for schooling in 1898. Plaster casts from Antiquity and the masterpieces in Vienna museums had a greater impact on him than any of the sculpture professors he met after his admission to the Akademie der Bildenden Künste in 1900.

Auguste Rodin visited Vienna in 1902, and Meštrović was swept up in the ensuing Rodin mania. His bronze *Portrait of Tolstoy* (1902) and *The Well of Life* are among 25 student works indebted to Rodin's modeling and figure composition techniques. Meštrović became a regular exhibitor at Vienna Secession shows in 1903. In 1904 he graduated and went to see Michelangelo's sculptures in Rome. By the time Meštrović moved to Paris in 1907, he had already abandoned Rodin's modeling method for one that mimicked stonework by cutting into the clay. Meštrović frequented the Musée du Louvre in Paris to absorb Greek, Assyrian, Babylonian, and Egyptian sculpture stored there, combining these lessons with whatever he found attractive in contemporaries like Aristide Maillol or Émile-Antoine Bourdelle, but the sway of Rodin remained strong. Meštrović's larger-than-life, marble *Psyche* (1927) shows the influence of both Rodin and Michelangelo, but the former's compositional style is still apparent in the *Atlantid* of 1946.

Between 1905 and 1914, Meštrović dreamed of making a great monument to the spirit of his oppressed homeland—the Vivodian Temple of Kosovo. Like the great cathedrals of the past, the Vivodian Temple was meant to employ generations of masons and stonecarvers over many decades. Meštrović grew up hearing the Vivodian Legend—that God offered medieval czar Lazar I a choice between a heavenly or earthly kingdom, that the czar chose heaven, and that thousands of his men were slaughtered by invading Turks at Kosovo on 20 June 1389. Whoever died fighting for Balkan freedom joined the Kosovo heroes in heaven.

Meštrović labored feverishly to sculpt the suffering widows and maidens, martyred heroes, caryatids, interior bas-relief panels, and a sphinx to fill his great temple commemorating the national tragedy. Larger-than-life, sometimes colossal figures, such as the three-times-life-size equestrian *Kraljević Marko*, emerged from his hand. The marble *Widows*, the famous *Banović Strahinja* (1908), and *Memories* were all intended for the temple.

At the Paris Salon d'Automne of 1908, Meštrović exhibited ten temple sculptures; he showed five more at the Salon National in Paris. He displayed nearly 60 sculptures at the 1909 Vienna Secession show, bringing this exhibit home to the Croatian capital of Zagreb in 1910.

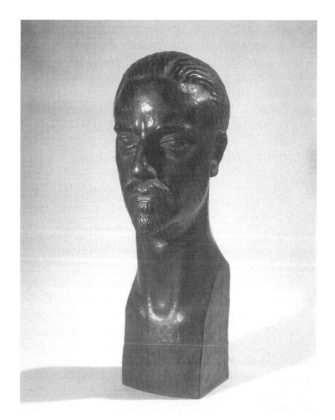

Sir Thomas Beecham, 1915
© Tate Gallery, London / Art Resource, NY

Meštrović became a European art celebrity and an important political figure at the 1911 International Exhibition in Rome when he snubbed the Austrian marquess to exhibit more than 70 pieces in the Kingdom of Serbia pavilion. Meštrović's work was awarded first prize.

Following the assassination of Archduke Francis Ferdinand at Sarajevo, Bosnia, in June 1914 Meštrović fled Split for wartime exile in Rome, where he renewed his acquaintance with Michelangelo's work; stays in London, Geneva, and Cannes, France, followed. Although he had finished a large wooden model of the Vivodian Temple of Kosovo in 1912, World War I ensured that it would never be built.

During the war, he abandoned heroism and embraced spiritual themes. The serene walnut *Madonna and Child* and the tormented *Christ on the Cross* (1914) are notable examples. Wooden relief panels of the period explore the attenuated forms of medieval Byzantine inspiration or Romanesque expressionism.

Meštrović had been a wartime member of the Yugoslav Committee on National Independence, but following the armistice, he tried to restrain Serbian and Croatian conflicts, and his moderate stance only made enemies on both sides. Meštrović retired from politics. The Račić Memorial Chapel in Cavtat, Croatia, a domed octagon that Meštrović completed in 1923, finally allowed him to realize some aspirations for the Vivodian Temple. He continued to integrate his sculptural influences in such monuments as *Gregory, Bishop of Nin*, *Gratitude to France* (1930; Belgrade), and *Tomb of the Unknown Soldier* on Mount Avala near Belgrade. *Croatian History*, a 1932 marble, is an important interwar work, as is the marvelous *Head of Moses* of 1926. In contrast, the lyrical marble nudes of 1927–40—*Dreaming*, *Resting*, *Waiting*, *Woman's Torso*, and *Woman Beside the Sea*—are refreshingly free from the burden of grand ideas.

Meštrović visited the United States in 1924–25; at this time the city of Chicago commissioned his equestrian *Indians* (1926–27) for Grant Park.

In 1941 Meštrović spent four months imprisoned by the Gestapo before the Vatican gained his release to Rome. With nothing to do in his Savska Sesta prison cell but suffer, draw, and think, Meštrović conceived some of his greatest and most profound creations, including *Job*, *St. Francis of Assisi Receiving the Stigmata* (1946), and *Supplication* (1946). Meštrović's masterpiece, the 5.5-ton Carrara marble *Pietà* of 1942–46 came directly out of this wartime experience.

Meštrović was appointed professor of sculpture at Syracuse University, New York, in 1946, and the following year he became the first living artist honored by the Metropolitan Museum of Art, New York City, with a solo exhibition.

STEPHEN MIRABELLA

See also **Bourdelle, Émile-Antoine; Central Europe; Maillol, Aristide; Rodin, Auguste**

Biography

Born in Vrpolje, Croatia, Austria-Hungary, 15 August 1883. Learned stone carving from his father; apprenticed to Pavle Bilinić in Split, Croatia, 1898; studied in Vienna under Otto Konig, 1898; admitted to Akademie der Bildenden Künste, Vienna, 1900; exhibited at the student annual exhibition and met Auguste Rodin, 1902; exhibited at Vienna Secession shows, from 1903; lived in Paris, 1907–09, and showed at two Paris Salons; major exhibitions at the Vienna Secession show of 1909, and in Zagreb, 1910; won first prize at the International Exhibition in Rome, 1911; exhibited at the Petit Palais, Paris, concurrent with Paris Peace Conference, 1919–20; designed and built Račić Memorial Chapel in Cavtat, Croatia, 1919–22; exhibition tour of United States, 1924–25; created monument, *Gregory, Bishop of Nin*, in Split, 1926; held solo exhibitions in Paris, Prague, Berlin, Munich, Vienna, and Graz, Austria, 1933; arrested by the Gestapo, 1941; released to Rome, 1942; moved to Syracuse University, United States, 1946; held solo exhibition at the Metropolitan Museum of Art, New York City, 1947; became a U.S. citizen, 1954; moved to the University of Notre Dame, South Bend, Indiana, 1955, where served as professor of sculpture. Died in South Bend, Indiana, United States, 16 January 1962.

Selected Works

1905   *Well of Life*; bronze; Theater Square, Zagreb, Croatia

1907   *The Maiden of Kosovo*, *Widows*, and *Memories*; marble; State Museum, Belgrade, Serbia

1910   *Kraljević Marko*; plaster; State Museum, Belgrade, Serbia

1915   Sir Thomas Beecham, Bt. (British Conductor); bronze; Tate Gallery, London, England

1917   *The Archers of Domagoj*; plaster; private collection, London, England

1917   *Crucifix* and *The Nativity (Madonna and Angels)*; wood; Meštrović Chapel, Split, Croatia

1919   *Archangel Gabriel*; marble; Brooklyn Museum of Art, New York City, United States

1920–22 *Our Lady of the Angels*; marble; Račić Memorial Chapel, Cavtat, Croatia

1926   *Head of Moses*; marble; Bezalel Museum, Jerusalem, Israel

1927   *Psyche*, *Daydreaming*, and *Mother's Offering*; marble; Meštrović Gallery, Split, Croatia

1932   *Croatian History*; marble; State Museum, Belgrade, Serbia

1942–46 *Pietà*; marble; Sacred Heart Church, University of Notre Dame, South Bend, Indiana, United States

1945   *Job*; bronze; Syracuse University, Syracuse, New York, United States

1946   *Atlantid* and *Supplication*; bronze; Notre Dame University, South Bend, Indiana, United States

Further Reading

Kečkemet, Duško, *Ivan Meštrović*, Zagreb, Croatia: Spektar, 1970; as *Ivan Meštrović*, New York: McGraw-Hill, 1970

Lauck, Anthony J., et al., *Ivan Meštrović: The Notre Dame Years* (exhib. cat.), Notre Dame, Indiana: Art Gallery, University of Notre Dame, 1974

Meštrović, Ivan, *Meštrović*, Zagreb, Croatia: Nova-Evropa, 1933

Schmeckebier, Laurence, *Ivan Meštrović, Sculptor and Patriot*, Syracuse, New York: Syracuse University Press, 1959

METAL CASTING

The basics of metal casting have been known for several millennia: the artisan makes a pattern or model and then takes an impression or mold of that pattern in refractory, heat-resistant material. After removing the pattern, the artisan then pours molten metal into the mold. When the metal is cool, the mold is discarded. This leaves only the metal casting, which is then *chased*, or cleaned, and polished.

Foundry technology includes mining, smelting, the refining of ore, furnace building and temperature capability, metallurgy, molding and pattern making, and the techniques for working different metals. According to archeological and trade-route records, the earliest sustained casting technology was developed in northern Turkey, then known as Anatolia, during the 5th millennium BCE. Foundry technology developed independently in both Yugoslavia and in central China during the 4th millennium BCE. The earliest known foundry technology in the Americas began in the 1st millennium CE, in northeastern South America. The first metals used commonly for implements and weapons were alloys of copper, called bronzes.

The Bronze Age lasted in Western culture from the 5th millennium BCE through the beginnings of the 1st millennium BCE, when it was supplanted with the Iron Age. In Asia the Bronze Age spanned the 4th through the 1st millennium BCE. Remarkably, the materials used for metal castings did not change drastically until the scientific developments of the 20th century, when ceramic-shell casting was invented during World War II.

There are two kinds of molding techniques: direct and indirect. Direct castings are one-time, or unique, castings. Indirect castings are multiple castings taken from one model.

In modern casts, green sand, a fine silica sand with high resistance to thermal shock, is the molding material used for sand casting, which can be used with both direct and indirect casting. Mixed with a small amount of water and clay or oil, green sand can be rammed against a pattern to hold a shape. When properly rammed, it retains a small amount of flexibility to allow for the pressure of the metal and the heat. The term *green* refers to this flexibility. For direct castings, especially of small pieces, the artisan uses Styrofoam or another combustible material, cutting and sanding the material into the exact shape desired. A Styrofoam cup is attached to the model for pouring the metal into. The artisan then packs the model into green sand, with the lip of the cup at the surface of the sand, and pushes gas vents into the sand with a rod. When molten metal is poured into the cup, the heat of the metal causes the Styrofoam to turn instantly into gas, which escapes through the vent holes. Note, however, that Styrofoam can be used only with metals that can be poured at temperatures above 600 degrees Celsius; at lower temperatures the Styrofoam will not turn directly to gas.

In indirect sand casting the artisan uses a pattern to create an impression in green sand. After removing the pattern, the artisan pours molten metal into the resulting cavity. For this process the pattern must be able to be cast in a two-part mold. A two-part mold consists of the top, or "cope," and the bottom, or "drag"; each holds the impression of half of the model. Copes and drags are rammed up inside of "flasks," which are open-sided steel squares that can be pinned together so that they do not move when the metal is poured into them. One can use this process for very large castings, depending on the size of the flask available.

Most castings must be hollow to be economical. A core is a mold of the interior of a casting. With a core in place, the molten metal will fill only the hollow space between the core and the mold. In sand casting, cores are often molded from fine silica sand that has been mixed with a catalyzing resin to give it strength. Cores can also be made from sand that has been coated with resin and then heated inside of a die form or core box. Baked cores, mostly used in industry, are much stronger than molded cores and can have a very fine surface. Because metal shrinks as it cools, cores need the flexibility of green sand to collapse slightly under pressure. The cores are shaken or chipped out after the metal has cooled.

The three methods for supporting cores in their proper positions include chaplets, core prints, and core pins. Chaplets are small spacers of the same metal and thickness as the casting, on which the core will rest. Chaplets will melt only partially into the poured metal and can be visible on the surface of the casting. A core print, which is only used for open-ended castings, is an indentation in the mold that holds an extension of the core. When the mold is closed, there should be no room for metal to flow in between the core print and the core. Core pins hold a core in place in an enclosed casting.

Solid-investment casting today uses plaster waste molds, although clay has also been used. Investment is an aggregate of materials that covers a model. It uses the *cire perdue* or lost-wax process. The artisan first makes a model out of wax, then fixes a system of *sprues*, or wax rods, to the surface of the wax model. Sprues are the channels through which molten metal will pass inside the mold to the mold cavity. The largest sprue, called the gate, extends from the base of the pouring cup to the casting. The gate must be large enough to allow a fast flow of metal. All other sprues are feeder channels extending from the gate to the surface of the wax model. Feeder sprues ensure a steady flow of metal to all parts of the casting. Wax sprues also form the vents through which gases escape. Vents must extend from any area on the model that could trap gas to above the level of the pouring cup to beyond the surface of the investment. If a core is to be poured, pins or short rods of the same metal as the casting will be inserted into the wax. The pins must be long enough to be securely gripped by both the inner and the outer investment.

When the sprue system is in place, the wax is treated with denatured alcohol or trichloroethane to remove grease, and possibly with a de-bubbler, or liquid surface-tension reducer. Investment is brushed onto the wax and sprue system. The investment is a mixture of one part plaster, one part grog, one part silica flour, and enough water to activate the plaster. The addition of a small amount of glue can improve the investment's adherence to the wax. After the surface is coated, the mold is quickly built up to a substantial thickness with investment mixed with coarse grog, and the final layer is reinforced with wire. Plaster investment cores consist of one part plaster to three parts "grog," or ground cement, mixed with enough water to activate the plaster. Cores are poured after the outer investment has hardened. Core vents made of wax rods are inserted into the core before the core is solid, to allow any gasses to escape freely. The fresh mold then bakes in a kiln at 170 to 225 degrees Celsius for up to three days. The wax will burn off, along with any carbon deposits left by the wax. While the mold is still warm it is placed into a large box and packed in with damp sand. The sand prevents any leaks from the mold and helps to prevent the mold from breaking under thermal shock. Molten metal is then poured into the mold. When the mold is cool, the plaster is chipped off and discarded, leaving only the casting. Ceramic-shell casting is capable of extremely fine surfaces and accurate detail. Models for ceramic shell are made with an attached sprue, cup, and gate system as in the solid-investment method. The wax is then dipped into a slurry, which is a mixture of a colloidal silica liquid binder and a fine refractory powder such as zircon, alumina, or fused silica mixed with water. While the model is wet it is *stuccoed* or coated with silica flour and then hung up to dry. The dipping-stucco-drying process is repeated several times. Increasingly coarse silica grains are used for the stucco, until a thickness of about 0.3 to 1.3 centimeters is formed. Ceramic shell may be used for cores in a hollow casting. Once the shell is thick and dry, it goes into a wax-burnout kiln. The kiln will heat to about 900 degrees Celsius within ten minutes, allowing the wax to become molten and run off without being drawn into the porous ceramic shell. The kiln then rapidly cools to about 170 degrees Celsius, and the shell will bake for three to four hours.

The shell is removed from the kiln and placed in a large box of damp sand, and metal is immediately poured into it. When the metal cools it shrinks slightly from the sides of the shell, allowing the shell to be easily knocked off with a hammer and chisel or a sandblaster. Ceramic shell is more accurate than most other methods of casting and can be used for any type of metal. It is frequently used in industry for machine parts that need a high level of surface accuracy.

Of the metal-casting techniques described here, ceramic shell is the most popular for industry and for artists because it allows for extremely complex and highly precise forms to be cast in a single pour. It is however very expensive to set up. Investment casting can require several piece-molds, which are then welded together. Investments also create a large amount of waste material. Sand casting using the indirect method requires two-part molds and severely limits the shape of the pattern of model to one with a single parting line. Sand casting is however more affordable and has a minimum of waste.

Artisans today make models and patterns from a wide variety of materials depending on the type of mold to be made and the type of metal to be poured. Historically, waxes modeled on armatures were used almost universally for model marking, with the exception of the early Chinese. Early Chinese foundries seemed to prefer models made of fired clay and stone, likely because these models could be used repeatedly, whereas waxes melt and deform with repeated handling. Impressions would be taken of a model with slabs of soft clay, and the clay impressions would be fired in a kiln. Metal would then be cast from the fired clay impressions. The ceramic molds were reusable, and allowed multiple identical castings. During the Shang Dynasty, which was the beginning of the Chinese Bronze Age, artisans there became capable of extremely complex sand casting. The largest known bronze in the world from this time was made by the Shang Chinese, who cast a *ting* or a large storage container using an ingenious process that cast some sections over and through other previously cast sections.

Early castings from the Greco-Roman age were sand molded or investment cast, although the Greeks and Romans used clay instead of plaster for the piece-molds. Marble sculptures that have survived from the Roman period are often slightly altered copies of Greek bronzes that have been lost or melted down for weaponry. The support posts included in many of the marble sculptures would not have been in the original bronzes, as the metal could support itself. Few artists' names are known from these times; the works were attributed to the patrons who commissioned them. Exceptions include Polyclitus of Argos, who is known for his lost treatise on ideal proportions, as well as for copies of his *Spear Bearer*, and Myron of Eleutherae for his *Discus Thrower*.

During the Italian Renaissance cast-metal sculptures represented the high point of that culture's artistic achievements. Sculptors often made direct lost-wax castings from full-scale models by using the investment method. Piece-molds would be taken from the model and lined with a thin layer of wax that would have the same thickness as the intended bronze. Core material would be used to back the thin layer of wax. The first heat would melt the wax and leave the cavity into which the metal would flow. After casting the pieces, workers welded them together and chased them.

Leonardo da Vinci redesigned both furnaces and pouring methods in preparation for an approximately 5.5-meter-high equestrian statue commissioned by the Trivulzio family in Milan. His process would have enabled him to cast the massive piece in one pour. The sculpture was never completed; nearly 200 years later the equestrian statue of *Louis XIV* by François Girardon was intended to be cast using a process similar to that devised by Leonardo, although it was only achieved as a small-scale version of the full-size bronze. Late Renaissance and Baroque bronzes continued to explore the compositional and technical possibilities of bronze casting.

Perhaps the most famous bronze sculptor of modern times was Auguste Rodin. He was prolific and used plaster investment casting to make his molds. Before casting in the molds, he would break them and reassemble them with steel reinforcements. The random fracture lines in the mold would transfer to the casting. When the waste mold was chipped away, the possibility of reproducing the casting exactly was lost, which is how Rodin guarded against unwanted reproductions.

AMBER GENEVA ERKILETIAN

See also **Polykleitos; Rodin, Auguste**

Further Reading

Agricola, Georg, *De Re Metallica*, translated by Herbert Clark Hoover and Lou Henry Hoover, New York: Dover, 1950

Ammen, C.W., *The Metalcaster's Bible*, Blue Ridge Summit, Pennsylvania: Tab Books, 1980

Bewer, Francesca, "Casting," in *The Oxford Companion to Western Art*, edited by Hugh Brigstocke, Oxford: Oxford University Press, 2001

Biringucci, Vannuccio, *Pirotechnia*, Venice: Roffinello, 1540; as *The Pirotechnia of Vannoccio Biringuccio*, translated and edited by Cyril Stanley Smith and Martha Teach Gnudi, New York: American Institute of Mining and Metallurgical Engineers, 1942

Kallenberg, Lawrence, *Modeling in Wax for Jewelry and Sculpture*, Iola, Wisconsin: Krause, 1981; 2nd edition, 2000

Mattusch, Carol C., *Classical Bronzes: The Art and Craft of Greek and Roman Statuary*, Ithaca, New York: Cornell University Press, 1996

Shapiro, Michael Edward, *Bronze Casting and American Sculpture, 1850–1900*, Newark: University of Delaware Press, and London: Associated University Presses, 1985

United States Navy Department Bureau of Ships, *Foundry Manual*, Washington, D.C.: s.n., 1944; revised edition, 1958

Young, Ronald D., and Robert A. Fennell, *Methods for Modern Sculptors*, San Rafael, California: Sculpt Nouveau, 1980

CONSTANTIN MEUNIER 1831–1905
Belgian

Dubbed the "artist of the Flemish collieries" and the Jean-François Millet of workers, Constantin Meunier is best known for his depictions of industrial and agricultural workers. He has long been considered one of Belgium's most important 19th-century artists, having produced almost 800 sculptures, paintings, and drawings over the course of his long career. The sheer volume of his artistic creations underscores the utter variety with which he produced his imagery.

His industrial subjects constitute, by far, the majority of his imagery from the final 25 years of his career. Meunier had begun his career as a painter of historical and religious subjects, having trained both as a sculptor and painter at the Brussels Royal Academy of Art and at the external studio of Charles-Auguste Fraikin. He later studied at various independent studios, most notably the Free Academy of Saint Luc, where he shared studio space with the Belgian realist painters Charles De Groux, Félicien Rops, and Louis Artan de Saint-Martin, who influenced his early style. Together, along with other artists, they formed one of the first of Belgium's independent exhibiting societies: the Free Society of Fine Arts, a group dedicated to the realist aesthetic.

Unlike many of his compatriots, Meunier came to his definitive imagery quite late in life. He stopped working in three dimensions almost entirely for a quarter of a century after his debut as a sculptor in 1851 and turned, instead, to painting. Meunier explained that it was chance that had taken him to the industrial sectors of Belgium and that gave him the impetus to return to sculpture. Despite his already advanced age of 50 and the need to support financially his pianist wife Léocadie and four children, he nonetheless completely transformed his subject and shifted his primary medium in the late 1870s.

Meunier's artistic production might be described as a "monument" to Belgian labor. Beginning in 1878, Meunier explored in myriad works each of his country's industries, and in the process, he created a new way to represent the modern world of labor and technology. His art is often characterized as realist, but this is far too limiting a designation. His good friend, the art critic and poet Émile Verhaeren, once wrote that Meunier's art was based in the direct experience of the activities of his subjects, which he then transformed; other critics, such as Octave Mirabeau, argued by contrast that Meunier's laborers might best be seen as the equivalents, in the modern world, of ancient gladiators and gods. Many of his sculptures, including his weary iron *A Puddler* (1885; Musées Royaux des Beaux-Arts de Belgique, Brussels) who sits slack-mouthed and empty-eyed, gasping for air, refer back to such diverse precedents as the work of ancient Greek and Roman statue makers and of Michelangelo. Their heroic nudity is not idealized, even if their features are generalized. Others, such as his monumental *The Hammerer*, are thoroughly modern in both substance and style.

Meunier's emergence as a sculptor, particularly of industrial subjects, at the Salon of 1884 and the Les XX exhibition in Brussels in 1885 was viewed almost unanimously as an important move on the artist's part. Whereas he had been a highly competent and often sought-after painter, his reputation soared as a result of this shift in medium and subject. He was, however, unable to support his large family. As a result, in 1887 he was hired to teach painting at the Art Academy in Louvain, Belgium, where he remained until 1894.

The period in Louvain was very important for Meunier. He eventually succeeded in becoming an artist whose works sold well in the Belgian and larger European art markets, both for private and public collections alike. These years were also marked by personal tragedy. In 1894, his sons Georges, a sailor, and Karl, a printmaker who had worked collaboratively with their father, both died unexpectedly. The remaining family returned to Brussels in 1896.

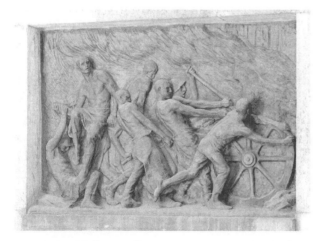

Relief from the *Monument to Labor*
The Conway Library, Courtauld Institute of Art

During his Louvain period, Meunier created many of his most important sculptures, including the life-size bronze *The Fire Damp*. This modern-day Madonna Dolorosa mourning her dead son presents a mother leaning over her son, who, laid out Christ-like, is a victim of a coal mine explosion. Meunier witnessed at least one explosion and its aftermath, and this grouping was a result of that tragic experience.

Other works that typify Meunier's aesthetic project are *The Old Horse of the Coal Mines* and *Head of Christ*. Rather than depict the horse as an athletic, galloping animal in the way that Edgar Degas or the British painter George Stubbs had done, Meunier's horse is presented half dead from starvation and years of labor, its back swayed and its head hanging as if holding it up would take too much energy. Perhaps more than any of Meunier's other sculptures, this small, pathetic horse captured the attention of all who viewed it. The same might be said of *Head of Christ*. Meunier continued to depict religious subjects throughout his career. Here, the artist presented not the stoic biblical figure described in the Gospels, but a man in mute anguish clutching his chest with his left hand. Meunier's pathos and sympathy for his subjects reflect, on the one hand, his desire to ennoble the working class and the animals who had made the economic boom in Belgium possible and, on the other, a late 19th-century attitude that saw the historical figure of Jesus as distinct from the divinity of Christ. It is for these reasons that Meunier was compared to Millet rather than Gustave Courbet.

It was in Louvain, and later in Brussels, that Meunier began to work, in earnest, on the sculptures that would become his *Monument to Labor*. Meunier worked on this project for at least 12 years, and perhaps much longer. As early as 1880, he had designed a large ensemble, a float, which was dedicated to industry for the 50th anniversary of Belgian independence. By 1884, he was beginning to refine his ideas for this massive project. A watercolor of a chimney from that year includes a representation of Meunier's 1884 painting of a glasswork factory, an image that ultimately was transformed into a monumental relief titled *Industry* for the *Monument to Labor*. In all, this ensemble includes the five life-size, freestanding bronze statues *The Sower*, *Maternity*, *The Ancestor*, *The Crouching Miner*, and *The Resting Blacksmith*, and the four large stone reliefs of *The Port*, *The Mine*, *Harvest*, and *Industry*.

Meunier composed his *Monument to Labor* as an alternation of static figures, who range in age from infancy to old age, and reliefs, in which the labor practices of four of Belgium's most important industries were represented. It is in this combination of action and stasis, of stone and bronze, and of youth and old age that Meunier's ensemble contains the universal signification of peace and fecundity and at the same time provides a depiction of work. The artist began this monument as an independent work. As early as 1896 he had begun to wonder how he might be able to complete it. Eventually, it was purchased by the Belgian government and installed, in 1930, near the port of Brussels in the Laeken neighborhood.

Meunier remained an active artist until the eve of his death. He was working on a maternal grouping for his monument to the novelist Émile Zola (completed in 1909 by Alexandre Charpentier; it was destroyed during World War II) when he suffered a fatal heart attack. His work is in major art collections worldwide. Posthumous retrospective exhibitions occurred in Vienna (1906), Prague (1906), Louvain (1909), and Ghent (1924).

SURA LEVINE

See also **Netherlands and Belgium; Relief Sculpture**

Biography

Born in Etterbeek, Brussels, Belgium, 12 April 1831. Brother, the engraver Jean-Baptiste Meunier, directed younger sibling to pursue art. Entered Royal Academy of Art, Brussels, 1845; studied under the sculptor Louis Jehotte from 1848; attended private studio of Neoclassical sculptor Charles-Auguste Fraikin from 1852; debuted as a sculptor in Brussels Triennial Salon, 1851; founding member of Société Libre des Beaux-Arts (Free Society of Fine Arts; 1868–75), Brussels; showed first industrial subjects at 1880 Triennial Salon, Ghent; exhibited almost yearly thereafter, at the Salons in Brussels, Antwerp, Ghent, and Paris; sent to Spain by Belgian government to copy a *Descent from the Cross* by a Flemish master, 1882–83; professor of painting at the Art Academy in Louvain, 1887–94; first major solo exhibition, which included sculpture, at Siegfried Bing's Art Nouveau Gallery, Paris, 1896; subsequent solo exhibition in Dresden, Germany, 1897; showed at Vienna Secession beginning in 1898; elected member of Belgian Royal Academy in 1899; moved to Ixelles, a suburb of Brussels, 1900; his home there became the Musée Constantin Meunier. Died in Ixelles, Belgium, 4 April 1905.

Selected Works

ca. 1880– 1930   *Monument to Labor*; collection of freestanding bronze statues and stone reliefs; bronze: *Maternity* (1893), *The Resting Blacksmith* (1901–02), *The Crouching Miner* (1903), *The Ancestor* (1903), *The Sower* (1904–05); stone:

Industry (1893), *Harvest* (1898), *The Port* (1901–02), *The Mine* (1905); Laeken, Port of Brussels, Belgium

1885   *Horse Belonging to a Nation*, Antwerp Port; bronze; Musées Royaux des Beaux-Arts de Belgique, Brussels, Belgium

1886   *The Hammerer*; plaster; The Carnegie Museum, Pittsburgh, Pennsylvania, United States; bronze cast: 1886, Musée Constantin Meunier, Brussels, Belgium

1886   *A Puddler*; bronze; Musée Constantin Meunier, Brussels, Belgium

1889   *The Fire Damp*; plaster; City Hall, Louvain, Belgium; bronze cast: 1889, Musées Royaux des Beaux-Arts de Belgique, Brussels, Belgium

1890   *The Old Horse of the Coal Mines*; bronze; Collection Maurice Tzwern Oeuvres d'Art, Brussels, Belgium

1893   *Woman of the People*; bronze; Musée Constantin Meunier, Brussels, Belgium

ca. 1897   *The Old Coal Miner*; bronze; private collection

1900   *Head of Christ*; bronze; J. Paul Getty Museum, Los Angeles, California, United States

Further Reading

Fontaine, André, *Constantin Meunier*, Paris: Alcan, 1923

Hanotelle, Micheline, *Paris/Bruxelles: Rodin et Meunier: Relations des sculpteurs français et belges à la fin du XIXe siècle*, Paris: Le Temps, 1982; revised edition, 1992

Levine, Sura, "Constantin Meunier's 'Monument au travail,' " in *Das Ernst Abbe-Denkmal*, edited by Stefan Grohé, Arnstadt, Germany: Rhino Verlag, 1996

Levine, Sura, "Monumental Transformations: The Changing Status of Constantin Meunier's 'Monument to Labor,'" Ph.D. diss., University of Chicago, 1996

Levine, Sura, "Constantin Meunier and the Antwerp Port Workers," *The Stanford University Museum of Art Journal* 26–27 (1996–97)

Levine, Sura, and Françoise Urban, *Hommage à Constantin Meunier, 1831–1905*, Antwerp: Pandora Petraco, 1998

Meunier, Constantin, *Constantin Meunier, 1831–1905: Skulpturen, Gemälde, Zeichnungen*, Hamburg, Germany: Ernst Barlach Haus, 1998

Sparrow, Walter Shaw, "Constantin Meunier: The Artist of the Flemish Collieries," *The Studio* 11/52 (15 July 1897)

Thiery, Armand, and Émile van Dievoet, *Catalogue complet des oeuvres dessinées, peintes et sculptées de Constantin Meunier*, Louvain, Belgium: Nova and Vetera, 1909

Treu, Georg Daniel Karl, *Constantin Meunier*, Dresden: Emil Richter, 1898

MICHELANGELO (BUONARROTI)
1475–1564 *Italian*

Michelangelo Buonarroti was the greatest sculptor of the 16th century, as Donatello was in the century before him and Bernini in the century after. Michelangelo's career spanned the final years of Lorenzo the Magnificent's Florence to the first stirrings of the Counter Reformation. He lived through the reigns of 13 popes and worked for 9 of them. Although his art occasionally has been criticized (he was accused of impropriety in the *Last Judgment* fresco), Michelangelo's influence and reputation have always been acknowledged. Many of his works—including the *Pietà*, *David*, *Moses*, and the Sistine Chapel ceiling—are ubiquitous cultural icons.

An often repeated cliché describes Michelangelo liberating a fully formed figure imprisoned within the roughly quarried block. Many of Michelangelo's sculptures reveal a more tortuous process of creation that frequently resulted in unfinished or abandoned blocks (e.g., a first version of the *Risen Christ*, Accademia *Slaves*, and the Florentine *Pietà*). After some fully finished early works (the Rome *Pietà*, *Bacchus*, *David*, and *Moses*), it seems that Michelangelo began exploring and perhaps purposely exploiting the suggestive power of the unfinished (*non-finito*), as we see especially in the allegories of *Dusk* and *Day* in the Medici Chapel. Whether rough or polished, finished or scarcely begun, Michelangelo had a nearly unparalleled ability to invest the resistant material of marble with life.

Michelangelo grew up in the village of Settignano on the outskirts of Florence, where he was first exposed to the local crafts of stone and marble carving. In this small world of interrelated and neighboring families, he learned the rudiments of sculpture and became acquainted with many of his future assistants. Michelangelo ardently believed that his family was descended from the medieval counts of Canossa. This belief in the antiquity and noble origins of his family fueled Michelangelo's lifelong ambition to improve their social and financial situation.

Through Michelangelo's grandmother, the Buonarroti were distantly related to the Medici, the de facto rulers of Florence. Michelangelo's father probably exploited this distant family tie in order to place his son in the entourage of Lorenzo the Magnificent (Lorenzo de' Medici). Here Michelangelo was introduced to some of the finest works of ancient and modern art and some of the most important literary and intellectual figures of the day, including Marsilio Ficino, Angelo Poliziano, Cristoforo Landino, and Giovanni Pico della Mirandola. Michelangelo spent nearly two years in the Medici household (*ca.* 1490–92). Almost unique among artists, he received the beginnings of a humanist education. He never mastered Latin, but he was exposed to a world of books, learning, and refined culture alongside two of his future patrons, Giovanni de' Medici (Pope Leo X) and Giulio de' Medici (Pope Clem-

ent VII). Michelangelo's skills as a letter writer and poet, and the subtlety of his thinking, bespeak the formative influence of these years. His fond recollection of his time in the Medici household understandably colored the stories related by his biographers, Giorgio Vasari and Ascanio Condivi, more than 50 years later.

Among Michelangelo's surviving early works are exercises in low relief (*Madonna of the Steps*) and higher relief (*Battle of the Centaurs*), respectively revealing the artist's emulation of Donatello and of Classical Antiquity. After the death of Lorenzo the Magnificent in 1492, Michelangelo actively sought patronage among the Strozzi and probably carved for them a life-size marble *Hercules* (lost). Without a regular artistic practice or steady patronage, however, Michelangelo's future and economic security remained tenuous. When the Medici were expelled from Florence in 1494, he elected to follow the family to Bologna, where he lived for nearly a year (1494–95) in the house of the Bolognese patrician Giovanni Francesco Aldovrandi, a position he secured because of his Medici connections. Aldovrandi encouraged Michelangelo's interest in vernacular literature, especially the works of Dante and Petrarch, and arranged for the 20-year-old artist to carve several small statuettes for the still incomplete tomb of St. Dominic (*St. Petronius*, 1494; *St. Proculus*, 1494; and *Angel with a Candlestick*, 1494–95).

Late in 1495 Michelangelo returned to Florence, which was then under the sway of the fiery Dominican preacher Girolamo Savonarola. In need of a patron, Michelangelo curried favor with Lorenzo di Pierfrancesco de' Medici, a member of the cadet branch of the Medici family, for whom Michelangelo carved a marble *St. John the Baptist* and *Sleeping Cupid* (1495; both lost). The cupid so successfully imitated the antique that Lorenzo suggested passing it off as authentic. This "forgery" and Lorenzo's recommendation opened doors to persons of wealth and power, including Cardinal Raffaele Riario, nephew of Pope Sixtus IV and one of the richest and most powerful men in the Roman curia. Thus armed with letters of introduction, Michelangelo, at 21, arrived in Rome for the first time, in the summer of 1496.

The ancient monuments of Rome must have been a revelation, inspiration, and challenge to Michelangelo, for he immediately attempted some extremely audacious works, beginning with *Bacchus*. He carved this *all'antica* (after the antique) figure at the behest of Cardinal Riario, but it ended in the collection of the Roman banker Jacopo Galli, who encouraged and supported the artist. Galli commissioned a *Cupid* and a *St. John* (*ca.* 1495–96; both variously but dubiously identified with surviving sculptures), and he guaranteed the contract for Michelangelo's commission to carve the *Pietà* for the French cardinal, Jean Villiers de La Grolais. A tour de force of aesthetic design and technical realization, the two-figure *Pietà* composition was carved from a single block of Carrara marble. It is the only work Michelangelo ever signed and is one of the best-loved religious images of all time.

Despite the success of the *Pietà* and evidence of an aborted painting commission for the Church of Sant'Agostino, Michelangelo had few opportunities in Rome. He therefore readily accepted a commission from Cardinal Francesco Piccolomini to carve some missing marble statuettes for the Piccolomini altar in Siena Cathedral. He completed the small figures *St. Peter* and *St. Paul* but his interest in the commission waned when in 1501 he was offered a large and partly worked marble that had lain abandoned in the workshop of Florence Cathedral for some 40 years. From the narrow block he carved the *David.* In this figure, Michelangelo successfully combined the Classical and Christian traditions, conceiving the youthful biblical hero on the scale of an ancient nude colossus and endowing him with imminent physical movement and intense mental alertness. With the twin successes of the *Pietà* in Rome and the *David* in Florence, Michelangelo firmly established his public reputation and would never again lack for commissions.

Between 1501 and 1508, Michelangelo sustained an astonishing level of productivity in a variety of media, which included the *David*, the *Bruges Madonna, St. Matthew*, marble tondi for the Taddei and Pitti families (*Taddei Madonna* and *Pitti Madonna*), a painted tondo for Angelo Doni (Galleria degli Uffizi, Florence), a bronze *David* (1502–08) sent to France (lost), a monumental bronze statue of Pope Julius II for Bologna (destroyed), and a commission for a giant fresco, *The Battle of Cascina* (never completed). The number, stature, and international character of Michelangelo's patrons during these years are equally impressive. They included a cardinal and a pope; Piero Soderini, the head of the Florentine government; four prominent Florentine families; the Florentine Cathedral Board of Works (Opera del Duomo); a company of rich Flemish merchants; and the French minister of finance. Condivi asserted that the artist even considered accepting an invitation from the sultan of Turkey to construct a bridge across the Bosphorus at Constantinople.

In 1505, at the recommendation of his friend and colleague Giuliano da Sangallo, Michelangelo was called to Rome to work for Pope Julius II. Together, the ambitious pope and equally ambitious artist conceived a giant tomb that would rival those of the Roman emperors. Thus began the long, convoluted history of a project that Condivi aptly called "the tragedy of the tomb." At least six designs, four contracts, and some 40 years later, a much-reduced but still grand monument was installed in San Pietro in Vincoli, the titular church of Pope Julius.

In characteristic fashion, Michelangelo began the tomb project in the marble quarries, supervising the selection and quarrying of the large quantity of material needed to construct the giant mausoleum. Returning to Rome eight months later, Michelangelo discovered that the pope's attention had turned elsewhere, mainly to war and the rebuilding of the venerated Old Basilica of St. Peter, then more than a thousand years old. Incensed that papal attention and resources had been deflected from the tomb project, Michelangelo left Rome for Florence despite the pope's intense displeasure and repeated efforts to lure him back. Not until Julius was on campaign in nearby Bologna was Michelangelo persuaded to appear before the pope and ask for forgiveness. Michelangelo then spent a trying year in Bologna (1507–08) casting a monumental seated bronze of Pope Julius, which just three years later was destroyed by an angry mob. Thus was erased a chapter in Michelangelo's career and his greatest achievement in the demanding medium of bronze.

Almost immediately after completing the statue in Bologna, Michelangelo was once again in Rome and once again given a task ill suited to a marble sculptor: the painting of the ceiling of the Sistine Chapel (1508–12). As with many commissions that Michelangelo initially resisted, once he reconciled himself to the task, he devoted immense energy and creative powers to carrying it out in spectacular fashion. The ceiling was officially unveiled on 31 October 1512, shortly before the death of Pope Julius in February 1513. For a brief period (1513–16) Michelangelo turned once again to the pope's tomb. During these years he carved the *Moses*, as well as the *Rebellious Slave* and *Dying Slave.*

The newly elected pontiff, Giovanni de' Medici (Pope Leo X), was Michelangelo's boyhood acquaintance from the Medici palace and the first Florentine ever elected pope. Although Leo's tastes ran to painting and precious objects, he commissioned Michelangelo to design a facade for the Medici Church of San Lorenzo in Florence. With little previous training in architecture, Michelangelo set out to create a magnificent all-marble facade that he promised would be "the mirror of architecture and sculpture of all Italy." A large wooden model was constructed (Casa Buonarroti, Florence), and tons of marble were quarried. The project taxed Michelangelo's organizational and logistical skills, proving that he was an engineer and capable businessman as well as an artistic genius. The ambitious undertaking, although never realized, prepared the way for Michelangelo's subsequent architectural projects.

The exceptional cost of the facade may have contributed to its suspension in March 1520, but equally important was the pope's urgent desire to turn Michelangelo's attention to the construction and adornment of a Medici mausoleum at San Lorenzo. The untimely deaths of the two young scions of the family, Giuliano de' Medici (*d.* 1516) and Lorenzo, Duke of Urbino (*d.* 1519), served as the immediate impetus to build the Medici Chapel. Statues of Dukes Giuliano and Lorenzo now grace the chapel's interior along with the *Medici Madonna* and the famous allegories *Night*, *Day*, *Dawn*, and *Dusk*. In the midst of this project, in 1523, Giulio de' Medici was elected Pope Clement VII. Clement was another boyhood acquaintance of the artist and a highly astute patron. In addition to the chapel, Clement commissioned Michelangelo to build the Laurentian Library, a reliquary tribune balcony on the inside facade of San Lorenzo, and a number of other minor projects. For 18 years (1516–34), Michelangelo devoted himself mainly to the Medici commissions at San Lorenzo. During these same years he carved *Risen Christ* and the highly enigmatic *Victory*.

The Sack of Rome in 1527 and the subsequent expulsion of the Medici from Florence resulted in a curtailment of work at San Lorenzo. During the unsettled years of Florence's last republic (1527–30), Michelangelo painted a *Leda* for Duke Alfonso d'Este of Ferrara (lost) and was commissioned for a never-realized statue of *Hercules and Cacus* that was intended as a pendant to his *David* in the Piazza della Signoria. In 1530 the Medici were restored to power, and Michelangelo turned once again to his Medici projects, albeit somewhat less enthusiastically. More work was relegated to assistants, and the artist spent more and more time in Rome. Between 1530 and his definitive move to Rome in 1534, Michelangelo carved the smallish figure *David/Apollo* for Baccio Valori and made a number of highly finished presentation drawings for his new friend, Tommaso de' Cavalieri. Increasingly disaffected with Florence, where the last vestige of republican liberty was erased when Alessandro de' Medici was declared duke in 1532, Michelangelo finally settled in Rome, where he spent the remaining 30 years of his life.

In 1534 the energetic and reform-minded Alessandro Farnese was elected Pope Paul III. Probably the greatest and most discerning of Michelangelo's many patrons, Paul lost no time in employing the artist's talents, first in the painting of the *Last Judgment* (1534–41), which adorns the altar wall of the Sistine Chapel. Shortly after completing the *Last Judgment*, Michelangelo painted two large frescoes, *Conversion of Saul* and *Crucifixion of Peter* (1542–50), for the Pauline Chapel at the Vatican. Paul III also patronized Michelangelo as an architect, appointing him in 1546 to direct the construction of St. Peter's Basilica and the Farnese Palace. In addition, he undertook to redesign and refurbish Rome's Capitoline Hill (Campidoglio, the work for which went from 1538 to beyond Michelangelo's death), the geographic and ceremonial center of ancient Rome. As with many of Michelangelo's architectural commissions, most of the Capitoline project was realized after the artist's death, but the force and clarity of his design ensured that the final result largely reflects his intentions. During these same years, Michelangelo also found time to complete the reduced but still impressive tomb of Pope Julius II.

With each successive pope, Michelangelo was confirmed in his position as supreme architect of St. Peter's Basilica, all the while taking on additional responsibilities from the popes and select patrons. During the reign of Pius IV (1559–65), Michelangelo designed the Porta Pia, transformed the Baths of Diocletian into the Christian church of Santa Maria degli Angeli, and designed the Sforza Chapel in the Church of Santa Maria Maggiore.

While working as an architect in the public sphere, Michelangelo also plumbed the depths of his personal faith in poetry, drawings, and a few sculptures. For an artist who early in his career proudly signed himself "Michelangelo scultore," in the last 30 years of his life, he completed only three sculptures: the *Rachel* and *Leah* for the tomb of Julius II and the bust of *Brutus*, which was carved for Cardinal Niccolò Ridolfi. The Florentine *Pietà* was destined for the artist's own grave but was given away broken and unfinished, and the *Pietà Rondanini* was worked so obsessively that it probably never could be brought to satisfactory completion. Noting this paucity, Vasari wrote, "There are few finished statues . . . and those he did finish completely were executed when he was young." As the artist grew older, drawing and poetry became increasingly important vehicles of creative expression. His late religious drawings, especially the series of haunting and intensely worked *Crucifixion* sheets, are the visual equivalent to his deeply felt penitential poetry.

Living nearly twice as long as the average life span of the period, Michelangelo outlived his entire family and many of his friends. At his side during his final illness were his friends Tommaso de' Cavalieri and Daniele da Volterra. He died on 18 February 1564, just two weeks shy of his 89th birthday.

WILLIAM E. WALLACE

See also **Donatello (Donato di Betto Bardi); Pietà; Renaissance and Mannerism; Tomb Sculpture**

Biography

Born in Caprese, Italy, 6 March 1475. Full name Michelangelo di Lodovico Buonarroti Simoni. Apprenticed to Domenico Ghirlandaio in Florence, 1488; in the Medici household (during the last years of Lorenzo the Magnificent), *ca.* 1490–92; studied anatomy by secretly dissecting corpses at Hospital of Santo Spirito; returned to Medici household for brief period, employed by Piero de' Medici; Medici expelled by republican government, 1494; fled to Bologna, 1494; returned to Florence, 1495, before moving to Rome, 1496–1501; returned to Florence, 1501–05; worked on Piccolomini sculptures, *David*, and other public and private commissions; in Rome, 1505, to design tomb of Pope Julius II, and again 1508–16, when he painted the ceiling of Sistine Chapel, 1508–12; in Florence, 1516–34, where he worked on Medici commissions at San Lorenzo; appointed military engineer to Florence, 1528; settled permanently in Rome, 1534. Died in Rome, Italy, 18 February 1564

Selected Works

ca. 1491   *Madonna of the Steps*; marble; Casa Buonarroti, Florence, Italy

1491–92 *Battle of the Centaurs*; marble; Casa Buonarroti, Florence, Italy

ca.   *Bacchus*; marble; Museo Nazionale del
1496–98 Bargello, Florence, Italy

1497–99 *Pietà*; marble; St. Peter's Basilica, Rome, Italy

1501–04 *David*; marble; Galleria dell'Accademia, Florence, Italy

1503–05 *Bruges Madonna*; marble; Church of Notre Dame, Bruges, Belgium

ca. 1504 *Pitti Madonna* (*Pitti Tondo*); marble; Museo Nazionale del Bargello, Florence, Italy

ca. 1504 *Taddei Madonna* (*Taddei Tondo*); marble; Royal Academy of Arts, London, England

1505–47 Tomb of Julius II; marble; Church of San Pietro in Vincoli, Rome, Italy

ca. 1513 *Dying Slave*; marble; Musée du Louvre, Paris, France

ca. 1513 *Rebellious Slave*; marble; Musée du Louvre, Paris, France

ca. 1515 *Moses*; marble; Church of San Pietro in Vincoli, Rome, Italy

ca.   *Risen Christ*; marble; Church of Santa
1518–21 Maria sopra Minerva, Rome, Italy

1519–34 Medici Chapel (the New Sacristy); marble; Church of San Lorenzo, Florence, Italy

ca.   *Slave (Atlas)*; *Bearded Slave; Awakening*
1520–23 *Slave; Young Slave*; marble; Galleria dell'Accademia, Florence, Italy

ca. 1530 *David/Apollo*; marble; Museo Nazionale del Bargello, Florence, Italy

ca.   *Victory*; marble; Palazzo Vecchio,

1532–34 Florence, Italy

ca. 1540 *Brutus*; marble; Museo Nazionale del Bargello, Florence, Italy

ca.   Florentine *Pietà*; marble; Museo
1547–55 dell'Opera del Duomo, Florence, Italy

ca.   *Pietà Rondanini*; marble; Castello
1555–64 Sforzesco, Milan, Italy

Further Reading

Ackerman, James S., *The Architecture of Michelangelo*, 2 vols., revised edition, London: Zwemmer, 1964

Bull, George Anthony, *Michelangelo: A Biography*, London: Viking, 1995

Buonarroti, Michelangelo, *Il carteggio di Michelangelo*, edited by Paola Barocchi and Renzo Ristori, 5 vols., Florence: Sansoni, 1965–83

Condivi, Ascanio, *Vita di Michelangelo Buonarroti*, Rome: Blado, 1553; as *The Life of Michelangelo*, translated by Alice S. Wohl, edited by Hellmut Wohl, Oxford: Phaidon, and Baton Rouge Louisiana State University Press, 1976

De Tolnay, Charles, *Michelangelo*, 6 vols., Princeton: Princeton University Press, 1943–62; especially vol. 3, *The Medici Chapel*, 1948

Einem, Herbert von, *Michelangelo*, Stuttgart, Germany: Kohlhammer, 1959; as *Michelangelo*, translated by Ronald Taylor, London: Metheun, 1973

Hirst, Michael, *Michelangelo and His Drawings*, New Haven, Connecticut: Yale University Press, 1988

Hughes, Anthony, *Michelangelo*, London: Phaidon Press, 1997

Poeschke, Joachim, *Die Skulptur der Renaissance in Italien*, vol. 2, *Michelangelo und seine Zeit*, Munich: Hirmer, 1992; as *Michelangelo and His World: Sculpture of the Italian Renaissance*, translated by Russell Stockman, New York: Abrams, 1996

Vasari, Giorgio, *Le vite de' più eccellenti architetti, pittori, e scultori italiani*, 3 vols., Florence: Torrentino, 1550; 2nd edition, Florence: Apresso i Giunti, 1568; as *Lives of the Painters, Sculptors, and Architects*, 2 vols., translated by Gaston du C. de Vere (1912), edited by David Ekserdjian, New York: Knopf, and London: Campbell, 1996

Wallace, William E., editor, *Michelangelo: Selected Scholarship in English*, 5 vols., Hamden, Connecticut: Garland, 1995

Weinberger, Martin, *Michelangelo the Sculptor*, 2 vols., New York: Columbia University Press, 1967

Wilde, Johannes, *Michelangelo: Six Lectures*, Oxford: Clarendon Press, and New York: Oxford University Press, 1978

DAVID

Michelangelo (Buonarroti) (1475–1564)

1501–1504

marble

h. 5.2 m (with base, approximately 7.0 m)

Galleria dell'Accademia, Florence, Italy

Immediately upon its completion, Michelangelo's *David* was lauded as an unrivaled feat of technical and creative prowess. Indeed, Giorgio Vasari's encomium was among the most exalted of any given in his 16th-century *Lives of the Painters, Sculptors and Architects*. The *David* remains today one of the most recognized sculptures in Western art, and its history is well documented.

The *operai* (building committee) of Florence Cathedral commissioned the statue from Michelangelo on 16 August 1501. The contract stipulated that *il Gigante* (the Giant) was to be completed in two years and that Michelangelo was to be paid 144 florins. As early as February 1502, the fee was raised to 400 florins and the deadline was extended.

The sculpture was originally intended for one of the buttresses on the apse of Florence Cathedral as part of a series of prophets begun early in the 15th century. The colossal block of marble (9 *braccia* high; 525 centimeters) was quarried in 1464 for Agostino di Duccio; the contract was terminated for unspecified reasons in 1466. In 1476, the *operai* reassigned the block to Antonio Rossellino, who also discontinued the project shortly thereafter. To what extent the two artists worked the block is a subject of some conjecture. We do know that when the revival of the Tribuna program was decided in 1501, a description of the block in a document dated 2 July refers to it as "badly begun" (*male abbozatum*). The history of this recycled marble block sets the framework for Michelangelo's subsequent triumph when confronted with such obstacles.

According to Vasari, in 1501 the *operai* had also considered both Leonardo da Vinci and Andrea Sansovino for the project. Yet after using carpenter's set squares to measure the block, it was Michelangelo who confirmed that it could still be successfully sculpted without attaching additional pieces. The assurance of a monolithic sculpture of such great size must have been instrumental in gaining the commission for Michelangelo. He made a small wax model and began to work the block on 13 September 1501. Scholars have, at various times, attempted to identify two wax figures in the Casa Buonarroti as Michelangelo's original model, and more recently, a small stucco figure was brought to light, but with little critical support.

As the figure neared completion, the city officials evidently felt that its exceptional quality could not be properly appreciated if placed high on a buttress of the cathedral. On 25 January 1504, a committee of the city's principal artists and government officials convened to determine the most appropriate site to display such a masterpiece. Various potential locations were proposed, including in front of the cathedral at ground level, under the central arch of the Loggia dei Lanzi, and finally, the chosen site, in front of the Palazzo della Signoria.

Michelangelo's *David* was immediately considered extraordinary for several reasons. First, Michelangelo was able to succeed with the marble block when others had tried before him and failed. Not only had the block already been worked, but Michelangelo was forced to overcome other technical difficulties, such as exceptional size. The scale of the figure was of considerable import; it set the standard for the many colossal statues that were to follow in the 16th century. Charles Seymour Jr. has argued most convincingly that when Michelangelo penned the phrase "*Davicte cholla fromba e io col larcho. Michelagniolo*" (David with the sling and I with the bow. Michelangelo), he was identifying himself with the young hero. Just as David overcame the giant with his sling, Michelangelo with his bow, the sculptor's drill, could triumph over the block of marble that had felled others (see Seymour, 1967b).

Michelangelo's statue also departed from the conventional depictions of David. The Bible describes David as both a boy (1 Sam. 17:33, 42) and as a "brave man and a warrior" (1 Sam. 16:18). Donatello and Andrea del Verrocchio clearly referred to the former in their earlier portrayals of the youth, whereas Michelangelo's *David* verges on maturity. Again unusual is the moment that Michelangelo chose to depict his hero. Rather than showing the victorious David standing over the decapitated head of Goliath, Michelangelo evoked the psychologically charged moment directly before the battle. He imbued his giant with a sense of poised anticipation; David stands in a Classical *contrapposto* pose (a natural pose with the weight of one leg, the shoulder, and hips counterbalancing one another) and evaluates the enemy.

The pronounced features of *David* and the deeply undercut hair serve to make him more readily visible at street level, far below his intended location on a cathedral buttress. The size of his head, hands, and feet are distorted for the same purpose. It is often noted that his right hand, in particular, is emphasized—this may refer to *manu fortis* (strong of hand), an appellation applied to David from the Middle Ages.

According to Saul Levine, *David* symbolized the impending threat of Cesare Borgia and the pro-Medici supporters against the freedom of the Florentine Republic (see Levine, 1974). Although the statue may have acquired these political overtones once placed in the Piazza della Signoria, it is doubtful that the sculpture was made with that intent, as Levine suggests. Certainly David's moral strength and courage are personified by his physical puissance; as such, he came to represent the courage and fortitude of the Florentine Republic.

The contemporary chronicler Luca Landucci reported that the statue was transported from the grounds of the Opera di Santa Maria del Fiore to the Piazza della Signoria in May 1504 using an intricate system of support and conveyance. It took the place of Donatello's *Judith Slaying Holofernes* (*ca.* 1459) on the *ringhiera*, or rostrum, in front of the Palazzo Vecchio. As is often the case with Renaissance sculpture, the pure white marble that we see today was not the original aesthetic. Payment documents to local craftsmen indicate that shortly after the sculpture was installed, the sling and tree stump were gilded, a gilt wreath decorated the head, and a garland of copper leaves was placed across the groin.

The *David*'s left arm was broken during a riot in 1527 and later repaired. The sculpture suffered from exposure to the elements over the centuries until 1873, when it was transferred to the Accademia delle Belle Arti. An act of vandalism in 1991 damaged a toe joint on the left foot; the fragments were immediately recovered and reattached. Despite these difficulties, the *David* continues to stand as a masterpiece of the Italian Renaissance.

JEANNINE A. O'GRODY

See also **Donatello (Donato di Betto Bardi); Verrocchio, Andrea del**

Further Reading

De Tolnay, Charles, *The Youth of Michelangelo*, Princeton, New Jersey: Princeton University Press, 1943; 2nd edition, 1969

The Digital Michelangelo Project (www.graphics.stanford.edu/projects/mich/)

Hirst, Michael, "Michelangelo in Florence: *David* in 1503 and *Hercules* in 1506," in *Scritti per Paola Barocchi*, Milan and Naples: Ricciardi, 1997

Lavin, Irving, "David's Sling and Michelangelo's Bow: A Sign of Freedom," in *Past-Present: Essays on Historicism in Art from Donatello to Picasso*, by Lavin, Berkeley: University of California Press, 1993

Levine, Saul, "The Location of Michelangelo's *David*: The Meeting of January 25, 1504," *Art Bulletin* 56 (1974)

Parks, N. Randolph, "The Placement of Michelangelo's *David*: A Review of the Documents," *Art Bulletin* 57 (1975)

Seymour, Charles, Jr., "Homo Magnus et Albus: The Quattrocento Background for Michelangelo's *David* of 1501–04," in *Stil und Überlieferung in der Kunst des Abendlandes*, vol. 2, Berlin: Mann, 1967a

Seymour, Charles, Jr., *Michelangelo's David: A Search for Identity*, Pittsburgh, Pennsylvania: University of Pittsburgh Press, 1967b

Smith, Graham, "'The Great Slinger Was Himself Slung': The Transfer of the *David* to the Academy in 1873," *Source: Notes in the History of Art* 18/3 (Spring 1999)

Weddingen, Tristan, "A Virtue of Necessity: Michelangelo's 'David' Difficilissimamente Facile," *Daidalos* 59 (1996)

Weil-Garris, Kathleen, "On Pedestals: Michelangelo's *David*, Bandinelli's *Hercules and Cacus*, and the Sculpture of the Piazza della Signoria," *Römisches Jahrbuch für Kunstgeschichte* 20 (1983)

MEDICI CHAPEL
Church of San Lorenzo, Florence, Italy, 1519–34

During Pope Leo X's pontificate (1513–21), he and his cousin Cardinal Giulio de' Medici commissioned tombs for family members Giuliano (*d.* 1478) and Lorenzo de' Medici (*d.* 1492), father and uncle to the pope (called the *Magnifici*), and for their cousins Giuliano, Duke of Nemours (*d.* 1516), and Lorenzo, Duke of Urbino (*d.* 1519) (called the *Capitani*). Although Michelangelo initiated plans in 1519 for the Medici Chapel tombs in the north transept of the Church of San Lorenzo in Florence, the election of Cardinal Giulio to the papacy in November 1523 allowed Michelangelo to turn uninterruptedly to the project.

A number of extant drawings reveal the development of the tombs. Michelangelo considered several options, including both a four-sided monument and two double tombs on each side wall, before deciding on a double tomb for the *Magnifici* and two wall tombs for the *Capitani*. In spring 1524, he oversaw the construction of at least one full-scale wooden architectural model of a wall tomb for the *Capitani*, complete with corresponding clay models of the sculptures. Michelangelo's detailed records from this period document all purchases and expenditures, which makes it possible to determine the materials used and total cost for the models. Shortly after working on the models, Michelangelo began to sculpt the marbles. He promised that he himself would carve the figures he considered most important: effigies of the two dukes, the four allegories representing the Times of Day, four river gods, and a Madonna and Child.

On the two wall tombs for the *Capitani*, seated effigies of the dukes reside in shallow niches above their carved marble sarcophagi. It is generally agreed that the effigies were not intended to be portraits but rather idealized images. Indeed, Michelangelo is said to have remarked that in a thousand years no one would remember the two dukes' visages anyway.

A male and female pair of allegorical figures representing the Times of Day each surmount the curved sarcophagi lids. *Night* and *Day* rest atop Giuliano's sarcophagus, while *Dawn* and *Dusk* lie on Lorenzo's. *Night* and *Day* in particular are among Michelangelo's most celebrated sculptures. It is generally believed that they were carved before the other two Times of Day, as their marble bases do not comply with the contours of the sarcophagus lid; it follows therefore that only after *Night* and *Day* were begun did Michelangelo modify the design of the sarcophagi to include the curved lids. *Night* is the only one of the four figures with attributes: she wears a diadem decorated with a star and crescent moon, leans against a mask, and has an owl and a cluster of poppies under her bent left leg, all of which allude to darkness and sleep. She is also the most highly finished of the four figures. Michelangelo scrupulously defined the powerful musculature of *Day* yet only roughly blocked out the figure's face from the marble. Compositionally, Michelangelo

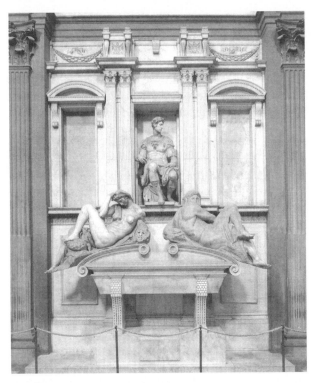

Medici Chapel, Tomb of Giuliano de' Medici
The Conway Library, Courtauld Institute of Art

clearly planned for the two sets of Times of Day to be complementary pairs. Whereas the emphatic torsion of *Night* is echoed in the figure of *Day*, *Dusk* and *Dawn* both reflect a more languid, relaxed state.

The double tomb for Lorenzo the Magnificent and his brother Giuliano on the entrance wall comprises an unfinished sculpture, the *Madonna and Child* (known as the *Medici Madonna*), flanked by statues of the Medici patron saints, *Cosmas* and *Damian*. Michelangelo himself carved the *Medici Madonna*, but at the urging of the pope he hired skilled colleagues to execute the saints in 1533; Giovan Angelo Montorsoli carved *Cosmas*, and Raffaello da Montelupo was responsible for *Damian*.

The elegant seated *Medici Madonna* provides a paradigmatic example of a figure contained within the confines of the marble block. The prescient young mother holds her active son, who straddles her left leg and twists back toward his mother's breast. The sculpture is the spiritual focus of the entire figural ensemble in the chapel: the priest faces it while performing the service behind the altar, and both dukes and patron saints likewise turn in her direction.

By June 1526, Michelangelo noted in a letter that he had begun all of the marbles except the four river gods and one of the *Capitani*. Work on the chapel then ceased from 1527 to 1530 during the expulsion of the Medici from Florence. By the time the project re-sumed, it no longer retained Michelangelo's absolute focus. The chapel remained unfinished when Michelangelo moved permanently to Rome in September 1534. The effigies of the two dukes were in place, but the four allegories were left on the chapel floor and the *Medici Madonna* was still in Michelangelo's studio. The sculptor never carried out beyond the sculpted model stage the four river gods that had been intended to lie on the floor below the Times of Day. He planned smaller allegorical figures for the niches flanking the dukes, to be carved by others, but these were never carried out. It was not until approximately 1545 that Cosimo I de' Medici instructed the artist Niccolò Tribolo to give the chapel some measure of organization, which included positioning the Times of Day and apparently the models of the river gods. The remains of the *Magnifici* were finally transported from the Old Sacristy to their double tomb in the chapel in 1559.

The collective group presents an exceptional opportunity to study Michelangelo's carving techniques. The incomplete sculptures left in various states of resolution offer abundant visual evidence of his use of the point and claw chisels and, in *Night*, his ultimate goal of highly polished surfaces.

Scholars have proffered countless readings to explicate the complexity of the iconographic program of the chapel, including political, philosophical, religious, and cosmological interpretations. It is generally held, however, that the essential concept is humankind's inability to conquer time and the resultant inevitability of death. Indeed, Ascanio Condivi, Michelangelo's biographer, wrote in 1553 that the Times of Day symbolized "the principle of time which consumes everything."

Among the more well-known interpretations regarding the symbolic nature of the Medici Chapel is that of Erwin Panofsky and Charles de Tolnay, who both argued for a Neoplatonic reading of the iconographic program. This suggests that the multiple levels of the tombs reflect the hierarchically arranged realms of the universe. The two dukes, whose immortalized souls are represented by their contrasting human characteristics, seek a higher sphere of existence and thus eternal life. Giuliano (*Vita Activa*) is depicted bareheaded, seated in an alert, open manner, and holding coins in his left hand, which could be interpreted to refer to a generous nature. Conversely, the more somber Lorenzo (*Vita Contemplativa*), whose face is cast in shadow by his fanciful zoomorphic helmet, leans his left elbow on a closed coin box. The active and the contemplative life, thus, are equally worthy of attaining higher spheres.

The Medici Chapel project constitutes one of the most renowned sculptural ensembles in Western art. The amount of extant supporting artistic and archival material pertaining to the project provides a remarkable account of Michelangelo's working methods while still leaving room for speculation regarding the incomplete nature of the entire program and its overall meaning. The chapel subsequently became a meeting place for aspiring artists from the newly formed Accademia del Disegno to meet and study Michelangelo's masterpieces in the honored tradition of inspiration and emulation.

JEANNINE A. O'GRODY

See also **Montorsoli, Giovan Angelo; Tomb Sculpture; Tribolo, Niccolò**

Further Reading

Balas, Edith, "The Iconography of Michelangelo's Medici Chapel: A New Hypothesis," *Gazette des Beaux-Arts* 120 (1992)

Beck, James H., Antonio Paolucci, and Bruno Santi, *Michelangelo: The Medici Chapel*, New York: Thames and Hudson, 1994

De Tolnay, Charles, *Michelangelo*, 6 vols., Princeton, New Jersey: Princeton University Press, 1943–62; especially vol. 3, *The Medici Chapel*

Gilbert, Creighton, "Texts and Contexts of the Medici Chapel," *Art Quarterly* 34 (1971)

Hartt, Frederick, "The Meaning of Michelangelo's Medici Chapel," in *Essays in Honor of Georg Zwarzenski*, compiled by Oswald Goetz, Chicago: Regnery, 1951

Hibbard, Howard, *Michelangelo*, New York: Harper and Row, 1974; 2nd edition, Cambridge, Massachusetts: Harper and Row, 1985

Panofsky, Erwin, "The Mouse That Michelangelo Failed to Carve," in *Essays in Memory of Karl Lehmann*, edited by Lucy Freeman Sandler, New York: Institute of Fine Arts, New York University, 1964

Wallace, William E., *Michelangelo at San Lorenzo: The Genius as Entrepreneur*, Cambridge and New York: Cambridge University Press, 1994

Waźbinski, Zygmunt, "La Cappella dei Medici e l'origine dell' Accademia del disegno," in *Firenze e la Toscana dei Medici nell' Europa del '500*, vol. 1, London: Routledge and Kegan Paul, and Florence: L.S. Olschki, 1983

Wilde, Johannes, "Michelangelo's Designs for the Medici Tombs," *Journal of the Warburg and Courtauld Institutes* 18 (1955)

MICHELOZZO DI BARTOLOMEO
1396–1472 *Italian*

Michelozzo di Bartolomeo was one of the most important sculptors and architects of Early Renaissance Florence. His role as a sculptor, however, has often been seen only in the light of his capacities as a metalworker and his collaboration with the leading sculptors Donatello and Lorenzo Ghiberti. Recent scholarship has tried to correct this view by citing the originality of Michelozzo's works in sculpture and architecture. Born in 1396, he belonged to the second generation of Renaissance sculptors with Filarete and Luca della Robbia. Most probably he was trained as a goldsmith; he is first documented as working at the Florentine mint in 1410. As an associate of Ghiberti from 1417 to 1424, Michelozzo took part in the creation of the north door of the baptistery and St. Matthew's tabernacle for the Church of Orsanmichele in Florence. The Madonna and the Annunciate Angel of St. Matthew's tabernacle have been attributed as his first independent works.

Although Michelozzo's share in the works of Ghiberti cannot be discerned clearly, the parts executed by him for the works commissioned from his joint workshop with Donatello have been established with some certainty, but the relative share is still much debated for single pieces. His association with Donatello started in 1424 or 1425, possibly after a stay in Venice. The first work executed in collaboration was the tomb of Baldassare Coscia, the antipope John XXIII. The monument incorporates the baptistery's architecture by linking the two-story elevation of the tomb to the structure's colossal inner columns. Although Donatello obviously was responsible for the general conception and the execution of the bronze effigy of the pope, Michelozzo's part consisted mainly in carving the three Virtues in niches on the high socle and in creating the Madonna and child lunette on the top.

From their second workshop at Pisa issued the tomb for Rinaldo Brancacci for the Church of S. Angelo a Nilo (1426–33) in Naples. This tomb for the one-time supporter of Baldassare Coscia was characterized by the necessity to respect Neapolitan conventions. Thus according to the tradition started by Tino di Camaino in the 14th century, three caryatids clad in flowing garments inspired by antique sculpture support the sarcophagus of the high, three-story tomb. Unexpectedly, however, these caryatids can be identified neither as Christian Virtues nor as allegorical personifications in any way because of the lack of any specific attribute. Michelozzo's share seems to have been more extensive here, because on the one hand he is made responsible for the architecture, which combines novel Classical elements (fluted double columns and composite order) with Gothic ones (curved gable), and on the other hand, he is held responsible for most of the sculptures, apart from the relief of the *Assumption* on the sarcophagus, which is surely by Donatello.

During his association with Donatello, Michelozzo independently created his most important work, the tomb of Bartolomeo Aragazzi, secretary to Pope Martin V, for the Pieve di S. Maria in Montepulciano. Also for Montepulciano he conceived the lunette over the central portal of the Church of Sant' Agostino. Although undocumented, the lunette showing the Madonna and Child with St. John the Baptist and St. Augustine has been generally accepted as a work by Michelozzo and dated to 1437 or 1438. While still in cooperation with Donatello, he worked on the exterior pulpit of the Cathedral of Prato, Italy, where his share was limited to casting the bronze capital (1433), which was designed and modeled by Donatello.

After the end of his common workshop with Donatello, which ran into financial difficulties several times, Michelozzo worked again for Ghiberti from 1437 to 1442. It remains unclear, however, which share he had in the creation of the second set of doors, the *Gates of Paradise* (completed in 1452). His influence has occasionally been discerned in the Isaac and Jacob panels.

In later works, his style changed, and he reverted from the programmatic imitation of antique sculpture back to the flowing lines of Ghiberti's sculptures. The terracotta St. John the Baptist is undocumented but generally accepted as his work. It was created probably for the chapel of St. John (1444), commissioned by Messer Antonio di Michele di Forese da Rabatta for the Church of Santissima Annunziata. Stylistically and conceptionally, it bears the greatest resemblance to the later silver statuette of St. John, commissioned from Michelozzo on 13 April 1452 for the central niche in the silver altar of the baptistery, Michelozzo's last documented sculptural work.

Although in 1446 he received a major commission—along with (Luca) della Robbia and Maso di Bartolomeo—to create a bronze door for the sacristy of the Florence Cathedral, the later execution was carried out by Luca alone. A considerable number of further sculptures has been attributed to Michelozzo, mostly reliefs of the Madonna and child. Of these, however, only the Madonna in the Bargello in Florence can claim to be an authentic work by Michelozzo, dating from the late 1430s. These attributions often serve to reconstruct an arbitrary late style that obviously did not exist, as Michelozzo seems to have abandoned sculpture in favor of his tasks as an architect.

Beginning in the 1430s Michelozzo was increasingly absorbed by his work as an architect, creating several of the most important buildings in early Renaissance Florence. In later years his reputation seems to have weakened and he went to Ragusa (Dubrovnik; 1461–64), and then on to Chios (Greece; 1464–67), working on fortifications there. After his return to Italy in 1467 and to Florence in 1469, he died in his hometown in 1472 and was buried in San Marco on 7 October.

JOHANNES MYSSOK

See also **Donatello (Donato di Betto Bardi); Filarete (Antonio di Pietro Averlino); Ghiberti, Lorenzo; Robbia, Della, Family; Tino di Camaino**

Biography

Born in Florence, Italy, 1396. Apprenticed as goldsmith; first mentioned as working at Florentine mint on 28 May 1410; worked as associate of Ghiberti, 1417–24; partnered with Donatello, 1424–35; became member of Stonemasons' and Carpenters' Guild, 1420, and began his career as an architect, chiefly employed by the Medici (Palazzo Medici, San Marco); second association with Ghiberti, 1437–42, to complete Aragazzi tomb; completed last sculptural work, 1452–53; Florence cathedral *capomaestro* (chief architect), 1446–51; accepted position in Ragusa (Dubrovnik, Dalmatia) to supervise strengthening city wall, 1461; contract extended, 1463; worked on the island of Chios (Greece), from 1464; returned to Italy, 1467, and settled in Florence, 1469. Died in Florence, Italy, 1472.

Selected Works

1424   Madonna and Angel; marble; Tabernacle of St. Matthew; Church of Orsanmichele, Florence, Italy

1424–28 Tomb of Pope John XXIII (with Donatello); marble and bronze, partially gilt; Baptistery, Florence, Italy

1427–38 Tomb of Bartolomeo Aragazzi; marble and bronze; fragments: Cathedral and Archivio Vescovile, Montepulciano, Italy; Victoria and Albert Museum, London, England

1428–38 Exterior pulpit (with Donatello); marble and bronze; Cathedral and Museo dell'Opera del Duomo, Prato, Italy

1430s   Madonna and child, terracotta with blue glass inlays; Museo Nazionale del Bargello, Florence, Italy

1437–38 Lunette with Madonna and child with St. John and St. Augustine; terracotta; Church of Sant' Agostino, Montepulciano, Italy

1444   St. John the Baptist; terracotta; Church of Santissima Annunziata, Florence, Italy

1452   St. John; silver; Museo dell'Opera del Duomo, Florence, Italy

Further Reading

Caplow, Harriet McNeal, *Michelozzo*, 2 vols., New York: Garland, 1977

Ferrara, Miranda, and Francesco Quinterio, *Michelozzo di Bartolomeo*, Florence: Salimbeni, 1984

Janson, Horst W., *The Sculpture of Donatello*, 2 vols., Princeton, New Jersey: Princeton University Press, 1957

Lightbown, Ronald W., *Donatello and Michelozzo: An Artistic Partnership and Its Patrons in the Early Renaissance*, 2 vols., London: Miller, 1980

Morolli, Gabriele, editor, *Michelozzo: Scultore e architetto (1396–1472)*, Florence: Centro Di, 1998

Poeschke, Joachim, *Die Skulptur der Renaissance in Italien*, vol. 1, *Donatello und seiner Zeit;* Munich: Hirmer, 1990; as *Donatello and His World: Sculpture of the Italian Renaissance*, translated by Russell Stockman, New York: Abrams, 1993

Pope-Hennessy, John, *An Introduction to Italian Sculpture*, 3 vols., London: Phaidon, 1963; 4th edition, 1996; see especially vol. 2, *Italian Renaissance Sculpture*

TOMB OF BARTOLOMEO ARAGAZZI

Michelozzo di Bartolomeo (1396–1472)
1427–1438; dismantled after 1616
Carrara marble, bronze
h. (disputed)
Fragments in Cathedral and Archivio Vescovile, Montepulciano, Italy; Victoria and Albert Museum, London, England

Michelozzo's most important work, his tomb for the papal secretary Bartolomeo Aragazzi in the Cathedral of Montepulciano, has been preserved only in fragments. Michelozzo began work on it in 1427 while Aragazzi was still alive (d. 1429). After several interruptions, the monument was set up in 1438. It represents the prototype of the "humanist tomb" (see Pope-Hennessy, 1996) because Aragazzi was a secretary and close counselor of Pope Martin V, and, as a Latin poet, he belonged to the circle of the humanist Poggio Bracciolini. Although Michelozzo received the commission for the tomb during his professional association with Donatello, the latter had no share in its design and execution. Stylistically as well as iconographically, it is, however, quite different from Michelozzo's previous works.

The monument was dismantled with the construction of the new cathedral in the early 17th century. The fragments preserved in the cathedral are the effigy of the deceased in the garments of a papal secretary, the base decorated with putti and garlands (now integrated into the high altar), two reliefs, two life-size standing figures in the round bearing candlesticks, and the figure of Christ in high relief (sometimes mistakenly identified as St. Bartholomew). A bronze epitaph panel remains in the Archivio Vescovile (Montepulciano, Italy). Further high-relief fragments of two adoring angels reside in the Victoria and Albert Museum.

The genesis of the monument can be traced to 1427, when evidently only the marble was purchased. The documents leave unspecified the point at which Michelozzo set to work, as well as when the bulk of the work was created. A letter by the Florentine chancellor Leonardo Bruni reporting his encounter with the monument's half-finished pieces on their transport to Montepulciano is undated. Most historians assume, however, that the parts of the monument date from the early 1430s, and therefore much of the work had been completed in advance of the hiatus that lasted until the establishment of the new contract with the heirs in 1437. This assumption is contradicted by the stylistic evidence of the sculptures, which, especially in the reliefs, show the influence of Donatello's *Cantoria* (singing gallery) and the pulpit in Prato, and thus can only date after their common stay in Rome (1432–33) that led both to an almost imitative approach to antique relief sculpture. Thus, substantial parts must have been created during the later phase at the end of the 1430s.

The formal reconstruction of the monument, attempted by several historians, is based on Bruni's letter and on the report of a visitation made in 1583. Consensus has been reached over the general form of the monument (the "cappella" mentioned in Michelozzo's tax return of 1469): a relatively shallow wall tomb that projected into the nave with pilasters or columns like the Brancacci tomb by Donatello and Michelozzo in Naples. Considerable disagreement persists, however, on the question of the original height. Taking into account that the monument had a proper altar and that the sarcophagus with the two reliefs served as a kind of altarpiece, a tall lower structure must be assumed. This possibility is corroborated by the further relief sculptures, the two angels and the blessing Christ, who originally continued the surge upward and redirected his gaze back down toward the effigy.

The monument's reconstruction is further complicated by its unusual iconography, especially that of the reliefs. The overall scheme embodied an eschatologi-

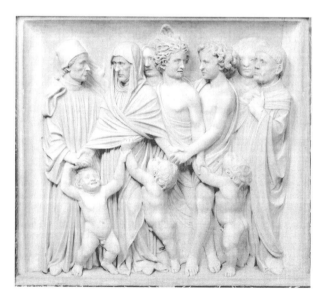

Relief from the tomb of Bartolomeo Aragazzi, Montepulciano, Italy
The Conway Library, Courtauld Institute of Art

cal program, focusing on the salvation of the deceased and his entry into paradise. The majestic figure of the standing Christ, adored by the two angels with arms crossed, must have been shown descending on clouds toward the tomb to raise the dead and to lead him into Paradise. His welcome there is the topic of the first relief, where Aragazzi, standing on the left, clutches the hand of a woman, perhaps his mother, in a *dextrarum junctio* (joining of the right hands) like married couples on antique sarcophagi, and he is greeted by several other members of his family, mostly clad in togas and accompanied by naked putti.

The second relief shows Aragazzi on the left kneeling in front of the Madonna and Child while his family surrounds the throne and putti dance merrily at the feet of the Christ child. The sarcophagus with the reliefs was originally flanked on each side by the two somber, life-size female figures standing on the sides or at a little distance in front of lateral pilasters. They have been identified as angels, although they show neither an attribute nor wings, but they do carry candlesticks. These two classicizing figures, along with the figure of Christ, are considered Michelozzo's best works, even if in their physique they are clearly based on Donatello's *Prophets of the Florentine* campanile (1416–36).

The reliefs, on the other hand, are qualitatively much weaker, only in part because of Michelozzo's forced attempt to imitate Roman reliefs as Donatello and Luca della Robbia did with their *Cantorie* for the Florence Cathedral. As with the life-size female figures, in the reliefs Michelozzo attempted to catch the low emotional pitch of Roman sarcophagi, a feature for which he often has been called a Classicist. Despite certain weaknesses, these reliefs constitute the closest approach to antique relief style before the High Renaissance. The effigy in the Cathedral of Montepulciano similarly betrays Michelozzo's approximation to antique sculpture. He used the technical as well as the expressive potential of Roman portraiture to render the features of the deceased clad in contemporary garments, probably basing the sculpture on a death mask. Some confusion persists over whether this was the only effigy to be shown on the sarcophagus or if indeed there was also a second effigy, the figure of Aragazzi's father Francesco. The sources allow different interpretations, however, and probably only the effigy of Bartolomeo Aragazzi was made.

The Aragazzi tomb was widely known in humanist circles and sparked a debate on this form of "memoria"; with the monuments to Leonardo Bruni and Carlo Marsuppini in the Florence Cathedral, the debate was finally decided in favor of tombs, giving the quattrocento humanist's tomb its definitive form.

JOHANNES MYSSOK

See also **Donatello (Donato di Betto Bardi); Robbia, Della, Family**

Further Reading

Clayton, Martin, "Michelozzo's Aragazzi Tomb: A Revised Reconstruction," *Studi di storia dell'arte* 5–6 (1994–95)
Pope-Hennessy, John, *An Introduction to Italian Sculpture*, 3 vols., London: Phaidon, 1963; 4th edition, 1996; see especially vol. 2, *Italian Renaissance Sculpture*

CARL MILLES 1875–1955 *Swedish, active in United States*

Carl Milles is regarded as one of Sweden's greatest sculptors. He found inspiration for his highly expressive works in archaic and Greek mythological sculpture and writings. His sculptures helped shape the course of German Expressionism and American sculpture during the first half of the 20th century.

Milles apprenticed as a cabinetmaker until the age of 20, during which time he also studied sculpture in night classes. His work, well received by his teachers, won him a scholarship to attend the Kungliga Tekniska Högskola (Royal Technical High School) in Stockholm. In 1897 he was bound for a job in Chile but stopped in Paris, where he decided to attend the Académie Colarossi. In 1899 he was admitted to the Salon. During this time he worked in the studio of Auguste Rodin and became influenced by Rodin's early work.

In 1902 Milles received praise and recognition for his sculpture of the Swedish hero Sten Sture, a monument at Uppsala (completed in 1925) for which he won a competition. He was also active in Munich between 1904 and 1906. His first major fountain, *Europa and the Bull*, was notable for its design. The subtlety of his trickling water effects and highly imaginative figures, such as the faun and troll, won Milles great praise.

Showing Rodin's influence, Milles's approach to sculpture was at first highly Impressionistic; he created sculptures that were intimate in size and free-flowing in form. He soon abandoned this style, feeling his work unsatisfactory and wanting a more free and personal style that was less derivative. In 1917 he and his son spent three days destroying all the sculpture left in his studio. His subsequent work is full of fantasy and humor. Still, his sculpture became more representative and formal with the inspiration of Greek and medieval art. The German sculptor and theorist Adolf von Hildebrand also influenced him. Milles's later work shows a more progressive pattern toward fluent and elaborate compositions, following von Hildebrand's theory that sculpture should emphasize clarity and form rather than meticulous detail.

Milles first visited the United States in 1929. In 1931 he was invited to exhibit his sculpture at the Art

Museum of St. Louis, Missouri, where he showed 44 works, well received by the public and critics alike. The exhibition led to an invitation to become a professor and artist in residence at the renowned Cranbrook Academy of Art in Bloomfield Hills, Michigan, after which became director of the department of sculpture there. His first work for Cranbrook Academy was the Jonah Fountain, which depicted the story of Jonah and the whale. Inside the bowl, small fish sent streams of water over the whale as it appeared to laugh at Jonah. The fountain, in the words of Milles, was "a joke for the children."

The year 1936 was a pinnacle one for Milles: he completed two exceptionally large works. The first, the Orpheus Fountain, consists of nine figures in a basin. The original was later sent to Stockholm; a replica of the fountain is located at Cranbrook. The second large work is a mammoth 11-meter-high American Indian, sculpted in alabaster and originally meant for St. Paul's Peace Memorial in Minnesota. In the same year, the Cranbrook Academy of Art acquired 66 of Milles's sculptures, bringing their unique collection of his works to a total of 70. The acquisition of these works established Cranbrook as one of the most important collections of sculpture in North America. The collection includes the equestrian group from Milles's renowned Folkunga Fountain (1927). In 1935 Cranbrook received a bronze replica of Milles's most famous work, *Europa and the Bull*, now overlooking the formal gardens.

Milles's creations did not go without controversy or criticism. Some perceived his *Meeting of the Waters*, a fountain symbolizing the joining of the Mississippi and Missouri Rivers and comprised of 19 nude figures, as being untrue to life. In 1952 Milles compromised and brought an artist from Sweden to apply fig leaves to some of the figures, thereby adding modesty to the fountain. In 1956 Milles's *The Sunglitter (Nereid on a Dolphin)* was removed from the hall of Detroit's Convention Hall and Exhibits Building to the less-traveled pool area. In 1962 the statue was placed in the Cobo Hall and later again in the popular cocktail lounge.

Many of Milles's works are found in the United States. For the 21 years that Milles lived and worked in the United States (becoming a citizen in 1945), he also amassed an extensive collection of books on Roman and Greek sculpture, from which he was said to have borrowed many of his ideas. In his last year at Cranbrook he completed *God's Hand*, a copy of which was later installed near the artist's former home in Millesgården, near Stockholm. Working in bronze, stone, and wood, he achieved high recognition for his ability to combine sculpture with architectural framework, which can be seen in many of his fountains. His work comprises arabesque angles and carries a strong sense of pantheism, with austerity, sensuality, anguish, and serenity. Milles returned to Sweden in 1951 and died in Lidingö in 1955.

CHRISTIAN CARDELL CORBET

See also **Fountain Sculpture; Hildebrand, Adolf von; Rodin, Auguste; Scandinavia: Sweden**

Biography

Born in Lagga, Sweden, 23 June 1875. Full given name Carl Emil Wilhelm Anderson. Studied cabinetmaking at Kungliga Tekniska Högskola (Royal Technical High School), Stockholm, 1895–97; sculpture at Académie Colarossi, Paris, 1897; admitted to the Salon, 1899, and the studio of Auguste Rodin, ca. 1900; lived in Munich, 1904–06; returned to Sweden, 1908; appointed professor at the Konsthögskola, Stockholm, 1920–31; moved to the United States, 1931; professor of sculpture at Cranbrook Academy of Art, Bloomfield Hills, Michigan, 1931–45; became a U.S. citizen, 1945; returned to Sweden, 1951. Died in Lidingö, Sweden, 19 September 1955.

Selected Works

1903	*Women in the Wind*; bronze; Lidingö National Museum, Stockholm, Sweden
1926	*Europa and the Bull* (fountain); bronze, granite; Halmstad, Sweden; replica: 1935, Cranbrook Art Museum, Bloomfield Hills, Michigan, United States
1930	Poseidon Fountain; bronze; Konstmuseum and Exhibition Hall, Gothenburg, Sweden
1932	Jonah Fountain; bronze and stone; Cranbrook Art Museum, Bloomfield Hills, Michigan, United States
1936	Orpheus Fountain; bronze; Concert Hall, Stockholm, Sweden; copy: 1988, Missouri Botanical Garden, St. Louis, United States
1936	Peace Memorial; Mexican onyx; City Hall, St. Paul, Minnesota, United States
1940	*Meeting of the Waters*; bronze; Aloe Plaza, St. Louis, Missouri, United States
1940	*Nature and Man*; wood; Time Life Building, New York City, United States
1947	*The Wings*; bronze; private collection, Stockholm, Sweden
1948	*God's Hand*; bronze, steel; Scarborough Sculpture Park, Scarborough, Ontario, Canada
1948	Resurrection Fountain; bronze; Falls Church, Virginia, United States
1955	The Fountain of the Muses; bronze; Falls Church, Virginia, United States

Further Reading

Brooklyn Museum, *Catalogue of an Exhibition of Sculpture by the Swedish Sculptor Carl Milles*, New York: Brooklyn Museum, 1932

Cornell, Henrik, and Dorothy Liljequist, *Millesgården: Its Garden and Art Treasures: A Photo Folio*, Stockholm: Albert Bonniers Förlag, 1960

McFadden, David Revere, *Scandinavian Modern Design: 1880–1980*, New York: Abrams, 1982

Milles, Carl, *Fountain of Faith*, Falls Church, Virginia: National Memorial Park, 1952

Rogers, Meryic R., *Carl Milles: An Interpretation of His Work*, New Haven, Connecticut: Yale University Press, 1940

ORPHEUS FOUNTAIN

Carl Milles (1875–1955)

1936

bronze, granite

h. 11.6 m

Concert Hall, Stockholm, Sweden

1988 replica installed at Missouri Botanical

Garden, St. Louis, United States

In 1926 Carl Milles entered a competition for a fountain to be erected in front and adjacent to the new Concert Hall in Stockholm, Sweden, designed by the noted architect Ivar Tengbom. The idea of the Orpheus Fountain came from Milles's strong interest in Greek mythology. Orpheus's music was said to be so beautiful and powerful that the animals, trees, and even rocks would dance as he played. Milles saw this figure as an opportunity to entertain as well as educate the viewer.

Milles won the competition for the fountain in 1930 with a first model consisting only of the figure of Orpheus. Throughout the creation process Milles greatly revised the design. The original study had only the Orpheus figure with abstract plant life surrounding his feet, in a granite basin. Milles then reworked the composition with the plant life and added eight additional subsidiary figures.

The Orpheus Fountain depicts Orpheus playing a lyre given him by the god Apollo. Orpheus, approximately five times life size, stands on a plant form, which in turn is mounted on the back of the figure of Cerberus, the three-headed dog. Cerberus stands on all four legs, clenching his teeth, through which water is dispersed as if he is drooling. Cerberus is also perched on a plant form, thus elevating the center point of the fountain.

The nude Orpheus, holding upright his large horned lyre, gazes down to the figures below while gracefully caressing the space between the horns on the instru-

ment, which is void of any representation of strings. The figure carries a strong sense of realism, sculpted with much greater detail than the other figures. Muscles are more pronounced as are Orpheus's fingers and toes. Milles gave the greatest detail to Orpheus's facial expression, which carries a look of both concern and concentration with finely detailed eyes and mouth. A wreath of poppy flowers sits on his head. The figure itself portrays great dramatic intensity and character.

The eight bronze figures arranged in the bronze basin are approximately double life size. Each of the figures has its own distinct personality; Milles is said to have created them from people with whom he was familiar, using their gestures as inspiration. He arranged the figures as though they are responding to Orpheus's music. One male figure holds a small bird in his hand while looking up toward Orpheus. Another woman plays with her hair. One of the figures is meant to represent an actual person, the composer Beethoven. This figure carries the strongest expression, with his head arched back, eyes closed, and hands tightly clenched as if to feel the power of the music. All of the figures stand in a standard position, with little regard to

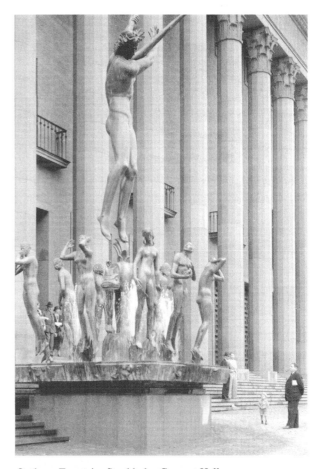

Orpheus Fountain, Stockholm Concert Hall
The Conway Library, Courtauld Institute of Art

movement and greater focus placed on their arms, hands, and heads as they respond to the central figure.

The Orpheus Fountain contains a variety of symbols that act as signs of intimate expression. Milles's own personality comes through clearly in the fountain, as it represents through the figures' various expressions and different emotions not only the artist's own sense of the incongruous but also the importance of music in his own and others' lives. The result is a fountain of intense freedom that represents and interprets the immediate and intense joy one feels when listening to powerful music.

When Milles finally completed the Orpheus Fountain in 1936, it was shipped to Stockholm, Sweden, where it was installed in the Concert Hall to great critical acclaim and admiration. The popularity of Milles's fountain, which was long a favorite work of the sculptor, helped solidify his importance in the art world. In 1988 a replica of the Orpheus Fountain was installed at the Missouri Botanical Garden, St. Louis, on loan from the Gateway Foundation.

CHRISTIAN CARDELL CORBET

See also **Fountain Sculpture**

Further Reading

The Journal and Catalog of the Exhibition Entitled Sculpture and Carl Milles, Baltimore, Maryland: Baltimore Museum of Art, 1940

Lidén, Elisabeth, *Between Water and Heaven: Carl Milles: Search for American Commissions*, Stockholm: Almqvist-Wiksell International, and Montclair, New Jersey: Schram, 1986

MINIMALISM

The history of modern sculpture, specifically in America and Europe, had long been seen as subservient to the development of a modernist paradigm in painting. The two-dimensional arts had arguably, since the 1850s, been self-consciously occupied with formal and particularly spatial concerns such as the flatness of the picture plane, an abstract iconography, and, in particular, a growing architectonic quality as evident in the work of Dutch De Stijl painter Piet Mondrian and the iconoclastic canvases of Russian Suprematist Kasimir Malevich. As Lucy Lippard—one of the first significant art critics of Minimalism in New York—noted in 1967, the relationship between painting and sculpture was changing radically in the face of a constellation of "new work" in both mediums that was reductive in terms of subject matter and minimal in form (whether through line, color, or shape). Moreover, this new work, be it painting or sculpture, resonated with a strong, almost stubborn, "object-like" quality that was reminiscent of the Dadaist Marcel Duchamp's tongue-in-cheek readymades from the 1920s. What marked the postwar Minimalist art as different, however, lay in the artist's and gallerist's utter disavowal of the work's underlying content. Unlike the Duchampian urinals and hat racks, no iconographic glyphs were waiting to be discovered, unlocked, as if the artist held a key to some mystical treasure box.

This attitude is reflected in the example of Frank Stella, an American Minimalist painter, who in 1959–60 began to paint measured, almost banal, black-and-white stripe paintings in which the width of the stripes—masked out with ordinary tape and painted with industrial enamel and house painters brushes—was predetermined by the width of the prefabricated wooden stretcher frame. Stella famously claimed that "what you see is what you see" when critics struggled to find some metaphysical content or poetry from his work.

This tendency toward reductivism, simplicity, order, rationality, and, perhaps most important, the utter dismissal of Abstract Expressionism's perceived overwrought emotionalism and excess subjectivity in both painterly gesture and symbolism came to characterize Minimalist sculpture, an "antimovement" movement that dominated postwar New York and California art of the 1960s and 1970s. Originally called "ABC Art," "Cool Art," "Idiot Art," and even "Know-Nothing Nihilism," the emotionally neutral name that would stick was coined by the English philosopher of aesthetics and modern art Richard Wollheim, who had described the painted surfaces of Andy Warhol, Morris Louis, and other modernists as *minimal*. The most deeply cherished aspect of modern painting, the mark of the artist's hand as inscribed on the canvas or in the bronze or marble object as surface texture, nuance, perceptible flourishes, marks, and signs of the artistic execution was voided in the hands of the Minimalists.

One of the key forerunners of the movement, American sculptor, art critic, and writer Donald Judd, emphasized the aesthetic in a factual, nondescriptive essay entitled "Specific Objects," published in *Arts Yearbook* in 1965. "Specific Objects," which was also the categorical name for the new work, were "not painting" but also "not sculpture"; the work rejected imagery, composition (that is, the aesthetic arrangement of shapes, colors, and forms), and instead focused on the constructed wholeness of "well-built" organized forms. Unlike traditional sculpture, the specific object refused to represent Nature; rather, the artist relied on industrial materials such as steel, lacquered iron, aluminum, Plexiglas, and unpainted wood to construct serial work of modular and usually cubic or geometric forms. The repetitive, redundant nature of the work (most of which was untitled to further eschew any referents to observable nature or ideas) pointed to a new language of sculptural form that puzzled, and even outraged, viewers, who were shocked by its utter banality and apparent simplicity. Much of Judd's early work comprised series of identical open or closed box-like forms of galvanized iron and colored Plexiglas that were either mounted in a row on the wall or placed directly on the gallery floor.

Judd's education in philosophy at Columbia University influenced him to incorporate the empiricism of David Hume in forcing sculpture to confront only what could be directly experienced, repudiating (painterly) illusionism and metaphor in favor of the concrete and the tactile qualities of shape, mass, weight, and scale. The poetry of the work, if one could argue for it at all, lay in the work's straightforward and functional relationship to materials.

One of the first exhibitions of the so-called Minimalist art was Robert Morris's 1964 show at the Green Gallery in New York, installed one year later at the Castelli Gallery in New York where it rapidly upstaged Pop's status as the new avant-garde. For the Green Gallery, Morris built a series of rectangular and L-shaped beams of painted white plywood and arranged them in a seemingly random fashion in the center of the room, or abutting the walls and ceiling, in an attempt to reshape the viewer's physical experience of the space. Morris claimed that his use of white neutralized the forms, and the arrangement represented an attempt to see how many different ways he could dispose the same form in the same space. In his essay "Notes on Sculpture 1–3," Morris reconfigured the traditional relationship of sculptural object to the beholder from one of contemplation and distance to one of physical engagement. He believed that the three-dimensional

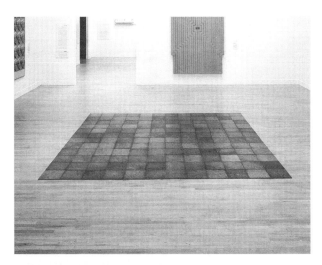

Carl Andre, *144 Magnesium Squares*, 1969
© Tate Gallery, London / Art Resource, NY, and Carl Andre / Licensed by VAGA, New York

work (or specific objects) and the viewer's body codetermined the nature of the space, and that the experience of the work was derived, as in psychology's gestalt theory, from a pseudoscience of perception and psychological phenomena. Gestalt psychology asserted that human perception and behavior comprised a constellation of *gestalts* (structures, configurations, or patterns) derived from the study of natural stimuli. Gestaltists conceived of consciousness as an autonomous, unified totality that was not made up of separate elements, but rather a whole whose "parts" had no singular existence. Following these ideas Morris claimed that the viewer would not view the L-beams as separate from each other and outside him or herself; rather, the viewer would perceive them according to gestalt consciousness. The arrangement of forms prevailed upon the viewer as a total visual and tactile experience.

Other important national exhibitions followed including "Primary Structures" at the Jewish Museum in New York in 1966 where Carl Andre's *Lever*—137 firebricks extending $34\frac{1}{2}$ feet along the floor—was first exhibited. Unlike Judd, who rarely made direct reference to artistic precedents in his curiously neutral but elegant pieces, Andre spoke of the work's relationship to Constantin Brancusi's monumental *Endless Column*, a sculpture also composed of repetitive, but carved units that extended into the sky with a vertical and priapic thrust that asserted not only the power of the artist but the smallness of the beholder. Andre's claim that he intended *Lever* to "dominate the floor" the way that *Endless Column* dominated the landscape or sky is only partially realized. There is nothing essentially monumental about *Lever*; one could imagine kicking the lowly firebricks out of order, or stumbling over them, like a rotted railroad track. Fundamental to the Minimalist aesthetic was the very ordinariness of these objects that could very easily be mistaken for a piece of furniture, a pedestal, or industrial leftovers. Nothing of the romanticism, the drama, or the primal symbolism of Brancusi remained. The rejection of not only craft but also traditional and precious materials proceeded to destroy the aesthetic framework for conceiving of the work as sculpture in its own right. In particular, Andre's zinc, lead, and copper planes (or *plains* as he titled them) laid directly on the floor like industrial carpets, where the viewer is encouraged to walk unencumbered across them, radically subvert the conventional role of sculpture as precious, or as an object to behold. This new role for sculpture notwithstanding, Andre's works (for example, *144 Magnesium Squares* [1969; Tate Gallery, London]) evoked a range of associations and resonance within the overtly politicized milieu in which they were made. Andre defined himself as an "artworker" or "artisan" with the freedom to employ himself as the primary tool to produce [artistic] goods for a consuming public, namely, gallerists and collectors (see Wood et al., 1993). He maintained that his pieces—which were not well suited for exhibition, buying, or selling—functioned as a critique of commodity culture, which on the heels of a flamboyantly well-liked and financially lucrative American Pop art, had been a source of dismay for Minimalists and feminists alike. Artists such as Andre, Judd, and Robert Smithson actively lobbied for the politicization of the institutions of the art world, claiming that the avant-gardism of Minimalism represented a kind of freedom of artistic agency and creativity.

This transgression of traditional aesthetics underscored Judd's dictum that the three-dimensional work comprise "real materials in real space" rather than the *illusion* of "real" objects that painting promised. Only by undoing the traditional language of sculpture and severing its connection to the two-dimensional arts could a new avant-garde of sculpture emerge. Other artists who embraced these ideas included Tony Smith, whose training as an architect informed his large-scale, often publicly placed pieces of minimally painted polyhedrons. Smith conceived of his pieces as whole and unified structures that explored spatial and conceptual dynamics. His well-known piece of 1962, *Die*, a 1.83 meter steel cube placed directly on the ground or sometimes on a barely noticeable platform, further eliminated the sign of the artist's hand. Unlike Judd and Morris, who constructed most of their own human-scale pieces, Smith provided the specifications to an industrial plant, where the work of steel could be cast and fabricated in an edition of three. Smith distanced himself from the work of art physically; his participation in the work functioned at the level of the concept, reducing, in effect, not only the evidence of his touch but also the artist's emotional relationship to the art object.

As early as 1963, Dan Flavin began working exclusively with industrially fabricated fluorescent tubes and fixtures in the making of his Minimalist pieces. Similar to his peers, he chose to use interchangeable, mass produced parts to create a whole object, gestalt, or environment; however, Flavin's work perhaps most successfully transformed a space through an ironically "immaterial" substance, that is, colored light. The tubes themselves, when installed in various combinations in the gallery space to articulate architectural space, filled the room with sometimes muted, sometimes glaring light of green, red, blue, yellow, and various spectral combinations. Flavin's choreography of the light from the tubes investigated the idea of sculpture as space rather than form (see Fineberg, 2000). Not a strict materialist, Flavin allowed a certain amount of iconography and history in his work; he built, in

particular, a piece entitled *Monument for V. Tatlin* (1968) in homage to the Russian Constructivist who embraced the importance of technology and industry to art. Moreover, the aesthetic use of light and its iconographical and associative allusions recalled the light-infused German Romantic canvases of the 19th century, or the sublime landscapes of American Regionalist painters of the same century. This sensibility separated Flavin somewhat from other Minimalists, linking him with Los Angeles artists such as James Turrell and Robert Irwin, who both explored the environmental and metaphysical aspects of light and space. Turrell, for example, defined his room-scaled work of color fields as "not minimalism, not conceptualism, but *perceptual* work" (see Fineberg, 2000).

The critical momentum and strict purity of Minimalism, however, did not last much beyond 1970. Often framed as an art of negation by critics who desired something more pluralistic and less reductive from art, Judd's prescriptive Minimalism, in the hands of practitioners such as Smithson, Richard Serra, Eva Hesse, Barry Le Va, Richard Tuttle, Bruce Nauman, Lynda Benglis, Sol LeWitt, and others was adapted through a more versatile language of forms and even, eventually, iconography. The Post-Minimalist, or Anti-Form group of artists retained the Minimalist artist's relationship to materials. While on the surface different from the historical understanding of the artist's intention, the effort entailed a conscious reinterpretation of a series of Anti-Form activities: to shape, form, drape, cut, stack, hang, cast, or weld usurped techniques of modeling and carving. The variability of hard and soft materials, relying upon gravity, time, and temperature as "tools" for manipulating sculpture, deeply and profoundly built upon key Minimalist theories.

Second- and third-generation Minimalists have continued to transform its original concepts, particularly in the early 1990s. California artist Rachel Lachowicz cast nondescript, geometric forms such as cubes, crates, and cages in blood-red lipstick, subtly playing with the incongruity of objective Minimalist structures and a particularly feminine, even frivolous substance, that is, lipstick. Lebanese-born artist Mona Hatoum built installations comprised of multiple rows of wire mesh lockers, dimly lit with bare light bulbs, and often rigged to move and make sounds with industrial motors, creating mysteriously beautiful and yet disturbing environments that referenced the refugee and war camps of the Middle East where she grew up. Hatoum's industrially influenced pieces evoke the scale and repetition of Minimalist structures intensified by iconography. British artist Rachel Whiteread has continued to sculpt quasi-Minimalist forms, often on a grand scale, by casting objects such as bathtubs, mattresses, fireplaces, and even the empty spaces inside of houses in materials such as wax, plaster, rubber, and fiberglass. The use of creamy white (or nearly translucent) substances remains minimal and reductive, but they also allow the viewer to bring his or her associations to these ghostly monoliths. Whiteread's sculptural casts suggest the frozen, negative imprint of a real room; however, voided of its contents and context, the work seems inaccessible, like a memory or a dream.

LYNN M. SOMERS

See also **Abstract Expressionism; Andre, Carl; Caro, Anthony; Contemporary Sculpture; Hesse, Eva; Judd, Donald; LeWitt, Sol; Morris, Robert; Serra, Richard; Smithson, Robert; Turrell, James**

Further Reading

Baker, Kenneth, *Minimalism*, New York, Abbeville Press, 1988

Battcock, Gregory, editor, *Minimal Art: A Critical Anthology*, New York, E. P. Dutton, 1968

Bochner, Mel, "Primary Structures," *Arts Magazine*, June 1966

Fineberg, Jonathan, *Art since 1940: Strategies of Being*, Upper Saddle River, New Jersey: Prentice Hall, 2000

Foster, Hal, "The Crux of Minimalism," *Individuals: A Selected History of Contemporary Art 1945–1986*, New York and Los Angeles, California: Abbeville Press and the Museum of Contemporary Art, Los Angeles, 1986

Judd, Donald, "Specific Objects," *Arts Yearbook* 8 (1965)

Lippard, Lucy, "As Painting Is to Sculpture: A Changing Ratio (1967)," *Changing: Essays in Art Criticism*, foreword by Gregory Battcock, New York: E.P. Dutton, 1971

McShine, Kynaston, *Primary Structures: Younger American and British Sculptors*, New York: Jewish Museum, 1966

Meyer, James, *Minimalism: Art and Polemics in the Sixties*, New Haven, Connecticut: Yale University Press, 2001

Robertson, Bryan, *The New Generation: 1965*, London: Whitechapel Gallery, 1965

Tuchman, Phyllis, "Minimalism and Critical Response," *Artforum*, May 1977

Wollheim, Richard, "The Work of Art as Object," *Studio International* 180/928 (December 1970)

Wood, Paul, Francis Frascina, Jonathan Harris, and Charles Harrison, *Modernism in Dispute: Art since the Forties*, New Haven, Connecticut, and London: Yale University Press and The Open University, 1993

Zelevansky, Lynn, *Sense and Sensibility: Women Artists and Minimalism in the Nineties*, New York: Museum of Modern Art and Harry Abrams, 1994

GEORGE MINNE 1866–1941 *Belgian*

George Minne's most essential sculptures might be limited in theme, yet his importance in turn-of-the-century sculpture and for the generation of artists who came to maturity in the early 20th century is uncontested. Throughout his career, Minne was viewed by his avant-gardist contemporaries as a premier European sculptor alongside Constantin Meunier and Auguste Rodin, although today his reputation has declined. After his initial training at the Fine Arts Academy in Ghent between 1879 and 1886, and still thinking he needed additional training from a master sculptor, Minne applied to Rodin to ask if he could become his pupil. The French sculptor declined, saying he believed Minne was already a mature artist. Thus, even after Minne had shown a number of his sculptures in official and independent exhibitions in the latter years of the 1880s and 1890s, he began additional studies for a year in 1895 at the Academy in Brussels.

Minne's sculptures of his most important, pre–World War I period almost exclusively comprise grieving or injured figures or androgynous figures that seem weighted down by emotion. The open expression of grief in some of these works, such as the more obviously medieval wooden sculpture *Three Holy Women*, hark back both visually and symbolically to the late medieval tomb figures of Claus Sluter, sculptor of the Burgundian court at Dijon, and the lime-wood sculptors of Germany. Others seem to evoke the larger ennui of the century's end.

Minne's concentration on emotion as the subject of his work permeates almost all of his sculptures until World War I. The emotional power of these works, including the many versions of a maternal figure mourning her dead child, was hailed by Belgian writers of the Symbolist aesthetic, such as Grégoire Le Roy, Maurice Maeterlinck, and Emile Verhaeren, as the visual equivalent of their neurasthenic and world-weary outlook. Throughout the 1880s, Minne was eagerly commissioned to illustrate their works. Belgian poet Charles van Lerberghe saw in Minne's sculptures a "primitive humanity." Fellow poet Verhaeren and the playwright Maeterlinck also recognized in Minne's art a kind of emotional disengagement from his epoch. In Verhaeren's words, "they come and go beyond [to] the other side where only the Idea . . . of that to be revealed . . . can live. . . . One imagines them more than one sees them." The stark emotionalism of these sculptures later gave way to more abstract, generalized images of pathos and pessimism.

Minne was embraced by avant-garde circles despite the ridicule he often received from more conservative art critics, who viewed his imagery as comprised of starving, hydrocephalic stick figures. Beginning in 1890, Minne showed with the most important independent exhibiting society, Les XX, in Brussels and, beginning in 1892, with Joséphin Péladan's Salon de la Rose + Croix in Paris. In the late 1890s and well into the 20th century, Minne also exhibited with the Vienna and Berlin Secessions, as well as at the Venice Biennials.

The sculptures he created in the final two decades of the 19th century are among Minne's most important subjects. These include the various versions of a mother weeping over her dead child, in which emotion is starkly rendered through the angularity of the bodies and their intertwining limbs, and *Fountain of Kneeling Youths*, which relies on a more abstracted emotional state of the psyche. Originally commissioned by Karl Ernst Osthaus for the entrance to his home and private art collection, Minne's figurative fountain comprises a group of identical figures set in a circle around a basin. They kneel, Narcissus-like, but, rather than glancing at their reflections, they cast their gazes down and inward while they close their arms tightly in across their chests. In choosing the chronological moment between childhood and adulthood, the figures here seem to suggest a kind of vulnerability that might be characterized as unprotected by age, experience, or innocence.

As is the case with all of his major subjects, Minne's working method was arduous and entailed continuous revisions that resulted in an increasingly abstract quality while maintaining a figural theme. He rendered his statues in a variety of media beginning, invariably,

with a series of drawings. Eventually he worked them up in clay and then had them cast into plaster. Ultimately, they were finished in bronze, stone, wood, and marble.

Minne's turn-of-the-20th-century work elicited a major influence on such emergent Art Nouveau and Expressionist artists as the Austrians Gustave Klimt, Egon Schiele, and Oskar Kokoschka and the German sculptors Wilhelm Lehmbruck, Ernst Barlach, and Käthe Kollwitz. The almost schematic postures of Minne's androgynous kneeling youths evoke the calm, pessimistic, and transcendent states of mind typical of turn-of-the-century Symbolist art. Yet underlying these poses, their repetition in a circle also suggests some other kind of emotionality. It was this latter element that was incorporated repeatedly into the statues and paintings of Minne's German and Austrian counterparts. In this sense, Minne's art is both a precursor to and an exemplar of the early-20th-century avant-garde.

In the years during World War I and its aftermath, Minne's artistic output was transformed definitively. During the war, Minne ceased to sculpt altogether and concentrated on drawing. Although in his earlier period Minne's figures were expressive in their content, he turned his attention to the representations of Christ and the nude in his postwar sculptures. These latter works were much sought after and brought him considerable fame and even a noble title, but they might best be characterized as far more decorative in execution.

Sura Levine

See also **Barlach, Ernst; Kollwitz, Käthe; Lehmbruck, Wilhelm; Meunier, Constantin; Netherlands and Belgium; Rodin, Auguste**

Biography

Born in Ghent, Belgium, 30 August 1866. Son of an architect; initially studied architecture himself; sculpture student at Académie Royale des Beaux-Arts in Ghent, 1879–86, where he worked with sculptor Louis van Biesbroeck and painter Théodore Caneel; at Académie Royale, Brussels, 1895–99; debuted at Ghent Salon with *The Wounded One*, 1887; befriended and provided illustrations for Symbolist writers Grégoire Le Roy (1889), Maurice Maeterlinck (1889), and Emile Verhaeren (1895); from 1890, exhibited with Les XX (The Twenty); earned membership, 1891; with the Libre Esthétique (Free Esthetic) in Brussels, beginning in 1898; with l'Association pour l'Art (the Association for Art) in Antwerp from 1892; at the Salon de la Rose + Croix in Paris, beginning in 1891; lived in Brussels, 1895–99, and moved to Sint-Martens-Latem near Ghent, 1899; taught drawing at Académie Royale des Beaux-Arts, Ghent, 1912–14 and 1918–

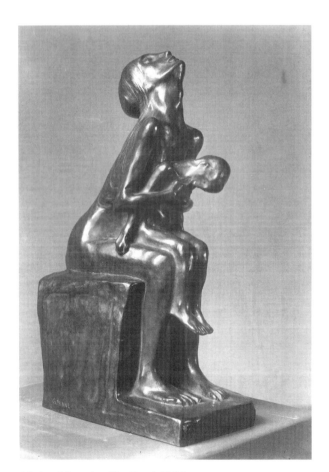

Mother Mourning Her Dead Child
© Musées Royaux des Beaux-Arts de Belgique, Brussels, and ACL Brussels

19; during World War I, lived with family in Wales; member of the Belgian Royal Academy, 1923; same year, awarded noble title of baron. Died in Sint-Martens-Latem, Belgium, 18 February 1941.

Selected Works

1886   *Mother Mourning Her Dead Child* (several versions); marble; Hessisches Landesmuseum, Darmstadt, Germany; bronze; Musées Royaux des Beaux-Arts de Belgique, Brussels, Belgium

1888   *Sorrow, Mother Weeping over Her Two Children*; bronze; Musées Royaux des Beaux-Arts de Belgique, Brussels, Belgium

1895   *St. John the Baptist;* stone; Museum voor Schone Kunsten, Ghent, Belgium

1896   *Three Holy Women*; wood; Musées Royaux des Beaux-Arts de Belgique, Brussels, Belgium

1897   *Boy Holding a Reliquary*; marble; Musées Royaux des Beaux-Arts de Belgique, Brussels, Belgium

1897   *Man with a Water Sack*; plaster; The Detroit Institute of Arts, Michigan, United States

1898   *Kneeling Youth*; plaster; private collection, Sint-Martens-Latem, Belgium

1898   *Solidarity*; bronze; Koninklijke Museum voor Schone Kunsten, Antwerp, Belgium

ca. 1898   *Fountain of Kneeling Youths*; plaster model; Museum voor Schone Kunsten, Ghent, Belgium; marble version: 1905, Folkwang Museum, Essen, Germany

1911   *Torso of a Man*; plaster; Musées Royaux des Beaux-Arts de Belgique, Brussels, Belgium

Further Reading

Alhadeff, Albert, "George Minne: Fin de siècle Drawing and Sculpture," Ph.D. diss., New York University, 1971

Alhadeff, Albert, "Meunier and Minne: Subterreanean Visions and the Blue Summits of the Soul," *Bulletin of the Detroit Institute of Arts* 65/1 (1989)

Boyens, Piet, *Sint-Martens-Latem: Kunstenaarsdorp in Vlaanderen*, Tielt, Belgium: Lanno Art Book Company, 1992

Draguet, Michel, *Splendeurs de l'idéal: Rops, Khnopff, Delville et leur temps*, Ghent, Belgium: Snoeck-Ducaju en Zoon, 1996

Hoozee, Robert, *George Minne en de kunst rond 1900*, Ghent, Belgium: Gemeentekrediet, 1982

Pudles, Lynne, "The Symbolist Work of George Minne," *Art Journal* (summer 1985)

Puyvelde, Leo van, *George Minne*, Brussels: Cahiers de Belgique, 1930

Verhaeren, Émile, "Constantin Meunier," *La Nation* (5 December 1891)

MINO DA FIESOLE 1429–1484 *Italian*

One of the best-known marble relief sculptors of his day, Mino da Fiesole was principally active in Rome and Florence, where he received commissions from several popes and the Medici family. His portrait busts, sacrament tabernacles, and carved tomb monuments were pioneering works of their kind. Until very recently his oeuvre was viewed as distinct from that of Mino del Reame (or Mino del Regno, which means "of the Kingdom," or Naples, reflecting his activity south of Rome), owing to the division of his career into two biographies by Giorgio Vasari (1550 and 1568), who also applied the sobriquet "da Fiesole." His identity was further clouded by Vasari's notion that his name might be Dino and because some sculptures are signed "Opus Nini" (the names Dino and Nino, both present in the earliest literature, appear to be variants); his origins as stated in Neapolitan documents, "da Montemignaio," refer to a Tuscan village near his birthplace (see Caglioti, 1987).

Nothing is known of his apprenticeship, although Vasari's description of him as a pupil of the delicate, more decorative Desiderio da Settignano, his almost exact contemporary, is questionable; he may possibly have trained with Bernardo Rossellino, whose activity in Rome as chief architect to Pope Nicholas V could have enticed the young Mino there. His first known work, a portrait bust of *Piero de' Medici* (an inscription reads "aged 37," hence 1453–54), reveals his achievement as a sculptor in the highly competitive artistic milieu of Florence and remains the earliest datable bust in modern history. The formal frontality of the intricately carved base is set off by a head of energetic and unyielding character. A series of other busts followed, some executed in Rome (*Niccolò Strozzi*) and Naples (possibly including *Astorgio II Manfredi, Lord of Faenza*, 1455; National Gallery of Art, Washington, D.C.), all sensitively combining individuality and commemoration. His early career was certainly spent in Rome, where he was awarded important commissions by the papal court, in particular by Cardinal Guillaume d'Estouteville, for whom he executed two major works, which are now both dismantled and partly destroyed: the monumental ciborium for the high altar of the Basilica of Santa Maria Maggiore and the slightly later altar of St. Jerome for the same church. The numerous sacred figures and narrative reliefs reveal his debt to both Classical relief sculpture and early Christian ivories.

The presence of dissimilar technical and stylistic elements, already evident in these works and long debated in the literature, should be considered in the context of workshop practice: Mino must have had two groups of assistants in Rome and Florence, each of which were distinct, prolific, and active during three decades. Moreover, his partnership with other Roman sculptors such as Paolo Romano, Giovanni Dalmata, and Andrea Bregno may be seen as a matter of practical expediency for the patron. Alone, Mino was a sophisticated artist capable of painstaking, inventive carving and remarkable expressiveness, qualities perhaps eclipsed by some of his eccentric, aloof-looking figures with their heavy-lidded eyes and abstract, patterned features. One weakness appears to have been with figures in the round, especially such colossal ones as *St. Peter* for the Vatican, which was commissioned in tandem with *St. Paul* by Paolo Romano and abandoned in 1463–64; it was only recently rediscovered in modified form. Mino was clearly more at home with the Florentine tradition of relief carving.

His return to Florence in 1464 may be associated with the premature death of Desiderio in January of that year. On 28 July he matriculated in the Arte della Pietra e del Legname and began receiving more significant church commissions, including altarpieces (at a time when it was customary in Florence to have them painted), such as those for Bishop Salutati in Fiesole Cathedral, which was combined with a tomb and bust and accompanied by Cosimo Rosselli's frescoes; and for Dietisalvi Neroni, which was left incomplete when the patron was exiled. A document of 1470 states that Mino's Florentine workshop was rented from the Badia (the Benedictine Abbey of Florence), with which he had an extended professional relationship, and by whose abbot and monks he was paid, mostly in kind, for the execution of two important works: the Tomb of Bernardo Giugni (completed in 1468) and the Tomb of Count Hugo of Tuscany, the founder of the Badia, commissioned in 1469 and cited by many critics from Vasari onward as Mino's masterpiece. A document of 1481 shows that upon conclusion of the contract in that year (when Mino was paid and the date of the inscription), the monks of the Badia had requested changes in design and material through the addition of a bench and elements made of marble, rather than a less expensive stone. As in the Giugni monument, the celebration of the civic virtues of its subject is evoked allegorically, and these are far more than imitations of the celebrated tombs by Rossellino and Desiderio da Settignano in Santa Croce (see Zuraw, 1998).

Mino's reliefs, such as the *Virgin and Child* within a tondo (Bargello, Italy; *ca.* 1470), often have a hieratic quality, and his style can be defined, in general, as linear and abstracted; his figures were sober and often attenuated. Some sketches discovered in 1905 on the walls of Mino's Florentine residence of 1480–84 are no doubt by him, revealing a self-assured hand, and there are six documentary references to his own preparatory drawings for sculpture. These, and a wooden model for a projected facade of Florence Cathedral that appears as a bequest in his will, are untraced. Mino's posthumous fame was somewhat compromised by his status as an "outsider" in Florence, yet for all Vasari's confusion regarding names and dates, the biographer was correct on most points of attribution. Like other Renaissance sculptors from Tuscany, Mino was very popular in the 19th century. The historically correct image of Mino is the fruit of very recent scholarship.

FRANK DABELL

See also **Desiderio da Settignano; Rossellino Family**

Biography

Born in Papiano, near Poppi, Italy, 1429. Nothing known of early training; first documented work, Florence, 1453–54, Naples, 1455–56, and Rome, 1463–64; mainly produced portrait busts after studying antique models in Rome; spent early career in Rome; worked on papal commissions and marble reliefs for Basilica of Santa Maria Maggiore; returned to Florence, 1464; studied at Arte della Pietra e del Legname, Florence; worked on tomb monuments and ecclesiastical commissions in Volterra, Prato, and Perugia; established successful workshops in Rome and Florence; restored antique statuary for Medici; traveled to Rome, 1473–80; collaborated on tomb of Pope Paul II; lived in Florence for remainder of life, working on tomb monuments for the Badia Fiorentina and sacrament tabernacle for the Church of Sant'Ambrogio. Died in Florence, Italy, 1484.

Selected Works

1453–54   *Piero de' Medici*; marble; Museo Nazionale del Bargello, Florence, Italy

1454   *Niccolò Strozzi*; marble; Skulpturensammlung, Staatliche Museen, Berlin, Germany

ca. 1458   *Shield-Bearing Angel*; marble; Church of San Giacomo degli Spagnuoli, Rome, Italy

1461–63   Ciborium, for Basilica of Santa Maria Maggiore; gilding, porphyry; fragments: Basilica of Santa Maria Maggiore, Rome, Italy; *Virgin and Child*: Cleveland Museum of Art, Ohio, United States; *Church Fathers*: Cathedral of Saint Wenceslas, Olomouc, Czech Republic

1463   Benediction pulpit of Pope Pius II (with collaborators); marble (lost)

1463   *St. Peter*; Aula Capitolare, Palazzo delle

Sagrestie, Saint Peter's Basilica, Rome, Italy

1464   Bust of Dietisalvi Neroni; marble; Musée du Louvre, Paris, France

ca. 1465   Chapel of Bishop Leonardo Salutati; marble; Fiesole Cathedral, Italy

ca. 1466   Altar for Dietisalvi Neroni (incomplete); marble; Church of the Badia Fiorentina, Florence, Italy

ca. 1468   Tomb of Bernardo Giugni; marble; Church of the Badia Fiorentina, Florence, Italy

1468–71   Blessed Sacrament tabernacle; marble; Volterra Cathedral, Italy

ca. 1471–81   Tomb of Count Hugo of Tuscany; marble; Church of the Badia Fiorentina, Florence, Italy

1474–75   Tomb of Pope Paul II (with Giovanni Dalmata); marble; divided fragments: Vatican Museums, Rome, Italy; Musée du Louvre, Paris, France

1481   Blessed Sacrament tabernacle; marble; Church of Sant'Ambrogio, Florence, Italy

Further Reading

Caglioti, Francesco, "Per il recupero della giovinezza romana di Mino da Fiesole: Il'Ciborio della neve,'" *Prospettiva* 49 (1987)

Cassidy, Brendan, "Two Trecento Angels at Volterra Disguised by Mino da Fiesole," *The Burlington Magazine* 136 (December 1994)

Pope-Hennessy, John, *An Introduction to Italian Sculpture*, 3 vols., London: Phaidon, 1963; 4th edition, 1996; see especially vol. 2, *Italian Renaissance Sculpture* (one of the best English-language summaries)

Sciolla, Gianni Carlo, *La scultura di Mino da Fiesole*, Turin, Italy: Giappichelli, 1970 (still useful although superseded)

Vasari, Giorgio, *Le vite de' più eccellenti architetti, pittori, e scultori italiani*, 3 vols., Florence: Torrentino, 1550; 2nd edition, Florence: Apresso i Giunti, 1568; as *Lives of the Painters, Sculptors, and Architects*, 2 vols., translated by Gaston du C. de Vere (1912), edited by David Ekserdjian, New York: Knopf, and London: Campbell, 1996

Zuraw, Shelley, "Mino da Fiesole's First Roman Sojourn: The Works in Santa Maria Maggiore," in *Verrocchio and Late Quattrocento Italian Sculpture*, edited by Steven Bule, Alan Phipps Darr, and Fiorella Superbi Gioffredi, Florence: Le Lettere, 1992

Zuraw, Shelley, "The Medici Portraits of Mino da Fiesole," in *Piero de' Medici "il Gottoso" (1416–1469); Kunst im Dienste der Mediceer; Art in the Service of the Medici*, edited by Andreas Beyer and Bruce Boucher, Berlin: Akademie Verlag, 1993a

Zuraw, Shelley, "The Sculpture of Mino da Fiesole (1429–1484)," Ph.D. diss., Institute of Fine Arts, New York University, 1993b

Zuraw, Shelley, *Masterpieces of Renaissance and Baroque Sculpture from the Palazzo Venezia, Rome* (exhib. cat.), Athens: Georgia Museum of Art, University of Georgia, 1996a

Zuraw, Shelley, "Mino da Fiesole" and "Mino del Reame," in *The Dictionary of Art*, edited by Jane Turner, New York: Grove, and London: Macmillan, 1996b

Zuraw, Shelley, "The Public Commemorative Monument: Mino da Fiesole's Tombs in the Florentine Badia," *Art Bulletin* 80 (1998)

BUST OF DIETISALVI NERONI

Mino da Fiesole (1429–1484)

1464

marble

h. 57 cm

Musée du Louvre, Paris, Fance

The bust of Dietisalvi Neroni is a powerfully expressive sculpture and a quintessential work by Mino da Fiesole, for both its stylistic and technical qualities and its approach to the subject, and it was the product of a culture that gave birth to the modern portrait bust. An inscription appears along its base: " + *Aetatis . Svæ . An* [abbr.]. *Age[n]s. LX Tyrc* [or *Tyro*; followed by a lacuna with room for at least ten other characters] *[F]aciv[n]dvm . I* [over an] *S . Cvravit . Dietisalvivs . Opvs Mini . MCCCCLXIIII* ." (Dietsialvi had this made in his sixtieth year . . . The work of Mino, 1464); the fragmentary central passage of the inscription is enigmatic, whereas the name of the sitter and his age are legible. Mino's signature and date are inscribed along the back in a significantly more classicizing and careful manner. The artist was at the midpoint of his career after a decade of activity in Rome and Naples; his sitter was likewise at the peak of his success.

The bust is slightly larger than life, and, as with several other figures carved by Mino, the sitter turns slightly to one side with a forthright gaze; the drilling of the pupils and precisely cut circle of the iris are typical of the artist. The regularity of certain elements, such as the vertical furrow in the brow and the flamelike locks of hair (flowing from a central point at the crown of the head) are also entirely characteristic. The mottled brown marble enhances the lifelike effect, and occasional imperfections provide added color and texture. The most recognizable element of Mino's sculptural vocabulary is the stylized drapery that falls in V-shaped folds and resembles pleats that have been starched or ironed too firmly. This classically inspired feature recurs throughout Mino's oeuvre, from his Roman reliefs to the allegorical figures on his tomb monuments in the Badia Fiorentina. As for the revival of antique forms, this sort of bust was preceded for 20 years or so by the classicizing portrait medals of the early Renaissance, with which humanists such as Leon Battista Alberti sought to emulate the heritage of ancient Rome. With the revival of the portrait bust, a sitter's civic virtues could be idealized in three dimensions. Mino's subject is represented *al-l'antica* (after the antique) through the form of the bust itself, the Latin inscription, the togalike dress that is fastened at the shoulder with a ribbon, and the full but sharply trimmed cut of his hair. The viewer can imagine that in such a portrait as this—at once combining vivid realism and symbolic presence—the artist has captured the sitter's personality.

Dietisalvi di Nerone di Nigi di Nerone (a variant is Diotisalvi; the family name Neroni was adopted during the 15th century) was born in 1403, the son of an influential wool merchant. He rose to become one of the most distinguished citizens of the Florentine Republic until his disgrace and exile in 1466. He was a member of the political and mercantile elite in the Florence of Cosimo de' Medici and held the position of Gonfaloniere di Giustizia and Accoppiatore—two of Florence's highest offices—several times during the 1440s and 1450s. He was the republic's ambassador to the papal court, Venice, France, Sicily, and notably Milan, where he befriended Duke Francesco Sforza. His brother Giovanni was archbishop of Volterra and Florence, although he fled to Rome after the decline of the family's fortunes and died there in 1473.

Having gained some popular support, Neroni, Agnolo Acciaiuoli, and Luca Pitti attempted to curtail the growing power of the Medici family between 1464, when Cosimo died, and 1466. The plot against Cosimo's son Piero backfired, and on 11 September 1466, members of the Neroni family and other notable citizens were exiled. Neroni took ultimate refuge in Rome, where he died on 28 July 1482 and was buried in the Church of Santa Maria sopra Minerva. His tomb, a curious mixture of Roman and Florentine styles, has an effigy that bears no resemblance to Mino's bust, and the epitaph bears erroneous dating.

Neroni was a Florentine patron of the arts on several fronts. As a leading citizen, he was on the Mercanzia's (merchant court) committee for Andrea del Verrocchio's bronze *Incredulity of Thomas* in 1463–66; he may have commissioned Michelozzo to design his palazzo, which is just behind the Palazzo Medici in the present-day via dei Ginori. Neroni was an important contributor to the new Church of San Lorenzo, his parish church and that of the Medici. During the early 1460s, the Neroni family, already patrons of a chapel in the south transept (next to the Medici sacristy), took over the double-bay chapel at the end of the north transept (its contemporary, carved marble altarfront with the Neroni arms survives) and built another chapel in the third bay of the south aisle. The latter was intended by Neroni as a burial chapel and destined as the setting for the extant marble altar with figures in half relief by Mino, now in the church of the Badia. This *Virgin*

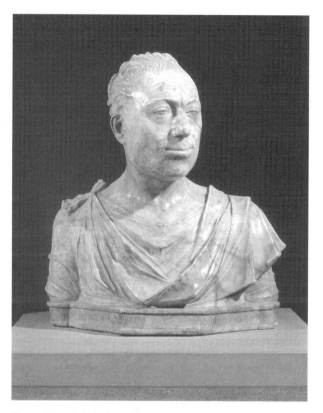

Bust of Dietisalvi Neroni
© Erich Lessing / Art Resource, NY

and Child Flanked by Saints Lawrence and Leonard (patron saints of the Neroni family and of the church and chapel, respectively) was commissioned in 1464. It was not yet complete in 1466 and was sold, upon Neroni's exile, to the Badia, where Giorgio Vasari first described it as being in 1550; the biographer makes no mention of the bust, which was probably destined for a domestic setting.

The network of Florentine patrons was often a closely knit one, and among Neroni's relatives by marriage were other men who had been portrayed by Mino, their busts dated here in parentheses: his brother Agnolo married a niece of Bishop Leonardo Salutati (*ca.* 1464); and his niece, Piera, was the wife of Carlo della Luna, first cousin of Rinaldo della Luna (1461), himself a first cousin once removed of Niccolò Strozzi (1454). As with all of these works, the modern viewer must rely on Mino's busts for what one imagines must be a faithful likeness. Of the two painted portraits of Neroni in Florence mentioned by Vasari, the putative frescoed figure by Alesso Baldovinetti in the Church of Santa Trinita (commissioned in 1471) was destroyed; the inclusion of Neroni in the scene of *Lorenzo the Magnificent with the King of Naples* (Palazzo Vecchio, Florence), painted by Vasari himself in 1556/58, is nothing more than a historical portrait made a century later, although it may be noted that Vasari made specific use of Mino's bust of Piero de' Medici for the tondo portrait in the neighboring room.

After Vasari's citation, Mino's portrait—only identifiable thanks to the inscription—vanished from history, as the Neroni family later became extinct. With typical appeal to 19th-century taste, the bust reemerged in Florence in about 1846, when it was purchased by Eugène Piot, from whom it was soon acquired by the painter Charles Timbal. Its last private owner, from 1872, was Gustave Dreyfus, whose celebrated collection (mostly of bronzes) was ultimately sold to the Kress Foundation; among the notable exceptions was this marble bust, left as a bequest to the Musée du Louvre, Paris.

FRANK DABELL

Further Reading

Arrighi, Vanna, "Diotisalvi Diotisalvi," in *Dizionario biografico degli italiani*, vol. 41, Rome: Istituto della Enciclopedia Italiana, 1991

Benigni, Paola, editor, *Palazzo Neroni a Firenze*, Florence: Edifir, 1996

Ganz, Margery A., "Perceived Insults and Their Consequences: Acciaiuoli, Neroni, and Medici Relationships in the 1460s," in *Society and Individual in Renaissance Florence: Essays in Honor of Gene A. Brucker*, edited by William Connell, Berkeley: University of California Press, 2002

Ginori Lisci, Leonardo, *The Palazzi of Florence: Their History and Art*, vol. 1, Florence: Giunti Barbera, 1985

Saalman, Howard, "San Lorenzo, 1462–66: The Neroni Ascendancy," in *Hülle und Fülle: Festschrift für Tilmann Buddensieg*, edited by Andreas Beyer, Vittorio Magnano Lampugnani, and Gunter Schweikhart, Alfter, Germany: Verlag und Datenbank für Geisteswissenschaften, 1993

JOAN MIRÓ 1893–1983 *Catalan*

Joan Miró's art expresses an iconographic abstract style that transformed the medium of sculpture particularly through symbolic and often totemic forms in three dimensions. Critics have described his work variously as childlike, sensual, playful, colorful, and even simplistic, but these terms belie a psychological interior that hints at the unconscious views people have of their own bodies, their relationship with the natural world, and the hidden aspects of sexual desire. That Miró was able to achieve this without a hint of pretension places him alongside other sculptural masters including contemporaries Constantin Brancusi, Henry Moore, Jean (Hans) Arp, Max Ernst, and Alberto Giacometti.

Although he is known primarily for his paintings and murals, Miró's sculptural work represents a crucial accomplishment in the field. Miró broke down pictorial conventions while constructing deceptively simple-looking sculptures. An early statement about intention, quoted in an article entitled "Je rêve d'un grand atelier," which was published in a 1932 edition of the French publication *Cahiers d'Art*, bespeaks his sculptural beginnings: "The more I work, the more I feel like working. I should like to try my hand at sculpture, ceramics, or graphic work, or to have a press."

As a young art student in 1912 in Barcelona, Miró was once blindfolded by his teacher Francesc Galí, who had him handle a variety of forms to understand the dimensions of shape through touch, thus solidifying an intuitive approach to building volume.

The region of Spain known as Catalonia also greatly influenced Miró. The Mediterranean scenery and nearby Tarragona countryside provided a visual foundation with other peripheral elements such as the Romanesque frescoes installed in the Art Museum of Catalonia, the Art Nouveau architecture by Antoni Gaudí, and the work of another Spanish painter (who had attended the same art school 12 years before)—Pablo Picasso.

One can perhaps best describe Miró's earliest sculptural work as assemblages or surrealistic sculptural objects with relief and form, but not volume. *Man and Woman*, for example, features two painted forms on a constructed wooden box with a chain dangling from

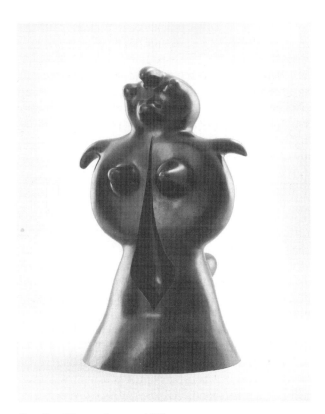

Standing Woman, bronze, 1969
Founders Society Purchase, W. Hawkins Ferry Fund
© 2001 The Detroit Institute of Arts and VAGA, New York, and 2003 Artists Rights Society (ARS), New York / ADAGP, Paris

two nails. The chain represents the connection of man and woman; the materials, found objects presented in an insouciant way, imply both vulnerability and strength. Another example from this early period, *Poetic Object*, features a mounted stuffed bird. The irony is that although the bird represents freedom, it has clearly lost its life and furthermore has been stuffed and mounted in order to be presented and considered "art."

Such themes were common to Late Modernism and were associated with the Dada movement. Francis Picaba and the avant-garde poets Guillaume Apollinaire and André Breton, also known as the Surrealists, were all friends, and although Miró never signed any official documents of the group, many critics consider him to be an especially intuitive Surrealist.

Later sculptural work derives from Miró's ceramic creations completed in the 1950s, which incorporated themes of nature by transforming abandoned pottery shards into witty biomorphic shapes. For Miró, however, form itself was never something abstract. He was always aware that the shapes he formed in clay, on canvas, or in other forms were always a token of something real, something from nature.

From 1945 to 1946 and again from 1953 to 1956, Miró explored the sculptural possibilities of clay, in collaboration with his friend Josep Llorens Artigas, creating a variety of pieces including cups and plates made from irregularly shaped broken pot fragments. In 1954 Miró created a series of seven assemblages he called "Projects for a monument," which combine disparate materials including a telephone bell, leather, and porcelain with stone, wood, and bronze into cement. The artist known for his distinctive pure hues thus found a way to put color in relief, a critical last step just prior to his full commitment to sculpture.

From 1964 to 1971 Miró concentrated mostly on sculpture with two main revolving themes: women and birds. Collectively, these works feature a bold use of curves and sensuous line. Volume is as key as color and surprise. The wit of the painted-bronze *Jeune fille s'évadant* (Girl in Evidence), for example, features a mannequin's painted red legs mounted on a marble block, with a block of blue for the midtorso, topped by a lollipop-shaped visage with an actual part of a water tap on the head. The piece manages to collectively reference primitive Mediterranean art; the *tribhanga* or ancient Indian sculptural pose that indicates a three-bend body pose whereby the human torso stands with hips, waist, and shoulders in perceived movement; and Duchamp's found objects-as-sculpture oeuvre.

Two large companion pieces of 1966, *Lunar Bird* and *Solar Bird*, represent the theme of night and day with contrasting color (one is black, the other white) and differing mediums (one in bronze, the other in marble). The sheer bulk of the two works plays against the imagery of a union between solitude (night) and universality (day) or the dualistic human emotions of loneliness and joy of being fully engaged in the light.

Contemporaries Alexander Calder, Magritte, and Jean (Hans) Arp embraced Miró. The works of Robert Rauschenberg, Jean Dubuffet, Jackson Pollock, Robert Motherwell, and Julian Schnabel, among many others, confirm also his legacy to both sculpture and painting.

JAN ARRIGO

See also **Arp, Jean (Hans); Assemblage; Brancusi, Constantin; Calder, Alexander; Dubuffet, Jean; Duchamp, Marcel; Ernst, Max; Giacometti, Alberto; Moore, Henry; Surrealist Sculpture**

Biography

Born in Barcelona, Spain, 20 April 1893. Studied art in Barcelona at Escuela de Artes y Oficios de la Lonja, 1907; studied at Francesc Galí's Escuela des Artes, 1912; fellow art student Josep Llorens Artigas became a lifelong friend and eventual collaborator on ceramic projects; joined Grupo Courbet (founded by Artigas), 1918; first solo exhibition same year; moved to Paris and befriended poets André Breton and Guillaume Apollinaire, 1920; influenced by Surrealism and Dada; made first bronze sculptures, 1946; retrospectives at the Museum of Modern Art, New York City, 1941 and 1959; received Grand Prix of Guggenheim Foundation, 1959; decorated the Labyrinth of Fondation Maeght, St.-Paul-de-Vence, France, 1964; awarded honorary doctorate, Harvard University, 1968; sculpture exhibitions at Art Institute of Chicago and Kunsthaus in Zurich, 1971–72; Fundació Joan Miró opened in Park of Montjuiec, Barcelona, 1975; sculptural exhibition, "Cent Sculptures 1962–1978," at Musée d'Art Moderne de la Ville de Paris, 1978. Died in Palma, Majorca, Spain, 25 December 1983.

Selected Works

1931   *Man and Woman*; oil on wood, nails, chain; private collection, Paris, France
1936   *Poetic Object*; stuffed bird, wood; Museum of Modern Art, New York City, United States
1954   Projects for a monument; bronze, stone, wood, cement, porcelain, leather, telephone bell; Fundació Joan Miró, Barcelona, Spain
1963   *La Fourche* (The Pitchfork); iron, bronze; Fondation Maeght, St.-Paul-de-Vence, France

1964	*Gargouille* (Gargoyle); ceramic; Fondation Maeght, St.-Paul-de-Vence, France
1966	*Lunar Bird*; bronze; Museum of Art, Philadelphia, Pennsylvania, United States
1966	*Solar Bird*; marble; Fondation Maeght, St.-Paul-de-Vence, France
1968	*Jeune fille s'évadant* (Girl in Evidence); painted bronze, pipe, molded plastic; Fondation Maeght, St.-Paul-de-Vence, France
1968	*Personage Totem*; ceramic, iron; Fondation Maeght, St.-Paul-de-Vence, France
1973	*Sobreteixim No. 7*; burlap, cloth, tapestry; private collection, Galerie Maeght, Paris, France
1977	*Personage Gothique*; bronze; National Gallery of Art, Washington, D.C., United States

Further Reading

Bernier, Rosamond, *Sculpture in Ceramic by Miró and Artigas*, New York: Pierre Matisse Gallery, 1956

Diehl, Gaston, *Miró*, New York: Crown, 1974

Greenberg, Clement, *Joan Miró*, New York: Quadrangle Press, 1948

The Marguerite and Aimé Maeght Foundation, Paris: Maeght Editeur, 1993

Miró, Joan, *Joan Miró: Selected Writings and Interviews*, edited by Rowell Margit, translated by Paul Auster and Patricia Mathews, Boston: G.K. Hall, 1986

Penrose, Roland, *Miró*, London: Thames and Hudson, and New York: Abrams, 1970

Sweeney, James Johnson, *Joan Miró*, New York: Museum of Modern Art, 1941

MISERICORD

When communities of monks, priests, or canons gather in the church choir for services, specially designed, high-backed seating provides not only a chair but also a support while standing and sometimes storage for service books. Generally constructed of wood and located on either side of the choir, choir stalls are arranged in rows with hinged seats and armrests that serve as partitions. When folded up, each seat reveals a small bracket on its underside upon which a cleric may lean while still appearing to stand. That bracket is the "mercy seat," or misericord, so called because of the relief it provides for the weary or infirm clergy (*pro miserere*). Because the part of the human anatomy that rests on the misericord is the backside, it was not the best place for revered religious subjects—the art under the seat was often delightfully irreverent, even obscene, during the Middle Ages. As Dorothy and Henry Kraus have noted, "the art of the misericord was born out of indulgence" (see Kraus and Kraus, 1975).

The choir-stall format became standard under Charlemagne; the oldest surviving examples date from the 12th century. The term *misericord* was first used in an 11th-century document from the German monastery Hirsau (in Swabia) and was also mentioned in a letter written by Peter Damian (988–1072) against the use of seats during the divine office. That the seating never lost the air of impropriety is clear from its nomenclature, "cheater seats" and "nodding seats" among them. Nevertheless, *scabella*, little seats attached to the larger one, are documented at the Abbey of Cluny, Burgundy, France, in 1121. Conditions of use posed certain artistic problems to the sculptors of misericords. Frequent daily manipulation of the seats and the weight concentrated on them mandated that the most durable wood, oak or chestnut, be used. The triangular shape of the bracket meant that the artist had to conform to a given shape in all compositions. English misericords developed distinctive supporters, winglike carvings on either side. Originally ornamental, the earliest supporters to develop the narrative of the central scene were those at Ely Cathedral, of 1339–41. Where they appear, the impact of English art is implicated, as in the misericords of Barcelona Cathedral, Spain. Surviving contracts reveal that highly regarded artists carved misericords as well as the more visible areas of the choir stalls, and numerous artists' signatures are recorded.

As with manuscript decoration, misericords provided a private place in which the imagination of patron and artist could run riot during the Gothic period. The most exuberant decoration for misericords occurred from the 13th to the 16th centuries, particularly in Great Britain, France, Flanders, and Spain. Whereas dignified coats of arms, foliage, saints, and apostles ornamented the high backs and other visible areas of the stalls, the hidden seats and sometimes the hand rests provided the field for satirical and salacious imagery. Of the nearly 8,000 misericords documented in France by the Krauses, only 3 percent had subjects drawn from scripture, and the majority of those are at Amiens and Auxerre Cathedrals. Misericord sculpture appropriated the entire gamut of medieval culture: labor, professions, games, the seasons, family life, courtship, proverbs, folk tales, and mythology. As documents for daily life in the Middle Ages, misericords rank high in preserving images of the way people lived, worked, and fantasized about sexual relations of all sorts. Couples dance, embrace, or share a tub or domestic tasks such as washing the dishes. At Ely, in England, a housewife uses a distaff to scare off a fox stealing a goose. At Astorga (León; *ca.* 1515–after 1525), in Spain, dogs play cards while one smokes a pipe with that new American import, tobacco. Several sites include scenes of clerics making improper advances from the confessional. The sculptors often represent themselves in the act of carving; in the Church of Saint-Martin-aux-Bois (Oise; 15th century), a misericord depicts God and the devil as sculptors putting the finishing touches on their creation, woman.

Much has been made of the freedom granted to the artists in carving these subjects, but the patron, with the control of payment, had the last say and also most likely made the initial selection of the decoration. Within a given ensemble of misericords, the subjects vary widely, owing in part to the number of artists involved in any project, the choice of the individual whose stall was being carved, and the range of available material. At the Church of Saint-Pierre of Saumur, France, a confraternity funded the misericords carved in 1474–78; these provide examples of sexual titillation and religious submission. Men and women together, wantonly drunk, contrast with images of Mary Magdalene as penitent. At the Church of Notre-Dame in Brou, near Bourg-en-Bresse in Burgundy, France, the local citizenry contracted local artists to carve new choir stalls in 1510, with the condition "that these artisans make the seats according to the desire of those paying for them." In this case, the misericords take the form of the burghers' heads. With the Reformation of the 16th century, the more raucous subjects ceased to be produced in favor of creating a more sober environment, as found in the choir stalls from the Chateau Gaillon, now in Saint-Denis, France, with fragments dispersed in various museums. Carved from 1508 to 1518 by Colin Castille of Rouen, the Italianate stalls have misericords representing saints' lives, musical recitals, and dancing putti set into elaborate vine scrolls. The contrast between modern modesty and the earthier medieval attitude to church decoration is exemplified by the story that in 19th-century Zamora, Spain, a dean felt impelled to take a hammer to a misericord that showed a monk and a nun in an immodest pose.

Although the clergy, in theory, were not to participate in the bawdy activities represented in misericords, the images certainly could have reflected their extramural experiences or class attitudes. Michael Camille indicates with acuity that by sitting on images of vice or of peasants, the cleric debases them (see Camille, 1992). Furthermore, the social commentary and critical attitude toward human behavior in the imagery often reveal a homiletic intent, just as do many proverbs.

ELIZABETH VALDEZ DEL ALAMO

Further Reading

Block, Elaine C., *Misericords in the Rhineland*, Lakewood, Ohio: Shelden, 1996

Bond, Francis, *Wood Carvings in English Churches*, London: Frowde, 1910; see especially vol. 1, *Misericords*

Camille, Michael, "Misericords and Posteriors," in *Image on the Edge: The Margins of Medieval Art*, Cambridge, Massachusetts: Harvard University Press, 1992

Grössinger, Christa, *The World Upside-Down: English Misericords*, London: Miller, 1997

Kraus, Dorothy, and Henry Kraus, *The Hidden World of Misericords*, New York: Braziller, 1975; London: Joseph, 1976

Kraus, Dorothy, and Henry Kraus, *The Gothic Choirstalls of Spain*, London and Boston: Routledge and Kegan Paul, 1986

Remnant, G.L., *A Catalogue of Misericords in Great Britain*, Oxford: Clarendon Press, 1969

Wood, Juanita Ballew, and Charles A. Curry, *Wooden Images: Misericords and Medieval England*, Madison, New Jersey: Fairleigh Dickinson University Press, 1999

FRANCESCO MOCHI 1580–1654 *Italian*

Francesco Mochi's career has often been presented as a tragic foil to the success of his contemporary Gianlorenzo Bernini. Showing early brilliance, Mochi created works in the first decade of the 17th century that presaged the Baroque style in sculpture. Mochi then produced his masterpieces, the equestrian monuments of Rannuccio and Alessandro Farnese, in Piacenza, where he spent nearly two decades. Returning to Rome, Mochi found the artistic scene dominated by the younger Bernini, whose exuberant, dynamic style had outstripped Mochi's early example. Although he received commissions from the highest ranks of Roman patronage in the 1630s, Mochi suffered a series of professional disappointments, with major works criticized or rejected and commissions withdrawn. His late sculptures display a harsh introspection and a severe, dry quality that seem the antithesis of Bernini's sensual, expansive style. The image of an artist out of touch with his times, producing haunting late works reflecting his own personal decline, has been challenged in recent literature, pointing the way to a more balanced consideration of Mochi's oeuvre and a fuller understanding of 17th-century Italian sculpture.

Mochi's early biographers report that he trained in the Florentine studio of Santi di Tito, a painter known for his clear presentation of religious narratives. Moving to Rome about 1600, Mochi came into contact with Camillo Mariani, from whom he learned a gracefully animated style and sensitivity to the nuances of emotion and expression. Strong support from Mario Farnese, Duke of Latera, led to Mochi's first independent commission, the *Annunciation* for Orvieto Cathedral. His first major Roman commission came from Maffeo Barberini, for a *St. Martha* for the Barberini chapel in Sant'Andrea della Valle. Mochi exploited the tension between figure and niche to enliven the narrative force of the sculpture and extend the drama into the viewer's space.

In 1612 Mochi was called to Piacenza by Rannuccio Farnese, Duke of Parma and Piacenza, and spent the next 17 years creating a pair of equestrian statues representing Rannuccio and his late father, Duke Alessandro Farnese. Mochi's monuments present two aspects of Farnese rule: Rannuccio is a calm, benevolent leader, leading his horse in stately movement; Alessandro is represented as a forceful general, moving forward in battle, with wind whipping through his cloak and the mane and tail of the horse. Particularly in the monument of Duke Alessandro Farnese, where figure and horse are presented with the same degree of energy, power, and motion, Mochi created an innovative monument imbued with the dynamism characteristic of Baroque sculpture.

Mochi's achievements seem even more heroic because midway through the production of the monument of Duke Rannuccio Farnese, the sculptor assumed responsibility for casting the bronzes. The casts of both horse and rider emerged with only minor flaws, and the Alessandro monument showed no casting flaws, proving Mochi's mastery of the specialized processes of bronze casting. Such independence and insistence upon controlling all aspects of production is a clear sign of Mochi's nature as a creative individual, intent on his own participation in every phase of the work. It was also extremely rare: Mochi is one of only two sculptors of the period known to have cast their own works.

Returning to Rome in 1629, Mochi carved *St. John the Baptist* in marble for the Barberini family, destined for the same Barberini chapel in Sant'Andrea della Valle as his *St. Martha*. The seated saint preaches, enumerating points by counting them on his fingers, a traditional gesture of eloquence. The intensity of the message is conveyed through the sinewy musculature, sharply focused gaze, turned head, and tensed energy that barely allows the saint to maintain his seated pose. For reasons that are unclear, *St. John the Baptist* was never put in place. Mochi was also chosen in 1629 for an even more prestigious commission, one of the four over life-size figures for the crossing piers of St. Peter's, a project overseen by Bernini. In his *St. Veronica*, Mochi brought to a niche figure the same energy and animation so ideally represented in the Alessandro Farnese monument. Like the *St. Martha*, *St. Veronica* challenges the boundaries conceptually and physically imposed by the niche as she runs forward to display the miraculous image of Christ's face on her veil. The figure has aroused strong response throughout its history. Mochi's 17th-century biographer, Giovanni Battista Passeri, offered the most damning and prevalent criticism: the *St. Veronica* seemed to deny the essential, static quality of statuary. Such forceful movement was considered indecorous in a marble statue.

Three late projects exhibit taut musculature, elongated proportions, and intensely observed psychology.

Two of these commissions ended in failure, and the statues remained in Mochi's shop at his death: the *Baptism of Christ*, a two-figured tableau for the high altar of San Giovanni dei Fiorentini; and *St. Peter* and *St. Paul* for San Paolo fuori le Mura. Mochi also carved a *St. Thaddeus* for Orvieto Cathedral, completed and installed in 1644. It develops the intensity of expression of Mochi's earlier *St. Philip*, also for Orvieto Cathedral, and the *St. John the Baptist*, while its harsher, more linear forms in the drapery patterns and hair exemplify his late style.

Mochi's work on a smaller scale can be appreciated in *Bust of a Youth*. This work displays great sensitivity of carving of the fleshy forms of the face, the animated, curling hair that is consistent throughout his oeuvre, and the intensity of focus of the head and glance, which engage the space around the figure.

Innovative in his approach to each of his subjects, Mochi consistently challenged the limitations of his materials and rethought the relationship between sculpture and setting. Given his fiercely independent nature and his desire to maintain control over the processes of production, it is not surprising that Mochi did not have a large workshop and consequently did not have a significant impact on later generations of sculptors. Mochi's creations stand apart from the work of his contemporaries, challenging our notions about Baroque sculpture and enriching our view of a period dominated by the impact of Bernini.

MARIETTA CAMBARERI

See also **Bernini, Gianlorenzo**

Biography

Born in Montevarchi, Italy, 29 July 1580. Father Lorenzo Mochi, a tailor, not Orazio Mochi, the sculptor. Studied in Florence with painter Santi di Tito; moved to Rome, *ca.* 1600, and may have trained with sculptor Camillo Mariani; Mario Farnese, Duke of Latera, wrote letters of support to Opera del Duomo, Orvieto Cathedral, 1603; moved to Orvieto, April 1603; returned to Rome, 1607; in Orvieto, 1608–10; spent time in Rome, 1609; completed works left unfinished by Mariani upon his death, 1611; went to Piacenza to work for Rannuccio Farnese, Duke of Parma and Piacenza, 1612; traveled to Padua and Venice to study equestrian monuments by Donatello and Verrocchio and bronze Horses of San Marco, 1616; granted citizenship in Piacenza, 1618; went to Rome, January 1621; returned to Piacenza, April 1621; back to Rome, 1629; lived in the parish of Sant'Andrea delle Fratte; member of the Accademia di San Luca from 1630, and elected *principe* for the year, 1633; went briefly to Orvieto, 1644. Died in Rome, Italy, 6 February 1654.

Selected Works

1605	Angel of the *Annunciation*; marble; Museo dell'Opera del Duomo, Orvieto, Italy
1609	Virgin of the *Annunciation*; marble; Museo dell'Opera del Duomo, Orvieto, Italy
1610	*St. Philip*; marble; Museo dell'Opera del Duomo, Orvieto, Italy
1610–17	*St. Martha*; marble; Barberini Chapel, Sant'Andrea della Valle, Rome, Italy
1620	Equestrian monument of Duke Rannuccio Farnese; bronze; Piazza Cavalli, Piacenza, Italy (narrative reliefs on pedestal, by 1629)
1625	Equestrian monument of Duke Alessandro Farnese; bronze; Piazza Cavalli, Piacenza, Italy (narrative reliefs on pedestal, by 1629)
ca. 1629	*Cardinal Antonio Barberini the Younger*; marble; Toledo Museum of Art, Ohio, United States
1629–40	*St. Veronica*; marble; St. Peter's Basilica, Rome, Italy
1630	*Carlo Barberini on Horseback*; bronze; Barberini Collection, Rome, Italy
1630	*St. John the Baptist*; marble, Hofkirche (Court Church, now Cathedral), Dresden, Germany
ca. 1630	*Bust of a Youth*; marble; Art Institute of Chicago, Illinois, United States
1634	*Baptism of Christ*; marble; Museo di Roma, Palazzo Braschi, Rome, Italy
1638–52	*St. Peter* and *St. Paul*; marble; Porta del Popolo, Rome, Italy
1644	*St. Thaddeus*; marble; Museo dell'Opera del Duomo, Orvieto, Italy

Further Reading

Borea, Evalina, *Francesco*, Milan: Fratelli Fabbri, 1966

Del Bravo, Carlo, *Francesco Mochi*, Montevarchi, Italy: Comune di Montevarchi, 1981 *Francesco Mochi, 1580–1654* (exhib. cat.), Florence: Centro Di, 1981

Lavin, Irving, "Duquesnoy's 'Nano di Créqui' and Two Busts by Francesco Mochi," *The Art Bulletin*, 102 (1970)

Montagu, Jennifer, "A Model by Francesco Mochi for the 'Saint Veronica,'" *The Burlington Magazine* 124 (1982)

Montagu, Jennifer, [review of *Francesco Mochi, 1580–1654*], *The Burlington Magazine* 125 (1983)

Pantaleoni, Gaetano, editor, *Il barocco del Mochi nei cavalli farnesiani*, Piacenza, Italy: Gallarati, 1975

Wardropper, Ian, "A New Attribution to Francesco Mochi," *The Art Institute of Chicago Museum Studies* 17 (1991)

Wittkower, Rudolf, *Art and Architecture in Italy, 1600–1750*, London and Baltimore, Maryland: Penguin, 1958; 6th edition, 3 vols., revised by Joseph Connors and Jennifer Montagu, New Haven, Connecticut: Yale University Press, 1999

ANNUNCIATION

Francesco Mochi (1580–1654)
1603–1609
marble
h. of Angel 1.85 m; h. of Virgin 2.10 m
Museo dell'Opera del Duomo, Orvieto, Italy

Francesco Mochi's *Annunciation* for Orvieto Cathedral, his first known, independent commission, aroused critical appreciation in its own day and in modern scholarship. Rudolf Wittkower, for example, called it "a fanfare raising sculpture from its slumber" (see Wittkower, 1999). There is little agreement, however, about its place in the history of sculpture. Characterized alternately as the culmination of Giambologna's elegant, courtly style, or *maniera*, and as a harbinger of the Baroque, the *Annunciation* displays elements of both styles but is best understood in its own place and context. It is the early masterpiece of a young, ambitious sculptor and the fruit of Mochi's training in Florence and Rome, and it fulfills, with innovation and virtuosity, the requirements of its commission and setting in Orvieto Cathedral.

Mochi was unknown and untested in 1603 when Mario Farnese, duke of Latera, wrote letters in his support to the governing council of Orvieto Cathedral. A Farnese recommendation would have carried weight at Orvieto, since a Farnese bishop consecrated the cathedral in the early 14th century and, in the late 1530s, Pope Paul III Farnese funded a renovation project that would set the stage for the placement of Mochi's *Annunciation* in the tribune of the church. The pope ordered that the medieval choir be removed from the first bays of the nave into the tribune, making the high altar visible and accessible to the congregation. Embellishment of the high altar and tribune led to the decision, in 1603, to replace the existing medieval *Annunciation* (*ca.* 1400; Museo dell'Opera del Duomo, Orvieto [artist unknown]) with a new marble group to be carved by Mochi. The group, placed at the liturgical and devotional heart of the church, would express the moment of the Incarnation of Christ, setting in motion a program already in place in the crossing and tribune. Marble relief altarpieces representing scenes of Christ's early manifestations on earth, the Visitation to the left of the tribune and the Adoration of the Magi to the right, which were carved in the mid 16th century, decorated the crossing. The story culminated in the monumental sacramental tabernacle on the high altar, where the Eucharist, the sacrificial Body of Christ, was housed.

In April 1603, the 22-year-old Mochi was sent to Carrara to obtain blocks for the figures. The *Angel* was finished in 1605 and the *Virgin* was carved in 1608–09. During this period, Orvieto was a major center for marble sculpture, increasing for Mochi both the prestige and the challenge of the commission. The 14th-century facade reliefs established a marble-carving tradition at the cathedral that was further developed in the 16th century by sculptors such as Raffaello da Montelupo, a collaborator of Michelangelo. Montelupo transmitted Michelangelo's ideals to the local sculptor Ippolito Scalza, who carved a four-figured, monolithic *Pietà* (1579; Orvieto Cathedral), which met the challenge of Michelangelo's failed, four-figured group (Museo dell'Opera del Duomo, Florence, Italy). A series of marble apostles for the nave of the cathedral was carved by artists such as Giovanni Battista Caccini and Pietro Francavilla (working on a model by Giambologna) in the years around 1600. Pietro Bernini and Stefano Maderno sought but failed to attain commissions, but Mochi carved two apostles.

Mochi's *Annunciation* is a scene of enormous energy, power, and dramatic intensity, and the statues expanded the expressive potential of marble statuary.

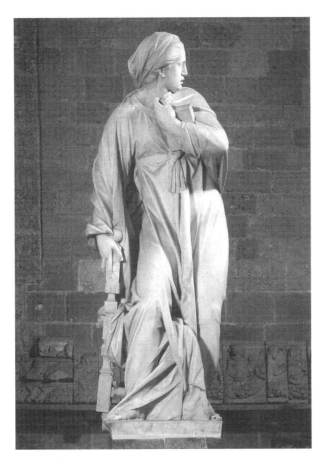

Virgin of the *Annunciation*
© Scala / Art Resource, NY

The *Angel* flies through clouds that serve as support for the figure but conceptually deny this function. His draperies swirl around him, conveying an unprecedented sense of motion and flight; this was Mochi's response to the challenge of Giambologna's bronze *Mercury* (1581), which he achieved in the heavier, obdurate medium of marble. The remarkable sense of naturalism of the *Angel* also characterizes the figure of the *Virgin* who responds with surprise, fear, and wonder. She nearly tips her chair as she rises, pulling her cloak around her as if to shield herself from the wind whipped up by the *Angel* and from his momentous salutation. The psychological insight, dramatic interaction between the two figures, and naturalistic details, like the clouds and the chair, impart to the group an almost pictorial character that recalls Mochi's training with the painter Santi di Tito. Mochi seems to have looked, for example, at Alessandro Allori's *Annunciation* (1580s; Accademia, Florence) for the pose and gesture of the *Angel*, his flight through the clouds, and the intimate setting of the room of the *Virgin* indicated by the contemporary chair.

Although Mochi drew upon both the sculptural and the pictorial traditions of the Florentine *maniera*, the dramatic, animated energy and interaction of the figures across space presage Baroque sculpture in Rome, which was exemplified by the younger Gianlorenzo Bernini. Mochi himself would develop these ideas in his equestrian monument of Alessandro Farnese and the *St. Veronica*.

Mochi signed the *Angel*, marking it as his masterpiece. He indicated that he wanted it placed on the balustrade of the tribune, which would have heightened the dramatic, physical impact and the startling immediacy of the figure in flight. The *Angel* was positioned there in a provisional setting that seemed too precarious to the cathedral council, and it was removed onto a solid pedestal inside the confines of the tribune in 1608.

Problems also arose regarding the placement of the *Virgin*. Cardinal Giacomo Sannesio, bishop of Orvieto, refused to allow the figure to be installed, perhaps because he disapproved of it. The members of the cathedral chapter, however, as patrons of the group, had seen and approved the model, and the figure was judged on completion to conform to the model. The council, determined that the bishop had no good reason for his objections and voted to appeal directly to Pope Clement VIII. Within a few months the figure was set into the church, completing the tableau as Mochi had planned it.

The *Annunciation* was recognized as a masterpiece in its own day and throughout the 18th century. Nineteenth-century critics, however, loathed it and the Baroque style it represented, and the *Annunciation* was removed to the cathedral museum just before 1900 as part of a sweeping renovation of the cathedral interior.

MARIETTA CAMBARERI

Further Reading

Cambareri, Marietta, "Francesco Mochi's *Annunciation* Group at Orvieto Cathedral," *Sculpture Journal* 5 (2001)

De Luca Savelli, Maddalena, in *Francesco Mochi, 1580–1654*, Florence: Centro Di, 1981

Wittkower, Rudolf, *Art and Architecture in Italy, 1600–1750*, London and Baltimore, Maryland: Penguin, 1958; 6th edition, 3 vols., revised by Joseph Connors and Jennifer Montagu, New Haven, Connecticut: Yale University Press, 1999

MODELING

Modeling is a process by which the sculptor builds up the form from a material that can be manipulated, as opposed to carving, in which the sculptor reveals the form by cutting away from a hard, inflexible material. A sculptor can model any material that can be made to take on the characteristic of a thick viscous liquid or a pastelike putty, although in practice it needs to be a material that will remain in a manipulable state for a reasonable length of time without the aid of dangerous components or extreme temperatures. Materials most used for modeling are clay, wax, and plaster of Paris, together with various derivatives or alternative materials with slightly different characteristics.

Ancient humans likely would have used whatever materials were available to express ideas that scholars today can only guess at. The materials may not have been durable, but that need not have been important. Durability comes with refinement of techniques and greater selectivity of materials, which inevitably leads the modeler to clay, the universal material for modeling. Almost every culture throughout history has produced decorative or sculptural objects made from clay, which is readily available in most parts of the world and is easily extracted and processed.

Clay is found in beds in the earth's surface laid down as the result of the erosion of igneous rock: basalt, granite, obsidian, and the hard, dense volcanic rocks. Fine particles are deposited on the beds of rivers, lakes, or seas over periods of many millennia and become mixed with different oxides, minerals, and organic matter to form sedimentary clay. Although one can refine sedimentary clay or add ingredients to suit the application, it is the basic material most used for modeling. One can use this highly versatile material in all states between liquid and solid to produce a wide variety of forms, textures, and surfaces; above all, it is seductively tactile.

Only relatively simple, structural forms in clay are self-supporting; more complex sculptures need an ar-

mature provided with anchor points to prevent the clay from sliding off. While work is progressing, one must keep the clay damp because it is prone to cracking as it dries; if overwetted, however, it will slump and distort. These technical limitations make clay essentially an intermediate material. One needs to fire the form to make terracotta or translate it into another material (e.g., stone, metal, concrete, or plastic) to render it permanent. It is relatively easy to take a mold from damp clay, and its pliancy at the modeling stage outweighs the minor disadvantages.

Historically, the use of modeled clay has been central to the development of sculpture. The speed and ease with which one can produce a tremendous range of forms, either as sketches or in detail, at small scale, as maquettes (or models), or at full scale, has helped sculptors develop their basic language of form. Modeled clay has been essential to the development of the work of individual sculptors (such as Gianlorenzo Bernini) and has consequently made a vast cultural contribution.

As the cultural climate changed in the second half of the 19th century, sculptors moved away from idealized representation. The bronzes of Auguste Rodin, who was at the forefront of the development of modern sculpture, demonstrate the expressiveness of his modeling and the vigor with which he used clay. The textures show quite graphically how he worked: the routes his fingers took over the surface, the added pellets, and the incised marks of the modeling tools. Another modeler, Alberto Giacometti, also reveled in expressive modeling of clay. His work of the 1960s shows clay both feverishly pummeled and tightly drawn in the same piece.

Wax, like clay, established itself over a long period and throughout many cultures as a modeling material. It is easy to imagine ancient peoples, having harvested and eaten wild honey, discovering that the leftover material (the beeswax) could be gently warmed and then formed into three-dimensional shapes. The tradition of using wax as an end material for sculpture is a long one, and numerous examples from many periods and cultures survive, despite its fragility and vulnerability to heat. Surviving wax sculptures include Renaissance maquettes, anatomical representations (in which sculptors used the semitranslucency of pigmented wax to eerie effect to imitate skin and flesh), and waxworks, such as those shown at Madame Tussaud's, London, from the 18th century on.

The sculptor models directly in wax. After the wax is softened by gentle heating in a container, the sculptor can model the wax in much the same way as clay, adding and manipulating pellets. As the wax cools, it hardens, giving rigidity to the form. The sculptor can further build up and texture the surface by brushing molten wax onto the cooled surface or by dipping it quickly into molten wax. The sculptor can also smooth and manipulate the surface by passing a blowtorch flame quickly across it; alternatively, the sculptor can use a warmed metal spatula. If the form needs to be changed radically, the sculptor can gently warm it until it becomes softened throughout so that all or major sections can be moved into a new position.

Modeled wax forms that are intended to be directly invested must be fairly even in cross section because large variations in mass will cause technical problems due to differential cooling of the casting. Filigree forms, low reliefs, or simple figurative forms are ideally suited to the technique. Due to the inherent structural weakness of wax, only small simple forms may be made without an armature; however, one can make armatures from copper wire or small-bore tubing, wooden sticks, or tubes of rolled paper to allow an increase in scale. Copper remains in the mold when the wax is melted, but it is compatible with the bronze; wood or paper will burn away. One can make larger or bulkier sculptures by building up the wax around a core of clay or the same type of investment material used to make the outer mold. One then coats the core with wax by dipping if it is small enough or by painting on molten wax. When a sufficient thickness has been built up, the sculptor can embellish details and textures by adding pellets, painting, or using a warmed spatula or blowtorch.

Wax is central to the *cire perdue* (lost-wax) method of metal casting, as an intermediary stage in the translation of a sculpture made in another material, for example, clay or plaster. The sculptor takes a mold made of plaster of Paris or a flexible mold material such as silicone rubber supported in a rigid mold from the original and reproduces a hollow form of the sculpture in wax—at which stage the sculptor can rework or change the form to some degree. The sculptor embeds the wax form in a new mold, called the *investment* or *investment mold*, made of a mixture of plaster of Paris and a refractory material such as ground ceramic. The investment mold is then gradually heated to red hot and held at that temperature until all remnants of the wax are burnt away, or lost, hence the name of the process, lost wax. Molten metal is then poured into the void left by the burnt-out wax.

Plaster of Paris is another material that is invaluable to sculptors. The use of plaster can be traced back to ancient Egypt, but it was in 19th-century Paris, due to the extensive gypsum deposits under the city, that the commercial production of the reliable material known today was developed. Gypsum is first heated and ground into a powder. It recrystallizes when water is added, heating up and expanding slightly to produce a hard, dense material similar to the original gypsum.

Several different grades are available, with different characteristics, but "fine casting" is the most useful for the sculptor. Its setting time is such that, when it is used as a modeling material, the sculptor has time to work in a considered way but at a brisk pace, although setting times can be accelerated or retarded.

When it is first mixed, plaster has a smooth, creamy consistency. At this stage one can dip a scrim in it, which will add reinforcement and texture when it is laid over the form. Initially, one can also pour, throw, or paint the plaster onto the form. As it sets, the mix becomes progressively stiffer, and one can scoop it up and smear or push it onto the surface by hand or with spatulas. One can still apply plaster when it has reached a crumbly, almost-set condition, when it can be ground onto the surface to add texture. The sculptor can carve, saw, or rasp back the hardened plaster to refine the form or change the texture and can repeat the process of mixing and adding. The work of 20th-century sculptor Elisabeth Frink, who produced a considerable body of her work by direct plaster modeling, shows this process clearly. Her monumental figures contain the sense of the physicality of working plaster—its bulk and weight—and the sheer effort expended in making the sculpture while the surfaces demonstrate plaster's hardness and the way it can take complex texture or a taut smoothness.

ANDREW NAYLOR

See also **Bernini, Gianlorenzo; Clay and Terracotta; Giacometti, Alberto; Metal Casting; Rodin, Auguste; Stucco (Lime Plaster); Wax**

Further Reading

Alec Tiranti Limited, *Sculptors' Catalogue*, London: Alec Tiranti, 2000

Lanteri, Edward, *Modelling*, 3 vols., London: Chapman and Hall, 1902–11; reprint of vols. 1–2, as *Modelling and Sculpting the Human Figure*, New York: Dover, 1985; reprint of vol. 3, as *Modelling and Sculpting Animals*, New York: Dover, 1985

Mills, John W., *The Encyclopaedia of Sculpture Techniques*, New York: Watson Guptill, 1989; London: Batsford, 1990

MODERNISM

In European sculpture as in the other arts, Modernism is the manifestation of a belief that the importance of a work should be determined not by a valuation of its quality but rather of its novelty or originality. A shared aesthetic dating from the time of Michelangelo, inherited by one generation and built upon and transferred to the next was substituted with the less certain and more fractious ideals of originality and innovation by the end of the 19th century. Already by 1830, however, the concerted maintenance of the Classical tradition found in the works of Antonio Canova, Bertel Thorvaldsen, and Hiram Powers had become increasingly defensive in tone. The Romantic forms of Antoine-Louis Barye and Jean-Baptiste Carpeaux asserted in their self-conscious avoidance of finish and the studied pose an attitude of proto-Modernism, which served as the foundation for the medium's most celebrated exponent of the late 19th century: Auguste Rodin.

The Modernist aesthetic in sculpture began in earnest only with the consummation of Rodin's reputation in 1900 when he exhibited *The Gates of Hell* and other major long-term projects at his first retrospective in Paris. Thereafter the work of Rodin served as a standard against which younger European and American sculptors' art was judged and against which many other sculptors rebelled. It is therefore within the context of an established order for art—the institution of the Paris Salon exhibitions and the schooling system of the École des Beaux Arts—that sculpture's avantgarde developed, rather than entirely outside of its sphere of influence. The frequent involvement of government bodies and wealthy private patrons in the development of major public sculptural projects was also a relatively constant tempering influence on the art form's Modernist development and expression. As a result, the rise of a Modernist aesthetic was slow and less explosive in the field of sculpture than in that of the less environmentally integrated medium of painting. The most influential Modernist sculptors tended to produce socially and politically acceptable adaptations of radical innovations already put forth in the pictorial language of two-dimensional media.

In France after 1900, the many students and assistants of Rodin (including Charles Despiau, François Pompon, Camille Claudel, and Malvina Hoffman) avoided the vanguard, but few young sculptors of the time could resist engagement with or fierce reaction against Rodin's influence. The succeeding generation of French sculptors still committed to figurative work took on a so-called archaizing, or Neoclassical style inspired in part by the simple, heavy forms of non-Western tribal sculpture and archaic Mediterranean art and in part by the surrounding early-20th-century exploration of abstract form. By 1905 Aristide Maillol and Emile-Antoine Bourdelle had developed a loosely shared "modern" ideal for the female figure, which remained the almost exclusive subject of Maillol's art until his death in 1944. In the process these idealized but abstracted female figures were adopted by Art Deco sculptors and designers, as in the archaizing style of Paul Manship, the Cubist-influenced portraiture and figures of Jacques Lipschitz, and even the ungainly women who constitute Gaston Lachaise's oeuvre.

The overriding importance of the role of the monument served to moderate and even to restrict the formal, expressive, and intellectual range of Modern sculpture during the first half of the century. This is particularly evident in the swift integration of abstracted forms within the agendas of socialist realism and German nationalism after 1920. If there was a sculptural revolution, or at least a swift transformation, after World War I, it came in the choice of materials, or media, used.

The vast expansion of available materials in the 20th century and at the same time a new premium on direct creation (rather than the transposition from clay or wax to marble or bronze, which had been virtually inevitable during the previous century) allowed sculptors to explore enormous ranges of technique, texture, and color in the creation of a Modern sculptural aesthetic. The very physical and plastic challenge of direct carving in stone served to facilitate these sculptors' Modernist ambitions. The first results of such efforts— among them Constantin Brancusi's *The Kiss* (stone, 1908), Ludwig Kirchner's *Dancing Woman* (wood, 1909), and the Cubistic work of Henri Gaudier-Brzeska (as, for example, *Birds Erect*, carved in limestone in 1914)—marked a kind of anti-Rodinesque turn that moved sculpture decidedly away from the tradition of modeling and into the possibilities posed by direct cutting. By the early 1930s the organic abstraction of Barbara Hepworth and Henry Moore had also benefited from this shift away from pliable media; the natural surface texture and color of stone were incorporated into the artistic process and affected the expressive outcome to an unprecedented extent.

Out of the utopian optimism of early Soviet ideals came a kind of line-based response to Cubism called Constructivism, in which the energy of the people's movement was expressed through the "pure" expression of form, untainted, it was thought, by the mundane values of bourgeois formalism. Constructivism simultaneously exploited the artistic potential of industrial and "modern" materials such as tin, wire, iron, plywood, glass, and steel. The sculptural programs of Constructivist artists such as Vladimir Tatlin, Naum Gabo, and Lazar El Lissitzky were mainly architectural and theoretical, however, and following the imposition of social realism on the Russian art world later in the 1920s, Tatlin and Gabo immigrated to western Europe to join with continuing abstract movements there.

By 1910 European sculptors had begun almost systematically appropriating the formal properties of painting, beginning with color. Between 1914 and 1924 there appeared another body of abstract and nonobjective formal constructions and assemblages by sculptors from a wide variety of schools and art centers, including Dada artist Kurt Schwitters, Cubist-influenced sculptor Alexander Archipenko, and Futurist Umberto Boccioni, who exploited the possibilities of color as an essential component of the three-dimensional form.

The introduction to sculptors of industrial welding techniques through the works made by Julio González and Pablo Picasso in the late 1920s further expanded the design vocabulary available to sculptors by creating a kind of three-dimensional line and plane. Already by the early 1930s this expansion of the plastic limits to sculpture spurred Alexander Calder and David Smith to conduct early experiments in mobile and line/plane-oriented assemblage.

Between 1921 and 1936, László Moholy-Nagy was developing in his *Space Modulator* and other less finished works a different concept of the role of sculpture in the 20th century, one that saw the structure as primarily an agent, or scaffold, for the casting of light and shadow to present kinetic, two-dimensional compositions on the walls of Modern architecture. His vision of the role of sculpture in the contemporary environment greatly expanded the formal potential of three-dimensional media and blurred still further the boundaries between the flat and the plastic arts.

Meanwhile a kind of fetishization of objects inspired in part by psychoanalysis, or at least its trappings, resulted in sculptural works by Surrealist artists, notably Alberto Giacometti, Hans Bellmer, and Salvador Dalí, and these received theoretical support from André Breton, who proposed that the artist is compelled to create the work of art out of a need to fill a void created by the early loss of an ideal. Such works as Giacometti's *Suspended Ball* (1930) and Bellmer's career-long *Poupée* series (*ca.* 1936–70) embody efforts to fulfill the promise of this theory. Indeed, Salvador Dalí's avowed ambition was to create an undeniable plastic presence from the impossible object of his fancy, and his own sculpture of the 1930s, such as the *Retrospective Bust of a Woman* (1933), conveyed an overriding intention to disorient the viewer by placing common objects in unexpected and implausible contexts.

This line of development for the aesthetic of the found object in sculpture is separate from that introduced by the Dada movement and Marcel Duchamp, who advocated a similar disconnection of form and function with the exhibition of his readymades such as *Coatrack* (1917) and *Fountain* (1917), but with a more detached and ironic motive. Duchamp maintained that the association of the artist with his work was misunderstood: the readymade became art not necessarily through a manipulation of its form but through the artist's very act of choosing it. This ironic denial of purpose in the use of the purposely built object resulted in an extensive series of aggressively nonsensi-

cal works of like kind, notably in the Dada exhibitions that took place throughout these years. In Cologne in 1920, for example, the Dada artist Max Ernst offered as an exhibit a small axe with which the spectators were invited to attack the other works on view. With the advent of World War II, the challenge of creating interest out of such contradictions, and the sardonic sense of humor that they required of an indulgent spectator (as, for example, Meret Oppenheim's *Object: Breakfast in Fur*, a fur-lined teacup, spoon, and saucer exhibited in 1936), seemed less relevant. New directions were sought out in new locations.

After World War II sculpture in Europe began to share many of the formal reworkings of earlier developments exhibited by painting, and by 1960 more attention was directed toward the United States as a center for innovative work in three-dimensional media. The line between painting and sculpture, already often obscured by artists in prewar Europe, was further explored in the constructions and assemblage art movements of the 1960s. Pioneered by Robert Rauschenberg in the 1950s with such pieces as *Odalisk* (1955) and *Bed* (1955), these works brought together a chaotic jumble of found objects, detritus, taxidermic trophies, collage elements, and traditional media in an effort to reanimate forms through unlikely juxtapositions. Forcing her found objects to conform to a more rigorous abstract conception, Louise Nevelson signaled a new approach to traditional Modernist formal concerns with such works as *Black Chord* (1964).

The next postwar Modernist trend came from, among others, Mathias Goeritz, a German living in Mexico, whose monumental nonobjective works in welded steel began a movement of sorts, known sometimes as primary structure. Ronald Bladen's *The X* (steel, 1967), a massive crossing of metal beams standing nearly 7.6 meters in height, represented this perspective on proto-Minimalist formalism at its literal, if perhaps not its artistic, height. The Minimalist movement in painting that developed in the same period was paralleled, and possibly better realized, in the work of the Minimalist sculptors working in the United States between 1960 and 1990. Most notable among these were David Smith, who launched during these years a series of primary structures in brushed stainless steel known as *Cubi*; Donald Judd, who refined the surfaces of his extremely Minimalist, cube-based forms and added a sleek somewhat decorative aesthetic to the process; and Richard Serra, the creator of numerous monumental leaning walls of cold-rolled steel or iron, which enjoyed the distinction of frequent protests against their ominous presence in public spaces. Another body of work with a radically different formal aesthetic, in the form of oversized objects from everyday postwar commercial life, brought the Pop artist

Claes Oldenburg to the public's attention. His enormous plastic *Giant Hamburger* (1962) in vivid synthetic colors or the awkwardly mobile *Ice Bag* (1970)—measuring some 4.6 by 5.5 by 5.5 meters—were elemental icons of contemporary life executed on a scale that made them impossible to ignore. And the Japanese-American sculptor Isamu Noguchi meanwhile worked in both small and monumental scale to create a synthesis of organic abstraction and Minimalism that proved especially popular in later 20th-century public and corporate architectural and urban environments.

Performance art, by its very nature an act in real space and time, must be considered in any discussion of Modernist trends in sculpture. Josef Beuys's *Coyote* (1974), for example, consisted of a week-long exhibition of himself, a coyote, and several square yards of felt sharing a New York gallery space. Installation art inevitably took on a three-dimensional form; such pieces as Edward Kienholz's *The State Hospital* (1966) and earlier examples of George Segal's life-size plaster-figure casts were efforts at making sculpture a more immediate experience for the spectator. The kinetic art movement, for which Jean Tinguely's deliberately disastrous mechanical monstrosity *Homage to New York* (1960) was a kind of humorously anarchic prototype, settled down and found places in corporate and public spaces throughout the United States. The later large-scale projects of Calder and George Rickey's mobile monuments in stainless steel were particularly common choices for public commissions.

The manipulation of the natural environment for formal and expressive purposes attracted many sculptors in a movement known as Earth art (also as Land art or Earthworks). Primary exponents of this trend include Robert Smithson, whose *Spiral Jetty* (1970) was an early, large-scale work in earth transformation. The east European émigré Christo (Christo Javacheff), perhaps the most celebrated of contemporary conceptual artists, has established his career on a series of wrapped monuments and objects that have frequently drawn attention to the artist and his publicized legal struggles to realize his visions.

It may be seen as ironic that even Conceptual art found an expressive outlet in sculpture during the late phases of the Modernist era. Joseph Kosuth's *One and Three Chairs* (1965) is representative of this paradox. The breakdown of theoretical and formal boundaries between the many informal schools of late-20th-century Modernism in sculpture led to a vulnerability of their one remaining shared premise: the principle that art must be valued mainly for its novelty. During the last three decades of the century, these disparate and sometimes very brief trends and movements in sculpture succeeded each other at a bewildering pace, lead-

ing ultimately to a temporary defeat of the tyranny of the new by so-called Postmodernist artists, architects, designers, and critics.

ANDREW MARVICK

See also **Archipenko, Alexander Porfirevich; Art Deco; Assemblage; Barye, Antoine-Louis; Bellmer, Hans; Beuys, Joseph; Boccioni, Umberto; Bourdelle, Emile-Antoine; Brancusi, Constantin; Calder, Alexander; Canova, Antonio; Carpeaux, Jean-Baptiste; Christo and Jeanne-Claude; Claudel, Camille; Constructivism; Dalí, Salvador; Despiau, Charles; Duchamp, Marcel; Ernst, Max; Gabo, Naum; Gaudier-Brzeska, Henri; Giacometti, Alberto; González, Julio; Hepworth, Dame Barbara; Hoffman, Malvina; Judd, Donald; Kienholz, Edward and Nancy Reddin; Lachaise, Gaston; Lipchitz, Jacques; Maillol, Aristide; Manship, Paul; Moholy-Nagy, László; Moore, Henry; Nevelson, Louise; Noguchi, Isamu; Oldenburg, Claes; Oppenheim, Meret; Performance Art; Picasso, Pablo; Postmodernism; Powers, Hiram; Schwitters, Kurt; Segal, George; Serra, Richard; Smith, David; Smithson, Robert; Tatlin, Vladimir; Thorvaldsen, Bertel; Tinguely, Jean**

Further Reading

Beardsley, John, *Earthworks and Beyond: Contemporary Art in the Landscape*, New York: Abbeville Press, 1984; 3rd edition, 1998

Causey, Andrew, *Sculpture since 1945*, Oxford and New York: Oxford University Press, 1998

Curtis, Penelope, *Sculpture, 1900–1945: After Rodin*, Oxford and New York: Oxford University Press, 1999

Elsen, Albert Edward, *Origins of Modern Sculpture*, New York: Braziller, and London: Phaidon Press, 1974

Janson, H.W., *Nineteenth-Century Sculpture*, edited by Phyllis Freeman, New York: Abrams, and London: Thames and Hudson, 1985

Read, Herbert Edward, *A Concise History of Modern Sculpture*, New York: Praeger, and London: Thames and Hudson, 1964; as *Modern Sculpture: A Concise History*, London: Thames and Hudson, 1987

Tucker, William, *Early Modern Sculpture*, New York: Oxford University Press, 1974; as *The Language of Sculpture*, London: Thames and Hudson, 1974

LÁSZLÓ MOHOLY-NAGY 1895–1946

Hungarian-American

The diverse production of the Hungarian-American artist László Moholy-Nagy is not easily classifiable. His search for a radically modern means of expression paid no regard to traditional divisions between the arts, and he was active as a painter, sculptor, photographer, designer, theorist, and educator. As an alternative to older ways of seeing and creating, Moholy-Nagy proposed a dynamic new vision that would put the artist in accord with the potential of the machine. In 1922 he stated: "The reality of our century is technology: the invention, construction and maintenance of machines. To be a user of technology is to be of the spirit of this century. It has replaced the transcendental spiritualism of past eras." Influenced by Marxist and Constructivist theories, Moholy-Nagy felt bound by the zeitgeist to work in the spirit of the engineer, applying new materials and new technologies (notably metals, plastics, motors, and artificial illumination) to productive ends. In this sense, the artist was no longer engaged in an isolated or introspective aesthetic quest but was to work actively to improve life through functional research.

During convalescence from injuries sustained during military service, Moholy-Nagy began to create Expressionist drawings and watercolors. But his true intellectual formation came after 1919, when he left Hungary for Vienna and Berlin. Here he mixed in Dadaist, Futurist, and Constructivist circles, met El Lissitzky, and abandoned figuration. His paintings became arrangements of abstract rectilinear forms, and he started to make constructions in wood and metal, their austere geometries expressing his fascination with the precise forms of machinery. In 1922 Moholy-Nagy produced a series of three paintings, titled *Em 1*, *Em 2*, and *Em 3*, each of different size. These were manufactured in enamel on steel in a factory, in accordance with the graph-paper blueprints that he supplied. The exactitude and anonymity of this process led him to speculate that such works could be ordered over the telephone. After thus demonstrating the possibility of unprecedentedly mechanized and depersonalized methods of creation, Moholy-Nagy began to predict the complete dematerialization of art into a play of pure light in the form of mixed-media spectacles.

In spring 1923, Moholy-Nagy was invited by Walter Gropius to teach at the Bauhaus, where he was put in charge of the metal fabrication workshop. Here he oversaw the production of prototypes for mass production, including a series of innovative lighting fixtures. With Josef Albers, he also took over the six-month *Vorkurs* (preliminary design course) required of all incoming students, shifting the curriculum from the mystical and Expressionist ideals of his predecessor Johannes Itten toward more practical studies, stressing such elemental issues as space, form, balance, and structure, as well as the intrinsic nature of materials.

Moholy-Nagy's preoccupation with light, movement, abstraction, and industrial production all played a part in the creation of the device known as the *Light Prop*, later termed the *Light-Space Modulator*. He had envisioned such an apparatus as early as 1922, but it was finally constructed in 1929–30 for the Deutscher Werkbund exhibition in Paris. At first glance, the work

is ambiguous: simultaneously a sculpture and machine, the *Light-Space Modulator* is an assemblage of metal, glass, wood, and plastic parts that rest upon a motorized base. At its center, held inside an open steel armature, is a large, perforated metal disk, surrounded by a screen of vertical rods, angled sheets of mesh, and other asymmetrical appendages. Its purpose was to throw complex, shifting patterns of light and shadow onto surrounding walls—a process Moholy-Nagy called "painting with light." Originally planning to synchronize its actions with a musical score, he recorded its effects in a film titled *Light Play: Black-White-Gray* (1930).

It is thus unclear whether the *Light-Space Modulator* was intended as a source of sculptural interest in itself or whether it was simply a functional prop—presaging more ambitious manifestations in which moving shapes and patterns would be projected onto buildings or clouds. Although critics like A.M. Hammacher have advanced the opinion that the productions of Moholy-Nagy "do not possess the convincing power that characterizes true works of art," perhaps the greatest innovation of the *Light-Space Modulator* was in demonstrating that sculpture could be open, transparent, and active. As Moholy-Nagy wrote: "This urge of mine to supersede pigment with light has its counterpart in a drive to dissolve solid volume into defined space. When I think of sculpture, I cannot think of static mass. Emotionally, sculpture and movement are interdependent."

After leaving the Bauhaus in 1928, Moholy-Nagy worked in Berlin, Amsterdam, and London, where he supported himself by doing commercial photography, documentary films, and set design. In 1936 he began to produce what he called "space modulators," using flat or curved planes of transparent Rhodoid plastic. These were again meant to be seen in the context of

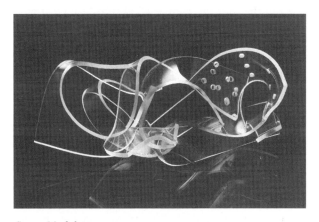

Space Modulator
Gift of W. Hawkins Ferry

projected light, casting patterns and colors on the white-painted boards to which they were attached. Feeling these were too static, Moholy-Nagy discontinued their production after 1944. At the invitation of Gropius, he emigrated to Chicago in 1937 and began making sculptures in sheets of twisted Plexiglas (such as *Leda and the Swan*). These manifest a new lyricism in their titles and in their Baroque interplay of voluptuous curves. After 1943 he added chromium steel rods to his compositions: *Double Form with Chromium Rods (Wire Curve)*, in which looping rods pierce two pieces of rounded Plexiglas, was meant to be suspended and mobile, producing changing effects of light and virtual volume.

Moholy-Nagy's work evinces the optimism of the early machine age, when technology seemed to be opening up new ways of seeing and being in the world. Yet his tireless promotion of abstraction was later influential in defining a mainstream of modern art and design in the postwar era. He was the forerunner of the kinetic sculpture of the 1960s and has been cited as a pioneer of minimal, conceptual, and even deconstructive tendencies in art (see Kaplan, 1995). To Postmodernists, his unmitigated technolatry may now seem misguided, and many will still be put off by the cool, impersonal, and mechanistic qualities of his work. Moholy-Nagy's methods and motivations were nevertheless materialistic and realistic rather than antihumanistic, for his ultimate goal was always social improvement.

CHRISTOPHER PEARSON

See also **Assemblage; Constructivism; Gabo, Naum; Modernism; Postmodernism; Tatlin, Vladimir Yevgrafovich**

Biography

Born in Bácsborsod, Hungary, 20 July 1895. Cofounder and Berlin representative of the avant-garde art group MA (Today), 1917; mixed in Dadaist, Futurist, and Constructivist circles; exhibited at Sturm Gallery, Berlin, 1922; taught at the Bauhaus (Weimar and Dessau), 1923–28, and experimented with photograms; directed metal workshop and foundation course; oversaw production of Bauhausbücher series; set up a practice in Berlin doing stage and exhibition design, typography, photography, advertising, and film, 1929–34; fled from Nazi regime to Amsterdam, 1934, and became director of a new periodical, *International Textiles*; moved to London and did first commercial film documentary, *Lobsters*, 1935–37; did commercial photography, documentary films, and special effects for Alexander Korda's film *Things to Come*, 1936; immigrated to America, 1937; founded the New Bauhaus in Chicago, 1937–38; started the School of Design, 1939 (later renamed the Institute of Design in 1944); director of American Designers Institute, 1943. Died in Chicago, Illinois, United States, 24 November 1946.

Selected Works

1921   *Nickel Construction*; nickel-plated iron; Museum of Modern Art, New York City, United States

1929–30 *Light-Space Modulator (Light Prop)*; motor, steel, plastic, wood; Busch-Reisinger Museum, Harvard University, Cambridge, Massachusetts, United States; replicas: 1970, Stedelijk Van Abbe Museum, Eindhoven, the Netherlands; Bauhaus Archive, Berlin, Germany

1936   *Space Modulator L3*; oil on perforated zinc and composition board, glass-headed pins; Museum of Modern Art, New York City, United States

1942   *Untitled (Space Modulator)*; oil on plastic; Museum of Modern Art, New York City, United States

1945–46 *Spiral* (replica); Plexiglas; Collection Hattula Moholy-Nagy, Ann Arbor, Michigan, United States

1946   *Space Modulator*; plastic, bent, scored, drilled; Detroit Institute of Arts, Detroit, Michigan, United States

1946   *Double Form with Chromium Rods (Wire Curve)*; Plexiglas, chromium-plated rods; Solomon R. Guggenheim Museum, New York City, United States

1946   *Leda and the Swan*; Plexiglas; Guggenheim Museum, New York City, United States; Instituto Valenciano de Arte Moderno, Julio Gonzalez Centre, Valencia, Spain

1946   *Twisted Planes*; Plexiglas, steel rods; Addison Gallery of American Art, Phillips Academy, Andover, Maine, United States

Further Reading

Caton, Joseph Harris, *The Utopian Vision of Moholy-Nagy*, Ann Arbor, Michigan: UMI Research Press, 1984

David, Catherine, editor, *László Moholy-Nagy* (exhib. cat.), Marseille: Musées de Marseille, 1991

Kaplan, Louis, *László Moholy-Nagy: Biographical Writings*, Durham, North Carolina: Duke University Press, 1995

Mansbach, Steven A., *Visions of Totality: Laszlo Moholy-Nagy, Theo Van Doesburg, and El Lissitzky*, Ann Arbor, Michigan: UMI Research Press, 1980

Margolin, Victor, *The Struggle for Utopia: Rodchencko, Lissitzky, Moholy-Nagy, 1917–1946*, Chicago: University of Chicago Press, 1997

Moholy, Lucia, *Marginalien zu Moholy-Nagy; Moholy-Nagy, Marginal Notes* (bilingual German-English edition), Krefeld, Germany: Scherpe, 1972

Moholy-Nagy, László, *Von Material zu Architektur*, Munich: Langen, 1929; as *The New Vision, from Material to Architecture*, translated by Daphne M. Hoffmann, New York: Brewer Warren and Putnam, 1932; 4th revised edition, New York: Wittenborn, 1946

Moholy-Nagy, László, *Vision in Motion*, Chicago: Theobald, 1947

Moholy-Nagy, László, *Moholy-Nagy*, compiled by Richard Kostelanetz, New York: Praeger, and London: Allen Lane, 1970

Moholy-Nagy, Sibyl, *Moholy-Nagy: Experiment in Totality*, New York: Harper, 1950; 2nd edition, Cambridge, Massachusetts: MIT Press, 1969

Passuth, Krisztina, *Moholy-Nagy*, Budapest: Corvina, 1982; as *Moholy-Nagy*, London and New York: Thames and Hudson, 1985

Senter, Terence A., "László Moholy-Nagy," in *The Dictionary of Art*, edited by Jane Turner, New York: Grove, and London: Macmillan, 1996

Suhre, Terry, *Moholy-Nagy: A New Vision for Chicago*, Springfield: University of Illinois Press, and Illinois State Museum, 1990

Weitemeier, Hannah, Wulf Herzogenrath, and Tilman Osterworld, *László Moholy-Nagy*, Stuttgart, Germany: Hatje, 1974

PIERRE-ÉTIENNE MONNOT 1657–1733

Franco-Roman

Pierre-Étienne (more commonly known as Pietro Stefano) Monnot was one of the leading sculptors in Rome bridging the 17th and 18th centuries. His work, highly admired by contemporaries, is emblematic of the transitional period of the late Baroque and is difficult to define stylistically. Careful study of his oeuvre reveals that Monnot was quite capable of adjusting the manner of his designs and carving to suit the purpose and requirements of a given commission or patron. For example, his public religious works, such as the tomb of Pope Innocent XI, are more traditional, declamatory, and classicizing in a post-Berninesque style, whereas his private religious reliefs, such as the *Holy Family with the Infant St. John the Baptist* (before 1733; Staatliche Museen, Berlin), convey a new, intimate, even sentimental mood and display softer modeling of the figures and drapery. In a similar manner, his portrait busts of aristocrats could follow the well-established form with a windswept *allonge* (long and curly) wig and contemporary armor, such as Landgrave Carl of Hesse-Kassel, or they could be more avant-garde, with a strictly Classical short hairstyle over a Roman cuirass, such as in the tomb of John Cecil, Fifth Earl of Exeter. Monnot employed this stylistic flexibility while maintaining an extraordinarily high level of quality in the carving and treatment of the marble.

These diverse sculptures reflect a number of influences that Monnot absorbed and adapted over the years

of his training. He received his first instruction in Besançon in the workshop of his father, the woodcarver Étienne Monnot, and studied under the foremost Baroque sculptor of Dijon, Jean Dubois, in 1676. Before moving permanently to Rome in 1687, Monnot must have visited Paris and may have even assisted one of the royal sculptors decorating Versailles. Although there is no documentary proof for such a sojourn, Monnot's later figures contain direct references to contemporary works by Pierre Puget and Antoine Coysevox and show the general stylistic influence of François Girardon. It is still unclear why Monnot never became a student at the Royal Academy in Paris and how he financed his travel and eventual emigration to Rome, ostensibly on his own.

His beginnings there are equally murky; his arrival in 1687 is documented, but his earliest figures are dated only 1692. Although not formally associated with the Royal French Academy in Rome, Monnot worked there at times and was well acquainted with its most talented young sculptors, Jean Théodon and Pierre Legros the Younger. In addition to the required study of antiquities, Monnot's Roman sculptures reflect the deep impact of the late Gianlorenzo Bernini and of Domenico Guidi, with whom he collaborated on at least one commission, the Capocaccia Chapel in the Church of Santa Maria della Vittoria. Several smaller works dated 1693 were made for Prince Livio Odescalchi, nephew of Pope Innocent XI and Monnot's most faithful Roman patron. In 1697 Monnot received widespread recognition for the *Two Angels Holding IHS-Monogram* he carved for the altar of the Chapel of St. Ignatius, Church of Gesù. Having competed successfully with the best in Rome, he subsequently received a steady stream of public and private commissions. Most notable among his Roman works are the tomb (1697–1701) of Pope Innocent XI, for Odescalchi in St. Peter's Basilica, and the *St. Peter* (1711) and *St. Paul* (1708) in the Lateran basilica. Both of these important public commissions were made after drawings by or in collaboration with the painter-designer Carlo Maratta, whereas Monnot's major independent works were executed for foreign patrons.

Perhaps unwilling to submit to the typically collaborative and committee-run sculptural projects in Rome, in 1699 Monnot managed to secure an important commission from John Cecil, who visited Italy repeatedly and was known as an avid collector. Monnot carved a large sepulchral monument for the earl of Exeter and his wife, the Countess Anne, with the couple recumbent before a towering pyramid, which he completed by 1704 in Rome and shipped to Exeter's heirs in England. The tomb and two portrait busts of the Earl and his wife are early examples of a more detailed classicism and were extremely influential for artists working in England, such as Michael Rysbrack, Peter Schee-makers, Henry Cheere, and James Gibbs. For the family seat at Burghley House, Monnot also provided a mythological fountain ensemble with a life-size *Andromeda and the Sea-Monster* as its centerpiece, the attribution of which, however, has been called into question.

After the death in 1713 of his supporter Odescalchi, Monnot actively sought princely patronage elsewhere in Europe and found it in Landgrave Carl of Hesse-Kassel. For him Monnot produced his final masterpiece, the so-called *Marmorbad*, or *Marble Bath*, an exceptional garden folly of lavish proportions and materials. Between 1714 and 1728 in a pavilion adjacent to Carl's summer residence, Schloss Orangerie, Monnot covered the walls with pastel-colored marbles and eight figurative reliefs representing scenes from Ovid's *Metamorphoses*. Around the walls and central octagonal basin, Monnot placed 12 large mythological sculpture groups that bear dates between 1692 and 1716, spanning his entire career and illustrating his evolution from a talented Baroque carver to a proto-Rococo master. Surrounded by allegorical references, portrait medallions of Landgrave Carl and his wife adorn two chimneypieces; reliefs of the *Seasons* and *Elements* decorate the ceiling. Both pantheon and panegyric, unique in its size and scope, the Marmorbad represents a stunning achievement for the mature sculptor, who subsequently returned to Rome and his family for the final years of his life.

Monnot's surviving tombs, portraits, religious and mythological statues, and small- and large-scale reliefs in marble, wood, terracotta, and wax represent an astonishing variety of sculptures of highest artistic quality in different materials. His autograph works are often easy to identify because he signed and dated them so frequently. His first biographer and friend, Lione Pascoli, recounts Monnot's enormous productivity and mentions his busy workshop, although few names can be directly associated with it. Because of his long absence in Germany late in his career, Monnot did not have any close followers in Rome. His unusual background and international clientele led to Monnot's relative obscurity among modern scholars. More recently, art historians have recognized that Monnot's stylistic flexibility and imaginative use of Classical models made him a trendsetter in the increasingly international world of European sculpture at the beginning of the 18th century.

STEFANIE WALKER

See also **Bernini, Gianlorenzo; Coysevox, Antoine; Girardon, François; Legros II, Pierre; Puget, Pierre**

Biography

Born in Orchamps-Vennes, France, 9 August 1657. Son of Étienne, a woodcarver in Besançon; younger brother Pierre-Josephe later his assistant. Studied in Dijon under Jean Dubois, 1676; returned to Besançon family workshop; moved permanently to Rome, 1687; collaborative commissions with the painter Maratti and the sculptors Guidi, Le Gros the Younger, and Rusconi, among others; Roman and foreign patrons included Prince Livio Odescalchi, Cardinal Savo Mellini, Luca Capocaccia, John Cecil, Fifth Earl of Exeter, and Landgrave Carl of Hesse-Kassel; member of the *Virtuosi del Pantheon* from 1695; worked in Kassel, Germany, 1714–28; returned to Rome, 1728. Died in Rome, Italy, 24 August 1733.

Selected Works

1686	*Scenes from Christ's Passion*; oak; Town Hall, Poligny, France
1695–97	*Adoration of the Shepherds* and *Flight into Egypt*; marble; Capocaccia Chapel, Church of Santa Maria della Vittoria, Rome, Italy
1697	*Two Angels Holding IHS-Monogram*; marble; high altar, Chapel of St. Ignatius, Church of the Gesù, Rome, Italy
1697–1701	Tomb of Pope Innocent XI; marble, bronze; St. Peter's Basilica, Rome, Italy
1698–99	Bust of Cardinal Savo; marble; Mellini Chapel, Church of Santa Maria del Popolo, Rome, Italy
1699–1704	*Andromeda and the Sea-Monster*; marble; Metropolitan Museum of Art, New York, United States
1699–1704	Narcissus and Phineus fountains; marble; Burghley House, Lincolnshire, England
1699–1704	Tomb of John Cecil, the Fifth Earl of Exeter, and his wife, Anna Cavendish, the countess of Exeter; marble; St. Martin's Church, Stamford, England
1714	Bust of Landgrave Carl of Hesse-Kassel; marble; Hessisches Landesmuseum, Kassel, Germany
1714–28	*Marmorbad*, including statue groups of *Leda and the Swan* (1692), *Bacchus* (1692), *Mercury and Cupid* (1698), *Apollo and Marsyas* (1698), *Venus and Cupid* (1708), *Narcissus* (1712), *Latona and Her Children* (1712), *Faun with a Lamb* (1716), *Bacchante* (1716), *Paris* (1720), *Aurora* (before 1733), *Minerva as Protector of the Arts* (before 1733), and

eight reliefs (1728) after Ovid's *Metamorphoses*; marble; Schloss Orangerie, Kassel, Germany

Further Reading

Bacchi, Andrea, "L'Andromeda di Lord Exeter," *Antologia di belle arti* 48–51 (1994)

Beaulieu, Michèle, "Quelques oeuvres romaines inédites du sculpteur Pierre Étienne Monnot conservées en France," *Bulletin de la Société de l'histoire de l'art français* (1962)

Burk, Jens Ludwig, "Pierre Étienne Monnot und die Entstehung des Kasseler Marmorbades—Neue Archivfunde," *Marburger Jahrbuch für Kunstwissenschaft* 25 (1998)

Dotal, Christiane, *Pierre-Etienne Monnot (1657–1733): L'itinéraire d'un sculpteur franc-comtois de Rome à Cassel au XVIIIe siécle*, Lons-le-Saunier, France: Musée des Beaux-Arts, 2001

Enggass, Robert, *Early Eighteenth-Century Sculpture in Rome: An Illustrated Catalogue Raisonné*, University Park: Pennsylvania State University Press, 1976

Fusco, Peter, "Pierre-Étienne Monnot's Inventory," *Antologia di Belle Arti* 33–34 (1988)

Honour, Hugh, "English Patrons and Italian Sculptors in the First Half of the Eighteenth Century," *Connoisseur* 141 (1958)

Raggio, Olga, "Sculpture in the Grand Manner: Two Groups by Anguier and Monnot," *Apollo* 106 (1977)

Schlegel, Ursula, "Bozzetti in Terracotta by Pietro Stefano Monnot," *Boston Museum of Fine Arts Bulletin* 72/367 (1974)

Schlegel, Ursula, *Die italienischen Bildwerke des 17. und 18. Jahrhunderts in Stein, Holz, Ton, Wachs, und Bronze mit Ausnahme der Plaketten und Medaillen*, Berlin: Mann, 1978

Walker, Stefanie, "The Sculptor Pietro Stefano Monnot in Rome, 1695–1713," Ph.D. diss., New York University, 1994

JUAN MARTÍNEZ MONTAÑÉS 1568–1649 *Spanish*

Juan Martínez Montañés, the greatest Spanish sculptor of the 17th century, was known to his contemporaries as the *Dios de la Madera* (God of Wood Carving). During his career he produced tabernacles, retables, and processional images with the idealized qualities of the Renaissance and the realism of the Baroque periods. His sculpture is known for its spirituality, which expressed the theology of the Counter Reformation. Montañés ran a large workshop in Seville and employed other artists to paint his sculptures.

In his early career, Montañés received numerous sculptural commissions. In 1597 he carved *St. Christopher* for the glover's guild in the Church of El Salvador in Seville. As a processional sculpture, the work had to provoke emotion in public. Therefore, it was made dramatic through its larger than life-size scale, imposing character, and glossy oil finish that glowed in the sunlight or candlelight. The Christ Child holds the orb symbolizing his role as *Salvador Mundi*, or Savior of the World. On 2 March 1598, two more processional sculptures were ordered for the churches of Nuestra Señora de la Encarnación and St. Michael. A catafalque, a temporary funerary structure designed to support a coffin, was built for Philip II. Montañés made several sculptures for the structure, including *Sevilla* and *Loyalty*, which were placed under the arches. His first recorded commission for a complete retable was for the Convent of La Limpia Concepción, Panama, in 1598. Many royal commissions for tabernacles and retables for the New World followed.

By the beginning of the 17th century, Montañés was an established master, and he received numerous commissions. Montañés sculpted *Christ of Clemency* for the Cathedral of Seville, which was later given to the Monastery of Santa María de la Cuevas. *Christ of Clemency* is based on the formula set forth by Francisco Pacheco, who was the inspector of paintings for the Inquisition in Seville. According to Pacheco, Christ should be in a standing position, as it would eliminate the curve of the body, which he thought lessened the dignity of the image. Pacheco suggested that artists should depict the feet crossed and use a total of four nails—one in each hand and one in each foot. In addition, the contract stipulated that the Christ figure should be alive with his eyes open and glancing downward on the faithful.

In 1604 Montañés sculpted a retable dedicated to St. John the Evangelist for the nuns of the Convent of La Limpia Concepción for the parish of San Juan, Seville, which included six sculptures in middle relief with God the Father in the pediment and Virtues at the summit. Also in 1604 Montañés sculpted the main retable for the Convent of Santa Clara at Cazalla de la Sierra with *St. Clara* in high relief, *Virgin*, and *God the Father*. The following year, *St. Joseph and the Christ Child* was ordered by the guild of ship carpenters for their confraternity dedicated to the saint in the Monastery of Nuestra Señora de la Victoria in Triana.

From 1606 to 1608, Montañés sculpted a two-story retable for the chapel in the Church of Nuestra Señora de Consolación in El Pedroso. He carved the Immaculate Conception for the center niche of the retable. The Virgin Mary is shown with her hands in prayer and the moon at her feet. She was flanked by sculptures in half relief of *St. James the Great* and *St. Bartholomew*, and paintings occupy the upper story.

In 1609 Montañés sculpted the retable for the Church of San Ildefonso in Seville. The *Two Trinities* is the only surviving image from the retable. This new iconographic type represents the earthly Trinity of Joseph, Mary, and Christ and the heavenly Trinity of the Holy Spirit, God the Father, and Christ.

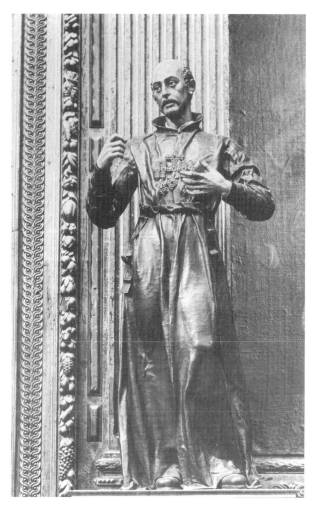

St. Ignatius Loyola
© Foto Marburg / Art Resource, NY

From 1609 to 1613, Montañés completed the main retable for the Jeronymite Convent of San Isidoro del Campo at Santiponce. St. Jerome is depicted in the round as a penitent saint with protruding veins, and the severe expression emphasizes the pain of mortification of the flesh. His features were probably exaggerated to inspire the public—the sculpture was meant to be taken out of the retable and carried in a procession. St. Isidore is represented on the second story; he was a Sevillian saint, and he completed the biographies of famous men that had been started by St. Jerome. St. John the Baptist and St. John the Evangelist flank the altar on either side. The Assumption of the Virgin and the four Cardinal Virtues are located at the top of the retable. On the sides are reliefs of the Adoration of the Shepherds, Adoration of the Magi, Resurrection, and Ascension. Angels were placed throughout the retable and a Crucifixion crowns it. Montañés also carved statues of Alonso Pérez de Guzmán, el Bueno, and María Alfonso Coronel kneeling in prayer for the monastery.

On 20 January 1610 Montañés was contracted to execute a small retable of St. John the Baptist for the Church of the Annunciation in Seville; it was later transferred to the Convent of Santa María del Socorro in Seville. The central image of the Baptism of Jesus has figures that project more than others in order to draw the attention of the viewer to the retable. It also has reliefs of the Nativity of St. John and the Visitation, as well as reliefs depicting St. John Taking Leave of His Parents, St. John Preaching, St. John in Prison, the Young Saint in the Wilderness, St. John Reproving Herod, and the Beheading of St. John.

Montañés sculpted *St. Ignatius Loyola* in 1610 and *St. Francis Borgia* in 1624 for the University Chapel of the University of Seville. The sculpture of Loyola commemorated his beatification. Similarly Montañés sculpted St. Francis Borgia to honor his beatification in 1624. These saints were depicted realistically and with intense spirituality. Borgia's lips are pressed together, and his hollow cheeks and protruding veins at the temples express his intense devotion.

In 1612 Montañés was contracted for the retable for the Franciscan Monastery of Nuestra Señora de Gracia at Villamanrique de la Condesa by Marchioness Beatriz de Zúñiga y Velasco. This retable included figures and scenes of St. John the Baptist and St. John the Evangelist, the Annunciation, St. Louis of France, St. Anthony of Padua, and St. Diego of Alcalà. Reliquary busts were placed above but have since disappeared. Montañés made an addition to the retable when the chapel was enlarged.

Montañés sculpted *Jesús de la Pasión* (Jesus of the Passion) for the penitential confraternity of La Pasión in the Church of the Divino Salvador in Seville. Penitential confraternities were dedicated to certain aspects of the Passion and staged public processions for Holy Week. Montañés heightened the realism in the sculpture in order to inspire devotion in the spectators. Christ is portrayed wearing the crown of thorns with blood dripping down his face as he bears the weight of the cross he carries. The figure was constructed with movable arms so that the confraternity could change his position.

From 1621 to 1622, Montañés worked on the retable of St. John the Baptist for the chapel in the convent of the Augustinian nuns of San Leandro, which was ordered by Juan Peñate de Narváez. On the first level was a relief of St. John the Baptist flanked by the Virgin Mary and St. Joseph. St. John the Baptist is set in the wilderness with his attribute of the lamb in a cloud and *Ecce Agnus Dei* (Behold the Lamb of God) written on a banderole in the upper right. *The Head of St. John the Baptist on a Platter* is placed between the two levels. A relief of the Baptism of Jesus flanked by St. Elizabeth and St. Zachariah occupies the second level. The individual figures gesture beyond their niches to interact with the faithful.

From 1621 to 1624 Montañés sculpted scenes from the life of the titular saint for the main retable for the Franciscan Convent of Santa Clara in Seville. Figures of the Virgin and child are flanked by those of St. Anthony of Padua and St. Bonaventure. Reliefs of *St. Francis Giving Her Habit to the Order* and *St. Clara Blessing the Bread* are on the sides of the retable. In the center, St. Clara holds the pyx containing the host, and she is flanked by figures of St. Agnes and St. Mary Magdalene and scenes of the Annunciation and Nativity. The Trinity and angels are located in the summit of the retable. A relief titled *St. Clara and Her Nuns* was removed in 1722. Montañés also executed retable-tabernacles of the Immaculate Conception, St. John the Baptist, St. John the Evangelist, and St. Francis of Assisi for the convent.

By the 1630s Montañés had entered the last phase of his career. From 1632 to 1633 he sculpted the retable of St. John the Evangelist as a companion to the retable of St. John the Baptist for the Convent of San Leandro in Seville. St. John the Evangelist is depicted writing his scripture in the center on the first level. *St. John the Evangelist in the Cauldron* is located between the stories, and the *Virgin and Child* occupies the summit. Four saints are depicted: St. Mariá Cleofás, St. Maria Salomé, St. James the Less, and St. James the Greater. These figures express a stronger emotion and are more coarsely carved than those in the retable of St. John the Baptist. In 1634 Montañés sculpted *St. Bruno*, patron saint of the Carthusian order, for the Charterhouse of Las Cuevas, Seville. In 1635 he was then called to court to assist with a bronze equestrian statue of Philip IV, now in the Plaza de Oriente at Madrid. Florentine Pietro Tacca was assigned to execute the statue, and Montañés made a model of the king's head. Diego Velázquez painted a portrait of Montañés working on the sculpture.

Montañés had a tremendous influence on sculpture and painting that lasted into the 18th century. He was extremely prolific, and many of his sculptures have survived. His student Juan de Mesa worked in Montañés's style for his entire career, and his follower Alonso Cano was also influenced by his work.

JENNIFER OLSON-RUDENKO

See also **Cano, Alonso; Mesa, Juan de; Spain: Renaissance and Baroque**

Biography

Born in Alcalà la Real (Jaén), Spain, before 16 March 1568. Apprenticed to sculptor in Granada; obtained license to practice sculpture, 1 December 1588; studied work of Pietro Torrigiani, Juan Bautista Vázquez, Jerónimo Hernández, and Gaspar Núñez Delgado; accused of killing Luis Sánchez and imprisoned, 1591; pardoned after paying fee, 1593; became member of Cofradiá del Dulce Nombre de Jesús, 1592; commissioned by Philip II and III to make tabernacles and retables for the New World; often handed commissions over to other sculptors. Died in Seville, Spain, 18 June 1649.

Selected Works

1597–98 *St. Christopher*; polychromed wood; Church of El Salvador, Seville, Spain

1598 Retable; polychromed wood; Convent of La Limpia Concepción, Panama

1603–06 *Christ of Clemency*; polychromed wood; Cathedral of Seville, Spain

1604 Main retable; polychromed wood; Convent of Santa Clara, Cazalla de la Sierra, Seville, Spain

1604 Retable of St. John the Evangelist; polychromed wood; Convent of La Limpia Concepción, Parish of San Juan, Seville, Spain

1605 *St. Joseph and the Christ Child*; polychromed wood; Monastery of Nuestra Señora de la Victoria, Triana, Spain

1606–08 Retable of the Immaculate Conception; polychromed wood; Church of Nuestra Señora de Consolación, El Pedroso, Seville, Spain

1609 Retable; polychromed wood; Church of San Ildefonso, Seville, Spain

1609–13 High altar; polychromed wood; Convent of San Isidoro del Campo at Santiponce, Seville, Spain

1610 *St. Ignatius Loyola*; polychromed wood; University Chapel, Seville, Spain

1610 Retable of St. John the Baptist; polychromed wood; Convent of Santa María del Socorro, Seville, Spain

ca. *Jesús de la Pasión* (Jesus of the Passion);
1610–19 polychromed wood; Church of El Salvador, Seville, Spain

1612 Retable; polychromed wood; Monastery of Nuestra Señora de Gracia, Villamanrique de la Condesa, Seville, Spain

1621–22 Retable of St. John the Baptist; polychromed wood; Convent of San Leandro, Seville, Spain

1621–24 Main retable, polychromed wood; Convent of Santa Clara, Cazalla de la Sierra, Seville, Spain

1624–25 *St. Francis Borgia*; polychromed wood; University Chapel, Seville, Spain

1632–33 Retable of St. John the Evangelist; polychromed wood; Convent of San Leandro, Seville

1634 *St. Bruno*, for Cartuja de las Cuevas, Seville, Spain; polychromed wood; Museo Provincial de Bellas Artes, Seville, Spain

Further Reading

Enggass, Robert, and Jonathan Brown, *Italy and Spain, 1600–1750*, Englewood Cliffs, New Jersey: Prentice Hall, 1970

Hernández Días, José, *Juan Martínez Montañés: 1568–1649*, Seville: Ediciones Guadalquivir, 1987

Palomino de Castro y Velasco, Antonio, *Las vidas de los pintores y estatuarios eminentes españoles*, London: Woodfall, 1744; as *Lives of the Eminent Spanish Painters and Sculptors*, translated by Nina Ayala Mallory, Cambridge and New York: Cambridge University Press, 1987

Proske, Beatrice Gilman, *Juan Martinez Montanés: A Commission for Santo Domingo*, Paris: Gazette des Beaux-Arts, and New York: Hispanic Society of America, 1960

Proske, Beatrice Gilman, *Juan Martínez Montanés: Sevillian Sculptor*, New York: Hispanic Society of America, 1967

RAFFAELLE MONTI 1818–1881 *Italian, active in England*

Raffaelle Monti was associated with the development of verismo sculpture in mid-19th-century Lombardy, but he worked for most of his life in England. He enjoyed great success in the 1840s and 1850s with his own brand of naturalism, characterized by virtuoso marble carving and the use of illusionistic effects; he was especially noted for the revival of the veiled figure. In his later career, he worked principally as a designer for silverware and the decorative arts.

Born at Iseo, near Lake Garda, Monti grew up in Milan, where his father, the sculptor Gaetano Matteo Monti, worked on public projects such as the Arco della Pace. At the Brera Academy Monti and his contemporaries, including Vincenzo Vela, Pietro Magni, and Giovanni Strazza—future leaders of the so-called School of Milan—were deeply influenced by the naturalism of the work of the Tuscan sculptor Lorenzo Bartolini, whose *Fiducia in Dio* was exhibited in Milan in 1837. Monti's own rejection of Neoclassicism was accompanied by an exploration of pictorial and decorative modes and an interest above all in the Baroque, an amalgam that distinguished his work from the more politically motivated realism of his contemporaries. Monti's early works were Classical in subject, including *Alexander and Bucephalus*, which won the gold medal at the Brera, and *Ajax Defending the Body of Patroclus*, which led to an invitation to Vienna. There, he worked for the imperial court, and in 1842 he com-

pleted, in collaboration with sculptor Ludwig Schaller, the pediment representing the *Apotheosis of Pannonia* for the National Museum, Budapest.

Monti returned to Milan in 1842 and in 1846 visited England, where the sixth duke of Devonshire purchased his figure of *A Veiled Vestal*. The sculptor's first recorded veiled statue, it employs the effect that was to bring Monti public success. The illusion created on the marble surface of form beneath transparent drapery derived from 18th-century Baroque sculpture, particularly the work of the Venetian Antonio Corradini. Monti's revival of the theme appealed to the Victorians' taste for novelty and ingenuity, and the work led to a number of imitations after it was shown at the Great Exhibition of 1851.

Monti returned to Italy and in 1848 assisted in the republican cause. As an officer in the Milanese National Guard, he took part in the insurrection of the Cinque Giornate against Austrian rule, but, after the defeat at Custozza, he returned to London, where he remained until his death. In the following years, he enjoyed great success in his adopted country. At the Great Exhibition of 1851, he showed nine works in marble—the largest contribution of any sculptor—that demonstrate in their variety of theme and treatment the eclectic nature of his production and his understanding of the different idioms of English taste in art. His subjects encompassed the Miltonic nude (*Eve after the Fall*), poetic romance (*Angelica and Medoro*), genre (*The Sister Anglers*), and Orientalism (*A Circassian Slave in the Market Place*), the latter another veiled subject. Monti's most impressive church monument is the tomb of Barbara, Lady de Mauley, a poignant effigy flanked by life-size kneeling angels in the meticulously worked style of Lombard funerary verismo.

The culmination of Monti's production of statuary on a grand scale was his involvement in the early 1850s with Joseph Paxton's Crystal Palace Company at Sydenham in London. At the exhibition site, transferred from Hyde Park, Monti produced a large array of figurative and decorative sculpture, including six colossal statues for the upper garden terrace, two figurative fountains in the north nave, and a full-scale polychrome reconstruction of the Parthenon frieze for the Greek court, as well as fountain and cascade figures and a variety of ornamental garden features. Few of these works survived the destruction of the Crystal Palace by fire in 1936 and the subsequent dispersals, but record photographs provide a glimpse of an output of remarkable inventiveness, combining historical and national styles on a monumental scale.

The vast scope of the Crystal Palace venture led to Monti's bankruptcy in 1854 and marked a change in the direction of his work toward more collaborative projects and increasingly to commissions for ornamen-

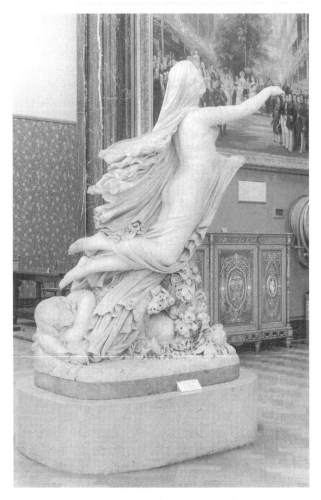

The Sleep of Sorrow and the Dream of Joy
© Victoria and Albert Museum, London. Photo courtesy The
Conway Library, Courtauld Institute of Art

tal sculpture on a small scale. He worked again with Paxton on the decoration of the great hall of the Rothschilds' country house, Mentmore, and executed the large relief featuring *Orpheus and Ossian* over the proscenium arch of the Royal Opera House, Covent Garden. From 1859 to 1861 Monti contributed a series of reviews of London art to the newly established French periodical, the *Gazette des Beaux-Arts*.

Monti's excursions into the field of the industrial arts, which began with his experiments with patented materials at the Crystal Palace, led to his involvement beginning in the late 1850s with Elkingtons, the Birmingham firm of metalworkers. The equestrian statue of Charles William Vane Stewart, third marquess of Londonderry, for the Durham marketplace, a rare civic monument by the sculptor, followed three years of experimentation with the electrotype process and was the largest statue to be cast by this technique. In the same period came the work with which Monti's name is most closely associated, *The Sleep of Sorrow and the*

Dream of Joy, a culmination of virtuoso carving skills and illusionism in marble and one of the sensations of the London International Exhibition of 1862. The group—an allegory of the Risorgimento—consists of a figure of *Sorrow* lying prostrate in a bed of roses while above her the veiled figure of *Joy* soars upward, seemingly weightless. The floating effect, achieved by masking the structure of the marble support with dexterous naturalistic carving, was another Baroque device, indebted to Gianlorenzo Bernini's *Apollo and Daphne* (1622–24). Monti also used the effect in the figures of *Night* and *Day* made in Parian ware. In the last 20 years of his life, Monti worked principally in the field of the applied arts, modeling figures for the company of Copeland Parian ware and designing many of the most impressive banqueting services and sporting trophies with which the silverware firm of C.F. Hancock is associated.

MARTIN GREENWOOD

See also **Bartolini, Lorenzo; Bernini, Gianlorenzo; Corradini, Antonio**

Biography

Born in Iseo (Ticino), Italy, 1818. Son of the sculptor Gaetano Matteo Monti (also known as Gaetano Monti da Ravenna). Studied with father and at Accademia di Belle Arti di Brera, Milan; pupil of Pompeo Marchesi; won gold medal at the Brera; worked in Vienna, *ca.* 1838–42; in Budapest, 1842; in Milan, 1842–46; visited England, 1846; returned to Milan and assisted in nationalist cause, 1848; took part in the uprising of the Cinque Giornate, March 1848, but after defeat at Custozza fled to England, where he remained until his death; exhibited at the Great Exhibition, London, 1851, and received a medal; exhibited six works at Royal Academy, 1853–60; executed statuary for the Crystal Palace Company, *ca.* 1852–55; contributed reviews of London art exhibitions to *Gazette des Beaux-Arts*, 1859–61; exhibited *The Sleep of Sorrow and the Dream of Joy* at London International Exhibition, 1862; employed principally as a designer of ornamental arts for Elkingtons, Copeland, and C.F. Hancock, 1860s and 1870s. Died in London, England, 16 October 1881.

Selected Works

ca.   *Alexander and Bucephalus*; plaster;
1836–38 Galleria d'Arte Moderna, Milan, Italy
ca. 1838 *Ajax Defending the Body of Patroclus*; material unknown (untraced)
1842   *Apotheosis of Pannonia* (with Ludwig Schaller); zinc; National Museum, Budapest, Hungary

ca. 1847 *A Veiled Vestal*; marble; Compton Place, Eastbourne, England

ca. 1849 Tomb of Barbara, Lady de Mauley; marble; St. Nicholas's Church, Hatherop, Gloucestershire, England

1850 *Eve after the Fall*, for Grittleton House, Wiltshire, England; marble; private collection

ca. Statuary and ornamental sculpture:
1852–55 colossal figures *South America, Italy, Spain, Holland*, and the *Zollverein*, a full-size polychrome reconstruction of the Parthenon frieze, *Eve* and *Veritas* for the sculpture court, and figures of Rivers and Oceans for the Crystal Palace, Sydenham, England; marble, stone, and other materials (mostly destroyed, some dispersed)

1858 *Orpheus and Ossian*; plaster; proscenium arch, Royal Opera House, Covent Garden, England

1861 Charles William Vane Stewart, Third Marquess of Londonderry; electroplated copper; Market Place, Durham, England

1861 *The Sleep of Sorrow and the Dream of Joy*; marble; Victoria and Albert Museum, London, England

1862 *The Poetry of Great Britain*; silver service; private collections

1870 *Nora Creina*; statuary porcelain (Parian ware); private collections

Further Reading

Atterbury, Paul, editor, *The Parian Phenomenon: A Survey of Victorian Parian Porcelain Statuary and Busts*, Shepton Beauchamp, Somerset: Dennis, 1989

Janson, Horst Woldemar, *Nineteenth-Century Sculpture*, New York: Abrams, and London: Thames and Hudson, 1985

Lankheit, Klaus, *Von der napoleonischen Epoche zum Risorgimento: Studien zur italienischen Kunst des 19. Jahrhunderts*, Munich: Bruckmann, 1988

Panzetta, Alfonso, *Dizionario degli scultori italiani dell'Ottocento*, Turin: Allemandi, 1989

Radcliffe, Anthony, "Monti's Allegory of the Risorgimento," *Victoria and Albert Museum Bulletin* 1/3 (July 1965)

Read, Benedict, *Victorian Sculpture*, London: Yale University Press, 1982

Ward-Jacason, Philip, "Monti Raffaelle," in *The Dictionary of the Art*, edited by Jane Turner, New York: Grove, and London: Macmillan, 1996

Williamson, Paul, editor, *European Sculpture at the Victoria and Albert Museum*, London: Victoria and Albert Museum, 1996

GIOVAN ANGELO MONTORSOLI ca. 1507–1563 *Italian*

Giovan Angelo Montorsoli was principally a sculptor who worked through Italy in the first half of the 16th century, first as an assistant to Michelangelo and then as an independent master with collaborators such as Bartolomeo Ammanati, Silvio Cosini, and Raffaello da Montelupo. Montorsoli carried out numerous commissions, mainly for the Servite order and for state governors. He was chiefly a marble sculptor, carving and executing decorative details of great virtuosity. His skill was remarkable, especially in marble reliefs, which are both narrative, such as the *Pastoral Scene* in the tomb of Jacopo Sannazaro, and decorative, such as the *Triumph* reliefs with putti and trophies, which are now in the atrium of the Palazzo Doria in Genoa. Montorsoli's role was considerable in the design of monumental structures, such as tombs, altars, and fountains, and of decorative complexes with marble and stucco decoration. The marble and stucco decoration of the presbytery and crypt of the church of San Matteo in Genoa, which was patronized by the Doria family, is a project of particular interest for its richness and antique-style taste. The presbytery ceiling and the cupola are covered with figural stuccowork and gold plating; the walls are enriched with polychrome marble incrustations and reliefs; and the apse is filled with niche figures.

In Montorsoli's monumental works, fountains have special importance because of their innovations in typology, especially in relation to the 16th- and 17th-century development of the Florentine fountain, for which they served as a model. Three fountains are particularly remarkable: first, the Triton Fountain because of its naturalistic settlement on a little island in a pool (*peschiera*); second, the Neptune Fountain because of its typological innovation (the latter is wholly based on figural and colossal sculpture, apart from the architectonic structure of the fountain, which is reduced); and third, the Orion Fountain for its enormous size and complexity of planimetric structure and for the richness of its sculptural decoration. The entire structure and decoration of this fountain is rigorously symmetrical but not monotone because of the small variations in the single elements of the whole complex. The larger lower basin is placed on a base of three steps of dodecagonal shape, and at the foot of the steps are four little basins. Four larger basins flanked by squatted sea monsters abut four angles of the larger receiving basin. On the edge of this basin recline four river god statues. The outer faces of the major basin are covered by decorative sculptures in relief, such as shells, cornices, and harpies-caryatids, and in the middle of each face is a narrative oval relief with representations of Ovidian mythological stories. In the center of the larger basin is a polygonal base with harpies on the corners, from which rises up a shaft decorated with a group of four triton-telamones that sustains the second circular basin. From this rises a shaft decorated with four full-length and seated female figures that sustains the third circular basin. On this, a group of four putti sustain the circular base of the *Orion* statue, which crowns the whole. Each sculptural group is related to the lower basins by water jets. The colossal work was commissioned from Montorsoli by the Senate of Messina.

Montorsoli also worked in portraiture. A constant characteristic of his style, not only of portraits but also of sacred, mythological, and decorative figures, is the stress on expressiveness, which tended toward the grotesque. This is clear, for example, in the funerary bust of Tommaso Cavalcanti, in the monstrous figure of Charybdis on the Neptune Fountain, and in the pathetic devotion of the *Saint Cosmas*, whose dynamic posture, especially in the upper part of the figure, functions to emphasize the inner tension of the saint.

Montorsoli was also active in other, not so prestigious, sectors of sculpture, such as votive wax portraiture, which was typical of the Florentine Church of Santissima Annunziata, as well as in terracotta sculpture and in the restoration of antique sculpture. In this field, Montorsoli's work is particularly remarkable for the extraordinary celebrity of two of the statues entrusted to his technical ability by Pope Clement VII at

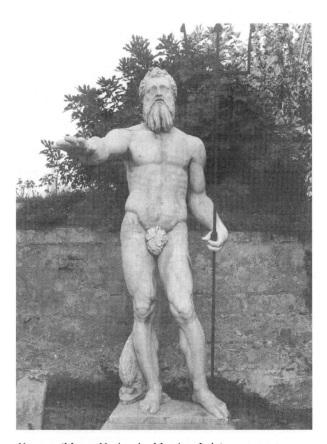

Neptune (Museo Nazionale, Messina, Italy)
© Alinari / Art Resource, NY

Michelangelo's suggestion: the *Laocoön* group and the *Apollo Belvedere*. Older sources also mention that Montorsoli was active in engraving and as an amateur poet.

Beginning in the 1530s, Montorsoli befriended the Florentine author Anton Francesco Doni, and this relationship is evident in a reciprocal exchange of letters and by the continuous praise of the sculptor in Doni's writings. The first and principal biography of the sculptor is contained in the second edition of Giorgio Vasari's 16th-century *Lives of the Painters, Sculptors, and Architects.* Vasari, who also knew the sculptor, composed a rich and precise biography emphasizing Montorsoli's diligence in art studies and his honesty and also dwelling particularly on his important role in the 1563 founding of the Accademia del Disegno in Florence, the first official art academy, established under Medici patronage for the education of young artists and to promote artistic production and the dignity of the figurative arts. A partial biography of Montorsoli is also contained in Raffaello Soprani's *Lives* (1674) concerning foreign artists working in Genoa. In all of the 16th- and 17th-century sources, a positive assessment of the artist can be credited primarily to his proximity to the great Michelangelo but also to his technical ability. On the contrary, judgment is fundamentally negative in Leopoldo Cicognara's *History of Sculpture* (1813–18) due to the general censure of Mannerism and Baroque pursued by the Neoclassical historiographer.

FRANCESCA PELLEGRINO

See also **Fountain Sculpture; Michelangelo (Buonarroti)**

Biography

Born in Montorsoli, near Florence, Italy, *ca.* 1507. Trained in Florence with sculptor Andrea di Piero Ferrucci; assistant to Silvio Cosini and Michelangelo and independent master with continual trips through Italy; worked in Florence, 1524–27, 1533, 1536–37, and in Rome, 1532–34, in both cases as a collaborator of Michelangelo; worked as an independent master in Paris for King Francis I, 1534; in Arezzo for the Servite order, 1536; in Naples, 1536–37, 1541–42; in Florence for the Servite order, for Cosimo I de Medici, grand duke of Tuscany, for Duke Alexander de' Medici, and for the Accademia del Disegno, 1527, 1533, 1561–63; principal works in Genoa for Prince Andrea Doria, 1539–41; in Messina for the city government, where he was chiefmaster of the cathedral and of the city, 1547–57; and in Bologna for the Servite order, *ca.* 1558–61; entered the Servite order at Santissima Annunziata in Florence, 1527; dispensed by Pope Clement VII; left the order in 1533 but forced by Pope Paul IV to reenter, 1557; cofounder of the Accademia del Disegno in Florence, 1563. Died in Florence, Italy, 31 August 1563.

Selected Works

ca. 1524–27, 1533–34	Medici Chapel (assistant to Michelangelo, with Niccolò Tribolo and Raffaello da Montelupo); marble; Church of San Lorenzo, Florence, Italy
ca. 1527– *ca.* 1532	Portraits of the Medici family (restoration); wax; Church of Santissima Annunziata, Florence, Italy
1532	*Apollo Belvedere* (restoration); marble; Vatican Museums, Rome, Italy
1532	*Laocoön* (restoration); marble; Vatican Museums, Rome, Italy
1532, 1534	Tomb of Julius II (assistant to Michelangelo); marble; Church of S. Pietro in Vincoli, Rome, Italy
1533, 1537–38	*Saint Cosmas* (under the direction of Michelangelo); marble; Medici Chapel, Church of San Lorenzo, Florence, Italy
1536/1537–42	Tomb of Jacopo Sannazaro (with Bartolomeo Ammanati and Silvio Cosini), including statues of *Apollo, Minerva, Saint James,* and *Saint Nazarius* and a relief of a mythological scene; marble; Church of Santa Maria del Parto, Naples, Italy
1539–40	*Andrea Doria* (begun by Baccio Bandinelli); marble (damaged); fragments: Palazzo Doria, Genoa, Italy
1540–41	Doria Family Church (with Silvio Cosini), including *Resurrected Christ, Saint John the Baptist, Pietà, David, Saint Andrew, Jeremy, Cantoria,* tomb of Andrea Doria, and *Triumph* reliefs (latter now in Palazzo Doria, Genoa, Italy); marble, stucco; decoration of the presbytery, transept altars, choir loft, and crypt; Church of San Matteo, Genoa, Italy
ca. 1540–43	*Reclining Pan,* for Palazzo Barberini, Rome, Italy; marble; Saint Louis Art Museum, Missouri, United States
ca. 1540–43	Triton Fountain; marble; Palazzo Doria, Genoa, Italy
1547–53	Orion Fountain (with Andrea and Domenico Calamech and Camillo Camilliani); marble, polychromatic stones, slate; Piazza del Duomo, Messina, Italy
1553–57	Neptune Fountain; marble (damaged in 1848, 1908, and during World War II); original statues of *Neptune* and *Scylla:* Museo Regionale di Messina, Italy; copies *in situ:* Piazza dell' Unità d' Italia, Messina, Italy
1558–62	*Resurrected Christ, Virgin with Child, Saint John the Baptist, Saint Laurence, Saint Sebastian, Adam,* and *Moses*; marble, encrustations of polychromatic semiprecious stones; high altar, Church of Santa Maria dei Servi, Bologna, Italy
ca. 1558, 1561	Funerary bust of Tommaso Cavalcanti; marble; Cavalcanti Chapel, Church of S. Spirito, Florence, Italy

Further Reading

Borghini, Raffaello, *Il riposo di Raffaello Borghini*, Florence: Marescotti, 1584; reprint, as *Il Riposo*, Hildesheim, Germany: Olms, 1969

Borntrager, Conrad M., "Works Attributed to Giovannangelo Montorsoli, O.S.M., in the United States," *Studi storici dell' Ordine dei servi di Maria* 38/1–2 (1988)

Elam, Caroline, "The Mural Drawings in Michelangelo's New Sacristy," *The Burlington Magazine* 123 (1981)

Ffolliott, Sheila, *Civic Sculpture in the Renaissance: Montorsoli's Fountains at Messina*, Ann Arbor, Michigan: UMI Research Press, 1984

Gorse, George L., "The Villa of Andrea Doria in Genoa: Architecture, Gardens, and Suburban Setting," *Journal of the Society of Architectural Historians* 44/1 (1985)

La Barbera Bellia, Simonetta, "Il restauro dell' antico in Montorsoli e la fontana di Orione," in *Argomenti di storia dell'arte*, Palermo: Istituto di Storia dell'Arte Medievale e Moderna della Facoltà di Lettere e Filosofia dell'Università di Palermo, I (1983)

Laschke, Birgit, *Fra Giovan Angelo da Montorsoli: Ein florentiner Bildhauer des 16. Jahrhunderts*, Berlin: Mann, 1993

Mösender, Karl, "Montorsoli, Giovanni Angelo," in *The Dictionary of Art*, edited by Jane Turner, New York: Grove, and London: Macmillan, 1996

Pope-Hennessy, John, *An Introduction to Italian Sculpture*, 3 vols., London: Phaidon, 1963; 4th edition, 1996; see especially vol. 3, *Italian High Renaissance and Baroque Sculpture*

Summers, David, "The Sculptural Program of the Cappella di San Luca in the Santissima Annunziata," *Mitteilungen des Kunsthistorischen Institutes in Florenz* 14 (1969–70)

Vasari, Giorgio, *Le vite de' più eccellenti architetti, pittori, e scultori italiani*, 3 vols., Florence: Torrentino, 1550; 2nd edition, Florence: Apresso i Giunti, 1568; as *Lives of the Painters, Sculptors, and Architects*, 2 vols., translated by Gaston du C. de Vere (1912), edited by David Ekserdjian, New York: Knopf, and London: Campbell, 1996

Verellen, Till R., "Cosmas and Damian in the New Sacristy," *Journal of the Warburg and Courtauld Institutes* 42 (1979)

HENRY MOORE 1898–1986 *British*

Forty years before the artist's death the New York Museum of Modern Art had already hailed Henry Moore as among "the foremost living British sculptor," and he could now be claimed as among most renowned sculptors of the 20th century. Influenced by such figures as Jean (Hans) Arp, Constantin Brancusi, and Pablo Picasso, Moore's voluminous oeuvre shows affinities with many modern tendencies, including abstraction, Primitivism, and Surrealism. Although Moore's methods were never doctrinaire, he was a longtime exponent of direct carving and truth to materials, inevitably displaying an acute sensitivity toward three-dimensional form. Critics often view his monumental sculptures, which trace an extraordinary range of expression between abstraction and figuration, as icons of existential mystery for a secular age.

Moore began his training under a tutor at the Leeds School of Art in his native Yorkshire. Here, he absorbed the ideas of the critic Roger Fry, particularly the supremacy of carving over modeling, truth to the nature of materials, and the expressive power of African tribal arts. In 1921 he won a scholarship to the Royal College of Art in London, where he spent much time in the British Museum studying pre-Columbian, African, and Oceanic sculptures. According to an article titled "Primitive Art" (he was ambivalent about the term) that he wrote for the *Listener* in 1941, such work "makes a straightforward statement, its primary concern is with the elemental, and its simplicity comes from direct and strong feeling." The "intense vitality" he sensed in Egyptian, Aztec, and Cycladic sculpture found a response in the powerful, blocky quality of many of his early works. Most notable among these is the stone *Reclining Figure* of 1929, inspired by an illustration of an ancient *Chacmool* figure excavated at Chichén Itzá in Mexico. The figure was Moore's first treatment of a theme to which he would return obsessively throughout his career.

While living in Hampstead and teaching at the Royal College of Art and then the Chelsea School of Art, Moore associated with many prominent British Modernists, including Ben Nicholson, Barbara Hepworth, Herbert Read, and Stephen Spender, as well as notable refugees from the continent such as Piet Mondrian and László Moholy-Nagy. In 1928 he received his first commission, a relief titled *West Wind*, for the new headquarters of the London Underground Railways. His first solo exhibitions had a mixed reception: Augustus John and Jacob Epstein bought his drawings, but one newspaper review of 1932 accused him of promoting a "cult of ugliness." Moore's goal at this time was to work with the inherent characteristics of individual pieces of stone or wood—as though the figures were latent within the block, waiting to be brought into being.

Growing fame followed from the publication in 1934 of a monograph on his work by Herbert Read (*Henry Moore, Sculptor*), as well as from Alfred Barr's borrowing (and later purchase) of the wooden *Two Forms* for his seminal show on *Cubism and Abstract Art* at the Museum of Modern Art in New York. At the same time, following Hepworth's lead, he began piercing holes in his forms, giving a new spatial complexity to the reclining figures of the later 1930s. Here, the female form becomes conflated with topographical features—rolling hills, eroded caves—and summons archetypal notions of the female principle in its manifestation as Earth Mother.

When his Hampstead home was damaged by a bomb in 1940, Moore moved to Perry Green, Much Hadham, Hertfordshire, where he later bought a large estate. At this time he made his famous and haunting series of drawings of Londoners sheltering in the Underground during the Blitz. Moore received an atypical commission in 1942 for a *Madonna and Child* for St. Matthew's Church, Northampton, a work whose conventional realism was seen as retrograde by some critics. Yet at the same time he began a series of *Helmet Heads* whose ambiguous but suggestive forms have been interpreted as an oblique comment on militarism. After the war Moore began a rapid rise to international celebrity, having a major retrospective at the New York Museum of Modern Art in 1946 and winning the sculpture prize at the Venice Biennale of 1948.

Moore now began to work principally in bronze, which allowed him to increase both the scale and the rate of his production. After about 1955 he would generally create a small-scale plaster maquette, which would be turned over to assistants for execution. This procedure ostensibly allowed him to appreciate the three-dimensional qualities of the proposed work more immediately than preliminary drawings would permit, but critics have sometimes characterized the resultant large bronzes as formulaic and inert. While Moore continued to produce many attenuated but more or less naturalistic human figures (for example, the bronze *Reclining Figure* of 1951), he abstracted much of his work of the 1950s from organic forms, inspired by the collection of bones, pebbles, shells, and gnarled pieces of wood he kept in his studio. His two works for the roof terrace of the Time-Life Building in London, a *Draped Reclining Figure* and an abstract pierced screen, exemplify the two sides of his production. His later sculptures become ever more colossal, from the travertine *Reclining Figure* at the UNESCO headquarters in Paris to the bronze *Reclining Figure* (1963–65) at Lincoln Center to the *Three Way Piece No. 2: Archer* in Toronto and the *Knife Edge* at the National Gallery in Washington, D.C.

Moore revealed his responsiveness to nature in his preference for siting his works in landscape, which can best be seen at the Yorkshire Sculpture Park near Wakefield, established in 1977. Moore once remarked, "Sculpture is an art of the open air. I would rather have a piece of my sculpture put in a landscape, almost any landscape, than in or on the most beautiful building I know." Similarly, he appreciated the effects of time and weathering on his pieces, which gave them an aura of antiquity as well as a direct connection to natural cycles. Moore particularly enjoyed seeing the use that sheep made of the sheltering forms of the large bronze *Sheep Piece* installed in a field at Much Hadham, England.

By the late 1970s over 40 shows a year were being devoted to Moore's work, including major retrospectives held at the Forte di Belvedere in Florence in 1972 and at the Metropolitan Museum of Art in New York in 1983. He donated many of his works to the Art Gallery of Ontario, and the Nelson Atkins Museum in Kansas City, Missouri, has an important group of his outdoor sculptures. In order to conserve his oeuvre and reduce his heavy tax burden, he established the Henry Moore Foundation at Much Hadham in 1977. In 1986, the year of his death, he deeded the estate at Perry Green to the trustees of the Henry Moore Foundation, which now holds a large collection of his sculptures, plasters, drawings, and prints. Although Moore stipulated that no further casts of his sculptures were to be made after his death, the large touring exhibitions that regularly show his work throughout the world assure his continuing fame.

Moore's approach ceased to appear avant-garde as early as the 1950s, when criticism from the Independent Group and later Pop exponents made his sculptures seem untenably elitist or portentous, cut off from the everyday concerns of real people. His mystical and synthesizing vision would indeed seem far removed from the present-day Postmodern concern with contingency and diversity. Yet the evident popularity of Moore's works confirms that they are not simply clinical investigations of form or materials: their themes are broad and universal—comprehending the female figure, the forms and processes of nature, change and metamorphosis, the family, and war and conflict. They suggest archetypes rather than conventional symbols; Moore believed that works of art, instead of aiming for "an empty immediacy, like a poster," should retain a certain mystery, evoking ineffable truths about life, nature, and being.

CHRISTOPHER PEARSON

See also **Arp, Jean (Hans); Brancusi, Constantin; England and Wales: 19th Century–Contemporary; Hepworth, Barbara; Modernism; Noguchi, Isamu; Picasso, Pablo; Public Sculpture**

Biography

Born in Castleford, West Yorkshire, England, 30 July 1898. Saw action in France during World War I and was gassed at Battle of Cambrai, France; attended Leeds School of Art, 1919–21; received scholarship to the Royal College of Art, London, 1921–24; impressed by Mesoamerican, Egyptian, and African works in the British Museum; part-time teaching appointment, Royal College of Art, 1925–32; traveling scholarship to Paris and Italy, 1925; first solo exhibition, Warren Gallery, London, 1928; settled in Mall Studios, Hampstead; head of new Department of Sculpture, Chelsea School of Art, London, 1932–39; moved permanently to Perry Green, Much Hadham, Hertfordshire, 1940. Appointed an Official War Artist and trustee of Tate Gallery, 1941; first retrospective exhibition, Temple Newsam, Leeds, 1941; won sculpture prize, Venice Biennale, 1948; donated over 200 sculptures and drawings to Art Gallery of Ontario, Toronto, 1974; established Henry Moore Foundation, Much Hadham, 1977, and Henry Moore Centre for the Study of Sculpture, Leeds, 1980; Perry Green Estate given to trustees of Henry Moore Foundation, 1986; Henry Moore Institute established in Leeds, 1993. Died in Perry Green, Much Hadham, Hertfordshire, England, 31 August 1986.

Selected Works

1928–29 *West Wind*; Portland stone; London Underground Headquarters, St. James's Park Station, London, England

1929 *Reclining Figure*; Hornton stone; City Art Gallery, Leeds, England

1931 *Mother and Child*; alabaster; Hirshhorn Museum and Sculpture Garden, Washington, D.C., United States

1934 *Two Forms*; Pynkado wood; Museum of Modern Art, New York City, United States

1935–36 *Reclining Figure*; elm wood; Albright-Knox Art Gallery, Buffalo, New York, United States

1938 *Reclining Woman*; Hornton stone; Tate Gallery, London, England

1939 *Reclining Figure*; elm wood; The Detroit Institute of Arts, Michigan, United States

1943–44 *Madonna and Child*; Hornton stone; St. Matthew's Church, Northampton, England

1951 *Reclining Figure*; bronze; Tate Gallery, London, England

1952–53 *Draped Reclining Figure*; bronze; Time-Life Building, New Bond Street, London, England

1952–53 *Time-Life Screen*; Portland stone; Time-Life Building, New Bond Street, London, England

Further Reading

Allemand-Cosneau, Claude, Manfred Fath, and David Mitchinson, editors, *Henry Moore: From the Inside Out*, Munich and New York: Prestel, 1996

Berthoud, Roger, *The Life of Henry Moore*, London and Boston: Faber and Faber, 1987

Garrould, Ann, Terry Friedman, and David Mitchinson, editors, *Henry Moore: Early Carvings, 1920–1940*, Leeds, West Yorkshire: Leeds City Art Gallery, 1982

Hedgecoe, John, *A Monumental Vision: The Sculpture of Henry Moore*, London: Collins and Brown, and New York: Stewart Tabori and Chang, 1998

James, Philip Brutton, editor, *Henry Moore on Sculpture*, London: Macdonald, 1966; New York: Viking Press, 1967; revised edition, New York: Viking Press, 1971

Lieberman, William S., *Henry Moore: 60 Years of His Art*, New York: Metropolitan Museum of Art, 1983

Melville, Robert, *Henry Moore: Sculpture and Drawings, 1921–1969*, London: Thames and Hudson, and New York: Abrams, 1970

Mitchinson, David, editor, *Henry Moore: Sculpture*, London: Macmillan, and New York: Rizzoli, 1981

Mitchinson, David, *Celebrating Moore*, London: Lund Humphries, and Berkeley: University of California Press, 1998

Packer, William, *Henry Moore: An Illustrated Biography*, London: Wiedenfeld and Nicolson, and New York: Grove Press, 1985

Sylvester, David, and Alan Bowness, editors, *Henry Moore: Complete Sculpture*, 6 vols., London: Lund Humphries, 1977–88

Wilkinson, Alan G., *The Moore Collection in the Art Gallery of Ontario*, Toronto: Art Gallery of Ontario, 1979; revised edition, as *Henry Moore Remembered*, Toronto: Art Gallery of Ontario, 1987

RECLINING FIGURE
Henry Moore (1898–1986)
1956–1958
Roman travertine
h. ca. 5 m
United Nations Educational, Scientific, and Cultural Organization Secretariat, Paris, France

Henry Moore's *Reclining Figure* is the focal point of the sweeping curve of the main facade of the United Nations Educational, Scientific, and Cultural Organization (UNESCO) Secretariat in Paris. Intended as a foil to the stark geometries of modern architecture, it rests on a massive three-legged pedestal at some distance from the building. This was the largest sculpture Moore had ever worked on, weighing about 39 tons (over 60 tons including the pedestal). Taking up the theme of the reclining female figure that he had been using since the late 1920s, Moore confronts us with a monumental presence, whose bulky lower limbs rise up like the face of a cliff. Its distinctively porous travertine recalls the art and architecture of Rome. Yet as an admixture of figure and landscape, the massy and simple forms of this palpably stony work have an almost geological power: pinnacles, hills, and eroded caves suggest themselves, and a long hole tunnels through the sculpture along its entire length.

When approached in 1955 to create a sculpture for the new UNESCO headquarters, Moore consulted with his friend Julian Huxley (director-general from 1946 to 1948) as to how the ideology of UNESCO might be defined and how this could be addressed through appropriate iconography. Through 1957 Moore produced numerous sketches and models suggesting ideas of international solidarity and education—a family group, a teacher instructing a child, a seated figure reading. In the end, he stripped away secondary figures and symbolic props to return to his well-tried formula of a single reclining figure.

UNESCO originally requested a bronze from Moore, and he made several studies with this medium in mind. After devoting much attention to creating an effective contrast between sculpture and ground, however, he concluded that the metal would become too black after weathering and would not appear distinctly against the dark glass of the building. At one point he even considered using a freestanding wall to create a neutral field behind the figure. His solution was to work in white travertine, a material that he had long hoped to use in the creation of a very large piece and that would stand out against the windows of the lower floors while matching the travertine cladding on the upper part of the headquarters.

Realizing that the unprecedented scale of the *Reclining Figure* would preclude shipping the uncut stones to England, Moore instead sent the plaster maquette to Italy. Four blocks of white travertine weighing a total of 60 tons had been quarried near Rome by the firm of Henraux. (This was the same quarry from which Michelangelo had selected stone in the 16th century.) The company owned large marble quarries at Querceta, near the Carrara Mountains, and this was where the carving took place. Working on and off, Moore and two assistants took nearly a year to complete the figure, which was then shipped to Paris in four pieces. Upon its unveiling, Moore found the sculpture too white, although he hoped that the Paris rains would mitigate this; he was to comment appreciatively on its weathering in later years. Moore also admired the way the architects sited his figure to face the sun, which, as he said, "brings a piece of sculpture to life."

As one of a number of new works commissioned for the Secretariat, Moore's *Reclining Figure* was part of an ambitious larger project. As Françoise Choay was to note, UNESCO was widely seen as "the most comprehensive experiment of our age in integrating the arts into architecture." UNESCO's parent agency, the United Nations (UN), had set a precedent in favoring nonfigurative (or at least nonnarrative) art in its commissions for the New York headquarters, as witnessed by the two large abstract murals designed by Fernand Léger on the walls of the General Assembly. This Modernist bias was due to the influence of Secretary General Dag Hammarskjöld, who often expressed the desire to have a work by Moore on the grounds of the United Nations. UNESCO followed this lead: its Committee of Art Advisers included Herbert Read and

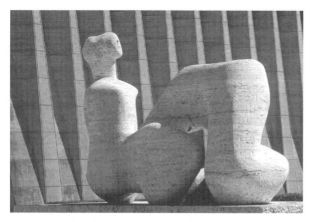

Reclining Figure
© Charles and Josette Lenars / CORBIS. Reproduced with permission from The Henry Moore Foundation, England

Georges Salles, both strongly committed to Modernism. In fact, the first six artists secured for UNESCO by the Committee were Jean (Hans) Arp, Alexander Calder, Joan Miró, Moore, Isamu Noguchi, and Pablo Picasso (Léger was also contacted but died in the summer of 1955). UNESCO's official literature states simply that "these artists were chosen not as representatives of any particular school of painting or national culture, but as internationally recognized figures in contemporary art," but the bias toward post-Cubist abstraction did not go unrecognized at the time.

Critical reaction to the new headquarters and its art was mixed. Some thought the project too conservative: Lewis Mumford called UNESCO "a Museum of Antiquated Modernities," and Reyner Banham complained of "this dated dream of [the] *Gesamtkunstwerk*" (total work of art) and termed Moore's figure an "eroded dowager." In 1959 *Life* magazine confirmed that the critical response had been to dismiss the works as "too passé" while reporting that public reaction to the indeterminate iconography of the UNESCO works was hostile—many finding the works "too modern and bizarre."

A decision to avoid specific ideological references led to Moore's choice of the reclining figure motif, which, as he said in 1962, "seeks to tell no story at all. I wanted to avoid any kind of allegorical interpretation that is now trite." Although ultimately deriving from his study of Aztec *Chacmool* figures, the iconography of the UNESCO *Reclining Figure* was seen as effectively neutral—or at least open-ended. Moore described it as one of a series that were "inspired by general considerations of nature, but which are less dominated by representational considerations, and in which I use their forms and their relationships quite freely." Perhaps conditioned by 19th-century paradigms of symbolic architectural decoration, commentators seemed puzzled by the lack of specific references in the *Reclining Figure*, and few were willing to hazard a guess as to what it might signify: the *Architectural Record* ventured to say only that it might "offer a symbolism that has something to do with what UNESCO stands for."

Yet Moore's *Reclining Figure* is not devoid of content. When read as an icon of artistic individuality in the context of the mechanistic ground of the headquarters' architecture, it embodies the ideology of "scientific humanism" (in the words of Huxley) underpinning the worldview promoted by UNESCO. In other words, free, isolated, and idiosyncratic expressions of the human spirit are seen to live in accord with—and are validated by—the neutral, functional background of modern technology. The display of modern art at UNESCO was at the same time a tacit claim for the universality of such a means of expression—a claim based on a Western liberal-humanist ideal that may no longer seem quite so neutral or universal as was once believed.

In the early 1980s, another work by Moore, the bronze *Reclining Figure: Hand*, was installed at the UN as a memorial to Hammarskjöld after the secretary general's untimely death.

CHRISTOPHER PEARSON

Further Reading

Banham, Reyner, "The Arts and Entertainment: Unesco House," *New Statesman* (6 December 1958)

Bowness, Alan, editor, *Henry Moore: Sculpture and Drawings*, 6 vols., London: Lund Humphries, 1944–88; see especially vol. 3, *Sculpture, 1955–64*

Burchard, John Ely, "Unesco House Appraised," *Architectural Record* 127 (May 1960)

Evans, Luther H., Françoise Choay, and Lucien Hervé, *Unesco Headquarters in Paris*, London: Tiranti, and Stuttgart: Hatje, 1958

Jouffroy, Alain, "Unesco," *Graphis* 15 (January/February 1959)

Marks, Edward B., *A World of Art: The United Nations Collection*, Rome: Il Cigno Galileo Galilei, 1995

Mumford, Lewis, "Unesco House: The Hidden Treasure," in *The Highway and the City*, by Mumford, New York: Harcourt, Brace and World, 1963; revised edition, London: Secker and Warburg, 1964

"Palace of Concrete," *Time* (8 December 1958)

Strachan, W.J., "Henry Moore's Unesco Statue," *The Studio* 156 (December 1958)

L'UNESCO: Foyer vivant des bonheurs possibles, Paris: UNESCO/Flammarion, 1991

The UNESCO Courier 11 (November 1958) (special issue on the new Paris headquarters)

MORGAN MADONNA (VIRGIN AND CHILD IN MAJESTY) *Morgan Master (fl.*
late 12th century)

ca. late 12th century

walnut, gesso, linen

h. 79.4 cm

Metropolitan Museum of Art, New York City, United States

The statue of the *Morgan Madonna* (also known as the *Virgin and Child in Majesty*) held in the Metropolitan Museum of Art is considered the finest example of a type of Romanesque sculpture known as the Throne of Wisdom, or *sedes sapientiae*. Numerous examples are documented or extant throughout Europe (the earliest from the mid 10th century), especially from the Auvergne region of France, the region in which the *Morgan Madonna* was made. Following iconographic convention, the Virgin Mary is seated frontally in a throne, as her body forms a throne for the Christ Child, whom she presents to the viewer. The child appears like a miniature adult, representing Divine Wisdom. The iconography derives from Early Christian and Byzantine art, where it is found in mosaics as early as the 6th century and is based on theological commentaries comparing the Virgin Mary to the throne of Solomon, the wise king of the Old Testament.

The Virgin's static posture, hieratic symmetry, and serene expression convey a majestic calm. The statue exudes authoritative power as it emphasizes the child. The Virgin's large hands with stiff horizontal fingers direct our view. The undulating drapery folds form concentric patterns leading from the Virgin's shoulders toward the child. The rigid, abstract forms enhance the statue's otherworldly aspect, as if it were a heavenly vision.

Several pieces of wood (walnut) have been doweled together, a frequent practice for this type of sculpture. The heads were carved separately. Aside from losses of the forearms and feet of the child, some cracks, and insect holes, the piece is in excellent condition. In the Virgin's left shoulder, concealed by a small fitted panel carved with drapery, is a small pyramid-shape cavity that at one time would have held a relic. On the center of the Virgin's chest a shallow rectangular cavity is covered with a fitted panel. It is doubtful that this was carved to conceal a relic, particularly since no other examples have such cavities in the front. Mobility is a key feature of the *sedes sapientiae* sculptures. Carved in the round and completely painted, they were routinely carried in processions and used in liturgical drama.

Some of the original raised decoration in gesso is preserved, particularly on the Virgin's sleeve hem and the upper edge of the throne, where a pattern of circles alternating with lozenges imitates cut gems. Quite a bit of the original polychromy (over linen) remains, especially on the cushion and arches of the throne. The Virgin's tunic has traces of bright red; her mantle has traces of lapis lazuli blue. The polychromy of the child's garments is the reverse. This color arrangement would have contributed to directing a viewer's attention to the Christ Child. The faces of both figures are sensitively modeled, whereas the polychromy there is mostly of a later date.

Owing to the exceptional quality of this sculpture, the carver has been named the Morgan Master by Ilene Forsyth, who has two other examples (the *Virgin and Child in Majesty* from Claviers and that from Saint-Victor de Montvianeix, now in the Metropolitan Museum of Art, The Cloisters, New York City) attributed to the artist. Many variants exist, although none of the related examples is dated. An approximate date to the second half of the 12th century is the generally held opinion. According to Little, the more humanizing qualities, especially in facial expression, indicate a late-12th-century date and signal this *Morgan Madonna* as probably the most mature work of the carver.

LESLIE BUSSIS TAIT

Further Reading

Europe in the Middle Ages, New York: The Metropolitan Museum of Art, 1987

Forsyth, Ilene H., *The Throne of Wisdom: Wood Sculptures of the Madonna in Romanesque France*, Princeton, New Jersey: Princeton University Press, 1972

Little, Charles T., "Romanesque Sculpture in North American Collections XXVI: The Metropolitan Museum of Art, Part VI, Auvergne, Burgundy, Central France, Meuse Valley, Germany," *Gesta* 26/2 (1987)

GIOVANNI MARIA MORLAITER 1699–1781 *Italian*

Giovanni Maria Morlaiter played a prominent role in the world of Venetian sculpture of the 18th century. He is credited with having inaugurated a more free yet elegant style, completely Rococo. Renowned among his contemporaries, and in demand among the international aristocracy, he was one of the most prolific sculptors of his time. He worked on all of the most prestigious artistic endeavors in Venice from the late 1720s, often collaborating with the architect Giorgio Massari.

Morlaiter completed his training with Alvise Tagliapietra. Also important to the formation of Morlaiter's artistic personality was his friendship with the painter Sebastiano Ricci in the years immediately preceding the latter's death in 1734. Morlaiter had an early interest in activities outside of Venice, particularly in Austria and southern Germany, an influence, as contemporary critics noted, that his works reveal. Personal contacts between Morlaiter and artists north of the Alps are documented in 1731 and 1732, when Georg Raphael Donner and Jacob Shoj came to Venice to purchase marble. Both artists came to Morlaiter, who was a prior at the College of Sculptors, to obtain permission to use the rough-hewn stonecutters' blocks.

The spirit of novelty that characterizes Morlaiter's language is noticeable even in his first works, which date from the 1720s and which oppose, with liveliness and compositional whim, the Classical current represented in Venice by Giovanni Marchiori and Antonio Gai. Nevertheless, Morlaiter's *Virtues* and the statues representing St. Joseph and St. Simon still indicate some uncertainties in the slightly clumsy arrangement of the starched and incongruent puffs of drapery. His dependence on the style of Tagliapietra, from which he derived the eccentric and serpentine physical characteristics of his figures, is also evident. The influence of his first teacher is visible in the first of two reliefs, depicting *Christ among the Doctors* (1733–35). The second relief, *Rest on the Flight into Egypt* (1735–38), is somewhat different and almost seems an homage to his friend Ricci, who had recently died. Morlaiter's style here reached its first maturity, rich in compositional momentum and refined details.

During this period Morlaiter created some of his most convincing works, characterized by an increasingly fervent painterlike quality and a lighter touch. Such is the case in the figures of *St. Benedict* and *St. Scholastica*—sculpted for the main altar of the Church of Santi Biagio e Cataldo at the Giudecca in Venice—and in the elaborated marble frame (*Glory of Angels*) for the painting of *St. Dominic* by Giambattista Piazzetta. The architect Massari entrusted the decorative sculpture of this church entirely to Morlaiter. It consists of six statues of *Prophets* and *Apostles* and eight reliefs of episodes from the life of Christ and represents one of the highest moments in the maturity of Morlaiter's art. The work is a clear example of his exquisite technique that translates in the marble a dynamic impetus, marked by light and shadow, and the formal elegance of Rococo painting, in harmony with the paintings and frescoes by Ricci, Piazzetta, and Giambattista Tiepolo that adorn the same church. The link with painting is even more evident in the series of models and sketches in earthenware and terracotta, now in the Museum of 18th-Century Venice at the Ca' Rezzonico, which testifies to Morlaiter's ability to capture with rapid and precise gestures the first ideas for a work.

In the 1750s, Morlaiter took part in the exchange of ideas between sculptors and painters both in various artistic collaborations and in the Venetian Academy, founded in 1756 but already active in 1750. He was among the academy's strongest backers. His statue of angels holding a crown, a project for which he once again worked with Massari, dates to these years. In these delicate figures, so close to the paintings of Giannantonio Guardi and Giambattista Pittoni, the sculptor bestowed a worldly character, suffused with subtle sensuality, on a sacred subject. This quality is even more evident in Morlaiter's portraiture. The busts of Pope Benedict XIV and Cardinal Rezzonico and the monument to Marshall von der Schulenburg (*ca.* 1756), for example, reveal his lack of interest in a psychological or realistic investigation of the person. The worldliness and sophistication of Morlaiter's style were particularly well suited to secular themes. Yet only a small part of this work is known today, to judge from the prestigious commissions received from the Saxon court and from Catherine II of Russia. Of these only the two allegories of the *Judgment* and of the *Fortress* of Gatchina remain.

From the end of the 1750s, the sculptor's style underwent a change. Works carried out in this period for Venetian churches, such as the *Virgin with Child* and the statue of *Blessed Gregorio Barbarigo*, demonstrate compositional rhythms that are not as busy as his earlier works, as well as a greater orderliness and scale. In the same year that Massari died, 1766, Morlaiter began his collaboration with the architect Bernardino Maccaruzzi, creating sculptures for the facade of the Church of San Rocco and later the sculptural decoration for the Scuola della Carità (School of Charity, now Gallerie dell'Accademia di Venezia, Venice). In the low relief of the facade of the Church of San Rocco, *St. Rocco Healing the Plague Victims*, one notices a certain strength in the decisive dynamic of the composition. However, the statues for the school, the *Charity towards God* and the *Charity towards Neighbor*, both seem routine, characterized by a heavy structure. Given his advanced age, Morlaiter may well have delegated the material execution of these sculptures to his son Gregorio and to craftsmen in the workshop he had maintained for some time together with other collaborators. In fact, Gregorio is said to have finished his father's last sculpture, the *Madonna of the Rosary* (ca. 1781; Church of San Geremia, Venice), which Morlaiter began in 1778, only three years before his death.

MONICA DE VINCENTI

Biography

Born in Venice, Italy, 13 July 1699. Son of a glass maker. In workshop of sculptor Alvise Tagliapietra, *ca.* 1710–15; two sons were artists, the painter Michelangelo (1729–1806) and sculptor Gregorio (1738–84); significant commissions throughout career in Croatia, Italy, and Russia; held various offices, including "Prior," 1731, in the College of Sculptors, Venice; also active in the Academy, Venice, which he helped to found, until 1774; turned down the office of Academy treasurer for last time due to his ill health, 1778. Died in San Moisè, Italy, 22 February 1781.

Selected Works

In addition to the finished works listed here, a collection of terracotta and earthenware *bozzetti* (small sculptures made as preparatory studies or models for full-scale works) is preserved in the Ca' Rezzonico, Venice, Italy.

1728–29	Four *Virtues*; marble; Church of Saint Ignatius, Dubrovnik, Croatia
1729	*St. Joseph* and *St. Simon*; marble; Christ altar, Church of San Vidal, Venice, Italy
1733–38	*Christ among the Doctors* (1733–35) and

Rest on the Flight into Egypt (1735–38); marble; Rosary Chapel, Church of Santissimo Giovanni e Paolo, Venice, Italy (damaged by fire, 1867)

1735	*St. Scholastica* and *St. Benedict*; marble; Name of Jesus altar, Church of Santissimo Pietro e Paolo, Fratta Polesine, Italy
1738–39	*Glory of Angels* (frame for Giambattista Piazetta's painting of St. Dominic); marble; altar of St. Dominic, Church of Gesuati, Venice, Italy
1743–55	*Apostles* and *Prophets*; marble; Church of Gesuati, Venice, Italy
1743–55	Episodes from the life of Christ; marble; Church of Gesuati, Venice, Italy
1746	Busts of Pope Benedict XIV and Cardinal Rezzonico; marble; choir, Padua Cathedral, Padua, Italy
1750– ca. 1753	Angels holding crown; marble; main altar, Church of Santa Maria della Fava, Venice, Italy
1761	*Virgin with Child*; marble; Church of the Zitelle, Venice, Italy
1761–65	*Blessed Gregorio Barbarigo*; marble; altar, Church of Saint Mary Zobenigo (also known as Santa Maria Giglio), Venice, Italy
1764–67	*Fortress* and *Judgment*; marble; Gatchina Palace, St. Petersburg, Russia
1766–68	*St. Rocco Healing the Plague Victims*; marble; facade, Church of San Rocco, Venice, Italy

Further Reading

De Grassi, Massimo, "Per il catalogo di Gian Maria Morlaiter: Una precisazione ed una aggiunta," *Arte Veneta* 47 (1995)

De Vincenti, Monica, "Gianmaria Morlaiter e alcune sue opere giovanili in Stiria e in Dalmazia," in *Francesco Robba and the Venetian Sculpture of the Eighteenth Century*, edited by Janez Höfler, et al., Ljubljana, Slovenia: Rokus, 2000

Guerriero, Simone, "I rilievi marmorei della cappella del Rosario ai SS. Giovanni e Paolo," *Saggi e memorie* 19 (1994)

Martinelli Pedrocco, Elisabetta, "Gianmaria Morlaiter scultore veneziano," *Atti dell'Istituto Veneto di scienze, lettere ed arti* 138 (1979–80)

Martinelli Pedrocco, Elisabetta, "Catalogo dei bozzetti del 'fondo di bottega' di Giammaria Morlaiter," *Bollettino dei Musei civici Veneziani* 26 (1981)

Pedrocco, Filippo, "Gli scultori del medio Settecento," in *'700 veneziano: Capolavori da Ca' Rezzonico* (exhib. cat.), edited by Filippo Pedrocco, Venice: Marsilio, 1998

Ress, Anton, *Giovanni Maria Morlaiter: Ein venezianischer Bildhauer des 18. Jahrhunderts*, Munich and Berlin: Deutscher Kunstverlag, 1979

Rossi, Paola, "Lavori settecenteschi per la chiesa di San Rocco: La decorazione della sagrestia e le sculture della facciata," *Arte Veneta* 35 (1981)

Rossi, Paola, "I Morlaiter a Santa Maria del Giglio," *Arte Veneta* 51 (1997)

Rossi, Paola, "La scultura a Venezia nel Settecento," in *Venezia: L'arte nei secoli*, edited by Giandomenico Romanelli, vol. 2, Udine, Italy: Magnus, 1997

Semenzato, Camillo, *La scultura veneta del Seicento e Settecento*, Venice: Alfieri, 1966

Tomic, Radoslav, *Barokni oltari i skulptura u Dalmaciji*, Zagreb: Matica Hrvatska, 1995 (with summaries in English and Italian)

ROBERT MORRIS 1931– *United States*

Although Robert Morris began his career as a second-generation Abstract Expressionist painter in the late 1950s, he gained recognition as a neo-Dadaist and Minimalist sculptor during the 1960s. No longer content to produce objects valued solely for their aesthetic qualities, Morris sought to make sculptures that engage the viewer both physically and philosophically.

In 1961 Morris produced a series of reductively shaped geometric sculptures. These protominimalist objects, such as the now-destroyed *Two Columns* and *Portal*, drew directly from the vocabulary of architecture, and, in their scale, they explicitly engaged the viewers' own bodies. Devoid of reference to the architectural orders and stripped of all decoration, Morris's *Two Columns* were rectangular solids 2.4 by 0.6 by 0.6 meters constructed from painted plywood. *Portal* illustrated the simplicity of post-and-lintel construction and invited interaction by walking through it. These sculptures forced viewers to consciously involve their own bodies in their aesthetic response to the rarified spaces of the art gallery and museum. Morris's works implicitly comment on the institutionality of the art world and critique the manner in which modern art is produced, collected, and exhibited.

Much of the work that Morris created during the early 1960s was destroyed after it was shown, then rebuilt for later exhibitions. Ironically, the monetary value of the object is based on the idea, whereas its philosophical value is based on its physical form. For instance, *Passageway* consisted of a corridor 15 meters long and 2.4 meters tall whose walls converged; this work revealed a nexus between dance, happenings, Fluxus (the Neo-Dada movement of the 1960s), and Minimalism. *Passageway* was billed as "An Environment" that was open to guests for several hours during 3–7 June 1961. The viewer became a performer who actively experienced the sculpture instead of passively looking at an object. By walking through *Passageway*, participants became increasingly aware of their bodies via the constriction of the space.

In the same year, Morris also built *Box with the Sound of Its Own Making*. Contesting the rules of high Modernism as established by Clement Greenberg, in which purity to the materials required the separation between the disciplines, this sculpture incorporates sound as an integral element. Whereas *Passageway* revealed intersections between the avant-garde trends of the 1960s, this sculpture exemplifies the indebtedness of these trends to the example of Jackson Pollock and Marcel Duchamp. Given that the *Box with the Sound of Its Own Making* continuously plays a recording of the measuring, cutting, assembling, and hammering of the object, it also responds to Pollock's foregrounding of the role of process. Just as we can imagine Pollock's body at work by looking at the arcs of dripped paint, we can imagine Morris's labor as a sculptor by listening to his body at work in his studio. Although twice the size, *Box with the Sound of Its Own Making* (25.4 by 25.4 by 25.4 c) recalls Duchamp's readymade *With Hidden Noise* (1916), which consists of an unknown sound maker enclosed by a ball of twine bound between two 12.7-centimeter metal plates. Both works require viewers to consider how they were made. The sound hidden within Duchamp's readymade produces an imaginative enigma; Morris's cube invites the imagination to visualize the object's construction.

In the latter half of the 1960s, Morris published a series of articles, "Notes on Sculpture," in *Artforum*, which not only offered a defense of Minimalism but also articulated his own theory of sculpture. Minimalism, for Morris, strives to give the viewer "strong gestalt sensations" through the experience of simple forms. For instance, with a cube, the viewer need not move around the piece to comprehend the other side.

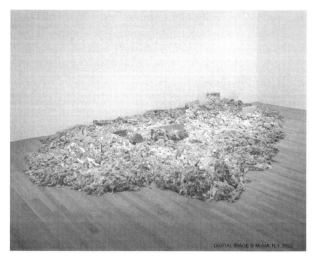

Untitled (*Threadwaste*), 1968, felt, asphalt, mirrors, wood, copper tubing, steel cable, and lead, 54.6 × 668 × 510.5 cm, The Museum of Modern Art, New York. Gift of Philip Johnson
© The Museum of Modern Art and SCALA/Art Resource, New York, (2003) Robert Morris / Artists Rights Society (ARS), New York

The viewer "sees" it with the mind's eye. In this sense, one's apprehension of the visual field is broader than that which the eye can see at one time. Now destroyed, Morris's *L-Beams* was an experiment with complex polyhedrons that also produces gestalt sensations. Grouped in a set of three—one upright, one laying down, and one forming an inverted V—*L-Beams* invoked a gestalt sensation because the totality of all three objects could be perceived at a single glance. Simultaneously, given the size of the objects together, 2.4 by 2.4 by 0.6 meters, the viewer's body was involved in the perceptual experience.

Drawing on these unitary relationships between the body and the mind, Morris dialectically undermines the uniform nature of gestalt experiences. For instance, *Mirrored Cubes* maintained the structural integrity of the cube, but the mirrored surfaces fractured the environment. These cubes produced numerous infinite regresses, multiple reflections of the viewer, and fragmented glimpses of the space in which they were placed. In this way, *Mirrored Cubes* dislocated the gestalt experience by simultaneously implying and denying it.

Further investigation of the limitations of gestalt perception and a continued desire to disrupt the commodification of art led Morris to experiment with thread waste and felt. By producing sculpture without use of rigid materials, such as metal or wood, Morris made process visible and further collapsed the barrier between the ends and means of art that began with *Box with the Sound of Its Own Making*. Unlike the a priori nature of additive and subtractive sculpture, in which the sculptor exerts his or her will on the materials, felt and thread waste are amorphous and force the sculptor to acknowledge chance and indeterminacy as essential for the finished sculpture. Scattering, piling, and hanging serve as the basis of Morris's process as he continues to move beyond making objects. What Morris calls his "anti-form" sculptures focus on dedifferentiation, in which wholeness is sensed instead of being perceived as a visual image. An installation such as *Threadwaste*, consisting of industrial packing materials (colored thread), mirrors, copper tubing, and felt, denies the gestalt by embracing the totality of the space. Its horizontal amorphousness fuses the traditional figure–ground relationships of sculptures. In this body of work, the ground *is* the figure. The entire visual field, even beyond one's peripheral vision, becomes part of the sculpture, which stretches like landscape across the horizon.

In the 1970s Morris's interest in horizontality and the viewer's perception of the visual field led him to produce several land art projects. *Observation* is Morris's best-known large-scale outdoor sculpture. This enormous work contains two concentric rings and a triangular-shaped passageway that cuts through the rings on the east–west axis. The inner ring contains a portal and three slender "windows." In the center of this space, given its high wall, the horizon is hidden from the viewer except for the narrow view from the "windows," which are aligned with the passageway and two sets of two 2.7-meter square steel plates placed in a V-form in the berm of the outer ring. These windows and V-forms mark the trajectory of the summer and winter solstices. This astronomical calendar intentionally evokes Stonehenge and forces the viewer to confront his or her body in relation to the passage of time.

In a return to the ideas he first explored in *Passageway*, Morris began producing elaborate, claustrophobic *Labyrinths* in the mid-1970s. The viewer is again required to enter the artwork (which is 2.4 meters tall and 9 meters in diameter) and move through it. In this case, a narrow passageway winds efficiently throughout the interior of the circle. Again, given the work's height, the viewer cannot see beyond the narrow passageway and must encounter his or her own body. As with all of Morris's sculpture, this work forces the viewer to examine the interplay between the mind and the body.

Morris's works of the 1980s and 1990s continued to explore the ideas that had preoccupied him through earlier decades of his sculptural endeavors. In addition, in more recent years, Morris has increasingly turned his attention to two-dimensional work.

BRIAN WINKENWEDER

See also **Andre, Carl; Bourgeois, Louise; Contemporary Sculpture, Duchamp, Marcel; Installation; Judd, Donald; Long, Richard; Minimalism; Modernism; Postmodernism; Serra, Richard; Smithson, Robert**

Biography

Born in Kansas City, Missouri, United States, 9 February 1931. Attended Kansas State Art Institute, 1948–50; enrolled in California School of Fine Arts, 1951; first solo exhibit at the Dilei Gallery, San Francisco, in 1957; studied art history at Hunter College, 1961–63, Master of Arts in art history, 1966; professor at Hunter College, 1967–present; had solo shows at Green Gallery, New York, 1963, 1964, and 1965, and collaborated in performance works with Yvonne Ranier, New York, 1963; other solo show at Leo Castelli Gallery, New York, 1967; received several art awards, including Simon R. Guggenheim International Award, 1967, and Guggenheim Memorial Foundation Fellowship, 1969; retrospective exhibition, Solomon R. Guggenheim Museum, 1994. Presently living in Gardiner, New York, with a studio in New York City.

Selected Works

1961   *Box with the Sound of Its Own Making*; walnut box, speaker, 3.5-hour recorded tape; Seattle Art Museum, Washington, United States

1961   *Passageway*; painted plywood (destroyed)

1961   *Portal*; wood (destroyed)

1961   *Two Columns*; wood (destroyed)

1965   *L-Beams*; wood (destroyed)

1965   *Mirrored Cubes*; Plexiglas mirrors on wood (destroyed)

1968   *Untitled* (*Threadwaste*); thread waste, asphalt, mirrors, copper tubing, felt; Museum of Modern Art, New York City, United States

1969   *Continuous Project Altered Daily*; earth, clay, asbestos, cotton, water, grease, plastic, felt, wood, thread waste, electric lights, photographs, tape recorder; temporary installation: Leo Castelli Warehouse, New York City, United States

1970   *Observation*; earth, wood, granite; Oostelijk Flevoland, the Netherlands (rebuilt in 1977)

1974   *Labyrinth*; plywood, Masonite; Guggenheim Museum, New York City, United States (other examples destroyed; some rebuilt)

1983   *House of Vetti*; felt, steel bracket, metal grommets; private collection

Further Reading

Battcock, Gregory, editor, *Minimal Art: A Critical Anthology*, New York: Dutton, 1968; London: Studio Vista, 1969

Berger, Maurice, *Labyrinths: Robert Morris, Minimalism, and the 1960s*, New York: Harper and Row, 1989

Compton, Michael, and David Sylvester, *Robert Morris*, London: Tate Gallery, 1971

Morris, Robert, *Robert Morris: The Mind/Body Problem* (exhib. cat.), New York: Guggenheim Museum Foundation, 1994

Lippard, Lucy, *Six Years: The Dematerialization of the Art Object from 1966 to 1972*, New York: Praeger, and London: Studio Vista, 1973

Robert Morris (exhib. cat.), Washington, D.C.: Corcoran Gallery of Art, 1969

Tucker, Marcia, editor, *Robert Morris*, New York: Praeger, 1970

VERA MUKHINA 1889–1953 *Russian/ Soviet*

Vera Mukhina's international recognition as a leading Soviet sculptor followed the installation of her vibrant and captivating group *Worker and Collective Farm Woman* atop the Soviet pavilion at the International Exhibition in Paris in 1937. Upon its immediate success, Mukhina commented, "The epoch itself gives birth to images that are in need of plastic realization." The messages of the Soviet Adam and Eve were manifold: an homage to emancipated labor, an allegorical embodiment of the achievements and values of the Soviet state, a romantic vision of the progress of humankind, and a glorification of the new harmonious man of the future. Familiar through numerous reproductions, it is no longer seen as an integral part of its original setting, but it cannot be dissociated from ideological overtones or assessed predominantly in terms of its artistic merit. The only major monumental project that Mukhina actually realized, it resulted from a single occasion when the grandeur of her conception correlated with the importance of the commission. Fantastic, megalomaniac, and costly, most of her later designs were too extravagant even by Soviet standards, and their extensive and deliberate use of allegory was not always compatible with the official principles of socialist realism.

With most of Mukhina's earlier achievements incorporated into the design of *Worker and Collective Farm Woman*, her previous work seemed a mere preliminary to this production. Throughout her career, she systematically explored only a handful of sculptural themes, including the female nude, articulation of the human figure in movement, construction of sculpture with multiple viewpoints, and adaptation of new materials to sculpture production. Her experiments with glass, wood, and steel demonstrate that a command of sculptural form for Mukhina meant not only exploring new plastic dimensions but also mastering as many new materials as possible. *Julia* (1926; State Tretyakov Gallery, Moscow) is an unusual study of the female nude, with shockingly strong muscles, a spiral composition, and an emphatic upward surge. Mukhina's favorite essay in representing figure in movement was *Wind* (1926; State Tretyakov Gallery, Moscow), a study of plastic forms in dynamic interrelationship. Its subject is clearly subordinate to the dramatic dialogue of volumes. *Bread* (1939; State Tretyakov Gallery, Moscow) continues the theme of the female nude, but its decorative lyricism belongs to a different epoch. With its complex juxtaposition of the figures of two girls holding a sheaf of corn, the group yields a number of accomplished profiles.

Although Mukhina was considered a major exponent of socialist realism in sculpture, her artistic principles took shape before the Bolshevik Revolution of 1917. Mukhina's early views did not manifest the radicalism typical of Russian artists of her generation. In moving away from naturalism, she did not enter the area of pure formal experiment. Although early in her career Mukhina drew on Cubism as a method of sche-

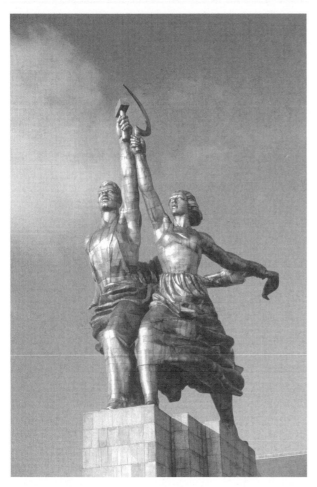

Worker and Collective Farm Woman
© Neil Beer / CORBIS, and The Estate of Vera Mukhina /
RAO, Moscow / VAGA, New York

matizing sculptural form by breaking it up into sharp-edged planes, her adoption of Cubist modeling was decidedly mechanistic. The straightforward imagery of a winged figure bearing a torch in *Flame of Revolution* (1922; Central Museum of Revolution, Moscow) makes the subject easily identifiable, distinguishing it from similarly angular works of Cubist sculptors.

More fundamental to the formation of Mukhina's approach to art was the training that she received in Émile-Antoine Bourdelle's studio. A former assistant of Auguste Rodin, Bourdelle rejected his older colleague's approach to subject matter based on direct observation. In seeking universal laws or structures behind appearances, he developed a method of constructing sculpture "from the inside." Clarity of construction, concision of expression, and observance of the laws of materials in creating a sculptural composition are the values that Mukhina absorbed in Bourdelle's studio. From there she also inherited the Romantic quality of her work.

Mukhina's principal requirement of sculpture was its readability. For her, sculpture's function was to move and instruct by appealing to the senses rather than the mind; its necessary prerequisite was not the mere inclusion of appropriate symbols but the construction of a captivating image. This view was consistent with the set of demands put on artists under Joseph Stalin's regime. In Mukhina's *Peasant Woman* (1927–28; State Tretyakov Gallery, Moscow), sculptural forms emerge from the decreasing volumes of a cylinder, a cube, and a pyramid. Its static composition, exaggerated volumes of arms and legs, and overall emphasis on earthly strength and health derive from the Russian folk sense of physical form but also give the work a distinctly monumental character.

The slogan of the 1937 International Exhibition in Paris, "art and technology in modern life," posed to its participants a technical as well as an artistic challenge. Mukhina's response was to create a composition based entirely on the properties of stainless steel, a material then novel to sculpture production. Constructed of relatively small rectangular plates welded to a double frame, *Worker and Collective Farm Woman* required no buttressing in the lower part. Mukhina's tour de force was a piece of flying drapery behind the group, which she referred to as a scarf. With the weight exceeding five metric tons, this ten-meter projection was not feasible in bronze, making its installation a major engineering achievement. The scarf served a dual function: relating the group to the architecture of the pavilion by emphasizing the horizontal rhythms in its composition and visually confronting the verticality of the Eiffel Tower across the Seine, which dominated the exhibition.

Monumental sculpture was traditionally conceived of in terms of static grandeur and dignity. In the design of *Worker and Collective Farm Woman*, Mukhina expanded the concept of monumentality by applying it to figures in movement. Her accomplished use of dynamic form in monumental compositions secured Mukhina's importance for the development of 20th-century sculpture.

ANATOLE TCHIKINE

See also **Bourdelle, Émile-Antoine; Russia and Soviet Union**

Biography

Born in Riga, Latvia, Russian Empire, 19 June 1889. After finishing secondary school, moved to Moscow, where she studied painting under K. Yuon, 1909–11, and I. Mashkov, 1911–12; also worked in N. Sinitsyna's sculpture studio, 1911; lived in Paris, 1912–14, where she attended Émile-Antoine Bourdelle's studio at the Académie de la Grande Chaumière and briefly studied Cubist painting under J. Metzinger and H. Le Fauconnier; visited Italy during the summer of 1914; on return to Moscow, worked as a nurse in a military hospital until 1918; also assisted Alexandra Exter as a theater designer in Aleksandr Tairov's Chamber Theatre, from 1916; participated in the realization of Lenin's Plan for Monumental Propaganda, 1918–20; member of the Monolith group of sculptors, 1919–20; member of the Four Arts society, founded in 1924; joined the Society of Russian Sculptors, 1926; taught in the Higher Artistic-Technical Studios, 1926–30; awarded a trip to Paris for *Peasant Woman*, 1928; exiled with her husband, a military doctor, to Voronezh, USSR, 1930, but allowed to return to Moscow in 1933; won a closed contest in 1936 for the decoration of the Soviet pavilion at the 1937 International Exhibition in Paris, with her model of *Worker and Collective Farm Woman*; awarded Stalin prizes for *Worker and Collective Farm Woman* (1941), the portrait busts of I. Khizhnyak and B. Yusupov (1943), the bust of A. Krylov (1946), *We Demand Peace!* (1951), and the monument to Gorki in Moscow based on I. Shadr's project (1952); became a founding member of the USSR Academy of Arts, 1947. Died in Moscow, USSR, 6 October 1953.

Selected Works

1916   *Pietà* (pity); clay (lost)
1922   *Flame of Revolution*; plaster; Central Museum of Revolution, Moscow, Russia
1926   *Julia*; wood; State Tretyakov Gallery, Moscow, Russia
1926   *Wind*; bronze; State Tretyakov Gallery, Moscow, Russia
1927–28 *Peasant Woman*; bronze; State Tretyakov Gallery, Moscow, Russia
1934–35 *Architect S. Zamkov*; marble; State Tretyakov Gallery, Moscow, Russia
1936–37 *Worker and Collective Farm Woman*; stainless steel; All-Union Agricultural Exhibition, Moscow, Russia
1938–39 *A. Gorki*; bronze; Nizhny Novgorod, Russia
1939   *Bread*; toned plaster; State Tretyakov Gallery, Moscow, Russia
1942   *B. Yusupov*; plaster; cast: 1947, bronze; State Tretyakov Gallery, Moscow, Russia
1942   *I. Khizhnyak*; plaster; cast: 1947, bronze; State Tretyakov Gallery, Moscow, Russia
1945   *A. Krylov*; wood; State Tretyakov Gallery, Moscow, Russia
1945–53 *P. Tchaikovsky*; bronze; outside the Great Hall of the Conservatory, Moscow, Russia
1947–50 *We Demand Peace!* (with Z. Ivanova, N. Zelenskaya, A. Sergeev, and S. Kasakov); plaster; State Tretyakov Gallery, Moscow, Russia

Further Reading

Iablonskaia, Miuda, *Women Artists of Russia's New Age, 1900–1935*, edited by Anthony Parton, London: Thames and Hudson, and New York: Rizzoli, 1990

Suzdalev, Petr, *Vera Ignatievna Mukhina*, Moscow: Iskusstvo, 1981

Vorkunova, Nina, *Simvol novogo mira: Skul'ptura "Rabochiy i Kolkhoznitsa" narodnogo khudozhnika SSSR V.I. Mukhinoy*, Moscow: Nauka, 1965

Voronov, Nikita, *Vera Mukhina*, Moscow: Izobrazitel'noe Iskusstvo, 1989

Voronov, Nikita, *Rabochii i kolkhoznitsa* (Worker and Collective Farmer Woman), Moscow: Moskovskii Rabochii, 1990

HANS MULTSCHER *ca.* 1400–*ca.* 1476
German

Hans Multscher ran a large workshop in the southern German city of Ulm. He likely completed his apprenticeship in the local Allgäu region of Germany, although his journey years almost certainly included travel to northern Europe, particularly northern France, Belgium, the southern Netherlands, and the Lower Rhine. Often called the early years, the period 1420–27 reflects Multscher's study and adaptation of Netherlandish realism inaugurated by the sculptor Claus Sluter and the painters Robert Campin and the van Eyck brothers. Netherlandish realism, which proliferated between 1390 and 1430, must be placed in the context of the artistic style that immediately preceded it, known as International Gothic. Characteristics of International Gothic include elongated and elegant figures mannered in a way as to display no substantial weight or three-dimensional space. In contrast, Claus Sluter and his Netherlandish contemporaries began to add weight, substance, and three-dimensionality to their figures. Surfaces of different materials also received careful attention, and painters began to capture, for example, the quality of velvet, metal, the wrinkled skin of an elderly person, and the glisten of a teardrop.

Netherlandish realism provided the background of Multscher's experience in northern Europe. Although he would only exploit the elements of realism to their fullest extent after he established his workshop in Ulm in 1427, his works prior to the workshop nevertheless incorporate a sense of monumentality and vigor. Of these earlier examples, Multscher's sculpture in Aachen best illustrates his stylistic connections to the work of Sluter, as well as his familiarity with architectural sculpture. A statue of the Virgin and Child (*ca.* 1420–25) betrays the influence of Sluter; the hard-edged drapery lines and overall angular qualities have become more curvilinear, and the body exhibits a gentle S curve from head to base. Simultaneously, the figure is weighty and three-dimensional, not elongated and frail. Similar in date to the statue of the Virgin and Child is a piece of architectural sculpture in the High Gothic choir of Aachen Cathedral. Here, an angel attached to a console recalls the angels from the Moses Well (*ca.* 1396–1405) by Sluter. Bold and substantial, yet elegant, the console angel at Aachen is a strong departure from earlier console and corbel sculpture from the International Gothic. That Multscher carved architectural sculpture suggests that he was familiar with the sculptural practices of a large cathedral workshop before he developed his own independent studio.

Man of Sorrows illustrates Multscher's shift from a softer style prevalent in his early works to a stronger sense of realism. The *Man of Sorrows* also reveals qualities that appear in a number of painted panels attributed to Multscher, including the Wurzach Altarpiece. One of Multscher's earlier painted works, the Wurzach altar, carries the following inscription: "Bitte Gott für Hansen Multscher von Reichenhofen bürger zu Ulm hat das werk gemacht da man zählt 1437" (Praise to God for Hans Multscher from Reichenhofen, citizen from Ulm, who made this work in 1437). Yet whether Multscher actually painted these panels or a painter executed them in a style unusually similar to Multscher's sculpture is unknown. In any regard, the panels of the Wurzach Altarpiece illustrate the new realism that is the hallmark of Multscher's sculpture and raise the question that this sculptor also may have been a painter.

More interesting, owing to the rarity of their type, are depictions of Charlemagne, the king of Hungary, the king of Bohemia, and two shield bearers located on the *Prunkfenster*, or "Grand Window" of the Ulm city hall. The compositional unity that exists between the figures and the architectural ornamentation suggests that Multscher designed the entire ensemble. Many sculptors, in fact, were skilled in designing and carving architectural ornament. Unique to Multscher are the depictions of the faces on these figures: the shield bearer with an eagle on his shield smiles so strongly that Multscher carved the teeth. Prominent wrinkles around the eyes, the furrow of the brow, and the smile lines around the figure's face give this once-painted work a true individual character of an older man. The second shield bearer is as individualistic; obviously younger, perhaps 20 years old, and has the full fleshy cheeks and tighter skin of youth. These shield bearers have the realistic features that best describe the work of Multscher; a variety of facial types, differences in age, and attention to the surfaces of different materials had replaced the generic shapes,

forms, and surfaces that artists used during the 14th century.

These elements, combined with Multscher's ability to harmonize the movement of the body with rich drapery patterns, have led many scholars to credit him with establishing Ulm as a leading artistic center during the 15th century. By 1450 the maturity and consistency of Multscher's style brought him many commissions. Among these mature works, Multscher created a series of limewood sculptures intended for the Sterzing altar and numerous wooden figures of the Virgin and Child and Virgin Enthroned. Multscher's legacy is measured not solely by the works he alone produced but also by his influence on those workshops that adopted a Multscheresque style during the latter part of the 15th century.

Kevin McManamy

See also **Germany: Gothic–Renaissance; Sluter, Claus**

Biography

Born in Reichenhofen, Bavaria, *ca.* 1400. Nothing known of background and training; apprenticeship possibly in Allgäu; presumed trips to northern France, Burgundy, and the Low Countries, perhaps related to his early artistic training; born a freeman (owing allegiance only to the emperor), he was admitted as freeman in Ulm and married Adeherd Kitzin, herself from a long-standing family of sculptors, 1427; owned home near Ulm Cathedral; eventually ran a large workshop in Ulm; referred to as *geschworener Werkhmann* (sworn artisan, or assessor for the trades of sculptor and carver for a city), an honorary office bestowed by Ulm city council, 1431. Died in Ulm, Germany, before 13 March 1476.

Selected Works

1427–30	*Prunkfenster* (Grand Window); stone; Ulm City Hall, Germany
1429	*Man of Sorrows*, for west doorway, Ulm Cathedral, Germany; sandstone (moved inside; copy *in situ*); Ulm Cathedral, Germany
1456–58/59	Sterzing altar; oil on painted panel and limewood; Church of Unserer Lieben Frau im Moos, Vipiteno (formerly Sterzing), Germany

Further Reading

Baxandall, Michael, *The Limewood Sculptors of Renaissance Germany*, New Haven, Connecticut: Yale University Press, 1980
Gerstenberg, Kurt, *Hans Multscher*, Leipzig: Insel-Verlag, 1928

Huth, Hans, *Künstler und Werkstatt der Spätgotik*, Augsburg, Germany: Filser Verlag, 1923; 2nd edition, Darmstadt, Germany: Wissenschaftliche Buchgesellschaft, 1967

Müller, Theodor, *Sculpture in the Netherlands, Germany, France, and Spain: 1400 to 1500*, translated by Elaine Robson Scott and William Robson Scott, Baltimore, Maryland, and London: Penguin, 1966

Tripps, Manfred, *Hans Multscher, Meister der Spätgotik: Sein Werk, seine Schule, seine Zeit*, Leutkirch, Germany: Heimatpflege Leutkirch, 1993

MAN OF SORROWS

Hans Multscher (ca. 1400– ca. 1476)

1429

sandstone

h. life-size

West doorway, Ulm Cathedral, Germany (copy in situ); original now inside

The "Man of Sorrows" is a particular depiction of Christ the victim, or the suffering Christ after the Crucifixion. In western Europe the depiction of the Man of Sorrows became common after 1350; some examples in eastern Europe are from an earlier date. Artists used many variations on the theme—Christ alone, Christ with the Virgin, Christ with the Virgin and John the Evangelist, Christ with angels, and in some cases, Christ with God the Father. Additionally, the objects of Christ's Passion—those items used during his torture, including whips, the sword or lance stabbed into his right side, and the crown of thorns placed on his head— are sometimes depicted. Certain works also depict Christ surrounded by angels, some of whom even hold the chalice or cup of wine to catch the blood that drips from his wounds, a reference to Christ's blood represented by the chalice of wine used during the mass. Such variations of the Man of Sorrows became common at the end of the 14th and beginning of the 15th centuries. Scholars have suggested that the Netherlandish examples of the dead Christ, specifically those painted by the Master of Flémalle, are likely predecessors of Hans Multscher's *Man of Sorrows*. Such claims are supported by Multscher's apparent importation of a modified version of Netherlandish realism into southern Germany based on, among others, the works of Netherlandish artists Claus Sluter and the brothers van Eyck.

In contrast to the painted examples by the Master of Flémalle, where God the Father holds Christ's lifeless body, Multscher's example depicts Christ as a dramatic seminude figure who stands agile and alive. The body clearly demonstrates *contrapposto* (a natural pose with the weight of one leg, the shoulders, and hips counterbalancing one another) in which the left leg supports most of the body and the right leg is more relaxed, with a slightly bent knee. *Contrapposto* in sculpture is primarily associated with Classical and Italian Renaissance sculpture. It is unclear if Multscher himself was directly influenced by Italian examples; certainly, one of his successors, Michael Pacher, incorporated Italian principles into his work only a few years after Multscher. Nevertheless, Multscher's use of *contrapposto* in his *Man of Sorrows* conveys a sense of life and movement of the body, truly a unique addition to the subject. Conversely, the figure of Christ affords a sense of imbalance and weakness; emaciated, with thin folds of skin connecting his shoulder to his arm and covering his torso only to reveal the bones underneath, Christ leans to the right as if teetering from lack of strength. His legs are thin and bony, while his hands have the appearance of an old man's. Disheveled drapery only incompletely covers his body, revealing both the embarrassment of his partially nude body and the wounds of his agony. More emotional than these details are the gestures of Christ himself. With his left hand he points to the cut in his side where he was stabbed (after which the wound was splashed with vinegar to cause more pain). His right hand is raised slightly to show the wounds caused by the nails driven through his hands to keep his body on the cross. Although Christ's mouth is not original (a repair was

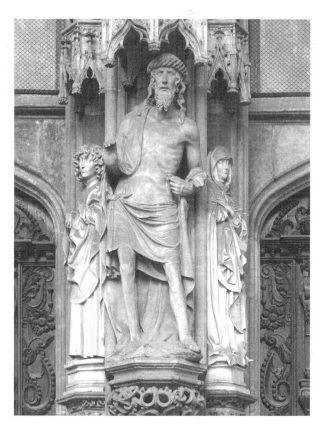

Man of Sorrows
© Erich Lessing / Art Resource, NY

made during the 18th or 19th century), his gaunt cheeks, sunken eyes, and furrowed brow reveal an intensity of sorrow, though interestingly, not pain.

Sorrow, not pain, aligns with the purpose of depictions of the Man of Sorrows. A form of *Andachtsbild*—a picture meant to invoke the contemplation of religious suffering and passion of faith—Multscher's *Man of Sorrows* is less an image about the infliction of pain than one that imparts to the viewer Christ's Passion and suffering that brought salvation to the world. Such a devotional image does not focus on a particular historical event, such as the Flagellation of Christ, which is recorded as happening at a specific place and specific time; rather, the image carries with it both an emphasis on the living Christ after the Crucifixion and the stage of death before the Resurrection. The duality of life and death implied in such an image reveals the mystery of eternal life. This shift from the less literal to the more abstract meaning of images occurred during the 14th and 15th centuries when a series of mystic writers began to espouse *devotio moderna* (modern devotion). *Devotio moderna* emphasized the meditation and contemplation of religious mystery by individuals, where they were to internalize the life and suffering of Christ through emotions. The location of Multscher's *Man of Sorrows* at the front entrance of Ulm Cathedral would have made the image patent to all who entered the building.

The artistic importance of Multscher's *Man of Sorrows* is no less significant than the spiritual message it imparted to those followers of the Christian faith. Multscher certainly was trained as an architectural sculptor of stone, yet he transformed the same talents into his wooden sculptures and imbued them, as he did here, with elements of realism and individuality not realized in prior sculpture. One needs only to imagine this *Man of Sorrows* with its original paint: white, gold, and dark blue colors on the drapery and the pigmentation of the skin would have contrasted greatly with the deep red, painted to show the blood where nails punctured Christ's feet and hands, where the lance pierced his side, and where the crown of thorns caused his head to bleed.

KEVIN MCMANAMY

See also **Germany: Gothic–Renaissance**

Further Reading

Paatz, Walter, *Süddeutsche Schnitzaltäre der Spätgotik: Die Meisterwerke während ihrer Entfaltung zur Hochblüte, 1465–1500*, Heidelberg, Germany: Winter, 1963

Schröder, Manfred, *Das plastische Werk Multschers in seiner chronologischen Entwicklung*, Tübingen, Germany: Kunsthistorischen Institut der Universität, 1955

MYRON 5th CENTURY BCE *Greek*

Myron is one of the most famous bronze sculptors from the Classical period. With Pheidias, Polykleitos, Lysippos, and Praxiteles, he is one of the sculptors most often mentioned by the ancient sources. Although he was born in Eleutherae, a small town on the frontier between Boeotia and Attica, his sculptural education was Athenian in terms of the quality of his style and the perfection of his technique. His son Lykios was also a sculptor working in Athens: two signed bases of his were found at the Acropolis. Myron's career began about 475 BCE and seems to have extended to early in the third quarter of the 5th century BCE. His best-known works date from 460 to 440, a period when he may have worked with his son.

None of Myron's original sculptures are preserved; all information comes from Roman copies and literary sources. Myron's works can be grouped into six categories: cult statues, heroes, mythological subjects (including *Athena and Marsyas* and *Perseus after Killing Medusa*), athletes, the wooden *xoanon* (small, roughly shaped image) of Hekate at Aigina, and animals (including a sea monster, a dog, a locust, and a cicada). Cult statues attributed to him include *Apollo* at Agrigentum, *Apollo* at Ephesus, *Dionysos* at Orchomenos, and *Zeus* and *Athena and Herakles*, which were displayed on a common base at the Heraion at Samos. Statues of heroes connected with Myron include *Erechtheus* at Athens, *Herakles* at Messana, and *Herakles* at Rome.

The *Diskobolos*, or discus thrower, is the sole work of Myron securely identified through copies. The only other work for which copies exist is *Athena and Marsyas*, although the evidence concerning the work is open to much interpretation. The statues of a "Satyrum admirantem tibias et Minerva" (a satyr marveling at the flutes and an Athena) mentioned by Pliny (*Naturalis Historia, ca.* 77 CE) most probably formed the group of the satyr Marsyas and Athena that Pausanias saw on the Acropolis of Athens, although he does not name Myron. It is not clear if Pliny is referring to the group here because he cites the statues separately (linked by "et" [and]). However, the group can be identified in a vase painting from about 430 BCE and from Roman coins of the Hadrianic period.

The scene that the sculptural group portrays occurs after Athena, who has been playing the double flutes, sees herself reflected in water with a distorted face and swollen cheeks and throws the instruments away. Marsyas, fascinated by the magic sound, tries to pick them up, but the goddess commands him to leave them alone. Myron's group shows Athena warning Marsyas not to pick up the flutes (it is unlikely that she is striking him, as Pausanias states). She is in a walking, chiastic position, moving away from the center, although turning her head back, looking at the flutes on the ground. Marsyas, seemingly surprised by the appearance of Athena, leans a bit backward. Although afraid of disobeying Athena, he cannot resist taking the flutes. The two figures form a V-shaped composition, outlined by two centrifugal axes. Their different characters are embodied by their faces (Marsyas's is very masklike), poses, and gestures. Marsyas, as a human, had the freedom to choose; the punishment would come later. This was a typical philosophical attitude of Classical thought. Viewers would have been familiar with such stories in theatrical productions; indeed, we know of a dithyramb (choral song in honor of Dionysos) about Marsyas by Melanippides.

In works such as *Athena and Marsyas*, as well as the *Diskobolos*, or even *Perseus after Killing Medusa*, poses acquired the meaning of temporal narration, an aspect of Myron's work perhaps influenced by painting and architectural sculpture. The conception in *Athena and Marsyas* is reminiscent of the west pediment of the Temple of Zeus in Olympia: the group underlines the dramatic difference between the "quiet" predominance of Athena and the "loud" vulgarity of the satyr, much as in the pediment the calm authority of Apollo dominates the struggle between Centaurs and Lapiths. In a deeper sense, both figures underline the gap between morality and immorality, intellectuality and ignorance, and rationalism and irrationality, all values of Classical art and thought. The representation of the group could also have a political message: displayed at the Acropolis, the statue of Athena perhaps represented the self-satisfaction of Athenians in the middle of the 5th century BCE following the victory of Athens over the barbarian Persians, a recurrent theme in the Periklean buildings at the Acropolis.

Myron also carved the statue of the victorious runner *Ladas*. The statue was admired for its realism in both modeling and pose. As one source describes it, the statue is "full of hope; and on the edge of his lips the breath from his hollow flanks is visible; soon the bronze will leap for the crown, nor will the base be able to hold it back. Oh, art is swifter than a breath of wind" (*Anthologia Graeca*). Another Myronian work that was famous for the same reason is a bronze cow on the Acropolis of Athens. Some 41 epigrams about it have been preserved, for example, "Seeing the heifer of Myron you would quickly cry out: Nature is lifeless but art is alive" (*Anthologia Graeca*).

Although the realism of *Ladas* and the bronze cow was probably exaggerated by poetic form, the expression of naturalism in Myron is discussed in almost all the sources. According to Pliny, whose history of sculpture is based on technical terms of art criticism, "Myron seems to have been the first to extend the rep-resentation of reality; he used more compositional patterns in his art than Polykleitos and had a more complex system of symmetry" (*Naturalis Historia*). Indeed, Myron was the first to deliver art from the conventions of the form; his system of proportions developed toward the depiction of momentary poses.

The reported association of Myron with Polykleitos is important for the history of art since they were contemporaries and bronze sculptors, referred to as pupils of the Peloponnesian sculptor Ageladas (who was mentioned also as the master of Pheidias). Their role in Classical art was different, and they were mentioned as rivals. Polykleitos's system of proportions emphasized the measured relationships among the various parts of the body (symmetry), whereas Myron's system revealed the compositional centers of motion (rhythm). In the end Myron's contribution seems more daring. As Quintilian mentions (*Institutio Oratoria, ca.* 95 CE), sculptures such as the *Diskobolos* should be appreciated not only in terms of the distorted pose (not upright) but also in terms of their novelty and difficulty. Myron was an intellectual, one of the leading figures of early Classical art. He most likely wrote a treatise about his work, similar to the *Canon* of Polykleitos, since it was a regular practice for Classical artists to write manuals about their own rules of art. Unfortunately, nothing of this work survives.

HARA THLIVERI

See also **Greece, Ancient; Lysippos; Pheidias; Polykleitos; Praxiteles**

Biography

Born in Eleutherae, Greece, early 5th century BCE. Worked from *ca.* 475 to *ca.* 440 BCE, mainly in Athens; pupil of Ageladas of Argos; an intellectual influenced by the Pythagorean school of philosophy and by Athenian drama; probably created his own system of proportions, recorded in a treatise; likely also worked with his son Lykios. Died in Greece, date unknown.

Selected Works

All works date from the 5th century BCE. No more specific date information available unless otherwise indicated.

1. Cult Statues:

   Apollo, at Agrigentum, Greece; bronze (lost)
   Apollo, at Ephesus, Greece; bronze (lost)
   Dionysos, at Orchomenos, Greece; bronze (lost)
   Hekate, at Aigina, Greece; wood (lost)

Zeus and *Athena and Herakles* group, at Samos, Greece; bronze (lost)

2. Heroes:

Erechtheus, at Athens, Greece; bronze (lost)
Herakles, at Messana, Greece; bronze (lost)
Herakles, at Rome; bronze (lost)

3. Mythological subjects:

ca. 450–440 BCE *Athena and Marsyas*, for Acropolis, Athens, Greece; bronze (lost)
Perseus after Killing Medusa, for Acropolis, Athens, Greece; bronze (lost)

4. Athletes:

ca. 460–450 BCE *Diskobolos*; bronze (lost); Roman copy in marble: *ca.* 130–150 CE, Museo Nazionale Romano, Rome, Italy
Ladas, at Argos, Greece (?); bronze (lost)
Pankratiasts (all-in wrestlers); bronze (lost)
Pentathletes, at Delphi, Greece; bronze (lost)
Victorious athletes (four statues), at Olympia, Greece; bronze (lost)

5. Animals:

Cow, for Acropolis, Athens, Greece; bronze (lost)
Dog; bronze (lost)
Sea-monster; bronze (lost)

6. Attribution uncertain:

Cicada; bronze (lost)
Locust; bronze (lost)

Further Reading

Bieber, Margarete, "Myron I," in *Allgemeines Lexikon der bildenden Künstler von der Antike bis zur Gegenwart*, edited by Ulrich Thieme, Felix Becker, and Hans Vollmer, vol. 31, Leipzig: Engelmann, 1931; reprint, Leipzig: Seemann, 1978
Carpenter, Rhys, "Observation on Familiar Statuary in Rome," *Memoirs of the American Academy in Rome* 18 (1941)
Daltrop, Georg, *Il gruppo mironiano di Atena e Marsia nei Musei Vaticani*, Vatican City: Monumenti, Musei e Gallerie Pontifiche, 1980
Dörig, Jose, "Myrons Erechtheus," *Antike Plastik* 6 (1967)
Furtwängler, Adolf, *Masterpieces of Greek Sculpture: A Series of Essays on the History of Art*, edited by Eugénie Sellers, London: Heinemann, and New York: Scribner, 1895; reprint, Chicago: Argonaut, 1964
Lippold, Georg, *Ladas*, Munich: Verlag der Bayerischen Akademie der Wissenschaften, 1949
Mattusch, Carol C., *Greek Bronze Statuary: From the Beginnings through the Fifth Century B.C.*, Ithaca, New York: Cornell University Press, 1988
Ridgway, Brunilde Sismondo, *The Severe Style in Greek Sculpture*, Princeton, New Jersey: Princeton University Press, 1970
Robertson, Martin, *A History of Greek Art*, 2 vols., London: Cambridge University Press, 1975; abridged edition, as *A Shorter History of Greek Art*, Cambridge and New York: Cambridge University Press, 1981
Stewart, Andrew F., *Greek Sculpture: An Exploration*, New Haven, Connecticut: Yale University Press, 1990

DISKOBOLOS (DISCUS THROWER)
Myron (5th century BCE)
Roman copy (Lancelotti version) after the original bronze of ca. 460–450 BCE
ca. 130–150 CE
marble
h. 155 cm
Museo Nazionale Romano, Rome, Italy

The *Diskobolos*, or Discus Thrower, by the Early Classical sculptor Myron was one of the most famous statues of antiquity. Its date, about 450 BCE, is attested partly by stylistic criteria and partly by the working life of Myron (*ca.* 475–440 BCE). Although the bronze original is lost, evidence for its appearance survives in Roman marble copies (in full size there are eight statues, three torsos, three heads, six arms and hands; in smaller sizes there are three statuettes and four torsos), ten gems, a sarcophagus, and three full-size reconstructions.

The *Diskobolos* is the only one of Myron's works that has been identified, following the discovery in Italy (1781) of the Lancelotti copy (Museo Nazionale Romano) and the evaluation of ancient literary sources. Lucian's accurate description of the statue (*Philopseudes*, 2nd century CE) leaves no doubt of the authenticity of the copy. Other information related to the *Diskobolos* is given by Quintilian (*Institutio Oratoria*, *ca.* 95 CE) and Pliny (*Naturalis Historia*, *ca.* 77 CE). The life-size statue represents a crucial moment before the throwing of the discus. According to Lucian's description, the athlete "is bent over, into the throwing position, is turned toward the hand that holds the discus, and has the opposite knee gently flexed, like one who will straighten up again after the throw." In all the copies the torso turns to the right and twists at the waist while the legs are set frontally. The right leg steps forward while the left leg behind is relaxed. The right arm is raised back with tensed muscles as the hand grasps the discus, while the left arm is lowered with slightly bent elbow.

Despite the well-established fame of the original statue, there is no information about its fate or its original location. It is quite possible that it was dedicated at a Panhellenic sanctuary, such as Olympia, since it probably represented a victorious athlete, the majority of which were dedicated in sanctuaries by victors in the games. That Pausanias (*ca.* 170 CE) reports the names of other victorious athletes portrayed by Myron and seen in Olympia but not the *Diskobolos* suggests that the statue may have been moved to Rome earlier, possibly by Nero during his trip to Greece in 66–67 CE.

Of the full-size copies preserved, the Lancelotti seems the most closely related to the original. Its superior quality is confirmed by the style of the head, whose excellence and fine execution relate closely to early Classical renderings. This is also the only head found intact with the body and the only one that represents the original position of turning back, as described by Philostratus: "The thrower must turn his head to the right and bend himself over so far that he can look down to the side" (*Images*, 3rd century CE). Compared with the other marble copies, the Lancelotti reveals a greater concern for anatomical forms and pose, with more emphasis on the development of the surfaces and less on the outlines. A Roman bronze statuette of a *diskobolos* found recently at Ampelokipoi in Athens (National Museum of Athens) has direct links to the Lancelotti copy. Despite the extremely poor condition of the surface, the high quality of this work is apparent both in the rendering of the pose and in the style, as well as because it never used the supports that were present in the marble copies.

Study of the *Diskobolos* of Myron involves facing the issue that very few original freestanding statues of the same era have survived. Nonetheless, the figure belongs to the tradition of bronze athletes in action that was established in Greek sculpture, mainly in Athens, in the late Archaic period and continued throughout the first half of the 5th century BCE, as these figures gradually explored three-dimensionality. The main character of these figures is conveyed by the alert pose and the individuality of the types. The small-proportioned bodies, the musculature, taut and rounded but not excessively so, and the close-fitting cap of hair are all typical features meant to represent the true appearance of the contestants in the games.

The motif of the *Diskobolos* was well known before Myron's sculpture: at least nine vase paintings and five coins from Cos dated to the first half of the 5th century BCE show almost the same pose. There has been much discussion as to whether the stance represents a realistic moment of discus throwing. It certainly cannot be said to have photographic realism. The main appeal of the pose is that the sense of movement is pervasive, through the rendering of *rhythmos*, an aesthetic term of ancient art criticism (originally meaning shape or

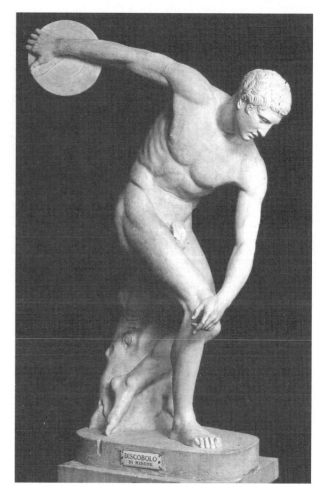

Diskobolos (Discus Thrower)
© Alinari / Art Resource, NY

pattern) that was associated with the sense of repetition and time. In a rhythmic composition the whole was arranged in definable schemes corresponding to the structural centers of movement. In the *Diskobolos* motion is activated by a number of circular or semicircular shiftings of the body around the fixed axis of the legs. The circularity of the outer scheme counteracts the tension of the contrasted axes, and the pose is organized around its own space. Nowhere in ancient Greek sculpture is there such an admirable conception of movement. Here, the need for balance feels urgent and inevitable. The poise of the arms freely in the air and the position of the legs, one crossed behind the other, one supporting and one relaxed, enhance the momentary balance of the pose. Movement is captured in a temporal halt, enabling viewers to fasten their vision on a particular position that characterizes the entire action of throwing the discus. The moment represented can be perceived either as a static unit or as a continuous process of repetition.

Approaching the middle of the 5th century BCE, artistic values such as symmetry, rhythm, and harmony all echoed the predominance of rational thinking. In the *Diskobolos* of Myron the calmness of the face and the well-balanced pose embody the controlled power and self-restraint of the mind (*sophrosyne*), that is, the knowledge that dramatizes the temporary freedom from material weight.

HARA THLIVERI

Further Reading

Barron, John, "The Fifth-Century Discoboloi of Kos," in *Essays in Greek Coinage, Presented to Stanley Robinson*, edited by Colin M. Kraay and G. Kenneth Jenkins, Oxford: Clarendon, 1968

Giuliano, Antonio, "L'identificazione del discobolo di Mirone," in *Scritti in onore di Giuliano Briganti*, edited by Marco Bona Castellotte, Milan: Longanesi, 1990

Howard, Seymour, "Some Eighteenth-Century Restorations of Myron's Discobolos," in *Antiquity Restored: Essays on the Afterlife of the Antique*, Vienna: IRSA, 1990

Pollitt, Jerome J., *The Art of Greece, 1400–31 B.C.: Sources and Documents*, Englewood Cliffs, New Jersey: Prentice Hall, 1965; 2nd edition, as *The Art of Ancient Greece: Sources and Documents*, New York: Cambridge University Press, 1990

Rausa, Federico, *L'immagine del vincitore: L'atela all'ellenismo*, Treviso, Italy: Fondazione Benetton, and Rome: Viella, 1994

Thliveri, Hara, "Evidence for the Discobolos of Myron and Its Place in Ancient Greek Art," Ph.D. diss., King's College, London, 1996

Thomas, Renate, *Athletenstatuetten der Spätarchaik und des strengen Stils*, Rome: Bretschneider, 1981

N

ELIE NADELMAN 1882–1946 *Polish, active in France and the United States*

Elie Nadelman's life and career were marked by the extremes of the early 20th century. After establishing himself in Europe, he came to the United States and became one of the preeminent sculptors of the 1920s. Nadelman's fascination with Greek sculpture was a lifelong affair, but what made his art more than a mere homage to Classicism was the manner in which he molded a modern sensibility into his work.

Nadelman was born and schooled in Warsaw; his artistic interests, however, quickly pushed him beyond the borders of Russian Poland. He attended the Warsaw Art Academy briefly before traveling to Munich for six months to view that city's art. It was there that he saw two things that would influence his future art: Classical Greek sculpture at the Glyptothek and 18th- and 19th-century dolls at the Bayerisches National-museum. In 1904 Nadelman traveled to Paris, where he then settled and began working on his drawings in earnest, working and socializing with artists such as Pablo Picasso and Henri Matisse. Nadelman took classes at the Académie Colarossi and turned his attention increasingly to the problems of mass, volume, and the relation of contours. His early drawings and sculpture were abstract in form, and he gave all his pieces the titles *Research in Volume* or *Accord of Forms*. As these titles indicate, Nadelman's artistic emphasis was entirely structurally oriented. This aesthetic has been called proto-Cubist and drew the attention of Leo Stein, the art collector, and his sister Gertrude Stein, the Modernist author, both of whom became cham-

pions of Nadelman's art. But unlike Picasso and other Cubists who continued to push abstraction further and further, Nadelman was wedded to form and Classical shapes. His sculptures of the period, such as *Standing Female Nude*, show his adherence to the ideals of ancient Greek art. Nadelman's subject matter revolved around the human figure. He worked primarily in marble and bronze, and he aimed toward achieving balance and proportion as markers of beauty. In 1909 he began to work on a series of idealized female heads. Although Classical in their facial features and hairstyles, these sculptures, with their exaggerated features and stylized expressionlessness, exuded a modern feeling.

Nadelman had tremendous success with his combination of Classicism and Modernism, and he attracted intellectuals as well as wealthy patrons. In 1911 Helena Rubenstein bought all of the pieces in Nadelman's solo exhibition at Paterson's Gallery in London. His art, however, grew increasingly out of step with newer art movements, such as Futurism and what would be later called German Expressionism. Artists of these movements tied social progress to artistic production; Nadelman's retrograde art was seen as emblematic of a cultural elite who valued the art of the past over the art of the present. This dispute became heated when, in 1912, Nadelman interrupted the Futurist Filippo Marinetti in a lecture he was giving about the need to eradicate art of the past. In 1914, however, such arguments and conversations were cut short as Europe erupted in war. Nadelman attempted to enlist in the Russian army, but, finding passage to the east impossible, he traveled first to London and then, with the help of wealthy benefactors such as Rubenstein, immigrated to New York City.

Although Nadelman's art was beginning to be viewed as passé in Europe, the American artistic community welcomed him with open arms. He was already a well-known figure—his drawings and sculpture had been exhibited in the pivotal Armory Show of 1913, and his writings had been published in Alfred Stieglitz's magazine *Camera Work*. Nadelman's first solo exhibition at Stieglitz's Photo-Secession Gallery initiated a new period of success. His sculpture, although continuing to exhibit a distinctly Classical tone in terms of proportion and style, began to reveal an increased interest in modernity. Nadelman's *Man in the Open Air* became an icon of the era. A male figure stands with his legs crossed, one arm behind his back and one leaning against a thin tree. The stance and proportions recall Greek masterpieces, but the finishing touches of a bowler hat and a bow tie update the piece. This combination of Old World style with New World flair struck a chord with Americans who, flush with money from booming industrialism and a soaring stock market, saw themselves as the epitome of all things modern. During the next decade, his art continued in this vein; he still produced the idealized female heads of bronze and marble, but he also sculpted such pieces as *Circus Girl* and *Orchestra Conductor*, which, with their contemporary dress and Classically inspired stances, made modernity eternal.

Nadelman also became interested in American folk arts. Together with his wife, Viola, he began collecting both European and American folk art in earnest. After buying an estate in 1920 in Riverdale-on-Hudson, New York, he began to build a museum on the property for his collection. In 1926 Nadelman opened to the public the Museum of Folk and Peasant Arts (later called the Museum of Folk Arts). His fortunes quickly changed, however, after the stock market crash of 1929. The Nadelmans lost much of their fortune and were forced to retreat to their Riverdale estate. Simultaneously, Nadelman's art began to fall from favor. The same optimism and decorative beauty that distinguished his art before 1929 seemed out of place during the Great Depression. Aside from two commissions for sculptural designs in New York City in the early 1930s (the Fuller Building and the Bank of Manhattan Company), Nadelman became increasingly isolated from the art community. In 1937 he was forced to sell his folk art collection and the museum. During the 1930s and 1940s, he stopped exhibiting his art but did not stop producing it. His later work consisted primarily of small plaster figures, which have a doll-like quality to them. These pieces (more than 500 in number) also resemble Greek artifacts, with their brittle and chipped

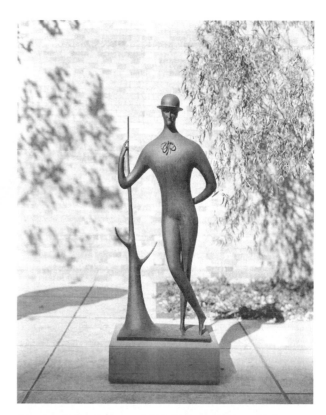

Man in the Open Air, ca. 1915, bronze, 138.4 cm high at base, 29.8 cm × 54.6 cm, The Museum of Modern Art, New York, Gift of William S. Paley (by exchange)
Photograph © Museum of Modern Art, New York

forms. These last sculptures, with their size and style, can be seen as the perfect combination of interests that had occupied Nadelman throughout his career: the timeless and the temporal, the Classical and kitsch.

ALEXIS L. BOYLAN

See also **Modernism; Picasso, Pablo**

Biography

Born in Warsaw, Poland, Russian Empire, 20 February 1882. Began studies at the Warsaw Art Academy, 1899, and returned there in 1901–02, after a period spent as a volunteer for the Imperial Russian Army; moved to Paris, 1904, and studied drawing at the Académie Colarossi; began to focus on sculpture in 1905 and exhibited works at the Salon d'Automne, Paris, 1905–07, and the Salon des Indépendants, Paris, 1907; first solo exhibition at the Galerie Druet, Paris, 1909; also participated in the Armory Show, New York City, 1913; at outbreak of World War I moved to New York City, 1914; exhibition at Alfred Stieglitz's Photo-Secession Gallery ("291"), 1915; continued to exhibit and moved to an estate in the Bronx, New York, 1920;

opened Museum of Folk and Peasant Arts to the public, 1926; lost fortune in the stock market crash of 1929; forced to sell folk art collection and museum, 1937; during World War II, served as air raid warden in Riverdale and did volunteer art instruction for patients at the Bronx Veterans' Hospital. Died in Riverdale, Bronx, New York, United States, 28 December 1946.

Selected Works

1907   *Head of a Man*; plaster (destroyed)
1909   *Classical Head*; marble; Yale University Art Gallery, New Haven, Connecticut, United States
1909   *Standing Female Nude*; bronze; Museum of Modern Art, New York City, United States
1913   *Head of a Man*; bronze; Hirshhorn Museum and Sculpture Garden, Washington, D.C., United States
1914–15 *Man in the Open Air*; bronze; Museum of Modern Art, New York City, United States
1915   *Wounded Stag*; bronze; Whitney Museum of American Art, New York City, United States
1919   *Circus Girl*; painted wood; Hirshhorn Museum and Sculpture Garden, Washington, D.C., United States
1919–21 *Orchestra Conductor*; painted wood; Hirshhorn Museum and Sculpture Garden, Washington, D.C., United States
1933   *Mrs. Clark*; marble; Sterling and Francine Clark Art Institute, Williamstown, Massachusetts, United States

Further Reading

Baur, John I.H., *The Sculpture and Drawings of Elie Nadelman, 1882–1946*, New York: Whitney Museum of American Art, 1975
Goodman, Jonathan, "The Idealism of Elie Nadelman," *Arts Magazine* 63 (February 1989)
Kertess, Klaus, "Child's Play: The Late Work of Elie Nadelman," *Artforum* 23 (March 1985)
Kirstein, Lincoln, *The Sculpture of Elie Nadelman*, New York: Museum of Modern Art, 1948
Kirstein, Lincoln, *Elie Nadelman*, New York: Eakins Press, 1973
Levin, Gail, and John B. Van Sickle, *Elie Nadelman, 1882–1946: Elie Nadelman's New Classicism*, New York: Salander-O'Reilly Galleries, 1997
Spear, Athena T., "Elie Nadelman's Early Heads (1905–1911)," *Allen Memorial Art Museum Bulletin* 28 (Spring 1971)
Stillinger, Elizabeth, "Elie and Viola Nadelman's Unprecedented Museum of Folk Arts," *Magazine Antiques* 146 (October 1994)

NANNI DI BANCO *ca.* 1370/80–1421
Italian

Nanni di Banco's exact date of birth is unknown. His father Antonio di Banco's marriage in 1368 can, however, serve as a useful indicator. In February 1405 Nanni matriculated in the Arte dei Maestri di Pietra e Legname (Guild of Stonemasons) in order to work together with his father in the Florence Cathedral construction, where he is mentioned for the first time in 1406/07 for work on the left half of the arch of the Porta della Mandorla. On 24 January 1408 he received, together with his father, the commission for the statue of the prophet *Isaiah* to be placed in one of the northern buttresses of the choir. He seems to have carved the figure largely without the collaboration of his father, for the final document from 15 December 1408, in which the latter received payment on behalf of his son, designates the statue as "facte per Iohannem eius filium in totum" (done entirely by his son Iohannes). In 1408 a figure of David was commissioned from Donatello as counterpart to the *Isaiah*. In this document Nanni is designated with the title of master for the first time. It remains controversial, however, whether this document concerns Donatello's figure of the youthful David located today in the Bargello, or whether it provides evidence for the ascription to Nanni of the figure of a prophet in the Florence Cathedral, or that of another prophet in the Museo dell'Opera del Duomo in Florence.

On 19 December 1408 Nanni is supposed to have begun work on a seated figure of *St. Luke* for one of the four niches in the entrance area of the cathedral facade begun by Arnolfo di Cambio. The other three figures, whose precise distribution on the facade is unclear, were ordered from Donatello (*St. John the Evangelist*), Bernardo Ciuffagni, and Niccolò di Piero Lamberti (*St. Mark*; all today in the Museo dell'Opera del Duomo, Florence). The influence of Antiquity is more notable in Nanni's *St. Luke* than in Donatello's *St. John the Evangelist*. Nanni's figure has more slender proportions and is more spacious and majestic; in addition, the opulent folding so prized in the International Gothic style—as can be seen in the other three figures—is markedly reduced. It probably took such a long time to finish this work—the final payment is dated 16 February 1413—because Nanni had been increasingly active with the Orsanmichele since 1410, where his reliance on the language of forms of Antiquity, already visible in the *St. Luke*, would again increase significantly.

Nanni must have begun with the over-life-size sculptures for Orsanmichele, commissioned by the great Florentine craft guilds, at almost the same time.

Since no written documents concerning them have been preserved, they can be attributed and dated solely based on stylistic properties. The three works clearly attributable to Nanni—*St. Philip* (Arte dei Calzolai [Guild of the Shoemakers]), *St. Eligius* (Arte dei Maniscalchi [Guild of the Farriers]), and the *Four Crowned Saints* (*SS. Quattro Coronati*; Arte dei Maestri di Pietra e Legname)—have been dated in the research in every possible sequence between 1409 and 1417.

The *Four Crowned Saints* group is often designated the first sculptural grouping of the Renaissance. The clear references to Antiquity in the garments, equilibrium, and shaping of the four saints' heads, which were just as pronounced in the figure of the apostle Philippus, have led some to speculate about Nanni's having taken a trip to Rome, although no documentary evidence of this can be found. A comparison of these sculptures with Donatello's *St. Mark* (1411) shows the very close relationship of the two sculptors to one another, who seem to have undergone comparable development. It is Nanni who deserves the credit for having spurred and fostered, already quite early, Florentine sculpture's turn toward antiquity. The younger Donatello, however, with whom Nanni had collaborated in the cathedral, responded to this stimulation in a more artistically successful and imaginative way.

Nanni's style took another decisive turn in 1414 with the commission for the pediment relief of the Porta della Mandorla for the Florence Cathedral. The theme of the relief is the Virgin Mary's Ascension and Lowering her Girdle to Thomas. The artist labored on this until his death in 1421 and seems to have largely completed it. With its dramatic dynamism and soft, flowing vocabulary of distinct forms, this very deep relief stands in sharp contrast to the preceding works in their nearness to Antiquity. Possible influences from theatrical performances of the Ascension, which are well documented in Tuscany in the 15th century, cannot be discounted. The stylistic change exhibited by the relief has been traced to the influence of Jacopo della Quercia, especially that of his *Fonte Gaia* in Siena, but it is also explained as a return to the formal repertoire of the Late Gothic and thus his conforming to the ambiance of the cathedral (see Paoletti, 1996; Dachs, 1996). Giorgio Vasari's suggestion, however, that the design can be traced back to Jacopo is not tenable. The relief is not solely Nanni's work, as the workshop, in which Luca della Robbia was perhaps working, participated in its creation. Six stone coats of arms from 1419 for the Arte della Lana (Wool Guild) also are attributable to the workshop.

Along with his sculpting activities, Nanni participated together with Umberto Brunelleschi and Donatello in the competition for the dome of Florence Cathedral in 1419, as is documented by receipts of payment for his drawings in this regard. In addition, he was quite active politically. As was his father before him, he was consul of the Arte dei Maestri di Pietra e Legname several times. Aside from that, he held the offices of Podestà of the Montagna Fiorentina and Castelfranco di Sopra from 1414 to 1416.

NICOLAS BOCK

See also **Architectural Sculpture in Europe: Middle Ages–19th Century; Donatello (Donato di Betto Bardi); Jacopo della Quercia**

Biography

Born Florence, Italy, *ca.* 1370–80. Came from a family of stonemasons. Matriculated in Arte dei Maestri di Pietra e Legname (Guild of Stonemasons), 1405; many other guild associations throughout professional life; along with Donatello and Lorenzo Ghiberti one of the most important sculptors of the early Renaissance in Florence; major works were produced for the Florence Cathedral and for the Church of Orsanmichele; occupied various official posts and was a key figure in matters concerning reception of Antiquity in sculptural arts of early Renaissance. Died in Florence, Italy, 12 February 1421.

Selected Works

1408   *Isaiah*; marble; Museo Nazionale del Bargello, Florence, Italy
1408–13 *St. Luke*; marble; Museo Nazionale del Bargello, Florence, Italy
1409–17 *Four Crowned Saints, St. Philip, St. Eligius*, and niche of the Guild of Stonemasons and Carpenters; marble with bronze additions; Church of Orsanmichele, Florence, Italy
1414–21 *Assumption of the Virgin*; marble; tympanum, Porta della Mandorla, Florence, Italy

Further Reading

Bergstein, Mary, "Nanni di Banco, Donatello, and Realism in the 'Testa Virile,'" *Source: Notes in the History of Art* 5 (1986)

Bergstein, Mary, "The Sculpture of Nanni di Banco," (dissertation), Columbia University, 1987

Bergstein, Mary, "The Date of Nanni di Banco's 'Quattro Santi Coronati,'" *The Burlington Magazine* 130 (1988)

Dachs, Monika, "Banco, Nanni di," in *Allgemeines Künstlerlexikon*, vol. 6, Munich: Saur, 1996

Dunkelman, Martha Levine, "Nanni di Banco," in *Italian Renaissance Sculpture in the Time of Donatello* (exhib. cat.), Detroit, Michigan: Founders Society, The Detroit Institute of Arts, 1985

Janson, Horst Woldemar, "Nanni di Banco's 'Assumption of the Virgin on the Porta della Mandorla' (1963)," in *Sixteen Studies*, by Janson, New York: Abrams, 1974

King, Catherine, "Narrative in the Representation of the Four Crowned Martyrs: Or San Michele and the Doge's Palace," *Arte Cristiana* 743 (1991)

Kreytenberg, Gerd, "Masaccio und die Skulptur Donatellos und Nanni di Bancos," in *Studien zu Renaissance und Barock: Manfred Wundram zum 60. Geburtstag: Eine Festschrift*, edited by Michael Hesse and Max Imdahl, Frankfurt and New York: Lang, 1986

Munman, Robert, "The Evangelists from the Cathedral of Florence: A Renaissance Arrangement Rediscovered," *Art Bulletin* 62 (1980)

Paoletti, John T., "Nanni di Banco," in *The Dictionary of Art*, edited by Jane Turner, New York: Grove, and London: Macmillan, 1996

Philipps, M., "A New Interpretation of the Early Style of Nanni di Banco," *Marsyas* 11 (1962/64)

Seymour, Charles Jr., "The Younger Masters of the First Campaign of the Porta della Mandorla," *Art Bulletin* 41 (1959)

FOUR CROWNED SAINTS AND NICHE OF THE GUILD OF STONEMASONS AND CARPENTERS

Nanni di Banco (ca. 1370/80–1421)

ca. 1409–1417

marble, with marble inlay and some bronze additions

h. of figures 185 cm

Church of Orsanmichele, Florence, Italy

Nanni di Banco's work for the Florentine Arte dei Maestri di Pietra e Legname (Guild of Stonemasons and Carpenters) at Orsanmichele (Florence, Italy) includes not only the four figures in the niche but also the half-length figure of Christ Blessing in the pediment, the scene of men working in the predella (a painted panel, usually small, belonging to a series of panels at the bottom of an altarpiece), and the niche itself. Although some elements of the ensemble are still Gothic in style, others reveal the transition toward the new style that we now call the Early Renaissance. Nanni's work, then, must be understood as one of a small group of revolutionary sculptures (including several others at Orsanmichele) that marked the change from Gothic to Renaissance and that helped to define the new style. Nanni's figures and niche are not securely dated, but evidence suggests they were created between 1409 and 1417.

The four crowned figures in the niche, patron saints of the commissioning guild, were stone carvers who, according to legend, lived during the late Roman Empire under the emperor Diocletian. They were converts to Christianity who were put to death when they refused imperial orders to make an idol of Aesculapius (the Roman god of healing) for his temple in Rome and to worship a figure of Apollo. A study of the four figures reveals curious disparities; the two figures on the left, for example, are each carved from a single block of stone, whereas the two figures on the right are carved from the same block. Stylistically, the figures change from Gothic to Renaissance as we read across the niche from left to right. The leftmost figure is still Gothic in style. His costume is the long, belted robe with broad folds typical of the Gothic period. His head, with its long hair, curling beard, and expression of pious satisfaction, is equally Gothic. Renaissance qualities are more evident in the other three figures who reveal the interest in antique models that will come to be such an important characteristic of the Renaissance. Their robes resemble togas, and their drapery is closer to ancient sculpture than to either medieval precedents or observation from nature. The crimping of the edge of the drapery of the saint on the far right—an effect resulting from cutting material on the bias—is also derived from a study of ancient sculpture. The serious demeanor, short hair, and distinctive stubble of the three figures on the right can all be found in Roman models. These changes suggest that Nanni designed and executed the four figures in sequence from left to right. Exactly why the artist turned to antique models for these three figures is not known, but there is a certain truthfulness to history in representing figures who lived during Late Antiquity with the costume and style of that period. It is possible, then, that the new Renaissance respect for historical accuracy seen in humanist writings played a role in Nanni's conception of this sculptural group.

The four large saints are shown as if they are engaged in a narrative moment. The open mouth of the figure on the far right and the oratorical gesture of his right hand suggest that Nanni is depicting the moment in the legend when the stone carvers are debating whether to sculpt a pagan idol or to follow the tenets of their forbidden faith. Nanni dramatizes their experience and involves the viewer in their search for a decision.

The four figures shown at work below, in the predella do not wear togas but rather the shorter, belted tunics of a Florentine 15th-century workman. Although it has been argued that the four figures refer to events in the saints' legend, they must also refer to the kinds of work undertaken by members of the sponsoring Florentine guild: laying stones and carving architectural ornament and figures, the very activities that have produced the splendid ensemble of which they are a part. This focus on everyday craftsmanship is new; an earlier predella made for the same guild had shown narrative scenes from the saints' legend. Earlier predellas at Orsanmichele had featured decorative patterns and coats of arms; it seems that it was Nanni who introduced the narrative predella in the sculpted niches at Orsanmichele.

Nanni's niche follows the basic Gothic formula seen in earlier examples at Orsanmichele, with foliate capitals, pinnacles, crocketing, and cusping in the arched opening. In this case, however, the enframing arch is rounded, not pointed. The elaborate working of the decorative elements and the complex stone inlay that decorates the niche, both of the highest quality and of unusual complexity among the niches at Orsanmichele, were probably meant as demonstrations of the kind of craftsmanship that could be expected from members of this guild.

The niche has two unexpected features. First, by hiding the supporting bases for the white marble figures behind the dark gray-veined marble ledge that forms the base of the niche, Nanni enhances the naturalism of his figures and heightens the sense that they could step out of the niche. This reading is encouraged by the manner in which feet and drapery overlap this edge. The second innovation is the sculpted cloth that is represented as if draped on the side pilasters and

across the back of the niche. As art historian Diane Zervas has emphasized, the illusion that this is cloth attached to the stone niche is heightened by the use of bronze nails. This motif, which helps to unify the figural grouping, is derived from a similar use of sculpted fabric in ancient Roman sarcophagi.

Like the other impressive guild niches at Orsanmichele, Nanni's complex exalts the importance of the guilds in the ostensibly republican government of the Florentine commune. Nanni's niche, figures, and predella relief all demonstrate that he is cognizant of the new developments revolutionizing art in general and sculpture in particular during the second decade of the 15th century.

DAVID G. WILKINS

Further Reading

Bergstein, Mary, *The Sculpture of Nanni di Banco*, Princeton, New Jersey: Princeton University Press, 2000

Butters, Suzanne B., *The Triumph of Vulcan: Sculptors' Tools, Porphyry, and the Prince in Ducal Florence*, 2 vols., Florence: Olschki, 1996

King, Catherine, "Narrative in the Representation of the Four Crowned Martyrs: Or San Michele and the Doge's Palace," *Arte Christiana* 79 (1991)

Pope-Hennessy, John, *An Introduction to Italian Sculpture*, 3 vols., London: Phaidon, 1963; 1985; 4th edition, 1996; see especially vol. 1, *Italian Gothic Sculpture*

Zervas, Diane Finiello (editor), *Orsanmichele a Firenze; Orsanmichele, Florence* (bilingual Italian–English edition), 2 vols., Modena: Panini, 1996

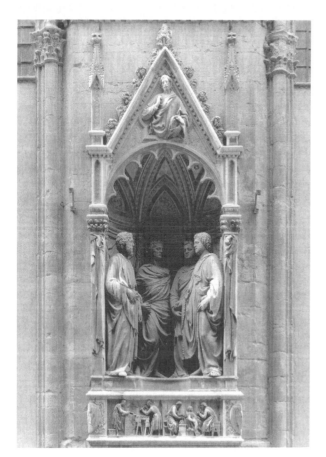

Four Crowned Saints
The Conway Library, Courtauld Institute of Art

NATABORI

Natabori refers to a Buddhist sculptural style prevalent during the 11th and 12th centuries in the eastern districts of Japan of the Late Heian and Kamakura periods. *Natabori*, or "ax-carved," sculptures are recognized by their seemingly unfinished surfaces. Made of wood, these Buddhist sculptures retain the rough-cut surface made by the round chisel employed by the sculptors, leaving an impressionistic flavor admired during this period in Japan.

At least two competing interpretations of these works have arisen. One theory holds that these works were in fact unfinished, that the production was aborted for some reason before smoothing the surface. The other theory maintains that the sculptors intentionally styled these ax-carved markings. This latter theory gains support by the appearance on many of these sculptures of a smoothed finish just beneath the modeled carvings.

Research shows that Japanese wood sculpture met with its first full development during the Early Heian period (794–894). *Natabori* sculptures may have developed from a tradition of wooden Buddhist images made for the smaller temples during this time. Scholars of Japanese art have classified the wooden sculptures of the Heian period into three subtypes: unpainted type, scented wood type, and painted type. *Natabori* sculptures are often made of one piece of wood and were not painted except in some nominal areas such as the hair, eyes, and lips, placing these works in the unpainted-type category of wood sculptures.

Various examples of *natabori* statues reveal a number of types of chisel marks that permit further classification of these wooden sculptures. The first type is characterized by deep, horizontal stripes applied regularly throughout the piece, as in the Eleven-Headed Avalokitesvara of Gumyoji Temple. This type perhaps best indicates the intention of the unfinished style in both the regularity and depth of these markings. The second type consists of a more random application of remarkable chisel marks. This style appears in the Eleven-Headed Avalokitesvara of Nichirinji Temple. The third type demonstrates a smaller number of, and weaker, chisel marks, as seen in the Avalokitesvara of Kosanji Temple. Some examples of this last type are believed to be from the Kamakura period (1185–1333). The varying styles and their dates seem to indicate a gradual formal tendency through the centuries toward abandoning the unique *natabori* style. However, the existence of few such statues and their relatively isolated locations in small temples in eastern provinces makes such an analysis questionable.

Chisel marks on the surface of Japanese wooden sculptures appear in the capital region as early as the 10th century. The markings often occur on the drapery of these Buddhist statues. Some researchers agree that wandering Buddhist monk sculptors introduced this carving method to the eastern provinces, where it was adopted as a stylizing tool for wood sculptures that lasted about two centuries. The popularity, then eventual decline and disappearance of the *natabori* sculptures may be closely linked to the political and religious tendencies of the Heian and Kamakura periods. Evidence shows that eastern provinces, such as the Kanto District, were extremely independent of central-government control during the 10th century. Such independence led to a development of a new culture. Scholars have suggested that the emergence and adoption of *natabori* sculptural techniques and styles in these areas of Japan reflect this political and social stance.

The Late Heian period (894–1185) was a grand aristocratic age lasting approximately three centuries. During this time Japan's court society celebrated a culture of elegance and refinement distinct from that of China. Such refined tastes continued through the Kamakura period, with numerous commissions for the rebuilding of great Buddhist temples such as the Todai-ji. With such a volume of Buddhist sculpture produced as graceful images of classically finished surfaces, *natabori* sculptures remained outside of the mainstream or traditional Buddhist sculpture.

Although the production of *natabori* sculptures continued into the Kamakura period, this was a time often referred to as the Japanese Renaissance, particularly in regards to sculpture. Followers of Jocho began looking back to the Nara period (710–94) for inspiration, thus ignoring the eclectic *natabori* style. Perhaps more threatening to continuing production of *natabori* sculptures was Buddhism itself. During the Kamakura period, Buddhism increased its influence on not only the nobility but also the common people's life, becoming the faith of all classes. The introduction of Zen Buddhism, which encouraged the worshiper to seek enlightenment from within rather than placing one's faith in something outside, nearly eliminated the need for additional statuary during the early part of the period.

Evidence exists of roughly carved statues dated after the Kamakura period, including those produced by monks as late as the Edo period (1603–1867). Thus, although *natabori* statues had a nominal influence on Japanese sculpture, it seems to have been a lasting one. A number of modern artists have employed the *natabori* carving technique to create abstract works. The technique allows artists to rely almost exclusively on the essential properties of the wood, allowing it to influence the outcome of their roughly finished product.

KATHY HORNBROOK

See also **Japan; Jocho**

Further Reading

Cunningham, Michael R. (editor), *Buddhist Treasures from Nara* (exhib. cat.), Cleveland, Ohio: Cleveland Museum of Art, 1998

Hiromitsu, Washizuka, *Enlightenment Embodied: The Art of the Japanese Buddhist Sculptor (7th–14th Centuries)* (exhib. cat.), New York: Japan Society Gallery, 1997

Kuno, Takeshi, *Natabori*, Toyko: Rokko Shuppan, 1976

Morse, Anne Nishimura, and Samuel Crowell Morse, *Object as Insight: Japanese Buddhist Art and Ritual* (exhib. cat.), Katonah, New York: Katonah Museum of Art, 1995

Nishikawa, Kyotaro, and Emily J. Sano, *The Great Age of Japanese Buddhist Sculpture, AD 600–1300*, Seattle: University of Washington Press, 1982

Yiengpruksawan, Mimi Hall, *Hiraizumi: Buddhist Art and Regional Politics in Twelfth Century Japan*, Cambridge, Massachusetts, and London: Harvard University Press, 1998

NATIVE NORTH AMERICA

Woodlands

Prehistory archaeologists use the term *Archaic* to describe a vast era of North American culture history stemming from as early as 8000 BCE to approximately 1000 BCE. Archaeologists note that this long episode is defined, still rather vaguely, less by what it is than what it is not. This era shows no evidence of agriculture, technology of pottery manufacture (with the exception of early fiber-tempered ceramics in the southeast), or large nucleated settlements (except until the Late Archaic period, 3000–1000 BCE). For many culture groups active at this time, a lifestyle of hunting and gathering skillfully adapted in detail to specific environmental and topographic features of a discrete territory characterizes the Archaic period. In some places in North America—the subarctic, for example—the outlines of these kinds of adaptations changed little until quite recently.

The ancient North American manufacture of lithics, blades, projectile points, and tools made of stone had always possessed a strong aesthetic dimension well beyond technical efficiency. The selection of colorful, highly lustrous, or exotic materials, decorative flaking for chipped stone tools, and eccentric nonfunctional shapes for evidently special, nonutilitarian tools becomes conspicuous in the archaeological record of the Midwest and southeast late in the Archaic period. One is hard pressed to categorize these creations as sculpture, however. Some in recent years have admired objects made with ground-stone technology, pecking, abrading, and polishing for their sculptural qualities. Atlatl (spear-thrower) weights, also known as bannerstones, exhibit a particularly high grade of finish and imaginative form. Knobbed crescent, notched double crescent, and butterfly shapes made from highly polished banded slate, speckled granite, and mottled chalcedony represent some of the more elaborate varieties of banner-stone. A bird-stone is evidently a kind of bar weight, lashed to the side of an atlatl rather than drilled through the center and pierced onto the shaft of the atlatl, as in the case of banner-stones. Bird-stones are so called because their polished forms resemble seated birds with pointed beaks and upright tails, some with telescopic pop-eyes. Although their effigy references are unmistakable, their symbolic significance remains clouded in speculation.

Unique among Late Archaic period cultures is the community reflected in the archaeological remains at the Poverty Point site, located in south-central Louisiana. Something of a planned community, the residents of Poverty Point built perishable domiciles atop a series of six concentric, crescent-shaped embankments, each about 25 meters wide and altogether stretching over a distance of approximately 1200 meters. The community garnered exotic materials from much of the eastern continent through trade: chert from the upper Mississippi valley, steatite from the Appalachians, and other varieties of stone obviously imported to this rock-poor environment. A sculptural tradition of sorts, more lapidary arts than sculpture, produced a series of remarkable effigy beads carved from very hard red jasper, including owls, insects, bivalve clams, and other less-recognizable creatures. Most measure less than 2.5 centimeters in size. The earliest human figurines produced in North America, roughly modeled in sandy clay, also come from the Poverty Point site.

Hopewell

Hopewell is certainly one of the most enigmatic and yet evocative artistic traditions of ancient North America. The term comes from the Hopewell site in south-central Ohio, which dates from approximately 200 BCE to 400 CE (the middle of the "Woodland" period, 1000 BCE–900 CE). Hopewell is a mortuary site consisting of approximately 22 burial mounds scattered within an oblong area surrounded by a low earthen embankment. Archaeologists found that the dead had been gathered together in perishable "charnel houses" resembling enlarged versions of wood and bark structures built by eastern Indians in more recent times. There, for some period of time, the dead were laid out in shallow crypts and surrounded by valuable possessions and offerings, or they were cremated in pits and artifacts likewise gathered together in caches and burned. At some moment, probably specified by a cycle of mortuary ritual, the charnel house itself was burned and buried beneath a domelike mound. The largest mound at the site, Mound 25, contained a remarkable assortment of sculptural objects included with the dead: stone pipes carved with the images of roseate spoonbills and ducks, flat cut-outs of pure, cold-hammered copper in the shape of serpents and eagles, and, most impressive, delicate sheets of nearly transparent, muscovite mica cut in the form of a graceful human hand and raptors' talons.

Several dozen sites in Ohio make up the Hopewell mortuary complex, most gathered along the Scioto River. Related but culturally independent mortuary complexes are scattered across the eastern woodlands region: along lower Ohio (Allison/Crab Orchard), the Illinois River (Havana), the lower Mississippi River (Marksville), the Tennessee River (Copena), the Gulf Coast (Porter, Santa Rosa, and Swift Creek), and even as far west as the lower Missouri River (Kansas City Hopewell). About all they share in common is some variety of mound burial and a propensity to procure exotic, presumably valuable materials for use as mortuary offerings. Elaborate, interregional procurement and exchange networks circulated distinctive "Hopewell" objects, or at least the ideas for them, among these regional mortuary complexes in varying degrees. Of particular significance were "effigy platform pipes," small, delicate smoking pipes made of soft stone and carved with remarkably observed animal effigies. Most have been recovered from the sites of the northern traditions—Ohio Hopewell, Crab Orchard, and Havana—although a small number of rather crudely carved, locally produced versions have been recovered in the south. In addition, at least two distinct traditions of human figurines modeled of fired clay existed. One was centered in the southeast but extended up through the lower Ohio region with figurines made without indications of gender or clothing, often posed in a stilted, half-seated position. Another tradition of figurine manufacture, shared between Ohio Hopewell and Havana, represents men and women elaborately dressed and ornamented and posed in several standing, seated, and kneeling postures. In at least two instances, the Turner site in Ohio and the Knight site in Illinois, several figurines of this latter style were interred together as a set, seemingly to depict an extended family group.

Mississippian

Corn agriculture had been introduced to eastern North America by as early as 600 CE, perhaps earlier. By 900 CE intensive cultivation of the American Bottoms region near present-day Illinois (some of the richest agricultural land in the world), led to growth of Cahokia, prehistoric North America's largest city. Cahokia and its satellite communities supported a population estimated at over 20,000 people. A 300-acre space enclosed by a palisade containing a large plaza and 17 platform mounds marked the center of town. The largest, Monk's Mound, measures 329 meters long by 216 meters wide at the foundation and is over 30 meters high. These flat-topped mounds functioned as elevated platforms for temples, charnel houses, and chiefly residences. Cahokia spawned a distinctive pattern of social organization of hereditary chiefdoms, which, combined with intensive corn agriculture and nucleated town planning with platform mounds, spread throughout the Southeast during the next 500 years. Archaeologists refer to this cultural pattern as "Mississippian."

Mississippian elite enlisted specialized artists for the production of elaborate ritual objects. A workshop affiliated with Cahokia created a series of small figurine sculptures and effigy smoking pipes from a locally quarried red bauxite. These compact, fully realized figural sculptures depict warriors and chiefs, some shown engaged in ritual activities, as well as figures apparently of mythical importance. A figurine recovered recently from the BBB Motor site (within the Cahokia precinct) shows a woman crouched, with a hoe, on the back of a coiled serpent whose tail sprouts gourd plants climbing up the woman's back. Trade dispersed these bauxite figurines and smoking pipes to several other Mississippian communities. Several were recovered from the "Great Mortuary" where the elite were buried at the Spiro site, in northeastern Oklahoma, and archaeologists excavated a crouching figure made of this distinctive red stone from the Moundville site in Alabama.

The Late Mississippian period (1200–1500 CE) saw the rise of several impressive Mississippian towns throughout the southeast, none of which approached the scale of Cahokia. Priests cared for the preserved remains of deceased chiefs in temples perched high on platform mounds. Ultimately, the human remains, temple goods, and offerings were interred within the mound itself. Alongside these human relics were housed large-scale stone and wooden effigies of more distant ancestors or lineage founders. At the Etowah site, in northwest Georgia, archaeologists excavating Mound C found a mammoth male and female pair of figures carved of white Georgia marble and painted with thick mineral pigments. Archaeologists have also excavated similar ancestor figures from the Angel site in southern Indiana and the already-mentioned Spiro site. Other related examples have no known provenance. All depict carefully rendered seated figures, the males wearing tight-fitting caps and females with long tresses.

Mississippian smoking pipes parallel these sculptural traditions. At least one of the bauxite figurines, the so-called Big Boy found at the Spiro site, was reworked as a smoking pipe some time after its fabrication as a figurine. Stone pipes range from hand-size to those far more massive and heavy. Several depict what appears to be a bound prisoner but may in fact represent a bundled chiefly corpse. Other stone pipes depict mythical creatures such as monstrous felines. Throughout North America tobacco is considered a sacred plant, and smoking is closely associated with religious ritual. Large-scale smoking pipes found in mortuary temple contexts would seem to function within the context of the ritual obligations of the semi-divine Mississippian elite.

Of course, archaeologists, for the most part, only recover the record of ancient arts fashioned in durable materials. Garcilaso de la Vega's account of De Soto's journey through the Southeast in 1540 hints at a vast Mississippian industry in more perishable wood. In his description of a Mississippian temple that was once located in present-day Georgia, he describes a number of monumental wooden sculptures: "twelve giants, carved in wood and copied from life, . . . two rows of statues [that were] figures of men and women," and rows of wooden chests, each with a "statue carved of wood and placed on a pedestal against the wall. This was a personal likeness of the man or woman within the chest and was made at the age he or she had attained death" (see Garcilaso de la Vega, 1951).

Archaeologists have recovered some wooden sculpture from Mississippian sites, including wooden figures and masks from the Spiro site preserved as a result of contact with salts from copper objects buried in the same "Great Mortuary." Oxygen-depleted muck also preserved wooden sculptural works from several prehistoric sites in Florida. Fort Center, a 7th-century charnel house complex of wood built out over a marsh, included several monumental figures of animals carved on top of piers or pilings. Many more diminutive wooden animal figures and masks evidently housed in a temple at the much later Key Marco site were preserved in mud after the temple collapsed.

Historic Woodlands

The rather abrupt discontinuity in the art historical record of sculptural production in the eastern Woodlands region reflects the destructive scale of postcontact epidemics. As Mississippian chiefdoms of the Southeast collapsed and dispersed, the production of ritual arts that had been in the service of the elite withered as well. The last remnant of Mississippian social organization died with the defeat of the Natchez chiefdom of the lower Mississippi valley by the French in 1729. This is not to say that Mississippian-related ideologies, cultural practices, or ritual patterns disappeared. Evidently, they were integrated into reorganized communities of dispersed Mississippian populations. But never again in eastern North America were the arts enlisted on such a vast scale in support of such a highly stratified social system. Remnants of Mississippian sculptural traditions are elusive among their historic period descendants. A Mississippian-style seated ancestor figure, now at the Smithsonian Institution in Washington, D.C., was collected among the Caddo, the direct descendents of the Spiro community in Oklahoma, but detailed knowledge of its significance was not collected with it.

The sculpture produced by the traditional tribes of the eastern woodlands and plains during the period of European colonization of North America does not include monumental works. Carving in stone, bone, and wood was confined for the most part to the ornamentation of utilitarian objects, spoons, bowls, smoking pipes, and clubs. While exhibiting remarkable sculptural qualities, they correspond more accurately to categories of decorative arts.

Figural sculpture, which was a strong component of precontact arts, persisted into the historic period only in the creation of small-scale wooden carvings of full-standing males and females, often dressed in miniature clothes. Invariably, they were associated with ritual practice. Many such figures surviving in museum collections were once part of sacred bundles, a collection of objects and natural materials employed with religious rites and prayers to maintain spiritual health and material success. The Potawatomi Human Clan Bundle linked to annual ceremonies conducted by clan members included some five carved figures, said to be the primordial ancestors of the clan. The Midewiwin Society, an initiatory organization of healers originating among the Ojibwa but spreading through the neighboring Great Lakes tribes, employed small human figures of wood for their ceremonies, but detailed information about their significance has eluded ethnographic inquisitors. Socially deviant religious practitioners of the Great Lakes tribes employed miniature figures to coerce sex from reluctant partners or to inflict disease and death upon their enemies.

The issues of spiritual health and healing are the primary concern of the Iroquois False Face Society. Members heal the sick, perform purification rites for the community in spring and autumn, and participate in the community-wide midwinter ceremonies. Their masks, with their twisted and distorted faces, derive from the originating tradition of the society, when the Great World Rim Dweller promised the Master of Life to help human beings if they would make masks in his image. Sculptors carve the masks from a living tree with appropriate accompanying rites. They consider the masks to be living things that require proper care. Mask owners feed the mask cornmeal and customarily place an offering of tobacco, in a small pouch, affixed to the back of the mask.

A wooden mask also plays a role in the Delaware Big House Ceremony, an annual ritual that ensures the ongoing health and well-being of the entire community. The ceremony requires 12 days of prayers (chanted and danced) and feasting at the Big House, a ceremonial structure. Two carved faces representing spirit powers decorate each side of the central interior support post. The mask, a humanlike face with sunken eyes and a furrowed brow, appears on the fourth day as a representation of a forest spirit, a kind of master of animals, called the Great Living Stone Face.

Southwest

The present-day Pueblo cultures of the American southwest evidently evolved from some of the earliest residents who settled the region as hunter-gatherer societies some 10,000 years ago. Pueblo traditions hold that their ancestors emerged there from a world beneath the terrestrial earth. Their transformation to settled agriculturists was gradual, according to the archaeological record. By the 10th century several groups had established permanent villages dependent on the cultivation of food plants—corn, beans, and squash—that had their origins among the civilizations to the south. The Hohokam cultural tradition migrated from Mexico, establishing colonies in southern Arizona as early as the 7th century. They brought with them sophisticated technologies for managing the meager water resources, some version of the Mesoamerican ball game, and other Mexican-related cultural traits. No evidence exists of the kind of monumental stone sculpture for which ancient Mexico is so famous, however. Instead, Hohokam artists produced small objects of stone and shell—ornaments, stone mortars perhaps for the preparation of pharmaceuticals, and other evocative objects—some carved in relief with images of horned toads, snakes, and other creatures more difficult to identify.

Sculptural creations by the Mogollon and Anasazi antecedents of the modern Pueblos are rare. Most were likely produced as components of shrines or offerings. Several caches, or collections, of wooden and stone figures of humans and animals found in New Mexico have been attributed to the Mimbres culture ("classic" Mimbres sites date between 900 and 1300). Most measure only a few centimeters in size, but an exceptionally well-preserved cache of wooden carvings included a figure over 64 centimeters high. The human figures have blocky reductive bodies with arms carved in shallow relief crossed over their torsos. This cache, at the Art Institute of Chicago, Illinois, also included a mountain lion and snakes fashioned of twisted twigs. They are brilliantly painted with white, black, and bluish-green mineral pigments. Archaeologists also report scattered finds of stone animal effigies from Anasazi-related sites, their rough but elegant forms pecked from soft sandstone.

These ancient remnants of ritual art probably relate to the modern Pueblo practice of creating shrines as part of an annual cycle of agricultural and world-renewal ceremonies. At Zuni Pueblo members of the Bow Priest or Warrior societies periodically constructed a shrine that included as its centerpiece a tall cylindrical figure with a conical cap and large, horizontal phallus. After the ceremonies were complete, the Bow Priests deposited the components of the shrine at an isolated outdoor location atop nearby Corn Mountain, where their sacred power, activated by prayers, infused the world while they eroded away to dust. These so-called War Gods have become controversial within the last few decades, since field anthropologists and traders had removed many from the site to place them in museum collections, thereby thwarting their ritual intent. The Zuni have been successful in reclaiming War Gods from museums and private collections.

Zuni and Hopi ritual includes performances by kachinas, masked impersonators of ancestral beings. Members conduct the performances in an annual cycle corresponding to the agricultural calendar. Hundreds of different kachinas exist, each with its own identifying features of appearance, including painted masks, made of leather, that fit over the entire head. Archaeologists date the origins of the kachina cult to the 13th or 14th century, as evidenced by wall paintings on ceremonial structures called kivas and the singular instance of the recovery of kachina masks from a 14th-century kiva at the site of San Lazero, on the Galisteo Plain of New Mexico.

Artists at both the Hopi and Zuni pueblos create kachina dolls, small representations of kachina dancers carved of cottonwood. Their detail faithfully reproduces all the attributes of kachina dress and mask. Their original function was in fact pedagogical, distributed to children, principally girls, to help instruct them about the kachinas. Up through the early 20th century, both the Hopi and Zuni communities attempted to restrict trafficking in kachina dolls to those within the community, but by the 1920s they were sold rather freely. Today, well-known artists make kachina sculptures as fine art sold in shows and galleries.

Pueblo communities of the American Southwest responded to visitors' appetites for purchasing "authentic" ritual sculpture by creating a tourist-art tradition of ceramic figurines. Ceramic artists of Cochiti Pueblo created expressive, whimsical hollow figurines intended for sale in Santa Fe. Teseque Pueblo specialized in smaller "Rain Gods," small seated figures holding pots on their laps. At least one trader attempted to market these innovative creations as "ancient Montezuma relics."

Northwest Coast

The northern Pacific coast of North America—present-day Washington, British Columbia, and southeast Alaska—is home to indigenous North America's greatest sculptural traditions. They consist principally of wood carving but include stone, bone, and horn on a lesser scale. The sculptural form is the result of a reductive carving process closely linked to traditions of surface ornament wherein the sculptor uses incising and relief carving illusionistically to describe positive form in relation to negative space. According to art historian Bill Holm, all the Northwest Coast sculptural styles derive at least partially from a system of two-dimensional design he calls the "form line tradition." This style of two-dimensional representation employs a small number of standardized elements situated within broad, form-defining outlines. When applied to three-dimensional representations of animal and human figures, the form lines organize the relationships between various anatomical parts. Most Northwest Coast sculpture combines a fully three-dimensional, illusionistic style of sculpture with more schematic form-line details.

The archaeological record reveals little about the early development of Northwest Coast wood-carving traditions due to poor preservation of wood remains. Bone and antler figurines, decorated combs, and other kinds of objects with surface ornamentation recovered from archaeological sites along the coast testify to the antiquity of carving traditions. A small figurine made of antler from the Glenrose site near present-day Vancouver dates to the second millennium BCE. Nearby, a multicomponent midden known as the Marpole site yielded a large number of sculptural objects made between 2500 and 1500 years ago. It included several delicate antler objects: a pestle with a handle carved as a large, heronlike bird and several miniature masks. The site produced three human figure bowls of stone, including an exceptionally large one. These three sculptures of seated figures that hold bowls on their laps are particularly significant because more than 50 other examples have been found elsewhere without archaeological context. Archaeologists speculate that they are ritual objects associated with shamanistic healing that evidently had been traded or reproduced among cultures up and down the coast. Examples have been found as far south as the Columbia River.

Some time during the 16th century, a mud slide buried a village now known as the Ozette site located on the northern coast of Washington State. This natural catastrophe preserved many architectural features, wooden objects, and other ephemeral materials. The population of the Ozette site was ancestral to modern-day Makah or Nuu-chal-nuth peoples. The site preserved several clubs carved with human and animal heads, and boxes made of cedar planks suggest early (southern) variants of the so-called form-line tradition. Perhaps most remarkable is a wooden food bowl carved in the form of a man reclining on his back, head slightly raised, knees bent, with the bowl hollowed out of his abdomen.

When James Cook visited the Nuu-chal-nuth village of Yuquat in 1778, he collected a number of objects startlingly reminiscent of the archaeological finds at Ozette. A bowl of alder wood carved in the form of a reclining woman (now at the British Museum, London) closely resembles the Ozette bowl. Cook also acquired several face masks and a series of small figural carvings. These latter miniature sculptures, such as a mother-and-child ensemble at the British Museum, offer no hint of any ritual significance. In expressive form and three-dimensionality they approach modern European canons of sculpture more closely than perhaps any other indigenous North American arts tradition. The English Modernist sculptor Henry Moore seemed to recognize this in sketches of the ethnographic collections he made at the British Museum during the 1920s.

John Webber, who accompanied Cook on his third voyage, made a sketch of the interior of a Nuu-chal-nuth house showing two large support posts, very likely of cedar, carved with human features. The domestic architecture of the Northwest Coast region included massive posts and beams of cedar and hand-hewn planks. Architectural decoration offered opportunities for monumental sculpture. A small model of a Nu-chal-nuth house post in the Berlin Ethnological Museum closely resembles the full-size examples illustrated in Webber's drawing. As is characteristic for the carving styles farther north in British Columbia, the massive figure fills out the cylindrical form of the support post with features carved in shallow relief.

The best-known examples of this volumetric sculptural tradition are the memorial poles, or totem poles, of the Haida and Tsimshian of British Columbia. Haida villages of the Queen Charlotte Islands consist of rows of houses arranged facing the beach. Many houses would include a large frontal pole placed vertically against the facade, with a circular doorway cut through the base. Artisans would carve the frontal pole with a vertical arrangement of animal and human figures, one perched on top of the other. The imagery illustrates a narrative about the ancestry of the house owner with representations of culture heroes and spirit beings that figure prominently in the origin stories of the resident family. Similar narrative carvings might adorn internal house posts. Villages would erect additional freestanding poles on the occasion of a memorial feast for a recently deceased chief, hence the term *memorial pole.* Other, shorter poles also located in front of houses would support the boxlike coffins of ancestral chiefs and their families. Freestanding memorial poles are more the standard for Tsimshian villages, located on the British Columbia mainland along the Skeena and Nass Rivers.

Farther to the north along the coastal panhandle region of southeast Alaska, the Tlingit created some of the most elaborate architectural decoration of house interiors. Like those of other Northwest Coast native cultures, the Tlingit winter house is a family possession inherited by titled chiefs through a system of matrilineal succession. Between 60 and 80, or more, family members lived in larger houses with living spaces arranged along the side walls around a central hearth. The senior chief occupied the rear of the house separated from the rest by an elaborately carved screen. Artists would carve the screen and the internal support posts with family crests and animal and human figures that played prominent roles in the mythic history of the clan. Chiefs commissioned house posts, screens, and other kinds of crest objects from established carvers. The well-known sculptural program for the Whale House of the Alaskan village of Klukwan is attributed to the Tlingit sculptor Kadjis-du-axtc, who is mentioned in field notes at the University of Pennsylvania Museum, Philadelphia. The same notes reveal that the house was dedicated with a lavish potlatch ceremony in the 1830s.

Like houses, canoes were also family property, and a prominent crest figure was positioned on the prow. Subsequently separated from the canoes, many now appear in museums as freestanding, crouching figures, such as the famous Otter Man sculpture at the University of Pennsylvania Museum. Surviving descendants of the families who commissioned these crests, however, may reassert claims of ownership and have successfully repatriated canoe prows. Art dealers removed and attempted to buy the contents of the Klukwan Whale House, but village residents who claimed ownership rights successfully thwarted the attempt.

Traditions of masks and mask making are very powerful on the Northwest Coast. Shamans among the Tlingit employ masks when healing the sick. Their masks, often used in sets of four, bring powerful spirit beings into play to assist with diagnosis of the ailment, often believed to have resulted from witchcraft. The carved features of the wooden masks often combine human and animal attributes. A Tlingit shaman also uses a rattle carved in the form of a shore bird (an oyster catcher) with the figure of a shaman shown in ecstatic transport or engaged in the act of torturing a witch.

While only Tlingit shamans use masks, other tribes of the Northwest Coast perform ceremonies using masks based on the concept of shamanism, or more properly, human control over powerful, sometimes malevolent, spirit beings. Ethnographers refer to these masked performances as secret society dances, since only those who organize them and are initiated into their secrets are supposed to know that the masked performers are not real spirit beings. Chiefs among the Tsimshian, dressed with frontlet headdresses and wielding a raven rattle that resembles the Tlingit shaman's rattle, present a performance in which they dance and call in *Naxnox*, or spirit beings, as an expression of the chief's spirit power. A number of masked dancers appear in the dance house when the chief beckons. The Tsimshian are well known for their masterly portrait masks: wizened, elderly women, with wrinkled faces or beautiful young slave girls (e.g. Portland Museum of Art, Oregon). While these masks would seem to be unlikely spirit representations, the old woman past childbearing age and the foreign slave from an alien tribe both lie outside common social relations and therefore represent potential danger and power. Haida chiefs of the Queen Charlotte Islands preside over similar ceremonies, and Haida carvers likewise produced a broad range of expressive face masks.

The Kwakiutl of southern British Columbia produced some of the most dramatic masks of the Northwest Coast region. Kwakiutl mask performances are linked to large feasts, or potlatches, hosted by wealthy families. A program of events scheduled over several days would include feasting, a formalized distribution of gifts to guests, speeches recounting the host family's ancestral legacy, and staged performances in which the host demonstrates the family's associations and mastery over powerful spirit beings, impersonated by masked dancers. The Kwakiutl regarded the Cannibal dance, or *Hamatsa*, as one of the most prestigious masquerades. Only families who possessed the dance through ancestral inheritance could perform it. After an elaborate dramatically performed fiction, in which the host's child or nephew is "kidnapped" by cannibal spirits and retrieved, family elders "cure" the child of cannibal power. At the end as many as four oversize masks representing dangerous cannibal birds with snapping beaks appear in the dance house.

Families commissioned Kwakiutl carvers to make hundreds of different kinds of masks, each a different spirit character stemming from distinctive family-owned masquerades. The masks are boldly carved and brightly painted, and some could be manipulated while worn to move their eyes, mouths, or other parts. A thunderbird "transformation mask" now in the Brooklyn Museum, New York City, splits down the middle to open wide and reveal a *sisiutl*, or double-headed serpent, inside.

Kwakiutl potlatches have been characterized as aggressive events in which the host belittles his rivals with outlandish displays of generosity. Some potlatches featured life-size wooden sculptures, called potlatch figures, which served as props during the speeches given by the host. They might depict esteemed ancestors to praise or antagonistic rivals to ridicule. Broadly carved, they often have exaggerated features in keeping with their dramatic intent.

European exploration of the Northwest Coast region by English, Spanish, and Russian expeditions revealed the economic opportunities of trade. Seaborne traders bartered for sea otter pelts, in great demand in China. The great early 19th-century whaling fleets that fished the North Pacific stopped for provisions on the Queen Charlotte Islands and the mainland. Haida sculptors of the Queen Charlotte Islands developed a trade in curios with the outland visitors, offering small sculptural works carved of argillite, a local black slate originally used for smoking pipes. The early generation of argillite carvers responded to opportunities of the market-place with exquisitely fashioned representations of the visiting sea captains, often with inlaid walrus ivory detail, or images of Haida prostitutes, another area of brisk trade. These images of Haida women are dressed in European-inspired fashion, often holding small handbags. Argillite carvers retained the smoking-pipe format, creating imaginative figural ensembles that combine ship parts, sea captains, prostitutes, and other elements more difficult to identity. These so-called ship pipes could not be smoked. Carving in this medium for outsiders continues to this day. Later artists focused their efforts on presentations of Haida myth and exotic (for the purchasers) cultural practice, miniature totem poles, and exquisitely carved dishes and miniature boxes. Charles Edenshaw, one of the best-known Haida artists from the turn of the 20th century, worked extensively in argillite but also created totem poles, sculptural tombstones, masks, headdresses, bowls, chests, and silver jewelry.

Northwest Coast sculptors such as Edenshaw, acknowledged masters within their communities, took commissions for many different kinds of objects, from monumental house posts with complex sculptural programs to small dishes and ladles, no less beautifully carved. Artists such as Edenshaw and later Kwakiutl carvers Willie Seaweed and Mungo Martin often themselves possessed chiefly titles confirmed through potlatch and the display of crest objects and masquerades. These three artists worked to preserve Northwest Coast cultural and artistic traditions endangered by government repression and population decline as the consequence of epidemic disease.

Twentieth Century

Official U.S. policy toward the native peoples of North America did everything in its power to absorb and obliterate native culture and art. As Richard Pratt, one of the most influential educators involved with formulating turn-of-the-20th-century Indian policy, put it, one must "kill the Indian to save the man." Traditional arts were threatened because they were tied so closely to cultural practice. As it turned out, the visual arts, among many other kinds of traditional practices, proved exceptionally adaptable to modern American life via the marketplace.

The market for Indian curiosities was already centuries old by 1900. As commercial mobility developed in the modern United States, opportunities to expand the market for native-made arts and crafts flourished as well. Not only did the railroad and steamship bring tourist consumers within reach of native communities, as in the case of the Southwest and the Northwest Coast, but native entrepreneurs used the railroad to find customers. Iroquois from New York State criss-crossed the country on the railroads to market Iroquois handicrafts during the early decades of the 20th century. The Southwest cultures demonstrated with compelling strength the dramatic ability of arts production to bring money to native communities; corporate interests such as the Santa Fe Railroad and the Fred Harvey Company, servicing the railroad travelers with restaurants and hotels, enlisted the help of artists to attract tourists. By the 1930s, with the more enlightened administration of the Bureau of Indian Affairs under John Collier, federal Indian policy embraced arts and crafts as a strategy for economic development within Indian communities. The bureau established the Indian Arts and Crafts Board as an instrument of economic policy.

Next to traditionally derived arts of pottery, textiles, and basket weaving, sculpture played a minor role in this transition from community-based arts to tourist consumerism. The Studio School, established in Santa Fe in 1934 as the first Native American arts school, produced few sculptors. Alan Houser, a Chiricahua Apache, was a brilliant exception. The Studio School trained him, as it did many others, to paint images of traditional dances in watercolors. He became interested in stone sculpture and bronze casting during the 1940s, eventually producing an impressive body of monumental works depicting idealized images of the traditional Apache. Inspired by such modern masters as Henry Moore and Jean (Hans) Arp, he also abstracted the human form with broad, organically inspired shapes. He was the first Native artist to have been recognized with the National Medal of Arts, in 1994.

The eccentric pottery figurines of Cochiti and the ubiquitous Rain Gods of Tesuque lay at the center of the arts-and-crafts trade during the turn-of-the-century era. Nonetheless, non-Indian promoters of native arts tended to dismiss these works as catering to the worst of tourist sensibilities. Two extremely significant Pueblo ceramic sculptors of the 20th century stem directly from this tradition, however. Helen Cordero, from Cochiti Pueblo, self-consciously revived the Cochiti figurine tradition in 1964 with the innovation of her Story Teller figures. These images of a seated elder with clusters of diminutive children hanging from every appendage have inspired countless imitations. Roxanne Swentzell of Santa Clara Pueblo trained in the arts of traditional pottery making within her community but attended the influential Institute of American Indian Arts in Santa Fe between 1978 and 1980. She creates surprisingly animated and lifelike figures, drawing from traditional Santa Clara myth and culture, as well as from more contemporary native life.

Sculptural arts in the Northwest Coast region had declined significantly during the first decades of the

20th century. Haida sculptor Bill Reid was instrumental in inspiring a contemporary revival of Northwest Coast Indian sculpture. He worked initially as a jeweler, producing diminutive works in gold and silver based on years of study with his maternal grandfather, Haida silversmith Charles Gladstone. Later in his life Reid produced several monumental commissions, among them *The Raven and the First Men* (University of British Columbia Museum of Anthropology) and *The Spirit of Haida Gwaii*, for the Canadian Consulate in Washington, D.C. Younger sculptors such as Robert Davidson, Haida, and Lysle Wilson, Haisla, represent the best of the present so-called Northwest Coast arts revival. Their work combines careful study of museum collections with sensibilities informed by the strengths and ironies of native experience today.

The mythic subjects in moose and deer antler of self-taught carver Stan Hill, Iroquois, have inspired several generations of younger artists. He draws his subjects from Iroquois mythology and folklore, with animal and human figures combined in an almost Surrealist sense of composition. His work relates to the spirit style of Ojibwa painter Norval Morriseau, although they arrived at their distinctive styles separately. Between the two of them, Morriseau and Hill defined the style and subject matter for dozens, if not hundreds, of native artists of the American Northeast working today.

As the 21st century, many prominent artists of native ancestry have graduated from university fine arts programs, where some serve as faculty. Their work sits comfortably within the contemporary art world, and the artists enjoy a broad knowledge of art history. Yet most articulate both in word and work a commitment to ancestral heritage, even if it is not readily visible to the casual viewer. Truman Lowe, Ho-Chunk or Winnebago, taught at the University of Wisconsin, Madison, from 1973 to 2000 and served as the chair of its art department. His wood constructions reflect experiences as a member of the Ho-Chunk community of Black River Falls, Wisconsin, as well as a broad interest in the greater history of Native American art. He draws inspiration from elder relations who were carvers and basket makers but also from ancient mound builders. One can compare his work with that of his contemporary Martin Puryear in the use of natural, unfinished wood to create evocative shapes, but Lowe's forms derive from traditional native architecture, canoes, mounds, shields, and other traditional sources. Like many artists of his generation, Lowe is a dedicated student of his ancestral legacy, but his work reflects a personal and forward-looking practice of making art.

DAVID PENNEY

See also **Mesoamerica**

Further Reading

Bolz, Peter, and Hans-Ulrich Sanner, *Native American Art: The Collections of the Ethnological Museum Berlin*, Seattle: University of Washington Press, 1999

Brose, David S., et al., *Ancient Art of the American Woodland Indians*, New York: Abrams, 1985

Carlson, Roy L. (editor), *Indian Traditions of the Northwest Coast*, Burnaby, British Columbia: Archaeology Press, Simon Fraser University, 1976

Garcilaso de la Vega, *The Florida of the Inca*, translated and edited by John Grier Varner and Jeanette Johnson Varner, Austin: University of Texas Press, 1951

MacDonald, George F., *Haida Art*, Seattle: University of Washington Press, 1996

Matuz, Roger (editor), *St. James Guide to Native North American Artists*, Detroit, Michigan: St. James Press, 1998

NEAR EAST, ANCIENT: NEOLITHIC

Sedentary life associated with agriculture promoted the development of sculpture during the Neolithic period, 8500–5500 BCE. The people of the ancient Near Eastern farming communities carved in stone and experimented with new materials such as clay and plaster to model human and animal images in the round and in relief.

During the Pre-Pottery Neolithic A period, 8500–8000 BCE, Levantine sites such as Salabiyeh, Nahal Ohren, and Gilgal perpetuated the former Mesolithic tradition of miniature stone carving, but with new motifs. Figures depicted women with the head barely disengaged from the shoulders and a trunk ending in two stumpy thighs. The figurines may also be viewed as representing a phallus, the nose and brows representing the foreskin and the thighs representing the testicles. The dual-gendered style continued in the sixth millennium at Shaar Hagolan, Israel, and could still be found at Tepe Yahya, Iran, in 4500 BCE.

In the seventh millennium BCE, stone female figurines were created across and throughout the Near Eastern region. In Mureybet, Tell Ramad, and Ras Shamra, Syria, the stylization was extreme. Omitting head, arms, and sexual features, the figures were reduced to a torso with squat legs and emphasized buttocks, producing a characteristic arched posture. Around 6300 BCE, tombs at Tell es-Sawwan, Iraq, included female alabaster statuettes with inlaid eyes and adorned with small bead necklaces. In the sixth millennium BCE, the theme of the pregnant woman cradling her womb was introduced at 'Ain Ghazal, Jordan, whereas Çatal Hüyük, Turkey, yielded examples of coital and double-headed figures.

Cursorily executed clay female figurines were a hallmark of the Neolithic period. The seated figures, a few centimeters high, were often reduced to a mere cone pinched at the base into pointed legs. Others displayed prominent breasts or attested pregnancy. Painted or impressed patterns suggest that some of the women were dressed. The clay figurines are found consistently mixed with ashes, charcoal, and other refuse, implying that they were thrown away because they had no intrinsic value or enduring use.

Thirty-two anthropomorphic plaster statues and busts, sometimes two-headed, were found in Ain Ghazal, Jordan, buried in two caches dated 6750 and 6570 BCE. Compared with the contemporaneous minuscule clay or stone figurines, the 35–100 centimeter high statues were monumental. The flat and oversize heads and necks and the torsos and legs were built separately around reed bundles and covered with a layer of plaster before being assembled for the final modeling. The facial features were striking. In particular, the nose was short and upturned; below the pronounced labial canal, the minuscule mouth was lipless. Bulging eyes, outlined with black bitumen, had sometimes diamond-shaped, feline pupils that cast an eerie glance. The statues showed few details except for buttocks and knees. The sex was not indicated. Fingers and toes were cut with slashes of inconsistent length and occasionally feature four to seven digits. The statues became more schematic over their 200-year evolution. Whereas two of the early figures had tiny arms holding their breasts, the later ones had no upper limbs. The red paint perhaps depicting garments disappeared. The busts also underwent greater stylization. At first, the head extended naturally from a human-shaped torso, whereas later, two heads projected from a shapeless base. Most important, an increase in size of both busts and statues may signify that the monumental quality of the figures gained importance over time.

Plastered skulls of men, women, and children are typical of the Levant during the Pre-Pottery Neolithic B period, between 7300 and 6300 BCE. At Nahal Hemar, Beisamun, Kefar Hahoresh, Israel; Jericho, Palestine; 'Ain Ghazal, Jordan; and Tell Ramad, Syria, the skulls were often buried under houses but occasionally belonged to living quarters. They were prepared by removing the flesh and the lower jaw from a human skull, covering the skull with plaster, and modeling the forehead, brows, eyes, nose, mouth, and chin. The fact that the chin was modeled over the upper teeth changed the proportions of the visage, giving it a puffy look. The plastered skulls shared some of the stylistic features of the statuary, namely, some exhibited the characteristic upturned nose. However, the treatment of the eyes was different. At Jericho, inlaid bivalve shells simulated the cornea's glossy surface. Otherwise, the eyes were depicted closed, creating an important departure from the staring statues.

Animal figurines, modeled in clay, 3 to 15 centimeters long, are familiar in sites from the Levant to Iran. They featured rams, goats, bulls, gazelles, boars, and dogs. The figurines were typically manufactured by pinching a coil of coarse clay into the head, limbs, and tail and attaching horns that had been made separately. The foreparts were exaggerated, with the head and neck bulging in front and contrasting with the small, tapering rear ends. In contrast, the horns are faithfully portrayed with the length and curvature typical of a specific species, reflecting a concern for verisimilitude. The animals stay firm on parallel legs, which suggests that they were meant to stand.

Reliefs are rarer than freestanding figures. In Turkey, Nevali Cori and Göbekli Tepe yielded monumental limestone pillars featuring lions and snakes, as well as humans. In buildings of Catal Hüyük, walls were decorated with reliefs modeled in clay over a vegetal core. The motifs featured women with legs and arms spread wide, leopards, and heads of bulls and rams fitted with actual horn cores.

The Neolithic sculptures were no doubt symbolic, but their significance remains enigmatic. The archaeological context suggests that each genre had a distinct purpose. For example, the plaster statues were buried in abandoned parts of the settlement, but the plaster skulls were with the living. Furthermore, the fact that each type of artifact has unique characteristics implies a different function; for instance, the stone figurines emphasized nudity, but clay specimens were clad. Clues to the significance of the sculptures may be derived from iconography and texts. The plaster statues presenting their breasts may be the prototype of the Bronze Age images of deities shown in the same posture. Finally, the Neolithic clay animal and human figurines may correspond to those prescribed in magical texts of the historic period.

DENISE SCHMANDT-BESSERAT

Further Reading

Bar-Yosef, O., "A Human Figurine from a Khiamian Site in the Lower Jordan Valley," *Paléorient* 6 (1980)

Broman Morales, Vivian, *Figurines and Other Clay Objects from Sarab and Cayönü*, Chicago: Oriental Institute of the University of Chicago, 1990

Cauvin, Jacques, *Naissance des divinités, naissance de l'agriculture: La révolution des symboles au néolithique*, Paris: CNRS Editions, 1997

Contenson, Henri de, and Patricia C. Anderson, *Aswad et Ghoraifé: Sites néolithiques en Damascène (Syrie) aux IXe et VIIIe millénaires avant l'ère chrétienne*, Beirut: Institut Français d'Archéologie du Proche-Orient, 1995

Garfinkel, Yosef, *The Yarmukians: Neolithic Art from Sha'ar Hagolan*, Jerusalem: Bible Lands Museum, 1999

Hauptmann, Harald, "Ein Kultgebäude in Nevali Cori," in *Between the Rivers and Over the Mountains*, edited by Marcella Frangipane, et al., Rome: Dipartimento di Scienze Storiche

Archeologiche e Anthropologiche dell'Antichità Università di Roma "La Sapienza," 1993

Mellaart, James, *Catal Hüyük: A Neolithic Town in Anatolia*, New York: McGraw Hill, 1967

Mellaart, James, *The Neolithic of the Near East*, New York: Scribner, 1975

Schmandt-Besserat, Denise, "Animal Symbols at 'Ain Ghazal," *Expedition* 39/1 (1997)

Schmandt-Besserat, Denise, "A Stone Metaphor of Creation," *Near Eastern Archaeology* 61/2 (1998)

Schmidt, Klaus, "Frühneolithische Tempel: Ein Forschungsbericht zum präkeramischen Neolitikum Obermesopotamiens," *Mitteilungen der deutschen Orient Gesellschaft* 130 (1998)

Walker Tubb, Kathryn, and Carol A. Grissom, "'Ayn Ghazal: A Comparative Study of the 1983 and 1985 Statuary Caches," *Studies in the History and Archaeology of Jordan* 5 (1995)

NEAR EAST, ANCIENT: MESOPOTAMIA

Ancient Mesopotamia covered the area of modern Iraq. Ancient Greek authors referred to the northern part of the country as Mesopotamia ("[land] between the rivers"), which was Assyria in Antiquity; today the term applies to the area covered by ancient Assyria (in earlier periods known as Akkad) and Babylonia (in earlier periods known as Sumer in the south). As the major contribution to Mesopotamian art, sculpture represented state and/or religious themes. The artistic iconography was the primary aim of the artist, and therefore it was not important to create, for instance, individual portraits or to mention artists in connection with their oeuvre.

Ubaid Period (*ca.* 4000–3500 BCE)

The Ubaid period (*ca.* 4000–3500 BCE) produced the earliest sculpted objects, which were found in southern Mesopotamia. These objects consist of carved stamp seals of stone with simple, often geometrical motifs and small figures that were sculpted in the round. No outstanding singular work emerged from the Ubaid, but general motifs influenced the sculpture of subsequent periods.

Sumerian Period (*ca.* 3500–3100 BCE)

The Sumerian period (*ca.* 3500–3100 BCE) comprises the Uruk period and the Jamdat-Nasr period, both named after main excavation sites. The Uruk period witnessed the invention of script and cylinder seals, which replaced stamp seals. Script and seals were important for organization and administration. Cylinder seals were essential for the Mesopotamian bureaucracy until the Achaemenid period (539–330 BCE). They serve as guides for the dating of archaeological finds from the ancient Near East. The large cylinder seals from the Uruk period portray scenes of captives and the "priest king," a bearded man who wears his hair in a bun and a bandage around his head and is dressed in a diagonally crossed skirt.

The development of (low-carved) reliefs resulted from carved vessels: carved stone bowls and pots were often decorated with animal figures that are attached, incised, or inlaid with colored stone. The most important vessel carved in relief is the *Vase of Uruk* (which was already broken and repaired in Antiquity), a cylindrical alabaster jug about 1 meter in height that is decorated with five panels (from bottom to top: water, plants, animals, people, and a cult scene).

The lion-hunt stela from Uruk is the first known stela (a carved and/or inscribed stone slab or pillar used for commemorative purposes) from Mesopotamia. Two narrative hunting scenes are depicted: in the upper scene the priest king kills lions with a spear and in the lower scene with oblique-shaped arrowheads, which at that time were archaistic. All of the relief carving was of little depth and avoided overlapping the figures. Human figures (for example, *Little King*) and small animals constituted the most popular sculptures carved in the round from this time. The finely carved female head known as the *Lady of Warka/Uruk* exemplifies taller statues.

Small sculpted figures, as well as the *Blau'sche Stones*, date from the Jamdat Nasr period. They represent the style of earlier reliefs and show for the first time a combination of picture and script. Seals from this period are small, squat cylinders that were worked with a drill, typified by the so-called pig-tailed figures. During the late Jamdat Nasr period, seal carving became highly schematized.

Early Dynastic Periods I, II, III (*ca.* 2900–2330 BCE)

From the Early Dynastic periods I, II, and III (*ca.* 2900–2330 BCE), sculpted objects were found in a large geographical area. Excavation sites ranged from Susa in Elam (Iran) via southern Mesopotamia to Tell Khuera in northern Syria. The center was the region of Diyala. Motifs and styles from this area were homogeneous and showed three groups of styles in chronological order: Early Dynastic periods I, II, IIIa, and IIIb. Cylinder seals are evidence of the development of cuneiform script, with depicted scenes enlarged for a personal name by a columnlike space. By this time, the use of seals was no longer limited to temple administration. The earliest seals of this period were carved in "brocade style": linear carved figures placed closely side by side and interlocking animal forms. The surface of the picture gives the impression of a pattern. Another style depicts semicouchant (half-lying, with head lifted up) animals incised with drills. Banquet scenes (people eating at tables or drinking from large vessels or cups) and contest scenes (a lion attacking a bull, both standing upright on their hind legs; sometimes involved human figures) became common subjects. In the middle, perforated quadrangular plaques with reliefs (the so-called *Weihplatten*) predominated the Early Dynastic period. They were adorned with two friezes with cult scenes (banquet, offering, and libation scenes). Closely related to the *Weihplatten* is the all-over inscribed stone plaque depicting the so-called *figure aux plumes*. Other sculpted objects are maces, such as Mesilims' with carved lions, and stelae such as the so-called *Geierstele* (stela of vultures) of Enannatum, a victory monument that features a historical inscription and four carved friezes showing Enannatum, his god Ningirsu, captured enemies, and vultures that carry away the heads and arms of dead enemies. Carved in low relief, overlapping was avoided. Proportionally, the figures correspond to those sculpted in the round, such as *Beterstatuetten*, which are 15 to 60 centimeters in height and made of light stone; the eyes and eyebrows are inlaid with bitumen and stone. The statuettes represent the dedicating person, who is clothed in a massive shaggy/tufted skirt or garment. The majority of the statuettes stand and clasp their hands in front of their breasts. Early Dynastic II statuettes (such as those from Tell Asmar) are geometrically shaped, are without volume, and have such unnatural proportions as massive shoulders and tiny hands. Large eyes, big noses, and duck-beak mouths characterize these faces. Early Dynastic IIIa statuettes are more three-dimensionally shaped; men wear smaller skirts with massive girdles and have a new kind of beard. Voluminous early Dynastic IIIb statuettes show figures sitting with thick skirts draped barrel-like around the bodies. Sculpted foundation figurines from foundation deposits confirm the enormous building activity during this period.

Akkad Period (*ca.* 2340–2198 BCE)

The influence of sculpture from the Akkad period (*ca.* 2340–2198 BCE) holds importance in the development of Mesopotamian art: statues were taller and slimmer, and the figures wore tight clothes (a new type of garment) that more naturally displayed the shape of body and muscles. The earliest depiction of garment pleats occurs during this period. Manishtusu's statues and bases, fragments of a monumental seated statue of Naramsin, and series of stelae also belong to this period. The latter show several friezes of historical scenes glorifying victories over captured enemies. The famous Sargon stela depicts the king under an umbrella among prisoners, while the Naramsin stela shows the over-life-size king in the mountains in triumph over his enemies after a victorious battle. Similarly, the *Enheduana Disk*, named after the high priestess, is a round object with a sculpted frieze depicting a cult scene. Glyptic art (carving of seals) concerns well-balanced groups and many subjects, such as frequent contest scenes. Seal carving was an important part of Mesopotamian sculptural work as seals always served as transmitters of the motifs of the current period. New presentations revealed greater gods marked by fixed attributes (for instance, Shamash, the sun god, stands with his right foot on top of a mountain; Ishtar, the goddess of love and war, is armed; Ea, the god of wisdom, is sitting in his ocean *apsû* [his cosmic subterranean water]).

Neo-Sumerian Period (*ca.* 2230–2000 BCE)

At Lagash, the most important excavation site from the Neo-Sumerian period (*ca.* 2230–2000 BCE), archaeologists have unearthed small animal sculptures, carved vessels, and a coherent group of statues made of diorite (a shiny black stone that was very precious because it was imported). Most of these statues represent the local prince Gudea, known by extensive inscriptions placed on the figure's arm, back, and skirt (seated statues show inscriptions on the throne as well). These inscriptions tell of Gudea's deeds for his god Ningirsu, in particular Gudea's construction of the temple of Eninnu. Gudea's innovations in internal affairs correspond to expressions or characteristics in the statues. For instance, one of the statues shows the local governor as an architect holding a sketch of the planned temple. Thus, he displays the current system of measures. Stelae of Gudea were carved in low relief, and the scenes arranged on friezes depict cult activities. "Basket-carriers," or peaked nails, the upper part of which are anthropomorphically shaped, and "nail figures" (human figures attached to conic pegs) belonged to foundation deposits. A different type of nail figure carries a basket on its head (for building bricks) supported by its arms.

Third Dynasty of Ur (2111–2003 BCE)

In the period of the Third Dynasty of Ur (2111–2003 BCE), the amount of glyptic art diminishes, but stone weights shaped like ducks remained popular. Names of sculptors such as Lu-Utu and Zi-kalam-ma are associated with this period. Low-relief stelae carved on both sides with cult scenes in several friezes are partially preserved and reconstructed, such as the stela of Urnammu. Figures sculpted in the round from the Isin-Larsa period include finely carved statues of Puzur-

Eshtar of Larsa and Ishtup-Ilum from Mari, which were made of dark stone.

Old Babylonian Period (1894–1595 BCE)

Sculptures carved in the round from the Old Babylonian period (1894–1595 BCE) have not survived, but statues (of governors) are mentioned in texts. For example, some years are named after the important event of the installation of a statue of a governor in a temple. Two smaller-than-life-size statues of gods, a goddess with a water bowl and a mountain god, can be traced to Mari. A new type of stela was created by Hammurabi of Babylon: the depicted scene is located at the rounded upper section, and the greater part of the long stone is carved with a royal inscription, which is prolonged by enumerated laws. The carved picture shows the king Hammurabi in front of the sun god Shamash, who carries responsibility for judicial affairs. The slim figures are differentiated and plastically carved, the clothes show the shape of the bodies, and the bulky forms of earlier periods no longer appear. The so-called introductory scene—a mediator deity leading a worshipper to a seated god—dominates the motifs of glyptics in the first half of the Old Babylonian period. Later, offering and adoration scenes (which often depict worshippers) become more common, followed by filling motifs and less important scenes, such as the motif of the hero who defeats animals and contest scenes from the Akkad period.

Representations of the traditional types of gods and cult scenes form the connection to the Neo-Sumerian tradition. During the Old Babylonian time, the use of cylinder seals increased enormously. The names of sculptors and seal cutters, such as Sin-imguranni, are known from texts.

Kassite Period (*ca.* 1415–1160 BCE)

From the Kassite period (*ca.* 1415–1160 BCE), no sculptures worked in the round are preserved, but a new genre of relief was the *kudurru* (boundary stone): irregular stelalike blocks of stone showing highly carved reliefs on all sides. The shapes of some *kudurrus* resemble Old Babylonian stelae, and the Old Babylonian tradition of long inscriptions was also appropriated. The depiction of symbols of the gods were new, as figural scenes were seldom represented in the past. Cylinder seals may be divided into three groups based on the depiction of human figures. Gods were rarely represented. A characteristic of the Old Kassite style is unnaturally long figures seen, for instance, in the architectural sculptures of the Karaindash temple: the facade was decorated with the motif of the "goddess

with the water bowl" and the "mountain god." The Younger, or Later, Kassite style had squatter proportions and more closed contours. The youngest/latest style of this period revealed more modeled features than the latter style, as depicted in some *kudurrus* and seals. The further development of this style led to the so-called grotesque style, which dominated Babylonian art during the 1st century BCE.

Assyrian Period (1350–612 BCE)

The Assyrian period (1350–612 BCE) encompasses art from the Old, Middle, and Neo-Assyrian periods. A cult vessel and a relief from the Ashur temple at Assur date from the Old Assyrian period (*ca.* 2000–1800

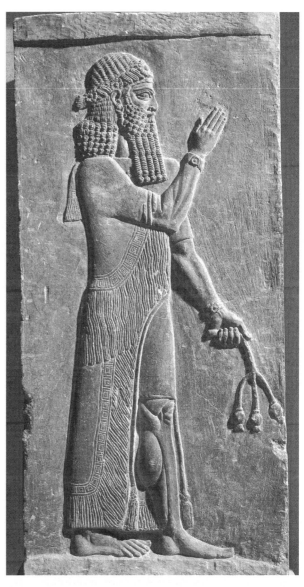

Relief from Palace of Sargon II, Khorsabad (Neo-Assyrian period, 721-705 BCE)
© Gianni Dagli Orti / CORBIS

BCE). No special style derives from the Middle Assyrian period (*ca.* 1350–1200 BCE), with only local ivories, stone vessels, and occasional objects of glass paste (such as masks) preserved as sculptures in the round. In Nuzi, excavated lion sculptures resemble the style of Old Babylonian art. Cult pedestals (altar-shaped bases with sculpted symbols of gods) from Assur were carved in a linear style and correspond to the style of the large cult basin from Assur. The so-called Nuzi glyptics of the Mitanni (people of northern Mesopotamia) employed a new material for cylinder seals. Small groups of figures resist a basic line arrangement (which was a northern Syria motif); rather, the remaining part of the picture was filled with small motifs.

Middle Assyrian cylinder-seal carving was based on one-frieze scenes of fine-modeled figures, and animal scenes were common. Contest scenes from this time show beasts standing diagonally instead of upright and on their hind legs. Sculptors who carved seals had their own guild and collaborated with goldsmiths; some cylinder seals were framed at both ends.

The Neo-Assyrian period (911–630 BCE) produced much sculpted work of stone and ivory. Rock reliefs in the mountains and huge stone panels from interior decorations of royal palaces of the Neo-Assyrian capital cities still exist. The capital cities were Nimrud/Kalhu (the northwest palace of Assurnasirpal II, 9th century BCE; the central palace of Tiglath-Pileser III, 8th century BCE; and the southwest palace of Esarhaddon, 7th century BCE, which featured the reliefs of Tiglath-Pileser III and possibly of the northwest palace), Dur Sharruken/Khorsabad (the new city founded by Sargon II, 8th century BCE), and Nineveh (the southwest palace of Sennacherib and the north palace of Assurbanipal, both dating from the 7th century BCE). Style and subjects correspond to statues (exclusively of the king, as statues of gods were intended for architectural context only, or are not preserved), stone bowls, throne daises (from Fort Shalmaneser of Shalmaneser III at Kalhu, 9th century BCE), cylinder seals, and works of bronze (such as the gates at Balawat). Polychromy (the process of adding color) enhanced the stone reliefs from palaces and ivories; the former sometimes showed traces of paint, and the latter showed traces of gold plating or inlays of glass or stone.

The palaces of the Assyrian kings were decorated with stone reliefs, which can be dated by motif, style (for example, by the use of foreground and background and the depth of carving; some reliefs stand out nearly three-dimensional, whereas others were carved shallower), and length and position of inscriptions. The depicted scenes manifest the program of the ruling king. The majority of scenes emphasize battles and sieges, showing foreign people bringing tribute, as well as hunting and cult scenes.

The general development of the Assyrian state is reflected in the state art of the reliefs; for example, Assurnasirpal's palace in Nimrud was depicted in one scene several times: two mythical winged figures pollinate a stylized palm tree, and a winged disk stands over the tree as a symbol of the god Assur. The latter scene is slightly modified: sometimes the king accompanies the tree scene and symbolizes his god-chosen, central role in the newly built state as well as his pledge to the state and his people, especially the agricultural aspect of his duty to protect the country. In other words, it was the king's responsibility—both stately and divine—to protect the crops. At the end of the Assyrian Empire, in Ashurbanipal's reliefs, this motif appears only as a decoration on the clothes of the king, whereas the subjects of his wall panels focus on the imperial economy of his reign, such as battle scenes reflecting conquests and lion hunts showing the force of the king. Huge apotropaic bull colossi with human heads as guardian figures stood at the gates of palaces. A letter from the royal correspondence describes Duianusi working at such a bull colossus for the new residential town of Sargon, Dur Sharruken. The transport of an unfinished bull colossus is depicted on a relief from Nineveh, and Neo-Assyrian kings such as Esarhaddon mention the sculptors' work in their royal inscriptions. Other sculptors (seal cutters or stone drillers, for instance) associated with this period are Qurdi-Nergal, Mannu-ki-abi, Dugul-ili, Bel-iddina, and Mannu-ki-Arbela. Bullutu, an engraver, and Iluremanni, a limestone mason from Nineveh, also contributed to the three-dimensional art of the time.

Stelae from this period resemble Hammurabis's stela (a small panel for a carved motif), which were allocated in the town or at strategically important points of the empire as victory monuments. Pillarlike stelae with steps at the upper end, such as the so-called *White Obelisk* and the *Black Obelisk* of Shalmaneser III, utilize dark stone and depict the defeated king of Judah in front of the king and all of the war booty (including animals). Ivories, mainly found at Nimrud, were carved as small objects (*pyxidae*, or round cases with a lid, and combs) or larger objects (heads of statues, such as the so-called *Mona Lisa* and *Ugly Sister*, and a scene of a lion killing a man), but most became carved panels that enhanced wooden furniture, as shown in the relief of Ashurbanipal in the "arbor" scene. Often, four or five panels were combined with a larger panel and attached to wooden furniture.

Ivory panels fell into four major carving styles: North Syrian, Phoenician (influenced by Egyptian motifs and techniques, such as cloisonné), South Syrian (a combination of the former two styles), and Assyrian.

The local Assyrian style borrowed from motifs of carved reliefs and is engraved in outline. The ivories of the other styles were carved as reliefs or as broken work (from two sides); common motifs of non-Assyrian origin are sphinxes, the "woman at the window" scene, the "figure holding a plant" scene, and the "cow suckling its calf" scene. Ivories popularly brought from Syria to Assyria as booty and tribute were sculpted in Syrian workshops.

Neo-Babylonian Period (626–539 BCE)

In the Neo-Babylonian period (626–539 BCE), the subjects and motifs of glyptic art strongly diminished, leaving behind little more than the typical scene of a worshipper before a symbol of a god. Stone sculptures carved in the round failed to survive, although texts describe impressive statues of gods and kings built of wood and plated in gold or silver. The only stone relief of this period is located in Lebanon (Nahr el-Kelb). Marked by a lengthy inscription, its picture avoids the contest tradition and instead depicts the cutting of trees (cedars) for the building of temples in Babylonia.

Neo-Babylonian royal, well-rounded stelae combine a picture and lengthy inscription but ceased development from the 9th century BCE (Marduk-zakir-shumi, prior to the first Neo-Babylonian king Nabopolassar) to the 6th century BCE (Nabonid, 555–539 BCE). The lack of other sculptural work results from a change in the art of relief-making: the former Assyrian stone reliefs were no longer produced. For the extensive construction program of the Neo-Babylonian rulers, mainly blue, white, yellow, and brownish orange glazed bricks—a part of them for three-dimensional reliefs—were used to decorate public buildings (such as Procession Street and the Ishtar Gate at Babylon). Assyro-Babylonian art is important in the tradition of art and the development of the epochs to follow.

The finest collections of Mesopotamian sculpture can be found at the British Museum, London; Musée du Louvre, Paris; Vorderasiatisches Museum, Berlin; Iraq Museum, Baghdad; Archaeological Museum, Istanbul; University of Pennsylvania Museum, Philadelphia; Metropolitan Museum, New York City; and Oriental Institute Museum, Chicago.

KARIN STELLA SCHMIDT

Further Reading

Amiet, Pierre, *L'art d'Agadé au Musée du Louvre*, Paris: Éditions Des Musées Nationaux, 1976

Amiet, Pierre, *Die Kunst des alten Orient*, Freiburg, Germany: Herder, 1977

Börker-Klähn, Jutta, *Altvorderasiatische Bildstelen und vergleichbare Felsreliefs*, Mainz, Germany: Von Zabern, 1982

von Braun-Holzinger, Eva Andrea, *Figürliche Bronzen aus Mesopotamien*, Munich: Beck, 1984

Collon, Dominique, *First Impressions: Cylinder Seals in the Ancient Near East*, London: British Museum, 1987

Harper, Prudence O., et al., editors, *Assyrian Origins: Discoveries at Ashur on the Tigris: Antiquities in the Vorderasiatisches Museum*, New York: Metropolitan Museum of Art, 1995

Matthiae, Paolo, *L'arte degli Assiri*, Rome: Laterza, 1996

Orchard, J.J., et al., *Ivories from Nimrud (1949–1963)*, London: British School of Archaeology in Iraq, 1967–92

Orthmann, Winfried, *Der Alte Orient*, Berlin: Propyläen, 1975

Schlossman, Betty L., "Portraiture in Mesopotamia in the Late Third and Early Second Millennium B.C.," *Archiv für Orientforschung (Vienna)* 28 (1981–82)

Spycket, Agnès, *La statuaire du Proche-Orient ancien*, Leiden: Brill, 1981

Strommenger, Eva, *Fünf Jahrtausende Mesopotamien: Die Kunst von den Anfängen um 5000 v. Chr. bis zu Alexander dem Grossen*, Munich: Hirmer, 1962

NEAR EAST, ANCIENT: IRAN

The ancient name of Iran was Elam. Sculpture from Iran consists primarily of religious and state art and was strongly related to Mesopotamian art.

Susa (*ca.* 3500–3100 BCE)

The center of early southwest Iranian art (*ca.* 3500–3100 BCE) was Susa (modern Shush) in Huzistan. Susa held its central position during the Proto-Elamite period (from *ca.* 3100 BCE), but Proto-Elamite finds come from a wide area, including Tepe Sialk and Tepe Yahya. Susa was an important location until the Neo-Elamite period, which ended about 600 BCE. The first cylinder seals appeared during the Proto-Elamite period, and the invention of cylinder seals possibly took place in Iran, rather than Mesopotamia. Glyptics were similar to contemporary Mesopotamian art; both areas shared the motif of the "priest king" figure who wears a skirt, a beard, and his hair in a bun.

Scenes of daily life, as well as contest scenes and the representation of captured persons, frequently mark the work of this period. The latter often show a row of strong men bent forward—this triumphal motif was common in western Iran until the Achaemenid period. The earliest sculptures, which were found in Susa, consisted of small figures carved in the round. The kneeling men and women were carved voluminously and out of proportion. Animal sculptures reveal more natural features. A lion-demon made of magnesite corresponds to depictions of local cylinder seals. Five standing "men with scars" and a "bull's man" of dark stone with inlays probably came from the south of Shiraz; the upper part of their bodies are scaly, and their faces show a deep scar. These statuettes have been interpreted as musicians and can be dated only approximately.

2500–*ca.* 1500 BCE

From about 2500 BCE, no sculptures in the round or reliefs have been excavated; however, a great number of bronze objects survive, particularly from the north. A sculpted female figure who wears jewelry, her arms stretched out sideward, comes from the north (Turang Tepe). This figure may be interpreted as a goddess, since this type of statue has been known for more than 1000 years.

The impact of the Mesopotamian Akkad period carries particular importance: at the end of Puzur-Inshushinak's reign, the Mesopotamian cuneiform script replaced the former Elamite *Strichschrift* (linear script). Mesopotamian influence can be identified in the figure of a seated goddess with a dedication of Puzur-Inshushinak. Reliefs produced during his reign show a kneeling god with a nail or peg accompanied by an interceding goddess in a pleated garment.

Statuettes from the Old Elamite period (figures often depicted wearing fringed-scarf garments) have been confirmed; written documentation also verifies the existence of governors' statues in bronze and stelae, the latter of which were probably carved with reliefs. Incised bowls and bowls with attached figures also survive. Cylinder seals are reminiscent of contemporary Mesopotamian seals because of their motifs; their engravings, however, are coarser. Adoration scenes are bordered by trees, and seals of officials show votive axes.

Middle Elamite Period (*ca.* 1500–1100 BCE)

From the Middle Elamite period (*ca.* 1500–1100 BCE), scattered pieces of stone statues of gods are known, as well as a bronze statue of Napir-Asu cast in two pieces. The naturally proportioned figure with a bell-shaped dress is a little smaller than life-size, and its surface is graphically incised. Untash-Napirisha's stela (12th century BCE) is only partly preserved. Its stylized smaller figures are of lower quality than major sculptures. The stela shows several panels featuring the king and his god and related scenes. Fragments of other sculpted finds in the Elamite style (including colored portrait heads made of clay) and statuettes have been preserved. A characteristic artistic feature up to the Neo-Elamite period is hair combed to the front, as shown by a copper head sculpture.

Rock reliefs from this period have been found at Kurangun and Naqsh-i Rustam. The latter was mostly destroyed by reworking of the relief during the Sasa-

nian period. Most of the cylinder seals of this period derive from Tchoga Zanbil; they were preferably cut of glass paste and blue glass (carved in the so-called *Kerbschnittstil*, a simple style with sharply curved outlines and flat surfaces), and are closely linked to Kassite seals from Mesopotamia. An exceptional bronze sculpture from this period is a full-cast ceremonial scene on a plaque titled *Sit Shamshi* ("survive"), which now resides at the Musée du Louvre, Paris.

Neo-Elamite

Neo-Elamite stone sculptures from the first half of the 1st millennium BCE are rare. Most of them were found at Susa; the dating of several of these finds (such as rock reliefs and bases of statues decorated with architectural buildings like towers) is difficult. A fragmentary plaque in relief from Susa shows a spinning woman and an accompanying servant. Another relief plaque, carved in lower relief than the other, is made of limestone. The perforation in the middle (for hanging on a wall) divides the two figures, an Elamite god and a human figure with an eagle's head and feet. The scene is surrounded by lotus buds in an Assyrian style. Both reliefs show stout figures. Also preserved are statues of women and the fragment of a relief of Atta-hamiti-Inshushinak (7th century BCE), which is carved in low relief. Details are incised graphically. The figure wears the typical caplike hairstyle. Rock reliefs from the Neo-Elamite period also include carved scenes found at sites near Malamir (which depict the worshipping king, queen, and a prince, as well as a procession of people) and Naqsh-i Rustam. Their style is already linked to Achaemenid art. Neo-Elamite glyptics were not well represented, and only a few cylinder seals from Susa made in a rough style of glass paste are known. Common motifs were banquet scenes, hunting scenes, and scenes that involve a "holy plant" and mythical beasts; the scenes were bordered by a ladderlike garland.

Northwestern Iran Luristan (*ca.* 1500–700 BCE)

From the area of northwestern Iran (for example, Marlik Tepe) and the site of Luristan from *ca.* 1500–700 BCE, two types of sculptures take precedence: ivories and the so-called Luristan bronzes. Local ivories dated to the 9th century BCE survive from Hasanlu. Some motifs originated in Assyria (such as battle scenes with chariots) and northern Syria (such as ornamental borders), but most reflect a local style. No Phoenician-influenced or imported ivories have been found. Ivories from Ziwije represent the Urartean style, marked by carving in low relief. Most ivories consisted of panels with scenes. Bronze objects discovered in a large bronze basin together with ivories also derive from Ziwije.

The oldest Luristan bronzes consist of cups (*ca.* 9th century BCE) decorated with a ritual banquet scene in relief and round plates often decorated with scenes inspired by Assyrian art. Most typical are standards with animals placed antithetically; later standards depicted a god between these animals, as well as pins with round or quadrangular pinheads. The latter show symmetrical motifs, many of them sculpted in open work, with the former scenes in relief.

The Medes in northern Iran are regarded as the founders of Ekbatana (modern-day Hamadan) and other cities (such as Nush-i Jan and Godin-Tepe) where official buildings were constructed with many columns; it was here that the forerunner of Achaemenid architecture developed.

Achaemenid Dynasty (559–330 BCE)

The main centers of the Persian Achaemenid Dynasty (559–330 BCE), which produced state art, were located in the center of Iran: Parsagadae, Susa, and Persepolis. Stone sculptural reliefs and sculpture in the round can be traced to Pasargadae and Persepolis, whereas multi-colored glazed bricks can be traced to Susa. In Cyrus II's residential town of Pasargadae, columns were used in the architecture of the official building. The relief of an apotropaic winged genius with an Egyptian crown that resembles Phoenician ivory works of the 7th to 6th century BCE flank the entrance. Other bas-reliefs copied Assyrian motifs, with details related to Greek art. Monumental statues of Darius I have been found in Susa. A series of statues were originally displayed at the entrances of official buildings. Glazed bricks were not found *in situ* but seem to have represented a procession of royal guards. The official buildings of Persepolis (founded by Darius I) show a variety of architectural sculpture. Marble columns on quadrangular or bell-shaped bases with floral motifs, such as that in Apadana, typified these buildings. The huge capitals featured either double volutes over wreaths of leaves or huge outstanding animal busts (bull, griffin, or fabulous beasts); the backs of two animals placed opposite one another hold the beams. Official buildings were marked by reliefs placed outside (such as at the front of the monumental staircase, entrances, or gates), the subject of which depicted processions and official acts (such as the New Year's festival) with the king and his god Ahuramazda in the scene's center. The sequence of friezes depicted long delegations from foreign countries who brought tribute and were subordinated to the Persian king. They are shown in a stereo-

typical sequence, foreigners distinguished and characterized by different clothing and attitude. The depiction of furniture may have derived from originals that were plundered by the Medes during the conquest of the Assyrian capital Ninevah in 612 BCE, stored at Ekbatana, and transferred to Achaemenid residential cities.

Symbolic animal contest scenes were also depicted in relief with elaborately carved details. The reliefs reveal a high standard, characterized by clear shapes of figures, naturalistic proportions, and fine modeling. It is attested that the sculpting of the half-round carved monumental guarding figures (winged bulls) at the entrances of official buildings, a motif originating from Mesopotamia, can be attributed to artists from many parts of the country, as well as to Greek artists. Some Achaemenid sculptors are known from texts: a contract of Cyrus II's reign found at Babylon mentions the slave Guzu-ina-bel-ashbat who was sent as an apprentice to the sculptor of the crown prince, Hashdaia, who was a slave himself. Another sculptor is Hanzan(a)i, who worked in the last quarter of the 5th century BCE at Susa. A horse's head of alabaster may be attributed to him.

Other reliefs are known from rock carvings in the mountains (such as the victory monument at Bisutun, which resembles Assyrian styles and shows Darius I in a triumphant pose) and from graves (such as rock graves at Naqsh-i Rustam) showing a cult scene over the entrance to the grave chambers (which depicts the worshipping King Xerxes in front of an altar and the suspended, winged sun disk of Ahuramazda).

Cylinder seals were still used for official administration, but stamp seals became more common. Motifs of cylinder seals were influenced by Mesopotamian seals. The main subject was the king (hunting or worshipping), often accompanied by Ahuramazda's winged sun disk. Some cylinder seals show two scenes next to each other. Stamp seals are divided in two major groups: one representing official art and traditional motifs, the other carvings in Greco-Persian style, which were influenced by Greek art.

Seleucid Dynasty (300–64 BCE)

The Seleucid Dynasty (300–64 BCE) experienced Hellenism, but Greek influences in Iranian art of this time are barely traceable. The primary sources come from Greek architectural art (ionic capitals at columns standing on Achaemenid bases at Failaka and a theater in Babylon). The capital of the Seleucid Empire was the newly founded town of Seleukeia on the Tigris (ancient Tell ʿUmar), and the plan of the city was Hippodamean. In 141 BCE, the city was captured by the Parthians, cementing a strong relationship between Seleucid and Parthian art. Most sculpted finds in a

Greek style are small objects, an outstanding example of which is a bronze statue of Hercules in a pose not frequently found in this area. The statue was erected in the temple of Apollo and is dated by its inscription in Greek and Pahlevi to 151/150 BCE.

Early Parthian Period (250–1 BCE)

Parthian art is divided either in two (Philhellenic period and Parthian period) or four groups, each of them represented by sculptures from different areas of the Parthian Empire: the Early Parthian period (250–1 BCE), found in Iran, which produced only a limited number of sculptures; the Middle Parthian period (1–150 CE), found in the western parts of the Parthian Empire; the Late Parthian I and II period (150–225 CE), found in the west and in the east (such as Hatra); and the Sub-Parthian period (230s CE), found only in Hatra.

From the Early Parthian period, most of the carved objects are reliefs, but during the following time from the Early Parthian to the Sub-Parthian period, the number of sculptures in the round increased, the largest number dating to the Late Parthian period. Sculptures include representations of gods, but most are official rock reliefs in the mountains and cult scenes. Early Parthian sculpture—known from two stelae from Assur and rock reliefs at Bisutun, Hung-i Nauruzi, and Bavian—show figures in profile (continuing the older local traditions), but also from the front, which was an elemental trait in Parthian sculpture from the second half of the 1st century CE. The figures are stylized and show geometrically shaped drapery folds. Preserved reliefs and statues, but no stone reliefs of the Middle Parthian period, can be found in the western part of the empire (Assur, Uruk, Kadhamin, Nisa, and Dura Europos), the static habit showing a distinctive rupture with Greek narrative style. In the second half of the 2nd century CE, figures in profile materialize again, but these figures were worked more naturally and the plasticity increased. The Late Parthian period (from Susiana, central Iran, and greater Mesopotamia) in its first phase was characterized by figures depicted from the front, by symmetrical figures that did not overlap, or by reliefs without depth or perspective. In its second phase, Late Parthian period art was influenced by Greco-Roman art. The Sub-Parthian style, characterized by stylized drapery folds and persons depicted from the front and standing on their right legs, was only practiced at Hatra in 240/41 CE.

Parthian art was also practiced in Palmyra and in the city-states in Commagene (the capital of which was Samosata), such as in Nemrud Dagh, the Hierotheseion of Antiochos I, and in Arsameia. Commagenian sculpture combined Hellenistic Roman (finely carved heads of figures and anatomical details) and oriental styles (figures shown from the front) and a Greco-Roman element was dominant, whereas the severe Parthian style was absent. The religious art at Nemrud Dagh was also concerned with royalty, such as the portrayal of the investiture. The intention of the Commagenean rulers to trace back their family trees to Darius I or Alexander the Great is shown by the clothing depicted in the reliefs.

Sasanian Dynasty (224–651 CE)

Sculpture from the Sasanian Dynasty (224–651 CE) is closely related to Achaemenid and Parthian art. Architectural sculpture in stone on the outside of buildings and stucco decoration inside was intended as mere decoration at Assur. Stone mosaics at Bishapur adopted from Syro-Roman art show local influence. The tradition of statues, reliefs, and rock reliefs continued, the latter for the first time found in western areas and later in the area of Kermanshah on the Silk Road. From the 3rd century CE, reliefs from Firuzabad, a monumental statue of Shapur I sculpted in stone at Bishapur, and rock reliefs from Naqsh-i Rustam survive. The 4th century CE produced triumphal scenes of kings at Bishapur. Hunting scenes, riders, and investiture scenes were sculpted at Taq-i Bostan in the 5th century CE: the right-angular rock relief was replaced by a grotto with sculpted wall decorations. From the 5th century CE, stuccowork enhanced not only wall decorations but also kings' busts, the latter of which would see adaptation to bronze in the 6th century CE. Stamp seals and cameos depicted mythical, banquet, and religious scenes, as well as horse riders. From the 6th century on, Iranian art developed without Hellenistic influences, as motifs and style began to borrow from Eastern and Northeastern art.

The preserved sculptures of this period can be seen in a wide array of international locations. A large collection of Elamite sculpture from Susa belongs to the Musée du Louvre, Paris. Most sculpture from Iran is stored or exhibited in the Iranian museums (particularly in Teheran; other finds are spread across significant museums of Europe and the United States). A vast amount of architectural sculpture from Persepolis as well as the rock reliefs in the mountains are still found at their original settings. Major works of Parthian art are also located in Iraq, primarily *in situ* or in the Iraq Museum, Baghdad.

KARIN STELLA SCHMIDT

Further Reading

Curtis, John (editor), *Mesopotamia and Iran in the Parthian and Sasanian Periods: Rejection and Revival c. 238 BC–AD 642*, London: British Museum Press, 2000

Curtis, Vesta Sarkhosh, Robert Hillenbrand, and J.M. Rogers (editors), *The Art and Archaeology of Ancient Persia: New Light on the Parthian and Sasanian Empires*, London and New York: Tauris, 1998

Gunter, Ann C., and Paul Jett, *Ancient Iranian Metalwork in the Arthur M. Sackler Gallery and the Freer Gallery of Art*, Washington, D.C.: Arthur M. Sackler Gallery and Freer Gallery of Art, Smithsonian Institution, 1992

Harper, Prudence O., Joan Aruz, and Francoise Tallon, *The Royal City of Susa: Ancient Near Eastern Treasures in the Louvre*, New York: Metropolitan Museum of Art, 1992

Mathiesen, Hans Erik, *Sculpture in the Parthian Empire: A Study in Chronology*, 2 vols., Aarhus, Denmark: Aarhus University Press, 1992

Matthiae, Paolo, *La storia dell'arte dell'oriente antico: I grande imperi*, Milan: Electa, 1996

Potts, Daniel T., *The Archaeology of Elam: Formation and Transformation of an Ancient Iranian State*, New York: Cambridge University Press, 1999

Roaf, Michael, "Sculptures and Sculptors at Persepolis," *Iran* 21 (1983)

Root, Margaret Cool,"Pyramidal Stamp Seals—The Persepolis Connection," in *Studies in Persian History: Essays in Memory of David M. Lewis*, edited by Maria Brosius and Amélie Kuhrt, Leiden, The Netherlands: Nederlands Instituut voor het Nabije Oosten, 1998

Vollkommer, Rainer (editor), *Künstlerlexikon der Antike*, 2 vols., Munich: Saur, 2001–02

NEAR EAST, ANCIENT: SYRIA

The collapse of the Hittite Empire caused the region of Syria to divide into smaller city-states: Neo-Hittite states in the north (such as Karkemish, Tell Tainat, Malatya, and Tell Fekheriyeh) and Aramaean states in the south (such as Tyros). These city-states had their own traditions and sculpture workshops. Influences between these workshops are identifiable. Sculptural motifs parallel finds from Mesopotamia, and their style bears a strong relationship to Hittite art and Egyptian influences.

Neo-Hittite Period (*ca.* 1200–850 BCE)

Neo-Hittite sculpture (*ca.* 1200–850 BCE) was mainly intended for an architectural context. Carved figures (apotropaic lions and mythical creatures) at gates or as bases for monumental statues of governors or gods characterize these works. Carved hunting, battle, cult, and dining scenes of local origin enhanced formerly undecorated bas-reliefs (*orthostats*) at city walls, gates, and palaces. Depicted gods, in particular, were closely related to Hittite tradition. Some cult scenes extend over several panels.

Late Hittite I–Late Hittite III

Three major style groups can be distinguished. Late Hittite I, found in Karkemish and Ain Dara, is discerni-ble by firm and compact figures worked in high relief. With scarcely modeled surfaces and blocklike figures, these works share the tradition of the Hittite Empire. The rough-worked bas-reliefs were possibly covered with stucco. The stylization of monumental sculptures had been a typical feature since *ca.* 1500 BCE (such as the blocklike seated figure of Idrimi of Alalakh) and continued until the 9th century BCE with over-life-size statues. These figures generally stood on beasts or on relief-carved bases; the columnar figures lacked proportion and were without necks, and their clothes were worked on the block in relief without depth. Late Hittite II sculpture is known from the workshop of Sam'al (Zincirli), which in all probability also worked at Sakcegözü; these sculptures show more differentiated surfaces. In the 8th century BCE, figures became more voluminous and had a more discernible contour, and the surfaces showed more detailed modeling. The influence of Assyrian art appears in the more natural proportions of these figures. Reliefs belonging to the Late Hittite III period were found at Karatepe and fall into one of two styles. The linear style was influenced by Phoenician art: surfaces of sculptures show very little modeling but many graphic details. The second style was influenced by the workshop of Sam'al and depicted fine-carved sculptures in high relief. Sculptures of the 8th century BCE (such as caryatids and a singular bird) of the Aramaean town of Guzana (Tell Halaf) were carved in a distinguished style characterized by more graphic representation. Of importance in Late Hittite III monumental sculpture is the finely carved head of a god excavated at the temple at Ain Dara.

Neo-Syrian Period (*ca.* 1150–540 BCE)

Neo-Syrian glyptic work, dated from 1150 to 540 BCE, relates strongly to Assyrian and Babylonian cylinder seals, but figures are more elongated and the "Syrian linear style" is characterized by a border of small triangles. Motifs and subjects borrowed from Hittite art and Egyptian influences are evident. At the western shore, stamp seals in the shape of Egyptian scarabs were used.

New Syrian cultural centers could be found in Tyros, Arslan Tash, and Aram (Damascus). The art and style was either local or strongly influenced by Phoenician art. Styles and workshops can be traced by the enormous number of carved ivories, the majority of which were transported as booty and tribute to Mesopotamia. In the 9th century BCE, the Assyrian state began to expand to the west, which caused the Syrian workshops to cease production.

The oasis Palmyra (ancient Tadmor), which is located on the desert road from the Euphrates River to Damascus and traces its importance as a commercial town back to the 19th century BCE, is now best known for its relics dating to the Hellenistic/Roman period. The Roman city was built over older Near Eastern structures and retained a variety of Near Eastern style and motif traditions, which were incorporated in Roman art and architecture. Religious and public buildings followed Hellenistic/Roman construction, but sculpted decorative details mostly followed local patterns, such as carved ornaments of Roman pillars. These local floral and geometric patterns originated in the traditional patterns of clothes and correspond exactly to the excavated textiles found in graves. Statues placed in niches or standing on bases and architectural reliefs were spread throughout the town, ranging from private "portraits" (the portrayed person is identified by an inscription, not by individual features) to religious scenes. The two types of portraits were worked either in a local style or in a Greek manner.

Within religious sculpture, cult statues of local gods reveal a Roman influence, but the carved stonework from the walls of shrines show figures from the traditions of the Parthian kingdom (men wearing Persian trousers and jewelry and holding Persian weapons). Tombs became the source of the majority of sculpted work, popularizing funerary motifs such as fully carved scenes of families or banquet scenes of local origin on reliefs. Three types of funerary sculpture were found in tower tombs and *hypogaiai* (underground rooms that were used as burial chambers), which were attached to the towers: the plaque with relief carving, the sarcophagus, and the funerary statue. The plaque was the most popular. In the latest stage, plaques held finely carved busts of the deceased, some of them dated from about 50/100 to 250/270 CE. The busts can roughly be grouped according to three major and several substyles. Characteristics include frontal views of all figures, a linear style, and carved details. Sculpted stone sarcophagi are borrowed from the West about 130 CE (earlier examples were uncarved). Roman sarcophagi, which were imported by workshops at the Syrian shore, also displayed motifs, scenes, and architectural patterns—some of which were uncommon—from Rome to Palmyra. All Palmyrene sculpture features fine, detailed work of a high technical standard and is evidence of the wealth of the settled clans of former nomads and mercantile inhabitants of Palmyra.

KARIN STELLA SCHMIDT

Further Reading

Assaf, Ali Abu, "Der Tempel von 'Ain Dara in Nordsyrien," *Antike Welt* 2 (1993)

Cluzan, Sophie, Eric Delpont, and Jeanne Monliérac, *Syrie: Mémoire et civilisation* (exhib. cat.), Paris: Imprimerie Chiffonleau, 1993

Colledge, Malcolm A.R., *The Art of Palmyra*, London: Thames and Hudson, 1976

Dentzer-Feydy, Jacqueline, and Javier Teixidor, *Les antiquités de Palmyre au Musée du Louvre*, Paris: Éditions des Musées Nationaux, 1993

Fontin, Michel, *Syrie, terre de civilisations*, Montreal, Quebec: Éditions de l'Homme, 1999; as *Syria, Land of Civilizations*, translated by Jane Macauly, 1999

Hawkins, John D., "The Neo-Hittite States in Syria and Anatolia," in *The Cambridge Ancient History*, edited by John Boardman et al., vol. 3, part 1, *The Prehistory of the Balkans, and the Middle East and the Aegean World, Tenth to Eighth Centuries B.C.*, Cambridge and New York: Cambridge University Press, 1982

Klengel, Horst, *Syria, 3000 to 300 B.C.*, Berlin: Akademie Verlag, 1992

Kühne, Hartmut, *Das Rollsiegel in Syrien: Zur Steinschneidekunst in Syrien zwischen 3300 und 300 vor Christus*, Tübingen, Germany: Universitätsbibliothek, 1980

Orthmann, Winfried, *Untersuchungen zur späthethitischen Kunst*, Bonn: Habelt, 1971

Ploug, Gunhild, *The Palmyrene Sculptures, Ny Carlsberg Glyptotek*, Copenhagen: Ny Carlsberg Glyptotek, 1995

Ruprechtsberger, Erwin M. (editor), *Palmyra: Geschichte, Kunst und Kultur der Syrischen Oasenstadt* (exhib. cat.), Linz, Austria: Gutenberg, 1987

Schmidt-Colinet, Andreas, *Palmyra: Kulturbegegnung im Grenzbereich*, Mainz, Germany: Von Zabern, 1995

NEAR EAST, ANCIENT: ANATOLIA

Located in present-day Turkey, Anatolia has a rich and varied history of sculpture dating from as early as the Neolithic period. The area's sculpture conveys the importance of this location as an early center of civilization that went through an extensive period of militarism. The history of this location can be broken into the following periods: Early and Middle Neolithic (*ca.* 7000–5000 BCE), Early to Middle Bronze Age (*ca.* 3000–1700 BCE), and Hittite (1700–1200 BCE).

Early and Middle Neolithic (*ca.* 7000–5000 BCE)

Evidence from excavations at Hacilar and Çatal Hüyük indicates that Anatolia was the site of a flourishing Neolithic culture between 7000 and 5000 BCE and may have been culturally the most advanced region of its time. The source of wealth in this area was trade, and items such as obsidian (important for the creation of Neolithic tools) provided an abundance of wealth for those who lived at these sites. Agriculture was established, and stoneware and ceramics were made as well. The 32-acre site of Çatal Hüyük (meaning "forked mound") was excavated in 1961, but excavations were stopped until the 1990s due to the technical inability to adequately preserve the findings. Dating from about 6500 to 5500 BCE, Çatal Hüyük is the largest Neolithic site so far discovered in the ancient Near East and seems to have been an early experiment in urban living.

It consisted of a mud brick and timber apartment complex without any roadways or pathways between buildings. Wooden ladders provided access to the communal flat rooftops.

Although little is known regarding the religious beliefs of the people who once lived at Çatal Hüyük, chambers identified within the complex may have functioned as shrines. These shrines stand out from other living areas of the structure because of their wealth of decoration, which consists of wall painting, plaster relief, and bovine skulls representing fertility and agricultural symbolism. Actual bulls' horns set into stylized plaster bulls' heads and plaster breasts project from the walls as images of male and female fertility and deities. These shrines also contain numerous small-scale terracotta or stone figurines thought to represent deities in male or female human form. Most of these figurines range from about 5 to 20 centimeters in height, although a few reach approximately 30 centimeters.

A particularly interesting sculptural find at this site is a group of clay Great Mother figures. These figures are sometimes painted with crosslike patterns, the significance of which is uncertain. One particular work from *ca.* 6500–5700 BCE (now in the Archaeological Museum in Ankara) is just over 15 centimeters high and likely represents a female goddess, or Great Mother, giving birth to a child. She is enthroned and flanked by a pair of armrests in the form of feline heads, and her pendulous breasts, sagging belly, and enlarged arms and legs emphasize her fertility. Although the figure is not well proportioned, attention to detail is evident in the arc-shaped indentations representing her navel and her knees. This figure typifies the fascination of the inhabitants of Çatal Hüyük with the forces of nature and fertility, as well as the special status accorded women because of their association with agriculture and reproduction. Most of these figures are female; few sculptural representations of male figures have been found. Animals in painted plaster relief have been discovered, such as a pair of plaster leopards with stylized painted spots measuring 69 by 165 centimeters long that decorate the wall at Shrine VIa.

Early to Middle Bronze Ages (*ca.* 3000–1700 BCE)

During the Early and Middle Bronze Age, a pre-Hittite group called the Hatti dominated Anatolia. Hattusas (located in central Turkey), later the capital of the Hittite Empire, was originally a Hatti settlement. During the 1930s, Turkish archaeologists discovered royal tombs at the site of Alaca Hüyük with caches of metalwork sculpture in gold, silver, and bronze, as well as

chalices inlaid with jewels and ceremonial standards representing cosmic symbols. This cache emphasizes a high degree of expertise, particularly in metalwork, including casting by the *cire perdue* (lost-wax) method, metal inlay, repoussé, filigree, and other methods. From Hasanoglan near Ankara, a statuette of silver inlaid with gold was discovered, perhaps from a tomb. It is a beautiful, stylized female image with a long, thin body, small, buttonlike breasts, and an emphasized pubic triangle and hips. The figure is nude with the exception of a pair of gold anklets around each ankle, incised bracelets on her wrists, and gold bands or sashes across her chest and back. Her head, of beaten gold, is highly stylized, with a long nose, thin lips, and large eyes and ears.

Hittite Period (1700–1200 BCE)

From about 1700 to 1200 BCE, the Hittites controlled Anatolia. The Hittite armies spread through Mesopotamia, sacking Babylon around 1595 BCE. During the 15th and 14th centuries BCE, the Hittites were one of the three most powerful cultures in the Near East, and during the 13th century BCE, they shared dominance with the Egyptians. The prominence of fortification and citadels constructed from large blocks of heavy stone allude to the Hittite preoccupation with military power. Sculptural discoveries in this area include stone relief sculpture that served as adornment for these architectural structures.

At Hattusas, near the modern-day Turkish village of Boghazköy on the Halys River, the height of the Hittite Empire transpired. The remains of palaces and temples, a high citadel, and a four-mile circuit of fortifications indicate that this was the home of a great imperial people. At the western entrance to the citadel at Hattusas, called the Lion Gate or Royal Gate, a pair of guardian lions flanks the entrance, their forequarters protruding from massive blocks of stone to either side of the entrance. Always shown awake, lions are a popular and familiar guardian image, and this 2.1-meter-high pair of lions would have intimidated the boldest intruder. The lions' front legs, heads, and chests were carved in high relief on exposed faces of natural rock, whereas details such as the mane and eyes were incised. The gate lions at Boghazköy have a perfected frontal view but not much profile. This frontal technique has an immediate and powerful effect on the viewer. Many other sites repeat the guardian theme; for example, at the Hittite site of Alaca Hüyük, a pair of sphinxes guards the entryway to the citadel.

Although animal images are frequently found, the Hittites' main concern was capturing images of human activity, particularly religious and militaristic themes. Low-relief sculptural images with military themes run along the lower portion of the Cyclopaean city walls at Hattusas. For example, an over-life-size image of a Hittite war god is represented on the King's Gate. Clad in a kiltlike outfit and an elaborate helmet in a style adopted from Mesopotamia, the figure brandishes a weapon and raises a fist. Stylistically, he is shown in a traditionally Mesopotamian composite view with a frontally facing chest and torso and a profile face and leg, rendered in the position from which his most salient features could be easily identified. The sculptor gave special attention to the muscles of his arms and legs in order to emphasize their power, whereas clothed areas remain flattened. The firm open stance and raised fist of the King's Gate figure, as well as his steady gaze, give him an appearance fitting of authority and divinity.

Temple architecture from Hattusas also includes low-relief stone sculpture (on walls) that is both religious and related to military conquest. At the rock-cut sanctuary of Yazilikaya to the northeast of Hattusas, walls contain relief sculptures of male and female deities, including a 3-meter-high image of the Hittite sword god and a procession of 12 gods as armed warriors. The armed warrior deities are rendered marching in procession, with overlapping legs providing a sense of rhythm and movement. They are dressed identically in belted kilts, shirts, and large conical hats or helmets and are brandishing weapons. They are shown in composite view, with profile head and legs and three-quarter–profile chest. Images of royalty from numerous sites include domestic scenes and family processions.

At the end of the 2nd millennium BCE, a time of crisis for all the Near East, the Hittite Empire disappeared under circumstances that are still unclear, leaving behind the remains of a powerful and intellectually brilliant civilization. The Phrygians invaded Anatolia from eastern Europe during the final centuries of the 2nd millennium BCE. Excavations of Phrygian sites have uncovered numerous tombs, including the alleged tomb of Midas, inside of which, enclosed by juniper logs and buried in rubble, were discovered wooden inlaid furniture and bronze vessels.

CATHERINE BURDICK

Further Reading

Akurgal, Ekrem, *Treasures of Turkey*, trans. by Robert Allen, Geneva: Editions d'Art Albert Skira, 1966
Akurgal, Ekrem, *The Art and Architecture of Turkey*, New York: Rizzoli International Publications, 1980
Gurney, Oliver Robert, *The Hittites*, New York: Penguin, 1990
Hanfmann, George M.A., *Sardis from Prehistoric to Roman Times: Results of the Archaeological Exploration of Sardis, 1958–1975*, Cambridge, Massachusetts: Harvard University Press, 1983
Lloyd, Seton, *Ancient Turkey: A Traveller's History of Anatolia*, Berkeley: University of California Press, 1989
Mellaart, James, *The Earliest Civilizations of the Near East*, New York: McGraw-Hill, 1965
Mellaart, James, *Çatal Hüyük: A Neolithic Town in Anatolia*, New York: McGraw-Hill, 1967

NEOCLASSICISM AND ROMANTICISM

The traditions of figurative sculpture in western Europe from the Renaissance onward could, in an extremely general sense, be considered Neoclassical, insofar as most accomplished and admired pieces were heavily influenced by Italian sculptors' rediscovery of Greek and Roman sculpture during the proto-Renaissance and early Renaissance periods. However, from the later 18th century into the 19th century, the practice of figurative style influenced by Classical Antiquity was newly reinflected by a number of factors aesthetic, intellectual, and political. The interplay and coincidence of these factors forged a new and different attitude toward the ubiquitous Classical inheritance that can be identified rightfully as a new phase in sculptural history. An important contribution to this sense of demarcation from previous eras was Neoclassicism's position, emerging out of complex interactions between the pure visual sensation of aesthetics and the philosophical and political aspirations of the 18th century Enlightenment. The precise nature of these interrelationships has been interpreted with different emphasis from generation to generation of scholars.

Influences that set Neoclassicism apart from earlier uses of Classical styles include the archeological discoveries at Herculaneum and Pompeii, which permitted a far more contextualized and interrelated knowledge of ancient styles than hitherto accessible. These recent discoveries gave impetus to an austere and archeological approach to quotation from the Classical in many art disciplines in the mid to late 18th century. Art theoretical writing of the 18th century also set Neoclassicism on a new and different course, favoring sculpture as a medium and identifying it as a witness to the glorious Classical past. Johann Joachim Winkelmann, writing during the mid 18th century, considered Greek Classical sculpture as one of the highest achievements in known human civilization, and his works stimulated a new cultural focus upon statuary. His fervent admiration for these works placed high Classical sculpture at the forefront of intellectual respectability for at least a century and a half, especially in German-speaking countries but also throughout the continuum of European culture. Moreover, his writings made a crucial link between the physical beauty of the Greek statue and its *virtu* as cultural treasure and moral guide. The terms of his praise set out clear possibilities for linking Classical sculpture to the growing intellectual movement of the Enlightenment. In the wake of such arguments, the finest sculptures from Greece and Rome could be seen as akin to or parallel to current radical intellectual thought of the period. This important shift in perception contributed to the growing credibility of the Neoclassical style among sculptors. Gotthold Ephraim Lessing's essay on the *Laocoön*, first published in 1766, was another highly influential mid 18th century theoretical text on aesthetics that employed Greek sculpture as a metaphor in discussing culture at the highest level of the ideal.

The formation of a circle of cultured émigrés (Winkelmann prominent among them) from the north—Germany, Scandinavia, and Britain—living in Rome during the 18th century coincided with and facilitated this renewed fascination with Classical culture. These men advocated a purist style in sculpture. Some of the earliest visual expressions of the Neoclassical style can also be sourced to northern artists. The Swedish sculptor Johan Tobias Sergel, another long-term Roman resident, although still relatively unfamiliar outside of a German-Scandinavian nexus, had an iconic presence among his contemporaries and exerted considerable international stylistic influence. He was one of the first sculptors to rigorously study known ancient visual precedents and make his own creative output—to a great degree—a series of variations upon respected early works. Moreover, it was expected that his erudite cross-references could be read as such by the educated eye. Not only did he emphasize a purity of visual Classical style but also his subjects drew lofty and sublime emotions from Classical legends and history, adding the sense of republican moral virtue that was a potent force itself in reconfiguring the bounds of what was considered appropriate and admirable in sculpture.

Erudition and archeology also produced an equally influential British Neoclassical stream, showcased most effectively by Josiah Wedgwood's high-profile porcelain factory. Major artists, male and female, produced designs in a purist Neoclassical style for commercial production, and the ware was exported internationally throughout the (then known) bounds of the cultured world. The Portland Vase directly expresses the historical and scholarly basis of the 18th-century Neoclassical: its association with aristocratic connoisseurship, especially as it had developed in English practice, and the attention to replicating Classical art with utmost fidelity and felicity. The most remarkable and prophetic aspect of Wedgwood's ceramic production in relation to the growing Neoclassical aesthetic was the conscious avoidance of current canons of beauty in hairstyling and body types in his molded figurative decorations. The Classical style and appearance of the colored jasperware is heightened by the strong contrast between figures and background, which references ancient carved gems and Roman decorative glass.

Politics also contributed to bringing a new interpretation of classicism to the fore. Although French court circles by the 1780s on the eve of the Revolution were already beginning to seek alternatives to the Rococo, Neoclassicism has been broadly associated in both contemporary minds and subsequent generations with (French) Revolutionary dissent. The definition of the Neoclassical style as a sign of the "revolutionary" appears as early as the mid 19th-century writings of Charles-Pierre Baudelaire. In the political and cultural flux after the Revolution of 1789, one can equally find—as Alison West rightly notes—counter texts by revolutionary writers that set out a minority counter position that has not survived into the art historical mainstream (see West, 1998). These radicals suggested that Neoclassicism was not an "accessible" style for the "people"; rather, it but was an elitist and obscure language for aristocratic connoisseurs. This argument is linked to a belief that the plain white marble of Neoclassical tradition represented a higher, more cerebral art than the verismo (realism) and color of such popularist plastic expressions as wax works, sideshows, and votive figures and, later in the 19th century, dress mannequins.

In the dominant interpretation, due to the linking of Greek and Roman art to the ideals of the Enlightenment through reading it as unquestionably masculine, rational, and ideal, the late 18th-century use of Greek or Roman style in sculpture began to have new resonance and gave out new and radical intellectual meanings. If the Neoclassical can be read in some ways as the anti-Rococo, one could uphold—especially in a French context—the direct linkage confidently stated by Fred Licht that Neoclassicism was the sculptural language of the French Revolution (see Licht, 1967). Surveying a wide range of works suggests that Licht's analysis is somewhat crude. Not only were elements of Neoclassicism surfacing during the Ancien Régime in France but also in sculpture (and other media) the style became important in contexts that were neither dissident nor revolutionary. Artists and architects in England, Italy, Germany, Sweden, Denmark, and Russia also experienced a heightened awareness of the Classical, but they worked in cultural climates that cannot be fully aligned to the deep political and social tensions of France. For instance, the Swede Johan Tobias Sergel enjoyed royal patronage, and some of the most severe and linear yet graceful expressions of Neoclassicism were created by German sculptors from about 1790 to 1840, again removed from the immediate political upheavals of the French Revolution.

Yet Licht's claim that there was a reforming, revolutionary impetus in the understandings and uses of Neoclassicism in late-18th-century France is broadly valid in terms of the change of sensibility and the new intellectual horizons. Sculptural reference to the Romans recalled the Roman republic and therefore governance without a monarch. Neoclassicism in painting was already established as the revolutionary style par excellence. Likewise, sculptural Neoclassicism was not the style associated directly with the throne, so it could be read as a visual symbol of the nascent middle classes. The revolutionary impetus was heightened during the late 18th and early 19th century through the frequent reading of Neoclassicism as an explicitly non-Christian style. Simultaneously Neoclassicism begot outstanding Christian sculptures such as Carlo Marochetti's *Assumption of the Magdalene* (1835–41) and Jean-Pierre Cortot's *Marie-Antoinette Succoured by Religion* (*ca.* 1827). Neoclassicism was also consistently read during this era, and by subsequent generations, as a "humanist" style, when such a description indicated straightforward praise. The style was considered humanist at its emergence by reflecting a tangible presence of the human body and the natural world (despite later advocates of experimental art often reading Neoclassicism as an arid, effete rejection of the "real"). If Neoclassicism was read as a "realist" style, it was equally seen as fundamentally opposed to the unnatural artifice of the Rococo. This appeal to the authority of the "laws of nature" was seen as a democratic overturning of the courtly and therefore a further link to the Enlightenment. The humanist impetus was understood to be ratified through sculptural Neoclassicism's placing of the human (usually male) body as the highest authority and caliber of aesthetic and moral rightfulness.

This nexus between the political and philosophical world of the Enlightenment, the "rights of man," and

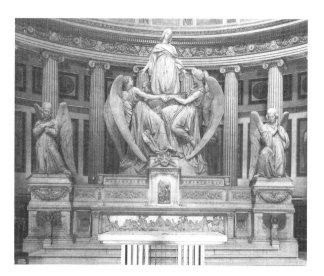

Carlo (Charles) Marochetti, *Assumption of the Magdalene*, High altar of the Church of the Madeleine, 1833–34, Paris The Conway Library, Courtauld Institute of Art

the art historical issue of Greco-Roman visual quotations was consolidated by the regime of Napoléon, for whose government the Neoclassical became almost the equivalent of a corporate logo. Myriads of classicizing busts, portraits, monuments, small trophies, and presentation gifts were distributed throughout the centers of civic bureaucracy and military infrastructure in his empire.

At the same time, the Neoclassical was accepted as the appropriate style for the British to commemorate those national heroes who distinguished themselves in fighting Napoléon. Indeed, as Benedict Read has put forward, the many memorials to heroes of the Napoléonic Wars brokered the ongoing Victorian British statue mania and fascination with erecting monuments to local worthies, which bore fruit in provincial as well as metropolitan communities (see Read, 1982). The association of Neoclassicism with Britain and (to the present day) British imperialism itself became ratified in a highly political context through the acquisition of the Elgin marbles, the arrival in Britain of which proved highly influential on sculptors across Europe. These connections have been spun out by contemporary poststructuralist and postcolonial scholars who suggest that the hierarchical ranking implied by the admiration of Classical art in the wake of Winckelmann could morph easily from the aesthetic to the racial (see Leoussi, 1998). Thus the Greek Classical inheritance was, first, not only robbed from the modern Greeks (seen as orientalized and Balkanized and therefore not "worthy" of their sculptural patrimony either actually or metaphorically), but, second, firmly coopted to denote the white Eurocentric upper-class male. Monuments such as G.F. Watt's memorial to Cecil Rhodes are seen by scholars to further demonstrate the imperialist and expansionist ambitions ascribed by postcolonialists to the original acquisition of the marbles. Such arguments carry the greatest fascination in that the Elgin marbles still can be read in the 21st century as symbolic of the *virtu* and identity of either modern Britain or modern Greece to the degree that a major political controversy continues to flourish over their rightful location. This ongoing dispute demonstrates the important role that the Neoclassical has played in the visual vocabulary of consolidating the modern nationalist (generally) republican state.

The Neoclassical was not tied solely to the new intellectual currents of the 18th century, nor did it speak only of imperial ambition. Bertel Thorvaldsen's Neoclassical style of exquisite clarity and grace could express the piety and domestic outlook of the middle classes in Denmark, a country not popularly associated with pan-European expansion. The spread of the Biedermeier style across central and northern Europe, into which Thorvaldsen's sculptures so effortlessly assimilated themselves, facilitated a truly international reiteration of Neoclassicism a generation after the French Revolution. This newly expanded audience was bourgeois as much as imperial. Pirated copies of Thorvaldsen's *Day* and *Night* in porcelain or plaster could be found on drawing room walls from Melbourne, Florida, to Melbourne, Australia, and from St. Petersburg, Florida, to St. Petersburg, Russia. Thorvaldsen also successfully claimed Neoclassicism—despite its Roman (both ancient and Catholic) and pagan roots—for Protestant Christianity. The hairstyles and features of his angelic figures are as clearly stylized in a Greek manner as those borne by the deeply classicizing pagan deities sculpted by Canova.

The new forces coming to bear on sculpture (both in the realm of critical theory and equally in practical execution and design) at this period justify distinguishing between the late-18th- to mid-19th-century interpretation of the Classical and that of previous generations. This demarcation is still valid to a substantial degree even when current scholarly judgments upon the Neoclassical style are rapidly transmuting in the wake of Postmodernism and a broadening of the canons of the artistically acceptable. No longer does art history follow a Darwinian narrative of perfectibility, enacted by a chain of ever more enlightened and radical masters, liberating visual arts from the mimetic. Neoclassical sculpture has been long co-opted into this adversarial construction of art history as first an offshoot of painter J.L. David's proto-Modernist "challenge" to the 18th-century Rococo—and by implication the feminized corruption of the Ancien Régime. Simultaneously 19th-century Neoclassical sculpture was the "other" against which Romantic and avant-garde "innovations" were showcased. Images of Hiram Power's *Greek Slave* (1844) or Gibson's *Tinted Venus* (1856) were included in undergraduate texts and courses to raise a laugh; Canova's nymphs merely demonstrated for docents and lecturers the sexual hypocrisy of academic art against the maturity of painters such as Edouard Manet.

Ironically, recent scholarly discussion suggests that the aim and concept of 18th- and 19th-century returns to the Greek and Roman were themselves extremely Romantic. The belief that one could—substantially by the magic potency and credibility of male scholarship and erudition—leap over an intervening millennium to reconstruct a bygone ethos, to communicate with the past, and thereby forge a more "pure" style, untainted by the triviality and corruption of the modern and everyday, is inherently Romantic. Likewise there is a Romantic impetus in the idea that through intense concentration and aesthetic/intellectual effort one could identify and commune with "the past" and the authority of the "source." The late-18th-century and early-19th-century practice of immersing oneself in the emotional experience of revisiting the "ancients," by visiting sculptural icons by torchlight or in a sculptural Walhalla, indicates the overlapping of the Romantic with the Classical. Collections of modern and historic sculptural icons in a sympathetic and suggestive architectural setting were assembled internationally. When these collections survive substantially intact, the interaction between the works and their setting suggests the intense emotional validation involved in Neoclassicism as well as the network of aesthetics and scholarship that distinguished the style at its most highly developed. Such pantheons were not only located in the mansions of European aristocracy but in the Congress building of the United States, the Hall of Fame for Great Americans, New York (erected 1900–01), and (in a more rudimentary form) in the office of the late-19th-century premier of New South Wales, Sir Henry Parkes, or, in an even more ad hoc fashion, in Cathedral Square, Christchurch, New Zealand. In the latter, sculptures with highly charged regional significance were erected over several decades in close proximity to engage in the type of visual and conceptual dialogue associated with these sculptural pavilions.

But while the center appears to crumble under the mutations and nuances of scholarly debate, Fred Licht's identification of the Neoclassical in sculpture as a protomodel of an identifiable "Modernist" style still holds basically true, insofar as Neoclassicism was a universalizing style, with its own dominant and self-reflexive values. It also was underpinned and interwoven with certain rhetorical and theoretical components and surrounded by intellectualizing discourse. Both these elements are harbingers of the Modern. The sense of mission and transformation in the declamatory statements made around Neoclassical sculpture undeniably preempt the Modernist experience. Well before the Romantic era, the "hostility to deception of any kind" identified by Hugh Honour establishes the sense of morality and critique of the conventional that sustained Modernism for two centuries (see Honour, 1972). Honour goes so far as to claim that Neoclassicism in sculpture and painting introduced the primacy of formalist values above illustration, thus establishing attitudes to art practice "that have so vitally sustained the 20th century artist."

However, one should not emphasize the Postmodern origins of the construction of Neoclassicism as a contested field. Sculptural Neoclassicism always was surrounded by controversy as to where a stance could be taken and values defended. It delivered up intense debates and anxieties from within its own parameters, especially when further archeological discoveries in the 19th century proved without a doubt that Greek practice favored polychromy. Nationalism provided another challenge as to how far one could express one's "national identity" through the favored style of the period, which deemphasized particularity and favored schematization. Canova's transnational popularity, and the inescapable influence of his taste and skill in reviving the Classical spirit, sat uneasily with the strongly patriotic sentiments governing the appreciation and patronage of sculptors by the French state. From Winckelmann onward, the supposedly analytical rigor of Neoclassicism was also laced with a certain erotic component, made manifest in Canova. From this sensuous undertone the legions of *filles de marbre* (erotic young female nudes) seen at the salon throughout the 19th century drew inspiration. Another variable available to Neoclassical sculptors was the choice of which Classical era or region one should reference, for the resulting effect could express vastly different characteristics if one looked either to Rome or to Athens.

Yet one can comb out the signs of Neoclassicism more easily after viewing a range of sculptures than from heeding the contested textual fields of history and criticism. There was a new stress upon going back to the original sources of Classical figuration. Artists were compelled to become jongleurs who balanced their desire for an original and striking statement with the scholarly basis of practice. Cohesiveness and credibility of the depictions of Greek or Roman precedent remained a clear signifier of the Neoclassical. Purity and simplicity of gesture and pose in bas-reliefs also were emphasized. From Wedgwood and John Flaxman onward, this linear clarity is a key distinction between the sculpture of the late 18th century and that of the previous generations. This clarity and precision in line moved through Flaxman into the graphic arts as well to become a central expression of taste at about 1800. The emergence of a value system in aesthetics that ranked the intellectual power and decisiveness of line above the sensuousness of color was particularly cogently expressed through Neoclassical sculpture. Canova set a precedent that the best Neoclassical sculpture was associated with a high level of executive precision and elegance and subtlety of surface finishing. Close adhesion to authentic historical principles in the treatment of hairstyles and personal features, including an archaicizing severity of profile, outline, and pose is another signifier. In the early period this authenticity was expressed as a self-conscious attempt to avoid Rococo or Baroque stylization within the Classical canon. Likewise any conscious reference to contemporary details of fashion was suppressed to as great a degree as possible. The able sculptor had to balance the illustrative demands of the function of portraiture with Neoclassicism's urge toward the primacy of the "type" above the particularized. The wig or no

wig debate extended to toga or no toga and into the appropriateness of nudity for memorializing a "Great Man." Both Napoléon and his adversary the Duke of Wellington appeared virtually naked in monumental statues. Even today, despite the relative liberation of social mores, these nude statesmen create faint disquiet, as if it were not only their bodies but also the state apparatus that is presented for promiscuous scrutiny by the public eye. At this point one senses the impossibility—in fact the Romantic nature of the dream—of detaching a sculpture or its style from the taste of the era in which it was created.

With female portraiture around 1790 to 1810, the sculptor's task was easier. Joseph Chinard's bust of *Madame Récamier* (1801) or Gottfried Schadow's *Princesses Louise and Friederike of Mecklenburg-Schwerin* (1797) indicate how far the Neoclassical (especially as defined by surviving ancient sculptures) had already shaped female costume. When fashionable women aspired to look like Greek or even Canovan sculptures, not only *figurantes* and *danseuses* wetted their draperies and wore *trompe l'oeil maillots* (chemise-style gowns) to resemble a living sculpture. Canova's *Pauline Borghese as Venus Victrix*, while extreme in its gesture of transposing a contemporary woman with a Classical ideal and coolly masking its provocative nature through using its Classical identity as justification, stands also as a reminder of the change in female personae permitted in the early Neoclassical era and the movement to more conventional female personifications within the general Neoclassical canon by the mid 19th century.

Neoclassicism became so dominant in sculpture that it substantially dictated the terms upon which its would-be dissenters would operate. Because of the centrality of Neoclassicism, the "anti-Classical" gesture in 19th-century sculpture was always somewhat diffused if not compromised. The stranglehold of the Classical style upon figurative European sculpture ensured that even those sculptors who were consciously dissident to the ethos of Classical tradition still greatly employed a Classically based figuration, as is seen in the work of François Rude. His sculptures on the Arc de Triomphe were antischematic in their primitive sublimity and emotional extremity and could therefore be termed as Romantic. Equally they were still firmly Neoclassical in the details of armaments and dress. Baudelaire went so far as to say there could be no Romantic sculpture, so firmly was Neoclassicism planted in the minds of French aesthetes and critics as inevitable for sculpture. Romantic sculpture is a more disparate entity in art history, having had far less historical attention as a movement than Neoclassicism. Much of what 20th-century historians have lauded as "Romantic" sculpture when originally created was seen by contemporaries as expressive products of individualism such as the work, of Antoine-Auguste Préault or even isolated marginal work, which hardly begot schools or influences. A high-profile example is the three-dimensional caricatures of Honoré Daumier, executed with a hasty impressionistic surface. They have assumed a greater celebrity and centrality for later generations than they ever had when new. Romantic sculpture is a far more arbitrarily constructed art historical genre than Neoclassicism. There is far less common ground or historical unity between such items as popularist realist genre pieces from Italian late-19th-century sculptors or Daumier's caricatures than there is between Neoclassical works produced in 19th-century cultures as diverse as Russia or Australia.

In Great Britain the realist mid 19th-century work of Thomas Woolner, especially his female figures, proved how difficult it was to detach the ethos of commonly held definitions of acceptable sculptural values from Classical stylization. With males, strength of character and a saturnine force that overturned the Classical were deemed acceptable, and Woolner was regarded as a master of such portrayals. The canons that governed the idealization of female figures were harder to subvert, especially when the Neoclassical image of woman tended to the more demure (or if sensual, a more passive eroticism than a generation previously). Woolner's female figures such as *Love* (1856) and *Elaine* (1868) remain firmly within a recognizable Classical stylization. Only rarely as in the *Lord's Prayer* (1867) or *Housemaid* (1893) at the end of his career did Woolner produce realist women who integrated the actuality of the period of origin with the authority and presence of the Neoclassical.

Another mid-19th-century sculptor whose works illustrate the inescapability of the Neoclassical, despite original and unusual subjects, is African American sculptress Edmonia Lewis. Whereas 20th-century critics may identify not only a Romantic impetus but also a non-Anglo-European position in such works as the *Marriage of Hiawatha* (*The Old Arrow Maker and His Daughter*; 1866) and the *Death of Cleopatra* (1876; the latter historical figure becoming linked explicitly to African American culture in the late 20th century), Lewis's *Poor Cupid* (1876) or copies after "masterpieces" indicated that Neoclassicism's homogenizing bent could substantially negate the issues of race and identity that are seen as fundamental to late-20th-century understandings of creative and cultural activity, no matter the gender or race of the artist.

Lewis is one of a number of notable female Neoclassical sculptors in 19th-century Europe, including her fellow (white) American Harriet G. Hosmer and the British Mary Thornycroft. Woolner, though often seen like Lewis as being somewhat beyond the Classical canon, equally interacted with and was shaped by the Neoclassical. His collections of bas-reliefs and busts of the eminent personalities of his era were drawn from the practice of David D'Angers, whose works he would have known through his colleague, Bernhard Smith, who had studied in Paris. The herm-type base, archaically Greek, a favored format in Woolner's male busts, resembles the busts of great Germans and international men of note created for the Neoclassical Walhalla of King Ludwig (1830–42) and again signified a return to a purist or archaically Classical prototype. The borders between the two styles are flexible. While Auguste Rodin's work is frequently read as towering Romantic individualism and the impressionist/dissonant sculpture par excellence, during the late 19th century conservative patrons could admire Neoclassical references and even divine a degree of artistic respectability in certain examples from his diverse oeuvre without having to acknowledge or validate his more experimental works.

It could be argued that no effective or cohesive answer to the dominance of sculptural Neoclassicism in the manner of a quintessential artistic countermovement arrived until the British New Sculpture movement of the 1870s and 1880s. With Edmund Gosse and Marion Spielman as polemicists and propagandists, New Sculpture openly attacked established precedent to a degree that confounds conventional truisms that Victorian art was conservative. Yet one of the key sources of New Sculptural support and development in Britain, Royal Academy president Frederick Leighton, was himself firmly identified with a new Victorian British Classical revival. In some ways the French never developed an oppositional movement to Neoclassicism so clearly unified as New Sculpture. The Romantic spirit manifested itself in great diversity in sculpture. The restoration of the Bourbon monarchy inspired a degree of motivation toward instituting the Troubadour style as a "Royalist" style as opposed to "Republican" Classicism, but this substitution was thwarted due to the change to the Orleanist monarchy. After the revolution of July 1830, the new regime was more favorable to Neoclassicism. The Troubadour style was essentially an *intimiste* style of fantasy boudoirs and reliquaries that could not match the grand public rhetoric already implemented by the Neoclassical, and it lacked the clear focus of the later New Sculpture. Sculptural dissonance through an imagined poetic medieval taste gained widespread plausibility at least a generation later than the Troubadour style in the wake of Pre-Raphaelitism and Symbolism and then more effectively in Britain and elsewhere in Europe rather than France.

Yet the picture is complicated because there were a number of differently intentioned Gothic styled expressions within the Romantic canon. One could contrast the sometimes otherworldly religiosity of Pre-Raphaelite or Troubadour works with the more ambiguous symbolism and formalist exaggerations of the extremes of New Sculpture. Across the German and Austro-Hungarian empires in the late 19th century, Gothic-style sculpture occupied a similar position to the Neoclassical as a public state-sponsored rhetoric in such projects as the completion of Cologne Cathedral (1870s) or the decorations for Parliament House in Budapest (1885–1904). Other major projects of similarly iconic centrality in these regions such as Wallot's Reichstag in Berlin (1894) simultaneously used a somewhat Baroque form of Classicism in their figurative decoration.

Many of the hallmarks of Romanticism in painting such as bold color and brushwork were by convention ruled out of the question for sculpture. Other Romantic elements, such as Orientalism and polychromy, when they appeared in sculpture, frequently diverted the piece in question to a more populist or a decorative arts genre. Charles-Henri Cordier's series of busts from the 1850s of North African subjects were intended for the Musée d'Histoire Naturelle in Paris as a "scientific" depiction of national and racial types. Yet the final works highlight the Romantic escapist elements of French Orientalism, through the intense and rich deployment of mixed media and decorative coloristic touches such as colored enamel highlights. Some early critics deplored the juxtapositions of different media and saw the works as populist and vulgar. The work of the *animalier* (animal sculptor) Antoine-Louis Bayre demonstrates the blurring between decoration and high art, as does the commercial production of a head by Albert-Ernest Carrier-Belleuse (itself after François-Joseph Bosio's Henri IV) as a child's doll.

Technology and scientific advances throughout the 19th century diversified the range of coloristic responses and media available to sculptors, thus facilitating an alternative to the Classical purity of white marble. Industrial processes made large-scale production of popular works more feasible. Editioning and circulation defined new intimate relationships of sculptor to market, which turned away from the publicly legible and morally didactic rhetoric implied by the sentiment and function of many iconic Neoclassical sculptures. The New Sculpture movement explicitly radicalized the statuette and *bibelot* as a gesture of defiance against the white marble sculptured Apollo. The avant-garde impetus of sculptors from Aimé-Jules Dalou to the British New Sculptors, who uncompromisingly depicted contemporary dress, eluded generations of 20th-century Modernist commentators, who persisted in reading these anti-Classical works as mimetic. Thus Modernists overlooked the transgressive qualities of

moving sculpture from the Neoclassically eternal to the current and documentary.

As the years passed the envelope of the "Neoclassical" as a visual style became increasingly flexible. The Rococo and Baroque insinuated itself gradually, especially in France, where the Salon gave a de facto encouragement to startling tours de force from Auguste Clésinger's *Femme piqué par un serpent* (1847) to the multiple figures in complex groupings of around 1900. The anecdotal and emotionally stirring as opposed to the conscious appeal to moral and intellectual ideas that marked early Neoclassicism became a dominant trend in 19th-century Neoclassical sculpture. Moreover, the wealth and ostentation of the French Second Empire favored a more dynamic neo-Baroque interpretation of the Classical, with a strong appeal to the emotions in both theme and bravura handling of media. Yet it is inaccurate to suggest that the Neoclassical became less important in sculpture throughout the 19th century. The era's widespread passion for accurate research and precedent ensured that Neoclassicism remained relevant. Visually well-educated sculptors became carefully attuned to the differences between early styles and periods. Neoclassicism became aligned with revivalist practices such as Gothic, Renaissance, and various regionally significant styles. Therefore it was frequently ratified in an academic or public state-sponsored context as long as such revivalist practices were dignified by the mainstream. Neoclassicism's position changed slightly as the 19th century progressed. It retained an ongoing relevance as one of a number of options rather than the sole centralizing ideal. As noted above, the aesthetic writings of Winckelmann and the concomitant validation they ascribed to Greek Classical sculpture were unchallenged as a cultural authority into the early 20th century.

Neoclassicism—or at least a broadly defined practice of drawing inspiration from the Classical past—was never entirely overwritten by Modernism. Perhaps this is a further indication of the significant resonances between Neoclassicism and the origins of Modernism. While such later works are far removed from late 18th-century Neoclassicism, it should not be forgotten that the Classical remained consistently an inspiration throughout the early to mid 20th century, although 20th-century expressions of Classical inspirations can vary. Some radical sculptors looked backwards and found justifying precedents in Archaic and Cylcadic Greek sculptures to present an abstracted and highly stylized interpretation of figurative sculpture. A more traditional Neoclassicist with a widespread but transient public recognition was Arno Brekker, a sculptor now firmly associated in popular and professional memory with Hitler's Third Reich. The association of Brekker's classicism to this regime was already ratified by the masculinist and imperial precedent provided by Napoléon's empire and the long-standing reading of the sources of Neoclassicism as the sources of Eurocentric cultural authority in the modern age. However, the internationally widespread cult of health and beautiful bodies (of which Brekker and his patrons were the most extreme and notorious expression) in the interwar period frequently referenced the Classical ideal and reinvigorated a fashionable and popular interest in Neoclassical sculpture. Art Deco was another manifestation of the Neoclassical, itself again inflected by a sense of patriotism when French sculptors in particular could claim the Neoclassical as a signifier or symbol of their national cultural identity.

JULIETTE PEERS

See also **Barye, Antoine-Louis; Canova, Antonio; Chinard, Joseph; Chinard, Joseph:** *Bust of Madame Récamier*; **Clésinger, (Jean-Baptiste) Auguste; Cordier, Charles-Henri-Joseph; Dalou, Aimé-Jules; Daumier, Honoré; David d'Angers; England and Wales: Baroque–Neoclassical; Flaxman, John; Germany: Baroque–Neoclassical; Hosmer, Harriet Goodhue; Italy: Neoclassicism–19th Century; Lewis, Mary Edmonia; Rodin, Auguste; Rude, François; Rude, François:** *Departure of the Volunteers of 1792 (La Marseillaise)*; **Schadow, Johann Gottfried; Sergel, Johan Tobias; Thornycroft Family; Thorvaldsen, Bertel**

Further Reading

Blühm, Andreas, et al. (editors), *The Colour of Sculpture, 1840–1910* (exhib. cat.), Zwolle, The Netherlands: Waanders, 1996

Curtis, Penelope (editor), *Patronage and Practice: Sculpture on Merseyside* (exhib. cat.), Liverpool: Tate Gallery Liverpool and National Museums and Galleries on Merseyside, 1989

Fusco, Peter, and H.W. Janson (editors), *The Romantics to Rodin: French Nineteenth-Century Sculpture from North American Collections* (exhib. cat.), Los Angeles: Los Angeles County Museum of Art, and New York: Braziller, 1980

Honour, Hugh, "Neo-Classicism," in *The Age of Neo-Classicism* (exhib. cat.), London: Arts Council of Great Britain, 1972

Hubert, Gerard, "Early Neo-Classical Sculpture in Italy and France," in *The Age of Neo-Classicism* (exhib. cat.), London: Arts Council of Great Britain, 1972

Leoussi, Athena S., *Nationalism and Classicism: The Classical Body As National Symbol in Nineteenth-Century England and France*, New York: St. Martin's Press, 1998

Licht, Fred, "Sculpture: 19th and 20th Centuries," in *A History of Western Sculpture*, edited by John Pope-Hennessy, London: Joseph, 1967

Read, Benedict, *Victorian Sculpture*, New Haven, Connecticut: Yale University Press, 1982

West, Alison, *From Pigalle to Préault: Neoclassicism and the Sublime in French Sculpture, 1760–1840*, Cambridge and New York: Cambridge University Press, 1998

NETHERLANDS AND BELGIUM

Early-14th-century sculpture in the Low Countries developed from many regional traditions, of which the two around the Scheldt and Meuse Rivers were the most prominent. Meuse valley sculpture was then under the influence of the French courtly style, with graceful, elongated figures and flowing draperies. This style found its prime expression in freestanding Madonnas; the white marble *Virgin and Child* (ca. 1330–50) by the Master of the Marble Madonnas in Antwerp Cathedral is a characteristic example, with its somewhat artificial drapery and Mannerist pose. The decorative S shape of her body and the dreamy face she presents to the Infant Christ, who meekly touches her cheek, stresses the figure's motherly attitude. Sculptors also used white marble for important tomb monuments, such as the two in Cologne Cathedral by Gilles de Liège to Walram von Jülich (d. 1349) and Wilhelm von Gennep (d. 1362). These tombs are stylistically comparable to the south portal (ca. 1330–40) of the Church of Notre-Dame, Dinant, which reinterprets the exterior reliefs of the chevet chapels (ca. 1320) of the Cathedral of Notre Dame, Paris.

Jean Pépin de Huy (active 1311–29) sculpted the recumbent statue of *Robert d'Artois* (1317–20), now at the Basilica of Saint-Denis, near Paris. The figure was originally polychromed by Pierre de Bruxelles, and the highly refined carving of the marble enhances its composition. Robert's mother, Mahaud d'Artois, commissioned the few other remaining works by this assumed Meuse-region artist, such as his 1329 *Madonna* at Gosnay, Pas-de-Calais.

In the Scheldt region, the *Virgin and Child* (ca. 1310–20) of the west facade of Tournai Cathedral opened the century with a statue much imitated throughout the region. Tournai became known for its remarkable sculpture in blue-gray limestone. The statues (1350–75) by Wouter Pans for the choir of Mechelen Cathedral, showing the influence of the school of Reims, and the porch statue of the *Madonna* on the Church of Onze-Lieve-Vrouw-ten-Poel, Tienen, also belong within this French stylistic context. Jacques de Baerze from Dendermonde (active 1384–99) similarly favored this courtly style when he carved the figures for his impressive altarpieces of the *Saints* and the *Passion* for Philip the Bold (Musée des Beaux-Arts, Dijon).

From the middle of the 14th century, increased realism and a sense of movement began to challenge the previous stylistic interests. The monumental alabaster statue of *St. Catherine* (1372–73) in the Church of Onze-Lieve-Vrouwe, Kortrijk, attributed to André Beauneveu (active ca. 1360–1400) and most likely commissioned by Louis de Male, is one of the most distinguished productions of its time, blending new conceptions of realistic expression and plasticity with the more traditional effect of verticality and slender proportions. His influence became widespread in the 14th century, from Bruges to the Meuse region. In the latter region, the *Coronation of the Virgin* (*ca.* 1380–90), in the Church of St. Jacques, Liège, constitutes a remarkable example in this new style, combining ample and soft draperies with a greater naturalistic rendition of the human body. Although now essentially known as a sculptor of tomb monuments for French high society in Paris, Jean (Hennequin) de Liège, a talented artist, also produced alabaster statuettes and altars.

By the 14th century, the growing urban centers created much demand for large-scale secular sculpture and city authorities commissioned monumental secular sculpture for such buildings as city halls with belfries and aldermen's halls. The former abbey Church of Sint-Bavo, Ghent, preserves one of the four guards in armor that were placed in 1338 on the corners of the belfry. Jean de Valenciennes and collaborators provided the Bruges aldermen's hall in 1376–79 with numerous statues, niches, and consoles (largely destroyed in 1792). In Brabant in particular, small architectural sculpture such as keystones, bosses, and gargoyles received much freer treatments in the new realistic mode.

In the 15th century, Brussels gradually rose in status in political, economic, and artistic matters. It was the city of Claus Sluter (who originally came from Haarlem), one of the most prominent sculptors in the Low Countries. The Duke of Burgundy recruited him for his numerous sculptural projects at and near Dijon, his main seat. There, Sluter introduced a new direction away from the international mannerist mode and toward a reinvigorating and original naturalism. He had widespread influence, although paradoxically rather little in the duchies of Flanders and Brabant. The eight figures of prophets together with five consoles, all that remain from the facade decoration of the Brussels Town Hall (*ca.* 1404–05), and strongly reminiscent of the Champmol sculptures by Sluter, have recently been attributed to the Master of Hakendover. This master is named after his wooden carved altarpiece at the Church of the Goddelijke Zaligmaker, Hakendover, which displays his talent for narrative description, just as in the stone sacraments tabernacle and the apostle statues at the Church of Sint-Martinus, Halle, usually attributed to the same hand. Much of the sculpture from this period in the northern Netherlands perished under the iconoclasts' hands. The extant early-15th-century architectural sculpture worth mentioning includes the historiated bosses (*ca.* 1412–20), probably by Jorijs de Beeldsnijder, in the choir of the Pieters church, Leiden.

Collaboration between painters and sculptors was frequent during this period because most sculptures were polychromed. Even such a prominent sculptor as Jan van Eyck is documented as having painted statues for the Bruges town hall. Jean Delemer's stout figures and deeply carved drapery in his *Annunciation* statues (1426–28), now in the Cathedral of Tournai, accord to the style that Robert Campin used in his panel painting. This is not surprising considering that the former polychromy of the statues is the only documented work by Campin. Jan van Eyck and Rogier van der Weyden similarly impressed their different stylistic preferences on contemporary sculptors, although painters were not systematically at the forefront of stylistic developments; destruction and lack of study of the sculpture make it difficult for firm conclusions to be drawn. Links on a functional level also frequently existed between painted and sculpted devotional objects. Such close interaction between painting and sculpture accounts for this high point in artistic endeavors in the Low Countries.

Painters occasionally also provided sculptors with designs for sculpture. The history of the Leuven town hall, preserved in great detail, is explicit in this respect. Jacob Schelewaerts, doctor in theology, and Jan van den Phalisen, priest of the Church of Sint-Pieter, devised the iconography of the facade decoration. The painter Hubrecht Steurbout provided the designs, which were translated into the third dimension by the master mason Mathijs de Layens in 1447–48.

In the second quarter of the 15th century, the International Gothic style largely made way for the Late Gothic realism that was favored particularly in Tournai funerary reliefs. These reliefs demonstrate a greater interest in a full rendition of space and plasticity of the figures. As the century drew to a close, they gradually became smaller in order to be included in the church's wall masonry, with a low relief often inspired on contemporary painting, particularly that of Rogier van der Weyden. Such a case is the funerary relief in Tournai Cathedral of Jean Lamelin (d. 1470), court chaplain to Philip the Good.

The center of production of freestanding tomb monuments gradually moved from Tournai to Ghent in the 15th century, although they were also produced elsewhere, as they were highly individualized projects. Avesne stone was more appropriate for the carving of the delicate figurative parts; Tournai blue stone was relegated to the structural parts. In more lavish monuments sculptors frequently imitated Sluter's weeping figures, carved for his tomb of Philip the Bold.

At the top end of sculptural production, brass monuments with spectacular decoration and profuse use of black marble, such as in the tomb of Mary of Burgundy (*ca.* 1490–1502), Church of Onze-Lieve-Vrouwe,

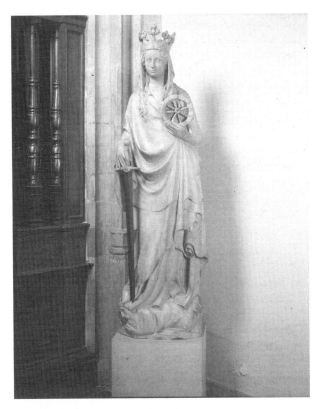

St. Catherine, attributed to André Beauneveu
Photo courtesy of Onze-Lieve-Vrouwekerk, Kortrijk and
ACL Brussels

Bruges, were complex collaborative projects between specialists of metal production (in this case, Renier van Thienen) who cast the monument with the wooden model carved by Jan Borman (active *ca.* 1479–1520). This tomb represents the summit of Gothic courtly naturalism, particularly in the facial expression of the *gisant* (reclining figure).

Rood lofts became particularly prominent church commissions by the late 15th century and achieved remarkable heights in a form that combines architecture and sculpture in an ornate way, with many statuettes decorating the architectural niches. Few survived the iconoclastic period, particularly as concerns their figurative sculptural content. A parallel production was that of "sacraments towers" and wall tabernacles. Generally near an altar, but separate from it, they contained the ingredients of the Holy Sacrament to be used by the priest during mass. The earliest surviving one is in the Church of Sint-Pieter, Leuven (*ca.* 1450), although most of the surviving ones date from the 16th century.

In the second quarter of the 15th century, Utrecht developed into an important center for sculpture production, exemplified by the limestone figures of saints (*ca.* 1455) attributed to Jan Nude in Utrecht's Centraal Museum, originally in the cathedral. Other rare surviv-

als from this period include figurative epitaphs and chimneypieces. Utrecht's leading position was intimately linked to the presence within its walls of Adriaen van Wesel (*ca.* 1417–*ca.* 1490). Although aware of developments in other centers such as Brussels, he elaborated a personal style full of courtly elegance and restrained pathos, well suited to small oak groups, such as the remaining fragments of the altarpiece from the Cathedral of 's-Hertogenbosch (1475–77, now in the Rijksmuseum, Amsterdam, and the Staatliche Museen, Berlin).

Master Arnt van Swol (i.e. Zwolle) (active 1460–92) worked in the manner of Adriaen van Wesel, at first at Kalkar, where his major works remain in the Church of St. Nikolai, then from 1484 at Zwolle. His inspiration was often drawn from Rogier van der Weyden's style, and he was to form a prolific school. Also worth mentioning is the anonymous sculptor active in northern Brabant named after the altarpiece group of the *Meeting of Sts. Joachim and Anne* (*ca.* 1460–70) in the Rijksmuseum, Amsterdam.

The 15th century as a whole in the Low Countries was characterized by a boom in sculptural production, not just in stone and bronze but particularly in elaborately carved wooden altarpieces. These wooden altarpieces were produced in mass and sold throughout Europe. To achieve this level of production, workshops used a strategy of consistency, following virtually unchanged formulas for design and iconography, regardless of the place (e.g. Antwerp or Brussels) or time of production (in the 15th or early 16th century). Only small expansions and adaptations of the formulas, which did not change the basic concept, concerned the increasing narrative and anecdotal aspect of early-16th-century work, the increasing architectural complexity of the altarpieces, and the adaptation from a late Gothic to a Mannerist to a Renaissance stylistic idiom.

Built up from numerous individually fashioned compartments that are usually closed by painted shutters (during nonfestive days), the altarpieces typically present a complex iconography narrating a logical series of biblical stories. On feast days, such as those of the patron saint of the church (for the high altar) or that of the relevant guild altar, the retable would be opened to display the sculptural parts. In these compartments, high-relief figures and some figures in the round, frequently polychromed, are positioned in perspectival space so as to suggest a realistic scene. A remarkable example is the Passion Altar from the Church of Sint-Genoveva, Oplinter (now in the Royal Museums of Art and History, Brussels). The workshop of Pieter Coecke van Aelst painted its wings; its nine sculptural compartments show the main stations of the road to Calvary. The St. Leonard altarpiece by Arnold de Maeler, in the Church of Sint-Leonard, Zoutleeuw, is also a fine example.

Jan Borman was the consummate woodcarver of the period. His St. George altar (1493, Royal Museums of Art and History, Brussels) displays his masterly rendition of space and action. Other important masters from the early 16th century included the Master of Elsloo, active probably at Roermond (ca. 1500–45), and Jan van Steffeswert (active in the early 16th century), who largely worked at Maastricht in an idiom that started to incorporate Renaissance details.

The Antwerp production of carved retables increased until the early 16th century, while that in Brussels—although not yet waning, as they both would later in the century—often concentrated on commissioned pieces rather than works made for the open market. Besides altarpieces, Mechelen also specialized in Virgin and Child statuettes (so-called poupées de Malines) and enclosed-garden ensembles (besloten hofjes), echoing in their more folkloristic aestheticism the earlier Utrecht production of pipeclay (white terracotta) figurines. The bread-and-butter production of alabaster reliefs, set in presmass (a mixture of plaster, animal glue, and oil) frames, also provided an important source of income.

Church furniture gradually became increasingly sculptural in its decoration. Sculptors covered choir stalls with reliefs representing daily life and illustrating proverbs, although they continued to decorate the most prominent parts with proper religious iconography. The stalls in the Cathedral of 's-Hertogenbosch (ca. 1430–60) rely directly on south Netherlandish stylistic precedent, although they also incorporate local interests, notably in the monumentality of bench-end reliefs. The sculptor Nicolaas de Bruyn and the joiner Geert Gorys produced the choir stalls at the Church of Sint-Sulpitius, Diest, in the 1490s. Another example, the Late Gothic choir stalls at the Church of Onze-Lieve-Vrouwe, Aarschot, date from the early 16th century.

Arnt van Tricht (active 1530s–70), possibly of Utrecht origin, spent most of his active life at Kalkar (near Kleve). At first a prolific woodcarver whose work frequently displayed innovative adaptations of Late Gothic models, he switched to stone relief carving with the advent of the Reformation, specializing in memorial tablets and chimneypieces. His Holy Trinity altarpiece in the Church St. Nikolai, Kalkar, is one of his most spectacular works.

In the first half of the 16th century, the Antwerp production of carved altarpieces gradually introduced Classical motifs amid its profusion of Gothicizing detail and Mannerist fanciful costumes and caricatured poses. The strong indigenous tradition of Gothic sculpture prevented a simple adoption of a foreign decorative vocabulary (whether Classical or contemporary Italian or French); instead, the main sculptors' workshops produced often idiosyncratic and eclectic sculpture, which has unhappily been termed Flemish Renaissance or Mosan Renaissance for the distinct Liège-region sculpture, for want of a better name.

The court at Mechelen became the preeminent center for the adoption of a new stylistic mode. There, foreign artists worked in the idiom of the Renaissance, largely imported from Italy, although frequently via complex routes and media (particularly prints). Conrat Meit executed the lavish tomb of Margaret of Austria (1526–32) in the Church of Saint-Nicolas de Tolentin at Brou, as well as the marble bust of the Virgin with the Christ Child, now in Brussels Cathedral. Jan Mone (ca. 1480–ca. 1549) carved alabaster altarpieces for the Church of Sint-Martinus, Halle (1533), and the chapel of the ducal palace in Brussels (1538–41, now in the Brussels Cathedral), as well as the tomb of Cardinal Guillaume de Croÿ (ca. 1528, now in the Capuchin church at Enghien).

In other circles, the Renaissance was also forcefully introduced via court circles. Lancelot Blondeel designed the spectacular mantelpiece executed by Guyot de Beaugrant in the aldermen's chamber of the Brugse Vrije (Bruges). The Grote Kerk at Breda contains some remarkable tomb monuments that also introduced the new Renaissance idiom, particularly the (about) 1526–38 tomb monument to Engelbert II van Nassau and his wife, until now unconvincingly attributed.

Jacques Du Broeucq, best known for his rood screen (now dismantled) at the church of Sainte-Waudru, Mons, and the master of Giambologna, replaced Jan Mone as court sculptor near the end of Mone's active life. He was part of a new generation of sculptors, including the internationally known artists Willem van den Broeck, alias Paludanus, and Jacques Jonghelinck, who interpreted the Classical tradition from a novel and archaeologically more accurate perspective. As part of his Classical interests, Jonghelinck was also a remarkable medalist.

Antwerp became the preeminent center of sculptural production in the Low Countries at the time of the architectural and sculptural activities of Cornelis Floris in the mid 16th century, remaining so until about the middle of the 18th century. Antwerp engaged in such export to other cities despite the guild system privileging artistic production within the city walls. The production of much sculpture in the southern Netherlands had become protoindustrial, aiming to satisfy the increasing demand emanating from a wide range of patrons, particularly from northern and central Europe. Other artists widely imitated Floris's workshop organization: many assistants worked under the guidance of a supervisor and to the designs of the master or some other artist's designs. Floris was not only responsible for the erection of the new town hall of Antwerp (1561–65) but also widely exported sculpture, particularly tomb monuments, of which those to the kings of Denmark were some of the most spectacular.

Although execution was generally (although not always) of decent quality, Floris's workshop system enabled the master to free himself from the hard manual work and to concentrate on designing. In addition, Pieter Coecke van Aalst, Hans Vredeman de Vries, and Floris published many of their designs in the form of illustrated treatises, pattern books, and loose prints, which display a repertory of motifs and ornaments for use in a variety of decorative schemes. Through these publications, the artists could significantly assert their reputation and social status. Such publications, together with the emigration of many sculptors during the religious wars of the late 16th century, helped widely disseminate the style of Flemish Renaissance sculpture throughout northern and central Europe.

In this context should be mentioned the De Nole dynasty of sculptors. They had moved from Cambrai to Utrecht (and later played an important role in the Baroque period in Antwerp) and had adopted the complex Renaissance decorative idiom in their many tomb monuments as well as in the well-known chimneypiece of the town hall at Kampen (1543–45).

Several prominent sculptors from what was effectively to become the separate northern Netherlands by the late 16th century spent a number of years in Italy, training in important workshops and acquiring skills as sculptors and as bronze casters. Because the Netherlands hardly had a market for such sculptors to make a living, most of them eventually emigrated. Willem Daniëlsz van Tetrode (*ca.* 1510–75) spent 20 years in Italy before returning home, eventually leaving for Cologne (in 1574) during the iconoclastic outbreak. He produced a number of mythological bronze and alabaster groups that show his interest in the antique and in strong musculatures. The Nijmegen-born Johann Gregor van der Schardt spent many years in Italian cities before being employed by Maximilian II in Nuremberg in 1570. There, he modeled several polychrome terracotta busts, including a self-portrait (now in the Rijksmuseum, Amsterdam), that display a remarkable naturalism. Hubert Gerhard, similarly trained in Italy, was active mainly in Munich and Augsburg as a sculptor in bronze (known especially for his monumental fountains), terracotta, and plaster. Adriaen de Vries, also of Dutch origin (The Hague), traveled to Italy early in life, working in Giambologna's and Pompeo Leoni's studios before building a career in Augsburg and Prague.

Hendrik I de Keyser continued the tradition of the late-16th-century Dutch sculptors, producing important works in bronze. His masterpiece is no doubt the mausoleum to William the Silent (1614–22), which signaled a high point in Dutch sculpture not to be equaled for several decades. He also produced the over-life-size statue of *Erasmus* at Rotterdam (1622). De Keyser's talents were many, and he was the first to introduce white Carrara marble to the northern Netherlands, which he used to carve the bust of *Vincent Jacobsz. Coster* (1608).

The revolts of the 1560s and 1570s and the consequent emigration of many sculptors led to a stagnation in the production of artistic goods (including its high-end sculpture). Only under the Archdukes Albert and Isabella (*r.* 1598–1621/1633), and especially during the Twelve Year Truce (1609–21), did a rebuilding and redecoration campaign of the mutilated or destroyed Roman Catholic churches begin. This campaign continued for the rest of the 17th century and provided sculptors with many important commissions. The monumental and sumptuous sculpture ordered to fill the churches anew emphasized and justified the new liturgy of the Counter Reformation. The prosperity that one could achieve as a sculptor gradually raised the status of the profession. The move from the stonecut-

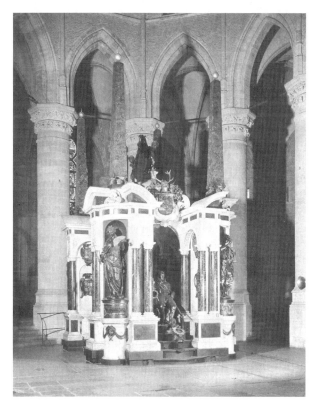

Hendrick de Keyser, Tomb of William the Silent, Prince of Orange
© Scala / Art Resource, NY

ters' guild to the artists' (St. Luke) guild was conspicuous in many cities and was accompanied by frequent disputes between the guild members.

The truce also coincided with Peter Paul Rubens's return from Italy (1608), and because he is generally credited with the introduction of the Baroque style in Flemish sculpture, this date marks the beginning of Baroque conceptions in Low Countries sculpture. Naturalism was a key concept of the new style. Rubens's influence was not a simple matter: patrons frequently requested his opinion, if not actual designs by him. The Jesuit church of Antwerp (now the Church of Sint-Carolus-Borromeus and once the most lavish church of the Low Countries), for example, was largely built following his ideas, as is attested by a series of designs he drew or painted.

Sculptors such as the De Nole family executed such sculptures, particularly the large-scale monumental projects, as did Hans van Mildert (1588–1638), a friend and frequent collaborator of Rubens. None of these sculptors, however, were of any consequence in terms of quality. Only with François du Quesnoy and Artus I Quellinus (Quellin) of the subsequent generation did a high level of sculpture production make a new start in the Low Countries. François du Quesnoy, however, spent little time in his home country, going to Rome at age 21. His presence in the north is traceable only in terms of models traveling back with his brother Hiëronymus II on François du Quesnoy's death in 1643, as well as casts, drawings, and prints after his statues. Artus I Quellinus, on the other hand, kept his workshop running, led by his brother-in-law Pieter I Verbrugghen (1615–86), while he was in Amsterdam sculpting the extensive Carrara marble decoration of the town hall on the Dam (now a royal palace).

Construction of the Amsterdam town hall began in 1648, to coincide with the peace treaty of Münster that ratified the separation of the northern Netherlands from the southern. It aimed to be the eighth wonder of the world. Built in the Baroque fashion with an immensely complex iconography drawing on biblical and Classical sources, it also emulated the Temple of Solomon. Its decoration therefore had to be durable and lavish. The court architect Jacob van Campen was responsible for the project, and the sculptural decoration was given to Artus I Quellinus, who gathered a large workshop around him, including his nephew Artus II Quellinus, Rombout Verhulst, and probably Bartholomeus Eggers (ca. 1630–92). The building's decoration took more than 15 years to complete, of which the two pediments, the eight high-relief gods framing the main floor, and the three reliefs in the justice chamber are the most well known. Quellinus's plastic style, combining northern naturalism with the High Baroque Classicism of du

Quesnoy, was also used in the Dutch Palladian buildings of the 1630s to 1660s.

Artus I Quellinus also restored the level of portrait sculpture to what it had been in the hands of a van der Schardt or a Hendrik de Keyser. Among his series of busts made during his work on the town hall is that of the burgomaster *Andries de Graeff* (1665, Rijksmuseum, Amsterdam). This figure also blends a high degree of naturalism and rendition of texture with the dignity afforded by the Classical idiom. Twenty years earlier François Dieussart had already introduced Roman Baroque Classicism in the numerous court portraits that he produced for the courts of northern Europe, including the court at The Hague.

Verhulst and Eggers later built their own careers in the northern Netherlands (as well as in northern Germany), especially with a series of monumental tombs to national heroes. Jacob van Campen designed the tomb of Admiral Maarten Tromp (1654–57, Oude Kerk, Delft), which was executed by Rombout Verhulst, apart from the low relief with the battle scene and the decorative sculpture created by Willem de Keyser (1603–after 1678), one of Hendrik's sons. Pieter Xavery (ca. 1647–after 1674) seems to have specialized in terracotta figures and groups, whereas Albert Jansz Vinckenbrinck (ca. 1604–64/65) preferred boxwood. Vinckenbrinck also created the intricate but monumental pulpit (ca. 1646–49) in the Nieuwe Kerk, Amsterdam. Most sculptors of the 17th and 18th centuries, however, both north and south, carved in ivory. Unfortunately, these works are primarily known from contemporary biographers, and it is today difficult to establish clear authorship because few of these pieces are signed. One exception is the 17th-century artist Francis van Bossuit, who specialized in ivory carving.

In Antwerp, together with Artus I Quellinus, Peter I Verbrugghen trained a whole generation of sculptors in Antwerp, including Peter II Verbrugghen (ca. 1640–91) and Mattheus van Beveren (1630–90). They were all active in a number of projects, carving and sculpting altars, confessionals, pulpits, choir stalls, pier statues, communion rails, rood lofts, and so on for the wealthy religious orders. Their strong family businesses enabled them to engage in huge collaborative projects, such as the high altar of the Church of Sint-Jacob in Antwerp. Similarly, collaboration with joiners and other sculptors facilitated the completion of large-scale paneling, incorporating fully three-dimensional sculptural confessionals. Dynasties of sculptors were common, and they vied for the same lucrative projects, thereby often creating controversies leading to court action. In this respect Lucas Faydherbe should be named, as he attracted an unrivalled number of lawsuits, mainly with his patrons. His association with Rubens nevertheless brought him much fame.

Faydherbe's training in Rubens's studio meant that it took him many years to free himself from the stylistic influence of Rubens, with his often heavy, genrelike figures, which are traditionally contrasted with the Classicism that Hiëronymus II du Quesnoy derived from his brother François. Scholars traditionally contrast Faydherbe's tomb monument to Archbishop Andreas Cruesen (1659–66) in the Cathedral of Saint Rombant in Mechelen to Hiëronymus du Quesnoy's monument to Bishop Antonius Triest (1651–54) in the Cathedral of Saint Bavo in Ghent, although the wishes of their patrons and actual similarity are rarely noted. Faydherbe did have a relatively large following, with sculptors such as Frans Langhemans (1661–ca. 1720) and Jan-Frans Boeckstuyns (ca. 1650–1734), unlike his contemporaries and rivals Hiëronymus II du Quesnoy, Nicolaas van der Veken (1637–1709), and Jan van der Steen (1633–1725).

In the Mosan region, sculptors such as Lambert Duhontoir (1603–61) and Robert Henrard (1617–76) worked in an academic Classicism akin to that prevalent at the French court. The more famous Jean Delcour adopted a fully fledged Baroque idiom, allegedly derived from Gianlorenzo Bernini during an assumed prolonged stay in Rome, although he seems to have had more contact with the work of Alessandro Algardi. His idiosyncratic understanding of the purpose, for instance, of a profusion of drapery, is most evident in works such as his *Dead Christ* (1696) in Liège's current cathedral.

The Late Baroque period in Antwerp, beginning about 1670, gradually increased the elegance and refinement of the previous Baroque vocabulary. One of the main exponents of the Late Baroque, Artus II Quellinus brought Flemish sculpture to new heights. He in turn trained the next generation of sculptors, including Alexander van Papenhoven. Other important sculptors included Guillielmus Kerricx, Peter I Scheemakers (1652–1714), Michiel I van der Voort, and Jan Peter I van Baurscheit (1669–1728) Henricus-Franciscus Verbrugghen (1654–1724) developed an idiosyncratic draftsmanship style that is perceptible in the realizations, both sculpted and architectural.

The end of the 17th century also marked the end of the prosperous business Flemish sculptors obtained from so many church authorities and related patrons. The restoration of the Catholic Church was nearing completion, and the fervor had evaporated. Moreover, the slackening economy of the southern Netherlands meant that patronage became rarer. Increasing numbers of sculptors thus emigrated and contributed significantly to the field of European sculpture, including Martin van den Bogaert, alias Desjardins, Gerard van Opstal, Philippe de Buyster, Sébastien Slodtz and Jean Warin in Paris, Peter II Scheemakers and Michael Rys-

brack in London, Gabriel Grupello in Düsseldorf, and Wilhelm de Groff and Aegid Verhelst in Munich. Others diversified their interests to include such activities as designing prints; an increasing number moved toward architecture. The export of garden sculpture, especially to England, remained an important source of revenue.

Classicizing tendencies or Rococo features in the early years of the 18th century were generally associated with new commissions for secular sculpture, while the few church commissions (notably from some wealthy abbeys that were being constructed) often maintained the traditional Baroque vocabulary so well adapted to the specificities of liturgical function and style of the Roman Catholic Church. This tradition for church commissions continued into the 19th century with such sculptors as Jan Frans van Geel (1756–1830) who had the versatility to adapt their style to the particular commissions, reinterpreting Baroque vocabulary in such a way that their early-19th-century pieces have not infrequently been mistaken for late-17th-century ones.

Gradually the preeminence of Antwerp as the sculptural center of the Low Countries began to wane as other regional centers took over, in particular Bruges, Ghent, and Nivelles. Iconographic and stylistic renewal on a local basis encouraged dispersal of skill and enterprise toward these other cities. The court in Brussels continued to be an important source for commissions, which Laurent Delvaux (based in Nivelles) was largely able to tap as the officially appointed sculptor. His initial career in England and Rome largely determined his highly Classical style, which he later infused with "northern" naturalism. The pulpit he carved for the Cathedral of St. Baro, Ghent (1741–45), where for the first time he included large blocks of Carrara marble, demonstrates this blending of traditions.

In the northern Netherlands local sculptors, of whom many were émigrés from the south, increasingly fulfilled many of the commissions emanating from the northern Netherlands. Jan-Baptist Xavery (1697–1742) is mainly remembered for his portrait sculpture, particularly his bronzed terracotta bust of the painter Balthasar Denner (Gemeentemuseum, The Hague), though he was a versatile sculptor in such other materials as ivory, boxwood, and marble. He was court sculptor to Stadholder Willem IV. His contemporaries were the productive sculptors Ignatius van Logteren (1685–1732) and his son Jan van Logteren (1709–45).

Just before the French Revolution, sculptors, increasingly geared toward the decoration of secular projects, adopted the strict Neoclassical style, thereby largely eliminating figurative elements. Sculptors such as Willem Hendrik van der Wall (1716–90) and Antho-

1179

nie Ziesenis (1731–1801) worked in the northern Netherlands, as well as, for a couple of years, the renowned French sculptor Étienne-Maurice Falconet. The 1773 decision by Maria Theresa to abolish the Jesuit order in the southern Netherlands marked the beginning of a dramatic period for sculptural production, not just for sculptors but also for past projects that had been destroyed. After the revolutionary wave, altars, pulpits, choir stalls, and many more church furnishings were slowly but gradually moved into the remaining parish churches. Overall, monastic buildings suffered most.

During the first half of the 19th century, Neoclassicism remained the dominant mode of expression in Netherlandish sculpture, varying from severe Greco-Roman interpretations of portraiture and mythological scenes to more sensuous and charming alternatives. Many sculptors perfected their training in Rome and Paris, and hence the dominant stylistic influence. Gilles-Lambert Godecharle (1750–1835) remains the best known of his generation. His remarkable models for the pediments of the Château de Laeken and the Palais de la Nation in Brussels (1781–84) survive, as does the plaster bust of his wife, *Jeanne Catherine Offhuys* (1807, all Royal Museums of Fine Arts Brussels).

Two other well-known Neoclassical sculptors spent most of their active life abroad. Mathieu Kessels (1784–1836) trained in St. Petersburg under Joseph Camberlain and in Rome under Bertel Thorvaldsen. On Kessels's death, the Belgian government bought up his complete studio contents to create a museum of sculpture. The contents included the full-size plaster model of his tomb of the comtesse de Celles, the marble of which he erected in the Church of S. Giuliano dei Fiamminghi, Rome. His contemporary Henri-Joseph Rutxhiel (1775–1837) enjoyed much success in Paris throughout his career, after training under Jean-Antoine Houdon. Paul Joseph Gabriel (1784–1834) spent several years in Rome before and after training under Pierre Cartellier in Paris. He was subsequently appointed royal sculptor to Willem I of Holland and city sculptor of Amsterdam.

Nevertheless, the strong hold of Baroque conceptions, in all its forms from Mannerism to Rococo, continued to enjoy patronage, particularly for religious commissions. Noteworthy examples are the naturalistic oak pulpits, of which Flemish sculptors made a specialty. The 1821 pulpit in the Church of Sint-Andries, Antwerp, by Jan-Baptist van Hool (1769–1857) and Jan-Lodewijk van Geel (1787–1852), takes the possibilities offered by a naturalistic, life-size, three-dimensional representation of a scene from the Gospel to its extreme.

Technically, the production of sculpture in the 19th century had not inherently changed since the 18th century. The academies continued to be the main outlets for sales during regular exhibitions for much of the century. The Geefs family rose to prominence in the 1830s; one of its many exponents, Guillaume Geefs (1805–83), was responsible for the 1833 tomb monument of Frédéric, comte de Merode in the Brussels Cathedral, which is noted for its naturalness and lack of idealization. Although creative originality still had to grow from an increasingly outdated Neoclassicism imported from France and Italy, signs of renewal, particularly the introduction of Romantic traits, began slowly to appear.

Belgium's independence in 1830 signaled the beginning of a gradual increase in interest by the state to promote sculpture, which took on many forms, including the erection of overtly propagandistic monuments to stress the historical continuity of the southern Low Countries in the new independent state. The over-life-size statue of *Général Augustin-Daniel Belliard* by Guillaume Geefs (1836, rue Royale, Brussels) began a long tradition reaching into the 20th century. Attention to historical accuracy and Romantic traits characterize even more Eugène Simonis's (1810–82) equestrian monument to *Godefroid de Bouillon* (1848, place Royale, Brussels). This mid 19th-century phenomenon has frequently been described as statuemania. National history of the Middle Ages and Renaissance in particular was a beloved subject matter to all those involved in the sculpting of religiously inspired, devout Neo-Gothic, or "troubadour"-style statues. Literary sources became highly fashionable.

The Musée de Peinture et de Sculpture (as the Royal Museums of Fine Arts of Belgium were called in the 19th century) received much attention, becoming the main national organ to promote the contemporary fine arts. Throughout the 19th century, its collections grew with works often purchased directly from the artists or at salons, and not infrequently complete studio contents, such as that of Kessels already mentioned.

The bourgeoisie followed state patronage as their income rose rapidly with industrialization. They avidly consumed, among others, domestic mythological and allegorical nudes. Charles-Auguste Fraikin (1817–93) became famous for his nudes, such as *L'Amour captif* (1845, Royal Museums of Fine Arts, Brussels, and Hermitage, St. Petersburg).

The increasingly widespread use of bronze, a material that faithfully reproduces malleable wax, allowed sculptors to move away from strict Neoclassical forms and to indulge in more mobile shapes and tactile surfaces. The reproducibility of the medium suited a bourgeois market well at a time that coincided with the internationalization that salons and world exhibitions encouraged.

The present-day Netherlands, the territory that was left after the separation of independent Belgium in 1830, continued to rely on the sculptors established in such cities as Antwerp and Brussels. Foreign training of Dutch sculptors was only one feature of sculptural production, which was dominated, as in Belgium, by the academies. Academies here, however, were mainly run by foreigners. Mechelen-born Louis Royer (1793–1868), for instance, became director of sculpture at the Amsterdam academy in 1837. He monopolized much of the market for historic pieces, arising from the increasing awareness of national identity after the collapse of the French regime in 1815. Romantic inspiration, for those who used that style, typically drew from Belgian precedent.

In the third quarter of the 19th century, the dominant academic style kept its momentum. Iconographies that did not fit into this model were often the only way for sculptors to produce entirely new works. Examples include images of Neapolitan youths introduced by François Rude after his years of exile in Brussels. In the works on this subject by Belgian sculptors, such as Antoine Sopers's (1823–82) *Jeune Napolitain jouant à la roglia* (1859) or Adolphe Fassin's (1828–1900) *Acquaiuolo napolitain* (1863, both Royal Museums of Fine Arts, Brussels), close study from life replaced traditional models. The result was a fine realism and elegance of line. At its opposite lay the crowning of Belgian Romantic sculpture: Antoine Wiertz's (1806–65) series *Les quatre âges de l'humanité* (1860–62, Musée Wiertz, Brussels), which is heavily indebted to Rubens. Rodin spent most of his time between 1870 and 1877 in Brussels executing public monuments but also portrait busts, as for instance of the sculptor Paul de Vigne (1876, Musée Rodin, Paris)

Beginning in the 1870s sculptors often combined study from life with a renewed interest in the use of terracotta and the lost-wax casting technique of bronze. The Compagnie des Bronzes in Brussels, a company much favored by prominent artists, revived the bronze casting technique. The Italian Renaissance became a frequent source of inspiration, notably for Julien Dillens (1849–1904) and Paul de Vigne (1843–1901). Charles Van der Stappen's (1843–1910) early work *David* (1878; Koninklijk Museum voor Schone Kunsten, Antwerpen) and Thomas Vinçotte's (1850–1925) *Giotto* (1874, Royal Museums of Fine Arts, Brussels) also belong to this circle.

The architect Pierre Joseph Hubertus Cuypers (1827–1921) introduced the Gothic Revival in Dutch sculpture from about 1850. This style particularly suited the decoration of his Roman Catholic churches, whereas his secular public buildings generally received decoration inspired by 17th-century precedent, especially Artus I Quellinus. In purely sculptural terms, the results were not always laudable. The Gothic Revival style in Belgian sculpture was virtually exclusively linked to church commissions, often intended to return to "indigenous" art and thereby eliminating Baroque church furnishings. However, some Neo-Gothic country houses also included sculpture among the decoration.

Despite the frequent re-Gothicization of churches, church furniture, including monumental altarpieces, represented such enormous investments that trade in existing 17th- and 18th-century structures frequently implied adaptations and additions that required the work of the sculptor to be blended in neatly. Sculptors such as the Antwerp-based De Cuyper brothers (unrelated to the Dutch Cuypers), who achieved high standards in 17th- and 18th-century terms (for instance, the 1845 antependium of the high altar of the Church of Sint-Paulus, Antwerp), filled an important market. These sculptors are just one name among creators of an enormous continuous production of devotional Neo-Baroque sculpture from the 17th century to at least World War I and that is therefore often deceptively difficult to date.

Cuypers's need for skilled masons and cabinetmakers to fulfill his numerous commissions led him to create workshops in Roermond (1853) and later in Amsterdam for the decoration of the new Rijksmuseum building (1876–85) and the Centraal Station (1882–89). With this, Cuypers intended also to revive the sculpture-as-craft tradition within the professions of stonemasonry and wood carving. The emphasis on modeling in clay and wax in the academies prevented them from being able to teach these more practical aspects of the sculpture trade. The outcome was overwhelming, and the Rijksmuseum buildingshed workshops were transferred to rooms in the Quellinus School, an arts-and-crafts school. The design of the sculptural elements, however, was generally done outside the Quellinus School by such artists as the Leuven professor François Vermeylen (1824–88) and the Moravian Ludwig Jünger (b. 1856). All of the sculptors involved in this project, including the only Dutch sculptor, Bartholomeus Johannes van Hove (1790–1880), were typical exponents of the academic style.

By the 1890s Cuypers's efforts at the Quellinus School paid off significantly. Some of the more famous sculptors of the time had enjoyed their training in that workshop. Sculptors such as Joseph Mendes da Costa (1863–1939) and Lambertus Zijl (1866–1947) built their reputation on decorative sculpture in the Nieuwe Kunst style, the Dutch interpretation of Art Nouveau. Mendes da Costa found inspiration in orientalism, whereas Zijl favored an abstracted medieval style that fitted into the architecture of Hendrik Petrus Berlage (1856–1934), with whom he often collaborated. The Amsterdam exchange (*ca.* 1898–1903) is probably the most famous of Berlage's projects. Zijl's independent sculpture often resembles George Minne's work in its angular and broadly modeled forms.

Just as the other branches of the arts and humanities, sculpture thrived in the last 20 years of the 19th century. Brussels became a major center of production, promoted by periodicals such as *L'Art moderne* and artists' groups such as Les XX. Constantin Meunier and Jef Lambeaux (1852–1908) achieved particular prominence, each with his own distinctive style. Meunier's *Grisou* (1889, Royal Museums of Fine Arts, Brussels) is his most famous of a whole series of statuettes and groups devoted to working-class iconography. Meunier later worked on a gigantic *Monument au Travail* (posthumously erected, now on the bassin Vergote, Laeken, Brussels), with four large reliefs and colossal figures.

Lambeaux's endeavors often returned to Giambologna's interest in the human figure in motion: the Brabo fountain (1887) on the Grote Markt, Antwerp, is a prime example. A representation of movement is also the main motif of a monumental relief by Lambeaux, housed in a special building, erected by Victor Horta in the Cinquantenaire park. Called *Les Passions humaines* (1889–99), it displays a complex iconography, including the ages of man, mostly as heroic nudes.

During the years that Art Nouveau flourished, George Minne developed an idiosyncratic style akin to contemporary Symbolist moods, with simple, fluid masses but with angular lines stressing the generally sorrowful circumstances of the iconography. His *Mère pleurant son enfant mort* (1886, Royal Museums of Fine Arts, Brussels) and his most popular work, the *Fontaine des agenouillés* (1899), demonstrate this style. Among his circle of Symbolists friends were the painter Fernand Khnopff (1858–1921) and for some time the sculptor Victor Rousseau (1865–1954).

During the height of Art Nouveau, sculptors too became increasingly interested in the decorative aspect of their work. The state encouraged polychromy and combinations of precious materials. Sculptors often integrated natural products from the Belgian colony (Congo), such as ivory, into their works to achieve unusual effects. The main exponent of this type of sculpture was Philippe Wolfers (1858–1929), a jeweler by training.

Auguste Rodin's loose modeling technique became the foremost source of inspiration for young Belgian sculptors of the early 20th century. Rik Wouters followed Rodin in favoring nervously modeled surfaces that allow complex playing with light. His stirring personal style has sometimes been labeled Fauvist, particularly works such as his *Torse de jeune femme* (1909) and his portrait of *Edgar Tytgat* (1910; both Royal Museums of Fine Arts, Brussels). His most daring composition, *Het zotte geweld* (1912, Middelheim, Antwerp), is based on the dancer Isadora Duncan, although he based most of his other work, such as *Hui-*

selijke zorgen (1913–14), on a synthetic view of his wife's image rather than harking back to historic precedent. The latter was a preference of Antoine Bourdelle that a sculptor such as Ernest Wijnants (1878–1964) followed in looking for inspiration in Greek, Egyptian, and Assyrian art. With the advent of abstraction, Wijnants nevertheless remained faithful to his figurative art.

In Dutch sculpture the architects J.L.M. Lauweriks and K.P.C. de Bazel began an antinaturalistic style. Their interest lay in Near Eastern, Indian, and Chinese aesthetic sculptural principles, which they combined with occult and masonic principles; theosophy was also an important source. Truthfulness to materials was essential. In sculpture, Johan Altorf (1876–1955) represented this strand. Later, Mendes da Costa and Zijl collaborated with the school of Amsterdam architects. They adapted the form of their sculptures to the architects' requirements in order to use rough materials they had not used before, such as hard stones and tropical woods. Ancient Egyptian and Assyrian works, with their compressed forms, proved to be the only viable models. They also used granite and basalt for independent sculpture. Concrete, too, was introduced in the 1920s, although the most influential technical change was the introduction of direct carving, following Adolf von Hildebrand's precepts, which Dutch sculptors started to practice after frequent periods in German workshops, where potential employment had attracted them during the economic crisis at home. Among the sculptors associated with the Amsterdam school were Hendrik van den Eynde (1869–1939), Hildo Krop (1884–1970), and John Raedecker (1885–1956).

Georges Vantongerloo (1886–1965) was among the first to move toward abstract sculpture, beginning about 1917. He was briefly associated with De Stijl, but he is chiefly remembered for raising abstract experimental sculpture on an international footing and becoming a pioneer of modern sculpture. Abstract sculpture in Belgium was hardly understood at the time, despite the great effort on the part of exhibition and conference organizers and art critics. Later, in France, where he spent the rest of his life, Van Tongerloo's interests changed, and he concentrated instead on open, dynamic works.

Paul Joostens (1889–1960) similarly started to produce abstract works from 1917, including collages and reliefs in Cubist and Dada stylistic modes. Oscar Jespers (1887–1970) was probably the most influential of this group of abstract sculptors during the 1920s. For a while influenced by Archipenko and other Cubists, although also inspired by Flemish Expressionism and Egyptian art, he nevertheless fused these sources into personal wholes as a result of his sense for plasticity.

Jozef Cantré (1890–1957) had knowledge of Ossip Zadkine's work in the Netherlands (where he stayed during World War I), with his preferences for a closeness to the human form. He shared Henri Puvrez's (1893–1971) interest in stylized shapes. Cantré and Puvez also followed Jespers in generally choosing the technique of direct carving, in wood or stone.

Another contemporary strand was that of the Animists Charles Leplae (1903–61) and Georges Grard (1901–84) based on more Classical premises. In their move away from the fragmentation that Expressionism implied, they followed French precedent in the work of Aristide Maillol and Charles Despiau. Leplae certainly was in contact with Despiau during a stay in Paris.

The great Flemish Expressionist painter Constant Permeke (1886–1952) also tried his hand at sculpture beginning about 1935. His sculptures directly reflect the power and monumentality of his painting.

Surrealism also appeared in sculpture, with Marcel Mariën (1920–93) exhibiting in 1937 *Surrealist Objects and Poems*. The fantastic was a beloved subject in Belgian sculpture; adherents to its theories included Pierre Caille (1912–96), Octave Landuyt (*b.* 1922), and Carmen Dionyse (*b.* 1921).

Such avant-garde strands were inappropriate for the numerous war memorials that World War I inspired; sculptors instead used the traditional prewar idioms of monumental sculpture to fill the cities of Belgium with memorials to war heroes. Conceived within the parameters of an architectural, site-specific, and historical framework, the works permitted little innovation, although the eventual outcome is still one of enormous diversity, mainly due to the large number of sculptors involved in these projects.

In the Netherlands of the 1920s, German Expressionism and Die Brücke influenced such groups as De Ploeg in Groningen and the work of the Rotterdam-based artist Hendrik Chabot (1894–1949). Abstraction, whether in Cubist or Constructivist forms, remained secondary, and by the 1930s, the Classical strand of such artists as Maillol and a type of expressive realism became prevalent. Numerous memorials to World War II also used these styles. The focus on the anatomy of the human body became an important element of the memorials, which continued to be erected for several decades after the war by such artists as Mari Andriessen (1897–1979).

After World War II, Dutch sculptors who achieved prominence had generally in part trained abroad. Ossip Zadkine and to a lesser extent Jacques Lipchitz became influential sources for a sculptor such as Wessel Couzijn (1912–84), who together designed the landmark Rotterdam war memorial to the merchant navy of 1951. Shinkichi Tajiri (*b.* 1923) rose to prominence with his 1949 entry to the Cobra exhibition, and his

Junk sculptures (1950–51), which used recycled materials, focused on material culture. Other Cobra artists included Karel Appel (*b.* 1921) and Lotti van der Gaag (*b.* 1923).

The internationalism of the Exposition Universelle in Brussels in 1958 prompted many sculptors to discard traditional styles and to follow (if not lead) the international trends. Assemblages made conspicuous advancements in the 1960s. The Antwerp-based G58-Hessenhuis group (which included Paul Van Hoeydonck [*b.* 1925] and Vic Gentils [1919–97]) advocated an antipainting style with reject objects. Van Hoeydonck increasingly made fully three-dimensional figurative assemblages that included mechanical parts. Gentils's experiments with pieces of burned wood may be compared to Nouveau Réalisme; he expanded these a few years later into large-size compositions, such as those made from piano parts. His *Chess Set* (1966–67, Middelheim, Antwerp) is an example. Pol Bury (*b.* 1922) added movement to his wooden and steel works, with a weird and estranging effect.

In the north, Joost Baljeu (1925–91), André Volten (*b.* 1925), and Carel Visser (*b.* 1928) produced three-dimensional abstract geometrical works inspired by De Stijl. A knowledge of Brancusi's work is discernible in their works as well. The scheme of setting aside a percentage of the cost of a building for art when constructing public edifices led some artists such as Peter Struycken (*b.* 1939) to engage in sculptural projects. In Belgium, monumental sculpture is particularly well represented by Olivier Strebelle (*b.* 1927) who made a specialty out of fluid bronze compositions.

During the 1960s ecology became one of the main themes permeating Happenings and other events of conceptualist artists such as Panamarenko (*b.* 1940) and groups such as Mass Moving. Panamarenko continued with his interest in technology, producing hot-air balloons, utopian airplanes, and racing cars. Marcel Broodthaers (1924–76) adapted forms of Nouveau Réalisme, Pop art, Conceptual art, and performance art to convey his criticism of the Belgian artistic scene. He also rejected American Pop and satirized it in works such as *Casserole and Closed Mussels* (1965), contrasting his humble possessions such as household goods and mussel shells with mass production and big business. Both Panamarenko and Broodthaers cultivated a mythology of the individual whose influence continued into the 1970s.

Environment-conscious artists such as Bernd Lohaus (*b.* 1940) tried to achieve a different spatial and territorial experience with wooden beams and blocks of stone. The heterogeneity of installations by Leo Copers (*b.* 1947) addressed contrasts between art and reality. Artists often intended a combination of materials to reflect the concept of an action or even the object itself. Richard Long thus became a model for such artists as Carel Visser.

Since the 1980s artists have diversified materials and concepts and have thus distanced themselves from reality. Intuition and unexpected associations create sculptural expressions that could convey powerful inner feelings, in a world between abstraction and new figuration. On a monumental scale, Guillaume Bijl (*b.* 1946) displayed life-size interiors of spaces in daily life. With these avant-garde interpretations of the sculptural medium, more traditional and Classical trends coexisted, such as the late portrait busts by Charlotte van Pallandt (1898–1997), although they generally relied on an older generation of sculptors because some academies (particularly at Arnhem and The Hague) had stopped teaching traditional sculptural techniques during the 1960s.

LÉON E. LOCK

See also **Assemblage; Bossuit, Francis van; Bourdelle, Émile-Antoine; Delcour, Jean; Delvaux, Laurent; du Quesnoy, François; Faydherbe, Lucas; Lipchitz, Jacques; Meunier, Constantin; Minne, George; Quellinus (Quellin) Family; Rude, François; Rysbrack, John Michael; Warin, Jean; Zadkine, Ossip**

Further Reading

Beelden in de late middeleeuwen en Renaissance/Late Gothic and Renaissance Sculpture in the Netherlands, Nederlands Kunsthistorisch Jaarboek/Netherlands Yearbook for History of Art 45 (1994)

Brand, Jan, Nicolette Gast, and Catelijne de Muynek, *Het Grote Gedicht, Nederlandse beeldhouwkunst 1945/1994*, Ghent: Snoeck Ducaju, 1994

Derom, Patrick, *The Statues and Monuments of Brussels*, Antwerp: Pandora, and Brussels: Patrick Derom Gallery, 2000

Jacobs, Lynn F., *Early Netherlandish Carved Altarpieces, 1380–1550: Medieval Tastes and Mass Marketing*, Cambridge: Cambridge University Press, 1998

Jolly, Anna, "Netherlandish Sculptors in Sixteenth-Century Northern Germany and Their Patrons," *Simiolus* 27/3 (1999)

Koopmans, Ype, *Muurvast en gebeiteld: Beeldhouwkunst in de bouw, 1840–1940; Fixed and Chiselled: Sculpture in Architecture, 1840–1940*, Rotterdam: Nai, 1994

Lawrence, Cynthia Miller, *Flemish Baroque Commemorative Monuments, 1566–1725*, New York: Garland, 1981

Leeuwenberg, Jaap, and Willy Halsema-Kubes, *Beeldhouwkunst in het Rijksmuseum*, The Hague: Staatsuitgeverij, 1973

Monumentale beeldhouwkunst in Nederland, Nederlands Kunsthistorisch Jaarboek/Netherlands Yearbook for History of Art 34 (1983)

Scholten, Frits, *Gebeeldhouwde portretten: Portrait sculptures: Rijksmuseum Amsterdam*, Amsterdam: Rijksmuseum Amsterdam, and Zwolle, the Netherlands: Waanders, 1995

Scholten, Frits, *Sumptuous Memories: Studies in Seventeenth-Century Dutch Tomb Sculpture*, Zwolle, the Netherlands: Waanders, 2000

Sculpture au siècle de Rubens dans les Pays-Bas méridionaux et la principauté de Liège, Brussels: Musées royaux d'Art et d'Histoire and Musées royaux des Beaux-Arts de Belgique, 1977

Steyaert, John William (editor), *Late Gothic Sculpture: The Burgundian Netherlands*, Ghent, Belgium: Ludion Press, 1994

Woods, Kim, "Five Netherlandish Carved Altar-Pieces in England and the Brussels School of Carving, c. 1470–1520," *The Burlington Magazine* 138 (1996)

Woods, Kim, "Newly Discovered Work in England by the Master of Hakendover, Oud Holland," *Oud Holland* 113/3 (1999)

Woods, Kim, "Some Sixteenth-Century Antwerp Carved Wooden Altar-Pieces in England," *The Burlington Magazine* 141 (1999)

LOUISE NEVELSON 1899–1988 *United States*

Rising to artistic prominence during the 1940s and 1950s, Louise Nevelson specialized in sculptures in wood, which became her exclusive medium. Her work from the 1940s contributed to the development of American abstraction, which after World War II shifted the center of international art from Paris to New York. Nevelson used the traditional subjects of the figure, still life, and landscape and incorporated aspects of Cubism and Surrealism into a language of geometric abstraction and radically simplified shapes. Similar to other Abstract Expressionist painters and sculptors, Nevelson relied upon an intuitive, rather than rational, approach to creating sculpture that was meant to evoke emotional and psychological responses.

Nevelson, whose father and brother were builders and managed a lumberyard, became interested in wood as a medium for her sculpture. She enjoyed the spontaneity and impulsivity that she could achieve with wood. In addition, on extended travels throughout Mexico and Europe, where she frequented museums and became acquainted with the landscape, she was greatly inspired by African and indigenous wooden sculptures and tribal aesthetics.

Nevelson's earliest works comprised small abstract "landscapes" and tabletop objects that incorporated found objects, such as discarded wooden materials that she encountered while walking through the streets of New York. She then arranged these sculptures in deep boxes constructed from salvaged wooden crates. By stacking the crates on top of each other, Nevelson formed large walls, and rather than polishing or staining the wood, she painted all the components black. This became a preferred color for her sculptures, and she described herself as "an architect of shadow."

In the mid 1950s, Nevelson began illuminating the bases of her sculptures and refining her structural assemblages. These distinctions marked a mature phase of her oeuvre. By using unorthodox methods of collage and incorporating a sense of randomness with her use of wood, Nevelson imbued her sculptures with a sense of inner luminosity. During this period the artist's rectangular box sculptures developed into the completion of her first large-scale wall piece.

By the late 1950s, Nevelson began constructing vertical sky columns using the intuitive approach and the incorporation of found wood objects that marked her earlier career. The construction and outcome of her vertical columns have an affinity with architectural models. This phase in Nevelson's career represented a refinement of past methodologies and an experimental process that allowed for innovative variations.

In the 1960s, Nevelson's ongoing curiosity and investigations led her to experiment with and incorporate transparent Plexiglas and metal into more anthropomorphic columns. These new materials challenged her familiarity with color, form, and shape. This shift also led to an inclusion of landscape in her sculptures. Her later work was comprised of random orderings of forms and patterns, which she stacked in Cubist-like grids. Throughout her oeuvre, Nevelson was able to join a sense of mystery, intuition, and adaptability with a formal relationship to geometry, structure, and order. In this respect, Nevelson shares the ability to fuse the subjective with the objective, the abstract with the figurative, in a manner similar to that of her peer Louise Bourgeois.

A Russian Jew whose family moved to Maine when she was just five, Nevelson had faced the pain of anti-Semitism during her young life. These difficulties came to influence her later work. In 1964 she created *Homage to 6,000,000*, a memorial to Jews killed in the Holocaust and a clear assertion of her own identity. Later, she was slated to donate a work to the Centre Georges Pompidou in Paris at the same time that the French government released a Palestinian terrorist. In protest, she withdrew her donation. In 1966 she returned to the abstract theme of remembrance with

Homage to the World, a monochrome, black-painted construction that spans an 8.7 meter wall. The idiosyncratic clusters of collected geometric forms registers not only a sense of dynamic rhythm but also a strange repetition that is nearly compulsive.

Honored by the Whitney Museum of American Art with a major career retrospective in 1967, Nevelson continued to work until her death in 1988. The Louise Nevelson Plaza in New York City stands as a tribute to her, and, in April 2000, the U.S. Postal Service commemorated her with stamps depicting five of her sculptures.

MIKI GARCIA

See also **Assemblage; Bourgeois, Louise; Contemporary Sculpture; Modernism; Women Sculptors; Wood**

Biography

Born in Kiev, Russia, 23 September 1899. Moved to Rockland, Maine, 1904; studied with Kenneth Hayes Miller at The Art Students League, New York City; trips to Europe and Mexico, 1919; moved to Munich, Germany, where she studied with Hans Hofmann, 1931; returned to United States and taught at Educational Alliance Art School, New York, as part of WPA-funded program, 1937; first exhibition, 1941; destroyed entire exhibition when no works sold; first major retrospective at the Whitney Museum of American Art, New York City, 1967. Died in New York City, United States, 17 April 1988.

Selected Works

1945   *Moving-Static-Moving Figures*; terracotta; Whitney Museum of American Art, New York City, United States

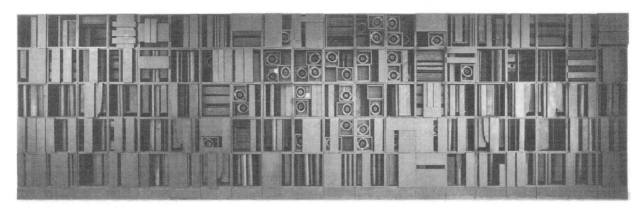

Homage to the World
Founders Society Purchase, Friends of Modern Art Fund and other Founders Society Funds
© 1985 The Detroit Institute of Arts, and (2003) Estate of Louise Nevelson / Artists Rights Society (ARS), New York

1956   *Sky Totem*; painted wood; Smithsonian American Art Museum, Washington, D.C., United States

1956   *First Personage*; painted wood; Brooklyn Museum of Art, New York, United States

1958   *Sky Cathedral*; boxes, wood, chair backs, finials, furniture legs, moldings, spindles, and other found objects; Museum of Modern Art, New York City, United States

1964   *Black Chord*; painted wood; Whitney Museum of American Art, New York City, United States

1966   *Homage to the World*; painted wood; The Detroit Institute of Arts, Michigan, United States

1967–68 *Transparent Sculpture I*; Plexiglas; Albright-Knox Art Gallery, Buffalo, New York, United States

Further Reading

"Black Sculpture: Painted Wood, 1958," *Art in America* 88/5 (May 2000)

Friedman, Martin L. (editor), *Nevelson: Wood Sculptures*, New York: Dutton, and Minneapolis, Minnesota: Walker Art Center, 1973

Lipman, Jean, *Nevelson's World*, New York: Hudson Hill Press, 1983

Lisle, Laurie, *Louise Nevelson: A Passionate Life*, New York: Summit Books, 1990

"Louise Nevelson: Sculpture and Drawing from the 1940s: Washburn Gallery," *Sculpture* 18/2 (March 1999)

NEW GUINEA

New Guinea is the largest island of Oceania. Located in the South Pacific between the equator and Australia, east of Indonesia, New Guinea is home to a great number of ethnic groups speaking nearly 800 languages. Today, the eastern portion of New Guinea constitutes the country of Papua New Guinea, while the western portion, Irian Jaya, is a province of the Republic of Indonesia.

A variety of prized sculptural traditions ranging from complete figures in the round to relief carving on shields and ceremonial house posts and lintels to elaborate mask constructions dominate the island's diverse art styles. Many of the art techniques and styles, primarily those of the east coast, have strong affinities with the islands of Melanesia. Publications discussing the art of Oceania often include New Guinea within the cultural and geographical delineation of Melanesia. In order to do greater justice to the vastness and diversity of both New Guinea and the Melanesian Islands, they are discussed separately in this volume.

The earliest migration into New Guinea and its smaller nearby islands may have taken place possibly 50,000 years ago during the last Ice Age. At that time the oceans were as much as 120 meters lower than they are now. The lower water levels exposed the continental shelves, which created the landmasses of Sahul and Sunda. Sahul included the regions of Australia, New Guinea, and Tasmania. Sunda encompassed the Malay Peninsula, the Philippines, Borneo, Sumatra, Java, and Sulawesi.

The first migration from Southeast Asia could have been accomplished 35,000 years ago on foot with the stretches of ocean and rivers—being of considerably less distance than today—separating Sahul and its nearby islands of New Britain and New Ireland being traversed by small canoes or rafts. The longer voyages to the Solomon Islands were accomplished as soon as 28,000 years ago and to the Admiralty Islands by approximately 20,000 years ago. Some evidence suggests that the earliest migrations into this region may have included groups from earlier populations established in Australia.

After the Pleistocene Era the rising ocean waters between 11,000 and 8000 years ago covered the exposed continental shelves creating the landmasses, as they are known today. This process not only increased the divide between the islands of Southeast Asia, New Guinea, and Australia but also shrank the size of the islands of Melanesia considerably. The greater distance between the islands and their smaller size would have made the prospect of ocean voyage less likely without increased maritime skill. Contact between these regions may have continued, although on a considerably smaller scale.

The second sizable migration into Oceania from Southeast Asia began possibly as early as 6000 years ago through 1000 years ago. Much of the evidence for these migrations is linguistic and connected to the dispersal of Austronesian speakers from Southeast Asia throughout Oceania. The seafaring migrations of these people and their contact and blending with the prehistoric settlements account for more than 1000 languages and cultures. In New Guinea the Austronesian settlements seem to have never reached the highlands, where the prehistoric populations may have been well entrenched and only established themselves along the coast and rivers. The resistance to these migrants seems evident in New Guinea, where the vast majority of the 800 languages spoken are non-Austronesian.

Pottery along the Sepik coast of New Guinea first appeared by approximately 3700 BCE. Linguistically and archaeologically, the origin of pottery in both Asia and Oceania has been linked to Austronesian languages, although New Guinea samples suggest that pottery in Oceania may have predated this Austronesian contact.

The artistic traditions that have developed over the last several millennia in New Guinea do not easily fit Western categories of visual art and art production. The most prolific art form is sculpture of both carved and constructed types. The sculptural elements of New Guinea art are evident in the forms of canoe prow and stern figures, paddles, carved door posts, lintels and roof finials, figurines, ceremonial and domestic suspension hooks, relief-carved shields, slit gongs, flute finials, masks and headdresses, and agricultural and house implements.

An important feature of sculpture in New Guinea and many areas of Oceania is the ephemeral aspect of the art. In many cases in addition to the wood carvings and sculptures most readily accepted by the Western eye as art, the attached ephemeral elements and their movements either in battle or through dance and ritual in conjunction with music and chant were the most important attributes given to a sculpture. Some of the many materials used in the construction and ornamentation of the sculptural arts include woods from various types of trees, their leaves, beaten bark, seeds, fruit, colored earth and clays, shells, birds-of-paradise and other bird plumage, pelts of tree-dwelling mammals, insects, and human hair. For many sculptures the loss of these elements or immobility due to a lack of use would render the sculpture irrelevant and powerless to the society. After a work of art has lost its ritual significance, some cultures will burn or discard it in the jungle to be reclaimed by the environment, which had provided the elements used for its construction.

Most representations of traditional art are either of a nature or of a human spirit, or some combination of the two. The nature spirits inhabit the different aspects of the environment and some animals. The human images commonly depict culture heroes, which can be in the form either of remembered real ancestors or of ancestors of mythical origin.

The production of wood carvings and sculptures with traditional stone, shell, or bone tools still continues in a limited fashion in some New Guinea highland communities. The Western introduction of iron tools greatly impacted the efficiency and elaborateness of sculpture. The ability to make more precise cuts in a timely manner allowed for a higher quantity of more intricately designed larger objects. For example, with iron tools Asmat artists could create taller *mbis* poles (mortuary poles) with more complex openwork.

With the long history of settlement, migration, and trade through the modern day, tracing specific iconographic patterns through time can be problematic. The great diversity of languages and worldviews also makes difficult the formation of broad generalizations to categorize sculpture types, their use, and their development across New Guinea. In an attempt to consider a variety of New Guinea art traditions this discussion delineates the island into several fairly homogenous regions.

Sepik Basin

The Sepik Basin of Papua New Guinea is the richest and most diverse art-producing region in Oceania. The Sepik River originates in the central highlands and covers nearly 700 miles before entering the Pacific Ocean on the island's north coast. The river's course and its many adjoining tributaries are the main propagating element in the high level of cross-cultural diversity reached in the region. The Sepik River functions as an internal life source, supporting at least 69 separate language groups and hundreds of ethnic groups that have traded goods, beliefs, and traditions along its shores and surrounding hills throughout its complex history. In addition to the internal developments, the Sepik River has allowed the infiltration of external influences at a less-restricted pace than other areas of the island that have less-hospitable terrain to traverse.

Within the great diversity of art produced, the Sepik people are known for their elaborate spiritual and social ceremonies that emphasize the importance of the deeply interrelated aspects of visual and aural art traditions. The Sepik approach to and interaction with their environment is holistic; therefore, the interdependence of visual and aural elements is integral to the success of Sepik ritual performance. The unity of the visual and aural in the Sepik Basin has centered on the use and production of musical instruments. Many ceremonies incorporate intricately carved musical instruments that are said to imitate the voices or noises of spirits and ancestors. Of particular importance are the sounds produced by the carved drums, hollowed log slit gongs, and the sacred bamboo flutes with their decorative figurative finials and woven masks.

The hand drum, commonly referred to as an hourglass drum because of its shape or as a dance drum, is primarily a secular instrument, although it also accompanies sacred instruments and chanting. All adult men make and own this type of wooden drum. Played by hand, it proliferates a rhythm at festivals. The drumhead is a stretched reptile skin in lowland areas and tree kangaroo skin in the highlands, secured with cane string. Small pieces of beeswax may also be placed on the drumhead to vary the sound. The body, averaging 60 to 90 centimeters high, may be heavily carved over the entire surface or be reserved to a central geometric band or bracelet with affinities to its owner. At the body's most central point is a simple wooden handle carved from the same piece of wood or a totemic symbol carved in the round, such as the fish-eagle, which the Sepik people hold in esteem for its great hunting and killing abilities.

The slit gong plays a central role in Sepik ceremonies and dances and also has an everyday secular function of transmitting messages to summon individuals from the bush or assemble village residents for a meeting. The slit gong is made of a large log hollowed out through a slit along one side, ranging 38 to 180 centimeters long and 15 to 60 centimeters in diameter. It is embellished with incised symmetric, geometric, and animal motifs. The crocodile is a commonly depicted animal, representing a water spirit. The curvilinear designs prevalent throughout Melanesia have found a bold and imaginative style in Sepik art. Some gongs also include painted designs in addition to or in place of the carving. Of the two prevailing styles of slit gongs, one has two three-dimensionally carved handles or lugs protruding at either end in the generalized form of an animal or ancestor figure, often with a long curving nose, a sign of virility. In the other style one entire end is carved into a loop-shaped face. Players strike various points along the edge of the slit with wooden hand beaters that are often carved with as much detail and care as the slit gong itself. The slit gong produces tones of immense resonance.

The most lavish instruments are the sacred flutes adorned with carved wooden figure stoppers and attached woven masks ornamented with clay, shells, beads, and cassowary feathers. The two most common sacred flutes are made of bamboo ranging from 90 to 240 centimeters long and about 5 to 8 centimeters in diameter. One type is played vertically and has no finger holes. In playing, the fingers partially cover the open end and form a mouthpiece to reproduce animal noises. The second type, the transverse flute, has two finger holes and can be manipulated to perform a greater variety of sound. These flutes are played in pairs at spirit-based ceremonies and at cult initiations for periods lasting continuously for two to four days and nights.

Flute figurines, often representing male ancestors and spirits, are placed into the upper ends of the flute while not in use, by way of a long shaft protruding from the bottom of the figure. The Biwat people use figures that embody formal characteristics found throughout the Sepik River region. An oversized head atop a proportionate body with an aggressive stance, for example, depicts the importance of the head as a center of spirituality and power. Several other types of small woven objects and masks attach at the midpoint of the flute shaft. The masks are made of carved wood or bone overlaid with objects important to the particular use of the flute. A common mask type is decorated with nassa and conus shells set in a black-ened compound of clay and vegetable oil while others may incorporate hair, flowers, plant fibers, and feathers into the design.

Sculptural aspects of architecture are also important throughout the Sepik Basin. The spirit house, or men's society house, is centrally located at the highest point in a village. The house is used for holding debates, ceremonial rituals, and storing sacred objects. Intricately carved posts and lintels support its steep thatched roof. The wood used for the posts and lintels and the images and figures carved on them often relate to local myths. For the Iatmul people the main post of the house is seen as the masculine father, while the king post is the feminine mother. Side supporting posts represent the totems of the clans that participated in the construction of the house.

The ceremonial figure central to the Arambak people, known as the *yipwon*, is closely related to the activities of the men's society. These wooden figures, comprising a face and repeated pairs of symmetrical hooks, range in size from small palm-size amulets carried by men to large sculptures of up to three meters tall that are stored within the spirit house. The large sculptures are used in ceremonies of ritual preparation for hunting expeditions and raids on enemies. After the leader of the expedition has rubbed the *yipwon* with a mixture of animal excrement and blood drawn from his penis, he plants the sculpture upright in a dirt mound in front of the spirit house. The direction the sculpture faces dictates the trajectory of the expedition.

The carved hardwood suspension hook used to suspend objects and food out of the reach of insects, snakes, and rodents are used in both private dwellings and the spirit house. The carved body of the hook is in the form of an ancestral figure, which protects the suspended items and their owner. In the spirit house predominantly male ancestor figures would suspend sacred objects, while female figures would have been delegated to domestic settings.

Another sculpturally ornate pair of objects carved by the Sepik people is the lime container and spatula. A wood or bone spatula, or dipping stick, accompanies a plain or incised gourd or bamboo container used for holding lime. The end of the spatula that is held in the hand commonly takes the form of a human or animal. The Sepik generally use the lime obtained from heat oxidized limestone or oyster shells to flavor betel nuts, as well as in some ritual ceremonies.

Gulf of Papua

The immense span of the gulf at the southeast end of Papua New Guinea encompasses several cultural groups with discernable stylistic continuities in their art production. The majority of their cultural traditions and arts were lost during the first half of the 20th century. Common art objects in this region include painted and relief-carved panels and woven fiber and beaten bark cloth masks. The wood panels and masks play an important role in the traditions and rituals of the men's houses. The variations in the styles of these objects tend to coincide with differences in language and associated rituals between groups.

Torres Strait

The peoples of the Torres Strait populate some 30 islands located between New Guinea and the Cape York Peninsula of Australia. Politically, these islands are linked to Australia. Common art produced on these islands include turtle shell and wood masks and wood and stone sculptures. Artists created elongated human figures from wood, bamboo, and plant fiber. Many of these figures and the masks were carried in ritual dances. The volcanic stone and coral sculptures of animals or humans were much smaller. These were primarily used as garden ornaments to procure rain and promote a bountiful harvest.

Massim

The Massim region at the southernmost tip of Papua New Guinea encompasses Milne Bay, the D'Entrecasteaux Islands, the Trobriands, the Woodlark Islands, the Marshall Bennett Islands, and the Louisiade Archipelago. Knowledge of the history of this region before Western contact is very limited. It is difficult to discern if the current Massim art styles derive directly from the few pieces of prehistoric artwork that have been found with curvilinear motifs.

The homogenous aspect of art found throughout the Massim region today can be linked to the *kula* tradition, a complex ceremonial trade system. The region exhibits a high level of skill in wood sculpture. The predominant style incorporates two-dimensional curvilinear ornamentation. Fully three-dimensional animal or human figures are primarily limited to the handles of lime spatulas.

Among the Massim objects incorporating the local art style are canoes, shields, adze handles, hunting tools, and household utensils. The *kula* sailing canoes used in inter-island trade are particularly laden with carved curvilinear decoration. The prows, splashboards, masts, and paddles are all richly carved.

Asmat

The sculpture of the Asmat people is the most widely studied art produced in Irian Jaya. Critics consider Asmat carving as having a more aggressive and combative style than is found in the other parts of New Guinea. The predominance of this style of carving descends from two factors: the central importance of head-hunting to the traditional culture and the belief that humankind was created from wood at the hands of a sculptor. The Asmat sculptors are best known for their immense carved mortuary poles, known as *mbis*, relief-carved shields, elaborate openwork canoe prows, and large figures.

The woods used in their art are predominately from the mangrove and sago palm trees, trees that are central to many areas of Asmat life. The Asmat consider the mangrove tree, which has a harder wood, to have male attributes and view the fruit of the mangrove as the head of the tree, equated with the human skull. The Asmat believe the power of a man to exist within the head. They thus see the "flying fox" fruit bat and other avian animals of the region who eat these fruits as eating the head of the tree. The analogy of the bat eating a head relates to the importance of head-hunting for the Asmat and is portrayed in the widespread use of bat motifs on shields and other war-related items. The Asmat see the sago palm as having female attributes. The soft red pith of the sago and the insect larvae living in the tree are the staple foods of the Asmat. They view the red color and nourishment of the sago pith as the menstruation of the tree.

Artists decorate the Asmat shield, carved from mangrove wood, with curvilinear raised relief and highlighted with red, black, and white paint. In addition to the fruit bat motif, artists commonly use a squatting figure with knees to elbows. The squatting figure relates both to the position people are born in and to the pose of the praying mantis. The praying mantis's practice of eating the head of the male of the species also relates to the cultural importance of head-hunting.

Asmat sculptors carve *mbis* poles from an inverted mangrove tree trunk with a protruding flat section of tree root carved with elaborate openwork. The *mbis* poles commemorate a death that must be avenged. Traditionally, the death of a fellow warrior in battle would be avenged by the taking of the head of an enemy warrior. Mangrove fruit or skulls are often hung from the extended tree root prow at the top of the pole. Only the multipiece canoe prows created along the Cenderwasih Bay rival the formidable and elaborate craftsmanship of the prows of the Asmat *mbis* poles and canoes.

JOHN L. MACHADO, Jr.

See also **Melanesia**

Further Reading

Gathercole, Peter W., Adrienne Lois Kaeppler, and Douglas Newton, *The Art of the Pacific Islands*, Washington, D.C.: National Gallery of Art, 1979

Kaeppler, Adrienne Lois, Christian Kaufmann, and Douglas Newton, *Oceanic Art*, translated by Nora Scott and Sabine Bouladon, New York: Abrams, 1997

Meyer, Anthony J.P., *Oceanic Art; Ozeanische Kunst; Art océanien* (trilingual English-German-French text), 2 vols., Cologne, Germany: Konemann, 1995; Edison, New Jersey: Knickerbocker Press, 1996

Newton, Douglas (editor), *Arts of the South Seas: Island Southeast Asia, Melanesia, Polynesia, Micronesia: The Collections of the Musée Barbier-Mueller*, Munich and New York: Prestel, 1999

Thomas, Nicholas, *Oceanic Art*, New York: Thames and Hudson, 1995

Wardwell, Allen, *Island Ancestors: Oceanic Art from the Masco Collection*, Seattle: University of Washington Press, 1994

NEW SCULPTURE

See **Art Deco; Frampton, George; Gilbert, Alfred; Leighton, Lord Frederic**

NEW ZEALAND

Before European settlement in the early 19th century, sculpture, especially wood carving, was the major art medium in New Zealand. Although colonists acquired Maori carvings for museum and private collections, they derived little artistic inspiration from them. As late as 1965 Peter Tomory claimed, "Our contemporary sculptors show no trace of Maori art in their work" (see Tomory, 1965). Instead, colonists looked at their own, largely British, sculptural traditions. With few exceptions, major sculptures before 1914 were commissioned from British artists and shipped to New Zealand. The exploding population of public monuments erected worldwide during this period affected New Zealand, although the country's modest population and economic base limited their numbers. Thomas Woolner's robustly realistic statue of colonizer John Robert Godley (1863–65) in Cathedral Square, Christchurch, is the earliest public monument and considered one of the finest. Each of the main urban centers—Auckland, Wellington, Christchurch, and Dunedin—boasts a Queen Victoria memorial, reflecting the close imperial links with Britain. Wellington's version (1902–04) by Alfred Drury is a typical example of the New Sculpture.

The earliest sculpture by New Zealand–based Europeans in the mid to late 19th century took the form of architectural carvings. Although not executed on a large scale or budget, the work of Louis John Godfrey (*fl.* 1862–87) in Dunedin and Anton Teutenberg (1840–1933) in Auckland is spirited, confident, and, in the use of New Zealand subjects, innovative. The work of Charles Kidson (1867–1908), who taught modeling and metalwork at the Canterbury College School of Art in Christchurch, shows the influence of the Arts and Crafts movement. His successor, Frederick Gurnsey (1868–1953), was New Zealand's most important ecclesiastical carver. Gurnsey's work combines the spiritual ideals of the Late Gothic Revival with a keen eye for indigenous flora and fauna.

Memorials commemorating the South African War and World War I provided new opportunities for New Zealand sculptors. Initially they faced governmental discouragement of—and disbelief in—the home product, a "colonial cringe" mind-set. The Auckland-based sculptor Richard Gross (1882–1964), who had studied with the British sculptor Albert Toft, executed several impressive memorials, notably the equestrian National War Memorial in Wellington (1932–59). He also established New Zealand's first sculpture foundry in the mid 1920s. William Thomas Trethewey (1892–1956) was the first New Zealand–born sculptor to attain national prominence. His Christchurch War Memorial (1933–37) incorporates New Sculpture realism with Art Deco stylization and is pacifistic in mood. Trethewey was the leading sculptor involved with the New Zealand Centennial Exhibition in Wellington (1939–40).

During the interwar years, some of New Zealand's most significant sculpture originated in the leading art schools. In Christchurch, Francis Shurrock (1887–1977) maintained the approach of his Royal College of Art teacher, Edward Lanteri, in requiring sound technical foundations. But he also encouraged experimentation and smoothed the path for the next generation's Modernism. In Dunedin, Robert Field (1899–1987) was more radical, certainly in his own work. His *Wahine* (1934) combines the massive limbs and simplified features of Henry Moore's sculpture with references to Maori greenstone tiki carvings. Less influential but equally impressive was the achievement of Margaret Butler (1883–1947). During her ten-year stint in Europe, she studied with Antoine Bourdelle; Charles Despiau also admired her work. After returning to New Zealand in 1934, she executed two busts of Maori, *La Nouvelle Zélande* and the *Maori Madonna* (both *ca.* 1937–38). Proficiently modeled and pensive in mood, they possess a distinctively New Zealand identity.

The 1950s witnessed a slow but unmistakable rise in the status of sculpture, long the poor relation of painting. In 1955 the Auckland City Art Gallery held the first major exhibition exclusively devoted to sculpture. The following year, a touring Henry Moore exhibition attracted 61,000 visitors and aroused considerable critical controversy in a culture hitherto resistant to Modernism. Several Auckland-based sculptors, all former Shurrock students, championed Moore and responded to his influence. They included Alan Ingham

(1920–96), who had worked in England as Moore's studio assistant; his brother-in-law, Russell Clark (1905–66), who executed several major semiabstract public sculptures in the early 1960s; and Molly Macalister (1920–79), whose over-life-size bronze *Maori Warrior* (1964–66) is an updated and indigenized version of Auguste Rodin's *Balzac*. Although their work seems derivative and cautious today, they increased public appreciation of modern sculpture and made it accessible to private collectors.

The Elam School of Art at the University of Auckland was at the forefront of New Zealand sculpture in the 1960s and 1970s. Its head, Paul Beadle (1917–92), made small-scale sculptures that eccentrically and wittily combine the influences of Celtic art, Ashanti bronzes, and modern Auckland life. Beadle was also New Zealand's foremost medalist. Michael Dunn has described Beadle's colleague, Greer Twiss (*b.* 1937), as "the major sculptor of his generation" (see Green et al., 1977). Twiss's bronzes of struggling athletes from the mid 1960s link stylistically with Kenneth

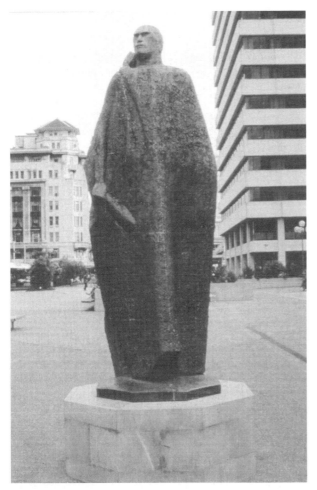

Maori Warrior
The Conway Library, Courtauld Institute of Art

Armitage and Alberto Giacometti but are distinctively "kiwi" in subject matter. His later sculptures use truncated forms, found objects, and abrupt dislocations in scale to create disturbing, surrealistic effects.

In the late 1960s, W.R. (Jim) Allen (*b.* 1922) made a more radical contribution to sculpture at Elam. Earlier sculptors always emphasized the object, however abstract. Allen, in contrast, was New Zealand's pioneering Post-Object artist, stressing concept and process more than product. He intended his installations, such as *Barbed Wire: Two Environments* (1970), to provoke and engage the viewer. They did not aim to be aesthetically pleasing, and because of their deliberately ephemeral nature, few have survived. Allen's status has nevertheless endured as a charismatic teacher and as "a catalyst for individual activity," as Dunn puts it (see Green et al., 1977). Allen's encouragement of diverse media such as installation, video, kinetic, and performance art inspired several leading younger artists, including Bruce Barber, Philip Dadson, and Peter Roche. Not all Elam-trained sculptors followed Allen, however. Terry Stringer (*b.* 1946) produces delicately cast figurative works, often domestic in scale; pleasurable objects on one level, they subtly disturb on another. Christine Hellyar's (*b.* 1947) cupboard installations of carefully arranged found objects and her latex casts of leaf forms could also be interpreted as a quiet reproach to the sculptural libertarianism of the 1960s.

In the mid 1960s, the influence of the constructed metal sculpture of Anthony Caro, together with that of American Minimalism, was also considerable, affecting both Elam-trained sculptors and students at the University of Canterbury School of Fine Arts in Christchurch. Several New Zealand counterparts to the British New Generation sculptors emerged, including John Panting (1940–74), Carl Sydow (1940–75), and Terry Powell (*b.* 1944). The Christchurch artist Neil Dawson (*b.* 1948) inherited some of their ideas, but his work is more playful and witty, incorporating the influence of the Pop artists Roy Lichtenstein and Patrick Caulfield. Dawson's sculpture has been called "three-dimensional drawing." By use of media such as wire mesh, cord, and crumpled foil, he "draws" architectural motifs and ripples of water. His 15-meter mixed-media *Globe* captured international attention when it was suspended over the Georges Pompidou Center, Paris, in 1989.

Dawson's elegance graphically contrasts with the work of the largely self-taught sculptor Don Driver (*b.* 1930). Prolific, inventive, and eclectic, Driver responds to such diverse sources as Kurt Schwitters, Mark Rothko, Robert Rauschenberg, and Donald Judd. Yet he gives his sculpture a decidedly kiwi inflection: his assemblages from the 1970s onward incorporate fertilizer sacks, pitchforks, and fluffy nylon bath mats to create surprisingly powerful, even beautiful, effects. Jeff Thomson (*b*. 1957) uses the quintessentially New Zealand material of corrugated iron for his sculpture, such as in his popular ironclad Holden automobile (1991) at the Te Papa Tongarewa Museum of New Zealand.

Len Lye (1901–80) is an isolated figure of genius in New Zealand sculpture. He is not a New Zealand sculptor per se; he spent his entire working life overseas, first in England and later in the United States. In the 1950s he became a major exponent of kinetic sculpture, but his work was not seen in New Zealand until shortly before his death. He bequeathed his works and archives to the Len Lye Foundation, which supervises the fabrication of his works. These include *Fountain* (1977), a motorized sculpture consisting of steel rods emanating from a container and creating a delicate spraylike effect. Lye's aim here was to portray energy, understood as the fundamental force of nature. Although Lye was in no position to make an impact on the work of New Zealand sculptors until the 1970s, Driver and Andrew Drummond (*b*. 1951) consider him a seminal influence. Lye's status was reflected in the dedication to him of the first book on New Zealand sculpture, Jim Allen and Wystan Curnow's *New Art* (1976).

The environment looms large for several New Zealand sculptors. The themes and materials of Drummond's sculpture link the human body to the land. Drummond's work underwent a transition from performance art in the late 1970s to carefully crafted sculptures such as *Listening and Viewing Device* (1994). This work, set on a hilltop in the Botanical Gardens, Wellington, comprises a copper cone suspended in a columned frame. The cone responds to the elements in magnifying sound and funneling vision, and the frame imparts a shrinelike quality to the work. Chris Booth (*b*. 1948) is a more active conservationist in his outlook and in his sculpture, which consists of assemblages made from stones, boulders, and wood, often set in their landscape of origin. His work has won warm praise from Maori for its integrity and understanding of the land.

In recent years, the work of Maori sculptors has received considerable attention. It would be inaccurate, however, to refer to "Maori sculpture." Like the sculptors of European origin already discussed, Maori practitioners do not constitute a coherent movement—and still less a style. They are diverse individuals, each taking as much or as little from their ancestral culture as they see fit. The interplay between traditional carvings and Western Modernism can first be seen in the primitivist sculpture of Arnold Wilson (*b*. 1928), one of the earliest Maori art school graduates, and in the larger constructions of his near-contemporary, Para-

tene Matchitt (*b*. 1933). Jacqueline Fraser (*b*. 1956), like Dawson, uses wire and plastic, but there the similarity ends. The delicate spirals and curves of her work subtly evoke Maori tiki motifs, and her media suggest traditional fibers and threads. Nonetheless, Fraser's work is more suited to the contemporary gallery context than it is to the Maori *marae* (meeting place). A younger artist, Michael Parekowhai (*b*. 1968), cleverly combines references to Marcel Duchamp's readymades with Maori sing-along culture in his installation *Ten Guitars* (1999).

New Zealand has sometimes undervalued its most talented sculptors. Butler was largely ignored on her return from France, and Lye soon realized that his future lay overseas. However, New Zealand sculpture witnessed great strides in the second half of the 20th century. The first came with the growth of Modernism in the later 1950s, and the second with the impact of Post-Object art 15 years later. Since then, the sculptural scene has been energetic and diverse, but no single figure, style, or movement has dominated. Never has New Zealand been more sculpture conscious. This applies to the gallery context, with such venues as the Govett Brewster Gallery, New Plymouth, and Artspace in Auckland providing arenas for contemporary practice, as well as dealer galleries, sculpture in public places, and the teaching, scholarship, and criticism of sculpture.

MARK STOCKER

Further Reading

Allen, Jim, and Wystan Curnow (editors), *New Art: Some Recent New Zealand Sculpture and Post-Object Art*, Auckland: Heinemann, 1976

Brown, Warwick, *Another 100 New Zealand Artists*, Auckland: Godwit, 1996

Cape, Peter, *Artists and Craftsmen in New Zealand*, Auckland: Collins, 1969

Dunn, Michael, "New Zealand: IV: Sculpture," in *The Dictionary of Art*, edited by Jane Turner, New York: Grove, and London: Macmillan, 1996

Dunn, Michael, *New Zealand Sculpture from 1860 to the Present*, Auckland: Bateman, 2001

Green, Anthony, et al., "Aspects of New Zealand Sculpture" (parts 1–9), *Education* 26/1–10 (1977)

Nicholson, Michael, "New Zealand Contemporary Sculpture: A Comprehensive Showing at Auckland City Gallery," *New Zealand Home and Building* 18 (July 1955)

Pitts, Priscilla, *Contemporary New Zealand Sculpture: Themes and Issues*, Auckland: Bateman, 1998

Sculpture 1986: Aspects of Recent New Zealand Art (exhib. cat.), Auckland: City Art Gallery, 1986

Stocker, Mark, *Francis Shurrock: Shaping New Zealand Sculpture*, Dunedin, New Zealand: University of Otago Press, 2000

Tomory, Peter, "New Zealand Sculpture," *Art and Australia* 3 (September 1965)

ELISABET NEY 1833–1907 *German, also active in United States*

Elisabet Ney was a sculptor with an independent spirit, both in her birthplace of preunified Germany and in the United States, where she spent the second half of her life. A strong-willed child, Ney became a sculptor over the objections of her parents at a time when few women entered "the manly art." A principled woman, she defied social convention by denying her married state and keeping her own name for the sake of her career and her personal and artistic freedom. A talented artist, she became court sculptor to the king of Bavaria and an honored sculptor of the Texas legislature. She lived a Bohemian life in Texas but eventually won the support of the citizenry she had at first shocked by her unusual behavior, career choice, and mode of dress. She became a well-known Neoclassical sculptor of ideal subjects as well as portraits, first of German royalty and European personalities and then Texas leaders. She even gleaned praise from sculptor Lorado Taft, who referred to Ney as "one of the best equipped of women sculptors" (see Taft, 1903).

Ney was the only daughter of a Prussian sculptor of gravestones and ecclesiastical statuary. Helping in her father's workshop as a child, she decided to become a sculptor. She desired to study with the eminent sculptor Christian Daniel Rauch in Berlin, but her Catholic parents were uncomfortable with her living in Protestant Berlin, so they compromised by allowing her to attend the Royal Bavarian Academy of Fine Arts in Munich. Ney was the first woman admitted to study sculpture at the academy in 1852. Although she entered on a probationary level, the academy accepted her at full status the following year.

After receiving her diploma from the Munich academy, Ney finally became a student of the aged Rauch. Through him, and later Karl Varnhagen von Ense, she toured the Berlin salons, meeting and sculpting the well-known and influential members of European artistic, political, and intellectual society who would become her friends. These portraits, such as those of naturalist Alexander von Humboldt and philologist Jacob Grimm from about 1858, reflect Ney's ability to integrate a Classical countenance with naturalistic elements and reveal Rauch's influence on her style.

Ney convinced the philosopher Arthur Schopenhauer to sit for a portrait bust to prove to Schopenhauer, who openly doubted women's talents, her artistic ability. She created an accurate but flattering likeness, imbued with heroic and intelligent character. The bust received favorable criticism and was a triumph for Ney. Almost immediately, she received a major commission to model a bust of King George V of Hannover. After completing this commission, Ney returned to Berlin a success and maintained a studio in the Lagerhaus, home of the studios of the most prominent sculptors in Berlin.

On the island of Madeira, in 1863, Ney married Scottish physician, scientist, and philosopher Edmund Duncan Montgomery, whom she had met ten years earlier. Ney opposed marriage on principle and denied their marriage publicly throughout her life. She spent the years following their marriage in art travels to Egypt, Greece, and Italy. During this time, she modeled a bust of Giuseppe Garibaldi and received a commission from King William I of Prussia to model a bust of Otto von Bismarck (1867). She also modeled her ideal pieces *Sursum*, or *Genii of Mankind*, and *Prometheus Bound*.

When Ney returned to the cultural center of Munich in 1867, she was a popular and successful portraitist

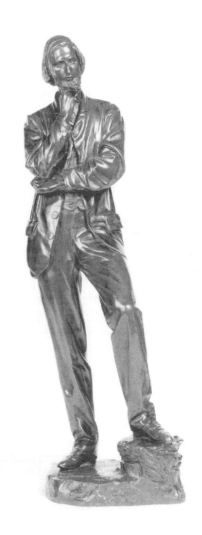

John William Spencer, 2nd Earl Brownlow, The Belton House, The National Trust
Photo courtesy Photographic Survey of Private Collections, Courtauld Institute of Art

so admired by King Ludwig II of Bavaria that he invited her to be his personal sculptor. He provided her with a villa at Schwabing and a studio in the royal palace. During her tenure, the king commissioned a full-length statue of himself for his castle in Linderhof. Modeling the king was a long and tedious process at times, with postponements and interruptions to the sittings. Ney's relationship with Montgomery, thought to be experienced without benefit of wedlock, eventually resulted in social ostracism. This exclusion, together with growing political tensions, forced Montgomery and Ney to immigrate to the United States in 1871, just after the outbreak of the Franco-Prussian War, leaving Ney's statue of Ludwig unfinished (the work was eventually completed in marble in 1903).

Ney and Montgomery first settled in Thomasville, Georgia, but purchased the Liendo plantation, near Hempstead, Texas, two years later. Ney produced little sculpture until she bought her studio in Austin, which she named Formosa after her studio in Madeira. Austin was the closest cultural center and the capital of Texas. There, she slowly formed significant friendships despite concerns over her unusual working attire (which included a tunic, leggings, and boots) and personal life. Through the Daughters of the Republic of Texas Ney received the commission to sculpt the statues of two Texas dignitaries, Sam Houston and Stephen F. Austin, for exhibition in the Texas State building at the World's Columbian Exposition, held in Chicago in 1893. Ney created her *Houston* and *Austin* as historical portraits, clothing them as pioneers in buckskin and including accoutrements befitting their accomplishments. The combined naturalism, accuracy, and easy countenance in these full-length models made them admired sculptures, and the artistic recognition she received, as well as her canvassing of potential patrons from legislators to women's clubs, brought Ney more portrait commissions, chiefly busts of prominent statesmen.

Ney's renewed artistic efforts paid off in 1901, when the Texas legislature voted appropriations totaling $26,500 for commissions for copies of her *Houston* and *Austin* for the Texas State Capitol Building, a copy of *Houston* for Statuary Hall in the U.S. Capitol in Washington, D.C. (as a companion to the *Austin* already commissioned by the Daughters of the Republic of Texas), and a memorial for the grave of General Albert Sidney Johnston. Ney used this major commission to fund two projects: the publication of her husband's philosophical texts and the execution of a statue in marble of her favorite literary heroine, *Lady Macbeth*, Ney's last work. With *Lady Macbeth*, Ney ventured beyond the stylistic elements of the Neoclassical and created an expressive, Romantic figure, full of inner turmoil and energy, which is made manifest in the twisting of the figure's head, torso, and arms and her tension-filled clasped hands. It represents a poignant end to a volatile artistic career.

Pride, eccentricity, and self-imposed exile from the European art world nonetheless cost Ney career opportunities and the worldwide acclaim her talent deserved. Her lack of ongoing artistic interaction with her European peers limited her opportunities as an artist; nevertheless, she continued to work (along with the majority of 19th century American sculptors) in the Neoclassical style well beyond its international decline.

CHARLENE G. GARFINKLE

See also **Neoclassicism and Romanticism; Rauch, Christian Daniel; Taft, Lorado; Women Sculptors**

Biography

Born in Münster, Westphalia (now Germany), 26 January 1833. Daughter and granddaughter of stone carvers. Studied with father and at private art school of painter Johann Baptiste Berdellé, 1852; first woman admitted to sculpture class at Royal Bavarian Academy of Fine Arts in Munich, 1852–54; studied with sculptor Christian Daniel Rauch at Berlin Academy, 1854–57; completed commissions after his death; studios in Berlin, Hannover, Münster, and Munich; traveled to London, Madeira, Rome, Naples, Egypt, and Greece, 1863–67; served as personal sculptor to King Ludwig II of Bavaria and maintained studio at Munich palace, 1867–70; exhibited at Berlin Exposition, 1856, Paris Salon, 1861, World's Columbian Exposition, Chicago, 1893, Louisiana Purchase Exposition, St. Louis, 1904; immigrated to United States with husband, 14 January 1871; stopped sculpting professionally, 1873; modeled only friends and family until commissions of 1890; opened studio Formosa (later Elisabet Ney Museum) in Austin, Texas, 1890; introduced art studies at University of Texas and in Texas public schools; president of Association of Texas Academy of Liberal Arts; revisited Germany 1895, 1902, and 1903. Died in Austin, Texas, United States, 29 June 1907.

Selected Works

1859	Bust of Arthur Schopenhauer; marble; Elisabet Ney Museum, Austin, Texas, United States; marble; Stadt- und Universitätsbibliothek, Frankfurt am Main, Germany
1859	Bust of King George V of Hannover; marble; Georg-August-Universität, Göttingen, Germany
1863–1903	Self-portrait; marble; Elisabet Ney Museum, Austin, Texas, United States

1864	*Sursum* (also known as *Genii of Mankind*); marble; private collection
1865	Bust of Giuseppe Garibaldi; marble; Fort Worth Art Museum, Texas, United States; bronze statuette (untraced)
1867	*Prometheus Bound*; plaster; Elisabet Ney Museum, Austin, Texas, United States; marble version: 1903, Bavarian royal castle, Linderhof, Germany
1869	*King Ludwig II of Bavaria*; plaster; Elisabet Ney Museum, Austin, Texas, United States; marble version: 1903, Bavarian royal castle, Linderhof, Germany
1881	Bust of Governor Oran M. Roberts; plaster; Elisabet Ney Museum, Austin, Texas, United States; marble version: Barker Texas History Center, University of Texas at Austin, United States
1891	*Sam Houston*; plaster; Elisabet Ney Museum, Austin, Texas, United States; bronze version: 1899, Elisabet Ney Museum, Austin, Texas, United States; marble versions: 1904, Statuary Hall, Capitol Building, Washington, D.C., United States; Texas State Capitol Building, Austin, Texas, United States
1893	*Stephen F. Austin*; plaster; Elisabet Ney Museum, Austin, Texas, United States; marble versions: 1904, Capitol Building, Washington, D.C., United States; Texas State Capitol Building, Austin, Texas, United States
1901	Memorial for General Albert Sidney Johnston; marble; State Cemetery, Austin, Texas, United States
1903	*Lady Macbeth*; plaster; Elisabet Ney Museum, Austin, Texas, United States; marble versions: 1905, Elisabet Ney Museum, Austin, Texas, United States; Smithsonian American Art Museum, Washington, D.C., United States

Further Reading

Burger, Renate, "Ney, Elisabet," in *Dictionary of Women Artists*, edited by Delia Gaze, vol. 2, London and Chicago: Fitzroy Dearborn, 1997

Cutrer, Emily Fourmy, *The Art of the Woman: The Life and Work of Elisabet Ney*, Lincoln: University of Nebraska Press, 1988

Fortune, Jan Isbelle, and Jean Burton, *Elisabet Ney*, New York: Knopf, and London: Harrap, 1943

Loggins, Vernon, *Two Romantics and Their Ideal Life: Elisabet Ney, Sculptor; Edmund Montgomery, Philosopher*, New York: Odyssey Press, 1946

Loggins, Vernon, "Ney, Elisabet," in *Notable American Women, 1607–1950*, edited by Edward T. James, Janet Wilson James, and Paul S. Boyer, vol. 2, Cambridge, Massachusetts: Harvard University Press, 1971

"Ney, Elisabet," in *Dictionary of American Biography*, New York: Scribner, 1928–58

Rutland, J.W., editor, *Sursum! Elisabet Ney in Texas: Letters in the Elisabet Ney Archive*, Austin, Texas: Hart Graphics, 1977

Taft, Lorado, *The History of American Sculpture*, New York and London: Macmillan, 1903; new edition, 1930

Taylor, Bride Neill, *Elisabet Ney, Sculptor*, New York: Devin-Adair, 1916; new revised edition, Austin, Texas: s.n., 1938

Wood, Sarah Lee Norman, "The Heroic Image: Three Sculptures by Elisabet Ney," (Master's thesis), University of Texas at Austin, 1978

NICCOLÒ DELL'ARCA *fl.* 1462–1494
Italian

Niccolò dell'Arca's name is taken from the Arca di San Domenico (shrine of St. Dominic) designed by Nicola Pisano (*ca.* 1279) for the Church of San Domenico Maggiore in Bologna. Niccolò updated the famous Arca in the 1470s. His origins are uncertain; he is variously referred to as Nicolaus de Apulia, Niccolò da Ragusa, and Nichollò de Bari, implying a southern home. Just as elusive are attempts to trace the eclectic elements of his style. Scholars have theorized that he worked on the massive triumphal arch at the Castello Nuovo in Naples during the 1450s and possibly came in contact with the Catalan sculptor Guillem Sagrera, or was trained by the Dalmatian sculptor Giorgio da Sebenico. Others maintain that his powerful style derives from a period in Siena and Florence, where he would have developed under the sway of Jacopo della Quercia and Donatello. Stylistic debts to Venice and France have also been suggested. The earliest document records the artist renting a workshop in Bologna on 5 April 1462. Niccolò made his will on 6 October 1484, died on 2 March 1494, and was buried in the Church of S. Giovanni Battista, the Celestine church in Bologna. A contemporary, Girolamo Borselli, described Niccolò as eccentric, barbarous in his habits, and obstinate. Borselli also revealed that the sculptor refused to accept any students; nonetheless, the monumental power of Niccolò's marble and terracotta sculpture was without equal in the region at the time and had a significant influence on later sculptors such as Michelangelo.

Niccolò was contracted in 1469 to update and complete the Arca di San Domenico. The lid of the sarcophagus was to include the marble figures of God the Father and the four Evangelists; a *Pietà* with adoring angels; a *Resurrection* relief; various saints, including Petronius, Dominic, Francis, Florian, Vitale, and Agricola; an angel with a candelabrum; and putti with swags. Although the superstructure was installed in 1473, Niccolò never completed the project. He may have worked on the shrine sporadically until his death in 1494, although he probably did not return to the Arca after 1473, or possibly 1478. For no apparent reason, he left several elements unfinished, including the *Resurrection* relief, the figures *Saint Proculus* (originally *Saint Vincent*) and *Saint Petronius* (which Niccolò had apparently begun), and a kneeling angel. In 1494 Michelangelo received the commission to complete the figures, an experience that had an undeniably profound impact on the young sculptor. The diminutive scale of Niccolò's figures on the Arca belies their tremendous force. They are not highly polished, nor do they overly concern themselves with meticulous detail. Particularly powerful is *God the Father*, with heavy brow and flowing hair, standing on a globe at the top of an elaborate pinnacle. The overall design, its garlands, and its finials have been traced to the tomb of Carlo Marsuppini (*ca.* 1453–59) by Desiderio da Settignano, and the candelabrum-bearing angel shares features with Luca della Robbia's figures for Florence Cathedral. The influence of Jacopo della Quercia also has been seen in the vigorous figures, but other elements suggest French or northern European exposure.

In 1478 Niccolò's large *Madonna della Piazza* was installed on the facade of the Palazzo del Comune in Bologna, adjacent to the Church of S. Petronio. Jacopo's style informs the heavy drapery, but the influence of Andrea del Verrocchio seems evident in the Christ Child, perhaps transmitted through Francesco di Simone Ferrucci.

Niccolò's famous terracotta *Lamentation* group, originally in the Church of S. Maria della Vita, Bologna, consists of five standing figures (the *Virgin, Saint John the Evangelist,* and three other women), a kneeling *Nicodemus* (traditionally called a self-portrait), and a recumbent *Dead Christ*. The original placement of the figures is uncertain, and with few exceptions the original polychromy is now gone. The group may have originally included *Joseph of Arimathea,* supposedly rendered with the features of Giovanni Bentivoglio II and perhaps deliberately destroyed in 1506 when the Bentivoglio were exiled from Bologna. The group is signed "Opvs Nicolai de Apvlia," on Christ's pillow. An inventory from 1601 provides a retroactive date of 1463 for the group. Although initially accepted, scholars have contested this date since 1942, when Gnudi argued for a date sometime after 1485 based on style (see Gnudi, 1942). If the earlier date is correct (as argued by Pope-Hennessy, Beck, and Salas), Niccolò's *Lamentation* formed the basis for the entire genre of monumental terracotta sculptural groups, which was particularly popular among artists from Emilia, such as Guido Mazzoni. The anguished faces, contorted bodies, and wildly billowing drapery of the two women to the far right par-

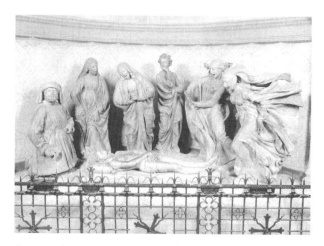

Lamentation
The Conway Library, Courtauld Institute of Art

ticularly exhibit an intensely emotive ultrarealism that has been compared to the dramatic Ferrarese paintings of Cosmé Tura, Francesco della Cossa, and Ercole de' Roberti.

Several other works, some of which are now lost, can be traced to Niccolò. Salas recognized the marble statue *St. John the Baptist* (signed "Nicolavs") at the Monastery of San Lorenzo el Real, Escorial, Madrid in 1967. A terracotta bust of St. Dominic, once above the vestry door of the Monastery of San Domenico, now resides in the Museo di San Domenico, Bologna, and a terracotta eagle (inscribed "Nicolavs F.") was placed over the entrance to the Church of S. Giovanni in Monte, Bologna.

It is primarily on the basis of three extant figural groups, those for the Arca di San Domenico, the *Madonna della Piazza*, and the *Lamentation*, that Niccolò dell'Arca's reputation rests. Despite the uncertainty of his name, dates, training, and origins, Niccolò was clearly a master of exceptional and eclectic talent. Whether working in terracotta, an essentially additive process, or marble sculpture, a detractive process, he was equally adept, and his monumentally powerful vision remains undiminished 500 years after his death.

ARNE R. FLATEN

See also **Desiderio da Settignano; Donatello (Donato di Betto Bardi); Jacopo della Quercia; Pisano, Nicola; Verrocchio, Andrea del**

Biography

Origins uncertain, probably from Apulia in southern Italy. May have worked on Castello Nuovo in Naples, 1450s; first record in Bologna, 1462; contracted work on Arca di San Domenico, Bologna, 1469; made bust of St. Dominic for monastery of San Domenico, 1474;

finished *Madonna della Piazza* for Palazzo del Comune, 1478; created eagle for Church of S. Giovanni in Monte, 1481. Died in Bologna, Italy, 2 March 1494.

Selected Works

1460s– *Lamentation*; terracotta; Pinacoteca
80s   Nazionale, Bologna, Italy
1469–   Arca di San Domenico; marble; Church of
73(?)   San Domenico Maggiore, Bologna, Italy
1474   Bust of St. Dominic; terracotta; Museo di
        San Domenico, Bologna, Italy
1478   *Madonna della Piazza*; marble; Palazzo
        del Comune, Bologna, Italy
1481   *Eagle*; terracotta; Church of S. Giovanni in
        Monte, Bologna, Italy
1492   *Adoration of the Magi*; terracotta (lost)
1492   *Annunciation*; terracotta (lost)
date   *St. John the Baptist*; marble; Monastery of
unknown S. Lorenzo el Real, Escorial, Madrid,
        Spain

Further Reading

Agostini, Grazia, and Luisa Ciammitti (editors), *Niccolò dell'Arca: Seminario di studi*, Bologna, Italy: Nuova Alfa, 1989

Beck, James, "Niccolò dell'Arca: A Re-examination," *Art Bulletin* 47 (1965)

Bottari, Stefano, *L'Arca di S. Domenico in Bologna*, Bologna, Italy: Patron, 1964

Gnudi, Cesare, *Niccolò dell'Arca*, Turin, Italy: Einaudi, 1942

Gnudi, Cesare, *Nuove ricerche su Niccolò dell'Arca*, Rome: De Luca, 1973

Pope-Hennessy, John, "The Arca di San Domenico—A Hypothesis," *The Burlington Magazine* 93 (1951)

Pope-Hennessy, John, *An Introduction to Italian Sculpture*, 3 vols., London: Phaidon, 1963; 4th edition, 1996; see especially vol. 2, *Italian Renaissance Sculpture*

Salas, X. de, "The St. John of Niccolò dell'Arca," in *Essays Presented to Rudolf Wittkower on His Sixty-Fifth Birthday*, edited by Douglas Fraser, Howard Hibbard, and Milton J. Lewine, vol. 2, London: Phaidon, 1967

NICHOLAS OF VERDUN *fl.* 1181–1205

French

Nothing is known about Nicholas of Verdun's life. Two treasures from the High Medieval period bear his name, the *Klosterneuburg Pulpit* and the Shrine of the *Virgin*, and a "Nicolaus de Verda" is purported to have been on the pedestal of one of two lost seated figures (St. Peter and a Queen Constance) in Worms. Nicholas's few remaining works reveal an affinity with the art of the Rhine-Maas region. They show Nicholas to be a leading personality in art at his time, a virtuoso of figural embossing in gold and in champlevé enameling. He was an innovator of a vigorous Classical direction of style known as *Muldenfaltenstil* (depressed fold style), which led painting and sculpture north of the Alps toward the Early Gothic style around the year 1200.

The *Klosterneuburg Pulpit* of the Klosterneuburg Abbey, Austria, was originally created as a cover for the ambo. Its chief ornament consists of 45 enamel tablets with scenic depictions from the life and Sufferings of Christ. An inscription provides information about the theological significance behind the images, the year in which they were created (1181), the patron (Provost Werner [1168–86]), and the artist, "Quod Nicolaus opus Virdunensis fabricavit" (Thus Nicholas of Verdun made the work). A second inscription explains that Provost Stephan von Sierndorf (1317–36) restored the work in 1331 and removed it from its original location, a chancel near the cross altar (*Kreuzaltar*) of the abbey church. The impetus for this was a fire in the abbey in 1330, during which "die gross taffl" (the big panel) barely escaped destruction. It was placed on the *Volksaltar* of the Collegiate Church until 1589, then replaced by modern decoration. It found its way in 1837 to its present location in the abbey's Leopoldskapelle (St. Leopold's Chapel).

Typologically, the organization of the images presents the Life and Sufferings of Christ as a harmonic and theologically significant unity. Events of the Old Testament are conceived as foreshadowing those of the New Testament and juxtaposed with them. The center row of three horizontally stacked rows shows a Life of Christ cycle from the Annunciation through Pentecost, images from the *sub gracia* (under Grace) era. A theologically meaningful corollary from both the time before the Old Testament (*ante legem*, or before the Law) and during the Old Testament (*sub lege*, or under the Law) is allocated to each scene above and below. The *Baptism of Christ* in the river Jordan, for example, correlates with the crossing of the Israelites through the Red Sea above. Below, it relates to an image of a temple implement, the brazen sea. Six tablets on the right edge break up this organizational pattern, depicting motifs from the Last Judgment. In 1331 two rows of representations, six pictures in total, were added to the series (the *Arrest of Christ* and the *Deposition*, with their preceding scenes). The scenes are compact and show an understanding of the subject matter. The figures, in their heavy and richly flowing garments, call to mind Classical models—the ivory diptych of the Nicomachi-Symmachi has been suggested for the *Queen of Sheba* (see Claussen, 1985). Despite the stylistic and technical perfection, one discerns the work of many masters.

The basilica-shaped Three Kings' Shrine bears no artists' inscription. However, parts of it can be safely attributed to Nicholas, as they correspond closely with the style of the pieces in Klosterneuburg and Tournai and are connected to both works through identical punch work. An energetic restoration returned the work, which was shortened in 1804–07, to its status as the largest extant medieval shrine. The front shows the worship of the Three Kings in the presence of a fourth king, the German anti-king, Otto IV (*r.* 1198–1216), and the Baptism of Christ. Above that is the *Maiestas Domini* (Majesty of God) and two angels with instruments of the Passion. The back shows the Flagellation and Crucifixion of Christ, and Christ crowning the martyrs Felix and Nabor, who are also buried in this shrine. The sides of the work feature 12 prophets below and the apostles above. A lost cycle of the Life of Christ on the roof surfaces completed the series.

The relics of the Three Kings were taken from Milan in 1164 and—according to a tradition dating to the 17th century—placed inside the shrine in 1191. From this it was long concluded that large portions of the gold work had already been completed by that time. Kroos demonstrates the problems with this assumption and suggests a later date for the commencement of the gold work, around 1198, beginning with the front and ending with the back (see Kroos, 1985). The relics could have been, as the contemporaneous case of the Charlemagne Shrine in Aachen exemplifies, placed in 1191 in the provisorily decorated wood casing, around which the metal structure was subsequently built. How long the work took remains an open question; records for the chapter of Cologne Cathedral from the 1240s indicate that six goldsmiths were engaged at that time. The prophets, with their powerful movements and their expressive, seemingly individualized faces, are among the most impressive images of man of the time; their stylization is reminiscent of Classical sculptures.

The Shrine of the *Virgin* in Tournai Cathedral, Belgium, is an architecturally decorated wood casing with a high roof. A now lost—and perhaps secondary—inscription listed 1205 as the year of origin and gave the name of the artist, "hoc opus fecit Magister Nicholaus de Verdun" (Master Nicholas of Verdun made this work). On the sides appear figures and scenes crafted in gold under tripartite arcades. The front shows the *Maiestas Domini* and angels with instruments of the Passion while the back portrays the *Worship of the Three Kings*. Along the left side are the *Annunciation*, the *Visitation*, and the *Birth of Christ*, and along the right side are the *Escape to Egypt*, *Offering in the Temple*, and the *Baptism of Christ*. On the ceiling, in part, are later scenes from the Passion.

Owing to its poor state of preservation, the shrine was thoroughly restored in 1890, making an art historical judgment difficult to render. The quality of manufacture is clearly divergent. The figures pale by comparison to the brilliantly embossed heads with their Classical pathos. Differences between this shrine and the work from Klosterneuburg are readily apparent, such as enamel here and embossing there. In addition, the Tournai shrine uses modern, Gothic forms, not solely in the architecture. However, there can be no doubt as the identity of the studio. Identical punch work also confirms the continuity on a technical level.

The Shrine of St. Anno, a type of sarcophagus with a saddle roof, was made for St. Michael's Abbey, Siegburg, near Cologne, to hold the relics of the founder, Archbishop Anno of Cologne, canonized in 1183. Around 1800 it was robbed of its embossed figures and reliefs, impeding a definitive judgment on the artistic authorship. The remaining decoration is of high quality and directly follows the Three Kings' Shrine in terms of style. It is therefore likewise linked to Nicholas of Verdun. Since "custos Heinricus," who was active at Siegburg until 1185 and obtained Anno's canonization, is depicted here, work on the shrine was usually presumed to have commenced about that time until Kroos, on the contrary, placed production before the early 13th century.

PETER DIEMER

Biography

All that is known for certain about Nicholas of Verdun is that he was a goldsmith, presumed to have been born in Verdun, with dated works from the years 1181 to 1205.

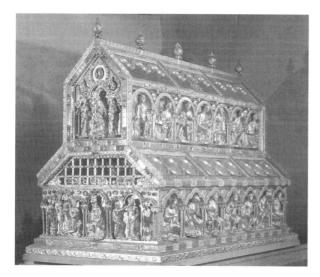

Three Kings' Shrine
© Erich Lessing / Art Resource, NY

Selected Works

Further Reading

Buschhausen, Helmut, *Der Verduner Altar: Das Emailwerk des Nikolaus von Verdun im Stift Klosterneuburg*, Vienna: Tusch, 1980

Claussen, Peter Cornelius, "Nikolaus von Verdun: Über Antiken- und Naturstudium am Dreikönigenschrein," in *Ornamenta Ecclesiae: Kunst und Künstler der Romanik in Köln* (exhib. cat.), 3 vols., edited by Anton Leger, Cologne, Germany: Schnütgen-Museum Stadt Koln, 1985

Claussen, Peter Cornelius, "Nicholas of Verdun," in *The Dictionary of Art*, edited by Jane Turner, New York: Grove, and London: Macmillan, 1996

Demus, Otto, "Zu Nikolaus von Verdun," in *Intuition und Kunstwissenschaft: Festschrift für Hanns Swarzenski zum 70. Geburtstag am 30. August 1973*, edited by Peter Bloch et al., Berlin: Mann, 1973

Kroos, Renate, *Der Schrein des heiligen Servatius in Maastricht und die vier zugehörigen Reliquiare in Brüssel*, Munich: Deutscher Kunstverlag, 1985

Legner, Anton (editor), *Monumenta Annonis: Köln und Siegburg: Weltbild und Kunst im hohen Mittelalter* (exhib. cat.), Cologne, Germany: Museums of Cologne, 1975

Röhrig, Floridus, *Der Verduner Altar*, Vienna: Herold, 1955

Schnitzler, Hermann, and Peter Bloch, *Der Meister des Dreikönigenschreins* (exhib. cat.), offprint from *Achthundert Jahre verehrung der Heiligen Drei Könige in Köln: 1164–1964*, Cologne: Bachem, 1964

Telesko, Werner, "Das theologische Programm des Kölner Dreikönigenschreins," *Jahrbuch des Kölnischen Geschichtsvereins* 68 (1997)

NIKE OF SAMOTHRACE Anonymous

3rd to 2nd century BCE

marble

h. 2.45 m

Musée du Louvre, Paris, France

This magnificent statue of the goddess Nike, or Victory, was discovered on the northern Aegean island of Samothrace in 1863. The *Nike of Samothrace*, a colossal statue (2.45 meters tall) beautifully carved from Parian marble, is shown in action, flying down to land on the prow of a warship. The strong wind and her forward movement press the fine material of her dress close to her body, revealing the rounded forms beneath. Although secured by a knotted belt just below the breasts, the dress has slipped off her right shoulder from the vigorous action of raising her right arm. The top edge of the garment clings suggestively to the upper curve of her right breast. A heavy mantle, which swathes much of the lower body in deep folds of material, flies up in waves on either side of the extended right leg and sweeps out in a mass behind. The massive wings, stretching up and back to steady the landing, are beautifully and meticulously detailed.

Nike of Samothrace is a marvelous example of the Hellenistic Baroque style in its colossal size, massive body forms, and powerful torsion, with hips and shoulders twisting on different axes. In addition to its powerful beauty and virtuoso carving, the *Nike of Samothrace* is an important and rare example of an original Hellenistic work with a known display context and an original setting that can be reconstructed with great precision.

The *Nike of Samothrace* stood on a hillside terrace in the Sanctuary of the Great Gods on Samothrace, a site of much royal activity in the Hellenistic period. The monument was framed in an exedra, or enclosure, that overlooked the sanctuary's theater to the sea below. The ship's prow on which the goddess lands was carved from gray marble with precise naval detail. Placed at an angle within the enclosure, the prow was set into a shallow basin or pool filled with water. In front of this was a second, lower basin in which stood large rocks, suggesting a shoreline or harbor. The dramatic natural setting, the reflective properties of the water, the vigorous forward action of Nike, and the violent movement of her drapery give the monument a distinctly theatrical quality, a hallmark of Hellenistic art. Here we see the winged goddess carried by a strong ocean breeze alighting on a ship's deck to crown its commander and crew—a glorious epiphany of naval victory.

Statues of Nike have a long history as war monuments. Precisely which victory the *Nike of Samothrace* celebrates is a matter of some debate. It was thought that the monument commemorated a victory of Demetrios Poliorketes over Ptolemy in 306 BCE, because a coin of Demetrios shows a very similar Nike landing on a ship's prow, her right arm extended up, holding a trumpet. After the discovery in 1950 of the open and empty right hand of the *Nike of Samothrace*, however, this association was mostly abandoned. Most scholars now favor a connection with the island of Rhodes and suggest that the monument was set up around 190 BCE to commemorate a victory over the Seleucid forces of Antiochos III by a combined Rhodian and Roman fleet. The argument for this Rhodian connection is based on the following evidence: the gray marble of the ship is said to be Rhodian; moreover, a very fragmentary inscription found with the base of *Nike of Samothrace* is thought to have letter forms similar to those on some

Rhodian inscriptions, a number of which preserve the name of the sculptor Pythokritos, who carved a ship's prow in relief at Lindos in the early 2nd century BCE. In addition, pottery found during excavation of the ex-edra has been dated to around 200 BCE, and stylistically, the statue is said to fit best around 200 BCE.

The evidence adduced for this Rhodian attribution, however, is at best inconclusive. First, the gray marble of the ship, even if Rhodian, is no guarantee of the origin of either the monument's sculptor or its dedicator. Here we should remember that the statue itself was carved from Parian marble. Second, there is no demonstrated connection between the fragmentary inscription and the monument. Third, on present evidence at least, the associated pottery is only broadly datable to the Hellenistic period. Fourth, stylistic assessments of the statue have been used to argue for dates ranging from the late 4th to the 1st centuries BCE. Though it is certainly possible that the monument represents a Rhodian commission, it cannot be demonstrated with certainty on the basis of the available evidence.

Although it is now widely accepted that the *Nike of Samothrace* was a Rhodian commission of the early 2nd century BCE, there are, in fact, other possible occasions for the monument's dedication. For example,

R.R.R. Smith has suggested the early or middle Hellenistic period as a date for the monument on the basis of a combination of historical probability and statue style. He argues that the style of the statue's drapery retains many of the formal qualities of the Classical period, which would suggest a date earlier, rather than later, in the Hellenistic period (see Smith, 1991, 1993). Within this time frame, a likely historical setting might be either the victory of Demetrios Poliorketes, mentioned above, or the great naval victory of the Macedonian king Antigonos Gonatas over the island of Kos in the 250s BCE. The fact that the Nike on the coins of Demetrios held a trumpet, whereas the *Nike of Samothrace* did not, only proves that the coins did not copy the monument.

Alternatively, as Antigonos is known to have set up a monument commemorating his victory over Kos on the island of Delos, a similar dedication on Samothrace is therefore possible and perhaps even likely. The Macedonian kings were great patrons of the Samothrace sanctuary and set up a number of dedications there while the island was under their control. Although any conclusions about the statue's date must remain provisional until full publication of the archaeology of this monument, it is certain that the *Nike of Samothrace* was a royal dedication. Its Baroque style was an expressive sculptural language invented specifically for this new genre of sculpture: the victory monuments of the Hellenistic kings. Precisely which Hellenistic king commissioned this magnificent statue, however, must remain a matter of debate.

SHEILA DILLON

See also **Greece, Ancient**

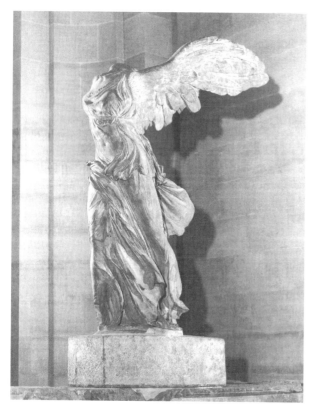

Nike of Samothrace
© Alinari / Art Resource, NY

Further Reading

Knell, Heiner, *Die Nike von Samothrake: Typus, Form, Bedeutung und Wirkungsgeschichte eines rhodischen Sieges-Anathems im Kabirenheiligtum von Samothrake*, Darmstadt, Germany: Wissenschaftliche Buchgesellschaft, 1995

Lehmann, Karl, "The Ship-Fountain from the *Victory of Samothrace* to the *Galera*," in *Samothracian Reflections: Aspects of the Revival of the Antique*, by Karl Lehmann and Phyllis Lehmann, Princeton, New Jersey: Princeton University Press, 1973

Pollitt, J.J., *Art in the Hellenistic Age*, Cambridge and New York: Cambridge University Press, 1986

Smith, R.R.R., "The Hellenistic Period," in *The Oxford History of Classical Art*, edited by J. Boardman, Oxford and New York: Oxford University Press, 1993

Smith, R.R.R., *Hellenistic Sculpture: A Handbook*, New York: Thames and Hudson, 1991

Stewart, Andrew, *Greek Sculpture: An Exploration*, 2 vols., New Haven, Connecticut: Yale University Press, 1990

Stewart, Andrew, "Narration and Allusion in the Hellenistic Baroque," in *Narrative and Event in Ancient Art*, edited by Peter J. Holliday, Cambridge and New York: Cambridge University Press, 1993

ISAMU NOGUCHI 1904–1988 *United States*

For Isamu Noguchi, sculpture was always more than an art of object making. He perceived sculpture not as isolated, static objects but rather as creations that engage and energize the spaces they occupy: "If sculpture is the rock, it is also the space between the rocks, and between the rocks and a man." The work he produced in the seven decades of his unusual career reflects this expansive artistic vision—from the innovative stage sets he designed for avant-garde choreographers such as Martha Graham to his frequent collaborations with architects such as Gordon Bunshaft and Louis Kahn and the numerous playgrounds, sculpture gardens, and courtyards he designed, some realized, some not. Whether creating solitary objects or large sculptural landscapes, Noguchi aspired for sculpture to fulfill spiritual needs. In this regard, he drew inspiration largely from ancient civilizations—temple structures, ancient Japanese gardens, Native American mounds, and other sculptural monuments of the past. Throughout his peripatetic career, Noguchi visited celebrated sculptural complexes of the past, drawn to the way the sculptures of early cultures were an integral part of their physical environment and culture.

His father an acclaimed Japanese poet and his mother an American schoolteacher, Noguchi felt connections to both American and Japanese culture while never feeling that he belonged fully to either. His artistic training began informally as a child when he was apprenticed to a local carpenter in Japan. From this experience, he gained satisfaction from working with his hands. His formal training began in the United States when, at 18 years of age, he was apprenticed to the sculptor Gutzon Borglum, famous for carving the faces of Mount Rushmore, South Dakota. In 1927, with a letter of recommendation from Alfred Stieglitz, Noguchi won a Guggenheim Fellowship. With this fellowship, Noguchi went to Paris and convinced Constantin Brancusi to entrust him with the task of cutting and polishing stones. From this consummate Modernist the young Noguchi learned how to carve stone using basic hand tools such as the ax and chisel. Brancusi encouraged direct contact with materials, extolling this method, known as *taille directe* (direct carving), over the clay modeling technique associated with Auguste Rodin. Although Noguchi spoke little French and Brancusi little English, Brancusi nevertheless conveyed the importance of avoiding unnecessary decorative embellishments, an admonition that mirrored the purity of Japanese aesthetics and philosophy. Above all, the six months spent in Brancusi's all-white studio affirmed Noguchi's commitment to abstraction.

Upon his return from Paris, Noguchi produced a tentative body of approximately 20 or so abstract sculptures and gouaches. Stung by their lackluster reception, in 1929 he turned his attention to portrait heads and busts of wealthy patrons and fellow artists such as R. Buckminster Fuller, Gabriel Orozco, Martha Graham, and George Gershwin. Noguchi generated portraits when he needed to make money in the early years of his career.

In the early 1930s Noguchi produced a few small, cylindrical terracotta figures inspired by ancient Japanese artifacts called *haniwa*, funereal figurines made of red clay, that he discovered for the first time at a museum in Kyoto, Japan's legendary historic city. He also envisioned many of his most ambitious and visionary projects in the 1930s, although many went unrealized, much to his frustration. In 1933, for example, he designed *Play Mountain*, his first children's playground. Although he continued to face obstacles, he maintained his dedication to children's playgrounds, devoting five years in the 1960s to one intended for New York City's Riverside Park, designed in collaboration with Kahn and, again, never realized.

Noguchi met fewer obstacles in his numerous stage designs for the theater. In 1935 Martha Graham invited him to design the set for her avant-garde dance *Frontier*. It was the first time Graham had invited an artist to create a set for one of her dances. Their frequent collaborations nourished a shared interest in primitive forms.

Throughout his career, Noguchi's practice also included the design of mass-produced objects, from tables to his well-known paper light fixtures. His first utilitarian, mass-produced object was an elegant nursery intercom, produced in 1937 largely in response to the Lindbergh kidnapping. A more explicit acknowledgment of Noguchi's concern for social welfare was his sculpture of a lynched black man, titled *Death* (also known as *Lynched Figure*). This small metal piece commented on the racial climate of the United States in the 1930s not only through its subject matter but also by means of a devastating racist review of Noguchi's work that it elicited. During World War II, Noguchi again confronted the social inequities of the United States in his voluntary incarceration in a Japanese-American internment camp in Poston, Arizona.

A body of biomorphic sculptures composed of interlocking parts made from flat sheets of marble or slate established Noguchi's reputation in the mid 1940s. Held together solely by gravity, these fragile life-size sculptures carry subtle existential undertones owing to their precarious method of construction (and in the case of *Humpty Dumpty*, reinforced by its title). Like much American art of the 1940s, Noguchi's biomorphic expressions reveal the contribution made by European Surrealist émigrés during their exile in the United States. On the basis of these works, the Museum of

Modern Art in New York City invited him in 1946 to join their exhibition, *Fourteen Americans*, which included David Hare, Arshile Gorky, and other major figures of postwar American art.

The *Akari* paper lanterns Noguchi introduced in 1951 provide one of the best examples of his ability to reconcile the past with the future. *Akari*, the name he gave his innovation, refers to the Japanese word for light. Now ubiquitous in the United States, the *Akari* lanterns presented an updated version of ancient Japanese paper lanterns used by cormorant fishers by employing electricity where once candles were used.

In 1964 Noguchi completed one of his most important public commissions—a sunken sculpture court for the newly created Beinecke Rare Book and Manuscript Library at Yale University. Bunshaft, a leading architect at Skidmore, Owings, and Merrill, designed the library. He also provided Noguchi with numerous opportunities to create sculpture for architectural settings over the course of their 30-year friendship. For the Beinecke, as with all their collaborations, Bunshaft involved Noguchi from the very beginning of the project to ensure that sculpture would be an integral part of the overall design, as opposed to a mere decorative afterthought. If ancient Japanese gardens can be classified as either one of two types, open (for strolling) and closed (for meditation), the Beinecke corresponds to a closed sculpture garden, intended solely for viewing from above. Made from white Vermont marble with pale gray streaks, the sunken courtyard consists of three geometric volumes—a circle, square, and pyramid—placed on a grid. Although the courtyard appears at first glance to be Noguchi's most pure geometric creation, the square rests precariously on a single point, the circle is missing its core, and the grid dissolves in the space enclosed by the three shapes. Like his interlocking sculptures of the 1940s, the Beinecke subtly evokes the fragile nature of life through its asymmetry.

Noguchi spent much of his energies in the 1960s on large-scale public projects such as the Beinecke. One of the other major commissions awarded to Noguchi was the Billy Rose Sculpture Garden in Jerusalem. Given Noguchi's conviction of the spiritual capacity of sculpture, the five acres of land he was offered in Israel presented an immensely desirable opportunity. Noguchi wanted to preserve the space's powerful dialogue between the sky and earth. The result is an understated composition with walls made of local stone that create niches of varying sizes to house a variety of sculptures and with olive trees interspersed throughout.

In the late 1960s Noguchi frequented the Italian quarries of Querceta, made famous by Michelangelo. Unlike his celebrated 16th-century predecessor, No-guchi used newly invented power tools and epoxy glue on the stones he gathered there. Connecting dark and light stripes of marble with internal rods, he also made a notable break from the strict reliance on gravity that characterized his earlier works.

In the 1970s Noguchi used industrial materials and advancements in technology and tools to create large-scale works, providing civic sites in Seattle, Cleveland, Honolulu, and Munich with large individual sculptures. He also involved himself in the creation of several large fountains both in the United States and Japan, prompted by an invitation to design a fountain for the 1970 exposition in Osaka, Japan. For the nine fountains of his exhibition in Osaka, he used computer technology and the best local engineers available to create a theatrical waterworks display. For Detroit, Michigan, he designed a massive stainless-steel ring 9 meters above the ground supported by two diagonal columns of steel. A complex lighting system theatrically illuminates the water at night.

In the final decade of his career, Noguchi created two spaces to permanently display his work—one in Mure, Japan, and the other in Long Island City, New York. Carefully tending to every detail, from the placement of his sculptures to the kinds of trees and plants in their gardens, he ensured that the two museums embody his long-espoused commitment to the integration of sculpture and spaces.

VERONICA C. ROBERTS

See also **Brancusi, Constantin; Modernism; Public Sculpture**

Biography

Born in Los Angeles, California, United States, 17 November 1904. Moved to Japan, 1906; returned to United States and attended high school in Indiana; apprenticed to sculptor Gutzon Borglum in Stamford, Connecticut, 1922; studied medicine, Columbia University, 1923–25; attended night classes at Leonardo Da Vinci Art School, New York City; received Guggenheim Fellowship and studied with Constantin Brancusi in Paris, 1927; traveled to Paris instead, worked for Constantin Brancusi; first solo exhibition, Eugene Schoen Gallery, New York City, 1929; traveled to Asia, 1931–32; returned to New York City, 1932; began designing public spaces and monuments, 1933; designed first stage set for choreographer Martha Graham, 1935; voluntarily spent six months in U.S. internment camp, Poston, Arizona, 1942; established studio at 33 MacDougal Alley, New York City, 1942; traveled to Europe, India, and Japan to study ancient art and monuments, 1948–49; established studio in Mure, Japan, 1972; Isamu Noguchi Museum opened to public in Long Island City, New York, 1985. Died in New York City, United States, 30 December 1988.

Selected Works

1929   *R. Buckminster Fuller*; chrome-plated bronze; Allegra Fuller Snyder, Pacific Palisades, California, United States

1931   *The Queen*; terracotta; Whitney Museum of American Art, New York City, United States

1933   Design for *Play Mountain* (unrealized), submitted to the New York City Parks Department

1934   *Death (Lynched Figure)*; Monel metal and rope; Isamu Noguchi Garden Museum, Long Island, New York, United States

1935   Set design for *Frontier* (choreographed by Martha Graham); rope; Martha Graham Center of Contemporary Dance, New York City, United States

1944–45   *Kouros*; marble; Metropolitan Museum of Art, New York City, United States

1946   *Humpty Dumpty*; slate; Whitney Museum of American Art, New York City, United States

1951–78   Designs for *Akari* (light sculptures); primarily paper and metal; Isamu Noguchi Museum, Long Island, New York, United States

1960–64   Sunken Garden; marble; Beinecke Rare Book and Manuscript Library, Yale University, New Haven, Connecticut, United States

1960–65   Billy Rose Sculpture Garden; Israel Museum, Jerusalem, Israel

1960–65   Design for Riverside Playground (unrealized), submitted to the New York City Parks Department

1973–78   Horace E. Dodge fountain; stainless steel; Philip A. Hart Plaza, Detroit, Michigan, United States

Further Reading

Apostolos-Cappadona, Diane, and Bruce Altshuler (editors), *Isamu Noguchi: Essays and Conversations*, New York: Abrams, 1994

Ashton, Dore, *Noguchi: East and West*, New York: Knopf, 1992

Friedman, Martin, *Noguchi's Imaginary Landscapes*, Minneapolis, Minnesota: Walker Art Center, 1978

Gordon, John, *Isamu Noguchi*, New York: Praeger, 1968

Grove, Nancy, and Diane Botnick, *The Sculpture of Isamu Noguchi: A Catalogue*, New York: Garland, 1980

Hunter, Sam, *Isamu Noguchi*, New York: Abbeville Press, 1978; London: Thames and Hudson, 1979

Noguchi, Isamu, *A Sculptor's World*, London: Thames and Hudson, 1967; New York: Thames and Hudson, 1968

Noguchi, Isamu, *Isamu Noguchi: The Sculpture of Spaces*, New York: Whitney Museum of American Art, 1980

Noguchi, Isamu, *The Isamu Noguchi Garden Museum*, New York: Abrams, 1987

KOUROS

Isamu Noguchi (1904–1988)
1944–1945
marable
Metropolitan Museum of Art, New York City

Noguchi first gained international recognition in the mid 1940s when he produced a group of abstract sculptures composed of interlocking marble and slate slabs. *Kouros* is one of the finest examples of this body of work, as demonstrated by its inclusion in the New York Museum of Modern Art's landmark 1946 exhibition, *Fourteen Americans*. Made of pink Georgian marble, *Kouros* (and the related works of this period) is roughly human scale. Its title, *Kouros*, refers to one of the earliest expressions of man in stone—the famous Greek statues of idealized male youths.

In *Kouros*, Noguchi combined his fascination with ancient art with his commitment to the modern, specifically abstraction, one of the defining movements of 20th-century art. The formal debt to Surrealist art in particular becomes evident in the group's biomorphic segments. These seminal works also demonstrate Noguchi's talent for creating dynamic contrasts. Noguchi alternated solids and voids and contrasted the flatness of the individual planes of stone with their three-dimensional profile.

In addition to fusing ancient and modern, they pay tribute to both Western and Eastern artistic traditions. The influence of Classical Greek Art and European Surrealism are plainly evident in *Kouros*. The work evokes Eastern art more subtly in its overall resemblance to a letter of calligraphy.

One of the unique aspects of these organic sculptures is their unusual method of construction. The interlocking segments of marble and slate rely solely on gravity as their adhesive. This technique, coupled with the fact that the majority of these biomorphic objects are made of slate, a delicate stone, powerfully asserts the fragility of humanity. Created at a time when World War II deeply affected people's understanding of their selves and the world, *Kouros* captures the acute instability that many must have felt.

VERONICA C. ROBERTS

See also **Kore and Kouros**

Further Reading

Ashton, Dore, *Noguchi: East and West*, New York: Knopf, 1992
Noguchi, Isamu, *A Sculptor's World*, London: Thames and Hudson, 1967; New York: Thames and Hudson, 1968

NOLE, DE, FAMILY *Netherlandish*

The earliest sources about the de Nole family concern its sculptural activity in Cambrai. However, none of the Cambrai-based de Noles have left us with any works, except for the wooden models (*ca.* 1551–52) by Guillaume de Nole for bronze statues of Justice and a donor, which hung until 1793 on the facade of the town hall of Cambrai. Jean and Robert de Nole, probably Guillaume's sons, were the foremost sculptors of their day at Cambrai. They actively involved themselves in the redecorating—both outside and inside—of the town hall of Cambrai, as well as in the production of major tomb monuments (e.g. for canon François Sarre and archdeacon Jehan Happe, both works formerly in the Cathedral of Cambrai).

Colijn de Nole, also probably Guillaume's son, left for Utrecht, the Netherlands, in 1530. There he set up a successful workshop delivering tomb monuments, chimneypieces, and festive decorations, often in collaboration with the city's master mason, Willem van Noort. Colijn is chiefly remembered for the magnificence of the sandstone chimneypiece he carved for the sheriff's courtroom in the (former) town hall at Kampen. This piece was assembled on site from parts carved at Utrecht. Indebted to the Fontainebleau school of architecture and decoration, Colijn may have acquired this knowledge through prints or possibly in person at Francis I's palace. He is also famed for his three-dimensional reinterpretations of prints by Cornelis Bos. Other works are attributed to Colijn on stylistic grounds, such as a *Virgin and Child* (date unknown) at the Catharijneconvent, Utrecht. His son Jacob continued the workshop and is recorded to have worked on the restoration of statues and a rood loft and in producing a tabernacle and tomb monuments. Only fragments of two tombs remain in the Cunerakerk at Amerongen and in the Catharijneconvent at Utrecht. The latter comes from Jan van Scorel's tomb, which included a portrait of van Scorel by Antonis Mor (now Society of Antiquaries, London).

The third branch of the de Nole family left Utrecht for Antwerp shortly after the effective separation of the independent northern and Spanish southern Netherlands in 1585, perhaps feeling that the market for sculpture would dwindle in the northern provinces as a result of Protestantism's rejection of images. Robrecht and Jan, later joined by Jan's son Andries, quickly established one of the most prominent sculpture workshops in Antwerp, really only rivaled by that of Peter Paul Rubens's friend and protégé Hans van Mildert. The de Nole's strong tradition for collaboration between family members was continued to such an extent that it is hardly ever possible, if even desirable, to segregate the individual contributions. This enabled the workshop, formally led by Robrecht, to handle large-scale projects, as delegation of work did not need formal subcontracting. Occurring within the family, it increased trustworthiness and reliability in an otherwise harsh business environment. The number of commissions was typically small, although the projects were mostly of considerable size, so that competition for them was fierce.

The Antwerp de Noles's numerous works, of which only a small number survive, included tomb monuments, epitaphs, freestanding statues, pier statues, altars, *altartuinen* (altar enclosures, literally "altar gardens"), armorial trophies, chapel gates, fountains, rood loft decoration, facade Madonnas, and crucifixes. Jan is also specially recorded as being active in the production of small-scale sculpture for *Kunstkammer*, including Madonnas and mythological figures, although none can today be attributed to him or to his family members. The works the de Noles produced in the early 17th century are unequal both in quality and in style, reflecting the large-scale operations of their business, as well as not infrequent collaboration with other workshops.

The de Noles were in contact with the wealthy and the mighty of their time, private patrons and city magistrates alike. Moreover, Robrecht was appointed court sculptor to the archdukes Albert and Isabella in 1604. Such a status implied important bargaining power for him and enabled him to develop excellent contacts with the court at Brussels.

The court architect Wensel Cobergher later contracted Robrecht's workshop for the sculptural decoration of his newly rebuilt pilgrimage church dedicated to the Virgin at Scherpenheuvel (Montaigu). Cobergher's strict instructions had to be followed by all those working under him. The high altar had to follow precisely the architect's drawing and the colored stone model that the sculptor produced after it. The contractual materials were particularly rich with white and colored marbles from both Italy and the Low Countries. Four niche statues of the Evangelists and seven (six extant) of prophets were also produced by them. Strict contract stipulations prevented them subcontracting to and collaborating with other workshops. Cobergher thus kept control over his design at every stage of production. These procedures obviously bear important consequences on the style of the work, which is in keeping with that of Cobergher's essentially High Renaissance conception of space and light.

A similar relationship can be surmised from the extremely lucrative project to decorate the Houtappelkapel of the former Jesuit church of Antwerp (now Sint-Carolus-Borromeuskerk). Rubens's authorship of the designs for it is only partly proven, although highly likely. Here too the execution is fine, although not of great inspiration, and the quality of the project should first of all be sought on an iconographic and architectonic level. Nevertheless, the sculptural vocabulary is quite separate from earlier and later projects of the de Noles, as it completely assimilates Rubens's Baroque forms and spatial conceptions. However, this project is unique in the oeuvre of the de Nole family, as Rubens normally favored working with his friend van Mildert.

If the Antwerp de Noles were by no means major artists, they were occasionally brought to a higher artistic level in collaborative projects (as with the Houtappelkapel), and theirs was among the first workshops to sometimes adopt a Baroque sculptural vocabulary borrowed from Rubens. Their fame is understood better in terms of their competence in the technical training of apprentices and especially that of the running of (arguably) Antwerp's largest and most prosperous sculpture firm, as borne out at Robrecht's death in 1636, when he owned substantial property and an art collection, including a painting by Correggio. Van Dyck also included a portrait of Andries in his *Iconography* of famous contemporaries first assembled in the 17th century.

LÉON E. LOCK

See also **Netherlands and Belgium**

Guillaume de Nole late 15th century–after 1550

Biography
Born probably at the end of the 15th century, location unknown. Possibly the father of Colijn, Jean, and Robert de Nole; active in Kamerijk (present-day Cambrai, France). Died after 1550, location unknown.

Selected Works
ca.   Models for Justice and a donor; wood;
1551–52 Musée Communal, Cambrai, France

Colijn (Colyn) de Nole early 16th century–after 1558

Biography
Born in Kamerijk, present-day Cambrai, France, date unknown. Probably the son of Guillaume de Nole. Moved to Utrecht, the Netherlands, 1530; member of the saddlers' guild (and not the guild of the stonecutters). Died in Utrecht, the Netherlands, after 1558.

Selected Works
1543–45 Chimneypiece; sandstone; Sheriff's courtroom, Old City Hall, Kampen, the Netherlands

Jean de Nole early 16th century–after 1599

Biography
Born probably in first quarter of 16th century, location unknown. Probably a son of Guillaume de Nole. Active in Kamerijk (present-day Cambrai, France). Died after 1599, location unknown.

Selected Works
No works of Jean de Nole have survived.

Robert de Nole early 16th century–after 1572

Biography
Born probably in first quarter of 16th century, location unknown. Probably a son of Guillaume de Nole and brother of Jean. Active at Kamerijk (present-day Cambrai, France). Died after 1572, location unknown.

Selected Works
No works by Robert de Nole have survived.

Jérôme de Nole *ca.* 1550s–after 1612

Biography
Born probably in 1550s, location unknown. Probably a brother of Claude and a grandson of Guillaume de Nole. Died after 1612, location unknown.

Selected Works
No works of Jérôme de Nole have survived.

Claude de Nole late 16th century–after 1616

Biography
Born probably in second half of the 16th century, location unknown. Last de Nole family member active in Kamerijk, present-day Cambrai, France. Probably a brother of Jérôme and a grandson of Guillaume de Nole. Died after 1616, location unknown.

Selected Works
No works by Claude de Nole have survived.

Jacob de Nole birth date unknown–1601

Biography
Born in Kamerijk, present-day Cambrai, France, date unknown. Son of Colijn de Nole and father of Jan.

Continued the Utrecht workshop of his father; member of the saddlers' guild in Utrecht; treasurer of this guild in 1569. Died in Utrecht, the Netherlands, 8 March 1601.

Selected Works
No works by Jacob de Nole have survived.

Robrecht (Colijn) de Nole before 1570–1636
Biography
Born in Utrecht, the Netherlands, probably before 1570. Son of Jacob de Nole and brother of Jan. Moved to Antwerp, with his brother Jan, *ca.* 1590; master in the Guild of St. Luke, 1591; member of the Masons' Guild by 1593; member of the chamber of rhetoric *De Olijftak* (The Olive Branch) from 1593; appointed court sculptor to the archdukes Albert and Isabella, 1604. Died in Antwerp, Belgium, July 1636.

Selected Works (collaborations among Robrecht, Jan, and/or Andries de Nole)

1596–98	Altar; polychromed wood; Presentation Chapel, Church of St. Jacob, Antwerp, Belgium
1598–1607	Altar of St. Annakapel; marble, alabaster; Church of St. Jacob, Antwerp, Belgium
1601–07	Tomb of Archduke Ernest of Austria; alabaster, marble, basalt; Brussels Cathedral, Belgium
1614–25	High altar, for Cathedral of St. Bavo, Ghent, Belgium; marble, alabaster (dismantled); fragments: Church of St. Gummarus, Lier, Belgium
1622	High altar; marble, alabaster; Church of Onze Lieve Vrouw, Scherpenheuvel, Brabant province, Belgium
1622–23	Two angels; Avesnes stone; Church of Onze Lieve Vrouw, Scherpenheuvel, Brabant province, Belgium
1622–23	*Moses, Isaiah, Ezekiel, David, Jeremiah,* and *Daniel*; Italian white marble; Church of Onze Lieve Vrouw, Scherpenheuvel, Brabant province, Belgium
1622–23	*St. Matthew, St. Mark, St. Luke,* and *St. John*; Avesnes stone; Church of Onze Lieve Vrouw, Scherpenheuvel, Brabant province, Belgium
1624–27	Chapel gates; wood, marble; Church of Onze Lieve Vrouw, Scherpenheuvel, Brabant province, Belgium
ca.	*St. Peter, St. Paul, St. John, St. Andrew,*
1628–32	*St. James the Minor,* and *St. Philip*; stone;

Cathedral of St. Rombaut, Mechelen, Belgium

1635–38	*St. Joseph*; plaster model; Musées Royaux des Beaux-Arts de Belgique, Brussels, Belgium
1635–47	Chapel decoration; white and colored marbles; Houtappelkapel, Sint-Carolus-Borromeuskerk, Antwerp, Belgium

Jan (Colijn) de Nole before 1570–1624
Biography
Born in Utrecht, the Netherlands, probably before 1570. Son of Jacob de Nole and brother of Robrecht. Moved to Antwerp with his brother Robrecht, *ca.* 1590; master in the guild of St. Luke by 1591; member of the masons' guild by 1593; dean of the guild of St. Luke in 1604; member of the chamber of rhetoric *De Olijftak* (The Olive Branch) from 1593. Died in Antwerp, Belgium, 14 September 1624.

Selected Works
(See above.)

Andries (Colijn) de Nole 1598–1638
Biography
Born in Antwerp, Belgium, 2 December 1598. Son of Jan de Nole and nephew of Robrecht; joined their sculpture workshop in Antwerp; traveled to Italy before 1621; master in the guild of St. Luke by 1621; dean of the guild in 1628. Died in Antwerp, Belgium, October 1638.

Selected Works
(See above.)

Further Reading

Banz, Claudia, "*Pax—Liberalitas—Pietas*: Anmerkungen zum Ausstattungsprogramm der Marienwallfahrtskirche in Scherpenheuvel," in *Albert and Isabella, 1598–1621: Essays,* edited by Werner Thomas and Luc Duerloo, Turnhout, Belgium: Brepols, 1998

Baudouin, Frans, *Pietro Pauolo Rubens,* Antwerp: Mercatorfonds, 1977

Casteels, Marguerite, *De beeldhouwers de Nole te Kamerijk, te Utrecht en te Antwerpen,* Brussels: Paleis der Academiën, 1961

Defoer, H.L.M., and P. Dirkse, "Het grafmonument van Jan van Scorel," *Oud-Holland* 100 (1987)

Fremantle, Katharine, *The Baroque Town Hall of Amsterdam,* Utrecht: Haentjens Dekker en Gumbert, 1959

Grieten, Stefaan, "De 17de-eeuwse afwerking van de Antwerpse kathedraal: Nieuwe gegevens over Hans en Cornelis van Mildert en over Robrecht en Jan de Nole," *Jaarboek* van het Koninklijk Museum voor Schone Kunsten Antwerpen (1993)

Meganck, Tine, *De kerkelijke architectuur van Wensel Cobergher (1557/61–1634) in het licht van zijn verblijf te Rome*, Brussels: Koninklijke Academie voor Wetenschappen, Letteren en Schone Kunsten, 1998

La sculpture au siècle de Rubens, dans les Pays-Bas méridionaux et la principauté de Liège, Brussels: Musée d'Art Ancien, 1977

Van der Stock, Jan, and Hans Nieuwdorp, "Het Christusbeeld van de Meir te Antwerpen; Een meesterwerk van de gebroeders De Nole uit de vergeethoek," *Revue belge d'archéologie et d'histoire de l'art; Belgisch Tijdschrift voor Oudheidkunde en Kunstgeschiedenis* 55 (1986)

JOSEPH NOLLEKENS 1737–1823 *British*

A major personality in the history of 18th-century English sculpture, Joseph Nollekens was one of the most prolific producers of busts and funerary monuments. Executing over 200 portraits of famous politicians and society figures during his career, Nollekens had no real rival in the carving of busts until the ascendancy of Sir Francis Chantrey Legatt. Nollekens played a role in sculpture comparable to that of Sir Joshua Reynolds in painting, and his studio became a fashionable setting for people of the highest rank. His style, a slightly mannered Classicism inflected by coy charm, exhibits the influences of both Antiquity and Italian sculpture of the 16th and 17th centuries. In his relatively rare, independent, mythological statues, his embellishments on Classical themes reveal a lyrical and inventive approach to the ancient past.

Nollekens exhibited an early talent for modeling and apprenticed with Peter Scheemakers in 1750. Participating with distinction in competitions at the Society of Arts from 1759 to 1762, Nollekens amassed sufficient cash premiums to fund his travel to Italy. Soon after arriving in Rome, Nollekens began copying, restoring, and selling antique fragments and statues, an undertaking surely supported by his associations with Thomas Jenkins, Gavin Hamilton, and Bartolommeo Cavaceppi, whose studio he entered in 1764. Apparently Nollekens participated in some of the common but deceitful practices of the day, such as staining his restorations with tobacco water to age them artificially. Among his first marbles executed in Rome was Nollekeus *Boy on a Dolphin*, with which copied a composition attributed to Raphael but probably originating with Cavaceppi. In his multiple versions of this thinly veiled homoerotic group, Nollekens showed himself to be a highly competent carver, sensitive to the textural differentiation of youthful flesh, hair, fish scales, and fins. His copy of the ancient *Castor and Pollux* also displayed his understanding and close study of the antique. Although accused by many contemporaries of possessing only a dull intellect, Nollekens acquired considerable antiquarian knowledge; his opinion of an-

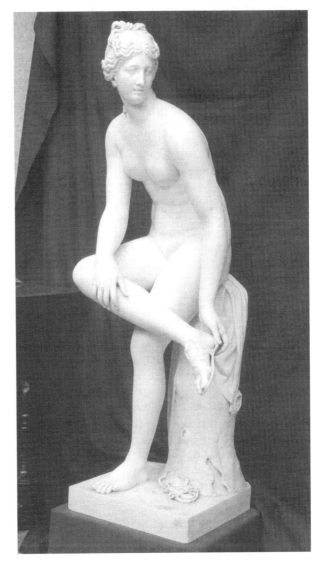

Venus
The Conway Library, Courtauld Institute of Art, Collection of J. Paul Getty Museum, Los Angeles

cient sculptures was solicited by such collectors as Charles Townley and Lord Bessborough and later by the House of Commons when it was deciding whether to acquire Lord Elgin's marbles for the nation in 1816.

Nollekens's earliest portrait commission was for a terracotta bust of the actor David Garrick in 1764 (Althorp, Northamptonshire, England). The subsequent marble depicts Garrick with a turned head, intense gaze, and bare chest terminated below the clavicle. Another bust produced in Rome, that of noted author and humorist Lawrence Sterne, is marked by a strong, detailed handling of facial features and deeply incised pupils to create an arresting, animated portrait. The Sterne bust was sent to London for exhibition, thus securing the sculptor's reputation as a portraitist back home. Although these two busts are more intimate than Nollekens's later, grander portraits, they exhibit the basic characteristics of his style in this genre: a preference for incised rather than blank eyes to maximize expressiveness, a turned rather than strictly frontal head, keenly observed facial features, and a more generalized treatment of the chest, whether draped or nude.

Nollekens returned to London in 1770, receiving a steady stream of commissions for busts and monuments. His tombs ranged from Rococo combinations of chubby, winged putti and portrait medallions to single standing figures in poses recalling the Apollo Belvedere or the Capitoline *Faun*, both 2nd century CE. Among his more accomplished memorials in a classicizing style are the monument to Mrs. Sophia Pelham, which exploits the antique formula of the veiled, virtuous wife leaning on a tree stump; the monument to Mrs. Howard, deceased in childbirth, showing the dying mother with a baby in her lap, supported by the bending figure of Religion, with both women clothed in ample, Classical drapery; and the monument to the Marquis of Rockingham representing Lord Rockingham in a *contrapposto* (a natural pose with the weight of one leg, the shoulder, and hips counterbalance one another) stance, surrounded by busts of his Whig associates.

As in Rockingham's mausoleum, Nollekens's portrait busts were sometimes displayed in groups conveying themes of friendship and political alliance. For instance, the Fifth and Sixth Dukes of Bedford commissioned a temple at Woburn Abbey in Bedfordshire to house the bust of Charles James Fox (1801) surrounded by six portraits of his friends and supporters, all by Nollekens. The sculptor had earlier executed a dramatic, masterful bust of Charles James Fox (1791), with his head sharply turned, wavy locks flowing, and loose drapery falling asymmetrically around his chest. The new bust type ordered for Woburn, with a more frontal pose and close-cropped hair, recalled Roman republican portraiture and may have been considered more compatible with Fox's liberal values. The differences between the busts of Fox also underscore Nollekens's change after 1800 to a broader, staid, and more recognizably Neoclassical portrait style.

The idea of a sculptural ensemble also informed Nollekens's most inventive and ambitious work, a narrative group for Lord Rockingham of three marble goddesses—*Venus*, *Minerva*, and *Juno*—to accompany a statue of Paris believed to be ancient. Together the four statues would have interacted across the space of a large room, through glance and gesture, to illustrate the story of the Judgment of Paris. An important precedent for this project occurred in the ancient *Niobe* group (ancient copies of 4th century BCE originals), which, until 1769, could be seen in the Villa Medici in Rome, displayed in a picturesque arrangement of sculpted figures, horses, and landscape elements to

convey a violent narrative. Similar groupings were found in 17th-century French garden sculpture, which the artist may have studied on his way to or from Italy. Nollekens's individual figures, especially *Venus*, reveal his profound interest in the serpentine, spiral compositions of Giambologna. Unfortunately, the conditions of British patronage offered Nollekens few opportunities for such original statuary with mythological themes. He executed a marble *Diana* for Lord Rockingham and *Venus Chiding Cupid* and *Seated Mercury* for Lord Yarborough, but the majority of his concepts for mythological groups were expressed in small terracotta sketches never realized on a larger scale. These models, which apparently gave Nollekens great pleasure, remained in his workshop until after his death in 1823, when they were sold at auction with the rest of his studio's contents.

PEGGY FOGELMAN

See also **Apollo Belvedere; England and Wales: Baroque–Neoclassical; Giambologna; Chantrey, Sir Francis (Legatt)**

Biography

Born in Soho, London, England, 11 August 1737. Son of Joseph Francis Nollekens, a genre painter. Apprenticed to sculptor Peter Scheemakers, 1750; studied drawing with William Shipley; also at Duke of Richmond's gallery of casts in Whitehall, from 1758; won series of prizes for models at Society of Arts, 1759–62; left London for Italy after 21 May 1762; arrived in Rome, 11 August of same year; entered studio of Bartolommeo Cavaceppi, 1764; also associated with Thomas Jenkins and Gavin Hamilton; shared studio with James Forrester, landscape painter, in via Babuino, 1765–70; bust of Lawrence Sterne shown in 1767, *Castor and Pollux* in 1768, at Society of Artists in London, through assistance of James "Athenian" Stuart; gold Medal at Academy of St. Luke for model of *Jupiter, Juno, and Io*, 1768; member of Florentine Academy, June 1770; left Rome, October 1770; stops in Genoa and Paris, reached Dover 24 December 1770; associate of Royal Academy, 1771; full member, 1772; exhibited regularly at Royal Academy, 1771–1816; received commission for Westminster Abbey *Monument to Three Captains*, 1782; summoned by Select Committee of the House of Commons to give his opinion of the Elgin marbles, 1816. Died in London, England, 3 April 1823.

Selected Works

1764–66 *Boy on a Dolphin* (after Cavaceppi); marble; versions: Burghley House,

Lincolnshire, England; Broadlands, Hampshire, England; Althorp, Northamptonshire, England; Ickworth, Suffolk, England

ca. 1764 Bust of David Garrick; marble; Althorp, Northamptonshire, England

ca. 1766 Bust of Lawrence Sterne; marble; National Portrait Gallery, London, England

1767 *Castor and Pollux* (after the antique); marble; Victoria and Albert Museum, London, England

1773 *Venus*; marble; J. Paul Getty Museum, Los Angeles, California, United States

1775 *Minerva*; marble; J. Paul Getty Museum, Los Angeles, California, United States

1776 *Juno*; marble; J. Paul Getty Museum, Los Angeles, California, United States

1778 *Diana*; marble; Victoria and Albert Museum, London, England

1778 *Venus Chiding Cupid*; marble; Usher Gallery, Lincolnshire, England

1782–88 *Monument to Three Captains*; marble; Westminster Abbey, London, England

1783 *Seated Mercury*; marble; Usher Gallery, Lincolnshire, England

ca. 1786 Monument to Mrs. Sophia Pelham; marble; Brocklesby Mausoleum, Great Limber, Lincolnshire, England

ca. 1788 Monument to the Marquis of Rockingham; marble; Rockingham Mausoleum, Wentworth Woodhouse, Yorkshire, England

1791 Bust of Charles James Fox; marble; Holkham Hall, Norfolk, England

ca. 1800 Sketch for a Monument to Mrs. Howard; terracotta; Victoria and Albert Museum, London, England

1801 Bust of Charles James Fox; marble; Temple of Liberty, Woburn Abbey, Bedfordshire, England; another marble version: *ca.* 1802, Victoria and Albert Museum, London, England

1803 Monument to Mrs. Howard; marble; Wetheral Church, Cumberland, England

Further Reading

Gunnis, Rupert, *Dictionary of British Sculptors, 1660–1851*, London: Odhams Press, 1953; Cambridge, Massachusetts: Harvard University Press, 1954; revised edition, London: Abbey Library, 1968

Kenworthy-Browne, John, "A Monument to Three Captains," *Country Life* 161 (27 January 1977)

Kenworthy-Browne, John, "Joseph Nollekens: The Years in Rome," *Country Life* 165 (7 and 14 June 1979)

Kenworthy-Browne, John, "The Temple of Liberty at Woburn Abbey," *Apollo* 130 (1989)

Penny, Nicholas, *Church Monuments in Romantic England*, New Haven, Connecticut: Yale University Press, 1977

Penny, Nicholas, "Lord Rockingham's Sculpture Collection and *The Judgment of Paris* by Nollekens," *J. Paul Getty Museum Journal* 19 (1991)

Physick, John Frederick, *Designs for English Sculpture, 1680–1860*, London: HMSO, 1969

Whinney, Margaret, *Sculpture in Britain, 1530–1830*, London and Baltimore, Maryland: Penguin, 1964; 2nd edition, revised by John Physick, London and New York: Penguin, 1988

Whinney, Margaret, *English Sculpture, 1720–1830*, London: HMSO, 1971; New York: Alpine Fine Arts Collection, 1984

NORWAY

See **Scandinavia**

BERNT NOTKE *ca.* 1440–1509 *German*

Bernt Notke was considered a key figure of his era. Scarcely settled in Lübeck, Germany, he obtained commissions for monumental objects, very likely as a protégé of clerical and secular dignitaries and without being a member of the guilds, which was unusual for that time. He executed his commissions with supreme artistic and technical quality. New standards in form, size, and technique were established by his first version of the *Dance Macabre* (1463; St. Mary's Church, Lübeck) and the *Triumphal Cross* (1477, Cathedral of Lübeck). To accomplish the extraordinary sizes of the monuments in sufficient time, a workshop was necessary. Notke signed two of his works, the retable of the high altar in the Cathedral of Århus, Denmark, on a border under the sculptures of the central shrine, and the Lübeck *Triumphal Cross* with two written documents in the hollowing of the figures of St. John and St. Mary, which accounts the workshop staff with their professions. Notably, Notke described himself only as the master who made the work.

There was no German medieval artist with a sphere of influence as great as Notke's. His works have been discovered in Germany, Denmark, Sweden, and Estonia. Because of economic and traditional artistic conditions in central Europe, Notke's contemporaries Tilman Riemenschneider or Veit Stoss could not penetrate these areas to such an extent.

The critical discussion regarding Notke's profession as a sculptor and a painter, however, remains highly controversial. The problem lay in the lack of a continuous style within Notke's oeuvre, which prevented him from achieving the financial success that more "consistent" artists—with a less revolving workshop staff—did. The polychromy of his works was the only consistent feature. No artist used mixed media such as parchment, textiles, wigs, and cords to the extent that Notke did. The *St. George and the Dragon* (1489) ensemble in the Cathedral of Stockholm, Sweden, is one such example. The piece is unique in both size and character. Although the work is freestanding, it is unlike the equestrian sculptural figures in northern Italy, which invite the viewer to circumnavigate and thereby see multiple viewpoints. The front of *St. George and the Dragon* is regarded as the main view; it is from this perspective that all of the sculpture's parts present a balanced form, which is believed to symbolize the fight between good and evil.

Resting on its left foreleg, the dragon bows its back and lifts its head up to the horse, who recognizes the dragon's strength and invincibility. The viewer is also made aware of the dragon's powerful nature by the tusk protruding from its forehead. Undaunted, the horse stands with raised forelegs about to fall upon the beast. The dragon's body, wings, and prongs embody a sea of flames, on top of which St. George appears with his sword raised. Neglecting the danger and standing upright in his saddle, the redeemer appears to take his time before administering the final and deadly stroke. It is not clear if the arm must be raised further in order to make the final push or if the sword is already in the proper position. Remarkably, there is no contact between the eyes of the man and of the dragon. To all appearances, St. George is interested in an event removed from the slaying of the tyrant that tormented the town of Silene.

The *Legenda aurea*, the medieval literary basis of this story, recasts as the happy ending in front of the gates of the town as witnessed by the king and queen. This scene was built onto two pillars at the crossing in front of St. George. At one pillar the over-life-size sculpture of the princess was mounted. Today she kneels behind the horse, her head turned slightly in devotion. The princess's parents were placed on top of their castle, originally on the opposite pillar; this group is now lost. In this scene, St. George has already ended the battle and is pondering his guidance of the princess back to town. Accordingly, the church visitors face the rear elevation, indisputably the most lackluster view, but in front of them are the princess, her parents, and St. George carrying out his deed of redemption.

In this work, Notke created a spatial ensemble that was without comparison. This conception of the placement of the sculptures remains unique. The knight on his horse—the remains of the original group—compels historians to find similarities to equestrian statues from northern Italy. Notke also may have conceived his iconography from the scenery of church plays based on the legend of St. George.

Originally, the ensemble was mounted in the crossing and had been surrounded by a railing in which the reliefs representing the life of the saint were incorpo-

rated; today they may be viewed in the basement. Researchers are confident that the equestrian group stood higher and was probably surmounted by a baldachin. An altar was linked to the monument, but nothing is known regarding its design. After the Reformation and the final burial of the donor, Sten Sture, the group was dismantled and portions of it erected in several places in the church. Following restoration of the cathedral in 1920, the remains of *St. George and the Dragon* were placed in the north aisle.

The splendor of Notke's creation had an overwhelming effect on his contemporaries and his posterity. The chronicler wrote that Sture had ordered an artist in Antwerp to create a work of art in a style that had never been seen in the Roman Empire; the artist was then put to death in order to prevent the creation of a similar work. As a national monument, *St. George and the Dragon* had never been forgotten, but it was never authenticated as Notke's. The attribution to Notke is based solely on stylistic grounds. Indirectly, his authorship is supported by an acquaintance of Notke. In a letter, the artist Hendryk Wylsnycks described himself as one who had helped in the execution of *St. George and the Dragon*.

ARNULF VON ULMANN

See also **Germany: Gothic–Renaissance**

Biography

Probably born in Lassahn, Pomerania, *ca.* 1440. Trained as apprentice, possibly in southern Netherlands; first documented works, 1471; established reputation as woodcarver and painter of altarpieces in Baltic area, 1471; purchased home in Lübeck, Germany, 1479; traveled widely to Sweden, Denmark, and Estonia, gaining commissions, often from high-ranking secular and clerical patrons; appointed director of Swedish State Mint, 1491–93; administrator of St. Peter in Lübeck and, by association, appointed master of works in Ziegelhof, Lübeck. Died in Lübeck, Germany, just before 15 May 1509.

Selected Works

Walter Paatz, in 1939, used stylistic grounds to assemble a vast oeuvre by Notke. After the restoration of three major works in the 1970s the oeuvre saw marked reduction.

1470　*Triptych of St. John's*; Museum für Kunst und Kulturgeschichte, Lübeck, Germany

1477　*Triumphal Cross*; polychromed wood, papier mâché, wigs, strings; Cathedral of Lübeck, Germany

1479 High altar; polychromed wood; Cathedral of Århus, Denmark

1483 *Triptych of Whitsuntide*; polychromed wood; Holy Ghost Hospital, Tallinn, Estonia

1489 *St. George and the Dragon*; wood, elk-antler, hair, other materials; Cathedral of Stockholm, Sweden (attributed)

Further Reading

Eimer, Gerhard, *Bernt Notke: Das Wirken eines niederdeutschen Künstlers im Ostseeraum*, Bonn: Kulturstiftung der Deutschen Vertriebenen, 1985

Freytag, Hartmut (editor), *Der Totentanz der Marienkirche in Lübeck und der Nicolaikirche in Reval*, Cologne, Germany: Böhlau, 1993

Hasse, Max, *Bernt Notke: St. Jürgen zu Stockholm*, Stuttgart, Germany: Reclam, 1962

Hasse, Max, "Bildschnitzer und Vergolder in den Zünften des späten Mittelalters," *Jahrbuch der Hamburger Kunstsammlungen* 21 (1976)

Karling, Sten Ingvar, *Medeltida Träskulptur i Estland*, Stockholm: Kungl. Vitterhets Historie och Antikvitets Akademien, 1946

Lumiste, Mai, and S. Globatchowa, "Der Revaler Totentanz von Bernt Notke: Forschungsberichte im Lichte einer neuen Restaurierung," *Zeitschrift des Deutschen Vereins für Kunstwissenschaft* 23 (1969)

Paatz, Walter, *Bernt Notke und sein Kreis*, 2 vols., Berlin: Deutscher Verein für Kunstwissenschaft, 1939

Paczkowski, Renate, *Bernt Notke: Eine Dokumentation*, Kiel, Germany: Stiftung Pommern, 1978

Petermann, Kerstin, *Bernt Notke: Arbeitsweise und Werkstattorganisation im späten Mittelalter*, Berlin: Reimer, 2000

Reinecke, Heinrich, "Buchbesprechung von Walter Paatz, Bernt Notke und sein Kreis," *Hansische Geschichtsblätter* 65/66 (1940/41)

Stoll, Karlheinz, Ewald M. Vetter, and Eike Oellermann, *Triumphkreuz im Dom zu Lübeck: Ein Meisterwerk Bernt Notkes*, Wiesbaden, Germany: Reichert, 1977

Svanberg, Jan, and Anders Qwarnström, *Saint George and the Dragon*, Stockholm: Rabén Prisma, 1998

Thorlacius-Ussing, Viggio, "Einige Arbeiten in Dänemark aus Bernt Notkes Werkstatt," *Acta Archaeologica* (1938)

Von Ulmann, Arnulf, " '. . . dem Original getreu nachgebildet . . .': Zu den lithurgischen Gewändern am Triumphkreuz von Bernt Notke, 1477," in *Unter der Lupe: Neue Forschungen zu Skulptur und Malerei des Hoch- und Spätmittelalters: Festschrift für Hans Westhoff*, Ulm, Germany: Süddeutsche Verlagsgesellschaft, and Stuttgart, Germany: Thorbecke, 2000

NOUVEAU RÉALISTE GROUP

See **Arman (Fernandez); Assemblage; Klein, Yves; Merz, Mario; Tinguely, Jean**

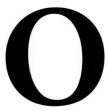

OBELISK

A four-sided tapered stone shaft, square or rectangular in section, usually monolithic and capped with a pyramidal tip, the obelisk form is closely associated with the history of ancient Egypt and is considered a hallmark of that kingdom's architectural decoration. The obelisk reached its full development as a type in that culture as early as the 3rd millennium BCE, but its use has extended both as a trophy and later as a memorial well into modern times. The term *obelisk* derives from a Greek word meaning "little spit" or "pointed instrument," in the sense of a metal skewer used for roasting meat. The ancient Greeks perhaps applied the term in a spirit of derision to these monuments seen as peculiar to Egypt. As an embellishment for architecture or as a freestanding memorial, the obelisk form can be considered an example of sculpture.

The obelisk was called *tekhen* in ancient Egyptian, a word derived from the verb "to pierce," presumably with the implication of piercing the sky. The shape evolved over time simply as an elevated base for its own apex in pyramid form. Egyptians considered the apex a separate part and gave it its own name, *benben*. The *benben* was originally a symbolic stone or cult object associated with the first mound of creation, the first emergence from the waters of chaos, and the first appearance of the sun god. An ancient cult object representing the *benben* was venerated at Heliopolis (near Memphis and modern Cairo) and considered to be imbued with the reproductive powers of the sun god. Obelisks continued in Egyptian history to be dedicated to the solar deities, with inscriptions often including the naming of the king with one of his epithets as "mighty

bull," alluding to the virility or the revitalization of the ruler. Gilding of the pyramid-shaped apex was intended to reflect (or capture) the rays of the sun. Pliny the Elder in *Natural History* (77 CE) states that the obelisk represents the sun's rays, which suggests that the Romans had some idea that the form was more than just a grandiose monument. Modern post-Freudian interpretations of the obelisk have rather expectedly seen it as a phallic symbol. The ancient Egyptians, it seems, were less obscure in the use of such symbolism, and the notion that the obelisk was an object of veneration associated with either "the time of creation" or the generative powers of the sun is a more likely explanation for the widespread use of the form, particularly in temple architecture.

In Antiquity obelisks were essentially of two types, differentiated by size, the larger for temples and the smaller for private tombs. Sculptors in ancient Egypt carved the largest examples from granite quarried at Aswan in the south. These obelisks had a nearly flawless constituency and consistent red-pink color. The oldest extant obelisk of great size is still standing at the site of the temple of Heliopolis in what is now a suburb of modern Cairo. Dedicated by King Sesostris I in the 20th century BCE, it attests to the early resolution of what continued to be the classic form for the monumental type. In Egypt only a few other complete major examples of the form still exist, principally in Karnak and Luxor Temples. Fragments of large obelisks also exist, preserved at temple sites and in the Cairo Museum. The famous unfinished example in the granite quarry at Aswan is of particular interest for technological reasons. The shaft was abandoned during quarrying due to a flaw in the stone and by this chance has provided the best evidence for the technique of removal from the quarry bed.

In general Egyptian usage, sculptors created pairs of obelisks to flank the entrances to temples; the temple pylon was a symbol of the horizon over which the sun rose. Although rare, single obelisks have been attested. Evidence of paired obelisks, in addition to numerous foundation emplacements for them still *in situ*, may be seen in an ancient depiction of Luxor Temple representing its own facade, found in a relief carving on an inner wall of the temple. Among the other ancient depictions of obelisks is an elaborate wall relief in Queen Hatshepsut's mortuary temple at Deir el Bahri on the west bank at Thebes, illustrating the moving of her giant monoliths by barge on the Nile. Depictions of the erection and the ritual of dedication of obelisks also appeared regularly in an abbreviated or symbolic way on temple walls and occasionally even in private tombs. With the exception of some Assyrian reliefs depicting the moving of large sculpture, preserved depictions of the moving of large stone objects appear only in Egypt.

The largest Egyptian obelisks exceeded 30 meters in height. The mechanics of quarrying and transporting these multiton monoliths in ancient times, with limited technological aid, almost defy explanation, although

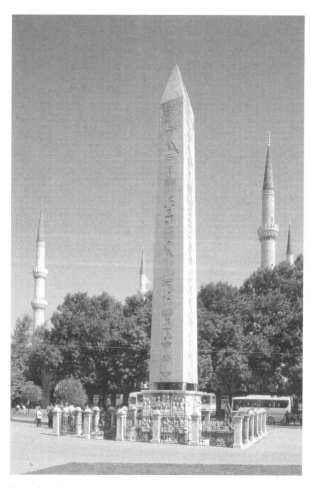

Base for Obelisk of Theodosius I depicting emperor watching a chariot race, Constantinople, *ca.* 390–91, Istanbul
© Archivio Iconografico, S.A. / CORBIS

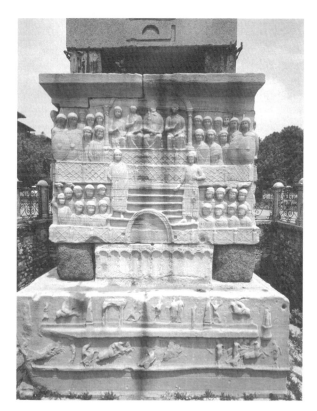

Obelisk of Theodosius, Constantinople, *ca.* 390–81, Istanbul
© Archivio Iconografico, S.A. / CORBIS

numerous theories have been put forward, particularly concerning the final erection of the stone shaft. Paintings on the walls of private tombs depicting the moving of monumental sculpture suggest that obelisks were moved on sleds, aided not by the roller or the wheel but perhaps by some lubricant under the sled runners. Massive corps of workers dragged the sleds. The most logical method suggested for the erection of an obelisk involves dragging it up a long gradual ramp of brick and rubble and carefully tilting and slipping it into place.

The largest known example of an ancient obelisk (approximately 32 meters high and weighing about 455 tons) now stands in the piazza of the Church of San Giovanni in Laterano in Rome. Tuthmosis III created it as a unique object for the temple at Karnak in the 15th century BCE, Constantine I moved it to Alexandria in 330 CE, and Constantinius II transported it to Rome around 337 and erected it in the Circus Maximus. It was rediscovered where it had fallen, and ultimately Dominico Fontana reerected it during the pontificate of Sixtus V in 1588. The history of this obelisk is typical of many others that were taken from Egypt in Antiquity, displayed in Rome (particularly in the Circus Maximus), knocked down or broken, and eventually buried and lost for centuries, only to be rediscovered and restored. The rediscovery of these ancient monuments gave rise to considerable imitation throughout Europe. Ancient obelisks of various sizes can be seen in Rome, where once more than a dozen stood. Ironically, more obelisks are preserved in the city of Rome today than in all of Egypt. Significant examples also exist in Constantinople and in Florence. Of the smaller class, obelisks can be found in such unlikely places as the English countryside (e.g., Kingston Lacey). A number of museum collections also contain examples of the smaller sizes in the range of approximately 1.8 to 2.4 meters, which were meant for the entrances of private tombs.

From Antiquity through the Middle Ages, the obelisk continued in use in Europe as a marker or memorial, never completely disappearing, even if the association with ancient Egypt was not clear. The Renaissance revival of interest in the form continued, and its widespread use in more recent times can be attested by examples in as varied locations as St. Petersburg, Russia; Potsdam, Germany; Dublin, Ireland; Bath, England; and Ramsgate, England. As a memorial, the uses of the form can be suggested by examples ranging from the tomb of George Villiers, Duke of Buckingham, in Westminster Abbey to the monument to Captain James Cook in Kealakekua Bay in the Hawaiian Islands.

Contemporary authors documented well the Renaissance interest in obelisks and the work of Fontana, and the literature on the modern collection and transport of ancient obelisks is equally vast. To that record may be added three significant examples removed from Egypt in the 19th century. In 1831 Mohamed Ali presented to the French nation one of the two obelisks, at that time still standing in front of Luxor Temple. It is now the centerpiece of the Place de la Concorde in Paris, where its modern base records in gilded relief the saga of its reerection. Two other examples, the so-called Cleopatra's needles, erected at Heliopolis under Thutmosis III, were taken to Alexandria during the reign of the Emperor Augustus to stand in front of the Caesarium, dedicated to the deified Julius Caesar. One of the pair that had fallen was ceded to the English in 1801 as a reward for liberation from the French, but it was not removed until 1877. The United States received the other obelisk still standing in Alexandria; it was removed from Egypt in 1879. Something of an adventure accompanied the voyage of each of these monoliths. The London obelisk, in a ship especially constructed for it, was almost lost in a storm at sea; the New York example had to cross the Atlantic and be transported across Central Park on an elevated railway built for the purpose. In Europe and the United States, however, the popular association of the obelisk form with memorial or mortuary monuments certainly predates these late arrivals to the Thames embankment in London and Fifth Avenue in New York.

The interest in Egyptian forms for decoration and memorial extends from the Romans to the interior decorating schemes of Giambattista Piranesi in the 18th century. A distinct "Egyptian revival" in the decorative arts as such never occurred because the memory of ancient Egypt was never completely lost in Europe. The most recent and intensified vogue in the last two centuries for Egyptianizing architecture, particularly in the designs for prisons, zoological parks, and cemeteries, had its modern origins in the reopening of Egypt as a result of the Napoleonic expedition at the end of the 18th century. Architects and sculptors took up the cavetto cornice, papyriform columns, and especially the obelisk form for their immediate connections with exotic Antiquity, intimations of eternity, and allusions to life after death. Freemasonry and Masonic symbolism also played some part in the choice of the obelisk as a memorial form. It became so popular in the 19th century that cemeteries in the United States abound with obelisks in various sizes, but the more monumental usage of the form was generally employed for important public memorials. One of the most prominent and obvious examples of the obelisk in the United States is the Washington Monument in Washington, D.C., where, at approximately 168 meters, the form has been taken to its ultimate expression in majesty and size. The association of such a monument with ancient Egypt in many minds is tenuous at best; the obelisk has simply become a generic memorial.

WILLIAM PECK

Further Reading

Carrott, Richard G., *The Egyptian Revival: Its Sources, Monuments, and Meaning, 1808–1858*, Berkeley: University of California Press, 1978

Curl, James Stevens, *The Egyptian Revival: An Introductory Study of a Recurring Theme in the History of Taste*, New York: Manchester University Press, 1982

Gorringe, Henry Honeychurch, *Egyptian Obelisks*, New York: Gorringe, 1882

Habachi, Labib, *The Obelisks of Egypt*, New York: Scribner, 1977; London: Dent, 1978

Iversen, Erik, *Obelisks in Exile*, 3 vols., Copenhagen: Gad, 1968

Pevsner, Nikolaus, "The Egyptian Revival," in *Studies in Art, Architecture, and Design*, by Pevsner, 2 vols., Princeton, New Jersey: Princeton University Press, and London: Thames and Hudson, 1968; 2nd edition, 1984

Roullet, Anne, *The Egyptian and Egyptianizing Monuments of Imperial Rome*, Leiden, The Netherlands: Brill, 1972

CLAES OLDENBURG 1929– *Swedish, active in United States*

Claes Oldenburg was the only major sculptor to emerge from the style known as Pop art in the 1960s. He drew from the familiar but elusive, commonplace experiences of everyday life to create meaning out of what is normally ignored as a neutral or invisible backdrop to private, social, and political events. Unlike other Pop artists, Oldenburg neither focused on the slickness and superficiality of commercial imagery such as advertisements and comics or pop-culture icons and celebrities, nor employed the cool impersonality of mass media techniques. Instead, he chose objects that we interact with directly, even intimately, every day and refashioned them in a highly personal manner using unexpected texture, material, and scale. Oldenburg has said that his art embodies a "love for the rejected, inexplicable, and simple." His preferred subjects—clothing, food, cigarettes, bathtubs, and the like—are loaded with personal and psychological resonances. They are the things we ingest, consume, wear, use, and touch; they are the link between our inner selves and the exterior world. Working from associations suggested by both the form and the meaning of these objects, Oldenburg anthropomorphized and eroticized them by creating metaphors of human bodies and body parts—connections made explicit in extensive drawings and notebook sketches. His sculptures are studies in contradiction: objects we expect to be hard are reconfigured as soft and vice versa; small, intimate objects are presented as large and hulking forms; normally private interactions become public experiences. As a result, the sculptures he created have the appeal of the familiar, yet at the same time seem utterly strange and even disturbing.

When Oldenburg first came to New York City to be an artist in the mid 1950s after a stint as a newspaper reporter in Chicago, where he grew up, he became associated with a group of artists that included Jim Dine, Red Grooms, Lucas Samaras, and Allan Kaprow, with whom he participated in performance-art Happenings. The Happenings were a kind of improvisational or Expressionist theater that developed out of what Kaprow famously described as the "legacy" of Jackson Pollock: the idea that painting must expand beyond the limiting frame of the canvas and engage directly with the larger environment. Oldenburg's sculptures from this period consisted mostly of props, remnants, or souvenirs from his performances. His working method was one of free association from the things he collected in the immediate environment, including tokens of popular culture, discount store trinkets, and street trash. The ray gun, with its rudimentary yet undeniable phallic form, became a recurring icon for Oldenburg, appearing in the shape of found objects, in drawings and rough papier-mâché sculptures, and as his alter ego. As Ray Gun, Oldenburg presented his first sculptural installation, titled *The Street*, at Judson Church in 1960, which echoed the visual and social chaos of his surroundings. Coarse silhouettes of figures made from ripped cardboard, burlap, paper, metal, and other material associated more with the detritus of urban life than with traditional sculpture hung from the walls and ceilings and lay across the floor. Within this space, he, along with his wife, Pat Muschinski, created the Happening *Snapshots from the City*—a series of "living pictures" for which performers covered in similar rough materials posed for brief illuminations of still tableaux.

In 1961 Oldenburg, under the name of the Ray Gun Manufacturing Company, rented a commercial storefront in the working-class neighborhood of New York City's Lower East Side to house a life-size installation project called *The Store*. The back room served as his studio, while the front offered roughly hewn, brightly painted plaster sculptures of the kind of objects that could be found for sale in the crowded, old-fashioned displays of local stores and sidewalk vendors; each object had typical retail prices such as $99.99. Clothes and shoes, machines and appliances, baked goods and raw meat became quirky, personal, even expressionistic versions of themselves. *The Store*—at once a studio, a museum, a gallery, and, indeed, a store—complicated established distinctions between art and everyday life, between high culture and low, and between the institutions and rituals of art and those of commerce. But *The Store* was not a unification of art and life, nor simply a process of making art more accessible to "the people." As Oldenburg insisted, a loaf of bread sculpture is not a loaf of bread. In fact, it was the very difference between his objects and those they represent, between his installation and a real store, that made the work carry meaning that was both psychologically compelling and socially revealing.

The following year, several sculptures based on the theme of the store were displayed at the uptown Green Gallery. It was here that Oldenburg began to make his so-called soft sculptures for which he is perhaps best known. Loosely stuffed painted canvas and vinyl sculptures on the scale of furniture and people were placed, dropped, and draped directly on the floor. In subsequent years, he shifted his attention from the milieu of thrift shops and open-air food markets to uptown department stores. The shiny vinyl of his mid–1960s sculptures suggests slickness and opulence, rather than the derelict or decayed. But even with the more mechanical items, the intimate, bodily connection is still present in the pendulous breasts in the blades of the hand mixer or the sensation of touching a soft typewriter or trying to talk into a soft pay phone.

Oldenburg left New York City in 1963 and 1964, going first to Los Angeles and then to Europe. In Los Angeles, he turned his attention to the American obsession with car culture and the private home. In the fascinating and funny installation *Bedroom Ensemble* of 1963, for which Oldenburg transformed the Sidney Janis Gallery in Los Angeles into a tacky, surreal bedroom, he turned assumptions about private and public space inside out. Objects that are expected to be soft and inviting—a bed, pillow, and linens—were reconfigured into hard, angular forms in garish materials, colors, and prints. What we think of as private tastes and intimate settings were revealed as mass-produced, prefabricated, and artificial.

His travels also brought about another shift in his working methods. He became intrigued by the relationship between everyday life and the forms and spaces of the city itself. In 1965 Oldenburg began a series he called *Proposed Colossal Monuments*, designs for fantastic sculptures on the scale of landscape and architecture. These were humorous and often contained piercing social satire, but at the same time, his use of the term "monument" was not entirely ironic. He wanted to develop a new sense of monumental themes for the contemporary world. In 1969 Oldenburg began to construct sculptures on a large scale. He moved his studio to an old factory building in New Haven, Connecticut, and began making sculptures at the Lippincott steel fabrication plant. His first monumental public sculpture was the 24-foot-high *Lipstick Ascending, on Caterpillar Tracks*, which consisted of a giant telescoping lipstick emerging from a military tank. Triggered by a comment made by counterculture social theorist Herbert Marcuse that Oldenburg's proposals would be subversive only if they appeared without notice, a group of graduate students at the School of Architecture at Yale University surreptitiously commissioned the sculpture for the campus. The lipstick monument is a powerful sculpture, attacking the macho posturing of warfare by feminizing a tank and literally deflating the phallic image of the proverbial big gun. Oldenburg's later large-scale sculptures, generally commissioned by museums, cities, and private companies for sculpture parks and public areas, tended to be more good-natured and less biting than the imaginary proposals, their humor relying more on their unexpected scale and striking coincidences of shape than on social ironies.

In the early 1970s Oldenburg reestablished a studio in New York City but continued working on large-scale projects, which were increasingly architectural in scale. He married Dutch art historian Coosje van Bruggen, who by the end of the decade became an important collaborator in the realization of huge civic projects, including several projects they made in collaboration with Los Angeles architect Frank Gehry during the 1980s. Oldenburg and Van Bruggen still live in New York City and continue to produce their large-scale sculptures around the world.

ELLEN TEPFER

Biography

Born in Stockholm, Sweden, 28 January 1929. Lived in New York City, Rye, New York, and Oslo, Norway, before settling in Chicago with his family, 1936, naturalized as U.S. citizen, 1953; attended Yale University, where he studied English literature, art, and theater, 1946–50; summer school at University of Chicago, 1948, and University of Wisconsin, 1949; worked as apprentice reporter at City News Bureau of Chicago and attended night courses at the Art Institute of Chicago before moving to New York City to pursue his art career in earnest, 1956; worked closely with first wife, Pat Muschinski, on performances and sculptures, 1960–69; married Dutch art historian Coosje van Bruggen, 1977, with whom he has collaborated on subsequent performances and large-scale projects. Currently resides with Van Bruggen in New York City, United States.

Selected Works

1960   *The Street*, for Judson Church, New York City, United States; mixed media installation (no longer extant)

1961–62 *The Store*, for storefront at 107 E. 2nd Street, New York City, United States; mixed media installation (no longer extant)

1962   *Giant Hamburger* (also known as *Floor Burger*), for Green Gallery, New York City, United States; canvas filled with foam rubber and cardboard boxes, painted with latex and Liquitex; Art Gallery of Ontario, Toronto, Canada

1963   *Bedroom Ensemble*, for Sidney Janis Gallery, Los Angeles, California, United States; wood, vinyl, metal, fake fur, muslin, Dacron, polyurethane foam, lacquer (no longer extant); replica: 1969, Museum für Moderne Kunst, Frankfurt, Germany

1965   *Proposed Colossal Monument for Park Avenue, New York: Good Humor Bar*; crayon and watercolor on paper; Collection of Carroll Janis, New York City, United States

1966   *Soft Toilet*; vinyl, Plexiglas, kapok on painted wood base; Whitney Museum of American Art, New York City, United States

1969   *Geometric Mouse, Scale A*; steel, aluminum; Walker Art Center, Minneapolis, Minnesota, United States

1969   *Lipstick Ascending, on Caterpillar Tracks*, for Beinecke Rare Book Library, Yale University, New Haven, Connecticut, United States; steel, aluminum, wood, painted with enamel (no longer extant); second version, 1974: Morse College, Yale University, New Haven, Connecticut, United States

1976   *Clothespin*; Cor-Ten, stainless steel; Centre Square Plaza, 15th and Market Streets, Philadelphia, Pennsylvania, United States

1977   *Mouse Museum*; corrugated steel room displaying collected items; installed at the Rijksmuseum Kröller-Müller, Otterlo, Netherlands, 16 June–29 July 1979; reinstalled at the Whitney Museum of American Art, New York, United States, 28 September–26 November 1978; other subsequent temporary reinstallations

1985   *Knife Ship I*; wood covered with vinyl, steel, aluminum, and motors; prop from *The Course of the Knife* (multimedia performance in Venice, Italy); installed at the Palacio de Cristal, Madrid, 18 June–9 September 1986

1988   *Spoonbridge and Cherry*; aluminum painted with polyurethane enamel, stainless steel; Walker Art Center, Minneapolis, Minnesota, United States

1994   *Shuttlecocks*; aluminum and fiberglass-reinforced plastic, painted with polyurethane enamel; Nelson-Atkins Museum of Art, Kansas City, Missouri, United States

Further Reading

Axsom, Richard H., and David Platzker, *Printed Stuff: Prints, Posters, and Ephemera by Claes Oldenburg: A Catalogue Raisonné, 1958–1996*, New York: Hudson Hills Press, 1997

Haskell, Barbara, *Claes Oldenburg: Object into Monument* (exhib. cat.), Pasadena, California: Pasadena Art Museum, and Los Angeles: Ward Ritchie Press, 1971

Haskell, Barbara, and John G. Hanhardt, *Blam! The Explosion of Pop, Minimalism, and Performance, 1958–1964*, New York: Whitney Museum of American Art, 1984

Kirby, Michael, and Jim Dine, *Happenings: An Illustrated Anthology*, New York: Dutton, 1965; London: Sidgwick and Johnson, 1967

Oldenburg, Claes, *Drawings and Prints*, London and New York: Chelsea House, 1969

Oldenburg, Claes, *The Mouse Museum, The Ray Gun Wing: Two Collections, Two Buildings* (exhib. cat.), Chicago: Museum of Contemporary Art, 1977

Oldenburg, Claes, *Claes Oldenburg: Multiples in Retrospect, 1964–1990*, New York: Rizzoli, 1991 (catalogue raisonné)

Oldenburg, Claes, *Claes Oldenburg: An Anthology* (exhib. cat.), New York: Guggenheim Museum, and Washington, D.C.: National Gallery of Art, 1995

Oldenburg, Claes, Coosje van Bruggen, and Germano Celant, *A Bottle of Notes and Some Voyages* (exhib. cat.), Sunderland, Tyne and Wear: Northern Centre for Contemporary Art, and Leeds, West Yorkshire: Henry Moore Center for the Study of Sculpture, Leeds City Art Galleries, 1988

Rose, Barbara, *Claes Oldenburg* (exhib. cat.), New York: New York Museum of Modern Art, 1970

Sandler, Irving, *American Art of the 1960s*, New York: Harper and Row, 1988

GIANT HAMBURGER (FLOOR BURGER)
1962
canvas filled with foam rubber and cardboard boxes, painted with Liquitex and latex
h. 132.1 cm; w. 213.4 cm
Art Gallery of Ontario, Toronto, Canada

The use of fabric and oversize scale, combined with a consumer-product theme, makes Claes Oldenburg's *Giant Hamburger*, also known as the *Floor Burger*, one of the most memorable artworks of 1960s Pop art. The artistic concepts generated from the *Giant Hamburger* anticipated formal developments in Oldenburg's independent sculptures, such as the soft sculptures and colossal public pieces. The use of the object as sculpture and the innovative treatment of material, theme, and installation mark this work as a seminal sculpture of the Modernist period.

Conceived and exhibited in 1962 at the Green Gallery in New York, a space considerably larger than the locations of Oldenburg's former installations, the *Giant Hamburger* developed as a later edition to Oldenburg's collection of materials for an exhibition known as *The Store*. In the fall of 1960 he began planning an environmental work consisting of store merchandise and clothing. Early the next year, he set up an actual store on the Lower East Side of Manhattan, producing his objects in the back rooms and selling them in the front. Opened to the public in December 1961, *The Store* contained sculptures of food, clothing, and other objects inspired by neighborhood merchandise and advertisements. The first public exhibition of *The Store* took place at the Martha Jackson Gallery in New York from May through June 1961 and attracted the attention of artists, collectors, and critics. The exhibition contained predominantly plaster reliefs, free-

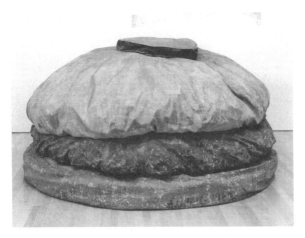

Giant Hamburger (Floor Burger)
© Art Gallery of Ontario, reproduced with permission of the artist

standing and free-hanging objects of food items, clothes, and other common merchandise that had the urban store as a reference point.

Oldenburg further developed the increasing complexities of ideas from *The Store* at the Green Gallery exhibition in the fall of 1962, when he first conceived of the *Giant Hamburger* and placed it among several large-scale sculptures of food items, including *Giant Ice Cream Cone* and *Floor Cake*. He compared the large sculptures lying on the floor of the gallery to the automobiles displayed in the shop windows near the gallery. His wife, Pat Muschinski, a painter, assisted in the construction of the sculptures. The exhibition introduced a series of new works by Oldenburg, marking the first appearance of his giant sculpture and soft sculpture, objects constructed in a fabric that allows them to change form and even collapse in defiance of their solidity. As both a giant sculpture and a soft sculpture, the *Giant Hamburger* embodied characteristics critical to Oldenburg's future artistic development.

The *Giant Hamburger* becomes a contradiction in its use of cloth to represent food and in its manipulation of scale. Oldenburg's work has often been interpreted as combining opposing elements that contain several levels of meaning. Thus, the *Giant Hamburger* is about art and fantasy, ambiguity and explicitness, eroticism and banality, mobility and permanence, life and disintegration. Ultimately, it is a commentary on the values of contemporary life. Through its monumental presence, yet collapsible reality, Oldenburg effectively captured its relevance to American life as an icon of popular culture.

Giant Hamburger also relates to Pop art's fascination with multiples. In 1962 Oldenburg again turned to the theme of the hamburger, creating *Two Cheeseburgers, with Everything (Dual Hamburgers)*, in plas-

ter. He duplicated the image, characterizing the endless commonality, expediency, and banality of consumer products, just as did Andy Warhol's soup cans. Among the most notable influences and inspiration for *Giant Hamburger*, aside from contemporary sources, were Marcel Duchamp and Jean Dubuffet. As with other key works from the 1960s, the *Giant Hamburger* adopts Duchamp's irreverence, humor, irony, the readymade, and the active engagement of art with life. Dubuffet's inspiration is evident in Oldenburg's use of distortion and thematic expansion and in the portrayal of an urban subject.

Perhaps the most enduring legacy of Oldenburg's sculpture is the impulse to integrate art and life, conceiving the gallery as conceptual space, acknowledging the persistence of art's relevance to popular culture, and further breaking down the barrier between high and low art. Scholars have viewed Oldenburg's works as antecedents to the Conceptual sculpture of the late 1960s, exemplified by artists Eva Hesse and Robert Morris. For Oldenburg, the object has a life of its own and reveals the ongoing confrontation between humankind and object.

ANTONIETTE GALOTOLA

Further Reading

Ashton, Dore, "Exhibition at the Green Gallery," *Studio International* 165 (January 1963)

Johnson, Ellen H., *Claes Oldenburg*, Baltimore, Maryland: Penguin, 1971

Oldenburg, Claes, "Extracts from the Studio Notes (1962–4)," *Artforum* 4/5 (January 1966)

Oldenburg, Claes, "Take a Cigarette Butt and Make It Heroic," *Art News*, 66/3 (May 1967) (interview with Suzi Gablik)

Oldenburg, Claes, and Emmett Williams, *Store Days: Documents from The Store, 1961, and Ray Gun Theater, 1962*, New York: Something Else Press, 1967

Rose, Barbara, *Claes Oldenburg: Notes*, Los Angeles: Gemini G.E.L., 1968

Tillim, Sidney, "Month in Review: The Stores," *Arts Magazine* 36/5 (February 1962)

PERE OLLER *fl.* 1394–1444 *Spanish*

Shortly after the untimely death of his father, King Alfonso (V) the Magnanimous of Aragon sent the sculptor Pere Oller to create the deceased king's tomb in the Cistercian Monastery of Poblet. This monument to Ferdinand of Antequera (Ferdinand I) was only one of the prestigious commissions documented for the artist, who worked in several cities in Catalonia during the first half of the 15th century. A substantial amount of his oeuvre survives, whether intact or in fragments, and his distinctive style makes his carving relatively easy to identify. In addition, modern scholarship has uncovered documents such as contracts that elucidate the conditions of many of the artist's commissions. These contracts have great historical importance because fewer detailed descriptions of sculptural projects from this time exist than do those of painting. Pere Oller's art is characteristic of the Gothic International style prevalent in his day, at once expressive and precious.

First documented on 4 May 1394, Oller is listed as a disciple (*deixeble del mestre*) of Master Pere Sanglada (Ça Anglada) in the contract for the choir stalls of the Cathedral of Barcelona. Judging from the salaries apportioned to Sanglada's students and assistants, Oller must have been at the beginning of his career. It is often noted that the relationship of his art to that of his teacher is evident. The training included exposure to artistic currents from northern Europe, for Sanglada went to Flanders to purchase the oak for the choir stalls, and his atelier included several sculptors from France. Oller specialized in alabaster carving, judging from his surviving work, and employed the fine stone of the Beuda quarry—a popular medium during the 14th and 15th centuries. He may have been from the city of Girona (Gerona), Spain, an important center for sculptural activity throughout the Middle Ages; at the

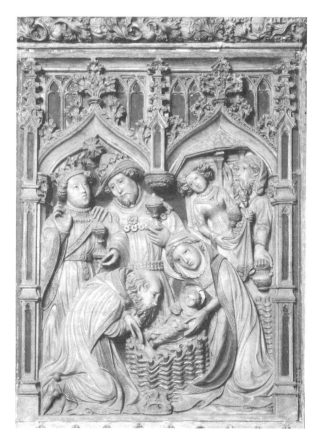

The Adoration of the Magi, detail from the high altar of Vic Cathedral, polychromed alabaster, 1420–1424.
© Archivio Icongrafico, S.A. / CORBIS

very least, he spent a significant amount of time there. Undocumented works in the Museo Provincial at Girona that are attributed to him include the relief *St. Matthew* for a keystone from the chapel in the house of Pía Almoina and *Madonna of Mercy (Virgin of Consolation)*, a small relief.

The contract, dated 22 August 1409, for the tomb of Cardinal Berenguer d'Anglesola of Girona identifies Oller as a master of images (*mestre de ymatges*). The cardinal, closely associated with the curia of the Avignon papacy, died in Perpignan, 23 August 1408. The prestigious commission one year later suggests that Oller was already highly regarded in his field. According to the contract, the artist had presented a drawing for the project and the executors of the cardinal's will made some changes. For example, Oller had suggested five mourners (*pleurants*) for the casket, and the executors mandated six. Other changes occurred during the course of production: for instance, Oller did not make an intended lid of black stone, probably Tournai marble, for the tomb is completely of Beuda alabaster, which was specified for the rest of the monument. In its final form, the effigy of the cardinal rests above the six mourners flanked by coats of arms, all under an elaborate Gothic arcade. The sepulchre was to be painted and inscribed with gold and azure. The executors gave Oller until Easter of 1410 to finish. Whether the tomb was painted and completed by that time is unknown, but other documents indicate that, in an elaborate ceremony of November 1411, the body was translated to the tomb.

The esteem in which his contemporaries held Oller is apparent by his commission to produce the tomb of Ferdinand of Antequera for the royal pantheon in Poblet. King Alfonso wrote a letter of presentation to the abbot on 21 January 1417, the primary document for this vanished monument. Poblet, as with all other monasteries in Spain, was nationalized by the *Desamortización* of 1835. Many of Poblet's artistic treasures, including Ferdinand's tomb, were dismantled, and elements have now been distributed among museums in Europe and the United States. Francesca Español Bertran has reconstructed something of the tomb's appearance on the basis of fragments she and others identified, all similar in style and dimension (see Español Bertran, 1998–99). She has also sorted out the enigmatic history of the monument, which was modified several times and even moved subsequent to its initial construction. The tomb represented the funeral cortege with mourners. A relief now in the Musée du Louvre in Paris, *Arms Bearers*, with knights holding the arms of Aragon and Sicily upside down and riding hooded horses, depicts the ceremony known as *Correr les armes* (literally "running the arms") that formed part of aristocratic funerals.

Stylistic analysis and identification of Oller's hand depend on his masterwork, the high altar of the Cathedral of Vic (Vich), Catalonia, Spain, for which the contract of 24 March 1420 survives. The sumptuous alabaster retable is so refined that it almost gives the impression of metalwork. The squared altarpiece subdivides into four registers and is surmounted by Gothic pinnacles. At the center is the figure *Saint Peter*, patron of the cathedral. Above him are the *Virgin and Child Enthroned*. To the sides are scenes of the lives of the Virgin and Christ, with the lives of Saints Peter and Paul, enclosed by ornamental architecture. On the lowest level under an arcade are *Apostles* and *Four Evangelists* writing their gospels; at the center, angels display the *Dead Christ*. The retable is polychromed and colored glass covers the backgrounds, in imitation of enamel technique. Oller's figures typically have oversized hands and heads on slender bodies concealed by ample, gathered robes. Feet and legs often set at odd angles cause the garments to fan outward or break into folds at the ground in such a way that disregards the integrity of the human form beneath. Decoratively curled hair and beards frame the figures' delicately carved faces. In narrative compositions, the compacted space produces odd juxtapositions of body parts, a device that lends theatrical expressiveness to the scenes. When seen at some distance from the altar, the effect is of dramatic animation. The combination of architectonic organization, dramatic storytelling, and decorative carving gives the sculpture of Oller its strength.

ELIZABETH VALDEZ DEL ALAMO

Biography

Born in the 14th century, location not documented. Trained in atelier of Pere Sanglada (Ça Angelada) together with more established artist Antoni Canet; worked in Catalonia (in present-day Spain); documented as working in Barcelona, 1394–99; resident of both Barcelona and Girona, 1409; sent to Poblet to execute sepulchre of Ferdinand of Antequera, 1417; completed before 1432; worked in Cathedral of Vic, 1420–24; documented working in Barcelona, 1439–ca. 1444. Died after 1444, location not documented.

Selected Works

1394–99 Choir stalls; Flemish oak; Cathedral of Barcelona, Spain
1409– Tomb of Cardinal Berenguer d'Anglesola;
ca. 1411 alabaster; Cathedral of Girona, Spain
ca. 1413 Sarcophagus lid of Pere Rovira; alabaster; Church of San Vicente, Besalú, Spain
1417– Tomb of Ferdinand of Antequera for

ca. 1432 Cistercian Monastery of Poblet, Spain (dismantled); alabaster; fragments: *Arms Bearers*; polychromed alabaster; Musée du Louvre, Paris, France; two *Mourners*; alabaster; Museo de Poblet, Spain; *Mourner*; alabaster; Metropolitan Museum of Art, New York City, United States; *Mourner*; alabaster; Helen Foresman Spencer Museum of Art, University of Kansas, Lawrence, Kansas, United States; *Mourner*; alabaster; Martin D'Arcy Gallery of Art, Loyola University, Chicago, Illinois, United States; *Mourner*; alabaster; present location unknown (formerly in the Terez collection, Barcelona, Spain, and the Echaurren collection, Madrid, Spain); Male head; alabaster; Museo de la Obra, Poblet, Spain
1420–24 High altar; alabaster, polychromed alabaster, colored glass; Cathedral of Vic, Spain
ca. 1420 Tomb of Canon Bernal Despujol; fragments in Museo Episcopal, Vic, Spain
1436–before 1450 Tomb of Sancha Ximenes de Cabrera; alabaster; Chapel of Santa Catalina y Santa Clara, Cathedral of Barcelona, Spain

Further Reading

Dalmases, Núria de, and Antoni José i Pitarch, *L'art gòtic s. XIV–XV*, Barcelona: Edicions 62, 1984
Duran i Sanpere, Agustí, *Los retablos de piedra*, 2 vols., Barcelona: Editorial Alpha, 1932–34; see especially vol. 2
Durán y Sanpere, Agustí, and Juan Ainaud de Lasarte, *Escultura gótica*, Madrid: Editorial Plus-ultra, 1956
Español Bertran, Francesca, "Clients and Patron in Catalan Gothic," and "Mourners from the Tomb of Fernando de Antequera: Pere Oller," in *Medieval Catalonia* (exhib. cat.), Barcelona: Generalitat de Catalunya, Departament de Cultura, 1992
Español Bertran, Francesca, "El sepulcro de Fernando de Antequera y los escultores Pere Oller, Pere Joan y Gil Morales, en Poblet," *Locus Amoenus* 4 (1998–99)
Manote, María Rosa, "Un relleu català al Museu del Louvre," *Daedalus* 1 (1979)
Manote, María Rosa, "Correr les armes, cerimònia dels funerals dels reis d'Aragò, representada en un relleu del monestir de Santa Maria de Poblet," *Lambard* 8 (1995)
Oliva Prat, Miguel, *Catálogo de la exposición de escultura gótica gerundense*, Gerona, Spain: Asociación Arqueológica de la Provincia de Gerona, 1973
Valero Molins, Joan, "El contracte del sepulcre del cardenal Berenguer d'Anglesola," *Locus Amoenus* 4 (1998–99)
Valero Molins, Joan, "L'activitat del taller de Pere Oller durant el seu període de maduresa artística," in *L'artista-artesà medieval a la Corona d'Aragó*, Lleida, Spain: Universitat de Lleida, Institut d'Estudis Ilerdences, and Fund. Publ. de la Dip. de Lledia, 1999

OLYMPIA, TEMPLE OF ZEUS

See **Temple of Zeus, Olympia**

MERET OPPENHEIM 1913–1985 *German, active in France and Switzerland*

Throughout her long career Meret Oppenheim produced works of art in a variety of media. Although she is best known for her assemblages, Oppenheim's drawings, paintings, and sculptures share equal importance in her artistic output.

Shortly after moving to Paris to study art in 1932, Oppenheim met Alberto Giacometti and Jean (Hans) Arp, who introduced her to the Surrealists who were part of André Breton's circle. Oppenheim's personality, intelligence, and sophistication appealed to the Surrealists, who invited her to attend their meetings at the Café de la Place Blanche. At this time, Oppenheim also spent many hours in Giacometti's studio while he worked on objects that gave visual expression to his inner reality. Giacometti spoke of his creations from this period, such as *Palace at 4 A.M.* (1932–33) as presenting themselves whole to his conscious mind from his unconscious mind, the various forms taking their place in space in relation to each other. The time Oppenheim spent observing Giacometti at work reinforced in the mind of the younger artist her own instinctual approach to artistic production.

In 1935 Oppenheim created her first important work of art, which came into being in true Surrealist fashion by a chance interaction among a group of individuals. While she was sitting in the Café de Flore with Pablo Picasso and Dora Maar, Picasso made note of Oppenheim's bracelet of fur-covered brass tubing and, pointing here and there, noted that anything could be covered with fur, to which Oppenheim responded by

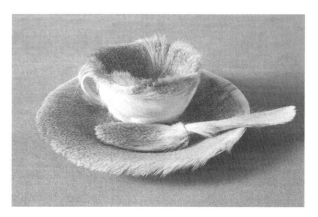

Object (Le Dejeuner en fourrure)
© 2003 Artist rights Society (ARS), New York / ProLitteris, Zürich; The Museum of Modern Art, New York / Licensed by Scala / Art Resource, New York

suggesting even the cup and saucer before her. Shortly after this meeting, Oppenheim purchased a large cup, saucer, spoon, and some gazelle fur, which she glued onto these objects. André Breton reputedly gave the work its subtitle, *Le déjeuner en fourrur*, or *Breakfast in Fur*, thus articulating the sexual nuances inherent in the work and at the same time relating it to Édouard Manet's *Déjeuner sur l'herbe* (1863).

Object: Breakfast in Fur brought Oppenheim instant fame, and it is often referred to as the most famous Surrealist object. Its genesis owes as much to the conversation between Picasso, Maar, and the artist as it does to Oppenheim's playful, whimsical approach to her materials—in this case, everyday objects whose ordinary function the artist's imagination had subverted by bringing them together in a startling combination. In so doing, Oppenheim created a visual metaphor that gave expression to unconscious desires and fantasies and, on an aesthetic level, to concerns that would preoccupy her for the remainder of her career: nature (the fur), culture (the dining implements), and gender dichotomies. (In accordance with Freudian dream symbolism, the Surrealists enjoyed the playfulness of words and objects associated with sexual imagery: here the vessel (the cup) can be read as the female (vaginal) element, and the spoon (tool or instrument) can be interpreted as the male (phallic) element). The genesis of *Object: Breakfast in Fur* finds an even earlier precedent than the conversation at the Café de Flore with Marcel Duchamp's famous subversion of the function of a urinal, which he turned upside down, titled *Fountain* (original lost; second version, 1951; third version, edition of eight signed and numbered replicas, 1964) and submitted for the first annual exhibition of the Society of Independent Artists in New York City in 1917.

From the mid 1930s to the mid 1950s, Oppenheim suffered a period of depression that inhibited the completion of her work. She continued to produce art, but many of these pieces were destroyed or left unfinished. In the late 1950s, well after she had recovered from her depression, Oppenheim began to revisit earlier ideas and sketches and used them to develop new works. This process of working—continuing to reinvestigate and repeat similar themes and iconographies using different formal approaches over a period of time—was similar to the Surrealists' devotion to unconscious processes such as condensation, projection, and sublimation. The later work of Oppenheim and second-generation Surrealist and Expressionist Louise Bourgeois reflected a kind of archaeological approach to artistic discovery in which the image is continually being reinvented in new plastic form. For instance, the form of the sculpture titled *The Green Spectator*, which was described by the artist as representing nature's indifference to both life and death, first appeared in drawings made in 1933. In 1978 an outdoor version of this sculpture was made for the Wilhelm Lehmbruck Museum in Duisburg, Germany. The austere form of *The Green Spectator* recalls representations of an ancient Egyptian horned goddess. The spirals in the upper part, or "head," may signify ears as well as snakes, the latter of which were closely related to mythological and Freudian images of Medusa (whose hair of snakes represented a terrifying image of female sexuality in the male unconscious) and to nature in Oppenheim's iconography. She made a drawing of Giacometti's ear, which was transformed into a stained glass window in 1932 (*Giacometti's Ear*). She then made a cast of the ear in bronze in 1959. *Primeval Venus* was developed in 1962 from a plaster model that the artist had made in 1933.

Primeval Venus, whose materials (terracotta and straw) refer to the earth and whose shape recalls images of prehistoric fertility goddesses, also relates to a slightly earlier performance event, titled *Spring Banquet*, which took place in a private residence in Bern, Switzerland, in April 1959. At this event, three couples partook of an exquisite feast laid out with tree anemones on the nude body of a woman. The couples, including the woman, consumed the food without utensils. Oppenheim has said that she chose a woman to support the feast because women are close to the earth and a source of nurture. She told Josephine Withers that it was "not just men and not a naked woman for men only, but a fertility rite for men and women. A different Easter" (see Withers, 1977).

With *Spring Banquet*, Oppenheim had created a piece of ephemeral sculpture using the human body in an early type of performance art. This event was also one of the earliest Happenings, a form of artistic expression that flourished in the 1960s and 1970s. Similar to Yves Klein's *Anthropométries of the Blue Period* (1960)—a performance in which naked women whose bodies had been covered with blue paint created paintings by writhing on bare canvases placed on the floor—*Spring Banquet* looks forward to the body art and performance art of the 1970s.

At Breton's request, Oppenheim permitted the recreation of *Spring Banquet* in the Surrealists' final joint exhibition, *Exposition inteRnatiOnal du Surréalisme (EROS)* in Paris in 1959. In his re-creation, Breton seated a group of mannequins dressed as men in evening clothes around a table on which lay a naked woman whose body had been painted in gold and laden with fruits. Breton named his work *Cannibal Feast*, most likely a reference to Salvador Dali's 1930s idea, *cannibalisme des objets* (cannibalism of objects). In the process of restaging the original meaning and context of *Spring Banquet* were obscured if not lost. Op-

penheim's intention had been transformed into a tableau whose subject was male pleasure (even consumption) in and of the female object.

The Surrealist approach to artistic creation was deeply embedded in Oppenheim's method of artistic production throughout her career, and she continued to produce visually provocative works, such as *Octavia* and *Geneviève*, until her death in 1985. In the early 1980s she designed two fountain sculptures for public spaces, *Fountain* in Bern, which created controversy in the press when it was unveiled in 1983, and *Spiral (Nature's Way)* in Paris, which is based on an earlier work of the same title.

GINA ALEXANDER GRANGER

See also **Bellmer, Hans; Bourgeois, Louise; Dali, Salvador; Duchamp, Marcel; Ernst, Max; Giacometti, Alberto; Klein, Yves; Modernism; Performance Art; Surrealist Sculpture**

Biography

Born in Berlin, Germany, 6 October 1913. Left secondary school to become a painter, 1931; moved to Paris, 1932, and enrolled at the Académie de la Grande Chaumière, attended meetings of the Surrealist circle of André Breton at the Café de la Place Blanche, starting in 1932; spent time in Alberto Giacometti's studio; invited to exhibit with the Surrealists in the Salon des Surindépendants, 1933, and in the group's other exhibitions, until 1937; made famous by *Object: Breakfast in Fur* at the *Fantastic Art, Dada, Surrealism* exhibition at the Museum of Modern Art, New York City, 1936; first solo exhibition, at Galerie Schulthess, Basel, Switzerland, with invitation text written by Max Ernst, 1936; began two years of study at the School of Arts and Crafts, Basel, Switzerland; exhibited *Table with Bird's Feet* as part of exhibition of fantastic furniture at René Drouin and Leo Castelli's gallery in Paris, 1939; moved to Basel, and began to study restoration; designed costumes and masks for Daniel Spoerri's production of Picasso's *How to Catch Wishes by the Tail*, in Bern, 1956; a major retrospective exhibition held at Moderna Museet, Stockholm, 1967, contributed significantly to her rediscovery; invited to exhibit in *Documenta 7* in Kassel, West Germany, 1982. Received Art Award of the City of Basel, 1975; awarded Art Prize of the City of Berlin, 1982. Died in Basel, Switzerland, 15 November 1985.

Selected Works

1933   Model for *Primeval Venus*; plaster and oil; Kunstmuseum, Solothurn, Switzerland

1935   *Object: Breakfast in Fur*; fur-covered cup,

saucer, and spoon; Museum of Modern Art, New York City, United States

1959 *Giacometti's Ear*; bronze; private collection

1959 *The Green Spectator*; limewood, oil, and sheet copper; Kunstmuseum, Bern, Switzerland

1959 *Spring Banquet*; event with nude woman, exquisite repast, and tree anemones; Bern, Switzerland

1962 *Primeval Venus*; terracotta, oil, and straw; Kunstmuseum, Solothurn, Switzerland

1969 *Octavia*; oil on wood, molded substance, and saw; private collection

1971 *Geneviève*; wooden board, two poles, and oil; Museum Moderner Kunst Stiftung Ludwig, Vienna, Austria

1971 *Spiral (Nature's Way)*; plaster model on plaster base, with four "heads" of movable glass, painted in oil; French Ministry of Culture, Paris, France

1978 *The Green Spectator* (outdoor version of *The Green Spectator* of 1959); green serpentine, front of the "head" gold-plated; Wilhelm Lehmbruck Museum, Duisburg, Germany

1983 *Fountain*; water, plants, concrete, and intermittent lighting; Waisenhausplatz, Bern, Switzerland

1985 *Spiral (Nature's Way)*; bronze; gardens of the Ancienne École Polytéchnique, Paris, France

Further Reading

Burckhardt, Jacqueline, and Bice Curiger, *Meret Oppenheim: Beyond the Teacup* (exhib. cat.), New York: Independent Curators, 1996

Chadwick, Whitney, *Women Artists and the Surrealist Movement*, Boston: Little Brown, and London: Thames and Hudson, 1985

Curiger, Bice, *Meret Oppenheim: Spuren durchstandener Freiheit*, Zurich: ABC, 1982; 3rd edition, 1989; as *Meret Oppenheim: Defiance in the Face of Freedom*, translated by Catherine Schelbert, Zurich: Parkett, and Cambridge, Massachusetts: MIT Press, 1989 (with a catalogue raisonné by Oppenheim and Dominique Bürgi)

Finkelstein, Haim N., *Surrealism and the Crisis of the Object*, Ann Arbor, Michigan: UMI Research Press, 1979

Helfenstein, Josef, *Meret Oppenheim und der Surrealismus*, Stuttgart, Germany: Hatje, 1993

Withers, Josephine, "The Famous Fur-Lined Teacup and the Anonymous Meret Oppenheim," *Arts Magazine* 51/3 (November 1977)

ORCAGNA (ANDREA DI CIONE) ca. 1315/20–ca. 1368 *Italian*

Andrea di Cione, called Orcagna, came from an established family of goldsmiths and painters. He had three brothers: Nardo and Jacopo were exceptional painters, and Matteo, a sculptor, may have worked with Orcagna on the tabernacle at the Church of Orsanmichele, Florence. Orcagna worked extensively as a painter, matriculating in the Arte dei Medici e Speziali (Painters' Guild) in Florence in 1343/44; by the 1450s he was among the most highly regarded artists in the city.

Orcagna's early work shows the decided influences of Maso di Banco and Taddeo Gaddi. Probably between 1348 and 1352 Orcagna worked on the extensive fresco cycles of *The Life of the Virgin* and *The Life of the Baptist* for the Cappella Maggiore at the Dominican Church of Santa Maria Novella in Florence. With the exception of 35 Old Testament busts by various artists in the vault, these frescoes are now covered by Domenico Ghirlandiao's cycles on the same subject (*ca.* 1486). Orcagna painted an altarpiece for the Strozzi Chapel (1354–57), also at the Church of Santa Maria Novella, which may reflect stylistic changes associated with his only documented sculptural project, the tabernacle at the Church of Orsanmichele. In 1352 he joined the guild of the stonemasons, presumably to allow him to accept the tabernacle's commission, and in 1455 he was named *capomaestro* (chief architect) of the Church of Orsanmichele. By 1357, while still engaged with the tabernacle, he began an association with the planning of the Cathedral of Florence, a project that seems to have occupied him intermittently for the remainder of his life. It has been suggested, probably correctly, that he designed the drum under the dome of the Cathedral of Florence, because the tabernacle's base shows a similar solution. In 1358 Orcagna became *capomaestro* of the Cathedral of Orvieto; he resided there sporadically between October 1359 and December 1360 and designed a mosaic of the *Baptism of Christ* for the pediment of the left portal of the cathedral. The *Madonna of Humility* panel (*ca.* 1365–67) probably represents Orcagna's latest surviving work.

According to Giorgio Vasari, the great biographer of Italian Renaissance artists, Orcagna was a student of Andrea Pisano (who was responsible for, among other projects, the first set of bronze doors for the Florentine Baptistery and several reliefs on the bell tower of the Cathedral of Florence, or *campanile*). Many of the tabernacle's reliefs suggest an affiliation with Andrea Pisano, but Orcagna's figures are generally heavier than those by Pisano, and the treatment of space and narrative technique is more pedantic. Although a fairly large body of attributed work has fleshed out much of Orcagna's development as a painter, very few sculptural projects or figures other than those at Orsanmichele are associated with the artist. Because of Orcagna's illness, the moneychangers' guild withdrew a commission for a triptych at Orsanmichele in 1368 and transferred it to his brother Jacopo. Orcagna probably died the same year.

ARNE R. FLATEN

Biography

Born in Florence, Italy, *ca.* 1315/20. Father a goldsmith, brothers Nardo and Jacopo painters, brother Matteo sculptor. Matriculated as painter in the Arte dei Medici e Speziali (Painters' Guild) in Florence, 1343/44; matriculated as stonemason, 1352; named *capomaestro* (chief architect) of the Church of Orsanmichele, Florence, 1355; *capomaestro* of the Cathedral Orvieto, 1358–60. Died in Florence, Italy, *ca.* 1368.

Selected Works

1352–60 Tabernacle for image of the Virgin; marble, stone, and polychrome glass inlay; Church of Orsanmichele, Florence, Italy
1359 *Baptism of Christ*; mosaic; Orvieto Cathedral, Italy

Further Reading

Cole, Bruce, "Some Thoughts on Orcagna and the Black Death Style," *Antichita viva* 22/2 (1983)
Kreytenberg, Gert, *Orcagna's Tabernacle in Orsanmichele, Florence*, New York: Abrams, 1994 (with photographs of all the reliefs and with schematic drawings)
Kreytenberg, Gert, "Andrea di Cione," in *The Dictionary of Art*, edited by Jane Turner, vol. 2, New York: Grove, and London: Macmillan, 1996
Pope-Hennessy, John, *An Introduction to Italian Sculpture*, 3 vols., London: Phaidon, 1963; 4th edition, 1996; see especially vol. 1, *Italian Gothic Sculpture*
Steinweg, Clara, *Andrea Orcagna*, Strasbourg, France: Heitz, 1929

TABERNACLE OF ORSANMICHELE

ca. 1352–1360

marble inlaid with colored stone and gold-glass panels

h. approx. 5 meters

Orsanmichele, Florence, Italy

The large marble tabernacle in the Orsanmichele is signed and dated "Andreas Cionis pictor Florentin oratorii archimagister extitit hui MCCCLIX" (Andrea di Cione, Florentine painter, was architect of this oratory, 1359) in an inscription on the base of the sarcophagus in the relief of the *Dormition*. Work on the shrine probably began about 1352, the year that Orcagna (Andrea di Cione) became a member of the Florentine stonemasons' guild, although the original plans for the taber-

nacle may have predated the commission for Bernardo Daddi's *Virgin and Child Enthroned with Angels* in 1346. Despite the presence of the date 1359 on the tabernacle, documents from the 1360s demonstrate that the bronze *cancello* (gate) and "candelieri e altre cose d'ottone per lo tabernacholo di Nostra Donna" (candlesticks and other items in brass for the tabernacle of Our Lady) were made later by the metalworkers Piero del Migliore and Benincasa di Lotto in order to complete the work.

Commissioned by Florence's most prestigious lay confraternity, the Compagnia della Madonna di Orsanmichele, the tabernacle was created to house and protect their new cult image of the *Virgin and Child* painted by Daddi. This painting was the second replacement of an original frescoed Madonna reputed to have manifested supernatural powers, which was probably destroyed by a fire at the grain market in 1304. The need to protect this sacred image housed in the secular context of Florence's grain market and the existence of the precedent artworks certainly influenced the eventual appearance of the tabernacle. It was necessary that Orcagna's design create an ambience that would encourage prayer and worship of the holy image within the bustling space of Orsanmichele.

A miniature of about 1340 in the *Biadaiolo Codex* illustrates Florence's grain market complete with the

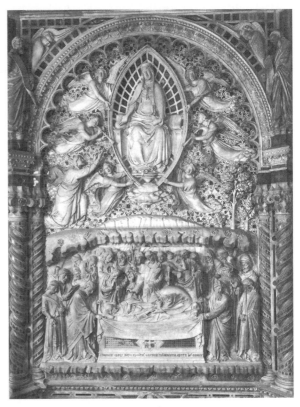

The Death and Assumption of the Virgin, from the Tabernacle
© Alinari / Art Resource, NY

new tabernacle built after the fire in 1304 to house a second image of the Virgin and Child. Although the drawing may be rather limited, it accurately portrays the general concept of the dimensions and composition of the original tabernacle, and its similarity to Orcagna's later design is apparent.

Comparisons have been made between the Tabernacle of Orsanmichele and Arnolfo di Cambio's altar baldachin (*ca.* 1284) in the Church of S. Paolo fuori le Mura in Rome. Despite the resemblance in their overall forms, the diverse function of altar ciboria renders improbable the suggestion that Orcagna's tabernacle is directly derived from Arnolfo's artwork. Mosaic decoration is, however, common to both Orcagna's shrine and the unfinished Florentine cathedral facade designed by Arnolfo di Cambio. In addition, the large-scale relief of the *Dormition*, which appears on the tabernacle dedicated to the Virgin, was also the subject of the lunette above the right portal of Santa Maria del Fiore. These similarities, together with the fact that 21 of the documented tabernacle officials also occupied active roles as cathedral *operai* (employees of the cathedral), treasurers, and purveyors and that Orcagna frequently played an advisory role at Florence Cathedral in the 1350s, indicate the close connections between the Compagnia and the city's Opera del Duomo.

The ciborium-like structure of Orcagna's tabernacle points to probable Roman prototypes, which preceded a reliquary ciborium of 1368–70 preserving the heads of Saints Peter and Paul in the Basilica of San Giovanni in Laterano. This shrine, attributed to the Sienese architect Giovanni di Stefano, is the only surviving Roman example of its type, but its later date excludes it from being one of the actual models that Orcagna may have known. The stone tabernacle, begun after 1341 to reserve the Blessed Sacrament above the high altar of the Church of Sant'Ambrogio in Florence, is an example of another Florentine tabernacle derived from these same sources. A generic resemblance between the mid-14th-century drawing for the Chapel in Piazza del Campo in Siena, for which the foundations were laid in 1352, and Orcagna's tabernacle is also worth mentioning.

Orcagna's tabernacle is remarkable not only for the lavishness of its sculptural detail but also for the sheer size and originality of its architecture. The freestanding, four-sided, three-tiered architectonic structure has a high parapet decorated with scenes from the Life of the Virgin, separated by bust-length reliefs of the Virtues, prophets, and saints. Above the parapet, three round arches frame the panel of *Virgin and Child*. The fourth arch is closed by Orcagna's large-scale reliefs of the *Dormition* and the *Death and Assumption of the Virgin*; below these is located the small door that leads to the interior of the monument. These scenes would

have been originally visible to the street through the open arch of the Loggia of Orsanmichele. The tabernacle is crowned by an octagonal cupola on a tall, arcaded drum, which is almost completely hidden behind gables on all four sides. The door on the back wall leads through a low narrow passage to a rectangular enclosure (2.34 by 2.29 meters) within the shrine; here a stairway ascends from one corner to spiral round between the back of Daddi's painting and the *Death and Assumption* relief to emerge in an octagonal enclosure beneath the cupola (2.5 meters high, 1.8 meters in diameter). This space once held the raised bronze grilles (now lost) that could be lowered by controlling mechanisms, located behind the roof gables, to enclose and secure the sacred image behind the three arched openings.

The entire architectural complex is lavishly decorated with finials and crockets on pinnacles and gables, gilded scallop shells on arches and cornices, and foliage in relief in trapezoidal frames on the balustrade. On the northern side are situated the *Birth of the Virgin* and the *Presentation*; the *Marriage* and *Annunciation* are on the west; the *Nativity* and the *Adoration of the Magi* are on the south; and the *Presentation of Christ in the Temple* and the *Annunciation of the Death of the Virgin* decorate the east. The *Death and Assumption of the Virgin*, with the translation of the girdle to St. Thomas the Apostle, is represented above these last two reliefs on the eastern side. All but two of the octagonal relief panels containing the Marian scenes repeat the framing motif of the drawn curtains at the sides of the miraculous painted panel within the tabernacle.

The compositional economy that Orcagna employed in these reliefs can be associated with the work of Andrea Pisano and Giotto. Orcagna's figures, too, are Giottesque in their weighty three dimensionality and their bulk, described by sweeping curves of drapery and cascading hems. The scenes are characterized by an emphasis on human interaction and contact; Orcagna's omission of halos on his biblical figures underscores this emphasis. Giotto's interest in realistic representation of depth and perspective fall second to Orcagna's focus on human interaction. The reliefs show strong stylistic affinities with similar scenes depicted by Giotto and Pietro Lorenzetti and Taddeo Gaddi's work in the Baroncelli Chapel in the Church of Santa Croce, Florence.

On three of the four sides of the balustrade, the octagonal panels narrating the Life of the Virgin are separated by a hexagonal panel representing a Theological Virtue. Half-length figures of the Cardinal Virtues accompanied by a pair of Attendant Virtues, according to a scheme derived from St. Thomas Aquinas, are represented on the base of the piers together with two figures of male saints or prophets. Above each of the four piers are three statuettes of apostles carrying books or scrolls bearing their contributions to the Creed. At the summit of the cupola stands the figure of St. Michael the Archangel brandishing a metal sword; he is surrounded on all four sides by metal winged angels in armor holding clubs or swords situated at the highest point on the gables. These warlike images appear alongside the repeated use of the lion, a well-known symbol of Florence, and the cross of the Florentine populace on the shields of the virtue *Fortitude* and two angels that flank the *Dormition*, indicating the Florentine commune's involvement alongside that of the confraternity and the historical context of the commission.

PIPPA SALONIUS

Further Reading

Cassidy, Brendan, "The *Assumption of the Virgin* on the Tabernacle of Orsanmichele," *Journal of the Warburg and Courtauld Institutes* 51 (1988)

Cassidy, Brendan, "The Financing of the Tabernacle of Orsanmichele," *Source: Notes in the History of Art* 8/1 (Fall 1988)

Cassidy, Brendan, "Orcagna's Tabernacle in Florence: Design and Function," *Zeitschrift für Kunstgeschichte* 61 (1992)

Fabbri, Nancy Rash, and Nina Rutenburg, "The Tabernacle of Orsanmichele in Context," *The Art Bulletin* 63/3 (September 1981)

Kreytenberg, Gert, *Orcagna, Andrea di Cione: Ein universeller Künstler der Gotik in Florenz*, Mainz: Zabern, 2000

Meiss, Millard, *Painting in Florence and Siena after the Black Death: The Arts, Religion, and Society in the Mid-Fourteenth Century*, New York: Harper and Row, 1964

Steinweg, Clara, *Andrea Orcagna*, Strassburg: Heitz, 1929

Pisetta, C., and G. Vitalli, "Il tabernacolo dell'Orcagna in Orsanmichele," in *Storia e restauro dell'architettura: Aggiornamenti e prospettive*, edited by Gianfranco Spagnesi, Rome: Centro di Studi per la Storia dell'Architettura, 1984

Zervas, Diane Finiello, "Orsanmichele and Its *Operai*, 1336–1436," in *Opera: Carattere e ruolo delle fabbriche cittadine fino all'inizio dell'Età Moderna*, edited by Margaret Haines and Lucio Riccetti, Florence: Olschki, 1996

Zervas, Diane Finiello, editor, *Orsanmichele à Firenze; Orsanmichele, Florence* (bilingual Italian-English edition), 2 vols., Modena: Panini, 1996

BARTOLOMÉ ORDÓÑEZ *ca.* 1480–1520

Spanish

Already in the 16th century Bartolomé Ordóñez's importance as a sculptor of reliefs was acknowledged, and he was one of the first artists in Spain to work in the Renaissance style. In spite of his historical significance, his oeuvre is small and he died leaving his most important projects, the double tomb of King Philip the Fair and Queen Joanna the Mad and the tomb of Cardinal Francisco Ximénez Cisneros, unfinished.

Little is known of Ordóñez's career before he was commissioned in 1517 to update the choir and retrochoir at Barcelona Cathedral with a series of reliefs, and the contract simply describes him as a master born in Burgos. Some have speculated that he worked on the tomb of Ferdinand and Isabella (1514–17; Royal Chapel, Granada, Spain) in Domenico Fancelli's studio in Carrara; others have alleged that he had previously served his apprenticeship in Burgos and then possibly traveled to Rome; and still others hypothesize that he was already working in Naples about 1515 (see Abbate, 1992; Negri Arnoldi, 1997; Lenaghan, 1998).

The progress of his career in the remaining three years of his life can be traced in more detail. To complete the reliefs for the cathedral, he entered into a partnership with another sculptor, Juan Petit Monet, who had long been active in Barcelona. In December 1517 Ordóñez was in Naples purchasing marble, presumably for the reliefs on the cathedral retrochoir. While there, he collaborated with Diego de Siloé and Girolamo Santacroce on the impressive marble altar in the Caracciolo Chapel in the Church of San Giovanni a Carbonara. Although the chronology of the work cannot be established definitively (*ca.* 1515–16 or 1517–19), most scholars agree that Ordóñez directed the project and carved the central relief of the Adoration of the Magi, two smaller reliefs, and perhaps more. Other works in that city have also been attributed to him, most notably the tomb of Andrea Bonifacio Cicaro. He had, however, only a limited time in Naples, at most a year and four months, in which to work on these projects. Nonetheless, the two works figure among the most important monuments of the Neapolitan Renaissance, and his example, along with that of Siloé, exerted a significant impact on subsequent local sculptors such as Santacroce and Giovanni da Nola (see Abbate, 1992; Negri Arnoldi, 1997).

By February 1519 Ordóñez had returned to Barcelona and had probably completed half of the retrochoir reliefs (installed 1562–64), as well as all those for the

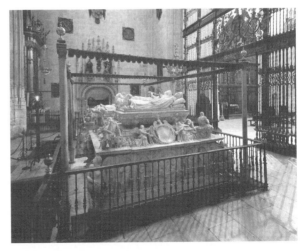

Sepulchre of Felipe I and Juana I
© Archivo Iconografico, S.A. / CORBIS

choir. These are among the first works in Spain to use Classical architectural forms and an Italian figure style in relief, and as such they doubtlessly had a significant impact. Then on 1 May 1519 Ordóñez received his most important commission to date: the tomb of Charles V's parents, Philip the Fair and Joanna the Mad. Significantly, Charles V and his advisers turned to Ordóñez within weeks of the death of the artist previously entrusted with the project, Fancelli. The speed with which they awarded the project suggests that the choice was obvious. Furthermore, the contract repeated verbatim the one that Fancelli had signed.

Charles V probably knew Ordóñez as the sculptor of the new reliefs in Barcelona Cathedral, particularly because the project had been undertaken in honor of the monarch's visit and plans to hold a meeting of the Order of the Golden Fleece in the choir. Any association with Fancelli on previous Spanish royal tombs might have strengthened Ordóñez's claim for the new commission, because in such a case, Charles V would be turning to one of the prominent members of the deceased master's workshop. At any rate, Ordóñez was by this time an established sculptor in Barcelona. Once Ordóñez had acquired this project, he subsequently received Fancelli's other projects: the tomb of Cardinal Francisco Ximénez Cisneros (awarded on 27 September 1519) and the Fonseca family tombs.

After dissolving his partnership with Monet, Ordóñez left for Italy, probably in the fall of 1519. He was working on the tombs of the kings (Philip and Joanna), Cisneros, and the Fonsecas when he died in Carrara early in December 1520. Although he had made substantial progress on these tombs in that year, Ordóñez left them unfinished. In his will (made on 5 December 1520), he ordered that his workshop should complete them under the direction of "Peter of Carona" (Pietro Aprile). According to the inventory of his studio after his death, the sculptor had carved the effigies of Philip and Joanna as well as other sections for that monument, but significant portions remained unfinished: the tondi on the base and at least two of the four large figures at the corners. More had been completed on the tomb of Cardinal Cisneros, with Ordóñez having overseen the effigy, the four principal reliefs, and the figures at the corners. Not all of this work however, can, be attributed to the master's hand because other documentation suggests that the four reliefs on the base were the work of Giangiacomo da Brescia and Santacroce. Although harder to interpret, the documents regarding the tombs in Coca suggest that this project also remained unfinished, and the ensemble—as finally installed by 1538—represents a compromise from the original intentions.

In spite of these difficulties, the documents have an important role in history because they reveal which portions were completed at Ordóñez's death and can thus suggest his role in the tombs' appearance. It is safest to attribute only the effigies to his hand but assume that he established the general composition for the monuments. In general, he adhered to Fancelli's models, but typologically, he created a more conventional rectangular base and made the tombs taller. With regard to figure style, Cisneros's tomb and that of Philip and Joanna suggest an artist creating more active figures who move freely and create more dramatic compositions. The four church doctors who sit on top of the base at the corner of the tomb of Cisneros draw on the comparable figures on Fancelli's tomb of Ferdinand and Isabella, but here they turn energetically and dominate the space as none of Fancelli's figures do. This tendency is more apparent in the comparable statues on the tomb of Philip and Joanna, although it should be remembered that they were finished only after Ordóñez's death. They lead the viewer's eye around the corner effectively and, unlike those on Cisneros's tomb, compose themselves at almost any angle from which they are considered. Moreover, two of them, the St. Andrew and St. Michael, draw on recent Italian models, Michelangelo's *Moses* (ca. 1515) and Raphael's *St. Michael* (1518). A similar progression is apparent in the bases' corners: On Cisneros's tomb, Fancelli's griffins are repeated, whereas on the king's tomb, sphinxes and tritons twist while putti clamber over them.

PATRICK LENAGHAN

See also **Fancelli, Domenico**

Biography

Born in Burgos, Spain, *ca.* 1480. Circumstances of training unknown; probably served as an apprentice in Burgos; perhaps worked in Domenico Fancelli's studio; probably traveled in Italy; first documented in Barcelona, May 1517; traveled to Naples, Italy, where he bought marble, 1517, and undertook several projects in 1518; returned to Barcelona, February 1519; predominantly worked on tomb sculpture; traveled to Italy, late 1519; Died in Carrara, Italy, December 1520.

Selected Works

1517–18   Tomb of Andrea Bonifacio Cicaro; marble?; Church of Santi Severino e Sosio, Naples, Italy

1518(?)   Altar (with Diego de Siloé and Girolamo Santacroce); marble; Caracciolo Chapel, Church of San Giovanni a Carbonara, Naples, Italy

1519   Reliefs for the retrochoir; marble; choir stalls; wood; Barcelona Cathedral, Spain

1519–20 Fonseca family tombs (presumably completed posthumously under the direction of Pietro Aprile; installed by 1538); Church of Santa María, Coca, Spain

1519–21 Tomb of Cardinal Francisco Ximénez Cisneros (completed posthumously under the direction of Pietro Aprile); marble; Church of San Ildefonso, Alcalá de Henares, Spain

1519–26 Tomb of King Philip the Fair and Queen Joanna the Mad (completed posthumously under the direction of Pietro Aprile); marble; Royal Chapel, Granada, Spain

Further Reading

Abbate, Francesco, *La scultura napoletana del Cinquecento*, Rome: Donzelli, 1992

Campori, Giuseppe, *Memorie biografiche degli scultori, architetti, pittori ecc, nativi di Carrara*, Modena, Italy: Vincenzi, 1873; reprint, Bologna, Italy: Forni, 1969

Carbonell i Buades, Marià, "Bartolomé Ordóñez i el cor de el catedral de Barcelona," *Locus Amoenus* 5 (2000–2001)

Gómez-Moreno, Manuel, *La escultura del renacimiento en España*, Florence: Pantheon Casa Editrice, 1931; as *Renaissance Sculpture in Spain*, translated by Bernard Bevan, Florence: Pantheon Casa Editrice, 1931; reprint, New York: Hacker Art Books, 1971

Gómez-Moreno, Manuel, *Las águilas del renacimiento español: Bartolomé Ordóñez, Diego Silóe, Pedro Machuco, Alonso Berruguete, 1517–1558*, Madrid: Consejo Superior de Investigaciones Científicas Instituto Diego Velázquez, 1941; reprint, Xarait Ediciones, 1983

Gómez-Moreno, María Elena, *Bartolomé Ordóñez*, Madrid: Instituto Diego Velázquez del Consejo Superior de Investigaciones Científicas, 1956

Lenaghan, Patrick, "Reinterpreting the Italian Renaissance in Spain: Attribution and Connoisseurship," *The Sculpture Journal* 2 (1998)

Marchamalo Sánchez, Antonio, and Miguel Marchamalo Main, *El sepulcro del cardenal Cisneros*, Alcalá and Madrid: Fundación Colegio del Rey, 1985

Negri Arnoldi, Francesco, *Scultura del Cinquecento in Italia meridionale*, Naples: Electa Napoli, 1997

Redondo Cantera, María José, *El sepulcro en España en el siglo XVI: Tipología e iconografía*, Madrid: Ministerio de Cultura, Dirección General de Bellas Artes y Archivos, Centro Nacional de Información y Documentación del Patrimonio Histórico, 1987

Wethey, Harold E., "The Early Works of Bartolomé Ordóñez and Diego de Siloé," *Art Bulletin* 25 (1943)

ORESTES AND ELECTRA

School of Pasiteles

1st century BCE

Parian marble

h. 1.5 m

National Archaeological Museum of Naples, Italy

A two-figure sculpture group of a male nude accompanied by a draped female whose arm encircles the young man is often identified as *Orestes and Electra*, who were the children of Agamemnon. The group was found in 1750 at Pozzuoli (ancient Puteolis), Italy, in the so-called Temple of Serapis (Serapide), now identified as the ancient city's *macellum*, or market. Some early sources on the *Orestes and Electra* mistakenly report that it was found at Herculaneum. The mistake is possibly due to the sculpture's placement in the Museo Ercolanese at Portici among the finds from Herculaneum and Pompeii. Finds from excavations conducted in the territory of the kingdom of Naples, which included Pozzuoli, were deposited in the Museo Ercolanese until the collection was transferred, beginning in 1805, to the new Museo Borbonico, the present-day National Archaeological Museum of Naples (see De Franciscis, 1963). The provenance of the group was eventually cleared by a letter, which notes its discovery.

The restorations on the sculpture, although minor, were done by Angelo Brunelli, a pupil of Antonio Canova; they included the right leg of Orestes (the left is reattached) and the left forearm, and Electra's right hand, fingers on her left hand, and a portion of the drapery hanging from her left wrist.

The unidentifiable artist is often associated with the school of the Greek sculptor and writer Pasiteles, who was active in the 1st century BCE in southern Italy.

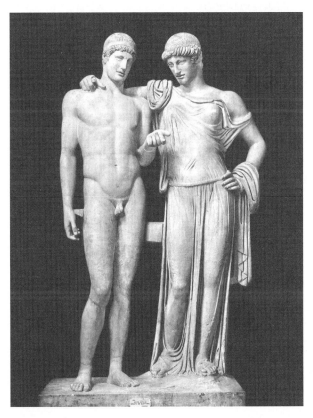

Orestes and Electra
© Alinari / Art Resource, NY

The Roman author Pliny the Elder, writing in the 1st century CE, tells of Pasiteles's interest in earlier models (see Ridgway, 1970). No sculpture signed by Pasiteles comes down to us, but two signed works from his school do, namely the *Stephanos Athlete*, or *Youth* (Villa Albani, Rome, Italy), signed by Stephanos, a pupil of Pasiteles, and another version of *Orestes and Electra* (Boncompagni-Ludovisi Collection, Rome, Italy) signed by Menlaos, a student of Stephanos. The identification of the Naples group with the school of Pasiteles is based on a comparison with the *Stephanos Athlete*. The *Stephanos Athlete* survives in multiple single-figure copies and as part of two-figure groups, paired typically with a male commonly identified as Pylades (*Orestes and Pylades*, Musée du Louvre, Paris, France; originally from the Borghese Collection in Rome, Italy). It is possible that the *Stephanos Athlete* was used as a type of "canon," much like the *Doryphoros* (ca. 440–435 BCE) of Polykleitos (see Borda, 1953). In the Naples *Orestes and Electra* group, the *Stephanos Athlete*, identified as the Orestes, is paired with a female figure, derived from the Roman *Venus Genetrix* by Arkesilaos, which in turn was modeled after the Classical Greek *Aphrodite Frejus* type. But in the Naples group, Electra has the head of a male figure like that of Plyades in the Louvre and the *Schloss Fasanerie* groups (see Zanker, 1974; Ridgway, 1984).

Categorizing the *Orestes and Electra* in terms of art historical style and period is problematic because of the mix of stylistic traits in the single group. The stylistic label typically attached to this piece is Severizing, meaning that it retains qualities of the Severe period (480–450 BCE), but this stylistic identification does not mean that it was created during the Severe period proper. Severe and Severizing are stylistic and periodic terms of debate between scholars, especially regarding their definitions. Problems have been raised concerning identification of Severe sculptures, especially if the sculptures were created by later Roman and Greek artists (see Ridgway, 1970; Fullerton, 1998). The Orestes in the Naples group is a good example of a Severizing work, retaining Severe qualities (see Ridgway, 1970) but combined with elongated proportions and a smaller head, qualities often attributed to the artist Lysippos. (4th century BCE). The body and drapery of the accompanying Electra represents the classicizing element of the group, but combined with a Severizing male head.

The *Orestes and Electra* group is not mentioned directly by any known source from antiquity. But on the basis of examples of similar sculptures and copies, this group exemplifies a type that appealed to Roman patrons for its inventive composition and blending of styles from different periods. During the 1st century BCE it became increasingly difficult to obtain original Greek art. To fill patrons' requests, artists in Italy, such as Pasiteles and his students, made sculptures that copied or manipulated elements from past styles. Pliny the Elder mentions artists who bought and made molds of original Greek sculpture (see Richter, 1955), making reference to Pasiteles. Pasiteles has been attributed as the first artist to use the pointing system, a mechanical method used to exactly reproduce earlier statues, which he would incorporate in his groups (see Richter, 1955). The similar sizes of the various copies of the *Stephanos Athlete* attest to this method (see Zanker, 1974).

The *Orestes and Electra* was found during a vital time for the discovery of antiquities in the Bay of Naples area and in a period of general increased interest in the cultures of ancient Greece and Rome on the part of people such as Johann J. Winckelmann. The discovery of the Naples group in Pozzuoli in the mid 18th century was no doubt overshadowed by the more extraordinary finds of Pompeii and Herculaneum. Winckelmann wrote about the finds in the Museo Ercolanese, but he makes no mention of the *Orestes and Electra*, even when mentioning other finds from Pozzuoli (see Winckelmann, 1783–84). For Winckelmann, the finds of cities such as Pozzouli were second only to the exceptional finds being discovered at Pompeii and Herculaneum.

Soon after its discovery, the group was identified as *Ptolemy and Cleopatra*, although it was eventually identified as *Orestes and Electra* (see Rochette, 1833), no doubt based in part on the identification that Winckelmann made of the Louvre (formerly Borghese) *Orestes and Pylades* (see Winckelmann, 1783–84). More recently, one scholar has taken up the issue of interpreting the various Pasitelian groups and proposes that the Naples group represents *Perseus and Andromeda* (see Simon, 1987).

LINDA NOLAN

See also **Canova, Antonio; Lysippos; Polykleitos**

Further Reading

Borda, Maurizio, *La scuola di Pasiteles*, Bari, Italy: Adriatica Editrice, 1953

De Franciscis, Alfonso, *Il Museo Nazionale di Napoli*, Cava dei Tirreni, Italy: Di Mauro, 1963

Dubois, Charles, *Pouzzoles Antique (Histoire et Topographie)*, Paris: Fontemoing, 1907

Fullerton, Mark, "Description vs. Prescription: A Semantics of Sculptural Style," in *Stephanos: Studies in Honor of Brunilde Sismondo Ridgway*, edited by Kim J. Hartswicke and Mary Carol Sturgeon, Philadelphia: University Museum, University of Pennsylvania, 1998

Richter, Gisela M.A., *Ancient Italy: A Study of the Interrelations of Its Peoples as Shown in Their Arts*, Ann Arbor: University of Michigan Press, 1955

Ridgway, Brunilde Sismondo, *Roman Copies of Greek Sculpture: The Problem of the Originals*, Ann Arbor: University of Michigan Press, 1984

Ridgway, Brunilde Sismondo, *The Severe Style in Greek Sculpture*, Princeton, New Jersey: Princeton University Press, 1970

Rochette, Raoul, *Monumens inédits d'antiquité figurée, grecque, étrusque et romaine*, Paris: Imprimerie Royal, 1833

Ruesch, A., et al., editors, *Guida Illustrata del Museo Nazionale di Napoli*, Naples: Richter, 1911

Simon, Erika, "Kriterien zur Deutung 'Pasitelischer' Gruppen," *Jahrbuch des deutschen archäologischen Instituts* 102 (1987)

Winckelmann, Johann Joachim, *Storia delle arti del disegno presso gli antichi*, edited by Carlo Fea, Rome: Pagliarini, 1783–84

Zanker, Paul, *Klassizistische Statuen: Studien zur Veränderung des Kunstgeschmacks in der römischen Kaiserzeit*, Mainz, Germany: Von Zabern, 1974

MARIE-CHRISTINE D'ORLÉANS 1813–1839 *French*

Although she produced sculpture only during the last five years of her short life, Marie-Christine d'Orléans created a few important works during the height of the French 19th-century Romantic period. Her principal sources were medieval history and, like other Romantics, she drew inspiration from the works of Lord Byron, Johann Wolfgang von Goethe, Friedrich von Schiller, William Shakespeare, and the life of Napoléon Bonaparte.

Marie-Christine d'Orléans, born Marie-Christine-Caroline-Adélaïde-François-Léopoldine, princess of Orléans, in Palermo, Sicily, on 12 April 1813, was the youngest daughter of Louis-Philippe, king of France, who reigned from 1830 to 1848, and Queen Marie Amélie. As did most girls of privilege, d'Orléans received her education from private tutors. At around the age of 12, she took drawing lessons with a family friend, Ary Scheffer, the German-born Romantic painter. Scheffer complained that d'Orléans's piety prevented her from learning how to draw from the nude, and thus her models were always heavily draped. Scheffer greatly admired the princess, however, and later became one of her first biographers. Her early oeuvre also consisted of lithographs and watercolors. Some scholars have noted that d'Orléans also studied privately with the French sculptor David d'Angers. In 1837 she married Alexander Frederick William, Duke of Württemberg, and gave birth to a son in the same year.

D'Orléans's most famous work was her *Joan of Arc at Prayer*, portraying a subject with which she identified and was fascinated by, and which was the sensation of the Salon of 1837. The work was commissioned by her father in 1835 for the palace at Versailles after the Swiss sculptor James (Jean-Jacques) Pradier's

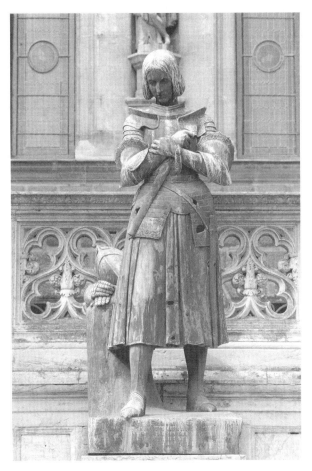

Joan of Arc at Prayer
The Conway Library, Courtauld Institute of Art

sculpted version of the same subject failed to please him. Crafted in the Troubadour style popular during the July Monarchy, countless reproductions were cast and sold, mainly through the important foundry Susse Frères (the most prominent foundry of the period), and these reproductions were enormously popular and widely known. Marble versions were produced by her *practicien* (marble carver) Auguste Trouchaud, based on d'Orléans's wax maquette. Her interest in having reductions of her work cast and sold showed that she wished to be taken seriously and that she wanted to establish herself as a professional sculptor. As daughter of the king of France, she hardly needed the income that the reductions would generate. One of these casts was known to have been used as the focus of a pilgrimage at Orléans, France, held annually on 30 May and marking the day when Joan of Arc was burned at the stake.

Joan of Arc was an extremely popular subject in France during this time, even though she was not canonized until 1920. D'Orléans's depiction of the saint is simply designed and motivated by pious devotion.

The saint's helmet and gloves are tossed aside, resting on a pedestal on her right. Her bowed head exemplifies religious devotion, as does the gesture of clutching the sword (an object that acts as a substitute for a crucifix). The delicate features, especially of the face and the hands that cross at the wrists, and the intense gaze, suggesting that the saint is listening to the voices that she claimed directed her, are a tour de force for sculpture of the period.

The work was later admired by Auguste Rodin, who believed (incorrectly) that the work was made with the help of the sculptor Antoine-Louis Barye. Barye was a friend of d'Orléans's brother, Ferdinand-Philippe, the Duke of Orléans, and certainly may have given the princess some advice or suggestions, but there is no evidence that he was in any way involved in its production.

Around the same time that *Joan of Arc at Prayer* was produced, d'Orléans also completed an equestrian monument of Joan of Arc that is now located in the town hall of Orléans. This work, depicting the heroic Joan of Arc on her warhorse compassionately observing a dying English solider underfoot, is a rare and early example of the depiction of a female hero in French sculpture. In fact, it was during the July Monarchy that France witnessed the origins of feminism not only with the sculptures of d'Orléans, but also with the writings of George Sand, the essays of Flora Tristian, and the paintings of Rosa Bonheur.

Unfortunately, most of d'Orléans's sculptures are now lost or destroyed, and her oeuvre was small owing to the brevity of her life. Always a delicate and sickly child, in 1839 she died of pulmonary disease at age 25; she was mourned publicly and eulogized in the press. One of her designs for a kneeling angel was completed posthumously as a collaborative work for the tomb of the Duke of Orléans, who also died prematurely during a riding accident. The tomb, at Chapelle Saint-Ferdinand, Neuilly (the site of the Duke's accident), was designed by Scheffer, and d'Orléans's *Angel* was completed by Henri de Triquête.

CATERINA Y. PIERRE

Biography

Born in Palermo, Sicily, Italy, 12 April 1813. Given name Marie-Christine-Caroline-Adélaïde-François-Léopoldine, princess of Orléans. Relocated to France with family, 1826; father crowned king of France, 1830; studied drawing with Ary Scheffer, *ca.* 1825, and sculpture with David d'Angers. Died in Pisa, Italy, 2 January 1839.

Selected Works

1835　　Equestrian monument of Joan of Arc; bronze; Hôtel de Ville, Orléans, France

1835–37　　*Joan of Arc at Prayer*; terracotta; Dordrechts Museum, Dordrecht, the Netherlands; marble version: Château, Versailles, Yvelines, France; bronze version: Hôtel de Ville, Orléans, France

1842　　*Angel* (completed posthumously by Henri de Triquête); marble; Chapelle Saint-Ferdinand, Neuilly, France

Further Reading

Art of the July Monarchy: France, 1830–1848 (exhib. cat.), Columbia: University of Missouri Press, 1990

Easterday, Anastasia Louise, *Charting a Course in an Intractable Profession: Women Sculptors in 19th-Century France*, Los Angeles: UCLA, 1997

Easterday, Anastasia Louise, "Labeur, Honneur, Douleur: Sculptors Julie Charpentier, Felicie de Fauveau and Marie d'Orléans," *Women's Art Journal* 18/2 (Fall 1997/Winter 1998)

Fusco, Peter, and H.W. Janson, editors, *The Romantics to Rodin: French Nineteenth-Century Sculpture from North American Collections* (exhib. cat.), Los Angeles: Los Angeles County Museum of Art, and New York: Braziller, 1980

Marie D'Orléans, *Une correspondance inédite de la Princesse Marie d'Orléans, Duchesse de Wurtemberg*, edited by Marthe Kolb, Paris: Boivin, 1937

Pingeot, Anne, et al., *Chefs d'œuvre de la sculpture du XIXᵉ siècle: "La sculpture française au XIXe siècle"* (exhib. cat.), Levallois, Paris: Publication Nuit et Jour, 1986

Waller, Susan, *Women Artists in the Modern Era: A Documentary History*, Metuchen, New Jersey: Scarecrow Press, 1991

Warner, Marina, *Joan of Arc: The Image of Female Heroism*, Berkeley and Los Angeles: University of California Press, and New York: Knopf, 1981

BORIS IVANOVICH ORLOVSKY (SMIRNOV) 1792–1837 *Russian*

By vocation Orlovsky was a monumental sculptor. He thought primarily in terms of enormous spaces and architectural-sculptural compositional groups, although his works also include a series of independent studio masterpieces. He was a man of extraordinary destiny and brilliant talent. A serf, he was sent by his owner in 1808 to learn the trade of marble cutting in Moscow at the studio of Santino Campioni. Working day and night, he learned, in his own words, "to carve marble as though cutting an apple." In 1816 he moved to St. Petersburg, with his master's permission, and started working in Agostino Triscorni's famous marble-cutting studio. Orlovsky's industry and passion for his work gained him a reputation as the best marble cutter in the capital. However, he had ambitions for independent creation and spent his spare time drawing and modeling.

Czar Alexander I and Ivan Martos, the rector of the St. Petersburg Academy of Arts, each played a

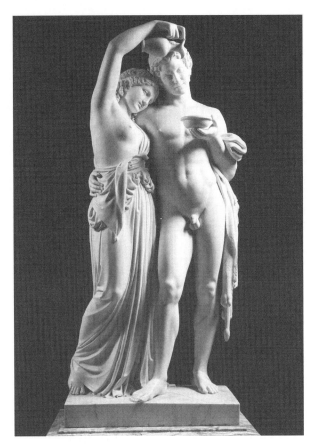

Faun and Bacchante
© The State Russian Museum / CORBIS

significant role in Orlovsky's life. In 1821, Orlovsky was assigned by Martos to sculpt a colossal marble bust of Alexander I that was commissioned by the merchants of St. Petersburg for the stock exchange. In 1822 Orlovsky executed several smaller versions of the bust. One of them was presented as a gift to the empress Elizaveta Alekseyevna. By the personal order of Alexander I, Orlovsky received freedom from his owner and was enrolled in the Academy of Arts. Within eight months the sculptor was sent to the studio of Danish sculptor Bertel Thorvaldsen in Rome on a stipend.

Orlovsky lived in Rome from March 1823 to December 1828 and was one of Thorvaldsen's favorite students. Orlovsky quickly achieved success. He copied works of ancient masters and also studied drawing. In addition, he worked for Thorvaldsen as a marble cutter, mainly on portrait busts. Thorvaldsen characterized him as "a man of very high morals and rare talent." In Rome Orlovsky created from plaster the statues *Paris, Satyr Playing the Pan-Pipes*, and the group *Satyr and Bacchante*. The composition of the latter reflects the influence of one of Praxiteles's early works from the 4th century BCE, *Satyr Pouring Wine*. Thor-

valdsen's perception of antique monuments clearly influenced Orlovsky's refined Roman sculptures. Closely connected with the Classical tradition, these works also display traits of Romanticism. Full of enchanting tranquility and genuine poetry, they belong to the idyllic current of Russian Classicism. The Roman statues were transferred to marble noticeably later, in St. Petersburg, and completed after Orlovsky's death by S.I. Galberg. Orlovsky also worked on a colossal marble bust of Alexander I (1827) in Thorvaldsen's studio. In 1834 this bust was exhibited in the Senate building in St. Petersburg.

The sculptor returned to his native land for a competition to construct monuments to Mikhail Illarionovich Kutuzov and Mikhail Bogdanovich Barclay de Tolly, Russian military leaders of the War of 1812. The participants of the competition were required to correlate the monuments with the architectural-sculptural ensemble of the Cathedral of Kazan, which had been built in the first decade of the 19th century. In addition, according to the dictate of Czar Nicholas I, the field marshals were to be depicted "on foot in uniforms" and modeled on Christian Rauch's monument to Field Marshal Blücher in Berlin. The depiction of contemporary clothing was counter to the Classical aesthetic, preventing the heroization of the leaders' images and necessitating a more true-to-life portrayal of the models.

Orlovsky handled the problems set before him brilliantly, organically inserting the statues into the ensemble of the square in front of the Cathedral of Kazan, bordering on Nevsky Prospekt. The statues stand on simple granite pedestals against the background of the portals of the cathedral's semicircular colonnade. Adjoining the ends of the colonnade, the monuments face each other across the center of the square. Orlovsky unified them through a pattern of rhythmic correspondences both with the surrounding architecture and with each other, but still as independent entities. A certain naturalism in the realization of the military leaders' images, far from lowering their demeanor, underscores their individuality. Kutuzov steps forward victoriously with his head proudly raised. With an unsheathed sword in his right hand, his left hand imperiously indicates the path ahead to the troops with his field marshal's staff. By contrast, Barclay de Tolly shows no assuredness of victory, standing with bent head, buried deep in thought, and drawing back his left hand holding the field marshal's staff. The artist, Romantic in temperament, saw in the military leader not only a celebrated war hero, but also a suffering human being, unfairly judged by his contemporaries. Orlovsky's interpretation results in a psychological sharpness unprecedented in monumental sculpture. The figures of the leaders are draped in military overcoats resembling

Roman togas. At their feet are French heraldic emblems—banners with poles crowned by images of eagles. The triumphant unveiling of the monuments took place on 25 December 1837, the 25th anniversary of the expulsion of the French from Russia.

During the same period, Orlovsky labored on a statue of an angel for the Alexander Column on Palace Square in St. Petersburg (the architect was August Ricard de Montferrand). The column, constructed in memory of Alexander I, with a height of 47.5 meters, dominates all the other buildings surrounding the square. It is a cylindrical monolith made out of red granite, installed without reinforcement on a four-sided base decorated with bronze reliefs. The column is completed by a capital with a semispherical top, on which there is a flying angel with a cross. The Roman columns of Trajan and Marcus Aurelius from the 2nd century CE served as a model for the architect. Nicholas I ordered Orlovsky to "give the statue the face of the late emperor Alexander."

Orlovsky made 14 models of different sizes before all of his and Nicholas I's requirements were satisfied. The angel, who flies in front of a triumphant chariot carrying an allegorical figure of Glory, tramples with a cross upon a snake, which personifies evil and treachery. The angel's silhouette is distinctly outlined against the background of the sky and can be seen from all possible angles. Adapting the precedent ensemble, Orlovsky harmoniously inserted a statue of an angel that is Romantic in spirit and Classical in form. It is a truly great monument, one in which the heroic theme is fulfilled in an allegorical religious image.

The Classical, Romantic, and realistic characteristics that appear in the sculptor's creations are united in the work *Jan Usmar, Stopping an Enraged Bull*, which he executed while a professor. Extolling the legendary Russian folk hero, Orlovsky made the bull the embodiment of a mighty elemental force. The dynamic of struggle, conveyed by the artist with original expression and plastic realization of the images, testifies to his indubitable realistic achievements. Orlovsky's creative practice shows a distinct tendency toward a reconciliation of Romanticism, proclaiming the freedom of feelings, with the world of Classical form, as well as a premonition of the era of realism. His Romanticism became the harbinger of a new realist art.

LINA TARASOVA

See also **Thorvaldsen, Bertel**

Biography

Born in Bolshoi Stolbetsk, Orlov province, Russia, 1792. Born to family of household serfs as the property of landowner N.M. Matsnevaya; Smirnov family sold to V.O. Shatilov, a Tula landowner, 1801. Studied and worked first in Moscow in the marble studio of Santino Campioni, then in St. Petersburg, in the marble studio of Agostino Triscorni; received freedom 2 April 1822; studied in the Academy of Arts, St. Petersburg, under Ivan Martos (1822); sent to Italy on stipend to studio of Bertel Thorvaldsen, 1823, by personal order of Czar Alexander I; student of Thorvaldsen in Rome, 1823–28; summoned to St. Petersburg, 1828, to take part in competition for creation of monuments to Field Marshals Kutuzov and Barclay de Tolly; received the title of academician for works executed in Rome, 1830; lecturer at Academy of Arts, 1831, professor, 1836. Died in St. Petersburg, Russia, 16 December 1837.

Selected Works

1822   Bust of Czar Alexander I; marble; Hermitage, St. Petersburg, Russia; version: Museum of the Russian Literature Institute of the Russian Academy of Sciences, St. Petersburg, Russia

1824   *Paris*; plaster (not preserved); marble version (rendered in 1838 by S.I. Galberg): State Russian Museum, St. Petersburg, Russia; another version in marble (rendered in 1838 by D.S. Savelyov): State Tretyakov Gallery, Moscow, Russia

1824–26   *Satyr Playing the Pan-Pipes*; plaster; Scientific Research Museum of the Russian Academy of Arts, St. Petersburg, Russia; marble version (begun by Orlovsky in 1829, completed by S.I. Galberg in 1838): State Russian Museum, St. Petersburg, Russia

1826–27   *Satyr and Bacchante*; plaster; State Tretyakov Gallery, Moscow, Russia; marble version (author's revision, 1837): State Russian Museum, St. Petersburg, Russia

1827   Colossal bust of Czar Alexander I; marble; State Russian Museum, St. Petersburg, Russia

1829–37   Monument to General Field Marshal M.I. Kutuzov; bronze, granite; Kazan Cathedral, St. Petersburg, Russia

1829–37   Monument to General Field Marshal M.B. Barclay de Tolly; bronze, granite; Kazan Cathedral, St. Petersburg, Russia

1831–34   Statue of an angel; bronze; Alexander Column, Palace Square, St. Petersburg, Russia

1831–36   *Jan Usmar, Stopping an Enraged Bull*; bronze (cast in 1911); State Russian Museum, St. Petersburg

1835   Bust of K.V. Meyer; plaster; State Russian Museum, St. Petersburg, Russia

1835–37   Statues of genii and military attributes; copper; Moscow Triumphal Arch, St. Petersburg, Russia

Further Reading

Petrov, V.N. (Vsevolod Nikolaevich), *Pamiatniki M.I. Kutuzovu i M.B. Barkliau-de-Tolli: Skul'ptor Orlovskii* (Monuments to M.I. Kutuzov and M.B. Barclay de Tolly: The Sculptor Orlovsky), Leningrad: Khudozhnik RSFSR, 1967

Romm, Aleksandr Georgievich, "Boris Ivanovich Orlovsky," in *Russkoe iskusstvo: Ocherki o zhizni i tvorchestve khudozhnikov, pervaia polovina XIX veka* (Russian Art: Essays on the Life and Creation of Artists of the First Half of the 19th Century), edited by A.I. Leonova, Moscow: Iskusstvo, 1954

Shurygin, IA.I., *Boris Ivanovich Orlovskii, 1792–1837*, Leningrad: Iskusstvo, 1962 Tarakanovskii, Georgii Georgievich, *Skul'ptor Boris Ivanovich Orlovskii* (The Sculptor Boris Ivanovich Orlovsky), Tula: Priokskoe Knizhnoe Izd-vo, 1986

Tesan, Harald, *Thorvaldsen und seine Bildhauerschule in Rom*, Cologne, Germany: Bühlau, 1998

OTTONIAN SCULPTURE

Ottonian sculpture was created during the Ottonian dynasty under the three German emperors Otto I, Otto II, and Otto III during the 10th and 11th centuries. This Saxon line of rulers can be traced from Henry I (*ca.* 876–936), father of Otto I the Great (912–973), and continued after the death of Otto III (980–1002) with the last Saxon ruler, Henry II (973–1024). As a stylistic term, Ottonian also has been applied to the period of Salic rule that followed Henry II, which began with Conrad II (*ca.* 990–1039) and continued with Henry III (1017–56) and Henry IV (1050–1106). This period closed with investiture dispute in 1075 that resulted in Henry IV's capitulation in 1077.

The term *Ottonian* was not coined until the 19th century, and it was not clearly defined until the 20th century. To this day, much discussion persists over its validity and extension. Although German art historians have defined the Ottonian epoch as the beginning of a proper German style that dominated European art (see Jantzen, 1959), others, primarily French and Spanish art historians, have tried to understand Ottonian art as part of the Pan-European pre-Romanesque art (see Focillon, 1938). However, both sides face serious problems regarding definitions because of regional limitation. Although several works from northern Italy (Milan) show clearly Ottonian characteristics, it is more difficult to maintain that the sculpture produced within the Italian region of the empire is Ottonian in style. The stylistic unity and elevated quality of the works set Ottonian sculpture as a "court style," which differs from the pre-Romanesque stylistic experiments in southern France and Catalonia.

In the Ottonian works of the late 10th century, the reappearance of monumental sculpture emerged (for example, the *Gero Crucifix* in Cologne and the Golden Virgin in Essen, Germany). Most pieces were fabricated in workshops belonging to monasteries, and commissions no longer depended directly and exclusively on the emperor and his court. However, patronage remained in most cases bound to the court, although it also included the higher clergy, who were mostly relatives of the emperor. In contrast to the following Romanesque period, Ottonian sculpture had a primarily liturgical function or was in some way related to the cult of relics, and thus it was often moveable. As a result, secure dates for single works are rare, and the dating of Ottonian sculptures is one of the main problems occupying current researchers. For several works, the dating oscillates more than 100 years, and thus a work considered Ottonian by one scholar may be labeled Romanesque by another.

Very few stone sculptures from this epoch have been preserved. The most important monumental works can still be found in the Rhineland region of Germany; this was an important area for sculptural production in stone and other media. Among the earliest sculptures from the Rhineland are draped figures and heads from the facade of St. Pantaleon in Cologne (*ca.* 984–91). The later relief fragments from St. Liudger in the choir of Werden Abbey near Essen (*ca.* 1060) show two standing bishops, seated apostles or prophets, and female figures depicting saints or sibyls under arcades. The fragments have been identified as either remnants of the tomb of St. Liudger or as parts of a choir screen and have been dated accordingly to around 1060.

Another sculptural center was at Hildesheim (Lower Saxony), which hosted not only the production of stone sculpture such as the tomb of Bishop Bernward (*ca.* 1020; St. Michael Cathedral, Hildesheim, Germany), but sculpture in different media as well. The most important works in stone at the end of the Ottonian period are the reliefs *Christ with Sts. Emmeram and Dionysius* at Regensburg (after 1049), which have sometimes been characterized as Romanesque. They are the only monumental stone sculptures of their time period that are preserved as part of the architecture in their original location.

One of the most important achievements of Ottonian sculpture was the revival of the Carolingian bronze technique. The door at the Cathedral of Mainz (*ca.* 1000; Mainz, Germany) portrays direct Carolingian inspiration in its plain, classicizing form and is derivative of the bronze doors of Charlemagne at Aachen. The masterpiece, however, is Bishop Bernward's door at Hildesheim (formerly St. Michael, now Cathedral of Hildesheim). Finished in 1015, it typologically depicts

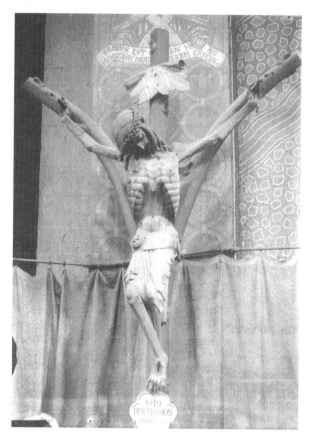

Crucifix in S. Maria im Kapitol, Cologne Cathedral, *ca.* 1304
© Foto Marburg / Art Resource, NY

on the left wing the story of Adam and Eve and on the right wing the Life of Christ. Although the idea for decorated doors can be traced to late antiquity examples from Rome and Milan and stylistic affinities have been identified in Carolingian miniatures, the vivid way in which the abbreviated biblical stories are told is fresh and original, including numerous figures that almost completely detach from the ground and thus create a highly plastic impression. From a technical point of view, the doors are an exceptional accomplishment because the two panels were each cast as one piece (approximately 4.7 meters high). In contrast, the third door created during the Ottonian epoch, the one at the Cathedral of Augsburg, was cast "Byzantine style" in 35 single panels. As with many Ottonian sculptures, the dating, and even more so the iconography, of this work, which shows panels with figures from the Old Testament and symbolic animals, is controversial.

Bishop Bernward also commissioned a second, even more exceptional, work in bronze, a monumental column (3.8 meters high)—known as the column of Bernward—that was inspired by the columns of the antique Roman emperors. The work depicted on the

shaft the story of Christ. The masterpiece of late Ottonian sculpture in bronze is the so-called *Werden Crucifix* (*ca.* 1060), a heavily stylized, under-life-size cross that expressively renders the anatomy of Christ in an extremely sharp and abstract manner.

The formative work of wooden sculpture during the Ottonian period in the Rhineland was the wooden *Gero Crucifix* (*ca.* 969–976) commissioned by Gero, archbishop of Cologne, for the Cathedral of Cologne (also known as the Cathedral of St. Peter and St. Maria), where it still remains. The cross was once located at the high altar over Gero's tomb. The dead Christ on the cross is shown in a naturalistic fashion, stressing the anatomical features of the heavy, hanging body of the Savior. In contrast to earlier sculpted crosses, it made no use of gold sheets covering the body but was instead painted, giving way to the expressive potentials of the wooden surface. The Gero Crucifix was extremely influential, as is witnessed not only in several further wooden crosses that clearly derive from the older one, but also by repetitions of the figure style in small works of precious metals.

Two further masterpieces in wood stand out at the end of the period: the wooden doors of St. Maria im Kapitol (*ca.* 1050; Cologne) depict scenes from the Life of Christ with small, completely rounded figures with very large heads that vividly exist within rectangular, crowded compartments. Much of the original polychromy has been preserved in this case, further adding to the animated impression. At the greatest distance from the genrelike narrative style of the Cologne doors is the Imad Madonna (*ca.* 1070) in Paderborn, commissioned by Bishop Imad. This was conceived as a remote cult image with an aloof expression of complete withdrawal. Inspired by Byzantine prototypes, it shows the rigidly frontalized Madonna with the Christ child sitting on her left knee. Just as in the Basel Antependium (see below), the elongated, geometrically abstracted forms, the calm pose, and the smooth finish of the wood create a courtly aura of extreme sophistication. Unlike the Golden Virgin at Essen, the Imad Madonna never received a cover of gold sheets and was naturalistically painted, similar to the Gero Crucifix.

The greatest continuation from the Carolingian tradition is illustrated in works made in precious metals and ivory. Not all of the pieces derive from Carolingian works, however, but can be traced back to either Early Christian examples, as were the Carolingian pieces before them, or are inspired by Byzantine works, sometimes created in the East only a few years before. One reason for this orientation surely was the intensified relations between the Saxons and Byzantium, which culminated in the marriage of Otto II to the Byzantine princess Teophanu (972), which also led to an intensified artistic exchange between the two empires. The reception of Byzantine works was further stimulated by an equal flowering of the arts in the East, which almost exactly paralleled that of the Ottonian period.

Of exceptional importance for the development of this sculpture was the Golden Virgin and child (*ca.* 1000; Essen Cathedral), which together with the Gero Crucifix inaugurates the renewal of monumental statuary. Made of a wooden core covered with thin, beaten gold sheets and decorated with enamel for the eyes, it shows the seated Madonna with the Christ Child on her lap. Although the forms are broad and heavy, the movement of showing the orb to the Child is stiff, and the gaze is frozen on the object, the Madonna nevertheless renders an impressive monumentality. The group held a depository for relics, much like the slightly earlier statue of St. Fides at Conques, but the Madonna's chief and new function was that of a cult image and not as a reliquary in human forms, as was the case of the St. Fides.

A later group of works in precious metals was either commissioned by or during the reign of Henry II. The central work of this group is the so-called Basel Antependium in Paris, which depicts Christ with St. Benedict and the three Archangels Michael, Gabriel, and Raphael beneath tall arcades (*ca.* 1020; Musée du Cluny, Paris, France). Although its dating is quite secure because of the inscriptions and the inclusion of the emperor and his wife Kunigunde at the feet of Christ, controversy has focused on where the work was created, whether in Fulda or Reichenau, and for which destination, the cathedral of Basel or Bamberg. Among the related works are the golden antependium and the ambo of the Palatine Chapel at Aachen, which, however, do not maintain the same level of quality. Like most works in precious metals of the Ottonian period, these were created with the *repoussé* technique (the method of producing relief metal by hammering and punching chiefly from behind) and additionally decorated with precious stones and enamels, such as the reliquary for the foot of St. Andrew (*ca.* 977–93; Trier, Germany) and book covers such as the one for the niece of Otto III, Evangeliar of Essen Abbess Theophanu (*ca.* 1050). These book covers continued the Carolingian tradition of sumptuous decoration in gold, filigree, and precious stones, often incorporating ivory panels of Carolingian or Byzantine provenance. Splendid golden crosses, such as the one of Duke Otto and Abbess Matilda at Essen (973–82) or the so-called Cross of Queen Gisela (*ca.* 1006) were produced with this technique of gold filigree as well. Bernward, Bishop of Hildesheim, was again responsible for the creation of a series of technically and qualitatively exceptional crosses and candlesticks that were cast in solid silver.

Despite the political turmoil between the fall of the Carolingian empire and the reestablishment of the empire in the West under Henry I, the production of ivory panels never seems to have stopped completely. Therefore, only a slow change toward Ottonian stylization and abstraction can be detected. Often older examples were still followed, and Carolingian pieces were sometimes copied faithfully. Nevertheless, some of the stylistically most innovative Ottonian works have been created in this medium. The most important early work in ivory is probably a series of almost square-shaped ivory panels (*ca.* 980; Metropolitan Museum of Art, New York, and other museums) commissioned from a Milanese workshop for Magdeburg Cathedral and showing scenes from the life of Christ. This may have served as an antependium, although other functions have been suggested, including an ambo or a chancel door. Other important centers of production were Cologne, Liège, and Trier.

Flat reliefs such as book covers were not the only objects created in ivory; rounded holy water buckets, called *situlae*—such as those in London (Victoria and Albert Museum) or Aachen (Schatzkammer)—were also produced in the medium. Stylistic relations to miniature painting are frequent, often leading to the assumption of a common local workshop for the production of ivories and book illuminations. As in book illumination, in some cases a marked artistic individuality is apparent, and a number of highly eccentric carvings has been attributed to a single sculptor, the so-called German Master and his workshop located in Trier or Echternach. Quite contrary to Ottonian stylization and courtly refinement, these works were boldly conceived and extremely expressive, rendering the human body in sometimes sturdy, sometimes elongated, contorted forms.

As in the Carolingian period, a considerable amount of sculpture must have been produced in stucco. Little of this is preserved. The most important monument in this media is the high altar ciborium of the Cathedral of Milan in Italy (before 1000). Like the wooden crosses, it is painted, which adds to the naturalistic appearance of the faces, and the figures are schematically frontalized or rendered completely in profile. Ottonian works had two main stylistic roots: on one hand the Carolingian heritage and its revival of late antiquity, on the other the influence from Byzantium. The monumental works of the following style, the Romanesque, emerged from serving a new function. In contrast to the mostly removable Ottonian sculptures, they were generally created in conjunction with the architecture, often to decorate the exterior of churches. This led not only to an increased production and diffusion of stone sculpture, but also to a greater monumentality of the works.

JOHANNES MYSSOK

See also **Gero Crucifix**

Further Reading

Beckwith, John, *Early Medieval Art*, London: Thames and Hudson, 1964; New York: Praeger, 1965; revised edition, London and New York: Thames and Hudson, 1969

Brandt, Michael, and Arne Eggebrecht, editors, *Bernward von Hildesheim und das Zeitalter der Ottonen* (exhib. cat.), 2 vols., Hildesheim, Germany: Bernward Verlag, and Mainz, Germany: Von Zabern, 1993

Focillon, Henri, *Art d'Occident: Le Moyen Âge, roman et gothique*, Paris: Colin, 1938; 4th edition, 1963; as *The Art of the West in the Middle Ages*, translated by Donald King, Ithaca, New York: Cornell University Press, 1980

Gaborit-Chopin, Danielle, *Ivoires du Moyen Âge*, Fribourg, Switzerland: Office du Livre, 1978

Jantzen, Hans, *Ottonische Kunst*, Munich: Münchner Verlag, 1947; revised edition, Hamburg: Rowohlt, 1959

Lasko, Peter, *Ars Sacra: 800–1200*, London and Baltimore, Maryland: Penguin Books, 1972; 2nd edition, New Haven, Connecticut: Yale University Press, 1994

Little, Charles T., "The Magdeburg Ivory Group: A Tenth-Century New Testament Narrative Cycle," Ph.D. diss., New York University, 1977

Panofsky, Erwin, *Die deutsche Plastik des elften bis dreizehnten Jahrhunderts*, 2 vols., Munich: Wolff, 1922; reprint, 1 vol., New York: Kraus Reprint, 1969

Wesenberg, Rudolf, *Frühe mittelalterliche Bildwerke: Die Schulen rheinischer Skulptur und ihre Ausstrahlung*, Düsseldorf, Germany: Schwann, 1972